It's a Crime
Women and Justice

Fourth Edition

❖

ROSLYN MURASKIN
Long Island University

PEARSON
Prentice Hall

Upper Saddle River, New Jersey 07458

Library of Congress Cataloging-in-Publication Data

It's a crime: women and Justice / [edited by] Roslyn Muraskin.—4th ed.
   p. cm.—(Prentice Hall's women in criminal justice series)
  Includes bibliographical references and index.
  ISBN 0-13-219349-3 (paperback)
   1. Female offenders. 2. Women criminal justice personnel. I. Muraskin, Roslyn. II. Series.

HV6046.I86 2005
364.3'740973—dc22   2005054971

Executive Editor: Frank Mortimer, Jr.
Associate Editor: Sarah Holle
Marketing Manager: Adam Kloza
Editorial Assistant: Kelly Krug
Production Management: GGS Book Services
Production Editor: Trish Finley
**Director of Manufacturing
and Production:** Bruce Johnson

Managing Editor: Mary Carnis
Production Liaison: Barbara Marttine Cappuccio
Manufacturing Manager: Ilene Sanford
Manufacturing Buyer: Cathleen Petersen
Senior Design Coordinator: Mary Siener
Cover Designer: Vicki Kane
Cover Image: Benny DeGrove/Getty Image Inc.
Printer/Binder: R. R. Donnelley & Sons

Pearson Education LTD
Pearson Education Singapore, Pte. Ltd
Pearson Education, Canada, Ltd
Pearson Education–Japan
Pearson Education Australia PTY, Limited
Pearson Education North Asia Ltd
Pearson Educación de Mexico, S.A. de C.V.
Pearson Education Malaysia, Pte. Ltd

10 9 8 7 6 5 4 3 2 1

ISBN 0-13-219349-3

Dedication

This fourth edition is dedicated to those women and men who continue to persevere to bring equality for all persons, regardless of gender, race, or creed.

And dedicated to four young girls, Lindsay, Nickia, Sloane, and Sydney, my granddaughters, who hopefully will never need to struggle as those before; as well as to two young boys, Benjamin and Zachary, my grandsons, who hopefully will be always supportive of the cause of women everywhere.

—Roslyn Muraskin

Contents

❖

Preface

---------------- ❖ ----------------

This is the fourth edition of *It's a Crime: Women and Justice*, an all-inclusive work on women and issues of justice. "Never doubt that a small group of thoughtful, committed citizens can change the world. Indeed, it's the only thing that ever has" (Margaret Mead). Over these many generations, dramatic social and legal changes have been accomplished on behalf of women's equality. Women have made these changes happen. They have not been passive, but rather have worked together to make changes, to create a better world where there are few constrictions. During the times of the American Revolution when America gained a new democracy, women had yet to gain the freedom they deserved as human beings. There continue to be women throughout today's world in the twenty-first century who strive for their own betterment and the betterment of society.

In "Phenomenal Woman," a poem that speaks to us of where we are as women at the dawn of the twenty-first century, Maya Angelou, who is referred to as a remarkable renaissance woman and is hailed as one of the great voices of contemporary literature, reminds us of our towering strength and beauty:

Pretty women wonder where my secret lies.
I'm not cute or built to suit a fashion model's
size
But when I start to tell them,
They think I'm telling lies,
I say,
It's in the reach of my arms,
The span of my hips,
The stride of my steps,

The curl of my lips.
I'm a woman
Phenomenally.
Phenomenal woman,
That's me.

I walk into a room
Just as cool as you please,
And to a man,
The fellows stand or
Fall down on their knees.
Then they swarm around me, A hive of honey bees.
I say,
It's the fire in my eyes,
And the flash of my teeth,
The swing in my waist,
And the joy in my feet.
I'm a woman
Phenomenally.
Phenomenal woman,
That's me.

Men themselves have wondered
What they see in me.
They try so much
But they can't touch
My inner mystery.
When I try to show them,
They say they still can't see.
I say,
It's in the arch of my back,
The sun of my smile,
The ride of my breasts,
The grace of my style.
I'm a woman
Phenomenally.
Phenomenal woman,
That's me.

Now you understand
Just why my head's not bowed.
I don't jump or shout about
Or have to talk real loud.
When you see me passing,
It ought to make you proud.
It's in the click of my heels,

The bend of my hair,
The palm of my hand,
The need for my care.
'Cause I'm a woman,
Phenomenally.
Phenomenal woman,
That's me.

According to Catherine MacKinnon,

> . . . equality in human societies is commonly affirmed but rarely practiced. As a principle, it can be fiercely loved, passionately sought, highly vaunted, sentimentally assumed, complacently taken for granted, and legally guaranteed. Its open detractors are few. Yet despite general consensus on equality as a value, no society is organized on equality principles. Few lives are lived in equality, even in democracies. . . . Social equality is hard to find anywhere. (2001, p. 2)

At the Seneca Falls Conference in 1848, women gathered together to declare that "we hold these truths to be self-evident that all *men and women* [emphasis mine] are created equal." In the *Declaration of Sentiments*, Elizabeth Stanton pointed out that the "history of mankind is a history of repeated injuries and usurpations on the part of men toward women, having in direct object the establishment of an absolute tyranny over her. To prove this, let facts be submitted to a candid world." It went into specifics:

- Married women were legally dead in the eyes of the law.
- Women were not allowed to vote.
- Women had to submit to laws when they had no voice in their formation.
- Married women had no property rights.
- Husbands had legal power over and responsibility for their wives to the extent that they could imprison or beat them with impunity.
- Divorce and child custody laws favored men.
- Women had to pay property taxes although they had no representation in the levying of these taxes.
- Most occupations were closed to women and when women did gain entry, they were paid only a fraction of what men earned.
- Women were not allowed to enter professions such as medicine or law.
- Women had no means to gain an education since no college or university would accept women students.
- With only a few exceptions, women were not allowed to participate in the affairs of the church.
- Women were robbed of their self-confidence and self-respect, and were made to feel totally dependent on men.

These were strong words. This was the status quo for women in the United States in 1848. In the words of Elizabeth Stanton:

> Now in view of this entire disenfranchisement of one-half the people in this country, their social and religious degradation—in view of the unjust laws . . . and because women feel

themselves aggrieved, oppressed and fraudulently deprived of their most sacred rights, we insist that they have immediate admission to the rights and privileges which belong to them as citizens of these United States.

That was then. The movement produced few results. Women did not receive the right to vote until the passage of the Nineteenth Amendment to the Constitution early in the twentieth century.

> Equal legal treatment for women, in their capacity as members of their gender, was not originally envisioned under either section of the Fourteenth Amendment. The ratification debates in Congress to the extent they considered women as such, centered on whether the Amendment would mandate women's suffrage. (MacKinnon, p. 15)

It was not until the early 1970s in the case of *Reed v. Reed* (404 U.S. 71 [1971]) that the guarantees of equal protection would be interpreted to stop different rights for different sexes. In the words of Supreme Court Justice Ruth Bader Ginsburg:

> I think about how much we owe to the women who went before us—legions of women, some known but many unknown. I applaud the bravery and resilience of those who helped all of us—you and me—to be here today. (1998)

The potential for progress in the realm of women's issues and the criminal justice system is possible because of the unremitting battles that women have continued to fight in striving for something called *equality or parity of treatment*. The legal history of women indicates that gender should not be a factor in determining the legal rights of women and men. Dating back to 1776 when this country was being formed and laws were being written by men, it was Abigail Adams, in a letter to her husband John, who insisted that if in the new American Constitution "care and attention are not paid to the ladies," they will foment a revolution. Women have been fomenting that rebellion ever since. The reader of this work will find that the struggle is yet to be won, even though women may have a voice and are being heard, though not always listened to.

This new edition presents the history, the theories, the issues concerning women and the law, women who are victims of violence, women and their health problems within the criminal justice system, issues of gender and race, women and prison issues, women in criminal justice professions, women, terrorism and beyond, and girls and delinquency.

The chapters in this work are written by the *Who's Who of Scholars in Justice Issues and Women*. This is the most up-to-date text written. The material and topics provide the best there is as they address the gender-based problems facing us in the twenty-first century.

Traditional literature ignores the role of women. There are those who will deprecate or ignore a woman's point of view entirely. For women, public denigration is not socially acceptable. Personal attacks should be a thing of the past, but are they?

> Sex equality as a principle has become firmly if incompletely entrenched in U.S. constitutional jurisprudence. At the same time, the solidity, meaning, vitality, and reach of sex equality as a constitutional principle are far from settled, its direction far from certain, its development far from over. (MacKinnon, p. 16)

Today, women and girls live the legacy of women's rights. It continues to be my fervent hope that this work will result in more meaningful and thought-provoking dialogue concerning the major tribulations women face in the criminal justice system. Indeed, *it's a crime* if we do not realize the significance of the role that women play. Basic human rights are fundamental to all, women and men alike. Women are simply human persons as much as men are. The vibrant material is presented in this text—hopefully, you will make it come alive.

Roslyn Muraskin
Long Island University

REFERENCES

Angelou, M. (1978). "Phenomenal Woman," copyright @ 1978 by Maya Angelou, from *And Still I Rise* by Maya Angelou. Used by permission of Random House, Inc.

Ginsburg, R. B. (1998). Speech delivered as part of Wilson lecture series: lawson@wellesley.edu.

MacKinnon, C. A. (2001). *Sex equality*. New York: Foundation Press.

Mead, M. (n.d.). Quote from the *Encyclopedia Britannica*.

Stanton, E. C. (1848). *The Declaration of Sentiments*. Seneca Falls, NY.

About the Author and Contributors

Roslyn Muraskin, Ph.D., is professor of criminal justice at the C.W. Post Campus of Long Island University. Her published works include *Key Correctional Issues* (2005), *Visions for Change: Crime and Justice in the Twenty-First Century* (2005) with Albert R. Roberts, and *The Mediafication of the Criminal Justice System: Myth or Reality* (in production). As editor of Prentice Hall's Women in Criminal Justice Series her published works include *Women in Law Enforcement Careers* (2005), *The Female Homicide Offender: Serial Murder and the Case of Aileen Wuornos* (2004), *The Incarcerated Woman: Rehabilitative Programming in Women's Prisons* (2003), *With Justice for All: Minorities and Women in Criminal Justice* (2003), and *Morality and the Law* (2001). Additionally, Dr. Muraskin serves on the Editorial Board of the *Encyclopedia of Criminology* and has written and spoken on numerous topics concerning gender and the law.

Dr. Muraskin serves as the director of the Long Island Women's Institute for the College of Management at Long Island University, as well as the executive director of the Alumni Chapter for the College of Management. She served in the capacity of associate dean of the College of Management (1990–1996) and as director of the School of Public Service.

She received her doctorate in criminal justice from the Graduate Center at the City University of New York, and her master's degree at New York University. She received her bachelor's degree from Queens College.

Dr. Muraskin's main research interests are those of gender and the law, in particular disparities in corrections as well as throughout the criminal justice system. She is a frequent lecturer on issues of gender and can be seen and heard on television and radio.

CONTRIBUTORS

Ina Allicott is a former Ronald E. McNair Post Baccalaureate Achievement scholar in sociology at Hampton University, and she is currently a graduate student in public health at the University of Pittsburgh.

Nawal H. Ammar, Ph.D., is a professor of justice studies at Kent State University, Kent, Ohio.

David V. Baker, Ph.D., J.D., is an associate professor of sociology in the Behavioral Sciences Department at Riverside Community College.

Cyndi Banks, Ph.D., is an associate professor of criminal justice at Northern Arizona University.

Asha Barber is a former Career Opportunities in Research Scholar in sociology at Hampton University, and she is currently a graduate student in marriage and family therapy at Michigan State University.

Thomas Bazley, Ph.D., is an instructor at the University of South Florida.

Barbara Bloom, Ph.D., is a faculty member of the Department of Criminal Justice at the California State University–Sonoma, Rohnert Park, California.

Ramona Brockett, Ph.D., J.D., is an assistant professor of criminal justice at the University of Maryland Eastern Shore.

Dale J. Brooker, Ph.D., is a faculty member of Saint Joseph's College of Maine.

Hoan Bui, Ph.D., is an assistant professor at the University of Tennessee, Department of Sociology.

Harold Chatman is a graduate of the criminal justice program at the University of Colorado at Denver and a police lieutenant with the Denver Police Department.

Meda Chesney-Lind, Ph.D., is a professor of women's studies at the University of Hawaii at Manoa.

Mona J. E. Danner, Ph.D., is an associate professor of sociology and criminal justice at Old Dominion University.

Elizabeth Piper Deschenes, Ph.D., is an associate professor of sociology and criminal justice at Old Dominion University.

Peter C. Ezekwenna, Ph.D., is an assistant professor in the Department of Mathematics and Computer Science at the University of Maryland Eastern Shore.

Mark A. Ferraiolo, graduated from Ithaca College, served in the U.S. Army (Special Forces) and currently works for Booz Allen Hamilton.

Laura T. Fishman, Ph.D., is an associate professor of sociology at the University of Vermont.

Cortney A. Franklin, M.A., is a doctoral candidate in the Criminal Justice Program at Washington State University.

Trudy-Ann Gayle is a former Career Opportunities in Research Scholar in psychology at Hampton University, and she is currently a graduate student in clinical psychology at the University of Rhode Island.

Rosemary Gido, Ph.D., is an associate professor of criminology at the Indiana University of Pennsylvania.

Jill Gordon, Ph.D., is an associate professor in the L. Douglas Wilder School of Government and Public Affairs at Virginia Commonwealth University.

Paula Gormley, ABD, is with the Graduate Center of the City University of New York.

Thomas E. Guild, J.D., is a professor of business law at the University of Central Oaklahoma.

Michael Hallett, Ph.D., is an associate professor and chair of the Department of Criminology and Criminal Justice at the University of North Florida.

Alex Heckert, Ph.D., is chair and professor of sociology at Indiana University of Pennsylvania.

Druann Maria Heckert, Ph.D., is an associate professor of sociology at Fayetteville State University.

Michele Inderbitzin, Ph.D., is a faculty member at Oregon State University.

Ida M. Johnson, Ph.D., is chair of the Women's Studies Department and an associate professor in the Department of Criminal Justice at the University of Alabama.

Ebone' Joseph is a former Ronald E. McNair Post Baccalaureate Achievement Scholar in sociology at Hampton University, and she is currently a graduate student in counseling at Regent University.

Janice Joseph, Ph.D., is a professor of criminal justice at the Richard Stockton College of Criminal Justice.

Mark M. Lanier, Ph.D., is an associate professor of criminal justice at the University of Central Florida.

Kimberly Kempf-Leonard, Ph.D., is a professor of criminology, sociology, and political economy, and director of the Center for Crime and Justice Policy in the School of Social Sciences at the University of Texas at Dallas.

Kim Lersch, Ph.D., is an associate professor in the Department of Criminology at the University of South Florida.

Arthur J. Lurigio, Ph.D., is the associate dean for faculty in the College of Arts and Sciences and professor of psychology and criminal justice at Loyola University, Chicago.

Faith Lutze, Ph.D., is an associate professor and director of the Criminal Justice Program at Washington State University.

Joan Luxenburg, Ed.D., L.C.S.W., is a professor and chair of the Sociology, Criminal Justice and Substance Abuse Studies Department at the University of Central Oklahoma.

Jennifer McMahon (Warner) is a doctoral student in the Sociology Department at the University of Georgia.

Stacy L. Mallicoat, Ph.D., is a faculty member at California State University in Fullerton.

Stephanie Amedeo Marquez, Ph.D., is a faculty member at Chapman University College.

Danielle McDonald is a doctoral candidate in criminology at Indiana University of Pennsylvania.

Zina T. McGee, Ph.D., is an endowed university professor of sociology at Hampton University, Hampton, Virginia, where she also serves as co-director of the Behavioral Science Research Center.

Michelle Meloy, Ph.D., is an assistant professor of criminology at Widener University.

Cheryl L. Meyer, Ph.D., J.D., is a faculty member at Wright State University in the School of Professional Psychology.

Susan L. Miller, Ph.D., is a professor of sociology and criminal justice at the University of Delaware.

Angela M. Moe, Ph.D., is a faculty member in the Department of Sociology at Western Michigan University.

Etta F. Morgan, Ph.D., is an assistant professor of sociology at Jackson State University.

Laura J. Moriarty, Ph.D., is an associate professor in the Department of Criminal Justice and assistant dean of the College of Humanities and Sciences at Virginia Commonwealth University.

Laura B. Myers, Ph.D., is a professor of juvenile justice at Prairie View A&M University, Prairie View, Texas.

Martin L. O'Connor, J.D., is an associate professor of criminal justice at the C.W. Post Campus of Long Island University.

Jonathan C. Odo, Ph.D., is an associate professor of criminal justice at the University of Maryland Eastern Shore.

Leslye Orlofff, J.D., is director of the Immigrant Women's Program, Legal Momentum, Washington, DC.

Barbara Owen, Ph.D., is in the Department of Criminology at California State University, Fresno, California.

Elicka S. L. Peterson, Ph.D., is an assistant professor of criminology and criminal justice at Appalachian State University in Boone, North Carolina.

Mark R. Pogrebin, Ph.D., is a professor and director of the Criminal Justice Graduate School of Public Affairs at the University of Colorado at Denver and Health Sciences Center.

Tara C. Proano-Raps has earned her doctorate in clinical psychology at Wright State University, School of Professional Psychology.

Christine Rasche, Ph.D., is an associate professor of criminal justice and sociology at the University of North Florida, Jacksonville, Florida, where she also serves as director of the Graduate Program.

Jennifer Ritchie is a graduate student in Loyola University Chicago's Department of Criminal Justice.

Lorena Roque is currently pursing a master's degree in criminal justice at Loyola University Chicago and has six years of experience working as an applied researcher and evaluator in the field of criminal justice.

Trina Rose is a doctoral student in the Department of Sociology at the University of Nebraska–Lincoln.

Jill Leslie Rosenbaum, Ph.D., is a faculty member at California State University, in Fullerton.

RoseMarie Rotondi is a graduate student at Rutgers University.

Jeffrey P. Rush, Ph.D., in his 16th year of university-level teaching, is currently an assistant professor of criminal justice at the University of Louisiana at Monroe.

Inger Sagatun-Edwards, Ph.D., is chair of the Justice Studies program at San Jose State University.

Elizabeth Schafluetzel-Iles has finished her master's degree from the University of Tennessee at Chattanooga. In the fall of 2005 she began service as an adjunct faculty member at UTC and also begin work on her Ph.D.

David Schulberg, J.D., is an adjunct faculty member at Long Beach Community College in California, and is a Ph.D. student at University at California, Irvine.

Magnus Seng, Ph.D., earned his doctorate from the University of Chicago in 1970 and joined the Loyola University criminal justice faculty in 1981.

Theresa A. Severance, Ph.D., is an assistant professor in the Department of Sociology, Anthropology, and Social Work at Eastern Connecticut State University.

Stacey L. Shipley, Psy.D., is the chief psychologist at the Social Learning Rehabilitation and Extended Treatment Program at North Texas State Hospital.

Robert Sigler, Ph.D., is a professor in the Department of Criminal Justice at the University of Alabama.

Alisa Smith, J.D., Ph.D., received her law degree in 1988 from Florida State University and her Ph.D. in criminology from Florida State University in 1998.

Ashley Smith is a Career Opportunities in Research Scholar in sociology at Hampton University and a health policy research intern at Harvard University Medical School.

Loretta Stalans, Ph.D., serves as professor of criminal justice and affiliated professor of women studies at Loyola University Chicago.

Lyn Taylor, Ph.D., is an associate professor of education at the University of Colorado at Denver.

Paul E. Tracy, Ph.D., is a professor of criminology, sociology and political economy, as well as director of the Crime and Justice Studies program in the School of Social Work at the University of Texas at Dallas.

N. Prabha Unnithan, Ph.D., is a professor and interim chair of the Department of Sociology at Colorado State University in Fort Collins.

Jody Clay–Warner, Ph.D., is an associate professor of sociology at the University of Georgia.

Elvira M. White, J.D., from the University of Maryland Law School, is a former criminal defense attorney and university professor and is currently a doctoral student at Prairie View A&M University, Prairie View, Texas.

Nanci Koser Wilson, Ph.D., is a professor of criminology at Indiana University of Pennsylvania, where she is also a member of the Women's Studies faculty.

Suzanne Zahrly is a graduate student and candidate for the master of science in criminal justice degree at the University of North Florida.

Barbara H. Zaitzow, Ph.D., is a faculty member in the Department of Political Science and Criminal Justice at Appalachian State University.

Acknowledgments

❖

My heartfelt thanks to all the contributors to the fourth edition of *It's a Crime: Women and Justice*. Their contribution has made this work the largest ever (with 50 chapters). This is by far the greatest work on women and justice and a credit to the fact that women are now not forgotten but studied as a matter of course in most universities and colleges. The contributors have worked hard and long but have made this their work of love. They are all to be commended for their superior contributions.

A big, big thank you to Sarah Holle, associate editor at Prentice Hall, who is always available. She is a wonderful person to work with, and I look forward to working on future projects with her. And to Frank Mortimer, the "man in charge" who has enough confidence in my abilities to allow me to write, publish, and work with Prentice Hall. I consider him a friend as well as a mentor. To Trish Finley, the production editor who is right there getting the job done, thank you.

My appreciation goes always to Long Island University, the C.W. Post Campus where I have worked for over 25 years, for their continued support and encouragement as I continue to work on projects. They are to be commended over the years for supporting me in my research endeavors.

Thank you also to all our students who love to follow the legal issues of women as they come to realize the plight that women and minorities have had to overcome.

And of course to the love of my life, my husband Matthew who continues to stand by me, as I write.

Roslyn Muraskin

SECTION I

Historical Development of Women's Issues

1

"Ain't I a Woman?"

Roslyn Muraskin

What is a woman? This is a question that has been asked over the many decades since the founding of this country. Women were never considered bright; rather they were emotional beings who were not logical. According to Schopenhauer, "[woman is] in every respect backward, lacking in reason and true morality . . . a kind of middle step between the child and the man who is the true human being."

Controversy still abounds even in the twenty-first century. Although women are involved in professions where once they were not allowed, the classification by gender, although slowly eroding, still does not give equality where equality is due. The women's movement has been the most integrated and populist force in this country. More than 200 years have passed since the Declaration of Independence declared that *all men are equal* (my emphasis). We still wait for the day when both women and men will be defined as persons; then equality will abound for all.

It was Justice David Bower who stated in 1908 that "the two sexes differ in the structure of the body, in the functions to be performed by each, in the amount of physical strength, in the capacity for long continuing labor. . . ." The physical structure of women and their ability to be mothers, and mothers only, as was always thought to be the case, had positioned women at such a disadvantage that any and all decisions from legislators was focused on *her* protection (Kerber & DeHart, 2004, pp. 8–9).

Sojourner Truth gave her famous "Ain't I a Woman?" speech at the Women's Rights Convention in 1815 in Akron, Ohio. Sojourner Truth, a Negro slave, stood at the podium and began to talk: "Well, children, where there is so much racket, there must be something out of kilter, I think between the Negroes of the South and the women of the North—all talking about rights—the white men will be in a fix pretty soon. But what's all this talking about?"

At this point Sojourner pointed to one of the ministers and stated: "That man over there says that women need to be helped into carriages, and lifted over ditches, and to have the best place everywhere. Nobody helps me any best place. And ain't I a woman?" She then raises herself to her full height, about six feet tall, and states: "Look at me! Look at my arm. I have plowed, I have planted and I have gathered into barns. And no man could head me. And ain't I a woman? I could work as much, and eat as much as a man—when I could get it—and bear the lashes as well! And ain't I a woman? I have borne children and seen most of them sold into slavery, and when I cried out with a mother's grief, none but Jesus heard me. And ain't I a woman?"

The women in the audience cheered. Sojourner then points to another minister: "He talks about this thing in his head. What's that they call it?" "Intellect," some woman whispers. "That's it, honey. What's intellect got to do with a woman's rights or black folks' rights? If my cup won't hold but a pint and yours holds a quart, wouldn't you be mean not to let me have my little half-measure full? That little man in black there! He says women can't have as much rights as men. 'Cause Christ wasn't a woman."

At this point she stands with outstretched arms and with eyes lit like fire: "Where did your Christ come from? From God and a Woman! Man had nothing to do with him!" There is alleged to be deafening applause at this moment. "If the first woman God ever made was strong enough to turn the world upside down all alone, these women together ought to be able to turn it back and get it right-side up again. And now that they are asking to do it men better let them."

HISTORICAL OVERVIEW

The search by women for equality is not a recent phenomenon. In 1776, Abigail Adams admonished her husband, John, to "remember the ladies" in the drafting of the Constitution. She insisted that

> in the new code of laws which I suppose it will be necessary for you to make, I desire you would remember the ladies and be more generous and favorable to them than your ancestors. Do not put such unlimited power into the hands of the husbands. Remember, all men would be tyrants, if they could. If particular care and attention is not paid to the ladies, we are determined to foment a rebellion, and will not hold ourselves bound by any laws in which we have no voice or representation.

Adams replied back to his wife:

> As to your extraordinary code of laws, I cannot but laugh. We have been told that our struggle has loosened the bonds of government everywhere; that children and apprentices were disobedient; that schools and colleges were grown turbulent; that Indians slighted their guardians and Negroes grew insolent to their masters. But your letter was the first intimation that another tribe, more numerous and powerful than all the rest, were grown discontented.

The wife, Abigail, responded:

> I cannot say that I think you are very generous to the ladies; for, whilst you are proclaiming power and good-will to men, emancipating all nations, you insist upon retaining an absolute

power over wives. But you must remember that arbitrary power is like most other things which are very hard, very liable to be broken; and not withstanding all your wise laws and maxims, we have it in our power, not only to free ourselves, but to subdue our masters, and, without violence, throw both your natural and legal authority at our feet.

Nowhere in the Constitution of the United States is the word *woman* used. The battle had begun.

The Declaration of Independence as signed in 1776 stated that all men are created equal and that the government derive their power from the consent of the governed. Women were not included in either concept. The only time the word *sex* is referred to is in the Nineteenth Amendment to the Constitution, signed in 1920, giving women the right to vote.

The original American Constitution of 1787 was founded on English law and did not recognize women as citizens or as individuals with legal rights. A woman was expected to obey her husband or nearest male kin—the power of the ballot having been denied to her. Women were not considered persons under the Fourteenth Amendment to the Constitution, which guaranteed that no state shall deny to "any person within its jurisdiction the equal protection of the laws." Women have historically been victimized by policies designed to protect them (Muraskin & Alleman, 1993).

SENECA FALLS

Constitutionally, no obligation existed for the government to provide any benefits beyond basic requirements. In 1848, a convention was held in Seneca Falls, New York, to mark the beginnings of the first organized feminist movement of the nineteenth century. The convention, attended by some 300 women, demonstrated a collective effort to achieve equal rights for women. Their focus was property and suffrage. They went so far as to adopt their own Declaration of Independence:

> We hold these truths to be self-evident; that all men and women are created equal; that they are endowed by their creator with certain inalienable rights; that among these are life, liberty and the pursuit of happiness; that to secure these rights governments are instituted, deriving their just powers from the consent of the governed. Whenever any form of government becomes destructive of these ends, it is the right of those who suffer from it to refuse allegiance to it, and to insist upon the institution of new government. . . . The history of mankind is a history of repeated injuries and usurpation on the part of men toward women, having in direct object the establishment of an absolute tyranny over her. To prove this let the facts be submitted to a candid world.
>
> He has never permitted her to exercise her inalienable right to the elective franchise.
> He has compelled her to submit to laws in the formation of which she has no voice.
> He has withheld from her rights which are given to the most ignorant and degraded men— both natives and foreigners.
> Having deprived her of this first right of a citizen, the elective franchise, thereby leaving her without representation in the halls of legislation, he has oppressed her on all sides.
> He has made her, if married, in the eyes of the law civilly dead.
> He has taken from her all rights in property, even to the wages she earns.

He has made her, morally, an irresponsible being, as she can commit crimes with impunity, provided they be done in the presence of her husband, he becoming to all intents and purposes, her master—the law giving him power to deprive her of her liberty, and to administer chastisement.

After depriving her of all rights as a married woman, if single, and the owner of property, he has taxed her to support a government which recognizes her only when her property can be made profitable to it.

He has denied her the facilities for obtaining a thorough education, all colleges being closed against her.

He allows her in church, as well as State, but in a subordinate position.

He has endeavored, in every way that he could, to destroy her confidence in her own powers to lessen her self-respect, and make her willing to lead a dependent and abject life. (Schneir, 1972, pp. 77–82)

So 300 women declared. They therefore resolved the following at Seneca Falls:

That all laws which prevent women from occupying such a station in society as her conscience shall dictate, or which place her in a position to that of men, are contrary to the great precept of nature, and therefore of no force or authority.

That the women of this country ought to be enlightened in regard to laws under which they live, that they may no longer publish their degradation by declaring themselves satisfied with their present position. . . .

That the same amount of virtue, delicacy, and refinement of behavior that is required of women in the social state, should be required of men, and the same transgression should be visited with equal severity on both man and woman. . . .

That the speedy success of our cause depends upon the zealous and untiring efforts of both men and women, for the overthrow of the monopoly of the pulpit, and for the security to women an equal participation with men in the various trades, professions, and commerce. (Schneir, 1972)

It did not happen then, and the struggles continued.

THE LEGAL SYSTEM

According to Catherine MacKinnon (2001), "[e]quality in human societies is commonly affirmed but rarely practiced. As a principle, it can be fiercely loved, passionately sought, highly vaunted, sentimentally assumed, complacently taken for granted, and legally guaranteed. Its open detractors are few. Yet despite general consensus on equality as a value, no society is organized on equality principles. Few lives are lived in equality, even in democracies" (p. 2).

Seneca Falls took place in 1848. The property rights of U.S. women in the nineteenth century as truly reflected in the declaration at Seneca Falls was set forth earlier by the legal scholar Blackstone, who wrote that by marriage, the husband and wife are one person in law. The very being of all women at this time was suspended during marriage. Laws were passed that gave the husband the right to give his wife "moderate correction"; he could hit her to restrain her but with nothing wider than his thumb.

A federal equal rights amendment was first introduced to Congress in 1923 and was submitted to the states continuously over a period of time for ratification until it finally failed in 1972. Stated simply:

- *Section 1.* Equality of rights under the law shall not be denied or abridged by the United States or by any other State on account of sex.
- *Section 2.* The Congress shall have the power to enforce, by appropriate legislation, the provisions of this Article.
- *Section 3.* This Amendment shall take effect two years after the date of ratification.

It never happened.

Jean-Jacques Rousseau, an eighteenth-century French philosopher, wrote in his work *Émile:*

> Men and women are made for each other then, but their mutual dependence is not equal. . . . We could survive without them better than they could without us. . . . Thus women's entire education should be planned in relation to men. To please men, to be useful to them, to win their love and respect, to raise them as children, care for them as adults, counsel and console them, make their lives sweet and pleasant; these are women's duties in all ages and these are what they should be taught from childhood. (Deckard, 1979, p. 217)

Oberlin College was the first college to admit women, in 1833. Until 1841, women could take only a shortened literary course, on the theory that the education of women had a different purpose than that of men. For many years women were not permitted to speak in class and were required to wait on male students. It was believed that women's highest calling was to be the mothers of the race and that they should stay within that special sphere in order that future generations should not suffer from want of devoted and undistracted mother care. If women were to enter the areas of law, religion, medicine, academics, government, or any sort of public character, the home would suffer from neglect. Washing men's clothes, caring for their rooms, serving the men at dining tables, remaining respectfully silent in public assemblages, the Oberlin coeds were being prepared for motherhood and to serve their men.

Elizabeth Blackwell was the first woman in the United States to get a medical degree, in 1849. She applied to 29 medical schools until one finally accepted her. She had to fight for the right to be present at the dissection of human organs, part of the training for any doctor.

In 1873, the U.S. Supreme Court upheld an Illinois state law prohibiting female lawyers from practicing in state courts (*Bradwell v. Illinois*, 1872). The Court in its *wisdom* (emphasis mine) noted that

> the civil war as well as nature herself, has always recognized a wide difference in the respective spheres and destinies of man and woman. Man is or should be women's protector and defender. The natural and proper timidity and delicacy which belong to the female sex evidently unfits it for many of the occupations of civil life. The constitution of the family organization, which is founded in the divine ordinance, as well as in the nature of things indicates the domestic sphere as that which belongs to the domain and functions of womanhood. The harmony of interests and views which belong or should belong to the family institutions, is repugnant to the idea of a woman adopting a distinct and independent career from that of her husband.

The Court continued by declaring that "[t]he paramount destiny and mission of woman are to fulfill the noble and benign offices of wife and mother. This is the law of the Creator. And the rules of civil society must be adopted to the general constitution of things, and cannot be based upon exception cases."

Justice Miller summed it up when he stated: "I am not prepared to say that it is one of her fundamental rights and privileges to be admitted into every office and position, including those which require highly special qualifications and demanding social responsibilities. In the nature of things it is not every citizen of every age, sex, and condition that is qualified for every calling and position." This decision demonstrated that law reflected society as it was meant to be since the founding of this country.

It took until 1860 in New York to pass the Married Women's Property Act, an attempt to give to women property that she owned as her sole and private property. Until this time a married woman was not entitled to own or keep property after marriage. This act stated "that which a woman married in this state owns at the time of her marriage, and the rents, issues and proceeds of all such property, shall not withstanding marriage, be and remain her sole and separate property."

The right to vote, which was not won until 1920, with the passage of the Nineteenth Amendment to the Constitution, was a struggle for women. In the case of *Minor v. Happersett* (1874), the U.S. Supreme Court denied women the right to vote. The argument then was "that as a woman born or naturalized in the United States is a citizen of the United States and of the State in which she resides, she has therefore the right to vote." The Court stated further that there is no doubt that women may be citizens. The direct question as presented was whether all citizens are necessarily qualified to be voters. "The Constitution has not added the right of suffrage to the privileges and immunities of citizenship as they existed at the time it was adopted" (*Minor*). In no state constitution was suffrage conferred upon women. It took the Nineteenth Amendment to the Constitution to grant women the right to vote. Neither John Adams nor those following him were willing to "remember the ladies." "Federal and state legislation prohibiting sex discrimination in selected areas does not fill the absence of a constitutional prohibition of discrimination on the basis of sex. Under the federal constitution and most state constitutions, women have not yet been raised to the status of constitutional protections enjoyed by males" (Thomas, 1991, p. 95). The Nineteenth Amendment did not automatically mean an end to women's oppression. It did not "negate the term 'male' in Section 2 of the Fourteenth Amendment. The lack of an explicit guarantee of sex equality has limited the U.S. Constitution as a vehicle for securing women's rights and social advancement" (MacKinnon, 2001, p. 16).

Even the language of the law referred to such terms as a reasonable *man, he*, and *his*. When a question about this is raised, the answer typically given is that the male terms used generally include females. As Justice Scalia has stated: "The word 'gender' has acquired the new and useful connotation of cultural or attitudinal characteristics (as opposed to physical characteristics) distinct to the sexes. That is to say, gender is to sex as feminine is to female and masculine is to male" (MacKinnon, 2001, p. 210).

Gender-neutral language does not solve the problem. Such gender-neutral language "serves only to reward the employers ingenious enough to cloak their acts of discrimination in a facially neutral guise, identical though the effects of [a facially neutral seniority] system may be to those of a facially discriminatory one" (Thomas, 1991).

RIGHT TO WORK

During the nineteenth century, differential treatment of women and men was challenged. A most striking incident was that of the protective state labor laws. In the early twentieth century, protective labor laws were allegedly enacted to protect both men and women from inhuman conditions. However, it was women who suffered. In the case of *Muller v. Oregon* (1908), a challenge was made to the Oregon statute prohibiting the employment of women in mechanical establishments, factories, or laundries for more than 10 hours a day. This law was upheld by the U.S. Supreme Court using a reasoning that was to haunt the advocates of women's rights for years to come.

Justice Brenner delivered the majority opinion of the Court:

> [W]omen's physical structure and the performance of maternal functions places her at a disadvantage in the struggle for subsistence. . . . This is especially true when the burdens of motherhood are upon her. [And] even when they are not, by abundant testimony of the medical fraternity continuance for a long time on her feet at work, repeating this from day to day, tends to injurious effects upon the body . . . the physical well-being of woman becomes an object of public interest and care in order to preserve the strength and vigor of the race. [As dictated by history] woman has always been dependent upon man. He established his *control at the outset by superior physical strength* [emphasis mine], and this control in various forms, with diminishing intensity has continued to the present. . . . She is properly placed in a class by herself, and legislation designed for her protection may be sustained, even when legislation is not necessary for men, and could be sustained.

THE RIGHT TO SERVE ON JURIES

And so it continued. Struggles ensued, with women bringing to court their case to serve on juries. In the case of *Hoyt v. Florida* (1961), Justice Harlan delivered the opinion of the Supreme Court. The issue was whether exclusion of women from jury service discriminated against a defendant's right to a fair trial. Justice Harlan stated:

> Manifestly, Florida's [law] does not purport to exclude women from state jury service. Rather the statute "gives to women the privilege to serve but does not impose service as a duty." It accords women an absolute exemption from jury service unless they expressly waive that privilege.
>
> It has given women an absolute exemption from jury based solely on their sex, no similar exemption obtaining as to men.
>
> Despite the enlightened emancipation of women from the restrictions and protections of bygone years, and their entry into many parts of community life formerly considered to be reserved to men, *woman is still regarded as the center of home and family* life [italics added].

In 1975, in *Taylor v. Louisiana* (1975), a male criminal defendant challenged his conviction on the ground that his jury had not been drawn from a fair cross section of the community. Women had systematically been excluded from jury lists. Using statistics to demonstrate that 54.2 percent of all women between 18 and 64 years of age were in the labor force, that 45.7 percent of women with children under the age of 18 were working, that 67.3 percent of mothers who were either widowed, divorced, or separated were in the workforce, and that 51.2 percent of the mothers whose husbands were gainfully employed were also working, the Court declared: "[I]f it was ever the case that women were unqualified to sit on juries or were so situated that none of them should be required to perform jury services that time is long past." A victory had been won.

GENDER AS A SUSPECT CLASSIFICATION

What has not been declared is that gender is a suspect classification. It was not until 1971 that the U.S. Supreme Court considered that many of the laws and official practices at all levels of government as practiced were in violation of the equal protection clause. The Fourteenth Amendment states that "[n]o state shall deny equal protection of the laws to any person." But what does that mean?

A rational relationship test was developed indicating that any classification "must be reasonable, not arbitrary, and must rest upon some ground of difference having a fair and substantial relation to the object of the legislation, so that all persons similarly situated shall be treated alike" (*Reed v. Reed*, 1971). There can exist no discrimination against women unless it is demonstrated that reasonable grounds exist for such discrimination.

Throughout the history of the courts, several classifications, including gender, religion, and national origin, have been labeled "suspect" classifications. What this means is that anytime a law is passed that discriminates in its language or is found to have a discriminatory effect on a suspect class of persons, the state has the burden not simply of showing that the law is rational, but must prove additionally that such a law serves a compelling governmental interest and that no other discriminatory law could accomplish the same or similar purpose. This is the principle referred to as a compelling state interest. We came close with the case of *Frontiero v. Richardson* (1973), but because there was a 4–4 plurality vote of the justices of the Supreme Court, such a decision of gender as a suspect classification never came about. With gender not being labeled a suspect classification, the government has the power to justify any type of discrimination as not being arbitrary and irrational. In the words of Justice Brennan: "There can be no doubt that our Nation has had a long and unfortunate history of sex discrimination. Traditionally, such discrimination was rationalized by an attitude of 'romantic paternalism' which in practical effect, put women, not on a pedestal, but in a cage."

If there had been just one more vote, the courts would have been obliged to treat gender classifications as they do race classifications. It was not to be. The rational basis for classifications is still based on the factor of women being dependent on their spouses, girls being dependent on parents for support, and men having more and better business experience than women. If the courts can determine that discrimination serves the purpose of the rational relationship test, it can and will stand. To this day there remains confusion regarding the standard of review in cases of gender discrimination. The issue remains whether gender and race classifications are ever constitutionally permissible. Are there instances in which it is proper to afford preferential treatment to one group above another? Clear answers do not exist. Each case is considered on an individual basis and on individual merit.

Even the Equal Rights Amendment (ERA) could not be passed. Concerns about family law, protective labor laws, the military, and the establishment of unisex bathrooms were enough to vote down the ERA. If ever there were stereotypical attitudes about women, one is found in the wisdom of many of the justices of the Supreme Court.

GENDER NEUTRAL

Admittedly, progress has been demonstrated, as, for example, in the changing roles of women and men that have led to gender-neutral, functional family laws. Today, the obligation of supporting a spouse is predicated on who can afford it, not simply on who needs it.

Women are not inferior to men. Nevertheless, in the twenty-first century there remains evidence of sexual discrimination, even with all the history and struggles to gain equality and similarly of treatment under the law. According to MacKinnon (2001), "[u]nless something is done, even if recent rates of measurable progress for elite women continue, no American now alive will live in a society of sex equality, nor will their children or their children's children" (p. 2).

In the 1970s there were feminists who both challenged the institutions and laws of the land that continued to deny women equality. There was a "barrage of test cases in state and federal courts challenging practices" denying women benefits as noted above as well as unequal age requirements with regard to marrying and drinking (Kerber & DeHart, 2004, pp. 17–18). What was won were equal pay for equal work, equal employment benefits as well as the ability to obtain credit but "building on the tactics and achievements of the civil rights movement . . . [women] discovered that guarantees of equality in a system structured with men's needs as the norm does not always produce a gender-neutral result" (p. 18).

There was an interesting article in *The New York Times* written by Maureen Dowd (March 26, 2005). The title was "Taming of the Shrews":

> Arabs put their women in veils. We put ours in the stock. Every culture has its own way of tamping down female power, be it sexual, political or financial. Americans like to see women who wear the pants be beaten up and humiliated. Afterward, in a gratifying redemption ritual, people like to see the battered woman rewarded.
>
> That's how Hillary Clinton won a Senate seat and a presidential front-runner spot. And that's how Martha Stewart won her own reality TV show and become a half-billion dollars richer while she was in prison.
>
> Maybe temperamental, power-mad divas always needed to be brought down a peg. They used to do it themselves. Judy Garland and Marilyn Monroe were gorgeous monsters, but were so destructive there was no need to punish them further.
>
> But Hillary and Martha—the domestic diva with the new ankle bracelet echoed Judy Garland on her Web site . . . that "there is no place like home"—are not self-destructive. They are brass-knuckled survivors who elicit both admiration and an enmity that Alessandra Stanley memorably dubbed "blondenfreude."
>
> From pornography to *Desperate Housewives* women being degraded has an entertainment value far greater than men being degraded. People like Hillary and Martha a lot more once they were "broken," like one of Martha's saddle horses, ice queens melted into puddles of vulnerability.
>
> Maybe it's because both women sometimes overreached, treated the help badly and displayed an unseemly greedy streak. Maybe it's because a dichotomy about their roles made them seem disingenuous: they gained renown for traditional feminine roles, and apron-and-hearth books, assuming guises to achieve male power and taking a route to the mahogany epicenter through the kitchen.
>
> Hillary was America's first lady, photographed smiling in her designer dress as she oversaw table settings and placement for state dinners, even though we knew she did not care about domestic piffle and was instead maneuvering to take over large chunks of domestic policy.

Martha was America's first lady of gold-leaf designer lifestyle nesting, even though we knew that her uber-nest was so scary that her husband had flown the coop. Though she was the ultimate professional homemaker and nurturer, she left her daughter out of the litany of things—cats, canaries, horses, chickens and dogs—she would miss in jail.

Obviously, many men are uncomfortable with successful women, so when these women are brushed back, alpha men can take comfort in knowing that alphettes are not threateningly all-powerful and that they had better soften those sharp edges.

After her husband's philandering with Monica, Hillary played the victim card all the way to the Senate. After her own bad judgment about her stocks, Martha metamorphised from jailbird to phoenix.

Why don't we need to see Oprah, another titan known by her first name, slapped back? Probably because Oprah never had an icy or phony side to her public persona and because her struggles in her childhood and with her weight take the edge off any animus that might be leveled at her for a net worth of $1.3 billion.

And what about Condi, who's now being touted for the Republican ticket in 2008? Perhaps she does not need to play the victim to make people feel better about her power because she was never seen as a termagant, pushing people around and bending them to her will. She always seemed subservient to President Bush and Vice-President Dick Cheney, a willing handmaiden and spokesperson for their bellicose bidding.

One Democratic image maker admiringly predicts that, having survived their virago and victim phases, our two most relentless blondes will outlast everyone: "When the world ends, there will be left only a few cockroaches, Cher, Hillary and Martha."

Unfortunately, the ideology of sexism is still embedded in our society. In a work written over 30 years ago, but which still holds true today, "the notion that women are inferior to or at least extremely different from men is taken as a self-evident truth" (Deckard, 1979, p. 6). She concludes, "Building a movement that is viable for an extended period of time is crucial. We cannot expect a quick and easy victory. But if we can avoid the mistakes of the suffragists, our chances of building a humane, nonsexist society are good. After all, women do constitute more than half the world's population" (p. 466). Remember, women are first humans and then female.

We have yet to reach the day when we can say honestly that women have been raised to the status of full constitutional protections as has always been enjoyed by the male sex. We must remember the words of Sojourner Truth: "Ain't I a woman?" We are constantly reminded of her statement and that of Abigail Adams, "remember the ladies," yet we are continuously reminded of the statement in the case of *Glover v. Johnson* (1975): "Keep it simple, they are only women."

REFERENCES

Deckard, B. S. (1979). The women's movement: Political, socioeconomic, and psychological issues. New York: Harper & Row.

Dowd, M. (2005, March 6). Taming of the shrews. *The New York Times*, Op-Ed. Retrieved from http://www.nytimes.com.

Kerber, L., & DeHart, J. S. (2004). *Women's America: Refocusing the past*. New York: Oxford University Press.

Letters of Abigail Adams. www.thelizlibrary.org/suffrage.

Mabee, C. (1993). *Sojourner Truth: Slave, prophet, legend*. New York: New York University Press.

MACKINNON, C. (2001). *Sex equality*. New York: Foundation Press.

MURASKIN, R., & ALLEMAN, T. (1993). *It's a crime: Women and justice*. Upper Saddle River, NJ: Regents/Prentice Hall.

SCHNEIR, M. (ED.). (1972). *Feminism: The essential historical writings*. New York: Vintage Press.

THOMAS, C. S. (1991). *Sex discrimination*. St. Paul, MN: West.

CASES

Bradwell v. Illinois, 83 U.S. 130 (1872).

Frontiero v. Richardson, 411 U.S. 677 (1973).

Glover v. Johnson, 478 F. Supp. 1075 (1975).

Hoyt v. Florida, 368 U.S. 57 (1961).

Minor v. Happersett, 88 U.S. 162 (1874).

Muller v. Oregon, 208 U.S. 412 (1908).

Reed v. Reed, 404 U.S. 71 (1971).

Taylor v. Louisiana, 419 U.S. 522 (1975).

2

Taming Women and Nature

The Criminal Justice System
and the Creation of Crime in Salem Village

Nanci Koser Wilson

Female-on-female violent crime is a rarity. Yet in 1692, in Puritan Salem Village, Massachusetts, hundreds of women were accused, and fourteen executed, for violent crimes, many of whose victims were female. Contemporary Americans view witchcraft as an imaginary offense, so this episode has been seen by most scholars as an aberration, atypical of U.S. criminal justice. But a careful examination of charges against these women reveals an offense that was not so imaginary after all—one for which women are still being brought to account. The Salem witches were persecuted because they were seen as wild women, in need of taming, just as was the rest of "nature." For the patriarchal mind, wild women and wild nature still pose a significant threat to orderly male-controlled production and reproduction, and are still sometimes met with a criminal justice response.

American women, like most women, are infrequent criminal offenders, especially against one another and especially in violent crime. The rarest criminal event is female-on-female violent crime. Yet in 1692, in Puritan Salem Village, Massachusetts, hundreds of women were accused, and fourteen executed, for violent crimes, many of whose victims were female.

The Salem witch hysteria has been seen by most historians as an aberration, a bump in our history, completely atypical of U.S. criminal justice. No longer believers in witchcraft, modern Americans are horrified that such an injustice could have occurred in relatively modern times. It is assumed that the witches were innocent of any crime, and (with the exception of Chadwick Hansen [1968]) scholars have sought explanations outside the phenomenon of witchcraft itself to account for the persecutions.

Yet if we examine carefully the charges against these women, we discover an offense that was not so imaginary after all, and one for which women are still being brought to account. The witches of Salem Village were thought to be disruptive of a natural hierarchy established by men at the behest of a male god. The image of divinely ordained masculine control of nature was captured for Puritans in the metaphor of the Great Chain of Being. This metaphor is still powerful today, with the exception that contemporary Americans have replaced the top rung in the hierarchy. Now, scientific technology reigns as god, and the only telos, or design, in nature is the continued unfolding of evolutionary process. The new divinity is as thoroughly masculinist as Yahweh and is capable of directing evolution by itself. A masculinist science embodies, as complete as did the old God, the American Dream of conquering wilderness, in its vision of total control over nature. In this vision, what counts is not so much more and more productivity (although this is certainly important) but human control of natural productivity.

This is well illustrated in modern agricultural practices. Bovine growth hormone does not produce more milk per cow over the entire span of a cow's life. Similarly, chemical fertilizers do not make the soil more fertile in the long run. Nor do dams create water, nor does experimentally induced laboratory growth replicate natural growth. At the core of all these ways of growing and knowing is the farmer's and the scientist's total control over (what are deemed to be) relevant conditions. It is apparent that this control is desired more than fertility itself. In the 1990s, this could be seen clearly in plans to "develop" wetlands as farms and shopping malls. Although the necessity to the hydrological cycle of these wetlands is now recognized, legislators and environmental agencies in state after state are permitting the development of wetlands upon the agreement by developers to create human-mode substitute wetlands as "replacement parts."

But as Lewis (1943/1988, p. 449) has noted, control over nature is really "a power exercised by some men over other men with nature as its instrument." Many feminist scholars believe that control over women was exerted to exploit their labor and was the first form of exploitation man invented, upon which he then modeled other forms of exploitation. Ecofeminists hold that the exploitation of nature and of women developed coterminously, nourishing one another. And many scholars have noted the centrality of conquest, especially the conquest of wilderness, to the development of the American character (Turner, 1920).

In the Salem witchcraft hysteria we see the convergence of all of these themes, as the Puritan criminal justice system created in the Bay Colony a frightful specter to contain their fears of wild nature—both in human females and in the nonhuman nature around them. In tracing witch-beliefs within the context of Puritan technology and examining the evidence brought against witches, we see a strong device for social control of natural forces—as Lewis (1943/1988) stated, the control of some men over other men (and all women), using nature as the tool. The relevance of Puritan cosmology and its use of criminal justice to achieve the ends of control and domination to contemporary gendered criminal justice can be seen as evidence for a consistent theme running through Western and American history.

PURITAN METAPHYSICS

According to a contemporary witch (Starhawk, 1989, p. 18), "witchcraft takes its teaching from nature." Further, witches understand nature as cyclical, spiral. "There is nothing to be saved from, no struggle of life against the universe, no God outside the world to be feared and obeyed; only the Goddess, the Mother, the turning spiral that whirls us in and out of existence, whose winking eye is the pulse of being" (p. 29).

Whether any Salem women understood themselves to be practicing an ancient religion centered on the immanence of divinity in the natural world (as Murray [1921] asserted of the European witches), or whether any of the accused believed themselves to be malefic witches (as Hansen [1968] maintains), it is clear that at one time such religions were strong competitors for Christianity. In Europe, that part of earlier nature-centered religion that could not be absorbed effectively into Christianity was vigorously suppressed. The struggle with these heretics left a legacy of witch-beliefs among European Christians, which, imported to the American continent with the Puritans, formed the basis for the Salem female crime wave of 1692.

Puritan metaphysics (like all such patriarchal systems) presented a markedly different view of nature to that embodied in nature-centered religions. Puritan cosmology was strongly hierarchical, and within its metaphysics, the ultimate source of life existed beyond it. Puritans saw the cosmos as a

> Vast chain of being! which from God began,
> Natures aethereal, human, angel, man,
> Beast, bird, fish, insect, what no eye can see,
> No glass can reach; from Infinite to thee,
> From thee to nothing—On Superior pow'rs
> Were we to press, inferior might on ours;
> Or in the full creation leave a void,
> Where, one step broken the great scale's destroy'd;
> From Nature's chain whatever link you strike,
> Tenth, or thousandth, breaks the chain alike.
>
> *(Pope, 1733)*

These lines from Pope, although written in the eighteenth century, reflect a "conception of the plan and structure of the world which, through the Middle Ages and down to the late 18th century, many philosophers, most men of science, and indeed, most educated men, were to accept without question" (Lovejoy, 1936/1953, p. 59). The universe was seen as a Great Chain of Being, "composed of an immense . . . number of links ranging in hierarchical order from the meagerest kind of existence, which barely escape non-existence, through 'every possible' grade up to . . . the Absolute Being."

For Puritans, each link in the chain fulfilled its nature and purpose partly by obeying the next highest link in the chain. Among human beings, a similar hierarchy had been ordained with "husbands superior to wives, parents to children, masters to servants, ministers to congregants, and magistrates to subjects. . . . In each of these relations, inferiors served God by serving their superiors. Men promised to ensure obedience in all their dependents, in return for God's promise of prosperity" (Karlsen, 1987, p. 164).

Although the Puritan God existed prior to his creation, and Puritan theology embraced a deity whose transcendence outshone his immanence, their theology was also strongly incarnational. Elements of the natural world reflected and sometimes revealed to humans a supernatural plan, and, on occasion, a struggle between supernatural forces. Both God and Satan, his fallen angel, took an intense interest in the created world.

Created below God in the hierarchy, but above all other things, angels were required to fulfill their place in the chain through obedience. Satan's obedience consisted precisely in his rebellion against his place. His desire to be "as God" included a struggle with the deity within nature itself. Satan not only attempted to seduce humans but also caused various natural disasters lower on the chain.

Long before Puritanism arose, European Christians had begun to understand Genesis 1:28[1] as a mandate to exploit all of nature below humans in the hierarchical chain (White, 1967); and this exploitation, of course, required the taming of wild nature—both human and nonhuman. Puritan theology thus fit neatly with the colonization of an uncivilized territory. The new immigrants found a land peopled by hunting and gathering groups who, for the most part, did not have established cities, agriculture, or a settled existence. Puritans viewed this land as a wilderness in need of taming, which would order it to God.

Part of this impulse was surely secular; but it had a sacred stamp and warrant. Strong strains in Judeo-Christian mythology emphasize the wilderness experience. The wilderness is a setting for man's struggle with his lower nature, a place of suffering and purification, from which he emerges dedicated completely to God and to His divine plan.

> [T]he desert wilderness . . . where the very existence of man is constantly threatened, is also the place specially chosen by God to manifest Himself as His "mighty acts" of mercy and salvation. Obedience to a divine call brings into this dreadful wilderness those whom God has chosen to form as His own people. . . . Failure to trust Yahweh in the wilderness is not simply an act of weakness: it is disobedience and idolatry. (Merton, 1978, p. 190)

This theme of wilderness was "taken over in the theology of radical Protestantism in the seventeenth century and hence entered into the formation of the Christian ideal of North American culture that grew up out of the Puritan colonies of New England" (Merton, 1978, p. 195).

The wilderness, once tamed, would become the orderly paradise the Puritan God commanded man to create. Importantly, a failure to conquer the wilderness was also a failure at individual salvation. If the Bay Colonists failed to establish the paradise of the "City on the Hill," this might be a sign that each Puritan was damned. Fearful for their own souls, frightened of wild nature both on its own terms and for the damnation that failure to tame it portended, Puritans attempted to contain their fears by sacrificing some of their middle-aged women. These women became the very emblem of their fears—of wilderness, of failure, and ultimately, of eternal damnation.

THE WITCHES AS WILD WOMEN

Although it has been suggested that "a genuine coven was meeting in the woods of Salem before the trials" (Starhawk, 1989, p. 21), evidence from the Salem trials does not support such a conclusion. What is more important are the witch-beliefs Puritans held which allowed for the persecutions.

Nature-focused religions had been of concern to the Judeo-Christian tradition since its inception. In the fifth century B.C., tempted to desert his patriarchal God during a time of great personal suffering, Job had proclaimed: "If I beheld the sun when it shined, or the moon walking in brightness; and my heart hath seen secretly enticed . . . this also were an iniquity to be punished by the judge; for I should have denied the God that is above" (Job 31:27–28).

Steeped in a tradition that had shaped its theology in direct contrast to animistic, nature-centered rival religions, the Puritans inherited a linear, hierarchical monotheism. While ancient religions had long since ceased to pose a genuine threat to the newer, patriarchal religion, during time of stress, the fear of heresy arose with new vigor.

Christianity met the challenge in two ways. It absorbed prior religions by building churches on the old sacred sites and by changing names of festivals while keeping their dates. It directly challenged such religions by turning its gods and goddesses into the Christian devil (Adler, 1986, p. 45). The witch persecutions were part of that transformation. What came to be called witchcraft included some elements of pagan belief systems, but "these survivals only became an organized system when the Church took the older beliefs and fragments and created an organized, systematic demonology, complete with new elements including the pact with the devil, the coven and the sabat" (Adler, 1986, p. 53; Trevor-Roper, 1970).

But witch persecutions were useful beyond the purposes of the Church in validating the new patriarchal religion. As Trevor-Roper (1970) notes, in the sixteenth and seventeenth centuries this new demonology acquired momentum. These were the centuries during which modern science was born and the Western worldview became more and more human-control oriented. The massive witch persecutions of the period also validated an increasingly centralized secular and male hierarchy in medicine, politics, and agriculture. The specter of possible resistance to this project of taming all of nature produced intense witch fears, culminating in the deaths of perhaps nine million persons (Daly, 1978, p. 183).

The struggle against wild nature as seen in untamed women produced important tracts whose dissemination was abided by the invention of printing. In *Malleus Malificarum of Instituris* (Kramer Sprenger, 1948; o.d. 1486), readers would learn precisely what to fear from women presumed to be in league with the devil. In books such as this and in the teachings of the clergy, witchcraft was invented.

The *Malleus Maleficarum* "explained and justified the Church's view that most witches were women" (Karlsen, 1987, p. 155). Women, the authors instructed, were more evil than men by nature, and because they were created inferior to men, were more susceptible to deception. Witches were also seen as dissatisfied with their place in the natural hierarchy. This made them angry and vengeful. Specific sorts of crimes were likely to be performed by witches, according to this tract. They were responsible for generative problems—they could cause men to be impotent, they could prevent conceptions and procure abortions in women. They also might kill newborns. They frequently attempted to dominate their husbands, which was a "natural vice" in women (Karlsen, 1987).

The witch-beliefs that the Puritans imported thus were strongly marked by fears of disruption of the Chain of Being, particularly of rebellion among women and damage caused to domesticated nature. The fear was that of tamed nature "going wild." Theologically and legally, the crime of witchcraft consisted in making a pact with the devil, whose supernatural power he lent to humans. With this power, a person could perform maleficium, that is, harm various parts of the natural order. She could cause disease, injury, or even death among humans and other animals. She could interfere with domestic processes such as dairying, brewing beer, and making cloth. Witches were also thought capable of causing disturbances in weather patterns—they could create droughts and storms at sea, for instance. Maleficium could be performed by look, by touch, and specifically, by curse.

Although invested with supernatural power, witches apparently refrained from certain kinds of harm, and specialized in others. They were not suspected of financial offenses such as theft, fraud, or embezzlement. In fact, they appeared unable to bring about good outcomes for themselves. It was not said that they increased the productivity of their own fields or domestic stocks; that they could weave superior fabrics or make finer butter, produce more food, or enhance the health of children, adults, or stock.

Rather, witches specifically engaged in actions that threatened to upset a natural hierarchy, to wreak havoc in domesticated nature—to unleash wild forces. The New England witch "was frequently suspected of causing illnesses or death, particularly to spouses or infants and young children." She also was likely to direct her malice toward domesticated animals—she could bewitch cows, horses, and swine—they would sicken and die, or simply wander off. She was often accused of "obstructing reproductive processes, either by preventing conceptions or by causing miscarriages, childbirth fatalities or 'monstrous' (deformed) births." She could procure abortions and cause impotence among men. She harmed domestic processes by spoiling beer in the brewing or making it disappear altogether. She could cause cows to stop giving milk and hens to lay fewer eggs. She could make spinning and weaving impossible (Karlsen, 1987).

If the Salem hysteria can be explained by Puritan uneasiness and fears during a period of political upheaval, as some have suggested (see, e.g., Erikson, 1966), it is clear from the nature of the accusations that these fears were of a specific sort. And if the high concentration of women among the accused can be explained in terms of misogyny and the desire to control women, as most feminist students of witchcraft have maintained (Daly, 1978; Ehrenreich & English, 1973; Karlsen, 1987), it is similarly clear from the nature of the accusations that women were thought to pose a particular kind of danger.

The Puritans had reserved an important and specific role for their women; and it is likely that female failure to fulfill their function was seen as extremely dangerous, in that one link in the Chain of Being broken, all else would disintegrate. Women were a part of wild nature that needed taming; once tamed, their role was to nurture. Men apparently realized that the creation of an inherently unfair and exploitative system carried within it the seeds of dissatisfaction and rebellion among the tamed. They expected women to rebel, and in their cosmology created an explanation for female dissatisfaction. Just as Eve had succumbed to the devil's wiles, so might other women. But Puritans did not fear self-aggrandizement on the part of the witches. Rather, they feared the vengeance of dissatisfied women. Insufficiently tamed women, it would appear, were the cause of fear. Untamed themselves, in league with the disruptive forces of wild nature, witches might unhook the carefully constructed Chain of Being.

ACCUSATIONS AGAINST THE SALEM WITCHES

The Salem hysteria began in the early months of 1692 when a number of young women were stricken with fits.[2] Reverend Samuel Parris's household contained a prepubescent daughter and a household servant, Tituba, from the West Indies. Elizabeth Parris, age 9, a number of preteen and teenage friends, and often, three older women gossiped and chatted in the Parris kitchen. Tituba, who knew the witchcraft of her native island, helped the girls to forecast their futures, focusing on the occupations of their future husbands. Later, Jonathan Hale was to blame the entire event on these seemingly innocent actions. He maintained that the girls in their "vain curiosity" had "tampered with the devil's tools" (as cited in Boyer & Nissenbaum, 1974, p. 23).

The most immediate result of this tampering was that the young girls became possessed. Their symptoms ranged from feelings of being pinched, pricked, and choked, to full-scale seizures. Two of the "circle girls" were epileptics (Gemmill, 1924, p. 48); the fits of the other girls were perhaps caused by ergot poisoning (Caporael, 1976) or the power of suggestion (Caulfield, 1943). Taken to the local doctor, they could neither be diagnosed nor cured by his arts, and he then declared that the cause was outside his profession. The appropriate jurisdiction was theological and legal.

Witchcraft was more than crime, although it was that—it was treason and heresy as well. And it was the most threatening offense in the Puritan world, because it was contagious. The authorities reacted promptly and predictably—they asked the girls to indicate who was bewitching them. Guided perhaps by the mother of one of the girls (Ann Putnam), who held grudges against some of her neighbors (Boyer & Nissenbaum, 1974; Gemmill, 1924), and by their own beliefs about just who a witch might be, the girls identified several local women—including, of course, Tituba, who confessed immediately. The hunt began.

In the pattern of the accusations, in the kinds of victims and offenders, and in the nature of the harm done, we begin to see what the Puritans feared. The power of maleficium was given by Satan himself, so Puritan officials were at pains to ascertain if the accused had actually made a pact with the devil. They looked for evidence of such a pact in confessions and in the testimony of witnesses that an accused had "signed the devil's book," had attended a witches' sabbath, or taken the devil's communion. Further, if a witness testified that an accused witch had urged her to engage in any of these actions, this testimony was evidence that the accused had attempted to seduce another human, drawing her, too, into the devil's snare, and therefore had obviously made a pact herself. Such evidence was produced for 77 percent of the accused women in our sample (see Table 1).

Entering into such a pact with the devil meant that a Puritan was in league with profane forces, unsanctioned authority. As a being who himself had rebelled against established authority, Satan was wild. Satan's fight with God was a rebellion against authority which

TABLE 1   Evidence of Pact

	Number	Percent
Confessing	7	20
Signing the devil's book	2	6
Attending the witch's sabbath	13	37
Taking the devil's communion	2	6
Seducing others	17	49
Total[a]	27	77

[a]In this and the following tables, totals will add to more than 100% because more than one form of evidence was brought for several of the witches.

TABLE 2   Evidence of Maleficium

	Number	Percent
Harming human beings	34	97
Assaulting circle girls	31	89
Assaulting others	20	57
Murdering	8	23
Harming domesticated nature	9	26
Damaging domestic production	1	3
Stopping domestic production	3	8.5
Damaging domesticated stock	9	26
Possessing supernatural powers	18	51
Flying through the air	6	17
Performing "impossible" physical feats	1	3
Predicting the future	2	6
Possessing poppets	7	20
Possessing familiars	10	29
Suckling familiars, having witch's teats	5	14

was carried out in the world—that is, within created nature. Thus, at the heart of the witches' crime was rebellion against hierarchical order and allegiance to an alternative force whose main purpose and power appeared to be the creation of chaos.

Maleficium directed at human beings was the most common charge in Salem, as it had been in England (Macfarlane, 1970, p. 154; Thomas, 1971, p. 539, who estimates that 70 to 80 percent of the victims were other humans). In our sample, 97 percent of the women accused were charged with assaulting or murdering humans (see Table 2).

Evidence for human harm began with and most usually involved evidence that the circle girls had been tortured by the accused. These girls were present in court and frequently went into fits when an accused entered the room. Eighty-nine percent of the accused women were charged with tormenting these girls. Since the medical profession had not been able to find a natural cause, these fits were continually attributed to supernatural actions by witches. Obviously, for Salem villagers, unexplained events were also uncontrollable events—and it was this lack of control that they feared. The first, and always the central, victims were the circle girls. They were the reliable indicators that an accused was actually a witch. In this regard, the age and gender of the victims and offenders is important.

There were ten circle girls; their ages ranged from 9 to 20, with a mean of 15.9 years (see Table 3). One of the oldest, Mary Warren, who was 20, was later accused of witchcraft herself, as were two of the older women present (Sarah Biber and Goody Pope). The accused were, for the most part, middle-aged women who were unmarried. Although the girls themselves could logically be accused, except for Warren (who confessed spontaneously, then later retracted her statements) they were not. Thus the pattern is that young, fertile, nulliparous women were assaulted by postfertile or unmarried women. Women who

TABLE 3   The Circle Girls

	Age
Elizabeth Parris	9
Abigail Williams	11
Ann Putnam	12
Mercy Lewis	17
Mary Walcott	17
Elizabeth Hubbard	17
Elizabeth Booth	18
Susan Sheldon	18
Mary Warren	20
Sarah Churchill	20

Note: In addition, three older women were often present: Sarah Bibber, Goodwife Pope, and Mrs. Ann Putnam (Gemmill, 1924).

were past the stage when their tamed fertility could be useful, apparently deliberately made fertile young women useless by making them wild.

The witches were thought to harm other humans as well, and 57 percent of them were accused of doing so, some (23 percent) to the point of death (see Table 2). These middle-aged women were also accused of harming domesticated nature. They were thought to be able to damage domestic processes. As Table 2 shows, 3 percent of our sample were accused of doing so. Mary Bradbury, for example, caused butter to go bad. They were also thought to stop production altogether, as when Elizabeth How caused the Perley's cow to stop giving milk. Altogether, 8.5 percent of the samples were so accused. They could damage or bewitch domestic stock, as 26 percent of them did. Sometimes the cattle, pigs, or draft animals sickened or died, and sometimes they went wild. One witch in our sample was accused of damaging an artifact—but, tellingly, one which kept tamed nature "inside": she was accused of using supernatural means to break a fence.

Evidence of maleficium also frequently took the form of testimony that the accused possessed superhuman powers. As can be seen from Table 2, such evidence was brought for 51 percent of the accused women. These women were thought to raise storms at sea, thus casting away vessels, as was thought of Mary Bradbury. They were believed to make hogs chase men, as Mary Parker was accused of doing. They were thought to create a light in a field that caused human accidents. Some of them, it was thought, could perform seemingly impossible feats, such as walking through the rain without becoming wet. Or, they could fly through the air or ride airborne on a broom. They could predict the future.

Some of the witches were believed to have worked their evil through a medium. They were accused of possessing "poppets"—small rag dolls in the image of an enemy, which when pricked with pins would cause the victim himself to suffer pain. Thirty-five percent of the women were accused of possessing "familiars," or suckling them. Familiars were small animals (dogs, cats, birds) that the devil sent to witches to aid them in doing their evil work. The familiar was believed to suckle the witch from a prenatural teat located somewhere on her body. Thus, when a witch was accused, a jury of same-gender townspeople was appointed to conduct a physical examination to determine if the witch possessed such a teat. The Salem villager who had a wart, mole, or hemorrhoid was in grave danger.

The role of the familiar was somewhat different from that of the poppet. Poppets were inert—the supernatural force somehow transferred itself from this image of the victim's body to the victim. Familiars had the added advantage that they could be sent on malefic missions—a small blue bird, a black puppy, or usually, a cat—would suddenly appear in the victim's home to torment him.

The witch's possession and use of natural and supernatural forces was threatening because it was assumed to be evil. Puritans were able to conceive of nature as saturated with supernatural forces only when such forces were evil. Why was this so?

The Puritan God was not within nature. He had made it, and existed outside and above it. As created, it was chaos and could only fulfill its telos when ordered into a Great Chain of Being, tamed and controlled from above, by man. In this manner all being was ordered to the Supreme Being in hierarchical fashion, through many layers of command and obedience. For the Puritans, there was thus only one appropriate relation to nature: to tame wild nature, order it to God, and nurture it in its tamed state. They could not conceive of working with nature, respecting its boundaries and limits, its right to be for itself. A careful observation of wild nature might allow one to predict its course. A respect for nature's own nature, for its limits and necessities, a capacity to "let grow and to make grow" (Mies, 1986) might yield human good by creating a harmonious relationship. Instead, for the Puritans, all of nature was first, wild: uncontrollable, unpredictable, unyielding, profane. Unless it was controlled and tamed, it was not only unfruitful, it was dangerous.

In possessing supernatural powers, it was thought that the witch used life forces to pervert the Chain of Being. She did not work against nature to control it. Rather than working to tame animals, she worked with wild animals to do evil. Rather than staying in her place, she flew through the air. Rather than contenting herself to whatever fate God ordained for her, calmly waiting for it to unfold, she attempted to discern the future.

Susanna Martin's case is quite typical.[3] This 72-year-old widow was accused by the circle girls, who ratified their accusations by falling into fits at her preliminary hearing. She did not help her case by laughing at their antics and declaring a lack of sympathy for them.

Martin was charged with assaulting the circle girls, and she was accused of harming others as well. Bernard Peach testified that she (or her spectral shape) entered his bedroom one Sunday night, took hold of his feet, and "drew my body into a whoope and lay upon me about an hour and one-half or two hours all of which time I could not stir or speak." He finally managed to bite three of her fingers. The next day he found her footprints and blood outside in the snow. She also apparently assaulted Elizabeth Brown, who when in her presence experienced a sensation "like birds pecking her leggs or picking her with the motion of their wings and . . . it would rise up into her stomach like a pricking payne as nayls and pinns . . . and it would rise up in her throat like a pullet's egg." She appeared in Jarvis Ring's bedchamber, lay upon him and bit his finger so hard that the mark "is still to be seen on the little finger on my right hand."

She was thought not only to have harmed humans, but to have harmed domesticated nature as well. In testimony against her, John Pressey claimed that she had bewitched his milk cattle and was capable of directing supernatural forces against him. On one occasion, he had become lost after dark and kept sighting a strange light. Frightened, he tried to strike the light with his stick, but after he gave it about "forty smart blows," he fell into a deep pit, yet "I do not know any such pit to be in the place where I was sliding into." Shortly thereafter, Susanna Martin appeared in exactly the place where the light had been. A few years later, she reviled him and his wife and claimed that he should never prosper. Specifically, she told them they would "never have but two cows" and "from that day to this we have never exceeded that number for something or other has prevented it."

John Kimball testified that he and the Martins had had a quibble about appropriate payment for a piece of land Kimball had bought from him. Kimball had offered them their choice of two cows and some other cattle but "did reserve two cows which I was not desirous to part with they being the first I ever had." Susanna threatened him in this way: "You had better [pay with those particular cows] for those will never do you no good." Kimball testified, "and so it came to pass that the next April following that very cow lay in the fair dry yard with her head to her side but stark dead; and a little while after another cow died and then an ox and then other cattle to the value of thirty pounds." In the same year Kimball desired to buy a puppy from her, but she would not let him have his choice from the litter, so he didn't agree to buy any. Upon hearing this, she said, "If I live, I'll give him puppies enough." A few days later he stumbled unaccountably upon some stumps in the woods. But soon he perceived the source of his difficulty—he was being attacked by several dark puppies, who were not hurt even when he cut them with his ax.

John Atkinson testified that Martin was angry with him because her son had traded one of their cows to him. When he went to the Martin place to receive the cow, she muttered and was unwilling that he should have the cow. When he took possession of it "notwithstanding the hamstringing and halting of her she was so mad that we could scarce get her but she broke all ropes fastened to her and we put the rope two or three times around a tree but she broke it and ran away and when she came down to the ferry we were forced to run up to our arms in water she was so fierce but after much ado we got her into the boat and she was so tame as any creature whatever."

On another occasion, William Osgood turned down the Martins when they asked him for a gift of beef. The next day one of his best cows went wild. And when Joseph Knight encountered her in the woods, his horses suddenly refused to cross a causeway—instead, they simply ran wild.

Other testimony suggested that she was a woman who could fly, walk in the rain without getting wet, and could change herself into the shape of a hog or a cat. And clearly she had made a pact with the devil because otherwise she would not possess such supernatural powers, nor would she have urged Mercy Lewis to sign the devil's book.

What did Puritans believe was the motive for such damage? The witches were asked repeatedly why they had bewitched the girls, but no satisfactory answer ever emerged. For other harms, a motive was sought and found. Usually, a witch who had harmed someone or someone's domestic production was seen to be displeased with that person. Just as Puritans believed that Satan was dissatisfied with his place, they believed some of their middle-aged women were similarly dissatisfied. Apparently, they were really frightened of this rebellion against authority and of the disruption in the Great Chain it signified.

This may explain why the officials were also interested in eliciting two other types of evidence. Table 4 shows that 34 percent of the women were accused of muttering after

TABLE 4 Evidence of Unseemly Behavior		
	Number	Percent
Muttering after begging	12	34
Using bad language/ill manners	8	23
Total	15	43

being refused some item for which they had begged, and 23 percent of possessing bad language or manners. Altogether, 43 percent of the women in the sample were accused of "unseemly behavior." Why were the Puritans interested in this type of evidence?

Muttering after begging might mean that the woman had actually placed a curse on the one who gave her offense. Some scholars have suggested that the real offense was not malefic witchcraft but abrasive behavior to the one who had refused, following on the heels of the refusal of neighborly aid. Thomas (1971) argues that in the most common situation, "the victim had been guilty of a breach of charity or neighborliness, by turning away an old woman who had come to the door to beg or borrow some food or drink, or the loan of some household utensil." Witch-beliefs implied that a neighborly obligation left unfulfilled might result in malefic witchcraft directed against the unneighborly person. Thomas suggests that the high percentage of women is most "plausibly explained by economic and social considerations, for it was the women who were the most dependent members of the community, and thus the most vulnerable to accusation" (Thomas, 1971, p. 553). Macfarlane's argument is similar, although he maintains that women predominated in the accusations because they were the most resistant to change, and their social position and power led to mounting hatred against them (Macfarlane, 1970).

These scholars refer to English witchcraft, but Boyer and Nissenbaum (1974) have made the same argument for Salem. They believe the accused were "on the move, socially and economically"; they were independent of the old social order. In their lack of willingness to accept their given station in life, they were typical of the emergent personality of citizens in a capitalist economy. The accusers represented the old order. "The social order was being profoundly shaken by a superhuman force which had lured all too many into active complicity with it. We have chosen to construe this force as emergent mercantile capitalism. Mather and Salem Village called it witchcraft" (Boyer & Nissenbaum, 1974, p. 209).

But this theory fails to explain why none of the men in our sample were accused of unseemly behavior and yet were accused of witchcraft. Nor does it explain why fewer than half of the accused female witches were accused of possessing bad manners, or why they were also accused of other depredations.

Rather, it seems the explanation may lie in the meaning of such behavior. Bad language or manners was evidence for rebellion against authority, the sign of a possible break in the Great Chain of Being. Six of the eight women accused of unmannerly behavior had been rude to a direct superior—a husband or a parent. The others were simply generally rude—but such testimony was always brought by a man.

The centrality of bad manners is demonstrated also by the evidence offered in defense of accused women. Testimony for Elizabeth How thus indicated that she was "neighborly," that she "carried it very well," that she never reviled anyone, that she had a courteous and peaceable disposition (Woodward, 1864/1969, p. 78). Wild women were dangerous. Just by looking, touching, or cursing, just by being in the same room with domesticated pubescents, they were thought to be able to make tamed nature go wild.

The males in this sample are quite different from the women who were accused. For all thirteen, evidence was brought that they had afflicted the circle girls, and five of them were accused of harming other humans. But only one of them harmed domestic nature in any way, and none was accused of unseemly, unmannerly, or unruly behavior. The most striking thing about the male witches is their atypicality. Apart from George Burroughs, a former Puritan minister who was believed to be the Satanic priest officiating at the sabbaths (where, of course, a priest was necessary) and a deputy sheriff (John Willard), who was probably accused because he was publicly sympathetic to those he was forced to jail, 72 percent (eight of eleven) of the accused men were relatives of accused female witches. Thus, as John Demos has suggested (1970, p. 1311), they "belonged to a kind of derivative category."

The only truly typical witch among the men was Samuel Wardwell. About 55 years of age at the time of the hysteria, Wardwell owned a little farm and "for many years had been a fortune teller, strolling about, reading palms and solving life's mysteries from the broken tea leaves in the bottom of the cup" (Gemmill, 1924, p. 185). His rather high success rate at this enterprise was part of his undoing. Accused and jailed, he promptly confessed. He claimed that he was able to control animal nature—he could banish wild creatures from his fields by "bidding the devil to take" them, and he could make domesticated stock "come round about and follow me." Wardwell later retracted his confession, whereupon he was tried, convicted, and hanged (Gemmill, 1924; Woodward, 1864/1969).

Reflection on the patterns formed by the evidence brought against witches and by their age and gender leads us to select as symbol and metaphor of witch fears the unfortunate Sarah Biber. A middle-aged woman who gossiped in the Parris kitchen with the circle girls, perhaps participating in their fortune telling, Biber was never accused of maleficium, or indeed of having made a pact with the devil. She was accused of "often quarreling with her husband," during which quarrels she "would call him very bad names," and of behaving in an unnurturing manner toward her children. "She wished that when her child fell into the river she had never pulled it out." Three of the four men who testified against her cited her "unruly, turbulent spirit" (Woodward, 1864/1969, pp. 203–205). Apparently, Sarah Biber's sole crime was her wildness.

WILDERNESS AND CRIMINAL JUSTICE

At its birth, philosophers justified the modern criminal justice system as a device to tame the naturally wild instincts of human beings. Its necessity was recognized when men became "weary of living in a continual state of war," as Beccaria wrote (1963, p. 11), following Hobbes's (1651/1947, p. 31) assumption that all mankind possessed "a perpetual and restless desire for power after power, that ceaseth only in death."

Contemporary criminologists often retain this frightening vision of nature as wildly dangerous. Travis Hirschi (1969, p. 31) finds no need to search for motivations to crime because "we are all animals and thus all naturally capable of committing criminal acts."

Our modern criminal justice system is permeated with this view—that only when nature is controlled is it safe. Erikson (1966) says of it that we have inherited from the

Puritans an assumption that "the convict's soul is permanently depraved and that sin is an inevitable part of his personal endowment." In light of this model of the convicted criminal as inherently wild, it "makes very little sense to . . . reform him. . . . The best one can do for him is to contain his reprobate spirit, in much the same way that one tames the wilder instincts of animals. . . . The object [of criminal justice] is not to improve his nature but to harness it so completely that it cannot assert itself" (p. 203).

What legacy then, did the witch hysteria of 1692 and the Puritan criminal justice system's handling of it bequeath to us? What did Puritans think their purpose was? How successful were they in achieving it? How successful is the contemporary criminal justice system in achieving this same purpose?

Puritans were intensely frightened by two kinds of wilderness—that in the forests surrounding them at the edges of their carefully cultivated fields and neat towns, and that which was within human nature (and especially female human nature). Both kinds of wilderness were evil precisely because they were wild.

"Seventeenth century writing is permeated with the idea of wild country as the environment of evil," Nash (1982, p. 36) tells us. "The new world wilderness was linked with a host of monsters, witches and similar supernatural beings" (p. 29). The wilderness was evil because it had not been ordered to the patriarchal God; it was seen not only as uncontrolled, but as the location of rival religion. A "dark wilderness cave" was believed to be the site of pagan rites, and the native Americans were "not merely heathens but active disciples of the devil" (pp. 33–36). For Puritans, "the untamed forests and the Indians that lurked in their shadows represented fallen nature inhabited by the powers of darkness" (Ruether 1983, p. 81). The wild evil of nature outside the village and farm was echoed in human nature as well. The Puritan mission thus involved both "an inner battle over that 'desolate and outgrowne wildernesse of humain nature' and on the New England frontier it also meant conquering wild nature" (Nash, 1982, p. 36). In the crime of witchcraft, these two wildernesses came together in wild women who used their evil power to make tamed nature wild, too. The Puritan "errand into the wilderness" (Miller, 1956) was a mission that would bring Godly order out of a natural chaotic fecundity. Only through a project of taming could they bring fertility under control.

The criminal justice response to witchcraft focused on women apparently because it was precisely among women that the relationship to nature was wrong. Fearful of the wild in nature and in human beings, knowing no way to deal with these fears other than by creating an orderliness based upon hierarchical control, Puritan justice announced in the witch trials that which it absolutely would not tolerate. The idea of women embodied, and some of their own middle-aged widows exemplified, what Puritans feared most. Where in the natural world there is harmony based upon each creature's capacity to be for-itself and simultaneously for-the-whole, the Puritan mind saw chaos. They sought to replace the "for-itself" and "for-the-whole" of nature with a system of nature-for-man and man-for-God, ordered in hierarchical neatness through a Great Chain of (Patriarchal) Being.

In the witches, Puritans saw wild creatures independent of the Great Chain, immersed in untamed natural processes: pure chaos, pure evil. What they tried to kill in Puritan women, all Puritan women, when they hanged the witches, was a particular relationship to the created world and its fertility—a metaphysic and an epistemology diametrically opposed to their own. Were they successful?

As a boundary maintenance device (Erikson, 1966), the witch trials were certainly successful. The Puritans sacrificed a few middle-aged widows, who were not particularly useful to them in any case. But the effect of trying, imprisoning, and hanging the witches was to send a message to all the Puritans, especially to the women. Henceforth, gossiping in a group of women, having a close or familiar relationship with animals, and observing nature's ways in a respectful manner that would allow prediction of the future would be dangerous. Fertility in women and in nature would be subjected to strict masculine design and control—and where it went wild, it would be criminally punished. Were the Puritans successful in bequeathing to their descendants a metaphysic, or epistemology, and a criminal justice system that would continue to control unruly feminine nature?

CONTEMPORARY WITCHCRAFT: THE CRIMINAL JUSTICE SYSTEM RESPONSE

> The . . . Great Chain of Being has been converted into a Becoming . . . [and] God himself is . . . identified with this Becoming. But the inversion . . . while it converts the Scale of Being into an abstract ideal schema, does not alter its essential character. (Lovejoy, 1936/1953, p. 326)

Americans no longer hunt witches in the fashion of their Puritan ancestors. But the fear of wild nature and the intense desire to tame it for human benefit (the source of the hysteria in Salem) is still strong. Having lopped off the top of the Great Chain of Being, postmoderns have neither God nor telos to guide and restrain their interactions with nature. Instead, a "neutral," scientific technology informs our actions. Nature now tends toward no other end than to be molded by men in power to their current benefit. For while the notion of the Great Chain of Being is now identified with evolution itself and inverted so that the tendency toward diversity and fullness is seen to arise from the bottom of the hierarchy, spontaneously rather than as a deliberate plan from the top, its danger to women and nature is not lessened, but perhaps increased. If there is a God in these first years of the third millennium, He is science: now seen as capable of altering evolution itself, to the special benefit of those men currently in power.

For the patriarchal mind, wild women and wild nature still pose a significant threat to orderly, male-controlled production and reproduction. Sometimes this threat is met with a criminal justice system response, as it was in Salem Village.

Human reproduction was a significant concern of the Puritan witch hunters, who blamed female witches for abortions (both spontaneous and induced), "monstrous births," and untimely deaths from disease in young children. Exertion of male control over human reproduction is still a vital concern, as evidenced in the following recent developments: the debate over the fate of frozen embryos and their possible use for stem cell research, proposed legislation to prohibit "partial birth" abortions and to protect the "unborn victims of violence," and the first homicide conviction of a crack-using mother.

While criminal charges of various sorts have for some time been brought against crack-using pregnant women whose fetuses are harmed, the May 2001 conviction of Regina McKnight was the first conviction for homicide (Firestone, 2001). The prosecutor noted that he wanted to send a message "not to use crack cocaine" (Gaston, 2001), but the message he appeared to send was that all women have a legal duty to maintain their health during pregnancy according to government standards. Consider, for example, whether use of a physician-prescribed Food and Drug Administration–approved drug, which killed a fetus, would result in a homicide charge against either the doctor or the drug company. The issue here is not drug use, but control of drug use.

The debate over partial birth abortions and that surrounding the use of embryos for stem cell research share a commonality. They reveal the extent to which, consciously or unconsciously, patriarchy denies woman's bodily integrity in its willingness to use her for male-controlled reproduction. Many proponents of stem cell research are antiabortion. Their justification for the seeming inconsistency is illuminating. They make the argument that stem cell research on frozen embryos that "will be discarded anyway" is appropriate because the embryos cannot be brought to viability. The inescapable conclusion is that a pregnant woman has an obligation to carry the child to term (and perhaps to rear it). But frozen embryos are deemed fair game even to experiment with. It is judged morally appropriate to use them for the benefit of other humans, even if they are "human life" (Wilson, 1996).

Here the issue clearly is not the status of the embryo as a "human being from conception." Rather, the issue is who gets to control its fate. If inside a woman, it is deemed "capable of viability." If in a petri dish where no woman can be used to bring it to term, it not only can be destroyed but can be used to make cells for other humans' health needs. The inconsistency becomes a consistency. One can use women as incubators; one can use embryos to harvest stem cells. These are both under patriarchal control. Like the Salem witches, postmodern women are not allowed to be free and in control of their own bodies.

Similarly, the proposed Unborn Victims of Violence Act of 2001 criminalizes "killing or injuring an 'unborn child' during the commission of a separate federal crime. The language of the bill defines 'unborn children' as members of the human species who reside in their mothers' wombs, regardless of their developmental stage" (Colb, 2001). It finds criminal wrong not just in violation of a woman's bodily integrity and security, which an assault charge would accommodate; rather, it focuses on the life she might possibly be carrying and makes criminally liable an assailant who may have no knowledge of his "victim's" existence.

In all of these instances an embryo inside a woman is controlled by other than the woman herself; its effect on her is deemed immaterial. Similar to the homicide prosecution of a crack user, the woman is not allowed to determine what to do. Clearly, the issue is as much control of her body as it is the fate of the fetus. And it is similar in regard to nonhuman nature—women are still told how to interact with nonhuman nature. As well (and consistent with patriarchy's general plan), senior men may tell junior men how to interact with nonhuman nature. Thus, Vice-President Cheney's views on the environment trump those of both deep and shallow ecologists.

Domestic production is still done by women under male control. Rather than working with nature to protect humans from food poisoning, our system features farmers who raise and sell dangerous food produced unnaturally and food experts who advise housewives to overcook meat and eggs. Corporate experts prescribe antibiotic soap for "safe" kitchens, ignoring the lessons Rachel Carson taught us regarding evolution of the microbe (see Wilson, 1998). Carson's vilification by patriarchal experts (Hynes, 1989) put her in the company of the Salem witches.

Patriarchy still does not allow women to work with nature, but instead, prescribes after-the-fact control of a nature spoiled by patriarchal uses. Even environmental law is after-the-fact control (Wilson, 2001). As in Salem, neither nature nor woman can be wild. As with stem cells, if there is a "need," a patriarchally controlled use for nature, it trumps any prior "right" of nature to bodily integrity and its own "purposes." Currently proposed uses include oil in ANWAR and the cloning of nonhuman animals. World trade also trumps ecoprotection.

As in Salem, the desire is total control, an orderly hierarchical arrangement of fecundity. The Puritans sacrificed some of their middle-aged women to further their project of taming. Today, it is still powerless women who suffer, although they may not be executed as witches.

Perhaps twenty-first-century Americans have no more need than did our seventeenth-century ancestors to punish wild women for its immediate effect. Perhaps, now as then, the crucial effect of the criminal justice process is a boundary maintenance that tames all women, bringing their fertility under control, ordering it into a neat hierarchical Great Chain of (patriarchal) Being.

NOTES

1. "And God said [to man], Be fruitful, and multiply, and replenish the earth, and subdue it: and have dominion over every living thing that moveth upon the earth."
2. Information on the specific charges leveled at the witches comes from Woodward's (1864/1969) *Records of Salem Witchcraft*. Woodward collected and compiled material from preliminary hearings which includes testimony of witnesses, victims, and the accused. Woodward's records are incomplete but provide us with a sample of forty-eight accused persons, thirteen men and thirty-five women. The tables in this section are based only on the women. Later, there is a separate discussion of the accused men.
3. Evidence on Susanna Martin's case comes from Woodward (1864/1969, pp. 193ff.) and Gemmill (1924, pp. 114ff.).

REFERENCES

ADLER, M. (1986). *Drawing down the moon*. Boston: Beacon Press.

BECCARIA, C. (1963). *On crimes and punishment*. New York: Macmillan.

BOYER, P., & NISSENBAUM, S. (1974). *Salem possessed*. Cambridge, MA: Harvard University Press.

CAPORAEL, L. R. (1976, April 2). Ergotism: The satan loosed in Salem? *Science, 192*.

CAULFIELD, E. (1943, May). Pediatric aspects of the Salem witchcraft tragedy. *American Journal of Diseases of Children, 65*.

COLB, S. F. (2001). Why the Senate should refuse even to consider the Unborn Victims of Violence Act of 2001. Retrieved from http://www.Findlaw.com/colb/20010606.html.

DALY, M. (1978). *Gyn/ecolgy*. Boston: Beacon Press.

DEMOS, J. (1970, June). Underlying themes in the witchcraft of 17th century New England. *American Historical Review, 75*.

EHRENREICH, B., & ENGLISH D. (1973). *Witches, midwives and nurses: A history of women healers*. New York: Feminist Press.

ERIKSON, K. (1966). *Wayward Puritans*. New York: Wiley.

FIRESTONE, D. (2001). Woman is convicted of killing her fetus by smoking cocaine. Retrieved from http://www.nytimes.com/2001/01/18/national/18FETU.html.

GASTON, E. (2001). Drug user convicted of abuse in fetal death. Retrieved from http://www. thesunnews.com/content/myrtlebeach/2001/05/17/localA01-2092156.htm.

GEMMILL, W. N. (1924). *The Salem witch trials*. Chicago: AC McClurg.

HANSEN, C. (1968, April). Salem witches and DeForest's Witching Times. *Essex Institute Historical Collections, 104.*

HIRSCHI, T. (1969). *Causes of delinquency*. Berkeley: University of California Press.

HOBBES, T. (1947). *Leviathan*. New York: Macmillan. (Original work published 1651)

HYNES, H. P. (1989). *The recurring silent spring*. New York: Pergamon Press.

KARLSEN, C. F. (1987). *The devil in the shape of a woman: Witchcraft in colonial New England*. New York: Norton.

KRAMER, H., & SPRENGER J. (1948). *Malleus maleficarum* (Montague Summers, Trans.). Magnolia, MA: Peter Smith Publishing. (Original work published 1486)

LEWIS, C. S. (1988). The abolition of man. In L. W. Dorset (Ed.), *The essential C. S. Lewis*. New York: Collier. (Original work published 1943)

LOVEJOY, A. O. (1953). *The great chain of being*. Cambridge, MA: Harvard University Press. (Original work published 1936)

MACFARLANE, A. (1970). *Witchcraft in Tudor and Stuart England*. London: Routledge & Kegan Paul.

MERTON, T. (1978). Wilderness and paradise. In *The Monastic Journey*. New York: Image Books.

MIES, M. (1986). *Patriarchy and accumulation on a world scale*. London: Zed Books.

MILLER, P. (1956). *Errand into the wilderness*. Cambridge, MA: Harvard University Press.

MURRAY, M. A. (1921). *The witch cult in western Europe*. New York: Oxford University Press.

NASH, R. (1982). *Wilderness and the American mind*. New Haven, CT: Yale University Press.

POPE, A. (1733). *Essay on man*.

RUETHER, R. R. (1983). Woman, body and nature. In *Sexism and God-talk: Toward a feminist theology*. Boston: Beacon Press.

STARHAWK. (1989). *The spiral dance: A rebirth of the ancient religion of the great goddess*. San Francisco: Harper & Row.

THOMAS, K. (1971). *Religion and the decline of magic*. London: Weidenfeld and Nicholson.

TREVOR-ROPER, H. R. (1970). The European witchcraze and social change. In M. Marwick (Ed.), *Witchcraft and sorcery*. New York: Penguin Books.

TURNER, F. J. (1920). *The frontier in American history*. New York: Krieger.

WHITE, L. JR. (1967, March 10). The historical roots of our ecological crisis. *Science, 155,* 1203–1207.

WILSON, N. K. (1996). An ecofeminist critique of environmental criminal law. In S. M. Edwards, T. D. Edwards, & C. B. Fields (Eds.), *Environmental crime and criminality: Theoretical and practical issues*. New York: Garland.

WILSON, N. K. (1998, November). *Food fights: Libeling, labeling and the social construction of food poisoning*. Paper prepared for presentation to the American Society for Criminology, Washington, DC.

WILSON, N. K. (2001). Environmental crime and justice. In M. A. DuPont-Morales, M. K. Hooper, & J. H. Schmidt (Eds.), *Handbook of criminal justice administration*. New York: Marcel Dekker.

WOODWARD, W. E. (1969). *Records of Salem witchcraft*. New York: DeCapo Press. (Original work published 1864)

3

Feminist Theories

Are They Needed?

Roslyn Muraskin

Historically, most criminological theories have been developed by and for men. It appears that "the extent of female crime is consistently obscured relative to the incidence, severity, and awareness of male criminality" (Shipley & Arrigo, 2004). As female crime increases, there exists the need to understand why. Are women as gentle as they have been described to be or are they capable of becoming hard-core criminals? The latter appears to be the answer. Feminism has challenged the overall *masculinized* nature of criminology by pointing to the repeated omission and misrepresentation of women in criminological inquiry. This chapter explores the thoughts of the theorists and how and if they apply to women.

If we look at the case of Andrea Yates who killed her five children and attempted unsuccessfully to present the defense of postpartum syndrome, do we conclude that she was/is mentally ill or a cold-blooded murderer who got up one day and set out to kill? "[W]hen women deviate substantially from their status as wife or mother, adopting instead a life of violent crime, they are deemed especially corrupt or evil" (Shipley & Arrigo, 2004). Of course in the case of Andrea Yates, the decision was overturned as a result of the failure of the prosecution's psychologist to give a truthful statement regarding the show *Law and Order*, where it was stated that there was a similar case presented, and that Yates was an ardent fan. Today, under psychiatric treatment, Yates awaits either a new trial or a new decision.

According to Belknap (1996), criminology is concerned with the development of those theories that show the cause and effect of crime. The field of criminal justice focuses on workers "in the criminal justice system and how decisions are made about victims and offenders" (p. xi). Belknap refers to invisibility as a universal criteria of women as offenders as well as victims.

When we review criminological theory with regard to women we look at biological influences whereas with men we have traditionally looked at economic and sociological factors. If we look at crime statistics, we tend to believe that black offenders are more likely to be sex offenders. When we talk about sexual victimization, we conclude that women need protection for their own good, and therefore women are not to work in those jobs which have physical attributes considered dangerous, such as policing.

James Messerschmidt (1993), in his work *Masculinities and Crime*, does some rethinking of feminist theories by addressing the impact of gender not merely on the criminality of women but that of men as well. His definition of social structure is "regular patterned forms of interaction over time that constrain and channel behavior in specific ways" (p. 378). In their research of both male and female offenders, Kathleen Daly and Meda Chesney-Lind (1988) spotlight women's individual pathways to breaking the law: street women, harmed and harming women, battered women, drug-connected women, and what they refer to as "other."

According to Sarri (1979), women's prior victimization places the human race at risk for offending as our prisons appear to be disproportionately populated with women of color. It appears that we as a society permit women to drift into the field of crime in order for them to survive, thereby ending up in correctional facilities that take better care of them than any welfare agency.

It is no secret who commits the majority of crime: men. It appears from all the research and the statistics provided that men and boys do perpetuate the more conventional crimes and the more serious of these crimes than women and girls, or so it appears historically. Gender has always been used by criminologists as the strongest indicator of who commits what crime. Theoretical works appear to have been gender blind, believing that men and boys should be the norm to be studied, not women and girls.

Traditionally, as men and boys have continued to be the "normal" subject studied, the gender content of women's legitimate and illegitimate behavior has been virtually ignored. The question often asked is "why is it that women do not offend?" Of course, they have and do. All this has resulted in an arrogant, biologically based misrepresentation of women. The fact that the study of women and girls has attracted the attention of criminologists as a special category explains the gendered nature of crime.

Feminism has challenged the overall masculinized nature of criminology by pointing to the repeated omission and misrepresentation of women in criminological inquiry.

Robert Merton's theory of anomie (1938) suggests that there is a lack of it in U.S. society because of the culturally defined goals (economic success as measured by monetary rewards) and the socially structured legitimate means (education and paid work) to achieve these goals. It is the "American Dream" to strive for economic success, while distributing unequally the legitimate opportunities to succeed. Though Merton's theory of anomie has attracted many to explain the class differences in crime, and it has been seen as "perhaps the consummate male theory of deviant behavior," anomie theory is clearly inadequate for comprehending the high gender ratio and gendered character of crime. Assuming that economic opportunities have been less available to women than men, and that women appear to strive for the same or similar goals as men, if we were to pursue the logic of Merton's argument, in reality there should be more crime by women and less by men.

If we turn to control theory of Travis Hirschi (1969), we find here, too, it is incapable of deciphering the gendered nature of crime. The majority of criminological theories uses conformity as the norm and concentrates on explaining criminal behavior. Such theorists generally inquire as to why people offend, and then proceed to use men and boys as their subjects as being the norm. Hirschi's control theory makes the assumption that crime is normal and it is conformity that becomes problematic. He differs from traditional criminology by asking why people conform. Society, according to Hirschi, has developed ways of controlling its members by inhibiting their "drive" to deviate.

Hirschi has identified four factors as being critical to the control of deviation: (1) *attachment* to parents, schools and peers; (2) *commitment* to conventional lines of action; (3) *involvement* in conventional activities; and, (4) *belief* in conventional values. In order to address the gendered nature of crime then, control theory would have to show that women and girls maintain higher levels of commitment to conventional activities, values, and people than do men and boys. As a result of such a commitment, women and girls would engage in higher levels of legitimate behavior. But no such data are presented by Hirschi. What is curious is that Hirschi started out by studying both boys and girls, but for some unexplained reason he concentrated his studies on boys and men. As the obvious substantially more law-abiding gender, especially considering Hirschi's "own argument that criminologists should reorient their thinking by making conformity, rather than criminality, the central object of study" (Hirschi, 1969), his theory as conceptualized becomes incapable of explaining why men and boys engage in more crime than do women and girls.

Next is labeling theory. Because of continuous labeling, primary deviants eventually accept their labeled identity as deviant, thereby acting in accordance with the societal reaction. This means that they are well on their way to a career in secondary deviation.

For labeling theorists to acquire a deviant self-image from labeling is determined by one's own power to counteract potential labeling contacts. According to Edwin Schur (1965), "those with the least power are most susceptible to deviating," while those with social power of sorts are the ones who will be much more able to "avoid initial identification as a deviator, and to avoid or reduce stigma even after being so identified," and to "influence the outcome in the course of official 'processing.'" Given the fact that men exercise greater power in society than women and following the logic of labeling theory, men should therefore have increased opportunity to counteract official labeling, thus resulting in a lower rate of crime than for women.

It was the work of Caesar Lombroso (1895) that set the stage for asking why it is that women do not offend. Lombroso is well known for his strict biological determinism, and thus his conception of the *born criminal*, or individuals whose atavistic qualities indicated a throwback to earlier evolutionary periods. It was Lombroso who collected data on a sample of men who were incarcerated and then compared them to a control group of soldiers. According to Lombroso, since the group of prisoners had more "atavistic" characteristics than did the soldiers—enormous jaws, high cheekbones, prominent superciliary arches, and handle-shaped ears—criminals could thus be identified and categorized simply from observing and counting their "degenerative physical stigmata" (Smart, 1976, p. 33).

Lombroso (1911) stated that "all statistics show that women are much less criminal than men." In the *Female Offender*, Lombroso and his son-in-law, William Ferrero (1895), concluded that women's lesser criminality is explained by their "piety, maternity, want of passion, sexual coldness, weakness and an undeveloped intelligence." It shows that when women do commit crime, it is significantly different from those of men, primarily because of women's biological makeup:

> That women are less often engaged in highway robbery, murder, homicide, and assault is due to the very nature of the feminine constitution. To conceive an assassination, to make ready for it, to put it into execution demands a certain energy and a certain combination of intellectual functions. In this sort of development women almost always fall short of men. It seems on the other hand that the crimes that are habitual to them are those which require a smaller degree of physically and intellectual force, and such especially are receipt of stolen goods, poisoning, abortion and infanticide. (Smart, 1976)

What Lombroso did was similar to all other criminological theorists: He constructed a general theory of crime based on men. Eventually he was to understand that such a theory could not be applied to both men and women. Lombroso maintained that "the born female criminal makes up for what she lacks in relative numbers by the excess vileness and cruelty of her crimes" (Smart, 1976, p. 3).

It was Sigmund Freud, both a physician and psychiatrist, whose theories based on the unconsciousness were a great influence on female criminality. His theory claimed that women were biologically inferior to their male counterparts. "In particular, he asserted that female offenders were passive, narcissistic, and masochistic as a result of a masculinity complex or as a consequence of penis envy" (Freud, 1963). It was Freud's belief that "women were unable to resolve the oedipal conflict, leaving them less in control over their impulses. As such, they were motivated by sentiments of 'jealousy, immorality, emotionalism, and bad judgment" (Flowers, 1994, p. 67). Additionally, Freud believed that anatomical deficiencies (e.g., relative size, strength, dexterity) predisposed women to immorality (Shipley & Arrigo, 2004).

It was William I. Thomas (1969) who linked "the social environment to a woman's proclivity for criminality." It was his belief that many of the gender differences were a direct result of "social and cultural influences rather than biological differences, although biology was seen as playing an important role. . . . [Thomas] argued that female criminality was a socially induced pathology, steeped in instinctive processes rather than biologically predetermined states. . . . the wish or desire for new experiences significantly impacted female criminality" (Pollock, 1999). "More specifically, he maintained that *wishes*, as derived from biological instincts, could be socialized to achieve appropriate goals. . . . [Thomas] alleged that the intense need to give and feel love frequently led women to adopt criminal patterns of behavior, especially in relation to sexual offenses (e.g., prostitution)" (Shipley & Arrigo, 2004. p. 5).

The socialists were the first to introduce the idea that crime under capitalism is, in part, correlated to economic conditions. It was in their eagerness to identify the economic forces that encouraged such crimes as prostitution, that socialist theorists denied women any role other that that of a passive victim. It was the assumption of the socialist movement, as well as other criminologists of the time, that any sex outside of marriage was both improper and degrading, and that no right woman would or could choose prostitution. Socialists focused on how a capitalist economic system could turn "good" women into "bad" women, thus damaging their prospects for marriage and proper childhood.

Bonger (1969), who was considered a socialist criminologist, proposed an explanation of why women commit less crime than men. In his discussion on strength and courage, he concluded that the average woman of our time has less strength and courage than the average man, and consequently, commits on the average fewer crimes than he. He also held the belief that women are not involved in what were typically sexual crimes because of their nature and their very being. He believed that when it came to sex, women were more passive while men were more active. Bonger failed to offer any reason for this theory other than to imply an inherent quality. This became apparent as well in his portrayal of women as lacking in courage, and therefore engaging in less property crime. Women would engage in areas of prostitution because of its profitability. Bonger felt that because working-class women work outside the home in the paid labor market, it was their children who became demoralized.

> The development of capitalism has led to the paid labor of married women, and consequently to one of the most important causes of the working class. When there is no one to watch a child, when he is left to himself, he becomes demoralized.

He concluded that if women were home, where they were supposed to be, children would not become demoralized, and young girls would not become prostitutes. Bonger did not regard wage labor by men and the onset of the dissolution of the family as the agency of child socialization. He objected to the removal of women from the family to work, but accepted men and husbands as having to go out to work, and therefore not the cause of any failures of the family.

In 1950, Otto Pollack addressed the high gender ratio of crimes in a manner that was significantly different than that of both Lombroso and Bonger. Lombroso and Bonger argued that women's biology created a "weaker sex" resulting is less crime being committed by women. Pollack argued that women's crime most likely equaled that of men's, but because of the biology of women interacting with certain social conditions, "the criminality of women is largely masked criminality" (Smart, 1976, p. 47). Pollack believed that women were addicted to crimes that were easily concealed (e.g., shoplifting, thefts by prostitutes, domestic thefts, abortion, and perjury). Accordingly, the crimes that women commit would be underreported. Also, because of the nature of women's biology, women were more prone than men to be deceitful. In Pollack's mind this criminal concealment on the part of women was a result of the biological fact that a man "must achieve an erection in order to perform the sex act and will not be able to hide his failure," yet for the woman:

> Lack of orgasm does not prevent her ability to participate in the sex act. It cannot be denied that this basic psychological difference may well have a great influence on the degree of confidence which the two sexes have in the possible success of concealment and thus on their character pattern in this respect. (Smart, 1976)

Additionally, Pollack felt that as women conceal their monthly menstruation, the biology of women and its impact on sexuality make the factor of concealment and misrepresentation in the eyes of women a socially required and commendable act, and must condition them to a different attitude toward sincerity than men. It was because of woman's social position in society that they more often than not were accomplices than perpetrators of crime. Pollack argued further that the division of labor placed women in the primary role of homemaker and mother, which furnished women the many occasions to commit crimes in ways and by means not available to men, thus lessening the public character of many crimes. It was this social position that helped keep women's crimes hidden from public view.

Another factor that entered into the picture was that of chivalry:

> One of the outstanding concomitants of the existing general protective attitude of man toward women . . . [is that] men hate to accuse women and thus indirectly to send them to their punishment. Police officers dislike to arrest them, district attorneys to prosecute them, judges and juries to find them guilty, and so on. (Pollack, 1950)

It was John Hagan's (1989) power-control theory that integrated some feminist insights into a framework for understanding youth crime by young girls, and developing a criminological theory that was to take gender seriously as an explanatory variable. Hagan asserted that working in a position of authority within the paid labor market would automatically translate into power and authority within the home. Though economic independence for women was a first step toward equality with men, it did not guarantee a reduction in gender power and authority within the home. The conclusion drawn was that the power-control theory and mother's liberation cause daughters to go out and commit crimes. Those women who defy traditional femininity by working outside the home in the paid labor market increase the chance that their daughters will become delinquent. In spite of women's labor force participation rate, it appears that this increase has not been evident.

If we compare Hirschi's control theory with Hagan's power-control theory the covert masculine nature of criminological theory becomes evident. In Hirschi's mind, his conforming boy is depicted as an admirable character who is energetic, intelligent, and denotes a rational being. But when we review the conforming girl in Hagan's theory we discover

> a grey and lifeless creature. She is passive, compliant and dependent. Gone is Hirschi's rational and responsible agent, intelligently evaluating the risks and costs of crime. Conformity is now described as "compliance". The law abiding female is biddable rather than responsible. Hagan's female seems unable to construct complex and caring relationships even with her mother who subjects her to her control. She is merely the "object" of her mother's instrumental training to be compliant. Hagan is explicit about the status of the female as a manipulated thing. (Hagan, 1989, pp. 788–816)

Summing up, both Hirschi and Hagan perpetuate what criminology has continuously done, and that is to devalue women and girls, and place a higher value on men and boys, even when both exhibit the same social behavior.

Others believe that women have not only been misrepresented in criminology's efforts to understand the gendered nature of crime, but for the most part, have been omitted entirely from criminological discourse. Understanding that theoretical criminology has been developed by and for men, the theories are not up to the analytical task of explaining female crime, if in fact we need separate theories. The theories as developed are reflective not of *all* human behavior but of male behavior alone. Regardless, it does not mean that those theories explain fully why men commit crimes.

Edwin Sutherland (1939) argued that through the use of interaction and communication within certain intimate personal groups, individuals learn the techniques, the motives, the needed drives, as well as the rationalizations plus the attitudes necessary to commit crime. Sutherland believed that criminal behavior is learned in the same manner that conforming behavior is learned. A particular person comes to engage in criminal behavior "because of an excess of definitions favorable to violations of law over definitions unfavorable to violations of law." Therefore, individuals become criminals because their associations with behavioral patterns which are criminal far outweigh their association with noncriminal behavior patterns in terms of frequency, duration, priority, and intensity. It was around 1947 that Sutherland attempted to explain why boys engage more frequently in criminal acts than girls. It was his argument that boys engaged in more crime than girls due to the differences in supervision of each. He asserted that as boys and girls live in the same poverty-ridden neighborhoods, social environment does not

> explain the relatively high rate of boy delinquency and relatively low rate of girl delinquency. The significant difference is that girls are supervised more carefully and the behavior in accordance with social codes taught them with greater care and consistency than is the case with boys. From infancy girls are taught that they must be nice, while boys are taught that they must be rough and tough; a boy who approaches the behavior of girls is regarded as a "sissy". This difference in care and supervision presumably rested originally on the fact that the female sex is the one which becomes pregnant. (p. 21)

Thus, Sutherland's work asserted that whether a boy turns to a life of delinquency rests on the assumption that socialization is grounded ultimately in the biological differences between men and women, boys and girls.

According to the works of Parsons (1964), "dichotomous sex roles structure the family," meaning that the "instrumental" role involves goal attainment, focusing on the relationship between family and society taken as a whole, whereas the "expressive" role involves the integration on both the internal structure and functions of the family. The family unit prepares children for adequate participation in society by teaching them the appropriate sex roles (i.e., masculine or instrumental and feminine or expressive). Therefore when children are socialized into their proper sex roles, society remains stable over generations.

Parsons used this functionalist perspective in the early 1940s to explain why boys turn to acts of delinquency. It was his thesis that in the family girls are more apt to be relatively docile, to conform in general according to adult expectations to be "good," whereas boys are more apt to be recalcitrant to discipline and defiant of adult authority and expectations. When a girl is physically able she begins a direct apprenticeship as a female adult, forming a feminine identification with the mother. It was Parsons's contention that women were inferior to men, and therefore to grow up like a woman was shameful for any man. It is this reaction-formation and resulting compulsive masculinity that creates a strong "tendency for boyish behavior to run in anti-social if not directly destructive directions, in striking contrast to that of . . . girls." Parsons's work was flawed as he was the first to attempt to connect masculinity with the gendered nature of crime.

In Albert Cohen's work *Delinquent Boys* (1955) he argued that a working-class delinquent subculture comes to pass in answer to discriminatory middle-class standards. According to Cohen's theory, teachers characteristically evaluate children entering school according to how their behavior approximates middle-class standards. Boys traditionally socialized in working-class families are relatively unprepared for the challenges set forth.

As individuals who constitute the working class, and have internalized middle-class standards as they see others doing, their status becomes unclear and they look for other means to adjust. "The obvious solution is the collective repudiation of middle class standards and adoption of their very antithesis—the public display of non-utilitarian, malicious, and negativistic delinquent behavior" (my notes).

According to Cohen who used himself and his wife as examples, "my skin has nothing of the quality of down or silk there is nothing limp or flute-like about my voice. I am at a total loss with needle and thread, my posture and carriage are wholly lacking in grace . . . my wife on the other hand, is not greatly embarrassed by her inability to tinker with or talk about the internal organs of a car, by her modest attainment in arithmetic or by her inability to lift heavy objects" (my notes).

Continuing, Cohen points out that because of the structure of the modern family and the nature of our occupational system, children of both sexes tend to form early feminine identification. The boy, however, unlike the girl, comes later under strong social pressure to establish his masculinity, his difference from female figures. Because his mother is the object of the feminine identification which he feels is the threat to his status as a male, he tends to react negatively to those conduct norms which have been associated with mother and therefore have acquired feminine significance. Since mother has been the principal agent of indoctrination of good, respectable behavior, goodness comes to symbolize femininity, and engaging in bad behavior requires denying his femininity and therefore asserting his masculinity. This is the motivation to juvenile delinquency, according to Cohen.

The conclusion to be reached is that when the nature of male sex-role socialization does not run efficiently, the problem associated with male anxiety within the home is solved by becoming a member of a street gang. The delinquent subculture is a tailormade answer to the problems of the male role, but is an unsuitable solution to correct problems of the female (Cohen). We understand how the delinquent subculture applies to men but not to women.

The conclusion reached is that when looking at middle-class-boy delinquency, it becomes an attempt to muddle through with a basic apprehension in the area of sex-role identification, whereas the incentive for working-class-boy delinquency is bending to evils created by his class position.

If we look at the theories of liberal feminism, we discover that women are discriminated against on the basis of sex and therefore are deprived of the same opportunities as men and kept outside the mainstream of society (e.g., politics, business, finance, medicine, law), all of which are fields now open to women. It is the very goal of liberal feminism to remove all sexist stereotypes that are promoted through sex-role socialization within the family, at school, and by the media and government, clearing the road for women's rapid integration into what has traditionally been regarded as the world of men.

It was the works of Freda Adler and Rita Simon that were credited with the "*female emancipation theory* of female criminality. This theory postulates that the rise in female crime is a result of the Women's Liberation Movement or increased opportunities" (Edwards in Shipley & Arrigo, 2004, p. 5). In a keynote address by Adler (1975) in Washington, DC at the National Conference on Women and Crime, she implied that "although males will commit by far the greater number of absolute offenses, females are surpassing them in rates of increase for almost every major crime." She continued, "it is apparent, that [women] are no longer willing to be second-class criminals, limited to 'feminine' crimes of shoplifting and prostitution, but that they are making their gains noticeable across the offense board." This factor becomes evident in the proceeding chapters on women and crime.

Adler's work was important at the time, as she argued that there existed a correlation between the Women's Liberation Movement and technology signifying that such a combination provided the capacity for violent crimes committed by women as being compatible with men (Adler, 1975, p. 6).

Other scholars have taken exception to the idea of female emancipation as causing women to go out and commit crimes. At the meeting of the American Association for the Advancement of Science in the 1970s, it was Denmark who declared:

> The female offender, whether acting by herself or with others, is not typically the emancipated intellectual striving for civil liberties. Her crime is rarely an assertion of civil rights, or an unconscious attempt at achieving her own or others' rights. She may feel dominated by men or even wish to imitate men or obtain male approval for her actions (as cited in Shipley and Arrigo, 2004, p. 6).

It was Simon (1975) who looked at female criminality as being analogous to male offenders. Simon suggested that "women have no greater store of morality than do men. Their propensities to commit crimes do not differ, but in the past, their opportunities have been much more limited" (Shipley & Arrigo, p. 6). Simon made a case for the increase in female crime having more to do with property offenses than their ability to commit crimes of violence.

Many of the feminists became outraged by Adler's and Simon's correlation between women's liberation and crime. Their frustration came about with the masculinization theory of Adler, and the opportunity theory of Simon which challenged the myth that the equalization of sexes diminishes crime. The critics "contended that many female offenders represented minority, poor, undereducated, and unemployed groups—constituencies that did not benefit from the increased opportunities afforded to women by the Liberation Movement" (Shipley & Arrigo, 2004, p. 6). It was their contention that the liberation movement had no connection to the rates of criminality of disenfranchised women.

There are a number of radical inspired feminist theories that "have challenged the liberal position and the social structure within which the liberal-feminist viewpoint operates. . . . radical feminists look at the function of patriarchy in society and the subservient roles that women play in relation to it. . . . They contend that individuals are socialized within 'core gender identities'. [It is the] Marxist feminists [who] tie the patriarchy of society to the economic structure of capitalism. Men are thought to control the economy and, as such, many of the property crimes committed by women are related to the unequal distribution of resources" (Shipley & Arrigo, pp. 6–7).

Meda Chesney-Lind (1998) has pointed out that factors like economic marginalization and victimization lead women to crime. To illustrate, she indicates that a disproportionate number of female criminals have histories that include drug-using parents, violent partners, childhood sexual abuse, and rape. Criminal roles represent care-taking which is demonstrated when a mother sells or prostitutes herself to feed her children, and no other options exist. Chesney-Lind argues that in most cases women offenders are socialized into exploitation. With no marketable skills and little education, these women find themselves structurally dislocated. Given the abusive and victimizing experiences that women endure, she questions "not why women murder but why so few murder" (p. 98).

In reviewing female violence and aggression studies, Shipley and Arrigo have found that "many theories about women's roles in crime relative to those of men stem from the notion that men are biologically more aggressive and more prone to violence. Commenting on the phenomenon of aggression, Berkowitz (1964, p. 104) defines it as 'the emotional state resulting from a frustration, presumably creating a readiness for aggressive acts" (p. 7). Closer study is needed to understand female violence and aggression.

As an example, again cited in Shipley and Arrigo's work,

> Eagley and Steffen (1986) undertook a meta-analytic review of sex differences in relation to aggression, finding that differences were inconsistent across studies. For example, whereas men were more likely to aggress in situations that produced pain or physical injury, the differences were less pronounced when it came to social or psychological harm. (p. 8)

Interestingly, women were more prone to guilt than men. Other researchers, such as Campbell, Muncer, and Gorman (1992), felt that aggression on the part of women "was more appropriately attributable to an expressive act or a cathartic discharge of anger" (p. 8). Others have speculated on what the true meaning of aggression denotes as applied to men and women. As an example, according to Fry and Gabriel (1994, p. 165) "a reluctance to focus on female aggression may be a reluctance to consider similarities between women and men." It is further suggested that "aggressive and violent behavior in men is valorized, whereas in women it is pathologized." They concluded that "aggression was a male-gendered category; one that was not amenable to understanding feminine identity and the existence of woman as synonymous with motherhood and pacifism."

There are other factors besides criminological theories that lead to criminality. According to Shipley and Arrigo (p. 9), "female deviance or criminality is frequently associated with broken homes." Researchers have found a strong correlation between women felons who are convicted, and those coming from broken homes. The U.S. Department of Justice Bureau of Justice Statistics (1992) found that more women living in jail or prison in 1989 lived with only one or neither parent as they were growing up. Flowers (1994) and others have found that there exists a relationship between female runaways, prostitution, and sexual abuse.

As summarized by Baskin and Sommers (1993),

> typically, then, the chain of events leading to criminalization is described as beginning with child physical or sexual abuse; this produces a vicious cycle that includes running away, institutionalization, return to the dysfunctional family, and ultimately street deviance, for example, prostitution and drug use. (p. 561)

One other factor of women turning to crime is their being abused by others. There are approximately 2.0 million husbands who abuse close to 1.8 million wives. There is recurring sexual and physical violence causing women to kill their significant others, whereas other researchers have found that women who abuse drugs wind up committing crimes as well. Research shows that minority women have more contact with law enforcement than white women, so the issues of race and gender have a causal effect on women and crime. As we will see in later chapters, specific gender defenses that have been used, such as postpartum syndrome, battered women's syndrome, premenstrual and postmenstrual syndrome, are noted as effective causes of women committing crimes. One other factor is that of mental illness. "Historically, women who commit offenses, particularly those considered violent, are viewed as more pathological than their male counterparts. Women who resort to violence are frequently considered *sick* rather than willful. . . . [W]omen who commit crimes are viewed as psychiatrically disordered as a result of gender typescripts. In other words, the stereotypes for women and the stereotypes for criminals do not produce a combined stereotype of the female criminal" (Shipley & Arrigo, 2004, p. 11). Other violent crimes and child maltreatment bear some relationship as well.

According to the late Ted Alleman (Muraskin & Alleman, 1993),

> the oppression of women becomes of secondary concern in traditional Marxism since women are seen as merely another class who would benefit from a socialist transformation of society. When analyzing the traditional Marxist literature from a broader socialist perspective it is clear that: (1) Marx and Engels as theorists, like everyone else, were products of their environment and cannot have been expected to totally transcend their time and place in history . . . and (2) the essence of Marxism is really its analytic method and not the attitudes of Marx and Engels concerning women and their social conditions. (p. 29)
>
> [B]y identifying the essence of female oppression to be the control men have over female sexuality, crime of and against women comes clearly into focus. Marx . . . saw prostitution as merely another example of the "universal prostitution of the worker." By not seeing women as an oppressed class in their own right, Marx . . . found no reason to pay special attention to women and crime. [However,] with a new sensitivity to the importance of gender as a causal variable, socialists are now able to trace the origin of crimes such as prostitution (male pimps manipulating and controlling the bodies of women) back to the rape and sexual abuse experienced in childhood by many prostitutes. (p. 31).

When we look at radical feminists we find that in the arenas of crime and criminal justice "radical feminists are successfully formulating into the law what were previously considered by many to be outlandish claims. By extricating themselves from their dependence on men, radical feminists have managed to expose the roots of female oppression" (Muraskin & Alleman, p. 33). Those thoughts allied with the word *feminist* result from the actions and efforts of radical feminism. Their position has been that men are the problem and men's dominance has to be removed.

The fact is that female participation in crime is on the rise and has been for some time. However, women do not act in a vacuum. All theories presented can be attributed to women and crime. Is there a need for a specific feminist theory of crime? We can only conclude no! Women commit crimes like men today.

As summed up nicely by Adler (1975):

> Women are no longer indentured to the kitchens, baby carriages, or bedrooms of America. . . . Allowed their freedom for the first time, women—by the tens of thousands—have chosen to desert those kitchens and plunge exuberantly into the formerly all-male quarters of the working world.
>
> There are now female admirals, longshorewomen, stevedores, and seagoing sailors[1] (tattoos and all); there are police women patrolling in one-person cars, women FBI agents and female sky marshals. Women can now be found clinging to telephone poles as installers and line workers; peering from behind acetylene welding torches and seated behind the wheels of

over-the-road tractor-trailer trucks. They can be found at work as forklift drivers and crane operators, pipe fitters and carpenters, mail carriers, and morticians, commercial airline pilots and jet-engine mechanics. Women now serve as Congressional pages.[2] They have run for, and won, a substantial number of powerful positions throughout the American political system; and ever-increasing numbers of women continue to become judges, lawyers and high level executives in industry and government.

In the same way that women are demanding equal opportunity in fields of legitimate endeavor, a similar number are forcing their way into the world of major crimes. . . . Like her sisters in legitimate fields, the female criminal is fighting for her niche in the hierarchy. . . . The mob, like other successful organizations, reacts to competition and accomplishment. They are not likely to ignore the increasing numbers of women who are using guns, knives, and wits to establish themselves as full human beings, as capable of violence and aggression as any man. (p. 3)

The whole realm of social existence is affected today by women's involvement in crime.

NOTES

1. And, of course, women fighting in war.
2. Women also serve in the Congress of the United States of America.

REFERENCES

ADLER, F. (1975). *Sisters in crime: The rise of the new female criminal*. New York: McGraw-Hill.

BASKIN, D. R., & SOMMERS, I. (1993). Females' initiation into violent street crime. *Justice Quarterly, 10*, 559–581.

BELKNAP, J. (1996). *The invisible woman*. Belmont, CA:Wadsworth.

BONGER, W. (1969). *Criminality and economic conditions*. Bloomington: Indiana University Press.

BONGER, W. (1969). *Race and crime*. Montclair, NJ: Patterson Smith.

CAMPBELL, A., MUNCER, S., & GORMAN, B. (1992). Sex and social representation of aggression: A communal-agentic analysis. *Aggressive Behavior, 19*, 125–135.

CHESNEY-LIND, M. (1998). *The female offender: Girls, women and crime*. Thousand Oaks, CA: Sage.

COHEN, A. (1955). *Delinquent boys: The culture of the gang*. New York: Free Press.

DALY, K., & CHESNEY-LIND, M. (1988). Feminism and criminology. *Justice Quarterly, 5*, 497-538.

EAGLEY, A. H., & STEFFEN, V. J. (1986). Gender and aggressive behavior: A meta-analytic review of the social psychological literature. *Psychological Bulletin, 100*, 309–330.

EDWARDS, S. S. M. (1986). Neither bad nor mad: The female violent offender reassessed. *Women's Studies International Forum, 9*, 79–87.

FERRERO, W. (1980) *The female offender*. Littleton CO: Fred Rothman. (Original work published in 1895.)

FLOWERS, R. B. (1994). *Female criminals, crimes, and cellmates*. Westport, CT: Greenwood Press.

FREUD, S. (1963). Some psychical consequences of the anatomical distinction between the sexes. In S. Freud, *Sexuality and the psychology of love*. New York: Collier Books.

FRY, D. P., & GABRIEL, A. H. (1994). On aggression in women and girls: Cross-cultural perspectives. *Sex Roles, 30,* 165–170.

HAGAN, J. (1989). *Structural criminology*. Cambridge: Polity Press and Newark, NJ: Rutgers University.

HIRSCHI, T. (1969). *Causes of delinquency*. Berkeley: University of California Press.

LOMBROSO, C., & LOMBROSO-FERRERO, G. (1972) *Criminal man, according to the classification of Cesare Lombroso*. Montclair, NJ: Patterson Smith (Original work published in 1911.)

MERTON, R. (1938). Social structure and anomie. *American Sociological Review, 3,* 672–682.

MESSERSCHMIDT, J. (1993). *Masculinities and crime*. Lanham, MD: Rowman & Littlefield.

MURASKIN, R. & ALLEMAN, T. (1993). *It's a crime: Women and justice* (1st ed.). Upper Saddle River, NJ: Prentice Hall.

PARSONS, T. (1964). *The social system*. New York: Free Press.

POLLACK, O. (1950). *The criminality of women*. Philadelphia: University of Philadelphia Press.

POLLOCK, J. M. (1999). *Criminal women*. Cincinnati, OH: Anderson.

SARRI, R. (1979). Crime and the female offender. In Edith S. Gomberg and Violet Frank (Eds.), *Gender and disordered behavior: Sex differences in psychopathology*. New York: Brunner/Mazel.

SCHUR, E. (1965). Crimes without victims: Our criminal society—*Deviant behavior and public policy*. New York: Random House.

SHIPLEY, S. L., & ARRIGO, B. A. (2004). *The female homicide offender: serial murder and the case of Aileen Wuornos*. Upper Saddle River, NJ: Prentice Hall.

SIMON, R. (1975). *The contemporary woman and crime*. Washington, DC: U.S. Government Printing Office.

SMART, C. (1976). *Women, crime and criminology. London:* Routledge.

SUTHERLAND, E. (1939). *Principles of criminology*. Philadelphia, Lippincott.

THOMAS, W. I. (1969). *The unadjusted girl*. Montclair, NJ: Patterson Smith. (Original work published 1923.)

4

"Mule-Headed Slave Women Refusing to Take Foolishness from Anybody"

A Prelude to Future Accommodation, Resistance, and Criminality

Laura T. Fishman

The system of slavery, a reflection of a patriarchal and racist social order, legitimized and facilitated not only the economic and racist oppression but the sexual exploitation of black slave women. An extensive review of the literature on slavery was used to address how slave women accommodated and resisted these multiple forms of oppression. The findings presented here indicated that as blacks, both sexes experienced the harsh and inhuman consequences of racism and economic exploitation. In response, there was a significant convergence in male and female involvement in such forms of "criminal" resistance as murder, assault, theft, and arson. These actions were employed to improve the slaves' lot in life and to express opposition to the slave system. Criminal resistance therefore set the stage for black women's participation in the criminal activities characteristic of today. Findings also suggested that in response to sexual exploitation, gender-specific forms of accommodation (e.g., acting as breeders and sex workers) were utilized to make slave women's lives bearable. It is concluded that these forms of accommodation served as a preface to black women's vulnerability to sex-oriented crimes within the context of twenty-first-century American society.

The slave system in the United States involved the forcible importation of black Africans for the express purpose of economic exploitation of their labor and bodies. Slavery was a form of involuntary servitude in which slaves were owned by others and were legal chattel. Thus, slaves were a privately owned commodity to be bought and sold and disposed of at the slave owner's will. As property, slaves were deprived of most human rights and freedom, while slave owners established for themselves the rights to the services of the slaves. Given this, black slave women were obliged to submit to their masters' orders and prohibitions and therefore to submit to whatever economic and sexual exploitation was imposed upon them. Not all women reacted to the events and demands that they encountered as stoic women who accepted their life conditions passively and helplessly. Instead, slave narratives documented how black slave women actively manipulated their environment while continuously attempting to survive the inhumane conditions of slavery. In this chapter I examine how the slave system, patriarchal in its culture and structure, by legitimizing and facilitating economic and sexual exploitation, shaped some of the black women's accommodations and resistance to the institution and, in turn, set the stage for black women's participation in criminal activities characteristic of today.[1]

Within recent years, the literature on African-American women had begun to look at the intersection of multiple structures of domination. A consistent theme in this literature (see, e.g., Dill, 1979, 1990; Lewis, 1990) suggested that the term *double jeopardy* described the dual discrimination of racism and sexism that subjugates black women. Beale (1979) contended that as blacks, they suffer all the burdens of prejudice and mistreatment that fall on anyone with dark skin. However, as women, they carry the extra burden of coping with both white and black men. King (1988, 1990) elaborated on this observation by suggesting that the reality of dual discrimination often entailed economic disadvantage. She contended that black women encountered multiple jeopardy: the simultaneous oppression of race, gender, and class. Under a system of slavery, therefore, black women were exposed simultaneously to the multiple oppressions of race, gender, and caste.

As a total institution[2] (Goffman, 1961), the slave system regulated every aspect of the slaves' lives from sunup to sundown (e.g., the types of work they performed; the quality and amount of food, shelter and clothing that they received; the reproductive rights of slave women). In her examination of the Auschwitz concentration camp, Pawelcznska (1979) offered some important insights into the resistance of prisoners. She observed that the formal norms and goals of the concentration camp were rendered dysfunctional to the survival of prisoners. For instance, she reported that if the prisoners abided by the rule "Thou shalt not steal" within the Ten Commandments, survival was questionable. In the face of scarce food and inadequate clothing and shelter, prisoners who did not steal would be most vulnerable to death by starvation or by exposure to harsh weather conditions. To steal, therefore, meant to survive. She also noted that a deeply internalized value system enabled many prisoners to survive biologically and morally, that is, to resist surrender and total submission.

Several recent research findings on the mechanisms of individual slave resistance to coercion complemented her findings. From the existing literature on slave narratives, we learned that resistance was made within the context of the slave women's particular social milieu.[3] Slave women were not only responding to their masters' values and norms, which were not, in many instances, suited to black survival, but also to stresses and strains that stemmed from their status as slaves, blacks, and women.

A number of studies reported that since black slave women shared in all aspects of the oppression of slaves in general, they participated in forms of resistance similar to those of black men. Knowing that they could not make themselves free, many investigators (e.g., Blassingame, 1972; Escott, 1979; Fox-Genovese, 1988, 1990; Genovese, 1974) reported that the vast majority of slaves struggled instead to lessen the extent of their enslavement by attempting to restrict abuses and improve their treatment. Resistance was expressed in many ways. For instance, these works indicated that such resistance was carried off both overtly in the form of slave rebellions and covertly in indirect attacks on the system, through resistance to the whip, feigning illness, conscious laziness, and other means of avoiding work and impeding production. The slave narratives also suggested that there were more extreme forms of resistance, such as murder, infanticide, assault, arson, theft, and abortion.

Within this context, then, Pawelcznska (1979) observed that not every situation in the concentration camps afforded prisoners the chance to give open battle or even to make a passive protest. Under the circumstances of the concentration camp, accommodations had to be achieved to make life more bearable and to survive. Recent research on the slave narratives (Beale, 1970; Blassingame, 1972; Rawick, 1972) has reported that slave women and slave men both accommodated to most aspects of the slave system. But as women, black slaves made some gender-specific forms of adaptation in order to improve their lot or to survive. Slave women outwardly accommodated to such forms of sexual oppression as breeding and prostitution. I will elaborate on these findings by describing how these forms of accommodation, functional for the perpetuation of slavery, served as a preface to black women's participation in sex-oriented crimes within the context of twentieth-century American society.

Almost no work has dealt explicitly with the more extreme forms of resistance as a precursor of current black female criminality. In the present study I examine these extreme forms of resistance as forms of "criminal resistance" that were utilized by black slave women as a means to express opposition to the slave system as well as to undermine the system that oppressed and exploited the slaves. I therefore use the concept crimes of resistance to broaden our analysis of crime, and I posit that crime itself can be a form of resistance insofar as it can be committed to improve one's social condition or to protest the existing social order.

However, it remains difficult to draw conclusions about the full range of patterns of accommodation and resistance employed by slave women. The literature can provide only a window on some of the kinds of accommodations and resistance strategies described by a unique population of black women and men. Information gathered here is derived primarily from the narratives of slaves who escaped to freedom through the underground railroad or by other means and from the oral history of slaves emancipated by the Civil War and whose testimonies were recorded at the end of the last century and the beginning of the twentieth century. There was consensus that these were the richest sources as to the very significant ways in which black female slaves accommodated to and resisted their condition (see, e.g., Escott, 1979; Hine, 1990; Lerner, 1972; Obitko, 1990; White, 1985). The reportings on these narratives provided an in-depth picture of the mechanisms of black slave women's accommodation and resistance, which laid the foundation for the criminal behavior of black women today.

THE SLAVE SYSTEM AND MULTIPLE OPPRESSION

As mentioned earlier, as a total institution, the slave system oppressed black women on the basis of their status as members of a degraded caste and on the basis of their race and gender. The slave and plantation system were patriarchal in structure and in culture. These systems were created by white men to benefit their monetary and personal needs. To a considerable extent, the types of jobs slaves did and the amount and regularity of labor they were forced to devote to such jobs—whether in the fields or in the masters' homes—were all dictated by the slaveholders. Given this, Fox-Genovese (1988) observed that black slave women, as workers in the fields or the Big House, were able to assume independent roles as working members of their households. As a consequence of their independence, they were able to obtain a modicum of freedom from domination of their men. It should be noted here, however, that slave women belonged to households that were not governed by their own husbands, brothers, and fathers but by their masters, and as the property of their masters, they belonged to a lower caste in which the members had no relational rights.

The treatment of slaves in terms of food, clothing, and housing was oppressive for men and women equally. Slave narratives were quite explicit about the poor quality of food, clothing, and housing that slaves were given. According to Burnham (1990), a slave woman's heavy workload, inadequate diet, and poor housing conditions constituted a serious threat to her health and life expectancy. Nevertheless, some slaves described the necessities of life as simple but supplied in adequate quantity. Others reported that food from the plantation was basically the same: cornmeal, fat pork, molasses, sometimes coffee, and depending on the master, greens and vegetables from a garden or animals hunted in the woods. As one woman said, "It warn't nothin' fine, but it was good plain eatin' what filled you up" (Blassingame, 1972). Several investigators (e.g., Blassingame, 1972; Burnham, 1990; Genovese, 1974) found that slaves resided in cramped and crowded living quarters. Shacks given to the slaves were likely to be 10 or 12 feet square with mud chimneys and no floors, doors, or windows. Because the majority of the huts contained no furniture, slaves had to sit on boxes or planks and slept on straw or dirty blankets. In addition, only enough clothing was issued for the barest level of survival. Women generally received one garment for summer and one for winter and a single pair of shoes.

Another aspect of slavery that made life onerous for male and female slaves were the harsh rules that constricted the bounds of daily life and the punishments meted out for any deviations from the rules. Most masters enforced the law strictly, rarely taking gender differences into consideration. A variety of punishments were inaugurated by slave owners, ranging from mutilation and extreme physical cruelty, to removing the slave from a work position, to selling the slave. Both Escott (1979) and Stevenson (1996) reported that the whipping of slaves was common practice, used almost universally for punishment of both female and male slaves. Punishment was meted to female slaves regardless of motherhood, pregnancy, or physical injury.

Physical coercion was not the primary territory of the male slaveholder. Jones (1985) and Fox-Genovese (1988) both observed that mistresses, in their role as labor managers, lashed out at slave women not only to punish them but also to vent their anger on slave women, who were even more oppressed than themselves. When punishing black women for minor offenses, mistresses were likely to use any readily available weapon: for example, forks, knives, or knitting needles (see, e.g., Blassingame, 1972; Burnham, 1990; Fox-Genovese, 1988; Genovese, 1974; White, 1985). According to Jones (1990): "Some of the most barbaric forms of punishment resulting in the mutilation and permanent scarring of female servants were devised by white mistresses in the heat of passion. As a group they received well-deserved notoriety for the 'veritable terror' they unleashed upon black women in the Big House" (p. 750). The slave narratives led to the conclusion that the poverty of living conditions and white violence aimed at slaves simply because of caste and race cut across gender differences.

Economic Exploitation as One Form of Oppression

They worked, in a manner of speaking, from can to can't, from the time they could see until the time they couldn't. [Abbie Lindsay, ex-slave from Louisiana (Lerner, 1972, p. 15)]

From the earliest moments of African slavery in the United States, the economic exploitation of black women became a permanent feature of the white patriarchal and capitalist society. A brutal kind of equality was thrust upon both sexes, a process dictated by the conditions of production. The plantation system did not differentiate between the sexes in exploiting slave labor. As noted by Higgenbotham (1990), slave women were first considered to be full-time laborers and then only incidentally, wives, mothers, and homemakers. As was the case with their male counterparts, slave women labored from sunup to sundown and sometimes beyond. Unremitting toil was the cultural birthright of slave women. Jones (1985) recorded an interview by a Federal Writers Project (FWP) worker in 1937 with Hanna Davidson, who spoke of her experiences as a slave in Kentucky: "'Work, work, work,' she said; it had consumed all her days (from dawn until midnight) and all her years (she was only eight when she began minding her master's children and helping the older women with their spinning). 'I been so exhausted working, I was like an inchworm crawling along a roof. I worked till I thought another lick would kill me'" (p. 13).

Slave women generally performed the same types of labor performed by men. Fox-Genovese (1988) observed that masters commonly assigned slave women to perform labor that was considered to be inappropriate work for white women. Slaveholders did not refrain, out of respect for female delicacy, from letting a slave woman exercise her full strength. The notion of a distinctive "women's work" disappeared as slaveholders realized that "women can do the plowing very well"; slave narratives reported that a great many women did plow. To harness a double team of mules or oxen and steer a heavy wooden plow was no easy feat, yet a substantial minority of slave women endured these rigorous activities.

Although black women generally worked "like men" in the fields, researchers (Fox-Genovese, 1988; Genovese, 1974; Higginbotham, 1992; Jones, 1985, 1990) contended that masters commonly differentiated the kinds and quantities of work that slave men and women were expected to perform. Some slave narratives reported that out in the field the men each had to pick 300 pounds of cotton, while the women were each responsible for picking 250 pounds per day. Work assignments for women and men also differed according to the size of the plantation and its degree of specialization. Often, the tasks that demanded sheer muscle power were reserved exclusively for men (clearing the land of trees, rolling logs, and chopping and hauling wood). However, plantation exigencies sometimes mandated women's labor in this area, too; in general, the smaller the farm, the more arduous and varied was women's fieldwork. For instance, Jones (1990) noted: "Lizzie Atkins, who lived on a twenty-five acre Texas plantation with only three other slaves, remembered working 'until slam dark every day'; she helped to clear land, cut wood, and tend the livestock in addition to her other duties of hoeing corn, spinning thread, sewing clothes, cooking, washing dishes, and grinding corn" (p. 743).

Black women also worked under the close supervision of whites (the master, overseer, or mistress) at a forced pace in the Big House. A division of labor based on gender and age was more apparent, reflecting slave owners' attitudes about the nature of domestic service. Women predominated as household workers and were assigned to such tasks as cleaning, laundering, caring for the master's children, cooking, ironing, spinning wool, sewing, and other numerous tasks. Although the household servants may have eaten better food and worn better clothes than the field slaves, their labor was an unbearable load. It was unending toil and trouble. They were at the constant beck and call of the owner or his wife, who demanded service from the time the slaves were awakened early in the morning until the household was ready for retirement. The master's house offered no shelter from the brutality of slavery, so it is not surprising that many black women preferred fieldwork to housework.

A consistent theme in the literature suggested that the sexual division of labor under slavery actually assumed two forms: one system of work forced upon slaves by masters who valued women only as work-oxen and brood-sows, and the other initiated by the slaves themselves in the quarters. But as Jones (1985) pointed out:

> However, slave women also worked on behalf of their own families, and herein lies a central irony in the history of their labor. Under slavery, blacks' attempts to sustain their family life amounted to a political act of protest against the callousness of owners, mistresses, and overseers. In defiance of the slaveholders' tendencies to ignore gender differences in making assignments in the fields, the slaves whenever possible adhered to a strict division of labor within their own households and communities. (p. 14)

According to some researchers (see Davis, 1971, 1981; Farnham, 1990; Fox-Genovese, 1988; White, 1985), after working in the field or in the master's house all day, black women returned to their cabins to care for their children, cook, wash, sew, knit, weave, or do other kinds of work before retiring for the evening. Thus Jones (1985) and Farnham (1990) contended that the slave narratives were at odds with some historians' observations that relations between the sexes approximated domestic sexual equality. Instead, slave narratives showed that the reverse situation occurred (i.e., men working in the home was but a "sometime" activity). For example, there was no evidence that men engaged in spinning, a job that occupied much of the women's time in the evenings, nor were husbands "equally" willing to wash clothes. Men were more likely to be involved in what has been termed "traditional men's work," collecting firewood, hunting, gardening, and constructing beds, tables, and chairs. In the absence of their men, women also performed male duties, such as gathering firewood.

Sexual Oppression as Gender-Specific Oppression

In addition to economic exploitation, women under slavery were oppressed sexually. As stated by Marable (1990): "Sexual oppression and exploitation refer not only to the obvious and well-documented fact of forced sexual intercourse with white masters, but also to those forms of exploitation resulting from the very fact of her female biological system" (p. 408). Controlling black women's reproduction was essential to the perpetuation of the slave system (see, e.g., Clinton, 1990; Collins, 1990; Davis, 1971, 1981; Hine, 1990; Marable, 1990). During the decades preceding the Civil War, black women came to be valued increasingly for their fertility. Those who conceived 10 or more children became a coveted treasure. Davis (1971, 1981) noted that the ideological exaltation of motherhood did not apply to slave women. In fact, in the eyes of slaveholders, slave women were not mothers at all. Instead, as "breeders," they were simply instruments ensuring the growth of the slave labor force. They were considered animals whose monetary value could be accurately calculated in terms of their ability to bear children. Finally, as "breeders" as opposed to "mothers," their children could be sold away from them like calves from cows.

Thus it was expected that slave women would bear children as frequently as possible and if they failed to give birth, they would be sold. Barren women were avoided by their communities and punished by their owners. Some slave owners voided blacks' marriages if they suspected that the men or women were sterile. Many masters did not wait for the slaves themselves to reproduce in sufficient numbers and took matters into their own hands (Clinton, 1990; Escott, 1979). Slaves reported that one way forced breeding occurred was by masters attempting to control mating by matching up couples. In addition to manipulating pair bonding, some masters rented or borrowed men for stud service, subjecting their female slaves to forced breeding or rape. These men were referred to in slave narratives as "stock men," "travelin' niggers," or "breedin' niggers." According to Sterling (1984): "On the Blackshear place, they took all the fine looking boys and girls that was thirteen years old or older and put them in a big barn. They used to strip them naked and put them in a big barn every Sunday and leave them there until Monday morning. Out of that came sixty babies" (pp. 31–32). And Escott (1979) noted that for a much smaller number of planters, intervention took more direct forms. Some masters supervised the pairing among their slaves and encouraged or even required a "fine and stout" man to marry a similarly built woman.

Many slaveholders also took control of reproduction by constantly subjecting black slave women to violent rape. As Angela Davis (1971, 1981) observed, the slave owner, like a feudal lord, manifested and reinforced his authority to have intercourse with all the females. Many women were severely punished or threatened with being sold South if they resisted this particular terrorization. White (1985) and Farnham (1990) reported that recourse to punitive measures was not the only method employed to encourage women to reproduce. As part of their manipulation of reproduction, some slave owners adopted the practice of rewarding prolific women. For example, each time a baby was born, the slave owners might reward the mother with bonuses. Sterling (1984) further elaborated: "The majority of planters utilized the carrot rather than the stick to increase their stock. A 'good breeder' was given a pig, a calico dress, or better rations. One planter ruled that 'women with six children alive are allowed Saturday to themselves'; another promised his house servant her freedom after she bore five children, one for each of his sons and daughters. Lulu Wilson was persuaded by a white dress" (p. 32). Other subtle, or perhaps not-so-subtle, inducements were to ensure that pregnant women did less work and received more attention and rations than did nonpregnant women. This technique was employed not only to ensure the good health of mother and fetus alike, but also served as a reward for overworked slave women to have children. On plantations where the workload was exhausting and backbreaking, a lighter work assignment could be enough of an incentive to get pregnant as often as possible.

Another form that sexual exploitation assumed with the institution of slavery was prostitution. Most frequently, prostitution assumed such forms as (1) regularly providing sexual services to enhance the profit of a master, (2) concubinage, and (3) acceptance of a trinket upon acquiescing to forced sex with white overseers and planters.

However, although brothels abounded in southern cities, most of the prostitutes were not black. White (1985) provided some evidence that there existed the "fancy trade," the sale of light-skinned black women for the exclusive purpose of prostitution and concubinage. Slaves selected for their grace, beauty, and light skin were shipped to the "fancy-girl markets" of New Orleans and other cities. Thus, whereas some women worked in bordellos, the majority became the mistresses of wealthy planters, gamblers, or businessmen. Generally speaking, reported Blassingame (1972), black slave women were literally forced to offer themselves "willingly" and sometimes received a trinket for their compliance rather than a flogging for their refusal and resistance.

Expediency governed the slaveholders' posture toward female slaves. When it was profitable for the masters to exploit them as if they were men, black women were regarded in effect as genderless, but when they could be exploited and punished in ways suited only for women, they were locked into their exclusively female roles (Davis, 1971, 1981). Slave women, therefore, could hardly shape their ways of acting according to the normative structure inherent in the model of white womanhood.

ACCOMMODATIONS AND BLACK FEMALE CRIMINALITY

The findings presented here remind us about the cruelty of bondage for slave women. Like their black brothers, black women were abused physically, exploited economically, denied physical comforts and rewards, separated at times from their loved ones, denied education, and deprived of basic freedoms. But black women suffered from the anguish of sexual subjection as well. They were used as sexual objects by their masters and became victims of forced "breeding." In the face of these difficult circumstances, black slave women engaged in overt compliance to their masters' demands and conformed to the norms imposed on them in order to mollify whites, avoid trouble, or gain some benefit.

Such accommodations helped to ease the pains of their existence and to make their lives bearable. Of particular interest is that these women not only accommodated to their economic exploitation (by complying with their masters' work ethics, by working long hours in the field or in the Big House, and then returning to their homes to do domestic chores), they also coped with their sexual exploitation by becoming what their masters desired ("breeders," sexual objects to be sexually abused, prostitutes, and concubines). However, there were rewards for their compliance. Thus many slave women did not resist these exploitations because it was futile, could offer them prestige and protection, or provide them with material advantages. Clinton (1990) reported that "'[a] woman's being a slave, don't stop her from having genteel ideas; that is, according to their way, and as far as they can. They know they must submit to their masters; besides, their masters, maybe, dress 'em up, and make 'em little presents, and give 'em more privileges, while the whim lasts.' The divorce records and wills of slaveowners provide testimony of the power and influence many black concubines possessed" (p. 233).

Many slave women, especially concubines and "yeller gals," who otherwise had limited opportunities within the severely circumscribed sphere of slavery, improved their status and that of their offspring through liaisons with their owners (see Blassingame, 1972; Clinton, 1990; Frazier, 1968; White, 1985). Within this context, subjecting slave women to sexual exploitation was "naturally" done by slaveholders and overseers. This form of exploitation was justified by the common belief that unlike the sexually virtuous white woman, black women were promiscuous Jezebels. On the other hand, any kind of sexual exploitation of mistresses, who were perceived as the embodiment of various otherwordly virtues, would be sacrilegious.

An important component of black womanhood is a strong work orientation and independence. Fox-Genovese (1988) contended that black women acted autonomously and self-reliantly in response to the circumstances of slavery, in order to effectively survive the system of slavery; black women took care of themselves because the circumstances of slavery forced them to do so. She argued further that the strongest case for the autonomy of slave women lay in their freedom from the domestic domination of their black men. However, slave women were not completely free of male domination. They were under the political and economic domination of their white owners. The power of the master constituted the fundamental condition of slave women's lives, however much it was hedged in by the direct and subtle resistance of the women themselves.

CRIMINAL RESISTANCE

Although black slave women accommodated to the harsh conditions of slavery, they did not passively accept the treatment dictated by their masters. Several investigators noted the significant role played by black female slaves in obstructing and thwarting the wishes and plans of their slave holders as well as the role they played resisting the slave system. This section is concerned with uncovering the more extreme forms of "criminal resistance"—murder, infanticide, theft, arson, assault—which female slaves employed to express their opposition to the slave system.

Within the more recent literature on slave women, there is consensus that since black women were equal to their men in the oppression they suffered, in some instances they asserted their equality aggressively by challenging the inhumane slave system (see Davis, 1971, 1981). Some researchers (Fox-Genovese, 1988; Genovese, 1974; White, 1985) contended that their forms of individual resistance differed somewhat from those of men, in part because of their childbearing and child care responsibilities. These responsibilities affected the female slaves' patterns of resistance. Differences in these forms of resistance also occurred as a consequence of slave owners' attitudes and beliefs about the significance of gender roles. For instance, slave narratives revealed that many slaveholders' notions of womanhood led them to reserve domestic tasks exclusively for women and specialized crafts—such as blacksmiths and carpenters—for slave men. Since these specialized crafts frequently required the men to move around the countryside, they were afforded greater opportunities to escape. In turn, as house servants, female slaves' proper "place" was in their masters' houses. Under these circumstances, they enjoyed far fewer opportunities for successful escape. Thus female and male slaves experienced some gender-specific opportunities for various forms of resistance which will be examined.

Characteristics of Female Slaves Who Resisted

In his extensive examination of slave narratives, Escott (1979) provided some important insights into characteristics of slaves who utilized some form of resistance. Escott noted that although field slaves engaged in more frequent forms of resistance, house servants also performed resistance activities. The differing roles of the sexes may account for a greater frequency of resistance performed by males. Escott's evidence showed that men were more likely to participate in those areas of resistance that required strength and endurance, such as joining in fatal confrontations with a white man. Women, on the other hand, were less likely to take part in this kind of action and approached parity with men in the area of theft. However, in two categories—verbal confrontations and striking the master—the women's resistance activities outnumbered that of the men. Most of the women who dared to strike the master were fieldhands and not house servants.

Theft: Emergence of Hustling as a Way of Life

The literature on slavery reported that stealing was commonplace among field and house slaves. Escott (1979) contended that theft was the most widespread practice of resistance and might better be called the appropriation or reappropriation of forbidden goods. Genovese (1974) reported that masters perceived theft as a normal feature of plantation life. To the slaveholders and whites generally, all blacks stole by nature. They convinced themselves that because slaves steal, they, as good fathers and mothers, merely had to take this in stride. They defined "a thieving Negro" simply as one who stole more than the average. He further stated: "Even on the best-managed plantations, which boasted well-fed slaves, the plundering of the hogpen, the smokehouse, the chicken coop, and the corncrib constituted a normal feature of plantation life" (p. 599). Acts of thievery generally were tolerated among masters and mistresses as long as the thief consumed her loot, but they were less tolerant when goods were used for trading purposes.

It was widely documented that cooks and house servants—mainly women—benefited from their position to supplement the diets of their families and friends from the storerooms of their masters (see, e.g., Burnham, 1990; Genovese, 1974). For instance, many female cooks smuggled extra rolls or meat to their homes in the slave quarters. This stolen food generally fed their families, runaways, or short-term fugitives hiding in nearby forests or swamps (Holt, 1994). Many former slaves described the pleasures of eating almost every kind of plantation produce: watermelons, eggs, chickens, sweet potatoes, hams, pig, cattle, and corn (Escott, 1979).

According to Genovese (1974), the main excuse given for stealing rested on the charge of underfeeding. Some, in fact, did not get enough to eat. Others said that even when they had no complaint about the amount of food issued, they resented the lack of variety and the assumption that they did not care about anything other than a full dinner pail of pork and cornmeal. "We had some good eats," remarked Walter Rimm of Texas, "but had to steal de best things from de white folks."

Some slaves justified thievery by arguing that they stole from each other but merely took from their masters. As reported by Genovese (1974), slave women figured that if they belonged to their masters, they could not steal from him. The act of "theft" in their view only transferred the masters' property from one form to another and the slave owner lost nothing in the process. In addition, they reasoned that if it was so wrong to steal, then why had their masters stolen the black people from their homeland in the first place? There was satisfaction to be gained from outwitting and outfoxing "Old Massa" in this fashion. Other slave narratives documented another satisfaction to be gained from theft. According to Lichtenstein (1988), some slaves perceived theft as the expression of the rights of parents to provide extra food for their children. Theft then functioned not only to feed the slave children but to undermine the control of slave diets as dictated by their slave owners. Finally, a few slaves explained that theft occurred at the instigation of their masters, who encouraged them to steal from neighboring farms and plantations (see Genovese, 1974).

For the many female slaves, stealing became a science and an art employed as much for the satisfaction of outwitting the slave owner as anything else (see Lichtenstein, 1988). To prevent detection, female slaves devised many strategies from putting pepper in the dog's eyes, to striking a single blow to silence their prey, to burying all the chicken feathers in the ground (Escott, 1979; Genovese, 1974). Genovese (1974) noted:

> Lewis Clarke told of a particularly adept woman whose overseer once almost caught her boiling a pig. Upon hearing his approach, she placed the pot on the floor, covered it with a board, and sat her young daughter upon it. It seemed the poor child had a terrible cold that just had to be sweated out of her. Quick thinking, but not so quick. Like many other slaves this woman had done her thinking in advance and tried to have a contingency plan for every emergency. (p. 606)

It is clear from slave accounts that one component of the hustling strategy emerged during slavery as a response to the harsh physical deprivations as well as the inhumane treatment of masters. For example, a female ex-slave's account revealed that the slaves' food allowance was not considered a gift to them from their masters and mistresses. Instead, she argued that this food allowance was given in exchange for the slaves' labor. Upon making this observation, she then came to the conclusion that, "if a slave did steal, he never take nothin' but what been belong to him" (see Lichtenstein, 1988, p. 259). Theft therefore became part of a slave's survival package, as income from theft had become an integral part of lower-income blacks females' survival package within twentieth-century American society. Several authors who studied the more current black lower-class community (Brooks, 1980; Fields & Walters, 1985; Glasgow, 1981; Valentine, 1978) suggested that most black males and females, being offered little from the community in the way of resources or controls, developed some knowledge of hustling in order to survive. They needed to combine income from intermittent employment, welfare, and hustling to maintain even a low standard of living. According to Fields and Walters (1985) and Valentine (1978), hustling referred to a wide variety of conventional, sometimes extralegal or illegal activities, designed to produce economic gain and was widely accepted and practiced in the slums and ghettos of larger cities. The findings presented here indicated that slavery was a precursor to hustling, which not only ensured survival but served as an active form of resistance to the slave system.

Homicide and Assault as Criminal Resistance

> "Fight, and if you can't fight, kick; if you can't kick, then bite," one slave advised her daughter. A sizable minority of "fighting, mule-headed" women refused to "take foolishness" from anybody. (Sterling, 1984, p. 56)

Insolence to the masters and overseers comprised only one aspect of slave resistance to slavery. Overt resistance in the form of assaultive and homicidal behavior made up another form of slaves' reactions to the system. This form of resistance strongly suggested that female slaves took their multiple oppression personally.

Frequently, violent confrontations that led to assault and homicide were spontaneous and unplanned when they occurred in the fields and in the Big House. The most common types of violent confrontations occurred as an outcome of vigorous altercations with the slave owners or overseers. Fights were often vigorous. Disagreements could escalate into physical battles. Any spark could set off the reaction (e.g., criticism for work the slave women knew had been done). A slave woman might submit to any and all abuse for years, then, suddenly fed up, fight any owner or overseer who attempted to criticize her. The slave women who struck back did not suffer a paralysis of fear; it was not unthinkable to stand up and fight (Escott, 1979; Jones, 1985; Lerner, 1972; Sterling, 1984).

Violence also frequently grew out of confrontations in the field over the amount and pace of work. According to Fox-Genovese (1988) and Stevenson (1996), field women fiercely defended their sense of acceptable workloads and violently resisted abuse of power, which for many meant any discipline at all. In some instances, reported Fox-Genovese (1988), some overseers rashly sought confrontations:

> Irene Coates remembered that one day when a group of women were hoeing, the overseer rode by and struck one of them across the back with a whip. A woman nearby said "that if he ever struck her like that, it would be the day he or she would die." The overseer overheard her and took the first opportunity to strike her with his whip. As he started to ride off, the woman whirled around, struck him on the head with her hoe, knocking him from his horse, and then "pounced upon him and chopped his head off." Then, going temporarily mad, she "proceeded to chop and mutilate his body; that done to her satisfaction, she then killed his horse." Her work completed, she "calmly went to tell the master of the murder." (p. 317)

Some women resorted to assault or murder in response to threats of whippings and actual brutal assaults perpetuated by masters, mistresses, and overseers. The following account revealed several incidents in which black women reacted violently (Obitko, 1990):

> There was Crecie, for example, who pulled up a stump and whipped an overseer with it when he tried to lash her; or Aunt Susie Ann, who pretended to faint while she was being whipped and then tripped the overseer so that he couldn't stand up; or Lucy, who knocked an overseer over and tore his face up so that the doctor had to tend to him; or the mammy who nursed a child but later, when he tormented her, did not hesitate to beat him until he wasn't able to walk; or Aunt Adeline, who committed suicide rather than submit to another whipping; or Cousin Sally, who hit her master over the head with a poker and put his head in the fireplace. (p. 988)

Not only did women attempt to protect themselves but they also resisted their slave-holders' meting out lashings to their children. These mothers considered protection of their children as an important obligation, and occasionally they were willing to risk death by trying to terminate these whippings by physically attacking the slaveholders (Holt, 1994). Slave women also sometimes violently resisted sexual exploitation. Since southern law did not recognize the rape of black women as a crime, often the only recourse slave women had was to fight off their assailants (Weiner, 1998). The following incident is from the life of Bishop Loguen's mother, who was the mistress of a white man near Nashville, Tennessee (Frazier, 1968):

> When she was about the age of twenty-four or five, a neighboring planter finding her alone at the distillery, and presuming upon privileges of his position, made insulting advances, which she promptly repelled. He pursued her with gentle force, and was still repelled. He then resorted to a slaveholder's violence and threats. These stirred all the tiger's blood in her veins. She broke from his embrace, and stood before him in bold defiance. He attempted again to lay hold of her—and careless of caste and slave laws, she grasped the heavy stick used to stir the malt, and dealt him a blow which made him reel and retire. But he retired only to recover and return with the fatal knife, and threats of vengeance and death. Again she aimed the club with unmeasured force at him, and hit the hand which held the weapon, and dashed it to a distance from him. Again he rushed upon her with the fury of a madman, and she then plied a blow upon his temple, which laid him, as was supposed, dead at her feet. (p. 56)

Fox-Genovese (1988) noted that some women reacted in a violent manner when they believed their masters had overstepped the limits of their authority that they could accept as legitimate. Finding themselves in an untenable situation, they frequently turned to violent resistance. Fox-Genovese recorded how one of Nancy Bean's aunts "was a mean, fighting woman": "Her master, presumably because he could not master her, determined to sell her. 'When the bidding started she grabbed a hatchet, laid her hand on a log and chopped it off. Then she throwed the bleeding right hand in her master's face'" (p. 329).

Specialization of skills according to gender offered female slaves some gender-specific opportunities to engage in homicide. For instance, gender conventions that assigned slave women to kitchens, to child care, and to nursing resulted in poisoning becoming an increasingly female activity. In the case of cooks and house servants, they had the greatest accessibility to the necessary ingredients for poisoning. Arsenic and other similar compounds were most frequently used. When they were not accessible, slaves were known to have resorted to mixing ground glass in the gravy for their master's table. Black slave women proved especially skilled at poisoning their masters, a skill that must have been transmitted down through the generations. Generally, these acts were calculated and initiated on an individual basis (Fox-Genovese, 1988, 1990; Genovese, 1974; White, 1985).

Periodically, the slaves on a plantation conspired to murder a master or overseer; such a murder reflected the collective judgment of the quarters. According to Genovese (1974), these actions struck at especially brutal whites, but in some cases slaves claimed the lives of reputedly kind masters and thereby suggested intense hostility toward slavery itself. In the face of the kinds of physical and sexual abuse that slaves encountered, it was not surprising to find that throughout slavery there was a persistence in the hostility of slaves and violence against slave owners and overseers as immediate oppressors.

Men and women conspiring together to kill overseers and their masters was not out of the ordinary. The literature on slave revolts occasionally mentioned that a woman was part of a conspiracy, but no documentation of the specific contribution of black women in these plots had been made. Obitko (1990) contended that if more males than females participated in rebellions, perhaps such a form of resistance presented the only successful manner in which the males could resist the forces of slavery. Black women, on the other hand, were constantly in a day-to-day manner resisting the conditions of slavery. Therefore, it could not be said that females did not participate in slave insurrections but that they simply found other means of resistance more effective.

Brutal resistance therefore was not the sole preserve of slave men. As documented here, slave women also physically fought their masters, mistresses, and overseers as well as rebelled and ran away. In many instances, these women refused to be broken no matter how many floggings they received. Instead, they continued to fight back in an uncompromising manner. Black slave women earned reputations as fighters. According to Obitko (1990), they were tough, powerful, and spirited. As pointed out, the black female directed most of her resistance against physical cruelty; some women would not submit to the whip, while others endured it until they reached a point when they would no longer tolerate their oppression.

Fox-Genovese (1988) contended that black women had to rely on themselves for protection against the attacks of masters and overseers. It was they who most likely had to defend themselves and their families since their men—brothers, fathers, and husbands—could offer them neither protection nor security. It therefore was expected that slave women would learn to defend themselves against abusive masters or mistresses, against attacks on their integrity or work ethics, and finally, against sexual violation of their bodies. In addition, women who knew that they were their masters' children had special reason to resent the orders of his overseers and drivers and to test the limits of their enslavement.

Arson as a Form of Criminal Resistance

Arson was another favored form of violent resistance. For the slaves, arson had much to recommend it as a way of settling scores. Arson required no great physical strength or financial resources and could easily be concealed. Genovese (1974) noted that next to theft, arson was the most common slave "crime," one that slaveholders dreaded almost constantly. All too frequently, slaveholders saw their gin houses, barns, or homes burned down, and in some cases, slaveholders saw the better part of a year's harvest go up in smoke.

From the literature we gleaned that women, to a lesser extent than men, did participate in arson (Escott, 1979; Giddings, 1984). As arsonists, women usually worked alone or at most in groups of two or three (Giddings, 1984): "In 1766 a slave woman in Maryland was executed for setting fire to her master's home, tobacco house, and outhouse, burning them all to the ground. The prosecutor in the case noted that there had been two other houses full of tobacco burnt 'in the country this winter'" (p. 39). As reported by Genovese (1974), an arsonist's display of resistance did not always win support or encouragement in the slave quarters. If the slave, for instance, burned down the master's house, the carriage-house, or some other building with little economic significance, the slaves might protect the arsonist. However, when a corncrib, smokehouse, or gin house was burned down, other slaves were not likely to feel any sympathy for the arsonist. Destruction of food stores meant that they would have less to eat. Destruction of cotton meant severe losses to their master and the potential sale of one or more members of the slave community, or even worse, bankruptcy and the breakup of the community together.

GENDER-SPECIFIC FORMS OF CRIMINAL RESISTANCE

As mentioned earlier, slave women performed a reproductive function vital to slave owners' financial interests and to the growth of the slave system in general. Yet slave women resisted slaveholders and overseers' attempts to exploit them sexually. As women, female slaves engaged in such forms of resistance associated with their sexuality and reproductive capacities as infanticide and abortion.

Possibly the most devastating means for undermining the slave system that slave women had at their disposal was infanticide. The frequency with which this occurred is by no means clear. Several historians contended that infanticide was quite rare and did not become a major problem for the slaveholders. It is important to note that the relatively small number of documented cases is not as significant as the fact that infanticide occurred at all (Genovese, 1974; Hine, 1990; White, 1985).

There was some consensus in the literature that the major motivation behind infanticide was that slave women preferred to end their children's lives rather than allow the children to grow up enslaved. Fox-Genovese (1988, pp. 315–316) observed that some women who could live with their own situation but could not accept what was done to their children, took some drastic measures. For instance:

> Lou Smith's mother told her of a woman who had borne several children, only to see her master sell them when they were one or two years old. "It would break her heart. She never got to keep them." After the birth of her fourth baby, "she just studied all the time about how she would have to give it up," and one day she decided that she just was not going to let her master sell that baby. "She got up and give it something out of a bottle and purty soon it was dead. 'Course didn't nobody tell on her or he'd of beat her nearly to death."

Hine (1990) contended that slave women did not perceive infanticide as murder but as an act that expressed a higher form of love and a clear understanding of the "living death" that awaited children under slavery. These acts also occurred in response to the slave owners abusing their children. Thus, reported White (1985): "An Alabama woman killed her child because her mistress continually abused it. In confessing her guilt, she claimed that her master was the father of the child, and that her mistress knew it and treated it so cruelly that she had to kill it to save it from further suffering" (p. 88).

Another motivation behind infanticide was that it was a response to the slave owners' threats to sell slave children. Many times, owners used the sale or the threat of sale of slave children as a means of manipulating their troublesome slaves. In turn, many slave women used their children to manipulate their masters. According to White (1985, p. 88), there was one documented instance in which a female slave was told that she must be sold following an incident in which she physically attacked her mistress. To maximize the harshness of the punishment, she was informed by her master that her infant would remain on the plantation. One of her older daughters recalled her mother's response: "At this, Ma took the baby by its feet, a foot in each hand, and with the Baby's head swinging downward, she vowed to smash its brains out before she'd leave it. Tears were streaming down her face. . . . It was seldom that Ma cried and everyone knew that she meant every word. Ma took her baby with her. . . ." And finally, infanticide occurred as a response to rape or forced pregnancy.

A second method of female resistance to slavery in general and to sexual exploitation in particular took the form of abortion. It was, however, almost impossible to determine whether slave women practiced abortion. These matters were exclusive to the female world of the slave quarters, and when the women needed abortions performed, they were attended to in secret. In a recent study of the black family, Gutman (1976) observed that the slave woman's decision to terminate her pregnancy was one act that was totally beyond the control of the master of the plantation. Gutman offered evidence of several southern physicians who commented upon abortion and the use of contraceptive methods among the slave population:

> The Hancock County, Georgia, physician E. M. Pendleton reported in 1849 that among his patients "abortion and miscarriage" occurred more frequently among slave than white free women. The cause was either "slave labor" (exposure, violent exercise, etc.) or "as the planters believe, that the Blacks are possessed of a secret by which they destroy the fetus at an early stage of gestation." All county practitioners, he added, "are aware of the frequent complaints of planters about the unnatural tendency in the African female population to destroy her offspring. Whole families of women. . . fail to have any children. (pp. 80–81)

Gutman also recounted a situation in which a planter had kept between four and six slave women "of the proper age to breed" for 25 years and that "only two children had been born on the place." When the slave owner brought new slaves, every pregnancy miscarried by the fourth month. Finally, it was discovered that the women were taking "medicine" supplied by an old slave woman to induce abortions. Hine (1990) suggested that if those women did not resist slavery by actually having an abortion, they resisted even more covertly by aiding those who desired them. It was possible that a sort of female conspiracy existed on the southern plantation.

White (1985) indicated some reasons why slave women might have practiced abortion. Certainly, they had reason not to want to bear and nurture children who could be sold from them at a slave master's whim. They had ample cause to deny whites the satisfaction of realizing a profit on the birth of their children. They may also have sought, as might any white or free black women, to avoid pregnancy and childbirth. Since obstetrics had not yet evolved into a science, childbirth was dangerous.

In these instances, contended Hine (1990), infanticide and abortion provided slave women with an effective means for gaining power over their masters and control over at least part of their lives. Slave women knew that if their infanticide and abortions were discovered, it was a crime against their masters' property. According to Giddings (1984), as documented in a slave narrative, the women understood the significance of their act. "If all bond women had been of the same mind," wrote the slave Jane Blake, "how soon the institution could have vanished from the earth" (p. 46).

In conclusion, slave narratives indicated that mothers cared dearly for their children and that infanticide and abortion constituted costly forms of resistance. Those who employed these forms of resistance did so at considerable pain to themselves, resisting from the very core of their experiences as women. Moreover, noted Giddings (1984), they were implicitly challenging their masters, who protected the sexuality and revered the motherhood of white women while denying these attributes of black women.

DISCUSSION

The findings presented here tell us that slave women were not sheltered from life's ugliness or dependent on their men for subsistence goods and service. Their society did not discourage them from taking initiatives in their quest for survival. The dehumanizing forces and the conditions of the slave system, as a total institution, warranted the rebelliousness and resistance that black women displayed. Coupled with the deplorable conditions created by the system was the unique position of women among the slaves—that is, they were valued as economic assets and exploited as sexual objects. By virtue of their participation in the slave economy and in reproduction, these women would not act the part of the passive female but could experience the need to challenge the conditions of their subjugation. They came to be active in such criminal forms of resistance as theft, murder, assault, and arson because of their social position, a position that encouraged women to be as assertive, independent, and risk taking as men. Within this context, the findings pointed out that slave women employed such forms of resistance as hustling and fighting in order to survive within the slave system as well as to undermine the system.

The findings presented here strongly suggested that some female offending could be interpreted as challenging patriarchal control and asserting independence, but much could be attributed to both economic necessity and rebellion. As suggested by King's (1988, 1990) observations, female participation in violent crimes as well as theft may stem from the frustration, alienation, and anger that was associated with gender and race. But it was through looking at the broader issues of multiple structures—in this case, caste, race, and gender as forms of oppression—that the resistance of black women had a more complex meaning.

It is important to note here that slave women's employment of resistance strategies was effective insofar as these strategies undermined the authority of slaveholders, gained the respect of their fellow slaves, and empowered the women themselves. In turn, these acts of resistance served as a mirror image of the slave system itself. Violence was a major dimension of slavery. Most white violence, directed at slaves, assumed the form of homicide, beatings, tortures, and rape. In turn, it was not surprising that black women responded to the pervasive violence by committing violent acts themselves. Theft was another major dimension of slavery. The form it assumed was the forcible kidnapping of African women and men in order to enslave them for the purposes of slaveholders. In turn, the findings indicated that slave women's reactions to the theft of their bodies included extended participation in theft from the masters' property.

From slave narratives, we also learned that black slave women had to perform socially and biologically determined gender-role-stereotyped work. Not only did they constitute an important and necessary part of the workforce but through their childbearing function, they became the one group responsible for the perpetuation of slavery. In turn, they were also utilized to satisfy the sexual needs of slaveholders and wealthy planters (i.e., they were sexually violated and forced into prostitution and concubinage). These accounts also revealed that in many instances, the accommodations women made to sexual exploitation could also be considered acts of resistance. To survive was to resist; and in order to survive, slave women complied to their masters' sexual violations. To participate in prostitution and rape meant nothing more than to survive, to try to adapt to conditions as they were. In this sense they may well have a great deal in common with inmates in concentration camps and other forms of total institutions.

Hooks (1981) broadened the analysis by pointing out that black slave women, engaged in various forms of accommodation and resistance associated with their sexuality and reproductive capacities, were reacting to the process of defeminization. She contended that slavery, a reflection of a patriarchal and racist social order, not only oppressed black men but oppressed and defeminized slave women. Black women were not permitted to conform to the dominant culture's model of "true womanhood," just as black men were unable to conform to the dominant culture's definition of "true manhood." The slave owners attempted to reestablish black women's femaleness by reducing them to the level of their biological being. Thus whites' sexual violations, enforced breeding, and other forms of sexual exploitation established black women as female animals. Slave women's resistance to the various forms of sexual exploitation posed an undermined threat to accept their defeminized status. They attacked the very assumption upon which the slave system was constructed and maintained.

Finally, the literature on slave narratives led to the conclusion that black women historically exhibited criminal behavior in response to the multiple oppressions they encountered. And in response to being black, women, and lower class, the kinds of crimes they engaged in during slavery and the twentieth century were both similar, yet different from black men's crimes. They might participate in aggressive crime, grand larceny, and sex crimes, but they tended to bring to these activities their gender identities as women. It is this identity that created a divergence from the kinds and manner in which black men committed crimes. Thus the findings here provide some important insights into how the "criminal" response of black women to slavery had persisted through the twentieth century.

NOTES

1. This chapter is adapted from the author's article "Slave Women, Resistance and Criminality: A Prelude to Future Accommodations," *Women and Criminal Justice, 7*, 35–65 (1995).
2. A total institution is one that completely absorbs and structures the identities and behavior of actors within it (see Goffman, 1961).
3. Fredrickson and Lasch (1989) corroborated the contention presented here that the social milieu in which slave resistance occurred typically was the plantation system, a total institution which for the most part resembled the prison system.

REFERENCES

BEALE, F. M. (1970). Double jeopardy: To be black and female. In T. Cade (Ed.), *The black woman: An anthology* (pp. 90–100). New York: New American Library.

BLASSINGAME, J. W. (1972). The slave community: Plantation life in the antebellum South. New York: Oxford University Press.

BROOKS, A. B. (1980). The black woman within the program and service delivery systems for battered women: A cultural response. In *Battered women: An effective response* (Chapter 2). St. Paul: Minnesota Department of Corrections.

BURNHAM, D. (1990). The life of the Afro-African woman in slavery. In D. C. Hine (Ed.), *Black women in American history: From colonial times through the nineteenth century* (Vol. 1, pp. 197–211). Brooklyn, NY: Carlson.

CLINTON, C. (1990). Caught in the web of the Big House: Women and slavery. In D. C. Hine (Ed.), *Black women in American history: From colonial times through the nineteenth century* (Vol. 1, pp. 225–239). Brooklyn, NY: Carlson.

COLLINS, P. H. (1990). *Black feminist thought: Knowledge, consciousness, and the politics of empowerment.* Boston: Unwin Hyman.

DAVIS, A. Y. (1971). Reflections on the black women's role in the community of slaves. *Black Scholar, 3*, 2–15.

DAVIS, A. Y. (1981). *Women, race and class*. New York: Random House.

DILL, B. T. (1979). The dialectics of black womanhood. *Signs: Journal of Women in Culture and Society, 4*, 543–555.

DILL, B. T. (1990). Race, class, and gender: Prospects for an all-inclusive sisterhood. In D. C. Hine (Ed.), *Black women's history: Theory and practice* (Vol. 1, pp. 121–140). Brooklyn, NY: Carlson.

ESCOTT, P. D. (1979). *Slavery remembered: A record of twentieth-century slave narratives*. Chapel Hill: University of North Carolina Press.

FARNHAM, C. (1990). Sapphire? The issue of dominance in the slave family, 1830–1865. In D. C. Hine (Ed.), *Black women in American history: From colonial times through the nineteenth century* (Vol. 2, pp. 369–384). Brooklyn, NY: Carlson.

FIELDS, A., & WALTERS, J. M. (1985). Hustling: Supporting a heroin habit. In B. Hanson, G. Beschner, J. M. Walters, & E. Bouvelle (Eds.), *Life with heroin: Voices from the inner city* (pp. 49–73). Lexington, MA: Lexington Books.

FOX-GENOVESE, E. (1988). *Within the plantation household: Black and white women in the old South*. Chapel Hill, NC: University of North Carolina Press.

FOX-GENOVESE, E. (1990). Strategies and forms of resistance: Focus on slave women in the United States. In D. C. Hine (Ed.), *Black women in American history: From colonial times through the nineteenth century* (Vol. 2, pp. 409–431). Brooklyn, NY: Carlson.

FRAZIER, E. F. (1968). *The Negro family in the United States*. New York: Macmillan.

FREDRICKSON, G. M., & LASCH, C. (1989). Resistance to slavery. In P. Finkelman (Ed.), *Rebellions, resistance, and runaways within the slave South* (pp. 141–156). New York: Garland.

GENOVESE, E. D. (1974). *Roll, Jordan, roll: The world the slaves made*. New York: Pantheon Books.

GIDDINGS, P. (1984). *When and where I enter: The impact of black women on race and sex in America*. New York: William C. Morrow.

GLASGOW, D. G. (1981). *The black underclass: Poverty, unemployment and entrapment of ghetto youth*. New York: Vintage Books.

GOFFMAN, E. (1961). *Asylums: Essays on the social situation of mental patients and other inmates*. Garden City, NY: Doubleday.

GUTMAN, H. (1976). *The black family in slavery and freedom, 1750–1925*. New York: Pantheon Books.

HIGGINBOTHAM, E. B. (1990). Beyond the sound of silence: Afro-American women in history. In D. C. Hine (Ed.), *Black women's history: Theory and practice* (Vol. 1, pp. 175–191). Brooklyn, NY: Carlson.

HIGGINBOTHAM, E. (1992). We were never on a pedestal: Women of color continue to struggle with poverty, racism, and sexism. In M. L. Andersen & P. H. Collins (Eds.), *Race, class, and gender* (pp. 183–191). Belmont, CA: Wadsworth.

HINE, D. C. (1990). Female slave resistance: The economics of sex. In D. C. Hine (Ed.), *Black women in American history: From colonial times through the nineteenth century* (Vol. 2, pp. 657–666). Brooklyn, NY: Carlson.

HOLT, S. A. (1994). Symbols, memory, and service: Resistance and family formation in nineteenth century African America. In L. E. Hudson, Jr. (Ed.), *Working toward freedom: Slave society and domestic economy in the American South* (pp. 192–210). Rochester, NY: University of Rochester Press.

HOOKS, B. (1981). *Ain't I a woman: Black women and feminism*. Boston: South End Press.

JONES, J. (1985). *Labor of love, labor of sorrow: Black women, work, and the family from slavery to the present*. New York: Basic Books.

JONES, J. (1990). "My mother was much of a woman": Black women, work, and the family under slavery. In D. C. Hine (Ed.), *Black women in American history: From colonial times through the nineteenth century* (Vol. 3, pp. 737–772). Brooklyn, NY: Carlson.

KING, D. K. (1988). Multiple jeopardy, multiple consciousness: The context of a black feminist ideology. *Signs: Journal of Women in Culture and Society, 14*, 43–72.

KING, D. K. (1990). Multiple jeopardy, multiple consciousness: The context of a black feminist ideology. In D. C. Hine (Ed.), *Black women's history: Theory and practice* (Vol. 1, pp. 331–361). Brooklyn, NY: Carlson.

LERNER, G. (ED.). (1972). *Black women in white America: A documentary history.* New York: Pantheon Books.

LEWIS, D. K. (1990). A response to inequality: Black women, racism and sexism. In D. C. Hine (Ed.), *Black women's history: Theory and practice* (Vol. 2, pp. 383–405). Brooklyn, NY: Carlson.

LICHTENSTEIN, A. (1988). "That disposition to theft, with which they have been branded": Moral economy, slave management and the law. *Journal of Social History, 21*, pp. 413–440.

MARABLE, M. (1990). Groundings with my sisters: Patriarchy and the exploitation of black women. In D. C. Hine (Ed.), *Black women's history: Theory and practice* (Vol. 2, pp. 407–445). Brooklyn, NY: Carlson.

OBITKO, M. E. (1990). "Custodians of a house of resistance": Black women respond to slavery. In D. C. Hine (Ed.), *Black women in American history: From colonial times through the nineteenth century* (Vol. 3, pp. 985–998). Brooklyn, NY: Carlson.

PAWELCZNSKA, A. (1979). *Values and violence in Auschwitz: A sociological analysis.* Berkeley: University of California Press.

RAWICK, G. P. (1972). *From sundown to sunup: The making of the black community.* Westport, CT: Greenwood.

STERLING, D. (1984). *We are your sisters: Black women in the nineteenth century.* New York: Norton.

STEVENSON, B. E. (1996). *Life in black and white: Family and community in the slave south.* New York: Oxford University Press.

VALENTINE, B. L. (1978). *Hustling and other hard work: Life styles in the ghetto.* New York: Free Press.

WEINER, M. F. (1998). *Mistresses and slaves: Plantation women in South Carolina, 1830–80.* Urbana: University of Illinois Press.

WHITE, D. G. (1985). *Ar'n't I a woman? Female slaves in the plantation South.* New York: Norton.

SECTION II

Women and the Law

5

Perpetrators and Victims
Maternal Filicide and Mental Illness

Stacey L. Shipley

This chapter will address maternal filicide as a result of postpartum depression or postpartum psychosis or other forms of psychotic illness such as schizophrenia, delusional disorder, bipolar disorder, or as a result of severe depression. The nomenclature of child murder such as neonaticide, infanticide, and filicide will be elucidated with the focus of the chapter remaining on maternal filicide. Discussion of a classification system, prevalence, motives, methods, victims, and the disposition of offenders will be offered. Specifically, altruistic filicide and acutely psychotic filicide will be explored by using the case example of Andrea Yates to illustrate how unidentified and untreated or undertreated mental illness can culminate into the occurrence of these tragic acts. Maternal filicide is in direct contradiction to society's firmly held notion that all mothers instinctually and unconditionally love, nurture, and protect their children. Women who kill their children as a result of an acute psychosis do not generally kill for the motives typically associated with murder such as punishment, revenge, and secondary gain. They often believe that they are being instructed by God or are in some way saving their children from unspeakable torment or disease and are driven by delusions and other perceptual disturbances. What are the legal implications for this type of crime? Whether or not these women belong in prison or a forensic psychiatric hospital and to what extent the media and public opinion influence their disposition will be examined. This chapter will discuss treatment implications for mental health professionals who will provide services to these women in a forensic setting (e.g., in jail or in a maximum-security forensic hospital). Women who kill their children due to psychosis often become very depressed and potentially suicidal after receiving psychiatric treatment in jail or a forensic hospital. Additionally, these women face unique issues such as grieving the loss of their children by their own hands, likely divorce, alienation from loved ones, and coming to terms with their mental illness under the harshest of circumstances. When their psychosis remits, these mothers are left asking, "How could

I have done such a thing?" Risk factors will be discussed and the importance of identifying those women who are most vulnerable to maternal filicide in order to provide successful treatment and prevention programs will be explored.

Child murder is so tragic and evokes such a strong response from the media and our communities that the women who commit these heinous acts are often demonized with little understanding of their actual plight. Women who murder their children vary in their motives and a rush to judgment and punishment often further exacerbates a horrible tragedy. The nation was horrified in June of 2001 at the news that Andrea Yates had drowned her five children in the bathtub of her Houston home. A collective reaction of "What kind of monster could have done such a thing?" and that someone had to pay for such brutal and senseless murders was heard across the country. As more information about the history of Mrs. Yates's mental illness, as well as her seemingly altruistic, albeit delusional, motives became apparent, it was impossible to compare her actions to the cold, calculated murder of one's children for personal or material gain or in some instances, revenge.

In October 1994, Susan Smith and her husband stood in front of media cameras and pled for the return of their two sons who had reportedly been kidnapped by an African American man with a gun. For nine days the country prayed for the safe return of the Smiths' children. It was later discovered that it was the tearful mother the public had seen on the news who was the actual killer. It was hard to imagine that a mother could drive her car into a lake with her two young boys strapped into their seats and watch as the car took several minutes to sink. When one thinks of murder for secondary gain, think of Susan Smith sending her car with her boys strapped inside deep into a lake. It was later revealed that Susan Smith had likely disposed of her sons in an attempt to further a romantic relationship with a man who did not want children. She viewed her children as a liability and she callously murdered them for her own personal gain. While it is clear that there is something deeply wrong with her character, she was not out of touch with reality due to mental illness. She knew the difference between right and wrong but was indifferent to the fate of her children in an effort to advance her own interests. She went to great lengths to hide her crime, which is not typical of severely mentally ill women, depressed or psychotic, who kill their children. The various categorizations of child murder based on age, motive, and impulse to kill will be discussed. However, this chapter seeks to increase the understanding of mentally ill mothers who kill their children from delusionally misguided altruistic motives. Consider the Andrea Yates case below:

On June 20, 2001, in Clearwater, Texas, Andrea Yates drowned all five of her children in the family bathtub after her husband Rusty left for work. Mrs. Yates had a long-standing history of mental illness, including four hospitalizations since 1999 and two attempted suicides, and she had had an outpatient prescription for Haldol, an antipsychotic medication used to help control hallucinations and other symptoms of psychosis (Gesalman, 2002; Manchester, 2003). She was suffering a severe postpartum psychosis with numerous delusions and hallucinations.

Andrea Yates was the valedictorian of her high school class, a champion swimmer, and went on to become an excellent nurse. She was an intelligent and gentle woman who by all accounts was a devoted mother who homeschooled her children, as well as providing them with Bible studies. She had been pregnant or breastfeeding almost continually for the seven years prior to the murder of her children (Spinelli, 2004). In addition to caring for Noah (age seven), John (age five), Paul (age three), Luke (age two), and Mary (six months), she was also caring for her beloved father, who was slipping away from Alzheimer's disease. He passed away six weeks after the birth of Mary, which was also a significant stressor for her. She was caring for her frail mother and her newborn, mourning the loss of her father, and home schooling her elder three children all while suffering from postpartum psychosis (Oberman, 2003). She had a family history of diagnosed and treated bipolar disorder and major depression (O'Malley, 2004; Spinelli, 2004). Each time she gave birth, she experienced a postpartum depression and her mental illness worsened with each subsequent birth.

Her first reported psychotic episode occurred after the birth of Noah in 1994. At the time, she refused to tell anyone of her experience because she had delusions that Satan would hear her and harm her children. After the first two pregnancies, she stopped jogging and swimming and with subsequent deliveries she became more depressed, psychotic, overwhelmed, and impaired. "Mood states of high energy and a hyperreligious focus on Satan and religious doctrine switched to documented worsening depression, psychosis, and suicide attempts. After her last two children were born, she had a total of four psychiatric hospitalizations. . . . After hospital discharge, a catatonic, psychotic Andrea Yates appeared to her friends and family like a 'caged animal,' staring for hours and scratching bald spots into her head. Discussions about Satan's presence were not uncommon in the Yates home, where a rigid religious belief system dominated the family's life" (Spinelli, 2004, p. 1554). She attempted suicide on two occasions after her fourth birth because she was trying to resist demonic voices or command hallucinations instructing her to kill her infant (Spinelli, 2004).

Each time she was discharged from the hospital, there was no family intervention. Mr. Yates indicated that she would begin to feel better and agree to have more children (Denno, 2003; Spinelli, 2004). She would frequently refuse medication because she was pregnant or lactating. According to Spinelli (2004), professional perinatal support and education were not available to teach her and her husband about the risks and benefits of pharmacotherapy during pregnancy and lactation, and the use of psychotropic medications for prevention of postpartum psychosis. Mrs. Yates's treating psychiatrist discontinued her Haldol two weeks prior to the event, resulting in her becoming floridly psychotic. She reported that Satan commanded her to kill her children to save them from the fires and torment of hell. She had delusional beliefs that she was influenced by the devil and that she had irreversibly damaged her children and the only way to protect their innocence and ensure their entrance to heaven was to kill them. It appears that everyone around her failed to appreciate the severity of her illness.

Andrea Yates was charged with capital murder with a maximum possible penalty of death, which the prosecution aggressively sought. While in jail, she requested a razor to shave her head and reveal the "mark of the beast-666" and reported "I am Satan" (Spinelli, 2004, p. 1549). The jury returned after three and a half hours with a verdict of guilty. During the sentencing phase, it took the jury only 35 minutes to decide on a sentence of life in prison. The Texas jury rejected her insanity defense despite the overwhelming psychiatric evidence. Manchester (2003) writes:

> In the United States, courts continue to evaluate postpartum depression defenses and other mental illnesses under the existing insanity defense [*M'Naghten test*]. The prevailing insanity defense test applied across United States jurisdictions is extremely narrow and makes proving legal insanity exceptionally difficult for even the most severely postpartum psychotic women. Therefore, the Yates case is most significant because it demonstrates the pressing need for

insanity defense reform to address the realities of postpartum psychosis and other mental illnesses. (p. 715)

In January of 2005, after Andrea had already been incarcerated for four years with deteriorating mental health, a Texas appeals court overturned her conviction based on the misleading and prejudicial information provided by an expert witness for the prosecution, Dr. Park Dietz. She currently remains in prison but will likely be granted a new trial. As much new information has come to light regarding Mrs. Yates's mental illness and its impact on her ability to appreciate the wrongfulness of her actions, one can only hope that a new jury will see that the justice rendered for someone like Susan Smith is not justice for Andrea Yates. She is a woman in deep torment due to her illness and the loss of her children, who is in need of intensive psychiatric treatment and therapy, not the harshest of punishments handed down to the most violent of offenders.

DEFINING CHILD MURDER

The killing of children by their parents is an almost unthinkable crime, particularly when the mother is the perpetrator. It is so antithetical to what it means to be mother, nurturing and the ultimate protector of her children. Fifty-seven percent of the murders of children under the age of 12 have been committed by the victims' parents (Dawson & Langan, 1994). According to the U.S. Bureau of Statistics (2002), out of all of the children under age five who were murdered between 1976 and 2000, 31% were killed by fathers; 30% were killed by mothers; 23% were killed by male acquaintances; 7% were killed by other relatives, and 3% were killed by strangers. The statistics on adult murder show that male perpetrators and victims outnumber females by a ratio of 5:1 or 6:1 (Jason, 1983; Marks & Kumar, 1993; Stanton & Simpson, 2002). When infants are killed within the first 24 hours, it is almost always by their mothers with equal number of male and female victims. For babies and children killed after one year, studies demonstrate that slightly more of the perpetrators are male or the numbers are almost even between male and females perpetrators and children are most frequently killed by one of their parents (Stanton & Simpson, 2002). In 1992, parents were responsible for 290 murders of their children to include adult children. Out of those, 121 (41.7%) were committed by mothers. Remarkably, infanticide and neonaticide is a common cause of childhood deaths (Dawson & Langan, 1994).

"Filicide" is often used as a generic term to describe the killing of children by their parents or stepparents and can include neonaticide, infanticide, and filicide (Stanton & Simpson, 2002). Dr. Philip Resnick, a forensic psychiatrist, was the first to categorize filicides based on the age of the child when they were killed (1969, 1970). He categorized neonaticide as the killing of a child directly after birth or shortly within the first 24 hours after birth. These perpetrators are typically young women who deny they're pregnant to themselves and others, and fear, not psychotic illness, motivates the crime (Oberman, 2003). Infanticide is the killing of a child up to one year by a mother who has not fully recovered from pregnancy and who typically suffers from some degree of mental disturbance often associated with postpartum mental illness (Bourget & Labelle, 1992). Filicide is the killing of a child older than one year and is very frequently associated with psychosis in the female perpetrator (Manchester, 2003). Pitt and Bale (1995) highlighted the characteristic differences between parents who commit infanticide as opposed to neonaticide. The results indicated that mothers in the neonaticide group were significantly younger than the mothers in the infanticide or filicide groups. The mothers in the infanticide or filicide groups were more likely to suffer from depression or psychoses and have histories of attempted suicide. "Eighty-eight percent of the infanticide mothers were married, while eighty-one percent of the neonaticide mothers were unwed" (Pitt & Bale, 1995, p. 378). Resnick (1970) found that the mothers involved in neonaticide are younger, often unmarried, and less frequently psychotic than mothers who commit filicide. He indicated that most neonaticides are carried out because the child isn't wanted due to illegitimacy, rape, or social stigma, rather than altruistic reasons.

"Studies have documented that neonaticide offenders are often single young women who deny the pregnancy and kill their newborn infants in an effort to avoid the social and parental pressure against an illegitimate child" (Manchester, 2003, p. 724). These young women may feel unable or unwilling to pursue alternatives such as adoption or abortion rather than murdering their newborns due to religion, culture, money, ambivalence, fear, denial, and immaturity (Oberman, 2003). It is fairly common for these women to make no plans for labor and often labor on the toilet and in silence. According to Oberman (2003), they may have a history of disassociative states related to a history of early abuse and chaotic family life and are frequently emotionally isolated from adults in their lives. The lack of mental illness in most perpetrators of neonaticide could be due to the possibility that newborns are more easily seen as objects as compared to older children, who are viewed as more valuable based on a more developed relationship (Gold, 2001). This also helps to explain why the murders of older children by their mothers are typically related to psychosis. Some researchers contend that the very young women who usually commit neonaticide are amenable to treatment, are not typically repeat offenders, and do not pose a threat to public safety, requiring rehabilitative services rather than prolonged prison sentences (Fazio & Comito, 1999; Schwartz & Isser, 2001). According to Schwartz and Isser (2001), "In the case of neonaticide, a delicate balancing act is needed to educate, rehabilitate, correct, and punish the woman who has killed her newborn" (p. 713)

Researchers have developed organized classification systems for child murder to improve mental health professionals' understanding of events leading up to these tragedies in the hope of intervening and educating to prevent future offenses (Pitt & Bale, 1995). These classifications have been based on interpretations of the perpetrator's motive, psychiatric history, psychosocial stressors, or source of impulse to kill (Lewis & Bunce, 2003). Resnick's (1969) seminal work reviewed 131 (88 mothers, 43 fathers) child murder cases from the international literature from 1751 to 1967 and proposed a classification system for filicide. He devised five categories based on motives for murder. His categories are: (1) altruistic filicide; (2) acutely psychotic filicide; (3) unwanted child filicide; (4) accidental filicide, and (5) spouse revenge filicide. He also introduced or coined "neonaticide" as a separate phenomenon and operationally defined it at that time.

1. Altruistic filicide can be separated into two subgroups, but is ultimately committed out of love or what is perceived by the parent as in the child's best interest. The first would involve an offense committed by a parent who believes he or she must relieve the child from some real or imagined (often delusional) condition, unbearable, inescapable torment or disease, or from the anticipated

suffering from the parent's suicide (McKee & Shea, 1998). The second is more typically associated with a major depression of the parent and involves a murder suicide, which was the most common (56% of maternal filicide reports). The parent believes that due to his or her deep love and devotion to the child, that the child would be better off dead or that the child would experience the same tortured existence as the parent or not be able to go on without the parent. Resnick indicated that the most dangerous period for the victim is the first six months and that when a mother commits suicide due to a postpartum depression, she typically sees the child as an extension of herself (Palermo, 2002). Scott (1973) separated this category into "primary" altruistic killings, which have also been termed as "mercy killings" where there is a real state of suffering (e.g., mental retardation or disease) and no evidence of secondary gain for the perpetrator. Wilczynski (1995, p. 368) states: "The much more common'secondary' altruistic killings involve no real degree of suffering in the child, and typically occur in the context of depression in the parent (virtually always the mother). These women expressed acute feelings of failure to measure up to society's standards of 'good' mothers or wives, such as one woman who regarded herself as a bad mother and wife, worried that the child was abnormal in some way, and felt that she did everything but it was never enough."

2. Acutely psychotic filicide would typically include parents who kill their children as a direct result of the delusions, hallucinations, or other forms of psychosis they experience, as well as epilepsy or delirium but did not include all psychotic child murders (24% of maternal filicide reports). This category includes those cases without a clear or discernable reality-based motive and the parent kills a child while under the pressure and effects of severe mental illness. The motives are typically tied closely to delusional beliefs or command hallucinations. Resnick (1972) found that three-quarters of the parents who killed their children presented with psychiatric symptoms prior to the homicide. Forty percent of these parents (almost always mothers) were seen by a physician shortly before committing the homicides.

3. Unwanted child filicide is carried out because the infant was never wanted or is no longer wanted by the parents unrelated to any mental illness or psychosis (11% of maternal filicide reports). Child murder for these reasons is frequently associated with extramarital affairs or illegitimacy (Resnick, 1969). It has been postulated that murder for this motive has decreased due to society's increasing acceptance and the growing commonness of unwed or single mothers in the United States, as well as women's increased presence in the workforce.

4. Accidental filicide is usually a result of an unintended homicide resulting from abuse that went too far or a "battered child syndrome" (7% of maternal filicide reports). The parent usually has a long history of abusing the child and in a rage strikes a fatal blow. It is most common for episodes of violent abuse to occur at mealtimes and bedtimes, as these are the times most associated with stress, arguments, and the need to discipline the child (Oberman, 2003).

5. Spouse revenge filicide is indicative of child murder that is perpetrated to retaliate against perceived rejection or wrongdoing by a spouse (Pitt & Bale, 1995). This has been referred to as the "Medea Complex" based on Greek mythology (Stern, 1948). After discovering her husband's betrayal through infidelity, she killed their two sons for revenge. The Medea Complex refers to maternal hatred for a child that can involve anything from rejection to murder (Simpson & Stanton, 2000). Resnick (1969) found that this group comprised only 2% of the maternal filicide reports.

Resnick (1969) found that the most common methods used by mothers committing filicide (infanticide) included strangulation, drowning, or gassing and that fathers typically used striking, squeezing, and stabbing. Head trauma was also a frequent cause. He reported that the most frequently diagnosed mental illnesses at the time of the offense, particularly for mothers, included schizophrenia, melancholia and manic-depressive disorders, and character disorders. An absence of psychosis was typical for the paternal offenders. The child's risk of murder was thought to be decreased as they aged. In 1999, out of the children that were killed by their parents, 42% were younger than one year and only 6 percent were older than four years (Gold, 2001). Resnick maintained that they were particularly vulnerable when bonding and maternal attachment had not yet been established (Palermo, 2002).

Approximately 30 years after Dr. Resnick began his research on parents who kill their children, he served as an expert witness for the defense in *Texas v. Andrea Pia Yates* and attempted to define "rationality within irrationality." To illustrate his aforementioned categories within the context of this case example, consider the following (as cited in O'Malley, 2004):

> According to Resnick, there are five classifications of parents who harm their children. This was not a case of spousal revenge: Andrea Yates believed Rusty Yates was a good husband. It was not a case of battered child syndrome: the Yates children weren't abused. It was certainly not an example of the children's being unwanted: Andrea Yates was a determined Supermom. Three of the five classifications did not apply, in Resnick's opinion. Yates, he said, did fit into the two remaining categories: "acutely psychotic" (no logical motive to do what she did–say, for insurance money) and "altruistic" (killing because she thought it was in the children's best interests). He classified Yates children's killings as "altruistic."
>
> "Mrs. Yates," he said, "had a choice to make: to allow her children to end up burning in hell for eternity or to take their lives on earth." By taking their earthly lives she achieved two good things: the children were happy through all eternity, and Satan was "eliminated for humankind. . . . She would give up her life on earth . . . *and her afterlife* for the purpose of eliminating Satan and protecting her children from the fate of eternal damnation." (p. 157)

To further elucidate the contrast between Andrea Yates, a mentally ill mother who killed for altruistic reasons, and Susan Smith, who appeared to kill for selfish ones, Dr. Resnick had been consulted by the defense team of Susan Smith, but concluded that he could not "be helpful to the defense with regard to an insanity defense in that case of child killing" (as cited in O'Malley, 2004, p. 157).

Scott (1973) developed a classification system with a sample of 39 maternal filicides that was more focused on the source of the impulse to commit filicide and included the following categories: (1) battering mothers, (2) mentally ill mothers, (3) retaliating mothers, (4) unwanted children, and (5) mercy killing. He contended that the origin of the impulse to kill was more objective than apparent motive, which was often overdetermined (Stanton & Simpson, 2002). He also expressed concern about the repercussions of speculating on motive for sentencing. Scott (1973) found that the diagnoses of the women who killed their children included personality disorders (43%), reactive depression (21%), or psychotic illness (16%). The psychotic illness group included postpartum psychosis, schizoid paranoid psychosis, and depressive psychosis. Regarding psychosocial stressors, he identified stress in the family, such as severe marital problems, housing problems, financial difficulties, and social issues such as being a young mother as risk factors (Palermo, 2002).

D'Orban's (1979) classification of maternal filicide was developed from her review of 89 cases of all English and Welsh women incarcerated at Holloway Prison over a six-year period convicted of murdering or attempting to murder their children. Information was available from psychiatric assessments, case records, and direct interviewing by the author in approximately half of all the cases. Her model is a modification of Scott's 1973 system and incorporated neonaticide basing classification on the source of the impulse to kill (e.g., parent, child, or situation). She had six categories which included: (1) battering mothers (36 cases, 40.4%), where the killing was an impulsive act triggered by the victim's behavior; (2) mentally ill mothers (42 cases, 27%), which included all psychotic, depressed, or suicidal women; (3) neonaticides (11 cases, 12.4%), which included newborns killed within 24 hours of birth; (4) retaliating women (9 cases, 10.1%), who took out aggression toward the spouse onto the child with the stimulus being revenge; (5) mothers of unwanted children (8 cases, 9%), "whose children died from passive neglect or active aggression" (p. 680); and (6) mercy killings (1 case, 1.1%), where the mother murders her child to end her child's suffering from a real illness without apparent secondary gain (McKee & Shea, 1998). Battering mothers and mentally ill mothers were the most common classifications in D'Orban's (1979) sample. The mentally ill mothers were most commonly married with the least marital stress, were older, attacked older children, and more commonly had multiple victims (Stanton & Simpson, 2002). D'Orban (1979) found that 60% of the sample was in contact with health workers or social workers and 17% of the mentally ill sample was specifically in contact with psychiatric services. The retaliatory groups were related to chaotic personalities, with high rates of suicide attempts and marital conflict but also were typically older, more frequently married, and were more likely to kill older children (Stanton & Simpson, 2002). Finally, Oberman (2003) indicated that the mentally ill mothers often murdered their children not only due to the mental illness, but their relative isolation in caring for the child also played a role. Once again, Andrea Yates was cited as exemplifying the case of a severely mentally ill mother left to care for five children with virtually no outside support. She was under the incredible stress of attending to the emotional and physical demands of her children, while experiencing a significant depressive and psychotic episode that would have inhibited her ability to meet those needs (Oberman, 2003).

Although the categories are similar to Resnick's (1969), these categories do not include paternal filicides and attempt to reduce misclassification from filicides that could fall into more than one category. "For example, her category of mentally ill mothers incorporates all psychiatrically impaired women and is distinguished from mercy filicides in that the child's suffering was from a real, not delusionally based illness. In Resnick's (1969) classification, a parent might be placed in either category depending on which motive seemed to the clinician to be more prominent" (McKee & Shea, 1998, p. 680). Both D'Orban's (1979) and Scott's (1973) classification systems are based on characteristics of the female parent as a result of most filicides being perpetrated by mothers of children who are under the age of 12 (McKee & Shea, 1998).

Bourget and Gagne (2002) conducted an eight-year review (1991 to 1998) of coroners' files in Quebec, Canada, and identified 34 cases of children murdered by their mothers. Their study revealed that most victims were less than six years old and there were numerous cases in which multiple siblings were murdered. Of the 34 victims, 19 were male and 15 were female and the ages ranged from approximately 4 weeks to 13 years (<1 year, 8 [23.5%]; 1–5 years, 17 [50%], 6–10 years, 7 [20.5%], >10 years, 2 [5.9%]). Twenty-four out of 34 offenses occurred in the family home (70.6%). The most common method was carbon monoxide poisoning (23.5%), followed by use of a firearm (17.6%), strangulation (14.7%), drowning (14.7%), stabbing (11.8%), beating (5.9%), and other (11.8%). In five of the cases, two siblings were killed; in one case, three siblings were killed; and in all six of these cases, the maternal suicide occurred immediately after the murders. There was no indication of family violence in any of the six cases and all six mothers had been previously treated for mental illness, five for depression, and one for psychosis. Three of these mothers had contacted a doctor or psychiatrist about their problems.

Out of 27 mothers (ages 19 to 49 years) in the sample, 15 of them attempted suicide after the filicide (11 of the 15 were successful). In the 11 cases involving 22 children of completed maternal suicide, a psychiatric motive was determined and 10 had prior treatment for mental illness (9 for depression, 1 for psychosis). Studies have shown that homicidal parents have high rates of suicide attempts; mothers are more likely to commit suicide after the act than fathers, and that suicide attempts by homicidal parents are often highly lethal and successful (Bourget & Gagne, 2002; Myers, 1970; Rodenburg, 1971; West, 1965). Bourget and Gagne (2002) identified a psychiatric motive for greater than 85% of the mothers, and the majority of the mothers had prior psychiatric treatment for a depressive or psychotic disorder. Eighteen of the women in this sample had a diagnosis of major depressive disorder and four had a diagnosis of schizophrenia or other psychotic disorder. There were diagnoses of substance abuse and almost half had contact with others about their problems to include medical or psychiatric staff (22%). Numerous researchers have identified major depression with psychotic features as the most common diagnosis in maternal offenders (Bourget & Gagne, 2002; Myers, 1970; Rodenburg, 1971; West, 1965).

In a study comparing parental and nonparental homicide, Bourget and Bradford (1990) determined that 30.8% of parents who commit filicide had a diagnosis of major depression compared with none of the nonparental perpetrators. Of the nine maternal filicides, five of the mothers were in a postpartum period of less than five weeks from delivery at the time of the offense. Greater than 46% of the parental offenders had a personality disorder, 23% had a substance abuse disorder, and 15.4% had an adjustment disorder. Most nonparental offenders had a personality disorder (53.2%), then substance abuse disorders (25.5%), and adjustment disorders (8.5%).

MENTAL ILLNESS AND MURDER

There are a variety of reasons that parents kill their children. Explanations range from postpartum depression or psychosis to schizophrenia. Postpartum depression is a mental disorder that occurs with new mothers shortly after they give birth. Postpartum mental illness is vastly underdiagnosed and can have devastating consequences for the mother, child, and parental relationship (Born, Zinga, & Steiner, 2004). According to the American Psychiatric Association's *Diagnostic and Statistical Manual of Mental Disorders*, Fourth Edition *(DSM-IV)* (American Psychiatric Association [APA], 1994), the severest form of postpartum depression, postpartum psychosis, often presents with episodes of delusions in which the mother feels that the infant is possessed or the mother has hallucinations that tell her to kill the child. Most incidents of postpartum depression do not include delusions or hallucinations, but there are suicidal ideation, obsessional thoughts of violence toward the child, and psychomotor agitation. Whereas the postpartum blues are very common (up to 80%), only about 0.2% of childbearing women will experience postpartum psychosis, which typically emerges within two weeks of the childbirth and frequently requires hospitalization (Dobson & Sales, 2000; Manchester, 2003). Postpartum blues peak three to five days after birth and involve a period of emotional lability with frequent crying, irritability, confusion, and anxiety that is transient and doesn't typically require treatment.

Postpartum depression has gained the acknowledgment of many in the mental health field. Some have hypothesized that environmental stressors associated with becoming a parent, along with the immediate demands required of the parent, can overwhelm and cause this disorder in even the most psychologically sound mother (Ewing, 1997). Hormonal changes have also been reported to be a major factor in explaining the incidence of severe depression and unusual actions by some mothers after the birth of their children (Ewing, 1997). According to Pruett (2002, p. 353), "The postpartum depression that often precedes an infanticide is a distinct, transitory illness that should be designated as such. Identifying mothers with postpartum depression who commit infanticide may not be easy . . . , but the possibility of early intervention and the potential role for hospitals and pediatricians to play in screening and intervention, render these mothers an important subgroup to identify."

Postpartum affective disorders are due in part to sensitivity to large changes in hormones such as progesterone, estrogen, and cortisol that occur near the end of pregnancy or after delivery of the child (Glover & Kammerer, 2004). Postpartum depression is more likely to occur in women who have experienced it with previous children and have a familial history of affective disorders. It usually begins in the first 6 to 12 weeks after delivery, although the onset can be later following a period of well-being (Born et al., 2004). The symptoms are similar to that of a major depressive episode but additional symptoms "include feelings of guilt or inadequacy about the new mother's ability to care for the infant, and a preoccupation with the infant's well-being or safety severe enough to be considered obsessional" (p. 31). Both anxiety and depression are as common during pregnancy as after childbirth (Glover & Kammerer, 2004). The prevalence of depressive symptoms in the first few weeks following childbirth is between 10% and 20% (Born et al., 2004). Fortunately, postpartum depression rarely results in maternal filicide (Gold, 2001). These women are more likely to seek help from their primary care physicians or their obstetricians than mental health professionals. "While severe depression and psychoses are easily recognized, milder or more insidious forms of depressive or other psychiatric illness are frequently missed" (Born et al., 2004, p. 29). The conditions can progress to the point of requiring hospitalization. Schwartz and Isser (2001) contend that postpartum depression and postpartum psychosis do not occur until several days to weeks after delivery and cannot account for neonaticide.

There is a strong genetic component to postpartum psychosis and there is a joint vulnerability with bipolar disorder. In other words, a family history of bipolar disorder is a strong risk factor for postpartum psychosis and research also indicates that this creates vulnerability to a puerperal trigger (Glover & Kammerer, 2004). Women with a genetic predisposition for a mental illness or a personal history of mental illness, a mood disorder in particular, are far more vulnerable to the flood of hormones associated with the postpartum period. Having symptoms of depression during pregnancy has been correlated with a reoccurrence of a bipolar depressive episode after delivery and approximately one in two women with bipolar disorder will have a relapse postpartum (Born et al., 2004; Chaudron & Pies, 2003). Early screening, identification, and intervention with those women at risk or who are already experiencing symptoms is imperative. In addition to the psychosis that is biologically driven, a woman with postpartum psychosis also experiences mood lability consistent with bipolar disorder.

Manic symptoms rather than depressive symptoms can result from a postpartum period as the primary symptoms in approximately 40% of cases (Huysman, 2003). These women typically have a genetic predisposition to mania, based on their family history. Mania is typically characterized by elation, a decreased need for sleep, irritability, agitation, poor, impulsive judgment, and severe hyperactivity. This period of mania or hypomania can last for hours, days, or weeks and can be followed by a period of depression. Often, these women find their increased productivity and extreme feelings of well-being as a positive, not alarming, experience and fail to immediately recognize it as symptoms of mental illness.

Postpartum psychosis occurs in only 1 in 500 to 1,000 childbirths, but the risk of reoccurrence is very high (Glover & Kammerer, 2004). It typically begins within the first 48 to 72 hours after delivery but the risk of onset is high for up to four months. Typically, the individual presents with lability of mood, rambling speech, disorganized behavior, and hallucinations or delusions. According to Born et al. (2004, p. 32), symptoms characteristic of this disorder include:

- Delusional beliefs, often related to the baby (e.g., infant death, denial of birth, belief that infant is possessed or has special powers)
- Hypervigilance about the baby
- Exhilaration and sleeplessness
- Psychomotor hyperkinesias and akinesia affecting expressive and reactive emotions
- Hypersensitivity to neutral comments
- Visual, tactile, olfactory, or auditory hallucinations
- Feelings of being perplexed, confused, or disoriented (organiclike presentation)
- Impaired cognition
- Deliriumlike symptoms
- Poor appetite
- Stupor
- Waxing and waning course with lucid periods

Women who experience postpartum psychosis also have more unusual psychotic symptoms, such as tactile, olfactory (e.g., smelling sulfur), and visual hallucinations consistent with an organic psychotic presentation (Wisner, Gracious, Piontek, Peindl, & Perel, 2002). The waxing and waning course of the illness would be consistent with a woman who looks stable one minute and can be floridly psychotic the next. When she appears confused or in a "zombielike" state or a lucid state that is different from her episodes of florid psychosis, the credibility of her psychosis may be called into question, particularly by individuals who are not aware of the unpredictable nature of the psychosis (Spinelli, 2004). This unpredictability necessitates that mothers be separated from their children while experiencing these symptoms and until thoroughly treated and mentally stable. She may be compelled, particularly by delusions or command hallucinations, to commit violent acts despite reasoned behavior in other contexts. "For example, in the case of Andrea Yates, the prosecutors concluded that she could not have been psychotic when she murdered her children because she was later lucid enough to call for help and to report her actions to the police" (Spinelli, 2004, p. 1551).

Postpartum psychosis severely impacts daily living and the risk for infanticide or suicide is high, frequently requiring inpatient hospitalization (Born et al., 2004; Chaudron & Pies, 2003). "Hospitalization is mandatory when parents express concern over harming their children and are overconcerned about their children's health" (Pitt & Bale, 1995, p. 384). The average length of hospitalization is approximately two months but a full recovery may necessitate more than a year (Born et al., 2004). It has been estimated that between 39% and 81% of these women may endure a relapse of illness not during a postpartum period. Specifically, the relapse rate for postpartum psychosis is 80% or greater (Altshuler, Hendrick, & Cohen, 1998; Gold, 2001; Stowe et al., 2001). The postpartum psychosis may also reoccur with each subsequent delivery (Spinelli, 2004). Some contend that a progressive postpartum depression can extend for months or even years after the postpartum period if not identified or treated (Huysman, 2003; Spinelli, 2004). Rates of infanticide that resulted from untreated postpartum psychosis have been estimated to be as high as 4% (Altshuler et al., 1998; D'Orban, 1979; Gold, 2001). Huysman (2003) describes the devastating effects of this phenomenon:

> We expect that a simple and time-limited postpartum depression will abate on its own or be treated in a timely fashion. The mother with *progressive* postpartum depression (PPPD), however, does NOT recover without treatment. She merely experiences a hiatus until her next episode. Subsequent episodes are very often triggered by rejections, separations, and losses, and recur throughout the woman's life. Usually the next episode is worse than the last. If this pattern goes unchecked, the mother will spiral into a cycle of illness that can destroy her life and her family. (p. 43)

Psychopharmacologic interventions before or after delivery can dramatically prevent the reoccurrence of postpartum mental illnesses, which occurs in 20% to 50% of cases (Spinelli, 2004). Research has demonstrated the efficacy of administering an appropriate antipsychotic, mood stabilizer, or antidepressant in the immediate postpartum period in preventing a relapse of postpartum psychosis, mania, or depression (Austin, 1992; Spinelli, 2004; Wisner & Wheeler, 1994). As compared to women with nonpostpartum psychosis, women with postpartum depression take longer to respond to psychotropic medication for depression and necessitate more antidepressant medications to gain a response (Gold, 2001). An increasing number of studies indicate that the use of antidepressant medication during the end of a pregnancy and after delivery produces minimal risk to the mother or baby (Altshuler et al., 1998; Gold, 2001; Wisner, Perel, & Findling, 1996). "The relatively low risk of the use of psychotropic medication during breast-feeding must be weighed against the risk of untreated postpartum disorder and the benefits of improvement in maternal mood" (Gold, 2001, p. 345). A family or personal history of mood disorder is the most important risk factor in determining the need for early medication management of postpartum depression (Spinelli, 2004). Despite the clear need, many women are unwilling to seek any help because they are ashamed of feeling depressed when they believe they should feel happy. They may also be unwilling to admit to having inappropriate and unnatural thoughts about harming their children, believing they have failed as mother and women (Gold, 2001). Their unwillingness to seek help and signs missed by medical or mental health professional who have contact with some of these women too often result in tragic consequences for the children.

SYMPTOMS AND MOTIVES

It is very uncommon for women to kill their children as a result of coldhearted, callous disregard, revenge, or some other self-serving motive. It is far more common that maternal filicide results from severe mental illness. Sadoff (1995) indicated that there is little evidence that these mothers kill in a callous, calculated manner but rather as a result of depression or psychosis, or in a disassociative state, or state of fear or panic. When women kill children that are over one year of age, depression and psychosis are often factors in the extreme emotional and impaired reality orientation that leads to this tragic event. Certainly, psychosis is more common in filicide as compared to any other form of child murder. Resnick (1970) found that psychosis was the primary factor in two-thirds of the women in his sample that committed filicide. These women kill their children based on altruistic beliefs of being merciful or ending real or imagined (delusional) suffering. Mood-congruent delusions or hallucinations may also result in a mother believing that she has irreversibly hurt or damaged her child or children in some way (Gold, 2001). Andrea Yates has reported that she believed she was possessed and was a "Jezebel" and that her poor mothering threatened her children's ability to go to heaven. She saw only two choices: either kill her children while some innocence remained, therefore allowing them entrance into heaven, or continue to damage them and ensure their eternal damnation. In her delusional state, her love for her children and her belief that she was saving them from eternal suffering led her to follow through on the grotesque act of drowning all five of her children. Some severely depressed and suicidal mothers will murder their child in order to prevent the child from the suffering associated with growing up motherless in a harsh, cruel world that will only cause them the same pain as what she endured.

In some instances, women experiencing ongoing grandiose delusions and a strong religious background may believe that she is being commanded by God to kill her children as a testament to her faith and to ensure entrance into heaven for both herself and her children. She may, in her delusional state and within the context of her strong religious upbringing, believe that she should not only do God's bidding without questioning, but that she has done a good thing that is in the best interest of her child. Certainly, the story of Abraham being instructed by God to kill his son has been referenced and may even serve as a model for this type of delusional belief. Consider many evangelical religions that encourage speaking in tongues, being filled by the Holy Spirit, and directly communicating with God. While these religions are in no way responsible for the actions or mental illness of these women, the norms of the church may make her perceptual disturbances more difficult to identify. If a woman casually described receiving instructions or directly communicating with God, she would likely not be challenged or questioned further and this could be missed as a sign of mental illness. Let me be clear, strong religious convictions or experiences do not equal mental illness; however, a woman who is predisposed to mental illness and begins to become symptomatic might be completely overlooked if her delusions and hallucinatory experiences occur in this manner. The psychotic woman with grandiose delusions of a religious nature may believe that otherwise meaningless things in her environment symbolize messages or are signs from God that require her action. Implications of this type of psychotic presentation will be further explored later in this chapter. In each of the aforementioned examples, these women's beliefs are not reality based and are directly resulting from their mental illness. The very act of the murders is so heinous that society immediately reacts to punish the monsters who could have committed such acts. Little is understood about the tragic, tortured, and often very psychotic motives that underlie these deaths.

Schizophrenics have been found guilty of infanticide. Depending on the defense team's strategy, many of these women will plead insanity due to their disorder. Most likely, these women would not be considered the victims of postpartum depression considering their past or current history of schizophrenia, although the symptoms are similar. However, women with chronic mental illness (e.g., schizophrenia) are more likely to commit infanticide due to postpartum stressors or symptom exacerbation at a time when they've discontinued their medication (Spinelli, 2004). Researchers have found that there exists increased risk for mental illness among mothers who kill their children, with major depression with psychotic features being diagnosed most frequently (Pruett, 2002). It is also very common for mentally ill mothers who kill based on altruistic, depressive, and psychotic motives to not attempt to conceal their crimes. In fact, it is not uncommon for these women to confess and to request punishment (Brockington, 1995; Gold, 2001). While they might understand that according to the strict letter of the law it was wrong, they may believe that they had no other choice, were acting in the best interest of their children, or were morally justified in answering to a higher power. In some cases, the mother may be so psychotically disorganized at the time of the crime that she could not appreciate the wrongfulness of her actions in any legal or moral context. Legal alternatives and ramifications will be further discussed below.

McGrath (1992) identified 115 mentally ill women who had killed their children over a period of 50 years that had been admitted to Broadmoor Hospital. Eighty-three percent of them had a major mental illness, specifically, 46% had affective psychosis and 37% had schizophrenia. Substance abuse had little impact and was not a factor in the maternal filicides. The majority of these women were married, and older (in their late 20s and 30s). Most presented as depressed at the time of the crime and had an altruistic motive. Suicide attempts were made in approximately half of the cases shortly after the offense. Almost half of the women had a previous inpatient psychiatric treatment and only 25% had no evidence of prior mental illness. Recidivism only occurred in one case, a woman who later killed her husband.

Myers (1970) found that from 1940 to 1965, 35 preadolescent victims were murdered by their mothers. In the vast majority of these cases, the mothers were determined to be overtly psychotic at the time of the offense. He found that the most common diagnosis was a psychotic depression, but that many suffered from schizophrenia. It was noted that the psychotically depressed mother will kill her child in attempt to "save" the child from a hostile, punitive world. Myers also noted that the schizophrenic mother may view the child as being defective, much as her own sense of self or her own body image is distorted. He indicated that the mother may repeatedly seek out a family physician or pediatrician with the unrelenting conviction that something is physically wrong with her child. Some maternal filicides have occurred as a result of a psychotically depressed mother enduring physical and emotional suffering and the delusion that she and her children are suffering from an incurable disease. These mothers are likely to contemplate or attempt suicide after killing their children to prevent them from suffering. Hypochondriacal or psychosomatic problems are not uncommon in these women. Myers also found in his sample that mothers may seek psychiatric consultation due to being obsessed with fears of harming their children or distressed by homicidal impulses toward them. Andrea Yates attempted suicide on one occasion because she was so distressed about her ongoing thoughts of harming her children.

When considering the mental state of these mothers, consider the following (as cited in Stanton & Simpson, 2002):

> Altruism has been seen as central as described by Baker (1902), "It may seem paradoxical, but it is not vice that leads to the death of the infant, rather it is morbid and mistaken maternal solitude" (p. 16). McGrath (1992) cited several examples of offenders' initial statements as recorded in police reports, several of which exemplify this perspective, e.g. "I have given her peace. . . . I loved him so" (p. 284). Resnick (1969) classified more than half his series as "altruistic filicide" or murders committed out of love. In this view, the murder would be seen as a rational act in the context of the mother's delusional perception of the world. (p. 10)

There are some women who, while in the grips of psychosis to include paranoid delusions, act violently toward their child out of fear. Some women have been known to kill an infant that they delusionally believed to be possessed by demons or to accidentally kill a child, while attempting to extricate an evil force within the child, without any other person's involvement and only based on their psychosis. Harder (1967) explained altruistic filicides as part of a gender role stereotype, whereby we view all women as nurturing caregivers devoted to protecting their children at all costs and must incorporate mothers killing their children into this schema (Stanton & Simpson, 2002). He further described the extreme of the maternal attentiveness as an example of reaction formation, in which the hostility toward the child is defended against by attempting to overnurture or care for the child (Stanton & Simpson, 2002). Additionally, the psychoanalytic viewpoint of mothers who kill their children as an extension of themselves involves her overidentifying with the child and that the aggression was actually directed toward herself (Stanton & Simpson, 2002). Tuteur and Glotzer (1959) described suicide–murder situations as an effort to erase the "total-all" or to completely annihilate the self due to a deep sense of rejection (as cited in Stanton & Simpson, 2002, p. 10). West (1965) states that homicide followed by suicide occurs in greater than 50% of the murders committed by women in England. According to Bourget and Bradford (1987), studies in the United States report that this occurs with less frequency, in the range of 10–13%. There is a high frequency of primary affective disorder in those individuals who commit murder-suicide, particularly in maternal filicide (Bourget & Bradford 1987). Finally, it has been suggested that mental illness may disinhibit filicidal

thoughts or create them. The preponderance of the evidence points to mental illness leading to maternal filicide rather than facilitating preexisting impulses.

Stanton, Simpson, and Wouldes (2000) undertook a qualitative study of filicide by
mentally ill mothers. Six women were identified and interviewed and each described an
intense investment in mothering their child or children. There were not significant external
stressors, but rather the experience of their mental illness was described as extremely
stressful. The motivations were described as altruistic or as an extension of their own suicides. These women, once stabilized with psychiatric and psychological interventions, further described feeling deep regret about the murders and feeling responsible, despite their
awareness of their mental illness at the time of the offense. This study sought to explain the
experience of these women from their own frame of reference. Each of the women in the
study suffered from a major mental illness to include severe mood or psychotic disorders,
which had required active, ongoing, inpatient and outpatient treatment for a year or longer.
The *DSM-IV* diagnoses given included major depressive disorder, schizoaffective disorder
(in either a manic or depressed phase prior to the killing), and schizophrenia. It was noted
that the women who described being manic prior to the filicide described mood incongruent delusions at the time of the filicide. Each described their experience of mothering as
changed with the onset of their mental illness, although they continued to love and care for
their children to the best of their ability. While they were so depressed, even minor events
could be experienced as extreme stressors.

Stanton et al. (2000, p. 1454) noted that being a good mother was important to all in
their study. One of the mothers stated, "You know, I've always sort of wanted to be the perfect Mother." It is not uncommon for mothers who commit maternal filicide to feel that
they must be perfect and see themselves as fatally flawed and perhaps their children by
extension. So many high-profile cases involve women who were caring for their children at
home full time with little support, as well as homeschooling them, and the like. These
women may also feel that they are inadequate in their marriages or that nothing they do can
match up to what is expected of them. In the study by Stanton et al. (2000, p. 1454), one
mother stated, "I expected so much of myself but when I look back now. . . . I mean I was
looking out the window and seeing, you know, the neighbors and everything doing really
well, but, and feeling that I wasn't, but I actually was. I was actually just doing so well and
I couldn't see it." Some of the women in the study described living with delusions of persecution, which caused ongoing, severe stress. One mother stated, "I thought people were
following me or vehicles were following me, or people were listening into where I was
staying or spying on me. It was terrible, yeah" (p. 1454). Another extremely difficult man-
ifestation of their psychosis was seeing signs and messages in otherwise benign things
around them. They described the challenge of psychotic reality where nothing was what it
seemed. One mother stated, "One of the things I used to do was like watch cars go past,
each color meant something different and each number plate meant something different
and they used to tell me things. The plates used to tell me things. I did that a lot. I hated it."

Stanton et al. found that the descriptions from women who were manic before they
killed their children were artificially positive. One woman reported, "Everything was so
good and wonderful. . . . Well, I felt I had it under control, really, I didn't realize."
A woman with this experience is unlikely to view her more euphoric feelings, a sense of
well-being, or increased productiveness as problematic or a sign of mental illness. The
researchers indicated that self-monitoring would have been impossible for the women who

experienced mania before the filicide due to symptoms such as grandiosity and euphoria. Finally, some of the depressed women in the study described thinking about the deaths for a few days or a few weeks prior to the event. Some of these women described feeling very worried about their children while depressed but with hindsight were clear that the concerns were not reality based. "The psychotic women described no warning at all and were adamant that if they had been asked about ideas of killing their children before the event they would have had no indication that it was likely or even possible" (p. 1455).

The methods of murder used by the six women in this study included stabbing ($n = 3$), jumping with her child from a high place, setting fire to the house, attempted drowning, and suffocation. There were multiple victims in some cases. These women did not express hostile or negative perceptions of their children, which are often seen in unwanted or abused child killings. Their perceptions were favorable or unremarkable. There was also a lack of significant premeditation or planning. The majority of the women were not able to give well organized accounts of what motivated them to kill, but altruism was prominent in the discernable accounts of motivation offered. Some of the women offered delusionally based mercy killings, "killing to protect or rescue the children from some awful fate that was indicated by their delusional system. They were clear about acting in the interest of their child(ren)" (p. 1456). Consider one of the participant's accounts:

A.   I thought that they [people in the mother's delusional world] were going to use my daughter as well, I don't know, and um . . .
B.   So you were kind of scared for her?
A.   Yeah, I thought she was going to go through what I had been through. I just thought that the devil was going to take [the baby] in a cot death, that I had to save her and return her to the angels because if he took her, she'd go to Purgatory, she'd be stuck there forever. (p. 1456)

Stanton et al. (2000) found that all of the women bitterly regretted the deaths of their children, grieved their loss, and desperately wanted what was done to be undone. They stated that the filicide was ego-syntonic as a result of their delusions, but was undoubtedly ego-dystonic once the woman stabilized or recovered from her illness. All of the women in the study were found Not Guilty by Reason of Insanity (NGRI) and were, therefore, not legally responsible, but still carried a tremendous burden despite their illness at the time of the crime. They questioned why it had to happen, and indicated it was something they would have to live with for the rest of their lives. When reflecting on what had happened at the time, the women in this study described having the intention to kill and not being out of control, although their actions were not reality based. None of these women attempted to avoid detection and had gone to the police, family, or neighbors to let them know what had happened. A woman stated, "Even though that is what I have been diagnosed as, and, I can't just say, Oh, I wasn't in my right mind, everything is fine. You know, I still blame myself and feel a lot of guilt. I really hate myself that I didn't get the right sort of help" (Stanton et al., 2000, p. 1457).

Finally, Stanton et al. (2000) concluded that impaired reality, disorganized thinking, and the instability of the women's mental states, not abuse or other psychosocial stressors, were the main factors for the mentally ill filicidal mother. "One might postulate that the intensity of the suffering perceived in a delusional state is of such a magnitude as to explain the filicide rationally. However, other features of the illness such as impaired impulse control, affective dysregulation, lack of cognitive flexibility, and unbalanced judgment are likely to contribute" (p. 1459).

Lewis and Bunce (2003) conducted a study to examine a sample ($n = 55$) of filicidal mothers and compared those with and without psychotic symptoms at the time of the filicide. The sample included all women referred for criminal responsibility or competency to stand trial evaluations from 1974 to 1996 at Michigan's Center for Forensic Psychiatry. The majority (52.7%) of these women had psychotic symptoms at the time of the offense. They found that the women with psychosis were more likely to have past and ongoing mental health treatment, to be older, unemployed, and more educated, and were divorced or separated. Their greater education but lesser employment may be a result of either being stay-at-home moms, homeschooling, or due to the progression of their psychotic illness. They were more likely to have more than one child and to not have had prior contact with Child Protective Services. Nonpsychotic mothers were more likely to be responsible for the beating deaths of their children. The mothers with psychosis more frequently confessed immediately after the homicide, used weapons, attempted suicide at the time of the crime, killed multiple children, and expressed homicidal thoughts or concerns regarding their children to psychiatrists and family before the filicide. Psychotic and nonpsychotic mothers were equally likely to have used alcohol or illegal drugs at the time of the offense. As one might expect, psychotic women were more likely to be adjudicated as incompetent to stand trial and to be found Not Guilty by Reason of Insanity than nonpsychotic women. Lewis and Bunce (2003) found that filicidal mothers were more likely to be psychotic if they had expressed homicidal ideation toward their children at least two weeks before killing them, and voiced concerns to their family about their children within two weeks of the filicide.

Similar to past studies, the most common diagnoses were schizophrenia, major depressive disorder with psychotic features, and personality disorder. Out of those women experiencing psychosis, 18 (62.1%) had command hallucinations; 23 (79.3%) had paranoid delusions (e.g., their children were going to be harmed by an external force, their children were at risk due to unfit mothering); 15 (51.7%) believed their children were dangerous (e.g., that they were possessed or were "monsters"); and 26 (89.7%) experienced auditory hallucinations (Lewis & Bunce, 2003, p. 463). Neither the gender of the victim nor the age of the victim was significantly associated with maternal psychosis. Lewis and Bunce concluded that maternal filicide was an extremely difficult event to predict and prevent.

Another explanation for why a mother would kill her child is Munchausen's syndrome by proxy (MSBP), which has not been addressed elsewhere in this discussion. Munchausen's is a disorder found in the *DSM-IV* as an appendix to factitious disorder. It differs from factitious disorder in that persons with Munchausen's syndrome have a psychological need to feign certain illnesses but for no external purpose, as is found with factitious disorder. In other words, they feel compelled to play the sick role and to acquire the likely attention accompanies that state. Patients with this syndrome have been known to inject themselves with poisons, urine, and feces so that they will become ill and be admitted to a hospital or otherwise receive medical attention. Munchausen's by proxy occurs when parents cause illness in their children through these means, requiring constant medical attention. In a very distorted and damaging way, they are meeting some type of psychological need with little evidence of direct external incentive. Although the incidences of MSBP are rare, there have been enough cases to support its existence (O'Shea, 2003). In most of the known cases, death is the ultimate fate of the children because the parents will stop at nothing to fulfill their own needs (Pitt & Bale, 1995). Sheridan (2003) found that mothers were the perpetrators in 76.5% of 451 cases reviewed. Lasher (2003) states that there is an underidentification of MSBP due to a lack of public awareness and professional expertise and that overall awareness must increase in order to protect victims. These women do not fit into the model of mentally ill mothers and would be more likely fall into the abuse filicide category. Usually their goal is to make the child sick but not to intentionally kill them; however, they take the ruse too far or for too prolonged a period.

MODE OF KILLING OR WEAPONS USE

Numerous researchers have discussed the very act of killing one's own child as offending our deepest level of humanity (Pruett, 2002). Considering the mode of killing and viewing crime scene photos or videos can traumatize and horrify even the most seasoned law enforcement, legal, and mental health professionals. A collective sense of outrage can create a rush to retribution without consideration of the myriad factors that led to these devastating crimes. No one in their rational mind could fathom that any mother could consider such carnage and death as being in the best interest of their children, yet, as previously described this is often the motive for the mentally ill filicidal mother. Oberman (2003, p. 493) states, "the thought of a mother killing her child evokes a deep sense of horror and outrage, as it represents a betrayal of the presumption of maternal love and altruism upon which civilization rests." It is not uncommon for the most shocking crime scenes to be a result of the most mentally ill or psychotic mothers. There are many factors involved in the prevalence and type of weapon use in maternal filicide and there are different patterns that emerge with psychotic mothers as compared to nonpsychotic mothers. As compared to murder in general, the typical means by which children are killed are less violent (Stanton & Simpson, 2002). Female offenders rarely use weapons and will typically use less violent means like drowning, suffocation, banging, hitting, or throwing. It is common for psychotic women to use more violent means than nonpsychotic women. Statistics show that in countries other than the United States, firearms are rarely if ever used as a means for maternal filicide (Stanton & Simpson). This should not be surprising as firearms are used more frequently in violent crimes in the United States, overall.

Unlike other types of maternal filicide, the psychotic mother intends to kill her child, albeit for delusional reasons, and takes some specific action to this end (Lewis & Bunce, 2003). She is driven by overwhelming feelings, impulses, or delusional ideas that make her impervious to actual reality as she is overtaken by her illness-driven reality. Lewis, Baranoski, Buchanan, and Benedek (1998) conducted a study to identify the factors associated with weapon use in a group of filicidal women ($n = 60$) who were evaluated at Michigan's Center for Forensic Psychiatry or through Connecticut's Psychiatric Security Review Board from 1970 to 1996. They defined weapon use as either with a gun or a knife and found that one in four women used a weapon. Thirteen percent of filicidal women used guns and 12% used knives. Psychosis was present in every woman who used a knife to murder her child and in seven out of eight of the women who killed her child with a gun.

Women experiencing psychosis were 11 times more likely to kill her child with a weapon than a nonpsychotic woman. Weapons were used almost exclusively with older children and were used infrequently in the deaths of infants or very young children. Weapons are typically used with children who are older than one year. Victims of filicide have been killed by diverse and sometimes bizarre methods (e.g., biting a child to death; forcing a child to eat pepper; overdosing the child on morphine rubbed on the nipples of the mother) (Lewis et al., 1998). When comparing filicidal mothers to filicidal fathers, Resnick (1969) noted that mothers tended to use more passive means of killing (e.g., smothering, drowning, gassing) than men (e.g., stabbing, striking, squeezing). Yet, other studies have also shown high rates of battering deaths for the victims of maternal filicide (Lewis et al., 1998).

Resnick (1969), utilizing cases from around the world including the United States, found that mothers committed filicide with guns as frequently as fathers (9% of the cases). Knives were used in just a slightly greater number of paternal filicides (14%) than maternal filicides (9%). The rate of weapon use Resnick (1969) found is somewhat higher than what is typically found amongst filicidal women (Lewis et al., 1998). D'Orban (1979) did not have any shooting deaths in any of her categories of maternal filicides from her British sample. She did find that three out of four stabbing deaths were perpetrated by mentally ill women.

Neonaticides are typically committed by drowning, beating, or strangling, without any weapon use (Lewis et al., 1998). Certainly the helplessness of the child would suggest that a weapon would not be needed to commit the murder. Psychotic women who used weapons were almost as likely to pick a knife as a gun, which is in contrast to statistics for murders of juveniles or children outside the home. Certainly, knives are more readily available in the home and could be considered as weapons of opportunity even for disorganized killers. Lewis et al. (1998) found that in the majority of cases where a child under 10 years was killed with a weapon, the mother had psychotic symptoms. They stated:

> In the majority of cases, there were delusions specifically about the victims which the mother described as terrifying. For example, one woman stabbed her infant 45 times because she had become convinced that the baby was possessed by the devil. It is not surprising that a mother, when confronted with a force which she believes is overpowering, uses a weapon rather than her own strength to confront it. Our study shows that the women who killed the youngest children with weapons were uniformly psychotic and a majority had command hallucinations and paranoid delusions. (p. 617)

Lewis et al. (1998) identified 36% of the filicides by psychotic women in their study involved a knife or gun, regardless of the age of the victims, while only 5% of the nonpsychotic women used a weapon to commit filicide. They noted that nonpsychotic women will kill by way of extreme and sometimes heinous forms of normal punishment or out of rage or frustration (e.g., a 25-year-old that beat her child to death after much prior abuse by "accident" because the child wet its pants). Weapon use by psychotic mothers is uncommonly related to punishment or anger, but rather it is typically related to delusions involving the child being in some type of suffering or danger or the child being dangerous (Resnick, 1969). Lewis et al. (1998) found that approximately 25% of filicidal women used weapons in the commission of their crime. However, the majority of women who had used weapons had a past history of mental illness (e.g., hallucinations and delusions) and about 75% were receiving treatment at the time of the filicides. Greater than half had expressed fears about their children to family members or clinicians and about an eighth had contacted the police to express their concerns. Stanton et al. (2000) found that mentally ill mothers were more likely to use violent methods of killing, have older victims, and kill multiple children as compared to nonmentally ill mothers.

A MOTHER'S BURDEN

"Hell awaits them when restored to reality" (Gold, 2001, p. 346). Mentally ill mothers who have killed because they believed they had no choice and that what they were doing was in the child(ren)'s best interest are dealt a crushing blow, when they become stabilized and realize the gravity of what they have done. Their experience of remorse, disbelief, and horror is often the most severe punishment inflicted upon them. While still in their psychotic, manic, or depressed states, they often do not appreciate the wrongfulness or senselessness of what has happened. For example, a woman who believes she has been instructed by God to commit such an act feels certain that it is God's will or a good thing and that she will be reunited with them in heaven or due to their resurrection. This type of delusion would prevent a mentally ill mother from appreciating what has happened. Lewis and Bunce (2003) found that it was not uncommon for the women in their sample to express sorrow, fear, or regret about what they had done, while at the same time maintaining that their children had died for the best at the time or shortly after the incident. She likely believes at the time that there was an unavoidable purpose for the death(s). Now, imagine the cold reality when you realize that all you believed (e.g., painful terminal illness, eternal torment in hell, demonic possession, a test by God) that led to the killing(s) was only a product of your mental illness. A biochemical or psychological mistake has cost you your child(ren), your freedom, likely your marriage, and much, much more. Again, imagine a woman who has defined herself as a "mother" and values this role above all others that define her. Now sit with the knowledge that your body and mind have betrayed you and what you believed were self-sacrificing or altruistic actions were actually the senseless murder of your children by your very own hands. It is an unfathomable pain and suffering the enormity of which most other persons will not have to contend with in a lifetime.

Another realization is the confusion, fear, and betrayal the child must have felt and having no tangible way of explaining or taking back what you have done. There is a domino effect of pain and confusion that leaves family members in shock and disbelief, wondering what they missed or how such a devoted mother could have taken the lives of her children. Stanton et al. (2000, p. 1458) state, "Having to live with having killed one's own child is a considerable burden for someone already struggling with a major mental illness." Study after study suggests that these women display significant remorse, even when their mental illness is only partially stabilized (Stanton et al., 2000; Schwartz & Isser, 2001).

Psychotic women who kill their children from motives such as saving or relieving their children from spiritual and other physical torture, suffering, and doom, or the belief that God instructed it are qualitatively much different from coldblooded murderers. A system of delusions leaves them believing that there are no other alternatives and they must act out of love for their children. Some argue that these women have lost their children and do not pose a significant threat to others as long as they are maintained on their medication and have a firm understanding of their mental illness and are committed to ongoing management of their mental illness. No measure of punishment such as extended incarceration or death will compare to the guilt they feel for what they have done. This way of thinking would not apply to the psychopathic killer who kills for personal or material gain. The psychopathic killer has only remorse for being caught and has no regard for the victim who has been objectified, murdered, and thrown away. The mentally ill maternal filicide offender who was devoted to her child does not demand the same type of justice as the quite different psychopathic or even revenge- or anger-motivated offenders. The mentally ill filicidal mother will punish herself extensively with her guilt. Ford (1996) asks the following difficult questions (as cited in Schwartz & Isser, 2001):

> If a mother is stunned and genuinely horrified by her own actions, is it necessary for the state to impose the longest or most severe penalties when she, herself, is her own worst punishing agent? . . . Generally, society considers random, repeated, and cold-blooded killers as the most dangerous to society. How much does a murdering mother's profile conform to this description? (p. 714)

RISK FACTORS

Due to the infrequency of child murder, accurate prediction is unlikely. Child murder is a rare and difficult event to predict but successful treatment and intervention programs are contingent upon identifying potential perpetrators. There are risk factors that make some women more vulnerable than others to maternal filicide. Wilczynski (1995, p. 365) found that numerous background stress factors to include: "financial, housing, marital problems, social isolation, psychiatric disorder, children who were regarded as particularly difficult to care for in some way, and the use of illegal or legal substances such as alcohol and prescription drugs were among the most common features of the cases" of child killing by parents in England in the 1980s and 1990s.

Research has shown that depression or anxiety during pregnancy, a family history of mental illness, an unwanted pregnancy, sleep deprivation, and significant psychosocial stressors, such as marital discord, are all risk factors for postpartum mental illness (Born et al., 2004). Warning signs for new mothers that might indicate the onset of a postpartum illness include the mother becoming quite unkempt while the child is excessively well groomed and dressed or the mother becomes hypersexual in a way that was uncommon for her previously (Huysman, 2003). Risk factors associated with mood disorders should be queried by obstetricians during their initial visit with an expectant mother regarding her experience and her family background. She should be queried, for example, about any substance abuse history, hypersexual behavior, unstable relationship history, unstable employment history, periods of depression, suicidal ideation, suicide attempts, violent acting out or aggression, grandiosity, family history of mental illness, and the like. The family might complain to the physician that the mother isn't sleeping or that she is obsessively worried about the baby. The mother may be unable to involve her husband or significant other in the new family dynamic with the infant (Huysman, 2003). Conversely, family members might report that the mother is unable to care for the child as a result of fearing she will harm the child or because she is always sleeping and unable to get out of bed. Huysman (2003, p. 102) reported that the families will often make excuses for the erratic behavior such as: "She must be jealous of the baby" or "She's too tired to have sex or even be affectionate." A woman who is suffering from postpartum depression can be overly preoccupied with her baby, or be abnormally angry, sad, or detached. Regarding infanticide that results from postpartum depression or psychosis, Huysman (2003, p. 103) stated, "it . . . crosses racial, cultural, and socioeconomic lines. It's not black, Hispanic, Asian, Native-American, or white; it's not rich or poor. PPD (postpartum depression), PPPD (progressive postpartum depression), and the infanticide cases that sometimes occur as a consequence of the illness when it is left untreated, does not discriminate."

Other signs of postpartum depression include panic attacks, severe anxiety, insomnia, disinterest in the child, spontaneous crying, trancelike states, vague comments to others about "not being well" (Huysman, 2003, p. 39), chronic irritability, and episodes of hyperactivity that include insomnia and increased energy. While postpartum psychosis is far more rare than postpartum depression, it is far more dangerous with approximately 4 percent of women who develop this disorder killing their children (Huysman, 2003). Maternal filicides that involve children older than one year reaches beyond the postpartum period; however, researchers have found that progressive postpartum depression involves a chemical imbalance that is triggered by the birth event that sets in motion a longstanding, serious mental illness that will likely wax and wane in its course if left untreated. As the mental illness progresses, an episode can be triggered by a psychosocial stressor such as a loss. Certainly, a genetically vulnerable woman would be at continued risk with each subsequent birth, particularly if untreated. In most cases, this mental illness is controllable if identified and effectively treated, especially on the front end.

The risk of postpartum illness is greater in women over 25 years of age who have a history of mood instability with 30% to 40% of these women having a postpartum episode (Huysman, 2003). Women with a family history of mood instability are also more vulnerable to progressive postpartum depression. The medical and psychological history of the woman's biological family will provide critical information about her level of risk for mental illness in general and her risk for postpartum illness. Certainly, a family history of mental illness, suicide, or substance abuse would indicate higher risk. A family may have a history of untreated depression or bipolar disorder. While the more severe manifestations often result in hospitalizations or, perhaps, some contact with the criminal justice system, this is not the case for more moderate symptoms or expressions of mood instability. Familial traits that could indicate a predisposition to psychotic or affective episodes of postpartum illness include "addiction to alcohol and/or drugs, family history of multiple marriages, compulsive gambling, poor judgment, indiscreet financial or sexual behaviors, impulsive or violent behavior, aggression, and inflated self-esteem or grandiosity. . . . At risk are mothers from families that displayed one or more of the following: unstable or chaotic lifestyles . . . too much dependence on one another or too much independence from one another, extreme rigidity, compulsive behavior, and frequent bouts of rage" (p. 55). Bear in mind, this list is not exhaustive and actually targets the more severe and overt signs of a family history of mood disorders or other mental illness.

Of those with clinical depression, individuals with marked anxiety and a hypochondriacal pattern or overconcern or exaggeration of somatic symptoms are more likely to attempt suicide (Huysman, 2003). A preexisting psychotic depression would make a woman extremely vulnerable to a progressive postpartum depression that would be more enduring and dangerous. Medical professionals are more likely to initially encounter these women than mental health professionals and should be well educated on this literature.

Command hallucinations and paranoid delusions correlate with a higher risk of violence in general; but delusions and paranoia about the child is a very significant risk factor for maternal filicide. Certainly psychosis as a component of a postpartum illness, affective disorder, or a psychotic illness greatly increases the likelihood that child murder will occur in these women. A severe delusional depression, where the children are a key focus of the delusional system, is a serious red flag. According to Laporte, Poulin, Marleau and Roy (2003), evaluating the dangerousness of filicidal women who are facing disposition includes whether or not delusions about the children exist, the age and number of children, availability of weapons, and the support available by having another responsible adult take care of the children until a mental health crisis or postpartum crisis is resolved. Due to the high lethality of firearms, women with a history of depression or postpartum mental illness should not have guns in the home.

Stanton et al. (2000) indicate that it is very difficult to predict risk and to prevent mentally ill filicide in mothers who described being devoted and are observed as very caring toward their children, providing little to no warning of filicidal urges. For these types of filicidal mothers, those at risk include mothers who have psychological significance or importance to the perpetrator, due to the nature of their motives (Bowden, 1990).

The majority of these women have a major mental illness that they are often trying to manage without treatment and are attempting to appear normal. They may be experiencing depression, psychosis, and they might be suicidal. These symptoms can lead to homicidal impulses even if for altruistic reasons or rationale. Certain women have a biological vulnerability based on a family history of mental illness, especially affective disorders. If a woman is experiencing postpartum mental illness, it is likely to become worse with each subsequent pregnancy and can extend far beyond the postpartum period. If a woman already has a genetic predisposition to mental illness, she may be particularly vulnerable to the huge influx of hormones, and the biochemical imbalance of an emerging mental illness may be set in motion.

When considering other categories of filicidal women such as battering mothers or fatal child abuse or retaliating women, threats to the husband–wife pair bond may end in violence toward the children by mothers (Stanton & Simpson, 2000). The loss of the father would certainly be a destabilizing event. Vulnerability factors include psychiatric history, social supports, and the nature and stability of significant or central interpersonal relationships.

THE RESPONSE OF THE CRIMINAL JUSTICE SYSTEM

The response of the courts to maternal filicide has a history of vacillating between leniency and retribution. What is the appropriate degree of culpability to attach to mentally ill mothers who kill their children for what they believe are altruistic reasons? The current response of society, the media, and the criminal justice system is punitive with mentally ill mothers often tried and convicted with the fervor given to any other coldblooded murder case. Certainly, the overzealous prosecution, conviction, and subsequent life imprisonment of

Andrea Yates, despite her well-documented history of mental illness and devotion to her children, illustrates this. It was only on a legal error that her conviction was overturned, although this decision remains in appeal. Sentences are often very inconsistent ranging from probation with counseling for some neonaticide offenders to commitment in a maximum-security forensic hospital as NGRI or life in prison with a guilty verdict. Prosecutors sought the death penalty for Andrea Yates, although the jury rejected it. Community outrage and public opinion during a time when it seems that everything is politicized has a tremendous impact on juror's verdicts and the severity of sentences. Jurors arrive at trials with preconceived notions about what type of woman could commit such a crime and what would constitute justice for such a seemingly heinous crime—child murder. Some might be able to set aside these ideas and some might not. Finkel, Burke, and Chavez (2000) indicate that public opinion changes over time based on cultural, legal, moral, historical, and psychological trends, as well as the cogent influence of media saturation of high-profile cases. Additionally, mandatory sentencing has become more common for the most serious offenses. Judges have much less discretion to take into consideration mitigating factors, particularly the severe mental illness of mothers who are found guilty of murder. While the victims of such crimes deserve justice, it should be a humane, well-informed justice.

The media can influence the leniency or severity of society and our criminal justice system, when conclusions are presented from outlier cases that give the impression that infanticide or filicide defendants are "getting away with murder," or "getting off light" (Finkel et al., 2000, p. 1115). With the 24-hour coverage on various cable news channels of high-profile cases, the offenders are tried in the media before ever stepping foot in the courtroom. This type of presentation can cause the public to believe that the outlier cases are more common than they are, creating outrage and a push for more punitive sentences. Public opinion or their constituents' views likely heavily influence our legislatures that pass bills regarding sentencing laws. People are very suspicious of insanity defenses, and successful Not Guilty by Reason of Insanity verdicts are rare and frequently result in lengthy incarceration in maximum-security forensic hospitals (Finkel et al., 2000).

McKee and Shea (1998) found that 75% of filicidal parents had exhibited psychotic symptoms prior to their child's homicide and that 40% had been seen by a psychiatrist shortly before the event. Twenty percent of the women in their study had a finding of legal insanity. Similar percentages have been found in other studies; for example, 27% in D'Orban's (1979) study, and 15% in Bourget's and Bradford's (1990) study. This is much greater than the rate of 0.1% for insanity acquittees in other criminal cases where the insanity plea was raised (McKee & Shea, 1998).

Finkel et al. (2000) explored the issue of specific symptoms and diagnoses, as well as adoption and abortion options as working against a climate of leniency. For example, as depression becomes more commonplace, most individuals know someone who has suffered depression, but would never commit filicide. These individuals know very little if anything about psychotic depression, which is much less common with a prevalence of 0.2%, and assume that a "depressed" individual should still know the difference between right and wrong and be able to control his or her impulses to follow the law, and therefore deny a verdict of legal insanity. Similarly, as options such as abortion and adoption are more common and safe, neonaticide offenders are viewed as ignoring other viable options and are treated more punitively. Although women have the option of abortion or adoption, these choices would have no bearing whatsoever on the motive of a psychotic infanticide offender. Regarding factors that work against mitigating infanticide, Finkel et al. (2000, p. 1121) state, "If manslaughter is a low probability verdict, and if exculpation to madness is low as well, then murder might be the default option." Finkel et al. (2000) found that neither depression alone nor childbirth, which may be associated with postpartum illness, have a mitigating effect on verdicts like NGRI or Guilty But Mentally Ill (GBMI).

Expert testimony on either of the aforementioned issues also does not have much of an impact, unless jurors are provided with evidence of psychosis at the time of the crime. In general, sentencing and treatment decisions are decided by the courts with little or no involvement from psychology or psychiatry. The courts and individuals who sit on juries are almost invariably undereducated about this devastating phenomenon. While it is still far more likely that an NGRI or GBMI verdict will not be reached, the chances are greater when psychosis is present, particularly when the act is seen as *bizarre*. Research has also shown that prospective female jurors are not more forgiving or lenient toward maternal infanticide offenders (Finkel et al., 2000). It is possible that the crime is so gender incongruent that some female jurors might judge more harshly.

The United States has extremely restrictive laws that govern infanticide or filicide cases the same as any other homicide. The United States does not have an infanticide statute. Traditionally, the older the child, the more likely the conviction rate. British law has specific infanticide laws, which some view as overly lenient, that take into consideration the very enormous possible impact of childbirth, depression, and other issues relating to the postpartum period. Around 1772 in England, public sentiment was shifting from being extremely punitive to being commonsense. "Put another way, commonsense justice seemed to buy the notion that depression and unsettling passions associated with child bearing took this crime out of murder and manslaughter categories and brought it much closer to insanity" (Finkel et al., 2000, p. 1119). Britain's law more closely equates infanticide to manslaughter with regard to penalties, rather than murder, which is much more common in the United States. In Great Britain, the Infanticide Act of 1922 and 1938 both maintained that postpartum psychosis was an appropriate cause to reduce charges for neonaticide and infanticide from murder to manslaughter. The diminished responsibility defense utilized in New South Wales allows for probation or for an individual to be sent to a psychiatric facility for treatment rather than to prison (Schwartz & Isser, 2001).

In approximately 30 countries throughout the world, to include Britain, Canada, and Australia, murder charges are ruled out for a lesser charge for women who kill their children within the first year after giving birth. This legislation implies that childbirth may have had a destabilizing effect on mothers, and that the infant homicide may have happened due to the resulting unstable psychological conditions, presenting a case for diminished responsibility for the crime (Marks, 2001). Their stance does not promote devaluing the lives of the infants, but rather reflects a greater understanding and mitigation for postpartum illnesses. Clearly, this should not take the place of prevention and education. Insanity defenses based on postpartum depression are not often successful. According to Gold (2001, p. 346), "This is, in no small part, because altruistic homicide, even in a psychotically disorganized individual, is voluntary, often premeditated, planned logically, and accomplished methodically, always in full consciousness, and perfectly remembered."

In a study that examined 32 adult women who killed their biological children in the province of Quebec from 1981 to 1991, 18 were found guilty (56%) and 14 received a medical disposition (Laporte et al., 2003). Out of those who were incarcerated, most received greater than two years, had a lower socioeconomic status, and were more likely to have a criminal and substance abuse history. The most common verdict was manslaughter; some received a second-degree murder verdict, and none of the women received a verdict of first-degree murder. Women who were given a medical disposition or those who had a successful insanity defense were more likely to have a psychiatric history; to suffer from psychotic symptoms; and were incorporated into the mental health system immediately after their offense. Most women with an NGRI defense had experienced psychotic symptoms at the time of the offense and were more likely to have attempted suicide after the offense. Laporte et al. (2003, pp. 96–97), stated that the most cogent arguments against sentencing women with postpartum depression to terms of incarceration are as follows: "1) an illness beyond their control caused these women's homicidal acts, 2) they have already suffered enough, 3) they have lost their offspring and have to live with the guilt related to their behaviour, and 4) they do not represent a threat to others as long as they do not have other children" (Ewing, 1997; Pitt & Bale, 1995).

Women who do not commit suicide following a depressive, typically psychotic filicide for altruistic reasons normally will make no attempt to hide the crime, will readily confess, and will often request punishment (Brockington, 1995; Gold, 2001; Lewis & Bunce, 2003). The actions of a mentally ill mother around the filicide may be quite confusing, particularly to a layperson who does not understand her mental illness. What may initially appear as a rational behavior that would suggest appreciation of wrongfulness (e.g., calling the police or 911) might actually be a product of psychotic illness. "For example, one might suggest that when a woman confesses or expresses regret that she killed her child, she recognizes that what she did was wrong. Instead, some confessions may be representative of underlying psychotic illness that interferes with full appreciation of wrongfulness" (Lewis & Bunce, 2003, p. 467). This type of maternal filicide offender at or shortly after her arrest will believe her actions were justified or she may have had no choice. Sometimes, her affect is even unusually jovial or elated based on her illness and belief that she just did a good thing for the child, God, or the world. Lewis and Bunce (2003, p. 467) found that the delusional thinking of the women in their sample could be based on "factors such as believing that their children were dangerous, inherently flawed, or at risk; that they, the mothers, were unfit in some way; or that they had helped the world or remaining family members by killing their children."

ISSUES FOR TREATMENT AS THE CURTAIN LIFTS

The treatment considerations discussed in this section will be specifically targeted for mentally ill mothers who have committed filicide or infanticide for altruistic reasons, rather than neonaticide or other categories of filicide. Suicide risk is high even at the time of the filicide or directly after. Yet, for those women who believe that they had to kill their children for some greater good, the reality of the senselessness of what they have done becomes apparent only when their mental illness has been stabilized. These women are at high risk of experiencing suicidal ideation or attempting suicide at that time. It is very common for these women to be placed on suicide watch in the jails or if they are in a psychiatric hospital setting to be placed on one-to-one observation status. In addition to medication management for their mood and psychotic symptoms, receiving support and having a mental health professional to talk to about what they are experiencing is important. Obviously, when such a woman is pretrial, what she should or would be advised or able to discuss about her situation is extremely limited. It would not be unexpected for a treatment provider in a jail or forensic hospital setting to be called as a fact witness at the criminal trial or competency hearing. Sometimes the woman believes she should be punished by death or desires suicide by capital punishment, and this deep sense of hopelessness and despair may contribute to an ongoing state of incompetency to stand trial until her mood stabilizes.

If a mentally ill maternal filicide offender is found NGRI and is likely committed to a maximum-security forensic hospital, treatment concerns and relevant issues can be more effectively observed and addressed. Grief is another cogent ongoing issue. As the curtain of psychosis or depression or mania lifts and the mother is left with the realization that her offspring are dead and she is responsible, the grief is usually unbearable. The loss of a child brings a void beyond compare under any circumstances. She will need to be informed about the emotions associated with grief, its nonlinear process, and the expectation that she will likely encounter head-on the grief of others associated with the children or family. Those women who had planned or attempted their own suicide in conjunction with the filicide but failed are likely to have survivor's guilt. Mental health professionals must be aware of the range of reactions from surviving family and friends including anger, fear, sadness, confusion, and the like and how their emotions and actions will impact the mental health of the mother/patient. These women may be extremely isolated from remaining family who are torn apart and in conflict about what has occurred. The shock, disbelief, and horror of what she has done is likely to give way to a deep, overwhelming remorse and sadness. Every woman is different, but for those who respond to treatment and emerge from their delusions and other symptoms, this type of reaction can likely be anticipated. She will not be able to grieve her children graveside but from a prison cell or hospital ward. She must grieve in a vacuum until and if she is eventually released to the community.

Mental health education is absolutely essential. Helping her to understand all of the signs, symptoms, and triggers of her illness, particularly those that led to the offense, is mandatory to get her mentally well, to reduce risk for relapse, and to protect society. She will need to understand and follow up with her treatment for the rest of her life to ever have an opportunity to safely reintegrate into society. These women struggle desperately with the question, "Why did this have to happen?" The whys and the what ifs are brutal and can lead to much depression and anguish. Depending on the nature of their mental illness, some women will respond much better than others to treatment. While many will respond very well to medication management, psychosocial rehabilitation, and psychotherapy, there may be some whose illness is treatment refractory and must remain in an institutional setting to prevent harm to self or others. The former is much more common and with ongoing treatment and a healthy support system, she can likely be safely reintroduced into the community at some point in the future.

For those women who had a strong religious component to their delusions that may have led to the crime itself, there often remains an anger and distrust of God or their previous faith. If at the time of the crime they believed they were serving the will of God or were instructed to not question the action of killing their children, they may fear any strong relationship with God or trust themselves to unquestioning faith in whatever they may have believed before. Certainly, due to their vulnerabilities for mental illness and the way their symptoms were previously demonstrated, they will have to be much more cautious and prudent in their involvement and expression of spirituality. For example, if a women who had previously been raised in a faith that believed and encouraged speaking in tongues, she may have been less inclined to interpret auditory hallucinations or hearing voices as a sign of mental illness, when it began. She may have viewed her experience of God having actually spoken to her and commanded her to do certain things as a wonderful blessing. To be clear, religion does NOT cause mental illness, but for those women who are susceptible or who are mentally ill, it is quite possible that their religious ideation will mask or become intertwined with their delusional system. This is a very personal and complicated issue but is a reality for those women whose delusions that led to the deaths of their children had strong religious meaning or components. This also has implications for educating church officials and congregations about signs of mental illness, including postpartum illnesses.

Many women who committed filicide were married at the time of the offense. This action almost invariably leads to divorce. While this may not come as a shock, it can still be traumatic for the recovering woman who is coming to terms with what she has done, the loss of her children, and now the loss of her marriage. She will often feel deep guilt and remorse about what she had done to their children, but cannot help also feeling a sense of abandonment at her darkest hour. She may no longer feel that she is the same woman or in the same frame of mind as she was when the filicides occurred and desperately long for some sense of normalcy or security in the face of such tragedy and chaos. Even when the spouse forgives his wife and understands the role of her mental illness, it is quite understandable that his feelings for her have changed in addition to the reality of a lengthy hospitalization or incarceration. In other instances, there may be only anger and confusion about what has happened or, perhaps, even some self-blame that he was unable to see, stop, or intervene in what has transpired. The families may be strongly divided about whether or not to support or shun the woman in question. If the woman is an insanity acquittee, there is also the question of the division of marital property and assets. As long as they remain married, he can also be responsible for her costly psychiatric care. While these issues pale in comparison to the loss of the children, there exists a harsh reality of the rest of the story long after the glare of unwanted media attention and public interest wanes.

Mentally ill women who killed for altruistic motives were typically devoted mothers prior to their emerging illness and subsequent filicides. If they primarily defined themselves or their role as wife and mother, how do they pick up the pieces and what kind of future might they have? If they remain delusional or unstable, they will be kept safely in the confines of a maximum-security hospital. Insanity acquittees who respond to treatment, at some point can and likely will be returned to the community. Facing the prospect that they are no longer mothers, wives, or that they may not be able to return to their communities or churches, what happens next? She may wonder if once returned home, nieces and nephews will fear her or if she will be a burden to those family members willing to accept her. Helping these women make realistic plans for the future and helping prepare them for the many changes they will encounter is yet another function of treating clinicians. The majority of these women were very vulnerable to their mental illness as a result of pregnancy and childbirth. Many infanticide offenders were experiencing postpartum illnesses and future childbirth would put them at high risk. So, the reality of never being a mother again is prudent but is often difficult to accept.

Whether the female offender is in prison or a psychiatric hospital, there is an inescapable stigma attached to killing children and they may suffer harsh reactions or treatment, particularly in a prison setting. This type of treatment, shame, and deep sadness are often rekindled when a story reemerges in the media, through television or in print. It is common for graphic details, pictures, and the names of all involved to be widely publicized. Coping with the reality of media coverage, including when and if they are ever released to the community, is another reality for which to prepare. Encouraging these women to find meaning in their tragedies and to have some hope for the future is a difficult but important role for mental health professionals involved in their treatment.

IMPLICATIONS

Early identification of signs of depression and psychosis is imperative in the prevention of maternal filicide (Myers, 1970). When a physician or a mental health professional has contact with a mother who is presenting with symptoms of severe depression or schizophrenia, he or she should not ignore the possibility of maternal filicide and inquire appropriately. Whether or not psychosis is present and the severity of the symptoms both have implications for the treatment, prognosis, and prevention efforts for potentially filicidal women (Lewis & Bunce, 2003). Preemptive action in these cases serves the best interest of the child and the mother. Identifying those women at risk, and providing early and appropriate treatment and ongoing management of the mental illness is critical. Education should be provided for mental health professionals, family members, general practitioners, emergency room doctors and nurses, pediatricians, obstetricians, police, child protective services personnel, members of the clergy, and social workers. A number of women who commit maternal filicide will come into contact with mental health professionals before the event, and the possibility of homicidal impulses or ideation should never be overlooked in depressed individuals, particularly mothers (Bourget & Labelle, 1992).

Regarding risk for postpartum mental illness, Spinelli (2004, p. 1554), states, "Since antepartum screening is the best strategy for identifying women at risk, the prenatal clinic is the optimum environment in which to use simple screening tools and objective mood scales. . . . Although these tools do not replace a diagnostic interview, they facilitate collection of focused information to identify women at risk in time for intervention." Physicians who treat women planning families should receive and offer education about risk for postpartum depression and available treatment routinely as part of their primary care. Physicians should also explain the risk versus the benefits of utilizing medication while pregnant or postpartum, based on the severity of the illness. If a woman has a severe depression, or has any history of severe mood instability to include depression or mania with associated psychosis, or schizophrenia, the severity of the illness would require psychotropic medications, and ideally therapy when stabilized. If pregnant, the stage of the pregnancy would have implications that the physician should advise her about. The more severe forms of the illness would not likely remit without pharmacotherapy.

Mental health and medical professionals should be particularly vigilant to hypochondriacal or psychosomatic concerns from the mother about her or her children's health. It is not uncommon for the mother to make numerous doctors' visits, often seeking second or third opinions because of her unshakable belief that she and her children are suffering from an incurable disease. It is critical that the aforementioned professionals be well educated that this is a risk factor for maternal filicide and to conduct the appropriate inquiries and risk assessments to prevent such a tragedy. For example, if a primary care physician notes that this is likely a psychiatric problem, he or she should not only suggest to the spouse that his wife be evaluated by a psychiatrist, but the medical professional should speak candidly about the correlation with maternal filicide and possible suicide risk. Many individuals do not trust mental health professionals and will balk at the idea of seeking mental health care. The contact with the medical personnel may be the solitary interface with a woman at high risk for maternal filicide. It is imperative that medical professionals are well aware of this literature and properly educate the women and families involved, as well as referring them to a mental health professional or seek immediate civil commitment if the mother is actually expressing homicidal impulses toward her children. The mother who is experiencing a major mental illness will likely have significant difficulty monitoring her parenting effectiveness and level of risk (Stanton et al., 2000).

Oberman (2003) suggests that in order to eliminate maternal filicide, we must first understand the individuals who commit the crime and the larger societal context in which it takes place. Women who experience postpartum illness should be approached as individuals and all possible causes for their illness should be explored. Medical professionals should not assume that a new mother's behavior, questions, or complaints are just related to her insecurities, fatigue, or hysteria (Huysman, 2003); but rather they should be able to ask the right questions and make appropriate referrals to mental health professionals if warranted. In addition to medication management and psychotherapy, those women need to have a strong emotional support system through their families, friends, communities, and churches. The lack of general education about mental illness by these individuals and institutions leaves a void in the prevention chain. Support groups and educational counseling have proven to be beneficial, particularly during pregnancy (Huysman, 2003).

Stanton et al. (2000) contend that psychotic forms of child abuse or murder should be explained separately from typical forms of abuse or murder. The unique and complex motives and the driving force of mental illness behind these tragedies make them qualitatively much different from murders resulting from anger, revenge, or some form of secondary gain. Lewis et al. (1998) indicate that most women who kill their children do not have a history of abusing them and, as such, programs focused on preventing child abuse will not be meeting the needs or effectively addressing the issues for these women that may lead to maternal filicide.

Those in contact with at-risk women should not be lulled into believing that a mother's devotion to her children would automatically preclude her from harming her baby or child. Research has demonstrated that a number of these women kill for motives that they believe are in their child's best interest, therefore, their apparent love and nurturance of their child does not reduce their risk. In fact, the risk may be increased due to the emotional investment in the child (Stanton et al., 2000). "Evident devotion to the child and parenting is not likely to be a protective factor" (p. 1459). These mothers often place undue pressure on themselves to be good or better mothers, further complicating their increased risk with additional stress. Aggressive treatment of psychotic symptoms and ensuring medication compliance in the mentally ill mother is critical in reducing the risk of weapon-related filicide deaths (Lewis et al., 1998).

The seemingly unthinkable act of a mother killing her child may prevent an otherwise prudent clinician from exploring the possibility of a female client committing filicide. Clinicians are trained to inquire about suicidal and homicidal ideation, but rarely do they inquire specifically about a mother's homicidal ideation toward her children (McKee & Shea, 1998). Resnick (as cited in McKee & Shea, 1998, p. 685) suggested that when a mother presents with suicidal ideation, the evaluating professional should always ask, "What are your plans for the children?" Lewis et al. (1998) describe using structured methods of assessing maternal feelings toward their children. For example, clinicians could ask a mother at risk if she ever has feelings of fearing her child or being fearful for her child in order to identify children at risk. Structured interviews should be designed to assess the mother's feelings about their children, her ability to care for them, and any fears she may have related to children. For those women who are identified as being at risk, home visits, which provide the opportunity to observe the mother interacting with her children, and clinical observations of the mother are recommended as methods of creating greater awareness of children at risk for maternal filicide (Lewis et al., 1998).

When the state (e.g., Child Protective Services) questions a parent's ability to raise his or her child as a result of mental illness or psychiatric vulnerabilities and characterological disorders, the parent's right to raise the child without interference is typically supported. A parent's right to privacy and overwhelmed family courts make it likely that parents at risk will proceed unchecked. Most parents with psychiatric vulnerabilities or mental illness do not harm their children. However, as children are increasingly suffering at the hands of their parents, it is crucial that we identify children who need protection from parents who cannot manage their aggressive or homicidal impulses and take action (Pruett, 2002).

Frequently women who were grossly psychotic at the time of the offense, at the time of arrest, and when first housed in the jail are stabilized and appear quite "sane" at their criminal trials. What impact does this have on the ability of jurors to imagine a woman so ravaged by mental illness that she would take the life of her own child? Particularly if there is a significant mood component to her illness, many of these women respond very well to appropriate pharmacological treatment and present a completely different and often stable picture at their criminal trial or other court hearings. Is it in the best interest of the client to remain unmedicated? If left untreated, these women will often not be restored to competency to even proceed to their trials. Clearly, it is a double-edged sword and raises many complex and ethical questions.

It is important that judges and the legal community be educated about the mental health issues surrounding postpartum depression or psychosis and other types of mental illness associated with filicide. Attorneys and judges should be educated about the potential altruistic motives for the crime that impact appreciation of wrongfulness, motivation for confessing, and the premeditation involved in the crimes committed by mentally ill mothers. A "delicate balance is needed to educate, rehabilitate, correct, and punish the woman who has killed" her child(ren) (Schwartz & Isser, 2001, p 713). Spinelli (2004) warns that postpartum depression or psychosis is severely minimized in the judicial process and is inadequately explained to jurors with devastating consequences for the mothers. Educating the legal communities and participants in the courtroom, including juries, is of critical importance. Professionals should be utilized and well trained to explain the biological and psychological factors to jurors and to use the courtroom as a classroom to help facilitate verdicts based on accurate understanding of the facts (Spinelli, 2004).

When considering the disposition and sentencing of mentally ill mothers, it is critical that juries and judges recognize the impact of incarceration or other options would have on the mental health of the defendant. These women are unlikely to receive adequate treatment and rehabilitation in the prison system. Unlike other Western countries that have infanticide laws that recognize the unique plight of mentally ill mothers and the potential impact of postpartum illnesses, the United States has no such law and sentencing and verdicts have recently been harsh. Schwartz and Isser (2001, pp. 715–716) suggest, "It would also help if legislators might be . . . enlightened enough to enact laws that would encourage the judiciary to examine mitigating circumstances and to exercise thoughtful judgment." Severe punishment is meant to be a deterrent but the mentally ill maternal filicide offender is acting with impaired reality testing and is often under the influence of severe depression, command hallucinations, delusions, and other types of perceptual disturbances. It is very unlikely that if they are ill enough to harm their children as a result of psychotic process or severe mental illness that the threat of severe punishment would have any impact on their decision making at the time of the offense. After the benefits of effective treatment, the mother is likely to agonize about how she could have believed what she did and committed the filicide as a result. To further illustrate the problematic nature of using punishment as retribution, Spinelli (2004, p. 1553), wrote, "In cases of infanticide, it often seems difficult to blame a single individual. Inevitably, clues and obvious signs were ignored, leaving one with a sense that there might be more than one blameworthy party."

The disparity between clinical insanity and legal insanity differs and the definition of legal insanity also differs based on the relevant country, state, jurisdiction, or judge. Filicidal mothers who are deemed to be NGRI are almost invariably treated within institutions due to the severity of their crimes, if not found guilty and sentenced to a term of incarceration. Therefore, they are typically not involved in community-based programming to help facilitate family reintegration upon their release (McKee & Shea, 1998). More attention is needed regarding incorporating their families into mental health education efforts and plans for the offender's safe reintegration into the family and community.

While the media can be used to villainize or convict mentally ill women, it could also be used as a powerful vehicle to educate the public about the role of mental illness and postpartum illnesses in some cases of child murder. This knowledge would be extremely powerful in preventing future tragedies. Rather than sensationalizing tragedies and further victimizing remaining family members, this medium could be used as a vehicle for an increased understanding, awareness, and prevention. Far too many people believe that mental illness and crime are things that happen to someone else. Most of the families who have endured the tragedy of maternal filicide would have never believed it could have happened to their daughter, sister, aunt, or cousin.

FUTURE RESEARCH

Future research on larger samples of filicidal women would facilitate a more robust and reliable set of predictive criteria to identify those women at higher risk for maternal filicide (Lewis & Bunce, 2003). They also suggest that research on women who do not kill children or have those impulses, but are mentally ill and are exposed to similar psychosocial stressors, would also be important in this endeavor.

McKee and Shea (1998) found from their sample of 20 women who had been charged with killing their children and been referred to a forensic psychiatric hospital for pretrial evaluation, 78% of the multichild families had sibling survivors that would likely require treatment for issues like posttraumatic stress disorder or major depression. They noted the complete absence of research on sibling survivors of filicidal parents and clearly this is a cogent area for future research. Further research on the impact of psychosis on weapon use in maternal filicide should be explored. Lewis et al. (1998) ask, what factors determine the method of filicide and what is the best way to address them for prevention?

CONCLUSIONS

Although paradoxical, the motivation of mentally ill mothers who kill for altruistic reasons is compassionate. As these women become stabilized through aggressive mental health treatment, they are often shocked and bewildered that they could have so dangerously miscalculated their situations or believed so fully their delusions. This chapter explored the definition of child murder specifically, discussing the different categories of filicide. The focus was then narrowed to mentally ill filicide offenders and the impact of their symptoms on their motives and methods was described. These mentally ill mothers are dealt a crushing blow when they become stabilized and realize the gravity of what they have done. Their experience of remorse, disbelief, and horror is often the most severe punishment inflicted upon them and this burden was described. Next, the risk factors associated with maternal filicide were discussed to help inform strategies for prevention and intervention. The response of the criminal justice system to include charges, pleas, verdicts, sentencing, punishment, and treatment was presented. Specific areas of concern that are prominent in the treatment of these women while awaiting trial in jail, or more commonly after having been found NGRI and while hospitalized in a maximum-security forensic psychiatric setting, were examined. Implications for treatment, education, prevention, intervention, the legal system, sentencing, verdicts, and the disposition of these women were discussed. Finally, suggestions for future research were offered. This chapter provided a comprehensive overview of the many issues and controversies that surround maternal filicide with the goal of education and prevention of these tragedies.

ACKNOWLEDGMENTS

I would like to thank Marcia Williams for her research contributions and Cindy Schiwart for her support for this project. I also deeply appreciate the ongoing encouragement of my friend Dawn Graney.

REFERENCES

Altshuler, L. L., Hendrick, V., Cohen, L. S. (1998). Course of mood and anxiety disorders during pregnancy and the postpartum period. *Journal of Clinical Psychiatry, 59*, 29–33.

American Psychiatric Association (APA). (1994). *Diagnostic and statistical manual of mental disorders* (4th ed.). Washington, DC: Author.

AUSTIN, M. P. (1992). Puerpal affective psychosis: Is there a case for lithium prophylaxis? *British Journal of Psychiatry, 161*, 692–694.

BORN, L., ZINGA, D., STEINE, M. (2004). Challenges in identifying and diagnosing postpartum disorders. *Primary Psychiatry, 11*(3), 29–36.

BOURGET, D., & BRADFORD, J. (1987). Affective disorder and homicide: A case of familial filicide theoretical and clinical considerations. *Canadian Journal of Psychiatry, 32,* 222–225.

BOURGET, D., & BRADFORD, J. (1990). Homicidal parents. *Canadian Journal of Psychiatry, 35,* 233–238.

BOURGET, D., & GAGNE, P. (2002). Maternal filicide in Quebec. *Journal of the American Academy of Psychiatry and the Law, 30*, 345–351.

BOURGET, D., & LABELLE, A. (1992). Homicide, infanticide, and filicide. *Psychiatric Clinics of North America, 15*(3), 661–673.

BOWDEN, P. (1990). Homicide. In R. Bluglass & P. Bowden (Eds.), *Principles and practice of forensic psychiatry* (pp. 507–522). London: Churchill Livingstone.

BROCKINGTON, I. F. (1995). *Motherhood and mental health.* Oxford: Oxford University Press.

CHAUDRON, L. H., & PIES, R. W. (2003). The relationship between postpartum psychosis and bipolar disorder: A review. *Journal of Clinical Psychiatry, 64*(11), 1284–1292.

DAWSON, J. M., & LANGAN, P. A. (1994). Murder and families. *Bureau of Justice Statistics Special Report.* July 1994. Washington, DC: Bureau of Justice Statistics.

DENNO, D. (2003). Who is Andrea Yates? A short story about insanity. *Duke Journal of Gender Law and Policy, 10*, 61–75.

DOBSON, V., & SALES, B. (2000). The science of infanticide and mental illness. *Psychology, Public Policy, & Law, 6*, 1098–1112.

D'ORBAN, P. (1979). Women who kill their children. *British Journal of Psychiatry, 134*, 560–571.

EWING, C. P. (1997). *The dynamics of intrafamilial homicide.* Thousand Oaks, CA: Sage.

FAZIO, C., & COMITO, J. L. (1999). Note: Rethinking the tough sentencing of teenage neonaticide in the United States. *Fordham Law Review, 67*, 3109.

FINKEL, N. J., BURKE, & CHAVEZ, L. J. (2000). Commonsense judgments of infanticide: Murder, manslaughter, madness, and miscellaneous. *Psychology, Public Policy, and Law, 6*(4), 1113–1137.

FORD, J. (1996). Note: Susan Smith and other homicidal mothers—in search of the punishment that fits the crime. *Cardoza Women's Law Journal, 3*, 521–549.

GESALMAN, A. B. (2002). Signs of a family feud: The trial of Andrea Yates tests the insanity defense as relatives try to cope with an "unspeakable" crime. *Newsweek*, January, 21, 2002.

GLOVER, V., & KAMMERER, M. (2004). The biology and pathophysiology of peripartum psychiatric disorders. *Primary Psychiatry, 11*(3), 37–41.

GOLD, L. H. (2001). Clinical and forensic aspects of postpartum disorders. *Journal of the American Academy of Psychiatry and the Law, 29*, 344–347.

HARDER, T. (1967). The psychopathology of infanticide. *Acta Psychiatrica Scandinavica, 43*, 196–245.

HUYSMAN, A. M. (2003). *The postpartum effect: Deadly depression in mothers.* New York: Seven Stories Press.

JASON, J. (1983). Child homicide spectrum. *American Journal of Disease of Childhood, 137*, 578–581.

LAPORTE, L., POULIN, B., MARLEAU, J., & ROY, R. (2003). Filicidal women: Jail or psychiatric ward? *Canadian Journal of Psychiatry, 48*(2), 94–98.

LASHER, L. (2003, April). Munchausen by proxy (MBP) maltreatment: An international educational challenge. *Child Abuse Neglect, 27*(4), 409–411.

LEWIS, C. F., & BUNCE, S. C. (2003). Filicidal mothers and the impact of psychosis on maternal filicide. *Journal of the American Academy of Psychiatry and the Law, 31*, 459–470.

LEWIS, C. F., BARANOSKI, M. V., BUCHANAN, J. A., & BENEDEK, E. P. (1998). Factors associated with weapon use in maternal filicide. *Journal of Forensic Sciences, 43*(3), 613–618.

MANCHESTER, J. (2003). Beyond accommodation: Reconstructing the insanity defense to provide an adequate remedy for postpartum psychotic women. *The Journal of Criminal Law & Criminology, 93* (2-3), 713–752.

MARKS, M. (2001). Parents at risk of filicide. In G. F. Pinard (Ed.), *Clinical assessment of dangerousness: Empirical contributions* (pp. 158–180). New York: Cambridge University Press.

MARKS, M. N., & KUMAR, R. (1993). Infanticide in England and Wales. *Medicine, Science and Law, 33*, 329–339.

MCGRATH, P. (1992). Maternal filicide in Broadmoor Hospital. *Journal of Forensic Psychiatry, 3*, 271–297.

MCKEE, G. R., & SHEA, S. J. (1998). Maternal filicide: A cross-national comparison. *Journal of Clinical Psychology, 54*(5), 679–687.

MYERS, S. A. (1970). Maternal filicide. *American Journal of Disorders of Childhood*, 120, 534–536.

OBERMAN, M. (2003). Mothers who kill: Cross-cultural patterns in and perspectives on contemporary maternal filicide. *International Journal of Law and Psychiatry, 26*, 493–514.

O'MALLEY, S. (2004). *"Are you there alone?": The unspeakable crime of Andrea Yates.* New York: Simon & Schuster.

O'SHEA, B. (2003, March). Factitious disorders: The Baron's legacy. *International Journal of Psychiatry in Clinical Practice, 7*(1), 33–39.

PALERMO, G. B. (2002). Murderous parents. *International Journal of Offender Therapy and Comparative Criminology, 46*(2), 123–143.

PITT, S. E., & BALE, E. M. (1995). Neonaticide, infanticide, and filicide: A review of the literature. *Bulletin of the American Academy of Psychiatry and the Law, 23*, 375–386.

PRUETT, M. K. (2002). Commentary: Pushing a new classification schema for perpetrators of maternal filicide one step further. *Journal of the American Academy of Psychiatry and the Law, 30*, 352–354.

RESNICK, P. J. (1969). Child murder by parents: A psychiatric view of filicide. *American Journal of Psychiatry, 126*, 73–82.

RESNICK, P. J. (1970). Murder of the newborn: A psychiatric review of neonaticide. *American Journal of Psychiatry, 126*, 1414–1420.

RESNICK, P. J. (1972). Infanticide. In J. G. Howells (Ed.), *Modern perspectives in psycho-obstetrics* (pp. 410–431). Edinburgh: Oliver & Boyd.

RODENBURG, M. (1971). Child murder by depressed parents. *Canadian Psychiatric Association Journal, 16*, 41–48.

SADOFF, R. L. (1995). Mothers who kill their children. *Psychiatric Annals, 25*, 601–605.

SCHWARTZ, L. L., & ISSER, N. K. (2001). Neonaticide: An appropriate application for therapeutic jurisprudence? *Behavioral Sciences and the Law, 19*, 703–718.

SCOTT, F. (1973). Parents who kill their children. *British Journal of Psychiatry, 13*, 120–126.

SHERIDAN, M. (2003, April). The deceit continues: An updated literature review of Munchausen syndrome by proxy. *Child Abuse & Neglect, 27*(4), 431–451.

SIMPSON, A., & STANTON, J. (2000). Maternal filicide: a reformulation of factors relevant to risk. *Criminal Behaviour and Mental Health, 10*, 136–147.

SPINELLI, M. G. (2004). Maternal infanticide associated with mental illness: Prevention and the promise of saved lives. *American Journal of Psychiatry, 161*(9), 1548–1557.

STANTON, J., & SIMPSON, A. (2002). Filicide: A review. *International Journal of Law and Psychiatry, 25*, 1–14.

STANTON, J., SIMPSON, A., & WOULDES, T. (2000). A qualitative study of filicide by mentally ill mothers. *Child Abuse & Neglect, 24*(11), 1451–1460.

STERN, E. S. (1948). The Medea complex: The mother's homicidal wishes to her child. *Journal of Mental Science, 94*, 321–331.

STOWE, Z. N., CALHOUN, K., RAMSEY, C., SADEK, N., & NEWPORT, D. J. (2001). Mood disorders during pregnancy and lactation: Defining issues of exposure and treatment. *CNS Spectrums, 6*, 150–166.

TUTEUR, W., & GLOTZER, J. (1959). Murdering mothers. *American Journal of Psychiatry, 116*, 447–452.

U.S. DEPARTMENT OF JUSTICE, BUREAU OF JUSTICE STATISTICS. (2002) Homicide trends in the U.S.: Intimate homicide. Available at: http://www.ojp.usdoj.gov/bjs/homicide/intimates.htm.

WEST, D. J. (1965). *Murder followed by suicide*. London: Heinemann.

WILCZYNSKI, A. (1995). Child killing by parents: A motivational model. *Child Abuse Review, 4*, 365–370.

WISNER, K. L., GRACIOUS, B. L., PIONTEK, C. M., PEINDL, K., & PEREL, J. M. (2002). Postpartum disorders: Phenomenology, treatment approaches, and relationship to infanticide. In M. G. Spinelli (Ed.), *Psychosocial and legal perspectives on mothers who kill* (pp. 36–60). Washington, DC: American Psychiatric Publishing.

WISNER, K. L., PEREL, J. M., & FINDLING, R. L. (1996). Antidepressant treatment during breastfeeding. *American Journal of Psychiatry, 153*, 1132–1137.

WISNER, K. L., & WHEELER, S. B. (1994). Prevention of recurrent postpartum major depression. *Hospital Community Psychiatry, 45*, 1191–1196.

6

Postpartum Syndrome and the Legal System

Tara C. Proano-Raps and Cheryl L. Meyer

❖

Postpartum syndromes are inconsistently acknowledged by the psychological and medical communities, resulting in a lack of definitive criteria for diagnosis. This lack of clarity can affect legal processes, particularly in criminal courts. In this chapter the current and historical status of postpartum diagnoses is examined, particularly as it relates to the admission of postpartum syndromes into evidence in criminal and civil courts. The authors of this chapter assert that gender inequality and cultural expectations of "good" women and mothers affect reactions to the use of postpartum syndromes in court processes. The politics of gender are addressed and solutions are offered for assisting, rather than pathologizing, women with postpartum syndromes.

On November 22, 1965, in Hawaii, Maggie Young drowned her five children, ages 8 months to 8 years, one by one in the bathtub. She then laid the bodies out on twin beds, four girls on one bed and the only boy on the other bed. Young was reportedly despondent over her perceived inability to care for her children. Earlier that year, she had been hospitalized for two months as the result of a "mental breakdown." Young immediately confessed to the killings and was committed to a state hospital. Approximately six months later, she escaped while on a pass and hung herself (Shapiro, 2001). During that same year, Andrea Yates was born.

Thirty-six years later, on June 20, 2001, Andrea Yates drowned her five children ages 6 months to 7 years, in their home in a Houston, Texas, suburb. Like Young, she reportedly held them under the bath water, one by one, first Luke, 2, then Paul, 3, and John, 5. Noah, age 7, walked in while his mother was drowning 6-month-old Mary. He asked his mother, "What's wrong with Mary?" According to Ms. Yates, she told Noah to get into the bathtub. He ran but she caught him and forced him under the water. She then called 911 and her husband Rusty, a NASA computer engineer, who had left for work just an hour earlier. When police arrived, they found the four youngest children wrapped in sheets on a bed and the oldest child still in the bathtub. All were dead. Ms. Yates reportedly told police that she had thought about killing the children for months because she believed that they had been permanently damaged as a result of her bad mothering (Thomas, 2001).

By all accounts, Ms. Yates was a compassionate, generous person and a loving mother. She was valedictorian of her high school class and was described as a "perfect" child. As both a child and an adult, she was eager to please. Previously a nurse, Ms. Yates quit her job to stay home with her children. She took care of her father when he was ill with Alzheimer's and home-schooled the children. However, at the time of the murders, Ms. Yates was suffering from severe postpartum depression, her second episode. She experienced her first episode in 1999, after the birth of her fourth child. She attempted suicide and was subsequently hospitalized. Through the use of psychotropic medications, Ms. Yates recovered, but in November 2001 the Yates had a fifth child and the postpartum depression appeared to return. In March, Ms. Yates's father died and she became even more withdrawn and robotic. The psychotropic medications were not as successful this time. Just prior to the killings, Ms. Yates's medications were changed and she was taken off her antipsychotic medication (suggesting that she may have had postpartum psychosis). A private person, she had been reluctant to seek counseling, although she told a friend that she was considering it (Thomas, 2001).

James Young, Maggie Young's husband, had the following to say about the Yates tragedy: "Medical science needs to recognize this condition earlier and help the mother before it develops into paranoid schizophrenia, as it did in the case of Maggie. . . . This ill woman [Yates] does not need to be sentenced to prison; certainly not charged with first-degree murder. . . . My wife was charged with first-degree murder. But Hawaii justice recognized her illness and gave her the medical help she needed. Unfortunately, she did not survive the cure" (Shapiro, 2001).

Like James Young, some people responded to Andrea Yates with compassion. Others reacted with anger. Most felt shocked and confused and asked themselves: "How could a mother do this to her children?" For many, the diagnosis of postpartum depression does not sufficiently explain the behavior of Andrea Yates. They want more details, a clearer understanding of how an apparently loving family could experience such tragedy. Andrea Yates has since gone to trial, the defense of postpartum did not work, and she was sentenced to a long period in a prison facility. Initially, she was tried for capital murder, but at sentencing, the assistant district attorney indicated that a prison sentence was fine. Since being convicted the decision has been overturned, due to a untruthful remark made by the psychiatrist for the defense. He had indicated in his testimony that Andrea Yates enjoyed watching the television show *Law and Order*, and one such segment was about a mother who drowned her children. That episode never took place, and therefore the decision was overturned. Rather than have her released, she is currently undergoing psychiatric treatment. Her husband has divorced her, and is looking forward to starting a new life.

In this chapter, we seek to discuss why postpartum syndromes are regarded with such suspicion by both professionals and laypersons and, in particular, how this can result in unjust legal outcomes for women with a postpartum syndrome. Initially, a brief history and description of postpartum syndromes is presented. Then we focus on the level of recognition and acceptance of postpartum syndromes by scientific communities and the resulting difficulty this can create in admitting postpartum syndromes into evidence in criminal courts. This is contrasted with the relative ease with which postpartum syndromes can be admitted into evidence in civil courts. An additional focus of this chapter is the politics of gender and the social construction of motherhood, which is used to explain why disparities in the legal system can continue to exist.

HISTORY OF POSTPARTUM SYNDROMES

Despite the heightened attention recently given to postpartum syndromes, they are not a new phenomenon. Hippocrates recorded the first known reports of postpartum syndromes over 2,000 years ago (Baran, 1989). In describing postpartum psychosis, he wrote that it was "a kind of 'madness,' caused by excessive blood flow to the brain" (Lynch-Fraser, 1983). Since that time, physicians have struggled with the etiology of the syndromes. For example, an eleventh-century gynecologist, Trotula of Salerno, provided an interesting explanation for postpartum syndromes, suggesting that postpartum blues resulted from the womb being too moist, causing the brain to fill with water, which was then involuntarily shed as tears (Steiner, 1990). However, it was not until the nineteenth century that physicians described the symptoms of postpartum syndromes in detail and formally began to theorize about a connection between physiological events and the mind (Hamilton, 1989). Marce termed this connection morbid sympathy and provided the first clear description of the syndromes (Hamilton, 1989). However, physicians were unable to agree upon a classification system or even a pattern of symptoms.

Once psychologists began to study postpartum syndromes, they too struggled with developing a classification system. Similar to physicians, psychologists found that postpartum syndromes defied easy definition and were too elusive, diverse, and inconsistent to classify (Hamilton, 1989). Therefore, in the early twentieth century, when it was suggested that there was not a connection between psychiatric disorders and childbirth, the argument persuaded the medical and psychological communities. When physicians began the task of creating a comprehensive list of all medical disorders, now known as the *International Classification of Diseases (ICD)*, they excluded the postpartum syndromes. Similarly, when professionals in the mental health field created their own comprehensive list, now called the *Diagnostic and Statistical Manual of Mental Disorders (DSM)*, which is published by the American Psychiatric Association, or APA (1994), they too excluded the postpartum syndromes. These exclusions were particularly damaging since these manuals are a means by which professionals within the two fields communicate, produce research, and develop treatments.

Subsequent revisions of both the *ICD* and *DSM* ultimately began to mention postpartum syndromes. The *ICD-10*, the latest version of the *ICD*, lists three specific levels of mental and behavioral disorders associated with the puerperium, or childbirth, ranging from mild to severe: postnatal depression, postpartum depression, and puerperal psychosis. However, physicians may use these diagnoses only for patients whose symptoms do not meet criteria for other disorders, such as depression (World Health Organization, 1992).

The *DSM-IV*, the latest version of the *DSM*, has increased the recognition of postpartum syndromes slightly. With regard to postpartum depression, the *DSM-IV* indicates that the onset of a mood disorder can be triggered by a birth, but postpartum depression is not a separate diagnosis. It can be used only to specify what triggered the onset of a mood disorder. This postpartum onset specifier in the *DSM-IV* can be applied if the onset of the depression is within four weeks after the birth of a child. This is perplexing given evidence suggesting that a postpartum depression may begin as late as several months after the birth of a child. The description of the postpartum onset specifier consists of approximately one page in the *DSM-IV* (APA, pp. 386–387).

Postpartum psychosis is listed under the catchall category "Psychotic Disorder Not Otherwise Specified" but not described or explained (APA, 1994, p. 315). The "category includes psychotic symptomatology (i.e., delusions, hallucinations, disorganized speech, grossly disorganized or catatonic behavior) about which there is inadequate information to make a specific diagnosis or about which there is contradictory information, or disorders with psychotic symptoms that do not meet the criteria for any specific Psychotic Disorder." Neither postpartum disorder is a specific diagnosis, but they are relegated to a more general status. This lack of *DSM-IV* categorization fosters the idea that postpartum syndromes are elusive and difficult to define, despite research which suggests that postpartum syndromes are discrete entities.

Popular literature also reflects this lack of clarity. In a content analysis of popular press articles about postpartum affective disturbance from 1980 to 1998, Martinez, Johnston-Robledo, Ulsh, and Chrisler (2000) found a surprising shortage of articles on postpartum depression or "baby blues." Moreover, the information in those articles was "often confusing and contradictory, and that the dominance of medical etiologies and treatments suggests that the postpartum period, like menstruation, menopause and childbirth, is another example of the medicalization of women's experience" (p. 49). Perhaps most disconcerting were their observations regarding the content of the articles.

> The popular press pathologizes and sensationalizes women's postpartum affective disturbances. The purpose of 32% of the PPD articles appeared to be to warn or scare readers, and three of the articles were written in reaction to recent cases of infanticide for which PPD was named as the defense. . . . Stories of women who have killed their children are attention grabbing and newsworthy, but infanticide is more likely a consequence of postpartum psychosis than of PPD. Articles that build stories around images of postpartum women as murderers may lead readers to believe that only "crazy" women experience postpartum blues and irritability or cause readers to link PPD and the baby blues to infanticide rather than to feelings of loss and anger. Furthermore, the stories about infanticide would not be problematic if the authors of the articles were careful to define and differentiate postpartum psychosis from PPD and the baby blues. Instead, the three are often discussed together in a way that blurs their definitions. This makes it difficult for readers to see the difference between feelings and experiences that are normal and common and those that are abnormal and infrequent. (pp. 51–52)

The case of Andrea Yates certainly reflects this confusion and inconsistency frequently seen in the media. Unfortunately, although the Yates case presents an opportunity to help educate the public about postpartum syndromes, many from the popular press have attempted to sensationalize the situation, which has not helped the public to distinguish between different types of postpartum syndromes or to develop empathy for women who suffer from postpartum syndromes.

Not surprisingly, this lack of clarity is also responsible for conflicting research findings (Thurtle, 1995). Additionally, the tendency of the *DSM* series to understate the importance and distinction of postpartum syndromes has probably been a significant cause of the lack of research because resources and funding are generally not available for onset specifiers. Since research provides a foundation for recognition, the paucity of research relating to postpartum syndromes has also probably contributed to their lack of recognition. This vicious cycle is especially problematic because treatment and prognosis for postpartum depression and psychosis may vary from other mood or psychotic disorders, so it is particularly important that research be conducted.

The use of *DSM* diagnoses in trials involving other reproductive health issues of women, such as menopause, illustrates the importance of clarity within the *DSM* (Bookspan & Kline, 1999). Although there was no *DSM* diagnosis of menopause, symptoms of menopause became associated with the *DSM* diagnosis involutional melancholia, agitated depression in a person of climacteric age. From this, a "menopause defense" was created. The first reported case citing the menopause defense occurred in 1900. In that case, a San Antonio gas company was unsuccessful in claiming that injuries a woman received when she fell into an uncovered trench were due to menstrual difficulties, not her physical injuries from the fall.

The menopause defense was used to persuade juries that menopausal plaintiffs were damaged people entitled to little or no recovery. In one case an insurer denied life insurance benefits to a common-law wife since, they argued, a menopausal woman could not be a wife. In another case, a woman injured in an auto accident spent 31 days in a hospital, yet when she sued the driver for negligence, the defendant attempted to deny liability, claiming her injuries were due to menopause. Interestingly, some of the women were not even menopausal. The defense was used primarily in civil cases such as divorce, workers' compensation, and negligence/personal injury cases. Bookspan and Kline (1999) indicate that the menopause defense was "a creation of a civil defense bar that seized upon a cultural stereotype of aging women and prevailing sexist norms. The defense predominantly was asserted by men, in male dominated courtrooms, to devalue female plaintiffs, cast blame upon them, and attempt to deny women compensation or other remedies. . . . The essential premise of this defense was that a woman approaching mid-life was either mentally ill, physically ill or both."

Between 1900 and the 1980s, Bookspan and Kline (1999) found over 50 reported appellate decisions using the menopause defense (an underestimate of the frequency of use, since most cases are not appealed). Some defendants were successful in reducing damages, others were not. Use of the defense waxed and waned until it finally disappeared in the 1980s. Bookspan and Kline indicate that the success of the defense was largely dependent on experts who applied the *DSM* diagnosis of involutional melancholia to plaintiffs. Coincidentally, involutional melancholia was dropped from the *DSM* in 1980, about the same time that the menopause defense disappeared from court records. The authors discuss how *DSM* recognition and social influences affected the use and success of the defense. Although there was no diagnosis of menopause, it was admitted into evidence at trials, generally at the expense of women. The lack of *DSM* clarity allowed for broad judicial discretion in the use of the menopause defense. The same lack of *DSM* clarity also allows for broad judicial discretion in the use of postpartum syndromes. Like postpartum syndromes, "even today, some doctors, therapists, and healthcare givers are woefully uninformed about menopause and are neither interested in nor motivated in researching this area" (Bookspan & Kline).

DESCRIPTION OF POSTPARTUM SYNDROMES

Despite the problems with classifying postpartum syndromes, three separate syndromes have reached some consensus in professional communities. From the mild to the moderate to the severe end of the continuum, the syndromes are termed postpartum or baby blues, postpartum depression, and postpartum psychosis, respectively (Lee, 1997).

Postpartum or baby blues is the least severe of the syndromes and occurs quite commonly, in from 50 to 80 percent of all mothers (Mauthner, 1998). Baby blues is described as a transient condition that typically occurs within the first week postpartum and usually lasts no more than 10 days. Symptoms include tearfulness, irritability, and mood swings (Lee, 1997). This condition could be the result of changing hormonal levels, medical procedures, or a reaction to the physical strains of childbirth (Lee, 1997).

Postpartum depression is often used as a catchall term for all three syndromes. In actuality, postpartum depression is a more severe form of postpartum blues, resembling the *DSM-IV* diagnosis criteria for a major depressive episode. Symptoms may include depression, insomnia, crying, irritability, subtle changes of personality, diminished initiative, and difficulty coping, especially with the baby (Baran, 1989; Hamilton, 1989; Jebali, 1993). Anxiety regarding how to cope with the baby is often present in postpartum depression. The depression may be related to medical issues or to sociocultural issues such as the conflict between women's expectations of motherhood and their actual experiences of motherhood. These women are often discouraged by their perceived weaknesses as a mother, with regard to issues such as childbirth, caregiving, and bonding with the child (Mauthner, 1998).

Postpartum depression develops slowly throughout the weeks following delivery (Hamilton, 1989), with the highest frequency of new cases occurring between the third and ninth months postpartum (Steiner, 1990). Most investigators estimate that the syndrome affects 10 to 20 percent of new mothers (Hamilton, 1989; Harding, 1989; Stern & Kruckman, 1983).

The most serious of all the syndromes is postpartum psychosis. In one such case, Angela Thompson went from being an honor society member, her school's first female senior class president, and an athletic and sociable person to a mother who drowned her second child, a 9-month-old son, in a bathtub after hearing voices telling her that her child was the devil (Japenga, 1987). After Thompson gave birth to her first child, she also suffered hallucinations, panic, and obsessions. She even attempted suicide by jumping out of a moving vehicle and then jumping from a bridge 30 feet high, which led to psychiatric hospitalization. Unfortunately, when she became pregnant with her second child, her doctors told her to forget about her previous psychosis, saying that it would not happen again (Brusca, 1990). Like Thompson, Sharon Comitz suffered a similar psychosis following the birth of her first child, but no one took notice of the repeated symptomatology with her second child until it was too late. Comitz had reported her fears of reoccurrence and of being left alone with the baby, but she was ignored.

In another case, Bethe Feltman, a Sunday school teacher and former grade-school teacher, murdered her two young children. She drugged both children and then strangled

3-year-old Ben and suffocated 3-month-old Moriah. When her husband arrived home that day, both children were dead and Mrs. Feltman was "incoherent." Mrs. Feltman had suffered from postpartum depression since the birth of her second child and had been hospitalized three times. She was released from the hospital on the last occasion just three days prior to the killings. She was scheduled to see a doctor the day after her children's deaths. In July 1998, Mrs. Feltman was declared insane and sent to a state psychiatric hospital. A psychiatrist testified that she was having auditory hallucinations and was almost catatonic at times. She is currently still in the hospital but is allowed home visitations every weekend (Blevins, 1998; "Colorado Man," 2001; Oulton, 1998).

Postpartum psychosis symptoms usually begin to appear within three weeks after delivery (Baran, 1989). Symptoms of postpartum psychosis include hallucinations, delusions, confusion, irritability, emotional lability, mania, obsessional thinking, feelings of hopelessness, insomnia, headache, agitation, violence, and early signs of depressive illness. Hamilton calls postpartum psychosis mercurial because of the rapidity with which moods and symptoms change (Hamilton, 1989). However, "the principal hazard of puerperal psychosis is violent, impulsive self-destruction. Infanticide is also a hazard, when the syndrome is unrecognized or disregarded and the [mother] is left alone with her child" (Hamilton, p. 94). However, instances of infanticide are rare in proportion to the number of women who suffer symptoms of postpartum psychosis.

PROPOSED CAUSES OF POSTPARTUM SYNDROMES

The cause of postpartum syndromes is unknown. There are, however, several theories as to why a woman develops postpartum syndromes. The medical model focuses on hormonal shifts that occur during and around the birthing process and on a woman's predisposition for mental illness. Certain hormonal levels, such as those of estrogen and progesterone, may drop by a factor well over 100 in the days after birth (Gitlin & Pasnau, 1989).

Although all women normally experience these severe changes in body chemistry, women who have previously experienced a mental illness or have a history of mental illness in their family may be at greater risk of developing a postpartum disorder. Harding (1989) indicates that "[t]he risk of developing a psychotic mental illness in the first 3 months after delivery is approximately 15 times as great as in nonpuerperal women, with nearly two of every 1000 women delivered requiring hospitalization for such a postpartum psychosis" (p. 110).

The goal of the medical model is to eliminate bias and subjectivity and to produce "value-free" findings; thus, when studying postpartum syndromes, women's accounts and subjective perspectives are virtually ignored (Mauthner, 1998). Mauthner argues that the devaluing of women's experiences accounts for part of the "mixed" and "inconclusive" results produced by postpartum syndrome studies. Since mothers' viewpoints are often excluded, and since most medical diagnoses, descriptions and explanations have been developed by men, it is likely that the medical model of postpartum syndromes has largely been constructed by men. This is problematic since important issues for women may be neglected. For example, medications are the treatment of choice according to the medical model. However, medications would not cure postpartum symptoms but rather, control the symptoms. This could create dependence issues, with women reluctant to discontinue medications lest the symptoms return. If the woman is breastfeeding, medications could actually increase her anxiety, as she may be concerned about the quality of her breastmilk. Most important, the issue of social support is ignored with a purely medical treatment.

Another limitation of the medical model is that it views postpartum syndromes as an illness, or, more specifically, a pathological condition relating to the individual mother's personality or inherent characteristics. Although having a medical label attached to their condition is comforting for some women, who believe that it relieves them of blame (i.e., the postpartum condition is something happening to them), other women feel helpless, as though their condition is beyond their control (Mauthner, 1998).

In contrast, feminist explanations for postpartum syndromes focus on sociological factors (Thurtle, 1995). Rather than identifying individual or personality factors related to the development of postpartum syndromes, feminist perspectives believe that postpartum syndromes are related to social and cultural issues. Feminists believe that the medical model, which views postpartum syndromes as an individual pathology, is limited because "it obscures the sociopolitical nature and context of women's distress" (Mauthner, 1998, p. 328). They believe that postpartum syndromes are related to women's inferior status in society and to "structural conditions and constraints such as the medicalization of child-birth, poor provision of state-funded child care, current labour market structures and policies, inadequate parental leave options, the loss of occupational status and identity, iso-lation and gendered divisions of household labor" (p. 329). Based on these conditions, feminists argue that it is normal for mothers to become depressed.

Also in contrast to the medical model, feminist sociologists and social psychologists have put much emphasis on mothers' accounts and experiences of postpartum syndromes. They have found that certain sociocultural factors such as single motherhood, lack of social support, and other stressful life events appear to increase women's risk for develop-ing a postpartum syndrome (Harding, 1989; Lee, 1997; Thurtle, 1995). Fox and Worts (1999) conducted interviews with 40 women who had just given birth for the first time and report that women with strong support from their partners were less likely to develop a postpartum syndrome. Further, for women in their study, the development of baby blues was related to a lack of social support and feeling overwhelmed by the responsibilities of motherhood. Sociological factors are given greater examination in a later section of this chapter. It is shortsighted to consider either approach independently, when it may be the unique interaction of medical and sociocultural factors that contribute to or precipitate postpartum syndromes.

THE LEGAL SYSTEM AND POSTPARTUM SYNDROMES

Postpartum syndromes have been admitted into evidence in both criminal and civil courts. Clearly, the use of postpartum syndromes in criminal cases has become more infamous. This could be due to the nature of the crime, usually infanticide (killing a child during the first year of life), or to the media frenzy that surrounds criminal cases involving the mental health of the defendant. The fact patterns of these cases are chillingly similar (see, e.g., Gardner, 1990). Generally, the defendant had no prior history of criminal activity and often went to great lengths, including using reproductive technologies, to become pregnant. In other words, often these were planned pregnancies or wanted children. In many cases, the women became psychotic, often perceiving the child as a source of evil, such as the devil.

The murders are particularly gruesome, including running over the child with the car, throwing the child in an icy river, and strangulation. Afterward, the mother either purportedly has no recollection of the event and reports the child missing or kidnapped or, like Andrea Yates, may call the police and report the murders.

It is difficult to estimate the frequency of infanticide in the United States. However, "in the United States and throughout the world, the population under one year of age is at great risk of death from homicide. Their killers are more likely to be their own mothers than anyone else" (Oberman, 1996, p. 3). Still, very few infanticide cases are tried, as many defendants plea bargain. Of those tried, few raise postpartum syndromes as a defense. Relatively speaking, only a small percentage of women who kill their children seem to involve postpartum syndromes (less than 5 percent; Meyer & Oberman, 2001).

In colonial times, women who killed their infants were often executed (Gardner, 1990). In the eighteenth century, juries became reluctant to impose such a harsh penalty, especially if women had committed infanticide due to social and economic hardship. This resulted in an increasing number of acquittals. In the twentieth century, postpartum syndromes became formally linked to infanticide under British law. The Infanticide Act of 1922 provided for a reduction in charge from murder to manslaughter for mothers who killed their newborns while suffering from the effects of childbirth. This act was amended in 1938 to include children up to 12 months of age and the effect of lactation. The English Infanticide Act served as a model for similar codes in numerous other countries, such as the Canadian Criminal Code provision that was enacted in 1948. There is no similar statute in the United States.

In the United States, postpartum syndromes can enter into the criminal proceedings at a variety of phases, including competency issues, pleading, or sentencing. At the outset, the competency of the woman to stand trial could be at issue. Competency refers to a defendant's ability to assist in her defense, including the ability to understand the charges against her and the rules of the court. Competency to stand trial is not an issue in most instances of postpartum syndromes since the majority of women are not continuing to experience postpartum effects at the trial. Moreover, this would probably be an ineffective defense strategy. Since the statute on murder never runs out, the defendant would simply remain in a treatment facility until competency could be achieved in order for a trial to take place. A treatment facility would be an inappropriate place for most defendants who previously had a postpartum syndrome, as postpartum syndromes are often transitory conditions.

More commonly, postpartum syndromes are used to attempt to exculpate a defendant. At issue is whether the defendant could have had the requisite mental state (mens rea) to commit murder. One way to challenge the mental state requirement would be through use of an insanity defense. Since most of these cases are not federal cases, the jurisdictional or state definitional test for legal insanity would be used. However, state definitions are incredibly inconsistent regarding insanity. In fact, three states do not have insanity statutes. The remaining states have adopted tests (criteria) to determine insanity. There are numerous tests used in the United States, but at least half of the states use a variation of the M'Naghten test (Melton, Petrila, Poythress, & Slobogin, 1997).

The M'Naghten test is a cognitive test that primarily addresses the question of whether the defendant knew that her actions were wrong at the time that she committed the crime. This is a relatively strict test of insanity, as even very debilitated persons generally know that their actions are wrong. Under the M'Naghten test, it is difficult to prove insanity for mothers suffering postpartum syndromes. For example, in *People v. Massip* (1990), the defendant threw her colicky baby into the path of an oncoming car after voices told her to do so. When the car swerved and missed the infant, the defendant put the infant under the front tire of her own car and ran over him, disposing of his body in the trash. Under M'Naghten, the jury found her guilty of second-degree murder.[1]

Other states have an additional component to their insanity test. This component can take various forms (Melton et al., 1997), but generally is a volitional component that focuses on whether a defendant could appreciate the wrongfulness of her conduct or could control her conduct. Such tests have a tendency to be more liberal than M'Naghten. For example, Angela Thompson, a nurse, claimed that voices told her to drown her 9-month-old son, and subsequently, she did so. The defendant was found not guilty of voluntary manslaughter and felony child abuse by reason of insanity but would probably have been deemed guilty by the M'Naghten test. A not guilty by reason of insanity (NGRI) verdict means that the defendant is not guilty of the crime but may be sentenced to a treatment facility until she is deemed safe to be released. Thompson was committed to an inpatient facility for 90 days. She was also required to meet other conditions placed on her by the court, such as receive outpatient follow-up with a psychiatrist for six years (Japenga, 1987).

As an alternative to the insanity defense, postpartum syndromes can assert diminished capacity, diminished responsibility, or automatism. These are used to attempt to mitigate or exculpate a defendant's responsibility for a crime. Evidence is admitted regarding whether the defendant had the capacity to form the required mental state necessary to be found guilty of the charge. However, only about half the states recognize diminished capacity defenses, and they are not generally successful.

Alternatively, the defendant may be found guilty but mentally ill (GBMI). In general, a GBMI verdict holds the defendant responsible for the murder but the mitigating role of illness is usually recognized in sentencing. The defendant may serve the same sentence length as if she were found guilty but may stay in a treatment facility until she has recovered enough to be transferred to a prison. In *Commonwealth v. Comitz* (1987), Sharon Comitz, who was discussed previously, pled GBMI to dropping her 1-month-old into the icy waters of a stream and then reporting the child's disappearance to police as a kidnapping. Only under hypnosis did she recall the killing. Under M'Naghten she would have been found guilty of murder, especially given the fabricated kidnapping. Comitz received an 8- to 20-year sentence. Less than half of the states have GBMI provisions, and support is dwindling. In any case, this may not be a very functional strategy for women suffering from postpartum syndromes, as they are generally recovered by the time of the trial.

As these verdicts indicate, the criminal cases involving postpartum syndromes as a defense are very similar, but the outcomes are quite disparate (see Brusca, 1990). Brusca indicates that these defendants must overcome skepticism about the diagnosis, which may stem from the public's lack of clear and consistent information (Martinez et al., 2000). In addition, "another obstacle faced by defendants who plead the postpartum psychosis defense is that the illness lacks the full acceptance of the medical and psychiatric communities. Postpartum psychosis is not accepted as a distinct and separate form of mental illness, and therefore is not listed in the psychiatric community's bible of disorders, the *DSM III-R*" (p. 1167). Brusca discussed these obstacles in 1990, before the most recent revision of the *DSM*, which provides more recognition of postpartum syndromes than the *DSM III-R*. Still, the present lack of precise definition perpetuates such obstacles and creates a situation where experts are left to do definitional battle in the courtroom. Brusca indicates that "this problem of the lack of medical acceptance will arise when defense attorneys try to establish proof of insanity, for which they must bring in a psychiatrist. Most psychiatrists are either not familiar with the illness, or are split down the middle on its diagnosis. Prosecutors are, therefore, likely to impeach any psychiatrist offering a postpartum psychosis diagnosis on the grounds that the psychiatrist is going against the weight of the psychiatric community" (p. 1167). The reality is that if there is debate over coverage of postpartum syndromes in the *DSM*, their validity and admissibility, it will almost always occur in criminal cases, not in civil cases.

THE USE OF POSTPARTUM SYNDROMES IN CIVIL CASES

The standard of proof and rules of evidence are not the same in criminal and civil cases, as illustrated in the well-publicized criminal and civil trials of O. J. Simpson. In criminal cases the standard of proof is that the prosecution must prove each element of the crime "beyond a reasonable doubt." In contrast, in civil cases the plaintiff can be successful if the "preponderance of the evidence" is in her favor. These standards can have a significant impact on what evidence is admitted into criminal and civil trials. In addition, admissibility of scientific evidence is determined by the Frye rule (*Frye v. United States*, 1923). Frye held that scientific evidence should not be admitted unless it has gained general acceptance in the field to which it belongs. Therefore, the medical or psychological community should generally accept a disorder before it can be admitted into evidence. Recently, federal and numerous state courts have shifted from Frye to the Daubert standard of admissibility (*Daubert v. Merrell Dow Pharmaceuticals*, 1993). Daubert usually requires a pretrial hearing regarding the degree of professional acceptance and recognition of evidence, such as a disorder, before it can be admitted into evidence. The judge then determines admissibility. Given the level of *DSM* recognition and acceptance for postpartum syndromes, coupled with the strict standard of proof in criminal courts, postpartum syndromes are less likely to be admitted into evidence in criminal courts than in civil courts.

In civil courts, the rules of evidence are much less stringent, as is the standard of proof. Although Frye may apply, the civil court has broader discretion. Recall that the menopause defense, which was used in civil cases, was admitted into evidence despite Frye. In custody matters, the trial court can allow in evidence regarding the mental health of parents. Mental health can be considered and weighed in relation to other factors in custody decisions. Postpartum syndromes have been raised as a health consideration in many custody cases. It is difficult to estimate how frequently the issue is raised because undoubtedly many mothers abandon their pursuit of custody after the father indicates that he intends to make mental health an issue. In addition, it is impossible to determine how heavily postpartum syndromes weigh in the decision because trial court transcripts are often inaccessible and opinions are generally not formally written. If custody awards are appealed, the court's opinion becomes more accessible. However, custody awards are appealed infrequently.

In custody disputes involving postpartum syndromes, the father generally asserts that the mother is an unfit parent, due to her history of postpartum mental illness, even though the mother may not be currently mentally ill and may have no other history of mental illness or unfit parenting. For example, in one of the first recorded cases (*Pfeifer v. Pfeifer*, 1955), the father appealed an order that gave care, custody, and control of the child to the mother, based solely on her potential threat to the child due to her history of postpartum psychosis. When the couple separated, Kent, their child, went to live with Mr. Pfeifer and the paternal grandparents. Ms. Pfeifer was recently recovered from postpartum psychosis, was trying to rebuild her life, and had no home to offer Kent. The paternal grandmother became Kent's primary caretaker. Mr. Pfeifer remarried and relocated, but Kent continued to live with his paternal grandparents. Ms. Pfeifer, who had also remarried, sued and eventually won custody of Kent. Mr. Pfeifer appealed the custody award, citing the mental instability of Ms. Pfeifer. At the time of the custody hearing the mother had been asymptomatic for five years and had no intention of having more children.

On appeal, the father claimed there had been no change in circumstances warranting modification of the original custody award. The court held that "the mother has remained in good mental health for more than two years without relapse; she has remarried, can offer the child a good home, and is willing to give up her profession to take care of him and her household. This change in the circumstance of the mother could in itself justify the change of custody ordered. Moreover, the father has also remarried and has moved out of the home of his parents to another neighborhood. The grandparents, with whom the child remained, have reached an age, which, notwithstanding their love and devotion, must make them less fit to educate a child of the age of Kent, and compared to them, the mother has, if she is not unfit to have custody, certainly a prior claim to the child" (*Pfeifer v. Pfeifer*, 1955, p. 56). Mr. Pfeifer's appeal was denied. However, several aspects of this opinion bear noting.

This case was appealed solely on the issue of postpartum psychosis. There was no other reason for Ms. Pfeifer not to be awarded custody. First, it was not Mr. Pfeifer who would have retained custody but the paternal grandparents. Had Mr. Pfeifer chosen to fight for custody, it is quite possible that the court would have reached a different opinion. Second, Mr. Pfeifer had led Kent to believe that his stepmother was his biological mother. The court felt that this posed a danger that Kent would never learn the identity of his real biological mother. This may have swayed the court's opinion. Third, Ms. Pfeifer's marriage was important to the court. It is questionable whether the court would have reached the same decision if Ms. Pfeifer had not been remarried. Fourth, the paternal grandparents were becoming too elderly to care for the child. Fifth, Ms. Pfeifer had no intention of bearing another child. Sixth, Ms. Pfeifer had been asymptomatic for five years. It would have been difficult to deny Ms. Pfeifer custody under these circumstances. In contrast, consider the following case.

Susan and Gary Grimm were married for 13 years and parented three children (*In re the Marriage of Grimm*, 1989). Gary's occupation is unclear, but Susan was a licensed practical nurse. After the birth of each child, Susan suffered from postpartum depression and was hospitalized for treatment. During these hospitalizations, Susan phoned home daily to speak with her children and had personal visits with them. Following the last hospitalization in 1985, the Grimms separated. During the separation the children resided with their father, while the mother lived nearby and visited daily. Susan organized, washed dishes, laundered and mended clothes, cooked for the children, and stayed with the children at night whenever Gary was working.

Eventually, the Grimms petitioned for dissolution and each sought sole custody of the children. The custody evaluation submitted to the court indicated that both Grimms were evaluated as excellent parents. Susan's treating psychiatrist testified that the depression was resolved and it had been two years since Susan's last postpartum hospitalization. However, the court placed custody with Gary. Susan appealed. The court affirmed the custody award.

It is clear that Susan Grimm's postpartum depression was an important factor in this custody award. Her treating psychiatrist was called to testify regarding her stability. Similar to *Pfeifer v. Pfeifer* (1955), Susan Grimm had not been hospitalized for a long period prior to the custody hearing. In addition, Susan had been and wanted to continue to be actively involved with the children's lives.

It is unclear why *Pfeifer* and *Grimm* were decided differently, especially in light of the fact that the courts have refused to allow testimony regarding postpartum depression to be persuasive in other civil matters. For example, in a 1997 adoption appeal, a biological mother who had given her child up for adoption asserted that postpartum depression rendered her incompetent to consent to the adoption. The Tennessee Appellate Court stated: "We do not dispute that [the mother] was probably depressed or emotionally distraught following this rather traumatic experience, but it is not unusual for there to be depression and distress following the birth of a child, even under the best of circumstances. If emotional distress meant that a parent was always incompetent to consent to an adoption, we would rarely have adoptions in this state" (*Croslin v. Croslin*, 1997, p. 10).

Similarly, the court did not find that postpartum depression nullified a woman's competency to consent to a postnuptial agreement. Kim and Anthony Latina had a 1-year-old son when Kim gave birth to a daughter, Jill, who was premature and had to be returned to the hospital daily for a short time after her birth. Kim was caring for both children and preparing to return to work while suffering from postpartum depression. Approximately three weeks after Jill was born, Kim had to be rushed to the hospital for severe hemorrhaging. Although she was not admitted to the hospital, the court acknowledged, "it was obviously a very frightening and traumatic experience" (*Latina v. Latina*, 1995, p. 19). A few days after Kim was rushed to the hospital, approximately one month postpartum, Anthony presented her with a postnuptial agreement to sign. Less than three months postpartum, Anthony presented Kim with a separation, child custody, and support agreement to sign. Kim signed both but later filed a motion to rescind the agreements based on a number of factors, including the impact of postpartum depression on her consent. Regarding the effect of postpartum depression on Kim's capacity to consent, the Delaware Family Court indicated:

> The break-up of a marriage never comes at a good time, and, as noted in many earlier opinions, usually separation agreements are signed in a highly charged atmosphere, thereby necessitating the precautions taken by the Delaware courts to ensure the agreements' fairness. However, if the courts could set aside agreements based upon their being signed during the emotional turmoil of a marriage splitting up, no separation agreement would ever be permitted to stand. Although the court recognizes Wife was extremely distraught and probably feeling somewhat vulnerable when she signed the agreement, the Court finds that Wife signed more because she did not understand the implications of the agreement than because she was coerced. It should be noted that the second agreement was signed by Wife approximately six weeks after the first agreement, by which time Wife's postpartum depression and concern for Jill's health should have lessened. (*Latina v. Latina*, 1995, p. 19)

All of these cases demonstrate a lack of a clear understanding of postpartum syndromes and are patronizing, and paternalistic. For example, the opinion in *Latina* indicates the court did not understand the etiology of postpartum depression, as it often begins weeks after a birth and can last for a year. Moreover, it is difficult to find other cases in which the court admitted in its opinion that a party was exposed to a recent trauma and yet proceeded to validate capacity to consent. Their inconsistencies simply reflect disparate treatment. How can a disorder be a key factor in one civil case but be easily dismissed in another? This is particularly confusing since court cases in which postpartum syndromes were given extensive consideration involved women who had been asymptomatic for several years. Conversely, the cases in which postpartum syndromes were easily dismissed involved women who made decisions in the midst of experiencing postpartum syndromes. Even more disconcerting is the fact that these cases generally resulted in hardships for women.

THE LEGAL DILEMMA

The current status of postpartum syndromes in the medical and psychological communities affects legal decisions. However, they are compounded by legal discrepancies in insanity criteria that foster subjectivity in insanity decisions. This can even be seen in cases that involve disorders that are recognized by the psychological/medical community, such as dissociative identity disorder (formerly multiple personality disorder) or posttraumatic stress disorder (PTSD). When asserted in court, the validity of these recognized disorders, and their exculpatory capability, often become the subject of dispute between experts. This dispute may be problematic for experts whose credibility and authority in the courtroom are already under scrutiny (see, e.g., Hagen, 1997). Experts are in an even more difficult situation when disorders are ambiguous, as in the case of postpartum syndromes.

One argument against routine recognition of postpartum syndromes in criminal courts is the even greater vagaries that could be created in the already ambiguous area of mental health defenses. Courts strive for bright lines, or clear criteria, on which to base decisions. Bright lines are rare but are desirable because they reduce disparate treatment that results from subjectivity. Recognizing postpartum syndromes in the legal system could create relatively fine lines and slippery slopes. For example, would a woman accused of child abuse now be able to assert postpartum syndromes as an exculpatory defense? Would the defense be available for other crimes, such as assault or shoplifting?

Although at first glance it appears that recognition of postpartum syndromes could lead to such unwieldy outcomes, it is unlikely. First, this has not been the case in England, where the defense is available but rarely used. Second, and more important, perpetrators with postpartum psychosis have very specific crimes and victims—harm to themselves or to their children. Additionally, the trigger does not have multiple origins as with PTSD, but is clearly due to one cause, pregnancy, and this cause is not likely to reoccur with any frequency in a defendant's lifetime and can be monitored. Third, the dangerousness is temporary. If anything, postpartum syndromes seem to have more specificity than already recognized defenses (such as PTSD and dissociate identity disorder) and represent much less threat to the integrity of the legal system.

Overall, recognition of postpartum syndromes in criminal cases would constitute a gender defense (Denno, 1994) and, in general, the court has not been responsive to recognizing or ameliorating gender biases against women in defenses. Criminal defenses, particularly with regard to murder, have always been more applicable to crimes committed by men ("irresistible impulse") than those committed by women. More men than women murder, but the fact that women represent a minority of murder defendants should not preclude their equal treatment under the law.

Courts could facilitate preventive action and clarification by the medical community if they acknowledged the importance of postpartum syndromes in their opinions. The courts have been able to address this issue directly in cases involving insurance and disability claims for postpartum syndromes. As far back as 1964, the court was asked to determine whether postpartum syndromes represented a sickness or mental illness (*Price v. State Capital Insurance Company*, 1964). If postpartum syndromes represent a sickness, the level of coverage under insurance and disability is generally expanded. Conversely, if they represent a mental illness, the coverage is generally restricted. The courts have held that the cause of postpartum syndromes has not been proven to be physical and the treatment is generally psychological; therefore, postpartum syndromes are excluded from coverage (see, e.g., *Blake v. Unionmutual Stock Life Insurance Company*, 1990). This is reinforced in court decisions regarding pregnancy. In pregnancy discrimination, "the cases define pregnancy in terms of a biological process that begins with conception and ends with delivery" (Greenberg, 1998, p. 227). The impact on consideration of postpartum syndromes is clear, since "by using a narrow, medicalized definition of pregnancy, they [the court] have excluded the time that women take to care for young children from the statute's protection" (p. 226).[2]

The idea that legal institutions influence the medical processes, and vice versa, is discussed at length in a thought-provoking law review by Noah (1999). He suggests "just as social forces have shaped medical practice, legal institutions influence both nosology and diagnosis. Law and medicine are not autonomous domains, fully insulated from one another in spite of numerous points of intersection concerning the definition and identification of disease. Instead, at these junctures, law and medicine are mutually constitutive or perhaps co-dependent" (p. 257). Noah outlines the dangers to both professions inherent in such co-dependence. For women, the danger is reflected repeatedly in court decisions regarding reproductive issues from contraception to postpartum and beyond.

THE MEDICAL AND PSYCHOLOGICAL DILEMMA

The lack of a clear definition of postpartum syndromes and inconsistencies in the medical and psychological literature probably become self-perpetuating by leading to the inaccurate education of health professionals. Small, Epid, Johnston, and Orr (1997) found that fourth- and sixth-year medical students had inaccurate or incomplete knowledge of postpartum syndromes. Medical students had a narrower view of the factors that contribute to postpartum depression than did women who had experienced the disorder. For example, students selected hormonal or biological factors and a "tendency to depression" as most influential in the development of postpartum depression. The women, however, identified social and experiential factors, such as lack of support, as contributing the most significantly to postpartum depression. The biological focus endorsed by the students suggests a likelihood to overlook the wide range of social, physical health, and life-event factors in diagnosis and treatment (Small et al., 1997). Indeed, Mauthner (1998) indicates that "the majority of research in the area of postpartum depression has disregarded mothers as a source of knowledge or understanding about their experiences" (p. 143).

If health professionals are unaware that factors such as lack of social support are common for women with postpartum depression, they will not realize that women with these factors are at greater risk for postpartum syndromes. Moreover, they will probably prescribe treatments that are not consistent with the woman's needs: for example, medications instead of counseling. As a result, women are disadvantaged on multiple levels: health professionals recognize only biological contributors to postpartum syndromes, reducing treatment effectiveness, while the court denies these biological components, preventing women from receiving disability or insurance coverage for postpartum syndromes.

SOCIOCULTURAL CONTEXT

Fortunately, in recent years there has been an increase in the recognition of sociocultural factors that influence the development of postpartum syndromes by some professionals, such as sociologists and psychologists and by feminists. As stated previously, feminist researchers and practitioners believe that postpartum syndromes are a natural response to a patriarchal society that devalues motherhood (Lee, 1997; Mauthner, 1998).

Examining the sociocultural context of postpartum syndromes involves considering the tremendous pressures that mothers face. For instance, gender roles in the United States dictate that women understand and love everything about motherhood (Cox, 1988; Mauthner, 1993). This value can be overwhelming to new mothers, who may be feeling unsure of their caregiving abilities. Women may feel inept and inadequate if they do not instinctively know how to care for their children (Thurtle, 1995).

Further, motherhood can be a stressful time for women because it entails the adoption of new roles and perhaps the loss of others. Despite the happiness that motherhood often brings, many new mothers experience grief due to their loss of freedom (Hopkins, Marcus, & Campbell, 1984). Activities of interest and important projects may need to be put on hold or may have less time allotted to them. Lee (1997) states that women's satisfaction with their new role of mother, and the quality of their relationship with their partner, both decline with the arrival of a child. She reports that the research results have unequivocally found that this decline in satisfaction is due to the "unexpected and inequitable division of household labour" (Lee, 1997, p. 101). In fact, Lee provides strong support evidence to support the sociocultural underpinnings of postpartum syndromes.

Motherhood can also be a difficult time, as many women feel societal pressure to make motherhood their primary role (Miles, 1988). This may have been true in the case of Andrea Yates, who not only quit her nursing job to stay home with her children but also home-schooled the oldest children (Thomas, 2001). Although Ms. Yates's feelings about her role as a stay-at-home mother are unknown, for many mothers, choosing whether to work outside the home is a no-win situation. Although U.S. society gives lip service to mothers who stay at home with their children, motherhood continues to be underappreciated. We often hear the question "Do you work or do you stay at home?", as if staying at home is not work. Therefore, working outside the home is many women's only opportunity to receive respect and recognition. However, they are then faced with stress related to juggling multiple roles and finding adequate childcare and may experience guilt about not staying at home with their children (Thurtle, 1995).

Mothers who decide to stop working outside the home may experience a loss of self-esteem related to loss of roles and the lack of importance given to mother's work. Additionally, these women may experience a further decrease in self-esteem, due to isolation and work that is repetitive and frustrating (Gove, 1972). As wonderful and exciting as children are, one can only imagine the time-consuming and monotonous work required of Andrea Yates to raise five children under age 7. Multiply this by the weight of the isolation that can easily occur for stay-at-home mothers, particularly those who home-school their children.

The pressure to be a perfect mother makes many women reluctant to disclose symptoms of postpartum depression. This, in turn, makes early detection difficult and may result in the increased severity of their symptoms, especially since lack of social support has been shown to contribute to depression (Inwood, 1985; Jebali, 1993; Lee, 1997). Mauthner (1999) interviewed 40 women with postpartum syndromes and found that many of them attributed at least a part of their condition to a conflict between their expectations (i.e., the mother they wanted to be) and their perceptions of themselves as mothers. Mauthner reports that the women's unrealistic expectations for themselves appeared to stem from the cultural context in which they lived as well as their interpersonal relationships. The women generally felt that admitting their needs and feelings was an indication of weakness or failure as a mother. This hesitancy to disclose symptoms of a postpartum syndrome is particularly evident in the case of Andrea Yates, who did not want to talk with a therapist and reportedly said that she felt "OK," even when family members began to notice serious symptoms (Thomas, 2001).

One of the strongest pieces of evidence in support of the influence of sociocultural factors is the decreased incidence of postpartum syndromes in non-Western cultures (Hayes, Roberts, & Davare, 2000). Stern and Kruckman (1983) point out that "recent cross-cultural studies of childbirth have emphasized that while childbirth is universally similar physiologically, it is differentially conceptualized, structured, organized, and experienced" (p. 1027). They believe that the development of postpartum syndromes in the United States results from a lack of several practices that are present in non-Western cultures: (1) social structuring of a distinct postpartum time period; (2) protective activities and rituals resulting from the presumed vulnerability of new mothers; (3) social seclusion; (4) a mandated period of rest; (5) instrumental assistance to the new mother; and (6) social recognition of a the new social status of the mother (i.e., rituals, gifts).

There are cultural differences in the structure and organization of the family and in role expectations for the new mother and significant others. For instance, in some non-Western cultures, women are considered quite vulnerable after pregnancy and are allowed a period of rest. Relatives support this rest period by fulfilling the new mother's normal duties. Additionally, while in the United States attention is typically paid to the newborn child, in some non-Western cultures much attention and importance is also lavished on the new mother. As with other major changes in the life cycle (i.e., puberty, death), pregnancy and childbirth are considered rites of passage and are marked by special ceremonies (Stern & Kruckman, 1983). The postpartum period of rest and support and clear recognition of the important status of motherhood may make women less likely to develop a postpartum disorder.

THE IMPACT OF INCREASED RECOGNITION OF POSTPARTUM SYNDROMES

Recognition of a condition that affects women solely or primarily creates the risk of pathologizing women with that condition. This phenomenon is seen with conditions such as premenstrual syndrome (PMS). Although the aim of increased recognition of PMS has been to provide more effective prevention and treatment for women, some argue that increased recognition has pathologized a normal life event so that it is seen as a defect in a woman's character (Rome, 1986). This viewpoint may then be used to patronize or discriminate against women in situations involving education or career, since women can be seen as incapable of handling these challenging situations. Additionally, some argue that increasing the role of the medical, psychological, and legal communities with regard to PMS has taken power away from women as diagnosis and treatment of this condition has come under the control of these professions.

Beaman (1998) discusses criticisms of "women's defenses," such as battered woman's syndrome, premenstrual syndrome, and postpartum depression, which recognize, within the legal system, women's unique biology and socialization. For instance, arguments against using battered woman's syndrome as a defense include the "tendency for the experiences of the abused women to be overshadowed by expert testimony; the negative ramifications of syndromization; and the boundaries imposed by creating the 'ideal' abused women" (Beaman, 1998, p. 88). Increasing the recognition of postpartum syndromes could potentially have the same medical, psychological, and legal consequences as increased recognition of other conditions affecting women.

Thus there are significant risks associated with increased recognition of postpartum syndromes. However, deciding to keep the status quo in an effort to avoid pathologizing women has its own risks: namely, the status quo involves no opportunities for the improvement of treatment or legal options for women. Further, the status quo already involves the pathologizing and paternalization of women.

Males control the medical, psychological, and legal systems in this country. Males have the power to invent and deny disorders, and they do so based on societal standards of male health. For instance, research has shown that the concept of a healthy male differs from the concept of a healthy female. In one classic study, mental health professionals were asked to select traits characteristic of either a healthy male, healthy female, or healthy adult person. Results showed that the participants' concepts of a healthy mature adult were similar to the concepts of a healthy male, but different from concepts of a healthy female (Broverman, Broverman, Clarkson, Rosenkrantz, & Vogel, 1981). Although this study was conducted two decades ago, in many respects men continue to be the standard against which women are compared.

As the Broverman et al. (1981) study demonstrates, women are already pathologized and have little control over the treatment of their bodies. The idea that recognition of postpartum syndromes will provide an excuse for the sexist practices happening in this society seems unfounded since sexism is already occurring. With regard to postpartum syndromes, sexism is seen in the medical and psychological communities. Health professionals indoctrinated in patriarchal practice choose conditions to which they want to devote resources. Thus, certain medical or psychological states receive more funding than others for research, education, or treatment. Because postpartum syndromes are conditions affecting women, there are no male norms with which to compare them. Not surprisingly, there appears to be less interest in the male-dominated health fields for these conditions. Sexism is also found in the legal arena, where postpartum syndromes are not dealt with in any uniform fashion.

We must increase recognition of postpartum syndromes if women are to receive the medical, psychological, and legal help that they need. Beaman (1998) states that women have different biologies, psychologies, and socialization than men and thus need different or new legal strategies. Some feminist scholars hesitate to use women's legal defenses because "different" has traditionally been seen as "inferior and in need of protection" (p. 89). They worry that these defenses would be seen as evidence of women's biological inferiority to men. However, Beaman (1998) argues that women's legal defenses should be designed carefully rather than discarded because if these women's conditions are minimized, researchers will continue to ignore them and women will continue to have inadequate treatment.

Some pathologizing might actually be necessary for women to receive treatment and recognition for medical and psychological conditions. Without pathologizing, health providers minimize women's syndromes, causing women to feel "crazy" for believing that something is wrong with them and leading to further problems as women's conditions go untreated. Indeed, Mauthner (1998) explored postpartum depression from the mothers' point of view and found that many women preferred that the severity of their depression be recognized, regardless of the pathology associated with this recognition. When others took their symptoms seriously rather than minimizing or trivializing them, the women said that their experience felt less "terrifying and abnormal" (Mauthner, 1998, p. 331).

Therefore, pathologizing may help normalize the experience of women suffering from postpartum syndromes. Additionally, pathologizing some types of postpartum syndromes and not others may decrease the overall level of pathology assigned collectively to these conditions. For example, pathologizing postpartum psychosis, which is a rare and serious disorder, may increase the distinction between this condition and less severe types of postpartum syndromes, which would then be able to be normalized.

Some may argue that even pathologizing one type of postpartum syndrome does an injustice to women. In response to this argument, it is important to remember that women with postpartum syndromes are already being pathologized. One has only to consider the negative comments made toward Andrea Yates (i.e., "monster," "bad mother") to recognize this. Increased recognition may pathologize postpartum psychosis by pointing out the danger of the condition but also increases awareness of the context in which these conditions develop—biological, psychological, and societal stressors, rather than "evilness" or "bad mothering." It would also allow greater opportunity for education and awareness.

CONCLUSIONS

If the medical, psychological, and legal communities would recognize the sociocultural factors that contribute to the development of postpartum syndromes, it would be possible to increase recognition and acceptance of these conditions without pathologizing women.

Women could receive the help that they need, without fear that their condition would be viewed as inherently pathological.

Sexism, along with racism and other forms of inequality, continues because people in power are rarely willing to reduce power differentials that could result in loss of their own power. Thus we cannot wait for professional communities or society as a whole to diminish sexism. It is time to empower women to take control of their bodies and the medical and psychological conditions affecting them. Women are currently relying on the paternalistic health care systems to equalize the power differential between men and women, neglecting to remember that these systems had a large role in creating inequality in the first place. If equality between men and women is to be gained, women must take an active role in defining and explaining conditions with which they are affected.

The lessons learned from the menopause defense discussed earlier in the chapter apply to postpartum syndromes and the legal system.

> The menopause defense resulted from a confluence of factors: a social climate that embraced menopause as illness; medical professionals eager to create and substantiate the perilous and evil manifestations of hormonal change; essentially unchallenged admission of expert testimony on menopausal syndrome; and unequal application of the eggshell plaintiff doctrine. The defense should have died in 1916 with the failed attempt to use it against Anna Laskowski. The stories of the women (and men) who followed Anna Laskowski reveal the misconstructions and inequalities that can result when negative social and cultural stereotypes supplant neutral decision-making. The stories also show when the intimate circumstances of women's lives become the source of public review and analysis by eager lawyers and acquiescent judges.
>
> Law develops over time in the context of theories and institutions that are controlled by the dominant political group. For the greater part of the Twentieth Century, women had little role and no power in the American judicial system. Since law is a manifestation of the sociocultural values of dominant political groups, the development, usage, acceptance, and decline of menopause as a legal defense is an example of power and perspective as law. Thus, the menopause defense, like a mirror, reflects prevalent societal attitudes toward women. Similarly, it symbolizes how, with the strike of a gavel, law can give voice to prejudice and stereotype. It took eighty years for the gavel to crack the social mirror that reflected a mad, diseased, and useless menopausal woman. It remains for society to erase the image totally. (Bookspan & Kline, 1999, p. 1318)

Therefore, although greater recognition is needed for postpartum syndromes, this must be done with the awareness of the gender inequalities that exist in the United States. If we do not also contextualize postpartum syndromes by recognizing their sociopolitical contributors, we are at risk for further pathologizing women, as seen in the case of the menopause defense.

Encouraging women to become active with decisions affecting their bodies and their lives does not negate the influence and responsibility that men as well as medical, psychological, and legal professionals have with regard to postpartum syndromes. Women do not exist in a vacuum; therefore, a condition that affects women affects their families, friends, work, and eventually, the larger society. The impact of one woman's behavior on society and the importance of societal response to her future is illustrated by Andrea Yates. People and institutions influence the fate of women with postpartum syndromes; thus each is instrumental in helping to ameliorate the disparate treatment experienced by these women.

Simple interventions could alter tragic outcomes. After Andrea Yates killed her children, James Young, Maggie Young's husband, indicated that he hoped that increased awareness of postpartum depression would result in better screening of expectant and new mothers (Shapiro, 2001). He stated: "Why not train obstetricians to screen mothers-to-be for their potential to suffer [postpartum mood disorders]? How about a simple interview?" Young suggested that pregnant women could be asked how they felt following earlier births. Perhaps even more important, their partners should be interviewed. After all, when someone is suffering from postpartum syndromes or some mental illnesses, it is often best to solicit additional viewpoints regarding the person's health. As Young suggested, earlier intervention could lead to more effective treatment.

In fact, efforts at intervention have been successful. Zlotnick, Johnson, Miller, Pearlstein, and Howard (2001) provided four sessions of interpersonal-therapy-oriented group intervention to pregnant women receiving public assistance who had at least one risk factor for postpartum depression. Three months postpartum, 33 percent of a control group of women had developed postpartum depression, whereas none of the women receiving treatment had developed postpartum depression. The treatment consisted of four 60-minute group sessions that focused on education regarding postpartum syndromes, issues, and concerns. Despite the fact that even relatively brief cost-effective interventions, such as the four-session therapy group in the Zlotnick et al. study, have been shown to be effective, they are rarely used.

EPILOGUE

Andrea Yates has just begun to weave her way through the criminal justice system.[3] Prosecutors have already indicated that they will seek the death penalty. There is no clear motive for her crime. It is likely, although not certain, that her defense attorney will use her diagnosis of postpartum depression in her defense. If so, this case has the potential to help educate both laypersons and professionals about the nature of postpartum syndromes and to replace feelings of anger and hostility with compassion and understanding for Andrea Yates and other women suffering a postpartum syndrome. On August 27, 2001, a coalition of activist groups, including the National Organization for Women and anti–death penalty groups, formed a coalition and voiced support for Andrea Yates. Beatrice Fowler of the American Civil Liberties Union was quoted as saying: "This case has touched a nerve. Every single woman I have spoken to has had the same reaction I had: What could she have possibly been going through for her to take that kind of action? It's not real" (Parker, 2001). Andrea Yates has focused attention on postpartum syndromes and their use in the legal system.

For those fortunate enough not to have had their lives touched by postpartum syndromes, perhaps the best model for their attitudes and sentiments should be those who have lived with postpartum syndromes: either themselves or a loved one. Rusty Yates, who presumably knows his wife better than anyone, has described the changes she experienced as a result of her postpartum depression and has stated unequivocally that his wife, as he knew her, "is not the woman who killed my children. . . she wasn't in her right frame of mind" (Thomas, 2001). And of course, Mr. Yates has now walked away, yet still indicating his feelings for his wife.

Mr. Yates is not alone in his feelings. James Young is supportive of both his late wife and Andrea Yates, stating: "I feel compelled to do what I can to help this woman who is a victim of postpartum depression and the terrible feelings of inadequacy she must have felt—the same feelings my late wife must have felt. Behavioral signs we all recognized in hindsight" (Shapiro, 2001). Additionally, Jeff Thompson, Angela Thompson's husband, supported his wife after the murder and stated: "Doctors are literally ignoring mothers to death on this thing" (Japenga, 1987). Further, Glenn Comitz, husband of Sharon Comitz, said that if they had understood his wife could have a second episode of postpartum psychosis: "We would have thought twice about having a second child, or have taken precautionary measures to control the situation" (Japenga, 1987). In fact, most of the husbands whose wives killed their child or children as the result of a postpartum syndrome were extremely supportive. If these men, who have lost more than most of us can even imagine, are able to look past their shock and sadness and recognize the need to help rather than blame women with postpartum syndromes, perhaps it is time for the rest of us to do the same.

NOTES

1. However, the judge rendered a judgment notwithstanding the verdict and found Massip not guilty by reason of insanity. The prosecution then appealed this judgment, but their appeals were eventually dismissed.
2. The statute Greenberg refers to is the Pregnancy Discrimination Act.
3. Andrea Yates was found guilty of murder, and sentenced to 40 years to life in a correctional facility. The jurors did not believe her postpartum syndrome defense, nor did they understand the charge of not guilty by reason of insanity.

REFERENCES

AMERICAN PSYCHIATRIC ASSOCIATION. (1994). *Diagnostic and statistical manual of mental disorders* (4th ed.). Washington, DC: Author.

BARAN, M. (1989). Postpartum illness: A psychiatric illness, a legal defense to murder, or both? *Hamlin Journal of Public Law and Policy, 10,* 121–139.

BEAMAN, L. G. (1998). Women's defenses: Contextualizing dilemmas of difference and power. *Women and Criminal Justice, 9*(3), 87–115.

BLEVINS, J. (1998, April 12). Mom not queried in deaths of kids. *Denver Post,* p. B-02.

BOOKSPAN, P. T., & KLINE, M. (1999). On mirrors and gavels: A chronicle of how menopause was used as a legal defense against women. *Indiana Law Review, 32,* 1267.

BROVERMAN, I. K., BROVERMAN, D. M., CLARKSON, F. E., ROSENKRANTZ, P. S., & VOGEL, S. R. (1981). Sex-role stereotypes and clinical judgments of mental health. In E. Howell & M. Bayes (Eds.), *Women and mental health* (pp. 86–97). New York: Basic Books.

BRUSCA, A. (1990). Postpartum psychosis: A way out for murderous moms? *Hofstra Law Review, 18,* 1133–1170.

CANADIAN CRIMINAL CODE. (1970). 2 R.S.C. 216.

COLORADO MAN KNOWS PAIN OF CHILDREN'S DEATH. (2001, June 21). Associated Press.

COX, J. (1988). The life event of childbirth: Sociocultural aspects of postnatal depression. In R. Kumar & I. F. Brockington (Eds.), *Motherhood and mental illness: Vol. 2. Causes and consequences* (pp. 64–77). London: Butterworth.

DENNO, D. W. (1994). Gender issues and criminal law: Gender crime and the criminal law defenses. *Journal of Criminal Law and Criminology, 85*, 80–173.

FOX, B., & WORTS, D. (1999). Revisiting the critique of medicalized childbirth: A contribution to the sociology of birth. *Gender and Society, 13*, 326–346.

GARDNER, C. A. (1990). Postpartum depression defense: Are mothers getting away with murder? *New England Law Review, 24*, 953–989.

GITLIN, M. J., & PASNAU, R. O. (1989). Psychiatric syndromes linked to reproductive functions in women: A review of current knowledge. *American Journal of Psychiatry, 146*, 1413–1422.

GOVE, W. R. (1972). The relationship between sex roles, marital status, and mental illness. *Social Forces, 51*, 34–44.

GREENBERG, J. G. (1998). The pregnancy discrimination act: Legitimating discrimination against pregnant women in the workplace. *Maine Law Review, 50*, 225.

HAGEN, M. A. (1997). *Whores of the court: The fraud of psychiatric testimony and the rape of American justice.* New York: Regan Books.

HAMILTON, J. A. (1989). Postpartum psychiatric syndromes. *Psychiatric Clinics of North America, 12*, 89–103.

HARDING, J. J. (1989). Postpartum psychiatric disorders: A review. *Comprehensive Psychiatry, 30*, 109–112.

HAYES, M. J., ROBERTS, S., & DAVARE, A. (2000). Transactional conflict between psychobiology and culture in the etiology of postpartum depression. *Medical Hypotheses, 55*(3), 266–276.

HOPKINS, J., MARCUS, M., & CAMPBELL, S. (1984). Postpartum depression: A critical review. *Psychological Bulletin, 95*, 498–515.

INFANTICIDE ACT OF 1938. (1938). 1 & 2 Geo. 6, Ch. 26, § 1.

INWOOD, D. G. (1985). The spectrum of postpartum psychiatric disorders. In D. G. Inwood (Ed.), *Recent advances in postpartum psychiatric disorders*. Washington, DC: American Psychiatric Press.

JAPENGA, A. (1987, February 1). Ordeal of postpartum psychosis: Illness can have tragic conse- quences for new mothers. *Los Angeles Times*, p. 1.

JEBALI, C. (1993). A feminist perspective on postnatal depression. *Health Visitor, 66*(2), 59–60.

LEE, C. (1997). Social context, depression and the transition to motherhood. *British Journal of Health Psychology, 2*, 93–108.

LYNCH-FRASER, D. (1983). *The complete postpartum guide: Everything you need to know about tak- ing care of yourself after you've had a baby*. New York: Harper & Row.

MARTINEZ, R., JOHNSTON-ROBLEDO, I., ULSH, H. M., & CHRISLER, J. C. (2000). Singing "the baby blues": A content analysis of popular press articles about postpartum affective disturbance. *Women and Health, 31*(2–3), 37–55.

MAUTHNER, N. (1993). Towards a feminist understanding of "postnatal depression." *Feminism and Psychology, 3*, 350–355.

MAUTHNER, N. S. (1998). "It's a woman's cry for help": A relational perspective on postnatal depres- sion. *Feminism and Psychology, 8*(3), 325–355.

MAUTHNER, N. S. (1999). "Feeling low and feeling really bad about feeling low": Women's experi- ences of motherhood and postpartum depression. *Canadian Psychology, 40* (2), 143–161.

MELTON, G. B., PETRILA, J., POYTHRESS, N. G., & SLOBOGIN, C. (1997). *Psychological evaluations for the courts: A handbook for mental health professionals and lawyers*. New York: Guilford Press.

MEYER, C. L., & OBERMAN, M. (2001). *Mother who kill their children: Understanding the acts of moms from Susan Smith to the "prom mom."* New York: New York University Press.

MILES, A. (1988). *The neurotic woman.* New York: New York University Press.

NOAH, L. (1999). Pigeonholing illness: Medical diagnosis as a legal construct. *Hastings Law Journal, 50*, 241.

OBERMAN, M. (1996). Mothers who kill: Coming to terms with modern American infanticide. *American Criminal Law Review, 34,* 1–110.

OULTON, S. (1998, September 2). A tragedy is retold on Web site Internet page dedicated to wife, dead children. *Denver Post,* p. B-01.

PARKER, L. (2001, August 28). Coalition supports Houston woman. *USA Today,* p. 1A.

ROME, E. (1986). Premenstrual syndrome (PMS) examined through a feminist lens. In V. L. Olesen & N. F. Woods (Eds.), *Culture, society, and menstruation* (pp. 145–151). Washington, DC: Hemisphere Publishing.

SHAPIRO, T. (2001, June 26). Father whose wife killed their five kids in Aiea in 1965 urges compassion. *Honolulu Star-Bulletin.*

SMALL, R., EPID, G. D., JOHNSTON, V., & ORR, A. (1997). Depression after childbirth: The views of medical students and women compared. *Birth, 24,* 109–115.

STEINER, M. (1990). Postpartum psychiatric disorders. *Canadian Journal of Psychiatry, 35,* 89–95.

STERN, G., & KRUCKMAN, L. (1983). Multi-disciplinary perspectives on post-partum depression: An anthropological critique. *Social Science and Medicine, 17* (15), 1027–1041.

THOMAS, E. (2001, July 2). Motherhood and murder. *Newsweek, 138*(1), 20–25.

THURTLE, V. (1995). Post-natal depression: The relevance of sociological approaches. *Journal of Advanced Nursing, 22,* 416–424.

WORLD HEALTH ORGANIZATION. (1992). *The* ICD-10 *classification of mental and behavioral disorders: Clinical descriptions and diagnostic guidelines.* Geneva: Author.

ZLOTNICK, C., JOHNSON, S. L., MILLER, I. W., PEARLSTEIN, T., & HOWARD, M. (2001). Postpartum depression in women receiving public assistance: Pilot study of an interpersonal-therapy-oriented group intervention. *American Journal of Psychiatry, 158*(4), 638–640.

CASES

Blake v. Unionmutual Stock Life Insurance Company, 906 F.2d 1525 (1990).

Commonwealth v. Comitz, 530 A.2d 473 (Pa. Super. 1987).

Croslin v. Croslin, 1997 Tenn. App. LEXIS 84.

Daubert v. Merrell Dow Pharmaceuticals, 509 U.S. 579 (1993).

Frye v. United States, 392 F. 1013 (D.C. Cir. 1923).

In re the Marriage of Grimm, 1989 Minn. App. LEXIS 143.

Latina v. Latina, 1995 Del. Fam. Ct. LEXIS 48.

People v. Massip, 271 Cal. Rptr. 868 (Cal. App. 1990).

Pfeifer v. Pfeifer, 280 P.2d 54 (Cal. App. 1955).

Price v. State Capital Insurance Company, 134 S.E. 2d 171 (Super. Ct. 1964).

7

The Effects of Specialized Supervision on Women Probationers

An Evaluation of the POWER Program

Arthur J. Lurigio, Loretta Stalans, Lorena Roque, Magnus Seng, and Jennifer Ritchie

❖

BACKGROUND

Punitive crime-control policies caused state prison populations to increase steadily from the mid-1980s to the beginning of the 2000s (Mauer & Chesney-Lind, 2001). In 1990, for example, 684,554 adult inmates were incarcerated in state prisons. By the end of 2002, the number of adult prison inmates had grown to 1,209,640, a 77 percent increase (Harrison & Beck, 2003); in midyear 2004, the adult inmate population was 1,410,404. Between yearend 1995 and midyear 2004, the number of persons incarcerated in the United States increased an average of nearly 4 percent annually (Harrison & Beck, 2005). Growth in state prison populations led to widespread prison overcrowding and an unprecedented flurry of new prison construction across the country (Harrison & Beck, 2002).

Throughout the era of burgeoning prison expansion, women constituted approximately 5 to 6 percent of the country's annual inmate population. However, the rate of growth in the number of imprisoned women vastly exceeded that of men. Since 1990, for example, the number of men in prison increased 77 percent whereas the number of women in prison increased 108 percent (Beck & Harrison, 2001). At the end of 2001, 76,200 women were incarcerated in state prisons, constituting 7 percent of the inmate population (Harrison & Beck, 2002). Since 1995, the women inmate population grew an average of 5 percent annually (Harrison & Beck, 2005).

The probation population has also grown dramatically since the mid-1980s, especially the number of women sentenced to probation. From 1990 to 2003, the number of adult probationers rose from 2,670,234 to 4,073,987, a 53 percent increase (Glaze & Palla, 2004). In 1990, 480,642 women were on probation. By the end of 2001, 865,205 women were on probation, an 81 percent increase. During the same time period, the number of men probationers increased only 40 percent (Glaze, 2002). At the end of 2003, the number of women probationers (933,100) was nearly 12 times higher than the number of women inmates (Glaze, 2003; Glaze & Palla, 2004). Nonetheless, much less is known about women probationers than about women inmates—a lack of knowledge that sorely limited the types of gender-sensitive programs that have been developed to serve this rapidly expanding population (Festervan, 2003). The research described in this chapter was designed to address gaps in knowledge regarding the supervision of women probationers.

Supervising Women Probationers

Many studies have shown that the experience of being in prison is markedly different for women and men (e.g., Greer, 2000; Pollock, 2002; Sharp, 2003). As the population of women prisoners grew, prison staff began attending to women prisoners' specific problems. For example, correctional administrators' awareness of women inmates' needs led administrators to modify prison environments and programs to make them more gender sensitive (see, for example, Pollock, 2002; Stinchcomb & Fox, 1999). In contrast, few researchers have studied probation officers' views on working with women probationers or whether probation officers' case management techniques have become more gender sensitive as more women have been placed on probation (Erez, 1989; Klosak, 1999).

In an Oregon Policy Group study (1995), probation officers indicated that women probationers have greater needs for services than men probationers in areas, such as parenting skills training, domestic violence interventions, and substance abuse treatments. Moreover, officers reported that these services are often unavailable in the community or are designed expressly for men probationers and are therefore less effective for women probationers. Similarly, Motiuk and Blanchette (1998) noted that risk assessment tools in probation are designed for men offenders and are inappropriate and ineffective for use with women offenders (see also Klosak, 1999).

In another study, Norland and Mann (1984) found that, although women probationers are less likely than men probationers to violate their probation conditions, probation officers considered women probationers more "troublesome" than men probationers. According to Norland and Mann, probation officers perceived that women probationers consume an inordinate amount of officers' time with their complaints about "minor problems" and are interested in forming dependent relationships with probation officers (p. 127). These perceptions made officers feel uncomfortable and overwhelmed. Furthermore, probation officers reported that women's problems focused "on family, children, and welfare" (p. 128)—problems they found difficult to address. Probation officers also reported that women probationers had greater needs for services than men probationers and had more emotional disorders that were "outside the scope of officers' competences" (p. 129). Norland and Mann's research raised important practical questions about managing women probationers, particularly the extent to which women's special needs and problems complicate their supervision. These findings and conclusions are consistent with those found in a national survey of probation officers. As stated in Bloom, Owen, Covington, and Raeder (2003),

> many staff interviewed in the focus groups report[ed] that the woman offender is often defined as inconvenient and difficult to work with in a system designed to supervise the behavior of men. Other[s] note[d] that working with the woman offender is seen as a low-status assignment. Attitudes toward female offenders were described as stereotypical and negative. (p. 24)

Probation Officers' Views in Cook County

Seng and Lurigio (in press) surveyed a large sample of probation officers in one of the largest probation departments in the United States: Cook County (Chicago), which is the site of the study presented in this chapter. Seng and Lurigio (in press) found that probation officers believed that women and men probationers have different needs and therefore require different supervision strategies. The multiple problems and challenges women clients present to their officers and the greater emotionality these clients express in their interactions with their officers often place great demands on officers' time, energy, and skills. For these reasons, Cook County officers—especially women officers—thought women probationers were more difficult to supervise than men probationers.

According to Seng and Lurigio (in press), the absence of affordable day care and the lack of financial and emotional support place heavy burdens on women probationers. Many women probationers probably view probation as just another challenge in their already challenging lives; however, many others might consider time with their officers as their only meaningful social contact and as a major source of social support. Whereas officers observed that the overall performance of men and women clients was similar, they viewed women as less likely to be arrested but as more difficult to supervise. They also reported when women and men broke the same types of rules (e.g., failure to report to their officers), they were likely to do so for different reasons, which were gender related (e.g., failure to report because of lack of childcare).

Probation officers' frustrations about being responsive to women's needs is reminiscent of the longstanding debate in the probation and parole literature, which began nearly 50 years ago, about the probation officer as caseworker or law enforcement agent (e.g., Glaser, 1964; Laningham, Taber, & Dinitz, 1966; Ohlin, Pivin, & Pappenfort, 1956). The debate has resurfaced more recently in the context of policies about probation officers' use of weapons (e.g., Keve, 1979; Sigler, 1988). Probation officers actually function in dual capacities (caseworker and enforcement officer); however, large caseloads interfere with their ability to perform both functions well. The compliance officer role is likely to predominate because supervision is probation's primary legal mandate, and officers are chiefly agents of the courts. Much of the debate about officers' roles has been waged without a consideration of how women probationers affect officers' professional orientations.

Officers in the Seng and Lurigio (in press) study also observed that the establishment of a specialized unit for women clients was a useful, albeit imperfect, mechanism for addressing services needs—more common among women than men probationers. Furthermore, officers reported that in the absence of specialization, an extensive and reliable resource network would help them handle women clients' problems more effectively.

The ability of officers to make effective referrals seems essential. In particular, officers need to assist women in taking the steps necessary to access and use available services. Furthermore, officers should be better prepared to broker services and to develop resources for their women clients in the areas of finance, housing, and health. Notwithstanding the issue of additional resources, officers are limited in their freedom to schedule more time for their women clients. The reporting requirements of large caseloads simply prohibit them from doing so on a regular basis.

CURRENT CHAPTER

The current chapter features research that evaluated the implementation and effects of a specialized program for women probationers (see Lurigio, Stalans, Roque, Seng, & Ritchie, 2004). As mentioned, we conducted the study in the Cook County Adult Probation Department (CCAPD). Cook County is the largest county in Illinois. The county includes the city of Chicago and 110 suburban communities and has a population that exceeds 5 million persons. CCAPD officers supervise an active caseload of nearly 32,000 clients, the vast majority of whom are convicted of felonies. Women constitute approximately 20 percent of the probation population. Of the 520 probation officers in the department, 315 were supervising probation caseloads at the time of the study. The other officers were assigned to various special units, for example, presentence investigations, court liaison, home confinement, victim assistance, or community service. Officers with special assignments were ineligible for the study because our goal was to investigate routine probation practices for women on standard probation supervision (SPS).

POWER PROGRAM

As we have noted earlier in this chapter, several probation agencies recognized that women offenders have different needs than their male counterparts and developed specialized units to supervise women probationers (Glaze, 2003). Consistent with this trend, the CCAPD created a specialized unit for women probationers. The specialized unit was proposed in July 2001 and began supervising clients in May 2002. The program was given the acronym POWER, which stands for Promotion of Women Through Education and Resources. Compared with SPS, the POWER program has several distinctive features. Specifically, all the program's probation officers are women and received training on gender-responsive supervision and support strategies. In addition to face-to-face contacts in the probation department, POWER officers hold monthly group meetings that can be counted as an officer contact. These group meetings are educational and focus on issues that women offenders should know about or address in order to achieve more positive, law-abiding lives. The first group meeting was held in July 2002.

Group meetings covered topics such as job readiness, HIV/AIDS education and prevention, financial stability, parenting, relationships, self-esteem, and substance abuse. The educational group meetings were also intended to serve as peer support group meetings (CCAPD memorandum). The program was designed to enhance both the quality and quantity of officer and probationer contacts. Officers were trained to spend more time with clients, assess their needs, and make referrals to gender-responsive agencies.

Objectives

A research team from Loyola University Chicago conducted a formal evaluation of the POWER program. The team compared a random sample of clients from the POWER program with a random sample of probationers on SPS. The evaluation included several outcome measures in order to examine how well the POWER program had met its goals. The evaluation tested the following hypotheses:

1. Compared with probationers on SPS, POWER clients will rate their probation officers higher on respectfulness, helpfulness, listening skills, and encouragement to meet their goals.
2. Compared with probationers on SPS, POWER clients will receive more referrals for services.
3. Compared with probationers on SPS, POWER clients will have more steps in their action plans and the action plans will state that they need substance abuse counseling when a substance abuse problem has been identified.
4. Compared with probationers on SPS, POWER clients will have a higher rate of participation in employment programs and a lower rate of positive drug tests.
5. Compared with probationers on SPS, POWER clients will have lower rates of violations of probation and new arrests while on probation.
6. Compared with probationers on SPS, POWER clients will have a lower total arrest rate and a lower arrest rate for drug crimes and prostitution.

Evaluation Methodologies

The evaluation of the POWER program began in May 2002. Evaluators were onsite to examine program operations and attended meetings with POWER Program and CCAPD administrative staff. With input from POWER program and CCAPD administrative staff, evaluators developed a comprehensive evaluation plan that explored program implementation and effectiveness. The study included samples of POWER clients who had only individual contacts with probation officers (POWER-IC) and those who had individual contacts with probation officers and participated in educational groups (POWER-EGP). Both these groups were compared with each other and with a sample of probationers on SPS. To enhance the validity and reliability of the findings, the evaluation team used several data-collection methods and information sources, including:

- Surveys of probationers and probation officers
- Interviews with POWER clients and probationers on SPS
- Analyses of criminal histories and event-record data
- Observations of educational and group sessions
- Interviews with probationers and probation officers

As shown in Table 1, the samples were similar on current employment and substance abuse problems. In the combined samples, 73 percent of women probationers were currently unemployed. Substance abuse problems were determined using multiple indicators such as court-ordered urine testing, court-ordered substance abuse treatment, substance

TABLE 1   Comparison of Samples on Key Characteristics

Characteristic	SPS Sample	POWER-IC Sample	POWER-EGP Sample
Substance abuse	56%	50%	45%
Currently unemployed	77	67	76
Current property offense	28	40	37
Drug offender*	72	56	53
Given jail time*	7	15	21

*Samples are significantly different at alpha = .05 ($p < .05$).

abuse mentioned in the action plans completed by the probation officer, and offenders' self-reports of substance abuse problems. About half of both samples (POWER and SPS) were identified with a substance abuse problem.

The two POWER samples were combined and compared with the SPS sample on court-ordered special conditions and length of probation sentence. Approximately half of each sample received a 24-month probation sentence. The samples were similar on court orders for mental health treatment, fines and court costs, and community service mandates. Overall, 1 percent of probationers were ordered to receive mental health treatment and 9 percent were required to pay court costs or fines. Furthermore, 19 percent were required to perform community service.

A higher percentage of the POWER clients than probationers on SPS were given jail time as a condition of their probation. While in jail, many of these probationers participated in drug treatment and other programs at the Department of Women's Justice Services, located in the Cook County Department of Corrections, before they began the community-supervision component of their probation sentences. In addition, judges ordered a higher percentage of the POWER sample (38 percent), compared with the SPS sample (28 percent), to pay probation fees, $X^2(1) = 4.04, p < .04$.

We created a measure of whether a probationer was a drug offender. A drug offender was defined as an offender who was placed on probation for drug possession or selling or had a previous arrest for drug possession or selling. A large percentage of woman probationers in our study were drug offenders. Table 2 shows that drug offenders were more prevalent in the SPS sample than in the POWER samples.

The SPS and POWER samples were similar on the percentages of probationers with at least one previous arrest for violent, property, or misdemeanor crimes not included in the "other" category. The sample of probationers on SPS, however, had greater experience in the criminal justice system. As presented in Table 2, they were more likely to have two or more arrests for any crime, a previous probation sentence or violation, at least two arrests for drug possession, an arrest for prostitution, and an arrest for drug selling. The mean number of total previous arrests for any crime was higher in the SPS sample (mean = 5.14) than the combined POWER sample (mean = 3.5), $t(340) = 4.20, p < .001$. The mean number of total previous convictions for any crime was higher in the SPS sample (mean = 1.58) than the combined POWER sample (mean = 0.66), $t(340) = 6.94, p < .001$. The POWER-IC sample did not differ from the POWER-EGP sample on any criminal history measure.

TABLE 2   SPS and POWER Samples' Criminal Histories

Criminal History Measures	SPS Sample	POWER-IC Sample	POWER-EGP Sample
Two or more previous arrests for any crime*	80%	62%	62%
Previous probation sentence*	84	30	41
Previous probation violation*	26	6	0
Previous arrests for drug possession*	56	39	35
Previous arrests for prostitution*	26	13	6
Previous arrest for prostitution or drug possession*	60	34	32
Previous arrest for drug selling*	22	13	15
Previous arrest for violent crime	38	42	35
Previous arrest for property crime	67	52	62
Previous arrest for misdemeanor not included in other categories	31	21	23

*SPS sample differs from POWER-IC and POWER-EGP samples at alpha = .05 ($p < .05$).

Small percentages (10 percent) of offenders overall in both the POWER and SPS samples were required to undergo court-mandated drug testing. The POWER-EGP sample had a greater percentage of drug offenders required to undergo drug testing (40 percent), compared with the POWER-IC sample (14 percent) and the SPS sample (11 percent), $X^2(2) = 12.06$, $p < .002$. The POWER sample overall, compared with the SPS sample, had twice as many offenders with a condition of drug testing, but the reverse was found for court-mandated substance abuse treatment. Twice the percentage of drug offenders in the SPS sample (33 percent) compared with the POWER-EGP (15 percent) and POWER-IC (18 percent) samples, were court-mandated to participate in substance abuse treatment, $X^2(1) = 7.84$, $p < .02$.

In summary, the POWER samples differed significantly from the SPS sample on criminal history. The SPS sample overall had a more extensive criminal record; however, both samples were similar on the number of previous arrests for violent and property crimes. The SPS sample had a greater percentage of drug offenders and was less likely to be in jail before starting their current probation terms. The majority of probationers in both samples were unemployed and about half of each sample had a substance abuse problem.

MAJOR FINDINGS

Mental Health Problems

Table 3 presents all study participants' responses to the mental health questions in the interview. As shown in Table 3, slightly over one-third of the sample thought that they needed mental health treatment at some point in their lives. However, three-fourths of the women who felt that they needed mental health treatment sought no help. Of those who

TABLE 3   Clients' Reports of Their Mental Health Status (Interview Data)

Client's Mental Health	Yes	No
Has a doctor or mental health care professional ever told you that you have a mental health problem?	9%	9%
Have you ever been in treatment for a mental health problem?	14	86
Have you ever taken medication for a mental health problem?	14	86
Have you ever felt that you needed mental health treatment because you felt depressed, nervous, or disconnected from reality?	38	62
Have you ever tried to kill yourself?	13	87
Have you ever thought about killing yourself but did not attempt to do it?	17	83

reported that they received mental health treatment, one-third sought treatment on their own, that is, before a mental health professional indicated that they needed to do so. Most of the probationers who sought treatment took medication for depression. A small percentage of clients (12 percent) reported trying to kill themselves and slightly more (17 percent) reported thinking about suicide but not making an attempt.

Another important aspect of women offenders' lives is social support. Women often place great importance on their relationships with others. As a result, lack of social support can be a barrier to achieving probation goals and leading a productive, law-abiding life. Social support can help women in a variety of ways, such as with childcare, financial support in emergencies, and a place to stay if their intimate partner becomes violent. Interviewees were asked to estimate the number of people who had close personal relationships with them and could help them in times of need. Table 4 presents the median number of people for each question; half had fewer than this number and half had more. Table 4 presents the percentage of interviewees who reported that they had "no one" for each of the social support questions.

Clients' Referrals and Use of Services

Based on interview and event-record data, nearly half the POWER clients, overall, received referrals. The three most common referrals were for employment, education, and substance abuse services; however, the majority of women also needed affordable housing but only 3 percent of them, based on event-record data, received referrals for housing services. The wide gap between clients' expressed needs for affordable housing and probation officers' referral rates is attributable, in part, to the limited number of affordable housing programs in Chicago. Nonetheless, lack of options to address women's needs is only a partial explanation for underreferrals; even in areas in which there are more services, such as substance abuse treatment, probation officers are still underreferring women who either want or need services.

Another explanation might be that probation officers are unaware of women's widespread need for affordable housing and other services. Moreover, probation officers might harbor misconceptions about probationers' willingness to follow through with referrals.

TABLE 4   Clients' Social Networks (Interview Data)

Client's Social Support	Median Number of People	Percent Having No Support
Can go to for a place to live	4	17%
Can turn to for financial help	2	16
Can discuss personal issues	2	9
Close women relationships	2	11
Close men relationships	1	17
Intimate relationships	1	30

Our interview data showed that, with the exception of educational referrals, in which only 52 percent pursued services, from 67 to 87 percent of women reported that they followed through on all other major referral categories. Training to enhance probation officers' awareness of women probationers' needs and motivation to address these needs might increase referral rates.

The POWER program was designed to increase referral rates by encouraging probation officers to incorporate referrals as part of their routine contact with clients. POWER probation officers have also established relationships with several community service providers. As a result, POWER-EGP clients were twice as likely to receive a referral, as were probationers on SPS. However, POWER-IC clients were referred for services at a much lower rate than POWER-EGP and SPS clients. The event-record data showed that twice as many probationers in the SPS sample (15 percent), compared with the POWER-IC sample (7 percent), received at least one referral. But the interview data showed the opposite results: POWER-IC clients were almost five times more likely to receive a referral than were probationers on SPS. The interview data, which were collected several months after the event-record data, indicated that POWER officers improved their referral rates for POWER-IC clients. Furthermore, the interview data showed that POWER probation officers significantly increased referral rates for affordable housing and employment services for both POWER-EGP and POWER-IC clients (Table 5). Probation officers might have increased their referral rates because they received information about women probationers' unmet needs based on a preliminary report that described the findings of the written survey of women clients. Thus, educating probation officers about the supervisory issues affecting women seemed to modify officers' behaviors favorably.

Group Observations

To evaluate the monthly group sessions and examine client–staff interactions, service delivery, and the effects of the program on clients we conducted several site visits, which were scheduled throughout the evaluation. These visits often involved systematic observations of group education sessions and special events, including a health fair, back-to-school jamboree, holiday events, and the program's graduation ceremony. In addition to

TABLE 5   **Probationers' Reports of Referrals and Use of Services**

Type of Service	Client Referred to Service (Survey) Valid Percent	Client Referred to Service (Interview) Valid Percent	Client Used the Service (Interview) Valid Percent	Client Used the Service (Survey) Valid Percent
No services	58%	41%	46%	50%
Employment	10	33	24	13
Housing	1	21	16	3
Educational	9	28	17	7
Substance abuse	12	26	26	13
Welfare/Public aid	1	10	10	10
Legal aid	0	7	7	2
Physical health	1	9	9	1
Mental health	2	8	8	4
Parenting	2	8	8	1
Domestic violence	0	8	8	0
Number of persons responding	146	88	88	146

assessing the content and quality of the sessions, we also explored whether clients were applying the information they learned in the program to their daily lives and if a peer support network was being developed for clients, which was one of the goals of the program.

POWER group sessions were held monthly during the first year of program implementation and addressed several topics (e.g., job readiness, employment training, financial independence, domestic violence, education, substance abuse, self-esteem, and HIV/STD education). Program staff employed a variety of instructional methods to promote learning and facilitate skills building (e.g., videos, extensive written materials, interactive training modules, and special fieldtrips). POWER probation officers led most of the sessions; however, consultants and guest speakers or "experts" (e.g., licensed health workers and financial and educational counselors) were also brought in to discuss particular issues.

Most of the group attendees were African American and ranged in age from their early 20s to late 60s. Evaluators observed that many clients would report up to 30 minutes before the designated group session's start time in order to meet with their probation officers and fulfill their monthly reporting requirements. A small number of probationers arrived late and others left before the group session concluded. The constant flow of activities and clients coming in at the start of sessions were a bit disruptive but had no negative effects overall on the dynamics of ongoing discussions; instead, the flow created an open and flexible program environment. Probation officers expressed no objections to the interruptions that occurred early in the sessions. They appeared to understand that some clients had to travel long distances and the vast majority of them relied on public transportation to take them to their probation appointments.

In general, POWER probation officers created a friendly, safe, and receptive atmosphere. The programming room was neat, clean, and decorated for special events. Clients mentioned that they preferred sitting in the conference room instead of the small cubicles where they usually meet with their probation officers. On particular occasions, such as holidays and graduation ceremonies, clients commented on how "special" they felt when they walked into the decorated conference room. Several mentioned that they did not feel like they were "meeting at the probation department" because of the festive environment. Interactions between clients and POWER staff members were very positive and respectful. Officers and clients were observed "chatting" or "hanging out" with one another in the lobby before group sessions started. Many of the women were overheard talking about their supportive relationships with other clients whom they had met during program sessions. Observations and discussions with clients and staff indicated that women attending the program had developed their own peer support network and looked forward to the next monthly meeting in order to see one another again. Many positive themes permeated evaluators' written impressions about the educational sessions:

- *Presentations were informative and enjoyable.* Clients seemed to enjoy sitting in sessions and learning from presentations. Clients were very vocal, joined discussions with great interest, and often shared their own knowledge.

- *Atmosphere was friendly.* Session participants were respectful to one another and allowed others in the group to voice their opinions about the topics being discussed.

- *Officers were sensitive to clients' emotions.* Clients participating in group sessions tended to become emotional. Probation officers were sensitive to the emotions triggered by certain discussion topics and encouraged clients to express their feelings freely during group sessions. Following group sessions, probation officers often made time for individual clients to discuss emotionally charged topics.

- *Presenters were knowledgeable about different topics.* Probation officers and guest speakers were knowledgeable about special topics (HIV/AIDS and STDs, finances, housing, and employment). Clients' questions were answered completely and information was presented in an understandable manner.

- *Groups develop and strengthen social networks.* Clients who regularly attended sessions reported that they forged strong ties with one another. Session discussions prompted clients to look for similarities in shared experiences and to identify with one another. This process also appeared to promote the development of meaningful relationships among clients, adding peer support to women probationers' experiences. In addition to talking about life experiences, many of the women "bonded" by sharing their experiences involving the criminal justice system, children, and family problems, and their strategies for better responding to problems and completing their probation sentences successfully.

- *Clients gain a sense of accomplishment and improve their self-esteem.* Clients were awarded graduation certificates for their regular participation in group sessions. During graduation ceremonies, women voiced their gratitude to the POWER program and their individual officers for helping them during their probation sentences. They expressed a sense of accomplishment and pride for having participated successfully in the program.

- *Time constraints and conflicts lowered client attendance.* Group attendance on some days was extremely low. Most women who were part of the POWER program could not attend because of conflicting work schedules, whereas some could not attend because of other obligations and commitments. For example, women who were enrolled in the Department of Children and Family Services' Welfare-to-Work program were mandated to participate in activities that often conflicted with POWER's schedule of group sessions.

- *Transportation delays created a lag in start times.* A majority of women who attended program sessions typically relied on public transportation. Because group attendance counted as a monthly visit for clients, probation officers had to record information in order to fulfill the monthly reporting requirements for all their clients. The brief check-ins with probation officers sometimes took longer than expected and transportation delays created a lag in session start times.

Program staff recognized these barriers and the following changes were implemented to remedy them:

- *Officers lowered the incidence of late start times.* Delays in start times appeared unavoidable because of transportation and client scheduling issues. To respond to those issues, the POWER officers adjusted the session rules and informed clients that they would be allowed a 10-minute grace period to join the group. If they arrived late, they would have to wait until after the group session to meet with their assigned probation officers and complete their monthly reporting requirements. In addition, they would receive no credit for group participation. The new "rule" appeared to lower the incidence of late arrivals.

- *Schedule conflicts reduced attendance.* A second session each month was added to the program schedule in order to accommodate clients who missed group meetings because of schedule conflicts. POWER clients were also placed in different tracks based on their ability to attend sessions. Clients who were employed and needed less assistance had no monthly attendance requirement. Clients who were deemed most in need of additional services were directed by their probation officers to attend monthly sessions.

- *Officers reduced the wait for checking-in/reporting.* The problem of delays in meeting with probation officers seemed unavoidable because monthly contact reports are required for probation clients. However, the POWER probation officers were able to reduce the time it took to capture necessary information from clients by creating sign-in sheets to record any new information that clients were required to report. This procedure streamlined the reporting process and sessions began in a timelier manner.

POWER Program Effects

Perceptions of Probation Officers.   Probationers, in general, rated their officers highly on a number of characteristics such as helpfulness, respectfulness, and goal setting. POWER clients rated their officers as more helpful than non-POWER clients did and women in the program greatly appreciated the support and advice of fellow probationers.

The program accords women with a sense of accomplishment and camaraderie. POWER officers have created a comfortable and safe atmosphere for women, encouraging them to express their feelings and to learn various strategies for improving their lives. Officers adjusted program procedures to alleviate the problem of late arrivals to groups and made program participation convenient and enjoyable for women.

Probation Outcomes.   The evaluation of the POWER program examined the performance of the program on critical process and outcome measures. The program was designed to increase referrals and enhance the quality of probation officers' supervisory sessions with women probationers for the purpose of helping clients lead positive and law-abiding lives. Thus, we examined whether the POWER program reduced unsatisfactory probation terminations, probation revocations, violations of probation (VOPs), and arrests while on probation.

The POWER program had no effect, overall, on reducing VOPs or missed appointments. However, POWER-EGP clients at the medium-risk level were less likely than clients on SPS to miss their office visits and were less likely than probationers in the POWER-IC and SPS samples to test positive for drug use. POWER-EGP clients had lower rates of unsatisfactory probation terminations and arrests for any crime. These findings appeared after we statistically controlled for differences among the groups on criminal history measures. The POWER-EGP, POWER-IC, and SPS samples were similar on rates of VOPs and revocations, and new arrests for drug possession and prostitution.

The POWER-EGP program's favorable effects were especially evident in two high-risk groups: offenders with previous incarcerations and drug offenders, defined as those who had a previous arrest or were sentenced to probation for drug possession or drug selling. Offenders with previous incarcerations who were supervised in the POWER-EGP program had a lower number of new arrests and were less likely to have their probations unsatisfactorily terminated than were probationers on SPS with previous incarcerations. Moreover, drug offenders in the POWER-EGP program had a lower mean number of new arrests and were less likely to have their probations unsatisfactorily terminated than were drug offenders on SPS. Research should address why the POWER program had more beneficial effects on new arrests and unsatisfactory terminations among drug offenders and those with previous incarcerations. We speculate that the effects might be attributable to women's participation in drug-treatment services in the Cook County Department of Corrections.

In summary, participation in the POWER program was related to several other favorable outcomes. Specifically, POWER-EGP clients were less likely to miss appointments and to test positive for drugs, compared with other types of clients. They were also less likely than those on SPS to be terminated unsatisfactorily and be arrested for new crimes. The POWER-EGP program was particularly effective for drug offenders and those with previous incarcerations (Figure 1).

MAJOR CONCLUSIONS AND RECOMMENDATIONS

Supervisory Issues

As Seng and Lurigio (in press) reported, caseload officers in the CCAPD are quite aware of the special needs of women probationers and the different strategies that are necessary for responding to those needs. Nonetheless, they often felt overwhelmed or ill equipped to

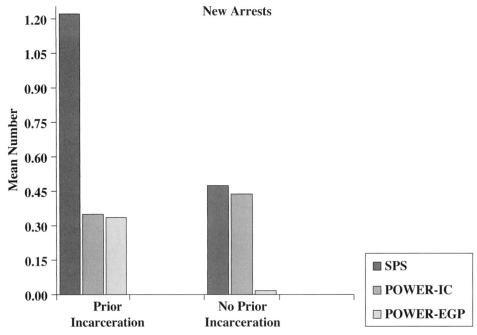

FIGURE 1   New Arrests Comparisons: Offenders with and without Previous Incarcerations

handle the challenges that are peculiar to working with female clients. In general, they believed that implementing a specialized supervision unit for women can be both a practical and an effective alternative to monitoring women on SPS. In officers' views, specialization should involve lower caseloads, the continued training of officers, and a wider and deeper array of services for women. These are the stated components of the POWER program. Therefore, the general mode of operations and staffing of the POWER program makes sense to caseload officers in the department and comports with the research literature that encourages the implementation of specialized caseloads for women probationers (Festervan, 2003).

Despite the apparent value of specialized caseloads, the size of the female population in the CCAPD is so large that specialized supervision is an unrealistic goal for all women on adult probation. The establishment of a specialized unit can address the needs of only a relatively small number of female clients and leaves the department with the responsibility for responding more effectively and efficiently to women on SPS. To improve the supervision of women in the POWER program and those on SPS, we recommended that the department provide more training for officers and more childcare and transportation assistance for clients.

Training should prepare officers to be more gender sensitive and responsive in all their activities and interactions with women probationers. Specifically, officers should be educated about more effective ways to communicate with women and to respond to their emotional needs and to be less inclined to perceive women in terms that are gender biased or stereotypical. Stereotypic responses were more common among male probation officers than among female probation officers, and male probation officers felt less capable of handling women clients' problems than female probation officers did (Seng & Lurigio, in press). Nonetheless, both male and female probation officers can be more helpful to their women clients when they become more cognizant of the wider circumstances that are affecting their clients' everyday lives (Bloom et al., 2003).

The vast majority of women probationers reported that CCAPD officers treat them respectfully, courteously, and professionally. They also indicated that their officers, especially those working in the POWER program, genuinely cared about them and work diligently to help them achieve their goals. Women in the POWER-EGP program seemed to value deeply their interactions with officers. Nonetheless, we still maintain that all probation officers can benefit from further education to enhance gender sensitivity in their assessment and supervision of female clients. Stereotypes are difficult to change and are likely to affect officers' supervisory styles and contacts with female clients. Thus, the CCAPD should consider adopting gender-sensitive training curricula. In particular, sensitively training for officers should directly and vigorously confront stereotypes about women offenders (Bloom et al., 2003).

Childcare rooms or facilities should be opened on or near the premises of probation facilities. Many women miss probation appointments or have their appointments disrupted because of childcare obligations, which they often bear without the assistance of partners or family members (Seng & Lurigio, in press). Childcare rooms could be stocked with toys, books, movies, and video games donated by local businesses. Student or community volunteers could be solicited to care for children during their mothers' sessions with probation officers. Such an arrangement would decrease the number of missed report days and help clients and officers concentrate on doing business instead of watching children. The time spent with women probationers is officers' greatest resource. Childcare settings would ensure that less of that time would be detracted from conducting intake interviews and routine visits and building a relationship with women clients—an important factor in their probation success (Festervan, 2003).

Women probationers and probation officers discussed problems with missed appointments that are the result of transportation issues. Most women have no cars and many have no money to pay for public transportation. Recognizing this need, the POWER program staff established a transportation fund that provided clients with tokens to help them afford the travel costs incurred in their visits to the probation department.

Group Sessions

Educational sessions seemed to be an effective component of the POWER program. Their benefits to women probationers were demonstrated through statistical comparisons of outcomes, women's self-reports, and researchers' observations. The group experience can be a powerful vehicle or mechanism for client change. Participation imparts knowledge; teaches skills; and conveys information about employment, educational, and other opportunities. Perhaps most important, groups broaden women's network of social support and convey a sense of community and communality. Decades of research on peer support and group therapy techniques have demonstrated the therapeutic value of group interactions for persons with a variety of medical and social problems.

The beneficial effects of the POWER-EGP program cannot be attributed solely to the educational group sessions. The POWER-EGP sample also obtained more resources than did the POWER-IC sample. Specifically, clients in the POWER-EGP sample were:

- four times more likely to receive a referral
- two times more likely to participate in job or educational training
- more likely to spend more contact time with their probation officer
- more likely to report that peer support was important

In part, clients in the POWER-EGP sample were given more chances to improve their lives because they were more likely to receive referrals to outside agencies for any kind of services, such as job or educational training, compared with POWER-IC clients and probationers on SPS. Although the benefits of POWER-EGP might be only partially attributable to the educational group meetings, the findings reinforce the importance of these meetings. Therefore, the program should try to engage all women probationers in educational group meetings, especially those who have previous arrests or current convictions for drug possession or sales. If possible, these sessions should be mandatory for program participants. Higher referral rates and the positive differences associated with these referrals (participation in job training and lower rates of positive drug tests) should be present among all clients in the POWER program, not just those involved in educational group meetings.

Of course, differences between POWER-EGP clients and those in the POWER-IC and SPS samples might be entirely or largely a function of selection bias. Women probationers who are chosen for groups or who volunteer to participate in groups might simply be a better risk and more likely to succeed on probation without any special interventions. Nonetheless, we statistically controlled for the risk of reoffending by holding criminal history constant among the three groups, which was a useful (but not a foolproof) method to alleviate the effects of selection bias.

Limited Resources

Because of limitations in resources and the growing and already considerable numbers of women on probation, the POWER program can continue serving probationers from select geographic areas of the city. Another option is for the program to be used selectively in a gradient of services for women. Women at the lowest level of service need can be monitored on SPS; those at a moderate level of service need can be monitored in the POWER-IC program. However, POWER-IC's usefulness or "valued-added" must be more clearly established relative to SPS before it can be considered a more intense and gender-responsive supervision option.

Another useful plan for conserving limited resources is for the POWER program to target drug offenders. As our results indicated, women with histories of drug offenses seem to profit most from the program's group interventions. Those with previous incarcerations also do particularly well in the POWER-EGP program. As we discussed above, we suspect—but were unable to verify—that these women were ordered to participate in jail-based drug treatment before their probation sentences began. The jail experience primes women to take advantage of subsequent probation services by engaging them in recovery and providing them with the skills necessary to benefit from group interactions. Hence, we recommend that the CCAPD further strengthen its relationship with the Department of Women Justice Services and encourage judges to order its services as a front-end condition of probation for POWER participants with drug histories. Such orders would ensure that women have a continual treatment experience—from more intensive inpatient treatment at the jail to less intensive outpatient treatment while on probation. This model of enhancing the effectiveness of specialized probation programming for women should be evaluated in other jurisdictions.

Referrals for Services

The data suggested that women probationers' needs for affordable housing, mental health, and domestic violence services are being inadequately addressed in probation action plans. Probation officers might believe that making referrals would enhance probationers' lives, if the court sanctioned unmotivated clients for repeated failures to follow through with the referrals. Thus, we recommend that the court mandate participation in social services as special conditions of probation.

The staff of specialized probation programs for women should survey service providers to ascertain whether they offer gender-exclusive or -responsive services. Officers should direct women to interventions expressly tailored to respond to their clients' individual needs. Several experts have offered guidelines on how to determine whether services are equipped to handle women's issues (e.g., Austin, Bloom, & Donahue, 1992; Chesney-Lind, 2000). Services that respond to the criminogenic needs of women offenders can help reduce the likelihood of rearrest and rule infractions. Further research is also needed to establish what occurs when clients receive referrals; how community agencies help or hinder them; what percentage of clients improve their life situations using referrals; and whether referrals are related to better compliance with probation conditions.

Finally, the staff of specialized probation programs for women should closely explore the referral process—from assessment, to action plans, to resource identification, to service brokerage and linkage, to actual use of and benefit from referrals. Our data demonstrated incongruence between clients' and officers' perceptions of needs as well as between reports of needs and evidence of referrals to meet those needs. We have no hard evidence to explain the gaps. Possibilities include officers' failures to assess women properly for services or document the referral in the record and offenders' failure to use or report the use of referrals in our interviews and surveys. Officers should not assume the offenders have the confidence, experience, or knowledge to navigate the complex service domain. Clients must be guided and supported throughout the readjustment and recovery process.

ACKNOWLEDGMENTS

The study reported here was funded by a grant from the Cook County Board of Commissioners. We are grateful for their support and the participation of the staff of the Cook County Adult Probation Department, especially those who worked in the POWER program. In particular, we acknowledge the invaluable assistance of Mike Bacula, the executive assistant of the department's chief probation officer; without him, this research could not have been completed successfully. The views expressed in this chapter are solely those of the authors and do not necessarily reflect the views of the board or department.

REFERENCES

Austin, J. B., Bloom, B., & Donahue, T. (1992). *Female offenders in the community: An analysis of innovative strategies and programs.* San Francisco: National Council on Crime and Delinquency.

Beck, A. J., & Harrison, P. M. (2001). *Prisoners in 2000.* Washington, DC: U.S. Department of Justice, Government Printing Office.

Bloom, B., Owen, B., Covington, S., & Raeder, M. (2003). *Gender-responsive strategies: Research, practice, and guiding principles for women offenders.* Washington, DC: National Institute of Corrections, U.S. Department of Justice.

Chesney-Lind, M. (2000). Successful gender-responsive programming must reflect women's lives and needs. *Women, girls, and criminal justice: Vol. 1, Number 1.* Kingston, NJ: Civic Research Institute.

Erez, E. (1989). Gender, rehabilitation, and probation decisions. *Criminology, 27,* 307–327.

Festervan, E. (2003). *Women probationers: Supervision and success.* Lanham, MD: American Correctional Association.

Glaze, L. E. (2002). *Probation and parole in the United States, 2001.* Washington, DC: U.S. Department of Justice, Government Printing Office.

Glaze, L. E. (2003). *Probation and parole in the United States, 2002.* Washington, DC: U.S. Department of Justice, Government Printing Office.

Glaze, L. E., & Palla, S. (2004). *Probation and parole in the United States, 2003.* Washington, DC: U.S. Department of Justice, Government Printing Office.

Glaser, D. (1964). *The effectiveness of prison and parole systems.* Indianapolis, IN: Bobbs-Merrill.

Greer, K. (2000). The changing nature of interpersonal relationships in a women's prison. *Prison Journal, 80,* 442–468.

Harrison, P. M., & Beck, A. J. (2002). *Prisoners in 2001.* Washington, DC: U.S. Department of Justice, Government Printing Office.

Harrison, P. M., & Beck, A. J. (2003). *Prisoners in 2002.* Washington, DC: U.S. Department of Justice, Government Printing Office.

Harrison, P. M., & Beck, A. J. (2005). *Prison and jail inmates at midyear 2004.* Washington, DC: U.S. Department of Justice, Government Printing Office.

Keve, P. W. (1979). No farewell to arms. *Crime and Delinquency, 25,* 11–23.

Klosak, J. M. (1999). *The course of their lives: Female offenders on probation.* Unpublished doctoral dissertation, University of Illinois at Chicago.

Laningham, D., Taber, M., & Dinitz, R. (1966). How probation officers view their job responsibilities. *Crime and Delinquency, 12,* 118–127.

Lurigio, A. J., Stalans, L., Roque, L., Seng, M., & Ritchie, J. (2004, August). *A process and outcome evaluation of the POWER program.* Chicago: Cook County Adult Probation Department.

Mauer, M., & Chesney-Lind, M. (2001). *Invisible punishments: The collateral consequences of mass imprisonment.* New York: Free Press.

Motiuk, L., & Blanchette, K. (1998). Assessing female offenders: What works? *International Community Corrections Journal, 10,* 6–9.

Norland, S., & Mann, P. J. (1984). Being troublesome: Women on probation. *Criminal Justice and Behavior, 11,* 17–28.

OHLIN, L., PIVEN, H., & PAPPENFORT, D. (1956). Major dilemmas of the social worker in probation and parole. *Nation Probation and Parole Association Journal, 2,* 46–53.

OREGON POLICY GROUP. (1995). *Intermediate sanctions for women offenders: Oregon Intermediate Sanctions for Female Offenders Policy Group.* Salem, OR: Author.

POLLOCK, J. M. (2002).*Women, prison, and crime.* Belmont, CA: Wadsworth.

SENG, M., & LURIGIO, A. J. (in press). Probation officers' views on supervising women probationers. *Women and Criminal Justice.*

SHARP, S. (2003). *The incarcerated woman.* Upper Saddle River, NJ: Prentice Hall.

SIGLER, R. T. (1988). Role conflict for adult probation and parole officers: Fact or myth. *Journal of Criminal Justice, 16,* 133–146.

STINCHCOMB, J. B., & FOX, V. B. (1999). *Introduction to corrections.* Upper Saddle River, NJ: Prentice Hall.

8

Abortion

Is It a Right to Privacy or Compulsory Childbearing?

Roslyn Muraskin

A bortion has been an issue that has dominated our system of laws for many years. When the first edition of this book was published in 1993, the controversy over the right of a woman to obtain an abortion was there. Today, there is even more focus on this issue. A very large conservative movement is afoot in the United States. The Supreme Court continues to face cases that restrict the rights of women over the control of their bodies. There continues to be public debate in state courts and the legislatures as well as among the justices of the Supreme Court regarding a woman's right to privacy. In this chapter, cases and their holdings are presented. Reproductive rights are the focus for recognition of the constitutional right to privacy; or stated otherwise, is there a constitutional right to privacy? The cases that are evidenced today are good examples of the court's ability to "protect" the rights of women. Viewed from another perspective the question becomes, is the unborn fetus a person, a person with rights? As of this writing, the U.S. Supreme Court has not made a determination as to when life begins. The fetus is not considered a person; still there is a strong faction attempting to overthrown the *Roe* decision and to give the fetus certain rights, such as proper medical care. Today the ruling of *Roe v. Wade* (1973) still pervades, giving women the right to abortion based on a sliding scale.

It is fair to say that abortion "has dominated the landscape of procreational discourse and policy in the United States during the twentieth" century and continues into the twenty-first century (MacKinnon, 2001, p. 1212). From Alice Walker, "[a]bortion, for many women, is more than an experience of suffering beyond anything most men will ever know; it is an act of mercy and an act of self-defense. To make abortion illegal again is to sentence millions of women and children to miserable lives and even more miserable deaths" (1989, pp. 691–692). To view abortion as a crime means that many women will die.

In MacKinnon's work of 2001, she describes a young black woman who had an illegal abortion during a time prior to *Roe*:

> We were very middle class 1950s . . . There was no spontaneous sex. . . . But on one occasion, in the fall, one of Joseph's apartment mates was away. . . . We were kidding around and we went to [his] room, and we started fooling around. . . . We fell into his bed and had sex, and my period did not come the next time. . . . I liked the guy, but when he started talking about marriage and babies and stuff I wasn't ready. I wanted to finish my education. . . . I decided to ask my stepmother in Des Moines if she could help me. . . . We must have done it on a Friday night. . . . We went to the poor section of town. I remember not seeing anyone—just looking straight ahead.
>
> It was a kitchen table, coat hanger abortion. It took maybe six minutes. I got on the kitchen table. I think my stepmother gave me a drink of brandy or something, and she said, "Now this may hurt a little bit." She held my hand and this woman stuck a piece of coat hanger into my vagina. She stuck the coat hanger in, a piece that had been sterilized or whatever the hell she had done, and then my stepmother said, "Okay, now you get dressed." And what you were supposed to do was leave that in there until you started to abort. And then I left. I remember walking out with this coat hanger between my legs. . . . That evening I started bleeding. . . . I got up very early in the morning and went to the bathroom and there was just this passage of blood and a clot that was slightly bigger than the clots I usually passed during my menstrual period. . . . I should have been more concerned. If for no other reason than for the physical reality. I could have died. I could have become sterile. . . . When I read about people on the kitchen table I say, "I had one of those." (As cited in Messer & May, 1994, pp. 17, 19–23)

This was then. In the 1970s it was estimated that the number of deaths from illegal abortions was eight times greater than that from legal abortion. Reproductive freedom has been joined with such rights as freedom of speech or assembly. There exist those who have come to the conclusion out of simple personal concern that if women do not control their bodies from within, they can never control their lives from the skin out. There are those who feel that women's role as the most basic means of production will remain the source of their second-class status if outside forces continue either to restrict or compel that production. Remember the words of Justice Miller in *Bradwell v. State of Illinois* (1872), where he stated that "[t]he paramount destiny and mission of woman are to fulfill the noble and benign offices of wife and mother. This is the law of the Creator."

The freedom for women to decide when to become a mother and under what conditions is an issue of great concern. Is abortion an issue that affects women only, and is it an example of sex discrimination? Are we to think primarily of the fetus and thus conclude that abortion is murder, thereby involving the criminal courts? Is abortion to be viewed from a religious perspective, thinking of how the legal codes of Western religions treat the subject? Is abortion a question of privacy? Should states be prevented from intruding into the affairs and personal decisions of their citizens? Does there exist under *Reed v. Reed* (1971) a compelling state interest to interfere with a woman's right to choose? If a woman is a victim of rape or sexual abuse, is she entitled to an abortion without interference from the state? Is it an issue of discrimination against the poor, who may need the state to subsidize abortions, or even racial discrimination because of the high proportion of minorities who choose to abort? The question that comes into focus is not "how can we justify abortion?" but "can we justify compulsory childbearing?" Is there a compelling interest on the part of the state to protect what the courts have refused to define as a person?

What are the issues that the courts have faced when we discuss the issue of abortion? There are two significant constitutional issues at stake in judicial bias against women. The first issue has to do with the right to privacy, implied by our Constitution in the Fourth Amendment. The other issue concerns the Fourteenth Amendment's right to due process and equal treatment. Is the issue simply one of female autonomy over her body? The conflict continues. It is an issue that comes back repeatedly to haunt the courts, the legislators, and the executive branch of government. When can a woman have a partial abortion? Whose rights are we protecting? The U.S. Supreme Court held that laws prohibiting abortion are unconstitutional. In *Roe v. Wade* (1973) the Court held that "no state shall impose criminal penalties on the obtaining of a safe abortion in the first trimester of pregnancy." Women cannot be charged criminally with obtaining an abortion, but there are administrative regulations and legal penalties that prevent her from doing so.

Abortion is an emotional, legal, religious, and highly volatile issue. In December 1971, the Supreme Court heard the *Roe v. Wade* case, brought to it by an unmarried pregnant woman from Texas who complained that the Texas statute permitting abortions only when necessary to save the life of the mother was unconstitutional. (This person has since indicated that women should not be given the option of abortions, that all life is precious, and therefore, if pregnant, a women should not have the right to choose.)

What was held in *Roe* was that a state may not, during the first semester of pregnancy, interfere with or regulate the decision of a woman and her doctor to terminate the pregnancy by abortion; that from the end of the first trimester until the fetus becomes viable (usually about 24 to 28 weeks), a state may regulate abortions only to the extent that the regulation relates to the protection of the mother's health; and that only after the point of viability may a state prohibit abortion except when necessary to save the mother's life. The Court further permitted the state to prohibit anyone but a licensed physician from performing an abortion.

The Court did not accept the argument that a woman has a constitutional right to have an abortion whenever she wants one and that the state has no business at all interfering with her decision. Rather, the Court established a sliding scale that balanced the right of the woman against the right of the state to interfere with the decision; it would have to prove that it had a compelling interest to do so. During the first three months of pregnancy, when continuing the pregnancy is more dangerous than ending it, the Court found no such compelling state interest for overriding the private decision of a woman and her doctor. When abortion becomes a more serious procedure, the Court found that the state's interest in the matter increases enough to justify its imposition of regulations necessary to ensure that the mother's health will be safeguarded. In the last trimester of pregnancy, the Court found that the state's interest in the health and well-being of the mother as well as in the potential life of the fetus is sufficient to outweigh the mother's right of privacy except where her life is at stake.

In the language of the *Roe* Court (1973):

> The right of privacy . . . is broad enough to encompass a woman's decision whether or not to terminate her pregnancy. The detriment that the State would impose upon the pregnant woman is apparent. Specific and direct harm medically diagnosable even in early pregnancy may be

involved. Maternity, or additional offspring, may force upon the woman a distressful life and future. There is also the distress, for all concerned, associated with the unwanted child and there is the problem of bringing a child into a family already unable psychologically and otherwise to care for it. In other cases as in this one, the additional difficulties and continuing stigma of unwed motherhood may be involved. All these are factors the woman and her responsible physician will consider in consultation.

The Court continued by indicating in *Roe* that the right to terminate the pregnancy at whatever time was not acceptable to the Court. They indicated further that the right to privacy was not absolute.

With regard to the argument presented that the fetus is a person, the Court went on to comment:

[I]n nearly all . . . instances [in which the word "person" is used in the Constitution] the use of the word is such that it has application only postnatally. None indicates, with any assurance, that it has any possible prenatal application. All this together with our observation . . . that through the major portion of the nineteen century prevailing legal practices were far freer than they are today, persuades us that the word person as used in the fourteenth amendment, does not include the unborn.

In answering the question of when life begins, the Court further stated:

It should be sufficient to note . . . the wide divergence of thinking on this most sensitive and difficult question.

In areas other than criminal abortions, the law has been reluctant to endorse any theory that life as we recognize it, begins before live birth or to accord legal rights to the unborn except in narrowly defined situations and except when the rights are contingent upon live birth. In short the unborn have never been recognized in the law as persons in the whole sense.

We repeat . . . that the State does have an important and legitimate interest in preserving and protecting the health of the pregnant woman . . . [a]nd that it has still another important and legitimate interest in protecting the potentiality of human life.

The Court had decided to allow the mother to abort at the end of the first trimester and then to allow her physician to decide medically if the patient's pregnancy was to be terminated after this period. The judgment was to be effected by a decision free from the interference of the state.

At the same time that the Supreme Court decided the *Roe* case, it decided a second case, that of *Doe v. Bolton* (1973), which involved a Georgia abortion statute that set forth several conditions that were to be fulfilled prior to a woman obtaining an abortion. These included a statement by the attending physician that an abortion was justified, with the concurrence of at least two other Georgia-licensed physicians; the abortion was to be performed in a hospital licensed by the state board of health as well as accredited by the Joint Commission on Accreditation of Hospitals; there was to be advance approval by an abortion committee of not less than three members of the hospital staff; and the woman had to reside in the state of Georgia.

The Court then held that these provisions were overly restrictive, thereby treating abortion differently from comparable medical procedures and thus violating laws that require the husband of a pregnant woman or the parents of a single mother to give their consent prior to having an abortion. Both of these requirements were struck down by the Supreme Court (*Planned Parenthood of Central Missouri v. Danforth*, 1976).

What, then, is to happen when husband and wife cannot agree? Who is to prevail? The courts have argued that the woman should. Since it is the woman who bears the child physically and who is affected more directly and immediately by the pregnancy, the balance would seem to weigh in her favor.

Until this point the state did not appear to have the constitutional authority to give a third party an absolute and possibly arbitrary veto over the decision of the physician and a parent. There has developed the question of the authority that a parent has over a child. It has been well understood that constitutional rights do not mature and come into being magically when one attains the state-defined age of majority. Minors as well as adults are protected by the Constitution and possess constitutional rights.

There does exist a suggested interest in the safeguarding of the family unit and of parental authority. The idea of providing a parent with absolute power over a child and its veto power will enhance parental authority or control where the minor and the non-consenting parent are so fundamentally in conflict that the very existence of the pregnancy already has fractured the family structure. The Court continues to review cases whereby the parent of the female will make the decision for her regardless of her wishes.

Two other important issues bearing on the ability of women to obtain abortions have been the right of hospitals to refuse to perform abortions and the right of Medicaid to refuse to pay for nontherapeutic abortions. In the case of *Nyberg v. City of Virginia* (1983), a federal court of appeals concluded that a public hospital may not refuse to perform abortions: "It would be a nonsequitur to say that the abortion decision is an election to be made by the physician and his patient without interference by the State and then allow the State, through its public hospitals, to effectively bar the physician from using State facilities to perform the operation." Theoretically, private hospitals may refuse to perform abortions, but it is not always easy to determine when a hospital is private. One needs to review whether it leases its facilities from the local government, whether it is regulated extensively by the state, whether it has received tax advantage, whether it has received public monies for hospital construction, and whether it is part of a general state plan for providing hospital services. Litigation and debate continue.

Under the decision in *Roe v. Norton* (1973), the Court concluded that federal Medicaid provisions prohibit federal reimbursement for abortion expenses unless a determination has been made that the abortion was medically necessary. The Court held that the government is not required by the Constitution to pay for any medical service, but once it does decide to do so, it must not unduly disadvantage those who exercise a constitutional right. Of late, laws have been passed that no birth control clinic that receives funding from the federal government may give information dealing with abortion, although that has not stopped those who are against abortion from using whatever tactics they deem necessary to prevent such information from being disseminated, including bombing abortion clinics.

Those who are against abortion state that when a woman chooses to have sex, she must be willing to accept all consequences. Those who are against abortion will defend the rights of the fetus to develop, to be given life, and to grow, regardless of the wishes of the mother. Those who are against abortion state that whatever the costs, even to those who are victims of rape and incest, there is a life growing, and it is murder to do anything but carry it to full term. Better that any number of women should ruin their health or even die than one woman should get away with not having a child merely because she does not want one.

There have been cases—in the state of Idaho, for example—that have attempted to make physicians criminally liable for performing abortions rather than lay the responsibility on the mother. Under the Idaho proposal, a man who had committed date rape, a term describing sexual assault by an acquaintance (although rape is still defined as rape), could conceivably force the woman to carry the child.

Further decisions have been made affecting the woman's right to choose. For example, in the case of *Bellotti v. Baird* (1979), the Court had voted by a majority vote of 8 to 1 that a state may require a pregnant unmarried minor to obtain parental consent for an abortion if it also offers an alternative procedure. In the case of *Harris v. McRae* (1980), the Court upheld by a margin of 5 to 4 the Hyde amendment, which denies reimbursement for Medicaid abortions. And in the case of *City of Akron v. Akron Center for Reproductive Health, Inc.* (1983), the Court voted 6 to 3 that states cannot mandate what doctors will tell abortion patients or require that abortions for women more than three months pregnant be performed in a hospital. In *Thornburgh v. American College of Obstetricians and Gynecologists* (1986), the Court voted 5 to 4 that states may not require doctors to tell women about risks of abortion and possible alternatives or dictate procedures to third-trimester abortions.

In the case of Ohio upholding a law that required a minor to notify one parent before obtaining an abortion, Justice Kennedy wrote that "it is both rational and fair for the State to conclude that, in most instances, the family will strive to give a lonely or even terrified minor advice that is both compassionate and mature." However, Justice Blackmun, who was the senior author of *Roe v. Wade* (1973), wrote in what has been described as a stinging dissent that Kennedy and his adherents were guilty of "selective blindness" to the reality that "not all children in our country are fortunate enough to be members of loving families. For too many young pregnant women parental involvement in this intimate decision threatens harm, rather than promises of comfort." He ended by stating that "a minor needs no statute to seek the support of loving parents. . . . If that compassionate support is lacking, an unwanted pregnancy is a poor way to generate it." And in *Webster v. Reproductive Health Services* (1989), the Court upheld 5 to 4 a Missouri law barring the use of public facilities or public employees in performing abortions and requiring physicians to test for the viability of any fetus believed to be more than 20 weeks old.

> Debate over these and other issues has spawned extensive litigation and put the Court in the position of reviewing medical and operational practices beyond its competence. We therefore believe that the time has come for the court to abandon its efforts to impose a comprehensive solution to the abortion question. Under the Constitution, legislative bodies cannot impose irrational constraints on a woman's procreative choice. But, within those broad confines, the appropriate scope of abortion regulation should be left with the people and to the political processes the people have devised to govern their affairs.

The Court stated that Missouri had placed no obstacles in the path of women seeking abortions. Rather, the state simply chose not to encourage or assist abortions in any respect.

Abortion remains as newsworthy and important a subject today. Perceptions of the abortion law differ. For the courts, it a constitutional issue. Others consider it an act of murder and believe that it should be turned over to the criminal courts. And indeed, there are those states who have at one time or other defined abortion as homicide. The focus is on the process. The issue is difficult because most people do not see it as a clear issue of law. Is the issue one that concerns a woman's right to privacy? Is it a case of sexual discrimination? Or are we to look at the issue from the view of the fetus and view it as an issue of murder? Should abortion be viewed from a religious perspective, thinking of how the legal codes of Western religions treat the subject? Is it simply an issue of privacy and telling the states that they cannot intrude into the private affairs of its citizens? Or do we view abortion as a matter of health, of preventing injuries and death to women who undergo abortions? The answer lies in the fact that there are no easy answers and no easy solutions. Abortion is an issue that explodes in the courts, in legislatures, and in the minds of citizens.

In the case of *Rust v. Sullivan* (1991), the Court upheld 5 to 4 the federal government's ban on abortion counseling in federally funded family-planning clinics. In the case of *Planned Parenthood of Southeastern Pennsylvania v. Casey* (1992), the Court decided against the constitutionality of a law passed in Pennsylvania:

Informed Consent

At least 24 hours before the abortion, except in emergencies, the physician must tell the woman:

- The nature of the proposed procedure or treatment and the risks and alternatives
- The probable gestational age of the unborn child
- The medical risks associated with carrying her child to term
- That government materials are available that list agencies offering alternatives to abortions
- That medical assistance benefits may be available for prenatal care, childbirth, and neonatal care

Parental Consent

If the woman is under 18 and not supporting herself, her parents must be informed of the impending procedure. If both parents or guardians refuse to consent, judicial authorities where the applicant resides or where the abortion is sought shall. . . authorize . . . the abortion if the court determines that the pregnant woman is mature and capable of giving informed consent.

Spousal Notice

No physician shall perform an abortion of a married woman . . . without a signed statement . . . that the woman has notified her spouse.

Exceptions

- Her spouse is not the father of the child.
- Her spouse, after diligent effort, could not be located.

- The pregnancy is the result of spousal sexual assault . . . that has been reported to a law enforcement agency.

- The woman has reason to believe that notifying her spouse is likely to result in bodily injury.

Reporting

Each abortion must be reported to the state on forms that do not identify the woman but do include, among other items:

- The number of the woman's prior pregnancies and prior abortions

- Whether the abortion was performed upon a married woman and if her spouse was notified

The Constitution has been interpreted in many cases to protect the woman from arbitrary gender-based discrimination by the government, yet the struggle continues. Cases continue to be heard by the courts. In no instance is reference made to women's rights. Rather, the cases are based on the constitutional theory of the right to privacy, which is subject to interpretation, there being no exclusive right of privacy mentioned in the Constitution. Of the Supreme Court justices, Justice John Paul Stevens has supported abortion rights; Justice Antonin Scalia looks to overturn the decision in *Roe v Wade* (1973) but has yet to do so; Justice Sandra Day O'Connor has taken the middle ground, as articulated in her dissenting opinion in *Akron v. Akron* as well as in the case of *Hodgson v. Minnesota* (1990), where she stated that the right to an abortion is a "limited fundamental right" that may not be "unduly burdened" absent a compelling government interest, but may be burdened less severely upon a rational basis (947 F.2d, at 689–91).

What becomes noteworthy about cases dealing with the issue of abortion is that the motivation of a woman becomes entirely "irrelevant" to a determination of whether such a right is "fundamental." The Supreme Court has refused to overrule the *Roe v. Wade* decision, although erosion has taken place. The Court in their "wisdom" has upheld state restraints on a woman's right to choose an abortion freely, as supported in their decision in *Planned Parenthood of Southeastern Pennsylvania v. Casey* (1992) by a 5 to 4 decision, but the courts have yet to turn back the clocks back to 1973, a time when states could make abortion a crime and punish both a woman and her physician. The Court in the case of *Planned Parenthood* did allow states to impose conditions on women seeking an abortion—an "informed consent" provision that includes a lecture to women in an effort to "educate" them about alternative choices to abortion, as well as a 24-hour waiting period to "think it over."

The decisions of the Court have given the states considerable leeway that can make abortions costlier and more difficult to obtain. Such requirements by the state certainly continue to prove difficult for the poor woman who lives and works far from abortion clinics. Even a waiting period as short as 24 hours will force some women who cannot afford to stay overnight to make two trips to the clinic. The issue of whether such a procedure will pose an undue constitutional burden to choose remains open. Has abortion become a question of sex equality? As indicated by Reva Siegel, "[a]bortion-restrictive regulation is state action compelling pregnancy and motherhood, and this simple fact cannot be evaded by invoking nature or a woman's choices. . . . A pregnant woman seeking an abortion has the practical capacity to terminate a pregnancy, which she would exercise but for the community's decision to prevent or deter her. If the community successfully effectuates its will, it is the state, and not nature, which is responsible for causing her to continue the pregnancy" (MacKinnon, 2001, p. 1248).

Partial birth abortions entail a still further controversial procedure. It is described as the extraction of all of the body of the fetus with the exception of the head from the uterus and into the vagina. Thereafter, the contents of the skull are taken from the fetus. The dead intact fetus is removed from its mother-to-be. Many states have enacted legislation that bans partial birth abortions except in cases where it can be confirmed that the mother's life was in danger. Such statutes have been found to be unconstitutional either because of its vagueness or because the statute is void for either being too vague, or putting too great a strain on the woman's right to terminate a preganancy. In *Carhart v. Stenberg*, 192 F.3d 1142, 76 A.L.R.5th 785 (8th Cir. 199), cert. granted inpart 2000 WL 21145 (U.S. 2000), the Eighth Circuit held a Nebraska statute banning patial birth abortions unconsitutional on the ground that the statute placed an undue burden on a woman's right to terminate a pregnancy because it would prohibit use of the dilation and evacuation procedure, which is the most common procedure for second-trimester abortions, as well as the dilation and extraction procedure, which is perhaps more commonly thought of as a partial birth abortion" (Bower, 2005, p. 1). By the year 1999, about 30 states had in fact enacted statutes restricting partial birth abortions, but the majority have been found to be unconstitutional either because of vagueness or because it misses the exception of protecting a woman's health. Yet, where we speak about constitutional protections, such procedures can be banned.

The following cases show the dilemma in granting women the right to a partial birth abortion:

- A statute regulating a method of abortion must include an exception where it is necessary in appropriate medical judgment for the preservation of the life or health of the mother (*Women's Medical Professional Corp.* v. *Taft*, [2000]).
- Illinois and Wisconsin partial-birth-abortion[1] statutes were unconstitutional; the laws lacked any exception for the preservation of the health of the mother and imposed an undue burden on a woman's ability to choose a dilation and evacuation (D&E) abortion, thereby unduly burdening the right to choose abortion itself (*Hope Clinic v. Ryan*, [2001]).
- Missouri Infant's Protection Act, which banned the intact dilation and extraction abortion procedure, was unconstitutional because it made no exception to protect the health of the pregnant woman (*Reproductive Health Services of Planned Parenthood of St. Louis Region, Inc. v. Nixon*, [2004]).
- Failure of the Partial-Birth Abortion Ban Act of 2003 to contain requisite exception for the preservation of the health of the woman warranted issuance of a temporary restraining order (TRO) against enforcement of the Act (*Carhart v. Ashcroft*, [2003]).
- Partial-Birth Abortion Ban Act of 2003 unconstitutionally restricted a particular abortion method without providing an exception permitting use of that method

when necessary to protect a woman's health; substantial evidence in record did not support congressional fact findings that the banned procedure was never necessary in appropriate medical judgment for the preservation of the health of the woman (*Carhart v. Ashfcroft,* [2004]).

- Any abortion regulation must contain adequate provision for a woman to terminate her pregnancy if it poses a threat to her life or health; an adequate health exception is a per se constitutional requirement (*Planned Parenthood of Idaho, Inc. v. Wasden*, [2004]).

And so the fight continues.

In the case of *New Mexico Right to Choose v. Johnson* (1999), the court held that a "prohibition by the New Mexico Human Services Department on using state funds to pay for abortion for Medicaid-eligible women who were not covered because of the Hyde Amendment violated the state ERA." Under the right to privacy, accessibility to the use of contraceptive devices cannot be made a crime, but then insurance companies typically do not cover such devices. Is this a form of discrimination against women?

There are those that argue that abortion is counter to the interests of feminists—that abortion is sexist in nature (Bailey, 1995). The argument goes that a new movement of pro-life feminists assert that abortion is an act of desperation. The argument continues that when women "murder" their own children, society has done a great disservice to women. There arises the question of whether the act of abortion is "an offensive and sexist notion that women must deny their unique ability to conceive and bear children in order to be treated equally" (Smolin, 1990).

There is still another issue that attaches itself to the question of abortion, and that is the issue of federal funding for stem cell research, related to abortion. "Stem cell science offers a wholly new approach to intractable diseases. . . . the issue is deeply controversial. Some opponents simply argue against fiddling with Mother Nature. Others view the use of embryonic stem cells—isolated from embryos—as murder, sure that the life of an individual begins at conception. Thus it is closely tied to the abortion debate, not soon to be resolved" (Cooke, 2001, p. 1). There are those who believe that this issue of stem cell research is tied to abortion, because these embryos are defined as humans with rights and privileges attached. President George W. Bush has indicated that he will allow federally funded research on existing human embryonic stem cells to go forward, but only on cells that already exist. The debate has once again become political. Rather than allowing research to go forward that may find the cures to various diseases, the mere fact that the president has put limits on the research means that research will slow down. According to an editorial by Clymer in *The New York Times* (August 10, 2001, p. A18), "[m]ost people might have trouble seeing a tiny clump of cells in a petri dish as a human being. But some abortion opponents do, and they have argued that the thousands of excess embryos created by fertility clinics every year should be protected and 'adopted' by childless couples. They deserve respect for their beliefs. But they should not be allowed to dictate public policy, especially in an area where the health of so many people might be in the balance. As supporters of the stem cell research keep pointing out, there is more than one way to be pro-life."

From the words of Justice Stewart speaking in the *Roe v. Wade* (1973) decision, "[I]n a Constitution for a free people, there can be no doubt that the meaning of 'liberty' must be broad indeed. The Constitution nowhere mentions a specific right of personal choice in matters of marriage and family life, but the 'liberty' protected by the Due Process Clause of the Fourteenth Amendment covers more than those freedoms explicitly named in the Bill of Rights" (p. 168). And as written by Justice Harlan, "[T]he full scope of the liberty guaranteed by the Due Process Clause cannot be found in or limited by the precise terms of the specific guarantees elsewhere provided in the Constitution. This 'liberty' is not a series of isolated points priced out in terms of the taking of property; the freedom of speech, press and religion; the right to keep and bear arms, the freedom from unreasonable searches and seizures and so on. It is a rational continuum which, broadly speaking, includes a freedom from all substantial arbitrary impositions and purposeless restraints . . . and which must also recognize what a reasonable and sensitive judgement must, that certain interests require particularly careful scrutiny of the state needs asserted to justify their abridgment" (p. 169).

According to the wording in the case of *Borowski v. Attorney-General of Canada* (1989), "[t]he Court must be careful not to create a time in a woman's life when, because of her unchosen biological capacities, she is outside the constitutional protection of the expansive equality rights." If we were to recognize the fetus as a person legally, and then grant legal rights over the woman's body, the woman would no longer have any legal and decision-making rights over her own body (Borowski).

As stated by Ellen Chesler (1992), "[I]t has been seventy years since Margaret Sanger claimed that science would make women 'the owner, the mistress of her self.'" The spirit of her words lives on. The struggles of women and their right to choose and not to be punished in criminal courts continue. The final decision is not yet in. But for those who enjoy a safe bet, it is that women during the twenty-first century will be limited in years to come to choose for themselves whether to have an abortion. That battles were fought and won in prior years does not mean that these decisions will remain. Battles won will still be fought.

NOTES

1.   D & X is deliberate dilation of the cervix usually over a sequence of days; instrumental conversion of the fetus to a footling breech; breech extraction of the body excepting the head; and partial evacuation of the intracranial contents of a living fetus to effect vaginal delivery of a dead but otherwise intact fetus *(American College of Obstetricians and Gynecologists, January 1997).*

REFERENCES

BAILEY, J. T. (1995). Feminism 101: A primer for prolife persons. In R. McNair (Ed.), *Profile feminism: Yesterday and today* (pp. 160, 163).

BOWER, C. (2005). American Law Reports ALR5th. (Copyright 2000–2004 West Group). Thomson/West.

CHESLER, E. (1992, August 2). RU-486: We need prudence, not politics. *The New York Times, Op-Ed. page.*

CLYMER, A. (1992, July 31). Lawmakers fear amendments on abortion rights. *The New York Times,* p. A11.

CLYMER, A. (2001, August 10). The stem cell battle moves to congress. *New York Times,* p. A18.

COOKE, R. (2001, August 10). Fundamentals of stem research. *Newsday,* p. A2.

MacKinnon, C. (2001). *Sex equality*. New York: Foundation Press.

Messer, E., & May, K. E. (Eds.). (1994). *Lilia, in back rooms: Voices from the illegal abortion era.* Amherst, NY: Prometheus Books.

Smolin, D. (1990). The jurisprudence of privacy in a splintered Supreme Court. *Marquette Law Review, 75*, 975, 995–1001.

Walker, A. (1989). What can the white man say to the black man? *The Nation, 75*, pp. 691–692.

CASES

Bellotti v. Baird, 443 U.S. 622, 99 S. Ct. 3035, 61 L. Ed. 2d 797 (1979).

Borowski v. Attorney-General of Canada, S.C.R. 342 (1989), 1279.

Bradwell v. State of Illinois, 83 U.S. 130 (1872).

Carhart v. Ashcroft, 287 F. Supp. 2d 1015 (D. Neb. 2003).

Carhart v. Ashcroft, 311 F. Supp. 2d 805 (D. Neb. 2004).

Carhart v. Stenberg, 192 F.3d 1142, 76 A.L.R.5th 785 (8th Cir. 199).

City of Akron v. Akron Center for Reproductive Health, Inc., 462 U.S. 416, 103 S. Ct. 2481, 76 L. Ed. 2d 687 (1983).

Doe v. Bolton, 410 U.S. 179, 93 S. Ct. 739, 35 L. Ed. 2d 201 (1973).

Harris v. McRae, 448 U.S. 297, 100 S. Ct. 2671, 65 L. Ed. 2d 784 (1980).

Hodgson v. Minnesota, 110 S. Ct. 2926 (1990).

Hope Clinic v. Ryan, 249 F. 3d 603 (7th Cir. 2001)

New Mexico Right to Choose v. Johnson, 975 P.2d 841 (1988), cert. denied, 562 U.S. 1020 (1999).

Nyberg v. City of Virginia, 667 F.2d 754 (CA 8 1982), dsmmd 462 U.S. 1125 (1983).

Planned Parenthood of Central Missouri v. Danforth, 428 U.S. 52 (1976).

Planned Parenthood of Idaho, Inc. v. Wasden, 376 F.3d 908 (9th Cir. 2004).

Planned Parenthood of Southeastern Pennsylvania v. Casey, 505 U.S. 833 (1992).

Reed v. Reed, 404 U.S. 71 (1971).

Reproductive Services of Planned Parenthood of St. Louis Region, Inc. v. Nixon, 325 F. Supp. 2d 991 (W.D. Mo. 2004).

Roe v. Norton, 408 F. Supp. 660 (1973).

Roe v. Wade, 410 U.S. 113, 95 S. Ct. 705, 35 L. Ed. 2d 147 (1973).

Rust v. Sullivan, 114 L. Ed. 2d 233 (1991).

Thornburgh v. American College of Obstetricians and Gynecologists, 476 U.S. 747, 106 S. Ct. 2169, 90 L. Ed. 2d 779 (1986).

Webster v. Reproductive Health Services, 492 U.S. 490, 109 S. Ct. 3040, 106 L. Ed. 2d 410 (1989).

Women's Medical Professional Corp. v. Taft, 114 F. Supp. 2d 644 (S.D. Ohio 2000).

SECTION III

Women: Victims of Violence

9

Fatal Attraction in Arizona

Glenn Close on Trial?

Mary Jackson and Cyndi Banks

On April 28, 1988, the *Arizona Republic* newspaper reported that a 28-year-old woman, Susan Brune, had been charged with the first-degree murder of her lover. It was alleged that she had shot him in the back. Readers were told that the investigating police officers had dubbed the homicide a "*Fatal Attraction* killing," alluding to a movie in which "actress Glenn Close's character stalks and tries to kill actor Michael Douglas' character after he breaks off an affair with her" (*Arizona Republic*, April 29, 1988).

In a series of news reports and one opinion article, the *Arizona Republic* tracked this story of a woman alleged to have murdered her lover through the criminal justice process. We explore and analyze the media depiction in one daily newspaper of Susan Brune, the *Fatal Attraction* killer, through eight articles with the aim of contributing to the current discourse on gender, media, and crime and to add to the cultural understanding of the relations between gender and the media. We argue that in the discourse that became the story of Susan Brune, the *Fatal Attraction* killer, the media, supported by the police and elements of the criminal justice system, reaffirmed patriarchal norms about the dangers of female sexuality and the empowerment of women, and appropriated the fantasy world of the movie *Fatal Attraction* to send a message that women who kill their lovers are obsessive, unnatural, and out of control.

We take our cue from Adrian Howe (1995) who accused the Australian media of denying the possibility of a fair trial to Lindy Chamberlain, alleged to have murdered her baby, by constructing her as "a dangerous, provoking counter-stereotypical woman who refused to play her assigned gender role" (p. 175). In the case of Susan Brune, the media repeatedly invoked the story of Alex Forrest in *Fatal Attraction* (the character played by

Glenn Close) to explain the motive and circumstances of the murder and obscured and rendered illegitimate other knowledge and explanations for her acts. The media created "the knowledge climate" about Brune and accordingly she was judged through "media-mediated messages which incriminated her long before the jury reached its media-contaminated verdict" (Howe, p. 179). However, we go further than Howe and suggest another view: that the unfairness in the trial of Susan Brune comprised not only prejudicial statements and reports in the media but included a persistent discourse in the media, on the part of the prosecution and the defense attorney that could have caused the jury to try, not Susan Brune, but Glenn Close playing Alex Forrest in *Fatal Attraction*. This seems to have had the effect of erasing the person of Susan Brune from the proceedings, making her invisible. How the jury came to focus on a symbolic Alex Forrest rather than Brune, and how the media, supported by the police, the prosecution, and the defense employed the fantasy world of *Fatal Attraction* to explain the deviance of Susan Brune is explored through an analysis of the *Arizona Republic*'s reporting of the case.

VIOLENT FEMALE OFFENDERS AND THE MEDIA

Recent research has examined how the media portray female offenders generally (Chesney-Lind, 1999; Frigon, 1995; Halkias, 1999; Meyers 1997; Naylor, 1995). Often focusing on a perceived breach of appropriate gender roles, the public's fascination with violent female offenders is a product of the media construction of gender. Chesney-Lind (1999) suggests that the majority of women's violence is trivialized but that women who commit crimes viewed as shocking and scandalous are "discovered" and sometimes demonized through media depictions.[1] As she puts it, "we witness the sporadic 'discovery' of rather heinous female offenders" (p. 133). In her discussion of women's violence, Margaret Shaw (1995) explains how male violence forms our only image of violence and that we lack the means to conceptualize women's violence other than by defining it as "unnatural" (p. 122). Demonizing the violent woman gives her the status of a folk devil sending a veiled threat to all women about the consequences of using violence and breaching gender expectations (Chesney-Lind, 1999, p. 133).

Studies of media portrayals of women who have killed their intimate partners through acts of self-defense reveal how the media judge such women (Meyers, 1997). In one study of a woman who killed her abusive husband, Meyers concludes that "the representation of women who fight back is tied to whether their actions are considered justified" (p. 71). The woman was a senior citizen, had had multiple marriages, and enjoyed a high social status. She claimed to have acted in self-defense in shooting her younger, stronger husband. Nevertheless, in media reports of the "discovery" of the crime, the wife was portrayed as a cold, calculating, premeditated murderer (Meyers, 1997). Meyers concludes that the press did not believe that the defendant was justified in acting as she did and instead portrayed her as having beaten the system and as having gotten away with murder. The woman explained that her husband had swindled her financially and subjected her to mental and physical abuse, yet the press concluded that she should have "known better" (p. 75). Similarly Wykes (1995), in charting media coverage of men and women who kill their intimate partners, concludes that "male killers get some positive press, although female killers get almost none" (p. 66) indicating a lack of understanding of their situation and a portrayal of such women as "wicked." By contrast, in the case of male murderers, Wykes found that the media often excused their actions and explained their conduct by blaming the victim.

A number of researchers have noted the failure of the news media to contextualize violent crimes involving women. The media does not usually investigate or document the social causes of intimate violence, focusing instead on individual explanations and the issue of accountability. In their classic study, Galtung and Ruge (as cited in Cohen Young, 1973, p. 66) identified a number of reasons for the personification of crime: the complexity that attaches to structural and social explanations of crime and that personification reflects a need to establish meaning and identification so that it is easier for the media to link a crime to a person than to any other agency. In a study of newspaper reporting of male homicide-suicide against their partners, Websdale and Alvarez (1998) found that these events were reported as a tragedy resulting from a single argument (p. 135). As they put it, "the reports fail to mention the well-documented role of domestic violence," terming this failure "internal myopia" (p. 140). The authors argue that internal myopia occurs when newspaper reporters fail to recognize a pattern occurring within the events they report. Similarly, Wykes (1995) found that the press generally depicted the crime of intimate murder as a tragedy initiated by the victim (p. 66). Websdale and Alvarez (1998) argue that more emphasis is placed on the event immediately preceding the crime and on the "vicious murder" of the victim than on the couple's history, which if properly scrutinized would reveal a pattern of mistreatment of the woman by the perpetrator (p. 138). This research underscores how, in focusing on the crime scene (forensic journalism), the media ignore the interpersonal characteristics of the victim–perpetrator relationship (pp. 139–140). Moreover, reporters seem unaware that they systematically ignore important facts when reporting these crimes:

> By using forensic journalism the social reality of homicide-suicide is framed through the immediacy of the crime scene including the relationships between the individuals involved ("situationally based explanations"), the deployment of the language of drama ("situationally based dramaturgical representations"), and a failure to discern structural patterns of the offense in their own journalistic coverage of the past cases of homicide-suicide ("internal myopia"). (Websdale & Alvarez, 1998, p. 138)

Websdale and Alvarez (1998) stress that this kind of reporting does not constitute an evil conspiracy on the part of the media to ignore important facts; rather, it is the result of the media focus on crime scene information (also see Chermak, 1998a; Sanders & Lyon, 1995) resulting from the existence of a media audience that is attuned to reading crime details. In delivering details of crime forensically the media is simply satisfying the public appetite for this kind of material (Websdale & Alvarez, 1998, p. 138).

GENDER, MEDIA, AND CRIME

Social construction feminism can serve as a theoretical window into issues of gender, media, and crime, helping to explain how gender influences media portrayals of women who commit crimes. Social construction feminism speaks to the issue of how the experience of gender is created and recreated through the interactions between men and women

(Lorber, 1998; West & Zimmerman, 1987). West and Zimmerman (1987) describe the social construction of gender as:

> An emergent feature of social situations: both as an outcome of and rationale for various social arrangements and as a means of legitimating one of the most fundamental divisions of society. (p. 126)

Thus, gendered assumptions organize social interaction and how individuals and groups understand gender legitimizes actions and responses to those actions. West and Zimmerman suggest that the act of identifying whether an individual is a man or a woman plays an important part in constructing the social interaction of gender (cited in Websdale & Alvarez, 1998, p. 146) and that once labels are applied, individuals are held accountable to either feminine or masculine characteristics and behaviors. Whether or not a person chooses to "do gender" in accordance with prevailing social norms, he or she is nevertheless evaluated and held accountable according to the adopted behaviors.

In his explanation of gender as an interaction, Messerschmidt (1997) discusses the notions of "hegemonic masculinity" and "emphasized femininity." He explains hegemonic masculinity and emphasized femininity as consisting of the ideal gender characteristics for a specific culture and time period (p. 9). His analysis as part of the "gender order" makes an important contribution to social construction feminism because these concepts reveal how specific gender ideals are constructed and maintained in society (p. 8). Messerschmidt and other social constructionists do not imply that we always do gender by participating in hegemonic masculinity or emphasized femininity, but they draw attention to the impact of these gender ideals on social interaction (p. 11). The author clarifies the power of hegemonic masculinity and emphasized femininity as follows:

> Hegemonic masculinity and emphasized femininity underpin the conventions applied in the enactment and reproduction of masculinities/femininities—the lived pattern of meanings, which as they are experienced as practices, appear as reciprocally confirming. (1997, p. 11)

Accordingly, our interactions are impacted by our own understandings of gender, as well as a perception of our location on the continuum between masculinity and femininity. We reproduce what we know and what we understand. In applying Messerschmidt's analysis, it is also important to consider other social influences and social contexts such as the media.

Lorber (1998) draws attention to how social construction affects our understanding of gender difference and how difference creates boundaries. In expressing sexuality as approved, tolerated, and tabooed, Lorber reveals that some sexual identities and practices are considered normal while others become viewed as abnormal and deviant (pp. 169–170). In doing gender correctly, according to the standards set by society, individuals are also expected to "do sexuality" in conformity with social expectations. How sexuality is done impacts the interpretation given of an individual's gender and provides another set of criteria that allows assumptions to be made about individual lives. Messerschmidt (1997) adds to our understanding the importance sexuality plays in the construction of gender by explaining that heterosexuality is deemed normative, and therefore "deviant" or subordinated sexualities are ridiculed, policed, and repressed (p. 10). How sexuality is constructed influences whether an individual is considered to be doing their gender correctly when they are doing their sexuality. In other words, if an individual is doing sexuality in what might be considered a normative way then that individual is considered to be doing their gender properly and in a way that allows the individual to do emphasized femininity or hegemonic masculinity. In examining gender and media cases, Chesney-Lind (1999) proposes that women who commit aggressive violent acts become demonized as examples of "bad women," and Meyers (1997) reveals how the older woman who killed her abusive husband found her actions under greater scrutiny because she did not act in the manner expected of her gender.

ANALYZING NEWSPAPER ACCOUNTS

The focus of our study is the media depiction of one woman living in Arizona who was convicted of killing her alleged abuser. One of the authors of this chapter, Mary Jackson, conducted a computer-aided library search of the *Arizona Republic* and located a series of articles that described the arrest and trial of Susan Brune. This type of focused, nonrandom research can capture the intersection of gender and crime in significant cases of media reporting as well as the impact this intersection has on meaning for the readership (Altheide, 1996; Silverman, 2000; van Zoonen, 1994). Our study examines these articles, attempts to tease out the media messages they communicate, and shows how, in the case of Susan Brune, the media put on trial not the real person of Susan Brune, but a *Fatal Attraction* killer—namely, the character of Alex Forrest in the notorious movie *Fatal Attraction.*

Current media research employs various methods such as content analyses of newspaper articles, an examination of the selection of stories placed in the news, and a form of structural analysis involving photographs (Cohen & Young, 1973). We analyzed the data from the *Arizona Republic* using a qualitative content analysis.[2] Berger (1998) characterizes content analysis as "a research technique that is based on measuring the amount of something" (p. 23). Qualitative content analysis allows for an understanding of meaning (Altheide, 1996; Miller, 1997; Silverman, 2000; Watson, 1997; Wimmer & Dominick, 1987) including latent meanings that quantitative content analysis does not take into account (van Zoonen, 1994, p. 69). Weber (1985) notes that "one important use of content analysis is the generation of culture indicators that point to a state of beliefs, values, ideologies, or other culture systems" (p. 10).

The framing of the articles we discuss is crucial in interpreting their meaning and effect and it also illuminates beliefs, systems, and culture (Goffman, 1974, p. 27). Goffman has drawn attention to the power of framing in media presentation in his investigation of how framing occurred in radio and newspaper accounts and in fictional plays. He suggests that the impact of framing and its power in influencing a text is unsettling: "the problem, in fact, is that once a term is introduced, it begins to have much bearing, not merely applying to what comes later" (p. 11). Immediately upon its introduction, the frame influences the entire meaning of the story for readers. Altheide (1996) expands on Goffman's explanation when he writes, "[f]rame refers to the particular perspective one uses to bracket or mark off something as one thing rather than another" (p. 31). One of the ways an article can be framed is by locating and referring to the same source at both the beginning and the end of the article. The information provided by the source can influence the themes covered and an examination of the framing of each article shows how framing influences themes. Frames provide a parameter that allows the article to tackle the material in a thematic manner. Altheide (1996) defines themes as "the recurring typical theses that run through a lot of the reports" (p. 31). In other words, the frame provides the structure for the themes to present a recurring message.

In this chapter, we pay attention to sources in examining the stories about Brune, noting Tuchman's (1971/1972) argument that a reporter solves the issue of determining what amounts to "truth" by basing the reporting on "credible" sources in order to counter any criticisms about lack of objectivity. Thus, reporting from convincing sources—among whom are official sources like the police and prosecutors, the "authorized knowers" (Chermak, 1998b, p. 89)—becomes in Tuchman's words "a strategic ritual" (p. 660) and the quoted or identified sources become "a set of building blocks" pulled together principally from reports based on such sources (Schlesinger & Tumber, 1994, p. 210). Ericson, Baranek, and Chan (1989) argue that reporters rely on their sources to such an extent that source reliance is essential to the act of reporting itself and that police spokespeople are therefore the real reporters (p. 6). However, reporters take these police scripts and edit them to determine what will be used and which aspects will be highlighted. This means that reporters are not just tools of the police but rather maintain an interdependent relationship with the police within the newsmaking process itself, especially in deciding how a report is to be framed for public consumption and newsworthiness. Reporters and their sources therefore work together to "construct order and effect change in everyday transactions and in the news texts which emanate from these transactions" (Ericson et al., 1989, p. 16).

In this discussion we state the headline of each report or article about Susan Brune. Headlines are important generally because they indicate the theme or frame of a story. In criminal justice stories the headlines not only grab the readers' attention but also influence their understanding of the topic (Altheide, 1996; Ericson, Baranek, & Chan, 1991; Silverman, 2000) and help create an image before the crime story is even read.

In our exploration of the series of articles written about Susan Brune, we also draw attention to how photographs are used to convey messages about morality and how they can be used to communicate states of emotion or the absence of emotion on the part of defendants in criminal trials. Photographs that accompany an article are influential in giving meaning to the story and creating a reality for the reader (Cheatwood & Stasz, 1979; Ericson et al., 1991). Pictures serve to animate the events described in texts and add a sense of objectivity as well as personalizing a story.

This is not the place to enter into an extended discussion of "newsworthiness" as a crucial concept in media production. However, Chermak (1994) has shown how novel and dramatic stories are most likely to be selected as crime news and that ordinary crime has little news value. The media choose crime stories that are unusual in some way because those stories sell newspapers. At the same time, a crime story must be made simple so that it can be placed within an already established framework that readers can follow (Chermak, 1994, p. 99). Ericson et al. (1991) explain that newsworthiness has little to do with the event itself but about what can be done with it in terms of the reporters' imagination (p. 243).

SUSAN BRUNE, THE *FATAL ATTRACTION* KILLER

In its first story about Susan Brune, the *Arizona Republic* reported that she had been dubbed by police "the *Fatal Attraction* killer" (Walsh, 1988, p. B1). The movie *Fatal Attraction* was released in September of 1987 and concerns the story of Dan Gallagher, played by Michael Douglas, a man with an attractive family but troubled about his own career advancement. Due to some feeling of discontent with his life, Gallagher has a one-night stand with a woman, Alex, played by Glenn Close, while his wife Beth is out of town. Alex becomes obsessed with Dan and begins to stalk and terrorize him and his family. His apartment is invaded and his car destroyed. Alex follows him to his new suburban home and abducts his daughter and murders her pet rabbit. Finally Alex attempts to kill Beth. At the end of the film, Beth and Alex (armed with a knife) fight to the death. Ultimately Beth is rescued by Dan when it appears that he has drowned Alex in the bathtub. However, she resurfaces with knife poised and it is at this point that Beth shoots her in the heart. As Berland and Wechter (1992) point out, the villainous Alex is "not only killed but killed twice" (p. 42). The movie became a box office hit—it was the third most-watched American movie of 1987 and after being released on video in June 1988 was voted the most popular video drama of the year (Thompson, 1992, p. 11). It generated intense debate in a period of changing gender relations, echoed in some movie theaters with audience shouts of "kill the bitch" obviously directed at Alex (Babener, 1992, p. 30). The film critic Richard Corliss hyped the movie as "the zeitgeist hit of the decade" (Rohrkemper, 1992, p. 84).

Babener (1992) argues that *Fatal Attraction* belongs to the movie genre concerned with "cautionary tales about life . . . paranoid fantasies about the threat to patriarchal authority posed by weakened manhood, female sexuality and feminists' empowerment in the volatile 1980s" (p. 25). For example, although it is the husband Gallagher who lapses in his marital fidelity, the movie casts all the blame for the violent events that follow onto the female character played by Glenn Close. She is constructed as a predator, seeking to capture Gallagher for herself and destroy his family. The film reverses gender expectations as Alex (note the masculine name) assumes a typically aggressive male role (she also smokes, drinks, and uses unladylike language) and Gallagher is portrayed as a damsel in distress. As Babener puts it, the film opposes "marital complacency and erotic escapism" (p. 28). The film condemns the latter and constructs Alex as "a vitriolic parody of feminist self-assertion and a *femme fatale* turned fiend" (p. 29). As the director intended, viewers seem to have identified mainly with the Gallagher character and his perceptions and viewpoint throughout the film. Given his patriarchal status within a family where his wife, Beth, privileges his career, indulges him, and generally fulfills all the stereotypes of the dutiful wife, the overall effect is to convey a message that patriarchal authority must be maintained against all challenges. Director Adrian Lyne presents his view of New York professional women in his depiction of Alex, describing them as:

> sort of pretending or trying to be men, sort of overcompensating for not being men. It's sad, you know, because it kind of doesn't work. . . . It's kind of unattractive, however liberated and emancipated it is. It kind of fights the whole wife role, the whole childbearing role. Sure you got your career and your success, but you are not fulfilled as a woman. (as quoted in Babener, 1992, pp. 28–29)

As will be seen, although Susan Brune was far from the type of urban professional woman depicted by Lyne (she worked as a food server), following the lead given by the police, the media constantly reported her as "the *Fatal Attraction* killer" and repeatedly emphasized the similarities between Brune and the character of Alex. Ultimately, we suggest, fantasy destabilized reality because Alex was put on trial and Susan Brune was expunged from the scene. Brune was read by the media as the exemplum of Lyne's anti-woman. The reality of the life of Susan Brune was ignored during her trial because the prosecution and defense both substituted the fantasy world of *Fatal Attraction* for the reality of Susan Brune. When the jury found Brune guilty of murder they too were shouting "kill the bitch."

A total of eight news reports and one opinion article were published about Brune in the *Arizona Republic* during the period from April 1988 to January 1989, at which point it was reported that she had been sentenced to imprisonment for life for the murder of her lover Gary Vargason. This analysis considers each news report and the opinion article with the aim of assessing the narrative about Susan Brune in terms of the interrelation between gender, violent crime by women, and the media reporting of such crime. This analysis addresses the issue of how meaning and value are articulated through this media discourse. In other words, as Hall, Critcher, Jefferson, Clarke, and Roberts (1978) ask, how events in the life of Susan Brune are "identified (i.e., named, defined, related to other events known to the audience) and assigned to a social context (i.e., placed within a frame of meanings familiar to the audience" (p. 54).

First Report of April 28, 1988: "Woman is held in fatal meeting with ex-lover"

Jim Walsh writes the first report of the alleged murder and all subsequent reports are authored by Brent Whiting. The fact that both reporters are male is particularly relevant because it is likely that their gender socialization causes them to reproduce dominant values including those which stereotype women who kill men.

Jim Walsh links the *Fatal Attraction* label to this murder in his first paragraph where he writes, "A 28 year old Fountain Hills woman has been charged with first degree murder after her former lover was shot in the back in what officers have dubbed a *Fatal Attraction* killing." Later in the piece a police officer, Sgt. Jay Ellison, "a spokesman for the Maricopa County Sheriff's Office," analogizes Brune's situation to that of Glenn Close in the movie *Fatal Attraction*. Sgt. Ellison is cited as a source five times in the report which bestows the status of authorized knowledge on his statements. The fact that a police source makes the analogy to the movie *Fatal Attraction* adds legitimacy to the notion that Susan Brune is another Glenn Close and that her motivation for the killing matched that of Glenn Close in the movie.[3] In effect, the reader is invited to construct a picture of this crime which parallels that in the movie because the reporter has recognized that establishing such a connection renders the story newsworthy. Thus, the newsworthiness of the *Fatal Attraction* label confers newsworthy status on the story and also fixes and defines Brune. From this time onward in the *Arizona Republic* reports of her story, Brune will be dubbed the "*Fatal Attraction* killer" as a means of maintaining the newsworthiness of the story.

Placed directly under the headline is a driver's license–sized photograph of Brune with a caption to the right reading, "Susan Brune is a real wreck" (Walsh, 1988, p. B1).

This photo caption is repeated in the final three lines of the article with a further quote from Cpl. Joe Rossano ("another spokesman for the Sheriff's Office"). Rossano is reported as saying, "She's real nervous." Thus, the article is framed at the beginning and end by descriptions of Brune from a police source promoting the view that she is "nervous" and "a wreck."

Walsh reinforces the police conception of Brune as a *Fatal Attraction* killer by introducing other sources to support the notion that events in the life of Alex Forrest in the movie and Susan Brune in reality are similar and perhaps even identical. For example, following the paragraph where Ellison compares Brune to the fictional character in the movie, Walsh introduces an unnamed Vargason relative who reveals that Brune was arrested the week before the murder, apparently for harassing Vargason (Walsh, 1988, p. B1). Following this account, Walsh uses Sgt. Ellison as a source to confirm that officers handled a situation involving Brune and the victim the week before the crime (p. B1). In reporting the relative's comment and supporting it with Ellison's information, Walsh creates a story-line analogous to the movie. Readers are invited to see Brune as a woman who was "obviously" obsessed with the victim.

Walsh now introduces a neighbor who suggests that the victim had a rocky relationship with his wife who left him (Walsh, 1988, p. B1), thus suggesting that the victim's marriage was troubled and that he was separated from his wife when Brune killed him. Later, Walsh reports Sgt. Ellison's statement that the victim wanted to terminate his relationship with Brune and return to his wife, again reinforcing the parallel with the events of the movie.

In its first six paragraphs, the article succeeds in depicting Brune as an obsessive woman who murdered her lover out of fear of losing him and it is only after this picture has been established that the real events surrounding the killing are presented. Sgt. Ellison relates that Brune "showed up" at the victim's house that evening, finding him in the back yard in a hot tub with another man and two women. Vargason requested Brune to leave but she asked to speak with him in the garage (Walsh, 1988, p. B1). During their meeting, the other persons in the hot tub heard shots and one ran to the garage to find the victim on the floor and Brune holding a gun. Brune was found two hours later less than a mile away from the victim's house with a gun believed to be the murder weapon (p. B1). Other than the bare facts given above, no information about the actual crime or the events leading up to it is made available. Critical for the reader is that at the beginning of the article the reporter suggests the motivation for the crime without providing any actual crime information or substantiated evidence about the crime. Instead, the crime is correlated to the fictional movie and the reporter relies on police and other sources to recreate an approximation of events and construct a picture of the crime.

After briefly stating the few known facts about the crime, the report underlines its already constituted depiction of Brune as "a woman obsessed with a man" when noting the victim's mother-in-law's statement that Brune had "harassed" Vargason.

Second Report of November 18, 1988: "Murder defendant called cold blooded"

This report concerns the opening arguments in Brune's trial and the headline has been selected from the prosecutor's address to the jury. The depiction of Brune as "cold blooded" is supplemented by a subheadline reading, "Woman likened to killer in movie by prosecutor" repeating the leitmotif of Susan Brune, the *Fatal Attraction* killer. In this report, themes begin to emerge about the crime following an immediate reference to the movie:

> Susan Lee Brune, a defendant in what investigators have called a *Fatal Attraction*-type killing, was described Thursday by a prosecutor as an obsessed woman who murdered her lover in cold blood when he tried to break off the relationship. (Whiting, 1988a, p. B1)

Not only is there a reference to the police investigators who tagged Brune with the movie label, but the label gains authenticity and legitimacy when the prosecutor adopts and reinforces this characterization, perhaps believing it will be helpful in securing a guilty verdict. The report cites only two sources, "prosecutor" Paul Ahler and Brune's attorney, "deputy public defender" Roland Steinle. Ahler explicitly states that Brune killed her lover because of her obsession with him, claiming "If she couldn't have him, then no one could" (Whiting, 1988a, p. B1). Ahler's announcement of Brune's motive links well with Whiting's introduction to the report, and both statements support the notion that Brune fits the image of the fictional stalker, Alex Forrest, of the movie *Fatal Attraction*.

Following Ahler, defense attorney Steinle attempts to counter the image of Brune as a stalker by arguing that she acted in self-defense. For the first time the reader learns that Brune will defend the charge as well as the basis of her defense—that she killed Vargason in self-defense after he threatened to beat her. Steinle attacks the image of his client as a stalker and the *Fatal Attraction* killer head on as he endeavors to present Brune as gullible and dependent and very much in love with the victim. Steinle explains, "She doesn't fit this profile that the state wants to portray of Glenn Close and *Fatal Attraction*" (Whiting, 1988a, p. B1). Following Steinle's refutation of the Glenn Close image, the reporter recites a version of the plot of the movie, inviting the reader to compare a fictional account on film to a set of real events: "the movie *Fatal Attraction* in which actress Glenn Close's character stalks and tries to kill actor Michael Douglas' character after he breaks off an affair with her." Reciting the plot of the movie will become another leitmotif in this narrative but interestingly after this report, other reports describe the movie plot differently. In later reports, the recurring characterization of the plot is "the case . . . has been called a *Fatal Attraction* slaying by sheriff's investigators, referring to a movie in which an obsessed woman seeks revenge on a married man after he ends their affair" (Walsh, 1988; Whiting, 1988a, 1988b, 1988c, 1988d, 1988e, 1988f, 1989). It is Brune/Close's state of mind that comes to be stressed rather than questions of fact such as whether Brune stalked and attempted to kill the victim. We suggest that the movie plot is recast in this fashion with the aim of simplifying the issue of guilt. Readers need only agree that Brune/Close developed an obsessive state of mind about her lover to hold the woman fully accountable. Questions of fact, such as whether or not she stalked and attempted to kill Vargason, are erased from the narrative and need no longer trouble readers.

The report continues with a physical description of Brune, a common gender-specific practice in media reporting. The specificity of the physical description recalls Websdale and Alvarez' (1998) forensic journalism. Whiting (1988a) describes her as follows:

> The blond, blue-eyed defendant, dressed in a white jacket and a burnt-orange patterned dress, sat impassively during Ahler's opening statement, sometimes whispering to Steinle. (p. B4)

"Blond, blue-eyed" suggests a "dumb blond" and therefore a woman of little intelligence. This would be consistent with her low-status employment as a food server. Her attire appears inappropriately colorful and inconsistent with the expectation that a defendant would wear a subdued outfit during the trial in such a serious case, again suggesting the absence of intelligence. Her impassivity suggests lack of emotion, supporting the prosecutor's argument that she acted like a calculating and cold-blooded killer when carrying out her crime. Similarly, Helen Benedict (1992) has pointed out that in cases of rape, women who remain calm in court are perceived as not having suffered sufficiently and therefore appearing as less of a victim (pp. 122–123). However, she notes that if a woman sobs or becomes hysterical during trial she is regarded as unstable and lacking in credibility. Overall, the media portrayal of Brune is one of a woman of little intelligence and emotion, and this depiction has the effect of directly contradicting the defense argument that she was sensitive and emotionally dependent on the victim. The report now cites the prosecutor's account of Brune having stalked Vargason and his wife and making threatening phone calls to other women in whom the deceased had shown an interest (Whiting, 1988a, p. B4). Ahler offers the torn-up photos of the victim that his wife found in Brune's car as evidence of Brune's obsessive feelings about the victim (p. B4). Steinle attempts to displace the image of Brune as the *Fatal Attraction* killer by describing his client as acting lovingly toward the victim and by casting the victim as a manipulative liar who cheated on his wife (Whiting, 1988a). He announces that Brune will give evidence that she shot Vargason after seeing "a look in his eye," one that she had observed previously during an incident where he had beaten her so badly that "one eye was closed for a week."

In this report the reader is presented with a choice: whether to believe that Brune is the *Fatal Attraction* killer, or accept her account that she killed him out of fear for her life based on Vargason's history of beating her. Nothing in this report or in the previous accounts of the killing suggests that Vargason had any history of abusing women, including his wife, and Brune's defense lawyer does not present any facts that the victim beat his wife or that his abuse of her was the cause of the breakdown in their relationship. The only information presented about the victim's character relates to his party with others in a hot tub, suggestive of sexuality rather than a history of violent attacks on women or his lies and manipulation of his wife. The account presented of Vargason therefore does not support the defense put forward by Brune.

Despite the fact that each attorney makes the same number of statements in the report, the prosecutor's statements frame the article because he is used as the first and last source. This gives greater weight to his account of events and tends to negate the arguments made by defense counsel. The report begins with the prosecutor describing Brune as an obsessed stalker like Alex Forrest, and ends with the prosecutor again raising the allegation of stalking, arguing that, "on at least two occasions, Brune even followed Kathy Vargason to church" (Whiting, 1988a, p. B4).

Third Report of November 29, 1988: "Slain man feared girlfriend, trial told"

Although there is no reference to Brune as the *Fatal Attraction* killer, the headline of this report not only questions Brune's statement that she feared Vargason but it reverses accounts to allege that he feared her. By recounting his alleged fear of Brune, it reminds the reader of the stalking allegation and the supposed *Fatal Attraction* connection.

Directly under the headline are two wallet-sized photographs of the female witnesses who testified for the prosecution. Located to the right of the photos is a much larger picture of Brune during her testimony supporting her chin with her hand and looking worried, distracted, and unfocused. In the photographs, witness Lori Ottenweiss displays a look of disbelief and irritation and wears a high-collared blouse. Alison Crenshaw, the other witness, points her finger like a gun and is looking determined. She too wears a high-collared blouse. Their style of dress conveys a message that they are both prim and proper, and contrasts with the text of the report that explains that both witnesses were partying with the victim nude in a hot tub on the day he was shot. In contrast to the photo of Brune, both women appear very focused.

In the first paragraph of his report, Whiting's (1988b) lead-in portrays Vargason as "in fear of" Brune:

> Witnesses testified Monday that hours before Gary Vargason was shot and killed, he told them that he was afraid of his girlfriend, Susan Lee Brune, and that he wanted to move away from her. (p. B1)

Whiting legitimizes this claim by citing the two female witnesses; however, he does not include a photograph of the male witness, Donald Rairigh, who testifies that the victim (who we are now told was a retired postal worker) disclosed to him that Brune had been threatening him (Whiting, 1988b, p. B1). Crenshaw adds credibility to the fear charge, explaining that the victim told her he had to get away from Brune (p. B1). Last, Whiting adds Lori Ottenweiss's claim that "Vargason told her that Brune had threatened to kill him" (p. B1). Thus, the cumulative weight of the evidence of all three witnesses adds legitimacy to the claim that the victim was indeed afraid of Brune and not the reverse. The ascending scale of charges from "being threatened" to "had to get away" ending finally with "had threatened to kill him" reinforces the truth of the claims.

Brief descriptions of the witnesses' backgrounds are given and the reader learns that Rairigh is a plumber, Crenshaw a hospital worker, and Ottenweiss (like Brune), a Fountain Hills resident (Whiting, 1988b, p. B1). The inclusion of personal facts about the lives of witnesses grants them a degree of authority and authenticity as members of a discrete community, and newspaper readers are more likely to accept the testimony of strangers if they can recognize characteristics within them that they consider comparable to themselves and their lives.

It is only after these claims about Brune have been heard that Whiting (1988b) reports a seedier side to the witnesses' lives when he recounts that the shooting occurred at a nude hot tub party that the witnesses had attended at the victim's house. The placement of this fact after the claims made against Brune significantly privileges their collective claims about Brune over any uncertainty about their own moral standards, obscuring a question that might ordinarily raise issues about a witness's credibility. At a later point, the report introduces an account of events surrounding the shooting that ignores the issue of witness credibility. For example, the nude hot tub party and the interaction between Brune and her victim are given little attention; instead the article focuses on the construction of Brune as a dangerous woman by making many references to the shots fired and the number of shots heard as well as to a claim from Rairigh that he saw Brune emerge from the garage holding a gun.

Whiting (1988b) refers only once to criminal justice sources, citing both the prosecutor and the defense attorney for their opposing views. Prosecutor Ahler again claims that Brune killed Vargason out of anger over the end of the relationship and Steinle contends that Brune killed the victim in self-defense. Ahler's and Steinle's views are presented in the body of the article, but only after the main thesis is offered and developed that Brune is a woman to be feared. By citing each attorney briefly and only once, the article directs attention away from issues related to legal legitimacy toward the witnesses' claims. While the first two reports mainly relied on criminal justice sources, this article focuses on the perceptions of noncriminal justice sources who are acquainted with Brune and the victim. Rairigh's claims frame the article, being the first and last speaker presented in the report, thus granting his account greater status and explanatory power.

At this point in the newspaper portrayal of the Brune murder case, Whiting's accounts of the three witnesses' testimony shapes the readers' understanding of the crime story. Whiting fails to provide any balance to these witness accounts by choosing not to include any statements from Brune's family or friends. As well, there is no report or investigation of her allegation of physical abuse.

Fourth Report of December 6, 1988: "'Either my life or his,' murder suspect swears"

With this report of the trial proceedings is juxtaposed an opinion article about the trial entitled "2 faces of a murder trial: Self defense vs. homicidal desire," placed directly beneath the report (Montini, 1988). Up to this point the media coverage has created a wholly negative image of Brune, but the content of the opinion article by *Republic* columnist E. J. Montini and the news report itself now focus on Brune's defense. Significantly, the words "self-defense" appear before "homicidal desire" in the opinion title and therefore both headline and title stress self-defense. Ericson *et al.* (1991) have pointed out how opinion columns are often wrapped with news stories to convey a certain version of events as part of an overall narrative told in an interesting and entertaining way (p.153). They also note that the techniques for producing impartiality include presenting the two sides of a story and creating items such as news features, editorials, and opinion articles that seem to separate fact from fiction (p. 168). Applying Ericson's insight to the media presentation of the Brune case would suggest that the opinion column and the report, taken together, are designed to project a high degree of media "objectivity" at a point where the substantive defense is being presented to the jury at the trial. The report annexes a photograph of Brune testifying. She is gesturing with her hand and appears quite intent and focused compared to previous images conveying messages of her passivity and lack of emotion.

The only cited sources in the report are Brune and her attorney. In a brief lead-in, Whiting reminds readers that Brune is on trial "for a so-called *Fatal Attraction* slaying" and it is only after this prompt to the reader's memory that he quotes Brune's statement to the court that she acted out in self-defense:

> It was either my life or his . . . I had to stop him so that he wouldn't beat me or take the gun away from me. I feared for my life and I defended my life. (Whiting, 1988c, p. B1)

Later in the report, Whiting recites the plot leitmotif, "the case . . . has been called a *Fatal Attraction* slaying by sheriff's investigators, referring to a movie in which an obsessed woman seeks revenge on a married man after he ends their affair" (Whiting, 1988c).

Brune is used as a source as she answers questions from her attorney, stating:

> I didn't think I shot him. He put his arms out gracefully . . . slid on the floor . . . and I saw orange splatterings from behind his back, and then I knew that I had shot him, but I didn't know how bad. (p. B6)

Her account of the shooting shows her as confused and is far from the image being portrayed of her as a calculating or cold-blooded murderer. The report cites Brune as telling the jury that Vargason told her that he would seek a divorce from his wife and marry her, but at other times he told her he planned to reconcile with his wife. According to Brune it was "an on-again, off-again affair" and Vargason was sometimes violent toward her. She explains how she pulled a gun from underneath her car seat, a gun she had taken from Vargason's truck a few days earlier. Brune explains that she was trying to leave the house when the victim became angry and hit her on the back of the head (Whiting, 1988c, p. B6). Only after the victim hit her, she says, did she get the gun, "I told Gary to get the hell away from me" (p. B6). According to Brune's account, she viewed the situation as life threatening, a claim that the police and prosecutor failed to acknowledge thus far in any of the media accounts.

The framing of the report is persuasive in Brune's defense because she is the first and final source in the report. Her concluding statement reinforces her belief that she was unaware that she had shot Vargason because she did not see blood on him but only later realized that she had in fact shot him because she saw "orange splatterings" on the garage wall, but that she still did not realize the severity of his injury.

The opinion piece refers early on to the nude hot tub party and notes that Vargason was there with other men and women when Brune arrived (Montini, 1988). Reporting on the demeanor of Brune when she testified, the author depicts her as emotional, "[she] spoke in low steady tones, with her voice occasionally cracking" (Montini). This time Brune is "appropriately" attired wearing a gray-knit dress with a beige shawl around her shoulders, an image of demure respectability. Now her hair is not labeled blond but instead is referred to as "brown" with "blond highlights" and she has "dark, deep-set eyes" suggesting a depth of emotion. Brune's claims about Vargason are given prominence with a full account of the perceived attack on her by Vargason. "He was going to hit me in the face, and I turned my head and he hit me in the back of the head" (Montini). After recounting Brune's story, Montini provides details of the prosecution's cross examination but the author is critical of the prosecutor's tactic in trying to provoke Brune's anger in order to "reveal" her obsession with Vargason. This tactic is described by the author as "a facet of criminal trials that most disturbs me. They often show how weakness, not strength, leads to violence" (Montini). The opinion piece seems sympathetic to Brune and does not refer to the *Fatal Attraction* label but continues to identify the narrative with that film. The piece does, however, portray Brune as emotional, suggesting the likelihood of obsession, and therefore contrasts with earlier reports that she is "cold-blooded." By drawing attention to her restrained style of clothing the article recalls her earlier, more flamboyant attire. This may signify to readers that Brune is a woman (like Alex Forrest in the movie) who can be both emotional and calculating. We suggest therefore that the attempt at this point in the narrative to buttress supposed media objectivity is unconvincing. The reports and opinion piece seem firmly attached to the notion that Susan Brune is Alex Forrest and that both women are *Fatal Attraction* killers.

Fifth Report of December 8, 1988: "'Fatal Attraction' image parried in murder trial"

The reporting of the trial continues in this fifth article with the expert testimony of a psychologist for the defense. The psychologist testifies that Brune is "a non-aggressive person," thus refuting prosecution attempts to portray her as the predator female of *Fatal Attraction*. The witness describes her as passive, with a dependent personality disorder, and as displaying naivete and immaturity. The term "gullible" is also used and the reader recalls that defense counsel has employed this term earlier. This witness is questioned directly about similarities between Brune's personality and that of Alex in the movie *Fatal Attraction*, demonstrating again how powerful the image of Brune as Alex Forrest has become and how the reality of Brune's life has been transformed into the fictional life of the Glenn Close character. The reader is also told that, although the psychologist was asked directly if Brune had the same personality as the woman portrayed by Glenn Close, the prosecutor objected to the question and the witness was not permitted to answer it. The defense attorney, however, later told reporters that had he been allowed to answer, the psychologist would have explained that the personalities were totally different.

It is at this point in the trial that the fantasy world of the movie *Fatal Attraction* takes on a bizarre form of reality. The defense counsel's questions for his own expert witness explicitly acknowledge the force of the *Fatal Attraction* label which has been so persistently attached to Brune through the efforts of police, media, and the prosecution and defense lawyers. The question as to whether Brune's personality resembled that of Alex Forrest brings the character directly into the trial. The issues now being put before the court and jury are not questions about "who is Susan Brune?" or about "what has she experienced in her life to make her shoot her lover?" Instead, the inquiry is focused on whether Susan Brune has a personality like that of the fantasy woman played by Glenn Close. The trial has ceased to be concerned with facts and defenses and has fixed on two issues: Is Susan Brune really Alex Forrest? If she is, should the jury convict Glenn Close for what she tried to do to Michael Douglas? As noted above, many theater audiences had already answered the second question. Adding yet more absurdity to this intrusion of the fantastic into Brune's trial, defense counsel now announces to reporters that he will argue that just as Brune was different from Glenn Close so too was Vargason different from Michael Douglas. It seems impossible for Vargason or Brune to escape from the frame of the movie. The report is framed by statements from the psychologist that favor the accused, including a reference in its conclusion to the psychologist addressing the prosecutor "sarcastically" as "*Dr.* Ahler" during his testimony. Nevertheless, we suggest that framing this report in favor of the accused does not help Susan Brune, who has all but disappeared from view as the subject of this trial.

Sixth Report of December 13, 1988: "Valley murder trial 'not a movie,' prosecutor says as case goes to jury"

As well as this headline, this report contains a subheadline entitled "Death trial in hands of jurors." A photograph of Brune appears in the article bearing the caption, "The defendant listens to closing arguments during her murder trial in Superior Court." It shows Brune sitting forward with the hands clasped and with her chin resting on her hands in an attitude of concentration. In the photograph her hair is clearly dark.

The report reveals that the prosecutor has changed tactics since his opening statement when he insisted that Brune was a *Fatal Attraction* killer. Now prosecutor Ahler objects to the defense counsel's comparison of the events of the murder to the movie and he stresses the reality of Vargason's death:

> They (defense attorneys) want you to believe that this is a movie. Well it's not a movie. It's not a made for television script. This is real. Somebody's dead. (Whiting, 1988e)

Immediately after this statement, Whiting (1988e) explains in the article how the case has been compared with the movie and restates the plot leitmotif of Brune as the "obsessed woman." Whiting also comments that the defense attorney has repeatedly referred to the movie to deny any resemblance between his client and Alex Forrest. Why has the prosecutor changed his tactics?

Also curious is the prosecutor's statement that the defense wants the jury to believe that the events are a movie. The defense lawyer was in fact trying to distance his client from the personality of Alex in the movie. It seems that the prosecution now believes that the defense has a better chance of acquittal if it can establish a link to the movie. This position runs contrary to most reactions to the movie which, as indicated above, firmly condemn Glenn Close and sympathize with Michael Douglas. One possible explanation for this change of tactic may be dictated by the character of Vargason which does not match that of Michael Douglas' character in the movie. The prosecutor acknowledges as much in his closing address when he speaks of "some out there who would say that Gary Vargason got what he deserved," when he describes Vargason as a "jerk," and when he assures jurors that "he was not asking for them to like Vargason for the way he treated other people" (Whiting, 1988e). He also takes care to describe Vargason as "living off women" and as "manipulating them." After initially following the lead of the police and media and framing the trial around the facts of the movie, the prosecutor has realized that reality does not in fact follow the script of the movie largely because Vargason lacks the sympathetic appeal of Douglas. This inconsistency might be enough for the jury to condemn Vargason for his sexual and moral misconduct and acquit Brune. Therefore, the prosecution strategy is now to acknowledge the moral deficiencies of the victim while at the same time insisting that in real life "you don't just get a gun and shoot someone" (Whiting).

The prosecution has therefore rewritten its script for the closing arguments. Instead of relying on the movie to direct the verdict, the prosecution now drags reality back into the courtroom because the movie does not accord with the prosecutor's truth statements to the jury. Unlike the Michael Douglas character, Vargason was not a partner in a stable marriage in which his wife reaffirmed patriarchal norms in her relationship with him. The jury could not readily identify with a husband who manipulated his wife and played nude in hot tubs with other men and women. Now it seems that both the defense and the prosecution want to cast out the movie; however, the media keep repeating the movie script and by now it is probably too late to recast the real-life movie with Susan Brune. For most readers, the series of media reports has established the movie as the reality.

Seventh Report of December 14, 1988: "Ex-lover convicted of murder"

This report appeared on the front page of the *Arizona Republic* in contrast to previous reports about the trial that appeared in the "Valley and State" section of the news.[4] Yet again, the lead-in links Brune to the movie *Fatal Attraction* and the plot leitmotif is restated. In the eyes of the media Brune remains "an obsessed woman who seeks revenge on a married man after he ends their affair" (Whiting, 1988f). The lead-in paragraph announces that the sentence of this obsessed woman has finally been determined by a jury comprising nine women and three men:

> A Fountain Hills waitress was convicted Tuesday of murdering her married boyfriend in what investigators have called a *Fatal Attraction* killing. (Whiting, 1988f, p. A1)

Significantly, it seems there is no longer any need to mention Brune's name. She is identified only by reference to her low-status occupation and to the movie. Her job as a "waitress" was mentioned in the first article and reappears in this report to frame her absent identity. Prosecutor Ahler is the first source and he announces that he will not seek the death penalty because there are no legal grounds for seeking it. Defense attorney Steinle describes his client as "devastated" by the verdict and firm in her belief that she acted in self-defense. In an ironic comment on the case, Ahler states that "the movie was not a factor in the case" (Whiting, 1988f, p. A6). Defense attorney Steinle makes the argument that because information about Vargason and the abuse he committed against a woman in another relationship was withheld, jurors could not understand the degree of harm Brune faced or the fear she had experienced (p. A6). Whiting frames the article by citing Ahler at both the beginning and end.

Eighth Report of January 14, 1989: "*Fatal Attraction* defendant sentenced to life imprisonment"

The final report of the Brune case covers her sentencing and provides another structural switch. The majority of articles about Brune had appeared on the front page of the B section of the newspaper while this article was buried in the back of the B section. The headline reflects the "media truth" that Brune was always a *Fatal Attraction* killer. As in the last report Brune's name is not mentioned; rather, she is simply "a Fountain Hills waitress." This concluding report employs the same lead-in and frame as the first report, thus framing the entire narrative of Brune's deviance as a *Fatal Attraction* killing (Whiting, 1989, p. B7). There can be little doubt now that Alex Forrest has been tried, convicted, and punished again.

The report cites Brune as denying the crime. "The Lord and I know that this wasn't true" (Whiting, 1989, p. B7). Whiting reports that at her sentencing Brune appeared in court carrying a Bible and this act might be interpreted as a symbol of her belief in her defense. Glassman, the psychologist who examined Brune and testified at the trial, provided an evaluation report attached to the presentence report where he explained that Brune had had a number of failed relationships he described as "shallow and superficial" (p. B7). In classifying Brune's romantic involvements in this way, Glassman continues the theme of the obsessive, unstable woman. In contrast to her claim that she committed the act out of fear for her life, he speculates that Brune's motive for the killing was that she could not handle losing yet another relationship: "Brune would find it psychologically damaging to undergo another failed relationship" (p. B7). This is the final statement in the narrative of Susan Brune, the *Fatal Attraction* killer.

DISCUSSION

This investigation of media reports of the arrest and trial of Susan Brune reveals that the reporting technique in linking Brune's real-life actions to a notorious movie had the effect of determining her guilt in advance of trial. A pattern emerges with each article. In most articles, a lead-in ties Brune to the movie *Fatal Attraction* and in the body of the article the reporter inserts the movie plot leitmotif concerning an obsessed woman who seeks revenge on a married man after he ends their affair. Brune's alleged obsession with her lover preoccupied the media as well as the prosecution and defense lawyers and both groups seemed to reinforce the notion that a woman cannot desire without being consumed by that desire, and perhaps even that a woman "free to pursue her desire is either mad or a controlling bitch whose freedom depends on depriving men of theirs" (Joshel, 1992, p. 61). In this plot, only Brune is culpable and only Brune is obsessed. In casting Brune as a woman obsessed, the media faithfully followed the plot line of the *Fatal Attraction* movie because, as Thompson (1992) notes, Alex's "obsessive nature quickly emerges as the central feature of her character, the central fact of the film" (p. 12). This focus on an alleged obsession negated all other explanations for her acts including her plea that she had only acted in self-defense and out of her fear of Vargason. The fact that her actions might have resulted from her fear of Vargason based on his prior acts of violence against her was never taken as a credible explanation for her violence against him.

Most of the media reports begin and end with statements and assertions by the prosecutor, a police officer, or witnesses against the defendant, thus shaping and framing the overall discourse in a way adverse to Brune. Knowledge of the person Susan Brune is almost completely absent. For example, only two references are made to her family, first that they attended court when the verdict was given, and second in the final report, where the reader learns that her father died of cancer when she was 16. Although Brune claimed that the crime was an act of self-defense and that she had been beaten by Vargason, there was no media investigation into the truth or otherwise of this claim.

Brune deviated from prescribed gender norms by doing her sexuality wrong. By entering into an affair with a married man, she was not doing her sexuality conventionally. Sexuality incorporates a continuum of acceptable sexual relationships and acts, and doing sexuality correctly means doing sexuality according to dominant norms. As Lorber (1998) points out, doing sexuality right is an important aspect of doing gender correctly and by preying on a married man, Brune did her gender wrong according to societal standards. As well, violence and aggression toward others are considered acts of masculinity while passivity is read as a characteristic of femininity (Lorber, 1998; Messerschmidt, 1997). Thus women who do their gender correctly do not participate in acts of aggression. They leave that for men. Social construction feminism provides a framework for revealing how Brune was demonized by the media for breaching expected gender norms. The media responded to Brune's violation of gender norms by using her story as a "cautionary tale" (Lorber, 1998; Messerschmidt, 1997) and she became the media's own pariah, sending a message to both women and men. For women, the message seems to be, "do not kill your boyfriend; if you do kill him and claim self-defense, your act will still be viewed as criminal." For men, the statement is less straightforward but seemingly encompasses a warning about the need to be careful in choosing girlfriends and wives.

Hall et al. (1978) explain how crime news operates to reaffirm "the consensual morality of the society" and how, in playing out stories of crime, the media enact "a modern morality play" in which the devil is cast out and order is restored through the work of the police and the judiciary (p. 66). As Halkias (1999) puts it, stories like that of Brune "present us with a compelling occasion to rearticulate social definitions of right and wrong, how we think the world should be, and how it is now" (p. 289). In judging Brune and ensuring that she was cast out of society for her transgression, the media was doing no more than affirming accepted stereotypes of how gender roles are to be enacted.

In its narrative of the *Fatal Attraction* killer, the *Arizona Republic* evidently shared the view expressed by Altheide (1985) that "our lives are awash in media" because from the outset the media capitalized on the name and plot recognition of the movie, following a path already marked out by the police (p. 37). It would seem that in taking its lead from the police the media sought first and foremost to make this a newsworthy story. Applying the *Fatal Attraction* label satisfied the newsworthy criteria and linked the story to a particularly notorious movie that pandered to the worst Jezebel stereotypes about an obsessed woman who kills her lover because she cannot have him for herself. Second, while reporting of the story continued in the media, the discourse about accountability for the murder came to be shaped almost entirely by reference to the fantasy world of the movie *Fatal Attraction*. Fancy subverted the reality of the story of Susan Brune and in the end, it seems that the order of things dictated that Glenn Close should be punished again for her obsession with Michael Douglas. The tale of Susan Brune is cautionary and warns against women deviating from accepted gender roles, but it is not the story of Susan Brune. Rather, we suggest, it is the story of the punishment of Glenn Close playing Alex Forrest, "the *Fatal Attraction* killer."

NOTES

1. See Cohen 1973a and 1973b for a discussion of moral panic and the media's process of discovery.
2. The *Arizona Republic* newspaper is the only Phoenix daily newspaper and covers the entire state of Arizona.
3. Ericson et al. (1989) provide the example of a police officer who explained he thought it important to assist the media in framing news stories: "you've got in a sense to assist the media person in getting the message out because you've got to sort of catch their fancy, whether it be a catchy phrase, or terminology, or whatever, so that they will get the message out" (p. 121).

4. This structural switch contradicts a study conducted by Chermak who found that the majority of media attention was focused on the discovery of crime, and that the verdict and sentencing generally received less media attention (Chermak, 1998b, pp. 92–93).

REFERENCES

ALTHEIDE, D. L. (1985). *Media power*. Beverly Hills: Sage.

ALTHEIDE, D. L. (1996). *Qualitative media analysis*. Thousand Oaks, CA: Sage.

BABENER, L. (1992). Patriarchal politics in *Fatal Attraction*. *Journal of Popular Culture, 26*(3), 25–34.

BENEDICT, H. (1992). *Virgin or vamp: How the press covers sex crimes*. New York and Oxford: Oxford University Press.

BERGER, A. A. (1998). *Media research techniques*. Thousand Oaks, CA: Sage.

BERLAND, E., & WECHTER, M. (1992). Fatal/Fetal attraction: Psychological aspects of imagining female identity in contemporary film. *Journal of Popular Culture, 26*(3), 35–45.

CHEATWOOD, D., & STASZ, C. (1979). *Visual Sociology*. In J. Wagner (Ed.), *Images of information* (pp. 261–270). Beverly Hills: Sage.

CHERMAK, S. (1994). Crime news in the media: Understanding how crimes become news. In G. Barak (Ed.), *Media Process and the construction of crime* (pp. 95–130). New York: Garland.

CHERMAK, S. (1998a). Predicting crime story salience: The effects of crime, victim, and defendant characteristics. *Journal of Criminal Justice, 26*(1), 61–70.

CHERMAK, S. M. (1998b). Police, courts, and corrections in the media. In F. Y. Bailey & D. C. Hale. (Eds.), *Popular culture, crime and justice* (pp. 87–99). Belmont, CA: West/Wadsworth.

CHESNEY-LIND, M. (1999). Media misogyny: Demonizing violent girls and women. In J. Ferrell & N. Websdale (Eds.), *Making trouble: Cultural constructions of crime, deviance, and control* (pp. 115–141). New York: Aldine De Gruyter.

COHEN, S. (1973a). Mods and rockers: The inventory as manufactured news. In S. Cohen & J. Young (Eds.). *The manufacture of news* (pp.226–241). Beverly Hills: Sage.

COHEN, S. (1973b). Sensitization: The case of mods and rockers. In S. Cohen & J. Young (Eds.), *The manufacture of news* (pp. 360–367). Beverly Hills: Sage.

COHEN, S., & YOUNG, J. (1973). Introduction. In S. Cohen & J. Young (Eds.), *The manufacture of news* (pp. 9–11). Beverly Hills: Sage.

ERICSON, R. V., BARANEK, P. M., & CHAN, J. L. (1989). *Negotiating control: A study of news sources*. Toronto: University of Toronto Press.

ERICSON, R. V., BARANEK, P. M., & CHAN, J. B. L. (1991). *Representing order: Crime, law, and justice in the news media*. Toronto: University of Toronto Press.

FRIGON, S. (1995). A genealogy of women's madness. In R. E. Dobash, R. P. Dobash, & L. Noaks (Eds.), *Gender and crime*. Cardiff: University of Wales Press.

GOFFMAN, E. (1974). *Frame analysis*. Cambridge: Harvard University Press.

HALKIAS, A. (1999). From social butterfly to modern-day Medea: Elizabeth Broderick's portrayal in the press. *Critical Studies in Mass Communication, 16*(3), 289–307.

HALL, S., CRITCHER, C., JEFFERSON, T., CLARKE, J., & ROBERTS, B. (1978). *Policing the crisis: Mugging, the state, and law and order*. New York: Holmes & Meier.

HOWE, A. (1995). Chamberlain revisited: The case against the media. In N. Naffine (Ed.), *Gender, crime and feminism* (pp. 175–182). Dartmouth, MA: Aldershot.

JAFFE, R. S., LANSING, S. (Producer), & Lyne, A. (DIrector). (1987). *Fatal Attraction* [Film]. (Available from Paramount)

JOSHEL, S. (1992). Fatal liaisons and dangerous attraction: The destruction of feminist voices. *Journal of Popular Culture, 26*(3), 59–70.

LORBER, J. (1998). *Gender inequality: Feminist theories and politics*. Los Angeles: Roxbury.

MESSERSCHMIDT, J. W. (1997). *Crime as structured action: Gender, race, class, and crime in the making*. Thousand Oaks, CA: Sage.

MEYERS, M. (1997). *News coverage of violence against women: Engendering blame*. Thousand Oaks, CA: Sage.

MILLER, G. (1997). Building bridges. In D. Silverman (Ed.), *Qualitative research: theory, method and practice* (pp. 24–44). London: Sage.

MONTINI, E. J. (1988, December 13). 2 faces of a murder trial: Self defense vs. homicidal desire. *Arizona Republic*, p. B1.

NAYLOR, B. (1995). Women's crime and media coverage: Making explanations. In R. E. Dobash, R. P. Dobash, and L. Noaks (Eds.), *Gender and crimes*. Cardiff, UK: University of Wales Press.

ROHRKEMPER. J. (1992). *Fatal Attraction*: The politics of terror. *Journal of Popular Culture, 26*(3), 83–89.

SANDERS, C. R.,& LYON, E. (1995). Repetitive retribution. In J. Ferrell & C. R. Sanders (Eds.), *Cultural criminology* (pp. 25–44). Boston: Northeastern Press.

SCHLESINGER, P., & TUMBER, H. (1994). *Reporting crime: The media politics of criminal justice*. Oxford: Claredon Press.

SHAW, E. (1995). Conceptualizing violence by women. In E. Dobash, R. Dobash, & L. Noaks (Eds.), *Gender and crime* (pp. 115–131). Cardiff: University of Wales Press.

SILVERMAN, D. (2000). *Doing qualitative research*. London: Sage.

THOMPSON, J. (1992). From diversion to *Fatal Attraction*: The transformation of a morality play into a Hollywood hit. *Journal of Popular Culture, 26*(3): 5–15.

TUCHMAN, G. (1971/1972). An examination of newsmen's notions of objectivity. *American Journal of Sociology, 77*, 660–679.

VAN ZOONEN, L. V. (1994). *Feminist media studies*. London: Sage.

WALSH, J. (1988, April 28). Woman is held in fatal meeting with ex-lover. *Arizona Republic*, pp. B1–B2.

WATSON, R. (1997). Ethnomethodology and textual analysis. In D. Silverman (Ed.), *Qualitative research* (pp. 80–98). London: Sage.

WEBER, R. P. (1985). *Basic content analysis*. Beverly Hills: Sage.

WEBSDALE, N., & ALVAREZ, A. (1998). Forensic journalism as patriarchal ideology: The newspaper construction of homicide suicide. In F. Bailey & D. Hale (Eds.), *Popular culture, crime, and justice* (pp. 123–142). Belmont, CA: West/Wadsworth.

WEST, C., & ZIMMERMAN, D. H. (1987). Doing gender. *Gender and Society, 1(2)*, 125–151.

WHITING, B. (1988a, November 18). Murder defendant called coldblooded. *Arizona Republic*, pp. B1, B4.

WHITING, B. (1988b, November 29). Slain man feared girlfriend, trial told. *Arizona Republic*, p. B1.

WHITING, B. (1988c, December 6). "Either my life or his," murder suspect swears. *Arizona Republic*, pp. B1–B2.

WHITING, B. (1988d, December 8). *Fatal Attraction* image parried in murder trial. *Arizona Republic*, pp. B1–B2.

WHITING, B. (1988e, December 13). Valley murder trial "not a movie," prosecutor says as case goes to jury. *Arizona Republic*, pp. B1–B2.

WHITING, B. (1988f, December 14). Ex-lover convicted of murder. *Arizona Republic*, pp. A1 and A6.

WHITING, B. (1989, January 14). *Fatal Attraction* defendant sentenced to life imprisonment. *Arizona Republic*, p. B7.

WIMMER, R. D., & DOMINICK, J. R. (1987). *Mass media research*. Belmont, CA: Wadsworth.

WYKES, M. (1995). Passion, marriage and murder: Analyzing the press discourse. In R. E. Dobash, R. P. Dobash, & L. Noaks (Eds.), *Gender and crime*. (pp. 49–76). Cardiff: University of Wales Press.

10

The Crime of Rape

Roslyn Muraskin

When Adam lost his rib, he gained a mate, but it has been a bone of contention ever since.

> My whole life has been invaded, violated. It didn't happen just to me, but to my husband and children.
>
> Rape, it shatters your sense of self; it leaves you with the feeling of having been defiled, of being stained, of being different.
>
> I am dirty. There are times when I wish the rapist had killed me, it would have been kinder.
>
> I have changed, the world has changed. I don't see things the way I used to.
>
> I am besieged by fear. I am afraid to stay home alone. I am afraid to go out alone.

When rape victims speak about their rape, as noted above, rape becomes a crime that says the victim no longer has the ability to control her own personal self. The victim experiences a diminishment in her ego defense. This act, more so than any other criminal act, deprives the victims and their relatives of the protective mantle of privacy, converting their private agony in finding themselves discussing what happened to them in private into a public forum.

The factor that there was a corroboration requirement that denigrated the testimony of women who claim to have been sexually violated is in and of itself indefensible. It evidenced an irrational belief in the dishonesty of women who *claimed* to have been sexually assaulted. Historically, women have always been considered the property of man. If she was raped at a young age, her father's property was said to have been defiled, and if the wife was raped, the husband's property was said to have been tarnished. Rape laws have always been premised on the assumption that women are liars, and therefore stricter standards of proof have been imposed. The woman's words were to be corroborated by other testimony; not so in cases of robbery, assault, arson, and so on. Judges were required to read the following cautionary instructions to the jury:

> A charge such as that made against the defendant in this case is one which is easily made and, once made, difficult to defend against, even if the person accused is innocent. Therefore the law requires that you examine the testimony of the female person named in the information with caution. (Judge Matthew Hale)

The dilemma of whether to report a rape is faced by thousands of rape victims. For many the answer is *no*. Although regrettable, the response is understandable. The rape victim has long been the victim of the popular but false belief that "she asked for it." Police, prosecutors, and medical examiners have been accused by many rape victims of insensitive and unsympathetic behavior. Social service agencies are often ill-equipped to deal with rape victims' special needs.

There has evolved a pattern—both the lack of support from the community and the low priority given rape cases by the police and prosecutors—that appears to alienate the victims. Those victims who do persevere to the trial stage historically have found themselves put on trial as the defense attorneys have grilled them about their own sexual behavior.[1]

What is rape? The definitions of forcible rape have varied from state to state. Two definitions that have been used include "carnal knowledge of a woman forcibly and against her will" and "sexual intercourse with a woman, not the wife of a perpetrator, forcibly and against her will or in circumstances under which she was incapable of giving consent." In nearly every state the way rape has been treated under the law has been different from the way other crimes have been treated. For reasons beyond understanding, most states traditionally have made it harder for a woman to establish that she has been raped than for any other person to establish that he or she has been the victim of some other crime such as robbery or assault. The reason given is the woman probably lied.

The rape laws as they have developed reflect fears: fears that vengeful women will charge innocent men against whom they bear grudges; that women who have consented to sexual intercourse and have become pregnant or have otherwise been found out by their husbands or parents will charge a man with rape so that they will escape some punishment; or, that some psychotic women who secretly wish to be raped will in fact believe that they have been. The other fear is that some women will simply bring rape charges to gain notoriety. This has resulted in our rape laws seemingly protecting the defendant, while ignoring the rights of the victim.

Understanding the words of Judge Hale, there existed under the common law the belief that chastity was a character trait. This fell under the belief that premarital sex was immoral. "Acts of previous illicit sexual relations, like other acts or moral turpitude, could thus be used to impeach the credibility of the complaining witness in a rape case" (Tanford, 1980, p. 544).

Traditionally, in order for innocent men to be protected, juries were instructed to scrutinize the testimony of a rape complainant closely, where the complaining witness and the defendant were expected to be chaste until time for marriage. The laws then developed not so much to protect the female but rather were developed to protect the property of the male. A woman was considered damaged goods if she was not a virgin. Men did not desire damaged goods.

It was believed that females were thought to have a definite character flaw. No "normal" woman would ever be raped. No "normal" woman exhibited a propensity to have sexual relations with anyone but her husband. Today, rape is still pretty much an unreported crime, but most courts and legislatures appear to have adapted to the times in that they realize that a woman who is unchaste or a woman who indulges in extramarital sexual relationships is no more likely to consent indiscriminately than a woman who is chaste.

In the past, the defendant in a rape case was to introduce testimony about the victim's sexual relations and was able to produce witnesses who would give testimony about the sexual reputation of the victim's chastity. If the woman was considered to be promiscuous, then how could she be believed?

Recent years have seen these laws reflecting the outmoded morality and unenlightened male-dominated legal system. Today, a growing awareness of women's equality has brought about the revision of the rape laws. It was always the woman on the witness stand who stood to be "raped" once more, this time by the criminal justice system. The myth is that women do not provoke rape, nor do they ask for it.

In the words of one woman:

> I had locked all doors because I was afraid, and I don't know how he got in; it was probably through the screen door. When I woke up, he was shaking my leg. His eyes were red, and I knew he had been drinking or smoking. I thought I would try to talk my way out of it. He started by saying that he wanted to sleep with me, and then he got angrier and angrier, until he started to say "I want pussy." Then, I got scared and tried to push him away. That's when he started to force himself on me. It was awful. It was the most humiliating terrible feeling. He was forcing my legs apart and ripping my clothes off. And it was painful. I did fight him—he was slightly drunk and I was able to keep him away. I had taken judo a few years back, but I was afraid to throw a chop for fear he would kill me. I could see he was getting more and more violent. I was thinking wildly of some way to get out of this alive, and then I said to him, "do you want money, I'll give you money." We had money, but I was also thinking that if I got to the back room, I could telephone the police—as if the police would have even helped. It was a stupid thing to think of because obviously he would follow me. And he did. When he saw me pick up the phone, he tried to tie the cord around my neck. I screamed at him that I did have the money in another room, that I was not going to call the police because I was scared, and that I would never tell anyone what happened. It would be an absolute secret. He said, "Okay," and I went to get the money. But when he got it, all of a sudden he got this crazy look in his eye, and he said to me, "now I am going to kill you." (New York Women Against Rape Conference, 1981)

Rape becomes an act of aggression where the victim has been denied her self-determination. Rape is an act of violence, an act of power. It is a form of mass terrorism; the victim of the rape is chosen indiscriminately, but the propagandists for male supremacy broadcast that it is women who cause rape by being unchaste or in the wrong place at the wrong time—in essence *by behaving as if they were free* (New York Women Against Rape Conference, 1981).

Rape is an unbelievably vicious and personal form of attack. Many a female victim fears her assailant will return (and some do). Many a victim is reluctant to return home or to return to her normal home life upon being raped. Rape victims oftentimes find themselves no longer trusting a man. Many a loving husband or boyfriend has abandoned his woman, knowing of her innocence after finding that he can't handle her having been raped.

Rape legislation has had a long-standing and sordid history as sexist legislation designed not to protect women, but rather to protect men's social and property interests in female chastity. Sometime back, two judges in separate cases made judicial decisions that would appear to "decriminalize" rape. In Wisconsin, the judge sentenced one of three boys involved in the gang rape of a sixteen-year-old girl to one year of court supervision at home. The judge *in his wisdom* explained that, after all, the boy was merely reacting normally to an environment of prevalent sexual permissiveness and provocative women's clothing. The judge continued, "I'm trying to say to women, 'stop teasing.'" In California, a judge voided the conviction of a man charged with raping a hitchhiker: "it may not speak well for the prevailing standard of morality in society, but women hitchhikers should anticipate sexual advances from men who pick them up" (Berger, 1977, p. 9).

Rape has become an instrument of forced exile. Rape has been known to drive a wedge through both community and family (Russell-Brown, 2002, p. 35). Mediation has been used as a tool in cases of acquaintance rape cases.[2] It is used to empower victims while addressing the needs of the offenders. Most rapes (as noted above) go unreported and are unsuccessfully managed by the criminal justice system. One out of every six women in the United States has been a victim of rape or attempted rape, and therefore other avenues, such as mediation, are looked for ("Indictments and Information XII," 2004).

Rape trauma syndrome requires only a general fit between the characteristics of the syndrome and the victim's syndrome. Women who suffer from the act of rape, and therefore from rape trauma syndrome, have recognizable reactions differing from other types of trauma. Anxiety and fear are common traits among those who have been raped. Rape trauma syndrome is the "acute phase and long-term reorganization process that occurs as a result of forcible rape or attempted forcible rape. It is an acute stress reaction to a life-threatening situation" (New York Jurisprudence, 2004).

A victim's reputation and sexual activities with men should be irrelevant. The concentration on the reputation of the victim, as if she were the one whose guilt or innocence was to be determined, has been a continuing indication of the bias against the rape victim in our current justice system. Whether the victim had a prior sexual relationship with the defendant should have little relevance to the issue of whether a current voluntary relationship existed. Even in the rape of a prostitute, a woman who engages in an established pattern of indiscriminate sex, she is entitled to claim rape. There are those courts as well as commentators who continue to express concern that many sexual offense accusations are made by psychologically disturbed individuals, and therefore such evidence should not be deemed reliable by the courts.

According to the rape shield laws, there must be:

- Evidence of prior sexual conduct or consensual sexual intercourse between the complainant and the defendant which tends to prove that the complainant consented to the conduct in issue.
- Evidence of an established pattern of prior sexual conduct on the part of the complainant which tends to prove that the complainant consented to the conduct in issue or such evidence, if known to the defendant at the time of the act or acts charged, which tends to prove that the defendant reasonably believed that the complainant was consenting.
- Evidence of prior sexual conduct on the part of the complainant so distinctive and so closely resembling the defendant's version of the alleged encounter with the complainant as to tend to prove that she consented to the conduct in issue.

- Evidence of prior sexual conduct on the part of the complainant which tends to prove that a person other than the defendant committed the act or acts charged or caused the complainant's physical condition allegedly arising from these acts. Such evidence shall include proof of the origin of semen, pregnancy, disease or injury allegedly resulting from these acts.
- Evidence of sexual conduct on the part of the complainant which tends to prove that the complainant has a motive for fabricating the charge or charges made.
- Evidence of sexual conduct on the part of the complainant offered as the basis of expert psychological or psychiatric opinion that the complainant fantasized or invented the act or acts charged.
- Evidence of prior sexual conduct on the part of the complainant which tends to show that the complaining witness has on direct examination, made a material misrepresentation as to the nature of her sexual experience on occasions other than that of the alleged offense. (Tanford, 1980, p. 544)

The rights of the rape victims as viewed by the courts recognize the need to protect a person who takes the stand from attacks designed merely to harass, annoy, or humiliate. "For many [women] the trauma of baring one's intimate past to the eyes of the world—turning one's bedroom into a showcase—overshadows the usual discomfort of testifying or having others testify, to one's biases, lies, or even conflicting criminal acts" (Tanford).

The victim of the rape is placed in a false light within the eye of the public. The result is that she is making a public disclosure of private facts that may have no relevance to the present case.

> Suppose that a victim has been "incautious" not in her actions preceding the rape (drinking, hitchhiking, walking alone at night), but her sexual habits and choices. Perhaps she has had extramarital affairs or borne children out of wedlock. Perhaps she has only had one or two premarital encounters but lives in a place where conventional morals are strongly enforced. Should the woman decide to go to court, she faces the prospect of having this personal data disclosed, sometimes directly, sometimes obliquely as reputation, unless of course she was "lucky" enough to have gotten attacked in a state with a stringent rape statute. Although it belies human experience to argue that women will tailor their lives to the image of the model rape complainant, just in case and thus be chilled in their primary conduct, it is not absurd to suggest that exposure of intimate facts in a public courtroom regardless of their degree of relevance imposes a truly harsh penalty on certain types of sexual choices. To say that the woman can always refrain from filing charges and thus avoid unwanted scrutiny is to her the option. (Tanford, 1980, p. 545)

But why should she be put to shame because she was the victim? "Bare the most personal parts of your life or abandon all hopes of legal redress. What the act of rape wholly denies, traditional rules of evidence punish: the right of women as well as men to sexual self-determination" (Berger, 1977, p. 42). Berger continues:

> To the extent that the prosecutrix in rape and related sexual crimes is uniquely subject to painful prejudicial attack on her private life and intimate conduct, one might argue that she has literally been denied the equal protection of the laws. Other complainants can go to court to seek redress for their victimization without incurring this heavy penalty. Rape targets, on the other hand, are

disproportionately discouraged from prosecuting their violators. As a result, they fail to receive the law's protection after the fact and probably (though it would be extremely hard to show) before as well, since knowledge of its inefficacy can be expected to lessen whatever deterrent effect the criminal sanction has in this area. Those victims who do invoke the legal process, paying the price in personal exposure, often find that their sacrifice has netted them absolutely nothing: the jury acquits the man of rape but convicts the woman of loose behavior. (p. 44)

With our system of justice an act of violence offends against the society at large, not simply the injured individual. As the state rather than the victim formally charges the defendant, there are some who would favor the use of an independent attorney, particularly in rape cases, to represent the victim. The fact that all sittings of the court are public gives the opportunity to be heard in public. To ban the public as has been done in some jurisdictions is to seemingly protect the complainant—the victim of the rape. Whatever way the case of rape is handled, it must be in a manner where the victim's dignity is preserved, where only pertinent information is presented, and where the decision to prosecute or not is in the hands of the victim.

The *moth-laden* rules of rape have changed. The law converts as well as mirrors cultural norms and expectations.

In Susan Brownmiller's work *Against Our Will*, published in 1975 but still quoted, the story is told of former Israeli Prime Minister Golda Meir who recalled:

Once in a cabinet we had to deal with the fact that there had been an outbreak of assaults on women at night. One minister suggested a curfew: women should stay home after dark. I said, "[B]ut it's the men who are attacking the women. If there is to be a curfew, let the men stay home, not the women."

The female victim is not to be raped by the criminal justice system.

NOTES

1. Rape shield laws, a recent phenomenon, prevent the questioning of the female victim about her prior sexual history, unless it has and/or is shown to have relevance to the case.
2. Where both victim and attacker know each other, but he attacks and she says no, it is still a crime of rape. There is no such crime as date or acquaintance rape. Most states recognize rape as being rape.

REFERENCES

BERGER, V. (1977). Notes on rape cases. *Columbia Law Review, 42.*

BROWNMILLER, S. (1975). *Against our will: Men, women and rape.* New York: Simon & Schuster.

NEW YORK JURISPRUDENCE. Indictments and information XII. 225 *Corpus Juris Secundum* (2004, June).

NEW YORK WOMEN AGAINST RAPE CONFERENCE, May 1981.

RUSSELL-BROWN, S. (2002). Rape as an act of genocide. *Berkeley Journal of International Law, 21,* p. 350.

TANFORD, A. J. (1980, January). Rape victims shield laws and the Sixth Amendment. 128 *University of Pennsylvania Law Review, 128,* p. 544.

11

Forced Sexual Intercourse in Dating

Testing a Model

Robert T. Sigler, Ida M. Johnson, and Etta F. Morgan

This chapter will attempt to introduce some degree of clarity in an area noted for its lack of clarity. Forced sexual intercourse is generally treated as a single phenomenon. The authors suggest that this term is used to label four types of behavior that are substantially different. Stranger rape occurs when someone who is not known or who is casually known to the victim uses force to gain sexual access. Courtship or date rape occurs when someone who is developing a legitimate relationship with the victim uses force to gain sexual access. Predatory rape occurs when someone uses force to gain sexual access while pretending to engage in a legitimate courtship or dating activity (the pretense is used to maneuver the victim into a vulnerable position). Spousal rape occurs when someone uses force to gain sexual access with a spouse or with someone with whom he has a relatively permanent relationship. The authors will argue that these are different sets of phenomena, which require different explanatory models and interventions. Each type will be defined with reference to the relevant literature when appropriate. Recommendations will be made for research foci for each type. Research evaluating one model for understanding forced sexual intercourse in a courtship context will be presented. The model suggests that this type of forced sexual intercourse is a dysfunctional aspect of the normal complicated dating and courtship process.

Forced sexual intercourse has been steadily growing in importance as an area of concern for scholars. The definition of women's roles and the social values that define the relationships between men and women have been changing. Social service and criminal justice agencies have responded to these changes by moving to adopt policies and practices that are more sympathetic to female victims of domestic violence, courtship violence, and forced sexual intercourse. In the process, rape—the intentional or planned use of physical force to obtain sexual access against the wishes of a woman who was not intimately involved with her assailant—has been redefined to the extent that rape is no longer an accurate characterization of the behaviors that can be addressed by the justice system on the complaint of a victim.

While one focus of this chapter is on the definition of types of forced sexual intercourse, it should be noted that the definition of rape that was common in the first half of this century has slowly evolved to include types of forced sexual intercourse which, in the past, were held to be of no interest to the justice system and to include offensive sexual behaviors less than intercourse. Sexual assault, the emerging concept, is broad, has been widely accepted, and specifies degrees of offensiveness. There is some recognition that offensive sexual behavior and forced sexual intercourse can be placed on a continuum based on degree of unacceptability of the offensive behavior. Although this evolution may have positive effects on the ability of the justice system to protect women from male offenders, it increases the confusion in definition that has characterized forced sexual intercourse by including a wide range of behaviors under one label. At the same time, the perspective that will be presented here suggests that the continuum of those behaviors identified as forced sexual intercourse is broader than generally accepted and may include offensive sexual behaviors that are tolerated by some of the victims. Specifically, some offensive sexual behavior occurs in the context of courtship and dating and is accepted, to some degree, by some of the victims.

Historically, theories that sought to explain rape focused on those cases in which a stranger sexually assaulted a relatively unknown victim. Sexual assaults were explained in terms of mental illness and generally asserted that rape was more a matter of serious mental defect or a matter of dominance and control of women than that of gaining sexual access.

Three major works, published in the 1980s, sought to explain the broader range of behaviors that had become defined as sufficiently unacceptable that they should be subjected to the control of the justice system. Sunday and Tobach (1985) addressed the sociobiological approach to violence against women, including rape. Ellis (1989) shifted the emphasis from predatory stranger rape to acquaintance rape and recognized the influence of the feminist perspective as originally advanced by Brownmiller (1975). He grouped explanations for forced sexual intercourse into three general theoretical perspectives: feminist theory, learning theory, and evolutionary theory. Baron and Straus (1989) also sought to present theories that reflected the broader definition of rape that had emerged by the 1980s. They grouped explanations for sexual assault into four general theoretical perspectives: gender inequality, pornography, social disorganization, and legitimate violence. Readers who seek more comprehensive coverage of these perspectives should review these three earlier works as well as Brownmiller's 1975 book, *Against Our Will: Men, Women, and Rape.*

THEORETICAL PERSPECTIVES

The Feminist Perspective

The feminist movement produced, or at least influenced, much of the reform in the manner in which society relates to women. Feminists argue that sexual assault is defined as a legitimate or normal product of male-dominated societies. From this perspective offensive behaviors that control women are defined as acceptable to the males who control the society. Feminist theorists argue that patriarchal societies define men as dominant over women. Women are assigned inferior social status, with relatively little power, while men are socially superior and dominate and control women (Dobash, 1979; Friedan, 1963). Men's power over women historically was defined as not subject to control by society in even the most severe of instances; thus it came to be perceived as a right or, at least, as a privilege exercised by men. In this context, forced sexual intercourse becomes more a matter of dominance and control than a matter of sex (Brownmiller, 1975; Goth, 1979; Holdstrom & Burgess, 1980; Riger & Gordon, 1981; Scarpitti & Scarpitti, 1977; Wald, 1997). Men (male-dominated society) use the fear of rape to allow men to assert their dominance over women and rape to control non-conforming women as a means of maintaining the patriarchal system of male dominance (Adamec & Adamec, 1981; Barry, 1979; Brownmiller, 1975; Goth, 1979; Persell, 1984; Riger & Gordon, 1981; Russell, 1975; Thompson & Buttell, 1984; Weis & Borges, 1977). Studies supporting the feminist perspective have tended to measure the incidence of rape in relation to incidents of violence in general (Baron & Straus, 1984; Benderly, 1982; Cauffman, Feldman, Arnett Jensen, & Arnett, 2000; Kutchinski, 1988; Sanday, 1981; Schwendinger & Schwendinger, 1985; Sigelman, Berry, & Wiles, 1984). Self-report studies that ask rapists to report their motivation tend to contradict the feminist model. They find that rapists report motivation by desire for excitement, risk taking, and sex (Scully & Marolla, 1984) and report high levels of deviant sexual fantasies (Walker & Meyer, 1981), with high levels of sexual arousal reported by date rapists (Yegidis, 1986). More recent research finds that sexually aroused males are more likely to report that they would be more likely to behave in a sexually forceful manner on a date (Cowling, 1998).

In the feminist model, behaviors, such as forced sexual intercourse, are defined as acceptable or justified. It is possible, however, to argue within the feminist perspective that the behaviors themselves are not defined as acceptable but, rather, they are defined as personal or private and not of interest to those outside the family. That is, men who force their wives or female friends to engage in sex are not defined as good or tolerated for the purposes of controlling women, but the offensive behavior that they exhibit is defined as private and personal and unsuitable for control by society.

The feminist perspective can be seen as an application of social learning theory. Some authors suggest that traditional gender roles and expectations define forced sexual intercourse as a normal aspect of male–female interaction, and thus encourage rape (Burt, 1980; Check & Malamuth, 1983b; Cherry, 1983; Curtis, 1975; Ewoldt, Monson, Langhinrichsen-Rohling, & Binderup, 2000; Hird & Jackson, 2001; Russell, 1975; Vogel, 2000; Weis & Borges, 1977). Norms that define masculinity in terms of dominance and control and femininity in terms of passivity and submission define the use of force by men to control women as gender-role expectations that support or encourage forced sexual intercourse (Gagnon & Simon, 1973). Mardorossian (2002) argues for the need to develop a more effective and focused theory of rape.

Social Learning Theory

From a learning theory perspective, forced sexual intercourse and the attitudes that support it are learned in the same ways that other behaviors are learned. Men who force women to have sex do so because they (and in some perspectives their victims) have learned that this is appropriate behavior. For the feminists, this learning is related to or associated with the set of values that supports the socioeconomic and political exploitation of women by men; nonfeminist social learning theorists see forced sexual intercourse as related to or associated with cultural traditions linked with interpersonal aggression, masculine roles, and sexuality.

Learning theory is a general term encompassing theories developed in a number of traditions including symbolic interaction and cognitive attitude theory; however, much of the work that addresses rape is derived from Bandura's (1973) drive-based, psychoanalytic modeling theory which addresses aggression. Ellis (1989, pp. 12–13) states that social learning theories of rape that assert that rape is a form of aggression state that these behaviors are learned in four ways: by imitating or modeling aggressive sexual behaviors that the learner has observed in real life or in media presentations (Huesman & Malamuth, 1986; Nelson, 1982); by observing sex and violence in the same context or presentation (Check & Malamuth, 1983a; Malamuth 1981, 1984, 1986, 1988; Malamuth, Briere, & Check, 1986); by repeating or portraying rape myths that make rape acceptable (Burt, 1980); and by desensitizing the learner to the victim's perspective through repetition of exposure to incidents of sex and violence or of violent sex (Donnerstein, Linz, & Penrod, 1987).

The Sociobiological Perspective

The sociobiological perspective asserts that humanity is a product of evolution in which both physical and social traits conducive to survival are selected and survive through a process of natural selection. Propagation is key to the survival of a trait, as a genetic predisposition can be passed on only through offspring. The linkage of sexual selection and rape with trait survival was first made by Deutsch (1944). Social traits that have been selected include female emphasis on child care and male emphasis on mating with as many partners as possible (Bateman, 1948; Chamove, Harlow, & Mitchell, 1967; Daly & Wilson, 1978; Hagen, 1979; Leshner, 1978; Smith, 1978; Symons, 1979; Trivers, 1972; Williams, 1975; Wilson, 1975). From a sociobiological perspective, men have a lower commitment to gestation than women (Quinsey, 1984) but have a disadvantage in that they cannot definitely identify their children (Daly & Wilson, 1978; Dawkins, 1976; Durden-Smith & deSimone, 1983), thus an inclination to impregnate as many females as possible has gene survival value. In this model, forced sexual intercourse increases the survival of a male's genes, thus selecting a tendency to rape (Gibson, Linden, & Johnson, 1980; Hagen, 1979; Quinsey, 1984; Symons, 1979). On the other hand, females who resist males who impregnate them and move on to other females are more likely to pass on their genes. The use of force to gain sexual access reduces the ability of a female to choose a mate who will stay with her after insemination. The absence of a male partner decreases the likelihood of survival of her children (Mellen, 1981; Richard & Schulman, 1982; Symons, 1979; Thornhill, 1980; Wilder, 1982). From this, rape would be a particularly effective strategy in modern times for men who have limited resources with which to attract a mate (Shields & Shields, 1983; Thornhill & Thornhill, 1983).

Social Disorganization and Legitimate Violence

Baron and Straus (1989) advance two additional theoretical perspectives for explaining rape: social disorganization and legitimate violence. Social disorganization occurs when social institutions and norms that regulate social conduct become ineffective (Blumer,

1937; Martindale, 1957; Mower, 1941; Thomas & Zaniecki, 1927; Wirth, 1940). When society's social control is weakened, deviant behavior and crime, including rape, are more likely to occur. Baron & Straus (1989) constructed a social disorganization index and discovered that when their measure of social disorganization is high, rates of rape are high.

Legitimate violence begins with the recognition that some theoretical perspectives define rape as normatively permitted rather than as beyond the control of society. Baron and Straus (1989) note that the feminists argue the presence of such norms (Brownmiller, 1975; Scully & Marolla, 1985).

Baron and Straus (1989) also note that a number of perspectives suggest that the legitimacy of rape might be supported indirectly. They cite violent subculture theories (Gastil, 1971; Hackney, 1969; Messner, 1983; Wolfgang & Ferracuti, 1967) and cross-cultural theories that demonstrate a link between types of violence (Archer & Gartner, 1984; Huggins & Straus, 1980; Lambert, Triandis, & Wolf, 1959) and between violence and sexual violence (Sanday, 1981) as well as between violence and sexual violence in the United States (Amir, 1971). These findings are taken by Baron and Straus to support a cultural spillover theory of criminal violence. As the extent to which society approves the legitimate use of violence in some areas increases, the use of violence in rape and in collateral areas, such as personal assault, increases.

MARITAL RAPE

Marital rape, more than any other form of forced sexual intercourse, tends to fall outside most theoretical models. The criminal status of forced sexual intercourse in marriage is still evolving. Historically, forced sexual intercourse in marriage was specifically excluded in definitions of rape to the extent that the "marital exemption" was an accepted legal principle (LaFave & Scott, 1972; Palmer, 1997; Yllo, 1998).

The rationales for the adoption of the marital rape exemption include the following: (a) the marriage contract, which some people would argue dissolves the woman's rights and enhances the rights of the husband as the head of the house. A woman's consent to marriage has been extended to imply consent to submit to the wishes of the husband and can be revoked only by divorce; (b) the legal definition of rape—historically, rape has been defined as a property crime and women were considered the property of their husbands or fathers. In *People v. Liberta* (1984) the court stated, "the purpose behind the proscriptions [against rape] was to protect the chastity of women and thus their property value to their husbands and fathers" (p. 567); and (c) marital unity—the belief that husbands and wives become one after marriage. If this is true, then a man cannot rape himself (Brown, 1995; Sitton, 1993). These rationales are no longer applicable to married women because the roles of women in society have changed dramatically.

Some contemporary theorists suggest that marital rape is not as serious as other types of rape (Sitton, 1993). It is argued that the closer the relationship between the victim and the perpetrator the more a victim feels violated both physically and mentally. In fact, the victim may be more traumatized because of the relationship. Additionally, some propose that having a marital rape classification would cause false rape claims to be made by angry wives who seek to damage or destroy their husband's reputation. Another issue raised in opposition to the inclusion of a marital rape classification was the possible impact on marital stability (Sitton). It is hard to imagine a marriage that is stable if the husband is raping his wife.

Regardless of which argument one examines concerning marital rape, the result is the same: women are not equal beings in our society. According to Sitton (1993), "throughout our legal and cultural tradition, the woman is either a virgin or a whore, alternatively someone to be placed on a pedestal or in the bedroom" (p. 268). Again, previous views and role expectations associated with women are no longer applicable. Fortunately, in *Trammell v. United States* (1980) the court ruled that women are not chattel and are no less than other human beings. Other reform measures toward gender equality have assisted in solidifying the legal status of women. Challenges to the marital rape exemption have been based on the constitutional right to privacy, a broad and private sphere interpretation of the Thirteenth and Fourteenth Amendments. For a more thorough examination of the arguments regarding marital rape based on the Constitution and its amendments see Dailey, 1986; *Merton v. State*, 1986; *People v. Liberta*, 1984; *Reed v. Reed*, 1971; and West, 1990.

The lines are clearly drawn from a social activist perspective: Forced sexual intercourse in marriage is either rape or a husband's privilege depending on the perspective of the speaker. It is more likely that this is an issue of public versus private interest rather than a matter of male rights. That is, few will actually believe that men who force their wives to engage in sex are behaving in a legally acceptable manner. The behavior is perceived as wrong but not a matter that should be resolved by the police and the criminal courts. Confusion is added by the prospect that there is an expectation of sexual access in marriage and a corresponding obligation of the wife to submit to her husband that is endorsed by both many men and many women (endorsement of "traditional values") (Bullough, 1974; Williams, 1979). Setting aside the legal arguments, the question of behavioral similarity remains: Is forced sexual intercourse in marriage the same as or more similar to the behavior exhibited when a stranger forces an unwilling victim, or the same as or more similar to forced sexual intercourse in a courtship setting? It is possible that forced sexual intercourse in marriage is not a matter of sexual access but a matter of power and domination. It is also possible that there are two types of forced sexual intercourse in marriage, the first reflecting power and dominance and the second reflecting forcing sexual access from an unwilling spouse.

STATE OF THE ART

The theories that have been developed to explain forced sexual intercourse tend to treat forced sexual intercourse as a single type of behavior. Because forced sexual intercourse is seen as a single phenomenon, scholars have sought to develop a single theory. The theories that have been developed tend to be most effective in explaining incidents of forced sexual intercourse in which a man intends to force a woman to have sex when she does not want to have sex, when physical force or the threat of physical force is used, and when the woman defines her victimization as rape. If the nature of the interaction between the victim and offender is such that forced sexual intercourse produces different sets of phenomenon, then a single model theory will not be sufficient to describe accurately the phenomena under study.

TYPES OF FORCED SEXUAL INTERCOURSE IN DATING

Some scholars have focused on the development of theoretical models that address forced sexual intercourse in dating or courtship settings. Most studies with a theoretical base attempt to identify factors that make types of assault more or less likely to occur. One effort (Shotland, 1992) develops a basic typology of date rape. Five different types of date rape are characterized, based on time, courtship violence, and degree of development of a relationship. Felson (1992) has developed a model that seeks to explain sexual assaults in terms of motives and goals. He identifies five paths using factors such as social identity, bodily pleasure, personal justice, domination, sexual relations, and harm to target.

The present theories that focus on rape are not effective in describing all of the events that presently are included under the terms *date rape*, *acquaintance rape*, and *marital rape*. In some incidents that are identified as date rape, a man intentionally forces a woman to have sex when she doesn't want to using substantial force, and the woman defines her victimization as rape. In other instances that are identified as date rape, the man may not intend to force the woman to have sex, the degree of force may be less substantial, and the woman may not define her victimization as rape. In the first instance, a rape has occurred that can be explained with one or more of the existing models; the incident just happened to occur in a dating context. In the second instance, the behavior is offensive and unacceptable by standards that are emerging today, but the behavior cannot be accurately explained with existing theories. The inability to describe the nature of the phenomena reduces the ability to effectively address what is clearly a contemporary social problem.

The data available from studies of forced sexual intercourse consistently have identified sets of incidents in which the forced sexual intercourse reported by victims is not identified as rape, beginning with Russell's (1984) early study. About one-half of the women who indicated that they had experienced incidents that met the legal definition of rape in use at that time did not respond affirmatively when asked if they had been raped. Similar results were reported by a leading study in the area of date rape. Koss, Dinero, Seibel, and Cox (1988) reported 23.1 percent of the women victimized by men they knew labeled their victimization as rape, and 62 percent of these victims indicated that they did not view their victimization as any type of crime. Similar results have been reported by Johnson, Palileo, and Gray (1992), Doyle and Burfeind (1994), Johnson and Sigler (1997), and other studies that report findings for women's characterizations of their victimization (Bondurant, 2001; Sawyer, Pinciaro, & Jessell, 1998).

A BEGINNING MODEL

We argue that all instances of forced sexual intercourse are not the same—that there are substantial differences among various sets of sexually offensive behaviors. While existing theories provide an effective basis for dealing with those cases in which a man intends to rape a woman who realizes that she is being raped, they are less effective in explaining many of the victimizations that are presently included under the labels of date or acquaintance rape.

At this point, we suggest that alternate models should be developed to explain different types of forced sexual intercourse. Based on the knowledge available today, four types of forced sexual intercourse can be identified that are substantially different from each other. These models are biased in that they assume that the victim is always a woman and the offender is always a man. While the same models might apply to homosexual relationships or to cases in which a woman victimizes a man, the limited information available in these areas makes it difficult to attempt model development. We identify four types of forced sexual intercourse: stranger rape, spousal rape, forced sexual intercourse in a dating or courtship context, and predatory rape.

Stranger rape occurs when a man who is unknown or known casually to the victim uses physical force or threat of physical force to secure sexual access against the wishes of the victim. Both the offender and the victim tend to identify the behavior as rape. This form of forced sexual intercourse has been studied more extensively than other forms of forced sexual intercourse and several models are available to explain the behavior, many of which suggest the behavior is not sexual in nature.

Spousal rape occurs when a man uses physical force or the threat of physical force against a woman to secure sexual access against her will from a partner with whom he has established a relatively permanent relationship. Definition of the behavior as rape will vary from offender to offender and from victim to victim. A relatively permanent relationship is defined as a relationship that includes sexual intimacy as a part of the relationship and is not limited to couples who share the same living area (cohabitation). Very little information is available about this form of behavior. Most of the literature that addresses this issue focuses on the legal and ethical dimensions of the issue rather than on understanding the nature of the interaction between the actors. Placing this behavior in the context of marital disputes and spouse abuse may be more effective than addressing the issue in the context of forced sexual intercourse as a sexual act, even when sexual access is the primary goal of the offender.

Forced sexual intercourse in a dating or courtship context occurs when a man uses physical force to secure sexual access without her consent from a woman with whom he is developing a relationship while the couple is engaged in a consensual intimate social context. Definition of the behavior as rape will vary from offender to offender and from victim to victim. This type of forced sexual intercourse applies only to events that occur as the relationship is developing. It is probable that sexual access is the primary motivator in these types of exchanges. In most cases, the man does not enter the exchange with the intent of using force. These events tend to be characterized as involving loss of control and may be better understood in the context of courtship than as independent acts of sexual assault.

Predatory rape occurs when a man pretends to engage in legitimate dating or courtship behavior with the intent of using force to gain sexual access against the will of the woman if he cannot gain consent. The offender will tend to identify his behavior as rape but the victim may or may not define the behavior as rape. In these cases, the offender is not seeking a personal or intimate relationship; rather, he is seeking sexual relief and has no concern for the feelings, rights, or needs of his victim. He intends to maneuver the victim into a comprising position so that she will not protest after the act has been completed and he will use almost any means necessary to achieve his goal. Very little is known about this behavior, thus the development of an accurate model is difficult. These men are identifiable in data that have been collected by the authors (Johnson & Sigler, 1997).

FORCED SEXUAL INTERCOURSE IN A COURTSHIP OR DATING CONTEXT

Sufficient data are now available to permit the development and testing of a model designed to explain the nature of forced sexual intercourse in a dating context. Although all factors that might operate in instances of forced sexual intercourse in these situations have not been clearly identified by contemporary efforts to examine forced sexual intercourse, sufficient information has been gleaned to permit the development of a tentative model that can be used to guide further research. The model addresses only behavior that has generally been characterized as date or acquaintance rape and does not address stranger rape, spousal rape, or predatory rape.

The model advanced here suggests that some forms of forced sexual intercourse should be examined in the context of courtship or dating. *Courtship* is defined as a set of activities that are undertaken with the intent of establishing a fairly permanent relationship. While some undetermined portion of dating is primarily temporary and recreational in nature, much of dating has a courtship function. Participants in recreational dating are, in many instances, evaluating their partners in terms of potential suitability as long-term partners. Dating is an activity that leads to courtship when a potential partner is identified. While this shift in emphasis is usually not formally noted, most of those who actively date are aware of the potential in their activity.

A couple progresses from casual dating to a committed, long-term relatively permanent relationship in a process that can be characterized by degrees of increasing intimacy. Both partners tend to assume that, at some point, sexual intimacy will become part of the relationship as the relationship matures. For most couples this assumption is not overtly recognized, the stages through which a relationship moves to maturity are unspecified, and the circumstances under which sexual intimacy will occur are unaddressed. The process, in terms of increasing commitment, is one of advancing and retreating as the relationship moves toward the development of a relatively permanent relationship. Forced sexual intercourse can occur when the process of relationship formation gets out of control.

In Western society, women are expected to control the degree of sexual intimacy at each stage in the development of the relationship. Men are expected to seek increasing degrees of sexual intimacy as a relationship develops and women are expected to resist male pressure until the relationship matures to the point at which the woman feels comfortable committing to sexual intimacy. Women have personal standards that must be met before they are willing to engage in increased sexual intimacy, particularly sexual intercourse. Couples generally do not discuss the conditions that must be met before complete sexual intimacy becomes part of the relationship. While these standards are individual, they can include such things as determination with a high degree of certainty by the woman that this man is the person with whom she wishes to establish a permanent relationship: he will not abuse her at some later date, he is as committed to her as she is to him, and he (as well as her friends, his friends, and significant others) will not label her negatively if she agrees to complete sexual intimacy. Men who are aware that such standards exist usually are not aware of the standards held by the person with whom they are seeking to establish a relatively permanent relationship.

"Real" men are expected to be aggressive. Men who express an unwillingness to be physically aggressive generally are negatively labeled. Aggression by men in the courtship process produces a situation in which men assertively attempt to move the courtship process to increasing levels of sexual intimacy while women resist these efforts in favor of a more deliberate and cautious development of the relationship. Men place pressure on women to move forward with commitment to the relationship while women want to move forward, but not as fast as the men are requesting. Moving toward sexual intimacy is an interactive process frequently involving trial and error, or advancing and retreating from complete sexual intimacy as the couple works to develop a long-term, stable, relatively permanent relationship. An out-of-control situation may develop that can produce forced sexual intercourse when unclear expectations result in unacceptable behavior, biological arousal reduces rational behavior for one or for both parties, or the level of male aggression is greater than the woman anticipated.

Some women consent to sexual intimacy when they do not really want to be intimate (Walker, 1997). There are a number of circumstances under which unwilling consent is given. This behavior may be more common in established sexually intimate relationships. Once a relationship has moved to a level including sexual intimacy, the man may desire sexual intimacy at times when the woman does not or more frequently than the woman prefers. Women sometimes will agree to sexual intimacy when they would rather not in order to meet the man's needs. In cases in which a relationship is developing, at times a woman may hesitate to commit to complete sexual intimacy although she has decided that she will become sexually intimate at some point in the relationship with the man she is dating. As the relationship develops, she may respond to the man's pressure to agree to sexual intimacy before she is certain that she is ready for the relationship to move to that particular level of intimacy. Men generally believe that, if they are persistent, some women will consent when they are not certain about their decision. Some men are not sufficiently sensitive to realize that they are forcing the women with whom they have a relationship to be sexually intimate.

The factors that have been advanced as important to a model which seeks to explain incidents of nonpredatory forced sexual intercourse include: (1) the relationship formation process in which couples become increasingly intimate, (2) role expectations for aggressive behavior in courtship (more rapid development of the relationship), (3) role expectations for women to resist male aggression in courtship (less rapid development of the relationship), (4) women control (decide) when the relationship will move to more intense levels of sexual intimacy, (5) women have standards (conditions) that must be satisfied before they agree to sexual intimacy, (7) some women will consent to sexual intimacy when they don't really want to be sexually intimate, and (8) men are aware that women will consent at times when they don't want to be sexually intimate, but men are usually not aware of or sensitive to the standards or conditions that women hold for their own commitment to sexual intimacy. When these factors are applied to instances of forced sexual intercourse in courtship and dating, a number of patterns emerge (Johnson & Sigler, 1997).

In some situations, both the man and the woman anticipate and are moving toward eventual complete sexual intimacy. They engage in preliminary sexually intimate behavior, and, at a point in the relationship, the situation gets out of control. The man forces the woman to have sex while they are engaging in consensual sexual activity. In these cases, it is probable that neither the man nor the woman will label the behavior as rape, psychological damage will be minimal, and both the man and the woman may choose to continue to develop a long-term relationship and have positive images of each other (Johnson & Sigler, 1997).

In some instances, the woman considers intense sexual intimacy a possibility at some point, but she has not committed to the development of a permanent relationship at that point. She engages in some exploratory sexual activity even though she may not antic-ipate a permanent relationship. During a period of intimacy, the man forces the woman to have intercourse. In these cases, both the woman and the man might or might not define the incident as rape. If the woman defines the incident as rape, she will terminate the relation-ship and have mixed or negative opinions of the man. Psychological damage will be moderate to high. If the woman does not define the incident as rape, she may continue the relationship and have mixed opinions of the man. Psychological damage will be low to moderate (Johnson & Sigler, 1997).

In some situations, the woman will hold a value that prohibits sexual intercourse before a firm permanent relationship is established, but she engages in some intimate sex-ual behavior in the process of seeking a relationship. During a period of consensual sexual activity the man forces the woman to have sexual intercourse. In these cases, the woman will define the incident as rape and the man may or may not define the incident as rape. The woman will terminate the relationship and have mixed but predominately negative opinions of the man in that there are characteristics that she found attractive that were not related to his sexual aggression. She will not continue the relationship and psychological damage, in most cases, will be high (Johnson & Sigler, 1997).

This model suggests that the development of an agreement to engage in consensual sexual intercourse in a dating or courtship setting is a negotiated process in which the woman grants sexual access to the man when specific personal conditions (personal stan-dards) are met. It is acceptable for men to actively pursue sexual intercourse, and this pur-suit is not channeled by the woman's conditions for agreeing to sexual intimacy because these conditions (woman's expectations) frequently are unclear.

The development of a relatively stable intimate relationship involves exploratory sexual behavior in which the couple approaches but does not necessarily engage in sexual intercourse. If this process gets out of control, forced sexual intercourse might occur because the man is larger and stronger or because the woman cannot manage to withdraw without permanently damaging a relationship she may want to preserve. When forced sex-ual intercourse occurs in this context, the woman may accept responsibility for the out-come, and the man might see this as an acceptable or anticipated outcome.

This model addresses only forced sexual intercourse that occurs during a legitimate pursuit of a relatively long-term relationship and does not address forced sexual inter-course labeled as predatory, blitz, or confidence rape. In the latter, a male predator engages in dating or courtship behavior to gain a position from which he can relatively safely force a woman to submit to sexual intercourse. He does not intend to develop a long-term rela-tionship but pretends to pursue a relationship in order to gain sexual access by trick or fraud. If his efforts to gain consensual sexual access are not successful, he might use what-ever degree of force is necessary to gain sexual access. The characterization of this behav-ior as courtship behavior provides some protection from sanctioning for the offender. It should be noted that research to date has not indicated that women are able to distinguish between the predatory rapist and the legitimate suitor until after they have been success-fully victimized, and it is possible that they may not be certain after their victimization. This behavior can be explained more successfully by traditional theories of rape than by a courtship model of forced sexual intercourse.

The model will not effectively address marital rape or rape that occurs in relatively stable relationships in which sexual intercourse has been accepted as a normal part of the relationship. While sufficient empirical attention has not been devoted to an examination of these phenomena to permit preliminary model development, it is probable that models that stress dominance and control rather than sexual access are more appropriate than other models. Power and dominance or sexual needs may drive the offender but the behavior occurs in the context of a relatively permanent relationship and may be better understood in the context of the dynamics of the relationship, particularly the dynamics of conflict resolution, than in the context of rape or the context of courtship and dating.

The courtship model advanced here will not effectively address situations in which sexual intercourse is a potential form of recreation rather than an activity that occurs in a relatively permanent relationship. In situations in which both the man and the woman define sexual intercourse as a recreational option in casual dating, the behavioral patterns might be similar but accelerated with different interpretations of expectations and processes held by the actors. If a man forces a woman to have sex in this setting, new models might need to be developed or traditional theories of rape may be more effective in understanding and investigating the behavior. Little empirical attention has been directed toward these phenomena, so any assessment is pure speculation at this point.

The model advanced here is a simplification of a very complex system of interactions that comprise dating and courtship. This model can be expressed in 13 propositions. The following research was designed to test these hypotheses.

METHODOLOGY

History of the Research

The first study in this line of research gathered data with a questionnaire that we administered to a random sample of classes (about 200 subjects). The results were sufficiently different from what had been expected that we conducted a validity assessment (administered a second questionnaire to the subjects asking if they had answered the first survey truthfully). The results were tentatively accepted as valid. We substantially revised the first instrument, dropping a number of variables that did not appear to be relevant and adding variables that appeared to be indicated by the original data. Results from the second, substantially larger sample were similar to the results in the first survey and supported some of the premises developed from the original data. A typology of forced sexual intercourse was developed and a model addressing forced sexual intercourse in dating or courtship was developed. The third study, reported here, expanded the second study by adding direct tests of the courtship model developed from the second study and by expanding the measurement of the impact of alcohol. The analysis presented here assesses the degree of support found for the forced sexual intercourse courtship model.

Design

A semistructured questionnaire was administered to a random sample of men and women attending classes. Fifty classes were selected from the list of all classes offered at the university during the spring semester of 1998. Of these classes, six were not "classes," per se, in that no students were registered (work such as thesis, dissertation, or independent study), and six instructors denied access to their classes—APR 431, GBA 490, HY 101,

HY 203, HY400, and MUA 364. Data were collected during regular class time from 32 of the remaining 38 classes in the classrooms assigned to the courses. In six classes (158 subjects) the instructors permitted the researchers to distribute the instruments with the verbal protocol and campus mail envelopes addressed to the researchers.

One hundred and two of the 158 mailed questionnaires were returned. Six instruments distributed in classes were returned blank. All other instruments were returned in usable form. The sample consisted of 668 subjects. No attempt was made to gather data from students who were absent on the day the instruments were administered.

Collection of Data

All class data collection was conducted by a male–female pair of researchers. Male subjects were asked to sit in the front of the room and female subjects were asked to sit in the back of the room to reduce stress and anxiety that might have occurred among the women if they had been observed by the men while answering the sensitive questions in the instrument. The female researcher gathered data from the female subjects, and the male researcher gathered data from the male subjects. In all data-gathering sessions human subject safety provisions were followed, and questions about the study were answered following the data collection.

The Instrument

The instrument was 14 pages long and was administered in two forms: one for women and one for men. The first page contained the human subject safety protocols and the beginning of the demographic section. The next section measured dating activity including reasons for dating, degree of sexual intimacy in dating, conditions under which consensual sexual intercourse occurs, and factors influencing the decision to be sexually intimate. The next section measured incidents of forced sexual intercourse, an expanded set of scales for measuring the nature of the impact of alcohol on forced sexual intercourse, incidence of other unacceptable sexual behaviors, and an extensive measurement of variables related to victimization for those subjects who were victims or offenders. The final section presented the formal propositions for endorsement for self and others in terms of percent of time the proposition was true.

The women's instrument and the men's instrument were identical for every scale. The only differences were the change of pronouns, and when appropriate, the target (your date). Men were asked about acts committed against women and women were asked about acts committed against them. The subjects appeared to understand the items and worked diligently until completion of the instrument in all classes.

FINDINGS

The Sample

The sample approximated the population with sample measures varying less than ±3% from population measures for race, gender, and class standing. The sample was 51% male, 14% African American, 78% White, and 6% other non-White. Freshman, sophomores, and juniors each constituted 22% with seniors representing 16% of the sample and with 13% of the subjects reporting that they were graduate students. The average age was 20 (mean = 22.02, median = 20, mode = 19).

TABLE 1   Reported Rates of Forced Sexual Intercourse

	Rates		
Type of incident	# subjects	%	# incidents
Attempted forced sexual intercourse on a date in 1997*			
Women	46	15.6%	242
Men	9	3.0	55
Forced sexual intercourse on a date in 1997*			
Women	20	6.8	209[a]
Men	2	0.6	3
Forced sexual intercourse not on a date in 1997**			
Women	8	2.7	17
Men	3	1.0	4
Forced sex on a date lifetime			
Women	33	11.2	55
Men	4	1.3	29
Forced sex not on a date lifetime*			
Women	25	9.2	49
Men	6	2.1	49
Total forced sexual intercourse*			
Women	56	17.4	330
Men	8	2.3	85

[a]Five women reported 174 incidents.
*$p \leq .001$.
**$p = .098$.

Rates of reported victimization for this study were similar to rates reported in the two prior surveys for this campus and for rates reported from other studies found in refereed sources (Sigler & Johnson, 1998). Approximately 17% of the women reported that they had been forced to have sex at some point in their life, 7% reported that they had been forced to have sex on a date in the prior year, and 3% reported that they had been forced to have sex not on a date in the prior year (see Table 1).

Testing the Propositions

The propositions were tested with two types of items. In the first third of the instrument, subjects were asked for their beliefs about a series of behaviors related to courtship (expressed as the percentage of time that they occurred) and for reports of their own behavior. Most of these statements had been used in the prior study with the structure of the item and its placement in the instrument retained from the second study instrument. At the end of the instrument, the subjects were asked to provide an endorsement of the specific propositions expressed in terms of the percentage of time that the proposition was true for both the subjects themselves and for people in general. The responses to these items are presented in Tables 2 and 3 and are the data presented to provide estimates of support for the propositions. Responses are expressed in terms of specific endorsements (true or false, yes or no) with nonresponse reported for each comparison so that the estimates of support are conservative. In addition, the mean percent of endorsement for the items and the percent of victims responding yes or true to the items are presented.

1. *Participation in sexual intercourse is fairly common.* Approximately 68% of the men and 66% of the women reported that they are presently sexually active, with men reporting that the sexual activity is consensual and wanted more frequently (mean = 86.3%) than women (mean = 56.7%) and less likely to be consensual but unwanted (mean = 10.5%) than women (mean = 26.9%). Both men and women endorsed the proposition as true for other people (86%) at higher levels than for themselves (64.5%).

2. *Women occasionally consent to sexual intercourse when they would prefer to abstain.* One-third of the men and half of the women reported that when they had sex the women consented even though they did not want sex (10.5% of the time for men and 26.9% for women) at that time. Approximately 80% of the subjects endorsed the specific proposition as true for others (half of the time other couples had sex) and 40% endorsed the proposition as true for themselves (41% of the time).

3. *Men know that women occasionally consent to sexual intercourse when they would prefer to abstain.* There is no indirect measure of this proposition. Approximately 78% of the subjects endorsed the proposition as true for others, with men reporting that this was true more often (55.5% of the time the couples had sex) than women (48.3%). Fewer subjects endorse the proposition as valid for themselves (40%).

4. *The decision to engage in sexual intercourse is something women control.* Relatively high percentages of subjects believe that both women and men control sexual access at times for both themselves and for others. Men believe that women control access more frequently (mean = 67.6%) than women (mean = 56.7%) while women believe that men control access more frequently (mean = 50.7%) than men (41.6%), with no significant differences for themselves in terms of frequency of occurrence (men control 50% and women control 64%). Approximately 81% of the subjects endorsed the specific proposition for others 59% of the time while 72% of the subjects endorsed the proposition as true for themselves 75% of the time.

5. *Sexual intercourse is something men seek to gain from women.* Approximately 88% of the subjects reported that other people believe that men seek to gain sexual access a little less than two-thirds of the time and 84% reported that this was true for them two-thirds of the time. Almost 87% of the subjects believe that men hope to gain sexual access on a date two-thirds of the time and 60% state that this is true for them 48% of the time. Approximately 77% of the subjects endorsed the proposition as true for others and 51% endorsed it as true for themselves.

6. *Men are expected to actively pursue women's consent to sexual intercourse.* Nearly 85% of the subjects stated that men attempt to talk their dates into sex a little more than half the time and 55% of the subjects stated that it was true for them a little more than a third of the time. Three-fourths of the subjects endorsed the proposition as true for others two-thirds of the time and 53% endorsed it as true for themselves two-thirds of the time.

7. *Women are expected to resist the efforts of men to gain sexual access until specific individual conditions exist, even though they plan to consent at some point in the relationship.* Approximately 80% of the subjects believe that women resist men's efforts two-thirds of the time. Almost 87% report that women have personal standards and 85% report that they or their dates have personal standards that must be met before the woman will consent to intimate sexual relations. Nearly 71% endorse the proposition as true 62% of the time for others and 57% endorse the proposition as true for themselves two-thirds of the time.

8. *The presence and nature of these conditions is usually not explicit.* About 80% of the subjects believe that women tell their dates what personal standards they hold for sexual intimacy 42% of the time and 87% of the subjects state standards are stated 46% of the time in their personal relationships. Approximately 61% of the subjects endorsed the proposition as true occurring 60% of the time for others while 45% of the subjects stated that the standards are not explicit 57% of the time in their own relationships.

9. *In the process of developing a relationship, men and women engage in exploratory sexual behavior.* Close to 85% of the subjects stated that other people engage in exploratory sexual behavior 72% of the time and 68% of the subjects report that this occurs in their own personal relationships 64% of the time. Three-fourths of the subjects endorse the proposition for other couples with the behavior occurring 80% of the time. For their own behavior, 67% of the subjects endorse the proposition as true and applying to 75% of their relationships.

10. *Gaining/granting sexual access is an interactive process involving some degree of trial and error.* There is no indirect measure of this proposition. Approximately 71% of the subjects endorsed the proposition as true for others occurring 70% of the time. Nearly 58% of the subjects endorsed the proposition as true for their own relationships 68% of the time.

11. *On occasion the trial-and-error process produces an out-of-control situation that leads to forced sexual intercourse.* Approximately 80% of the men and 84% of the women reported that men are likely to lose control in sexually intimate situations (42% of the time for men and 48% for women). For their own behavior, 7% of the men report losing control on at least one occasion while 26.7% of the women report an out-of-control event. Nearly 18% of the women and 4% of the men stated that unwanted sex occurred when the man lost control, and 9% of the women and less than 1% of the men stated that force was used in these cases. About 83% of the subjects stated that women lose control in intimate exchanges reporting that it occurs about a third of the time (men 33.8%, women 38%). Close to 25% of the women reported that they had lost control (men for their dates, 22.6%); 25.2% reported that this had led to unwanted sex (men, 8.2%),

and 6.8% reported that the men had used force (men, 1.2%). Almost 67% of the subjects endorse the proposition as true for others 35% of the time with 11% of the men and 22% of the women indicating that the proposition was true for them occurring a third of the time.

12. *If both actors anticipate sexual access, the question is one of timing, and they engage in some exploratory sexual behavior leading to an out-of-control situation, neither the man nor the woman will define the incident as rape.* About 61% of the subjects endorsed the proposition as true for others occurring 55% of the time. A third of the subjects reported that it was true for them occurring 60% of the time.

13. *If the woman does not anticipate sexual access at that point in the relationship but engages in some exploratory sexual activity leading to an out-of-control situation, the woman and the man may or may not define the incident as rape.* Approximately 62% of the subjects endorsed the proposition as true for others occurring 54% of the time. A third of the subjects reported that it was true for them occurring 60% of the time.

14. *If the woman chooses not to engage in sexual intercourse but engages in some exploratory sexual behavior in the process of seeking a relationship and the situation gets out of control, she will define the incident as rape, and the man may or may not define the incident as rape.* Nearly 65% of the subjects endorsed the proposition as true for others occurring 61% of the time. A third of the subjects reported that it was true for them occurring 63% of the time. The percent of the time that the statements or propositions were true for victims is reported. Almost all of the victims (base 56) responded to the behavior and belief items. The level of endorsement for all of the items was higher for victims than for women in the sample. A third of the victims chose to not complete the proposition section. Those who did consistently endorsed the propositions as true at higher rates than women in the sample.

TABLE 2   **Endorsement of General Statements Related to Forced Sexual Intercourse by Sex**

	Proposition is						victim[a]		
	no/never		true/yes		no response				
Proposition	#	%	#	%	#	%	# true	Mean	Mean[b]
Proposition 1									
Sexually active									
Men	92	27.0%	231	67.7%	36	5.3%	na	na	na
Women	94	29.2	212	65.8	16	5.0	na	na	na
% time wanted consensual sex									
Men	23	6.7%	234	68.6%	84	24.6%	na	na	86.3*
Women	24	7.5	216	67.1	82	25.5	53	94.6	69.5

(continued)

TABLE 2 (Continued)

| | Proposition is | | | | | | victim[a] | | |
| | no/never | | true/yes | | no response | | | | |
Proposition	#	%	#	%	#	%	# true	Mean	Mean[b]
Proposition 2									
% time consensual unwanted sex*									
Men	120	35.2%	120	35.2%	101	29.6%	na	na	10.5*
Women	66	20.5	159	49.4	97	30.1	52	92.9	26.9
Proposition 4									
% time women control sexual access									
Men	1	0.3%	307	90.0%	33	9.7%	na	na	67.6*
Women	1	0.3	300	93.2	21	6.5	54	96.4	56.7
% time men control sexual access*									
Men	32	9.4%	276	80.9%	33	9.7%	na	na	41.6*
Women	12	3.7	287	89.1	23	7.1	53	94.6	50.7
% time for subjects women control sexual access									
Men	26	7.6%	260	76.2%	55	16.1%	na	na	66.2
Women	20	6.2	242	75.2	60	18.6	54	96.4	63.4
% time for subjects men control sexual access									
Men	71	20.8%	219	64.2%	51	15.0%	na	na	49.1
Women	58	18.0	191	59.3	63	19.6	54	96.4	50.3
Proposition 5									
Men hope to gain sexual access from women on date									
Men	9	2.6%	287	84.2%	45	13.2%	na	na	64.9
Women	6	1.9	296	91.9	20	6.2	55	98.2	64.1
For subjects men sought to gain sexual access from women on date*									
Men	110	32.3%	180	52.8%	51	15.0%	na	na	47.1
Women	68	21.1	220	68.3	34	10.6	54	96.4	48.4
Sex is something that men seek to gain from women									
Men	4	1.2%	295	86.5%	42	12.3%	na	na	61.9
Women	4	1.2	296	91.9	22	6.8	54	96.4	63.5
Men are expected to seek sex from women									
Male	9	2.6%	285	83.6%	47	13.8%	na	na	68.7
Female	9	2.8	281	87.3	32	9.9	53	94.6	66.2
Proposition 6									
Men actively seek to talk women into sex									
Men	7	2.1%	279	81.8%	55	16.1%	na	na	54.8
Women	5	1.6	290	90.1	27	8.4	53	94.6	53.8

For subjects men tried to talk date into sex*

Men	129	37.8%	159	46.6%	53	15.5%	na	na	39.6
Women	86	26.7	207	64.3	29	9.0	54	96.4	36.7

Proposition 7

What % of time do women resist men's efforts to gain sex

Men	11	3.2%	268	78.6%	62	18.2%	na	na	63.3
Women	9	2.8	270	83.9	41	12.7	52	92.9	63.5

What % of women have personal standards that
must be met before they will agree to sex

Male	2	0.5%	296	86.8%	43	12.6%	na	na	67.3
Female	5	1.6	286	88.8	31	9.6	52	92.9	64.4

Do you (does your date) have standards*

Men	0	0%	296	86.8%	45	13.2%	na	na	68.4
Women	12	3.7	271	84.2	39	12.1	56	100	na

Proposition 8

How often did you (your date) tell standards

Men	0	0%	294	86.2%	47	13.8%	na	na	43.5
Women	0	0	287	89.1	35	10.9	54	96.4	49.4

How often do women tell dates standards*

Men	30	8.8%	252	73.9%	59	17.3%	na	na	41.6
Women	11	3.4	278	86.3	33	10.2	53	94.6	42.0

Proposition 9

Couples engage in exploratory sexual behavior*

Men	5	1.5%	287	84.2%	54	15.8%	na	na	71.6
Women	11	3.4	276	85.7	35	10.9	51	91.1	72.3

Subjects engage in exploratory sexual behavior

Men	24	7.0%	233	68.3%	84	24.6%	na	na	67.2
Women	27	8.4	218	67.7	77	23.9	51	91.1	61.7

Proposition 11

How likely are men to lose control*

Men	10	2.9%	273	80.1%	58	17.1%	na	na	41.9
Women	6	1.9	272	84.5	44	13.7	55	94.6	47.8

Male date lost control*

Men	267	78.3%	24	7.0%	55	16.1%	na	na	na
Women	190	59.0	86	26.7	46	14.3	53	94.6	na

Unwanted sex occurred*

Men	171	50.1%	15	4.4%	155	45.5%	na	na	na
Women	141	43.8	60	18.6	121	37.6	33	na	na

He used force*

Men	173	50.7%	4	0.3%	164	48.1%	na	na	na
Women	145	45.0	30	9.3	147	45.7	19	na	na

(continued)

TABLE 2   (Continued)

| Proposition | Proposition is | | | | | | victim[a] | | Mean[b] |
| | no/never | | true/yes | | no response | | | | |
	#	%	#	%	#	%	# true	Mean	
How likely are women to lose control									
Men	0	0%	280	82.1%	61	17.9%	na	na	33.8**
Women	0	0	273	84.8	49	15.2	54	44.3	38.0
Female date lost control*									
Men	209	61.3%	77	22.6%	55	16.1%	na	na	na
Women	206	64.0	81	25.2	35	10.9	27	na	na
Unwanted sex occurred*									
Men	237	69.5%	28	8.2%	76	22.3%	na	na	na
Women	174	54.0	81	25.2	67	20.8	28	na	na
She used force*									
Men	193	56.6%	4	1.2%	144	42.2%	na	na	na
Women	175	54.3	22	6.8	125	38.8	28	na	na

[a]Mean % of support for those victims who endorsed the proposition as valid; missing cases ranged from 0 to 5 (8.9%).

[b]Mean % of support for those subjects who endorsed the proposition as valid; victims are included.

*$p \leq .01$ level for t-test or Pearson's test for chi-square.

** $p \leq .05$ level for t-test or Pearson's test for chi-square.

TABLE 3   **Endorsement of Specific Propositions Related to Forced Sexual Intercourse by Sex**

| Proposition | Proposition is | | | | | | victim[a] | | Mean[b] |
| | false | | true | | no response | | | | |
	#	%	#	%	#	%	# true	Mean	
Proposition 1									
Sex is common									
Men	3	0.01%	292	85.6%	46	13.5%	na	na	75.6
Women	2	0.01%	288	89.4	32	9.9	49	87.5	76.2
Sex is common for subject									
Men	59	17.3%	228	66.9%	54	15.8%	na	na	67.1
Women	74	23.0	199	61.8	49	15.2	46	82.1	62.1

Proposition 2

Women consent when prefer to abstain*

| Men | 17 | 5.0% | 265 | 77.7% | 59 | 17.3% | na | na | 49.4 |
| Women | 6 | 1.8 | 277 | 86.0 | 39 | 12.1 | 46 | 82.1 | 52.0 |

Subjects consent when prefer to abstain

| Men | 142 | 41.6% | 134 | 39.3% | 65 | 19.1% | na | na | 40.2 |
| Women | 134 | 41.6 | 137 | 42.5 | 51 | 15.8 | 44 | 78.6 | 41.7 |

Proposition 3

Men know that women consent when prefer to abstain

| Men | 5 | 1.5% | 263 | 77.1% | 61 | 17.9% | na | na | 55.5** |
| Women | 13 | 4.0 | 256 | 79.5 | 53 | 16.5 | 43 | 76.8 | 48.3 |

For subjects men know women consent when prefer to abstain*

| Men | 119 | 34.9% | 151 | 44.3% | 69 | 20.2% | na | na | 49.0 |
| Women | 136 | 42.2 | 117 | 36.3 | 69 | 21.4 | 40 | 71.4 | 47.4 |

Proposition 4

Women control sexual access

| Men | 11 | 3.2% | 274 | 80.4% | 56 | 16.4% | na | na | 62.7 |
| Women | 8 | 2.5 | 266 | 82.6 | 48 | 14.9 | 46 | 82.1 | 55.9 |

For subjects women control sexual access*

| Men | 44 | 12.9% | 234 | 68.6% | 63 | 18.5% | na | na | 76.1 |
| Women | 24 | 7.5 | 248 | 77.0 | 50 | 15.5 | 46 | 82.1 | 76.8 |

Proposition 5

Men seek to gain sexual access from women

| Men | 21 | 6.2% | 261 | 76.5% | 59 | 17.3% | na | na | 61.1 |
| Women | 17 | 5.3 | 254 | 78.9 | 51 | 15.8 | 45 | 80.4 | 61.6 |

For subjects men seek to gain sexual access from women

| Men | 91 | 26.7% | 184 | 54.0% | 66 | 19.4% | na | na | 51.7 |
| Women | 97 | 30.1 | 157 | 48.8 | 68 | 21.1 | 41 | 73.2 | 51.7 |

Proposition 6

Men expected to actively pursue women's consent

| Men | 20 | 5.9% | 250 | 73.3% | 71 | 20.8% | na | na | 63.7 |
| Women | 15 | 4.7 | 253 | 78.6 | 54 | 16.8 | 41 | 73.2 | 63.6 |

For subjects men expected to pursue women's consent

| Men | 78 | 22.9% | 191 | 56.0% | 72 | 21.1% | na | na | 63.2 |
| Women | 86 | 26.7 | 162 | 50.3 | 74 | 23.0 | 39 | 69.6 | 67.6 |

Proposition 7

Women resist men's pursuit until personal conditions are met

| Men | 18 | 5.3% | 236 | 69.2% | 87 | 25.5% | na | na | 62.1 |
| Women | 15 | 4.7 | 235 | 73.0 | 72 | 22.4 | 40 | 71.4 | 61.7 |

(continued)

TABLE 3   (Continued)

Proposition	Proposition is						victim[a]		
	false		true		no response				
	#	%	#	%	#	%	# true	Mean	Mean[b]
Proposition 7 (cont.)									
For subjects women resist men's pursuit until conditions are met									
Men	60	17.6%	189	55.4%	92	27.0%	na	na	63.9**
Women	48	14.9	188	58.3	86	26.7	39	69.6	73.1
Proposition 8									
Conditions are not explicit									
Men	24	7.0%	204	59.8%	113	33.1%	na	na	62.0
Women	18	5.6	201	62.4	103	32.0	37	66.1	57.9
For subjects conditions are not explicit									
Men	69	20.2%	156	45.7%	116	34.0%	na	na	58.2
Women	68	21.1	147	45.7	107	33.2	38	67.9	57.0
Proposition 9									
Couples engage in exploratory sexual behavior									
Men	11	3.2%	254	74.5%	76	22.3%	na	na	80.3
Women	6	1.9	255	79.2	61	20.8	41	73.2	80.7
Subjects engage in exploratory sexual behavior									
Men	28	8.2%	233	68.3%	80	23.5%	na	na	75.3
Women	34	10.6	215	66.8	73	22.7	41	73.2	74.8
Proposition 10									
Approaching sexual intercourse is a trial-and-error process									
Men	14	4.1%	246	72.1%	81	23.8%	na	na	70.4
Women	10	3.1	229	71.1	83	25.8	40	71.4	70.1
Subjects approaching sexual intercourse is trial and error									
Men	49	14.4%	206	60.4%	84	24.6%	na	na	68.4
Women	59	18.3	180	55.9	89	27.6	39	69.6	67.7
Proposition 11									
Trial-and-error process can lead to forced sexual intercourse									
Men	28	8.2%	229	67.2%	84	24.6%	na	na	35.1
Women	23	7.1	218	67.7	81	25.2	39	69.6	34.6
Subjects' trial and error has led to forced sexual intercourse**									
Men	220	64.5%	38	11.1%	83	24.3%	na	na	37.5
Women	168	52.2	71	22.0	83	25.8	39	69.6	29.6

Proposition 12

If both believe trial and error leads to forced sex not labeled rape

Men	35	10.3%	205	60.1%	101	29.6%	na	na	50.6**
Women	26	8.1	201	62.4	95	29.5	36	64.3	60.4

For subjects if both believe trial and error leads
to forced sex, not labeled rape*

Men	138	40.5%	98	28.7%	105	30.8%	na	na	59.0
Women	95	29.5	115	35.7	112	34.8	34	60.7	62.5

Proposition 13

If woman does not anticipate sex at that point both may define forced sex as rape**

Men	30	8.8%	203	59.5%	108	31.7%	na	na	49.5**
Women	23	7.1	211	65.5	88	27.3	43	76.8	58.4

For subjects if she does not anticipate sex at that point both may define forced sex as rape*

Men	129	37.8%	99	29.0%	113	33.1%	na	na	58.8
Women	80	24.8	139	43.2	103	32.0	39	69.6	64.6

Proposition 14

If woman wants to remain a virgin but does trial and error she will label forced sex rape, he may label it rape**

Men	29	8.5%	209	61.3%	103	30.2%	na	na	62.1
Women	14	4.3	224	69.6	84	26.1	41	73.2	60.1

For subjects if she wants to remain a virgin but does trial and error she will label forced sex rape, he may label it rape.

Men	128	37.5%	97	28.4%	116	34.0%	na	na	60.1
Women	75	23.3	152	47.2	95	29.5	39	69.6	65.8

[a]Mean % of support for those victims who endorsed the proposition as valid; missing cases ranged from 7 (12.5%) to 18 (32.1%).

[b]Mean % of support for those victims who endorsed the proposition as valid; victims are included.

*$p \leq .01$ level for *t*-test (five additional comparisons were significant when subjects who believed the propositions were false (–0%) were included).

**$P < .05$ level for *t*-test.

SUMMARY

Forced sexual intercourse has been perceived as a single phenomenon throughout history. There has been a great deal of evolution in the reaction of the justice system with many acts of forced sexual intercourse that were considered private matters becoming criminalized. All forms of forced sexual intercourse have been defined as parts of a social problem that has emerged because changing social values regarding the roles of women and men in society and in intimate relationships have created a change in the degree of public interest in women's victimization.

Before effective responses to all forms of forced sexual intercourse can be developed, these phenomena must be understood. A first step in increasing understanding of the phenomena is to recognize that the same behaviors may be different phenomena in different social contexts. Some forms of forced sexual intercourse occur between relatively intimate partners and that one form of forced sexual intercourse might be substantially different from other forms of forced sexual intercourse. That is, types of forced sexual intercourse must be examined in the social context in which they occur.

Rape consistently has been evaluated in terms of aggression, dominance, control, and violence rather than in terms of sexual access. Historically, rape has been a crime that has been condemned, if not effectively prosecuted. Reforms in the past decade have introduced changes in the law that create different levels of sexual assault and that make cases of sexual assault easier to prosecute successfully. Social concern that accompanied reform efforts on intimate violence as well as on forced sexual intercourse has focused attention on the prevalence and nature of forced sexual intercourse.

Most theories that attempt to explain rape treat rape as a single phenomenon. All forms of forced sexual intercourse are seen as the same thing. The feminist perspective argues that rape is a characteristic of male-dominated patriarchal societies. Threat of rape functions to control and dominate women, forcing them into passive-submissive roles.

Learning theories, from a number of perspectives, specify that the use of force in sexual encounters is learned in the same way that other behaviors and values are learned. The most prominent of these are drive-based, psychoanalytic theories that are related to the work of Bandura (1973). Most other learning theorists, sociologists, and criminologists have not applied their perspectives directly to the explanation of forced sexual intercourse.

Sociobiologists argue that males who use force in sexual intercourse will be more likely to pass on their genes to future generations in that access to the greatest number of partners maximizes gene survival. Women, on the other hand, maximize the transmission of their genes to future generations by attracting males who will remain with them after insemination to care for the children. Baron and Straus (1989) added models based on social disorganization and on legitimate use of violence to other existing traditional models to advance an integrated model to explain rape. While their model effectively combines the elements of many of the traditional theories, it still treats rape as a single phenomenon in which a male intends to use force to obtain sex from an unwilling resisting female who sees herself as being raped.

The argument advanced in this chapter is that there are types or sets of related forms of forced sexual intercourse that are sufficiently different as to require separate explanatory models if the phenomena are to be effectively understood and examined. In rape, a man forces a woman whom he does not know or whom he does not know very well to have sex with him. In spousal rape, a man who is in a fairly long-term sexual relationship with a woman forces her to have sex. In predatory rape, a man pretends to engage in a legitimate dating relationship with a woman in order to manipulate her into a position in which he can force her to have sex with him. In courtship and dating forced sexual intercourse, a man and a woman are developing a long-term relationship. In the process, one or both of the actors loses control and the man forces the woman to have sex.

An expanded model for forced sexual intercourse in dating or courtship has been developed that can be used to frame future research in this area. This model assumes that the process of establishing a relatively permanent or long-term relationship involves progressively more intimate interaction as the relationship matures with sexual intercourse anticipated at some point in the relationship. The point at which sexual intercourse becomes part of the relationship and the conditions that must be met before this level of commitment to the relationship is accepted is determined by the woman. As the relationship moves to increasingly intimate contact, the potential for loss of control and the use of force increases. In these cases, neither the man nor the woman is likely to define the behavior as rape.

Substantial support was found for the model. All of the propositions were endorsed as true in some cases by 60 to 89% of the subjects. It is noted that fewer subjects indicated that the propositions were true for themselves than for the general public in every instance (39 to 66%—forced sex occurred for about 16%). Similar results were found when the beliefs and reported behaviors implied by the propositions were examined with some interesting variations from instances in which the measures addressed broader parameters. Both men and women were believed to control sexual access at times (men 85% true and women 92% true). The means are relatively complementary with women believed to control access 60% of the time and men believed to control access 46% of the time. For telling standards, the subjects endorsed the proposition stating that the standards were not explicit at a higher rate for others (60%) than for themselves (45%), but when asked about their behavior they report that they tell (are told) standards more often (true 87%) than others tell (true 80%).

Support for the most confusing issue in this line of research—why don't women label some cases of forced sexual intercourse as rape?—was assessed (see Table 3). Three specific propositions regarding labeling were offered to and endorsed by the subjects. These scales are preliminary at best and must be refined in future research before we will be confident that we have identified the primary variables. These data simply provided some support for the contention that when force is used in an out-of-control increasingly intimate environment, some women and some men may not label the use of force as rape.

This model will be refined and assessed through empirical examination. As the model develops, a more thorough and accurate understanding of the use of force in intimate relationships will emerge. As conceptualization of the phenomena becomes more thorough and accurate, more effective responses will be developed for the justice system, and more effective educational materials can be developed to reduce the victimization of women at the hands of those with whom they seek to develop long-term, relatively permanent relationships.

REFERENCES

ADAMEC, C. S., & ADAMEC, R. E. (1981). Aggression by men against women: Adaptation or aberration. *International Journal of Women's Studies, 1*, 1–21.

AMIR, M. (1971). *Patterns in forcible rape.* Chicago: University of Chicago Press.

ARCHER, D., & GARTNER, R. (1984). *Violence and crime in cross-national perspective.* New Haven, CT: Yale University Press.

BANDURA, A. (1973). *Aggression: A social learning analysis.* Upper Saddle River, NJ: Prentice Hall.

BARON, L., & STRAUS, M. A. (1984). Sexual stratification, pornography, and rape in the United States. In M. N. Malamuth & E. Donnerstein (Eds.), *Pornography and sexual aggression* (pp. 185–209). Orlando, FL: Academic Press.

BARON, L., & STRAUS, M. A. (1989). *Four theories of rape in American society: A state level analysis.* New Haven, CT: Yale University Press.

BARRY, K. (1979). *Female sexual slavery.* Upper Saddle River, NJ: Prentice Hall.

BATEMAN, A. J. (1948). Introsexual selection in drosophila. *Heredity, 2,* 349–368.

BENDERLY, B. L. (1982). Rape free or rape prone. *Science, 82(3),* 40–43.

BLUMER, H. (1937). Social organization and individual disorganization. *American Journal of Sociology, 42,* 871–877.

BONDURANT, B. (2001). University women's acknowledgement of rape: Individual, situational, and social factors. *Violence Against Women, 7*(3), 294–315.

BROWN, E. (1995). Changing the marital rape exception: I am chattel; hear me roar. *American Journal of Trial Advocacy, 18*(3), 657–671.

BROWNMILLER, S. (1975). *Against our will: Men, women, and rape.* New York: Simon & Schuster.

BULLOUGH, V. L. (1974). *The subordinate sex: A history of attitudes toward women.* Baltimore: Penguin Books.

Burt, M. R. (1980). Cultural myths and supports for rape. *Journal of Personality and Social Psychology, 38,* 217–234.

CAUFFMAN, E., FELDMAN, S., ARNETT JENSEN, L. & ARNETT, J. (2000). The (un)acceptability of violence against peers and dates. *Journal of Adolescent Research, 15*(6), 652–673.

CHAMOVE, A., HARLOW, H. F., & MITCHELL, G. D. (1967). Sex differences in the infant directed behavior of preadolescent rhesus monkeys. *Child Development, 38,* 329–355.

CHECK, J. V. P., & MALAMUTH, N. M. (1983a). Can participation in pornography experiments have positive effects? *Journal of Sex Research, 20,* 14–31.

CHECK, J. V. P., & MALAMUTH, N. M. (1983b). Sex-role stereotyping and reactions to stranger vs. acquaintance rape. *Journal of Personality and Social Psychology, 45,* 344–356.

CHERRY, F. (1983). Gender roles and sexual violence. In E. R. Allgeier & N. B. McCormick (Eds.), *Changing boundaries: Gender roles and sexual behavior* (pp. 245–260). Palo Alto, CA: Mayfield.

COWLING, M. (1998). *Date rape and consent.* Brookfield, VT: Ashgate.

CURTIS, L. A. (1975). *Violence, race, and culture.* Lexington, MA: Lexington Press.

DAILEY, A. (1986). To have and to hold: The marital rape exemption and the Fourteenth Amendment. *Harvard Law Review, 99,* 1255.

DALY, M., & Wilson, M. (1978). *Sex, evolution, and behavior.* North Scituate, MA: Duxbury Press.

DAWKINS, R. (1976). *The selfish gene.* New York: Oxford University Press.

DEUTSCH, H. (1944). *The psychology of women: Vol. 1. Girlhood.* New York: Bantam Books.

DOBASH, R. E. (1979). *Violence against wives: A case against the patriarchy.* New York: Free Press.

DONNERSTEIN, E., LINZ, D., & PENROD, S. (1987). *The question of pornography.* New York: Free Press.

DOYLE, D. P., & BURFEIND, J. W. (1994). *The University of Montana sexual victimization survey executive summary.* Missoula, MT: University of Montana.

DURDEN-SMITH, J., & deSIMONE, D. (1983). Sex and the brain. New York: Warner.

ELLIS, L. (1989). *Theories of rape: Inquiries into the causes of sexual aggression.* New York: Hemisphere.

EWOLDT, C. A., MONSON, C. M., LANGHINRICHSEN-ROHLING, J., & BINDERUP, T. (2000). Youth dating violence. *Adolescence, 35,* 455–465.

FELSON, R. B. (1992). *Motives for sexual coercion.* Annual meeting of the American Society of Criminology, Tucson, AZ.

FRIEDAN, B. (1963). *The feminine mystique.* New York: Norton.

GAGNON, J. H., & SIMON, W. (1973). *Sexual conduct: The sources of sexuality.* Chicago: Aldine.

GASTIL, R. D. (1971). Homicide and a regional culture of violence. *American Sociological Review, 36,* 412–427.

GIBSON, L., LINDEN, R., & JOHNSON, S. (1980). A situational theory of rape. *Canadian Journal of Criminology, 22,* 51–63.

GOTH, A. N. (1979). *Men who rape: The psychology of the offender.* New York: Plenum Press.

GROSS, A. M., WEED, N. C., & LAWSON, G. D. (1998). Magnitude scaling of intensity of sexual refusal behaviors in a date rape. *Violence Against Women, 4*(3), 329–343.

HACKNEY, S. (1969). Southern violence. *American Historical Review, 74,* 906–925.

HAGEN, R. (1979). *The bio-social factor.* Garden City, NJ: Doubleday.

HICKMAN, S. E., & MUEHLENHARD, C. L. (1999). By the semi-mystical appearance of a condom: How young women and men communicate sexual consent in heterosexual situations. *Journal of Sex Research, 36*(3), 258–272.

HIRD, M. J., & JACKSON, S. (2001). Where "angels" and "wusses" fear to tread: Sexual coercion in adolescent dating relationships. *Journal of Sociology, 37*(1), 27–43.

HOLDSTROM, L. L., & BURGESS, A. W. (1980). Sexual behavior of assailants during reported rapes. *Archives of Sexual Behavior, 9,* 427–439.

HUESMAN, L. R., & MALAMUTH, N. M. (1986). Media violence and antisocial behavior: An overview. *Journal of Social Issues, 42,* 1–6.

HUGGINS, M. D., & STRAUS, M. A. (1980). Violence and the social structure as reflected in children's books from 1850 to 1970. In M. A. Strauss & G. T. Hotaling (Eds.), *The social causes of husband-wife violence* (pp. 51–67), Minneapolis: University of Minnesota Press.

HUMPHREYS, T. P. (2001). *Sexual consent in heterosexual dating relationships: Attitudes and behaviours of university students.* Dissertation, University of Guelph, Guelph, Canada.

JOHNSON, D. G., PALILEO, G. J., & GRAY, N. B. (1992). Date rape on a southern campus: Reports from 1991. *Sociology and Social Research, 76*(2), 37–41.

JOHNSON, I. M., & SIGLER, R. T. (1997). *Forced sexual intercourse in intimate relationships.* Brookfield, VT: Ashgate.

KOSS, M. P., DINERO, T. E., SEIBEL, C. A., & COX, S. (1988), Stranger and acquaintance rape: Are there differences in the victim's experience? *Psychology of Women Quarterly, 12,* 1–24.

KUTCHINSKI, B. (1988). Towards an exploration of the decrease in registered sex crimes in Copenhagen. *Technical Report of the Commission on Obscenity and Pornography,* vol. 7. Washington, DC: United States Government Printing Office.

LAFAVE, W. R., & SCOTT, A. W. (1972). *Handbook on criminal law.* St. Paul, MN: West.

LAMBERT, W. W., TRIANDIS, L. M., & WOLF, M. (1959). Some correlates of beliefs in the malevolence and benevolence of supernatural beings: A dross cultural study. *Journal of Abnormal and Social Psychology, 58,* 162–169.

LESHNER, A. L. (1978). *An introduction to behavioral endocrinology.* New York: Oxford University Press

MALAMUTH, N. M. (1981). Rape proclivity among males. *Journal of Social Issues, 37*(4), 138–157.

MALAMUTH, N. M. (1984). Aggression against women. In N. A. Malamuth & E. Donnerstein (Eds.), *Pornography and sexual aggression.* Orlando, FL: Academic Press.

MALAMUTH, N. M. (1986). Predictors of naturalistic sexual aggression. *Journal of Personality and Social Psychology, 50,* 953–962.

MALAMUTH, N. M. (1988). Predicting laboratory aggression against female and male targets: Implications for sexual aggression. *Journal of Personality and Social Psychology, 50,* 330–340.

MALAMUTH, N., BRIERE, J., & CHECK, J. V. P. (1986). Sexual arousal in response to aggression: Ideology, aggressive, and sexual correlates. *Journal of Personality and Social Psychology, 50,* 330–340.

MALAMUTH, N., FESBACK, S., JAFFE, Y. (1977). Sexual arousal and aggression: Recent experiments and theoretical issues. *Journal of Social Issues, 33,* 110–133.

MARDOROSSIAN, CARINE M. (2002). Toward a new feminist theory of rape. *Signs: Journal of Women in Culture & Society, 27*(3), 743–776.

MARTINDALE, D. (1957). Social disorganization: The conflict of normative and empirical approaches. In H. Becker & A. Boskoff (Eds.), *Modern sociological theory in continuity and change* (pp. 340–367). New York: Rinehart & Winston.

MELLEN, S. L. (1981). *The evolution of love.* San Francisco: Freeman Press.

MESSNER, S. F. (1983). Regional and racial effects on the urban homicide rate: The subculture of violence revisited. *American Journal of Sociology, 88,* 997–1007.

MOWER, E. R. (1941). Methodological problems in social disorganization. *American Sociological Review, 6,* 639–649.

NELSON, E. (1982). Pornography and sexual aggression. In M. Yaffee & E. Nelson (Eds.), *The influence of pornography on behavior.* London: Academic Press.

OSMAN, S. L. (1999). Belief in token resistance and type of resistance as predictors of men's perceptions of date rape. *Journal of Sex Education and Therapy, 24*(3), 189–196.

PALMER, S. (1997). Rape in marriage and the European Convention on Human Rights. *Feminist Legal Studies,* 5, 91–97.

PERSELL, C. H. (1984). *Understanding society.* New York: Harper & Row.

QUINSEY, V. L. (1984). Sexual aggression: Studies of offenders against women. In D. Weisstub (Ed.), *Law and mental health: International perspectives* (Vol. 1). New York: Pergamon Press.

RICHARD, A. F., & SCHULMAN, S. R. (1982). Sociobiology: Primate field studies. *Annual Review in Anthropology, 11,* 231–255.

RIGER, S., & GORDON, M. T. (1981). The fear of rape: A study in social control. *Journal of Social Issues, 37*(4), 71–92.

RUSSELL, D. E. (1975). *The politics of rape: The victim's perspective,* New York: Stein and Day.

RUSSELL, D. E. H. (1984). *Sexual exploitation: Rape, child sexual abuse, and workplace harassment.* Beverly Hills, CA: Sage.

SANDAY, P. R. (1981). The socio-cultural context of rape: A cross-cultural study. *The Journal of Social Issues, 37,* 5–27.

SAWYER, R. G., PINCIARO, P. L., & JESSELL, J. K. (1998). Effects of coercion and verbal consent on university students' perception of date rape. *American Journal of Health Behavior, 22*(1), 46–53.

SCARPITTI, F., & SCARPITTI, E. (1977). Victims of rape. *Transaction, 14,* 29–32.

SCHWENDINGER, J., & SCHWENDINGER, H. (1985). Homo economics as the rapist in sociobiology. In S. R. SANDAY & E. TOCH (Eds.), *Violence against women* (pp. 85–114). New York: Gordian Press.

SCULLY, D., & MAROLLA, J. (1984). Convicted rapists' vocabulary of motives: Excuses and justifications. *Social Problems, 32,* 530–544.

SCULLY, D., & MAROLLA, J. (1985). Riding the bull at Gilly's: Convicted rapists describe the rewards of rape. *Social Problems, 32,* 251–262.

SHIELDS, W. M., & SHIELDS, L. M. (1983). Forcible rape: An evolutionary perspective. *Ethnology and Sociobiology, 4,* 115–136.

SHOTLAND, R. L. (1992). A theory of the causes of courtship rape. *Journal of Social Issues, 48,* 127–144.

SIGELMAN, C. K., BERRY, C. J., & WILES, K. A. (1984). Violence in college students' dating relationships. *Journal of Applied Social Psychology, 14*, 530–548.

SIGLER, R. T., & JOHNSON, I. M. (1997). *Forced sexual intercourse in intimate relationships*. Brookfield, VT: Dartmouth/Ashgate.

SIGLER, R. T., & JOHNSON, I. M. (1998). Examining courtship, dating, and forced sexual intercourse: A preliminary model. *Free Inquiry in Creative Sociology, 26*(1), 99–110.

SIGLER, R. T., & JOHNSON, I. M. (2000). Forced sexual intercourse among intimates. *Journal of Family Violence, 15*(1), 95–108.

SITTON, J. (1993). Old wine in new bottles: The "marital" rape allowance. *North Carolina Law Review, 72*(1), 261–289.

SMITH, J. M. (1978). *The evolution of sex.* New York: Cambridge University Press.

SUNDAY, S. R., & TOBACH, E. (1985). *Violence against women: A critique of the sociobiology of rape.* New York: Gordian Press.

SYMONS, D. (1979). *The evolution of human sexuality.* New York: Oxford University Press.

THOMAS, W. I., & ZANIECKI, F. (1927). *The Polish peasant in Europe and America.* New York: Knopf.

THOMPSON, W. W. E., & BUTTELL, A. J. (1984). Sexual deviance in America, *Emporia State Research Studies, 33*, 6–47.

THORNHILL, R. (1980). Rape in Panorpa scorpionflies and a general rape hypothesis. *Animal Behavior, 28*, 55–59.

THORNHILL, R., & THORNHILL, N. W. (1983). Human rape: An evolutionary analysis. *Ethnology and Sociobiology, 4*, 137–173.

TRIVERS, R. (1972). Parental investment and sexual selection. In B. Campbell (Ed.), *Sexual selection and the descent of man* (pp. 136–179). Chicago: Aldine.

VAN WIE, V. E., & GROSS, A. M., (2001). The role of women's explanations for refusal on men's ability to discriminate unwanted sexual behavior in a date rape scenario. *Journal of Family Violence, 16*(4), 331–344.

VOGEL, B. L. (2000). Correlates of pre-college males' sexual aggressions. *Women and Justice, 11*(3), 25–47.

WALD, A. (1997). What's rightfully ours: Toward a property theory of rape. *Columbia Journal of Law & Social Problems, 30*(3), 459–503.

WALKER, P. A., & MEYER, W. J. (1981). Medroxyprogesterone acetate treatment for paraphiliac sex offenders. In J. R. HAYS (Ed.), *Violence and the violent individual.* New York: Spectrum.

WALKER, S. (1997). When "no" becomes "yes": Why girls and women consent to unwanted sex. *Applied and Preventive Psychology 6*(3), 157–166.

WEIS, K., & BORGES, S. S. (1977), Victimology and rape: The case of the legitimate victim. In D. R. Nass (Ed.), *The Rape Victim* (pp. 35–75). Dubuque, IA: Kendall/Hunt.

WEST, R. (1990). Equality theory, marital rape and the promise of the Fourteenth Amendment. *Florida Law Review, 42*, 45.

WILDER, R. (1982, July). Are sexual standards inherited? *Science Digest, 69*.

WILLIAMS, G. C. (1975). *Sex and evolution.* Princeton, NJ: Princeton University Press.

WILLIAMS, J. E. (1979). Sex role stereotypes, women's liberation, and rape: A cross-cultural analysis of attitudes. *Sociological Symposium, 5*(1), 61–97.

WILSON, E. O. (1975). *Sociobiology: The new synthesis.* Cambridge, MA: Belknap Press of Harvard University.

WIRTH, L. (1940). Ideological aspects of social disorganization. *American Sociological Review, 5*, 472–482.

WOLFGANG, M., & FERRACUTI, F. (1967). *The subculture of violence.* London: Tavistock.

YEGIDIS, B. L. (1986). Date rape and forced sexual encounters among college students. *Journal of Sex Education and Therapy, 12*, 51–54.

YLLO, K. (1998). Wife rape: A social problem for the 21st century. *Violence Against Women, 5*(9), 989–1085.

CASES

Merton v. *State*, 500 So.2d 1301-05 (Ala. Crim. App. 1986)
People v. *Liberta*, 474 N.E.2d 567, 576 (1984)
Reed v. *Reed*, 404 U.S. 71, 92 S. Ct. 251, 30 L.Ed.2d 255 (1971)
Trammell v. *United States*, 445 U.S. 40, 52 (1980)

12

Guiding Philosophies
for Rape Crisis Centers

Stacy L. Mallicoat, Stephanie Amedeo Marquez, and Jill Leslie Rosenbaum

❖

Due to the significant levels of underreporting to official agencies compared to its prevalence rate, rape crisis centers in the community serve as a valuable resource for victims of sexual assault. The rape crisis movement began as a small grassroots organization during the 1970s to help address the physical and psychological needs for victims of sexual assault. A prominent component of these early agencies was its feminist orientation toward changing the rape culture of society. As home to one of the original centers in the United States, California has remained at the forefront of this movement. Focus groups conducted with 12 agencies throughout California indicate that while rape crisis centers differ in terms of organizational structure and program design, they share a guiding philosophy, which stresses the importance of social change and victim advocacy. This chapter traces the evolution of rape crisis centers in California and discusses the relationship between their philosophy and issues of job satisfaction, burnout, and retention.

BACKGROUND

With statistics indicating that a sexual assault occurs every two and a half minutes (Rape, Abuse and Incest National Network [RAINN]), and American women experience a one-in-four risk of being raped during their lifetime, rape crisis services play an important role in victim advocacy. In 2003, California's 85 rape crisis centers provided 24-hour services to over 34,000 people statewide, with an additional 586,000 people attending rape prevention programming (California Coalition Against Sexual Assault [CalCASA]). On a National level, research indicates that 198,850 people were victims of rape, attempted rape, or sexual assault in 2003 (Bureau of Justice Statistics, 2003). A comparison of these statistics to official police records indicates that rape continues to be underreported and documents the importance of rape crisis services in the community. The current rape crisis movement developed in response to the perceived need for prevention, community awareness, and amelioration of victims' pain.

The original rape crisis center was a small, grassroots organization. It was grounded in the philosophy of the 1970s women's movement. Collins and Whalen (1989, p. 61) describe the goal of the early rape crisis movement as "to change the society that permitted and encouraged the oppression of women and sexual violence against them." One of the original rape crisis centers in the United States was located in Berkeley, California, and the state has continued to be at the forefront of this movement. These early grassroots centers were not professional or clinical mental health organizations. Instead, they were mainly run by volunteers and they often recruited staff from the ranks of sexual assault survivors. The philosophical orientation toward "changing rape culture" advocated by the feminist movement was a prominent characteristic of each of these centers, in California and elsewhere.

The rape crisis center movement grew extremely rapidly. By 1976, there were approximately 400 centers nationwide. Three years later, their numbers had more than doubled to about 1,000 (Gornick, Burt, & Pittman, 1985). In 1979, an association named the National Coalition Against Sexual Assault (NCASA) was formed. Its initial meeting, held in Geneva, Wisconsin, was attended by members from more than 40 centers in 25 states (Koss & Harvey, 1991). Several attendees are now directors of rape crisis centers in California, and they have continued to keep California in the forefront of the movement by their efforts.

During the 1980s, the early model of the grassroots, volunteer, self-help organization began to be transformed. This was likely driven by reductions in funding during that decade. Rape crisis centers became increasingly affiliated with other agencies, including hospitals, police departments, and city government. They also began to connect to other nonprofits and to engage in fundraising activities, which necessitated closer connections to other community groups. As a result, professional staffing became necessary. Today, most client service providers have higher educational attainment than the general public. Yet, perhaps due to the tightened budgetary purse string, the grassroots flavor is often maintained, mainly by a deep reliance upon volunteers often drawn from the ranks of survivors. Such volunteers are critical to the agencies' ability to continue to staff various programs, notably the crisis hotline, in an era of constrained funding.

Gornick et al. (1985) suggested that this transformation from grassroots neighborhood "center" to rape crisis "agency" was at least partially due to the requirements of federal funding, for such organizations were often required by the government to incorporate, add boards of directors, and initiate other structural changes. Although the functions of the new-style "rape crisis agencies" may have shifted somewhat from organizing political action to providing direct services, the broader philosophy of the women's movement, which conceived of its mission as ameliorating or eliminating sexual assault, remained.

It is impossible to categorize these widely divergent agencies along any single criterion. As Gornick et al. (1985) pointed out, these agencies vary among many dimensions in organizational structure alone. These include (1) direct services versus community education/political action; (2) the number and types of direct services provided; (3) the degree of political, social, or feminist change advocated; (4) the independence or dependence of the center in terms of other institutions such as hospitals, the YWCA, or domestic violence shelters; (5) the diversity and amount of clients served; (6) the total staff size; (7) the ratio of paid-to-volunteer staff; and (8) the size of the budget. Add to this the number of differing funding sources and the issues of developing a typology of rape crisis centers begins to crystallize.

The transition stage of moving from a grassroots center to a multiprogram service agency is a difficult one. A review of rape crisis centers in California by Marquez and Rosenbaum (1997) found that several centers were grappling with the changes that such a transition requires. Some have struck a balance between the two styles, maintaining a small, professional staff responsible for several program components, while still using the services of a large volunteer cadre of survivors and women from the social community. Other agencies had clearly completed this transition, for they had evolved into large, almost corporate agencies with multiple sources of funding and myriad service provisions that allowed them to operate at a highly professional level.

At the same time, a key factor influencing the ability of small grassroots centers to do effective work in the community while operating on a shoestring budget is the multifaceted nature of many of the communities in which these centers are operating. Many centers are located in diverse ethnic communities, highlighting the need for programs and outreach to reflect the cultural differences. Additionally, many centers are serving different populations within the same community. Marquez and Rosenbaum (1997) discuss one such agency whose attempts to deliver professional and highly responsive services in a college town with at least 15,000 high-risk coeds is combined with their outreach effort to large numbers of women in isolated farming communities in the surrounding area. Thus, this agency is simultaneously serving a large population of students as well as a large group of Spanish-speaking and largely transient farm workers. Agencies who are responsible for serving multiple populations are not uncommon, particularly in smaller communities. The need to multitask to fulfill the needs of the community impacts all components of the agency, ranging from the organizational design, to the services provided by the agency. Such characteristics have significant impacts on the professionals working within these systems.

Notwithstanding differences, it is safe to say that all the rape crisis centers share one overriding attribute—a guiding philosophy. This attribute is characteristic of highly effective human service providers. According to Koss and Harvey (1991), it is the most important attribute an agency can have. Their philosophy stresses the importance of social change and prioritizes victim advocacy; it is essential to guide program development and ensure consistency between values and actions. A programmatic philosophy can provide the capacity for internal change and can enhance adaptability.

METHODS

In an effort to develop an understanding of rape crisis centers in California, 12 focus groups were conducted at rape crisis centers throughout the state. Centers were selected using purposive sampling techniques; that is, the centers were selected specifically to ensure that the sample would reflect the range of rape crisis centers. The goal of targeting for specific conditions such as geographical diversity is to maximize the capacity of the research to yield findings capable of being interpreted within multiple settings. According to Patton (1987, p. 53), "When selecting a small sample of great diversity, the data collection and analysis will yield two kinds of findings: (1) high quality, detailed descriptions of each case which are useful for documenting uniqueness, and (2) important shared patterns which cut across cases and which derive their significance from having emerged out of heterogeneity." Centers were chosen for their diversity, for they include centers serving both large and small cities, rural and urban neighborhoods, and dominant culture and minority culture communities.

The second level of sampling involved the selection of focus group participants. "Sometimes individual people—program participants, clients, or students—are the unit of analysis. This means that the primary focus of data collection will be on what is happening to the individuals in the program" (Patton, 1987, p. 50). Focus group participants included workers from all units that provide services to sexual assault survivors, and they ranged in the amounts of time spent in the agency. While volunteers represent an important component of community agencies in general, and for rape crisis centers specifically, the decision was made to include only direct service providers in this study as the goal was to see how professionals dealing with sexual assault perceive the nature of their jobs. According to Patton (1987, p. 54), in "direct contrast to maximum variation sampling is the strategy of picking a small homogeneous sample. The purpose here is to describe some sub-group in depth."

RESULTS

Marquez and Rosenbaum (1997) interviewed 95 workers from 12 agencies. These agencies were located in nine different counties across the state of California. Nearly all of the workers in the sample (96%) were female. Three-fourths work full time, while nearly half (48%) had some supervisory responsibilities. On average, staff members worked for their agencies in their current position for about three years and approximately eight years in client services. Nearly half (46%) were single, while 38% had children at home. Their average educational attainment was 16 years. About 47% of participants had a personal history of sexual assault.

These demographics suggest that rape crisis centers constitute very unique work settings. First, the workforce is overwhelmingly female. Many workers saw this as an advantage of their job and one of the main reasons for retention. Several noted the benefits of "having a supportive workplace, feeling supported by other women, and having a family oriented workplace that is flexible in terms of needs of children." Largely underinvestigated are the 4% of rape crisis workers who are male. In this female-oriented environment, the male service crisis provider must work both for and with women as colleagues, must provide services for a largely female clientele, and must adhere to or at least tolerate an extremely feminist agency philosophy. The reactions of male workers within such an environment are worthy of further investigation.

Equally striking are the high levels of sexual assault reported among rape crisis workers (almost 50%, or twice as high as the usually reported figure of one in four). These can be explained in at least three ways. First, previous sexual assault victims may be drawn to this work. Second, staff members are often recruited from volunteers, many of who are working through their own rape trauma. Finally, workers may feel particularly safe in reporting sexual assaults within this setting, leading to a higher reporting rate within this population, rather than a higher incidence rate.

Respondents were asked questions on several topics relating to their employment as rape crisis workers. A key theme of these discussions focused on the relationship of workers to a rape crisis philosophy. The concept of a rape crisis philosophy is uniquely connected not only to issues of job satisfaction, burnout, and retention, but also to the kinds of outcomes that these centers hope to achieve in working with clients.

Philosophy of Rape Crisis

To elicit an understanding of the rape crisis philosophy, focus group participants were asked, what makes the area of rape crisis victim services important to you? The responses to this question presented some of the most valuable information for this research. The high levels of solidarity, of concern with the meaning of their work, and of consensus on the importance of what these centers were doing immediately became evident. The level of commitment of the workers became clear in their responses—to rape crisis work in general, to their specific agency, and to other workers. This strong sense of solidarity appears to be largely responsible for the high retention rates found among workers who remain past a short-term period, and for the success of rape crisis agencies in general. This strong organizational philosophy and unity regarding goals suggests that rape crisis work is distinctive among American occupations. In fact, the literature on occupations suggests only two types of work subcultures manifesting an equivalently strong philosophy and esprit de corps: the police, and various branches of the armed services (Golembiewski, 1998).

In response to the question about what makes this work important, participants most frequently emphasized the impact of their services on both individuals and on the community. Many workers weighed these impacts equally, and several argued that these two types of service were intertwined. That is, individual rape survivors are also seen as members of a community—a hometown, or perhaps an ethnic or racial community. Even more important, workers see themselves as serving both the specific community of sexual assault survivors and the broader community of women. These attitudes help shape the services that these workers try to provide to both individuals and communities.

The most important services that workers felt they could provide to individuals were advocacy and empowerment. These services, workers argued, were highly interrelated and equally weighted. In promoting advocacy, workers felt that it was necessary to "meet the needs of individuals in crisis" and to "ensure the victim isn't alone." The first goal of advocacy is facilitated when the agency is able to "provide a safe place for the victim to come to or to call or to turn to," or when victims "have a real person on the telephone hotline at all times." The second goal is achieved when the rape crisis worker becomes "a timely, personal first responder" who accompanies the victim to the hospital, to police interviews, and to court. Similarly, workers viewed empowerment by "reducing trauma" for rape crisis survivors. Reducing trauma includes providing knowledge, to let the victim/survivor know that "what she's feeling is normal." In sum, staff members described their main objectives in dealing with individuals as (1) letting clients know what services exist; (2) helping clients see that these services will allow them to feel better; and (3) allowing clients to make their own choices to promote empowerment.

Equally important in the rape crisis philosophy, and embodied as one of its original goals, is the notion of community impact. In fact, one mission of rape crisis centers since their inception has been to change society and its relationship toward issues of sexual assault. Focus group participants felt that social change was readily affected by mobilizing the community. Specifically, they emphasized four basic goals in community work: (1) to prevent sexual assault, (2) to influence public policy on sexual assault, (3) to make a difference in the community, and (4) to ensure that services for rape victims exist. In fact, many argued that the very existence of rape crisis services makes a difference to a community. However, the rape crisis philosophy goes further than this, for it tries to promote other forms of active community participation, such as connections with other social welfare agencies, community education, and outreach programs.

Job Satisfaction, Burnout, and Retention

Much of the literature on employees in human service occupations discusses the relationship between job satisfaction, burnout, and retention. Although these occupations tend to experience high levels of burnout and have issues with retention, those who remain in these settings tend to express high levels of job satisfaction. Sharma et al. (1997) found that child welfare workers expressed high levels of job satisfaction and that much of this satisfaction was due to the structural organization, rather than the intrinsic value they received from the work. These workers indicated that low pay and lack of promotion opportunities did impact their feelings of job satisfaction.

Like many human service occupations, the rape crisis workers in this study expressed high levels of job satisfaction. However, the cause of this satisfaction appears to differ from those themes in the literature. In these settings, extrinsic motives such as salary appear to have less of an effect in determining overall job satisfaction than they do in other work environments, further emphasizing the uniqueness of the rape crisis center as a workplace. Focus group participants who indicated high levels of job satisfaction frequently expressed "a feeling of accomplishment." Here, high levels of intrinsic rewards create high levels of job satisfaction for the rape crisis worker, in spite of relatively low salaries and high rates of burnout. While salary level did not appear to have a strong effect on job satisfaction, some extrinsic measure did prove to be important. For instance, the worker's perception of the prestige of the agency in the community proved to be germane in determining overall job satisfaction and leadership of the agency.

Directly linked to measures of job satisfaction is the issue of burnout. Due to the intensive nature of human service occupations, these workers tend to experience higher levels of burnout, compared to other occupations. While the condition has long been recognized in nonprofit settings, the study of "burnout" is a relatively recent phenomena. Until the 1970s, a review of the literature would have revealed no entries listed under the term "burnout." A psychologist named Freudenberger studying the emotional and physical effects of chronic drug addicts borrowed this word from clients; they had used it to describe the effects of chronic drug abuse (as cited in Coomez & Michaelis, 1995). The term quickly gained currency in a wide number of fields, and mainly in human services. Between 1980 and 1985 alone, there were more than 300 professional articles using the word "burnout" in their titles. There are two main reasons for this. First, human service providers have long been noted for an occupational predisposition to early onset of adverse reactions to work. Second, the term "burnout," unlike earlier labels such as "incompetence" or "ineptitude", does not imply that the person affected is to blame.

Focus group participants indicated high levels of burnout similar to other human service occupations. Of the three dimensions of burnout, physical exhaustion played the strongest role for these rape crisis workers, although mental exhaustion also had a strong impact. However, this finding is unique considering the high levels of job satisfaction. Additionally, these findings differed from those found in other studies. For instance, these workers did not indicate feelings of worthlessness or weakness, common predictors of burnout in human service occupations. Even more surprising, rape crisis workers indicated a number of characteristics that suggest a resistance to the threats of burnout, such as "being happy"—a pattern not usually found with other human service workers. Thus rape crisis workers in California are indeed unusual, for high levels of burnout coexist with high levels of job satisfaction.

Various studies have looked at the relationship of job measures to levels of burnout. Romano (1995) suggested that time off or "flex time" had positive effects in reducing burnout. Schulz, Greenley, and Brown (1995) studied the effect of organizational and managerial techniques. Much debate has been presented on the opposing ideas of "overinvolvement" versus "debriefing." Researchers warning of the dangers of overinvolvement advocate "distance" from the workplace, including distance from both client and coworkers (Koeske & Kelly 1995). By contrast, those who emphasize a more community-based orientation (Medvene, Volk, & Meissen, 1997) and the related idea of culturally sophisticated workplaces (Gant, 1996) argue the opposite view: They believe that burnout can be reduced by talking to and bonding with colleagues, thereby keeping compassion and empathy alive.

If burnout is inevitable among human service providers (Golembiewski, 1998), the sources of relieving stress become crucial (Kafry & Pines, 1978, 1980). To assess the aspect of stress relief among rape crisis workers, focus group participants were asked about the strategies they employ to reduce the levels of stress as a result of their occupational demands. "Maintaining an esprit de corps" was defined as the most important stress reduction technique for the majority of rape crisis workers in this study. Other techniques included "maintaining a therapeutic distance from the job," "maintaining supportive relationships with managers," and "balancing work with a variety of outside interests."

The issue of retention is intrinsically related to levels of burnout. Several factors appear to impact retention rates in rape crisis centers. One is that retention has a bimodal pattern—that is, there is a high turnover rate among new workers, and a high retention rate among those workers who persist through the earliest phases. Several respondents offered explanations for the high turnover rate among new volunteers. Many volunteers start this work "full of excitement because of our training, and think they are going to change the world. Then on the hotline you hear hard stuff. They get vicarious traumatization instead of the rewards of changing the world." Another observed that volunteers "want to help and don't feel it's happening because so many of the clients you never see again." Additionally, these high levels of burnout for volunteers have a significant impact for staff members who are regularly involved in the training and management of a volunteer workforce. However, it appears that the training of many volunteers produces interesting unintended consequences, for it has increased the dissemination of information on rape crisis into the communities. Here, the community component of the rape crisis philosophy is fulfilled, albeit indirectly.

Agencies experiencing high rates of retention credited their success to several factors. Most important, many argued, was the "unique overall philosophy" or the "feminist management philosophy" found in these centers. A number of respondents also cited the possibilities for "increased knowledge and personal growth." Others reported more practical factors, including salary increases, good benefits, and enough time off.

The centers and participants of this study exhibited high levels of worker solidarity. Clearly a strong advantage of working in a rape crisis center is the bonding that unites these workers. Indeed, the cohesiveness and congeniality found in these centers is impressive, for such solidarity is not the rule in other workplaces. This level of worker solidarity was interlinked with their high levels of commitment to the rape crisis philosophy and serves as a common link in analyzing issues of job satisfaction, burnout, and retention.

CONCLUSION

Like many human service professions, rape crisis workers and their agencies provide a valuable service to their communities. Indeed, the growth of rape crisis centers in California since their inception in the 1970s provides evidence of their value.

In considering questions of staffing, levels of job satisfaction, retention, and burnout relative to comparable jobs in other human service agencies, rape crisis workers in this study were found to be quite unique. California rape crisis workers simultaneously report high levels of job satisfaction and high levels of burnout, a situation posited by the literature to be impossible. The high levels of burnout are regarded in the literature as endemic to human services. The coexistence of high job satisfaction with high levels of burnout is explainable by the unique nature of the rape crisis philosophy, which produces strong solidarity among the workers. Thus, the dissatisfaction with low salary levels, coupled with high-intensity emotional interactions with clients are counterbalanced by the workers' recognition of the meaningfulness and value of their work. Such differences from the national norm and from the overall literature on job satisfaction can be best attributed to the uniqueness of rape crisis centers as workplaces.

Across varying organizational structures and communities of service, the strength of these agencies lies in their unique connection to a rape crisis philosophy. This philosophy is twofold as it focuses on providing services for victims and survivors of sexual assault as well as maintaining a commitment toward social change for their communities. While this study has produced a number of valuable findings for workers in rape crisis work environments, additional research should continue to explore the role of the rape crisis philosophy to adequately provide services for victims and effect successful social change at the community level.

REFERENCES

Bureau of Justice Statistics, U.S. Department of Justice. (2003). *National Crime Victimization Survery*. Retrieved from http://www.ojp.usdoj.gov/bjs/cvict.htm

California Coalition Against Sexual Assault website, retrieved from http://www.calcasa.org

COLLINS, B. G., & WHELAN, M. B. (1989). The rape crisis moment: Radical or reformist? *Social Work, 34,* 61–63.

GANT, L. M. (1996, March). Are culturally sophisticated agencies better workplaces for social work staff and administrators? *Social Work, 4*(2).

GOLEMBIEWSKI, R. T. (1998, January/February). Estimates of burnout in public agencies. *Public Administration Review, 58*(1).

GOMEZ, J. S., MICHAELIS, R. C. (1995, January–March). An assessment of burnout in human service providers. *Journal of Rehabilitation, 61*(1) 23–26.

GORNICK, J., BURT, M. R., PITTMAN, K. J. (1985). Structures and activities of rape crisis centers in the early 1980's. *Crime and Delinquency, 31,* 247–268.

KAFRY, D. & PINES, A. (1980). The experience in tedium in life and work. *Human Relations, 33*(7), 477–503.

KOESKE, G. F., KELLY, T. (1995, April). The impact of overinvolvement on burnout and job satisfaction. *American Journal of Orthopsychiatry, 65*(2).

KOSS, M. P., HARVEY, M. R. (1991). *The rape victim: Clinical and community interventions,* 2nd ed. Newbury Park, CA: Sage.

MARQUEZ, S. ROSENBAUM, J. (1997). *Transition to outcomes-based evaluation rape crisis intervention.* California Office of Criminal Justice Planning.

MEDVENE, L. J., VOLK, F., & MEISSEN, G. J. (1997). Communal orientation and burnout among self-help group leaders. *Journal of Applied Social Psychology, 27*(3), 262–278.

PATTON, M. Q. (1989). *How to use qualitative methods in evaluations.* Newbury Park, CA: Sage.

RAPE, ABUSE AND INCEST NATIONAL NETWORK website, retrieved from http://www.rainn.org

ROMANO, C. (1995, July). Time for a sabbatical? Employee sabbaticals and leaves of absences. *Human Resources Focus, 72*(7).

SCHULZ, R., GREENLEY, J. R., BROWN, R. (1995, December). Organization, management, and client effects on staff burnout. *Journal of Health and Social Behavior, 36*(4).

SHARMA, J., MCKELVEY, J., HARDY, R., EPSTEIN, M.H., LOMAX, R.G., HRUBY, P. J. (1997). Job satisfaction of child welfare workers in an urban setting: Status and predictors. *Journal of Child and Family Studies, 6*(2).

13

The Historical Role of
and Views toward Victims
and the Evolution of
Prosecution Policies
in Domestic Violence

Paula Gormley

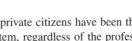

From colonial America until today, private citizens have been the primary gate-keepers to the criminal justice system, regardless of the professionalization of the components of the system. This chapter will provide a brief discussion about the process by which citizens, especially victims, used the criminal justice system in domestic violence. Furthermore, criminal justice actors' historical perceptions toward victims, although seemingly borne from desperate attempts to curb intimate violence among the poor, appear to have greatly influenced current views toward, and ultimately prosecution policy in, domestic violence. Several of these policies will also be discussed. Perhaps the most remarkable aspect about perceptions toward victims and offenders is how such perceptions have thrived over decades to become the images perpetuated by the rhetoric, both public and private, informing current stereotypes about battering relationships.

A discussion about prosecution responses to domestic violence should consider both the history of prosecution in the United States and the contexts in which criminal justice personnel socially constructed domestic violence. Prior to the existence of the office of the public prosecutor, victims, and often offenders, controlled the flow of cases through the system. Victims had status as being parties to their own cases and acted on their own behalves during the course of a prosecution. No separate victims' rights movements existed in the American colonies, and the Bill of Rights made no mention of crime victims' rights (Cassell, 1994). And prior to the 1880s, case law had not yet established the primacy of the public prosecutor (Steinberg, 1984).

PRIVATE PROSECUTION

Due to the limitations on policing (e.g., lack of professionalization, no warrantless misdemeanor arrests) and the private nature of domestic violence, prosecution usually was left in the hands of the victim and the victim's kin. The private citizen initiated the complaint and was responsible for pressing the local court, typically through financial incentive, for case conclusion. Until the late 19th century, the size of court dockets was directly influenced by the entry of private citizens' complaints. Private prosecutors, when retained by either or both parties to a case, paid the justice's fees, attended pretrial hearings before justices and grand juries, organized witnesses' appearances (Steinberg, 1984), and tried cases (Cardenas, 1986).

Justices of the peace (also known as alderman and magistrates) were the primary arbiters of low-level criminal offenses. They typically heard complaints, brought cases before grand juries, and decided case outcomes. Justices often relied on arbitration practices such as issuing peace bonds to adjudicate matters rather than criminal sanctions that perpetuated their disdain for overly retributive responses (Steinberg, 1984). Peace bonds, which were financial sureties made to the court, helped promote peaceable relations between two parties. If an assaulter violated a bond, she or he forfeited the bond to the court. Wives requested a surety bond for assaultive husbands to guarantee that they would appear at the next court date and keep the peace in the interim (Cole, 1999). By requesting peace bonds, women hoped to scare their husbands into nonviolence with the threat of prosecution.

In Baltimore, women chose which justice's services they would procure based on the severity of the justice's sanctioning style. When conducting an initial investigation into the veracity of the charges, justices could legally imprison the accused. The justices often used this time as a proxy cooling-off period by keeping batterers incarcerated for sometimes as long as 30 days. Since justices varied in these approaches, women who sought light punishments would complain to the justice whose "sentences" were below the norm. Women who were angrier or more economically independent could see another justice of the peace who generally imposed longer periods in jail (Parker, 1997).

Victims therefore possessed tremendous discretion over whether to file a complaint, with whom to file a complaint (which the victims determined by how much punishment they believed the offender should receive), how quickly the case should be moved through the system, and whether reconciliation should be made prior to adjudication.

The constituents of the justice of the peace courts were overwhelmingly poor and the least empowered (Parker, 1997). In Philadelphia, judges discouraged men from initiating prosecutions for assault and battery by calling the use of the law a process for women and children. Grand jurors, judges, and journalists marveled at the ease with which those who were excluded from public life could make use of the system. Although assault and battery were the most frequent charges in cases brought before the aldermen in Philadelphia in the late 1840s, grand jurors were concerned that the "miserable outcasts of society" were abusing their rights to complain against each other (Steinberg, 1984).

The decline in private prosecution in the late 19th century was attributed to a convergence of factors. Courts were being overwhelmed with private litigation, which was especially troubling because cases were often dismissed by grand juries, who considered most cases petty and frivolous, or were otherwise settled between parties prior to adjudication (Steinberg, 1984). Private prosecution was increasingly viewed as encouraging vindication of purely personal grievances ("Private Prosecution," 1955–1956). As their fees depended upon citizens' case initiation, justices of the peace routinely accepted cases without discerning the truthfulness of the charges alleged (Cole, 1999; Steinberg, 1984). Additionally, Beccaria's increasingly popular notion that crime was not a private concern between the aggressor and victim but a societal concern influenced criticism toward the allowance of the victim to control prosecution decisions (Cardenas, 1986).

In Philadelphia, lawmakers were disappointed with the ineffective way in which law enforcement quelled breaches of public order. Since the police were not successful at procuring convictions of accused rioters during the 1840s and 1850s, they were subsequently granted arrest powers. Police professionalization facilitated a later increase in the authority of public prosecutors and greater professionalization in the criminal justice overall (Steinberg, 1984). Prosecutors, as representatives of the state, could use their power to ensure justice for the innocent and punishment for the guilty, while crime victims were to be pushed to the periphery as witnesses for the state (Cardenas, 1986).

When prosecutors did finally enter the public arena in the late 19th century, specialized courts were created as places where victims could bring grievances to the criminal justice system, albeit under a civil regime. These specialized courts still exist in many jurisdictions. In domestic violence, they may operate as forums in which victims can implement restraining orders.

DOMESTIC RELATIONS COURTS

Prosecutors may have been reluctant to bring domestic cases to a grand jury out of concern for preventing a situation of destitution created by jailing the offender who was typically the husband and breadwinner. In San Diego in the late 19th century, prosecutors preferred to avoid prosecuting domestic violence cases since married women were financially dependent upon their husbands. Jailing a husband could lead to poverty (Parker, 1997).

Courts of domestic relations, alternately known as family courts, emerged as adult extensions of juvenile courts. Family courts had legal authority over domestic assault and nonpayment of child support, but lawyers were generally absent from these courts (Pleck, 1987). The fact-finder and final arbiter was typically the judge who often decided cases based on the recommendations of psychiatrists and social workers (Gordon, 1988; Pleck, 1987). Defining negligent husbands as family supporters provided the courts with the legal leverage to impose some burden on husbands to support their families (Igra, 2000).

Judges believed that relatives who engaged in crime against each other should not be punished as common criminals since private combatants were deemed merely ignorant, mentally deficient, or lazy. Wife beaters were characterized as drunkards who beat their wives in moments of passion with little thought to consequences. The official policy of domestic relations courts was to preserve the family by curative rather than punitive approaches, through reconciliation. Family violence was considered a domestic difficulty rather than criminal law violation. Since few courts granted divorces, family courts did what they could to keep the family intact. Wives who persisted in pressing their complaints at family court were persuaded to withdraw their complaints and get a promise from parties that they will do all they can to correct their relationship and not resort to the courts to resolve their familial problems (Pleck, 1987). Judges therefore sent families home after reasserting the husband's authority in the household and urging wives to become more subservient, compliant, and economically dependent. In essence, judges and reformers attempted to influence lower-class and immigrant families (the predominant clients of the system) to accept a middle-class paradigm of the family dynamic (Pleck, 1987).

In pre-World War II New York City, women used the Domestic Relations Court to seek financial support from husbands who deserted them. This court, founded in 1910, was designed as a collection agency for economic marital conflicts and was intended to protect taxpayers' pocketbooks. The typical complainants were poor, and courts that could force husbands to pay support could thereby prevent the family from becoming welfare customers. However, the court, whenever possible, availed itself to women's free labor by requiring them to expend the time in tracking down and monitoring delinquent husbands as proof that the women actually were in dire need of court assistance (Igra, 2000).

Around World War II, a family courthouse was built in Philadelphia on Vine Street to house domestic and juvenile cases. In this court, women (the most common complainants) brought suits in one of three ways. Unmarried women sought financial support from the fathers of their children (considered criminal and handled by the criminal division); married women sought financial support against their husbands (handled in the domestic relations division); and women charged assault and battery (considered criminal and typically brought by wives against husbands) (Levenstein, 2003).

The domestic events leading to each of these alternatives may not necessarily have been mutually exclusive. Women often had to make a decision whether to seek support, thereby leaving them without protection from violence, or press criminal abuse charges and potentially be left without financial support of their husbands who were sentenced to jail. The choice of intervention was often contingent upon the woman's level of desperation. Since the outcomes of assault and battery were so unpredictable due to the lack of policy guidelines for judges, it was usually the most severely abused women with nowhere else to turn who availed themselves of the court process to charge their husbands. And the most destitute women typically pressed for financial support from the courts since a court order could make a positive difference. For employed women, the financial support order could not compensate for the finances missed due to missed work days (Levenstein, 2003). In New York City, women frequently chose to charge nonsupport rather than assault because the legal community considered the former more serious (Ramsey, 2002).

Efforts to reform the family were also made through threatening, cajoling, jailing, and making home visits. Social workers attempted to quell violence in the home by influencing battering husbands. But men were rarely willing to meet with caseworkers and were more defensive about their own behavior. In search of any ways to influence troubled families, social workers turned their focus on those most open to influence: the women (Gordon, 1988). Woman-blaming became pervasive as workers realized they could influence their clients. Social workers placed with women the responsibility for getting along with a violent man. Social workers even went so far as to attribute women's placement of responsibility on their husbands as the result of infantile blaming, a denial of adult responsibility, and masochistic.

After the 1930s, divorce ultimately became more common among the poor. But caseworkers, in their attempts to discourage single-female-headed households and destitution, tried to continue ignoring wife beating, or when they couldn't, defined it as a problem for women to manage. Women who left the home to raise children on their own were labeled as morally bad.

DOMESTIC HOMICIDES

Extremely cruel or irresponsible men threatened the public order in a paternalistic patriarchy where obedience to the husband meant protection for the wife (Cole, 1999). Uncontrolled violence exceeded the ideal of a family man who disciplined his wife in the course of maintaining family stability. Such extreme cruelty was not tolerated by the criminal justice system. Cases where extreme cruelty was prosecutable exemplified how prosecutors attempted to satisfy an increasingly punitive public who desired to impose accountability upon prosecutors to ensure that defendants did not escape their deserved heavy punishments (Ramsey, 2002).

Domestic murderers made easy political targets since they were considered unmanly, marginal individuals and often possessed little economic or social standing (Cole, 1999). Such targets for prosecution were therefore politically uncontroversial. In New York City in the late 19th century, although male-on-male homicides outnumbered domestic homicides, men who were streetwise tough were less likely to be viewed as misaligned with masculinity norms and more likely to be spared the death penalty than domestic offenders (Ramsey, 2002). More than half of the men convicted of killing female intimates shared a heavy reliance on alcohol and the meager earnings of women. Between 1879 and 1893 in New York City, 17 of the 34 males convicted of first-degree murder killed female intimates, although wife killing accounted for only 14 percent of homicides committed by men. In 1889, 4 men convicted of murdering their wives or lovers in New York City were hanged in one day (Ramsey, 2002).

Today, the death penalty does not appear to be sought in domestic homicides to the same extent as in the past. Rather, the death penalty tends to be reserved for murders committed in the course of another felony (Ramsey, 2002). Current policy discussions in domestic violence seem more likely to consider the virtue of mandatory arrest. Questions still turn on whether mandatory arrest actually reduces recidivism (however recidivism is defined), who (offender or victim) most benefits from mandatory arrest, whether mandatory arrest is useful in light of victim cooperation issues, and whether alternatives to mandatory arrest can be successfully applied.

The shift in prosecutorial approaches to punishment in domestic violence cases evokes questions regarding cause. Is domestic violence recognized as so commonplace that to harshly punish domestic violence offenders would be politically and fiscally untenable? Has the paradigm shift in viewing women as equally capable as men created a shift in norms of femininity and masculinity? Has domestic violence come to be seen as less reprehensible because it is understood to be normative behavior in families? The answers to these questions may provoke thinking about changes in the law on domestic violence and the differences in how prosecutors view victims, offenders, and the relationships among them as we enter the 21st-century policymaking era.

DEVELOPMENT OF CURRENT PROSECUTION ISSUES IN DOMESTIC VIOLENCE

During the 1970s, the grassroots battered women's movement was the key to effecting changes in criminal justice responses to domestic violence. Historically, police were unwilling to arrest offenders, and prosecutors were reluctant to accept "unexceptional" cases where evidentiary problems plagued successful conviction. Witnesses, other than the victim and perhaps the children of the parties, often did not exist. Prior abuse documentation, such as medical reports, police reports, photographs, or bruises, was nonexistent. Before mandatory arrest laws, police responses to domestic violence often consisted of temporarily separating the conflicting parties (Goolkasian, 1986).

The Minneapolis Domestic Violence Experiment (MDVE) facilitated policy changes in police procedure across the United States. A major finding of this study was that arrest significantly reduced recidivism in misdemeanor domestic violence cases compared to police advisement, including mediation on the scene, and separation of the offender from the scene for at least eight hours (Sherman & Berk, 1984). In response to this study, the United States attorney general recommended that arrest become the standard response to misdemeanor domestic violence cases (Goolkasian, 1986). As gatekeepers to the criminal process, victims again made determinations whether to institute formal proceedings against batterers by deciding whether or not to involve law enforcement.

The five studies that replicated the MDVE did not fully support arrest as the most effective police response to categorically reduce domestic violence recidivism. The Omaha, Nebraska (Dunford, Huizinga, & Elliot, 1990), and Charlotte, North Carolina (Hirschel & Hutchinson, 1992), replication studies found that arrest was not a more effective deterrent to repeat abuse than advisement, separation, and court citation. In the Milwaukee, Wisconsin, study (Sherman & Smith, 1992), the researchers found that repeat violence was significantly higher among black, unmarried, and unemployed offenders, and for suspects who were arrested and held for 3–11 hours. The study refuted the idea that mandatory arrest policies created long-term deterrence, at least in inner-city poverty areas like Milwaukee's. The Colorado Springs experiment (Berk, Campbell, Klap, & Western, 1992) also supported the findings that arrest may lead to increased violence for "bad risks" (i.e., unemployed and unmarried suspects).

Another unforeseen consequence of mandatory arrest laws has been that many women are getting arrested along with their partners. In responding to domestic violence emergency calls, the police may not easily differentiate, or care to differentiate, between the perpetrator and victim since both may not be clearly definable in many cases (Sontag, 2002). Most domestic physical assaults consist of pushing, shoving, grabbing, slapping, and hitting (Tjaden & Thoennes, 1998, 2000), and determining a clear victim can prove daunting. The result is that the case falls onto the prosecutor's shoulders to disentangle culpability issues.

The Effect of Victim Cooperation on Prosecution

The debate about whether the prosecutor should pursue a case that the victim wants dropped has existed since at least the late 19th century with the creation of the public prosecutor's office (Ramsey, 2002). Victims' ambivalence about prosecution and their role as witnesses have often discouraged prosecutors from taking action. Some battered women are reluctant to cooperate with prosecution because of their emotional or financial attachment to the abuser, mistrust or lack of information about the criminal justice system, or the delay and inconvenience of court appearances. Reluctance might further stem from the batterer's threats of further retaliation for taking legal action (Goolkasian, 1986). When a victim does cooperate with the prosecution, the likelihood of prosecution going forward is seven times higher than if the victim does not cooperate (Dawson & Dinovitzer, 2001). Victim cooperation, therefore, seems paramount for case processing.

In their study of Sacramento County domestic violence cases, Kingsnorth and MacIntosh (2004) found that victim support for prosecution may be a function of the level at which charges are filed. Filing a case as a felony rather than misdemeanor or probation violation reduced the odds of victim support by 29 percent. The researchers attributed the lack of support for felony filings as a twofold concern. First, victims' primary motivation for seeking formal intervention is to end the abuse rather than punish the abuser. Second, felony conviction imposes greater costs on offenders (e.g., longer sentences and increased fines) that may ultimately be transferred to victims and their children.

In her study of prosecutors who handle sexual assault cases, Frohmann (1997) showed that prosecutors construct discordant locales by ascribing the stereotypical characteristics of a neighborhood to the actors who move through the neighborhood (i.e., victims and defendants) and the people judging the actors (i.e., jurors). Prosecutors can thus categorize actors, locations, and actions to determine whether these categorizations challenge or fit existing normative aspects of the behavior in question. Such decisions have the purpose of providing prosecutors with the authority to determine whether the facts of a case will be believed by jurors. "The organizational concern with convictability renders discordant locales a legitimate and frequent unofficial justification for case rejection" (p. 552), but would not appear on official written case rejection accounts. Rather, reasons given typically would be insufficient evidence and the victim's unwillingness to cooperate.

Prosecutors have claimed that many victims do not want to prosecute their batterers since the victims suffer from some mental illness or are too easily influenced by the batterer that prevents victims from knowing what they really want. Victims are deemed too fragile, mentally ill, indecisive, or uncooperative to protect themselves or help with prosecution. Prosecutors who are confronted with painful stories of abuse may not be emotionally prepared to help the victim and may instead develop feelings of grandiosity (Mills, 2003). This assertion only complicates an already complex set of circumstances.

A prosecutor's characterization of a victim as uncooperative may therefore provide the rationale for dismissing a case or rejecting a charging decision. In jurisdictions where a case's convictability is paramount, decisions based on whether a prediction of a jury returning a guilty verdict become all important. Those cases deemed unconvictable will be rejected from the system. The concern for convictability creates an environment where prosecutors must anticipate how others (i.e., jury and defense) will respond to a case (Frohmann, 1997). Prosecutors must grapple with the issue of the level of harm caused to a victim against this convictability standard. For jurors in domestic violence cases, the question foremost in their minds may be why the victim did not leave the relationship. If a victim chooses to remain in an abusive relationship, she may be considered masochistic (Dodge & Greene, 1991), at least partially responsible for the battering she suffers, or emotionally disturbed (Ewing & Aubrey, 1987).

In their interviews of municipal court professionals (prosecutors, judges, and defense attorneys), Hartman and Belknap (2003) learned that battered women were often viewed as pathetic, stupid, or even deserving of the abuse they experienced when they stayed with the defendant. They were simultaneously viewed as "vindictive, crazy, or falsely charging domestic violence to meet their own selfish needs" (p. 363). Prosecutors may deem relationships that have high levels of intimacy as indicative that the victim will not pursue prosecution. Level of intimacy has been measured by sexual intimacy at the time of the incident (Schmidt & Steury, 1989) and the relationship of victim to batterer, such as marital status (McLeod, 1983; Rauma, 1984) or cohabitation with the offender (Schmidt & Steury, 1989). Schmidt and Steury found that in 45 percent of the noncharged cases, victim's wishes were indicated as the primary reason for not prosecuting. These researchers acknowledged that they did not know whether the victim's change of heart to follow through reflects the victim's true desire or the influence of the defendant or prosecutor. While prosecutors disagree about how much a victim's wishes should influence the decision to file charges, some prosecutors' offices who have succeeded in reducing case attrition agree that once a charge is filed with the court, the decision to go forward must rest with the prosecutor and not the victim (Smith, Davis, Nickles, & Davies, 2001).

No-drop policies were adopted in prosecutors' offices in response to mandatory arrest policies.[1] No-drop policies prevent victims from dismissing charges, and in some instances, victims are advised that if they do not appear in court, a judge may assess court costs against them (Cahn & Lerman, 1991). However, Ford and Regoli (1992) acknowledge that even with no-drop policies, the victim retains control of the prosecution through a refusal to present oneself as a persuasive witness. In her experience as a prosecutor, Hanna (1996) recounted that, although her office adopted a hard no-drop policy, she rarely initiated contempt orders for abused women who refused to come to court. Hanna acknowledged that she frequently had difficulty reconciling her responsibility to prosecute with her concern that forcing victims to participate in the prosecution process would disempower them from responding to the abusive relationship on their own.

Evidence-based prosecution has followed upon the heels of no-drop prosecution in another effort to manage victim cooperation dilemmas. Evidence-based prosecution is unique in that it proceeds as a homicide case. In other words, prosecution is based on a presumption that the victim will not testify for the state at trial. Prosecutors thus try to prove the charges without the victim's testimony. Examples of evidence that aid in the investigation and prosecution of a case are photographs (e.g., injuries, property damage, crime scene), physical evidence (e.g., weapons, alcohol/drug abuse, victim's diary, clothing, phone pulled from wall, animal abuse), eye witnesses, excited utterances by the victim, abuser's statements, and expert medical opinion (Markarian, 2003). Although beneficial for prosecution, evidence-based prosecution requires additional training for police officers as well as cooperation of judges who decide whether to admit such evidence as part of the prosecution's case.

San Diego's prosecutor's office has practiced an evidence-based prosecution policy. According to San Diego City Attorney Casey Gwinn, "Ultimately, we have taken the decision away from the victim, because when the victim had the decision, we were drawing a target on her chest" (Atkinson Hudson, 2003, p. 13). However, Ford and Regoli's (1992) experiment on prosecutors' decisions in misdemeanor domestic violence cases indicated that any prosecutorial action on a case (i.e., accepting charges and proceeding through an initial hearing in court) significantly reduced by at least 50 percent the chance of further violence within six months of the time a case was settled, regardless of the type of case disposition (dismissal, acceptance of diversion agreement, conviction, finding of not guilty). Regarding the dismissal treatment, those victims who were permitted to drop charges and actually did drop them were significantly more likely to be battered than women in the other treatments. On the other hand, victims who were permitted to drop the charges but remained committed to the prosecution of the batterer had a less than 10 percent chance of being battered again within six months of settlement.

Smith et al. (2001) found that evidence-based prosecution fit office practices better than no-drop prosecution, which may be considered expensive. In one of the sites they studied, the researchers estimated that each misdemeanor prosecution averaged $1,000.[2]

Victim Empowerment and Case Processing

Mills (1998) believes that criminal justice personnel should hear the victim's story and take into account her particular circumstances, while considering her empowerment as the most important goal of prosecution. This means that the victim should decide whether she would like to actively pursue arrest and prosecution or have prosecutors pursue charges on her behalf and without her active participation. Some indices of empowerment Mills describes are: a victim's feeling of control over the case, the victim's feeling of alliance with the prosecutor, the victim's perceived ability to assert her own will, and the victim's belief that the court process can be used to improve the victim's relationship and avoid future incidents of violence.

Other Prosecutorial Considerations

Prosecutors employ at least some informal procedures to encourage victim participation in the domestic violence prosecution process. Victim support can take the form of domestic violence advocacy units within the prosecutor's office and victim/witness units that serve the needs of victims of different crime types. Victim support services range from referrals to social service agencies, court accompaniment, court preparation, education in getting criminal/civil remedies, and supportive counseling (Rebovich, 1996).

The abundance or reduction of organizational resources may provide a strong impact on how cases within a jurisdiction are pursued (Rosett & Cressey, 1976). Prosecutor offices, often dealing with finite budgets, must decide how expeditiously their resources are to be expended. A filtering process thus operates to remove those cases which the prosecutor feels will not be passed on to the next level (Cole, 1973) since standards of proof become more exacting at successive stages of the criminal process (Rosett & Cressey, 1976). The standard of proof for an arrest (probable cause) is less stringent than the standard required to convict an accused offender (beyond a reasonable doubt). Prosecutors agree that the availability of resources has a definite impact on how domestic violence cases should be handled (Rebovich, 1996). The problem of limited resources is one of the reasons why prosecutors possess discretion in charging and one of the most compelling reasons for decisions to limit prosecutions to the most "valuable" domestic violence cases (Ellis, 1984). Domestic violence cases must compete with cases that command more urgent political responses (Buzawa & Buzawa, 1996) (e.g., drug offenses, terrorism) where offenders are considered highly threatening to social order. Political prioritization of criminal justice responses may also be given to cases where victims are viewed as innocent and respectable (Karmen, 1996), such as child victims.

Throughout history, the role of the victim in domestic violence has helped shaped criminal justice responses. The responses, however, may not have considered the victim's best interests. In fact, debate today often surrounds exactly what response does serve the best interests of the victim. Domestic violence provides an extraordinarily complex set of interrelationships compounded by fiscal, emotional, and child care concerns. In terms of deterring future violence, criminal justice policy may need to consider the particular circumstances of each battering relationship rather than apply a single response set to all cases.

NOTES

1. No-drop prosecution policies were developed in response to victims' reluctance to cooperate in a prosecution strategy. Two types of policies exist. For hard no-drop policies, prosecutors are encouraged to pursue domestic violence cases regardless of the victim's wishes. For soft no-drop policies, prosecutors have the option to drop a case, with sufficient justification, if a victim desires dropping the case (Mills, 2003).
2. The research sites were San Diego, Everett, Washington, Klamath Falls, Oregon, and Omaha, Nebraska.

REFERENCES

ATKINSON HUDSON, D. (Executive Producer). (2003, January 23). *The Oprah Winfrey show* [television series]. Chicago: Harpo Productions, Inc.

BERK, R., CAMPBELL, A., KLAP, R., & WESTERN, B. (1992). The deterrent effect of arrest in incidents of domestic violence: A Bayesian analysis of four field experiments. *American Sociological Review, 57,* 698–708.

BUZAWA, E., & BUZAWA, C. (1996). *Domestic violence: The criminal justice response* (2nd ed.). Thousand Oaks, CA: Sage.

CAHN, N., & LERMAN, L. (1991). Prosecuting woman abuse. In M. Steinman (Ed.), *Woman battering: Policy responses* (pp. 95–112). Cincinnati, OH: Anderson Publishing/Academy of Criminal Justice Sciences.

CARDENAS, J. (1986). The crime victim in the prosecutorial process. *Harvard Journal of Law and Public Policy, 9,* 357–398.

CASSELL, P. (1994). Balancing the scales of justice: The case for the effects of Utah's victims' rights amendment. *Utah Law Review, 1994,* 1373–1474.

COLE, G. (1973). *Politics and the administration of justice.* Beverly Hills: Sage.

COLE, S. (1999). Keeping the peace: Domestic assault and private prosecution in antebellum Baltimore. In C. Daniels & M. Kennedy (Eds.), *Over the threshold: Intimate violence in early America* (pp. 148–172). New York: Routledge.

DAWSON, M., & DINOVITZER, R. (2001). Victim cooperation and the prosecution of domestic violence in a specialized court. *Justice Quarterly, 18*(3), 593–622.

DODGE, M., & GREENE, E. (1991). Juror and expert conceptions of battered women. *Violence and Victims, 6*(4), 271–283.

DUNFORD, F., HUIZINGA, D., & ELLIOT, D. (1990). The role of arrest in domestic assault: The Omaha Police experiment. *Criminology, 28*(2), 183–206.

ELLIS, J. (1984). Prosecutorial discretion to charge in cases of spousal assault: A dialogue. *Journal of Criminal Law and Criminology, 75*(1), 56–102.

EWING, C., & AUBREY, M. (1987). Battered women and public opinion: Some realities about the myths. *Journal of Family Violence, 2,* 257–264.

FORD, D., & REGOLI, M. J. (1992). The preventive impacts of policies for prosecuting wife batterers. In E. Buzawa & C. Buzawa (Eds.), *Domestic violence: The changing criminal justice response* (pp. 181–207). Westport, CT: Greenwood.

FROHMANN, L. (1997). Convictability and discordant locales: Reproducing race, class, and gender ideologies in prosecutorial decisionmaking. *Law & Society Review, 31*(3), 531–555.

GOOLKASIAN, G. (1986). *Confronting domestic violence: A guide for criminal justice agencies.* (NIJ Contract No. J-LEAA-0011-81). Washington, DC: U.S. Government Printing Office.

GORDON, L. (1988). *Heroes of their own lives: The politics and history of family violence.* New York: Penguin Books.

HANNA, C. (1996). No right to choose: Mandated victim participation in domestic violence prosecutions. *Harvard Law Review, 109*(8), 1849–1911.

HARTMAN, J., & BELKNAP, J. (2003). Beyond the gatekeepers: Court professionals' self-reported attitudes about and experiences with misdemeanor domestic violence cases. *Criminal Justice and Behavior, 30*(3), 349–373.

HIRSCHEL, D., & HUTCHINSON, I. (1992). Female spouse abuse and the police response: The Charlotte, North Carolina experiment. *The Journal of Criminal Law & Criminology, 83*(1), 73–119.

IGRA, A. (2000). Likely to become a public charge: Deserted women and the family law of the poor in New York City, 1910-1936. *Journal of Women's History, 11*(4), 59–74.

KARMEN, A. (1996). *Crime victims: An introduction to victimology* (3rd ed.). Belmont, CA: Wadsworth.

KINGSNORTH, R., & MACINTOSH, R. (2004). Domestic violence: Predictors of victim support for official action. *Justice Quarterly, 21*(2), 301–328.

LEVENSTEIN, L. (2003). Hard choices at 1801 Vine: Poor women's legal actions against men in post-World War II Philadelphia. *Feminist Studies, 29*(1), 141–163.

MARKARIAN, A. (2003). OPDV bulletin: Evidence-based prosecution of domestic violence cases. Retrieved July 16, 2004 from http://www.opdv.state.ny.us/public_awareness/bulletins/fall2003/prosecution.html

MCLEOD, M. (1983). Victim noncooperation in the prosecution of domestic assault. *Criminology, 21*(3), 395–416.

MILLS, L. (1998). Mandatory arrest and prosecution policies for domestic violence: A critical literature review and the case for more research to test victim empowerment approaches. *Criminal Justice and Behavior, 25,* 306–318.

MILLS, L. (2003). *Insult to injury: Rethinking our responses to intimate abuse.* Princeton, NJ: Princeton University Press.

PARKER, L. (1997). A "Brutal Case" or "Only a Family Jar"? Violence against women in San Diego County, 1880-1900. *Violence Against Women, 3*(3), 294–319.

Pleck, E. (1987). *Domestic tyranny: The making of social policy against family violence from colonial times to the present*. New York: Oxford University Press.

Private prosecution: A remedy for district attorneys' unwarranted in action. (1955–1956). *Yale Law Journal, 65*, 209–234.

Ramsey, C. (2002). The discretionary power of "public" prosecutors in historical perspective. *American Criminal Law Review, 39*, 1309–1397.

Rauma, D. (1984). Going for the gold: Prosecutorial decision making in cases of wife assault. *Social Science Research, 13*, 321–351.

Rebovich, D. (1996). Prosecution response to domestic violence: Results of a survey of large jurisdictions. In E. Buzawa & C. Buzawa (Eds.), *Do arrests and restraining orders work?* (pp. 176–191). Thousand Oaks, CA: Sage.

Rosett, A., & Cressey, D. (1976). *Justice by consent*. Philadelphia: Lippincott.

Schmidt, J., & Steury, E. (1989). Prosecutorial discretion in filing charges in domestic violence cases. *Criminology, 27*(3), 487–510.

Sherman, L., & Berk, R. (1984). The specific deterrent effects of arrest for domestic assault. *American Sociological Review, 49*, 261–272.

Sherman, L., & Smith, D. (1992). Crime, punishment, and stake in conformity: Legal and informal control of domestic violence. *American Sociological Review, 57*, 680–690.

Smith, B., Davis, R., Nickles, L., & Davies, H. (2001). *An evaluation of efforts to implement no-drop policies: Two central values in conflict*. Final report (Grant No. 98-WT-VX-0029). American Bar Association Criminal Justice Section: United States Department of Justice.

Sontag, D. (2002, November 17). Bad love: Why battered women return again and again to their assaulters and what that means for the law. *The New York Times Magazine*, pp. 52–57, 62, 84.

Steinberg, A. (1984). From private prosecution to plea bargaining: Criminal prosecution, the district attorney, and American legal history. *Crime & Delinquency, 30*(4), 568–592.

Tjaden, P., & Thoennes, N. (1998). *Prevalence, incidence, and consequences of violence against women: Findings from the National Violence Against Women survey*. Washington, DC: National Institute of Justice.

Tjaden, P., & Thoennes, N. (2000). *Full report of the prevalence, incidence, and consequences of violence against women*. Washington, DC: National Institute of Justice.

14

The Impact of Law Enforcement Policies on Victims of Intimate Partner Violence

Susan L. Miller and Elicka S. L. Peterson

❖

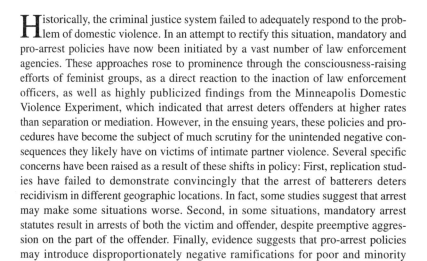

Historically, the criminal justice system failed to adequately respond to the problem of domestic violence. In an attempt to rectify this situation, mandatory and pro-arrest policies have now been initiated by a vast number of law enforcement agencies. These approaches rose to prominence through the consciousness-raising efforts of feminist groups, as a direct reaction to the inaction of law enforcement officers, as well as highly publicized findings from the Minneapolis Domestic Violence Experiment, which indicated that arrest deters offenders at higher rates than separation or mediation. However, in the ensuing years, these policies and procedures have become the subject of much scrutiny for the unintended negative consequences they likely have on victims of intimate partner violence. Several specific concerns have been raised as a result of these shifts in policy: First, replication studies have failed to demonstrate convincingly that the arrest of batterers deters recidivism in different geographic locations. In fact, some studies suggest that arrest may make some situations worse. Second, in some situations, mandatory arrest statutes result in arrests of both the victim and offender, despite preemptive aggression on the part of the offender. Finally, evidence suggests that pro-arrest policies may introduce disproportionately negative ramifications for poor and minority women.

In this chapter, changes in law enforcement policies since the 1980s are reviewed with a focus on their impact on battered women, including the results of research conducted to evaluate pro-arrest policies. The impact of these policies on victims—particularly poor and minority women—will then be discussed, along with possible ramifications arising from cultural and gendered differences in how intimates engage in relationships with one another. Finally, we offer a brief review of alternatives to arrest, as well as supplemental policies and programs when arrests are made that may improve the experiences of battered women in the criminal justice system.

Historically, the crime of intimate violence has been shrouded in secrecy, and largely viewed as a private matter rather than a social problem (see Erez, 2002; Hawkins & Humes, 2002; Straus & Gelles, 1986; Straus, Gelles, & Steinmetz, 1980; Worden, 2000). Both legal and social institutions reinforced the "hands-off approach" that characterized early responses to woman battering. However, since the 1970s, efforts initiated by the battered women's movement have successfully propelled the issue of intimate violence into the national spotlight (see Block & Christakos, 1995; Dobash & Dobash, 1977; Schechter, 1982). Much research and political activism has focused on identifying the correlates of abuse, providing services for victims, creating and strengthening domestic violence legislation, and generally improving the criminal justice system's responses to woman battering (Erez, 2002; Sherman, 1993; Stanko, 1995). One of the most compelling criticisms concerning the handling of woman battering has been leveled against police officers' failure to arrest perpetrators and adequately protect victims of domestic violence. Consequently, innovative laws and policy initiatives were introduced in the 1980s in an effort to improve criminal justice response to domestic disputes (Fagan & Browne, 1994). At the forefront of this shift was a move toward mandatory and pro-arrest policies. This chapter focuses on the problems that prompted these policy innovations, the pro-arrest strategies themselves, and a review of the current status of such strategies. Special attention is paid to the differential impact these policies may hold for lower-class and minority victims of domestic violence. It concludes with a brief review of alternative approaches to arrest-centered policies and their value to battered women.

THE CRIMINAL JUSTICE RESPONSE TO WOMAN BATTERING

In the past, responding to domestic disputes evoked deep feelings of frustration both from the law enforcement officers responding to these calls, and the battered women seeking their protection (see Belknap, 1995). Mediation or separation were common modes of police response, leaving batterers unpunished for their actions, and victims without adequate protection (Grant & Curry, 1993; Stanko, 1982, 1985; Wilson, Johnson, & Daly, 1995). Official responses were justified by a combination of cultural norms and gender role expectations, despite considerable evidence that unchecked intimate violence escalates in frequency and intensity, sometimes with lethal consequences for victims (Campbell et al., 2003; Browne & Williams, 1993; Browne, Williams, & Dutton, 1999; Felson & Ackerman, 2001; Peterson, 1999, 2002; Webster, 2003; Wilson et al., 1995; Zahn, 2003).

For years, battered women faced police officers who routinely supported offenders' positions and challenged the credibility of victims—often trivializing their fears and even blaming them for their own victimization (Gil, 1986; Karmen, 1982). Police officer training manuals of the time reinforced such behavior, stressing the use of family crisis intervention or separation tactics (International Association of Chiefs of Police, 1967; Parnas, 1967). Such policies sanctioned wide discretion for police officers, including officer reluctance to initiate criminal justice proceedings when they believed a reconciliation might occur, making arrest actions futile (Field & Field, 1973; Lerman, 1986). Not only did the police fail to formally respond to battering by invoking arrest, but other components in the system responded similarly (see, e.g., Bowker, 1982; Field & Field, 1973; Ellis, 1984; Klein, 1981; Laszlo & Mckean, 1978). Overall, the failure of the criminal justice system to appropriately respond to women battering perpetuated the silence surrounding intimate violence.

Statistics indicate that when police retain the discretion to arrest in domestic assault incidents, officers generally do not arrest.[1] In fact, Buel (1988) assessed three different studies and found that police arrest rates for domestic violence incidents ranged from 3 to 10 percent. In Milwaukee, although research showed that 82 percent of battered women desired arrest of their abusers, the arrest rate was only 14 percent (Bowker, 1982). Similarly, in Ohio, police arrested only 14 percent of the time, despite the fact that, in 38 percent of these incidents, victims were either injured or killed (Bell, 1984). To make matters worse, research showed that even officers in jurisdictions with pro-arrest policies failed to arrest batterers (Balos & Trotzky, 1988; Ferraro, 1995; Lawrenz, Lembo, & Schade, 1988; Maxwell, Garner, & Fagan, 2001).

As a result of inadequate responses by law enforcement to treat battering as a serious offense, class-action suits were introduced against police departments by victims (Martin, 1978; Paterson, 1979). Battered women who felt unprotected by police have received some satisfaction from this kind of court action, arguing successfully that the equal protection clause of the Fourteenth Amendment is violated when police treat women who are assaulted by an intimate partner differently from people assaulted by strangers. (For a discussion of domestic violence as a human rights violation, see Hawkins and Humes, 2002; for a discussion of domestic violence as a hate crime, see Isaacs, 2001).[2] Class-action suits, political activism by feminists, and victims' advocacy groups proved instrumental in challenging the efficacy and unresponsiveness of police departments (Schechter, 1982). The stage was set for researchers to explore new and different responses to battering, including advocating for pro-arrest and mandatory arrest policies.

MANDATORY ARREST POLICIES

Movement away from discretionary arrest policies and toward mandatory or pro-arrest policies was attractive for a variety of reasons. First, the psychological benefit to battered women cannot be overstated: Arrest demonstrates an official willingness to assert that battering will not be tolerated. Second, some police officers believe mandatory arrest laws assist in clarifying police roles by providing more guidance and training (Loving, 1980). Third, evaluations of jurisdictions that enact mandatory arrest laws indicate that rather than making police officers more vulnerable, police injuries decrease (National Criminal Justice Association, 1985); this decrease may be due to the advance notice or warning about the consequences of abusive behavior once mandatory arrest policies are in effect. Fourth, the onus of responsibility is transferred to police and does not remain solely on the battered woman's shoulders. Thus, many believe that officer-initiated arrest empowers victims (Buel, 1988):

> Arrest can kindle the battered woman's perception that society values her and penalizes violence against her. This perception counteracts her experience of abuse. . . . When a battered

woman calls the police and they arrest the man who beats her, her actions, along with the officer's actions, do something to stop her beating. . . . Now her actions empower. The woman may begin to believe in herself enough to endeavor to protect herself. (Pastoor, 1984)[3]

A fifth advantage of mandatory arrest policies is the feeling that more equitable law enforcement will result than is possible through a discretionary-based arrest system. Buel (1988, p. 224) argues that mandatory arrest that is conducted whenever specific, objective conditions are met will "ensure that race and class distinctions are not the basis for determining how police intervene in family violence situations."[4] Sixth, strong police action can contribute to purposeful follow-up by the other components of the criminal justice system.

Finally, some early research findings indicated that recidivism of batterers dramatically decreased after mandatory arrest policies were initiated. For instance, homicides decreased from 12 or 13 annually to 1 in the initial six months of 1986 in Newport News, Virginia (Lang, 1986); in Hartford County, Connecticut, the number of calls for police service for domestic violence incidents decreased by 28 percent (Olivero, 1987). Without question, the most influential research findings supportive of mandatory arrest policies were attributed to Sherman and Berk's (1984) Minneapolis Domestic Violence Experiment (MDVE).

The MDVE consisted of manipulating types of police response to misdemeanant domestic assault in order to measure their efficacy in reducing recidivism.[5] The finding from this study that almost singularly influenced a paradigm shift in law enforcement policies was that arrest was twice as effective as a deterrent for batterers than traditional police strategies of separation or meditation (Sherman & Berk, 1984).[6] Subsequent national surveys of police departments indicated that the number of jurisdictions supporting arrest for minor domestic assault began increasing almost immediately in the wake of the MDVE—from 10 percent in 1984 to 31 percent in 1986—with 11 states explicitly attributing these policy shifts to the publicized accounts of the success of the Minneapolis experiment (Cohn & Sherman, 1986).[7]

NEW CONCERNS ABOUT MANDATORY ARREST POLICIES

Mandatory arrest policies appear to solve many of the dilemmas faced by battered women. In fact, it is difficult not to embrace such a transformation in police procedures related to woman battering. However, despite the good intentions of researchers and practitioners in initiating such policies, there are at least three considerations that limit unconditional acceptance of the interpretation that mandatory arrest deters battering or eliminates disparity in police response to domestic violence. First, there are methodological problems associated with the original, first-wave research conducted under the auspices of the Minneapolis Domestic Violence Experiment (Binder & Meeker, 1996; Sherman & Berk, 1984). This is important in that the MDVE was the cornerstone for additional evaluations of mandatory arrest policies. Second, there are problems identified with the National Institute of Justice–funded replication studies, including contrary results reported in second-wave studies (Dutton, Hart, Kennedy, & Williams, 1996). Third, it now appears

likely that there are unintended negative consequences of mandatory arrest policies for battered women, particularly women of color or women from lower socioeconomic groups
(Erez, 2002; Lee, Sanders, Thompson, & Mechanic, 2002; Miller, 1989, 2001; Rasche,
1995; Senturia, Sullivan, Ciske, & Shiu-Thornton, 2003; Worden, 2000; Wright, 1998).
These concerns have sparked serious, ongoing debate over the use of mandatory arrest in
attempting to deter subsequent acts of intimate violence.

METHODOLOGICAL PROBLEMS

Since the Minneapolis Domestic Violence Experiment remains the seminal study that
informed public policy on police response to domestic violence, it is necessary to review
both the experiment and its findings. Methodological problems associated with the MDVE
are now legion (see, e.g., Binder & Meeker, 1988; Fagan, 1989; Lempert, 1984), with the
most salient concerns arising over sampling issues. More specifically, the deterrent effect
attributed to mandatory arrest was based on a small number of follow-up interviews completed by the battered women: Sherman and Berk (1984, p. 265) reported a 62 percent
completion rate for the initial face-to-face interviews, but this dropped to a 49 percent
completion rate for the biweekly follow-ups in six subsequent months (161 respondents
from a sample of 330 victims). While Sherman and Berk (1984) contend that the experi-
mental design of the research had no impact on victim participation during the follow-up
phase, it is unknown whether further violence occurred that was undisclosed in follow-up
interviews, or simply lost due to case attrition. If these problems did exist, a research artifact may have been created during the follow-up stage, or the observed deterrent effect
may have been only temporary, and contingent upon pending charges (Jaffe, Wolfe,
Telford, & Austin, 1986).

Another factor confounding a clear interpretation of the MDVE results is the possibility that victims may be reluctant to request police service after experiencing the consequences of official intervention once mandatory arrest policies are effected (Sherman &
Berk, 1984). This dynamic might mask continued violence in follow-up interviews and in
official records, demonstrating a deterrent effect in reporting practices that may not reflect
an actual reduction in the number of battering incidences (Berk & Newton, 1985). In fact,
Buzawa (1982) contends that once a woman loses control over the outcome of a domestic
dispute, she may be deterred from calling the police.[8] Battered women who call the police
for help may desire only the cessation of the immediate abuse; in such situations, arrest
would be viewed as an undesirable option. Another possibility confounding interpretation
is that battering may escalate as a result of arrest—silencing victims through increased
intimidation, threats, or retaliation from the abuser (Campbell, 1992; Goolkasian, 1986;
Felson & Messner, 2000).[9]

Findings of a deterrent effect also may be the result of displacement in cases where a
violent relationship has terminated, and the batterer simply moves into a another violent
relationship with a new partner (Fagan, 1989; Reiss, 1985). This displacement effect is
related to selective attrition problems identified by Elliott (1989), which may occur if
arrest affects the termination of the relationship, thereby limiting the deterrent interpretation of lower recidivism rates after pro-arrest policies are enacted. Ford (1984) offers

support for this hypothesis through evidence that arrest may be correlated with breaking up, which is one successful way of stopping further violence. A displacement effect might also take the form of violence shifting to other family members. Finally, if a relationship remains intact, but the couple moves away from the area, their absence in official records may be misleading if it is interpreted as the result of a deterrent effect (Lempert, 1984). Overall, the controversy over the existence of a significant deterrent effect attributable to mandatory arrest continues to spur considerable debate as well as research (see, e.g., Barnard, Vera, & Newman, 1982; Binder & Meeker, 1992; Fagan & Browne, 1994; Kuhl & Saltzman, 1985; Maxwell et al., 2001; Greenfield, Rand, & Craven, 1998).

Given the plausibility of alternative explanations for the reported deterrent effect, as well as the methodological issues reviewed here, many researchers have suggested caution in adopting such dramatic policy shifts based on the "success" of the Minneapolis experiment (Binder & Meeker, 1988; Elliott, 1989; Gelles & Mederer, 1985; Lempert, 1984; Zorza, 1994; Zorza & Woods, 1995).[10]

FAILURES AND PROBLEMS WITH REPLICATION STUDIES AND OTHER PRO-ARREST EVALUATIONS

In this section, we present a discussion of subsequent research on the impacts of mandatory and presumptive arrest policies in a number of jurisdictions in an effort to shed further light on the efficacy and costs of this response to domestic violence. Researchers examining the impact of pro-arrest policies in London, Ontario, found that the numbers of cases in which the police initiated criminal charges of domestic abuse increased dramatically (2.7 percent in 1979 to 67.3 percent in 1983), that the numbers of cases dismissed or withdrawn decreased substantially, and that victim self-reports revealed a decrease in subsequent violence for the year following the policy change and police intervention (Jaffe et al., 1986). However, despite this apparent success, results from an officer survey indicated that only 21 percent of the police surveyed believed the new policy was effective in stopping intimate violence, with 32 percent reporting that they thought women stopped calling the police after the policy was enacted (Jaffe). Elliott (1989) addressed this seeming contradiction, maintaining that the study was plagued by serious methodological problems (mainly the absence of a control group and an unrepresentative sample of victims) that call into question the findings suggesting the new arrest policy was a success. In light of these problems, it is difficult to conclude with any confidence that the pro-arrest policies in Ontario facilitated victim reporting, or that there is support for the notion that a deterrent effect was realized.

Buzawa and Buzawa (1993, 2003) contend that police officers are generally distrustful of law enforcement policy directives designed by anyone other than police personnel. This distrust is manifested in officer circumvention of laws or policies, which renders external efforts to effect change useless through officer subversion (Buzawa & Buzawa, 2003). Research that evaluates the impact of a presumptive arrest policy adopted by the Phoenix, Arizona, police supports the idea that police circumvent policy (Ferraro, 1989b): Despite both a new law and departmental policy, arrests were made in only 18 percent of the domestic assault cases. Ferraro (1989b) suggests that much of this noncompliance on the part of officers was related to legal, ideological, and political considerations that led them to ignore the policy change. In this analysis, Ferraro gathered detailed qualitative data from victims that provided explanations as to why some battered women—especially poorer women—would be less inclined to call the police. In particular, women reported that they would not seek police help if it meant their partners would be arrested, or might create a financial hardship for the family, including a possible loss of employment.

In 1987, the District of Columbia's police department enacted new legislation that directed officers to arrest batterers. However, an evaluation conducted two years later showed that police failed to enforce the guideline, continuing to resort to mediating domestic disputes, and keeping arrests at a minimum (Baker, Cahn, & Sands, 1989). These findings are based on interviews with almost 300 victims who sought protection at either the Superior Court or the Citizens Complaint Center. As in evaluations conducted in other jurisdictions, police circumvented the pro-arrest policy. In the DC study, only 5 percent of the cases resulted in arrest, even in situations where the complainant was injured seriously enough to require medical treatment, or had been threatened with guns, knives, or other weapons.[11] The most commonly cited reasons offered by police to explain their failure to arrest were that they believed nothing could be done (23.7 percent), that the police regarded the case as "domestic" or the couple lived together (and, thus, the police did not want to get involved; 22.6 percent), or that they chose to instruct the victim to explore civil remedies through the Citizens Complaint Center (20.1 percent).

Based on the questions and concerns generated by Sherman and Berk's Minneapolis Domestic Violence Experiment, the National Institute of Justice (NIJ) funded six different replication studies to explore the deterrent effects of police response to battering (U.S. Department of Justice, 1985).[12] It was hoped that these new studies would address and correct some of the important issues and problems raised by the Minneapolis experiment.[13] Overall, these replication studies achieved equivocal results, and, in fact, suggested that arrest may have no effect or even might escalate violence (see Garner, Fagan, & Maxwell, 1995; Berk, Campbell, Klap, & Western, 1992a, 1992b; Dunford, 1990; Dunford, Huizinga, & Elliott 1990; Hirschel, Hutchinson, & Dean 1992a, 1992b; Pate, Hamilton, & Annan, 1992; Sherman, Smith, Schmidt, & Rogan, 1991; Sherman et al., 1992; Sherman, Schmidt, et al., 1991).[14]

The NIJ-funded replication studies evaluated various interventions, with results demonstrating different outcomes. For instance, the Milwaukee project used three treatment responses: arrest with a mean jail detention of 11.1 hours, arrest that resulted in an average release time of 2.8 hours, and a warning in lieu of an arrest. An analysis of 1,200 cases revealed no significant differences in arrest effects after a six-month follow-up period, although a slight deterrent effect was noted after 30 days (Hirschel et al., 1992). The researchers concluded that arrest impacts batterers differently, producing a greater deterrent effect on those with a greater stake in conformity due to employment than on those who were unemployed, and thus had little stake in conformity (Sherman, 1992).

Another replication study, the Omaha Police Experiment, followed the design of the MDVE by randomly assigning cases to one of three police interventions: separation, mediation, or arrest. They developed two types of outcome measures: official recidivism and victim reports of subsequent violence (Dunford et al., 1990). Victims were interviewed twice over a six-month period, with an overall completion rate of 73 percent ($n = 242$).

Several comparisons between the MDVE and Omaha experiments concerning the victim interview data are important to highlight. First, the proportion of initial interviews completed in Minneapolis was 62 percent, while in Omaha the proportion was 80 percent. Second, the proportion of the sample completing the six-month follow-up interview in Minneapolis was 49 percent, while in Omaha the proportion was 73 percent. Finally, only the Omaha experiment employed the use of face-to-face interviews with victims. Thus, with better reporting, less attrition in the sample, and a qualitative component to aid in assessing findings, the researchers concluded that there is virtually no difference in the prevalence or frequency of repeat offending resulting from arrest (Dunford et al., 1990). The Omaha researchers also sought to determine if *any* of the interventions (separation, mediation, or arrest) could delay subsequent violence for a longer period of time than the others. After conducting time-to-failure analyses, they determined that there was no significant difference between the possible police responses (Dunford et al., 1990). The conclusions reached by the Omaha Police Experiment researchers provide ample caution against adopting mandatory or presumptory arrest policies in other jurisdictions if their findings were supported in the remaining five sites.[15]

Similar to the findings obtained in Milwaukee and Omaha, the Charlotte study found arrest actually increased domestic violence recidivism rather than deterring it. The Charlotte replication assessed three forms of law enforcement response: immediate arrest, issuing a citation for court at a later date, and taking no formal action other than separation and advising. An analysis of 650 cases revealed an increase in the proportion of repeat arrests across every category. Hirschel et al. (1992a) offered several reasons why the Omaha, Milwaukee, and Charlotte experiments failed to find evidence supporting arrest as an effective deterrent: The crux of the problem was that the majority of the offenders in the replication studies had previous criminal records; as such, arrest likely failed to deter because it was not a new experience to these batterers. This confounding effect may have been exacerbated by the fact that many of the sampled offenders were either chronic abusers or had criminal histories, making a deterrent impact from arrest even more unlikely, especially as such arrests commonly result in a relatively short amount of jail time. Moreover, the data revealed that few offenders were found guilty and sentenced to jail at any rate, further reducing any potential deterrent effect. In light of these observations, Hirschel et al. (1992b) criticized these studies for failing to recognize the possibility that arrest may produce only a deterrent effect in certain types of abusers.

Researchers in Colorado Springs and Metro-Dade found limited support for the MDVE findings, but only in the victim interview data, in which the response rate was low (Schmidt & Sherman, 1996). Sherman (1992) suggested that a higher response rate among the more stable, employed group of criminals in the Colorado sample might have provided stronger support for presumptive arrest. However, Hirschel, Hutchinson, & Dean (1992b) argued that extensive comparisons conducted on interviewed versus noninterviewed cases showed the two groups to be similar enough to counter criticisms of sampling bias. But a stronger criticism confounding interpretation of results in the Colorado experiment was that the majority (58 percent) of domestic violence in the sample reflected incidents in which offenders harassed or menaced victims in a nonviolent manner (Sherman, 1992). It is likely that this might produce results different from that of the physical attacks required for arrest in other replication studies.

Overall, the bulk of research on the subject indicates that mandatory and pro-arrest policies *do not* provide the anticipated panacea to intimate violence for a variety of reasons. In fact, many have argued that such policies are fraught with unintended negative consequences for victims that render them worse than ineffective. Buzawa and Buzawa (2003) have cited several reasons for not supporting mandatory arrest policies, including the argument that the benefits do not outweigh the costs with respect to increased conviction rates. Attempts to limit discretion in any setting rarely meet with success, and in the case of mandatory arrest, the police do not have a monopoly on retaining their control—victims may refuse to comply with prosecutorial efforts, or, when forced to comply, may be deliberately vague in an effort to thwart prosecution efforts (Ferraro, 1989b).

Other drawbacks of mandatory and pro-arrest policies are a cause for concern, as well. Police may engage in arrest-avoidance techniques that would limit assistance to some victims, while forcing assistance on others (Buzawa & Buzawa, 2003). In cases in which a victim does not desire an arrest, mandatory policies perpetuate the belief that police disregard victims' preferences. Another concern is that increased arrest rates in the wake of these reforms are at least partially attributable to "dual arrests" of both the male offender and his female partner, especially in light of the tendency for intimates to file charges and countercharges (Johnson, 1995; Martin, 1997; Miller, 1989, 2001), without making an assessment of which partner was the primary aggressor in the violent incident (for a detailed discussion of the issue of dual arrest and arrests of female victims, see Miller, 2005; see also Renzetti, 1999, for a discussion of feminist response to the violence of women). These last two reservations involve the potential for police to misuse their arrest power; critics also note that police may make more trivial arrests of victims more often when they are repeatedly called to the same house for domestic disturbances (Buzawa & Buzawa, 1996).[16]

RACE AND CLASS IMPLICATIONS

Obviously, one potential problem with mandatory arrest policies is that they almost certainly produce unanticipated and negative consequences for women. But due to limited opportunities, resources, and alternatives, men who abuse women from minority or lower socioeconomic groups may be disproportionately arrested in jurisdictions favoring pro-arrest policies, creating additional problems for these battered women (Wright, 1998). Given this likelihood, a discussion acknowledging the differential concerns of battered women from minority and low-income groups has surfaced in the domestic violence literature.[17] Much of this literature indicates that policies designed to assist battered women may prove to be inadequate or inappropriate based on the differing cultural or community needs of poor and minority women. Lockhart (1985) goes so far as to contend that mainstream research on battering necessarily suffers from major shortcomings in design due to its failure to take into account the radically different experiences of such disenfranchised groups.

Hagan and Albonetti (1982) report that blacks and lower-socioeconomic status individuals are more likely than whites and higher-socioeconomic status individuals to perceive injustice operating against them by police, juries, and court personnel. Indeed, minority groups have a long history of uneasy relations with police (see Miller & Meloy, 2005; Overby, 1971; Rossi, Berk, & Edison, 1974; Stack, 1974). If a legacy of distrust exists between the minority community and law enforcement agents, minority women may not embrace the new arrest policies. As such, some minority group women may object "to mandatory arrest laws because they are viewed as providing police with yet another means of harassing minority group men rather than as protection for battered women" (Goolkasian, 1986, p. 37). There is evidence that black women may be ambivalent about seeking relief from the criminal justice system; they call the police more often, but often are less than satisfied with the outcome when they do (Avakame, Fyfe, & McCoy, 1999). Further, some studies suggest that the interests of battered women are suppressed and marginalized by community concern over incarcerated men (Williams, 1981; Wright, 1998). This creates a situation in which black women who call for police intervention resulting in arrest may face community disapproval, or even punishment through withholding of material and emotional support, or refusing to shelter the woman or assist with childcare (Wright, 1998).

McLeod (1984) discusses two competing hypotheses concerning disproportionate representation of minority citizens and calls to the police: first is the differential participation hypothesis, which states that statistics accurately reflect that minorities are more involved in domestic violence incidents; and second is the differential notification hypothesis, which suggests that these statistics are misleading in that they reflect reporting rates, not participation rates. Research conducted by Block (1974) supports the latter interpretation— she found that black victims have higher reporting rates than whites with assault and battery incidents, and as such, are overrepresented in official statistics. Hindelang (1976) also claimed the statistics are misleading in that they reflect only assaults known to police.

With any assessment of pro-arrest policies, it is necessary to discern whether or not there are class differences in victim reporting of intimate violence to the police. Schwartz (1988) challenged the pervasive argument that there are *not* class differences in intimate violence vulnerability.[18] He argues that this issue is largely ignored by feminists conducting research on battered women because they do not want to advance the myth that battered women are primarily located at the lower end of the socioeconomic spectrum. Schwartz contends that since feminist ideology embraces framing the issue within a context that insists all women are equally oppressed and vulnerable to victimization in a patriarchal society, they refuse to investigate class distinctions. Feminists (and other researchers) are able to effectively criticize the methodology of studies that do find greater incidence rates among lower class women. Schwartz contends that this is very easy to do (for example, citing reporting artifacts—data sources oversample poorer persons, who are more likely to use services such as the police, courts, shelters, or other social service agencies; see Okum, 1986, p. 48).[19]

While this debate is far from settled, social class remains inextricably linked to race in the study of intimate violence because nonwhites are overrepresented in lower socioeconomic groups, and socioeconomic status greatly affects options (Lockhart, 1985, 1987). Women with more income have greater access to resources to assist them in keeping their abuse private, such as private physicians and safe shelters, which results in their being able to escape the detection of law enforcement, hospital emergency rooms, and social service agencies (Asbury, 1987; Block, 2003; Prescott & Letko, 1977; Stark, Flitcraft, & Frazier, 1979; Washburn & Frieze, 1981).

Another aspect related to class is that "lower-class people are denied privacy for their quarrels: neighborhood bars, sidewalks, and crowded, thin-walled apartments afford little isolation" (Eisenberg & Micklow, 1977, p. 142). An inability to afford privacy likely exacerbates the negative impact of mandatory and pro-arrest policies on minority and poor women, who may have fewer opportunities and alternatives available for settling disputes privately (Stanko, 1985). Further, the economic consequences of arrest may be devastating for lower socioeconomic households. If the batterer is jailed, income will likely be lost, thus increasing the probability that a woman may not call the police if arrest is imminent. Thus, it seems clear that limited alternatives exist for economically disadvantaged battered women, especially women from minority groups, who are faced with the dilemma of being dependent on the police for assistance when their partners engage in violence against them.

A BRIEF REVIEW OF ALTERNATIVES AND SUPPLEMENTS TO ARREST

Early efforts of the battered women's movement were aimed at assisting the victims of domestic violence through establishing shelters and crisis lines. Not all of these programs received unanimous support: Shelters have been criticized—mostly by profamily groups—as instrumental to the dissolution of families, though empirical assessments refute these contentions (Stone, 1984).[20] By the early 1980s, domestic violence legislation was enacted in most states (Langan & Innes, 1986; Lerman & Livingston, 1983; Mahoney, 1991; Morash, 1986). Included were a variety of programs and legal remedies: civil protection orders, legal advocacy, and job-training programs in women's shelters. However, not all of these options have been successful in aiding victims of domestic violence. Ironically, recent research on the decline of female-perpetrated intimate partner homicide suggests that these advances in assisting battered women have resulted in an unintended effect of which men are the beneficiaries. There is considerable evidence that the lives of batterers are being spared through women taking advantage of domestic violence services to reduce their exposure to violence before situations escalate to a lethal conclusion (Dugan, Nagin, & Rosenfeld, 1999, 2003; Dugan, Rosenfeld, & Nagin, 2003; Peterson, 1999; Rosenfeld, 1997).

Grau, Fagan, and Wexler (1984) report that restraining orders designed to provide civil court alternatives to formal sanctions are largely ineffective. Based on 270 victim interviews in four states, they contend that civil protection orders do little to prevent or reduce future violence. Further, the potential assistance of orders is limited by a number of implementation problems including long waiting periods, little or no protection afforded cohabitators and other unmarried partners, circumvention by police officers failing to enforce the orders, and an overall lack of coordination and integration of civil and criminal remedies (Grau et al., 1984). Harrell and Smith (1996), Klein (1996), and others have reported that, despite the lack of effectiveness of civil restraining orders in protecting victims from future violence, they serve an important symbolic role. These problems are particularly important given Harrell and Smith's (1996) finding that the majority of women who seek restraining orders were more seriously abused by their partners.

More recently, attention has shifted toward exploring the relationship dynamics of battering, concentrating on providing treatment for offenders. Many of these intervention or treatment efforts apply a feminist, antisexist, psychotherapeutic approach that challenges male batterers to examine traditional gender role socialization (see, e.g., Adams, 1989; Dobash, Dobash, Emerson, Cavanagh, & Lewis, 2000). Evaluations of counseling programs indicate much variability in recidivism rates—as low as 2 percent in programs in which batterers were eager to participate (Dutton, 1987) to as high as 39 percent (Gondolf,

1984). Some of this variability is attributed to small sample sizes and different measures of recidivism. Deterrence may be most effective when both social *and* legal penalties are utilized (Fagan, 1989). For instance, one study that followed batterers who were arrested and participated in court-mandated counseling demonstrated low recidivism rates (as measured by partner reports) after 30 months (Dutton, 1986b). Gondolf (1998) examined batterer treatment programs of varying interventions and lengths, and concluded that shorter programs may be just as effective as longer, more intensive programs. His research used a 15-month follow-up period, and he argues for the use of much longer follow-ups to determine the true efficacy of treatment programs.

Law enforcement policy changes cannot exist in a vacuum. Arrest is only the initial step in the criminal justice system continuum and assistance can easily be circumvented by unresponsiveness from other key players in the system (Dutton, Hart, Kennedy, & Williams, 1996; Elliott, 1989). There has been some demonstrated success in reducing battering through innovative programming that provides a combination of services, including policies that involve prosecutors taking responsibility for initiating prosecution, rather than the victim (see Lerman, 1981–1992 for a comprehensive review of these types of programs). Fostering links between the criminal justice system and social service agencies would likely be helpful, as well, especially for women with limited opportunities to explore other alternatives (see Hirschel et al., 1992a, 1992b). It has been suggested that a collaboration of legal sanctions and social services, such as court-mandated counseling, generally tend to complement one another, and correct power imbalances between victims and offenders with a minimum of coercion (Dutton, 1986a; Miller & Wellford, 1997). Third-party mediation programs are also being used as a method to formally mediate interpersonal disputes with the assistance of a trained mediator who strives to develop a way to solve disputes nonviolently. Prosecutor's offices have introduced pretrial mediation programs as an alternative to formal criminal processing. The idea behind mediation is to informally educate both the victim and the offender about more effective methods for resolving conflict and to inform both parties about their legal rights. Some preliminary evaluations of mediation programs indicate they offer similar reductions in recidivism as more formal case processing (Bethel & Singer, 1981–1982). However, mediation programs have been criticized for their failure to assign blame, and for allowing violence to be seen as part of a dysfunctional family, rather than as violence directed against women (Lerman, 1984).

Many prosecutor's offices have adopted a "pro-prosecution" policy to augment pro-arrest, which entails aggressive prosecution of domestic violence cases, even without victim cooperation, and the enhanced use of civil protection orders (Rebovich, 1996). However, prosecutors feel that protection orders are not very effective and that violators receive minimal punishment (Rebovich, 1996). Prosecutor's offices are very supportive of domestic violence diversion programs, offender counseling programs, and victim advocacy programs (Rebovich, 1996). Research in Indianapolis, however, found that court-mandated counseling as a condition of either probation or diversion was no more effective in reducing recidivism than prosecution with conviction using presumptive sentencing (Ford & Regoli, 1992).

Despite training to this end, it is still very rare for police to refer battered women to outside agencies (Donlon, Hendricks, & Meagher, 1986; Loving, 1980). Consistent police training for handling domestic violence cases, proper control over training course content, and funding support for this training are virtually nonexistent (Buzawa & Buzawa, 2003; and see Sorenson, 2003, for a discussion of difficulties funding domestic violence programs more generally). Cromack (1996) asserts that interagency cooperation is necessary in order to effectively deal with domestic violence; for instance, some police trainings use role-playing exercises while civilian volunteers act as peer advocates (Defina & Wetherbee, 1997).

Another potentially fruitful avenue to explore involves the procedure of arrest itself. Paternoster, Brame, Bachman, and Sherman (1997) found that when police acted fairly, the rate of rearrest for domestic violence was significantly lower, regardless of the outcome. McCord (1992) calls for examining the sequence of domestic violence, in which an offender leaves a violent partnership to begin a relationship with a new target. She also believes that researchers have overlooked important victim characteristics, such as education, occupation, and family or emotional resources, that may affect relationship durability following interventions or arrests (McCord, 1992).

Overall, it seems clear that in order to devise ways to deter domestic violence, policies, experiments, and ideas need to take into account both victim and perpetrator characteristics, displacement concerns, interagency and coordinated community responses, treatment programs, and issues of procedural justice.

CONCLUSIONS

Mandatory arrest policies and laws may exacerbate an already difficult social problem, despite good intentions and its intuitive appeal. Given inconsistent research findings and the negligible deterrence effects found in the policy evaluation research, it appears that many battered women may not benefit from mandatory arrest policies, and that these policies might be particularly detrimental for battered women of color or women from lower socioeconomic groups. In addition, if victims are arrested for their use of self-defensive violence, arrest policies serve to increase the harm for battered women. As such, expansion of state authority to intrude into people's lives may be unwarranted in the area of domestic violence, unless a victim specifically requests such action. Efforts to improve police responses must be embedded within the context of emerging knowledge about a range of intimate violence responses, and extend to the entire criminal justice system. Otherwise, operational changes that dictate police response to battering incidents will remain largely fractured, rhetorical, and ineffective.

N O T E S

1. However, see Smith's (1987) analysis of interpersonal violence that found particular extralegal factors, such as race, gender, victim preference, economic status of neighborhoods, and the demeanor of combatants toward officers influenced police arrest decisions.
2. For more details on litigation by battered women, see Eppler, 1986; Moore, 1985; Mahoney, 1991.
3. However, an alternative interpretation challenging Pastoor's empowerment hypothesis has been raised by MacKinnon (1983), who argues that police intervention likely increases dependency on the state by battered women. Additionally, MacKinnon argues that manipulating police

responses fails to address "the conditions that produce men who systematically express themselves violently toward women, women whose resistance is disabled, and the role of the state in this dynamic" (MacKinnon, 1983, p. 643). In a similar vein, see Rifkin (1980) for a discussion of the limitations of a system of law that remains embedded in patriarchal foundations that do not challenge sexual stratification in society.

4. Buel (1988) contends that officers disproportionately arrest batterers who are black and/or poor, and that mandatory arrest would reduce this inequity in police response.

5. The Minneapolis Domestic Violence Experiment randomly assigned police officers to deliver one of three possible responses to misdemeanant domestic assaults: mediation, separation, or arrest. During a six-month follow-up period, both victim and police reports indicated that arrest deterred offenders significantly more than alternative interventions (Sherman & Berk, 1984).

6. At least one effort to replicate this finding in a nonexperimental setting has been successful (Berk & Newton, 1985).

7. However, a reexamination of the mandatory arrest policy enacted in Minneapolis revealed that, despite the policy, out of 24,948 domestic assault calls in 1986, less than 3,635 resulted in arrest. Instead, officers continued to use mediation techniques to handle cases (Balos & Trotsky, 1988; see also Belknap, 1995; Belknap & McCall, 1994; Sherman, 1993; Buzawa & Buzawa, 2003).

8. Buzawa's (1982) position stems from an examination of aggregate domestic assault arrest data from Detroit after an aggressive arrest policy was enacted. Considerably *fewer* calls for police assistance were made by victims *after* the policy was in place. Buzawa concluded that this victim deterrence effect may be even more pronounced in jurisdictions with mandatory arrest policies, because victims would have even less power over the outcome (Buzawa, 1982).

9. One method of testing this hypothesis would be to assess the frequency of calls to domestic violence hotlines or shelters to determine if victim reliance on such services increases in response to mandatory arrest policies. This would likely indicate that battered women still seek help, but not in the form of official intervention.

10. However, it is not always feasible to postpone such decisions while awaiting the results of replication studies due to public sentiment and political pressures (see Sherman & Cohn, 1989).

11. In fact, the police filed a report in only 16.4 percent of the incidents, arrests were made only in cases where the victim suffered broken bones or was hospitalized for her injuries, and only 27.2 percent of the abusers were arrested even having threatened or attacked their partner with weapons, even in cases where the weapon was visible to the police. "When the incident included an attack on a child, arrests were made only 11 percent of the time. However, when the incident included damage to the victim's car, the police made arrests in 25 percent of the cases. . . . The single factor most highly correlated with whether an arrest is made is *whether the abuser insulted the police officer.* The arrest rate for such incidents was 32 percent" (Baker et al., 1989, pp. 2–3; emphasis in original).

12. The National Institute of Justice was the original funding source for the Minneapolis Domestic Violence Experiment (Sherman & Berk, 1984).

13. The replication sites were: Dade County, Florida; Atlanta, Georgia; Charlotte, North Carolina; Milwaukee, Wisconsin; and Colorado Springs, Colorado.

14. Mandatory arrest policies are designed to usurp officer discretion through dictating arrest action, while presumptive arrest policies are designed to strongly influence officer discretion in the direction of arrest.

15. Moreover, Dunford et al. (1990) report that victim-based measures of repeat violence at the Omaha site indicate that police action—whether arrest, separation, or mediation—had no impact on subsequent violence in misdemeanor cases.

16. Statutes that guide police to distinguish between the primary physical aggressor and the party who used violence in self-defense may be a fruitful avenue to pursue. However, these changes

may not be enough to solve the problem of dual arrests. Hooper (1996) explains that the self-defense and primary aggression paradigms were developed to accommodate male (to male) violence and may not be the most helpful for women's violence, which is essentially different from men's violence. Women's violent acts are often not immediately precipitated by the violent acts of their partners (Hooper, 1996). Rather, domestically violent women can be viewed as caught up in a pattern of violence that they did not initiate and do not control (Hamberger & Potente, 1994). Better training and education of police officers in both the dynamics of domestic violence and in communication with victims may help with the dual arrest problem (Saunders, 1995).

17. See, for example, Lockhart (1985, 1987), Ashbury (1987), and Coley and Beckett (1988) for research focusing on black women; Scarf (1983) on battered Jewish women; and Carroll (1980) for a comparison of battered Mexican American and Jewish families; Lobel (1986) and Renzetti (1987) for ramifications of domestic violence for lesbians; and Feinman (1987) and Hallum (2003) on battered Latino women.

18. Schwartz (1988) tackles the issue of differential representation of minority and lower-class citizens reflected in victimization surveys. Essentially, he argues that there is evidence suggesting that the National Crime Survey (NCS) is more likely to be biased in favor of showing more *middle-* and *upper-class* women's victimizations, rather than overrepresenting lower classes, citing Sparks's (1981) research: "[he] argues that black and lower-class persons systematically underreport assaults in NCS interviews, and that any findings which show a greater incidence of victimization of lower-class persons are in fact stronger than would be indicated by these data" (Schwartz, 1988, p. 378).

19. There exists even more of a split in the discourse between feminist and more mainstream analyses regarding the issue of class differences in intimate-violence victimizations. Several researchers refuse even to raise the issue, maintaining that the question is not only inherently sexist, but also a form of victim-blaming, by token of its assumption that victimization might somehow result from the personal characteristics of victims (see, e.g., Wardell et al., 1983; Klein, 1981; Davis, Hatch, Griffin, & Thompson, 1987; Dobash & Dobash, 1979; Stark et al., 1979). However, see Breines and Gordon (1983) for an opposing—and perhaps more courageous—discussion.

20. Stone (1984) conducted interviews of shelter residents in an effort to determine whether shelters truly promote the dissolution of marriages. This research is important, given a history of pro-family criticism that shelters persuade battered women to leave their spouse and family. Stone (1984) found that women who had decided to file for a divorce had made this choice *prior* to seeking shelter. Further, the vast majority of the battered women indicated that the shelter provided an opportunity to recover from physical and emotional trauma in a safe place where they could think and make rational decisions about their futures.

REFERENCES

ADAMS, D. (1989). Stages of anti-sexist awareness and change for men who batter. In L. J. Dickstein & C. C. Nadelson (Eds.), *Family violence: Emerging issues of a national crisis* (pp. 63–97). Washington, DC: American Psychiatric Press.

ASBURY, J. (1987). African-American women in violent relationships: An exploration of cultural difference. In Robert L. Hampton (Ed.), *Violence in the black family.* Lexington, MA: Lexington Books.

AVAKAME, E. F., FYFE, J. J., & MCCOY, C. (1999). Did you call the police? What did they do? An empirical assessment of Black's theory of mobilization of law. *Justice Quarterly, 16,* 765–792.

BAKER, K., CAHN, N., & SANDS, S. J. (1989). *Report on District of Columbia police response to domestic violence.* Washington, DC: The D.C. Coalition Against Domestic Violence and the Women's Law and Public Policy, Georgetown University Law Center.

BALOS, B., & TROTZKY, I. (1988). Enforcement of the domestic abuse act in Minnesota: A prelimi-nary study. *Law and Inequality, 6*, 83–125.

BARNARD, G. W., VERA, A., & NEWMAN, G. (1982). "Till death do us part?": A study of spouse mur-der. *Bulletin of the American Academy of Psychiatry and Law, 10*, 271–280.

BELKNAP, J. (1995). Law enforcement officers' attitudes about the appropriate responses to woman battering. *International Review of Victimology, 4*, 47–62.

BELKNAP, J., & MCCALL, K. D. (1994). Woman battering and police referrals. *Journal of Criminal Justice, 22* (3), 223–236.

BELL, D. J. (1984). The police response to domestic violence: An exploratory study. *Police Studies*, 23–30.

BERK, R. A., & NEWTON, P. J. (1985). Does arrest really deter wife battery? An effort to replicate the findings of the Minneapolis spouse abuse experiment. *American Sociological Review, 50*, 253–262.

BERK, R. A., CAMPBELL, A., KLAP, R., & WESTERN, B. (1992a). Bayesian analysis of the Colorado Springs spouse abuse experiment. *Journal of Criminal Law & Criminology, 83*, 170–200.

BERK, R. A., CAMPBELL, A., KLAP, R., & WESTERN, B. (1992b). The deterrent effect of arrest in inci-dents of domestic violence: A Bayesian analysis of four field experiments. *American Sociological Review, 57*, 698–708.

BETHEL, C. A., & SINGER, L. R. (1981–1982). Mediation: A new remedy for causes of domestic vio-lence. *Vermont Law Review, 6*(2), 7(1).

BINDER, A., & MEEKER, J. W. (1988). Experiments as reforms. *Journal of Criminal Justice, 16*, 347–358.

BINDER, A., & MEEKER, J. W. (1992). Implications for the failure to replicate the Minneapolis exper-imental findings. *American Sociological Review, 58*, 886–888.

BINDER, A., & MEEKER, J. W. (1996). Arrest as a method to control spouse abuse. In E. S. Buzawa & C. G. Buzawa (Eds.), *Domestic violence: The criminal justice response* (pp. 129–140). Thousand Oaks, CA: Sage.

BLOCK, C. R. (2003). How can practitioners help an abused woman lower her risk of death? *National Institute of Justice Journal, 250*, 4–7.

BLOCK, C. R., & CHRISTAKOS, A. (1995). Intimate partner homicide in Chicago over 29 years. *Crime & Delinquency, 41*, 496–526.

BLOCK, R. (1974). Why notify the police: The victim's decision to notify the police of an assault. *Criminology, 11*, 555–569.

BOWKER, L. H. (1982). Police service to battered women: Bad or not so bad? *Criminal Justice and Behavior, 9*, 476–486.

BREINES, W., & GORDON, L. (1983). The new scholarship on family violence. *Signs: Journal of Women in Culture and Society, 8* (3), 490–531.

BROWNE, A., & WILLIAMS, K. R. (1993). Gender, intimacy, and lethal violence: Trends from 1976 through 1987. *Gender & Society, 7*(1), 78–98.

BROWNE, A., WILLIAMS, K. R., & DUTTON, D. G. (1999). Homicide between intimate partners: A 20 year review. In M. D. Smith & M. A. Zahn (Eds.), *Homicide: A sourcebook of social research* (pp. 149–164). Thousand Oaks, CA: Sage.

BUEL, S. M. (1988). Recent developments: Mandatory arrest for domestic violence. *Harvard Women's Law Journal, 11*, 213–226.

BUZAWA, E. S. (1982). Police officer response to domestic violence legislation in Michigan. *Journal of Police Science and Administration, 10*(4), 415–424.

BUZAWA, E. S., & BUZAWA, C. G. (1993). The impact of arrest on domestic violence. *American Behavioral Scientist, 36*, 558–574.

BUZAWA, E. S., & BUZAWA, C. G. (Eds.). (2003). *Domestic violence: The criminal justice response* (2nd ed.). Thousand Oaks, CA: Sage.

CAMPBELL, J. (1992). "If I can't have you, no one can": Power and control in homicide of female partners. In J. Radford & D. E. H. Russell (Eds.), *Femicide: The politics of woman killing* (pp. 99–113). New York: Twayne.

CAMPBELL, J. C., WEBSTER, D., KOZIOL-MCLAIN, J., BLOCK, C. R., CAMPBELL, D., CURRY, M. A., et al. (2003). Assessing risk factors for intimate partner homicide. *National Institute of Justice Journal, 250*, 14–20.

CARROLL, J. C. (1980). A cultural-consistency theory of family violence in Mexican American and Jewish-ethnic groups. In M. A. Straus & G. T. Hotaling (Eds.), *The social causes of husband-wife violence* (pp. 68–81). Minneapolis: University of Minnesota Press.

COHN, E. G., & SHERMAN, L. W. (1986). Police policy on domestic violence: A national survey. *Crime Control Reports (vol. 5)*. Washington, DC: Crime Control Institute.

COLEY, S. M., & BECKETT, J. O. (1988). Black battered women: A review of empirical literature. *Journal of Counseling and Development, 66*, 266–270.

CROMACK, B. (1996). The policing of domestic violence: An empirical study. *Policy and Society, 5*, 185–199.

DAVIS, N. J., HATCH, A. J., GRIFFIN, C., & THOMPSON, K. (1987). Violence against women in the home: A continued mandate of control. *Violence, Aggression and Terrorism, 1*(3), 241–276.

DEFINA, M. P., & WETHERBEE, L. (1997). Advocacy and law enforcement: Partners against domestic violence. *FBI Law Enforcement Bulletin, 66* (10), 22–24.

DOBASH, R. E., & DOBASH, R. P. (1977). Love, honor and obey: Institutional ideologies and the struggle for battered women. *Contemporary Crises, 1*, 403–415.

DOBASH, R. E., & DOBASH, R. P. (1979). *Violence against wives: A case against the patriarchy.* New York: Free Press.

DOBASH, R. P., DOBASH, R. E., EMERSON, R., CAVENAGH, K., & LEWIS, R. (2000). Confronting violent men. In J. Hanmer & C. Itzin (Eds.), *Home truths about domestic violence: Feminist influences on policy and practice—A reader*. New York: Routledge.

DONLON, R., HENDRICKS, J., & MEAGHER, M. S. (1986). Police practices and attitudes toward domestic violence. *Journal of Police Science and Administration, 14*, 187–192.

DUGAN, L., NAGIN, D., & ROSENFELD, R. (1999). Explaining the decline in intimate partner homicide: The effects of changing domesticity, women's status, and domestic violence resources. *Homicide Studies, 3*, 187–214.

DUGAN, L., NAGIN, D., & ROSENFELD, R. (2003). Do domestic violence services save lives? *National Institute of Justice Journal, 250*, 20–26.

DUGAN, L., ROSENFELD, R., & NAGIN, D. S. (2003). Exposure reduction or retaliation? The effects of domestic violence resources on intimate partner homicide. *Law & Society Review, 37*, 169–198.

DUNFORD, F. W. (1990). System-initiated warrants for suspects of misdemeanor domestic assault: A pilot study. *Justice Quarterly, 7*, 631–653.

DUNFORD, F. W., HUIZINGA, D., & ELLIOTT, D. S. (1990). The role of arrest in domestic assault: The Omaha police experiment. *Criminology, 28* (2), 183–206.

DUTTON, D. (1987). *The prediction of recidivism in a population of wife assaulters*. Paper presented at the Third International Family Violence Conference, Durham, NC.

DUTTON, D. (1986a). The outcome of court-mandated treatment for wife assault: A quasi-experimental evaluation. *Violence and Victims, 1*, 163–176.

DUTTON, D. (1986b). Wife assaulters' explanations for assault: The neutralization of self-punishment. *Canadian Journal of Behavioral Science, 8* (4), 381–390.

DUTTON, D., HART, S. D., KENNEDY, L. W., & WILLIAMS, K. R. (1996). Arrest and the reduction of repeat wife assault. In E. S. Buzawa & C. G. Buzawa (Eds.), *Domestic violence: The criminal justice response* (2nd ed., pp. 111–127). Thousand Oaks, CA: Sage.

EISENBERG, S. E., & MICKLOW, P. L. (1977). The assaulted wife: "Catch 22" revisited. *Women's Rights Law Reporter, 3*, 142.

ELLIOT, D. S. (1989). Criminal justice procedures in family violence crimes. In L. Ohlin & M. Tonry (Eds.), *Family violence* (pp. 427–480). Chicago: University of Chicago Press.

ELLIS, J. W. (1984). Prosecutorial discretion to charge in cases of spousal assault: A dialogue. *Journal of Criminal Law and Criminology, 75* (1), 56–102.

EPPLER, A. (1986). Battered women and the equal protection clause: Will the constitution help them when the police won't? *The Yale Law Journal,* 788–809.

EREZ, E. (2002). Domestic violence and the criminal justice system: An overview. *Journal of Issues in Nursing, 7,* 1–30.

FAGAN, J. (1989). Cessation of family violence: Deterrence and dissuasion. In L. Ohlin & M. Tonry (Eds.), *Family violence* (pp. 377–425). Chicago: University of Chicago Press.

FAGAN, J., & BROWNE, A. (1994). Violence between spouses and intimates: Physical aggression between women and men in intimate relationships. In A. J. Reiss, Jr. & J. A. Roth (Eds.), *Understanding and preventing violence: Vol. 3. Social influences* (pp. 115–292). Washington, DC: National Academy Press.

FEINMAN, C. (1987). Domestic violence in Australia. Paper presented at the Annual Meeting of the American Soceity of Criminology, Montreal.

FELSON, R. B., & ACKERMAN, J. (2001). Arrest for domestic and other assaults. *Criminology, 39,* 655–675.

FELSON, R. B., & MESSNER, S. F. (2000). The control motive in intimate partner homicide. *Social Psychology Quarterly, 63,* 86–94.

FERRARO, K. (1989a). The legal response to women battering in the United States. In J. Hamner, J. Radford, & E. Stanko (Eds.), *Women, policing, and male violence* (pp. 155–184). London: Routledge & Keegan Paul.

FERRARO, K. (1989b). Policing women battering. *Social Problems, 36* (1), 61–74.

FERRARO, K. (1995). Cops, courts and woman battering. In B. R. Price & N. J. Sokoloff (Eds.), *The criminal justice system and women: Offenders, victims, and workers* (pp.262–271). New York: McGraw-Hill.

FIELD, M. H., & FIELD, H. F. (1973). Marital violence and the criminal process: Neither justice nor peace. *Social Service Review, 47,* 221–240.

FORD, D. A. (1984). *Prosecution as a victim power resource for managing conjugal violence.* Paper presented at the annual meeting of the Society for the Study of Social Problems, San Antonio, TX.

FORD, D. A., & REGOLI, M. J. (1992). The preventive impacts of policies for prosecuting wife batterers. In E. S. Buzawa & C. G. Buzawa (Eds.), *Domestic violence: The changing criminal justice response* (pp. 180–207). Westport, CT: Greenwood Press.

GARNER, J., FAGAN, J., & MAXWELL, C. (1995). Published findings from the spousal assault replication program. *Journal of Quantitative Criminology, 11,* 3–28.

GELLES, R., & MEDERER, H. (1985). *Comparison or control: Intervention in the cases of wife abuse.* Paper presented at the annual meeting of the National Council on Family Relations, Dallas, TX.

GIL, D. G. (1986). Sociocultural aspects of domestic violence. In M. Lystad (Ed.), *Violence in the home: Interdisciplinary perspectives* (pp. 124–149). New York: Brunner/Mazel.

GONDOLF, E. W. (1984). *Men who batter: An integrated approach to stopping wife abuse.* Homes Beach, FL: Learning Publications.

GONDOLF, E. W. (1998). Do batterer programs work? A 15-month follow-up of multi-site evaluations. *Domestic Violence Reporter, 3* (5), 65–80.

GOOLKASIAN, G. A. (1986). *Confronting domestic violence: A guide for criminal justice agencies.* Washington, DC: U.S. Government Printing Office.

GRANT, B., & CURRY, G. D. (1993). Women murderers and victims of abuse in a southern state. *American Journal of Criminal Justice, 17,* 73–83.

GRAU, J., FAGAN, J., & WEXLER, S. (1984). Restraining orders for battered women: Issues of access and efficacy. *Women and Politics, 4* (3), 13–28.

Greenfield, L. A., Rand, M. R., & Craven, D. (1998). *Violence by intimates: Analysis of data on crimes by current or former spouses, boyfriends, and girlfriends.* Washington, DC: U.S. Department of Justice.

Hagan, J., & Albonetti, C. (1982). Race, class, and the perception of criminal injustice in America. *American Journal of Sociology, 88* (2), 329–355.

Hallum, A. M. (2003). Taking stock and building bridges: Feminism, women's movements, and Pentecostalism in Latin America. *Latin American Research Review, 38,* 169–186.

Hamberger, L. K., & Potente, T. (1994). Counseling heterosexual women arrested for domestic violence: Implications for theory and practice. *Violence and Victims, 9* (2), 125–137.

Harrell, A., & Smith, B. E. (1996). Effects of restraining orders on domestic violence victims. In E. S. Buzawa & C. G. Buzawa (Eds.), *Do arrests and restraining orders work?* (pp. 214–242) Thousand Oaks, CA: Sage.

Hawkins, D., & M. Humes. (2002). Human rights and domestic violence. *Political Science Quarterly, 117,* 231–257.

Hindelang, M. J. (1976). *Criminal victimization in eight American cities: A descriptive analysis of common theft and assault.* Cambridge, MA: Ballinger.

Hirschel, J. D., Hutchinson, I. W. III, & Dean, C. W. (1992a). The failure of arrest to deter spouse abuse. *Journal of Research in Crime & Delinquency, 29,* 7–33.

Hirschel, J. D., Hutchinson, I. W. III, & Dean, C. W. (1992b). Female spouse abuse and the police response: The Charlotte, North Carolina Experiment. *Journal of Criminal Law & Criminology, 83,* 73–119.

Hooper, M. (1996). When domestic violence diversion is no longer an option: What to do with the female offender. *Berkeley Women's Law Journal,* 168–181.

International Association of Chiefs of Police. (1967). *Training key 16: Handling disturbance calls.* Gaithersburg, MD: International Association of Chiefs of Police.

Isaacs, T. (2001, Summer/Fall). Domestic violence and hate crimes: Acknowledging two levels of responsibility. *Criminal Justice Ethics,* 31–43.

Jaffe, P., Wolfe, D. A., Telford, A., & Austin, G. (1986). The impact of police charges in incidents of wife abuse. *Journal of Family Violence, 1,* 37–49

Johnson, M. P. (1995). Patriarchal terrorism and common couple violence: Two forms of violence against women. *Journal of Marriage and the Family, 57,* 283–294.

Karmen, A. (1982). Women as crime victims: Problems and solutions. In B. R. Price & N. J. Sokoloff (Eds.), *The criminal justice system and women* (pp. 185–201). New York: Clark Boardman.

Klein, D. (1981). Violence against women: Some considerations regarding its causes and its elimination. *Crime and Delinquency, 27* (1), 64–80.

Klein, A. (1996). Re-abuse in a population of court-restrained male batterers: Why restraining orders don't work. In E. S. Buzawa & C. G. Buzawa (Eds.), *Do arrests and restraining orders work?* (pp. 192–213). Thousand Oaks, CA: Sage.

Kuhl, A., & Saltzman, L. E. (1985). Battered women in the criminal justice system. In I. L. Moyer (Ed.), *The changing role of women in the criminal justice system* (pp. 180–196). Prospect Heights, IL: Waveland Press.

Lang, P. (1986, July 21). How to stop crime the brainy way. *U.S. News and World Report,* 55–56.

Langan, P. A., & Innes, C. A. (1986). *Preventing domestic violence against women.* Special Report. Washington, DC: U.S. Department of Justice, Bureau of Justice Statistics.

Laszlo, A. T., & McKean, T. (1978). Court decision: An alternative for spousal abuse cases. In *Battered women: Issues of public policy* (pp. 327–356). Washington, DC: U.S. Commission for Civil Rights.

Lawrenz, F., Lembo, J. F., & Schade, T. (1988). Time series analysis of the effect of a domestic violence directive on the numbers of arrests per day. *Journal of Criminal Justice, 16,* 493–498.

LEE, R. K., SANDERS THOMPSON, V. L., & MECHANIC, M. B. (2002). Intimate partner violence and women of color: A call for innovations. *American Journal of Public Health, 92*, 530–534.

LEMPERT, R. (1984). From the editor. *Law and Society Review, 18* (4), 505–513.

LERMAN, L. (1982). Criminal prosecution of wife beaters. *Response, 4* (3), 1–19.

LERMAN, L. (1982, May/June). Court decisions on wife abuse laws: Recent developments. *Response.*

LERMAN, L. (1984). Mediation of wife abuse cases: The adverse impact of informal dispute resolution of women. *Harvard Women's Law Journal, 7*, 65–67.

LERMAN, L. (1986). Prosecution of wife beaters: Institutional obstacles and innovations. In M. LYSTAD (Ed.), *Violence in the home: Interdisciplinary perspectives* (pp. 250–295). New York: Brunner/Mazel.

LERMAN, L. (1992). The decontextualization of domestic violence. *Journal of Criminal Law and Criminology, 83* (1), 217–240.

LERMAN, L., & LIVINGSTON, F. (1983). State legislation on domestic violence. *Response, 6*, 1–28.

LOBEL, K. (1986). *Naming the violence: Speaking out against lesbian battering.* Seattle: Seal Press.

LOCKHART, L. L. (1985). Methodological issues in comparative racial analyses: The case of wife abuse. *Social Work and Abstracts, 21*, 35–41.

LOCKHART, L. L. (1987). A reexamination of the effects of race and social class on the incidence of marital violence: A search for reliable differences. *Journal of Marriage and the Family, 49* (3), 603–610.

LOVING, N. (1980). *Responding to spouse abuse and wife beating: A guide for police.* Washington, DC: Police Executive Research Forum.

MACKINNON, C. (1983). Feminism, Marxism, method, and the State: Toward a feminist Jurisprudence. *Signs, 8*, 635.

MAHONEY, M. R. (1991). Legal images of battered women: Redefining the issue of separation. *Michigan Law Review, 90*, 1–94.

MARTIN, M. E. (1978). Double your trouble: Dual arrest in family violence. *Journal of Family Violence, 12* (2), 139–157.

MAXWELL, C. D., GARNER, J. H., & FAGAN, J. A. (2001). *The effects of arrest on intimate partner violence: New evidence from the spouse assault replication program series—Research in brief.* Washington, DC: National Institute of Justice.

MCCORD, J. (1992). Deterrence of domestic violence: A critical review of research. *Journal of Research in Crime & Delinquency, 29* (2), 229–239.

MCLEOD, M. (1984). Women against men: An examination of domestic violence based on an analysis of official data and national victimization data. *Justice Quarterly*, 171–193.

MILLER, S. L. (1989). Unintended side effects of pro-arrest policies and their race and class implications for battered women: A cautionary note. *Criminal Justice Policy Review, 3*(3), 299–316.

MILLER, S. L. (2001). The paradox of women arrested for domestic violence: Criminal justice professionals and service providers respond. *Violence Against Women, 7*(12), 1339–1376.

MILLER, S. L. (2005). *Victims as offenders: The paradox of women's violence in relationships.* New Brunswick, NJ: Rutgers University Press.

MILLER, S. L., & MELOY, M. L. (2005). Women's use of force: Voices of women arrested for domestic violence. *Violence Against Women, 11*(7).

MILLER, S. L., & WELLFORD, C. F. (1997). Patterns and correlates of interpersonal violence. In A. P. Cardarelli (Ed.), *Violence between intimates: Patterns, causes, and effects* (pp. 16–28). Boston: Allyn & Bacon.

MOORE, T. (1985). Landmark court decisions for battered women. *Response, 8*(5).

MORASH, M. (1986, June). Wife battering. *Criminal Justice Abstracts*, 252–271.

NATIONAL CRIMINAL JUSTICE ASSOCIATION. (1985). Domestic violence arrests deter batterers: Police agencies report. *Justice Bulletin, 5* (3).

Okum, L. (1986). *Women abuse: Facts replace myths.* Albany: State University of New York Press.

Olivero, A. (1987, November 16). Connecticut's new family violence law may be one of the toughest—but is it tough enough? *Hartford Advocate,* 6.

Overby, A. (1971). Discrimination against minority groups. In L. Radzinowicz & M. E. Wolfgang (Eds.), *The criminal in the arms of the law* (pp. 569–581). New York: Basic Books.

Parnas, R. E. (1967). The police response to the domestic disturbance. *Wisconsin Law Review, 31,* 914–960.

Pastoor, M. K. (1984). Police training and the effectiveness of Minnesota "domestic abuse" laws. *Law and Inequality, 2,* 557–607.

Pate, A., Hamilton, E. E., & Annan, S. (1992). *Metro-Dade spousal abuse replication project: Final report.* Washington, DC: Police Foundation.

Paternoster, R., Brame, R, Bachman, R., & Sherman, L. W. (1997). Do fair procedures matter: The effect of procedural justice on spouse assault. *Law & Society Review, 31*(1), 163–204.

Paterson, E. J. (1979). How the legal system responds to battered women. In D. M. Moore (Ed.), *Battered women* (pp. 79–100). Beverly Hills, CA: Sage.

Peterson, E. S. L. (1999). Murder as self-help: Women and intimate partner homicide. *Homicide Studies, 3,* 30–46.

Peterson, E. S. L. (2002). *Varieties of self-help in intimate partner homicide.* Paper presented at the annual meeting of the American Society of Criminology, Atlanta, GA.

Prescott, S., & Letko, C. (1977). Battered: A social psychological perspective. In M. M. Roy (Ed.), *Battered women: A psychosociological study of domestic violence* (pp. 72–96). New York: Von Nostrand Reinhold.

Rasche, C. E. (1995). Minority women and domestic violence: The unique dilemmas of battered women of color. In B. R. Price & N. J. Sokoloff (Eds.), *The criminal justice system and women* (pp. 246–261). New York: McGraw-Hill.

Rebovich, D. J. (1996). Prosecutorial responses to domestic violence: Results of a survey of large jurisdictions. In E. S. Buzawa & C. G. Buzawa (Eds.), *Do arrests and restraining orders work?* (pp. 176–191). Thousand Oaks, CA: Sage.

Reiss, A. J., Jr. (1985). Some failures in designing data collection that distort results. In L. Burstein, H. E. Freeman, & P. H. Rossi (Eds.), *Collecting evaluation data: Problems and solutions.* Beverly Hills, CA: Sage.

Renzetti, C. (1999). The challenge to feminists posed by women's use of violence in intimate relationships. In S. Lamb (Ed.), *New versions of victims: Feminist struggle with the concept* (pp. 42–56). New York: New York University Press.

Renzetti, C. (1987). *Building a second closet: Official responses to victims of lesbian battering.* Paper presented at the annual meeting of the Academy of Criminal Justice Sciences, San Francisco, CA.

Rifkin, J. (1980). Toward a theory of law and patriarchy. *Harvard Women's Law Journal, 3,* 83.

Rosenfeld, R. (1997). Changing relationships between men and women: A note on the decline of intimate partner homicide. *Homicide Studies, 1,* 72–83.

Rossi, P., Berk, R. A., & Edison, B. (1974). *The roots of urban discontent.* New York: Wiley.

Saunders, D. G. (1995). The tendency to arrest victims of domestic violence: A preliminary analysis of officer characteristics. *Journal of Interpersonal Violence, 19* (2), 147–158.

Scarf, M. (1983). Marriages made in heaven? Battered Jewish wives. In S. Heschel (Ed.), *On being a Jewish feminist.* New York: Schocken Books.

Schechter, S. (1982). *Women and male violence: The visions and struggles of the battered women's movement.* Boston: South End Press.

Schmidt, J. D., & Sherman, L.W. 1996. Does arrest deter domestic violence? In E. S. Buzawa & C. G. Buzawa (Eds.), *Do arrests and restraining orders work?* (pp. 43–53). Thousands Oaks, CA: Sage.

SCHWARTZ, M. D. (1988). Ain't got no class: Universal risk theories of battering. *Contemporary Crisis, 12*, 373–392.

SENTURIA, K., SULLIVAN, M., CISKE, S., & SHIU-THORNTON, S. (2003). Cross-cultural issues in domestic violence. *National Institute of Justice Journal, 250*, 35–36.

SHERMAN, L. W. (1992). *Policing domestic violence.* New York: Free Press.

SHERMAN, L. W., & BERK, R. (1984). The specific effects of arrest for domestic assault. *American Sociological Review, 49*, 261–272.

SHERMAN, L. W., & COHN, E. G. (1989). The impact of research on legal policy: The Minneapolis Domestic Violence Experiment. *Law and Society Review, 23*(1), 117–144.

SHERMAN, L. W. (1993). *Policing domestic violence: Experiments and dilemmas.* New York: Free Press.

SHERMAN, L. W., SCHMIDT, J. D., ROGAN, D. P., GARTIN, P. R., COHN, E. G., COLLINS, D., et al. (1991).From initial deterrence to long term escalation: Short custody arrest for poverty ghetto domestic violence. *Criminology, 29*, 821–850.

SHERMAN, L. W., SCHMIDT, J. D., ROGAN, D. P., SMITH, D. A., GARTIN, P. R., COHN, E. G., et al. (1992). The variable effects of arrest on criminal careers: The Milwaukee domestic violence experiment. *Journal of Criminal Law and Criminology, 83.*

SHERMAN, L. W., SMITH, D. A., SCHMIDT, J. D., & ROGAN, D. P. (1991). *Ghetto poverty, crime and punishment: Legal and informal control of domestic violence.* Washington, DC: Crime Control Institute.

SMITH, D. A. (1987). Police responses to interpersonal violence: Defining the parameters of legal control. *Social Forces, 65*(3), 767–782.

SORENSON, S. B. (2003). Funding public health: The public's willingness to pay for domestic violence prevention programming. *American Journal of Public Health, 93*,1934–1938.

SPARKS, R. (1981). Surveys of victimization—An optimistic assessment. In M. Tonry & N. Morris (Eds.), *Crime and justice: An annual review of research* (Vol. 3, pp. 1–60). Chicago: University of Chicago Press.

STACK, C. B. (1974). *All our kin: Strategies for survival in a black community.* New York: Harper & Row.

STANKO, E. A. (1982). Would you believe this woman: Prosecutorial screening for "credible" witnesses and a problem of justice. In N. H. Rafter & E. A. Stanko (Eds.), *Judge, lawyer, victim, thief: Women, gender roles and criminal justice* (pp. 63–82). Boston: Northeastern University Press.

STANKO, E. A. (1985). *Intimate intrusions: Women's experience of male violence.* London: Routledge & Kegan Paul.

STANKO, E. A. (1995). Policing domestic violence: Dilemmas and contradictions. *The Australian and New Zealand Journal of Criminology, 28*(3), 31–43.

STARK, E., FLITCRAFT, A., & FRAZIER, W. (1979). Medicine and patriarchal violence: The social construction of a "private" event. *International Journal of Health Services, 9*, 461–493.

STONE, L. H. (1984). Shelters for battered women: A temporary escape from danger or the first step toward divorce? *Victimology, 9*(2), 284–289.

STRAUS, M. A., GELLES, R., & STEINMETZ, S. K. (1980). *Behind closed doors: Violence in the American family.* New York: Anchor Press.

STRAUS, M. A., & GELLES, R. (1986). Societal change and change in family violence from 1975 to 1985 as revealed by two national surveys. *Journal of Marriage and the Family, 48*, 465–479.

U.S. DEPARTMENT OF JUSTICE. (1985). *Replicating an experiment in specific deterrence: Alternative police responses to spouse assault: A research solicitation.* Washington, DC: U.S. Department of Justice, National Institute of Justice.

U.S. DEPARTMENT OF JUSTICE. (2000). *First response to victims of crime: Handbook for law enforcement officers on how to approach and help.* Washington, DC: Office for Victims of Crime.

WARDELL, L., GILLESPIE, D., & LEFFLER, A. (1983). Science and violence against wives. In D. Finkelhor, R. Gelles, G. Hotaling, & M. Straus (Eds.), *The dark side of families: Current family violence research* (pp. 69–84). Beverly Hills, CA: Sage.

WASHBURN, C., & FRIEZE, I. H. (1981). *Methodological issues in studying battered women.* Paper presented at the First National Conference for Family Violence Researchers, University of New Hampshire, Durham, NH.

WEBSTER, N. (2003). Reviewing domestic violence deaths. *National Institute of Justice Journal, 250,* 26–32.

WILLIAMS, L. (1981, January/February). Violence against women. *The Black Scholar,* 18–24.

WILSON, M., JOHNSON, H., & DALY, M. (1995). Lethal and nonlethal violence against wives. *Canadian Journal of Criminology, 37,* 331–361.

WORDEN, A. P. (2000). The changing boundaries of the criminal justice system: Redefining the problem and the response in domestic violence. *Journal of Criminal Justice, 2,* 215–266.

WRIGHT, A. E. (1998). Not a black and white issue: For battered and abused Latinas and black women, dialing 911 may be risky business. *The Progressive Women's Quarterly, 7,* 42–48.

ZAHN, M. A. (2003). Intimate partner homicide: An overview. *National Institute of Justice Journal, 250,* 2–3.

ZORZA, J. (1994). *Must we stop arresting batterers? Analysis and implications of new police domestic violence studies.* New York: National Center on Women and Family Law.

ZORZA, J., & WOODS, L. (1995). *Mandatory arrest: Problems and possibilities.* New York: National Center on Women and Family Law.

15

The Limitations of Current Approaches to Domestic Violence

Hoan Bui

Using data drawn from a sample of abused immigrant women, the present study examines the experience of abused women with domestic violence interventions. The study reveals the limitations of current approaches to domestic violence in serving the needs of abused women. Emphasizing law enforcement and separation as a way to protect women's safety, current approaches to domestic violence deal only with the offender and disregard women's need for family relationships. Abused women often have to bargain with their partner for safety, and with their children or the extended family for emotional support and family relationships, but mandatory arrest and mandatory prosecution policies have taken away women's bargaining chips. Findings from the study suggest the importance of reconceptualizing abused women's needs to include both personal safety and family life. The study also points to the need of broadening domestic violence approaches by providing abused women with more options to deal with domestic abuse and by addressing women's inferior status as the root cause of the problem.

INTRODUCTION

Major changes in societal responses to domestic violence have occurred since the definition of domestic violence as a private family matter shifted to a view of domestic violence as a crime. In response to the criticism that the criminal justice system failed to protect women's safety, new approaches to domestic violence have emphasized arrests, prosecutions, and punitive sanctions. These approaches, which focus on the victim and the assailant within the context of criminal laws, have been created within the framework of specific deterrence that relies on legal sanctions and pain of punishment, including shame as well as a loss of freedom or personal prestige, to prevent undesirable behaviors. Women's advocate groups, which supported and lobbied for the criminalization of domestic violence, have expected that it would serve the goal of protecting women victims through the mobilization of legal institutions to take actions (Fagan, 1988). Pro-arrest and mandatory arrest policies have been regarded as a positive feature because they could make the police more responsive to family violence, address the problem of victims' noncooperation, and increase the probability of arrests as well as the likelihood of sanctions (Hoyle & Sanders, 2000). Mandatory arrest policies have also been viewed as relieving women victims from the burden of making arrest decisions in front of their assailants (Wanless, 1996). Prosecution innovations, including prosecutor-filing charge and no-drop-charge policies, which emphasize aggressive prosecution practices, have been designed to increase the percentage of cases formally prosecuted and ensure appropriate court treatment of domestic violence cases (Fagan, 1988). Advocates for battered women have also asked criminal justice agencies to refocus their efforts on the protection of domestic violence victims through the coordination of extralegal and legal services. However, victim assistant programs affiliated with criminal justice agencies have been geared to sustaining victims' commitment to prosecution efforts because the effectiveness of interventions is measured mainly in terms of criminal justice sanctions, namely the number of arrests, prosecutions, and convictions (Corcoran, Stephenson, Perryman, & Allen, 2001; Fagan, 1988).

The move toward the criminalization of domestic violence has emphasized sanctions and control of the offenders but overlooked the reality of women's lives, particularly family relationships and family dynamics. Established within the social organization of the legal system, criminal justice interventions have been modeled on cases involving strangers whose nature is different from the nature of domestic violence that occurs between intimate partners. In addition, criminal justice interventions may not appeal to all women who come from different social backgrounds (Radford & Stanko, 1991). Studies found that arrest was supported by abused women who wanted their husbands/partners to be arrested and punished, and who wanted a separation from their abusers (Hoyle & Sanders, 2000). However, other women who need safety protection and help to improve their family lives may not favor arrests or prosecutions that they perceive as a potential threat to family relationships and economic security. In fact, the intimate relationship between the victims and the assailants in domestic violence cases and the adversarial nature of the American legal system have created an inherent paradox for many abused women who attempt to use the criminal justice system to solve family problems, because a woman's adversary in the court is also her husband/partner at home (Jones, 1994).

The deterrence framework of domestic violence policies has facilitated empirical studies that emphasized the outcomes of criminal justice interventions at the expense of the intervention process and its impact on any aspect of women's family life (Lewis, Dobash, Dobash, & Cavanagh, 2000). With few exceptions, prior studies of the effect of domestic violence interventions tended to focus on the deterrence aspect of arrests and prosecutions measured by the absence of physical reoffending, but they largely ignored other forms of emotional and psychological abuse that might occur as a result of criminal justice interventions and might cause the same or even more devastating effects than the original physical attacks. The emphasis on outcomes also led to the tendency to view women survivors of domestic violence as passive recipients of legal interventions (Lewis et al., 2000). Women, in fact, are not passive. They are seen as active agents who can engage in a complex process of negotiation and strategic resistance (Kandiyoti, 1991). Abused women may actively participate in the negotiation to secure their safety, but the process of negotiation may not be the same for all women because of their different experiences with class, race/ethnicity, and gender relations. This study focuses on the experience of Vietnamese immigrant women and examines their strategic responses to domestic violence interventions. The goal is to improve understandings of the effect of domestic violence policies on women's safety and family lives.

RESEARCH METHODS

Feminist Standpoint Approach

The present study relies on qualitative analysis of women's voices to understand the impact of domestic violence interventions on family life. "Giving voice" has become a defining characteristic of the feminist standpoint approach, which focuses on gender differences in social situations and the importance of women's experiences in understanding social problems (Gorelick, 1991; Harding, 1991). Rooted in the symbolic interactionist tradition, the giving voice approach recognizes the hierarchy of credibility in the creation and dissemination of knowledge and emphasizes the actor's interpretation and understanding of the situations (Gorelick, 1991, McCall & Wittner, 1990). Qualitative analysis stresses the importance of social interactions, social processes, and the meaning of human behavior within its situational and structural context (Merriam, 1998; Strauss, 1987). By recognizing the significance of subjective interpretations of human experiences, qualitative analysis of women's experiences through their own voices allows not only an understanding of multiple realities of women's experiences but also the construction of a holistic reality based on women's differences (Blumer 1969; Lincoln & Guba, 1985). Indeed, women's experiences of and responses to male domination are not uniform because they are influenced by men's and women's different social positions in terms of race, class, and gender. The recognition of the interplay between class, race/ethnicity, and culture within the context of immigration resettlement and adaptation will facilitate an understanding of how gender, class, race/ethnicity, and culture affect women's experiences with domestic violence policies. A focus on women's accounts also allows an understanding of how individuals may use the law, purposefully and actively, as a strategic process of challenge and resistance (Lewis et al., 2000).

Sample and Data

Data for the study were drawn from in-depth interviews with a sample of abused Vietnamese immigrant women who had experience of abuse by an intimate partner, such as husband, ex-husband, boyfriend, or ex-boyfriend. These women were selected in four Vietnamese communities with different sizes across the United States, including Orange County (CA), Houston (TX), Boston (MA), and Lansing (MI). A majority of the participants (23 women) were recruited through referrals from various types of victim service agencies, including women's shelters as well as health and legal services. The rest of the sample was recruited through two Vietnamese radio talk shows on women's issues in

Houston and Orange County (7 women) and the snowball technique (4 women). These efforts yielded a sample of 34 abused Vietnamese immigrant women (10 in Orange County; 9 in Houston; 8 in Boston; 7 in Lansing). Interviews with the participants were conducted in 2000. Depending on the situation, each interview lasted between two and three hours. A majority of the interviews (28) were conducted face-to-face; 6 women were interviewed via telephone upon their requests. The Vietnamese language was used in most interviews; Vietnamese mingled with English was used in one interview.

The demographic characteristics of the participants were marked by economic struggles and cultural isolation. All were born in Vietnam, but in terms of ethnicity, 4 were Vietnamese Amerasian[1] and 1 was Chinese Vietnamese. The age of the participants ranged from 20 years old to 58 years old. Most of these women came to the United States as adults, in their 20s or older; only 8 women were under 20 years old at the time they arrived in the United States. The participants left Vietnam in different situations and by different means, including escapes by boats and official departures with government permissions. They arrived in the United States under different status, including refugees, dependents of husbands or parents, and out-of-country brides sponsored by husbands. Their residency in the United States ranged from 1 to 28 years. Of 34 women, 14 had already obtained American citizenship, 13 were American permanent residents, and 7 were legal aliens. In terms of educational achievement, more than half of the participants (20) had no formal education in the United States, but they had vocational and/or English training; 6 women had a college degree or some college education in the United States; the rest of the women had high school or less than high school education. Regarding English proficiency, only 3 women considered their English skills as strong or good; two-thirds of the women (21) reported weak English skills. Despite their lack of English proficiency, the majority of the participants worked (24 women), and most participants who were employed worked in manual jobs (18 women); only 2 women were professionals.

More than half of the participants (18) started their intimate relationships in the United States, others in Vietnam or in refugee camps. Most of them had same-ethnic husbands/partners, and 5 had husbands/partners who came from different racial/ethnic backgrounds, including Anglo-American, Chinese, Iraqi, and Laotian. The lengths of their relationships ranged from 1 to 35 years. At the time of the interviews, less than half of the participants (16) were legally married or had a live-in boyfriend; 12 participants were separate from their partners, either legally or because of a restraining order; 6 participants were divorced. Most participants (30) had children, and the majority of these women had children under 18 years of age.

BARGAINING FOR PERSONAL SAFETY AND FAMILY LIFE

Laws prohibiting domestic violence in the United States have been considered a resource for women to deal with abuse by an intimate partner (Bowman, 1992; Stark, 1993; Wanless, 1996). Calling the police when violence occurs, working with the criminal justice system to make the abusers responsible for their violent behavior, or obtaining a restraining order to prevent future attacks are a few ways women can respond to violence at home. Using the legal approach to deal with domestic abuse, however, may not be easy for many abused women. Economic dependency, language barriers, fear of reprisal, immigration status, and attachment to the family are among the reasons why many women do not seek help with law enforcement agencies (Abraham, 2000; Bui, 2001). For the study participants who had contacts with the criminal justice system as victims of intimate-partner violence, calling the police was initially not a practical approach to deal with domestic abuse, but it was the last resort when other forms of assistance failed to solve the problems. Before seeking help from law enforcement agencies, these women had strategically dealt with abuse in different ways. Some had accepted certain levels of oppression in exchange for family relationships, economic security, or a legal status in the United States. They had also tried different coping mechanisms, including reaching out to the extended family, friends, or religious leaders. When these mechanisms failed and violence escalated, concerns for their personal safety and the safety of their children as well as a desire to express agency caused them to report abuse. When contacting law enforcement agencies, these women had different expectations for interventions. Depending on their own circumstances and the resources available to them, they invoked different levels of interventions to bargain for their safety. They made decisions by considering the consequences of various legal interventions, including their personal safety, family economy and relationships, the welfare of their children, and their relationship to the extended family. Their strategic decisions were shaped by their cultural milieu and the constraints of race, class, and gender.

Bargaining with the Abuser

For many participants who called the police to report abuse incidents, seeking help with law enforcement agencies often excluded a desire for punishment but a hope for an improvement of family relationships. These women believed in police power and attempted to take alliance with the police to change family dynamics and their husbands' behavior. They considered the act of calling the police as a way to empower themselves, to challenge their abusive husbands/partners by sending a message that they could get their abusers arrested. As these women explained:

> I thought that the presence of the police would deter him. . . . I wanted the police to write a report on the incident and keep it in the file. I thought that when he knew that his name was in the police record, he wouldn't use force against me. (Lan)[2]

> My experience of abuse began in Vietnam after he was released from the re-education camp, and his abuse continued in the U.S. One time, he attempted to choke me when I was sleeping. That made me feel fear for my life and I had to report his abuse to the police. . . . He was not arrested because when the police came my daughter denied everything. I didn't want him to be arrested, but I wanted to warn him. I wanted him to know that I would make him arrested if he abused me, and he knew I would do it. . . . After this incident I only threatened to call [the police] by picking up the phone but I didn't actually call. That was enough to make him feel scared and stop hurting me. (Hong)

However, these women did not fully invoke law enforcement resources to include arrests. They only wanted the police to stop the violence, order their abusers to temporarily move out of the premise for the sake of their safety, calm down their abusers, or explain to their abusers that using force against wives/partners was wrong. Of 24 women who had contacts with the police, 17 women did not want arrests, and 5 women could not decide whether they wanted an arrest.

Besides the perception that the presence of the police at the time of the incident would be effective enough to stop the violence and prevent their husbands/partners from doing harm, other reasons for these women's disinterest in arrests were a desire to maintain family relationships and concerns with negative effects of criminal justice interventions on the family economy. In fact, some of them could not find suitable jobs because of language barriers, low levels of education, and a lack of vocational and English skills. Because these women depended on their husband's financial support, they feared the possibility that the arrest of their husbands/partners would negatively affect the family income. Even women who had high levels of education and held decent jobs felt ambivalent about arrests. They were concerned with possible financial losses resulting from family breakups following criminal justice interventions. However, a more important reason was a desire to maintain family relationships. Growing up in the Vietnamese family traditions that emphasized close family ties, women's domestic responsibilities, and the authority of parents over children, these women often relied on their husbands/partners who had the ultimate power in the family and the responsibility to make important decisions about the future and the discipline of children. Consequently, they were concerned with the possibility that the arrest of their husbands/partners would diminish the authority of the father over children, making the task of parenting more difficult. In addition, a need for emotional support to avoid loneliness caused by language barriers, cultural differences, and a lack of extended family ties forced many women to avoid situations that could cause their husbands/partners to "lose face" with other family members and friends, leading to strained family relationships and family breakups.

As cases moved to the judicial system, many participants continued engaging in the process of assessing their own circumstances and available resources to decide the course of their actions. Under the deterrence framework, prosecution serves as a resource for women to deal with abuse because it sends a message to their abusers that violence is not tolerated, and because abusive husbands/partners will be deterred by subsequent punitive sanctions (Corsilles, 1994). The experience of the women participants, however, indicated that the effectiveness of prosecution varied with women's ability to use the power of prosecutions, which in turn depended on family dynamics, resources available to them, and the support they received during the judicial process. Prosecutions could improve a woman's status and family relationship when her abusive husband/partner had a stake in conformity and was aware that she had the assertiveness, independence, and resources to invoke the authority of the law to fight domestic abuse.

Supportive services for victims of domestic violence often had an important role in improving women's independence and strengthening their ability to use criminal justice interventions. Most women participants were disadvantaged, educationally and/or economically, but some of them received the financial assistance, legal counseling, and emotional support that they needed to empower themselves and change family dynamics. These women appeared in court after they received assistance that helped them overcome economic dependency, protected them from the manipulations by their abusers, and provided them with information about different types of resources available to them. Contrary to the common wisdom that only women who wanted to testify against their husbands/partners would attend trials, these women went to court, often accompanied by staff from victim service agencies, to help their husbands/partners by asking the court for lenient treatments. They considered their acts as a way to empower themselves by building an alliance with the court and victim assistance programs and to send a message that they could have some control over the relationship (see similar findings in Ford & Regoli, 1993). A woman participant talked about her experience as follows:

> After I bailed my husband out of jail, he asked me to go to the court and request that charges against him be dropped. I followed the advice of my counselor [a victim advocate] and told him that I could help him if he showed remorse . . . that means he must take responsibility for his behavior by pleading guilty and I would ask the judge to give him a light sentence. . . . I wanted my husband to understand that I could have my say in the case. At first, he was angry and did not believe I could do this. However, when he found out I did get help from legal and victim services, he seemed to be afraid of me, and he agreed with my plan. . . . He pleaded guilty, got probation, and was ordered to attend counseling. That's what I wanted for him. . . . He made good progress. . . . He has stopped hitting me. (Hue)

However, not all women had the assistance that could facilitate their use of criminal justice resources. Instead, emotional and economic dependency often led to fear of losing family relationships and financial security, making many women participants disinterested in prosecutions, which they considered a threat to family relationships. In addition, women who came to the United States under the family reunification program often viewed participation in the prosecution as an indication of ungratefulness to their husbands who had sponsored them to this country. Women whose husbands/partners were not American citizens were concerned with negative effects of prosecutions on their husbands' or partners' applications for citizenship. These women either asked the prosecutor to drop the case or ignored the court request for their appearance as witnesses.

Beside arrests and prosecutions, the use of restraining orders is also considered an important way of protecting women's safety. In principle, the effect of restraining orders relies on the requirement of physical separation between the two parties of a family conflict. Restraining orders can prevent abusive husbands/partners from approaching and attacking their victims at home or elsewhere. They can also have a deterrent effect because the violation of a restraining order can be treated as contempt of court, a criminal offense that can result in arrest and even incarceration. Literature suggests that a restraining order is a useful tool for women to monitor the behavior of their husbands/partners because of its unique operation (Lewis et al., 2000). Abused women, in principle, hold the decision to request, maintain, or terminate the orders, and they can decide, on the basis of their judgments about their own safety and/or their children's safety, when they need to invoke this form of protection to prevent any contact with their partners.

Data from the study indicated that the preventive effect of restraining orders, like those of arrests and prosecutions, rested on family dynamics and the ability of women participants to make decisions regarding the implementation of restraining orders to bargain for their safety. Besides the legal threat of arrest for violations, the requirement of separation also caused abusive husbands/partners difficulties. When abusive men were ordered to move out, they faced housing problems, lacked of care and daily services from their wives/partners, and lost face with other family members and friends who became aware of the problem. Within this context of family dynamics, many women participants used the restraining orders not only to protect their safety but also to pressure their husbands/partners to change behavior. They believed that men who experienced difficulties resulting from the restraining order would learn the "lesson." Some women participants allowed their husbands/partners to return home without officially terminating the order. They were aware of the legal prohibition of contacts when the restraining order was in effect, but they attempted to negotiate with their husbands/partners to secure their safety while maintaining their family lives by relying on the deterrence of arrest in case of violations and by taking advantage of their husbands' or partners' stake in conformity as well as difficulties resulting from being out of the home. The experience of Xuan illustrated women's strategic use of a restraining order to protect their safety and at the same time maintain family lives. Xuan's husband, who was a former captain in the South Vietnamese military force, was not successful with adapting to American life, both economically and culturally. On the other hand, Xuan was relatively more successful and eventually became the main family provider. Xuan's husband frequently used violence against her because of his sexual jealousy, but she did not report it until he began threatening to kill her. Xuan talked about her experience with the restraining order as follows:

> He was arrested when I called the police to report the abuse. . . . He had to move out because I requested a restraining order, and this caused him a lot of difficulties. He had to rely on his friends for housing because he couldn't afford to rent his own apartment. . . . When he got sick, the children asked me to let him return home. . . . I agreed but didn't ask [the judge] to remove the order. I wanted to prevent him from hitting me again. I told him that if he hit me again, I would call the police and he would be charged with more severe offenses. . . . He seemed to learn the lesson. He knew that I was not afraid of calling the police, and I was ready to file for a separation or divorce.

Not all women participants who used restraining orders, however, had the same positive experience. Many felt obliged to terminate the restraining orders because they faced the threat of losing family relationships, or because they experienced economic insecurity. Forced separations required by restraining orders often affected family income and women's financial situations because the departure of a husband/partner, even temporarily, meant the departure of his income. Women who were homemakers and had children were most vulnerable to family separations because abusive men often failed to pay for child support until the court intervened. In addition, the amount of support tended to cover a small proportion of family expenses while public assistance was not available to many women participants because of their immigration status.[3] Some men who were forced to move out not only failed to provide cash to support their children but also stopped buying health insurance for them. In many cases, restraining orders also caused housing difficulties to some women who did not share homeownership with their husbands/partners, or whose names were not included in the leasing contracts. When abusive men owned or leased housing facilities, forced separations required by restraining orders often meant that abused women had to move out and find housing elsewhere. In addition, women who were emotionally dependent often deferred to their husbands' or partners' demand that the restraining orders be lifted. Those who lacked a network of family and friends particularly felt threatened by a possibility of divorce when they learned that their husbands/partners were having a relationship with other women during the separation. The need for the father's presence at home was also a reason behind women's decision to terminate restraining orders or not to report husbands' or partners' violations of no-contact requirements.

Bargaining with the Extended Family

In addition to their abusers, many participants also had to negotiate with other family members during the criminal justice process. Because the concept of the family in Vietnamese traditions includes both the immediate family and the extended family, the confrontational nature of criminal justice approaches to domestic violence often created problematic relationships between these women and members of the extended family on both sides. In addition, collectivism underlying Vietnamese traditions meant that what happened to a person also affected other members in his or her family. Thus, a woman's report of abuse to the police and the subsequent arrest of her husband/partner could jeopardize her relationship with her in-laws who often resented and blamed her for causing troubles to their sons (or brothers). She was also pressured by her husband's family to drop charges or not to testify for the court. Because disregarding these demands could result in more hostility and alienation from the family circle, many women were forced to satisfy these requests with an expectation that they would have a peaceful relationship with their in-laws. As a woman explained:

> I called the police to request a PPO [restraining order] to separate from him [her husband]. . . . I only wanted him to leave me alone but I didn't want him to be arrested or to be prosecuted and go to court. His family already hated me because I called the police. . . . I didn't want to suffer from his abuse, but I also didn't want other people to hate me and blame me for his involvement with the law. When his family asked me to drop the charge against him. I agreed, but the judge didn't approve my request. He was sentenced to two-and-a-half years [in prison]. . . . His lawyer filed an appeal, and I went to the second trial to ask the judge to acquit him. (Hanh)

Besides in-laws, many women participants also had to defer to the wishes of their own parents or their children who did not support the use of criminal justice interventions to solve family problems. Some parents who held a traditional view of family relationships and women's responsibilities were concerned with the possibility of family shame and family breakups resulting from criminal justice interventions. Growing up in a family tradition that emphasized filial piety, many women felt obligated to obey their parents, especially when their parents were the only source of support in time of crisis. Hue, a participant, explained her situation as follows:

> My mother didn't want me to call the police because she thought this would make other people aware of the problem. . . . After I reported the abuse and my husband was arrested, my mother was worried about the possibility that my husband would be convicted and sentenced to prison and my son would become fatherless. My husband also asked me to drop charges. . . . I went to the court and requested that charges be dropped to make my mother feel comfortable. (Hue)

Some participants also had to negotiate with their children during the criminal justice process. Children who did not understand the dynamics of abuse could take the side of their fathers and blamed their mothers for causing family problems. For example, two young children of a woman blamed her for the family problem because they thought that her "big mouth" caused her husband to use force against her. Another woman had a strained relationship with her daughter who blamed her for causing her husband's arrest and worsening family problems by reporting abuse incidents to the police. Other children might not agree with their fathers' use of force against their mothers, but they did not want their fathers to be arrested and jailed. Influenced by filial piety traditions in Vietnamese culture, many children wanted their mothers to help their fathers avoid criminal justice sanctions. Under emotional pressure of their children, many women agreed to drop charges, withdraw from the process, or terminate restraining orders.

THE LIMITATIONS OF DOMESTIC VIOLENCE POLICIES

The relationship between the offender and the victim in domestic violence cases, the emphasis on dealing with individual offenders at the expense of family relationships, and lacks of supportive services for abused women could make criminal justice interventions a barrier to women's efforts to combat domestic violence. The experience of participants in the present study indicated that mandatory-arrest and mandatory-prosecution policies often disempowered abused women by leaving them with no choice and no control of the direction of the criminal justice process. In addition, increased emotional abuse was often a price many abused women had to pay for their physical safety. Criticisms, degradations, and humiliations were new forms of abuse perpetrated by husbands/partners who were deterred by criminal justice interventions from using force against their wives/partners. Intensified family conflicts caused by criminal justice interventions often led to family breakups and women's economic insecurity.

Women's Disempowerment

For many participants, criminal justice interventions were an impediment to their efforts to combat domestic violence. Although they wanted to end violence, they often had to calculate the costs and benefits of various intervention types in light of their own circumstances. When the cost of interventions outweighed the benefits, such as causing more violence, economic hardship, or family breakups, they were less concerned with deterrence than they were with protecting their own safety as well as the financial security of their children. Consequently, many participants resisted criminal justice interventions that gave them little or no control over the direction of the case. To prevent interventions perceived as having a potential of causing more problems to family relationships, these women resorted to different strategies, including explicitly asking the police not to make arrests, changing the story by denying the abuse, or even lying to the police by saying that they had used force, but not their husbands/partners. The experience of Phuong indicated a woman's effort to prevent arrest caused by both her fear of retaliation and negative effects of arrest on the family economy. Phuong had experienced severe forms of abuse by her husband in Vietnam, in the refugee camp, and in the United States. Since she arrived in the United States, Phuong did not work because she had to take care of her disabled child who became paralyzed shortly after birth. Her husband worked only sporadically, holding no job for more than six months because he lacked both English and vocational skills. Phuong was concerned with the possibility that a combination of her husband's immigration status and his arrest would make it difficult for him to remain on his current job, or to find other jobs.

Consequently, she was determined to prevent the police from arresting her husband by lying to the police. Phuong talked about her experience as follows:

> After listening to my story [about the abuse by her husband], the officers asked my husband to stand facing the wall and handcuffed him immediately. I begged the police three times not to arrest my husband, but they did not agree. Finally, I told them that I had hit my husband, but he hadn't hit me. At that point, the officers gave my husband two options: either leaving the apartment that night, or being arrested.

Another woman, Diep, who was highly educated with a college degree, had to hire a lawyer not for her legal protection, but for helping her live-in boyfriend avoid prosecution. Concerned with the possibility that a prosecution would damage her boyfriend's reputation, make him angry, and have negative effects on their plan for a wedding and official marriage, Diep tried to drop the case by contacting the prosecutor several times. Because the prosecutor repeatedly refused to talk with her, Diep had to hire a lawyer who finally was able to convince the prosecutor to grant her boyfriend the diversion option. The indifference of criminal justice agencies to the needs of abused women and women's desperate strategies to prevent arrests and prosecutions could reinforce men's dominance when abusive men were aware that their wives/partners could not build an alliance with law enforcement agencies and also feared arrests and prosecutions. Mandatory arrest and mandatory prosecution policies could cause women who did not want arrests and prosecutions to stop reporting abuse incidents. As Ly explained why she stopped calling the police for help:

> Since the new law [mandatory arrest], I stopped calling the police because I [financially] depended on him and I didn't want him to be arrested. . . . After I gave birth to my son, I got fat and couldn't work in the coffee shop. . . . I didn't have any vocational skills and I didn't want to work as an assembler because day care costs would consume all my earning. . . . I'd rather stay home to take care of my baby.

Courts' organizational goals and lack of supportive services from the court could negatively affect women's bargaining power during the criminal justice process. Research showed that language barriers and lack of knowledge about court proceedings were among the difficulties that immigrants faced in court (Davis, Erez, & Avitabile, 1998). Data for the study indicated that most women participants had limited English proficiency but only a few were able to obtain interpretation assistance, which was often determined by court organizational goals. Under mandatory prosecution policies, the court's organizational goal was to seek prosecutions and bring more domestic violence offenders into the court system. Women who wanted to drop charges were not considered useful witnesses and, consequently, were unlikely to receive interpretation assistance during case proceedings. A participant, Xuan, talked about her experience as follows:

> The court didn't provide me with a translator. . . . I asked the victim advocate agency for help, but they told me that they couldn't help me when I wanted to drop the charge. They said they could help me to testify against him [her husband], and file for divorce or child custody.

Without interpretation assistance provided by the court, women had to rely on the help of relatives or friends and often became victims of false interpretations. Distortions by relatives and friends who changed details about the incidents to help the abusers reinforced abusive men's dominant position by undermining the credibility of women who reported abuse. In addition, women who did not have interpretation assistance at all were unlikely to understand the court process and outcomes. Consequently, these women often became victims of manipulation by their abusive husbands/partners who lied about case dispositions to avoid taking responsibilities for their abusive behavior, or who attempted to take away their custody right and refuse to pay for child support. For example, a study participant did not know that her husband had been placed under probation until she was contacted by a probation officer because she failed to understand the court process due to the language barrier and because her husband lied about the court disposition.

Increasing Emotional Abuse and the Likelihood of Family Breakups

Criminal justice policies that emphasize the punishment of individual offenders and overlook the relationship between the offender and the victim in domestic violence cases could put abused women in difficult situations. While arrests and prosecutions could not guarantee women's safety, they could cause abused women to become a target of intensive emotional abuse and retaliation by abusive husbands/partners as well as resentment by other members of the extended family. Interviews with the participants showed that emotional abuse by husbands/partners tended to increase after criminal justice interventions. Abusive husbands/partners often considered women's reports of abuse incidents as a challenge to their power and authority. Although abusive men often used both physical and emotional abuse to exert their control, most domestic violence policies only intervened in cases of physical violence. Consequently, abusive husbands/partners who felt angry or humiliated by arrests and court hearings but were deterred from using force, particularly during the criminal justice process or their probation terms, often turned to emotional abuse. Although emotional attacks did not cause physical injuries, they did cause mental injuries, pain, and fear among their victims. A woman participant explained her experience as follows:

> After I bailed him out, he didn't talk to anyone in the family for almost two weeks. . . . He made me feel guilty for his arrest. . . . It was a very tense period, and I felt scared all the time, not knowing when his anger would explode. . . . When he started to talk again, he began criticizing me on almost everything, even things he wouldn't mind before. He criticized me for not making money and compared me with other women. That hurt me a lot.

In many situations, emotional abuse became unbearable and caused family breakups when abused women felt that they could no longer endure humiliations, criticisms, and debasements by their abusive husbands/partners. Influenced by Vietnamese family traditions that emphasized the ideology of marriage, the subordination of women to men, and the presence of the father in the family, Vietnamese immigrant women often tried to stay in the relationship, partly because they were concerned about the future of their children, and partly because they had economic and emotional ties with their husbands/partners. Divorce was often viewed as the very last resort when physical or emotional abuse reached a level that threatened a woman's safety, caused severe damage to her self-esteem, and strained family relationships to the point where family members could not carry on their normal lives. Abusive men could also initiate a separation or divorce because of the humiliation caused by the criminal justice process. Women's reports of abuse to a criminal justice agency could stir distrust in men who believed in the supremacy of their gender and considered domination and domestic violence as a private family matter totally different from street crime. Combined with the breach of trust that threatened the relationship was the embarrassment and insult experienced by arrested husbands/partners who felt that they were treated like street criminals. As a woman participant talked about her experience,

> When the criminal justice process was over and shortly after he [her live-in boyfriend] participated in a program for batterers, he was often irritated and easily got angry with me. He blamed me for his arrest. . . . He felt humiliated by the arrest and his participation in the counseling program with other batterers who were alcoholic, drug addicts, and macho men. He said he was highly educated, not a bad person, but he was treated like street criminals. . . . He didn't trust me as he used to. . . . He no longer discussed with me about the marriage and the wedding. . . . I wanted to maintain the relationship because I wanted my son to have a family and a father, and I felt very disappointed when he told me that he could not continue the relationship without thinking about the incident and the problem.

Family breakups were also a consequence of using restraining orders. In many situations, separations required by restraining order, which was designed to protect women's physical safety, created opportunities for abusive men to abandon the family or cut off the relationship with their wives/partners. Several participants' husbands/partners formed new relationships during forced separations required by restraining orders, which led to the breakups of the original families to the disappointment of women who had expected that criminal justice interventions would improve family relationships.

CONCLUSIONS

The experiences of women participants in the present study indicate that current domestic violence policies overlook the reality of women's lives, family relationships, and family dynamics, and they can become a barrier to women's efforts to combat domestic violence. Arrests or prosecutions can become a threat to family lives when punishing the offender also has negative effects on the victim financially or emotionally. This is particularly true with immigrant women who experience legal dependency, fear of deportation, as well as economic and cultural isolations. While criminal justice interventions have been designed to protect women's safety, many abused immigrant women are deterred from reporting abuse incidents by the fear that prosecutions and subsequent convictions may cause their husbands to refuse to help them complete the paperwork for legal status (Bui, 2001). Victim service agencies created to support abused women and help them combat domestic violence also pay little attention to the family unit as a whole. Although many abused women want to improve family relationships, victim service agencies tend to emphasize leaving the abusive relationship as the best way to protect women's safety. By setting up shelters and providing legal counseling for divorce and child custody, victim service programs encourage women to pursue legal remedies and avoid violence by getting away and staying away from their abusers (Hoyle & Sanders, 2000; Peled, Eisikivits, Enosh, & Winstok, 2000).

Women want to stop violence but not at all costs. Their desired solutions to the problems vary with their own experience with race, gender, and class relations. For many women, staying with the abusive husband/partner is the result of a rational decision-making process based on weighing the perceived costs and benefits in the context of a multidimensional relationship. Some resist leaving because it is contrary to the ideology of marriage and the norm of heterosexuality (Ferraro & Pope, 1993). The need for family relationships is particularly great among immigrants not only because of the immigrant community's traditional value that emphasizes women's subordination and the importance of marriage for women, but also because of social isolation resulting from the process of immigration to the United States (Bui, 2001). For immigrant women who left behind the network of the extended family in their country of origin and who are culturally and economically isolated, family relationships are important because the family is their only available source of support during financial and emotional crises. Economic isolation also causes immigrant women to depend, totally or partially, on their husbands/partners to meet the financial needs of everyday life. Because women are not a homogeneous group in their circumstances and needs, it is important to broaden the goals of domestic violence interventions to include stopping the violence, improving family relationships, and preserving the family life of those who are in need. Criminal justice approaches are unlikely to alleviate the problems but likely to deepen the sense of powerlessness and exacerbate the frustration when the result of interventions is in contrast to the victim's wishes (Erez & Belknap, 1998). When interventions do not provide options for women who wish to end the violence while staying with their partners, abused women often have to make a choice between personal safety and family life.

The criminalization of domestic violence has been an important step in recognizing intimate-partner violence as a social problem, but criminal justice interventions alone will not be effective in combating the problem without additional supportive actions aimed at improving women's status and changing family dynamics. Although criminal justice interventions have addressed an important aspect of gender inequality, which was the practice of the state that condoned men's violence against women, the larger social structure that permeates men's control of women still exists. Arrests and prosecutions of men who batter women cannot change women's economic dependency, or give abused women social resources to enhance their economic status and change the dynamics of intimate relationships (Ferraro, 1993). In fact, abused women are often disadvantaged in intimate relationships because of a social structure and culture that emphasizes men's power and control. Women's economic dependency as well as women's roles and responsibilities, which are culturally created, are often impediments to women's efforts to escape abuse. In order to effectively deal with domestic violence, public policies need to address the structural aspect of the problem. Empowerment, which has been considered an important approach to help domestic violence victims improve their ability to control the environment and achieve self-determination, should be a major component of domestic violence policies (Peled et al., 2000). The empowering of battered women is to be achieved not through obedience to the expectation of service providers but through the acknowledgment of women's needs (Mills, 1996). As such, the task of empowerment should focus on providing abused women with support and resources to alleviate negative impacts of structural inequalities, improve their ability to take control of the situation, and help them make the choice appropriate to their own circumstances.

NOTES

1. The term "Vietnamese Amerasian" is used to indicate a person whose mother is Vietnamese and whose father is an American who served in American missions in Vietnam. In 1987, the Congress passed into law the Amerasian Homecoming Act allowing Vietnamese Amerasians who were born between 1962 and 1976 in Vietnam to settle in the United States under the sponsorship of American government.
2. To protect the anonymity of the participants, all names used in this report are pseudonyms.
3. The Illegal Immigration Reform and Responsibility Act of 1996 provides that legal aliens (who do not have American citizenship) do not qualify for most welfare benefits, except for refugees who could receive public assistance for no more than a total of five years.

REFERENCES

ABRAHAM, M. (2000). *Speaking the unspeakable: Marital violence among South Asian immigrants in the United States*. New Brunswick, NJ: Rutgers University Press.

BLUMER, H. (1969). *Symbolic interactionism: Perspective and method*. Upper Saddle River, NJ: Prentice Hall.

BOWMAN, C. (1992). The arrest experiments: A feminist critique. *Criminal Law & Criminology, 83*, 201–206.

BUI, H. (2001). Immigration context of wife abuse: A case of Vietnamese immigrants in the United States. In R. Muraskin (Ed.), *It's a crime: Women and justice* (3rd ed., pp. 394–410). Upper Saddle River, NJ: Prentice Hall.

CORCORAN, J., STEPHENSON, M., PERRYMAN, D., & ALLEN, S. (2001). Perceptions and utilization of a police-social work crisis intervention approach to domestic violence. *Families in Society, 82*, 393–398.

CORSILLES, A. (1994). No-drop policies in the prosecution of domestic violence cases: Guarantee to action or dangerous solution? *Fordham Law Review, 63*, 853–881.

DAVIS, R., EREZ, E., & AVITABILE, N. (1998). Immigrants and the criminal justice system: An exploratory study. *Violence & Victims, 13*, 21–30.

EREZ, E., & BELKNAP, J. (1998). In their own words: Battered women's assessment of the criminal processing system's responses. *Violence & Victims, 13*, 251–268.

FAGAN, J. (1988). Contributions of family violence research to criminal justice policy on wife assault: Paradigms of science and social control. *Violence and Victims, 3*, 159–186.

FERRARO, K. J. (1993). Cops, courts, and woman beating. In P. B. Bart & E. G. Moran (Eds.), *Violence against women: The bloody footprints* (pp. 165–176). Newbury Park, CA: Sage.

FERRARO, K. J., & POPE, L. (1993). Irreconcilable differences: Battered women, police, and the law. In N. Z. Hilton (Ed.), *Legal response to wife assault: Current trends and evaluation* (pp. 96–123). Newbury Park, CA: Sage.

FORD, D. A., & REGOLI, M. J. (1993). The criminal prosecution of wife assaulters. In N. Z. Hilton (Ed.), *Legal response to wife assault: Current trends and evaluation* (pp. 127–164). Newbury Park, CA: Sage.

GORELICK, S. (1991). Contradictions of feminist methodology. *Gender & Society, 5*, 459–477.

HARDING, S. (1991). *Whose science? Whose knowledge? Thinking from women's lives*. Ithaca, NY: Cornell University Press.

HOYLE, C., & SANDERS, A. (2000). Police response to domestic violence: From victim choice to victim empowerment? *British Journal of Criminology, 40,* 14–36.

JONES, A. (1994). *Next time, she'll be dead: Battering and how to stop it.* Boston: Beacon Press.

KANDIYOTI, D. (1991). Bargaining with patriarchy. In J. Lorber & S. Farrell (Eds.), *The social construction of gender* (pp. 104–118). Newbury, CA: Sage.

LEWIS, R., DOBASH, R. P., DOBASH, R. E., & CAVANAGH, K. (2000). Protection, prevention, rehabilitation or justice? Women's use of the law to challenge domestic violence. *International Review of Victimology, 7* (Special Issue), 179–205.

LINCOLN, Y., & GUBA, E. (1985). Postpositivism and the naturalist paradigm. In Y. Lincoln & E. Guba (Eds.), *Naturalistic inquiry* (pp. 14–46). Newbury Park, CA: Sage.

McCALL, M., & WITTNER, J. (1990). The good news about life history. In H. Becker & M. McCall (Eds.), *Symbolic interaction and cultural studies* (pp. 46–89): Chicago: University of Chicago Press.

MERRIAM, S. (1998). *Qualitative research and case study applications in education.* San Francisco: Jossey-Bass.

MILLS, L. (1996). Empowering battered women transnationally: The case for postmodern interventions. *Social Work, 41,* 261–268.

PELED, E., EISIKIVITS, Z., ENOSH, G., & WINSTOK, Z. (2000). Choice and empowerment for battered women who stay: Toward a constructivist model. *Social Work, 45,* 9–25.

RADFORD, J., & STANKO, E. (1991). Violence against women and children: The contradictions of crime control under patriarchy. In K. Stenson & D. Cowell (Eds.), *The politics of crime control* (pp. 188–202). London: Sage.

STARK, E. (1993). Mandatory arrest of batterers: A reply to its critics. *American Behavioral Scientist, 35,* 651–680.

STRAUSS, A. (1987). *Qualitative analysis for social scientists.* New York: Cambridge University Press.

WANLESS, M. (1996). Mandatory arrest: A step toward eradicating domestic violence, but is it enough? *University of Illinois Law Review, 2,* 533–586.

16

When the Victim Recants

The Impact of Expert Witness Testimony in Prosecution of Battering Cases

Alisa Smith and RoseMarie Rotondi

The effects of battering are, in some form, admissible as evidence in all 50 states to assist battered women who kill their abusers (Breyer, 1992; Dutton, 1996a, 1996b; Parrish, 1995).[1] These effects have been admitted to provide juries with contextual and background information on battered women. Expert testimony has been permitted to explain why some women stay in abusive relationships, to educate jurors on the psychological affects of battering, and to identify the behavioral responses of battered women in these relationships (Breyer, 1992; Schuller & Vidmar, 1992). In the last decade, evidence about battering and its effects has begun to be used as a tool in the prosecution of batterers as well. Twenty-seven states have held this type of evidence admissible against batterers.[2]

Although the effects of battering on those who kill their abusers and the impact of this evidence in trial courts has been widely studied by legal and criminological scholars (Blackman & Brickman, 1984; Ferraro, 2003; Follingstad, Brodino, & Kleinfelter, 1996; Follingstad et al., 1989; Follingstad, Shillinglaw, DeHart, & Kleinfelter, 1997; Schuller & Hastings, 1996; Schuller, Smith, & Olson, 1994; Schuller & Vidmar, 1992), much less attention has focused on its use by prosecutors against batterers. In fact, discussions about experts in the prosecution of batterers has been limited to reviews of the literature and evidentiary discussions by legal scholars (e.g., Dutton, 1996a, 1996b; Mangum, 1999; Parrish, 1995; Rogers, 1998; Schroeder, 1991). This limited study of the topic, however, has revealed that members of the courtroom workgroup (judges, prosecutors, and defense lawyers) along with expert witnesses and advocates believe that testimony about battering directly impacts deliberations as well as case outcomes (Dutton, 1996b). No research, however, has investigated prosecutor awareness of the availability of this testimony, the extent to which experts are used to prosecute batterers, whether prosecutors believe expert testimony impacts case outcomes, and most important, whether expert testimony about battering does impact juror decision making (Sigler & Shook, 1997). This research is intended to begin to fill this void.

BATTERING AND ITS EFFECTS: A BRIEF REVIEW OF THE LITERATURE

Twenty-seven states, including New Jersey, in some way, have admitted evidence about battering and its effects in the prosecution of batterers. Although there is not a "defense" per se of battering and its effects, battered victims may introduce this testimony along with other defenses such as self-defense, duress, or insanity. Battering and its effects have been introduced to educate jurors about the situational context of battering and to explain victim behaviors (Custer, Foreman, Ikeda, Matthews, & Morena, 2001; Dutton, 1996b; Walker, 1979, 1984). Generally, when prosecutors introduce this type of evidence against a batterer, the testimony is introduced to place the event or behavior in its "social framework," situation, or context (Monahan & Walker, 1998). Monahan and Walker (1987, p. 559) define social framework evidence as "[g]eneral research results [that] are used to construct a frame of reference or background context for deciding a factual issue crucial to the resolution of a specific case."

In the defense of battered women who kill, experts have been permitted to assist jurors in understanding the dynamics of battering (e.g., Kromsky & Cutler, 1989; Mather, 1988); specifically, to illustrate the impact of intimate violence, to explain the cyclical nature of domestic violence, and to describe seemingly unique behavioral responses of the battered victims. Since its admission in defense of battered women, a large number of studies have examined the impact of expert testimony on juror decision making (Blackman & Brickman, 1984; Follingstad et al., 1989; Follingstad et al., 1997; Kasian, Spanos, Terrance, & Peebles, 1993; Schuller, 1992; Schuller & Hastings, 1996; Schuller et al., 1994). Most studies found expert testimony resulted in greater leniency toward battered women who killed their abusers (Kasian et al., 1993; Schuller, 1992; Schuller et al., 1994; Schuller & Hastings, 1996).

Consistent with this body of research, it is expected that expert testimony in the prosecution of batterers would have the same effect—that is, the introduction of expert testimony would (in opposition to leniency toward the battered-victim defendant) result in less leniency toward the batterer-defendant. This hypothesis is correspondingly consistent with the findings from Dutton's (1996b) three-day focus group where it was concluded that expert testimony on the effects of battering was necessary to educate jurors and impact their deliberations. Dutton's group also identified several potential barriers to the use of experts by prosecutors. A lack of understanding among prosecutors on the potential uses of an expert and the lack of available expert witnesses for trial presentations were identified as impediments to using these experts (Dutton, 1996b).

METHODOLOGY

State v. Frost and the Admission of Expert Testimony on Battering

In 1990, in *State v. Frost* a New Jersey appellate court held evidence of battering and its effects admissible to explain a victim's seemingly inconsistent behavior following an attack by her abuser in his prosecution. Specifically, the *Frost* court ruled that this evidence was admissible to bolster the credibility of the victim during trial and that expert testimony was admissible even when victim credibility is not attacked or challenged. Other courts that have admitted this type of testimony have limited its admissibility to certain circumstances or have otherwise circumscribed the scope of its introduction (see Parrish, 1995, for a comprehensive review of the cases and evidentiary rulings). The *Frost* decision provides New Jersey prosecutors with wide latitude in using expert testimony in the prosecution of batterers.

The Prosecution Survey

To fill the current void in the literature on the use of experts by prosecutors, short interviews with trial prosecutors assigned to domestic violence cases were conducted in 12 of the 21 counties in New Jersey during the fall and winter of 2000. The office of the prosecutor was contacted in each county. A domestic violence prosecutor was identified and a telephonic interview attempted. When prosecutors indicated they were too busy to be interviewed telephonically, an offer was made to provide the interview instrument via facsimile to allow the opportunity for completion of the questionnaire. Several attempts to complete the interview were made by telephoning the office and leaving messages a minimum of three times per office. Following these attempts, 12 prosecutors participated. This amounts to a 57% response rate.

The interviews were intended to assess whether trial prosecutors[3] were familiar with the *State v. Frost* decision, whether the prosecutors understood the potential usefulness of expert testimony, and whether experts had been utilized in the prosecution of batterers. Prosecutors were also questioned about whether they thought trial judges would be willing to permit experts to testify and whether they believed expert testimony would influence a jury. Finally, prosecutors were asked what barriers, if any, prevented the use of experts in prosecuting batterers.

Table 1 provides a snapshot of the offices that participated in this study. Most created a specialized domestic violence unit in the 1990s and provided training to the prosecutors assigned to the unit. Only two offices did not have a specialized unit for domestic violence.

TABLE 1 Prosecution Offices		
Specialized domestic violence units	10 yes	2 no
If yes, unit created	1990 to 1993	6
	1994 to 1999	4
Average number of cases prosecuted		
	150 to 500 cases	4 offices
	600 to 1,000 cases	2 offices
	1001 to 2,000 cases	2 offices
	Unknown	4 offices
Specialized training	Office seminars	2 offices
	Attorney general	4 offices
	National training	5 offices

One of these offices handled domestic violence cases as part of a family unit, and these prosecutors were especially assigned to this unit and received training on domestic violence cases. In the other office, domestic violence cases were randomly assigned among the five lawyers in the office. Each lawyer got special domestic violence training. Nine out of the 10 offices with a specialized domestic violence unit provided domestic violence training to its members. The single office that did not provide training reported that it encouraged the prosecutors to take the training offered to the local police concerning domestic violence. Training included special seminars by the prosecutors' offices, the state attorney general's office, and the National College of Domestic Violence Attorneys.

The two offices without specialized units were unaware of the number of domestic violence cases prosecuted by their offices. The specialized units reported a great disparity among the offices in the numbers of cases prosecuted. This may reflect the diversity of the offices located in urban and suburban environments. The prosecutors reported, on average, handling between 150 to 2,000 domestic violence cases a year. These numbers included the handling of disorderly conduct, contempt, and violations of temporary restraining order cases. Most prosecutors estimated that between 1 and 20% of cases go to trial, and that a large percentage of victims are reluctant to prosecute.[4]

Juror Decision Making

To explore the significance of expert testimony on juror deliberations, a hypothetical domestic violence incident and trial scenario was developed that varied on the extent of injury to the battered victim and the introduction of expert testimony. The hypothetical was followed by a series of questions about the juror (respondent) decision of guilty or not guilty as well as the factors that influenced that verdict or decision.[5] The hypothetical scenario and survey was distributed to 100 students in introductory courses not involving criminology at a college in the state of New Jersey. In all four variations, the following facts were revealed to the respondents:

1. Mr. Doe is charged with battery against his wife. Battery, in this case, is defined as follows: Mr. Doe intentionally touched or struck Mrs. Doe against her will; and Mr. Doe intentionally caused bodily harm to Mrs. Doe.

2. Jane and Joe Doe have been married for ten years. They have three children. Jane and Joe are both school teachers.

3. The police arrived at the Doe residence in response to a noise complaint by a neighbor. Upon their arrival, the police noticed a lamp broken on the living room floor and books scattered across the hallway.

4. The police testified at trial that Mrs. Doe said that she and Mr. Doe had an argument, and that Mr. Doe pushed her down. Mr. Doe agreed that they had an argument but stated that Mrs. Doe fell down by accident. Mr. Doe apologized for the noise. Mrs. Doe said she did not want her husband arrested.

5. The police arrested Mr. Doe. Mrs. Doe testified at trial that the argument was a misunderstanding and she denied that Mr. Doe pushed her down. She testified that it was an accident and that she fell. When confronted with her prior statement, Mrs. Doe said she never made that statement to the police.

There were four variations of this scenario—injury/expert; no injury/expert; injury/no expert; and no injury/no expert. In the two vignettes with no injury, the respondents were informed that "[t]he police did not see any visible injury to Mrs. Doe." In the other two vignettes—the injury scenarios—the respondents were informed that "[t]he police also viewed a red mark on Mrs. Doe's arm and a swollen, bloody lip." The expert scenarios included the following paragraph:

> The prosecutor called an expert on battering to testify. The expert testified that there was a history of violent acts between Mr. and Mrs. Doe. The expert testified that battering victims are reluctant to tell others about the violence, and either hope the situation will change or fear that things would get worse if reported. The expert testified that after a 50-minute interview with Mrs. Doe and information about the incident as outlined above, it was determined that Mrs. Doe's conduct was consistent with that of someone who is repeatedly battered.

The no-expert vignettes did not include this paragraph.

The Student Sample

The study ($n = 100$) was comprised of a group of 100 nonrandom students taking introductory courses in social work, sociology, and business in two state colleges in New Jersey (the courses were not taught by the authors). The students were advised that participation was requested, but not mandatory, and that survey responses would be kept confidential as well as anonymous. The students were advised that the professors administering the surveys were not involved in the research project. None of the students declined to participate. As expected, most were noncriminal justice or law and society majors and they were predominantly first- or second-year students. This was the intended sample for this project as it may best represent the public at large.

The snapshot of the 100 students is shown in Table 2. More than half the respondents were female, Caucasian, single, and had no legal training and no experience with domestic violence. However, 33% did report some type of experience with domestic violence and of those 33%, 9% reported being victims of domestic violence, 15% reported being a witness to domestic violence, and 3% reported being a victim and witness of domestic violence.

Hypotheses

Prosecution Study.   It was expected that prosecutors would report an underutilization of experts in the prosecution of batterers. It was also expected that trial prosecutors, similar to the findings of the Dutton (1996b) focus group, comprised of senior prosecutors, judges, defense attorneys, expert witnesses, and advocates, would identify funding and the availability of experts as the two most prominent barriers to the use of experts.

Impact on Juror Decision Making.   Since much violence is progressive (Walker, 1979, 1984), it is important to assess the significance of using expert testimony in less serious (in terms of injury and criminal charge) prosecutions. This also best represents the

TABLE 2   Snapshot of Sample ($n = 100$)

Demographic Characteristic	Percentage
Sex	
Female	55.0%
Male	45.0
Race/Ethnicity	
White/Caucasian	78.0%
Black	
African-American	11.0%
Muslim	1.0
Haitian	1.0
Asian	3.0%
Hispanic	
Hispanic	3.0%
Mexican	1.0
Cuban	1.0
Portuguese	1.0
Marital status	
Single	82.0%
Married	8.0
Partnered	8.0
Divorced	1.0
No answer	1.0
Legal/Criminal justice training	
No	80.0%
Yes	20.0
Experience with domestic violence	
No	66.0%
Yes	34.0
Victim	9.0%
Witness	15.0
Victim and witness	3.0
Accused	1.0
Profession/Education	5.0

real-life scenario where prosecutors may be least likely to engage the use of experts because prosecutors are more likely to consult experts when prosecuting "serious" crimes—such as those involving near death or serious bodily injuries. From a policy perspective, if using experts in less serious cases educates juries and perhaps increases the chance of conviction before more serious injuries occur, the successful prosecution of minor crimes actually may prevent future violence (Kelling & Coles, 1996).[6] Some support is lent to this idea by research that has found batterers more empowered and more likely to continue to engage in violence when the court system fails battered women (Ptacek, 1999). Thus, it was expected that expert testimony would have a more significant impact on verdicts involving the no-injury scenarios.

That is, jurors deciding the case involving more serious violence would be more likely to discount the importance of recantations and render verdicts based on the seriousness of the injury (usually supported by photographs, scarring, and hospital records). Expert testimony, therefore, would impact cases more significantly where there was not any sign of physical injury. In this study, minor injury compared to no injury was examined. In other words, serious or severe injury was not utilized by any scenario.

RESULTS

Prosecution Offices

Every prosecutor interviewed was familiar with the *Frost* decision. Each also demonstrated knowledge about the dynamics of battering and the potential for educating juries about battering and its effects. Since these prosecutors indicated extensive training in the area of domestic violence, the ubiquitous knowledge of *Frost* as well as the use of expert testimony may be the result of this training. Despite the universality of knowledge, only three prosecutors actually used an expert during the prosecution of a batterer. Two others had planned to use an expert, but the defendants entered guilty pleas. As expected, the types of cases where prosecutors considered the use of experts involved serious charges (e.g., batterers charged with homicide).

Several barriers to using experts were identified by these prosecutors. Consistent with Dutton's (1996b) findings, two of the most common barriers were the lack of available, qualified witnesses and the lack of adequate funding to hire experts. Some prosecutors indicated that local shelter staff, who were qualified to testify as experts, were uncomfortable in this role. A third barrier, inadequate time to prepare witnesses for trial, was also mentioned by a number of prosecutors. These barriers may particularly affect the use of experts in less serious cases where caseloads are much higher and the time to prepare trials more limited. A final, practical barrier was that many cases simply end by negotiated plea, and therefore there are fewer trials of less serious matters.

Juror Decision Making

Table 3 presents the findings from the survey based on the domestic violence vignettes. Overall, 33% rendered not guilty verdicts ($n = 33$) and 67% guilty verdicts ($n = 67$). Differences in verdicts across experience with domestic violence, gender, and race were not statistically significant. In comparing across the four vignettes, however, statistically significant differences emerged (chi-square = 0.032; phi = 0.032). Respondents were more likely to render guilty verdicts when they were presented with expert testimony on battering and its effects. Of those rendering guilty verdicts, almost 60% were provided with the expert testimony. Similar, but less pronounced was the effect of injury on respondents'

TABLE 3　Verdicts across the Four Vignettes ($n = 100^{*}$)

	Injury/ Expert	Injury/ No Expert	No Injury/ Expert	No Injury/ No Expert
Not Guilty	16.0%	40%	24%	52%
	($n = 4$)	($n = 10$)	($n = 6$)	($n = 13$)
Guilty	84%	60%	76%	48%
	($n = 21$)	($n = 15$)	($n = 19$)	($n = 12$)

*Chi-square = 0.032; phi = 0.032.

verdicts. Of those respondents rendering guilty verdicts, almost 54% were presented with "visible" physical injury to the victim.

In examining the verdict results of those with the physical injury scenario, there were significant differences based on whether respondents were presented with expert testimony. In the injury/expert vignette, respondents were significantly more likely to render guilty verdicts (84%) than not guilty verdicts (16%). In the injury/no expert vignette, respondents were also significantly more likely to render guilty verdicts (65%). The margin, however, of guilty (65%) to not guilty (35%) was much narrower. An examination of the no-injury vignettes also demonstrated the influence of expert testimony on juror verdicts. Respondents were significantly more likely to render verdicts of guilty (76%) when there was an expert. In the no injury/no expert vignette, respondents were more likely to render not guilty verdicts (52%). The verdict patterns in this study demonstrate the potential importance of using expert testimony, particularly in cases involving no visible signs of injury and to a lesser extent, in those cases with a visible sign of injury.

In a qualitative examination of the "reasons" for the respondents' verdicts, it becomes even clearer that the use and nonuse of expert testimony significantly influenced case outcomes. Statistically significant differences were also found across verdicts and respondents' reasons for their verdicts (chi-square = 0.000; phi = 0.000). Respondents rendering not guilty verdicts stated the following reasons for their decisions: insufficient evidence ($n = 12$), refusal to press changes ($n = 11$), victim not credible ($n = 7$), and defendant credible ($n = 1$). Respondents rendering guilty verdicts gave the following reasons for their decisions: victim credible ($n = 25$), sufficient evidence ($n = 16$), the expert testimony plus the evidence ($n = 12$), and a history of abuse as indicated by the expert ($n = 9$).

The respondent rationales for their verdicts lend support to the hypothesis that expert testimony impacts case outcomes. Some respondents explicitly noted the influence of expert testimony on their decision-making process:

> He did battered [sic] her, but she did not want him to get in trouble. Based on the expert's statement I concluded that he is guilty.

> The expert on battering, when she said that she never made the statement of him pushing her. If she was really being honest, she could have said that she made up the comment because she was angry at him.

> The wife lied about the accident and changed her statement. The expert testified that their [sic] was a history of violent acts. Someone has to stop it.

> Because of the expert that said her conduct was consistent with that of a battered person.

> Mrs. Doe's original statement at the time of the argument, and the testimony of the expert on battering.

In other respondent explanations, the influence of expert testimony was implicit:

> When women are abused, most of the time, they are afraid to speak up, worrying about what might happen to the children.

> He is known to beat her. It has to stop. Someone has to do something about him. [The testimony concerning a history was provided by the expert witness in the hypothetical vignette.]

> The fact there was a history of violence between the Doe's [sic], and the fact Mrs. Doe gave conflicting statements.

Interestingly, many respondents, without the benefit of the expert testimony, highlighted similar factors as those finding guilt with the expert, but came to the opposite conclusion. For example, many respondents reasoned that the batterer was not guilty based on the changes in Mrs. Doe's testimony or conflicts in her testimony.

> If Mrs. Doe said the abuse never happened then nothing can be done. Unfortunately, the wife could be lying and justice will never be served.

> I feel that he did it but since his wife changed her testimony he will not be charged.

> Without the testimony of the other party involved, there is no way to prove that Mr. Doe hit his wife.

The visible, physical injury of the victim was also significant in influencing verdicts and as expected, physical injury made the lack of expert testimony less significant to juror outcomes. Respondents were more likely, even without expert testimony on the dynamics of battering, to find the batterer guilty, disregard her recantation or denial, and base their decision on the evidence of injury.

> The woman was touched without her consent.

> Whether caused directly or indirectly by Mr. Doe he led to the injuries caused to his wife.

> He is guilty because I feel that the facts point to his guilt and Mrs. Doe is scared to say her husband did it.

On the other hand, respondents presented with no injury and no expert testimony were more likely to render not guilty verdicts and reasoned that there was simply insufficient evidence of guilt or that the victim was not credible.

> Mrs. Doe didn't seem to know what happened. It seemed like she was not being truthful. She acted confused—her story changed.

> Mrs. Doe might have been upset about the argument and believed she was pushed when she actually just fell. She had no bruises and didn't testify against her husband.

My verdict is not guilty because there is not enough evidence to support the case. If there were visual marks on Mrs. Doe it may be a different story.

For some respondents, the availability of expert testimony also was insufficient to justify a guilty verdict. This was especially the case for respondents presented with no physical injury to the victim.

Just because he may have a history of hitting her doesn't necessarily mean he hit her this time. For this charge—not guilty, no evidence [no visible injury vignette].

I think that Mr. Doe is most certainly guilty of domestic violence, but with the information provided and Mrs. Doe's statement I don't believe that he could be found guilty [visible injury vignette].

Not enough evidence [no visible injury vignette].

Mrs. Doe said nothing happened [no visible injury vignette].

Not enough information and she denied it, it was the first time reported [no visible injury vignette].

CONCLUSION

The study findings suggest that prosecutors may benefit, in terms of greater conviction rates, from utilizing experts in the prosecution of batterers. Expert testimony on battering and its effects may be particularly helpful in influencing juror understanding of domestic violence when a victim recants or denies the violence and there is little or no physical injury visible. Based on the interviews with prosecutors, this tool is underutilized for two primary reasons—inadequate financial support and the unavailability of experts. To increase conviction rates for these cases, prosecutors might benefit from developing relationships with experts and investing in their use. Since battered women shelter advocates may be reluctant to become involved in litigation, other avenues to locate available, willing, and qualified experts from academic institutions should be explored. The instant study did not examine whether the "type" of expert (i.e., academic versus nonacademic) influences outcome. Future research should investigate potential distinctions and differences on this characteristic on case outcomes.

The findings from the "juror decision making" component of this study suggest that the use of an expert may significantly contribute to the successful prosecution of less serious domestic violence cases. As expected, expert testimony was influential in the cases with and without injury. Eighty percent of respondents presented with evidence of injury as well as expert testimony rendered guilty verdicts, and 76% of respondents not presented with injury evidence, but presented with expert testimony rendered guilty verdicts. Only 60% of respondents presented with evidence of injury to the victim and no expert testimony rendered guilty verdicts. This represents a 16% differential between respondents presented with expert testimony and those not presented with expert testimony. Only 48% of respondents presented with the no physical injury vignette and no expert testimony rendered guilty verdicts. The pattern suggests that expert testimony may increase the rate of conviction where there is little or no physical injury to the victim. Fewer and fewer respondents found the batterer guilty when there was no expert testimony available and when there was no physical injury to the victim.

Many of the respondents provided with the expert testimony relied on that information to render guilty verdicts. Twenty-seven percent of those presented with an injury to the victim and expert testimony relied on the description of the scene, injury to the victim, and victim reluctance to prosecute to determine guilt; an additional 30% explicitly noted the expert testimony as a reason for their decision. Almost half (48%) of the respondents presented with no injury to the victim and expert testimony indicated that the expert testimony influenced their decision of guilt. On the contrary, those without the benefit of the expert testimony were most likely to render not guilty verdicts based on the victim's refusal to testify, denial of the incident, or the perceived lack of credibility of the victim. The recantation or denial of violence was also a significant or pivotal factor in determining guilt by respondents and that likewise, the presentation of expert testimony mediated the importance of that particular factor. Respondents presented with the expert testimony were more likely to interpret the recantation as symptomatic of battering and its effects, while those without the expert testimony were more likely to find that the evidence was insufficient to convict or that the victim was simply not credible.

Although these findings suggest expert testimony is likely to increase the chance of obtaining convictions, there are several, significant limitations to this research. First, this was a preliminary study with a small sample size. In addition, the participants were college students and the findings are not generalizable to broader populations. Third, though cost-effective, the survey format does not adequately replicate or simulate true trial conditions and all the variables that must be controlled in that setting to fully distill the impact of expert testimony on case outcomes. Mock trials, using variation on injury to victim and presentation of expert testimony, may better test the hypotheses. Further, the hypothetical expert testimony, used as the basis for this study, does not replicate the wide variation of its uses and limitations across jurisdictions in the United States thereby creating further generalizability limitations. Finally, although the findings suggest an increase in conviction rates as a result of expert testimony, the findings may not be interpreted as inexorably leading to an overall decrease in domestic violence.

NOTES

1. A debate about the use of the term "battered woman syndrome" by legal as well as psychological scholars has emerged. The term "battered woman syndrome" was coined by Lenore Walker in her 1979 and 1984 books *The Battered Woman* and *The Battered Woman Syndrome* (Walker, 1979, 1984). The term "battered woman syndrome," which has been associated with psychological ailments, has been widely criticized and a growing number of academics, legal scholars, and lawyers have rejected it in favor of "battering and its effects" as a more appropriate and comprehensive characterization of the behaviors and responses of intimate violence victims (Dutton, 1996b). Dutton's (p. 4) focus group determined that "the concept of battered woman syndrome is inadequate to convey the information that is available for the purpose either to assist the fact-finder in understanding the evidence or to determine a fact in issue." For purposes of this research and its discussion, the term "battering and its effects" has been adopted.

2. *Brandon v. State*, 839 P.2d 400 (Alaska Ct. App. 1992)(dicta only); *People v. Humphrey*, 921 P.2d 1 (Cal. 1996); Cal. Evid. Code §1107 (West 1993); *State v. Borelli*, 628 A.2d 1105 (Conn. 1993); *State v. Rhone*, 566 So. 2d 1367 (Fla. 1990); *Pruitt v. State*, 296 S.E. 2d 795 (Ga. Ct.

App. 1982); *State v. Clark*, 926 P.2d 194 (Haw. 1996), approving, *State v. Cababag*, 850 P.2d 716 (Haw. Ct. App. 1993); *People v. Server*, 499 N.E. 2d 1019 (4th Dist. 1986); *Isaacs v. State*, 659 N.E. 2d 1036 (Ind. 1995); *Dausch v. State*, 616 N.E. 2d 13 (Ind. 1993); *State v. Griffin*, 564 N.W. 2d 370 (Iowa 1997); *State v. Clements*, 770 P.2d 447 (Kans. 1989); *Dyer v. Commonwealth*, 816 S.W. 2d 647 (KY 1991); *Commonwealth v. Goetzendanner*, 679 N.E. 2d 240 (Ma. App. Ct. 1997); *People v. Christel*, 537 N.W. 2d 194 (Mi. 1995); *State v. Merrill*, 1991 Minn. App. Lexis 790 (8/13/91) (unpublished opinion); *State v. Stringer*, 897 P.2d 1063 (Mont. 1995); *State v. Doremus*, 514 N.W. 2d 649 (Neb. 1994); Nevada Rev. Stat. §48.061 (1993); *State v. Searles*, 680 A.2d 612 (NH 1996); *State v. Baker*, 424 A.2d 171 (NH 1980); *State v. Frost*, 577 A.2d 1282 (NJ Super. Ct. App. Div. 1990); *People v. Hryckewicz*, 634 NYS 2d 297 (NY App. Div. 1995); *People v. Taylor*, 552 N.E. 2d 131 (NY 1990); *State v. Pargeon*, 582 N.E. 2d 665 (Ohio Ct. App. 1991); *State v. Milbradt*, 756 P.2d 620 (Ore. 1988); SC Code Ann. §17-23-170 (Law Co-op 1995); *Scugoza v. State*, 949 S.W. 2d 360 (Tex. Ct. App. 1997); *State v. Ciskie*, 751 P.2d 1165 (Wash. 1988); *State v. Bednarz*, 507 N.W. 2d 168 (Wisc. Ct. App. 1993); *Barnes v. State*, 858 P.2d 522 (Wyo. 1993); *Frenzel v. State*, 849 P.2d 741 (Wyo. 1993).

3. In other words, those attorneys handling the domestic violence cases, not the appointed officials or supervisors in the prosecutors' offices.

4. One prosecutor estimated that 90% of domestic violence cases go to trial in his county.

5. Prior to distributing the survey to the sample of 100 students, a pretest was provided to a non-random group of students in a criminal justice course. The students were not identified by the instrument and participation was voluntary. Students were advised of dual purposes for the survey: first, it was anticipated that the survey would engender discussion about domestic violence; and second, survey creators wished to critique the validity of the instrument for its improvement prior to distribution to the sample for study. Students were not asked to complete the demographic information on the survey, but they were asked to read the vignettes, answer the first two questions on the survey—the verdict and the reason for their decision—as well as to critique the follow-up demographic questions on the survey. The survey was modified based on the findings of this pretest and student critique.

6. This idea is consistent with the "broken windows" theory discussed in Kelling and Coles (1996).

REFERENCES

BREYER, H. (1992). The battered woman syndrome and the admissibility of expert testimony. *Criminal Law Bulletin, 28*(2), 99–115.

BLACKMAN, J., & BRICKMAN, E. (1984). The impact of expert testimony on trial of battered women who kill their husbands. *Behavioral Sciences and the Law, 2*, 413–422.

CUSTER, H., FOREMAN, B., IKEDA, K., MATTHEWS, V., & MORENA, N. (2001). *Community policing to reduce domestic violence, trainer lesson plan.* Washington, DC: Federal Law Enforcement Training Center.

DUTTON, M. A. (1996a). *The validity and use of evidence concerning battering and its effects in criminal trials, expert testimony trend analysis.* Washington, DC: U.S. Department of Justice.

DUTTON, M. A. (1996b). *Impact of evidence concerning battering and its effects in criminal trials involving battered women* (edited by Malcolm Gordon, NIMH for the National Clearinghouse for the Defense of Battered Women). Washington, DC: U.S. Department of Justice.

FERRARO, K. J. (2003). The words change but the melody lingers: The persistence of battered woman syndrome in criminal cases involving battered women. *Violence Against Women, 9*(1), 110–129.

FOLLINGSTAD, D. R., BRONDINO, M. J., & KLEINFELTER, K. J. (1996). Reputation and behavior of battered women who kill their partners: Do these variables influence juror verdicts? *Journal of Family Violence, 11*(3), 251–267.

FOLLINGSTAD, D. R., POLEK, D. S., HAUSE, E. S., DEATON, L. H., BULGER, M. W., & CONWAY, Z. D. (1989). Factors predicting verdicts in cases where battered women kill their husbands. *Law and Human Behavior, 13*, 253–269.

FOLLINGSTAD, D. R., SHILLINGLAW, R. D., DeHART, D. D., & KLEINFELTER, K. J. (1997). The impact of elements of self-defense and objective versus subjective instructions on jurors' verdicts for battered women defendants. *Journal of Interpersonal Violence, 12*, 729–747.

KASIAN, M., SPANOS, N. P., TERRANCE, C. A., & PEEBLES, S. (1993). Battered women who kill: Jury simulation and legal defenses. *Law and Human Behavior, 17*, 289–312.

KELLING, G. L., & COLES, C. M. (1996). *Fixing broken windows: Restoring order and reducing crime in our communities*. New York: Free Press.

KROMSKY, D. F., & CUTLER, B. L. (1989). The battered woman syndrome: A matter of common sense. *Forensic Reports, 2*(3), 173–186.

MANGUM, P. F. (1999). Reconceptualizing battered woman syndrome evidence: Prosecution use of expert testimony on battering. *Boston College Third World Law Journal, 19*, 593–620.

MONAHAN, J., & WALKER, W. L. (1987). Social frameworks: A new use of social science in law. *Virginia Law Review, 73*, 559–598.

MONAHAN, J., & WALKER, W. L. (1998). *Social science in law: Cases and materials*, 4th ed. New York: Foundation Press.

PARRISH, J. (1995). *Trend analysis: Expert testimony on battering and its effects in criminal cases*. Washington, DC: U.S. Department of Justice.

PTACEK, J. (1999). *Battered women in the courtroom: The power of judicial responses*. Boston: Northeastern University Press.

ROGERS, A. (1998). Prosecutorial use of expert testimony in domestic violence cases: From recantation to refusal to testify. *Columbia Journal of Gender and Law, 8*, 67.

SCHROEDER, J. M. (1991). Using battered woman syndrome evidence in the prosecution of a batterer. *Iowa Law Review, 76*, 553.

SCHULLER, R. (1992). The impact of battered woman syndrome evidence on jury decision processes. *Law and Human Behavior, 16*, 597–620.

SCHULLER, R., & HASTINGS, P. A. (1996). Trials of battered women who kill: The impact of alternative forms of expert evidence. *Law and Human Behavior, 20*, 167–187.

SCHULLER, R., SMITH, V. L., & OLSON, J. M. (1994). Jurors' decisions in trials of battered women who kill: The role of prior beliefs and expert testimony. *Journal of Applied Social Psychology, 24*, 316–337.

SCHULLER, R., & VIDMAR, N. (1992). Battered women syndrome evidence in the courtroom: A review of the literature. *Law and Human Behavior, 16*(3), 273–291.

SIGLER, R. T., & SHOOK, C. L. (1997). Judicial acceptance of the battered woman syndrome. *Criminal Justice Policy Review, 8*(4), 365–382.

WALKER, L. (1979). *Battered woman*. New York: Harper & Row.

WALKER, L. (1984). *The battered woman syndrome*. New York: Springer.

CASES

State v. *Frost*, 577 A.2d 1282 (N.J. 1990) *cert. denied*, 604 A.2d 59 (1990)

17

Beyond Shelter: Expanding Spheres of Influence for Reducing Violence against Women

A Case Study of Hubbard House in Jacksonville, Florida

Michael Hallett and Suzanne Zahrly

Given the overwhelming barriers to escape, it is amazing that women do survive battering relationships. . . . The shelter network operates like a modern version of the Underground Railroad acting as a referral and support system for women who need to take radical steps to escape from abusers who are determined to own and control them, and who need to protect themselves and their children.[1]

THE VOCATION OF SHELTER WORK

Women survivors of domestic violence often face complex challenges as they negotiate familial dislocation and poverty while assessing available community resources. Domestic violence shelters often provide a spectrum of services from immediate short-term respite from violence to longer-term assistance with job placement, referrals for medical and other family care, and legal assistance. These resources beyond shelter often prove transformative and emancipatory, particularly when shelter staff view their undertaking as providing a "helping situation" for "survivors" rather than services for "victims" of domestic violence (Krishnan, Hilbert, McNeil, & Newman, 2004).

Survivors of domestic violence reach shelters in varying states of exhaustion, isolation, confusion, or injury and often face a diverse set of challenges unique to their particular circumstance (Ferraro, 1997). "Research on women's attempts to leave their violent intimate relationships suggests that these attempts are affected by a variety of complex, interrelated, and explanatory variables" (Krishnan et al., 2004, p. 166). In all too many cases, however, the benevolent but limited resources available to survivors of domestic violence prove inadequate for surmounting the broader challenges of homelessness, pending financial crisis, medical issues, and child care faced by displacement in a shelter. In order to truly help battered women survive, shelter work must go beyond the important provision of respite from immediate harm to helping women improve their lives overall. As one of the nation's leading researchers on domestic violence concludes, "our findings seem to reinforce the importance of advocacy and emotional support across the spectrum of issues battered women face" (Gondolf, 2005, p. 367).

This chapter presents the story of one domestic violence shelter, Hubbard House, in Jacksonville, Florida, and its evolution from a shelter devoted to providing temporary respite from violence, to a full-service advocacy center broadly engaged in seeking to empower battered women by transforming their circumstances in the larger community. While some research on the operation of domestic violence shelters reveals how uses of surveillance and referral processes can be disempowering to women seeking refuge therein, this chapter documents the agenda of an activist shelter organization engaged in mitigating the violence in women's lives well beyond the provision of temporary respite from physical violence.

Moving beyond a grassroots, service-oriented operation to include enterprises such as operating a thrift store, running a batterers intervention program with court cooperation, opening the first on-site child care program for a shelter in the state of Florida, offering a child violence program for children exposed to violence, and mounting aggressive fund raising, public education, and even a state legislative campaign—all became responsibilities made possible through adoption of a more "corporatist" operating model than was possible or thought preferable initially. Reflections on the benefits and burdens of this expansive agenda from key stakeholders are provided.

THE SOCIAL CONDITION OF BATTERED WOMEN

By virtue of requiring sanctuary from violence away from their normal place of residence, victims of domestic violence often experience a profound sense of displacement and isolation during their time in shelter. To be "homeless" involves more than just loss of a place of residence; it also involves dissociation from known routines and trusted friendships, lack of access to personal effects and property, and potentially a sense of abandonment and hopelessness (see Baum & Burnes, 1993). Moreover, women in the somewhat "institutional" context of a domestic violence shelter become "subjects" and *subject to* institutional rules and categories, staff expectations and work routines, and sources of information for continued grant funding. For example, as documented by Pitts, Hatty, & Schwartz (2000), institutional rules and regulations regarding sexual behavior, private medical information and birth control data, staff work routines and expectations, suddenly govern the daily lives of women in shelters seeking refuge from domestic violence. The semi-public context of a shelter often compromises very private information, and makes "public work" of very private experiences and sensibilities. In short, when they leave abusive relationships, as a group battered women experience significant declines in income, reduced access to friends and family, and what amounts to a new set of power and control relationships to be negotiated *within the confines of the shelter* (Pitts et al., 2000). Importantly, the services available to women at this critical juncture and the attitudes and resources of shelter staff can play a determinative role in shaping the "help-seeking behaviors" of survivors of domestic violence (Krishnan et al., 2004). As research by Demie Kurz (1998) demonstrates: "the best way to get battered women the services they need is for organizations to have advocates who are trained to look out for their interests."

FEMINIST THOUGHT AND THE SHELTER MOVEMENT

> Staff members generally view their shelters as more than places where abused women can be safe and receive material assistance. Idealists, they try to implement in their programs egalitarian and feminist principles. Most shelters have adopted the goal of empowering their clients. They believe one reason why victims allow batterers to control their lives is that they have been made to feel incompetent and unworthy. . . . Shelter counselors encourage women to be assertive, determine their own objectives, and make independent decisions. (Shostack, 2001, p. 5)

The complexities of helping women escape patriarchal and abusive relationships while embedded in the context of a culture saturated with violent and sexist social understandings of women (and men) are reflected in the several "waves" of feminist thought. So-called liberal feminists focused on empowering women through the political process by acquiring for women the right to vote. Once the political right to vote was achieved, women's lack of political representation in Congress or even more especially in local politics convinced some activists, "socialist/Marxist feminists," that economic equality would first be required before women could hope to become political equals to men. The passage of the Equal Pay Act of 1970, which forbade unequal pay for equal work in instances where the qualifications for male versus female employees were the same, also failed to result in economic equality for women and men. Gender role socialization in the dominant heterosexual and patriarchal culture often leads women to "choose" to enter traditional service occupations with lower pay than those typically chosen by men, such as clerical work or "motherly" occupations such as elementary education or nursing. In each of these cases, the work of employees, almost exclusively women, is understood to be that of a nurturer or "assistant," in concert with the gender role expectations of women in our broader culture.

"Radical feminists" began to assert that heterosexist relations between men and women, specifically the sexualization of women in marriage and heterosexual relations, was carried over into the workplace and other social institutions, such as education, law, and economics. The "family role" of women as mothers, caregivers, and support system for husbands left women undereducated, underpaid (or more often unpaid), and dependent. That is, the social role expectations of women in the dominant patriarchal culture left them marginalized and unequal due to prevailing heterosexist expectations structuring relationships between men and women. What became necessary, radical feminists believe, is consciousness raising about the myriad ways heterosexuality marginalizes women and a corresponding redefinition of traditional gender role expectations. Finally, more recent feminisms have emerged highlighting racial and ethnic distinctions within the larger patriarchic social structure, as among black feminist and Jewish feminist writers such as Patricia Hill Collins or Tillie Olsen.

Thus, a legitimate set of questions face the staff of every domestic violence shelter: How can we best help women? Is it enough simply to provide shelter, without looking toward the broader social, political, economic, and cultural context? If the goal is to empower women to take care of themselves and to be assertive, to what extent is this going to be possible as women leave shelter and return to the broader social expectations that structured their relationships in the first place?

FOUNDING AND EVOLUTION OF HUBBARD HOUSE

Originally conceptualized in the mid-1970s as a "Women's Shelter and House of Refuge" for victims of both rape and domestic violence, the founding members of Hubbard House were closely allied with the Jacksonville Women's Movement, or JWM (Warren, 1996). "In March 1974, the Jacksonville Women's Movement Rape Task Force became the Women's Rape Crisis Center (WRCC)," when it opened a rape hotline (p. 76). Described as politically active and sometimes provocative, the Jacksonville Women's Movement organized around the issue of rape and other forms of violence against women—broadly construed— to include economic oppression and lack of equality in the workplace, as well as violence and rape against married women by their husbands. What was most necessary for improving the safety of women overall, these early activists believed, was consciousness raising, grassroots activism, and dialogue with women. Initial hotline contacts led to invitations for discussion group meetings and networking among women in similar circumstances. As a result of this, "discussion circles" were formed—where reanalysis of the status of women in American society could be related directly to the situation of individual women in Jacksonville, Florida. Women's issues in the broadest sense would be discussed, as well as means of helping women directly with these broader, immediate concerns: child care, economic dependency and job training, education, and of course, physical and sexual violence against women in the home and in society itself (i.e., marital rape). As described in Louise Stanton Warren's wonderfully written account of the early years of Hubbard House, *A House on Hubbard Street*, "Hubbard House was a local expression of the Women's Shelter Movement of the 1970s" (Warren, 1996, p. 12). As such, the internal debates of activists within the women's movement circulated and resolved themselves in unique ways in the Jacksonville context. Specifically,

> While some people regarded NOW as a left-leaning, liberal organization, the women of JWM worried that NOW was too traditional, too much a part of the existing political structure. For instance, JWM saw the hierarchical structure of NOW, with presidents and secretaries, dues and rules of procedure, as too traditional, too male, too much of the form by which they believed men governed themselves and subjugated others in the process. (Warren 1996, p. 15).[2]

Thus, a key organizational issue facing Hubbard House as it matured was how to reconcile the nonhierarchical aspirations of many of its founders, who were deeply committed to nontraditional authority structures and grassroots efforts at social transformation, with the very real demands of staff management, federal regulations imposed upon nonprofit organizations accepting governmental funding, and the corresponding requirement that a governing board of directors be separate from the operational staff. Early employees of Hubbard House praised the "egalitarianism" and "equality" that characterized daily operations as a major reason for working at Hubbard House over many years (Warren, 1996, p. 105).

Over time, however, palpable differences emerged between staff and board. Moreover, there were groups willing to help the advancement of Hubbard House, but which clearly "did not want to be labeled feminist" (Warren, 1996, p. 115). Finally, when Hubbard House accepted a sizeable grant from United Way in January 1978, the sense that the "countercultural stance" adhered to by many of the founders was being met with "disapproval," eventually leading to a "full-scale insurrection" between administrators and staff (Warren, 1996, p. 125). As described by Warren:

> This demarcation between staff and board was a newly sharpened knife to the hearts of the women who had begun and operated Hubbard House and who would no longer be part of its governance. Many Hubbard House founders saw themselves shifted to what they considered an inferior role in the project. . . . While Hubbard House staff balked at the new policies and the board apprehensively picked its way toward the future, they were nonetheless always allied in one struggle: to preserve the feminist soul of the organization and the sisterhood that had brought it so far. . . . Many of the original women felt Hubbard House was losing its feminist philosophy. They feared Hubbard House would forget its commitment to support and to empower women. (Warren, 1996, pp. 25–26)

HUBBARD HOUSE TODAY: FROM CONSCIOUSNESS RAISING TO CORPORATE STRATEGY

With growing awareness that expanding the services of Hubbard House was going to require broader types of cooperation with outside agencies, by the mid-1980s the organization's newest executive director was reaching out and developing a growing list of partnerships with the local police department (of which the Jacksonville Women's Movement had been openly critical in the past), the state attorney's office, United Way, a local hospital, and members of the general public. A more focused concentration on "media relations" emerged. "By the end of 1985, Hubbard House was taking on a different feel. It was a feeling of being widely accepted and appreciated, not only with members of the community or individual police officers, but also with government institutions and social service organizations" (Warren, 1996, p. 149).

At this writing in mid-2005, Hubbard House operates an amazing array of programs under a multimillion-dollar annual budget. Analysis of several years of the organization's annual reports reveals also that a feminist consciousness is still very much alive if not a predominant feature of its public relations activity. An expansive and aggressive capital campaign including several local foundations, prominent businesses and citizens, including the Jacksonville Jaguars Foundation, an important move in the community, given the National Football League's public avowals to reduce domestic violence committed by its own players. In fact, the Jaguars Foundation and the Weaver family (who own the Jaguars) "have been absolutely instrumental in helping Hubbard House help women in this community" (Warren, personal communication, 2005). Today, instead of a consensus model of operational governance at Hubbard House, however, there are clear lines of demarcation between board members and staff members, lists of staff hours and duties, and rules for residents and their children that govern their stay and also structure the services they receive. Fundraising efforts include an annual breakfast, a golf tournament raising $70,000, a tennis tournament, 310 students in an antiviolence school program, 557 children enrolled in their day care program, 34,802 hours of counseling offered, 1,150 women sheltered, 5,607 total clients served (including children of victims), hotline calls, batterers intervention services, and goods delivered to people through Hubbard House's own thrift store. Beyond direct residential services for survivors of abuse, Hubbard House today has over 1,300 volunteers, all of whom must pass a criminal background check and submit to an interview/selection process. All volunteers must sign in and receive and wear an identity badge while on the premises. While the informality of the early women's rape crisis center is gone, far more women are served by the new Hubbard House and far more services provided than would have been imagined possible by the organization's founders.

Interestingly, Hubbard House's annual reports prominently feature statements from women who are called "clients," but that arguably reflect the original and broad social ambitions of Hubbard House:

> The police took me to the hospital and a Hubbard House advocate met me there at 3 am. I was no longer alone.
>
> The first time I called, I was too scared to give my name. I just wanted someone to talk to.
>
> I came in my nightgown right from the hospital. I had nothing—they gave me what I needed. Thank you Hubbard House.
>
> They gave me a voucher (for the thrift store) and I was able to go in and pick what I needed. No one else knew I wasn't a regular shopper.
>
> I came in with a real bad attitude about the program denying any violence I've committed, but eventually the facilitators and other men helped me to face the choices I'd made. [This from a court-ordered participant in the batterers intervention program—exposure this person would never have gotten otherwise. 88% of program completers are not rearrested within three years.]

Most impressively, the now 10-year operation of the Domestic Violence Intervention Project (DVIP), which coordinates state attorney, local police, local judges, victim advocates, and nonprofit service providers by reaching out to victims of domestic violence as soon as they come up in police reports, has improved system responsiveness to victims. Designed as an early intervention project, the DVIP seeks to utilize Hubbard House's now close relationship with local law enforcement authorities to provide both consciousness raising and direct services to victims of domestic violence. The program is credited with helping prevent already abusive relationships from becoming more abusive or the violence within those police-identified relationships from escalating to a point of lethal violence. In the case of the batterers intervention project, a state-certified program operated in cooperation with local judicial authorities, over 600 batterers have participated in the program. One of the program's stated goals is to ask a new social question: Why won't he stop, instead of why won't she leave?

THE NEW WOMEN'S SHELTER MOVEMENT: FEMINISM ALIVE AND WELL AS THE STRUGGLE CONTINUES

Perhaps the most important lesson revealed by this brief recounting of the evolution of Hubbard House was offered by its current CEO, Ellen Siler:

> You know, I think what happened is that as Hubbard House expanded and more and more women came forward for help, we had to make some priority decisions. This happened long before I got here; however, I think it was the right decision. Clearly, the decision to accept monies from United Way—with all of its corresponding restrictions and rules—was a turning point. While by accepting the funding from United Way, Hubbard House could not continue to operate in the original ways its founders intended, far more good was able to be accomplished for far more women than was true before.

In addition, a recently departed development officer, Melanie Patz, explained:

> There is no question that the corporate structure enabled Hubbard House to do more outreach than was possible before. I think there was a sense that, look: we need to focus on the very real needs of these women who are reaching out to us right now. We may not be talking as much about gender equity for women, even as we may still believe in that. Be we're focused on these women, these victims of domestic violence who need help. We're focused on safety for women—while also operating the thrift store, the batterers intervention project to help change the consciousness of male batterers. It's not like we've forgotten our roots—we've just had to have the maturity to make some very serious choices. The other thing that happened is that the Jacksonville Women's Center was able to take up the mantle of feminist grassroots social transformation previously held by the founders of Hubbard House. So, it's not like that agenda has died within the community. What you have here is a dynamic situation of dire needs—and an organization striving to meet those needs, even while having to be flexible and bend to the strictures of the larger context. . . . I believe it was the right decision—especially given that there is still an outlet for the previous agenda. What's important is that both agendas have survived and still exist in the community.

Finally, Hubbard House's executive director during the years of key transformation very much considers herself a committed feminist today. As she left Hubbard House in the mid-1990s she wrote again, as she frequently did, to the local paper. Many in the community assumed Ms. Rita De Young's activism must be a result of her own abuse—an interesting misconception. In regard to the changes made by Hubbard House staff and the decision to "reach out" to the local police and state attorney's office, she stated:

> By changing our approach to the sheriff's office and the state attorney, we actually made women safer in our community. We made it safer for them to access our services and we made ourselves safer by being able to rely on the help. . . . In regard to the decision to accept funding from United Way, there was a definite struggle with this decision. Accepting funding from United Way required a new structure with a separate board of directors that could not include staff as well as some real outside oversight that we'd never had before. Some really did feel that we were losing our feminist identity . . . and some eventually left the organization or fell by the wayside. . . . But I never felt that Hubbard House had lost its feminist moorings.

The last of De Young's frequent editorials to the local newspaper read:

> My involvement in the women's movement following my divorce merely reflected the grow-
> ing awareness in the 1970's that (in many respects) women were second-class citizens in a
> male-dominated society. Some of us began working to change that reality, and Hubbard House
> was one venue in which to accomplish it. We viewed the oppression of women in a political
> and social context and became aware of a continuum of abuse. Our personal experiences with
> societal oppression were the basis for empathizing with those who had experienced more
> extreme forms of abuse such as rape and battering. We believe that the victimization of any
> woman impacts all women. Certainly, some of the founders of Hubbard House were survivors
> of domestic violence but, through the grace of God, many of us were not.

CONCLUSION: MAKING CHOICES, STAYING ENGAGED

As revealed by the example of Hubbard House, many domestic violence shelters
begin as small grassroots organizations driven by a few charismatic leaders devoted to a
particular set of ideals. As the organization experiences growth in requests for service,
however, new sets of priorities face its leaders—and require the ability to adapt to changing circumstances. Interestingly, much the same problem faces any successful corporation.
A series of natural challenges face any organization, particularly as it evolves and becomes
more successful. Core values are ultimately what anchor any organization through
changing circumstances. As aptly put by business guru Jim Collins: "The notion of preserving your core ideology is the central feature of enduring companies" (Collins,
2001, p. 195).

ACKNOWLEDGMENTS

Thanks to Ellen Siler, Rita De Young, Melanie Patz, and especially Louise Stanton Warren
for their assistance in writing this chapter.

N O T E S

1. Kathleen Ferraro, "Battered Women: Strategies for Survival," quoted in *Violence Between
   Intimate Partners: Patterns, Causes, and Effects* (pp. 124–140), by Albert Cardarelli (Ed.),
   1997, Boston: Allyn & Bacon.
2. Additional political fissures present in the community that affected the development of Hubbard
   House were the use of the shelter site as a meeting place for lesbian groups ("Critics alleged lesbians were using refuge houses to change the sexual preference of abused women" [Warren,
   1996, p. 23]), the cross-membership of Hubbard House supporters and staff with local pro-
   abortion and women's rights demonstrators, and the Vietnam War. An initial HUD grant in 1974
   for the proposed House of Refuge was rescinded, allegedly (but never officially) because of lesbian sentiments expressed in literature available through the Jacksonville Women's Movement
   on display at Hubbard House. (See Warren, 1996, throughout.)

REFERENCES

BAUM, A. S., & BURNES, D. W. (1993). Facing the facts about homelessness. *Public Welfare, 51,* 20–27.

COLLINS, J. (2001). *Good to great: Why some companies make the leap and others don't.* Boulder, CO: HarperCollins.

FERRARO, K. (1997). Battered women: Strategies for survival. In A. Cardarelli (Ed.), *Violence between intimate partners: Patterns, causes, and effects* (pp. 124–140). Boston: Allyn & Bacon.

GONDOLF, E. (2005). Reflection on "The effect of batterer counseling on shelter outcome." In Raquel Kennedy Bergen, Jeffrey Edleson, & Claire Renzetti (Eds.), *Violence against women: Classic papers.* Boston: Allyn & Bacon.

KRISHNAN, S. P, HILBERT, J. C., MCNEIL, K., & NEWMAN, I. (2004, June). From respite to transition: Women's use of domestic violence shelters in rural New Mexico. *Journal of Family Violence, 19*(3), 165–173.

KURZ, D. (1998). Women, welfare, and domestic violence. *Social Justice, 25*(1), 105.

PITTS, V., HATTY, S., & SCHWARTZ, M. (2000). *Power, gender and place: The surveillance of women in a homeless shelter.* Paper presented at the 2000 meetings of the American Society of Criminology. Used with permission.

SHOSTACK, A. (2001). *Shelters for battered women and their children: A comprehensive guide to planning and operating safe and caring residential programs.* Springfield, IL: Charles Thomas.

WARREN, L. S. (1996). *A house on Hubbard Street.* Jacksonville, FL: Olivette-Crooke.

18

Resistance, Compliance, and the Climate of Violence

Understanding Battered Women's Contacts with Police

Angela M. Moe

Much debate surrounds the issue of how police ought to respond in domestic violence cases. Coinciding with the movement toward increased community policing strategies are heightened efforts to develop and implement responsive as well as effective mechanisms for handling domestic violence cases. Unfortunately, the perspectives of battered victims are too often excluded from these discussions. This chapter attempts to expand current understanding of how domestic violence victims regard law enforcement intervention. Drawing from 19 interviews with residents of a domestic violence shelter in the Phoenix metropolitan area, battered women describe for themselves why it was often difficult and unsafe for them to call the police, the ways in which they would have liked law enforcement to respond to their circumstances, and how they felt about the police response. The findings suggest that victims of domestic violence could be better served through heightened and diversified police intervention.

INTRODUCTION

Concern over the police response to domestic violence is ongoing. Despite the unlikelihood that arrest serves as a preventative or deterrent measure for abusers (Dunford 1992; Dunford, Huizinga, & Elliott, 1990; Police Foundation, 1992; Sherman, 1992), victim advocates, criminal justice practitioners, and lawmakers continue to regard law enforcement intervention, particularly arrest, as a central tenet to our society's response to domestic violence.

The purpose of this chapter is to consider the police response more closely, and from the perspective of the victims involved with such intervention. The specific research questions guiding this inquiry are twofold. First, what are the contexts in which female victims of domestic violence find themselves at the time they call the police? This question requires consideration of both the circumstances surrounding a woman's decision to call the police and her desire for certain interventions to occur in doing so. Second, how do women perceive police responsiveness to their circumstances? This question involves an inquiry into how police respond to female victims and how these victims respond in turn to them and to law enforcement generally. To answer these questions, I interviewed 19 female residents of a domestic violence shelter. Their narratives are quite telling in terms of the current police response to domestic violence, and make a valuable contribution to the discussion of how police can and ought to improve their intervention in these situations.

UNDERSTANDING DOMESTIC VIOLENCE

For the purposes of this chapter, domestic violence is defined as a pattern of acts committed by a person against his or her intimate partner with the expressed or implied intent of exerting power and control over that person. This abuse may result in physical, sexual, emotional, or financial harm. Domestic violence can occur between married and unmarried couples; between intact, separated, or divorced couples; and between heterosexual, gay, or lesbian couples. Further, the vast majority of violence is perpetrated by men toward women (Tjaden & Thoennes, 2000a). For this reason, female pronouns are used throughout the following pages as a means of referencing domestic violence victims, and male pronouns are used to reference their perpetrators.

The central tenet of battering is coercive control. Control is often accomplished in part by isolating a victim from her family, friends, and employment contacts (Ferraro, 2001; Kurz, 1998; Raphael, 1996). Possessiveness and jealousy are also important tactics abusers use to establish and maintain control over their partners. Batterers often control all aspects of their partners' lives, becoming possessive and jealous of activities their partners undertake that seem to undermine their control (Ferraro, 2001).

Batterers often regulate their partners' activities through financial and property abuse as well (Ptacek, 1999). In many abusive relationships, the batterer controls the flow of household money and may be the sole wage-earner (Mrsevic & Hughes, 1997). In such instances, women are dependent on their abusers for money and financial support. Even in instances where women are earning incomes, batterers may order them to turn over their paychecks or harass them at work so much that they lose or quit their jobs (Browne, Salomon, & Bassuk, 1999). Likewise, violence and destruction of household items and material assets, particularly those that belong to the victim, is a common form of abuse. Not only is property damage economically hurtful, it also sends a powerful message to victims of what their abusers are capable of, and what may subsequently occur to them through physical assaults.

Sexual abuse also reinforces a batterer's power and control in an abusive relationship (Ptacek, 1999). Sexual abuse can include such actions as rape, unwanted fondling, and forced prostitution or pornography. Much research has indicated a high correlation between relationships that are physically abusive and relationships that are also sexually abusive, specifically in terms of rape (Campbell & Soeken, 1999; Meyer, Vivian, & O'Leary, 1998; Russell, 1982).

Physical battering serves as reinforcement for all of the coercive control strategies described above. A batterer resorts to violence, or threats thereof, as needed to establish dominance and control in a relationship. For couples who marry, physical abuse often begins shortly after the exchange of vows when women are legally united to their batterers as well as often being deeply in love with them. At this stage, abuse is often downplayed by both victim and perpetrator. Attacks are seen as isolated events and many women internalize the emotional harm caused by them (Dobash & Dobash, 1979; Ferraro, 1997). Batterers may apologize to their partners, buy them gifts, and make promises to never hit them again. Women sometimes reason that they must have done something to deserve an attack and that they can curb the abuse by altering their own behavior. In time, violence generally increases in severity and diversity—for example, mental and sexual abuse may occur in addition to physical assaults (Dobash & Dobash, 1979).

Despite the dynamics of domestic violence, most female victims do eventually leave their batterers (Campbell, Miller, & Cardwell, 1994) even if it takes several attempts to do so. For many, a vital step in leaving is knowing help is available and receiving empathetic assistance from social and institutional sources, particularly the police.

POLICING DOMESTIC VIOLENCE

The police response to domestic violence historically has been one of inaction. Prior to the 1970s, incidents of battery were regarded as isolated events involving families whose privacy ought to be respected (Dobash & Dobash, 1979; Schechter, 1982). Few laws existed that provided for the arrest and prosecution of batterers. In most instances, domestic assaults were handled as misdemeanors. Arrests usually occurred only in instances where victims were willing to press charges or after officers witnessed an assault (Schechter, 1982; Wallace, 1999).

In the mid-1980s a series of events facilitated widespread reform in law enforcement policies and practices regarding domestic violence. Among them was Sherman and Berk's (1984) police experiment in Minneapolis, Minnesota, which found that arresting batterers reduced recidivism. Despite the mixed results of several replications of this study, policymakers and police administrators concluded that arresting batterers was the most appropriate means of responding to domestic violence.

Expensive lawsuits against police departments who failed to protect abused women also contributed to the willingness to adopt stricter arrest policies. Among the better-known litigants was Tracy Thurman, who sued several individual police officers as well as the City of Torrington, Connecticut, alleging that the police repeatedly failed to arrest her husband despite her numerous complaints. During a final assault, which occurred in front of police, Thurman suffered permanent injuries and disfigurement. She was subsequently awarded $2.3 million in damages (Ferraro, 1996; Wallace, 1999).

Throughout the 1980s and early 1990s, mandatory and pro-arrest policies were implemented in police departments across the country (Davis & Smith, 1995). These policies mandated that upon establishing probable cause, responding officers ought to determine which of the two parties is primarily responsible for the abuse and arrest him or her. However, it remains unclear as to how effective pro-arrest policies are at protecting women. Several researchers have documented a continued avoidance toward intervention in domestic violence situations, even upon a victim's request (Buzawa & Austin, 1993; Erez & Belknap, 1998; Ferraro, 1989; Johnson, 1990; Websdale, 1995; Websdale & Johnson, 1997). Further research has suggested that police are more lenient in making arrests during domestic violence calls as compared to other violent interpersonal crimes between nonintimates (Eigenberg, Scarborough, & Kappeler, 1996; Fyfe, Klinger, & Flavin, 1997).

A number of studies suggest that these differences are due to situational influences, such as the officer's beliefs about the likelihood of future violence between a couple and the ability of the justice system to stop it, the seriousness of the assault, the victim's willingness to cooperate with the criminal justice system, the suspect's demeanor, and whether the suspect was present at the time the police arrived at the scene (Dolon, Hendricks, & Meagher, 1986; Dutton, 1988; Feder, 1996, 1999; Kane, 1999; McKean & Hendricks, 1997). Another study suggests that the race of the perpetrator and victim may impact how officers interpret these situational cues (Robinson & Chandek, 2000). Individual characteristics and beliefs of the responding officers have also been found to impact not only the extent to which police are willing to arrest batterers, but also how willing they are to offer support, empathy, and community resources to victims (Feder, 1997; Saunders, 1995; Stith, 1990). Departmental policies and political affiliations have also been correlated to the frequency and nature of referrals police officers make on behalf of domestic violence victims (Belknap & McCall, 1994).

Even in cases where arrests are made, recidivism is high among batterers (Dunford, 1992; Dunford et al., 1990; Police Foundation, 1992; Sherman, 1992). Certainly recidivism cannot be fully attributed to the arrest itself. The court and correctional systems have much room for improvement in terms of the aggressiveness with which abusers are prosecuted, the extent to which intervention programs are regulated, the level at which probationed offenders are monitored, and the treatment of and services offered to victims (Cretney & Davis, 1997; Ptacek, 1999; Wan, 2000, 2001).

Regardless of the roles courts and corrections play in responding to domestic violence, victims are most likely to interact directly with the frontline of the criminal justice system, the police, and base their opinions of the entire justice system on these contacts. Indeed, battered women are more likely to call the police upon their first victimization (Bachman & Coker, 1995), when injuries occur or after an attack is particularly more severe than prior assaults (Bachman & Coker, 1995; Johnson, 1990), when dependent children witnessed the assault, and when the abuser was intoxicated prior to the assault (Johnson, 1990). They are subsequently less likely to call when they believe that their abusers will not be arrested or that arrest will not stop the abuse (Baker, 1997; Hoyle & Sanders, 2000), and when they are too fearful of, dependent upon, or emotionally attached to their abusers (Baker, 1997; Erez & Belknap, 1998).

Given these circumstances, community-policing strategies are well poised to offer appropriate strategies for responding to domestic violence. Establishing citizen–police partnerships and enhancing community-based problem solving could help reduce this marginalization while enhancing police intervention (Jolin & Moose, 1997). Recent scholarship has documented the effectiveness of proactive and interventionist police approaches in this regard (Buzawa, Hoteling, & Klein, 1998; Feder, 1997; Jones & Belknap, 1999). Efforts by police agencies to coordinate with community domestic violence services such as legal advocacy centers, shelters, and support programs, as well as other aspects of the criminal justice system, have increased the level of satisfaction and confidence abuse victims express toward the police, despite recidivism (Baker, 1997; Davis & Taylor, 1997). Even the efforts of individual officers to provide greater crisis intervention beyond arrest have garnered widespread praise by victims and victims' advocates (McKean & Hendricks, 1997).

Unfortunately, well-coordinated police–community responses to domestic violence remain few and far between. The call for further reform remains constant (Davis & Smith, 1995; Melton, 1999). Battered women continue to rely on police intervention despite its shortcomings. In many cases, police officers are the first and perhaps only authorities made aware of such abuse. Their actions likely impact a woman's future decisions to seek help through other legal or formal means, as observed below.

METHODS

Data were gathered for this research via qualitative semistructured interviews of 19 women residing in a domestic violence shelter in the Phoenix metropolitan area of Arizona. Qualitative semistructured interviews were appropriate for several reasons, not the least of which was flexibility. Participants were able to contribute in ways they felt were most relevant to their circumstances while staying within their personal boundaries of comfort and safety. Because of the dangerous and vulnerable positions many of the participants were in at the time of the interviews (e.g., in hiding and fearing for their lives), it was not only desirable but also necessary to allow for such flexibility.

Moreover, qualitative semistructured interviews worked especially well in this study because the participants shared myriad experiences with abuse and help-seeking that would have been difficult to account for through quantitative measures. While this study was subsequently weakened because of shortcomings in reliability and generalizability, it produced a deeply rich, detailed, descriptive, and diverse set of narratives that would not have been possible through alternative means of data collection (Kvale, 1996; Lofland & Lofland, 1995).

Perhaps the greatest benefit of this method was its ability to emphasize the epistemic privilege, or the specific vantage point, of the subjects (Collins, 1989; Hartsock, 1987; Narayan, 1988; Smith, 1987). Assuming that members of marginalized groups can offer meaningful accounts of the ways in which the world is organized according to the oppressions they experience, it would behoove scholars, practitioners, and policymakers to account for the perspectives of groups impacted by criminal justice practices. Thus, in turning to the vantage points of battered victims, we may better understand the ways in which police interventions in domestic violence impact the respective parties. That said, the interview schedules for this research included a number of questions regarding the women's experiences with abuse, violent victimization, and help-seeking. These were informed by existing literature on women's victimization and were intended as a starting point in what frequently became free-flowing discussions about the participants' lives.

Participants were recruited between the months of July and November 2000 from a domestic violence shelter in which I worked as a volunteer and fill-in staff member.

Helping out at the shelter enabled me to negotiate approval for conducting research with relative ease. It also allowed me to establish cordial relationships with the women whom I later asked to participate. Many expressed a great deal of comfort and trust with me because they knew I understood the circumstances in which they were living.

All of the interviews were conducted at the participants' convenience within private rooms at the shelter. The interviews lasted between 20 minutes and two hours, with an average of 55 minutes. The interviews were audiotaped upon each participant's approval and expressed understanding that the recording could cease at any time at their request. These recordings were later transcribed verbatim and coded for emerging and recurring themes. All of the interview transcripts were held in the strictest of confidence and are identifiable only through assigned numbers and pseudonyms, most of which were chosen by the participants themselves. All interviewees were given a remuneration of $10 cash for their involvement, and access to their transcript. As a final note, 20 women were actually interviewed at the shelter. However, one woman's transcript was excluded from the present inquiry because she had not been battered by an intimate partner, but rather by her parents.

PROFILE OF RESPONDENTS

The women were very diverse in terms of race, ethnicity, age, and educational attainment. While 9 (47%) of the women identified themselves as white, 4 (21%) identified themselves as African American, 2 (11%) as American Indian, and 2 (11%) as Latina. Two other women identified themselves as biracial, being American Indian/white and African American/white, respectively. In terms of age, 5 (26%) women were between 18 and 25, 10 (53%) women were between 26 and 35, and 4 (21%) women were between 36 and 45. Eight (42%) women reported that they had obtained less than a high school education. However, 5 (26%) indicated that they had either graduated from high school or obtained a GED, and 5 (26%) women reported having completed at least some college. One woman had two undergraduate degrees. A commonality among the women was motherhood, as 16 (84%) had children. These mothers had an average of 2.4 children each. All but one of the children were minors and the majority of these kids were living at the shelter. Four of the women who had children with them were also pregnant at the time of the interviews.

The women reported suffering severe and multiple forms of abuse. Eighteen (95%) women stated that they had been physically assaulted and 7 (37%) stated that they had been sexually assaulted. Most frequently accompanying physical abuse was emotional abuse, which encompassed verbal threats, insults, degradation, and psychological terrorism. Sixteen (84%) of the women reported this form of abuse. Thirteen (68%) women described financial/property abuse; they had quit their jobs because of the emotional toll the abuse was taking on them, been unable to work due to injuries, forced to quit because of their abuser's control tactics, or suffered in some other way that affected their economic stability.

Despite these abuses, the women exhibited a great deal of help-seeking in an effort to escape and prevent further assaults. Among the most common efforts was utilization of the law or criminal justice system. Thirteen (68%) women stated that they had either called the police or had someone else call for them at least once. Eleven (58%) used other legal tactics such as filing for divorce or obtaining a protective order. Another common strategy was moving out of a shared residence or otherwise moving away from the abuser, which 16 (84%) women attempted to do prior to entering the shelter. In addition, 13 (68%) had contacted friends or relatives for assistance, advice, or support; 6 (32%) had gone to their doctors or to emergency rooms for medical services; and 2 (11%) had consulted their clergy or spiritual advisors for guidance.

FINDINGS

Police Response in Context

Because so many of the women had dealt with the police at some point during their abusive relationships, much discussion ensued during the interviews as to their experiences with law enforcement. Three overarching themes were illustrated throughout the narratives. First, women were very fearful of calling the police. Their abusers often threatened them or prohibited them from making such calls or asking others to make such calls. Second, those who did call the police were discouraged when their abusers were either not arrested or when they, the victims, were arrested in lieu of or along with their abusers. Such responses discouraged women from relying on the police for assistance. Third, when arrests were made, women felt like they had only been granted a temporary reprieve from the violence. In no cases did arrest stop or deter the abuse. Within this context, some of the women recognized the ways in which prosecutors and judges failed to respond to their victimization. These findings suggest the need to reevaluate police responses to domestic violence, and the ways in which legal and extralegal mechanisms may enhance such intervention.

Safety Concerns

To understand why battered women call the police, what their expectations are of the police, and how they respond to police intervention, we must begin with a comprehension of the circumstances surrounding incidents in which law enforcement is called. As indicated earlier, women are more likely to call the police after the first time they are assaulted or injured, when their children witnessed the attack, or when their abusers were intoxicated (Bachman & Coker, 1995; Johnson, 1990). They may not call during or after every single attack.

The women in this study seemed to call when they truly felt that law enforcement could do something to stop the abuse. They also called when they felt extremely vulnerable, such as after their lives had been threatened. Most of the women did call the police at least once during their relationships, and many stated that they would have called more often had they felt able and safe to do so. A few women never called the police either because they did not believe anything could be done to stop their abuse or because they never felt like they had the opportunity to call.

This form of help-seeking was deemed incredibly dangerous as women were threatened and beaten for even attempting to get to a telephone. Terri, a 38-year-old white woman, described a situation in which she had tried to call the police:

> I tried the last time to call the police and he ripped both the phones out of the walls so badly that we had to buy new phones. He was always threatening to kill me. It was almost a weekly

thing. That time he sat on my upper body and had his thumbs in my eyes and he was just squeezing. He was going, "I'll gouge your eyes out. I'll break every bone in your body. Even if they do find you alive, you won't know to tell them who did it to you because you'll be in intensive care for so long you'll forget."

Patsy, a 26-year-old American Indian woman, was also threatened so that she would not leave or call the police:

Yeah, like telling me he would chop me up. He told me I was never going to leave him. He had me by my throat and he told me that I was never going to leave him. He told me if I was ever going to leave him it would only be in a body bag, chopped up, and he would throw me in the trunk of his car. He told me that he's beat up people. I was like new to it all so I was freaking out. He's told me that if I ever called the cops that he would only be in jail for a certain amount of time but they would let him out eventually.

Such threats and coercion gave some women very good reasons not to call the police regardless of the circumstances. Those who did call faced great peril. Retaliatory assaults as well as alternative forms of abuse, such as property destruction, were reported by women who had previously called the police. It is easy to understand, then, why the subsequent response by law enforcement becomes such an important factor in women's future decisions. To many of them, it was simply not worth the risk.

Failure to Arrest

Despite well-founded concerns about their safety, 13 (68%) of the women did assume the risk and called the police. All of these women stated that the reason they assumed the risk was to have their batterers arrested; subsequently, it was very upsetting when an arrest was not made. Six of the 13 (46%) women who called police reported that their batterers were not arrested on at least one occasion. Four of these women stated that their abusers had never been arrested.

Not surprisingly, many women felt that calling the police did nothing to improve their situation, and they felt like the police did not care about them or their safety. Lydia, a 27-year-old Latina, summed up many women's feelings toward the police: "They didn't care that my life was in danger." The following narratives illustrate the severity of this situation and are suggestive of the increased danger women encounter after police leave the scene without making an arrest:

I called the police the last two times and he didn't get arrested. They came out, took a report, and left. I'm still trying to get him arrested. . . . They just left me there with him. There was a lot of evidence and they didn't even file a report. They said, "He has a different side to the story and there's nothing we could do." I was in the hospital. The ambulance came and they didn't even file a police report. [Samantha, 20 years old, white]

[Q: Did you ever try to call the police?] Yes. Nothing happened. He'd be gone and they'd say, "Well he's not here now." They told me to get the order of protection. They didn't show up for two hours. Police don't care. They do their own thing. They don't care. No matter how hard. . . I got locked in the apartment once and his friend guarded the door.

> I couldn't leave or nothing and they're like, "He's not hurting you." I just couldn't go anywhere. [Q: How many times do you think you called the police?] I called the police all the time at first . . . 20 or 30 times, and then I just said, "Forget it. They're not helping me." I've had like 15 restraining orders against him. [Q: And he's never been arrested?] Never. [Cynthia, 31 years old, white]

> I called the police the last time that we got into this. The police officer came and I was upstairs and he asked my husband, "Is everything okay?" and he's like "yeah" and he left. I see the police officer driving off and I'm like, "That's really nice" [in a sarcastic tone]. My daughter said, "The policeman was here but daddy told him everything was okay so he left.". . . They came out and just asked him if everything was okay. [Q: So you hadn't really had a chance to explain the situation?] Right. I called back a few days later and talked to the officers. I explained to them what had happened. He didn't really give me any feedback. [Melissa, 25 years old, African American/white]

Clearly, much frustration was expressed about the perceived lack of care or attention shown by police officers in these instances. While certainly there is always another side of every story and perhaps arrests were not merited in some of these cases, to these women, the only side that mattered was their own. Indeed, it was their safety that was at stake, not to mention the well-being of the children exposed to such violence. Calling the police was regarded as a way of helping ensure this safety and well-being, even if temporarily. Being denied assistance was subsequently interpreted as a lack of interest or concern on the part of the very officials obliged to extend such help.

Victim Arrests and Dual Arrests

Whereas many women complained that the police did nothing, others complained of being arrested instead of or along with their abusers. Again, in some instances both parties are indeed mutually combatant, justifying the use of dual arrests. However, dual arrests are generally discouraged, as in most cases one party is the primary aggressor. The primary aggressor instigates the majority of conflicts, inflicts more physical assaults, and causes more injuries than the other person. Thus, many police departments encourage their officers to do what they can to determine who the primary aggressor is in a relationship and to arrest only that person.

As one would imagine, victims who are arrested develop very negative impressions of the police and are not likely to call them in the future for fear of being arrested again. Such was the case for Amanda, a 26-year-old white woman:

> He assaulted me and my mom at the front office of the apartment complex where we were at. Called the police and the police took us both to jail. He said that I hit him but there was no marks but there were marks on me so they took us both to jail for 24 hours. They then let me go and let him go without any charges. After that I told my mom, "I'm never going to call the cops again." If I'm gonna get arrested, I might as well just stay here. I hate them. How dare they tell me that if I called again I'd go to jail!

While only Amanda and one other woman interviewed had been arrested, both of these women felt that they had acted in self-defense and that their arrests were unjustified. Both of these women were released quickly after their arrests and neither faced criminal charges.

Arrest as a Reprieve

For those whose abusers were arrested, very little deterrent value was observed. In fact, none of the women reported that the abuse ceased after their partners were arrested. They continued to be abused, stalked, and in the best cases, harassed. Rather than serve as a deterrent, arrest seemed more likely to offer women a reprieve from their abuse, allowing them time to think, act, and plan for the future without the fear of assault. Such reprieves were appreciated, even if they were only temporary. As Amanda explained with regard to an assault early on in her relationship:

> They arrested him and took him to jail and I had to go to the hospital that night. They thought I had a severe head injury cause he banged the side of my head a couple of times. Now I see spots. [Q: How long did he spend in jail?] Twenty-four hours. He came home and he acted like . . . it's hard to explain. He was mad but nice at the same time. He was upset that he had to spend the night in jail and that he did nothing wrong, but then he started being nice like he was before. It was okay for the first couple days and then after that he started doing the same old things again.

Some women stated that having their partners arrested gave them time to move out of a shared residence. Nina, a 34-year-old white woman, described an incident during which police intervention enabled her to flee the state with her children:

> We drove right into a police station and he followed, cut us off right in front of the police department. They ran us both through. They said that he was very violent and said to get as far from Arizona as we could, told us exactly which direction to take and just let me go and just held him for three or four hours.

Nina was not able to remain separated from her boyfriend as he eventually found her even though she had moved to another state. Arrest did not seem to protect women for any length of time. In the best scenarios, it provided a temporary respite from abuse.

Failures of the System Following Arrest

Of course, the police response to domestic violence cannot be divorced from how such cases are handled within the court system. It is often not up to police to decide how long an individual will be detained or incarcerated. Thus, many women's dissatisfaction with arrest may be best understood as dissatisfaction with the criminal justice process following arrest. As Patsy, cited earlier, explained:

> I called the police. My manager at the apartments where we were moving out of called the police. The manager of the apartments that we moved into, she called the police. He's went to

jail. He's got out. I was scared to press charges on him because he used to tell me some crazy stuff. I was like, "What if he does that stuff to me?" I never showed up. . . . [Q: Can you even count how many times he went to jail?] Probably four times. [Q: Was he pretty much out the next day?] Yeah, or the same night after he got into court. Well it took like five or six hours for him to get out, but yeah, he got out. They would let him out and he would be like pounding on the door. I was like, "Oh God." I had an order to protection on him, everything. He just kept on coming around. He just kept on looking for me. He ripped up the paper. He ripped it up and said, "Whatever." He was just there. I wanted to get the hell out but he would just beat me up again.

Even in cases where abusers were adjudicated, women reported that their partners faced only minor penalties. Diversion is amply available for first-time domestic violence offenders in Arizona under the state's domestic violence statute (Arizona Revised Statutes [ARS], 1980). Under the law, first-time offenders may complete a treatment program in exchange for a suspended sentence. The utility of such programs has been a matter of great controversy (Hollenhorst, 1998; Orme, Dominelli, & Mullender, 2000), and for the women in this study, the programs did not even seem pertinent to domestic violence. As Nina, cited earlier, noted: "He said it seemed like it was an alcohol and drug treatment program rather than anger management. He refused to go." Even in the most serious of incidents, abusers did not appear to face many repercussions in the criminal justice system. In one of the most brutal assaults reported, the sentence served was 37 days in jail and three years house arrest. The victim in this case had sustained four bone fractures in her face, a broken nose, a broken rib that cut into her lung and kidney, a bruised collarbone, and 47 slashing stab wounds that left scars across her arms, chest, abdomen, and legs.

DISCUSSION AND CONCLUSION

The experiences and feelings expressed by the women in this study are valuable for what they contribute to our understanding of how battered women perceive the law enforcement response to domestic violence, as well as how the police response to such abuse may be improved. The women in this study seemed to call the police with the expressed purpose of having their abusers arrested. Most were willing to cooperate with investigative and prose-cutorial efforts, despite their recognition that their abusers would likely recidivate. To the extent possible and within the confines of the law, their wishes ought to be respected. If a victim requests that her abuser be arrested and probable cause merits such arrest, an arrest should be made.

This of course begs the question, why should arrests be made if recidivism is so likely? The answer is twofold. First, arrest may prevent future violence for some people and there is no way to determine ahead of time with any certainty whether it will deter an individual. In short, it is worth a try if a victim requests such action. Second, domestic vio-lence *is* a crime. It ought to be treated like other criminal offenses are treated. Failing to respond to domestic violence as a crime only reinforces batterers' beliefs that they can do what they want to do to their partners without repercussions. Police officers are obligated to respond to domestic violence. Those who fail to arrest or who make unjustifiable dual or victim arrests under these circumstances need to be held accountable for their actions. Additional training and accountability measures within police departments may go a long way toward increasing arrest rates of primary aggressors in domestic violence situations, as well as decreasing the amount of frustration victims often feel after calling for assistance.

That said, domestic violence is not like many other crimes because of the dynamics involved between the offender and the victim. The main reason the women in this study did not call police or cooperate with authorities was out of fear for their safety. Based on these findings, it would seem that further efforts ought to be made to increase the likelihood that women will have the opportunity, capability, and confidence to call for assistance. Knowing arrests are likely to be made, or that other services will be offered, would help more victims feel confident that their needs will be addressed. Efforts to enhance victim's access to the police such as preprogrammed 9-1-1 cellular phones, which some departments and victim service agencies now have available, will increase the capability victims have to call for help at any time.

Perhaps the most needed reform is greater cooperative relations among the community, victim services, and law enforcement. Clearly, arrest is no panacea for domestic violence; however, the women in this study were relieved to have the reprieve from violence that arrest provided. A number of pragmatic efforts could be made to enhance the services offered to victims at the scene. Most of these are consistent with the community policing goals of partnership and problem solving (Jolin & Moose, 1997).

For instance, many police departments are working closely with local advocacy groups and victim service agencies to develop crisis response teams. Crisis response teams are groups of social workers, victims' advocates, and volunteers that either accompany or follow responding units to domestic violence calls to offer services, referrals, transportation, support, and crisis counseling to victims and their children. Coordination among these teams and patrol officers not only ensures victims' needs are better met, but also reduces the burden officers typically have to deal with both the offender and the victim under extremely tense circumstances (Tjaden & Thoennes, 2000b; Whetstone, 2001).

In addition to wider implementation of crisis response teams, community task forces are being formed in some cities to address domestic violence on a larger scale. These task forces typically bring various parties together, including law enforcement administrators, prosecutors, judges, probation officers, victims' advocates, shelter representatives, family counselors, educators, and even clergy members. These groups meet periodically to address the needs of the community as they relate to domestic violence. In this way, police departments may become better informed of the services available to victims and hence, better equipped to call upon particular persons or agencies when specific needs arise (Babcock & Steiner, 1999; Shepard & Pence, 1999). Stopping domestic violence is no easy task. However, providing victims with resources to live safe and productive lives can be accomplished through cooperative efforts of law enforcement, the court system, corrections, social services, victim services, and society generally.

REFERENCES

ARIZONA REVISED STATUTES (ARS). (1980). *Domestic violence*, 13-3601.

BABCOCK, J. C., & STEINER, R. (1999). The relationship between treatment, incarceration, and recidivism of battering: A program of evaluation of Seattle's coordinated community response to domestic violence. *Journal of Family Psychology, 13*, 46–59.

BACHMAN, R., & COKER, A. L. (1995). Police involvement in domestic violence: The interactive effects of victim injury, offender's history of violence, and race. *Violence and Victims, 10*, 91–106.

BAKER, P. L. (1997). And I went back: Battered women's negotiation of choice. *Journal of Contemporary Ethnography, 26*, 55–74.

BELKNAP, J., & McCALL, K. D. (1994). Woman battering and police referrals. *Journal of Criminal Justice, 22*, 223–236.

BROWNE, A., & SALOMON, A., & BASSUK, S. S. (1999). The impact of recent partner violence on poor women's capacity to maintain work. *Violence Against Women, 5*, 393–426.

BUZAWA, E., & HOTELING, G., & KLEIN, A. (1998). What happens when a reform works? The need to study unanticipated consequences of mandatory processing of domestic violence. *Journal of Police and Criminal Psychology, 13*, 43–54.

BUZAWA, E. S., & AUSTIN, T. (1993). Determining police response to domestic violence victims. *American Behavioral Scientist, 36*, 610–623.

CAMPBELL, J., & MILLER, P., & CARDWELL, M. M. (1994). Relationship status of battered women over time. *Journal of Family Violence, 9*, 99–111.

CAMPBELL, J. C., & SOEKEN, K. L. (1999). Forced sex and intimate partner violence. *Violence Against Women, 5*, (1999): 1017–1035.

COLLINS, P. H. (1989). The social construction of black feminist thought. *Signs, 14*, 745–773.

CRETNEY, A., & DAVIS, G. (1997). Prosecuting domestic assault: Victims failing courts, or courts failing victims? *Howard Journal, 36*, 146–157.

DAVIS, R. C., & SMITH, B. (1995). Domestic violence reforms: Empty promises or fulfilled expectations? *Crime and Delinquency, 41*, 541–552.

DAVIS, R. C., & TAYLOR, B. G. (1997). A proactive response to family violence: The results of a randomized experiment. *Criminology, 35*, 307–333.

DOBASH, R. E., & DOBASH, R. P. (1979). V*iolence against wives*. New York: Free Press.

DOLON, R., HENDRICKS, J., & MEAGHER, M. S. (1986). Police practices and attitudes towards domestic violence. *Journal of Police Science and Administration, 14*, 187–192.

DUNFORD, F. W. (1992). The measurement of recidivism in cases of spouse assault. *Journal of Criminal Law and Criminology, 83*, 120–136.

DUNFORD, F. W., HUIZINGA, D., & ELLIOTT, D. S. (1990). The role of arrest in domestic assault: The Omaha Police Experiment. *Criminology, 28*, 183–206.

DUTTON, D. G. (1988). Research advances in the study of wife assault: Etiology and prevention. In D. Weisstub (Ed.), *Law and mental health: International perspectives*. New York: Pergamon.

EIGENBERG, H. M., SCARBOROUGH, K. E., & KAPPELER, V. E. (1996). Contributory factors affecting arrest in domestic and non-domestic assaults. *American Journal of Police, 15*, 27–54.

EREZ, E., & BELKNAP, J. (1998). In their own words: Battered women's assessment of the criminal processing system's responses. *Violence and Victims, 13*, 251–268.

FEDER, L. (1996). Police handling of domestic calls: The importance of offender's presence in the arrest decision. *Journal of Criminal Justice, 24*, 481–490.

FEDER, L. (1997). Domestic violence and police response in a pro-arrest jurisdiction. *Women and Criminal Justice, 8*, 79–98.

FEDER, L. (1999). Police handling of domestic violence calls: An overview and further investigation. *Women and Criminal Justice, 10*, 49–68.

FERRARO, K. J. (1989). Policing woman battering. *Social Problems, 36*, 61–74.

FERRARO, K. J. (1996). The dance of dependency: A genealogy of domestic violence discourse. *Hypatia, 11*, 77–91.

FERRARO, K. J. (1997). Battered women: Strategies for survival. In A. Corderelli (Ed.), *Violence among intimate partners: Patterns, causes and effects*. New York: Macmillan.

FERRARO, K. J. (2001). Woman battering: More than a family problem. In C. M. Renzetti & L. Goodstein (Eds.), *Women, crime and criminal justice: Original feminist readings*. Los Angeles: Roxbury.

FYFE, J. J., KLINGER, D. A., & FLAVIN, J. (1997). Differential police treatment of male-on-female spousal violence. *Criminology, 35*, 455–473.

HARTSOCK, N. (1987). The feminist standpoint: Developing a ground for a specifically feminist historical materialism. In S. Harding (Ed.), *Feminism and methodology*. Milton Keynes, Great Britain: Open University Press.

HOLLENHORST, P. S. (1998). What do we know about anger management programs in corrections? *Federal Probation, 62*, 52–64.

HOYLE, C., & SANDERS, A. (2000). Police response to domestic violence: From victim choice to victim empowerment? *British Journal of Criminology, 40*, 14–36.

JOHNSON, I. M. (1990). A loglinear analysis of abused wives' decisions to call the police in domestic-violence disputes. *Journal of Criminal Justice, 18*, 147–159.

JOLIN, A., & MOOSE, C. A. (1997). Evaluating a domestic violence program in a community policing environment: Research implementation issues. *Crime and Delinquency, 43*, 279–297.

JONES, D. A., & BELKNAP, J. (1999). Police responses to battering in a progressive pro-arrest jurisdiction. *Justice Quarterly, 16*, 249–273.

KANE, R. J. (1999). Patterns of arrest in domestic violence encounters: Identifying a police decision-making model. *Journal of Criminal Justice, 27*, 65–79.

KURZ, D. (1998). Women, welfare, and domestic violence. *Social Justice, 25*, 105–122.

KVALE, S. (1996). *Interviews: An introduction to qualitative research interviewing*. Thousand Oaks, CA: Sage.

LOFLAND, J., & LOFLAND, L. H. (1995). *Analyzing social settings: A guide to qualitative observation and analysis* (3rd ed.). Belmont, CA: Wadsworth.

McKEAN, J., & HENDRICKS, J. E. (1997). The role of crisis intervention in the police response to domestic disturbances. *Criminal Justice Policy Review, 8*, 269–294.

MELTON, H. C. (1999). Police response to domestic violence. *Journal of Offender Rehabilitation, 29*, 1–21.

MEYER, S. L., VIVIAN, D., & O'LEARY, D. K. (1998). Men's sexual aggression in marriage. *Violence Against Women, 4*, 415–435.

MOE WAN, A. (2000). Battered women in the restraining order process: Observations on a court advocacy program. *Violence Against Women, 6*, 606–632.

MOE WAN, A. (2001). Strategies of survival: Studying the link between women's victimization and offending. Ph.D. dissertation, Arizona State University.

MRSEVIC, Z., & HUGHES, D. M. (1997). Violence against women in Belgrade, Serbia. *Violence Against Women, 3*, 101–128.

NARAYAN, U. (1988). Working together across difference: Some considerations on emotions and political practice. *Hypatia, 3*, 31–47.

ORME, J., DOMINELLI, L., & MULLENDER, A. (2000). Working with violent men from a feminist social work perspective. *International Social Work, 43*, 89–105.

POLICE FOUNDATION. (1992, October). Spouse abuse research raises new questions about police response to domestic violence. *Police Foundation Reports*, 1–6.

PTACEK, J. (1999). *Battered women in the courtroom: The power of judicial responses*. Boston: Northeastern University Press.

RAPHAEL, J. (1996). *Prisoners of abuse: Domestic violence and welfare receipt*. Chicago: Taylor Institute.

ROBINSON, A. L., & CHANDEK, M. S. (2000). Differential police response to black battered women. *Women and Criminal Justice, 12*, 29–61.

RUSSELL, D. E. H. (1982). *Rape in marriage*. New York: Collier Books.

SAUNDERS, D. G. (1995). The tendency to arrest victims of domestic violence: A preliminary analysis of officer characteristics. *Journal of Interpersonal Violence, 10*, 147–158.

SCHECHTER, S. (1982). *Women and male violence: The visions and struggles of the battered women's movement.* Boston: South End Press.

SHEPARD, M. F., & PENCE, E. L. (Eds.). (1999). *Coordinating community responses to domestic violence: Lessons from Duluth and beyond.* Thousand Oaks, CA: Sage.

SHERMAN, L. W. (1992). *Policing domestic violence: Experiments and dilemmas.* New York: Free Press.

SHERMAN, L. W., & BERK, R. A. (1984). The specific deterrent effects of arrest for domestic assault. *American Sociological Review, 49,* 261–272.

SMITH, D. E. (1987). *The everyday world as problematic: A feminist sociology.* Toronto, Canada: University of Toronto Press.

STITH, S. M. (1990). Police response to domestic violence: The influence of individual and familial factors. *Violence and Victims, 5,* 37–49.

TJADEN, P., & THOENNES, N. (2000a). *Extent, nature, and consequences of intimate partner violence: Findings from the National Violence Against Women Survey.* Washington, DC: U.S. Department of Justice, NCJ 181867.

TJADEN, P., & THOENNES, N. (2000b). The role of stalking in domestic violence crime reports generated by the Colorado Springs Police Department. *Violence and Victims, 15,* 427–441.

WALLACE, H. (1999). *Family violence: Legal, medical, and social perspectives* (2nd ed.). Boston: Allyn & Bacon.

WEBSDALE, N. (1995). Rural woman abuse: The voices of Kentucky women. *Violence Against Women, 1,* 309–388.

WEBSDALE, N., & JOHNSON, B. (1997). The policing of domestic violence in rural and urban areas: The voices of battered women. *Policing and Society, 6,* 297–317.

WHETSTONE, T. S. (2001). Measuring the impact of a domestic violence coordinated response team. *Policing, 24,* 371–398.

19

Battered Immigrant Women's Domestic Violence Dynamics and Legal Protections

Nawal Ammar and Leslye Orloff

❖

INTRODUCTION

All immigrants feel estranged because of the unfamiliar context of their new homeland. In their new setting immigrants have to adjust to new norms, values, lifestyle, and often a different language. However, women who immigrate from one country to another due to marriage, seeking an education, or in an attempt to improve their life chances by finding work, often encounter qualitatively different hardships than men. For many women immigrants, the mobility amplifies the gender asymmetry that already existed in their homeland (Abraham, 2000b; Acevedo, 2000; Ahmad, Riaz, Barata, & Stewart, 2004; Ammar, 2000; Raj & Silverman, 2002). Battered immigrant women's gender and ethnicity leave them vulnerable. However, their experience of being in a battering relationship is further complicated by lack of legal immigration status they can acquire on their own which often makes them more dependent on their abusers, who are usually the citizens or legal immigrants.

In the United States, demographic, legal, and philosophical changes have all contributed to the emerging of battered immigrant women as a significant concern in the justice system and with service providers. This chapter considers the unique dynamics of domestic violence among immigrant women, presents an overview of the major factors making the issue of battered immigrant women a significant one in the United States, examines the persistent problems this group of women continues to encounter as they work to become domestic violence survivors, and explores the future needs of this population. The chapter uses as a basis for its discussion data from the census review of the available academic and legal literature and information from advocacy caucuses that began in the early 1990s in preparation of the passage of the Violence Against Women Act (VAWA) in 1994 and the reauthorization of VAWA 2000.

RESEARCH FINDINGS AND THE UNIQUE DYNAMICS OF VIOLENCE AMONG BATTERED IMMIGRANT WOMEN

While immigrant populations in the United States are diverse and have varied experiences, there is sufficient evidence to show that battered immigrant women share some commonalities in their encounter of domestic violence (Menjivar & Salcido, 2002; Raj & Silverman, 2002). Reliable statistics indicating the prevalence of domestic violence among immigrant women are not available (Goldman, 1999; Raj & Silverman, 2002). Even when such rates become available they are likely to underreport domestic violence, since reporting crime rates among recent immigrants is generally low (Menjivar & Salcido, 2002).

Although we don't have a reliable understanding of occurrence rates of domestic violence among immigrant women, research shows that this is a group that faces a unique dynamic of violence. Abusers of immigrant spouses and intimate partners often use immigration-status-related abuse to lock their victims in abusive relationships (Abraham, 2000a, 2000b; Aguilar-Hass, Dutton, & Orloff, 2000; Ahmad et al., 2004; Dutton, Orloff, & Aguilar-Hass, 2000; Orloff, Dutton, Aguilar-Hass, & Ammar, 2003; Raj & Silverman, 2002). For immigrant victims, this form of power and control is particularly malicious and effective. The fear induced by immigration-related abuse makes it extremely difficult for a victim to leave her abuser, obtain a protection order, access domestic violence services, call the police for help, or participate in the abuser's prosecution. Immigration-related abuse results in the abuser's control of whether or not his spouse or partner attains legal immigration status in this country, whether any temporary legal immigration status she has may become permanent, and how long it may take her to become a naturalized citizen.

In addition to deterring a victim from seeking help to counter abuse, immigration-related abuse could be used to interfere with the victim's abilities to survive economically apart from her abuser (Aguilar-Hass et al., 2000; Dutton et al., 2000). Controlling the legal immigration status of the battered immigrant woman hinders her access to authorization that allows immigrant victims to work legally in the United States. Moreover, abusers of immigrant victims who are the mothers of their children often keep the victim from attaining legal immigration status, and then try to raise her lack of legal immigration status in order to win custody of the children despite his history of abuse (Ammar, Orloff, Aguilar-Hass, & Dutton, 2004).

Some examples of immigration-related abuse include, but are not limited to:

- Threatening to report her or her children to the Department of Homeland Security
- Telling her that if she calls the police for help he will have her deported
- Not filing papers to confer legal immigration status on her and/or her children
- Threatening to withdraw or withdrawing immigration papers he filed for her and/or her children
- Making her come to the United States on a visitor's or fianceé visa although she is already married to her spouse

- Not giving her access to documents that she needs for her application for lawful immigration status
- Hiding from her notices to appear before an immigration judge to defend against her deportation. (Ammar, 2005)

CHANGES CONTRIBUTING TO THE SURFACING OF BATTERED IMMIGRANT WOMEN AS A SOCIAL PROBLEM

Demographic, legal, and social changes in the past two decades have converged to make the issue of battered immigrant women of concern to service providers, legal advocates, victim advocates, and others working in the justice system. While an argument for a chronological order of the onset of each of these changes can be made, it is more important to underscore that their convergence in the early 1990s is the significant element for battered immigrant women.

Demographic Changes in Immigration and Battered Immigrant Women

Today, immigration is a major contributor to the population growth in the United States. The United States experienced a steady rise in absolute levels of immigration each decade during the last 65 years (Nowak, 2004). Since the 1990s more females than males have immigrated to the United States (Greico, 2002). This immigration pattern, combined with a persistent annual rate of natural increase (births minus deaths), has lead to the estimation that 60 percent of the population increase in the United States between 1994 and 2050 will be attributed to immigration (Nowak, 2004).

Since the 1970s the rate of immigrants entering the United States has increased three-fold, and the 1990s witnessed the largest influx of immigrants to date (Fix & Passel, 2001). The change has not only been in the numbers of immigrants but also in their primary destinations once they arrived in the United States. In the 1990s, as in every year since 1971, the primary destination states for legal immigrants were California (291,216, or 28%), New York (114,827, or 12%), Florida (90,819, or 9%), Texas (88,365, or 9%), New Jersey (57,721, or 5%), and Illinois (47,235, or 5%) (Ammar, Orloff, Dutton, & Aguilar-Hass, in press; Greico, 2002b). Recently the immigration dispersal pattern shows new growth states receiving immigrants—many have not seen this immigrant population growth for over 100 years (Fix, Passel, & Sucher, 2003; Saenz, 2004). Among the top receiving states are North Carolina, Georgia, Nevada, Arkansas, Utah, and Tennessee (Fix et al., 2003; Saenz, 2004). This demographic shift of immigration has created new demands on services in general and services that are culturally appropriate in particular. One example of such need resulting from the dramatic growth of the immigrant population in new destination states has been the need for interpretation into languages other than English and for bilingual social services, health care, and justice system personnel (Orloff et al., 2003). As of 1990, there were 31.8 million foreign language speakers who spoke a language other than English in the home (Fix & Passel, 2001). The number of countries with at least 100,000 foreign-born persons residing in the United States grew from 20 in 1970, to 27 in 1980, to 41 in 1990 and has continued growing (Fix et al., 2003). Such service delivery issues are magnified in the cases of immigrant women facing domestic violence. While we can't assume that immigrant women encounter intimate partner violence at a higher frequency than other women in the United States, the fact that the dynamics of the battering are more acute is a valid supposition (Ammar, 2000; Ammar et al., in press; Morash, Bui, & Santiago, 2000; Orloff et al., 2003). Battered immigrant women's immigration results in isolation, subjugation to threats of deportation that trap her in an abusive relationship, and the pressures of acculturation that often aggravate the conditions leading to the increase in the severity of domestic violence (Morash et al., 2000; Orloff et al., 2003; Raj & Silverman, 2002). In addition to the common factors leading to violence in all women's lives, immigrants are particularly vulnerable because of certain cultural understandings regarding domestic violence that silence the victim, call on her to subsume her individual needs for the larger protection of the family or community, and limit her access to the outside world (Ammar et al., in press; Dutton et al., 2000; Orloff & Kaguyutan, 2002; Raj & Silverman, 2002). Strategies about how to provide effective services and care to recent immigrant victims were only recently studied and understood (Rodriquez, 1995). Most service providers lack even the basic information about immigrant victim's legal rights and the tools to completely serve non-English-speaking clients, or address certain culturally based needs. This has become more problematic, especially in the new destination states that have not interacted with a critical mass of new immigrants for over one hundred years.

Change in Immigration and Domestic Violence Laws and Battered Immigrant Women

Change in immigration laws is another factor that has thrust the issue of violence against immigrant women to the forefront as a social problem in the last three decades. The history of immigration law in the United States has often been analyzed to reflect the U.S. views of race and class (Vellos, 1997). Immigration laws, however, have also often reflected an asymmetry favoring males. The early history of immigration laws have at their core the legal principle of "coverture," a legal principle under which "the very being or legal existence of the woman is suspended during the marriage, or at least incorporated and consolidated into that of the husband" (Orloff & Kaguyutan, 2002). Subsequent immigration laws such as the Immigration and Nationality Act of 1952 (INA), and the Immigration Marriage Fraud Amendment (IMFA) of 1986 (part of the Immigration Reform and Control Act [IRCA] of 1986) all maintained the coverture principles even though on their face these laws appeared to be gender neutral (see Orloff & Kaguyutan, 2002). The INA of 1952 (and its amendments of 1965 and 1976) gave women citizens and legal permanent residents the same rights as their male citizen counterparts to pass on their nationality or legal permanent residency (green card) to their spouses, children, and certain other immediate family members.

The 1986 IMFA sought to limit immigration fraud where noncitizens marry U.S. citizens just to obtain legal immigration status. In an attempt to control fraudulent marriages, the IMFA added to the burden of immigrant women by requiring that immigrant spouses who gained residency based on marriage to a U.S. citizen or lawful permanent resident submit to a two-year conditional residency requirement before being granted full lawful permanent residency (Orloff & Kaguyutan, 2002). Within 90 days of the end of the two-year conditional residency the couple must jointly petition to adjust the status of the "immigrant" spouse to permanent residency, which puts the immigrant spouse on the formal road to ultimately gain them U.S. citizenship. The citizen or permanent legal resident spouse is under no obligation to file or to support the joint petition. If a couple fail to file jointly, the dependent spouse loses legal permission to reside in the United States, becomes undocumented, and is subject to deportation (Orloff & Kaguyutan, 2002). The 1986 IMFA included some provisions to alleviate the dependency of the women on their husbands (e.g., extreme hardship, good faith, and good cause waivers) (Orloff & Kaguyutan, 2002). However, these provisions required strict standards (in the case of extreme hardship) or unrealistic expectations of the battered woman initiating the divorce (in the case of good faith and good cause waiver), making both provisions highly unlikely to be effectively used by battered immigrant spouses and obtainable only in exceptional cases (Locke, 1997).

The IMFA provisions as they stood created a structure where the woman had two choices. First, she could endure the abusive relationship until her two-year conditional status was removed. Alternatively, she would have to divorce her abuser prior to the completion of the two-year conditional status and risk deportation if immigration authorities did not grant her waiver request and allow her to stay in the United States (Shetty & Kaguyutan, 2002)[1]. In 1990 the "battered spouse waiver" amendment was added to the list of waivers available under the 1986 IMFA. The amendment no longer required the immigrant spouse to initiate the divorce, nor required a divorce for a "good cause" (Orloff & Kaguyutan, 2002). The amendment also exempted women who had been subject to battery or "extreme cruelty" from the joint petitioning process after the two years of conditional residency status. This reform allowed abused immigrant spouses with conditional residence to obtain full lawful permanent residence without waiting two years and without their abusers' cooperation.

The 1990 reforms, while very significant, helped only abused immigrant women whose abusive citizen or legal resident spouses had been willing to file an immigration case. Victims whose spouses had never filed immigration papers, immigrant spouses whose abusers were not citizens or lawful permanent residents, and victims abused by boyfriends remained trapped by immigration laws in abusive relationships.

The immigration provisions of the Violence Against Women Act, or VAWA (1994 and 2000) were specifically designed to offer the immigration relief protection to a broader range of battered immigrant women. The Violence Against Women Act of 1994 was signed into law on September 13, 1994, as part of the Violent Crime Control Act of 1994. The VAWA immigration provisions defined domestic violence as battering or extreme cruelty. This definition of domestic violence was broader than most state domestic violence laws, following more closely the international law definition of domestic violence. The definition under VAWA and implementing regulations includes being the victim of any act or threatened act of violence, including any forceful detention, which results or threatens to result in physical or mental injury (Orloff & Kagutuyan, 2002). The definition also includes psychological and sexual abuse and exploitation, including rape, molestation, incest (if the victim is a minor), or forced prostitution domestic violence.

The VAWA of 1994 contained several provisions designed to prevent abusers from using immigration as a tool to control their victims. Specifically, the act enabled battered immigrants to attain lawful permanent residency (green cards) without the cooperation of their abusive spouse. VAWA self-petitions and VAWA cancellation of removal are two such forms of relief (Pendleton & Block, 2001). The filing of a self-petition could occur without the cooperation of the abusive spouse, but until VAWA 2000 this was available only while the battered immigrant woman was married to the citizen or legal permanent resident spouse. Other proof requirements for a VAWA self-petition case included proving the abuser's immigration status, having suffered abuse or extreme cruelty, having entered the marriage in good faith, and proving that she has resided with the abuser for a period of time (Orloff & Kaguyutan, 2002). VAWA cancellation of removal (or, as formerly known, suspension of deportation) is the second VAWA remedy designed as a defense from deportation for battered immigrants who may not be eligible for self-petitioning. Once placed in deportation proceedings before an immigration judge, a woman can request that she not be removed from the United States if she can meet the same proof requirements of the self-petition, can prove that she would suffer extreme hardship if deported, and that she has been continuously present in the United States for three years (Orloff & Kaguyutan, 2002; Orloff & Kelly, 1995).

VAWA 1994 provided funding that emphasized enforcement as well as social and educational programs of crime prevention to improve services to battered women including battered immigrant women (see Orloff & Kaguyutan, 2002; Orloff & Kelly, 1995). The act also provided incentives for agencies seeking funding to have in place mandatory or pro-arrest policies, prohibit dual arrest, and prohibit mutual protection orders (Orloff & Kaguyutan, 2002).

On October 28, 2000, VAWA was reauthorized and expanded to create broader protections for victims of domestic violence, sexual assault, and stalking, trafficking and other violent crimes. VAWA 2000 made it easier for many more battered immigrant women to leave their abusers, receive culturally competent services, and to help prosecute their abusers. It created special rules for noncitizen battered women and children to allow them to remain in the United States. It changed the old law under which battered immigrant women could be deported if they divorced their abusers prior to filing their VAWA immigration case (Orloff, 2001; Orloff & Kaguyutan, 2002).

Two new nonimmigrant visas for immigrant victims were created under VAWA 2000. The first nonimmigrant visa is the U-visa, also known as the Crime Victim's Visa. An applicant must prove that she has been a victim of a serious crime listed in the statute; has suffered substantial physical or mental abuse as a result of the crime; has information about the crime; and can provide certification from a federal or state official (e.g., police, prosecutor, judge, immigration authority), a law enforcement official, or a judge that she has been, is, or is likely to be helpful in investigating or prosecuting the crime (Orloff, 2003, Chapter 6). The other type of nonimmigrant visa is the T-visa (Trafficking Victim Visa). An applicant must prove that he or she has been a victim of a severe form of trafficking and has either complied with any reasonable request for assistance in the investigation or prosecution of trafficking or has not yet turned 15 years old. To obtain the T-visa the victim must also prove that she will suffer extreme and unusual hardship if she is removed from the United States (Orloff, 2003, Chapter 6). If either the U-visa or the T-visa is approved, the applicant may be eligible to apply for lawful permanent resident status under certain circumstances (Orloff, 2001).

In addition to the protections offered under immigration laws, VAWA and a number of other pieces of legislation passed between 1994 and 2005 granted access to limited public benefits for battered immigrant victims (e.g., public housing, welfare, Medicaid). These laws also guarantee all immigrant victims access to shelter services, police protection, emergency Medicaid, and other services necessary to protect life and safety; victim compensation; and legal assistance (Orloff, 2003, Chapter 8). Limited access to legal assistance was also granted.

Philosophical Changes and Domestic Violence

Historically many laws either legitimized or minimized the negative impact of women battering in the United States (Browne, 1995). Early British Common Law established the rule of thumb that "allowed husbands to beat their wives with rods no larger than the thickness of their thumbs" (Belknap, 1985; Dobash & Dobash, 1979) In the 1920s the coverture doctrine gave a "husband the right to 'chastise' or even kill his wife if he deemed it necessary punishment" (Orloff & Kaguyutan, 2002; Stone, 1977). The various efforts of advocates on behalf of women generally and domestic violence victims in particular culminated in making the 1970s the critical decade of recognizing women battering as a societal problem (Belknap, 1986). However, issues related to battering and minority women did not crystallize in the academic literature and in advocacy until the early to mid-1980s. Various issues hindered the development of such studies and systematic advocacy. The primacy of concerns for racism over sexism have led to the scant focus and research interest in women battering among women of color researchers and advocates (Richie, 1985). Underreporting of violence in the home generally and in minority communities in particular (Carter, 1985; Skurnik, 1983) reduced the availability of data. Furthermore, debates about whether the dynamics of domestic violence within minority communities are different from those in the mainstream have created a focus on "cultural issues" rather than on collecting empirical data (Abraham, 2000a; Phoenix, 1987).

The 1980s witnessed the emergence of a systematic research on minority women in the United States and domestic violence (Agozino, 1997; Burns, 1986; Coley & Beckett, 1988; Fenton, 1998; Hampton, 1986). This research showed that minority women face the battering in much the same way as white women: A broken bone is a broken bone regardless of the racial makeup or language spoken by the victim or perpetrator. However, minority women find themselves facing different problems after the battering which may be different from their white sisters (Aguilar-Hass et al., 2000; Dasgupta & Warrier, 1996; Kulwicki & Miller, 1999; Peeks, 2002; Srinivasan & Ivey, 1999). During this period women of color began a critique of the prevailing feminist perspectives (Brewer, 1989; Hull, Scott, & Smith, 1982; Rosaldo, 1980). The critique saw the concerns of mainstream feminism as confined, restricted, and related only to women of privilege as defined both by race and class (Collins, 1986, 1990; Crenshaw, 1991, 1994). One concept of this critique has been the analytic concept of "intersectionality" (Crenshaw, 1994) or as stated by Abraham (2000a, 2000b) "ethno-gender." Intersectionality takes into account the multiple aspects of identity that some individuals have and argues that in many cases gender identity is influenced by other dimensions such as class, national origin, ethnicity, and race. Hence, the experience of gender for women of color must be understood in terms of the intersection of the multilayers that make identity. More directly related to domestic violence, Crenshaw argues (1994, p. 97) that the "ways in which the location of women of color at the intersection of race and gender makes their actual experience of domestic violence . . . qualitatively different than that of white women."

The same is true for battered immigrant women whose experience with domestic violence and whose struggle to survive domestic violence victimization is directly affected by their multiple layers of identity. According to the 2000 Census, the largest foreign-born populations living in the United States are from three countries: Mexico (9.2 million), the Philippines (1.4 million), and India (1 million) (Greico, 2003). For immigrant women from these countries and other immigrant communities of color their identity is also influenced by the intersection of ethnicity, class, and gender.[2] Battered immigrant women's identities, whether or not they are women of color, are further shaped by one more component, namely the immigration experience.

In addition to the focus on battering in the minority community by researchers and advocates, the 1990s saw a global resurgence of human rights protections. The last decade of the twentieth century saw the breakup of the Soviet Union, the creation of Special Courts to hold accountable the former Yugoslavians, Rwandan leaders held accountable, and the defeat of apartheid in South Africa. The extension of human rights protections on the basis of gender, age, sexual orientation, and cultural identity was most notable in countries of the European Union, rather than in the United States. However, in the United States VAWA 1994 and VAWA 2000 were pieces of U.S legislation (the other being the Americans with Disabilities Act of 1990) where human rights protections dominated constitutional interpretations (Anker, 2002; Orloff & Kagutuyan, 2002; Wolchok, 1997). Legal protections for battered immigrant women and their children under VAWA 1994 and 2000 were expanded to cover protections of women not on the basis of citizenship, but on the basis of their "humanity and vulnerability" (Perilla, 1999). Hillary Clinton's speech in the Fourth United Nations Conference on Women in Beijing, China, underscored such a shift when she stated, "Women's rights are human rights and human rights are women's rights." This shift in understanding the legal parameters affecting battered immigrant women as vulnerable human beings whose rights lie in their humanity rather than in the privilege of their citizenship was further advanced by advocates and lobbyists who worked and continue to work tirelessly to enhance immigrant women's safety.

PERSISTENT PROBLEMS AND BATTERED IMMIGRANT WOMEN

Despite the overreaching legislative and philosophical changes, battered immigrant women still encounter persistent problems unique to them due to their immigration status and national origin. Advocates and researchers have indicated four main barriers that still impede battered women's ability to either leave their abuser or stop the abuse (Abraham, 2000a; Abu-Ras, 2003; Aguilar-Hass et al., 2000; Ammar, 2000; Dutton et al., 2000; Peeks, 2002; Rodriguez, 1999; Srinivasan & Ivey, 1999). These barriers include fear of deportation, economic security, fear of losing custody, and language access.

Deportation

Fear of deportation (removal from the United States) is the principal barrier to immigrant victims' seeking any type of aid after experiencing abuse, including assistance from shelters, advocates, hospitals, and the police (Aguilar-Hass et al., 2000; Ammar et al., in press; Orloff et al., 2003). This fear of deportation affects both immigrant victims of domestic violence who have legal permission to live and work in the United States, and those who are undocumented. As a result, many battered immigrants believe that they have no legal right to protection from their abuser. The eligibility of many immigrant victims of domestic violence to reside legally in the United States is directly tied to the immigration or citizenship status of their abusive spouse. These and other immigrant domestic violence victims fear deportation because the abuser uses threats of deportation to keep victims of physical and sexual abuse from seeking help. National Institute of Justice (NIJ) (2003) research conducted across the United States found that 65% of the 157 battered immigrant women interviewed reported that their abuser has used some form of a threat of deportation. These are quotes from battered immigrant women describing this immigration-status-related abuse:

- He makes threats to report me to the INS if I don't do what he wants.
- He said that I was going to be deported; the INS would send me to Mexico.
- If I ever challenge him, he will divorce me, and then I will lose my green card.

Many victims who qualify for VAWA, battered spouse waivers, or the crime victim U-visa have no knowledge that options exist to attain legal immigration status without dependence on their abusers. To ameliorate this unique threat to battered immigrant women, legal changes alone are not enough. Reaching battered immigrants and women in the immigrant communities with the information is essential if legal changes are to be effective. Some of the strategies for reaching the battered immigrant women include:

- identifying and training immigrant women who can ensure leadership in their communities on domestic violence and the spread of the word on how to access help.
- presenting media campaigns on non-English-speaking programs through distributing pamphlets written in various languages at places immigrant women frequent (such as grocery stores, laundromats, health care clinics, and community centers).
- creating programs to enhance awareness of the issue by educating community leaders and organization members, shelter workers, police officers, judges, and health care and other service providers.
- educating immigrant community organizations, community leaders, and community members about the issues.

As a matter of federal law (the Personal Responsibility and Work Opportunity Reconciliation Act of 1996) all services of domestic violence advocates, shelters, and other victim services are to be provided without any requirement that service providers ask questions regarding the victim's immigration status (Orloff & Kaguyutan, 2002). If abusers are to be stopped from using deportation threats to lock their victims in abusive relationships and avoid prosecution it is imperative that all service providers, including police officers and justice system personnel, understand that their role is to protect the victims and not to act as immigration officers. This is particularly important in light of the rise in anti-immigrant sentiment in the United States post-2001.

Economic Security

Economic security, including cash, housing, and health care, is often an issue of significant concern and vulnerability for immigrant women (Dutton et al., 2000; Orloff, 2001). Research has found that more than two-thirds of battered immigrant women who stayed with their abusers reported a lack of money as the primary reason for not leaving a violent home (Dutton et al., 2000). Economic dependence on the abuser dramatically limits an immigrant victim's options for physical and legal separation from her abuser. The immigrant victim of domestic violence often has less vocational skills than her abuser, which could be due to her husband's isolation tactics or the general gender asymmetry in most cultures between men and women's education (Menjivar & Salcido, 2002). When immigrant victims leave abusive partners who have been financially supporting them, they often have less access to the public benefits safety net than other battered women (Orloff, 2001).

Economic survival, however, can be easier for documented women than for undocumented immigrant women. Undocumented immigrants, if they work, do so in the underground economy, often taking jobs that earn below the minimum wage. These jobs regularly do not include benefits such as medical insurance, paid vacation, sick leave, and pensions (Orloff & Kagutuyan, 2002). To address this issue and to provide immigrant victims who qualify for immigration benefits with a chance to sever economic dependence from their abusers, both VAWA and U-visa immigration relief enable a battered immigrant woman to obtain legal work authorization (Orloff, 2001; Orloff & Kagutuyan, 2002). Many battered immigrants who qualify for VAWA are additionally granted special access to public benefits that they can use to help sever economic dependence on their abusers. This access to benefits is particularly important as an option to rely on if their abuser interferes with their ability to work.

Since economic concerns make it difficult for an immigrant woman to leave her abuser successfully, it is extremely important to educate service providers, advocates, and immigrant community organizations about the opportunities available that can help battered immigrant women gain financial independence. It is also essential for this life-saving information about economic security options to reach battered immigrant women themselves.

Custody and Fear of Losing Children

Many battered immigrant women are the primary caretakers of their children and are concerned that, if they leave their abusers, it will have a negative impact on their children (Dutton et al., 2000; Orloff & Kaguyutan, 2002). Abusers of battered immigrant women often intimidate them by threatening to take the children if the immigrant victim leaves the marriage. Even if the battered immigrant woman succeeds in being awarded custody by the court, battered immigrant women fear that the children will be harmed during visitations (Ammar et al., 2004). The fear that abusers will redirect the violence against the children is a legitimate concern since in 60% of households where women face abuse, children are also abused (Ammar et al., in press; Pendleton & Maher, 2000). Thus, these concerns complicate a battered immigrant's decision making about whether leaving her batterer will reduce or increase the safety of her children (Aguilar-Hass et al., 2000; Ammar et al., 2004; Dutton et al., 2000).

Battered immigrant women need to be informed about laws that create a preference for placing children in the custody of nonabusive parents. Both citizen and foreign-born children need the protection of these important laws, although the vast majority of abused immigrants have U.S.-citizen children. A study about the co-occurrence of battery and children witnessing abuse among battered immigrant Latina women found that 80% of the children are American born (Ammar et al., 2004). The American Bar Association (ABA) Center on Children has urged courts to offer the same protection to children of immigrant parents recommended by the American Psychological Association. The ABA states that "custody, preference should be given to the non-violent parent whenever possible, and unsupervised visitation should not be granted to the perpetrator until an offender-specific treatment program is successfully completed, or the offender proves that he is no longer a threat to the physical and emotional safety to the children and the other parent" (Garlow, 2000).

Language Access

While there are no definitive statistics on the level of English spoken by immigrant women, it is clear from both the countries of origin (Greico, 2003) and the experiences of victim advocates over the last two decades that most immigrant women in the United States are not fluent in English. This inability to speak English creates a linguistic barrier to fully understand the norms of the larger society. Very often an immigrant woman's spouse serves as a translator or even her language teacher (Ammar, 2000; Orloff et al., 2003). Language barriers are exacerbated when the person who provides linguistic interpretation is abusing the immigrant woman. Battered immigrant women's need to seek assistance outside their immigrant community—such as from shelters, victim service programs, legal service offices, police departments, prosecutor's offices, and courts—is hampered when these services do not have employees who can speak their native languages and do not provide interpreters.[3] The absence of interpreters and bilingual staff at police stations, social service organizations, courts, and lawyers' offices complicates a victim's efforts to obtain help. These linguistic limitations can seriously cripple a woman's ability to escape the harms of domestic violence (Abraham 2000a, 2000b; Ammar, 2000; Orloff et al., 2003).

Language is a particularly significant barrier to obtaining police assistance during an abusive incident. In a study of Latina battered immigrant women, the overwhelming majority (75.6%) of participants spoke little or no English and most of the police officers responding to the victim's 911 calls did not speak the victim's language (Orloff et al., 2003). Research has found that when police respond to calls from immigrant victims they most often do not speak the victim's language and do not bring an interpreter (66% of the times in Orloff et al. [2003], and 75% of the times in an NIJ [2003] study). Orloff and colleagues' study and the NIJ study showed that when battered immigrant women whose English is not fluent called the police there were negative aspects of the encounter such as not talking to the victim who called 911 for help; not arresting the abuser; not taking the woman seriously; talking down to her; and believing the abuser's claims because he spoke better English. Employing trained interpreters and bilingual police officers would increase access to protection for immigrant victims of domestic violence. The current lack of competent linguistic support for domestic violence victims throughout the legal and social service systems in many jurisdictions makes reporting the violence, seeking help, and leaving their abusers difficult for battered immigrant women. The NIJ (2003) study showed that according to the battered immigrant women, language barriers were problematic in courts, shelters, and nonresidential services but not as acute as with police encounters.

NEED FOR SYSTEMIC REFORM

The barriers explored above should not be understood as the result of the immigrant women's culture and their inability to adjust to the U.S. mainstream norms and values (Dasgupta & Warrier, 1996; Rodriguez, 1995; Warrier, 2000). Rather, these barriers present conceptual and political challenges for restructuring both service delivery and policy development in a way that is able to gauge the extent by which the United States can respond to the needs of its multicultural societal fabric. Thus far the engagement regarding multiculturalism and diversity has revolved around the differences among clients (in this case, battered immigrants). This depiction of difference has resulted in mainstream services dealing stereotypically with battered immigrant women (and other minorities) by turning them away because of "these women's" disproportionate need. In order to curb domestic violence in the United States where immigrants and their children contribute to the nature of multiculturalism, the systems must change to be responsive to all victims regardless of the language they speak or whether they are citizens or noncitizens. Changes must be made not only in the justice system but for all service providers who serve victims. Real reforms will require collaboration and broadening of cooperation between mainstream domestic violence services and immigrant community-based programs that have gained the trust of the women in immigrant communities. This requires mainstream agencies to make available culturally specific services by partnering and sharing funding with culturally competent immigrant community-based programs in addition to hiring bicultural or bilingual staff. This broadening requires an engagement between the mainstream agencies and immigrant women's community-based organizations, and serious discussions about the intersection of race, class, gender, and the future we want for all women. By sharing funding opportunities and resources in true collaborations this restructuring would empower all agencies to deliver better services to their clients and empower all women.

FUTURE NEEDS AND BATTERED IMMIGRANT WOMEN

The Violence Against Women Act (VAWA) of 2000 expires in September 2005. A reauthorization of the bill is in process. Advocates are working on securing improvements that will better serve battered immigrant women as part of VAWA 2005. The improved protections for battered immigrants being sought in VAWA 2005 focus on three categories of problems.

Stopping the Deportation of Immigrant Victims of Domestic Violence, Sexual Assault, and Trafficking

Changes in immigration enforcement post September 11, 2001, have resulted in many battered immigrant women who are legally eligible for VAWA, T-visa or U-visa protection being detained and removed from the United States before they can learn about or apply for immigration benefits. Many are removed without having an opportunity to see an immigration judge. Immigration authorities have begun to seek out and try to pick up undocumented immigrant victims at shelters and at courthouses when they come to court seeking protection orders. Other immigrant victims have been picked up at the courthouse when they were to attend a custody hearing that would otherwise have resulted in their abuser being denied custody of the children. In some cases even immigrant victims who have pending and approved cases for VAWA-related immigration relief are being picked up by immigration authorities who detain and seek to deport them.

As illustrated in the following examples—in which the victims' names have been changed to protect their identities—the reports to immigration authorities usually come from the abusive spouse or partner who has legal immigration status or is a U.S. citizen. Rainy, an immigrant subject to deportation, had an abusive U.S. citizen spouse who withdrew the immigration petition he had filed on her behalf, as he had threatened to do on many occasions. Her husband then arranged for INS officials to arrest Rainy at the home the couple shared. Immigration authorities initially refused to set bond for Rainy, but after much advocacy demonstrating that her husband had used immigration laws as a tool of abuse, INS agreed to release Rainy on her own recognizance. INS also agreed to terminate its case against her. Since then, Rainy has been residing at a shelter, and is accessing domestic violence support services, including one-on-one counseling (*Northwest Immigrant Advocate Newsletter*, 2002, p. 4).

In Pennsylvania, a battered immigrant woman named Helga was abused severely by her husband who is a lawful permanent resident (has a green card). He constantly threatened to kill her, and reminded her that control over her immigration status is completely in his hands. After nearly killing her, he was finally arrested. Despite his arrest, he called immigration authorities and turned her in because he had never filed any petitions for her immigration. He knew she had remained undocumented. In fact, the INS detained her. Despite her detention, from jail Helga fully participated throughout in her abusive husband's prosecution. Helga was able to file for interim relief under the crime victim U-visa protections of VAWA and she was ultimately released from INS detention (Schakowsky, 2003).

Guaranteeing Economic Security for Immigrant Victims and Their Children

A second goal of VAWA 2005 reauthorization for immigrant victims is to expand upon the access to legal work authorization, public benefits, and legal services corporation-funded representation that is currently available in limited form to some immigrant victims of domestic violence, sexual assault, and trafficking. Under current law, some immigrant victims (T- and U-visa applicants) receive legal work authorization shortly after filing their applications once the Department of Homeland Security has determined that they have filed a valid case. VAWA self-petitioners and VAWA cancellation applicants have to wait often six months and sometimes up to a year before they receive full approval of their case and legal permission to work. VAWA 2005 will grant applicants for VAWA immigration relief early access to work authorization so that they can more quickly sever economic dependence on their abusers.

In 1996, battered immigrants who were VAWA self-petitioners and VAWA cancellation applicants were granted access to the public benefits safety net. Since 1996, new forms of immigration protections were added to cover more immigrant victims, but access to public benefits for these victims was not addressed. Furthermore, immigrant victims who entered the United States after August 1996 are required to wait five years before they can access benefits. Access to public benefits offers crucial life-saving assistance that helps immigrant victims remove themselves and their children from violent relationships. VAWA 2005 will ensure that all immigrant victims of domestic violence, sexual assault, or trafficking who qualify for VAWA or U- or T-visa relief, can access the public benefits they need—including Medicaid, Temporary Assistance to Needy Families (TANF), Supplemental Security Income (SSI), Food Stamps, and the State Child Health Insurance Program (SCHIP). Additionally, VAWA 2005 will include provisions that will ensure that legal services programs funded by the Legal Services Corporation (LSC) can use any source of funding including LSC funds to represent any victim of domestic violence, sexual assault, or trafficking without regard to the victim's immigration status.

Extending Immigration Relief to All Victims of Family Violence

The third significant need that advocates will be working to address in VAWA 2005 is ensuring that immigrant victims of family violence who have been left out of the protections of VAWA will be granted access to immigration relief and public benefits. To this end, immigrant victims of elder abuse who are battered or subjected to extreme cruelty by their U.S. citizen children will receive protection. Immigrant victims of child abuse and incest will no longer be cut off from applying for VAWA's immigration protections if they are unable to escape the abuse and file for relief before the date on which they turn 21 years of age. Adopted children who are abused will no longer be required to reside for two years with their abusive adoptive parent in order to obtain lawful permanent residency based on the adoption. Finally, VAWA's immigration protections are being improved to ensure that children of immigrant victims have access to legal immigration status along with their mothers. These extensions of VAWA remedies recognize the interconnectedness of women's lives, emphasize the importance of protecting all family members, and address the multiple forms of violence against women.

CONCLUDING REMARKS

We have highlighted in this chapter the interrelated concerns that battered immigrant women experience as victims of violence against women. The added dimension of deportation is a tool of battery that uniquely amplifies the needs, fears, and problems that battered immigrant women face requiring specific remedies and better understanding by service providers, legal advocates, and victim advocates. While demographic, legal, and philosophical changes have contributed to making the particular context in which assistance is most effectively offered to battered immigrant women better understood, the experiences of advocates and findings of researchers show that more is needed to ensure safety for this group of women. Some of these needs require legislative changes; others require a restructuring of service delivery and justice system approaches to include collaboration and creating contexts of multicultural competency. To be effective and have ongoing impact, system reforms must be accompanied by ongoing training of justice system personnel, advocates, attorneys, and service providers.

As of the writing of this chapter, advocates have been working hard to include the needed law reforms and increased access to funding to help immigrant victims in the reauthorization of VAWA 2005. Legal changes and access to funding are central tools in addressing the needs of battered immigrant women, especially in providing economic benefits and independence from the abuser. However, gaining legal rights alone is not sufficient to transform the social reality of battered immigrant women in the United States. Olsen (1991) argues that considering the "underlying commitments" these rights entail are as essential for effecting change. To further transform the conditions of battered immigrant women, a modification of organizational structures, social norms, and values toward immigrants in ways that fully address the intersection of violence, race, immigration status, and gender are needed.

NOTES

1. In the case of divorce she would have to be the first to file for divorce.
2. Despite the repeated claims that immigration imports poverty, Chapman and Bernstein (2002; p. 2) note that "Over the period 1994–2000 period, poverty rates fell much more quickly for immigrants than for natives. According to an example about the national poverty rates, they noted that this rate for recent immigrants (those here for 10 years or less) fell about four times as fast as for natives (11.6 percentage points for immigrants versus 2.9 points for natives); the rate for all immigrants fell 2.7 times as fast as that of U.S. natives. Based on such data they argue that immigration's role on poverty in the United States has been exaggerated and has crowded out other, more fundamentally economic factors, such as inequality and unemployment, from the discussion. These factors hurt the economic prospects of all low-wage workers, regardless of nativity."
3. The Department of Justice recognizes that "[I]n certain circumstances, failure to ensure that LEP [limited English proficient] persons can effectively participate in or benefit from federally assisted programs and activities may violate prohibition under Title VI of the Civil Rights Act of 1964, 42 U.S.C. 2000d and Title VI regulations against national and origin discrimination." 67 Fed. Reg. 41455, 21 (2002).

REFERENCES

Abraham, M. (2000a). *Speaking the unspeakable: Marital violence among South Asian immigrants in the United States.* New Brunswick, NJ: Rutgers University Press.

Abraham, M. (2000b). Isolation as a form of marital violence: The South Asian immigrant experience. *Journal of Social Distress & the Homeless, 9,* 221–236.

Abu-Ras, W. M. (2003). Barriers to services for Arab immigrant battered women in a Detroit suburb. *Journal of Social Work Research and Evaluation, 4,* 49–66.

Acevedo, M. J. (2000). Battered immigrant Mexican women's perspectives regarding abuse and help-seeking. *Journal of Multicultural Social Work, 8*(3/4), 243–282.

AGOZINO, B. (1997). *Black women and the criminal justice system: Towards the decolonisation of victimisation.* Sydney: Ashgate.

AGUILAR-HASS, G., DUTTON, M. A., & Orloff, L. E. (2000). Lifetime prevalence of violence against Latina immigrants: Legal and policy implications. *International Review of Victimology, 7,* 93–113.

AHMAD, F., RIAZ, S., BARATA, S., & STEWART, D. E. (2004). Patriarchal beliefs and perceptions of abuse among South Asian immigrant women. *Violence Against Women, 10,* 262–282.

AMMAR, N. H. (2000). Simplistic stereotyping and complex reality of Arab-American immigrant identity: Consequences and future strategies in policing wife battery. *Islam and Christian-Muslim Relations, 11,* 51–70.

AMMAR, N. H. (2005). *Evaluation of the HHS-funded grant entitled: "Preventing family violence in underserved and diverse communities."* The National Network to End Violence Against Immigrant Women. Submitted to the Administration for Children and Families/U.S. Department of Health and Human Services. Grant #90EV0253.

AMMAR, N. H., ORLOFF, L., DUTTON, M. A., & AGUILAR-HASS, G. (in press). Calls to police and police response: A case study from the Latina immigrant women in the U.S. *Journal of International Police Science and Management.*

AMMAR, N. H., ORLOFF, L. E., AGUILAR-HASS, G., & DUTTON, M. A. (2004). *Children of battered immigrant women: An assessment of the cumulative effects of violence, access to services and immigrant status.* A paper presented at the International Family Violence Conference, September 19–25, San Diego, CA.

ANKER, D. E. (2002). Refugee law, gender, and the human rights paradigm. *Harvard Human Rights Journal, 15,* 133–154.

BELKNAP, J. (1985). Perceptions of woman battering. In I. L. Moyer (Ed.), *The changing roles of women in the criminal justice system* (pp. 181–201). Prospect Hill, IL: Waveland Press.

BELKNAP, J. (1986). *The invisible women: Gender, crime and justice.* Albany, NY: Wadsworth.

BREWER, R. (1989). Black women and feminist sociology: The emerging perspective. *The American Sociologist, 20,* 57–70.

BROWNE, A. (1995). Reshaping the rhetoric: The nexus of violence, poverty, and minority status in the lives of women and children in the United States. *Georgetown Journal on Fighting Poverty, 3,* 17–23.

BURNS, M. C. (Ed.). (1986). *The speaking profits us: Violence in the lives of women of color.* Seattle, WA: Center for the Prevention of Sexual and Domestic Violence.

CARTER, D. (1985). Hispanic perception of police performance: An empirical assessment. *Journal of Criminal Justice, 13,* 487–500.

CHAPMAN, J., & BERNSTEIN, J. (2002). *Immigration and poverty: Disappointing income growth in the 1990s not solely the result of growth of immigrant population.* (Briefing Paper #130, 1–8). Washington, DC: Economic Policy Institute.

COLEY, S. M., & BECKETT, J. O. (1988). Black battered women: A review of empirical literature. *Journal of Counseling and Development, 66,* 266–270.

COLLINS, P. H. (1986). Learning from the outsider within: The sociological significance of black feminist thought. *Social Problems, 33,* 514–532.

COLLINS, P. H. (1990). *Black feminist thought: Knowledge, consciousness and the politics of empowerment.* Boston: Unwin Hyman.

CRENSHAW, K. (1991). Demarginalizing the intersection of race and sex: A black feminist critique of antidiscrimination doctrine, feminist theory and antiracist politics. In K. Barlett & R. F. Kennedy (Eds.), *Feminist legal theory: Reading in law and gender* (pp. 57–80). Boulder, CO: Westview Press.

CRENSHAW, K. (1994). Mapping the margins: Intersectionality, identity politics, and violence against women of color (pp. 93–118). In M. Albertson-Fineman & R. Mykitiuk (Eds.), *The public nature of private violence.* New York: Routledge.

DASGUPTA, S. D., & WARRIER, S. (1996). In the footsteps of "Arundhati"; Asian American women's experience of domestic violence in the United States. *Violence Against Women, 2*, 238–259.

DOBASH, R. E., & DOBASH, R. (1979). *Violence against wives.* New York: Free Press.

DUTTON, M. A., ORLOFF, L. E., & AGUILAR-HASS, G. (2000). Characteristics of help-seeking behaviors, resources and service needs of battered immigrant Latinas: Legal and policy implications. *Georgetown Journal of Poverty Law and Policy, 7*, 245–305.

EREZ, E., AMMAR, N., ORLOFF, L., PENDLETON, G., & MARIN, L. (2003). *Violence against immigrant women and systemic responses: An exploratory study.* A report submitted to the National Institute of Justice. Washington, DC. Grant #98-WT-VX-0030.

FENTON, Z. E. (1998). Domestic violence in black and white: Racialized gender stereotypes in gender violence. *Columbia Journal of Gender and Law, 8*, 1–38.

FIX, M., PASSEL, J. S., & SUCHER, K. (2003). Trends in naturalization. *Immigrant Families and Workers: Facts and Perspectives*, Brief No. 3. Urban Institute. Retrieved January 20, 2005, from http://urban.org/url.cfm?ID=31084705.

FIX, M. E., & PASSEL, J. S. (2001). U.S. immigration at the beginning of the 21st century. *Testimony before the Subcommittee on Immigration and Claims Hearing on the U.S. Population and Immigration Committee on the Judiciary U.S. House of Representatives.* Retrieved September 2003 from http://www.urban.org/url.cfm?ID=900417.

GARLOW, B. (2000). *Applying the immigration provisions of the Violence Against Women Act.* Washington, DC: American Bar Association, Domestic Violence and Immigration.

GOLDMAN, M. (1999). The Violence Against Women Act: Meeting its goals in protecting battered immigrant women. *Family and Conciliation Courts Review, 37*, 375–392.

GREICO, E. (2002a). Immigrant women. Migration Information Source. Retrieved February 27, 2005, from http://www.migrationinformation.org/Feature/display.cfm?ID=2.

GREICO, E. (2002b). Settlement patterns of foreign born in the United States: Results from the Census. Migration Information Source. Retrieved February 27, 2005, from http://www.migrationinformation.org/Feature/display.cfm?ID=61.

GREICO, E. (2003). Characteristics of the foreign born in the United States: Results from the Census, 2000. Migration Information Source. Retrieved February 27, 2005, from http://www.migrationinformation.org/Feature/display.cfm?ID=71.

HAMPTON, R. L. (1986). Family violence and homicides in the black community: Are they linked? *U.S. Department of Health and Human Services, report of the Secretary's Task Force on Black and Minority Health* (pp. 69–97). Washington, DC: U.S. Government Printing Office.

HULL, G. T., BELL SCOTT, P., & SMITH, B. (Eds.). (1982). *All the women are white, all the blacks are men, but some of us are brave: Black women's studies.* Old Westbury, NY: Feminist Press.

IMMIGRANT WOMEN PROGRAM, LEGAL MOMENTUM. (2005). Evaluation of the HHS funded grant 2005. Preventing family violence in underserved and diverse communities. *The National Network on Behalf of Battered Immigrant Women.*

KULWICKI, A. D., & MILLER, J. (1999). Domestic violence in the Arab American population: Transforming environmental conditions through community education. *Issues in Mental Health Nursing, 20*, 199–215.

LOCKE, T. L. (1997). Trapped in domestic violence: The impact of United States immigration laws on battered immigrant women. *International Law Journal*, 589–624.

MENJIVAR, C., & SALCIDO, O. (2002). Immigrant women and domestic violence: Common experiences in different countries. *Gender and Society, 16*, 898–920.

MORASH, M., BUI, M., & SANTIAGO, A. (2000). Gender specific ideology of domestic violence in Mexican origin families. *International Review of Victimology, 2*, 67–91.

NORTHWEST IMMIGRANT ADVOCATE NEWSLETTER. (2002). Volume 9, p. 4.

NOWAK, M. (2004). Immigration and U.S. population growth: An environmental perspective. *Negative Population Growth, Special Report.* Retrieved February 2005 from http://www.npg.org/specialreports/imm&uspopgrowth.htm.

OLSON, F. (1991). Statutory rape: A feminist critique of rights analysis. In K. Barlett & R. F. Kennedy (Eds.), *Feminist legal theory: Reading in law and gender* (pp. 305–318). Boulder, CO: Westview Press.

ORLOFF, L. (2001). Life saving welfare safety net access for battered immigrant women and children: Accomplishment and next steps. *William and Mary Journal of Women and the Law*, 597–620.

ORLOFF, L. (2003). *Breaking barriers*. Washington, DC: Legal Momentum.

ORLOFF, L. E., CUNDARE, J., & ESTERBROOK, E. (1999). *New dangers for battered immigrants: The untold effects of the demise*. Washington, DC: AYUDA, Inc.

ORLOFF, L. E., DUTTON, M. A., AGUILAR-HASS, G., & AMMAR, N. (2003). Battered immigrant women's willingness to call for help and police response. *UCLA Women's Law Journal, 13*(1), 43–100.

ORLOFF, L. E., & KAGUYUTAN, J. K. (2002). Offering a helping hand: Legal protection for battered immigrant women: A history of legislative responses. *American University Journal of Gender, Social Policy and the Law, 10*, 95–183.

ORLOFF, L. E., & KELLY, N. (1995). A look at the Violence Against Women Act and gender-related asylum. *Violence Against Women, 1*, 380–400.

ORLOFF, L. E., & LITTLE, R. (1999). *Somewhere to turn: Making the domestic violence services accessible to battered immigrant women. A "how to" manual for immigrant battered women advocates and service providers*. Washington, DC: AYUDA, Inc.

PEEKS, A. (2002, Fall). The undocumented Latina battered woman: Impediments to help seeking. *The Journal of Psychotherapy Integration*, 1–17.

PENDLETON, G., & BLOCK, A. (2001). Applications for immigration status under the Violence Against Women Act. In *Immigration and Nationality Handbook* (Vol. 1, 2001–2002 ed.). American Immigration Lawyers Association.

PENDLETON, G., & MAHER, H. (2000). *Domestic violence and immigration issues in the criminal justice system*. Washington, DC: American Bar Association, Commission on Domestic Violence.

PERILLA, J. I. (1999). Domestic violence as a human rights issue: The case of immigrant Latinos. *Hispanic Journal of Behavioral Sciences, 21*, 107–133.

PHOENIX, I. (1987) Theories of gender and black families. In G. Weiner & M. Arnot (Eds.), *Gender under scrutiny* (pp. 50–61). London: Hutchinson.

RAJ, A., & SILVERMAN, J. (2002). Violence against immigrant women: The roles of culture, context and legal immigrant status on intimate partner violence. *Violence Against Women, 8*, 367–394.

RODRIGUEZ, R. (1995). Barriers to domestic violence relief and full faith and credit for immigrant and migrant battered women. *Clinical Supplement of the Migrant Clinicians Network, 2*.

RODRIGUEZ, R. (1999). The power of the collective: Battered migrant farmworker women creating safe spaces. *Health Care for Women International, 20*, 417–426.

RICHIE, B. (1985, March/April). Battered black women a challenge for the black community. *Black Scholar, 16*, 40–44.

ROSALDO, M. Z. (1980). The use and abuse of anthropology: Reflections on feminism and cross-cultural understanding. *Signs, 5*, 389–417.

SAENZ, R. (2004). *Latinos and the changing face of America at the turn of the century*. New York: Russell Sage Foundation, Population Reference Bureau.

SCHAKOWSKY, J. (2003). Schakowsky delivers keynote address to National Network to End Violence Against Immigrant Women. *Press Release*, 1–6.

SHETTY, S., & KAGUYUTAN, J. (2002). Immigrant victims of domestic violence: Cultural challenges and available legal protections. *National Resource Center on Domestic Violence*, 1–11.

SKURNIK, J. (1983). Battering: An issue for women of color. *Off Our Backs, 13*, 8.

SRINIVASAN, S., & IVEY, S. L. (Eds.). (1999). Domestic violence. In S. Kramer, S., Ivey, & Y. W. Ying, *Immigrant woman's health: Problems and solutions* (pp. 179–193). San Francisco: Jossey-Bass.

Stone, L. (1977). *The family, sex and marriage in England.* New York: Van Nostrand Reinhold.

Vellos, D. (1997). Immigrant Latina domestic workers and sexual harassment. *American University Journal of Gender and the Law, 407,* 414–418.

Warrier, S. (2000). *(Un)heard voices: Domestic violence in the Asian American community.* San Francisco: Family Violence Prevention Fund.

Wolchock, C. (1997). Demands and anxiety: The effects of the new immigration law. *A.B.A. Human Rights,* 12.

20

Sexual Harassment and the Law

Violence against Women

Roslyn Muraskin

Sexual harassment remains one of the most pervasive features of our legal system. "Sexual harassment law addresses sexual subordination as sex discrimination" (MacKinnon, 2001, p. 908). Sexual harassment is "a problem with a long past but a short history" (p. 908). There are arguments that females have more equality than ever before, and in some cases this may be true, but unfortunately, females are being victimized in more areas than ever before. As women gain more equality, they become harassed by employers in a manner that is akin to rape and cases of domestic violence. A strategy needs to be developed that provides law enforcement personnel with a better understanding of the types of crimes committed against women.

Historically, women have been discriminated against by the law, often by policies designed to protect them. During recent decades, women have found themselves in courts of law arguing for equality. The history of women's struggles has taught us that litigation becomes merely a catalyst for change. It does not guarantee results.

Sexual harassment's problem "is probably as old as sex equality. Its known past encompasses feudalism, which entitled lords to the first night of sex with vassals' new wives; American slavery, under which enslaved women of African origin or descent were routinely sexually used by white masters" (MacKinnon, 2001, p. 208).

In 1913, Rebecca West stated: "I myself have never been able to find out precisely what feminism is. I only know that people call me a feminist whenever I express sentiments that differentiate me from a doormat." Women's basic rights are inextricably linked to our treatment by and with their participation in today's political world. Due to the fact that the lives of women are reflections of what they do, what they say, and how they treat each other, women as participating members of the human race are ultimately responsible for human affairs.

Throughout this work, we note that there is no way to allow both sexes to enjoy automatically equal protection of the law unless we are committed to the elimination of all gender discrimination. The criminal justice system has slowly come to grips with the needed understanding of women and justice. Today, courts need time for discovery of evidence and the opportunity to hear expert testimony in all cases of sexual violence.

According to the Equal Employment Opportunity Commission:

> Harassment on the basis of sex is a violation of [Title VI]. Unwelcome sexual advances, request for sexual behaviors, and other verbal or physical conduct of a sexual nature constitute sexual harassment when (1) submission to such conduct is made either explicitly or implicitly a term or a condition of an individual's employment, (2) submission to or rejection of such conduct by an individual is used as the basis for employment decisions affecting such individual, or (3) such conduct has the purpose or effect of unreasonably interfering with an individual's work performance or creating an intimidating, hostile, or offensive working environment. [29 C.F.R. § 1604.11(a) (1998)]

Crimes such as rape, domestic violence, and sexual harassment are all part of the continuum of violence against women. Rape is not a crime of sex; it is a crime of power. It is "an act of violence, an assault like any other, not an expression of socially organized sexuality" (MacKinnon, 1979, p. 218). The fact that rape is acted out in sex does not mean that it is an act of male sexuality. Rape is an act of violence. The act of sexual harassment has drawn parallels to the crime of rape. If sex or a sexual advance is imposed on a woman who is in no position to refuse, why is that act any different from the act of rape? Sexual harassment may be a lesser crime in the minds of many, including the courts, but nevertheless, it is an act of violence against women. Sexual harassment is gender discrimination, and laws are needed to remedy such disparities. There is a current of public discussion about the cases of women accused and sometimes convicted of assaulting and killing partners who have battered them. The actual volume of cases is small, but the attention given these cases illuminates the larger problem for which they have come to stand: the common disparity of power between men and women in familial relationships.

The laws of sexual harassment in the United States are deemed an exception. "Unlike the criminal law of rape, sexual harassment grew directly out of women's experiences of sexual violation, rather than from ruling men's notions of that experience. It sees sexual abuse as sex-based abuse: victims are understood to be violated as members of their gender group" (MacKinnon, 1979, p. 913). Further, if a crime of sex is one of power, then taken together, rape, domestic violence, and sexual harassment eroticize women's subordination. This continues the powerlessness in the criminal law of women as a gender (MacKinnon, 1979, p. 221).

From a historical point of view, there existed under the English common law the rule of thumb, which allowed a husband to beat his wife with a stick no wider than his thumb. The husband's prerogative was incorporated into the laws of the United States. The sad fact is that several states had laws on the book that essentially allowed a man to beat his wife with no interference from the courts. Blackstone referred to this action as the power of correction. For too many decades women have been victims of sexual assaults. Each act of "sexual assault is recognized as one of the most traumatic and debilitating crimes for adults" (Roberts, 1993, p. 362). The victimization of women has been more prevalent and problematic for the criminal justice system.

As pointed out by Susan Faludi (1991): "Women's advances and retreats are generally described in military terms: battles won, battles lost, points and territory gained and surrendered. In times when feminism is at a low ebb, women assume the reactive role—privately and most often covertly struggling to assert themselves against the dominant cultural tide. But when feminism becomes the tide, the opposition doesn't simply go along with the reversal, it digs in its heels, brandishes its fists, builds walls and dams."

In past decades we have seen sexual assault reform legislation, resulting "in several long-overdue improvements in the criminal justice processing of sexual assault cases for example, passage of rape shield laws, confidentiality laws to protect communications between the victims and their counselors, and laws designed to preserve medical evidence" (Roberts, 1993, p. 370). In addition, we have seen the establishment of victim assistance programs.

SEXUAL HARASSMENT

The female represents half of the U.S. population. She is deserving of the same rights and opportunities as are afforded males. There exists the rhetoric of gender equality, but it has yet to match the reality of women's experiences. Women who find themselves in the position of being sexually harassed indicate the forms that it takes:

> Wolf whistles, leering, sexual innuendo, comments about women's bodies, tales of sexual exploits, graphic descriptions of pornography, pressure for dates, hooting, sucking, lip-smacking, and animal noises, sexually explicit gestures, unwelcome touching and hugging, excluding women from meetings, sabotaging women's work, sexist and insulting graffiti, demanding "Hey, baby, give me a smile," sexist jokes and cartoons, hostile put-downs of women, exaggerated, mocking "courtesy," public humiliation, obscene phone calls, displaying pornography in the workplace, insisting that workers wear revealing clothing, inappropriate gifts (for example lingerie), inappropriate invitations (for example to go to a hot tub or nude beach), discussion of one's partner's sexual inadequacies, lewd and threatening letters, "accidentally" brushing sexual parts of the body, pressing or rubbing up against the victim, leaning over or otherwise invading a victim's space, sexual sneak attacks (such as grabbing breasts or buttocks on the run), indecent exposure, soliciting sexual services, demanding sexual services, stalking a victim, [and] sexual assault. (MacKinnon, 1979, p. 915)

Why are females forced to tolerate such action that is unwanted, in order to survive economically? The case of Anita Faye Hill, in the hearings to confirm Judge Clarence Thomas to serve as an associate justice of the U.S. Supreme Court in 1991, brought to light the terms of sexual harassment, words that gained new meaning for women. Her testimony with regard to Justice Thomas's treatment of her as sexual mistreatment while employed as his assistant helped to bring forth charges of sexual harassment from thousands of women who now understood the meaning of such actions.

Although we do not have a federal equal rights amendment, there are states that recognize its potential value. As an example, the use of male terms to indicate both sexes has been under examination for some time. There are those who choose to use gender-neutral terms. But gender discrimination is masked when gender-neutral terms are used. Words are meant to have definitive meaning. "Words are workhorses of law" (Thomas, 1991, p. 1160). Sexual harassment has become a major barrier to women's professional lives and personal development and a traumatic force that disrupts and damages their personal lives. For ethnic-minority women who have been sexually harassed, economic vulnerability is paramount. Women feel powerless, not in control, afraid, and not flattered by sexual harassment. We need to understand that so much of the harassment that occurs is not sexual. The first case before the Supreme Court was that of *Meritor Savings Bank, FSB v. Vinson*, a 1986 case, in which it was decided that gender harassment is sexual discrimination and illegal under Title VII of the Civil Rights Act of 1964. *Meritor* (1986) recognized two types of sexual harassment: quid pro quo and hostile environment. "When sex is exchanged, or sought to be exchanged, for a workplace or educational benefit, called quid pro quo [emphasis mine] . . . and when conditions of work are damagingly sexualized or otherwise harmful, called hostile environment" (*Barnes v. Costle*, 1977, p. 909).

Throughout this country, committees have been established to combat the charges of sexual harassment. It was almost as if the Thomas–Hill hearings brought people "out of the closet." Cases that followed include *Wagenseller v. Scottsdale Memorial Hospital* (1985) in Arizona, where the Arizona Supreme Court overruled earlier law and recognized a public policy exception to discharge at will in the case of an emergency room nurse who allegedly was terminated because she refused to "moon" on a rafting trip.

A worker who continually harasses female coworkers and is discharged does not have a right to reinstatement for failure of the employer to follow the notice provisions of the contract (see *Newsday, Inc. v. Long Island Typographical Union*, 1991). In the case of *Ellison v. Brady* (1991), the trial court had dismissed as trivial "love" letters that the plaintiff had received from a coworker along with persistent requests for dates. The Ninth Circuit disagreed, however, stating that the perspectives of men and women differ. Women, as indicated by the courts, have a strong reason to be concerned about sexual behavior, as they are potential victims of rape and sexual assault.

A court in Florida ruled in the case of *Robinson v. Jacksonville Shipyards, Inc.* (1991) that a display of nude women can lead to the creation of a hostile environment and is therefore deemed an act of discrimination. In the case of *Continental Can Co., Inc., v. Minnesota* (1980), the Minnesota Supreme Court upheld an action to stop harassment by fellow employees. In yet another case, *E.E.O.C. v. Sage Realty Corp.* (1981), the court held that an employer may impose reasonable dress codes for its employees, but the employer cannot require its employees to wear "revealing and sexually provocative uniforms" that would subject the employee to a form of sexual harassment. This constitutes gender discrimination.

The case of *Nichols v. Frank* (1994) involved Teri Nichols, who was deaf and mute. The night-shift supervisor (Francisco) with whom she worked had authority to grant employees leave as well as overtime pay. He was the only supervisor available able to communicate in sign language. At one point after asking Nichols to do some copying for him, "Francisco started kissing Nichols and indicated that he wanted her to perform oral sex on him. She refused his advances, but ultimately complied because she was afraid she would lose her job if she refused. According to Nichols, 'I remember that when this first happened I was just in shock. I was nervous. I was upset. I wasn't happy doing it, and I was hoping it would never happen again. And I just kept that all to myself. But then there was repeats and repeats and repeats, and I was more upset and . . . I didn't want to do it again and again for him, and I didn't know how to say, 'Stop, just stop.'" The court concluded that "a supervisor's intertwining of a request for the performance of sexual favors with a discussion of actual or potential job benefits or detriments in a single conversation constitutes quid pro quo sexual harassment."

In the cases of *Burlington Industries v. Ellerth* (1998) and *Faragher v. Boca Raton* (1998), the court decided a chaotic body of law in the area of sexual harassment, making it easier for women whose bosses harass them to sue them under Title VII of the 1964 Civil Rights Act. Patricia Ireland, former president of the National Organization for Women (NOW), stated that "the boss who paws, propositions and warns of retaliation takes away a women's dignity . . . even if he doesn't take away her job" (1998).

In the *Burlington* case the claim was that the female endured a steady stream of sexual harassment from her supervisor's boss, "including pats on the buttocks, offensive sexual remarks and the threat that he could make her work life 'very hard or very easy.'" Despite the employer's argument that she suffered no tangible job loss, the U.S. Supreme Court decided that her case could go forward because it was the employer's burden to prove that reasonable steps had been taken by the company and that the complainant had failed to follow proper reporting procedures.

While in *Faragher*, the complainant, Beth Faragher, claimed that while working at a remote lifeguard station she was harassed by male supervisors, "who repeatedly touched her, called her and other women 'bitches and sluts,' made comments about her breasts and threatened 'date me or clean toilets for a year.'" It was the city's claim that she was not entitled to damages, as she failed to go over her supervisors' heads and report the harassment. The U.S. Supreme Court reinstated her damages award, deciding that the city had not taken reasonable steps to prevent and correct the harassment. In the words of Patricia Ireland, "women's rights need to be written into the Constitution. . . . [w]ithout it . . . women do not have a constitutional right to bodily integrity."

Addressing violence against women requires a national commitment. A summary of the data amassed about gender violence was included in the dissenting opinion of the Supreme Court's David Souter in *United States v. Morrison* (2000, pp. 1761–1763):

> Three out of four American women will be victims of violent crimes sometime during their lives.
>
> Violence is the leading cause of injuries to women ages 15–44.
>
> As many as 50% of homeless women and children are fleeing domestic violence.
>
> Since 1974, the assault rate against women has outstripped the rate for men by at least twice for some age groups, and far more for others.
>
> Battering is the largest cause of injury to women in the United States.
>
> An estimated 4 million women in the United States seek medical assistance each year for injuries sustained from their husbands or other partners.
>
> Between 2000 and 4000 women die every year from domestic abuse.
>
> Arrest rates may be as low as 1 for every 100 domestic assaults.
>
> Partial estimates show that violent crime against women costs this country at least $3 billion a year.
>
> Estimates suggest that we spend $5 to $10 billion per year on health care, criminal justice, and other social costs of domestic violence.

The incidence of rape rose four times as fast as the total national crime rate over the past 10 years.

According to one study, close to one-half million females now in high school will be raped before they graduate.

One hundred twenty-five thousand college women can expect to be raped before they graduate.

Three-fourths of women never go to the movies alone after dark because of the fear of rape, and nearly 50% do not use public transit alone after dark for the same reasons.

Forty-one percent of judges surveyed a Colorado study believed that juries give sexual assault victims less credibility than other victims of crime.

Less than 1% of rape victims have collected damages.

An individual who commits rape has only 4 chances in a 100 of being arrested, prosecuted and found guilty of any offense.

Almost one-fourth of convicted rapists never go to prison and another one-fourth received sentences in local jails, where the average sentence is 11 months.

Almost 50% of rape victims lose their jobs or are forced to quit because of the crime's severity.

The attorneys general from 38 states urged Congress to enact a civil rights remedy, permitting rape victims to sue their attackers because "the current system of dealing with violence is inadequate." (Muraskin & O'Connor, 2002, p. 432)

Due to these findings, Congress found it necessary to pass the Violence Against Women Act (VAWA) in 1994. This act provided for "substantial sums of money to States for education, rape crisis hotlines, training criminal justice personnel, victim services and special units in police and prosecutors' offices to deal with crimes against women. The act specifically provided incentives for the enforcement of statutory rape laws, the payment of the cost of testing for sexually transmitted diseases for victims of crime, and studies of campus sexual assaults, and the battered women's syndrome" (Muraskin & O'Connor, 2002, p. 434).

In a Supreme Court case, *Pennsylvania State Police v. Nancy Drew Suders*, argued on March 31, 2004, and decided on June 14, 2004, a female who was a former employee of the state police sued, alleging that she was sexually harassed by her supervisers resulting in constructive discharge, in violation of Title VII. The facts of the case are as follows:

"In March 1998, the Pennsylvania State Police (PSP) hired plaintiff-respondent Suders to work as a police communications operator for the McConnellsburg barracks, where her male supervisors subjected her to a continuous barrage of sexual harassment" (*Pennsylvania*, p. 2343). During June 1998 Suders informed the Equal Employment Opportunity officer of her need for help, but nothing was done. After a few months of constant harassment and nothing happening, she complained again to the officer, was told to file a complaint, but not told how to file. Two days later, Suders' supervisors arrested her for theft of her own computer-skills exam papers. Suders had removed the papers after concluding that the supervisors had falsely reported that she had repeatedly failed, when in fact, the exams were never forwarded for grading" (p. 2343). She resigned her post at this point. "The constructive discharge here at issue stems from, and can be regarded as an aggravated case of, sexual harassment or hostile work environment." For such an atmosphere to exist there must be offending behavior that is "sufficiently severe or pervasive to alter the conditons of the victim's employment and create an abusive work environment" (p. 2399) and taken from the case of *Meritor* previously discussed. Justice Ginsburg delivered the majority opinion for the court. They agreed with the Third Circuit that "the case, in its current posture, presents genuine issues of material fact concerning Suders' hostile work environment and constructive discharge claims. We hold, however, that the Court of Appeals erred in declaring the affirmative defense described in *Ellerth* and *Faragher* never available in the constructive discharge form. [W]e vacate the Third Circuit's judgment and remand the case for further proceedings consistent with this opinion" (p. 2342).

Justice Thomas, in writing his dissent,[1] stated that "the Court has now adopted a definition of constructive discharge, however, that does not in the least resemble actual discharge. The Court holds that to establish constructive discharge a plaintiff must show that the abusive working environment became so intolerable that [the employee's] resignation qualified as a fitting rule" (p. 2342). He continued by stating that "[b]ecause respondent has not produced sufficient evidence of an adverse employment action taken because of her sex, nor has she proffered any evidence that petitioner knew or should have known of the alleged harassment, I would reverse the judgment of the Court of Appeals" (p. 2359).

And in the case of *Jackson v. Birmingham Board of Education*, argued on November 30, 2004, and decided on March 29, 2005, here a "former coach of [a] girls' high school basketball team sued the board of education, alleging that it retaliated against him in violaton of Title IX" (p. 1497).

The Supreme Court with Justice O'Connor held that:

1. retaliation against a person because that person has complained of sex discrimination is a form of intentional sex discrimination encompassed by Title IX's private cause of action;

2. coach stated claim of discrimination on the basis of sex that was actionable under Title IX;

3. coach could assert retaliation claim even though he was not victim of discrimination that was subject of his original complaints; and

4. Board of Education had sufficient notice that it could be subjected to private suits for intentional sex discrimination in form of retaliation.

The case was reversed.

Justice Thomas filed a dissention opinion along with Chief Justice Rehnquist and Justices Scalia and Kennedy. "The Court holds that the private right of action under Title IX of the Education Amendments of 1972. . . . Extends to claims of retaliation. Its holding is contrary to the plain terms of Title IX, because retaliatory conduct is not discrimination on the basis of sex" (*Jackson*, p. 1497).

Legal scholars such as Catherine MacKinnon, a law professor at the University of Michigan Law School and visiting professor at the University of Chicago Law School, and activists such as Susan Brownmiller are credited with initiating a view of sexual harassment that has changed radically the way that sexual harassment complaints are treated under the legal system. Shifting the focus of sexual harassment from the belief that males' sexual pursuit of a woman in the workplace or the classroom is essentially biological and that sexual harassment is therefore a "normal" consequence of attraction between the sexes, MacKinnon, Brownmiller, and others advocate a "dominance" approach. Sexual harassment is gender discrimination. It occurs in the workplace wherever women are situated in an attempt to keep them in their place (Corgin & Bennett-Haigne, 1998).

MacKinnon has asked the question as to whether "sexual harassment cases conceive gender horizontally in terms of sameness and difference, or vertically as hierarchy" (2001, p. 914). "One way women have been stigmatized as inferior is through the identification of a sometimes erroneous, usually exaggerated, always exclusive set of feminine needs. Women's sexuality has been a prime example. It has been hard to avoid branding women as inferior, long enough to balance a grasp of her dignity with an analysis of her enforced inferiority, in order to address the specificity of her situation" (MacKinnon, 1979, p. 144).

LITIGATION

Men who harass are not pathological but rather, people who exhibit behaviors that have been characteristic of the masculine gender role. The first litigation of sexual harassment claims did not occur until the mid-1970s. Title VII of the Civil Rights Act prohibiting sex discrimination in the workplace was followed eight years later by Title IX of the 1972 Higher Education Amendment, prohibiting gender discrimination in educational institutions receiving federal assistance. But in much of the early adjudication of gender discrimination, the phenomenon of sexual harassment was typically seen "as isolated and idiosyncratic, or as natural and universal and in either case, as inappropriate for legal intervention." It was in 1980 that the Equal Employment Opportunity Commission, in its guidelines on discrimination, explicitly defined sexual harassment under Title VII as a form of unlawful, gender-based discrimination.

As the law has been interpreted, prohibition against sexual harassment in the workplace technically covers any remark or behavior that is sufficiently severe and pervasive that not only the victim's but also a "reasonable person's" psychological well-being would be affected. A 1991 landmark ruling by the Court of Appeals for the Ninth Circuit in California held that the "appropriate perspective for judging a hostile environment claim [was] that of the 'reasonable woman' and recognized that a woman's perspective may differ substantially from a man's." While the 1991 Ninth Circuit Court ruling acknowledged that men and women may interpret the same behavior differently, in application this legal understanding was overshadowed by a grave misunderstanding of the nature of sexual harassment as experienced by its victims. The people doing the judging were in no position to understand the position of those being judged. The powerful were making judgments against the powerless.

But in the case of *Harris v. Forklift Systems, Inc.* (1993) the U.S. Supreme Court specified and refined its standards for hostile environment cases. "The U.S. Supreme Court decided in Harris that an environment of sexual harassment, to be actionable, had to be objectively hostile—one a 'reasonable person,' under all the circumstances, would find hostile or abusive—as well as hostile to the plaintiff herself. It also held that a hostile environment did not need to seriously affect a worker's psychological well-being to be discriminatory" (MacKinnon, 2001, p. 955).

Rape, Sexual Harassment, and the Criminal Justice System

Like the crime of rape, sexual harassment is not an issue of lust; it is an issue of power. Sexual harassment does not fall within the range of personal or private relationships. It happens when a person with power abuses that power to intimidate, coerce, or humiliate someone because of gender. It is a breach of trust. In voluntary sexual relationships, freedom of choice is exercised in deciding whether to establish a close, intimate relationship. This freedom of choice is absent in sexual harassment (Paludi, 1992). Sexual harassment may be understood as an extreme acting out of qualities that are regarded as supermasculine: aggression, power dominance, and force. Men who harass are not pathological but rather, people who exhibit behaviors characteristic of the masculine gender role in U.S. culture. Most sexual harassment starts at the subtle end of the continuum and escalates over time. Each year, 1 percent of women in the U.S. labor force are sexually assaulted on the job. Yet cultural mythologies consistently blame the victim for sexual abuse and act to keep women in their place. Scholars have identified several similarities in attitudes toward rape and sexual harassment, especially revealing cultural myths that blame the victim:

1. Women ask for it.

    Rape: Victims seduce their rapists.

    Sexual harassment: Women precipitate harassment by the way they dress and talk.

2. Women say no but mean yes.

    Rape: Women secretly need and want to be forced into sex. They don't know what they want.

    Sexual harassment: Women like the attention.

3. Women lie.

    Rape: In most charges of rape, the woman is lying.

    Sexual harassment: Women lie about sexual harassment to get men they dislike into trouble.

Women who speak about being victims of sexual harassment use words such as *humiliating, intimidating, frightening, financially damaging, embarrassing, nervewracking, awful,* and *frustrating.* They are not words that are used to describe a situation that one enjoys.

Historically, the rape of a woman was considered to be an infringement of the property rights of men. Sexual harassment needs to be viewed in the same light. The message is that further changes are needed. We can no longer blame the messenger. We need to understand the message. There is no question that what is referred to as "women's hidden occupational hazard," sexual harassment, is gender victimization. The fact that sexual harassment exists demonstrates that it must be understood as part of the continuum of violence against women. In a typical sexual harassment case, the female accuser becomes the accused and the victim is twice victimized. This holds true in cases of rape and domestic violence as well as in cases of harassment. Underlying the dynamics of the situation is the profound distrust of a woman's word and a serious power differential between the accused and the accuser. As indicated, sexual harassment is the most recent form of victimization of the woman to be redefined as a social rather than a personal problem, following rape and wife abuse.

Sexual harassment continues to be a major barrier to women's professional and personal development and a traumatic force that disrupts and damages their personal lives. For ethnic-minority women who have been sexually harassed, economic vulnerability is paramount. Women feel powerless, not in control, afraid. There is nothing flattering about sexual harassment. Their emotional and physical well-being resembles that of victims of other sexual abuses (i.e., rape, incest, and battering). It must be stopped.

Women's issues infuse every aspect of social and political thought. It was Gloria Steinem who noted that cultural myths die hard, especially if they are used to empower one part of the population. The struggle of women continues under the law. There is no way to allow both sexes automatically to enjoy the equal protection of the laws unless we are committed to the elimination of all gender discrimination. Sexual harassment is gender discrimination. The criminal justice system over these many years has slowly come to grips with the need to understand women in the context of justice and fairness.

Women continue to represent half the population. They are owed the same rights and opportunities as are afforded to men. For justice to be gained, the fight for freedom and equality must continue. Prevention is the best tool that the criminal justice system has to offer as long as it takes the action mandated by legislators. Dominance takes several forms. As stated so succinctly by Catherine MacKinnon in 1979: "Sexual harassment (and rape) has everything to do with sexuality. Gender is a power division and sexuality is one sphere of its expression" (pp. 220–221). There is no logic to inequality.

NOTE

1. The appeals court ruled that a constructive discharge, if proved, constitutes a tangible employment action that renders an employer strictly liable and precludes recourse to the *Ellerth/Faragher* affirmative defense.
   Note: Both *Ellerth* and *Faragher* decided on the same day that an employer is strictly liable for supervisor harassment that culminates in a tangible employment action, such as discharge, demotion, or undesirable reassignment.

REFERENCES

CORGIN, B., & BENNETT-HAIGNE, G. (1998, August 12). Sexual harassment: Open season on working women. Retrieved from: http://www.now.org/nnt/03-97/sexual.html.

FALUDI, S. (1991). *Backlash: The undeclared war against American women*. New York: Crown.

IRELAND, P. (1998). Sexual harassment: Open season on working women. *NOW Times*.

MACKINNON, C. (1979). *Sexual harassment of working women*. New Haven, CT: Yale University Press.

MACKINNON, C. (2001). *Sex equality*. New York: Foundation Press.

MURASKIN, R., & O'CONNOR, M. (2002). Women and the law: An agenda for change in the twenty-first century. In R. Muraskin & A. Roberts (Eds.), *Visions for change: Crime and justice in the twenty-first century* (3rd ed.). Upper Saddle River, NJ: Prentice Hall.

PALUDI, M. A. (1992). Working nine to five: Women, men, sex and power. In R. Muraskin (Ed.), *Women's agenda: Meeting the challenge to change*. New York: Long Island Women's Institute, College of Management, C. W. Post Campus of Long Island University.

ROBERTS, A. (1993). Women: Victims of sexual assault and violence. In R. Muraskin & T. R. Alleman (Eds.), *It's a crime: Women and justice*. Upper Saddle River, NJ: Prentice Hall.

THOMAS, C. S. (1991). *Sex discrimination*. St. Paul, MN: West.

CASES

Barnes v. Costle, 561 F.2d 983 (D.C. Cir. 1977).

Burlington Industries v. Ellerth, 123 F.3d 490 (1998).

Continental Can Co., Inc. v. Minnesota, 297 N.W.2d 241 (Minn. 1980), 242.

E.E.O.C. v. Sage Realty Corp., 507 F. Supp. 599 (D.C. N.Y. 1981), 243.

Ellison v. Brady, 924 F.2d 872 (9th Cir. 1991), 119.

Faragher v. Boca Raton, 111 F.3d 1530 (1998).

Harris v. Forklift Systems, Inc., 510 U.S. 17 (1993).

Jackson v. Birmingham Board of Education, 125 S. Ct. 1497 (2005).

Meritor Savings Bank, FSB v. Vinson, 477 U.S. 57, 106 S. Ct. 2399, 91 L. Ed. 2d 49 (1986), 239.

Newsday, Inc. v. Long Island Typographical Union No. 915, U.S. 111, S. Ct. 1314, 113 L. Ed. 2d 247 (1991), 195, 241.

Nichols v. Frank, 42 F.3d 503 (9th Cir. 1994).

Pennsylvania State Police v. Nancy Drew Suders, 124 St. Ct. 2342 (2004).

Robinson v. Jacksonville Shipyards, Inc., 760 F. Supp. 1486 (M.D. Fla. 1991), 241.

United States v. Morrison, 120 S. Ct. 1740 (2000).

Wagenseller v. Scottsdale Memorial Hospital, 147 Ariz. 370, 710 P.2d 1025 (Ariz. 1985).

SECTION IV

Women and Health Problems

21

Legal and Social Welfare Response to Substance Abuse during Pregnancy

Recent Developments

Inger Sagatun-Edwards

Maternal drug use during pregnancy raises complex legal and ethical questions, pitting the rights of the pregnant woman against the rights of the fetus. Important constitutional issues are involved in this debate. This chapter discusses the background and history of the legal response to these issues, including (1) criminalization or prosecution of women for substance abuse during pregnancy; (2) child welfare laws and juvenile court involvement for the purpose of protecting the child (or fetus); (3) civil commitment of pregnant substance-abusing women; and (4) social services and medical treatment interventions. Often two or more of these approaches may be combined. The most relevant recent Supreme Court and appellate court cases and state legislation are included in this discussion. This chapter concludes that criminal prosecution of fetal abuse does not protect the well-being of the fetus enough to warrant the violation of important constitutional rights for the mother, and that these issues should best be handled in the dependency court and social welfare/medical system.

This chapter discusses the main legal and social welfare approaches to the issues related to drug use in pregnancy: (1) prosecution of pregnant women who use drugs based on the application of various criminal laws; (2) juvenile dependency court involvement for the protection of the fetus or child after birth; (3) civil commitment of pregnant women to drug treatment facilities to protect the fetus; and (4) pure medical and social welfare treatment approaches. First, I will briefly summarize the current state of knowledge about the effects of prenatal drug use on the child, and the issue of the legal status of fetal rights.

EFFECTS OF MATERNAL SUBSTANCE ABUSE DURING PREGNANCY

Despite recent studies that have failed to show catastrophic effects of prenatal cocaine exposure, popular attitudes and public policies still reflect the belief that cocaine is a unique dangerous teratogen. Many findings once thought to be specific to in utero cocaine exposure have now been found to largely correlate with other factors, including prenatal exposure to tobacco, marijuana, or alcohol, and the quality of the child's environment.

During the late 1980s crack cocaine emerged as the most frightening enemy in the "war on drugs," with a media frenzy over the alleged crack epidemic (Humphries, 1998). Early medical studies concluded that crack cocaine had very negative effects on the fetus (Chasnoff, Burns, Burns, & Schnoll, 1986; Howard, Kropenske, & Tyler, 1986; Petitti & Coleman, 1990; Weston, Ivens, Zuckerman, Jones, & Lopez, 1989).

However, both early estimates of the widespread nature of maternal drug use during pregnancy and the conclusion that poor fetal outcomes are caused solely by illegal drugs later came under attack. The extent to which the children's medical problems are actually due to illegal drugs is very difficult to determine. Many drug users are polydrug abusers, mixing illegal drugs with legal drugs such as cigarettes and alcohol, all known contributors to poor fetal outcomes (Montgomery & Ekborn, 2002; Wang, Zuckerman et al., 2002). Often the use of illegal drugs, alcohol, and tobacco are compounded by family poverty, poor nutritional status and general health, and little or no prenatal care (Frank, Augustyn, Knight, Pell, & Zuckerman, 2001). According to Ira Chasnoff, an early researcher in this area, the home environment is *the* critical determinant of the child's ultimate outcome (Chasnoff, 2002). In an editorial for a specialized volume in the *Journal of the American Medical Association*, Zuckerman, Frank, and Mayes (2002) concluded that while there are small, but identifiable effects of cocaine/crack exposure on certain newborn outcomes, there is less consistent evidence of negative long-term effects up to the age of six years. Only 1 out of 10 studies included in the special volume found a negative association between toddlers' developmental test scores and prenatal exposure to cocaine (Singer, Arendt, & Minnes, 2002). A more recent follow-up study by Singer et al. (2004) through four years of age found that prenatal cocaine exposure was associated with an increased risk for specific cognitive impairments and lower incidents of IQ above the normative mean at four years, but not with lower full-scale IQ scores (Singer et al., 2004). Another large sample observed longitudinally found that infant prenatal exposure to cocaine and to opiates was not associated with mental, motor, or behavioral deficits after controlling for birth weight and environmental risks (Messinger et al., 2004).

Zuckerman and colleagues (2002) caution that we, as a society, have tended to focus on the negative effects of prenatal exposure to cocaine or other illegal drugs, rather than the adverse effects of prenatal tobacco and alcohol exposure. Often the tendency to ignore the effects of other risk factors is coupled with a moral bias against poor (and minority) women who use illegal drugs during pregnancy (Murphy & Rosenbaum, 1999).

TRADITIONAL FETAL RIGHTS

Whether a fetus has any legal rights is a controversial issue. Traditionally, laws have sought to protect children from harm after their birth. The nonrecognition of the fetus as a legal entity is embodied in the "born-alive rule," which states that the fetus has to be born alive as a precondition to legal personhood. Increasingly, however, the born-alive rule in child abuse and child neglect laws has come under attack. In *Commonwealth v. Cass* (1984), the court held that a viable fetus was a person within the protection of the state's vehicular homicide statute. Many states have recently enacted fetal homicide laws, which create a separate crime for actions taken against a woman that result in the death of—or harm to—her fetus, These laws treat the fetus as an individual apart from the woman. Fifteen states now have fetal homicide laws where fetuses are victims at any stage of development, and 12 states have fetal homicide laws where fetuses are victims at only specific stages in the development (Katz, 2004).

The most recent case involving fetal homicide laws is that of Laci Peterson. Scott Peterson was convicted in November 2004 of first-degree murder for killing his wife, and second-degree murder for killing his unborn child. At the federal level, on April 1, 2004, President Bush signed into law the Unborn Victims of Violence Act (2004). This law, also known as *Laci and Conner's Law* (after the Laci Peterson case), amends Title 18 of the United States Code by defining a violent attack on a pregnant woman as two distinct crimes: one against the woman herself, and the other against her newborn child. The law applies only to offenses over which the U.S. government has jurisdiction and exempts abortion as a context in which the fetus is declared a "person."

Ironically, *Roe v. Wade* (1973) has been used to argue in favor of the fetal rights movement. In *Roe v. Wade* the U.S. Supreme Court held that after the first trimester of pregnancy, the interests of potential life become important, and that after viability, the state has a legitimate and important interest in the unborn. Thus, both proponents and opponents of the criminalization of fetal abuse can draw on different parts of *Roe v. Wade* to support their cause. *Webster v. Reproductive Health Services* (1989) subsequently rejected the rigid trimester scheme for establishing viability, thus giving ammunition to those that argue that states may constitutionally prosecute pregnant women who abuse substances known to harm fetuses.

In civil law, fetal rights have already been well established. A majority of states consider fetuses that have died in utero to be a person under wrongful death statutes, and therefore parents may sue people who harmed the fetus in utero, causing the death (McNulty, 1987–1988). Courts have also long recognized "wrongful life" actions. However, most of these cases involve harm caused by a third person, not the mother, and are therefore not directly applicable to the issue of maternal substance abuse during pregnancy. De Ville and Kopelman (1999) have pointed out that even the use of terminology suggests different approaches to this issue, thus the terms "unborn child" and "expectant mother" elicit different feelings and content than the terms "fetus" and "pregnant woman." The choice of terms reflects an underlying ideology that may affect how a legal policy is implemented and received.

THE LEGAL RESPONSE TO SUBSTANCE ABUSE DURING PREGNANCY

Even though legislators have debated the question of how to deal with the problem of women's substance abuse during pregnancy, as of now no state has yet specifically criminalized drug use during pregnancy "(State Policies in Brief," 2005). Instead, prosecutors have attempted to rely on a host of criminal laws already on the books to attack prenatal substance abuse. Several states have expanded their civil child neglect and abuse statutes for juvenile court to include prenatal substance abuse, so that prenatal drug exposure can provide grounds for termination of parental rights because of child abuse and neglect. Additionally, some states have authorized protective custody and civil commitment orders while the woman is still pregnant for the purpose of protecting the fetus (Coffey, 1997; "State Policies in Brief," 2005). A number of states require health care professionals to report or test for prenatal drug exposure, while other states have placed a priority on making drug treatment more readily available to pregnant women without involvement of either criminal or civil law.

Criminalization of Substance Use during Pregnancy

Generally, women have been charged with one of three types of crime: (1) criminal child endangerment or child abuse and neglect, (2) fetal murder/manslaughter, and (3) drug delivery and distribution to minors. These prosecutions typically have involved creative applications of existing statutes. In all child abuse cases, prosecutors have equated a viable fetus with a child and argued that drug use during pregnancy constituted child abuse. In the drug delivery cases, women have been accused of delivering drugs to a minor through the umbilical cord. And in the homicide cases, prosecutors have argued that a stillborn birth, presumably due to drug use during pregnancy, constitutes fetal homicide (Harris & Paltrow, 2003).

Most prosecutions under existing law have ultimately been unsuccessful, with the notable exception of South Carolina (*Whitner v. State of South Carolina* [1997] and *State of South Carolina v. McKnight* [2003]). The courts have concluded that these laws were not meant to apply to the situation of drug use during pregnancy, and prior to the South Carolina Supreme Court cases, cases that were successfully prosecuted at the trial level had been thrown out by either the appellate or superior court of the relevant state. Many of these attempts to prosecute women criminally for illicit drug use during pregnancy foundered on the question of nonrecognition of fetal rights as discussed above, the perception that existing laws were not intended to include fetal abuse, the consideration that the constitutionally protected maternal rights to privacy were more important than the state's interest in protecting the unborn, and on strong opposition from leading medical and public health groups.

Prosecution under Child Endangerment Statutes.   Until the *Whitner* case, prosecutions based on criminal child abuse and neglect statutes had infrequent success. Courts repeatedly held that a fetus is not a "child" within the meaning of statutes prohibiting acts endangering the welfare of children. An example of such a decision is a case from the Supreme Court of Kentucky, *Commonwealth of Kentucky v. Connie Welch* (1993), where the high court concluded that its drug delivery statutes and child endangerment statutes did not intend to punish as criminal conduct self-abuse by an expectant mother potentially injurious to the baby she carries.

In a departure from the above, *Whitner v. South Carolina* (1997) upheld the prosecution of a woman who ingested crack cocaine during the third trimester of her pregnancy under child abuse and endangerment statutes by concluding that a fetus does have legal rights on its own. In this case, the South Carolina Supreme Court held that a viable fetus is a "person" under the state's criminal child endangerment statute, and that substance abuse during pregnancy endangering or likely to endanger the life, comfort, or health of a viable fetus could constitute child abuse (Dailard & Nash, 2000). The Court argued that the consequences of abuse or neglect that take place after birth often pale in comparison to those resulting from abuse suffered by the viable fetus before birth. In reaching this conclusion the Court relied on the harms reported by early articles in *The New England Journal of Medicine* (see, for example, Chasnoff, Burns, Schnoll & Burns, 1985; Volpe, 1992).

Whitner and a woman in a parallel case, *Crawley v. Evatt* (1977), subsequently appealed their cases to the U.S. Supreme Court on the grounds that they had been indicted for child abuse for giving birth to a child who had cocaine in its system, when the child abuse statute did not apply to a fetus. Several prominent national and state medical, health, social welfare, legal services, substance abuse treatment organizations, and social policy organizations wrote briefs to the U.S. Supreme Court in support of Whitner's and Crawley's petition for a writ of *certiorari* urging the Court not to let the decision in South Carolina stand. They warned that the *Whitner* decision would deter pregnant women from obtaining adequate prenatal care, including substance abuse treatment, and that it would seriously compromise the doctor–patient relationship (Olshansky, Davis, Paltrow, Paul-Emile, & Wise, 1997; Tracy, Frietsche, Abrahamson, Boyd, & Risher, 1997). The U.S. Supreme Court declined to grant *certiorari*, and the decision of the South Carolina Supreme Court therefore stands *(Whitner, cert. denied*, 1998).

A subsequent U.S. Supreme Court case affirmed that there are important legal barriers to prosecutions of pregnant substance abusing women (*Ferguson et al. v. City of Charleston et al.*, 2001). Ferguson was 1 of over 40 women (all but 1 were African American) arrested under a collaborative policy between law enforcement officials in Charleston and the Medical University of South Carolina (MUSC). Pursuant to the policy, the hospital tested pregnant women suspected of drug abuse and reported positive tests to the police. When Ferguson delivered her child, they tested her without her consent and found traces of cocaine in her bloodstream. She was given a choice of a residential drug treatment or arrest and prosecution. Unable to enter the program, she was arrested for failure to comply with the order to receive drug treatment.

In 1993, nearly two years after Ferguson's arrest, the Center for Reproductive Law and Policy in New York filed a class action suit in federal district court in South Carolina against the hospital and the City of Charleston, demanding $3 million in damages for the violation of several constitutional rights (Gagan, 2000). In particular, the petitioners alleged that the warrantless and allegedly nonconsensual drug tests were unconstitutional searches. The defendants successfully argued that the testing fell within the "special needs" exception to the Fourth Amendment requirements. This means that a court can excuse the warrant and probable cause requirements in situations in which the existence of special needs beyond the normal need for law enforcement makes the warrant and probable cause requirements impracticable. When special needs are deemed to exist, the court conducts a reasonable analysis, balancing the government interests at stake against the individual's privacy interests (Gagan, 2000). In the district court, the jury found that the plaintiffs, by signing MUSC's consent to medical treatment forms, had waived the right to privacy. In the subsequent appeal to the Fourth Circuit, the court dodged the issue of consent, holding instead that the warrantless testing of pregnant women's urine when the indicia of possible cocaine use were present constituted reasonable special needs searches and therefore did not violate the Fourth Amendment (*Ferguson v. City of Charleston*, 1999, p. 476).

The U.S. Supreme Court granted *certiorari* on the special needs exception only. The case was argued in October 2000, and in March 2001 the U.S. Supreme Court reversed the decision of the Fourth Circuit. The Court held that the MUSC policy of conducting warrantless, nonconsensual drug tests on pregnant women, and turning in positive results to the police violates the Fourth Amendment. The five-justice majority said that the law enforcement purposes behind the policy take it outside the scope of prior rulings in which the Court has been willing to uphold searches conducted under policies with the usual Fourth Amendment requirements in order to serve special needs beyond the normal need for law enforcement. Given the extensive involvement of law enforcement officials at every stage of the policy, this case, the Court majority argued, simply did not fit within the closely guarded category of special needs. The Court found that in balancing the intrusion on the individual's privacy interest against the special needs that supported the program, in this case the invasion of privacy was much more substantial than in previous special needs cases.

The *Ferguson* case was primarily a Fourth Amendment case, and did not deal directly with the issue of criminalizing maternal substance abuse. After its ruling in 2001 the U.S. Supreme Court ordered a lower court to consider the hospital's argument that the women had consented to the tests. A divided panel of the U.S. circuit of appeals ruled last year that most of the women who sued did not know that they were being tested. This ruling could be interpreted as requiring patient consent for every test or procedure, and the hospital in South Carolina appealed to the U.S. Supreme Court for a second time. In June 2003, the U.S. Supreme Court justices refused to hear the second appeal without comment.

Following the *Whitner* decision prosecutors in South Carolina also charged Brenda Kay Peppers with child abuse for delivering a stillborn with traces of cocaine in its system. Peppers accepted a plea agreement and then challenged her conviction on constitutional grounds before the South Carolina Supreme Court (*State v. Peppers*, 2001). Several medical associations submitted a brief on her behalf and urged the court to revisit its *Whitner* decision (Goldberg, Abrahamson, Appel, & Waldman, 2001). In July of 2001, the South Carolina Supreme Court dismissed the case on procedural grounds, claiming that the original plea agreement was legally flawed without addressing the substantive issues raised in the *amici curiae* for Pepper.

It remains to be seen what the far-reaching consequences of these decisions will be, and whether other courts will follow suit to specifically include fetal abuse in child abuse and child neglect statutes, and possibly child homicide laws. In 2000 Misti Harris was charged with criminal child abuse in Kentucky after a social worker revealed to the state that Harris had used drugs while she was pregnant. The trial court dismissed the charges based on the findings in *Commonwealth v. Welch* (1993). However, citing *Whitner*, the prosecutors decided to appeal the dismissal of the case to the Kentucky Court of Appeals. The Drug Policy Alliance submitted an *amicus curiae* brief on Harris's behalf (Goodwin, Appel, Abrahamson, & Paltrow, 2002).

In New Jersey, a trial judge sent a pregnant woman who had used drugs during pregnancy to a long prison term because he felt compelled to ensure that she remained drug-free during her pregnancy. On appeal, the appellate court in New Jersey held that a drug-addicted pregnant woman cannot be sentenced to a lengthier prison term merely to protect her unborn fetus (*State v. Ikerd*, 2004). In 2004, Texas made it a felony to smoke marijuana while pregnant, with a prison sentence of 2 to 20 years ("Women and Pregnancy," 2004). Likewise, state lawmakers recently amended Texas law to redefine the term "individual" to mean "a human being who is alive, including an unborn child at every stage of gestation from fertilization to birth" (McBride, 2005). In one county, the district attorney interpreted the civil child abuse law to mean that physicians were required to report all pregnant drug-abusing women to local law enforcement officials. This resulted in the arrest of over a dozen women who allegedly used an illegal drug while pregnant. However, in 2005, the Texas attorney general concluded that the county district attorney's interpretation of the Texas law was wrong, and that physicians were not required to report ("Letter to Texas District Attorney," 2005).

Prosecution under Homicide Laws.   Within one year of the Whitner decision, the prosecution in a Wisconsin case urged the court to adopt the reasoning in Whitner as applicable to a case in which a mother had attempted to kill her unborn child by excessive consumption of alcohol (Wisconsin v. Deborah J.Z., 1999). This case can be distinguished from other maternal substance abuse cases in that the mother clearly stated her intention to harm her fetus. The defendant in Deborah J.Z. filed a motion to dismiss the attempted first-degree murder charges, but the trial court denied this motion (p. 491). On appeal, however, the court rejected the reasoning of Whitner and held that the unborn child was not a "human being" for the purpose of the attempted first-degree intentional homicide and first-degree reckless injury statute (p. 494).

In a new landmark case (*State of South Carolina v. McKnight, 2003*) the Supreme Court of South Carolina upheld the conviction of fetal homicide for a woman who delivered a stillborn baby after using drugs during pregnancy. Upon conviction (after the jury deliberated for 15 minutes), Ms. McKnight, who had no other arrest history, was sentenced to 12 years in state prison without any chance for parole. Her arrests and conviction provoked an outcry from members of the medical community and others who questioned the constitutionality of using homicide statutes to prosecute women who experience stillbirths ("SC Supreme Court Hears Appeal," 2002).

McKnight subsequently appealed her conviction to the South Carolina Supreme Court with an *amicus* brief to the Court on her behalf from the South Carolina Medical Association and other public health organizations. The brief provided extensive medical and scientific evidence that McKnight's cocaine use did not cause her stillbirth and that the prosecution of her case might deter other women from seeking prenatal care. Moreover, there was a very clear legislative history that the state's homicide by child abuse laws was not intended to punish pregnant women—including those using illegal drugs. Nevertheless, in January 2003, the South Carolina Supreme Court affirmed the lower court's decision to make McKnight the first woman ever convicted of homicide as a result of her behavior during pregnancy. In 1992 the South Carolina legislature had made it a felony to cause the death of a child younger than 11 through child abuse or neglect under circumstances manifesting an extreme indifference to human life (Bhargava, 2004).

Since the Court had already previously ruled that a viable fetus is legally a person (in *Whitner*), the Court now applied the homicide law to a viable fetus.

Several medical, public health, and advocates for women organizations petitioned the United States Supreme Court for a writ of *certiorari*. They argued that punishing a pregnant woman as a murderer based on findings that her conduct or circumstances contributed to a stillbirth violates the Eight Amendment of cruel and unusual punishment. Further, that a criminal punishment in the event of stillbirth constitutionally infringes on fundamental autonomy interests, that the connection between stillbirth and use of cocaine could not be conclusively proven, and that the conviction was wholly without precedent in Anglo-American law (Paltrow, Goldberg, & Wise, 2003). In late 2003, the U.S. Supreme Court denied *certiorari* by declining to hear the appeal of Regina McKnight (*McKnight v. State of South Carolina*, 2003).

Prosecution under Controlled Substance Statutes.   Many criminal prosecutions have been based on other existing criminal laws that prohibit drug use, sale, possession, or delivery of drugs to minors, which apply to all adults, males and females. *Johnson v. Florida* (1992) was the first case of this kind that was prosecuted successfully at the trial level using a "delivery of drugs to a minor" statute to apply to drugs being transferred through the umbilical cord at birth. The mother appealed and the appellate court affirmed her conviction. The Florida Supreme Court, however, reversed the conviction on a variety of grounds, including legislative intent. The Court held that the legislature did not intend the word "deliver" to include the passage of blood through the umbilical cord. The decision noted that drug abuse is a serious national problem and that there is a particular concern about the rising numbers of babies born with cocaine in their systems as a result of maternal substance abuse. But the court pointed out the negative aspects of prosecuting pregnant substance abusers. Women who are substance abusers may simply avoid prenatal care for fear of being detected when the newborns of these women are, as a group, the most fragile and sickest and most in need of hospital neonatal care.

Most decisions from higher courts since the Florida Supreme Court reversal in *Johnson* have followed the same path—the courts have consistently refused to apply drug delivery statutes to pregnant women. However, in 2004, after the Texas legislature amended the Texas law to have an "individual" mean "a human being who is alive, including an unborn child at every stage of gestation from fertilization until birth," two women were convicted in trial court of a charge of delivery of a controlled substance to an unborn child after admitting they smoked crack or methamphetamine. Both women later filed appeals with the Amarillo's Seventh Court of Appeals (McBride, 2005).

Constitutional Issues Raised by Criminalization.   Proponents of criminalization believe that even under strict scrutiny standards the state's interests in protecting the health and the life of the unborn child take precedence over maternal privacy rights;—rights that have been firmly established in a series of previous decisions by the U.S. Supreme Court (*Eisenstadt v. Baird*, 1972; *Griswold v. Connecticut*, 1965; *Roe v. Wade*, 1973). Robertson (1989), for example, maintained that meeting obligations to the unborn child may require limitations on the mother's conduct that would not be there if she were not pregnant. Opponents of criminalization argue that prosecution of a woman's substance abuse during pregnancy violates a woman's rights to equal protection under the law (Sagatun-Edwards, 1997). Because evidence of a newborn's positive toxicology screen is used only in cases against women, women would be punished because of their drug use and their ability to get pregnant. A statutory requirement that women resolve all health care decisions in favor of the fetus would hold women to a much higher standard than men.

The Harvard Law Review Association (1998) provided an in-depth analysis of the policy considerations that legislatures and courts should take into account when deciding whether to enact criminal fetal abuse statutes or to read fetal protection into existing legislation. The long-established constitutional rights of the individual to control procreative and familial decisions should also apply to the maternal decisions potentially infringed upon by fetal abuse legislation. Broad fetal abuse statutes that are patterned on child abuse statutes, those that make neglecting or abusing a crime without specifying what constitutes neglect or abuse, would be unconstitutional. They would be void for vagueness, and they require an infringement on maternal rights not justified by the fetal protection they offer; thus they would not be narrowly tailored enough to survive strict scrutiny. However, even if that could be done, the authors conclude that a fetal abuse statute may provide a powerful incentive to women to stay away from doctors in order to avoid detection and prosecution, and statutes that criminalize pregnant women's conduct actually may thwart rather than serve the state's interest in protecting the fetus (p. 1008).

Juvenile Court (Civil Court) Involvement

Criminal prosecution is not the only method states have employed in an attempt to reach women who put their unborn children at risk by using drugs during pregnancy. States have also used child welfare statutes that provide for the temporary or permanent removal of children who have been abused or neglected by their parents or guardians to separate mothers from their children at birth—based on substance abuse during pregnancy (Clarke, 2000). Until very recently, civil child abuse and neglect proceedings dealt with the child after he or she is born; thus, they did not implicate the same constitutional issues of privacy, bodily integrity, and personal autonomy that are raised when mother and child are one entity (Coffey, 1997). However, as of March 2005, 14 states now consider substance abuse during pregnancy to be child abuse under civil child-welfare statutes: Colorado, Florida, Illinois, Indiana, Maryland, Minnesota, Nevada, Ohio, Rhode Island, South Carolina, South Dakota, Texas, Virginia, and Wisconsin ("State Policies in Brief," 2005). Other states have also addressed the issue of a pregnant woman's use of drugs in their civil child welfare statutes without necessarily equating it to child abuse: Arizona, California, Iowa, Massachusetts, Michigan, Oklahoma, and Utah. Some states also include fetal alcohol syndrome or evidence of a pregnant woman's alcohol use in their definitions of neglected or abused children, such as Indiana, Utah, and Wisconsin (Paltrow, Cohen, & Carey, 2000).

While the stated purpose of the criminal court is to punish the offender, the stated purpose of the juvenile court is protection of the child. Issues of concern for juvenile court or family court jurisdiction are the criteria for testing, whether positive tests should be included under mandatory reporting laws for child abuse and neglect, and the criteria used to remove a child from the mother.

Entry to Juvenile Court and Testing.   The first point of entry of drug-exposed infants and their families into the juvenile court system is often right after birth. Some states specifically require physicians to test and report pregnant women to child protective services for illicit substance abuse when toxicology tests on newborns are positive. Many hospitals now perform neonatal toxicology screens when maternal drug use is suspected. As of March 2005, four states (Iowa, Minnesota, North Dakota, and Virginia) now require testing when abuse is suspected ("State Policies in Brief," 2005). Typically, hospital protocols dictate that such screens are performed when the newborn shows signs of drug withdrawal, when the mother admits to drug use during pregnancy, or when the mother has had no prenatal care (Robin-Vergeer, 1990). There are several problems with such testing: the invasion of privacy, unreliability of the results, and racial and social class biases in both the testing procedures and the reports of the testing (Chasnoff, Landress, & Barrett,1990; Gomby & Shiono, 1991). Note that after *Ferguson*, testing without the woman's consent for the purposes of criminal prosecution is unconstitutional.

As of this date, no states require mandatory testing for drugs of all pregnant women. Minnesota is a state that early chose universal screening of neonates while limiting maternal testing to women with pregnancy complications that suggest drug use (Sagatun-Edwards, Saylor, & Shifflet,1995). Minnesota's child abuse statute defines neglect to include a positive toxicology test of the mother at delivery (Minn. Stat Ann., 626.556(2) C (7)). In South Carolina, drug tests on the woman herself may be the basis for a presumption of child neglect (S.C. Code Ann., 20-7-736(G)). In *Marchwinski, Konieczny, and Westside Mothers v. Howard* (2000), Michigan welfare recipients challenged the constitutionality of a new law authorizing drug testing without any suspicion of substance abuse (p. 1135), and the court found that the law was unconstitutional. Most states condition testing on a physician's suspicion of prenatal drug use, based on obstetric complications or assessment of mother and baby.

Mandatory Reporting under Child Abuse and Neglect Reporting Laws.   Based on a positive toxicology test, the hospital may report the case to the child protective services, which in turn may ask the court to prevent the child's release to the parents while an investigation takes place. If further investigation reveals a risk to the child, the court may assume temporary custody of the child, and in the most serious cases, parental rights may be terminated (Sagatun-Edwards et al., 1995).

As of March 2005, nine states now require reporting to Child Protective Services when substance abuse during pregnancy is suspected: Arizona, Illinois, Iowa, Massachusetts, Michigan, Minnesota, North Dakota, and Virginia ("State Policies in Brief," 2005). If the results on a toxicology screen of either mother or child are positive, the physicians are required to report the results to the Department of Health or Child

Protective Services, and local welfare agencies are then mandated to investigate and make any appropriate referrals.

In California, the Perinatal Substance Abuse Services Act of 1990 emphasizes the desirability of medical services and drug treatment, and it does *not* endorse mandatory reporting of positive toxicology screens. This law modified the existing child abuse reporting laws in California to specify that a positive toxicology screen at the time of delivery of an infant is not in and of itself a sufficient basis for reporting child abuse or neglect. Instead, any indication of maternal substance abuse shall lead to an assessment of the needs of the mother and her infant. Any indication of risk to the child as determined by the assessment shall then be reported to county welfare departments (Perinatal Substance Abuse Services Act of 1991, effective July 1, 1991; Sect. 11165.13 of the California Penal Code, 1991). In Wisconsin, although its Children's Code includes a new category for "unborn child abuse," the statute requires reporting only after the birth of a child (Paltrow et al., 2000).

Legal Criteria for Removing a Child from the Parents.   In determining what to do with a child, social services and juvenile courts in all states must now follow the directives of Public Law 105-89, or the Adoption and Safe Families Act of 1997. Under this law children's safety is now the paramount concern that must guide all child welfare services. State welfare agencies are mandated to make reasonable efforts to prevent a child's placement in foster care, and if foster care is necessary, the state must make efforts to reunite the family during specified time periods, with court hearings every 6 months. If such reunification is not possible, the law further requires permanency planning for the child, which may include termination of parental rights to make adoption possible (Sagatun-Edwards & Saylor, 2000a). This act creates a 12-month time frame for making decisions about a child's permanent placement, and a 15-month time frame for petitioning for termination of parental rights [Pub. L. No. 105-89, 111 Stat. 2115 (1997), sect. 675(5) C,E.].

Substance abuse during pregnancy is not specifically addressed in the act, except that it calls for expansion of child welfare demonstration projects, including projects that are designed to "identify and address parental substance abuse problems that endanger children and result in the placement of children in foster care, including placement of children in residential facilities" (Sect. 301 of the Adoption and Safe Families Act of 1997). However, the short time frame allowed for reunification services makes it difficult for pregnant substance abusing women to deal successfully with their addiction issues in time.

CIVIL COMMITMENT: PLACING THE FETUS IN PROTECTIVE CUSTODY

Outside the criminal context, the state may institute civil confinement for persons who present a danger to themselves or others. This procedure is called civil commitment and results in confinement in a hospital or treatment facility for varying lengths of time. As of March 2005, three states have enacted laws specifically authorizing civil commitment or detention in a noncriminal setting of substance abusing women during their pregnancy in order to protect their fetuses from harm: Minnesota, South Dakota, and Wisconsin ("State Policies in Brief," 2005). Constitutional requirements for civil commitment are clear and convincing evidence that an individual is mentally ill or dangerous to herself or others (*Addington v. Texas*, 1979). The laws allowing for the civil commitment of pregnant drug users therefore are based on the claim that a woman is a danger to another "person," the fetus.

In 1998 the Wisconsin state legislature amended its child protection laws so that women who abuse alcohol or drugs during pregnancy can be confined for the duration of their pregnancies [Wisconsin Stat. Sect. 48.01.347 et seq. (1998)]. The purpose of the Wisconsin law is "to provide a just and humane program of services to children and unborn children and the expectant mothers of those unborn children" [Wisconsin Stat. Sect. 48.01 (1998)]. The statute defines "unborn child" as a "human being from the time of fertilization to the time of birth," and stresses that provisions of the law are intended to apply throughout an expectant mother's pregnancy (Sect. 48.01–02). It is in the best interest of the "unborn child" to order the mother who abuses drugs and/or alcohol during pregnancy to receive treatment, including inpatient treatment. This treatment may include, but is not limited to, medical, psychological or psychiatric treatment, as well as alcohol or other drug abuse treatment or other services that the court finds necessary and appropriate (Sect. 48.01).

This modification to the Wisconsin's child abuse and protection laws followed a 1997 Wisconsin Supreme Court ruling that declared that the then current child abuse laws could not be used to confine a pregnant woman who had tested positive for cocaine (*Angela M.W. v. Kruzicki*, 1997). Soon after this decision, the Wisconsin legislature amended the statute to permit such detentions under state law.

South Dakota enacted similar legislation on July 1, 1998, which gives relatives the power to place pregnant women in custody for up to nine months [*South Dakota Codified Laws* (2s), 34-20A-63, 1998]. Minnesota also authorizes the emergency admission or pregnant women for mandatory drug treatment for as long as the duration of a pregnancy (Dailard & Nash, 2000). In 1996, Norway passed a civil law that provides that pregnant women can be confined to a locked residential drug treatment facility for the duration of their pregnancy if they refuse voluntary treatment and all other attempts to treat their substance abuse have failed. The legislation is based on the notion that if a woman foregoes the right to an abortion, she has a duty to protect the fetus (Sagatun-Edwards, 1999).

De Ville and Kopelman (1999) point out that by defining a fetus from conception as a "child" the Wisconsin legislature shifted the balance from a woman's privacy rights versus the fetus to balancing a woman's rights against a child's rights. De Ville and Kopelman argue that the Wisconsin civil commitment law is flawed in that it does not guarantee the evidentiary protection that is typically required when individual rights are abrogated. The varied effects of using drugs during pregnancy and the lack of clear knowledge about such effects makes it difficult to ever reach the standard of clear and convincing evidence for fetal injury.

SUBSTANCE ABUSE TREATMENT AND PRE- AND POSTNATAL CARE

Opponents and proponents of criminalization and/or juvenile court involvement alike agree that the most effective solution to the problem of prenatal drug abuse is drug treatment and rehabilitation. The major problem is that appropriate drug treatment programs have not always been available or affordable, and when they are available there are long waiting lists to get in.

However, in recent years, a number of states have placed a priority on making drug treatment more available to pregnant women. As of 2005, 18 states have either created or funded drug treatment programs specifically targeted to pregnant women: Arkansas, California, Colorado, Connecticut, Florida, Illinois, Kentucky, Louisiana, Maryland, Minnesota, Missouri, Nebraska, North Carolina, Ohio, Oregon, Pennsylvania, Virginia, and Washington. Six states give pregnant women priority access to state-funded drug treatment programs: Arizona, Georgia, Kansas, Missouri, Oklahoma, and Wisconsin ("State Policies in Brief," 2005). Although some of these states also include "fetal abuse" in their civil child neglect and abuse laws, most have taken nonpunitive steps to increase access to information and treatment for pregnant women and mandated education for the public and medical providers on substance abuse and pregnancy. For example, the state of Washington treats perinatal substance abuse as a public health issue, and made pregnant women a priority for treatment of chemical dependency. The state of Oregon treats alcohol abuse and drug dependency as an illness rather than a crime, and the Oregon legislature has rejected several bills aimed at criminalizing drug use during pregnancy (Jones, 1999). Several states have passed legislation that prohibits discrimination against pregnant women seeking drug treatment, and enhanced criminal penalties for people who sell or give drugs to pregnant women (Paltrow, et al., 2000).

An intervention study for substance-abusing mothers in juvenile dependency court found that providing enhanced services to substance abusing families had a significant positive impact (Sagatun-Edwards & Saylor, 2000b). Another study that provided residential treatment for pregnant crack users pointed to the importance of early interventions for this population (Fiocchi & Kingree, 2001). A 1998 study from Florida found that cocaine-exposed babies who stayed with mothers who were capable of caring for them fared better developmentally after a year than cocaine-exposed babies in state care (Bland, 2003). A recent review of interventions for drug-abusing mothers and their drug-exposed infants found that interventions that helped the mother toward abstinence and increased her self-esteem were the most beneficial for optimal infant development and healthy mother–child interactions (Bowie, 2005).

CONCLUSION

A wide variety of legal responses to maternal substance abuse has been discussed. Substance abuse during pregnancy has been consistently prosecuted in only one state, namely South Carolina. The fact that most states have steered away from criminalizing substance abuse during pregnancy in their legislation is remarkable, considering the media-fueled "crack baby" hysteria of the late 1980s. According to Paltrow and colleagues (2000), the trend is for states to have chosen treatment, education, and prevention over criminal sanctions, thus regarding drug use during pregnancy as a public health problem rather than a crime. While the health of a fetus is important, criminalizing fetal abuse will not serve the intended purpose. It would probably jeopardize, rather than secure, the fetal health. Women at risk would not seek medical advice for fear of being punished and of losing their children. The mother's constitutional guarantees of right to liberty and privacy would be violated. Prosecutions of conduct during pregnancy is simply a wrong policy; it is unconstitutional, sexist, and serves no social policy purpose.

Protection of children after birth is important. Any interventions on behalf of the drug-exposed infant must be predicated on other indications of future harm, not the past prenatal use. Such indicators might include the mother's failure to care for siblings even when services are offered, and consistent unwillingness to participate in a drug treatment program and parenting classes. The goal should always be to provide pregnant women with effective drug treatment and comprehensive pre- and postnatal care so that they may maintain custody of their own children. Intervention should be limited to protect children who are at great risk, so that loss of constitutional rights and societal costs may be prevented. Reports to the Child Protective Services should be only a last resort, and mothers should not be detained simply for failing treatment. Civil commitment should be used only when there is clear and convincing evidence of harm.

In general, the best policy to be followed is to treat perinatal substance abuse as a public health problem. Free and nonpunitive prenatal and postnatal care ideally should be available to all. Government expansion of educational and medical services aimed at all pregnant and especially substance-abusing women will avoid the infringement on maternal privacy rights, and in the long run prove less costly and intrusive than criminal liability or long-term juvenile court intervention.

REFERENCES

ADOPTION AND SAFE FAMILIES ACT OF 1997, Pub. L. No. 105–89, 111 Stat. 2115; 42 U.S.C., section 675 (5).

BHARGAVA, S. (2004). Challenging punishment and privatization: A response to the conviction of Regina McKnight. *Harvard Civil Liberties Law Reviews, 32*, 513–540.

BLAND, K. (2003, September 13). CPS reform: Hard choices; lawmakers struggle over policy on drug babies. *The Arizona Republic*, pp. 1–3.

BOWIE, B. (2005). Interventions to improve interactions between drug abusing mothers and their drug-exposed infants: A review of the research literature. *Journal of Addictions Nursing, 15*, 153–161.

CHASNOFF, I. (2002, February 25). *Testimony to the U.S. Sentencing Commission regarding drug penalties* (p. 2). Washington, DC.

CHASNOFF, I. J., BURNS, K. A., BURNS, W. J., & SCHNOLL, S. H. (1986). Prenatal drug exposure: Effects on neonatal and infant growth and development. *Neurobehavioral Toxicology and Teratology, 8*(4), 357–362.

CHASNOFF, I. J., BURNS, W. J., SCHNOLL, S. H., & BURNS, K. A. (1985). Cocaine use in pregnancy. *New England Journal of Medicine, 393*(11), 666–669.

CHASNOFF, I. J., LANDRESS, H. J., & BARRETT, M. E. (1990). The prevalence of illicit drug or alcohol during pregnancy and discrepancies in mandatory reporting in Pinellas County, Florida. *The New England Journal of Medicine, 322*(17), 1202–1206.

CLARKE, A. (2000). FINS, PINS, CHIPS, AND CHINS: A reasoned approach to the problem of drug use during pregnancy. *Seton Hall Law Review, 29*, 634–693.

COFFEY, C. (1997). *Whitner v. State*: Aberrational judicial response or wave of the future for maternal substance abuse cases? *Journal of Contemporary Health, Law & Policy, 14*, 211–255.

DAILARD, C., & NASH, E. (2000, December). State response to substance abuse among pregnant women. *The Guttmacher report on public policy* (pp. 1–4). New York: Alan Guttmacher Institute.

DE VILLE, K., & KOPELMAN, L. (1999). Fetal protection in Wisconsin's revised child abuse laws. *Journal of Law, Medicine & Ethics, 27*(4), 332–349.

FIOCCHI, F., & KINGREE, J. B. (2001). Treatment retention and birth outcomes of crack users enrolled in a substance abuse treatment program for pregnant women. *Journal of Substance Abuse Treatment, 20*(2), 137–147.

FRANK, D., AUGUSTYN, M., KNIGHT, W. G., PELL, T., & ZUCKERMAN, B. (2001). Growth, development, and behavior in early childhood following prenatal cocaine exposure. *Journal of the American Medical Association, 285*, 1613–1625.

GAGAN, B. (2000). *Ferguson v. City of Charleston, South Carolina*: "Fetal abuse," drug testing and the Fourth Amendment. *Stanford Law Review, 53*(2), 491–514.

GOLDBERG, D., ABRAHAMSON, D., APPEL, J., & WALDMAN, A. (2001). Brief as *amici curiae* in support of appellant, Brenda Peppers; in the Supreme Court of the State of South Carolina; *State of South Carolina v. Brenda Kay Peppers* (case no. 98-30-0809).

GOMBY, D., & SHIONO, P. (1991). Estimating the number of substance-exposed infants. *The Future of Children, 1* (1), 17–26.

GOODWIN, M., APPEL, K., ABRAHAMSON, D., & PALTROW, L. (2002). Brief of *amicius curiae* to Commonwealth of Kentucky Court of Appeals, *Commonwealth of Kentucky v. Misti Harris* (2002-CA-907, action no. 02-CR-00008).

HARRIS, L., & PALTROW, L. (2003). The status of pregnant women and fetuses in US criminal law. *Medical Student Journal of the American Medical Association, 289*, 1697–1699.

HARVARD LAW REVIEW ASSOCIATION. (1998, March). Maternal rights and fetal wrongs: The case against the criminalization of "fetal abuse." *Harvard Law Review, 101*, p. 994–1015.

HOWARD, J., KROPENSKE, V., & TYLER, R. (1986). The long term effects on neurodevelopment in infants exposed pre-natally to PCP. *National Institute of Drug Abuse Monograph Series, 64*, 237–251.

HUMPHRIES, D. (1998). Crack mothers at 6. *Violence Against Women, 6*(1), 45–61.

JONES, K. (1999). Prenatal substance abuse: Oregon's progressive approach to treatment and child protection can support children, women, and families. *Willamette Law Review, 35*, 797–823.

KATZ, N. (2004, October). Fetal homicide laws—What you need to know. About Women's Issues. Retrieved April 11, 2005, from http://womenissuesabout.com/cs/parentingfamily/a/aafetal homicide.htm.

Letter to Texas District Attorney Randall Sims on the arrest of pregnant women for child abuse. (March 1, 2005). Washington, DC: Drug Policy Alliance. Retrieved April 2, 2005, from http://www.drugpolicy/library/paltrowtxltr.cfm.

MCBRIDE, J. (2005, March 31). Potter County defends conviction of mothers for abusing crack. *Amarillo Globe-News*, pp. 1–2.

MCNULTY, N. (1987–1988). Pregnancy police: The health policy and legal implications of punishing pregnant women for harm to their fetuses. *Review of Law and Social Change, 16*(2), 277–319.

MESSINGER, D., BAUER, C., DAS, A., SEIFER, R., LESTER, B., LAGASSE, L., et al. The maternal lifestyle study: Cognitive, motor, and behavioral outcomes of cocaine-exposed and opiate-exposed infants through three years of age. *Pediatrics, 113*(6), 1677–1685.

Minnesota Statutes Annotated. (1990). Section 626.6661. Sub. 1 (West Supp.).

Minnesota Statutes Annotated. (1990). Section 626.556. Sub. 1 (West Supp.).

MONTGOMERY, S., & EKBORN, A. (2002). Smoking during pregnancy and diabetes mellitus in a British longitudinal birth cohort. *British Medical Journal, 321*, 27.

MURPHY, S., & ROSENBAUM, M. (1999). *Pregnant women on drugs: Combating stereotypes and stigma.* New Brunswick, NJ: Rutgers University Press.

OLSHANSKY, B., DAVIS, L., PALTROW, L., PAUL-EMILE, K., & WISE, C. R. (1997). Reply brief in support of petition for a writ of *certiorari. Whitner v. South Carolina*, and *Crawley v. Moore*, no. 97-1562, U.S. Supreme Court, October Term.

PALTROW, L., COHEN, D., & CAREY, C. (2000). *Year 2000 overview: Governmental responses to pregnant women who use alcohol or other drugs.* New York: National Advocates for Pregnant Women, and Philadelphia: Women's Law Report.

PALTROW, L., GOLDBERG, D., & WISE C. R. (2003). In the Supreme Court of the United States *Regina D. McKnight v. State of South Carolina*: On petition for a writ of *certiorari.* Attorneys for the petitioner.

PERINATAL SUBSTANCE ABUSE SERVICES ACT OF 1991. (1991). Sacramento, CA: California Senate.

PETITTI, D., & COLEMAN, M. (1990). Cocaine and the risk of low birth weight. *American Journal of Public Health, 80*(1), 25–28.

ROBERTSON, J. (1989, August). *American Bar Association Journal, 38.*

ROBIN-VERGEER, B. I. (1990). The problem of the drug exposed newborn: A return to principled intervention. *Stanford Law Review, 42*(3), 745–809.

SAGATUN-EDWARDS, I. (1997). Crack babies, moral panic, and the criminalization of behavior during pregnancy. In E. Jensen J. Gerber (Eds.), *The construction and impact of the war on drugs.* Cincinnati, OH: Anderson.

SAGATUN-EDWARDS, I. (1999). *Report to the Fulbright International Committee on the legal response to maternal substance abuse in Norway.* Oslo, Norway: Fulbright Association.

SAGATUN-EDWARDS, I., & SAYLOR, C. (2000a). Drug-exposed infant cases in juvenile court: Risk factors and court outcomes. *Child Abuse and Neglect, 24*(7), 925–937.

SAGATUN-EDWARDS, I., & SAYLOR, C. (2000b, Fall). A coordinated approach to improving outcomes for substance-abusing families in juvenile dependency court. *Juvenile and Family Court Journal,* 1–15.

SAGATUN-EDWARDS, I., SAYLOR, C., & SHIFFLETT, B. (1995). Drug exposed infants in the social welfare system and the juvenile court. *Child Abuse and Neglect: The International Journal, 19*(1), 83–91.

SC Supreme Court hears appeal: Don't punish women for stillbirth. (2002, November 6). National Advocates for Pregnant Women. Retrieved April 11, 2003, from http://www.advocatesforpregnant women.org/issues/mcknightnov2002.htm.

SINGER, L., MINNES, S., SHORT, E., ARENDT, R., FARKAS, K. M., LEWIS, B., et al. (2004). Birth outcome from a prospective, matched study of prenatal crack/cocaine use. *Journal of the American Medical Association, 291,* 2448–2456.

SINGER, L. T., ARENDT, R., & MINNES, S. (2002). Cognitive and motor outcomes of cocaine-exposed infants. *Journal of the American Medical Association, 287*(15), 1952–1960.

South Dakota Codified Laws (2s), 34-20A-63–70, 1998.

State policies in brief as of March 1, 2005: Substance abuse during pregnancy. (2005, March). *The Alan Guttmacher Report on Public Policy.* New York: Alan Guttmacher Institute.

TRACY, C., FRIETSCHE, S., ABRAHAMSON, D., BOYS, G., & RISHER, M. (1997). On petition for writ of *certiorari. Whitner v. State of South Carolina,* no. 97-1562, U.S. Supreme Court, October Term.

UNBORN VICTIMS OF VIOLENCE ACT. (2004). Pub. L. No. 108–212, Title 18, chapter 90, section 1841.

VOLPE, J. J. (1992, August). Effects of cocaine use on the fetus. *The New England Journal of Medicine, 327,* 399–407.

WANG, X., ZUCKERMAN, B., et al. (2002). Maternal cigarette smoking, metabolic gene polymorphism and infant birth weigh. *Journal of the American Medical Association, 287* (2), 198.

WESTON, D. R., IVENS, B., ZUCKERMAN, B., JONES, C., & LOPEZ, R. (1989). Drug exposed babies: Research and clinical issues. *National Center for Clinical Infant Programs Bulletin, 9*(5), 7.

Wisconsin Statutes subsections 48.01.347 et seq.; 1996 Wisconsin Laws 292 (A.B. 463, enacted June 16, 1998).

Women and pregnancy. (2004, June 22). *Drugs, police and the law.* Washington, DC: Drug Policy Alliance. Retrieved April 2, 2005, from http://www.drugpolicy.org/law/womenpregnan/.

ZUCKERMAN, B., FRANK, D., & MAYES, L. (2002). Cocaine-exposed infants and developmental outcomes: "Crack kids" revisited. *Journal of the American Medical Association, 287*(15), 1–2.

CASES

Addington v. Texas, 441 U.S. 418, 420 (1979).

Angela M.W. v. Kruzicki, 561 N.W.2d 729 (Wis. 1997), rev'd *Angela M.W. v. Kruzicki*, 541 N.W.2d 482 (Wis. Ct. App. 1995).

Commonwealth of Kentucky v. Connie Welch, 864 S.W.2d 280 (1993).

Commonwealth v. Cass, 392 Mass. 799, 467 N.E.2d 1324 (1984).

Crawley v. Evatt, Mem, Op. No. 97-MO-117 (S.C. Dec. 1, 1997).

Eisenstadt v. Baird, 405 U.S. 438 (1972).

Ferguson et al. v. City of Charleston et al., 121 S. Ct. 1281; 149 L. Ed. 2d 205; 2001 U.S. LEXIS 2460; 69 U.S.L.W. 4184.

Ferguson v. City of Charleston, 186 F.3d 469 (4th Cir. 1999).

Griswold v. Connecticut, 381 U.S. 479 (1965).

Johnson v. Florida, 602 So. 2d 1288 (Fla. 1992).

Marchwinski, Konieczny, and Westside Mothers v. Howard, 113 F. Supp. 2d 1134, (2000).

McKnight v. State of South Carolina, 576 S.E.2d 168 (S.C. 2003), 124 S. Ct. 101 (S.C. 2001); U.S. Supreme Court denied *certiorari*, Oct. 6, 2003.

Roe v. Wade, 410 U.S. 113 (1973).

State of South Carolina v. McKnight, 576 S.E.2d 168 (S.C. 2003), *cert denied*, 124 S. Ct. 101 (2003).

State v. Ikerd, 369 N.J. Super. 610; 850 A.2d 516; 2004 N.J.

State v. Peppers, Opinion No. 25330 (S.C. Sp. Ct.) July 23, 2001; Case no. 98-GS-30-0809.

Webster v. Reproductive Health Services, 492 U.S. 490 (1989).

Whitner v. State of South Carolina, 328 S.C. 1; 492 S.E.2d 777 (S.C. 1997); *cert. denied*, 118 S. Ct. 1857 (1998); 1998 U.S. 3564.

Wisconsin v. Deborah J.Z., 596 N.W.2d 490 (Wis. Ct. App. 1999).

22

Living and Dying with HIV/AIDS

The "Inside" Experience of Women in Prison

Mark M. Lanier and Barbara H. Zaitzow

The growing influx of ill and generally unhealthy female offenders into American prisons has resulted in many challenges for those who live and work in prison settings. In particular are the health needs of imprisoned women with HIV/AIDS. Women prisoners need the same preventive measures and the same level of care, treatment, and support as male prisoners. In addition, however, there is a need for initiatives that acknowledge that the problems encountered by women in the correctional environment often reflect, and are augmented by, their vulnerability and disadvantaged life experiences many of them have suffered outside prison. The need for prison systems to take immediate action to develop and implement effective HIV/AIDS programming options for all women prisoners is the focus of this chapter.

INTRODUCTION

The recent imprisonment binge has resulted in 2.1 million people filling our nation's jails or prisons—the highest number in our history and the highest rate of incarceration in the world. Prison populations have multiplied in recent decades, primarily because incarceration has been the central tactic of the "war on drugs" in the United States despite the fact that crime has been plummeting for the past decade and 70% of the people behind bars are nonviolent offenders. And we continue to invest in harsh, mandatory sentences although they are completely ineffective in the war on drugs. One of the casualties of this war has been women offenders. Since 1995, the annual rate of growth in the number of female inmates has averaged 5.2%, higher than the 3.5% average increase for males. Women accounted for 6.9% of all inmates at year-end 2003, up from 6.1% at year-end 1995 and 5.7% at year-end 1990 (Bureau of Justice Statistics, 2004).

A by-product of the recent "confinement era" within criminal justice is the influx of ill and generally unhealthy female offenders into this nation's correctional institutions (Lanier & Paoline, 2005). In addition to tuberculosis (TB), one of the pressing public health concerns facing correctional systems today is human immunodeficiency virus (HIV) and acquired immune deficiency syndrome (AIDS). While no segment of the incarcerated population is immune to this infection, an alarming number of female inmates have been shown to test positive for HIV at higher rates than male inmates (Maruschak, 1999). The high rates of HIV infection and AIDS among women offenders are essentially the result of intravenous drug use, trading sex for drugs and money, sexual abuse, living under conditions of poverty, and other gender-specific conditions of their lives, which make them more prone to HIV infection (DeGroot, Leibel, & Zierler, 1998).

The problem of HIV infection and AIDS is especially serious for incarcerated women, who often have less access to services for treatment and prevention than men (Lanier, Braithwaite, & Arriola, 2001). It is critically important to review the health care needs of women prisoners and the correctional system's ability to deliver adequate services. Continued indifference will have great economic and social costs to society for current and future generations. As noted by Acoca (1999), "health care issues are a tsunami and will engulf social justice, and many other issues, within the next decade if we don't make them a priority" (p. 35). The purpose of this chapter is to address the special needs of incarcerated women relating to HIV/AIDS infection, identify some of the barriers to meeting these needs, and articulate an initial strategy for effectively overcoming these barriers.

INCARCERATED WOMEN

The number of women in state and federal prisons is at an all-time high and growing fast, with the incarceration rate for females increasing at nearly twice that of men. There were 101,179 women in prison in 2003, 3.6% more than in 2002 (Bureau of Justice Statistics, 2004). That marks the first time the women's prison population has topped 100,000, and continues a trend of rapid growth. The prison figures, however, do not fully reflect the number of people behind bars. About 80,000 women were in local jails last year, along with more than 600,000 men. Since 1995, the number of women incarcerated grew an average of 5%, compared to an average annual increase of 3.3% for men.

Moreover, the impact on women of color has been disproportionately heavy (Lanier et al., 2001). For African American women, the incarceration rate is eight times that for white women; for Latinas, it is almost four times greater (Beck, 2000)—circumstances that reflect issues not only of ethnicity, but also of poverty. Despite the fact that female prisoner population growth outpaced that of males, females comprise less than 7% of the imprisoned offenders (Gilliard, 1999, p. 4).

CHARACTERISTICS OF INCARCERATED WOMEN

Like their male counterparts, female inmates are young (about two-thirds are under 34 years old), minority-group members (more than 60%), unmarried (more than 80%), undereducated (about 40% were not high school graduates), and underemployed (Beck & Mumola,

1999). Unlike men, large majorities are unmarried, mothers of children under 18, and daughters who had grown up in homes without both parents present. Moreover, a distinguishing characteristic of incarcerated females is their significantly increased likelihood of having survived sexual and/or physical violence, particularly by a male relative or intimate partner. Research also shows that women in prison have experienced unusually high rates of extremely abusive discipline from parents, involvement in drugs, and prostitution, whether they were imprisoned for these crimes or not (Harlow, 1999).

Whether as a direct consequence of abuse or other contributing factors, female inmates may suffer from a loss of self-respect, hiding their pain in substance abuse (McKinney, 1994). A significant number of female inmates report having substance abuse problems. Before their incarceration, women prisoners used more drugs and used those drugs more frequently than did men in prison. Women prisoners are also more likely to report that they were under the influence of drugs at the time of their current offense and to claim that they committed the offense to obtain money to buy drugs (Greenfeld & Snell, 1999).

A consistent pattern in the convictions that result in prison time for women are not primarily violent or dangerous crimes; yet, women convicted of violent offenses are mostly accessories in crimes committed by men or defending their lives against abusive partners (Harlow, 1999). Instead, women tend to be convicted of nonviolent offenses, primarily drug related and to a lesser degree, larceny.

The growth of the female prison population corresponds directly to the mandatory minimum sentencing laws in effect since the early 1980s and continuing into the 1990s. Longer sentences, especially for drug crimes, and fewer prisoners granted parole or probation are the main reasons for the expanding female (as well as male) prison population. Since more women are convicted for nonviolent, drug-related crimes than for any other crime categories, these sentencing policies have had a particularly profound effect on women. Unfortunately, the rise in imprisonment of women for drug-related crimes has not been met by a rise in addiction treatment and rehabilitation programs for these women.

MEDICAL SERVICES FOR WOMEN IN PRISON

Health services delivery within prisons has been increasingly strained over the last decade resulting primarily from (1) more inmates coming into the prisons and (2) new inmates being less healthy than their counterparts of just a decade ago. While improvements in the provision of medical services for incarcerated women have been noted, the implementation of innovative in-house medical treatment for women has not kept pace with the diverse needs of the ever-increasing population.

Women often require more medical attention than men, and women's prisons have to deal with a greater demand for adequate health care. In particular, women experience health problems related to their reproductive systems, which is especially true of those who enter prison pregnant and requiring prenatal care. A host of other problems related to health care exists in women's prisons, including the availability of specific medications (Zaitzow, 1999). Because the number of women in prison is less than that of males, policymakers believe that installing extensive medical services in the prison cannot be justified. Consequently, women inmates requiring greater medical attention than the prison provides must be transported to hospitals that could enhance access to care. Furthermore, when the prisons are located in rural areas, transporting inmates to urban medical centers can be problematic, thereby posing greater risks for the inmate-patient.

Women in prison complain of lack of regular gynecological and breast exams and argue that their medical concerns are often dismissed as overexaggerations. Additionally, many imprisoned women are survivors of physical and sexual abuse and have lacked previous health care in their communities, two factors that put them at even greater risk for having high-risk pregnancies and for developing life-threatening illnesses such as HIV/AIDS, hepatitis C, and HPV/cervical cancer. Moreover, despite being imprisoned and presumably safe from harm, in multiple prisons throughout the United States women are victims of sexual abuse by prison staff, at times during routine medical examinations.

Pregnant women who are incarcerated face even more difficulties in receiving quality care. Their pregnancies are often considered to be high risk and many are complicated by drug and alcohol abuse, smoking, and sexually transmitted infections (e.g., HIV, hepatitis B). These factors, if combined with poor social supports and histories of abuse, put these women and their newborns at even greater risk for increased perinatal and postnatal morbidity and mortality. While model programs do exist where pregnant, incarcerated women learn about appropriate prenatal care and parenting skills during their prison sentence, unfortunately, these programs are few and far between and do not reach the thousands of pregnant women in U.S. prisons.

The impact of imprisonment on the health of women and, in particular, on women infected with HIV/AIDS, is marked. In a prison system primarily designed for men, women's health needs are often not adequately addressed by prison policy, programs, and procedures. As such, medical issues that relate to reproductive health and to the psychosocial issues that surround imprisonment of single female heads of households are often overlooked. Even as the number of women in prison has risen rapidly, women's multifaceted needs are easily forgotten or, at best, put on the back burner of priorities in corrections. In all areas of medical need, prisons fail in prevention, screening, diagnosis, treatment, continuity of care, alleviation of pain, rehabilitation, recovery, and concern.

HIV/AIDS IN CORRECTIONAL FACILITIES

HIV/AIDS infection among the incarcerated population is nearly five times higher than in the total U.S. population (Maruschak, 1999). In 2000, the highest rates of HIV infection for inmates occurred in the Northeast, where 5.2% of the prison population was HIV-infected, followed by 2.3% in the South, 1.1% in the Midwest, and 0.09% in the West. A greater percentage of female (3.6%) than male (2.2%) inmates were HIV-infected (Centers for Disease Control and Prevention, 2001). It was estimated that incarcerated women had an HIV prevalence double that of incarcerated men and 35 times that of nonincarcerated women. This high-prevalence level in the female prison population may be attributed to the high-risk behaviors the women engaged in, many of which caused or contributed to their incarceration (Lanier et al., 2001). Many are imprisoned for drug-related crimes and, therefore, may be injection drug users or prostitutes who sell sex for drug money (Madhani, 2000). It is apparent that many incarcerated women have AIDS, a significant number are HIV-positive, and many more are at risk.

Of course, the likelihood of infection depends largely on sets of behaviors known to place a person at risk. HIV/AIDS is transmitted in only one of three ways: (1) by sexual activity with an infected person; (2) through contact with infected blood by sharing an intravenous needle with an infected person; and (3) from an infected mother to a newborn infant. The Centers for Disease Control and Prevention, or CDC (2001) concluded that the high rates of HIV infection and AIDS among women offenders are essentially the result of intravenous drug use and sexual activity with male injecting drug users. It is important to note that the results of the CDC's study are based on the information provided to them by jurisdictions that are required by law or simply willing to respond to the limited scope of the survey. Some components of the data necessary to calculate cumulative totals (i.e., current cases, cases among released individuals, and deaths while in custody) have not been available from every jurisdiction for each year of the survey. This suggests that the number of HIV and AIDS cases may be much higher than corrections officials are reporting. Additional cases may be concealed by the lengthy incubation period of the disease (sometimes as long as several years). Moreover, although levels of activity vary among facilities, many inmates continue to engage in the types of high-risk behavior—illicit sex and drug injection—during incarceration that pose a significant danger of viral transmission. Thus, it is likely that there are many more AIDS cases than have actually been detected at this time.

SPECIAL NEEDS OF WOMEN PRISONERS WITH HIV/AIDS

Incarcerated women and prison officials face many challenges related to HIV/AIDS. By definition, the common condition of imprisonment is that there is very little choice in every aspect of life. Additionally, issues and concerns become magnified within the prison environment. Crowded conditions, the forced close environment, the highly regulated living conditions, and the inability to control their own risk through personal decision making affect all inmates. When the concern is HIV infection, the implications are even more serious (Zaitzow & West, 2002).

This is especially true for medical care, where prison authorities have a financial interest in limiting choice. The cost of HIV/AIDS care in prisons is now rivaled by the costs and controversies surrounding management of hepatitis C, which affects 30% of prison inmates, and the cost of current psychotropic agents for the large number of individuals with mental illness who are imprisoned in the United States (Reindollar, 1999). The ability to make the most basic decisions about HIV antibody testing, HIV status disclosure, prevention education, or medical treatment often is denied to prisoners. Some persons infected with HIV may be asymptomatic, not even knowing they have the virus. Others may know they are HIV-positive but may appear just as healthy as noninfected inmates. Still others, however, may have developed AIDS or other health problems as a result of the virus and may need substantial medical treatment. Inmates in the terminal stage of AIDS will need intensive medical care. Since HIV compromises the body's ability to fight infection and resist disease, those who are infected, in whatever stage of the disease, must be removed from inmates with contagious illnesses and other conditions that might overwhelm their suppressed immune systems. However, when segregation is used to isolate HIV-infected inmates, these inmates need proper care. They should not be denied services or programming available to the general prison population (Zaitzow, 1999).

Judy Ricci, an HIV-positive inmate at the Central California Women's Facility, knew that she was watching end-stage liver disease slowly kill a fellow HIV-positive inmate. The following is from Ricci's October 2000 testimony about the horrific medical treatment of women prisoners in a California prison:

> The first woman that died on September 6, 1999, I had seen this woman running around for months. She had pieces of Tampax and Kleenex stuffed up in her nose to stop the flow of blood. Her stomach (she was a little skinny woman) looked like a basketball.
>
> Her eyes were literally the color of a pumpkin. I had never approached this woman, because while I knew what she had . . . I didn't want to break her confidentiality and I didn't want to offend her. But I couldn't help asking her, "Do you need some help?". . . As a person who was informed, I could see and I knew what was happening to her, and it hurt that much worse, but anybody, even an untrained eye, could see that she was going to die. How did they release her from the hospital in this condition? (Greenspan, 2001)

Medical providers had failed to realize that the woman's co-infection with hepatitis C had reached a critical point. Ricci made the above statement at a state legislative hearing in October 2000. She proceeded to share additional insights:

> Since I have been here, I have met literally hundreds of women who are infected with hepatitis C. I met them because I am really open about my disease. I like to talk about HIV and hepatitis C. I like to learn about it because I believe my survival depends upon it. I like to share the information that I have with other women who may not be able to read it so that they can survive. I have met a lot of women who have been incarcerated 10 or 15 years and are just finding out this year or last year that they are hepatitis C positive. And guess what? It was in their file for 10 years! How do you let somebody run around not knowing that they have a life threatening communicable disease? What if that woman goes home and transmits that disease to someone else in ignorance? That whole idea breaks my heart. I don't want anybody to live with what I live with. I mean, I am healthy today. I am running around. I'm jazzy today. In two years, I could be falling apart and I wouldn't wish my disease on another person.
>
> Something like 88% of our HIV-positive women also have hepatitis C because it was transmitted by IV drug use. So TB meds are really liver toxic. The second woman who died, I believe died because she was given TB medication. She never had TB. If a person is not having symptoms, they are not spitting blood, they don't have a fever, they don't have night sweats and you suspect that they have an active TB infection, then you isolate them. You should do a culture. This woman stayed for 14 days in isolation and when she came back her stomach was already distended. They offered to drain her stomach in our infirmary. Our infirmary has no emergency equipment. It's got a couple of gurneys and a curtain. She asked for a six-month chrono [for compassionate release] because it became apparent to her that she was going to lose her life. And this was denied. [She died on October 22, 1999.]
>
> You know, 54% of our female population has hepatitis C. If we have 3,600 women, then 54% is 1,944 women. We are always hearing that we're just prisoners and CDC [California Department of Corrections] doesn't have money for hepatitis C treatment. How come they returned $1.7 million dollars in 1998 that was designated for hepatitis C research and treatment in CDC? They didn't know what to do with it? (Greenspan, 2001)

Counseling issues must be handled with much care and sensitivity, depending on whether the inmate is uninfected but at risk for HIV infection, HIV-positive but asymptomatic, or has full-blown HIV infection or AIDS. The concerns expressed most frequently by

HIV-positive women inmates are fear of becoming ill, fear of transmitting HIV to their sexual partners and children, difficulty in communicating with potential sexual partners while remaining sexually active, and being unable to bear children for fear the offspring will become infected (Zaitzow & West, 2002).

Even uninfected inmates have concerns related to HIV infection that may be addressed through counseling. Programs for the "worried-well" may serve to address the fears of women who are not infected, but who interact daily with women who are. One uninfected inmate, when asked about her biggest AIDS-related fear, stated:

> I wouldn't want to die up here. My biggest fear . . . is getting sick and dying up here, because when you get sick . . . by the time you get in to see your doctor . . . then by the time they make arrangements for your [AIDS] test, you're gone. (West, 1996)

Unlike women in the other groups, those who have symptomatic HIV infection and AIDS must deal with grief over the loss of their previous body image, sexual freedom, and potential for childbearing. They must also address the imminent loss of their own lives. Grief and other emotions triggered by the HIV/AIDS diagnosis can be profound. Moreover, there may be as many as 80,000 mothers in local, state, and federal jails and prisons, and their dependents may total 150,000 people (Johnston, 1995). The legal and practical restrictions imposed on women prisoners infected with HIV/AIDS as they try to maintain relationships with their children significantly affect their physical and emotional well-being. The dramatic growth in the number of women in correctional settings during the past decade who either have tested positive for HIV/AIDS or are presumed to have HIV/AIDS, and their need for gender-specific services, has prompted researchers and advocates to call for increased attention to correctional programming for women and increased use of community-based interventions and alternatives.

DOING INFECTED TIME: ISSUES AND CHALLENGES

While prisoner advocates assert that women prisoners have a harder time getting treatment than men do, it is difficult to generalize about HIV/AIDS care in prison because it is not standardized across the nation. Each state system has its own set of policies and procedures for treating inmates, and the federal prison system operates under its own guidelines as well. Even within each state, the quality of treatment programs varies widely from facility to facility.

Women's struggles to change their conditions often lie in filing lawsuits rather than with directly confronting prison officials. In 1995, women at the Central California Women's Facility in Chowchilla, California, filed a class action suit demanding immediate improvement in life-threatening medical care. In 1996, seven women in Michigan filed a suit on behalf of all women prisoners in the state charging the Department of Corrections with sexual assault and harassment, violations of privacy, and physical threats and assaults. In 1998, six women in New York filed a class action suit against routine body searches by male guards. In Washington, "consensual sex" between women prisoners and prison employees is not outlawed, but front-page news about such incidents led state legislators to propose a ban (still not enacted). The power of media became evident in 1999, when

Geraldo Rivera's report on official sexual misconduct in prison was repeatedly cited during a House debate. In Wisconsin, a phone call from an anonymous prisoner to a woman reporter at the *Milwaukee Sentinel* about the asthma death of Michelle Greer led to an investigative report. It turned the story into a minor sensation, and forced the state Department of Corrections to take action and the state Assembly to hold investigative hearings. The reporters eventually examined every prisoner death since 1984, prompting lawmakers to require better training for medical staff, improved medical record keeping, and the creation of an independent panel of medical experts to review prison deaths. Perhaps because of the efficacy of lawsuits and the attendant publicity, those who file suits are often subject to administrative retaliation, or even worse, purposeful medical neglect.

In order to understand the seriousness of the problems confronting women prisoners with HIV/AIDS, meet Rosie.

Rosemary Willeby, aka "Rosie," died on October 22, 1999, while in the custody and care of the Central California Women's Facility (in Chowchilla, California). Rosie was coinfected with HIV/hepatitis C, and her death was preceded by an act of gross medical malpractice followed by months of pain, suffering and medical neglect.

On April 6, 1999, Rosie was summoned to her facility yard clinic. A mask was placed over her face. She was made to sit in a wheelchair, was wheeled to the infirmary, and from there was transported to an isolation room at the Valley State Prison for Women (the prison across the street). The order for her transfer and treatment was signed by the Chief Medical Officer (CMO). Her medical records state that she was complaining of "night sweats" and running a high temperature, thus was thought to have an active TB infection. However, no notations were made (before or after April 6) of complaints of night sweats, and her temperature was recorded as 97.1 upon her entry to Valley State.

Rosie did not have a temperature, night sweats or TB! TB medications are extremely hepatoxic, and Rosie had a pre-existing liver condition. It is reasonable to assume that a doctor would want to confirm the presence of an active TB infection before administering liver toxic medication to a patient with liver disease. But no sputum test was done, no x-ray taken, no test to confirm or deny the presence of an active TB infection. Rosie was pulled off all anti-HIV meds, and forced to take four types of toxic anti-TB meds for fourteen days. This caused a massive liver injury that ultimately led to her demise.

Rosie's remaining six months of life were spent in agony. Her abdomen was just beginning to swell upon her return to CCWF. Within four months, she resembled a woman in her third trimester of pregnancy. Her lower extremities began to swell also, making it painful and extremely difficult to walk, so swollen she could no longer wear a pair of shoes.

To add insult to injury, she lost her independence over her last few months, unable to even dress herself without assistance. During this time, Rosie received no special care in regards to her liver, besides diuretics. It was suggested to her that she allow a doctor to drain her abdomen in the prison infirmary, which she refused, as it is not set up to deal with life-threatening emergencies should something go wrong. She begged to be sent to the hospital to be drained, begged to see a specialist, and was denied.

As it became apparent that Rosie's days were numbered, the folks from "Women's PLAN" [Women's Positive Legal Action Network] started putting in a request for compassionate release for her, supplemented with letters from Rosie's family, professionals in the community, as well as from inmates who witnessed her daily struggle. It would have been necessary for the CMO to lend his signature to a document confirming the gravity of Rosie's condition and estimating her remaining life to be six months or less. He "could not find it in his heart" to sign such a document at that time, but said he would consider it if her condition worsened by October 10, and ordered that she be frequently measured and weighed to document increases in girth and poundage. And so it went. From 43 inches, to 53, to 59 inches. From a normal weight of 130, to 180. On October 11, Rosie finally collapsed and was taken to the Madera Community Hospital where she remained until she expired on October 22, 1999.

Rosemary's commitment offense was the sale of one ten dollar piece of crack. Her term was, for the most part, already served. The atrocity that led to her demise aside, what threat would have been posed on the community had she been allowed to die with some dignity and in some relative comfort with her family? Since when in America, does the sale of $10 worth of crack warrant the death penalty?

In the telling of Rosie's story, this author is suggesting that she was not only the victim of medical malpractice, abuse, and neglect—but of murder as well!!! With the telling of Rosie's story, and with increased awareness of medical atrocities going on inside California prisons— let the horror stories stop!

Please! Make them stop! ("A woman Inside the Central California Women's Facility," 2001)[1]

HIV/AIDS TREATMENT IN PRISON

While a complete HIV/AIDS cure or preventive vaccine remains elusive, medical advances have greatly increased the longevity of AIDS patients. The most successful treatment innovation to combat HIV and AIDS is the "cocktail" approach (AEGIS, 1997). Previously, people with AIDS had only one drug option: zidovudine, or AZT. Today, there are 9 separate drug combinations that can work in more than 100 different combinations (Leland, 1996, p. 64). The greatest gains have been made by using different combinations of drugs that attack HIV at different stages of its replication process (Markowitz, 1996). With these types of treatments AIDS-related illnesses (including opportunistic infections and cancers) and deaths have decreased by approximately half. Consequently, survival and delay of AIDS progression are significantly improved among those patients receiving combination therapy (U.S. Department of Health and Human Services, 1997).

Prison environments are not the ideal location for people living with AIDS (Leland, 1996, p. 67). Prisoners with AIDS become sick at twice the rate of those on the outside (Hope & Hayes, 1995, p. 12). Also, among prison populations there is a greater likelihood that a person's HIV status is unknown, and it is this group of patients (those unknowing) that are most likely to come in too late for effective treatment (AEGIS, 1997). Efforts to treat HIV and AIDS within prisons have been severely hampered by uneven medical care and a short supply of the promising new drug combination treatments described above. Unfortunately, most prison systems are following old treatment protocols that do not take advantage of the new combination drugs, especially protease inhibitors (Purdy, 1997, p. 1). More important, resistance to AZT is almost certain to develop when given the monotherapy (one drug at a time) commonly used in prison settings (Markowitz, 1996, p. 4).

The quality of treatment also varies from prison to prison and state to state, often depending on whether court actions have forced improved medical care (Purdy, 1997, p. 28). Some prison systems continue to put HIV-positive prisoners in isolation or special units, depriving them of limited programs and recreational opportunities available to other inmates (Berkman, 1995, p. 1618). Other correctional systems do not permit prisoners to participate in clinical studies, denying them the potential benefits of promising new treatment approaches (Stein & Headley, 1996, p. 3). In addition, now that treating HIV and AIDS is becoming as complex as treating cancer, with drugs and dosages carefully calibrated to each patient's medical condition, specialists are required. Unfortunately, many infected inmates are being treated by primary-care doctors and see a specialist only occasionally, if at all (Purdy, 1997, p. 1). The best medical care providers should deliver AIDS care, not those lacking specialization (Voelker, 1996, p. 438). Dr. Altice of Yale Medical School, who treats inmates in Connecticut's prisons, stated that "[p]rison doctors around the country are not trained specialists. We used to say that AIDS treatment is primary care. This is no longer true. We would no more have the average primary care provider deliver chemotherapy to cancer patients, than we would have the same people provide complex HIV treatment" (cited in Purdy, 1997, p. 28).

Of additional concern is the fact that the recent combination therapies require incredibly demanding regimes, sometimes as many as 30 or 40 pills a day, distributed over a strict timetable (Leland, 1996, p. 69). Some drugs have to be taken with food, others on an empty stomach (p. 69). Most correctional systems are crowded and must operate on a strict timeline, making this type of specialized care difficult and often impossible.

Finally, the organization of health care systems within prisons operates according to a sick-call model. In other words, they respond to discrete and immediate health problems such as injuries and specific illnesses (Smith & Dailard, 1994). Systems designed in such a way lack the flexibility that HIV-positive persons require.

Just to provide one illustration, consider the fact that since inmates are not trusted with the responsibility of controlling their own medication, prisoners who require medication on a regular basis must follow a rigorous procedure. AIDS patients who are incarcerated will require this medical attention several times a day. Concerns have also been raised because inmates going to the medical dispensary numerous times daily to receive medication pose a security risk (Purdy, 1997, p. 28). Consequently, correctional medical staff may have difficulty accepting or understanding the need for the large number of pills required or the frequency with which they must be administered (Kelly, 1995, p. 67). As a result, prisoners often miss doses of medication (Smith & Dailard, 1994, p. 82).

When patients divert from the required medical regimen, they risk cultivating a strain of the virus that's resistant to one or more of the drugs (Leland, 1996, p. 69). These drug-resistant viruses threaten the general and prison public health as well as that of the HIV-infected patient. This growing concern is illustrated by the increasing spread of multidrug-resistant tuberculosis (Linsk, 1997, p. 70). Therefore, adherence to drug regimes is critically important (Purdy, 1997, p. 28), despite the difficulty imposed on correctional administrators.

Making sure that inmates get uniform care is a problem not only when they are released but also when they move from one prison to another. A prisoner's medical records may fail to follow her as she moves through the prison system, and prison health care providers rarely coordinate treatments with community-based physicians once a prisoner is released (Smith & Dailard, 1994, p. 82). Continuity of care is critically important to prisoners with HIV, but the concerns and realities presented here make it difficult to provide consistent treatment (Smith & Dailard, 1994, p. 82).

POLICY RECOMMENDATIONS

Several policy recommendations must be taken into consideration for the development of correctional policies and practices for women (and men) with HIV/AIDS. Incarcerated women face myriad social, economic, psychological, and medical problems. Infection and the threat of infection with HIV and AIDS create additional stress. Obviously, sane, humane, and realistic care of women infected with HIV is necessary. However, it is also critical that effective preventive programs are implemented and evaluated. Based on the variety of policies and practices currently in use throughout the U.S. correctional systems, several areas of continued attention are needed to develop a comprehensive and sustained strategy to actively promote the health of incarcerated women.

1. Continue to educate and communicate with inmates and staff in all correctional institutions.
   - Implement a comprehensive HIV/AIDS education and training program (e.g., AIDS Education and Counseling [ACE]).
   - Safer sex negotiation, skill-building, and self-esteem workshops to improve their abilities to make informed sexual choices.
   - Provide individual and/or group counseling for HIV-infected inmates— peer-led counseling groups, drug treatment and AIDS education, and counseling.
   These are the most effective tools in dealing with anxiety and curtailing risky behavior associated with transmission of communicable diseases.
2. Institution staff must implement the required health and safety programs concerning air- and blood-borne pathogens and must implement universal precautions as well.
   - There is a need to develop policies and procedures that teach officers how to conduct searches in a manner that minimizes their likelihood of injury.
   - Improve the prison's physical plant in terms of ventilation and equip staff with appropriate barrier masks and respirators whenever TB outbreaks are noted.
   - Correctional staff need to follow all prescribed infection control guidelines issued by the Centers for Disease Control and Prevention.
3. Inmates should be screened for communicable diseases at booking or admission to, during, and upon release from a facility, and there should be annual examinations of correctional employees for communicable diseases.
   - Early identification of HIV-infected inmates is important. Recent scientific advances have contributed to a significant reduction in the fatality rate among HIV/AIDS-infected individuals who receive these medications in a timely fashion.
   - As the frequency of transmission of HIV/AIDS and other communicable diseases to other inmates and staff within the institution has yet to be determined,

continued monitoring is recommended for the health and safety of all who live or work in penal settings.

4. Correctional management teams, comprising custody and medical management, must make informed decisions about the numerous treatment approaches that are now available for HIV/AIDS (such as protease inhibitors).

   • These treatment regimens are very costly but they have become a part of the minimal standard of practice in treating HIV/AIDS. Therefore, we are obligated by the correctional health care standards (continuity of care and special medical needs) to make these regimens available. They include on-site gynecological and obstetric care, along with HIV care from nurses and HIV specialists who are available several times weekly to respond to the needs of HIV-infected and at-risk women.

   • Guidelines are needed to determine which protease inhibitors to stock and use in treatment initiated in the institution, and to develop effective communications with treating physicians on the outside to facilitate continuity. Needed are state-of-the-art drug treatments, which include access to a combination of drug therapy; antiviral medication monitoring; and postexposure to prevention methods (i.e., dental dams, bleach).

   • Establish contacts—and perhaps contracts—with community organizations (e.g., In-Prison Hospice and Hospice Services) that may be able to assist inmates and their family members with "death with dignity" issues and correctional staff with their continued exposure to inmate deaths.

5. Alleviate prison overcrowding, since it is a significant contributor to the spread of TB.

   • Refer TB- and HIV-infected inmates to community-based service agencies upon release. It has been suggested that many of the women currently serving prison terms could safely and more economically serve their sentences in community-based programs. Female offenders may, indeed, be an ideal population for community-based correctional programs in light of the fact that they (1) commit crimes that, while unacceptable, pose little threat to public safety; (2) are less likely to reoffend; and (3) respond favorably to community-based programs. Health-related programs for women inmates must be integrated into the release plans in which prison-based assistance can be linked to the free community.

   • Discharge programming planning that includes (a) educational and marketable skills development to provide women with the wherewithal to stay out of prison; and (b) the coordination of child care with drug abuse treatment services, safe housing, and medical and educational services.

The prison setting provides a unique opportunity to present HIV/AIDS-related information, to study the results of that presentation, and to modify attempts based on deficits that may be revealed upon evaluation (Martin, Zimmerman, Long, & West, 1995). Women inmates need the same preventive measures and the same level of care, treatment, and support as male prisoners. In addition, however, there is a need for initiatives that acknowledge that the problems encountered by female inmates in the correctional environment often reflect, and are augmented by, their vulnerability and abuse many of them have suffered outside prison. The task of protecting women prisoners from HIV transmission, therefore, presents different—and sometimes greater—challenges than that of preventing HIV infection in male prisoners.

SUMMARY AND CONCLUSIONS

Prisons, designed to confine and punish, frequently fail to provide the level of health services required by patients with HIV/AIDS. As with other chronic illnesses, HIV/AIDS requires health services that are expensive in terms of staff effort, laboratory testing, and medication. Effectively protected from public scrutiny, the prison health care system is uncoordinated, underfunded, and has almost zero accountability, thus escaping outside attention to serious failures of care. An HIV-positive prisoner at the California Institution for Women commented:

> We do not expect things to be pleasant or comfortable. But it is also not meant for those of us with HIV, to be faced each day of our sentence with contempt and abuse just because we have a virus. There is such a vast gap between us and the control of our health, our sanity and our sense of still being a human being. We are still a part of humanity that fears, and loves, and feels pain, both physical and emotional. We have families but many of us are separated from them. We do have real needs to be treated as you would treat someone who is not afflicted with the virus. No one should be treated this way, yet sadly we are, daily. . . . Doesn't anyone care? Many of us will die, we know that, and we do our best to accept the inevitable. But we also have the right to die with dignity and to know that everything was done to prolong our lives and give us some quality of life, even inside the prison walls.

To navigate the bureaucracy, lawyers are as necessary as doctors, but they too are handicapped. In any case, under rulings of the United States Supreme Court, no remedies are available unless prisoners can meet the monumental standard of showing that there was "deliberate indifference to serious medical needs." Advocates want to see women prisoners treated by the standards of acceptable medical care in the outside community.

Women prisoners often come from marginalized, socially deprived, and often high-risk backgrounds for HIV/AIDS. Many of them may already be infected with HIV on entering a prison. Prison medical care should be tailored to the special needs of women in prison, and be equipped and staffed to recognize and manage the diseases that facilitate HIV transmission or accompany AIDS. Most important, the correctional authorities and their health staff should take advantage of the women's stay in custody by providing education on prevention and on how to stay healthy that is tailored to the needs of the different age, racial, and ethnic groups as well as professions (e.g., prostitution). Prison may be a unique moment in these women's lives in which they have access to such care and counseling.

In 2001, the Centers for Disease Control and Prevention issued a report on treatment of HIV/AIDS in the nation's prison system. In its introduction, it explained why this is an issue that should concern us all:

> Conventional wisdom holds that prisons and jails are walled off and separate from the community. More and more, however, people are recognizing that this is not true. Many ties

connect the community with prisons and jails. For one, inmates are constantly moving back and forth between corrections and the community. Problems or risky behaviors begun in prison or jail return with inmates to the community after release (CDC, 2003).

Even if inmates receive treatment while imprisoned, that care will be for naught unless systems are in place to ensure their care continues outside prison walls. If we truly wish to improve the provision of health care to incarcerated populations and, in particular, HIV/AIDS-infected women prisoners, then we must commit further to the continuity of care that is necessary when women return to their communities. Here, partnerships between prison systems and the free-world communities they serve must be forged in order to realize the multifaceted goals related to the challenges faced by these women. One recently completed pilot program—the Corrections Demonstration Project—funded by the CDC and the Health Resources and Services Administration (HRSA) addressed this suggestion. The program sought to link community care providers with recently released inmates so that the level of care received while incarcerated could be maintained once released (Lanier & Paoline, 2005; Lanier & Potter, 2005). Remember, most prisoners are released from prison and return to their respective communities in the less-confined world. Without programs to address the unique physical, emotional, sexual, and drug-related problems of female inmates and prisoners in general, our prisons will be returning high-risk (not in a criminal sense) individuals to the free community.

NOTE

1. Stories of negligence and abuse are repeated again and again across the nation. In some cases, inmates with HIV may be sent to the nearest outside hospital, whether or not it has an infectious-disease specialist. Nevertheless, many inmates in state and federal prisons simply go untreated and find themselves in prison infirmaries or hospitals, where they are left to die. This is unacceptable. For more stories, go to http://www.prisons.org/regardin.htm.

REFERENCES

Acoca, L. (1999). Getting healthy, staying healthy: Physical and mental health/substance abuse. In *National symposium on women offenders* (pp. 33–36). Washington, DC: U.S. Department of Justice.

Aegis: International Association of Physicians in AIDS Care. (1997). Policy prescription for HIV. *American Medical News*, April 28.

A woman inside the Central California Women's Facility. (2001). Retrieved from http://www.prisons.org/hivin.htm.

Beck, A. (2000). *Prisoners in 1999.* Washington, DC: U.S. Department of Justice.

Beck, A. J., & Mumola, C. (1999). *Prisoners in 1998.* Washington, DC: U.S. Government Printing Office, p. 9.

Berkman, A. (1995). Prison health: The breaking point. *American Journal of Public Health, 85* (12), 1616–1618.

Bureau of Justice Statistics. (2004). *Prisoners in 2003.* Washington, DC: U.S. Department of Justice.

Centers for Disease Control and Prevention. (2001, August). HIV/AIDS counseling and testing in the criminal justice system. Retrieved from http://www.thebody.com/cdc/counseling.htm/

DeGroot, A. S., Leibel, S. R., & Zierler, S. (1998). A standard of HIV care for incarcerated women: A northeastern United States experience. *Journal of Correctional Health Care, 5* (2), 139–176.

GILLIARD, D. (1999). *Prison and jail inmates at midyear 1998*. Washington, DC: U.S. Department of Justice.

GREENFELD, L. A., & SNELL, T. L. (1999). *Women offenders* [NCJ 175688]. Special Report. Washington, DC: Bureau of Justice Statistics.

GREENSPAN, J. (2001, July/August). Positive women prisoners speak out. Retrieved from http://www.thebody.com/whatis/women_prison.html.

HARLOW, C. (1999). *Prior abuse reported by inmates and probationers*. Washington, DC: U.S. Department of Justice.

HOPE, T., & HAYES, P. (1995). A clear pattern of neglect: Prisons and the HIV crisis. *Gay Community News, 20*(4), 12–15.

JOHNSTON, D. (1995). Child custody issues of women prisoners: A preliminary report from the CHICAS project. *Prison Journal, 75*, 222.

KELLY E. (1995). Expanding prisoners' access to AIDS-related clinical trails: An ethical and clinical imperative. *Prison Journal, 75*(1), 48–69.

LANIER, M., & PAOLINE, E. III. (2005). Expressed needs and behavioral risk factors of HIV positive inmates. *International Journal of Offender Therapy and Comparative Criminology, 49*(5), 561–573.

LANIER, M., & POTTER, R. H. (2005). HIV/AIDS and correctional populations in the twenty-first century: The Corrections Demonstration Project. In R. Muraskin & A. R. Roberts (Eds.), *Visions for change: Crime and justice in the twenty-first century* (4th ed., pp. 483–509). Upper Saddle River, NJ: Prentice Hall.

LANIER, M., BRAITHWAITE, R., & ARRIOLA, K. J. (2001). New directions for incarcerated women with HIV in the twenty-first century: The Corrections Demonstration Project. In R. Muraskin & A. R. Roberts (Eds.), *Visions for change: Crime and justice in the twenty-first century* (3rd ed., pp. 439–462). Upper Saddle River, NJ: Prentice Hall.

LELAND, J. (1996). The end of AIDS? The plague continues, especially for the uninsured, but new drugs offer hope for living. *Newsweek, 128*(23), 64–71.

LINSK, N. L. (1997). Of magic bullets and social justice: Emerging challenges of recent advances in AIDS treatment. *Health and Social Work, 22*(1), 70–75.

MADHANI, S. J. (2000, Summer). HIV in prisons: Women and men of color disproportionately impacted. *Treatment Alert*, 1–2.

MARKOWTIZ, M. (1996). *Protease inhibitors*. New York: Aaron Diamond AIDS Research Center.

MARTIN, R., ZIMMERMAN, S., LONG, B., & WEST, A. (1995). A content assessment and comparative analysis of prison-based AIDS education programs for inmates. *Prison Journal, 229.*

MARUSCHAK, L. (1999, August). HIV in prisons, 1997. *Bureau of Justice Statistics Bulletin*. Washington, DC: U.S. Department of Justice.

MCKINNEY, J. D. (1994). *A descriptive case study of the impact of social learning experiences on adult female inmates*. Paper presented at the annual meeting of the American Society of Criminology, Miami, FL.

PURDY, M. (1997). As AIDS increases behind bars, costs dim promise of new drugs. *New York Times, 146*, p. A-1.

REINDOLLAR, R. W. (1999). Hepatitis C and the correctional population. *American Journal of Medicine, 107*(6B), 100S–103S.

SMITH, B., & DAILARD, C. (1994). Female prisoners and AIDS: On the margins of public health and social justice. *AIDS and Public Policy Journal, 9*(2), 78–85.

STEIN, G. L., & HEADLEY, L. D. (1996). Forum on prisoners' access to clinical trials: Summary of recommendations. *AIDS and Public Policy Journal, 11*(1), 3–20.

U.S. DEPARTMENT OF HEALTH AND HUMAN SERVICES. (1997). Study confirms that combination treatment using a protease inhibitor can delay HIV disease progression and death. *NIAID News*. Washington, DC: U.S. Department of Health and Human Services.

VOELKER, R. (1996). Can researchers use new drugs to push HIV envelope to extinction? *Journal of the American Medical Association, 276*(6), 435–438.

WEST, A. (1996). *Prison-based AIDS education: A comparative assessment of program impact with male and female inmates*. Unpublished doctoral dissertation, Indiana University of Pennsylvania, Indiana, PA.

ZAITZOW, B. H. (1999, November/December). Women prisoners and HIV/AIDS [Special issue]. *Journal of the Association of Nurses in AIDS Care, 10*(6), 78–89.

ZAITZOW, B. H., & WEST, A. D. (2002). Doing time in the shadow of death: Women prisoners and HIV/AIDS. In S. Sharp (Ed.), *The incarcerated woman: Rehabilitative programming in women's prisons* (pp. 73–90). Upper Saddle River, NJ: Prentice Hall.

23

Women, AIDS, and the Criminal Justice System

Joan Luxenburg and Thomas E. Guild

❖

Women as offenders and women as victims have played a significant role in the shaping of criminal justice policy to deter the spread of AIDS. For the woman as offender, we look at prostitutes and their association with the AIDS epidemic. For the woman as victim, we look at the offense of sexual assault and the controversy surrounding mandatory HIV testing (and disclosure).

In the misguided belief that female prostitutes transmit the virus to their male clients, several states have enacted AIDS-specific statutes that target prostitutes for HIV-antibody testing as well as for enhanced criminal penalties for HIV-positive prostitutes who know their serostatus and continue to engage in prostitution. With no scientific evidence indicating that prostitutes are a vector for transmission of the virus, they are incarcerated for periods longer than necessary.

The criminal justice system has targeted sexual assault defendants for mandatory HIV-antibody testing and disclosure to victims. With further expansion of these laws, women as the victims of rape will be granted medical information regarding their rapists. This seemingly necessary intrusion into the rights of defendants has been challenged unsuccessfully on constitutional grounds.

The epidemic of acquired immune deficiency syndrome (AIDS) has had an impact on every facet of the criminal justice system (Blumberg, 1990b). We address two legal issues surrounding AIDS that are very specific to women. One topic (prostitution) involves women as criminal offenders. The other topic (sexual assault) involves women as the victims of crime. Although men are also arrested for prostitution, the offense is clearly a female-dominated activity. In 1999, of the approximately 64,000 arrests for prostitution and commercialized vice, almost 61 percent were of females. Similarly, we recognize that males are the victims of rape. However, only an estimated 10 percent of rapes occur to males (*Face-to-Face*, 1990). This percentage may be larger, since overall, 3 to 10 rapes go unreported for every 1 rape that is reported (President's Commission on the Human Immunodeficiency Virus Epidemic, 1990).

Our focus on prostitution and AIDS will deal with whether prostitutes are at greater risk than other sexually active women for contracting the AIDS virus (also known as the human immunodeficiency virus [HIV]) and whether prostitutes are vectors for transmitting the virus to their customers. We examine legislation that targets prostitutes for mandatory HIV-antibody testing or that targets HIV-antibody-positive prostitutes for enhanced criminal penalties. For the issue of sexual assault, we look at the debate over requiring HIV-antibody testing of accused or convicted rapists and disclosure of such test results to the alleged or proven victims.

WOMEN AND AIDS

Women's concerns in the AIDS epidemic had gone virtually ignored until 1990. During the 1980s (the first decade of the AIDS epidemic), the public minimized the role of women and their relationship to this public health crisis. Women were merely viewed as the principal caregivers for persons living with AIDS (PLWAs), for example, as nurses in hospitals or as mothers welcoming their homosexual sons home to spend their remaining days with family. This picture changed when in 1990, AIDS was recognized as the leading cause of death among black women in New York and New Jersey, and it was predicted to become by 1991 the fifth-leading cause of death among U.S. women of childbearing age ("AIDS Deaths Soaring," 1990; "More Women Getting AIDS," 1990). During the summer of 1990, the World Health Organization (WHO) estimated that 3 million women and children would die of AIDS during the 1990s, a figure representing more than six times their numbers of AIDS deaths in the 1980s ("More Women, Children," 1990). The rising death rate for women with AIDS became apparent. Whereas only 18 women between the ages of 18 and 44 in the United States died of AIDS during the year 1980, for the year 1988 the number was 1430 ("AIDS Deaths Soaring," 1990). Prior to 1983 only 90 women 13 years and older in the United States had been diagnosed with AIDS (Miller, Turner, & Moses, 1990, pp. 50–51). However, by November 1990, the cumulative figure for all females in the United States (regardless of age) was 16,394 (Oklahoma State Department of Health, 1991).

In recognition of the increase in the number of women with HIV infection, World AIDS Day (held December 1, 1990) proclaimed its focus to be on women and AIDS. Earlier that year, the Sixth International AIDS Conference (held in San Francisco in June) became a forum for the Women's Caucus of the AIDS Coalition to Unleash Power (ACT-UP) to voice their grievances about women's issues related to HIV infection. By November 1990, the American Civil Liberties Union (ACLU) added to its staff a lawyer assigned to work exclusively with issues involving HIV infection among women and children (Herland Sisters Resources, 1990).

In the 1990s, women were among the new wave of HIV infection. By the end of the year 2000, 20 percent of PLWAs in the United States were females (Centers for Disease Control and prevention [CDC], 2001a). Of the 774,467 cumulative reported cases of AIDS in the United States (1981 to 2000), 134,411 were among women. Of the cumulative 448,060 deaths from AIDS during the same period, 66,448 were among women. Of the approximately 40,000 new HIV infections occurring in the United States annually, 30 percent are among women. Of these annual new infections for women, 75 percent were from heterosexual exposure and 25 percent were from injection drug use (CDC, 2001b).

PROSTITUTION AS A TRANSMISSION CATEGORY

The AIDS literature on prostitution has concentrated almost exclusively on female heterosexual prostitutes rather than on male (homosexual) prostitutes. Because the clientele of male prostitutes are principally males, the AIDS literature treats male prostitutes for discussion under the heading of "Homosexuals" (CDC, 1987b; Turner, Miller, & Moses, 1989, p. 14). Stereotypically, prostitutes have been cast as injection drug users (IDUs) or the sexual partners of IDUs when, in fact, only a small percentage may fall into the category of IDUs. In actuality, street prostitution accounts for an estimated 20 percent of all prostitution; and an estimated 5 to 10 percent of prostitutes are addicted (Cohen, Alexander, & Wofsy, 1990, p. 92; Leigh, 1987, p. 180). It is likely that those who are addicted (to injection drugs or to crack) disregard safer sex practices in order to support their habits. For HIV-infected women in general, by the end of the 1980s, 75 percent had acquired the virus through injection drug use or through sexual relations with IDUs ("AIDS Deaths Soaring," 1990).

Self-reported findings suggest that prostitutes may be more likely to use a condom with their customers rather than with their regular sex partners (Cohen et al., 1990; Miller et al., 1990; Rowe & Ryan, 1987, pp. 2–20). However, when Project AWARE (Association of Women's AIDS Research and Education) conducted its San Francisco General Hospital comparison of prostitutes and other sexually active women, it found a slightly lower seropositive rate for prostitutes (Leigh, 1987). The association between HIV-antibody-positive status and injection drug use (rather than with prostitution) was clearly found in the CDC-coordinated seroprevalence studies of prostitutes in 10 U.S. cities, including New York, San Francisco, Jersey City, Miami, and Los Angeles (CDC, 1987a).

Although our discussion focuses on street prostitution, it is worthwhile to note seroprevalence findings from other types of prostitution. In a study of New York City call girls, one in a sample of 80 was HIV-antibody positive, and that person was an IDU (Geraldo, 1990). When Nevada conducted testing of all prostitutes employed in legal brothels, not a single case of HIV-antibody-positive results occurred in over 4,500 tests of approximately 500 prostitutes (Hollabaugh, Karp, & Taylor, 1987, p. 135). Licensed houses of prostitution in Nevada (in addition to screening prospective employees for injection drug use) are required by law (since March 1986) to conduct preemployment HIV-antibody screening and monthly testing after employment; and employment is denied to HIV-antibody-positive applicants (CDC, 1987a; "Infection Not Reported," 1987).

Several years into the AIDS epidemic, the CDC had not reported any documented cases of HIV transmission from a female prostitute to a male customer through sexual contact (Cohen et al., 1990). Probably the most common means of an infected prostitute transmitting the virus to another person is through sharing infected injection drug paraphernalia (AIDS and Civil Liberties Project, 1990). In the United States, female-to-male transmission of the AIDS virus through sexual contact is less efficient than is male-to-female transmission (Eckholm, 1990a). For the period 1981 to October 1985, the CDC concluded that only one-tenth of 1 percent of all U.S. cases of AIDS were the result of female-to-male sexual transmission (Schultz, Milberg, Kristal, & Stonebruner, 1986, p. 1703). In January 1988, only 6 of the 11,000 cases of AIDS in New York City traced back to female-to-male sexual contact, although it was impossible to ascertain from the published data whether prostitutes were involved (AIDS and Civil Liberties Project, 1990). Randy Shilts (1987, pp. 512–513) reported on a case of a San Francisco injection drug-using prostitute who continued working while carrying the AIDS virus for 10 or 11 years until her death in 1987, yet during that period, only two male heterosexual contact cases of AIDS had occurred in San Francisco.

In a CDC study of spouses of transfusion-acquired PLWAs, 16 percent of wives were infected, while only 5 percent of husbands were infected; and although 10 percent of those studied had more than 200 sexual contacts with an infected partner, the uninfected spouse remained seronegative (Stengel, 1987). It must be remembered that the chances of becoming infected are greater for repeated sexual contact (e.g., with a spouse), as opposed to a one-time encounter (e.g., with a street prostitute). The ACLU estimated that 200,000 female prostitutes participate in some 300 million sexual transactions per year in the United States, yet the incidence of males contracting the AIDS virus from prostitutes in the United States was virtually nil (AIDS and Civil Liberties Project, 1990, p. 102). Early reports among U.S. servicemen are probably most responsible for having implicated prostitutes in the spread of the AIDS virus (Redfield et al., 1985). Critics of these reports were quick to reply that military men would be reluctant to report injection drug use or homosexual behavior (Potterat, Phillips, & Muth, 1987).

AIDS LAW AND PROSTITUTES

The ACLU's position on coercive measures against prostitutes is that such measures are futile and serve to drive the disease farther underground (AIDS and Civil Liberties Project, 1990). History reveals that government crackdowns on prostitutes to stop the spread of other sexually transmitted diseases (STDs) have been ineffective (Brandt, 1985, 1988, p. 370). Nevertheless, prostitutes have been the target in several states for mandatory HIV-antibody testing and for enhanced criminal penalties for HIV-antibody-positive prostitutes who continue to practice their trade while knowing their seropositive status.

By 1990, approximately 22 states had criminalized the act of knowingly exposing another person to the AIDS virus ("More States," 1990). From the authors' own observations in Oklahoma, the utility of an AIDS-specific law seems questionable. The Oklahoma law (Okla. Stat. Ann. tit. 21, § 1192.1), which took effect July 1, 1988, states:

A. It shall be unlawful for any person to engage in any activity with the intent to infect or cause to be infected any other person with the human immunodeficiency virus.

B. Any person convicted of violating the provisions of this section shall be guilty of a felony, punishable by imprisonment in the custody of the Department of Corrections for not more than five (5) years.

In January 1990, the first person to be charged under this new law was a 34-year-old Tulsa prostitute, Lynnette Osborne (aka Lynette Love). Osborne had apparently been reported to police by other prostitutes who work in the same general location (Tulsa's red light district). Four undercover Tulsa police officers had interactions with Osborne, resulting in four counts of soliciting between October 1989 and January 1990. Upon Osborne's arrest (under the then-new law), a search warrant was issued allowing authorities to test her blood for the HIV antibodies (Brus, 1990; "Charge Filed," 1990). Unfortunately, the Osborne case did not lend itself to us for analysis of the first trial of its kind in Oklahoma, because the defendant pled guilty in February 1990 to all four felony counts in exchange for four three-year prison terms, to run concurrently ("Prostitute Goes to Jail," 1990).

Several states enacted AIDS legislation that specifically targeted prostitutes. Among the earliest laws was Florida's 1986 statute, which mandated that convicted prostitutes be tested for HIV antibodies (and other STDs). In that state, engaging in prostitution after having been informed of one's seropositivity resulted in a misdemeanor, separate from the charge of prostitution (Bowleg & Bridgham, 1989; CDC, 1987a). Georgia law provided that a person who was aware of his or her seropositivity and subsequently offers to engage in sexual intercourse or sodomy for money, without disclosing (prior to the offer) the presence of the HIV infection, was guilty of a felony punishable upon conviction by not more than ten years. Georgia law also permitted HIV-antibody testing by court order for anyone convicted of or pleading no contest to any HIV-transmitting crime, including prostitution (Bowleg & Bridgham, 1989). Idaho law mandated HIV-antibody testing for defendants being held in any county or city jail who are charged with certain offenses, including prostitution (Bowleg & Bridgham, 1989).

Illinois law required HIV-antibody testing for those convicted of a sex-related offense, including prostitution, solicitation, patronizing a prostitute, and operating a house of prostitution (Thomas, 1988). One may question the relevance of testing the operator of a house if he or she is not exchanging his or her own bodily fluids with the customers. Similarly, the state of Washington's law required anyone convicted of prostitution or "offenses relating to prostitution under chapter 9A.88 RCW" to submit to HIV-antibody testing. Included (in 9A.88 RCW) were the offenses of "promoting prostitution" and "permitting prostitution." Under this law, even persons who engaged in no actual sexual act, but who advanced prostitution, were required to take the HIV-antibody test (Weissman & Childers, 1988–1989).

Michigan's law provided that those convicted of crimes capable of transmitting the AIDS virus (including prostitution) would be examined for HIV antibodies upon court order unless the court determined such testing to be inappropriate (Bowleg & Bridgham, 1989). Nevada law required anyone arrested for prostitution to be tested for HIV antibodies. If the arrest resulted in a conviction, the defendant was requested to pay $100 for the cost of the testing. After receiving notification of a positive test, if the person were subsequently to be arrested and found guilty of another charge of prostitution, the new conviction would be for a felony punishable by one to 20 years in prison and/or a $10,000 fine. Rhode Island and West Virginia each enacted laws requiring any person convicted of prostitution to be tested for HIV antibodies (Bowleg & Bridgham, 1989).

California's law required convicted prostitutes (and certain other sex offenders) to be tested for HIV antibodies. If a prostitute received positive test results and later received a subsequent conviction for prostitution, the subsequent conviction would be for a felony.

Despite California's law, some counties in that state opted not to conduct such testing. For instance, the Alameda County Health Department declined to test convicted prostitutes, partly because that county's budget did not permit it. Alameda County's policy came into the public limelight surrounding the highly publicized case of an Oakland prostitute, Linda Kean. Kean had posed for a picture in a *Newsweek* article in which she claimed to be an HIV-antibody-positive heroin-using prostitute who continued to service customers (Cowley, Hager, & Marshall, 1990). A zealous Oakland vice-squad sergeant, Mike Martin, read the *Newsweek* article and promptly arrested Kean for attempted murder, after he witnessed her getting into a car with a suspected customer. Robert Benjamin, director of the Communicable Disease Division of the Alameda County Health Department, referred to Kean's arrest as "scapegoating" and a "witch hunt." According to Benjamin, it is the customer's personal responsibility to use a condom. Benjamin further pointed out that testing prostitutes for HIV antibodies would send a "false message," suggesting to the public that those prostitutes who are still on the street have a clean bill of health.

In the 1990s, state supreme courts in California and Illinois upheld the constitutionality of laws involving mandatory HIV-antibody testing of convicted prostitutes, and at least two states passed laws requiring such testing for merely accused (not yet convicted) prostitutes (Anderson, 1998). In upholding the Illinois law, the state supreme court opined that such a warrantless and suspicionless search was allowable because the intrusion on the offender's privacy was minimal and convicted offenders have a diminished expectation of privacy. Further, the government's "special need" in protecting the public health overrides the individual's interest in requiring individualized suspicion that the prostitute might be HIV positive ("AIDS Testing for Convicted," 1992).

Critics of AIDS-specific laws targeting prostitutes suggest that enhancing penalties for subsequent convictions of HIV-antibody-positive prostitutes is an unproductive, punitive strategy aimed at a politically powerless group who show no epidemiological evidence that they are contributing significantly to sexual transmission of the AIDS virus. The laws clearly originated from a false perception that prostitutes pose a major risk to their customers.

ALTERNATIVES TO COERCION

The government's paternalistic concern can be helpful in assisting grassroots efforts to educate disenfranchised segments of the population to reduce risk behaviors. Among IDUs, the Community Health Outreach Worker (CHOW) has been most successful in educating this population; CHOWs are usually recovering addicts indigenous to the community and ethnically matched to the population they try to reach. CHOWs provide referrals for drug treatment programs, condoms, instructions for cleaning drug paraphernalia, and so on. Several organizations, such as Cal PEP (California Prostitutes Education Project), have utilized prostitutes and ex-prostitutes in a similar manner (Geraldo, 1990). Funding and expansion of such programs appear to be worthy areas in which the government can invest its resources wisely. Education with dignity appears to have worked in Pumwani, a crowded slum in Kenya, where in 1990 some 400 prostitutes could be found working on any given day (Eckholm, 1990b). More than 80 percent of Pumwani prostitutes had tested positive for HIV antibodies. Knowing that HIV reinfection or other STDs could worsen their health, these woman had cooperated with health officials and began using condoms, reportedly 80 percent of the time (Eckholm, 1990b). Since African prostitutes are transmitters of the AIDS virus, thousands of new HIV infections were being avoided by these efforts. Only about 30 percent of the male truckers at a nearby weighing station (outside Nairobi) reported that they "sometimes" used the free condoms handed to them; and one in four of those drivers (who consented to testing) showed HIV antibodies (Eckholm, 1990b). Stubborn male customers are not confined to Pumwani. In the United States, there is a need to educate the clients of prostitutes as well as to monitor these men to learn the incidence and prevalence of HIV infection among them (Miller et al., 1990). Although noncoercive government intervention shows promise for persuading prostitutes to reduce high-risk behaviors, the strategy may work only because we are dealing with consensual (although commercialized) sexual relations. For nonconsensual sexual relations, coercive measures may be appropriate.

AIDS LAW AND SEXUAL ASSAULT

By the mid-1990s, at least 45 states had enacted legislation that required either accused or convicted sexual offenders to submit to HIV-antibody testing (Stine, 2000). Prior to the enactment of AIDS-specific laws to address this topic, courts found themselves inconsistently deciding whether or not to permit testing of defendants accused of sexual assaults. In 1987, a Texas court of appeals ruled that a district court did not have the statutory (or constitutional) power to order an HIV-antibody test for a defendant charged with aggravated sexual assault, nor did the district court have the authority to release the results to alleged victims on a "need to know basis" (*Shelvin v. Lykos*, 1987). Subsequent to this appellate decision, Texas passed legislation (during a second special session in 1987) granting statutory power to trial courts to order such tests and to disclose the results to alleged victims [Tex. Crim. Proc. Code Ann., Art. 21.31 (Vernon 1988); Thomas, 1988]. According to the Texas law, a person indicted for sexual assault and aggravated sexual assault could be directed by a court to be examined and/or tested for STD, AIDS, or HIV antibodies. The court could direct such examination and/or testing on its own motion or at the request of the alleged victim. The results were not to be used in any criminal proceeding regarding the alleged assault. The court was not allowed to release the results to any parties other than the accused and the alleged victim.

In New York State, before similar legislation was introduced and defeated, that state's courts appeared to favor the victim's need to know over the defendant's right to privacy. In 1988, the New York Supreme Court ruled that it was not violative of a defendant's right to privacy for the state to divulge a rape defendant's HIV-antibody test results to the victim when such testing is done during routine processing of the person into the prison population (*People of New York v. Toure*, 1987). Further, the Court, in its balancing test, decided that the fears and health concerns of the victim outweighed the minimal intrusion to the defendant. Similarly, a county court decided in New York in 1988 that a defendant who had pled guilty to attempted rape could be ordered to submit to HIV-antibody testing and that the victim had a right to know the results (*People of New York v. Thomas*, 1988). In that case, the court concluded that the testing was not an unreasonable search and seizure under the Fourth Amendment and that the intrusion to the defendant was minimal.

Two New York City cases gained national attention in 1990 on the issue of the victim's need to know the accused sexual offender's HIV-antibody status. In one case, a 17-year-old Columbia University coed was raped at knife-point in her dormitory room by former Columbia University security guard, 28-year-old Reginald Darby (Glaberson, 1990; Salholz, Springen, DeLaPena, & Witherspoon, 1990). In this case a Manhattan assistant district attorney plea-bargained a first-degree rape case for a reduced sentence, contingent upon the defendant's submitting to an HIV-antibody test and making the results available to the district attorney's office and to "other appropriate parties." The reduced sentence was for no more than 5 to 15 years, rather than the maximum sentence of $8\frac{1}{3}$ to 25 years. One legal expert on women's rights criticized such agreements as creating a "windfall" for defendants and their attorneys (Glaberson, 1990). It was feared that rape defendants and their attorneys would have additional leverage for striking plea agreements and could even imply an AIDS risk where there was none. Clearly, AIDS-specific legislation was seen as preferable to this type of plea bargain. However, bills requiring HIV-antibody testing of rape defendants (and disclosure to victims) were defeated in New York's legislature in 1990 (Glaberson, 1990); and a principal opponent to the proposed laws was the Lambda Legal Defense Fund, a gay rights organization (*Face-to-Face*, 1990). Lambda's position was that no one should be "forced" to take an HIV-antibody test. However, subsequently Lambda reportedly was willing to support such testing when the rape victim is pregnant (*Face-to-Face*, 1990). The other New York City case to gain attention in 1990 involved a victim of a 1988 burglary and rape, whose assailant was apprehended at the scene by police after he fell asleep in the victim's bed. The defendant (32-year-old Barry Chapman), an IDU and career offender on parole for rape and burglary, was eventually convicted. The victim, who had witnessed a hypodermic needle fall out of Chapman's jacket when police searched it, wanted him tested. Chapman refused two requests, by the Manhattan District Attorney's office, to be tested. Even after Chapman died of AIDS in Sing Sing Prison in 1990, the victim remained unaware of the cause of death, until CBS News obtained the autopsy report and informed the victim. More than two years after her attack, the victim continued to test negative for HIV antibodies.

New York eventually enacted a testing law for those convicted of felonies involving "sexual intercourse" or "deviate sexual intercourse" if the victim requests the HIV test (Fishbein, 2000). New York's law was enacted in 1995 in response to a mandate by the federal government, contained in the 1990 Crime Control Act. The act requires that states provide mandatory HIV testing schemes for convicted sex offenders at the request of their victims (Fishbein, 2000).

In 1988, when Connecticut failed to pass a bill that would have forced rape defendants to be tested, those opposing the measure pointed out the unclear message that would result from a negative test (Hevesi, 1988). Because of the long "window period," the time between becoming infected and actually showing antibodies to the virus, a negative test does not rule out the presence of the virus in the rapist. For this reason, the victim is probably the most logical one to be tested (and retested every six months). With regard to repeated testing of the rapist, legislation can be worded to include this. For instance, Kansas law provided that if the mandated test results were negative for persons convicted of offenses capable of transmitting the AIDS virus, the court would order the person to submit to another HIV-antibody test six months after the first test (Bowleg & Bridgham, 1989).

This second test may actually be of dubious usefulness to the victim, because a positive test for the offender at this juncture may be the result of sexual activity after incarceration.

By late 1990, very few states provided for HIV-antibody testing of those merely accused of sexual assault (prior to conviction). Colorado law provided that those who, after a preliminary hearing, are bound over for trial for sexual offenses (involving penetration) would be ordered by court to be tested for HIV antibodies. The court would report the test results to victims upon the victim's request. If the accused voluntarily submitted to an HIV-antibody test, such cooperation would be admissible as mitigation of sentence if the offense resulted in conviction [Colo. Rev. Stat. 8B, § 18-3-415 (1990)]. Florida law provided that any defendant in a prosecution for any type of sexual battery, where a blood sample is taken from the defendant, would have an HIV-antibody test. The results of the test could not be disclosed to anyone other than the victim and the defendant [Fla. Stat. Ann. 14A, § 381.609 3(i)(6) (West 1990); "Rape Suspect," 1990]. Idaho law required the public health authorities to administer an HIV-antibody test to all persons confined in any county or city jail who were charged with "sex offenses" (Bowleg & Bridgham, 1989).

In 1993, New Jersey enacted two laws in order to comply with the mandate of the 1990 Crime Control Act. The laws authorized mandatory HIV testing for accused or convicted sex offenders. A case involving three juveniles (arrested under these statutes in 1994) reached the New Jersey State Supreme Court after the juveniles had challenged the constitutionality of the statutes. The New Jersey Supreme Court upheld the constitutionality of the statutes. In so doing, the Court explained that for the accused, a "formal charge" requires the state to establish "probable cause" to believe that bodily fluids could have been transferred from the accused to the victim. Such probable cause, the Court felt, would be necessary to support the state's compelling interest in such testing (Runke, 1999).

The length of time between testing the accused or convicted offender and notifying the victim (where allowed) is a crucial consideration. A case profiled on national TV (*Face-to-Face*, 1990) illustrated the problem of timing. The case involved a victim of a rape and attempted murder in a suburban Seattle park who was three months' pregnant at the time of the knife-point attack. The conviction took place two days before the victim gave birth to a baby girl (six months after the attack). However, it took another six months until the victim was notified of the negative test results. The victim wanted to know the defendant's HIV-antibody status prior to his conviction, to decide whether to terminate the pregnancy. However, Washington was not one of the states where an accused rapist could be required to be tested prior to conviction.

The President's Commission on the Human Immunodeficiency Virus Epidemic, in its June 1988 report, made several recommendations concerning HIV-antibody testing (and disclosure) in cases of sexual assault. Among its recommendations, the commission favored mandatory testing "at the earliest possible juncture in the criminal justice process" (Blumberg, 1990b, p. 76) and that there be disclosure to those victims (or their guardians) who wish to know.

As of the late 1990s, the CDC had no documented case of a rape victim becoming infected with the AIDS virus as a consequence of a sexual assault (Blender, 1997). According to Mark Blumberg, who has written extensively on AIDS and the criminal justice system, the risk of HIV infection to female survivors of rape is remote. Most rape victims have been subjected to vaginal, rather than anal intrusion, and (citing a 1988 *JAMA* article) Blumberg asserts that the chances are 1 in 500 for a female to contract the AIDS virus from a single male-to-female episode of vaginal intercourse (Blumberg, 1990a, p. 81). Nevertheless, rape has taken on an added threat to life in the AIDS epidemic and consequently, places its survivors in a tormented frame of mind.

SUMMARY AND CONCLUSIONS

Since no scientific evidence implicates U.S. female prostitutes significantly in transmission of the AIDS virus through sexual contact with their male customers, it may be futile, politically and legally, to use punitive legislative measures to "control" such activity. Coercive and punitive measures are unlikely to alter the behavior of women engaged in consensual sexual relations with their customers, especially where such activity constitutes their livelihood. Where they exist, it is unlikely that punitive strategies will stop the spread of the AIDS virus when such strategies target prostitutes.

> Noncoercive measures such as education would contribute at least as much to public health as coercive measures against such prostitutes. Since data indicate that transmission via injection drug use is a greater risk than sexual transmission as far as female prostitutes are concerned, education in this area as well as distribution of clean needles might do more to assure public health than all the coercive and punitive measures presently on the books.

Of course, proponents of punitive legislation might point out that even if the risk of sexual transmission is small, all possible measures must be taken to check the AIDS virus. They might also argue that since many female prostitutes live a somewhat urban nomadic lifestyle, statistics and documentation on their transmission role may be extremely difficult to gather.

As far as state legislation requiring either accused or convicted sexual assault offenders to submit to HIV-antibody testing, several problems are raised. First, if we are testing accused persons on an involuntary basis, we are eviscerating the presumption of innocence for the criminally accused. To conduct such testing, the government ought to have a compelling governmental interest before infringing on a criminal defendant's fundamental constitutional right to be presumed innocent. The right of a victim to obtain such information seems to fall short of such a compelling state interest. As for defendants who are convicted of sexual assault, convicts have traditionally lost many civil libertarian protections after conviction, and it seems more within the U.S. constitutional tradition to then use coercive HIV-antibody testing. The contribution to public health and the victim's peace of mind seem to be sufficient justification for such postconviction testing and limited disclosure.

Clearly, the AIDS health crisis is a serious epidemic. Rational and effective policies should be followed with a purpose of safeguarding both individual constitutional rights and public health in the United States.

REFERENCES

AIDS AND CIVIL LIBERTIES PROJECT, AMERICAN CIVIL LIBERTIES UNION. (1990). Mandatory HIV testing of prostitutes: Policy statement of the American Civil Liberties Union. In M. Blumberg (Ed.), *AIDS: The impact on the criminal justice system* (pp. 101–107). Columbus, OH: Merrill.

AIDS deaths soaring among women. (1990, July 11). *Daily Oklahoman*, p. 5.

AIDS testing for convicted prostitutes upheld. (1992, July 30). *Chicago Daily Law Bulletin*, p. 1.

ANDERSON, S. (1998). Individual privacy interests and the "special needs" analysis for involuntary drug and HIV tests. *California Law Review, 86*(1), 119–177.

BLENDER, A. N. (1997). Testing the fourth amendment for infection: Mandatory AIDS and HIV testing of criminal defendants at the request of a victim of sexual assault. *Seton Hall Legislative Journal, 21*, 467–501.

BLUMBERG, M. (1990a). AIDS: Analyzing a new dimension in rape victimization. In M. Blumberg (Ed.), *AIDS: The impact on the criminal justice system* (pp. 78–87). Columbus, OH: Merrill.

BLUMBERG, M. (ED.). (1990b). *AIDS: The impact on the criminal justice system*. Columbus, OH: Merrill.

BOWLEG, I. A., & BRIDGHAM, B. J. (1989). *A summary of AIDS laws from the 1988 legislative sessions*. Washington, DC: George Washington University, Intergovernmental Health Policy Project, AIDS Policy Center.

BRANDT, A. M. (1985). *No magic bullet: A social history of venereal disease in the United States since 1880*. New York: Oxford University Press.

BRANDT, A. M. (1988, April). AIDS in historical perspective: Four lessons from the history of sexually transmitted diseases. *American Journal of Public Health, 78*(4), 367–371.

BRUS, B. (1990, January 22). Tulsa official hopes arrest to slow AIDS. *Daily Oklahoman*, p. 1.

CENTERS FOR DISEASE CONTROL AND PREVENTION. (1987a, March 27). Antibody to human immunodeficiency virus in female prostitutes. *Morbidity and Mortality Weekly Report, 36*(11), 159.

CENTERS FOR DISEASE CONTROL. (1987b, December 18). Human immunodeficiency virus infection in the United States: A review of current knowledge. *Morbidity and Mortality Weekly Report, 36*(5–6), 8.

CENTERS FOR DISEASE CONTROL. (2001a, June–1). HIV and AIDS, 1981–2000. *Morbidity and Mortality Weekly Report, 50*(21), 430.

CENTERS FOR DISEASE CONTROL. (2001b, April 4). 20 Years of AIDS: A glance at the HIV epidemic. Retrieved June 15, 2001, from http://www.cdc.gov/nchstp/od/20years.htm.

Charge filed under anti-AIDS law. (1990, January 21). *Sunday Oklahoman*, p. A18.

COHEN, J. B., ALEXANDER, P., & WOFSY, C. (1990). Prostitutes and AIDS: Public policy issues. In M. Blumberg (Ed.), *AIDS: The impact on the criminal justice system* (pp. 91–100). Columbus, OH: Merrill.

COWLEY, G., HAGER, M., & MARSHALL, R. (1990, June 25). AIDS: The next ten years. *Newsweek*, pp. 20–27.

ECKHOLM, E. (1990a, September 16). AIDS in Africa: What makes the two sexes so vulnerable to epidemic. *New York Times*, p. 11.

ECKHOLM, E. (1900b, September 18). Cooperation by prostitutes in Kenya prevents thousands of AIDS cases. *New York Times*, p. 46.

Face-to-Face [Television broadcast]. (1990, December 10). Columbia Broadcasting System.

FISHBEIN, S. B. (2000). Pre-conviction mandatory HIV testing: Rape, AIDS and the Fourth Amendment. *Hofstra Law Review, 28*, 835–867.

Geraldo [Television series]. (1990, May 11). Have prostitutes become the new Typhoid Marys? *Tribute Entertainment*.

GLABERSON, W. (1990, July 9). Rape and the fear of AIDS: How one case was affected. *New York Times*, p. A13.

HERLAND SISTER RESOURCES. (1990). ACLU AIDS project to focus on women and children with AIDS. *Herland Voice, 7*(10), 4.

HEVESI, D. (1988, October 16). AIDS test for suspect splits experts. *New York Times*, p. 30.

HOLLABAUGH, A., KARP, M., & TAYLOR, K. (1987). The second epidemic. In D. Crimp (Ed.), *AIDS: Cultural analysis/cultural criticism* (pp. 127–142). Cambridge, MA: MIT Press.

Infection not reported among legal prostitutes. (1987, November 18). *AIDS Policy and Law*, pp. 2–3.

LEIGH, C. (1987). Further violations of our rights. In D. Crimp (Ed.), *AIDS: Cultural analysis/ cultural criticism* (pp. 177–181). Cambridge, MA: MIT Press.

MILLER, H. G., TURNER, C. F., & MOSES, L. E. (1990). *AIDS: The second decade*. Washington, DC: National Academy Press.

More states establishing laws allowing AIDS assault cases. (1990, October 22). *Daily Oklahoman*, p. 20.

More women, children expected to die from AIDS. (1990, July 29). *Edmond Sun*, p. A9.

More women getting AIDS, study says. (1990, November 30). *Daily Oklahoman*, p. 6.

OKLAHOMA STATE DEPARTMENT OF HEALTH. (1991, January). *Oklahoma AIDS Update, 91*(1), 6.

POTTERAT, J. J., PHILLIPS, L., & MUTH, J. B. (1987, April 3). Lying to military physicians about risk factors for HIV infections [To the Editor]. *Journal of the American Medical Association, 257*(13), 1727.

PRESIDENT'S COMMISSION ON THE HUMAN IMMUNODEFICIENCY VIRUS EPIDEMIC. (1990). Sexual assault and HIV transmission: Section V of Chapter 9. Legal and ethical issues. Report of the President's Commission on the Human Immunodeficiency Virus. Submitted to the President of the United States, June 24, 1988. Reprinted in M. Blumberg (Ed.), *AIDS: The impact on the criminal justice system* (pp. 73–77). Columbus, OH: Merrill.

Prostitute goes to jail in AIDS case. (1990, February 14). *Daily Oklahoman*, p. 31.

Rape suspect due AIDS test. (1990, July 23). *Daily Oklahoman*, p. 7.

REDFIELD, R. R., MARKHAM, P. D., SALAHUDDIN, S. Z., WRIGHT, D. C., SARNGADHARAN, M. G., & GALLO, R. C. (1985, October 18). Heterosexually acquired HTLV-III/LAV disease (AIDS-related complex and AIDS): Epidemiologic evidence for female-to-male transmission. *Journal of the American Medical Association, 254*(15), 2094–2096.

ROWE, M., & RYAN, C. (1987). *AIDS: A public health challenge: State issues policies and programs: Vol. 1. Assessing the problem*. Washington, DC: George Washington University, Intergovernmental Health Policy Project, AIDS Policy Center.

RUNKE, J. P. (1999). Fourth amendment balancing act: Special needs of rape victims justify court-ordered HIV testing of the accused. *Seton Hall Law Review, 29*, 1094–1121.

SALHOLZ, E., SPRINGEN, K., DELAPENA, N., & WITHERSPOON, D. (1990, July 23). A frightening aftermath: Concern about AIDS adds to the trauma of rape. *Newsweek*, p. 53.

SCHULTZ, S., MILBERG, J. A., KRISTAL, A. R., & STONEBRUNER, R. L. (1986, April 4). Female-to-male transmission of HTLV-III [To the Editor]. *Journal of the American Medical Association, 255*(13), 1703–1704.

SHILTS, R. (1987). *And the band played on: Politics, people and the AIDS epidemic*. New York: St. Martin's Press.

STENGEL, R. (1987, June 8). Testing dilemma: Washington prepares a controversial new policy to fight AIDS. *Time*, pp. 20–22.

STINE, G. J. (2000). *AIDS update 2000*. Upper Saddle River, NJ: Prentice Hall.

THOMAS, C. (1988). *A synopsis of state AIDS laws enacted during the 1983–1987 legislative sessions*. Washington, DC: George Washington University, Intergovernmental Health Policy Project, AIDS Policy Center.

TURNER, C. F., MILLER, H. G., & MOSES, L. E. (1989). *AIDS: Sexual behavior and intravenous drug use*. Washington, DC: National Academy Press.

VERNON. (1988). *Final authorization of state hazardous waste management program revisions.* Texas: EPA Federal Register.

WEISSMAN, J. L., & CHILDERS, M. (1988–1989). Constitutional questions: mandatory testing for AIDS under Washington's AIDS legislation. *Gonzaga Law Review, 24*, 433–473.

CASES

People of New York v. Thomas, 529 N.Y.S. 2d 439 (Co. Ct. 1988).

People of New York v. Toure, 523 N.Y.S. 2d 622 (Sup. 1987).

Shelvin v. Lykos, 741 S.W.2d 178 (Tex. App.-Houston 1987).

SECTION V
Gender and Race

24

Systemic White Racism and the Brutalization of Executed Black Women in the United States

David V. Baker

No criminal justice research has comprehensively studied the historical contexts of racialized, sexist oppression of executed black women in the United States. To better understand the contexts in which black female executions have taken place, this chapter examines the systemic white oppression of executed black women from the earliest periods of American history to the present. The most consistent factor giving rise to black female executions throughout United States history is that criminal justice authorities have executed black women for challenging their racist and sexist exploitation by white men. Colonial and antebellum slavery institutionalized the sexualized persecution of slave women who most often retaliated against the oppressive brutality by killing their white masters. White lynch mobs effectively augmented the legal killing of black women in postbellum society and lowered black female execution rates. Reduced to a peonage state in the apartheid of Jim Crow, black women's crimes of resistance against white male brutality paralleled those of slave women decades earlier. Despite delusionary expansion of civil rights and sovereignty of black people over the confines of segregation in the modern era, the racialized sexism of American criminal justice has rendered black women ever more vulnerable to death as punishment.

INTRODUCTION

A major shortcoming of the research record on race and capital sentencing in the United States is that criminal justice researchers have limited their investigations mostly to the decades following the U.S. Supreme Court decision in *Gregg v. Georgia* (1976). As a result, criminal justice researchers have ignored the historical contexts in which death penalty jurisdictions have executed most condemned prisoners in the United States; authorities put to death 92 percent of the executed prisoner population in the United States before *Gregg* (Espy & Smykla, 2004). Death penalty researchers have overlooked the social, political, and economic conditions giving rise to racism in capital sentencing; that is, much about the *historical maturation* of race and capital punishment remains elusive to criminal justice researchers. This dearth of research on the racial history of capital punishment is perhaps explainable since most criminal justice researchers no longer accept the notion of race discrimination in the U.S. justice system (Milovanovic & Russell, 2001; see also, Georges-Abeyie, 1990; Langan, 1994).

Still, considerable research exists showing an inextricable link between the execution of black persons in the modern era of capital punishment and the execution of black persons in earlier periods of United States history—especially in cases involving white victimization by black males (Aguirre & Baker, 1991). Although little criminal justice research has ferreted out this historical connection, legal scholars and social historians have added much to our understanding of the contextual backdrop of racism in capital punishment (McFeely, 1997). Scholars argue that to appreciate the modern relationship between race and criminal law, criminal justice researchers must study the historic connection between race, crime, and criminal law since United States society has yet to escape its colonial and early national past (Finkelman, 1993, p. 2,064). For example, "few have systematically studied the use of capital punishment against African Americans in bondage, nor have such executions been analyzed within the context of the general history of capital punishment" (Schwarz, 1996, p. 63; see also Aguirre & Baker, 1999; Vandiver & Coconis, 2001). Noticeably important to such scholarship is the recognition of a formidable "nexus between the brutal centuries of colonial slavery and the racial polarization and anxieties of today" (Higginbotham, 1978, p. 391). Criminal justice researchers must recognize the *historical* and *contextual* dimensions of race and punishment because, as Hawkins (1987) maintains, the "variations in levels of punishment by race must be more fully analyzed and explained within the context of the larger structural forces from which they emanate and in their proper temporal perspective. Such a historical-contextual analysis would allow for more attention to the political economy of criminal punishment" (p. 719). Understanding why race remains an important factor in erroneous capital convictions, for instance, entails a broader discussion on the *historical context of race* in the criminal justice system to the development of certain laws (Rizer, 2003, p. 847). What is more, the failure of justice researchers to consider *contextual factors as historical trends* often results in misspecifications of the relationship between racial inequities and criminal justice outcomes (Green, 1998; see also Fagan, 2005).

Similarly, criminal justice researchers have afforded scant attention to gendered racism in capital punishment; and what research investigators have done on gender issues in capital sentencing is limited typically to the modern era (Bohm, 2003; Crocker, 2001; Howarth, 1994, 2002; Morgan, 2003; Rapaport, 2000, 2001; Rueter, 1996; Schmall, 1996; Schulberg, 2000, 2003; Shapiro, 2000; Streib, 2003). Few scholars have linked the atrocities committed against black women by contemporary justice practitioners to comparable forms of mistreatment experienced by black women to the centuries of black oppression preceding the modern era in capital punishment (Baker, 1999; Harries, 1992; Johnson, 1995; Streib, 1990). As bell hooks (1981) explains, "sexism looms as large as racism as an oppressive force in the lives of black women" (p. 15). Despite death penalty jurisdictions executing 83 percent of black women put to death in the United States before the end of slavery (Espy & Smykla, 2004), criminal justice researchers have not studied female executions during slavery beyond constructing descriptive profiles of the historical data (Streib, 1990). Analyses of black female executions are devoid of a historical-contextual connection between earlier and later execution periods, and thus criminal justice researchers have failed to account for the execution of black women as fitting all too well into the United States justice system's historical legacy of devaluing black women. One researcher describes the dilemma confronting black women in criminal justice research this way:

> Black women in American society have been victimized by their double status as blacks and as women. Discussions of blacks have focused on the black man; whereas discussions of females have focused on the white female. Information about black females has been based on their position relative to black males and white females. Consequently, black women have not been perceived as a group worthy of study. Knowledge about these women is based on images that are distorted and falsified. In turn, these images have influenced the way in which black female victims and offenders have been treated by the criminal justice system. (Mann, 1989, pp. 105–106)

No criminal justice research has comprehensively studied the historical contexts of racialized, sexist oppression of executed black women in the United States. To better understand the contexts in which black female executions have taken place, this chapter examines the systemic white oppression of executed black women from the earliest periods of American history to the present. The most consistent factor giving rise to black female executions throughout U.S. history is that criminal justice authorities have executed black women for challenging their racist and sexist exploitation by white men. Colonial and antebellum slavery institutionalized the sexualized persecution of slave women who most often retaliated against the oppressive brutality by killing their white masters. White lynch mobs effectively augmented the legal killing of black women in postbellum society and lowered black female execution rates. Reduced to a peonage state in the apartheid of Jim Crow, black women's crimes of resistance against white male brutality paralleled those of slave women decades earlier. Despite delusionary expansion of civil rights and sovereignty of black people over the confines of segregation in the modern era, the racialized sexism of American criminal justice has rendered black women ever more vulnerable to death as punishment.

RACIAL CONTROL, SYSTEMIC WHITE RACISM, AND THE DEATH PENALTY

The United States is a societal system of white domination and black subordination. In it, whites maintain their social dominion over black lives with institutional and individual devices of disenfranchisement. The criminal justice system is one such institutional apparatus of white social control over black people. As Quinney (1977) explains, the coercive force of the state, as embodied in law and legal repression, is the traditional means of maintaining social dominance over disparate groups. The function of the justice system is to maintain the social arrangement of differential power relations between the whites and black people. The power to define social behavior as criminal resides with whites, thus, crime is any social behavior engaged in by blacks that whites perceive as threatening to their social, political, or economic interests. Staples (1975) explains the arrangement this way: "The ruling caste defines those acts as crimes that fit its needs and purposes and characterizes as criminal individuals who commit certain kinds of illegal acts, while similar acts are exempted from prosecution and escape public disapprobation because they are not perceived as criminal or a threat to society" (p. 18). State-sanctioned violence is fundamental to maintaining the social arrangement; that is, legitimated forms of violence are integral to the United States system of white control, domination, and exploitation of black people (Benjamin, 1991). The official, yet often coercive and violent tasks of law enforcement officers, prosecutors, judges, juries, and even state executioners in the criminal justice system is to protect white interests. To Kennedy (1997), "sentencing a person to death as punishment for crime is a unique flexing of state power" (p. 311). In flexing its power, the state disproportionately executes black people whose acts victimize white persons or threaten their institutions (Bowers & Pierce, 1980).

White racism is *systemic* to the societal arrangement in the United States of white dominion over black people. Sociologist Joe R. Feagin (2001) defines systemic racism as the "diverse assortment of racist practices; the unjustly gained economic and political power of whites; the continuing resource inequalities; and the white-racist ideologies, attitudes, and institutions created to preserve white advantages and power" (p. 16). Undeniably, white racism is systemic to the imposition of death as punishment in the United States. The deeply embedded racist relations of American society have produced a criminal justice system privileging white Americans to decency, fairness, and equitable treatment, while concomitantly leaving black Americans disentitled to impartiality and evenhandedness. Abolitionist Frederick Douglass recognized the disenfranchising effects of systemic white racism in the American criminal justice system generations ago when he noted, "justice is often painted with bandaged eyes. She is described in forensic eloquence as utterly blind to wealth and poverty, high or low, black or white, but a mask of iron, however thick, could never blind American justice when a black man [or woman] happens to be on trial" (cited in Baker & Davin, 2001). Systemic white racism results in differential punishments of blacks and whites. In both its legal and extralegal forms, U.S. society engages the brutality of lethal punishment against black persons to maintain white dominion over its social, political, and economic interests. The purpose of this chapter is to explain how systemic white racism has characterized the four-hundred-year history of putting black women to death in the United States.

SLAVERY IN THE UNITED STATES

The trans-Atlantic slave trade lasted from 1502 to 1888 with most slaves transported from the West African coastal nations of Senegambia, Benin, Wolof, Dahomey, and Lagos. The trade supplied 2.4 million African slaves to Brazil, 1.7 million to the British Caribbean, 1.5 million to the French Caribbean, 871,000 to Spanish America, 500,000 to the Dutch Caribbean, 400,000 to British North America, and 28,000 to the Danish Caribbean. Still, 4 million other Africans never survived the Atlantic crossing (Smallwood, 1998). Yet even here, at the dawn of American slavery, the experiences of black women were different from others. Traders, for instance, did not place female slaves in ship holds with shackled males. More exactly, slavers positioned female slaves on quarterdecks where they could move freely and were more accessible to the sexual perversions of officers who "were permitted to indulge their passions" (Johnson, 1995, p. 15, note 84). Rape was a common torture for disobedient slave women (hooks, 1981). Traders also branded slaves once aboard ship and they would ruthlessly beat slave women that resisted being strip naked for the practice. Crewmembers particularly "ridiculed, mocked, and treated contemptuously" slave women with children (hooks, 1981, p. 19). Often, slavers sadistically abused slave children just to watch their mothers' anguish; and if a child died from the cruelty, slavers forced the mother to throw the child overboard or suffer even more brutality. Slavers were no less barbaric in their treatment of captured pregnant slave women. As bell hooks (1981) explains:

> [T]he American slave ship Pongas carried 250 women, many of them pregnant, who were squeezed into a compartment of 16 by 18 feet. The women who survived the initial stages of pregnancy gave birth aboard ship with their bodies exposed to either the scorching sun or the freezing cold. The numbers of black women who died during childbirth or the number of still-born children will never be known. (pp. 18–19)

Accessible and unshackled female slaves posed a formidable threat to seamen, however; slave women recurrently incited and aided in seditious acts aboard ship. Although unsuccessful, a mutiny of the *Roberts* in 1721 resulted in a female and two male slaves killing several sailors and wounding many others. Apparently, the woman assisting the male slaves served as a lookout, alerted the male slaves to the number of sailors on the deck, and stole all the weapons used in the revolt. Nothing is said in the historical record about the punishment garnered on the male slave participants, but the ship's captain severely punished the female slave: "The Woman he hoisted up by the Thumbs, whipped, and slashed her with Knives before the other Slaves till she died" (Johnson, 1995, p. 15, note 84). In another incident in 1785, slave women attacked a ship's captain and tried to throw him overboard but his crew saved him. A similar incident had taken place aboard the *Thames* years earlier.

The first Africans arrived in Virginia in August 1619 when the colonial government of Jamestown traded food and other supplies for some 20 African captives aboard a Dutch warship (Bush, 1996). Apparently, Virginia's governor sent the *Treasurer* to the West Indies to obtain and deliver goods. The *Treasurer* met a Dutch warship once at sea and together the ships attacked a Spanish frigate carrying more than 100 Africans and stole the slave cargo. While heading back to Virginia the ships separated during a storm and only the Dutch warship made it to Jamestown where it traded its cargo of Africans for supplies. It is noteworthy that one of the captives was a woman named Isabella who later gave birth to the first child of African descent born in the British mainland colony (Reiss, 1997).

Social historians continue to debate the legal status of the first Africans as *slaves* or *indentured servants* (Higginbotham, 1978). Three forms of labor developed in colonial America: *free labor* involved a contractual arrangement of work for wages, *chattel slavery* had no contractual arrangement, and *temporary (indentured) servitude* involved a contractual arrangement for a term of years—usually from 4 to 7 years or until age 21 as repayment for the ocean voyage across the Atlantic to the English colonies (Jordan, 1968). Both black and white persons were indentured servants during the early colonial period. With little distinction made between them, early colonists held white and black servants in equal contempt and assigned them the same basic tasks (Bennett, 1982). But the legal status of whites was clear to the early colonists: Poor white laborers came to the colonies as tenants, bondservants, and apprentices—but not as slaves. Masters owned poor white *labor*, but not poor white *persons*. The first Africans were most likely indentured servants, but they did not become part of a servant class as equals. African servitude was most probably lifelong since the earliest Africans came to the British mainland colonies involuntarily and sold into service without written contracts limiting their service (Higginbotham, 1996). The early colonists had well-established notions of Africans as culturally and racially inferior persons, and thus, Higginbotham finds no reason to believe that the early colonists discarded "their historical tendency of associating blackness with inferiority in favor of a more enlightened view" (p. 19).

The concerted efforts of colonial legislatures, judicial officers, and regional sheriffs and local constables formed the justice system of institutionalized slavery. Colonial and antebellum governments adopted codes to protect slavery mostly against exigencies involving insurrection (Kennedy, 1997; Morris, 1996; Nash, 1988; Reiss, 1997). The codes safeguarded the institutionalization of slavery by imposing the death penalty for anyone concealing slaves for purposes of escape, conspiring with slaves for purposes of insurrection, circulating seditious literature among slaves, and for anyone engaged in slave stealing (Bowers, 1984). It was a capital offense in Louisiana "to use language in any public discourse, from the bar, the bench, the stage, the pulpit, or in any place whatsoever that might produce insubordination among slaves" (Stampp, 1956, p. 211). Moreover, colonial legislatures quickly developed statutory *slave codes* to control Africans and protect the proprietary and possessory slave interests of the owner class. Slave codes were the mainstay of the new slavocracy and regulated every aspect of slave life to ensure white dominion. The codes reflected the racial and cultural bias of the master-owning class toward Africans as a subhuman genus. The statutes defined slaves as freely alienable (devisable) property, mandated slavery as lifelong and inherited, and prohibited the unsupervised movement of slaves. Barred from owning personal or real property, slaves could not marry, learn to read or write, or make civil contracts, and the law prohibited them from bearing witness against whites in court. The codes called for the harshest penalties for their violation (Jones, 1993). The codes required increasingly more severe punishments for disobedient slaves as the institution expanded throughout the colonies, and the judiciary enforced their harsh provisions. In 1692, Virginia established separate criminal courts to adjudicate capital cases involving slaves because of a "growing belief of white legislators and judges that the government had to employ greater force to preserve slavery and protect slave owners" (Reiss, 1997, p. 71; see also, Johnson & Wolfe, 2003). No court recognized the *benefit of clergy* for slaves convicted of capital crimes until 1732, and no slave could plead self-defense against the brutality of white owners until 1792. Not until the antebellum period did slave law "distinguish between first- and second-degree murders in convictions of slaves." Capital slave offenders could not appeal their convictions until 1848, and even then, the historical record in Virginia reveals only one such case. In many capital cases involving slave women, judges overruled recommendations of leniency and mercy and sentenced female slaves to death. This was the case in Mississippi's hanging of a young slave girl named Eliza for assaulting her mistress with intent to kill. There, the jury recommended that the governor grant her mercy because of the child's age—she was probably 14 years old—but the judge demanded her execution. One newspaper reported that during Eliza's execution "the struggles of the culprit were protracted and severe, as if she died of strangulation rather than dislocation of the neck and the head of the spine" (Shipman, 2002, p. 153). Carrying out the perverted judicial punishments were sheriffs, and as Eliza's case shows, as executioners their actions often proved grossly inadequate. But at other times sheriffs were all too skillful at their tasks—sheriffs conducted at least five slave executions before 1785 in which they publicly displayed the head and torso of the executed slaves (Reiss, 1997).

SLAVE WOMEN EXECUTIONS IN COLONIAL AND ANTEBELLUM SLAVERY

Slave historians distinguish *colonial* slavery from *antebellum* slavery to acknowledge the variant forms of slavery that developed in discrete regions of the United States at differing times and for separate reasons (Berlin, 1998, 1980; Wright, 1991). In colonial slavery, three different slave systems developed in the British mainland colonies during the seventeenth and eighteenth centuries. Virginia and Maryland were the first colonies to institutionalize slavery in the Chesapeake region in the early 1600s where planters centralized slaves on small tobacco plantations. Slavery was without plantations in the New England and Middle colonies where most slaves worked as domestics and skilled and unskilled industrial workers. Slavery expanded into the Carolina and Georgia low country during this period where planters concentrated bonded workers on large tobacco and rice producing plantations. In contrast, slavery declined in the northern regions during the antebellum period while southern states developed a plantation economy based on large-scale cotton production. Slavery expanded beyond the coastal regions westward where its geographical boundaries took on the dimensions upon which the Civil War was fought.

It is difficult to develop much of an understanding about the legal frameworks in which slaves lived out their lives in the early colonial period because not much exists in the historical record about the treatment of slaves at that time (Bush, 1996). There is so little in the record on early colonial history that one legal historian refers to the period as "the dark ages of American law" (Friedman, 1985, p. 33). One reason for the dearth of information on slave women executions before emancipation is that the white-owned press made almost no mention of the events (Shipman, 2002). Even so, historical inventories reveal that colonial authorities used the death penalty against female slaves sparingly in comparison to the antebellum period. Death penalty jurisdictions executed more than *three times* as many slave women in antebellum slavery than in colonial slavery. Beginning with the Massachusetts hanging of a young slave woman named Marja for arson in September 1681, officials executed 40 slave women before 1789 and 124 slave women from 1790 to emancipation (Espy & Smykla, 2004). Undoubtedly, authorities executed far more slave women than the historical record otherwise reveals. In his analysis of county court proceedings in colonial Virginia, Schwarz (1996) verified 152 actual hangings out of 567 cases where officials sentenced slaves to death between 1706 and 1784. Authorities may have condemned as many as 945 slaves and actually hanged some 800 slaves over the period. But Schwarz identifies only 2 female slave executions occurring in 1737 and 1746.

The record also shows that Virginia authorities hanged 635 slaves between 1785 and 1865, but the record does not distinguish between male and female slave executions.

Death penalty jurisdictions put to death more than two-thirds of executed slave women for murder, conspiracy to commit murder, and attempted murder during colonial and antebellum slavery. Most slave women executed for murder killed their masters, their masters' mistresses, or some member of their masters' family including children. Of the 118 slave women identified by Streib (1990) as executed for murder, 67 murdered a member of their master's family, 35 murdered unrelated victims, and 7 slave women murdered their own children. Missouri hanged a 19-year-old slave girl named Mary for drowning and beating one of her owner's children (Streib & Sametz, 1989). Virginia executed Jane Williams for slashing to death with a hatchet the wife and infant of her master Joseph P. Winston. The Winstons apparently treated Williams badly and had threatened to sell her without selling Williams's child. An estimated 6,000 people watched Williams's hanging. Mississippi hanged a slave woman named Nancy for poisoning two members of her owner's family (Shipman, 2002).

Slavery institutionalized the sexual victimization of slave women who often resorted to violent retaliation for the sexualized brutality received from white masters. Celia's hanging in Missouri was one such case. Seventy-year-old Robert Newsome bought 14-year-old Celia and forced sexual relations upon her immediately and repeatedly. One night when Newsome went to Celia's cabin to abuse her, she struck him with a stick and killed him instantly. Celia was pregnant for the third time by Newsome and was very ill when he last approached her. At her trial, the court was concerned only with whether Celia had a right to defend herself against her master's assault. The trial judge made it clear that Celia did not have that right. To the court, Celia had no sexual rights over her own body because she was Newsome's property and she ought to have submitted to Newsome's demands. Celia was guilty of murder and hanged four days before Christmas in 1855 (Higginbotham, 1996). Incestual victimization provoked one slave woman to kill her master, Jacob Bryan, whom she battered to death with a hoe. Bryan was the slave woman's father and the father of four of her children (Shipman, 2002).

Poisoning was a major offense for which authorities often executed slave women. Many of the alleged poisonings and related attempted murders by slave women resulted from unintentional acts, however; even if poisoning was "well-suited to women's resistance because of their duties as cooks and nurses on the plantation" (Johnson, 1995, p. 22). Cases of poisoning typically involved an accusation of poisoning food prepared by the slave for the owner's family that most likely resulted from a lack of safe food preparation methods than intentional harm (Streib, 1990). Other cases involved slaves unknowingly administering poisonous medicine or unlawfully administering medicines. Schwarz (1996) identifies 179 Virginia slaves tried for poisoning offenses against whites between 1706 and 1784. Although authorities acquitted 28 of these slaves tried for poisoning, court records reveal that Virginia actually executed 14 slaves for poisoning over this period. A woman named Eve was one of the slaves burned to death for poisoning her master, Peter Montague, with a glass of milk. Executioners afterward quartered Eve's burnt body and displayed it publicly (Schwarz, 1996). Another slave woman was burned to death for murder years earlier who officials publicly displayed after quartering her body.

Arson was a crime appealing to slave women since they often "did not have the physical strength to confront their white enemies," and arson was a "powerful way to deprive whites of their property and injure their economic well-being" (Schwarz, 1996, p. 115–116). Slave women burned their masters' houses, jails, shops, wheat stacks, and agricultural buildings such as mills and barns. Massachusetts burned-at-the-stake a slave woman named Maria for attempted arson of her master's home (Johnson, 1995, p. 23). Virginia hanged a slave woman named Violet for burning her master's house, and the August County court that convicted Violet demanded that her "severed head was to remain on display on a pole near Staunton" (Schwarz, 1996, p. 115).

Slave rebellion was a concern among white planters as early as 1642. As noted, a crucial component of slave codes was to deter insurrections by imposing harsh punishments. Authorities acted swiftly and viciously to counter upheavals, often hanging the bodies of insurgents in chains or impaling their decapitated heads "upon a pole in some public place as a gruesome reminder to all passers-by that black hands must never be raised against whites" (Jordan, 1968, p. 114). The slaves that participated in Nat Turner's rebellion suffered beheading and their skulls were positioned on polls on public roads; someone sewed Turner's dried skin into souvenir purses (Marable, 1985). Slave rebellions took on a variety of forms including "malingering; self mutilation; suicide; destruction of [slave] owner's crops, tools, and livestock; running away; or criminal activity like stealing and violent insurrection" (Reiss, 1997, p. 198). Slaves manifested their resistance to bondage through assaulting or poisoning overseers or owners, breaking tools, pilfering, and burning barns (Reich, 1989). Slave insurgents often strangled, clubbed, stabbed, burned, shot, or poisoned their masters, mistresses, overseers, and even whole families (Jordan, 1968). Slave women's resistance included controlling reproductive functions and inducing abortions (Johnson, 1995). Infanticide was also part of the resistance by black women to slavery (Bridgewater, 2001). It is interesting that, although punishment was severe for slave women that committed infanticide, death penalty jurisdictions executed only white women for concealing the birth or death of her infant (Espy & Smykla, 2004).

Executions for slave revolts appear to be more a product of masters' fears of slave insurrections than from genuine threats of open rebellion, however. Even if slave society feared a *race war* and acted purposely to pass laws to "crush any possible slave revolt, and to punish disobedience and rebellion with brute force," actual slave insurrections were extraordinary (Friedman, 1985, p. 220). But slave insurrections were infrequent and posed very little challenge to slavery in the United States (Cooper & Terrill, 1996). In fact, Bell (1987, p. 247) argues that "slave owners used the threat of violent slave revolts as the 'common danger' to gain support for slavery among whites, including those who opposed the institution on moral grounds and those in the working class whose economic interests were harmed by the existence of slave labor." Surprisingly, Louisiana is the only state that executed a slave woman for insurrection even though colonial officials executed 24 male slaves for insurrection (Espy & Smykla, 2004). But mere rejoicing at freedom was enough to execute slave women. In March 1865, the townspeople of Darlington, South Carolina, hanged 17-year-old Amy Spain for treason and "conduct unbecoming a slave" for clasping her hands and crying, "Bless the Lord the Yankees have come!" when she heard that the Union army was quickly approaching (Shipman, 2002).

Runaway slaves posed a far more menacing problem to southern planters than open slave rebellions. Running away was a crime for which masters imposed harsh punishments, including branding recaptured slaves (Finkelman, 1993). Slaves often ran away from abusive masters or to "avoid punishment or to get revenge for punishments already received" (Stampp, 1956, p. 113). Despite fugitive slave laws providing for the return of slaves even if they reached free states, between 40,000 and 100,000 slaves escaped from slavery (Schaefer, 2004). Slave masters hired slave catchers to find fugitive slaves and in some cases would pay the capturers more reward money for killing fugitive slaves than for taking them alive (Hadden, 2001). Bounty hunters and paddy rollers recaptured or killed roughly half of all runaway slaves. Laws regarding fugitive slaves imposed legal duties to "justices of the peace, prison keepers, constables, and sheriffs" to capture runaway slaves, and government officials could sell at public action captured and unclaimed runaways (Schwarz, 1996, pp. 124–125). Slave codes prescribed particularly harsh punishments for runaway slaves.

> A first attempt led to up to 40 lashes; an *R* was branded on the right cheek for a second offense; an ear was cut off plus 40 lashes for a third attempt; castration was performed if the slave tried a fourth time (a female fourth-time offender had her left ear cut off and an *R* branded on her left cheek); and a fifth offense resulted in execution or incision of the Achilles. (Reiss, 1997, p. 194)

One aspect of the fugitive slave problem was that slave women rarely joined runaways. A review of newspaper notices calling for the return of fugitive slaves shows that just over three-quarters of all runaways were men in South Carolina, and almost 90 percent of all fugitive slaves in Virginia were men (Johnson, 1995). Similar patterns existed in Alabama and Louisiana where men represented 84 percent of fugitive slaves in Alabama and 68 percent of fugitive slaves in Louisiana. Slave women were less likely to run away, however, because of their "restricted mobility associated with childbearing and child-rearing responsibilities" (Johnson, 1995, p. 22). Most fugitive slaves were between 16 and 35 years old, the ages when most slave women were either pregnant, nursing an infant, or caring for a young child.

White planters treated slave women harshly. A staunch reality of slave life for bonded females was that they were at once agricultural workers and the primary mode for increasing domestic slave populations, especially after Congress prohibited traders from importing slaves after 1808. Planters valued slave women that produced children— child-producing female slaves were generally worth 25 percent more than childless slave women (Reiss, 1997). Planters considered female slaves *breeders*, but not *mothers* since slave women had no legal control over their own children (Bridgewater, 2001). Masters considered a slave woman a "good breeder" if she had 15 to 20 pregnancies during her productive years (Reiss, 1997). Still, planters expected pregnant slave women to maintain their normal work schedules and production yields. Planters did not exempt pregnant women or mothers with infants from fieldwork. Consequently, miscarriages among slave women were common and infant mortality high. Slave mothers often left their infants lying on the ground next to them as they worked while other mothers worked with their babies fastened to their backs. Some slave women left their infants in the care of young children or older women, and nursing mothers were frequently unable to feed their babies and suffered the excruciating pain of swollen breasts. Undaunted, overseers regularly punished nursing mothers that fell behind in their work. As one slave narrative explains, "I have seen the overseer beat them with raw hide, so that the blood and milk flew mingled from their breasts" (Davis, 1981, p. 9). Planters treated disobedient pregnant slave women harshly but guardedly to ensure the survival of unborn infants. One account explains that "a woman who gives offense in the field, and is large in a family way, is compelled to lie down over a hole made to receive her corpulency, and is flogged with the whip or beat with a paddle" (Davis, 1981, p. 9).

Given the occupational distribution of plantation slaves in the United States, planters regularly consigned slave women to domestic work as house servants—some 17 percent of female slaves were domestics (Fogel, 1989). Consequently, many slave women worked in close proximity to their white owners who often sexually abused and raped them. Sexual relations with their white owners was a routine feature of life for slave women that was "both deeply traumatic and destructive of family life" (Fogel, 1989, p. 181). Most slave women victimized by white sexual aggression were unmarried. Sexual assaults on slave girls as young as 12 years old were common. Married slave women largely escaped white rape because white men knew slave husbands would revenge the rape of their wives—they "would rather die than stand idly by" (Fogel, 1989, p. 166). White rape of bonded women was pervasive in the southern slavocracy. One crude measure of the prevalence of white rape of slave women is that the father was white in *one out of every six* female-headed households—roughly 10 percent of slave children in 1860 were mulatto (Fogel, 1989; see also Aptheker, 1993, pp. 25–35). Owners' perversions toward slave women rendered them powerless not only to resist the sexual advances of masters, but also those of masters' sons and overseers. Vulgarly, one southern planter declared that white rape of slave women explained the "absence of Southern prostitution and the purity of white women" (Kolchin, 2003, p. 124).

Sexual control over slave women was critical to slavery. Owners relied upon the routine sexual abuse of slave women as much as they did other forms of brutality. As a result, slave law did not recognize slave women's rights to control their own bodies (Higginbotham, 1996; Morris, 1996). White slave owners sexually attacked females with legal impunity—the rape of slave woman was simply not a crime, even if raped by another slave. One scholar explains, "Forced sexual exploitation of the black woman under slavery was no offhand enterprise. Total control over her reproductive system meant a steady supply of slave babies, and slave children" (Brownmiller, 1975, p. 153; see also Roberts, 1993). Also, the notion that "sexual coercion was an essential dimension of the social relations between slave master and slave—the right claimed by slave owners over the bodies of female slaves was a direct expression of their presumed property right over black people as a whole" (Davis, 1981, p. 175).

The rape charge demonstrates the status differences between white women and black women during slavery. Scholars can find no reported cases of a white man prosecuted for the rape or attempted rape of a slave woman (Higginbotham & Jacobs, 1992). Indeed, one of the more troubling historical facts about rape and capital punishment in the United States is that *no court has ever called for the execution of a white man convicted of raping a black woman* (Klarman, 2001, p. 104, note 322; *see also* Marable, 1985). But as Flowers (1988) notes: "Black rapists have been far more likely to be put to death when their victims were white females rather than black females, whereas the death penalty has been imposed on white rapists exclusively when their victims were also white" (p. 169). To Davis (1981), the fraudulent rape charge stands out as one of the most formidable artifices invented by racism in criminal justice system history. Even today, justice professionals view the rape of black women as far less serious than the rape of white women although black women are

12 times more likely than white women to suffer rape. Judicial bias toward black female rape victims explains the less serious punishments afforded rapists of black women (Macnamara & Sagarin, 1977; Wriggins, 1983). Ironically, the scarcity of workers and black females caused white colonial planters to "encourage, persuade, coerce immigrant white women to engage in sexual relationships with black male slaves as a means of producing new workers" (hooks, 1981, p. 15). And in many black rape cases involving white women in colonial Virginia, white townspeople often testified that white women encouraged and consented to sexual relations with male slaves (noted in Aptheker, 1993, p. 29).

It is not surprising to find absent in the historical record white prosecutions for raping slave women since southern slave law prohibited slaves from testifying against whites in court. Slave women had no rights that white men could violate (Higginbotham & Kopytoff, 1989b). What is more, "the assumption of promiscuous Negro sexuality and the assertion of white male dominance over blacks in the sexual sphere would have inclined white male prosecutors not to prosecute, and white male juries not to convict." White men generally viewed black women as "jezebels," "sexual temptresses," and "the embodiment of female evil and sexual lust" (Tarpley, 1996, p. 1,353; see also Bridgewater, 2001). White masters also worried little about fathering mulatto children since state laws defined children born to slave women as slaves (Higginbotham & Kopytoff, 1989b). Finkelman (1993) explains that rather than discouraging relations between slave women and white men, and discouraging miscegenation, such laws had the opposite effect and encouraged white men to sexually exploit slave women:

> By predetermining the status of a possible offspring, white men might be less concerned about the outcome of their sexual adventures. Slave owners were unlikely to bring bastardy charges against white fathers, because the masters after all, would gain the value of a new slave. Furthermore, the main social (as opposed to moral) reason for bastardy laws was to make sure that illegitimate children would be fed, clothed, housed, educated, and prepared for adult life. The 1662 law obviated all these problems for the bastard children of slave women and white men: the owner of the woman would pick up the tab, and be handsomely recompensed by the value of the new slave. Thus, rather than discouraging immoral relations between slave women and white men, as well as discouraging miscegenation, this law could have easily led to the opposite result. (p. 2084; see also Kennedy, 2003, pp. 45–48)

Tarpley (1996) explains that the racism of slavery also empowered white women to brutalize black women sexually involved with their husbands (see also Fede, 1996; Salmon, 1986). In many slaveholding households, white women whose husbands sexually assaulted female slaves tortured and persecuted slave women. In one case:

> A white mistress returned home unexpectedly from an outing, opened the doors of her dressing room, and discovered her husband raping a thirteen-year-old slave girl. She responded by beating the girl and locking her in a smokehouse. The girl was whipped daily for several weeks. When older slaves pleaded on the child's behalf and dared to suggest that the white master was to blame, the mistress simply replied, "She'll know better in the future. After I've done with her, she'll never do the like again through ignorance." (hooks, 1981, pp. 36–37)

Analysis of female slave executions cannot account for the informal agents of slave control resulting in executions carried out by masters, overseers, and slave patrols—what

Genovese (1974) calls "the complimentary system of plantation justice" (see also Hindus, 1980). As Flannigan (1974) points out, "*private* rather than *public* authority was the most efficient form of repression in the antebellum South" (p. 540). Interestingly though, the research record is mostly silent on private slave executions despite the notion that slave law sanctioned and encouraged masters to privately punish slaves rather than seek public prosecution (Higginbotham & Jacobs, 1992). Slave law enforcement mostly took place on plantations since it was relatively expensive and time-consuming to prosecute slaves publicly. Social historians allude to a handful of private slave executions, however, and many concede that punishments meted out to plantation slaves were horrific (Mann, 1993). Planters often branded, stabbed, tarred and feathered, burned, shackled, tortured, maimed, mutilated, crippled, whipped, hanged, beat, and castrated slaves (Schwarz, 1996; see also Blassingame, 1972). Slave owners reserved the most severe punishments for slaves attempting insurrection or escape, and masters often held out insolent slaves as examples to other slaves by forcing them to witness the punishment (Adamson, 1983; Higginbotham & Jacobs, 1992). Some slaves committed suicide in response to their oppression and maltreatment, but their numbers are unknown and historians consider such events rare (Quarles, 1987).

One of the substantive issues concerning social historians of slavery about the complementary system of plantation justice is the degree of authority society allocated to slave masters and third parties in controlling slaves (Morris, 1996). Slavery was a prime concern of colonial and state criminal justice systems, and "masters and overseers had the basic job of controlling the slaves and policing slave society" (Friedman, 1993). Although slave codes imposed a duty upon slave masters to punish and control their slaves, historians of slavery have mostly limited their discussions on the relationship between state and private interests in controlling slavery to the criminal liability of slave masters and third parties for the death of a slave. As Stampp (1956) explains: "Overseers sued masters for their wages when discharged for cruelty; masters sued overseers for injuring slave property; occasionally the state intervened to prosecute an overseer for killing or maiming a bondsman" (p. 183). Yet, the frequency with which masters brought civil suits against overseers for severely wounding or killing slaves attests to the commonality of abuse against slaves on plantations (Higginbotham & Jacobs, 1992).

Most slave codes decriminalized the use of violence against slaves by masters in the early colonial period. For example, as early as 1705 in Virginia "if anyone with authority correcting a slave killed him in such correction, it shall not be accounted felony, and the killer would be freed as if such accident had never happened" (Morris, 1996, p. 164). In the antebellum period, state governments expanded their control over slavery as it developed and became more institutionalized and the rights of slave owners to commit violent acts against slaves became far more restrictive. In 1798, for example, Georgia's constitution included the following provision: "Any person who shall maliciously dismember or deprive a slave of life shall suffer such punishment as would be inflicted in case the like offence had been committed on a free white person, and on the like proof, except in case of insurrection by such slave, and unless such death should happen by accident in giving such slave moderate correction" (Morris, 1996, p. 172). Friedman (1993) points out that appellate cases reported from slave states turn up more than a few instances where authorities tried whites for killing or abusing slaves. Virginia, in fact, executed two white men as early as 1739 for whipping a slave to death. In that case, Essex County officials hanged Charles

Quinn and David White for killing a slave belonging to Colonel Braxton (Higginbotham & Jacobs, 1992). One can argue that the idea behind more restrictive codes limiting violence that master could imposed upon slaves was to maintain and expand the slave system by making it less brutal. This argument holds if courts strictly enforced laws against slave brutality. Morris (1996) questions the historical record, however:

> Almost all homicides of slaves, from the colonial period to the end of slavery, ended in acquittals, or at most in verdicts of manslaughter, which meant that there had been some legal provocation from the slave. There were also killings that never led to criminal actions. Still, in theory some protection for the lives of slaves existed because people could be punished for their homicides. Occasionally they were. To that limited extent the law mediated or controlled some of the violence created by a social relationship based on the violent control of labor power in a biracial society. But the master-slave relationship was so delicate that it was intruded upon only in extreme or unusual circumstances. Those circumstances could be quite indeterminate and imprecise. (p. 181)

The vulgarities of plantation justice toward slave women were not limited to planters. Medical practitioners often perfected novel surgical techniques on slave women before performing the procedures on white women, and often without anesthesia. The most notorious practitioners was James Marion Sims, a founder of modern gynecology, who purchased slave women expressly for perfecting gynecological surgery in the nineteenth century. Sims was primarily a plantation physician who experimented on female slaves inflicted with vesicovaginal fistulas. The infliction amounts to tears from the vagina to the bladder (or develop between the bowels and the vagina), and the women continually drip urine from their vaginas. The condition results from difficulty in childbirth. In 1845, owners of the Westcott plantation summoned Sims because a young slave woman named Anarcha had been in labor for three days without delivering. Given the prolonged delivery, Anarcha sustained several fistulas that Sims attempted to correct surgically without anesthesia even though it had recently become available. Sims probably did not know that anesthesia had been developed at the time he operated on Anarcha, but this is doubtful since Sims used anesthesia on white women undergoing the same surgery. Sims subscribed to the notion that, unlike white women, African women had a physiological tolerance to pain. Sims operated on Anarcha more than 30 times without anesthesia since postoperative infections kept frustrating the surgeries when sutures became infected and the fistulas remained open. Sims successfully repaired the fistulas after using silver sutures that resisted infection. Sims operated on at least 10 more slave women over several years, perfecting the surgical technique. He also performed surgery on another slave woman named Lucy without anesthesia who nearly died from postoperative blood poisoning. White physicians also used dead slaves for autopsies, and if there were no available cadavers, practitioners stole slaves from their graves (Roberts, 1997; see also Axelsen, 1985; Barker-Benfield, 1976; Lerner, 2003; Randall, 1996; Roberts, 1993a).

Jurisdictional authorities often compensated slave owners for the economic loss of a slave sentenced to death—what Phillips (1915) called *the voucher system*. Compensation laws appeared early in slavery with Virginia adopting the first of provision in 1705. Virginia law required justices "to set a value for the slave and the master's reimbursement from the public purse" when sentencing a slave to death. Compensating slave owners for the loss of executed slaves served two functions: (1) it prevented owners from concealing slaves accused of capital crimes; and (2) it shifted the cost of public justice to the public at large and thereby balanced the slave owner's interests against that of public safety (Friedman, 1987; Hindus, 1980; Morris, 1996). Stampp (1956) explains, "Since the execution of a slave resembled the public seizure or condemnation of private property, most of the states recognized the justice of the owner's claim" (p. 199). Virginia allocated some $12,000 for the reimbursement of executed slaves in 1839, and authorities often did not reimburse slave owners for the full value of an executed slave because they viewed slave crime as the result of the owner's failure to properly manage their slaves. An 1824 Alabama law provided that juries should assess the value of the slave when trying a slave for a capital offense, and that the owner was entitled to claim up to one-half of that amount (Friedman, 1987). South Carolina paid a flat rate of $200 per slave, but the state did not reimburse slave owners at all for the loss of an executed slave convicted of murder or rebellion. Death penalty data confirm that none of the 72 slave executions conducted in South Carolina before 1843 for murder or slave revolt involved slave owner compensation (Espy & Smykla, 2004). Hindus (1976) explains that not until 1855 did South Carolina's legislature vote to compensate owners one-half the economic value of slaves executed for murder and rebellion. Colonial and state governments reimbursed 14 owners for the execution of slave women. Jane Williams's owner, for example, received $500 from Virginia authorities for her execution.

BLACK WOMEN EXECUTIONS IN RECONSTRUCTION

Death penalty jurisdictions executed far fewer black women during Reconstruction than in colonial and antebellum slavery. Mostly southern jurisdictions hanged six black females for murder between 1866 and 1877. In one case, some 5,000 people watched Louisiana officials hang 24-four-year-old Alcee Harris on a gallows set up outside the courthouse in November 1875. Authorities executed Harris for soliciting a friend, Toney Nellum, to kill her husband because he was going to kill her after they had been quarrelling.

The dramatic decrease in black female executions during Reconstruction may be the result of what some scholars insist was a period of positive social relations and a growing complacency in criminal justice policy toward "dangerous classes" (Turner, Singleton, & Musick, 1984). Actually, emancipation ushered in one of the most chaotic and turbulent periods in U.S. history. One backdrop to the racial violence of Reconstruction was that the Civil War had devastated the southern economy by destroying much of its agricultural infrastructure. The fighting left barns and dwellings burned; bridges demolished; fences, tools, and livestock destroyed; and widespread destruction of work animals, farm buildings, machinery, levees, and canals. The loss of life also had a profound effect upon the availability of labor; more than 260,000 southern whites and 37,000 southern blacks died in the war (Foner, 1988).

Reconstruction brought a pronounced political freedom to the former slaves. As one scholar puts it, "the explicit purpose of Reconstruction was to uplift the recently freed black population and prevent the political, economic, and social restoration of white supremacy after the defeat of the slave masters in the Civil War" (Raskin, 1995, p. 522). Easing the progress of black enfranchisement in southern society was the passage of the

Reconstruction Amendments to the federal Constitution; namely, the Thirteenth Amendment abolishing slavery in 1865, the Fourteenth Amendment granting citizenship to the former slaves in 1868, and the Fifteenth Amendment prohibiting racial discrimination in the right to vote in 1870—even if the amendment did not provide for the voting rights of black women. One of the more important legislative moves by Congress to promote and protect black equality was enactment of the Civil Rights Act of 1875 providing that:

> All persons with the jurisdiction of the United States shall be entitled to the full and equal enjoyment of the accommodations, advantages, facilities, and privileges of inns, public conveyances on land or water, theaters, and other places of public amusement; subject only to the conditions and limitations established by law, and applicable alike to all citizens of every race and color, regardless of any previous condition of servitude. (Perea, Delgado, Harris, & Wildman, 2000, p. 140)

As a result, blacks made significant social gains in the decade immediately following the Civil War: Blacks gained greater control over their labor, commanded higher wages, and they had more freedom of movement and were legally afforded equal access to public accommodations. Black literacy rates increased dramatically. As one scholar puts it, "in no other period of American history has either the absolute or relative rate of black literacy and school attendance increased so much as in the fifteen years after 1865" (Bell, 2004, p. 62). The black literacy rate rose from 10 percent in 1860 to 30 percent in 1880, and the number of black children in school increased from 2 percent to 34 percent during the same period. The former slaves gained greater participation in the political processes of the South as well. Black voters rallied majorities in several southern states; 16 blacks served in Congress, several blacks served as lieutenant governors, and several others held state offices (Cooper & Terrill, 1996). Some 20 percent of black farm operators owned their own land by 1880 (Bell, 2004). Black participation in southern political and economic life had profoundly changed since slavery. Foner (1988) describes Reconstruction as "a massive experiment in interracial democracy without precedent in the history of this or any other country that abolished slavery in the nineteenth century."

The newfound political rights of nearly 4 million freed blacks threatened white southern society, however. Poor whites particularly viewed the gains made by blacks during Reconstruction as rebellious and launched violent retaliations against black gains (McPherson, 1999). The demise of slavery brought about critical developments in black *political rights*, but blacks found improving their *social rights* a far more formidable task (Siegel, 1997). In effect, legal emancipation did not move southern society appreciably toward racial equality during Reconstruction. The South remained as segregated and racially unequal as it had during slavery. The Reconstruction amendments had introduced an ambiguity into black–white race relations, and keeping "blacks in their place" had become more difficult to enforce and often resulted in chaotic and unpredictable forms of racial domination over blacks. To white planters, the loss of millions of bonded workers profoundly threatened the southern lifestyle. Most southern states limited black rights by adopting laws similar to those used to regulate blacks in antebellum slavery—*black codes*. By 1866, all southern states had enacted these codes to regulate black lives, with Mississippi and South Carolina enacting the first and harshest codes (Higginbotham, 1996). Many states sought to keep blacks subordinated to whites by imposing discriminatory measures in the codes such as precluding blacks from voting, serving on juries, and testifying in court cases involving whites (Foner, 1988).

A dramatic increase in black female prison populations in southern states immediately following the Civil War is relevant to lowering black female execution rates during the period. Before emancipation, southern states rarely incarcerated slaves since planter production needs made few slaves eligible for public punishment. After 1865, however, newly freed black women swelled the ranks of southern prison populations where they comprised between 40 and 70 percent of women committed to southern penitentiaries. One reason for elevated black female incarceration rates was that black women had significant contact with whites as domestic servants and housemaids that made them particularly susceptible to crime accusations. Although imprisoned black women mostly committed property crimes, violent crimes were particularly common to black women, including historically executable offenses like accessory to murder, attempted murder, murder, manslaughter, assault, arson, and robbery. One scholar explains why black women precipitated violent crime during this period:

> Some black women born in the South may have been affected by the generally higher level of violence in that region. Some black women. . . may have been responding defensively against men who were themselves prone to violence. And some were perhaps predisposed to violent reactions owing to the stress generated by their dislocation, isolation, and economic marginality. All three factors may have operated simultaneously at times to make black women more likely to engage in crimes of violence. (Rafter, 2004, p. 145)

Black women had little property value after emancipation, but southern justice systems quickly recognized the pecuniary benefit of black women prisoners as lessees to private and public industries. Black female prisoners comprised large numbers of leased prison work gangs for mining and railroad interests and on prison farms. One reason for the development of the convict lease system in southern states was that state resources became heavily burdened. Leasing convicts to the highest bidder eliminated the government necessity to maintain control over managing the prisoners since the lessor assumed total responsibility for the prisoners in the lease system (Rafter, 2004). Lessors treated leased prisoners exceptionally poorly and the average lifespan for leased prisoners was five years. Alabama's leasing system killed nearly half of its prisoners in 1870. In one instance, 128 prisoners died in an Alabama mine explosion. The systematic exploitation, brutalization, and degradation of prisoners involved in the convict lease system, and later chain gangs, resulted in their suffering the extreme hardships of overwork, beatings, whippings, squalid living conditions, and poor diets. Chain gangs, including female chain gangs, continue to operate in many states (Peloso, 1997).

The reduction in black female executions in Reconstruction mostly resulted from white violence directed toward black people generally as a corresponding means of imposing capital punishment (Aguirre & Baker, 1991; Clarke, 1998; Jordan, 2000; Ogletree, 2002). Racial violence was an insidious and pervasive feature of everyday life for blacks during Reconstruction. Litwack (1979) has characterized the racial violence of Reconstruction this way:

> How many black men and women were beaten, flogged, mutilated, and murdered in the first years of emancipation will never be known. Nor could any accurate body count or statistical

breakdown reveal the barbaric savagery and depravity that so frequently characterized the assaults made on freemen in the name of restraining their savagery and depravity—the severed ears and entrails, the mutilated sex organs, the burning at the stake, the forced drownings, the open display of skulls and severed limbs as trophies. . . . Neither a freedman's industriousness nor his deference necessarily protected him from whites if they suspected he harbored dangerous tendencies or if they looked upon him as a "smart-assed" nigger who needed chastisement. (pp. 276–277)

In opposition to the federal civil rights reforms, southern whites intimidated blacks by employing selective and deliberate strategies of vigilante groups, namely the Ku Klux Klan, the Red Shirts, and the Knights of the White Camellias. Assaulting, murdering, lynching, and politically repressing blacks continued throughout Reconstruction. Many of the violent acts against blacks resulted from disputes arising from blacks' efforts to break the types of controls white masters had over slaves. Many of the assaults and murders experienced by blacks during Reconstruction, however, involved blacks "attempting to leave plantations, disputing contract settlements, not laboring in the manner desired by their employers, attempting to buy or rent land, and asserting that 'he was a freeman and he would not be tied like a slave'" (Foner, 1988, p. 121). In Texas, some 1,524 acts of violence against blacks took place between 1865 and 1868. Nearly 200 of these incidents involved the victimization of black women, 15 of which resulted in their murders. White mobs whipped, flogged, beat, assaulted, castrated, and murdered black children as well (see Carrigan, 2004). Whites murdered 295 blacks in Caddo Parish in Louisiana between 1865 and 1876. Rioting white mobs in cities in Tennessee and Mississippi "raped black women as they went on an antiblack rampage" during this period (Feagin, 2000, p. 58). Social historians have lauded the effects of politically instigated racial violence as far more damaging to southern blacks during Reconstruction than the racial violence associated with lynching during the early decades of Jim Crow.

> In Louisiana, during a six-month period in 1868, Democrats slaughtered nearly half as many Republicans, both black and white, as were lynched in the whole South in the fifty years after 1882. During and shortly after the 1874 election campaign in Vicksburg, Mississippi, Democrats killed three times as many blacks as were murdered in the South during the 1920s. Over Easter weekend of 1873, Democrats massacred more blacks in the tiny hamlet of Colfax, Louisiana, than were lynched in the South in any year after 1881. (Kousser & Griffin, 1998, pp. 173–174).

Scholars point out that the vulnerability of black women to white male sexual violence was even greater in the postbellum period than it had been during slavery. Davis (1981) speaks of the brutal effect the Southern criminal justice systems during Reconstruction had upon black women:

> The sexual abuse they had routinely suffered during the era of slavery was not arrested by the advent of emancipation. As a matter of fact, it was still true that colored women were looked upon as the legitimate prey of white men—and if they resisted white men's sexual attacks, they were frequently thrown into prison to be further victimized by a system which was a return to another form of slavery. (pp. 89–90)

Attesting to the brutality suffered by black women in this period is the hanging of the youngest black female juvenile put to death in the United States. She was a 13-year-old girl named Susan executed in Kentucky in February 1868 for the killing of a white child under her care as a babysitter. Susan's death was horrific; she "writhed and twisted and jerked many times" before dying. Many of the townspeople took pieces of the hanging rope as souvenirs after authorities cut down Susan from the gallows. Maryland also hanged 17-year-old Mary Wallis for murder in February 1871.

BLACK WOMEN EXECUTIONS IN JIM CROW

From the end of Reconstruction to the early days of the civil rights movement, mostly southern jurisdictions put to death 27 black women for crimes of murder, robbery-murder, and accessory to murder. Several cases exist of black women killing their spouses in retaliation for domestic maltreatment. A crowd of about 100 people gathered outside the Lunenburg County jail in April 1881, for example, to watch the hanging of Lucinda Fowlkes for murdering her husband with an ax because he was mean to her and consistently beat and abused her. South Carolina hanged Lucinda Tisdale in June 1882 along with her sister's husband, Anderson Singleton, for the murder of Lucinda's sister. Virginia officials hanged Margaret Lashley in January 1892 as an accessory to murder for her role in the killing of Margaret's husband by James Lyles, her boyfriend. Georgia officials hanged Amanda Cody with her male lover, Florence English, for the murder of Amanda's husband Cicero in November 1895. Other cases involved the execution of young black girls for killing young white girls. Some 3,500 people witnessed Georgia officials hang 18-year-old Margaret Harris in October 1883 for the murder of a young girl named Lela Lewis. Alabama hanged 19-year-old Pauline McCoy in January 1888 for murdering Annie Jordan for her shoes. And in October 1892, South Carolina hanged 14-year-old Milbry Brown for killing a white child (Shipman, 2002). Yet, most black women executed during this period were domestic servants and housemaids, and thus one can reasonably conclude that their offenses included crimes of resistance against male aggression similar to that experienced by slave women.

Postbellum southern white society harbored a gross intolerance toward marginalized persons, and the legal system was the single most effective apparatus for ensuring white supremacy. Jim Crow segregation began to take hold as an institutional means of subordinating blacks with the collapse of Reconstruction, and by 1890 southern society had fully entrenched legal segregation of blacks from white society. One scholar describes the legalism of white racism of post-Reconstruction period this way:

> Congress permitted the white South to reduce blacks to a state of peonage, to disregard their civil rights, and to disenfranchise them by force, intimidation, and statute. So did the Supreme Court. Writing into Constitution its own beliefs in the inferiority of blacks, the late-nineteenth-century high court tightened every possible shackle confining the ex-slaves. (Sitkoff, 1981, pp. 3–4)

Jim Crow segregation was not limited to the South. Litwack (1961) describes the segregation of most northern blacks:

> In virtually every phase of existence, Negroes found themselves systematically separated from whites. They were either excluded from railway cars, omnibuses, stagecoaches, and steamboats or assigned to special "Jim Crow" sections; they sat, when permitted, in secluded and

remote corners of theaters and lecture halls; they could not enter most hotels, restaurants, and resorts, except as servants; they prayed in "Negro pews" in the white churches, and if partaking of the sacrament of the Lord's Supper, they waited until the whites had been served the bread and wine. Moreover, they were often educated in segregated schools, punished in segregated prisons, nursed in segregated hospitals, and buried in segregated cemeteries. (p. 97)

A series of U.S. Supreme Court decisions effectively dismantled the federal civil rights protections put in place during Reconstruction and ushered in the constitutionalization of white hegemony in the United States. *Plessy v. Ferguson* (1896) constitutionally recognized an 1890 Louisiana statute separating blacks and whites on passenger trains, while *Williams v. Mississippi* (1898) legitimated black voting restrictions with poll taxes, literacy tests, secret ballots, multiple-box laws, and residency requirements. The court struck down the provisions of the Civil Rights Act of 1875 in *The Civil Rights Cases* (1893) as beyond the power of Congress to enact under the Thirteenth and Fourteenth Amendments since *private* discrimination was not tantamount to state action controlled by the amendments (Perea et al., 2000, p. 141). As a result, Jim Crow effectively replaced *laissez-faire* segregation and brought about a complete legal domination of black persons. Jim Crow brought on a social instability and a renewed legal domination of black persons reminiscent of slavery. Social relations had become ambiguous, chaotic, and once again unpredictable.

Whites again had the full force of law behind them in the systematic domination of blacks. As a result, the need for random violence against blacks diminished. The racism inherent in Jim Crow is undisputed, but that it was an instigator of lynching and other forms of violence against blacks is not supportable. Jim Crow did not reach its height until the 1890s, and the general increase in violence against blacks from Emancipation through the 1890s is more a case of chaotic uncertainty and deinstitutionalization of race relations in the South than one of Jim Crow. In fact, Jim Crow provided stability (although purely racist) to race relations—one that would systematically, comprehensively, and legally subject blacks to white dominion in all arenas of social life. Before Emancipation, the institutionalization of slavery provided a stabilizing force in race relations. During Reconstruction and the deinstitutionalization of slavery, black–white relations were unstable. The reinstitutionalization of slavery with Jim Crow segregation provided a certain stability to race relations in southern states, yet in a manner to continue white domination.

Jim Crow was nevertheless a bloody era in U.S. history for black people—legal and extralegal forms of the death penalty killed more than 8,100 black persons during the period. Death penalty jurisdictions killed 4,707 black prisoners (Espy & Smykla, 2004) and lynch mobs killed 3,445 black victims (Zangrando, 1980). Paterson (1998) identifies torture, mass attendance, and burning as the three main indicators of the ritualistic character of black lynchings. Indeed, black lynchings were a fundamentally different, socially constructed event from white lynchings in that the violence waged against white victims seldom involved tortured or mutilation (Brundage, 1993). Black lynchings were augmented with brutality and ritualistic savagery and entailed "a bestiality unknown even to the most remote and uncivilized parts of the world" (White, 1969, p. 81). Lynch mobs burned to death black men, women, and children, cremated their bodies after death, and often beat and dismembered the bodies of their victims. Of the 416 blacks killed between 1918 and 1927, lynch mobs burned 42 alive, burned 16 after death, and beat to death or cut to pieces 8 others (White, 1969). Reminiscent of James Byrd's killing in Texas in 1998, lynch mobs often tied their black victims to the backs of automobiles and dragged them through city streets until they were unconscious. Mobs tied down and castrated many other victims with knives or axes (Marable, 1985). In Georgia in 1930, white persons "jabbed a black man named James Irwin in the mouth with a sharp pole, cut off his toes and fingers, removed his teeth with wire pliers, saturated his body with gasoline and lighted his body on fire, and then shot him more than a hundred times" (Raper, 1933, pp. 6–7). A Florida mob lynched a young black man named Claude Neal for murder in 1934 after subjecting him to 10 hours of grievous torture involving castration and self-cannibalism (Snead, 1986). Referencing Claude Neal's lynching, McGovern (1982) details that Neal's assailants cut off his penis and testicles and afterwards forced him to eat them before they lynched him. Newspaper accounts illustrate the savagery of black lynchings and the taking of body parts as souvenirs in Luther Holbert and his wife's lynching in Vicksburg, Mississippi. Holbert's wife was most likely innocent of any wrongdoing; even so, the mob burned them for the alleged murder of a white planter named James Eastman (White, 1969).

Nearly 92 percent of all people lynched in the United States between 1918 and 1927 were black—including 11 black women of whom 3 were pregnant (Marable, 1985). Racial violence in the postbellum period was not exclusively a southern phenomenon of black victimization—"Jewish and Chinese merchants, Mormon missionaries and Catholic priests, Italian sugarcane workers and Hispanic cowhands all fell prey to lynch mobs" (Brundage, 1993, p. 91). Carrigan (2003) identifies 597 Mexicans lynched by white mobs mostly in California and Texas from 1848 to 1928. Roughly 3 percent of the 2,364 black lynching victims identified in 10 southern states between 1882 and 1930 were women; although mobs lynched 5 white females, there is no confirmation that the white female lynching victims suffered the savagery inflicted upon the lynched black women (Tolnay & Beck, 1995). Like black men, black women suffered inhumane treatment at the hands of white lynch mobs. One of the most monstrous acts of savagery involved the 1918 lynching of Martha Turner and her unborn child:

> An unscrupulous farmer in south Georgia refused to pay a Negro hand wages due him. A few days later the farmer was shot and killed. Not finding the Negro suspected of the murder, mobs began to kill every Negro who could even remotely be connected with the victim and the alleged slayer. One of these was a man named Hayes Turner, whose offense was that he knew the alleged slayer. . . . To Turner's wife, within one month of accouchement, was brought the news of her husband's death. . . . Word of her threat to swear out warrants for the arrest of her husband's murderers came to them. "We'll teach the damn' nigger wench some sense," was their answer, as they began to seek her. Sunday morning, with a hot May sun beating down, they found her. Securely they bound her ankles together and, by them, hanged her to a tree. Gasoline and motor oil were thrown upon her dangling clothes; a match wrapped her in sudden flames. . . . "Mister, you ought to've heard the nigger wench howl!" a member of the mob boasted to me a few days later as we stood at the place of Mary Turner's death. . . . The clothes burned from her crispy body, in which, unfortunately, life still lingered, a man stepped towards the woman and, with his knife, ripped open the abdomen in a crude Caesarean operation. Out tumbled the prematurely born child. Two feeble cries it gave—and received for answer the heel of a stalwart man, as life was ground out of the tiny form. Under the tree of death was scooped a shallow hold. The rope about Mary Turner's charred ankles was cut, and swiftly her

body tumbled into its grave. Not without a sense of humor or of appropriateness was some member of the mob. An empty whiskey-bottle, quart size, was given for headstone. Into its neck was stuck a half-smoked cigar—which had saved the delicate nostrils of one member of the mob from the stench of burning human flesh. (White, 1969, p. 27)

Faced with defeat of the Civil War, economic insecurities, religious fundamentalism, and a collective loss of honor attributed to the masterless slaves, southern society unleashed black lynchings as a "hatred, fear, loathing, and horror of Afro-Americans" that attained "levels of emotional, political, and religious intensity that are hard to imagine" (Patterson, 1998, p. 192). Black lynchings entailed ritualistic hatred and public hysteria that often culminated in "public spectacles of mockery, humiliation, and torture" (Brundage, 1993, p. 92). Thousands of people traveled great distances to witness the lynching of James Irwin in Ocilla, Georgia. Some 400 people participated in the lynching of Claude Neal in 1934. Most were after body parts that they could claim as souvenirs and sell to their friends. Moreover, public officials rarely held white mobsters involved in black lynchings criminally liable for murder. One analysis of newspapers reports from the Tuskegee Institute found that less than one-tenth of 1 percent of all white people involved in lynchings since 1900 ended in murder convictions, and there is no record of white executions for black lynchings. Only in Alabama, Georgia, Oklahoma, Virginia, Minnesota, and Texas did officials attempt to convict lynching participants. Some scholars explain that public officials were powerless in punishing whites that lynched blacks largely because they were answerable to white constituencies. Lynching was not regarded as a lawless act, however; it was understood as "law enforcement by informal means, a community-sanctioned extension of the criminal justice system . . . a legitimate, at times even gallant, defense of all that whites held sacred" (McMillen, 1989, p. 239). Coroners' juries often found that lynched blacks *died at the hands of parties unknown.*

Several factors made courts ineffective in gaining convictions of persons that participated in lynchings: divided responsibility between peace officers, judges, and grand and trial juries; an indifference of court officials to white criminality directed toward blacks; the widespread feelings among white men that white women should be shielded from court testimony; the disinclination of local jurymen to indict or convict their neighbors; and promises made the mob by officers and leading citizens to prevent further outbreaks (Raper, 1933). Law enforcement officers often aided white mobs in lynching blacks. Sheriffs' deputies were part of the townspeople and harbored hatred toward blacks. In one instance, police directed traffic while whites dragged the corpse of a black lynching victim through the city streets. As an excuse to intervene, police often reported that the mob had taken them by surprise, or that "they were unwilling to shoot into the crowd lest they kill innocent men, women, and children" (Raper, 1933, p. 13).

Scholars have put forward several explanations for the decline of black lynchings after the 1890s. One explanation is demographic changes in the distribution of the black population resulting from its attempts to escape the racial violence and the worsening agricultural conditions in the South. From the early 1920s through the 1960s, for example, nearly two million southern rural blacks migrated to the industrial northeast and western states. The search for improved economic opportunity in the urban industrial north resulted from increasing demands for unskilled labor after the First World War shut off European immigrant labor (Franklin & Moss, 2000). Blacks remained largely disenfranchised, segregated, and economically victimized during Jim Crow principally because southern states denied blacks job opportunities associated with the economic investment of northern industries and federally funded employment programs in southern states. Local officials appointed to administrate government work programs awarded positions exclusively to whites. Other scholars claim that black lynchings decreased as southern states became less isolated from the industrial north and Europe. Myrdal (1944) specifically notes that rural electrification, radio, paved highways, automobiles, motion pictures, educational improvements, and even intercollegiate athletics provided alternatives to traditional beliefs and routinized behavior of southern life. Journalists, business managers, and public officials also moved to curtail any evidence that would tarnish the image of southern states to northern investors who were extremely important to the region's economic growth (Reed, 1972). Public disclosure of the brutalities associated with black lynchings scared northern investors who demanded that southern society end the practice. Mechanization in agriculture, industrial expansion, and black migration produced considerable socioeconomic change in southern states that, in turn mandated mechanisms of social control other than the brutality of lynching (Zangrando, 1980). There was also a growing concern to secure federal antilynching laws, although Congress never enacted any legislation (Grant, 1975). Whatever caused the demise of lynchings in the United States, one scholar makes it clear the law had little or nothing to do with it:

> Throughout the Progressive Era, lynching remained a brutal crime that went largely uninvestigated, unprosecuted, unpunished, and undeterred by the agents of law at every level of government. State and local officials did not enforce existing law, and federal officials failed to enact any new legislation. Thus, lynchers never faced any serious deterrent from the government and could murder black people openly, notoriously, and boldly, without fear of reprisal. . . . This failure of the state and federal governments to protect blacks from lynching is part of a larger and more persistent failure of American law to find sufficient ways to defend black life and to ensure the promise of the Reconstruction Amendments to make African Americans full citizens. (Holden-Smith, 1996, pp. 39, 78)

BLACK WOMEN EXECUTIONS IN THE MODERN ERA

American society was a violent place for black people during the early civil rights movement ushering in the modern era. Still looming in our collective memory is the white violence precipitated against black persons involved in nonviolent protests for social, political, and economic equality. Forty years ago, for example, the country watched televised broadcasts of nightstick-wielding Alabama state police and mounted sheriff deputies brutally beating hundreds of peaceful civil rights marchers at the Edmund Pettus Bridge in Selma. The marchers had just made the 54-mile trek from Montgomery protesting the Jim Crow policies prohibiting black voting rights and the vicious police killing of Jimmy Lee Jackson weeks earlier. Also present are the images of whites humiliating and taunting blacks at lunch counter sit-ins, black students escorted to college classrooms by national guardsmen, and white terrorist attacks against freedom riders. The civil rights movement saw the Montgomery bus boycott protesting segregation in the aftermath of Rosa Parks's refusal to relinquish her bus seat to a white man. And who can forget the angry white mobs attacking school buses carrying black children to newly desegregated white schools? The rise of Black Nationalism, the Student Nonviolent Coordinating Committee, the Southern

Christian Leadership Conference, and the Congress of Racial Equality brought organization to black protest against white dominion. Whites invoked a horrific toll against black Americans in the long struggle for civil rights with sadistic beatings and the outright murder of hundreds of civil rights activists. Like black lynchings decades earlier, we will never have an actual accounting of the black Americans killed in the struggle. Still unsettled is the brutal killing of young Emmett Louis Till, the white firebombing of the 16th Street Baptist Church in Birmingham killing four young black girls (Denise McNair, Carole Robertson, Cynthia Wesley, and Addie Mae Collins); the murder of NAACP official Medgar Evers and that of Vernon Dahmer; and the killings of Michael Schwerner, Andrew Goodman, and James Chaney involved in southern black voter registration.

Still today, white Americans sadistically victimize black people. One only need consider the 1981 random lynching of young Michael Donald, the monstrous killing of James Byrd in 1998, and the young white supremacist that shot and killed basketball coach Richy Byrdsong in front of his three children to grasp the magnitude of violence whites inflict upon black Americans. Whites plague the black community by burning crosses, burning churches, racially motivating attacks against blacks in public places and on black students, throwing nooses around black teenager's necks, shouting racial slurs, randomly killing black men, holding a knife to young black girls' throats, and targeting and killing young black children (Leadership Conference on Civil Rights, 2004). White Americans commit thousands of hate crimes every year against black Americans. The latest government reports show that not only are hate crimes increasing over previous years, but that most victims are black and most offenders are white (U.S. Department of Justice, 2003). Schoolchildren report that they are the victims of hate language, and many of the thousands of Internet hate sites involve online games allowing young children to shoot and kill black people. Law enforcement insensitivity to black hate crime often encourages white violence. As Maroney (1998) points out, "[t]oo frequently victims of bias-motivated vandalism, hateful graffiti, threats, or assaults do not receive the police attention they merit" (p. 568). State and federal prosecutors, who are predominantly white males, are incredibly selective in prosecuting hate crimes. One report shows that the U.S. Department of Justice prosecuted only 22 of the more than 8,000 hate crimes reported in 1997 (Lieberman, 2000; see also Alfieri, 1995, 1998; Davis, 1998; Johnson, 1993;Lee, 1996). Scholars investigating the "disproportionate-enforcement" phenomenon are showing that the justice system is more likely to arrest, convict, and punish blacks as bias-criminals than whites even though most hate crime victims are black with white perpetrators (Bell, 2002; Lawrence, 2003).

Direct police violence against black citizens remains pervasive and widespread as well (Bandes, 1999; Cohen, 1996; Geller & Toch, 1996; Koepke, 2000; Leadership Conference on Civil Rights, 2000; Troutt, 1999). Unjustified shootings, severe beatings, fatal chokings, and unnecessarily rough treatment of detainees occur in police departments throughout the country (Human Rights Watch, 1998). Evidence suggests that police misconduct is highly institutionalized in large metropolitan police departments and that police aim their wrongdoing particularly at blacks (Human Rights Watch, 1998). Racism is central to police brutality because police consider black persons more dangerous than white persons. Black women are the victims of police violence: two white Los Angeles police officers shot and killed Eula Love, a black woman with intellectual disabilities, and four white Riverside California, police officers shot and killed Tyisha Miller, an unconscious black woman. Black women often encounter institutionalized racism when white police show little interest and often take no action when black women are rape victims. Police often fail to support black female rape victims. At an April 2000 conference in Santa Cruz, California, professor and social critic Angela Davis (2000) told a horrific story of black female victimization by a white police officer:

> Many years ago when I was a student in San Diego, I was driving down the freeway with a friend when we encountered a black woman wandering along the shoulder. Her story was extremely disturbing. Despite her uncontrollable weeping, we were able to surmise that she had been raped and dumped along the side of the road. After a while, she was able to wave down a police car, thinking that they would help her. However, when the white policeman picked her up, he did not comfort her, but rather seized upon the opportunity to rape her once more.

Equally troubling are a series of reports by Human Rights Watch reminiscent of the sexual atrocities experienced by plantation slave women (1996a, 1996b, 1998a, 1998b, 1998c, 1999; see also Geer, 2000; Laderberg, 1998). These reports reveal that the sexual assault of female inmates by male guards, staff, and wardens is commonplace in today's prisons. While all female inmates are potential victims of violent assaults by prison officials, black women are more prone to sexual violence since they constitute a disproportionate number of the female prison population—*in many states the black female incarceration rate is between 10 and 35 times that of white women* (Human Rights Watch, 2002). Male prison staff subject female inmates to rape, sexual assault, and unlawful invasions of privacy including prurient viewing during showering and dressing. Female inmate sexual abuse includes the atrocities of forced abortions, prisoners left stripped and bound for weeks, and inmates taken off the grounds to work as prostitutes. Prison staff regularly sell female inmates as sex slaves to male inmates when temporarily held in male detention centers. Male officers vaginally, anally, and orally rape female prisoners (Dinos, 2001). Indisputably, prison life for black women inmates amounts to "a climate of sexual terror."

Black resistance to racial inequality in the early civil rights period had some success in compelling legislative and legal reforms. Congress passed the 1964 Voting Rights Act ensuring black voter rights and the 1965 Civil Rights Act prohibiting discrimination in employment, housing, and public accommodations. One of the more significant legal challenges to Jim Crow disenfranchisement was the U.S. Supreme Court's holding in *Brown v. Board of Education* (1954) overruling the long-standing *Plessy* (1896) doctrine of "separate, but equal." The Court in *Brown* argued that segregation in public education is inherently unequal and constitutionally prohibitive. In most regards, however, these reforms have had little impact upon the burden of blackness in United States society. Sociologist Joe R. Feagin (2000) reminds us that

> Civil rights laws and desegregation decisions have been overwhelmed by the massiveness of racial discrimination. . . . [T]hese laws were crafted by the liberal wing of the white elite—mostly in the face of grass roots protests in the period from 1954 to 1972—with only modest concern for the group interests of African Americans. The laws were never intended to uproot systemic racism. While they have gotten rid of legal segregation, they are for the most part ineffective in regard to much informal discrimination and segregation. (p. 242)

One reason for the "massiveness of racial discrimination" in American society today is that the federal government has backpedaled on civil rights and failed to implement needed reforms. The federal government has failed to reduce entrenched discrimination, expand rights for disadvantaged groups, and promote access to federal programs and services for underserved populations on such issues as voting rights, equal educational opportunity, affirmative action, fair housing, environmental justice, racial profiling, hate crimes, immigration, women's rights, and gay rights (Leadership Conference on Civil Rights, 2003; U.S. Commission on Civil Rights, 2004). Mistakenly then, most Americans believe that the aims of the civil rights movement alleviated the inequities suffered by racial minorities and that they are no longer denied equal participation in societal institutions. Certainly the continued debate regarding white persons as the new victims of *reverse discrimination* and disadvantagement has fostered and encouraged this misconception. The socioeconomic status of black women in this country directly reflects the costs of these failed reforms. While blacks made civil rights and economic gains in the early periods of the civil rights period, these gains were significantly reversed in the 1980s. Current population reports reveal that the social conditions of unemployment and poverty clearly overburden black women. Black women fall far below national averages in their levels of educational attainment, placement in the occupational structure, and income and poverty levels. More than one-third of black female-headed households live in poverty, and black women are *three times* more likely than white women to live in poverty.

Unquestionably, continued marginalization of black women in American society places them at risk of contact with the criminal justice system. The criminal justice system controls *1 in 100* young white women, but *1 in 37* young black women. The incarceration rate of black women is *five times* that of white women, and black women are roughly 40 percent of female inmate population in the United States (Harrison & Beck, 2004). Black women also represent over 40 percent of the women in federal prisons. Evidence suggests that black female offenders are mostly poor, uneducated, and unskilled. Black female crime is often related to meeting the economic needs of their children since most black women are caring for dependent children when arrested (Johnson, 1995). Institutionalized gendered racism against black women by justice administrators results in higher incarceration rates of black women for violent crimes even though white women actually commit more violent crime than do black women—it is significant that two-thirds of females on probation are white and not black. Black women experience higher rates of violent victimization than white women—the black female homicide rate is *three times* the rate of white women. The impact of public policy reforms producing such draconian measures as mandatory minimum sentencing, three-strikes laws, and reductions in the availability of parole and early release programs have had a perverted effect upon black women and their communities. The human costs of these measures, "weakened lives, wrecked families, troubled children, according to Human Rights Watch (2003), are incalculable, as are the adverse social, economic and political consequences of weakened communities, diminished opportunities for economic mobility, and extensive disenfranchisement."

Criminal justice figures stand in the face of a national black female population of 13 percent. Black women are 27 percent of female defendants sentenced to death in the United States since 1973. Thus, black women constitute *twice* their proportionate representation in capital sentencing cases. Black women are 32 percent of the 52 females residing on death rows across the country—nearly *three times* their proportionate representation in the overall society (Fins, 2005). Death penalty jurisdictions have executed 10 females since 1976. Since Ohio's execution of Betty Butler in June 1954 for murder, however, authorities have executed 1 black woman—Oklahoma put 41-year-old Wanda Jean Allen to death by lethal injection for murder in 2001. Despite 1 black female execution over the last several decades, Wanda Jean Allen's execution epitomizes many of the jurisprudential issues facing condemned black women. Wanda Jean Allen is one of the most controversial figures regarding imposition of the death penalty to black women because, as one commentary put it, her case represents "an unflinching investigation of the role poverty, mental health, race, and sexuality play within the criminal justice system" (HBO Documentary). Prosecutorial racism, incompetent defense lawyers, innocence, and judicial override also inform the vulnerability of black women to execution.

Wanda Jean Allen

Oklahoma officials executed Wanda Jean Allen at the state penitentiary in McAlester at mid-morning on January 11, 2001. Allen was the second of eight children born to a mother who suffered from alcoholism and mental retardation, and who drank during her pregnancy with Wanda. Acting as a surrogate mother to her younger siblings after her father abandoned the family, Wanda regularly stole food and clothing for the children that led to juvenile arrests. Unsurprisingly, Wanda Jean performed poorly in school and at the age of 15 officials diagnosed her within the upper range of mental retardation. While serving a prison term for an earlier manslaughter conviction, Wanda Jean met Gloria Leathers with whom she began a lesbian relationship. Wanda's previous killing involved a case so dubious that she was able to plead guilty and received the minimum sentence. After their release from prison, they lived together but had a violent and turbulent relationship. In December 1988, the two women had a dispute at a grocery store over a welfare check. A police officer escorted the women to their house and watched as Gloria collected her belongings and moved out. Accompanied by her mother, Gloria went to the police station to file a complaint against Wanda who followed them hoping to talk to Gloria. One account has it that Wanda Jean shot Gloria in the abdomen with a .38-caliber handgun as she exited the car she drove to the police station. Wanda Jean's account is that she shot Gloria after Gloria attacked her with a rake. Gloria died two hours after police arrested Wanda. After a short deliberation, the jury convicted Wanda of first-degree murder and recommended the death penalty. Wanda's crime was most likely a heat of passion crime that does not usually call for the death penalty. Lawyers for Wanda lost her initial appeal for a rehearing and a subsequent appeal affirmed the denial of postconviction relief. The U.S. Court of Appeals for the Tenth Circuit also denied Wanda Jean's appeal in January 2000, and the Oklahoma Pardon and Parole Board denied recommending clemency to the state's governor.

Race and the Death Penalty

Though Wanda Jean Allen is the only black woman executed in the United States since Butler's execution, race discrimination in capital sentencing still accounts for the black disparity among female death-row inmates. Capital punishment underwent a series of constitutional challenges beginning in the early 1970s. Despite the U.S. Supreme Court's creation of a rational structure of procedural safeguards designed to curb racial discrimination in capital sentencing, the strategies have failed to correct for racial inequality in the imposition of the death penalty to black persons. In the first historical instance in which the U.S. Supreme Court undertook the issue of racism in capital sentencing, the Court held in *Furman v. Georgia* (1972) that imposition of capital punishment as then administered contravened constitutional protections against cruel and unusual punishment because it was arbitrary and capricious in its application. Here, the justices made it clear that death penalty jurisdictions were to devise procedural strategies to restrict unbridled discretion of juries in remanding prisoners to death. In *Gregg v. Georgia* (1976), the Court affirmed the death sentence of Troy Gregg because the Court affirmed the procedural safeguards adopted in Georgia's capital punishment statute intending to prevent arbitrary and discriminatory imposition of the death penalty. A final challenge to race discrimination in capital sentencing came when Warren McCleskey, a black man who had killed a white police officer, claimed that Georgia administered its capital sentencing process in a racially discriminatory manner. McCleskey proffered the results of one of the most methodologically powerful studies of racial bias in capital sentencing. McCleskey claimed that race had infected the administration of the death penalty in Georgia in two distinct ways: that jurisdictions were more likely to sentence murderers of whites to death than murderers of blacks; and that jurisdictions were more likely to sentence black murderers to death than white murderers. McCleskey alleged that Georgia's system of imposing the death penalty discriminated against him as a black man who killed a white man. The question in *McCleskey v. Kemp* was whether a complex statistical study indicating a risk that racial consideration enters into capital sentencing determinations is constitutional. The majority of justices held that the statistical study did not prove that Georgia's capital punishment system is unconstitutional—to establish that only a "pattern" of racial discrimination in imposing the death penalty to a select group of defendants is not sufficient to support an equal protection claim.

The research record on capital sentencing since *McCleskey* shows a continued pattern of racial discrimination in capital punishment. The record reveals that death penalty jurisdictions continue to sentence black defendants to death at significantly higher rates than white defendants, and that black defendants are particularly at risk of capital sentencing and actual execution when they victimize white persons. Selective prosecution of capital cases, prosecutorial misuse of peremptory challenges, and judicial override by trial judges, prosecutorial misconduct, and ineffective defense lawyers are the most important reasons why black defendants are denied fairness and evenhandedness in capital sentencing today.

Poverty and the Death Penalty

Wanda Jean Allen was a poor black women. Poor blacks overwhelmingly populate state and federal death rows. Condemned black prisoners are 42 percent of death-row inmates including 66 percent of federal and 71 percent of the U.S. military's death-row populations. As early as 1967, the President's Commission on Law Enforcement and Administration of Justice (1967) recognized discriminatory patterns in capital sentencing in the United States: "The death sentence is disproportionately imposed and carried out on the *poor*, the Negro, and the members of unpopular groups." Poverty is an aggravating factor for capital defendants because poor blacks cannot afford private attorneys who often succeed in mitigating capital sentences (Lofquist, 2002). Poor black defendants accused of capital crimes must rely on court appointed lawyers or public defenders—90 percent of death-row inmates had appointed lawyers (Bright & Keenan, 1995). Fogelman (2002) explains the inherent deficiencies in legal representation for indigent defendants.

> Furthermore, the poor are often represented by inexperienced lawyers who view their responsibilities as a burden and who have no real inclination to assist their clients. Other significant problems that plague indigent defense services include fee caps for appointed counsel; enormous caseloads and overworked public defender offices; low prestige and a lack of public support; and insufficient funding to pay necessary expert witnesses. Compounding these obstacles facing defendants, some defense attorneys often fail to request aid to which indigent defendants are entitled under certain circumstances. Because the indigent disproportionately receive appointed counsel, they risk being stuck with an attorney who is incapable of zealously advocating on their behalf, and, in some instances, who will fall asleep during trial, thus depriving them of their Sixth Amendment rights.

The Sixth Amendment right to counsel does not always equate to competent counsel for poor black defendants. The U.S. Supreme Court in *Gregg* touted bifurcated trials in capital cases as a procedural device calculated to eradicate capricious and arbitrary imposition of the death penalty. Bifurcated trials give defense lawyers an opportunity to present mitigating evidence to persuade juries to spare the convicted defendant's life. Yet, as Justice Marshall noted, federal reporters are filled with stories of lawyers who failed to present mitigating evidence on behalf of their clients simply because the lawyer did not know what to offer, how to offer it, or because the lawyer had not read the state's sentencing statute (Marshall, 1986). More recently, Justice Ginsburg noted, "I have yet to see a death case among the dozens coming to the Supreme Court on eve-of-execution stay applications in which the defendant was well represented at trial" (cited in Williams, 2002, p. 1189). Ineffective defense lawyers perpetuate race discrimination in capital sentencing when they fail to challenge procedures that preclude fairness to black defendants in capital trials. Often race discrimination claims are unsuccessful for black defendants because defense lawyers fail to raise the claims at required times. Defense lawyers often fail to present evidence in domestic murder cases involving black women in abusive relationships. In the case of Louise Harris, for example, defense counsel failed to provide the jury evidence that Louise had a long history of abuse and trauma:

> She had been sexually assaulted at age 11; she had witnessed her older sister die suddenly of a seizure in her arms, leaving Louise, at age 14, to raise her younger siblings; she had seen her younger brother being pulled from a lake after he drowned, and she had been the one to discover the body of her father, who was murdered. She had also been beaten severely and regularly by her first husband, John Wesley Robinson; she had been abused for years by her common-law husband Jesse Lee Hall and then by her husband Isaiah Harris, resulting in multiple trips to the hospital; and she was also abused by the man from whom she had sought comfort, Lorenzo McCarter. This abuse and trauma resulted in Louise suffering from Post-Traumatic Stress Disorder, Battered Women's Syndrome and Dissociative Disorder. (American Civil Liberties Union, 2004)

Wanda Jean Allen's defense counsel failed to introduce well-documented evidence of her mental retardation and thus the court never fully litigated the issue. Moreover,

Wanda's defense counsel tried repeated to have the court remove him from the case because he believed he was unqualified to conduct a capital defense. Defense lawyers in Sabrina Butler's case, a black woman that spent five years on Mississippi's death row for the killing of her infant son, failed to support their contention with adequate evidence that the child's injuries resulted from Sabrina's attempts to resuscitate the child. A jury later acquitted Sabrina of murder at a second trial when the defense lawyer proffered corroborated evidence from a neighbor who tried to help Sabrina revive the child, and an admission from the autopsy physician of shoddy work. Frances Elaine Newton, a black woman convicted of shooting her husband and two children to collect a life insurance policy, repeatedly requested that the trial court dismiss Ron Mock as her count-appointed attorney. Not only has the state executed seven of Ron Mock's previous death penalty clients, but the Texas Defenders Service (2000) found that he failed the newly required certification exam to become eligible for appointment to capital murder cases.

Racist Prosecutorial Discretion

The adversarial nature of criminal proceedings ostensibly offers impartiality in state prosecutions. Yet the selective prosecution of blacks raises the specter that prosecutors are racist in which criminal cases they chose to prosecute (Heller, 1997; Vorenberg, 1981). Arguably, state and federal prosecutors possess unbridled discretion in filing criminal charges against persons accused of crime. While courts impose formidable restrictions on the discretionary powers of police, sentencing judges, parole boards, and correctional officers, courts are unwilling to restrict prosecutorial discretion (Benson, 1991). The charging discretion of prosecutors remains largely unregulated, unreviewable, and for the most part, there is no public accountability (Davis, 1998; see Cole, 1970; "Developments in the Law," 1988; Oberman, 1996). Prosecutors alone determine the seriousness of criminal charges brought against suspects. One of the more disturbing examples of this bureaucratic authoritarianism of racist prosecutors against black women is the disparate prosecution of drug-addicted black mothers giving birth to babies that test positive for drugs. Racist public health officials prove much more likely to report drug-addicted black mothers to police than drug-addicted white women, and as a result, poor black mothers have become the primary targets of racist prosecutors "not because they are more likely to be guilty of fetal abuse, but because they are black and poor" (Roberts, 1991, p. 1422). Medical practitioners with affluent white female patients rarely remand drug-addicted mothers to law enforcement because, as Roberts (1991) puts it, "they have a financial stake both in retaining their patients' business and securing referrals from them and because they are socially more like their patients" (p. 1433). Prosecutors punish drug-addicted black mothers by depriving them custody of their children, jailing them during pregnancy, and prosecuting them after delivering their babies (Roberts, 1991).

Jurisdictions commonly consign decisions to seek the death penalty exclusively to the discretion of prosecutors (Johnson, 1994; Tabak, 1999), and no jurisdiction has implemented guidelines to control how prosecutors decide on seeking the death penalty (Ragone & Williams, 1995). Nearly all state prosecutors are exclusively white in most death penalty states (Pokorak, 1998), and certainly the pervasiveness of white prosecutors presupposes an unconscious racial bias toward black people that influences charging decisions in capital cases. White prosecutors have undoubtedly absorbed the cultural stereotype of *black inferiority* and perceive black defendants as more *violent* and more *dangerous* than white defendants ("Developments in the Law," 1988; Pokorak, 1998). Prosecutorial decision making fraught with racial bias surely challenges the idea that white prosecutors seek the death penalty *objectively*. Prosecutors deny that race bias effects prosecutorial decision making (Little, 2004); even so, Nunn (2000) explains that state prosecutors are a major source of racism in the criminal justice system:

> Though prosecutors assert that there is no racial bias in the exercise of prosecutorial discretion, they have done little to verify this belief, or dispel the concerns of others. Prosecutors have rarely commissioned studies, promulgated internal guidelines, or made attempts to keep voluntary statistics on prosecutorial racial bias. Few prosecutors have taken it upon themselves to maintain a dialogue on these issues within their offices. There is little effort to sensitize prosecutors or provide diversity training. Even more disappointing than the lack of prosecutorial effort to determine the extent of racial bias in prosecutorial decision-making, is that prosecutors actively oppose the efforts of others to do so. Prosecutors have vehemently opposed legislative attempts to gather information regarding bias in the imposition of death sentencing and in automobile stops. (p. 1498; see also Johnson, 2001)

Many commentators deny that conscious racism permeates prosecutorial decision making (Tonry, 1995), but other critics concede that prosecutors suffer from unconscious racism when seeking capital charges against black defendants (Davis, 1996; Johnson, 1988). Pokorak (1998) explains it this way:

> [U]nconscious bias may creep into the prosecutors' decisions to seek the death penalty. The predominantly white prosecutors may perceive violent crimes against whites as more serious than similar crimes against minorities and thus seek the death penalty more frequently against defendants accused of killing white victims. Conversely, white prosecutors may have an unconscious perception of blacks as inferior and may view violent crimes against blacks as less serious and less worthy of the death penalty than similar crimes against whites. (p. 1811; see also "Developments in the Law," 1988)

One result of racist prosecutorial discretion in selecting capital cases is that 81 percent of all capital cases tried by prosecutors involve white victims, while nationally only half of all murder victims are white (Death Penalty Information Center, 2005a; U.S. General Accounting Office, 1990). Execution data show similar disparities. Since 1976, death penalty officials have executed 12 white defendants for killing blacks but 199 black defendants for killing whites (Fins, 2005)—revealing that authorities are nearly *17 times more likely to execute black defendants with white victims than white defendants with black victims*. Only 35 cases exist historically in the United States where state jurisdictions executed white prisoners for killing blacks (Carter Center Symposium on the Death Penalty, 1997). Federal prosecutors are excessive in selecting blacks for capital punishment as well—nearly three-quarters of federal and U.S. military death row inmates are black (Fins, 2005). Some scholars suggest reforming prosecutorial discretion with race impact studies by prosecutors (Davis, 1998), and others have recommended jury nullification (Butler, 1995; Scott, 1989; see also Kennedy, 1997; Leipold, 1997; Scheflin, 1972) and the hiring of more black prosecutors (Howard, 1999).

Prosecutorial Homophobia

An important feature of systemic racism in the criminal justice system is prosecutors' marginalization of black female defendants. Prosecutors use sexuality to malign and disparage female defendants to juries. Indeed, the criminal justice system is a major location of homophobic-based oppression in U.S. society. Homophobia enters the decision making of white prosecutors in selecting capital cases and it is all too often central in the capital trials of black women. Prosecutors use the transgression of feminine stereotypes to show the dangerousness of female capital defendants and that lesbian killers deserve the death penalty. Prosecutors used sexual orientation to prejudice juries in at least three cases of female death-row inmates studied recently by the American Civil Liberties Union (2004). One result of prosecutors exploiting lesbianism to denigrate women in capital cases is that lesbians disproportionately occupy death row. While more than half the women on death row are lesbian (Brownworth, 1992), a national study shows that only 0.32 percent of the total U.S. population is lesbian (Laumann, 1994). This means that lesbians are represented on death-row more than *81 times* their proportionate representation in the overall society. One scholar explains that 40 percent of women accused of murder contend with prosecutorial assertions of lesbianism to purposefully masculate and dehumanize them (Streib, 1994). Prosecutors resort to marginalizing prejudices and stereotypes to render female defendants more executable to jurors. Wanda Jean Allen's lesbianism overwhelmed the state's case with erroneous assertions that Wanda dominated her lover, when in fact Wanda and Gloria Leathers most often mistreated each other. Prosecutors urged the trial court's rejection of defense motions outlining Leather's violent nature (American Civil Liberties Union, 2004). The prosecution inaccurately yet purposefully portrayed Wanda as wearing "the pants in the family" and that she was the masculine one in the relationship. The state attorney also solicited testimony from Wanda's mother that Wanda used the male spelling of her middle name. Wanda's sexuality played a prominent role in her trial and "evidences again that when a woman acts out from society's gender expectations, she faces harsher penalties" (Kopec, 2003, p. 362).

> Allen was convicted on the basis of a rash of stereotypes about lesbians which, combined with stereotypes about black people and poor people, played off juror biases to portray Allen as an aggressive offender so dangerous to society that the only recourse was execution. One observer proposed that had Allen been a middle class, white heterosexual woman who killed her boyfriend, the jury would probably have been more sympathetic and Allen's sentence would have been considerably lighter. (Kohn, 2001, p. 264)

Executing Mentally Retarded Defendants

Although the ruling came too late for Wanda Jean Allen to contest her mental impediments at trial, the U.S. Supreme Court declared in June 2002 that the execution of mentally retarded defendants is unconstitutional. In *Atkins v. Virginia* 2002, the Court held that imposition of the death penalty on mentally retarded persons constitutes cruel and unusual punishment (Grunewald, 2002; Steiker, 2002). The Court's ruling in *Atkins* overruled *Penry v. Lynaugh* (1989) where the Court argued that executing mentally retarded inmates was not violative of the federal Constitution. In *Penry*, the Court found that only Maryland

and Georgia prohibited executing mentally retarded inmates. But in *Atkins* the Court found that U.S. society had reached a national consensus against executing mentally retarded inmates since most death penalty states and the federal government now prohibited executing mentally retarded defendants. The Court surmised in *Atkins* that it was time to stop a practice that most Americans found repugnant.

The impact of *Atkins* on capital punishment in the United States remains uncertain, however. One concern is whether state procedures used for determining retardation fall in line with *Atkins*. Another question is whether pretrial hearings before a judge on the determination of mental retardation violate the Court's holding in *Ring v. Arizona* (2002) that only a jury can decide critical issues in death penalty cases. Still another concern is the establishment of a legal standard for determining mental retardation since *Atkins* did not provide a standard (McDonough, 2003). The actual number of death-row inmates across the country affected by *Atkins* is unknown—one estimate predicts that about 25 percent of North Carolina's death-row population may be implicated. In any event, one concern that legal scholars and the Supreme Court has not addressed is the impact of *Atkins* on black defendants. Imposition of the death sentence has had a perverse effect on black capital offenders with mental retardation—blacks represent 64 percent of executed mentally retarded prisoners and roughly half of executed black mentally retarded prisoners killed white people.

"The Judge as Lynch Mob"

The U.S. legal system traditionally has assigned responsibility for expressing community sentiment on death in capital cases to juries. As White (1989) explains, "Throughout its history, the jury determined which homicide defendants would be subject to capital punishment by making factual determinations, many of which related to difficult assessments of the defendant's state of mind. By the time the Bill of Rights was adopted, the jury's right to make these determinations was unquestioned" (p. 11). But when an Alabama jury sentenced a black woman named Louise Harris to life in prison for killing her husband, the presiding judge overruled the jury recommendation and sentenced Harris to death. In June 2002, however, the U.S. Supreme Court ruled the practice of judicial override unconstitutional—judges can no longer make the ultimate sentencing decision in capital cases. Justice Ginsburg argued for the majority in *Ring v. Arizona* that trial judges violate capital defendants' Sixth Amendment right to a jury trial when judges, rather than jurors, impute death. In part, the *Ring* case stems from states that incorporated judicial override into their death penalty schemes (Burnside, 1999; Erlich, 1996; Russell, 1994; Silverstein, 2001; Tran, 1997). Judicial override allowed trial judges to disregard jury recommendations and to use their own biased discretion in sentencing capital offenders to death.

Nowhere in *Ring* did the Court consider the factual data that trial judges are noticeably more likely to override jury recommendations in capital cases involving black defendants. Yet judicial override has had an adverse effect upon black capital offenders—overall, 55 percent of capital defendants sentenced to death through judicial override are black and 75 percent of the victims in override cases are white. Several studies document specific incidences of state trial judges exhibiting racial bias in capital cases and found it to be a common feature of state court systems (Ifill, 1997). One study finds that even though black and white judges convict black defendants more often than white defendants, the interracial disparity is greatest for white judges (Johnson, 1985).

Judicial override was a controversial issue because it was unclear if the Supreme Court would apply *Ring* retroactively to include defendants that had their death sentences imposed by trial judges rather than juries—that is, whether defendants affected by judicial overrides would have their sentences reduced to life imprisonment or receive new sentencing trials with new juries. Death penalty scholars estimate that the Court's decision affects some 800 condemned prisoners that judges sentenced without the protections extended in *Ring*. Finding *Ring* retroactive would surely impact black inmates disproportionately since condemned blacks are 46 percent of death-row inmates in Alabama, 53 percent in Delaware, 35 percent in Florida, and 33 percent in Indiana. Then, in June 2004, the U.S. Supreme Court held in *Schriro v. Summerlin* that *Ring* does not apply retroactively to defendants already sentenced to death by judges rather than juries. In the immediate future, some 100 defendants, most of them black inmates, will proceed to execution despite fundamental flaws in their Sixth Amendment right to a jury trial.

Prosecutorial Lawlessness

Prosecutorial lawlessness in capital cases is the product of systemic white racism in the justice system. Scholars have studied appellate court reviews of thousands of capital cases and found that courts reverse most capital sentences because of prosecutorial misconduct (Scheck, Neufeld, & Dwyer, 2000; Williams, 2000). Liebman, Fagan, West, & Lloyd, (2000) and associates studied capital cases nationally and learned that nearly all death penalty jurisdictions in the United States have excessive error rates mostly stemming from severe forms of prosecutorial misconduct (see also Center for Public Integrity, 2003). Some 30 percent of capital cases in Ohio study involve severe ethical issues of prosecutorial misconduct (Brewer, 2001). A study of wrongfully convicted capital defendants found that prosecutorial misconduct was one of the most significant factors leading to conviction in seven defendants' cases in Illinois (Warden, 2001). While these studies did not separately study the reversible error involved in female capital cases, Streib (2003) calculated an error rate in female capital cases at 58 percent.

One of the most common forms of prejudicial error in capital cases is prosecutorial suppression of evidence that defendants are innocent of the capital offense or that defendants do not deserve the death penalty. That is, state prosecutors frequently suppress exculpatory evidence, knowingly use false testimony, intimidate witnesses, give improper closing arguments, give false statements to the jury, and fabricate evidence. A *Chicago Tribune* investigation found hundreds of homicide cases in which the prosecutors concealed or fabricated evidence (Armstrong & Possley, 1999). A Texas study of cases involving serious prosecutorial misconduct revealed that state prosecutors have "used threats against defendants or their family members to coerce confessions" (Texas Defender Service, 2000; see also Bright, 1995; White, 2001). Undoubtedly, prosecutorial misconduct weighs most heavily against black offenders since blacks are so overrepresented as capital defendants (Kroll, 1992). Other studies have focused on prosecutors' use of racist remarks while trying capital cases involving black defendants (Johnson, 2001). The literature reveals that courts are frustrated over the frequency in which prosecutorial misconduct occurs, yet courts are unwilling to overturn cases on grounds of racial bias and, in the alternative, assess the relative weight of the statements to other evidence or otherwise explain away the prosecutors' remarks (Earle, 1992; Lyon, 2001). One commentator identified the problem of prosecutorial racism this way:

> Many courts refuse to recognize the more discrete and arguably more insidious uses of racism that occur during the criminal trial. Instead, they choose to focus solely on overt expressions of racial bias. Nonetheless, the subtler racial references made by a prosecutor are more difficult to detect, and are precisely those that are most difficult to prove. Thus, in order to protect a defendant's due process right to a fair trial, courts must look beneath the surface to discover the race-based stereotypes on which prosecutors so cleverly rely. (Richelle, 1993, p. 2357)

Prosecutorial misconduct is a problem in capital cases because efforts to deter the misdeeds of state and federal prosecutors have proven largely unsuccessful. For example, the U.S. Supreme Court held in *Brady v. Maryland* (1963) that prosecutors are under a constitutional duty to disclose evidence favorable to the accused. The above noted studies attest to the ineffectiveness of *Brady*. Moreover, prosecutors rarely face criminal charges for misconduct, as attested to by the fact that of those documented cases of prosecutorial misconduct, not one prosecutor was ever convicted of criminal conduct or even disbarred (Gordon, 2003). Adding to the problem of prosecutorial accountability for misconduct is that they enjoy absolute immunity from civil liability (Weinberg, 2003; see also Romney, 2005). Prosecutors found to engage in misconduct are often elevated to the bar as judges (Brown, 2000).

Excluding Black Women Jurors

State and federal prosecutors use the peremptory challenge as a procedural devise to remove potential jurors during *voir dire* for unexplained reasons. While prosecutors must give a reason when challenging jurors for cause, the peremptory challenge requires no justification and is "exercised without a reason stated, without impunity, and without being subject to the court's control" (Siebert, 1999, p. 308). It is the capricious nature of the peremptory challenge, however, that effectively masks racial discrimination in jury selection by allowing prosecutors to intentionally discriminate against black and female jurors (Broderick, 1992; Griffin, 1997). The U.S. Supreme Court first visited racial discrimination in jury selection in 1880 in *Strauder v. West Virginia* when the Court invalidated a state statute prohibiting blacks from serving on grand or petit juries. The Court reasoned that "the very fact that colored people are singled out and expressly denied by a statute all right to participate in the administration of the law, as jurors, because of their color . . . is practically a brand upon them, affixed by the law, an assertion of their inferiority" (p. 308). A century later in *Batson v. Kentucky* (1986), the Court reaffirmed its position in *Strauder* and argued that prosecutors are prohibited from using the peremptory challenge to strike potential jurors solely on account of race because it denies the defendant the protection that a trial by jury is intended to secure under the Constitution. The Court expanded *Batson* to include women in *J.E.M. v. Alabama* (1994).

Regardless of the Court's holdings in these and other cases involving prosecutorial abuse of the peremptory challenge, state attorneys continue to use the peremptory challenge in capital cases to openly discriminate against black women in jury selection. For example, veteran prosecutors in Philadelphia use training tapes to instruct new assistant district attorneys how to exclude *young black women* from juries. One prosecutor believed that black women who dye their hair blonde are undesirable as jurors because they are "not cognizant of their own reality and experience." The same prosecutor found white women that wear "Jheri curls" unsuitable for jury service (Page, 2005). Most recently, former Alameda County prosecutor claimed that he conspired with a trial judge to exclude *black women* from capital juries over a 20-year period from the 1970s to the early 1990s because they are reluctant to support the death penalty for black defendants (Kravets, 2005; Sample, 2005; Zamora, 2005). Many courts still hold that striking black women as jurors does not amount to racist exclusion. In one case, a trial judge told a defense lawyer objecting to a prosecutor striking black women: "You have got women on the jury. What function does a Black woman fulfill that the White woman doesn't?" (Babcock, 1993). Prosecutors prefer white jurors to black jurors in capital cases because they believe that white juries are more prone to convict black male defendants (Baldus, Woodworth, Euckerman, Weiner, & Broffitt, 2001; Broderick, 1992; Griffin, 1997; Johnson, 1985; Underwood, 1992). Some research shows that black women on capital juries does not measurably influence sentencing outcomes, but in most cases systemic white racism pervades jury decisions since most white juries are far more punitive toward black defendants generally, but they are particularly punitive in their sentencing decisions against black defendants that kill whites (Bowers, Steiner, & Sandys, 2001; Dieter, 1998). Still, it is difficult to make the case of racial discrimination when prosecutors abuse peremptory challenges because courts allow "almost any conceivable justification for peremptory challenges, however arbitrary or irrational, while ignoring evidence that such challenges were exercised in a racially discriminatory manner" (Conrad, 1998, p. 190; see also Mintz, 1987; Savage, 2005). Federal prosecutors repeatedly use peremptory challenges as well to exclude black jurors in capital cases (Walker, Spohn, & DeLone, 2000). In *Batson v. Kentucky*, Justice Marshall called for the elimination of peremptory challenges because he doubted that prosecutors could ever overcome their racist use of the device. He argued that:

> A prosecutor's own conscious or unconscious racism may lead him easily to the conclusion that a prospective black juror is sullen, or distant, a characterization that would not have come to his mind if a white juror had acted identically. Prosecutors' peremptories are based on their seat-of-the-pants instincts as to how particular jurors will vote. Yet seat-of-the-pants-instincts may often be just another term for racial prejudice. Even if all parties approach the Court's mandate with the best of conscious intentions, that mandate requires them to confront and overcome their own racism on all levels—a challenge I doubt all of them can meet. (Batson v. Kentucky, 1986, Marshall dissenting, p. 105).

Executing Innocent Black Defendants

The escalating rate of executions in the United States significantly increases the possibility that authorities may execute an innocent defendant. That possibility has become so disconcerting to the legal community that the American Bar Association (1997) called for death penalty jurisdictions to halt executions until authorities can ensure fairness and impartiality in its administration (see also McAdams, 1998). Social critic Alan Berlow (1999) has identified several facets of the process under which the criminal justice system imposes the death penalty that have increased the prospect that wrongfully convicted prisoners will be executed. Death-qualified juries, a "take-no-prisoners" mentality of jurists and politicians, the lack of resources required to fund public-defender organizations, an ever-increasing public condemnation of heinous criminality, an indifference of jurists to the possibility of wrongful convictions, the incompetence of defense counsel, the lawlessness of police officers and prosecutors in suppressing exculpating evidence, and the increasing complexity of the appeals process have all added to the equation that the U.S. criminal justice system's mechanism of imposing death as punishment is faulty, impractical, and ineffectual.

One of the more troubling studies on wrongful executions has identified some 350 cases in which U.S. jurisdictions have wrongfully convicted capital defendants (Bedau & Radelet, 1987; Radelet, Lofquist, & Bedau, 1996; Scheck et al., 2000). Of these cases, authorities sentenced 159 defendants to death; they actually executed another 23 prisoners, and 22 other prisoners came within 72 hours of their executions before lawyers established their innocence. Predictably, black defendants constitute a significant proportion of the hundreds of cases of wrongfully convicted defendants. In fact, 43 of the 101 capital defendants released from death rows across the country since 1971 have been black defendants. This number suggests a strong probability that jurisdictions erroneously convict black defendants more than white defendants.

One of the more significant statements questioning capital sentencing in the United States since the U.S. Supreme Court declared all state death penalty laws unconstitutional came when Illinois Governor George Ryan commuted the death sentences of all 167 condemned death-row inmates to prison terms in early January 2003. Four of the commuted sentences involved three black women (Dorothy Williams, Latasha Pulliman, and Jacqueline Williams) and one Latina (Bernina Mata). Ryan became concerned with Illinois's death penalty scheme when he took office as the state's governor. Ryan was troubled that in the time since Illinois had reaffirmed capital punishment, state authorities had conducted 12 executions and exonerated 13 death-row inmates, with one exonerated inmate coming with 48 hours of execution. As a result, Ryan called for a state moratorium on capital punishment in January 2000 and ordered a blue-ribbon commission to study the death penalty in Illinois. The commission issued more than 80 recommendations which the state legislature failed to adopt and reform death penalty law in Illinois and Ryan acted on his last day in office to commute the death sentences of all condemned inmates on the state's death row.

CONCLUDING REMARKS

A substantive conclusion that one can make from the historical-contextual analysis of the racialized, sexist oppression of executed black women in the United States put forth in this chapter is that criminal justice investigators must recognize black women "as a group worthy of study." While much of the discussion in this chapter attempts to isolate the racist conduct of justice practitioners peculiar to black women, often the white racism systemic to black oppression throughout our nation's history becomes blurred between black women and black men. Indeed, white people have directed much of their racial violence and brutalization to black people generally without regard to gender differences. Yet, as this chapter shows, there is much about racist relations in the context of criminal justice history in the United States that are specific to black women. As noted, one historically consistent factor giving rise to black women executions is that criminal justice authorities have executed black women for challenging their racist and sexist exploitation by white men. While colonial and antebellum slavery fully institutionalized the sexualized persecution of slave women, the perversion of sexual violence against black women continued during Reconstruction and Jim Crow. Today, as in the past, white violence remains manifested in the gross indifference criminal justice officials afford black female rape victims in relation to white female rape victims. The transparency of the racialized, sexist oppression of black women in the U.S. criminal justice system today is the blatant disregard justice officials have toward safeguarding the most fundamental rights of black women accused of capital crimes. White racism is *systemic* to prosecutorial selection of which cases involving black women are triable as capital cases, to prosecutors' blatant abuse of the peremptory challenge in gaining advantage of racist white jurors, to racist judges overriding jury recommendations of leniency, to the racist (and criminal) misconduct of prosecutors in failing to meet *Brady* safeguards, and the ineffectiveness and often racist disregard of defense lawyers toward black capital defendants. Moreover, the historical-contextual analysis furthers our understanding of black women executions in a societal system of white domination and black subordination. The analysis depicts in a graphic sense the brutality of black female executions rooted in our society's racist social fabric, and that these roots are so deeply buried in our racist relations that they prevent change in the treatment of black women in our society generally and its justice practitioners specifically.

REFERENCES

ADAMSON, C. (1983). Punishment after slavery: Southern state penal systems, 1865–1890. *Social Problems, 30,* 557–569.

AGUIRRE, A. JR., & BAKER, D. (1991). *Race, racism and the death penalty in the United States.* Berrien Springs, MI: Vande Vere.

AGUIRRE, A. JR., & BAKER, D. (1994). *Perspectives on Race and Ethnicity in American Criminal Justice.* New York: West.

AGUIRRE, A. JR., & BAKER, D. (1999). Support for the death penalty: A gender-specific model. *Springer Science, 43*(3–4), 163–179.

ALFIERI, A. (1995). Defending racial violence. *Columbia Law Review, 95,* 1301–1342.

ALFIERI, A. (1998). Race trial. *Texas Law Review, 76,* 1293–1369.

AMERICAN BAR ASSOCIATION. (1997). Resolution 107, ABA House of Delegates.

AMERICAN CIVIL LIBERTIES UNION. (2004, December). *The forgotten population: A look at death row in the United States through the experiences of women.* Retrieved from http://www.aclu.org/DeathPenalty/DeathPenalty.cfm?ID=17085&c=68.

AMERICAN CORRECTIONAL ASSOCIATION. (1998). *The female offender: What does the future hold?* Retrieved from http://www.ojp.usdoj.gov/reports/98Guides/wcjs98/chap2.htm.

AMNESTY INTERNATIONAL. (2003, April 23). *Death by discrimination: The continuing role of race in capital cases.* Retrieved from http://web.amnesty.org/library/index/engamr510462003.

APTHEKER, H. (1993). *Anti-racism in U.S. history: The first two hundred years.* Westport, CT: Praeger Press.

ARMSTRONG, K., & POSSLEY, M. (1999, January 10–14). Trial and error: How prosecutors sacrifice justice to win (Series: Tribune Investigative Report: The failure of the death penalty in Illinois. Parts I–V), *Chicago Tribune*.

AXELSEN, D. (1985). Women as victims of medical experimentation: J. Marion Sims on slave women, 1845–1850. *Sage, 2*, 10–13.

BABCOCK, B. (1993). A place in the palladium: Women's rights and jury service. *University of Cincinnati Law Review, 61*, 1139–1180.

BAKER, D. (1999). A descriptive profile and socio-historical analysis of female executions in the United States: 1632–1997. *Women and Criminal Justice, 10* (3), 57–93.

BAKER, D. (2003). The role of profiling in American society, criminal profiling, purposeful discrimination in capital sentencing. *Journal of Law and Social Challenges, 5*(1), 189–223.

BAKER, D., & DAVIN, R. (2001). *Notable selections in crime, criminology, and criminal justice.* Guilford, CT: McGraw-Hill/Dushkin.

BALDUS, D., WOODWORTH, G., ZUCKERMAN, D., WEINER, N., & BROFFITT, B. (2001). Use of peremptory challenges in capital murder trials: A legal and empirical analysis. *University of Pennsylvania Journal of Constitutional Law, 3*, 3–170.

BANDES, S. (1999). Patterns of injustice: Police brutality in the courts. *Buffalo Law Review, 47*, 1275–1341.

BANKER, F. (1995). Note: eliminating a safe haven for discrimination: Why New York must ban peremptory challenges from jury selection. *Journal of Law and Policy, 3*, 605–636.

BARKER-BENFIELD, G. (1976). *The horrors of the half-known life: Male attitudes toward women and sexuality in nineteenth-century America.* New York: Harper & Row.

BEDAU, H., & RADELET, M. (1987). Miscarriages of justice in potentially capital cases. *Stanford Law Review, 40*, 21–90.

BELL, D. (1987). *And we are not saved: The elusive quest for racial justice.* New York: Basic Books.

BELL, D. (2004). *Race, racism and American law.* New York: Aspen.

BELL, J. (2002). *Policing hatred: law enforcement, civil rights, and hate crime.* New York: New York University Press.

BENJAMIN, L. (1991). *The black elite: Facing the color line in the twilight of the twentieth century.* Chicago: Nelson-Hall Publishers.

BENNETT, L. (1982). *Before the Mayflower: A history of black America.* New York: Penguin Books.

BENSON, D. (1991). Capital sentencing evidence after *Penry* and *Payne*. *Thurgood Marshall Law Review, 17*, 1.

BERLIN, I. (1980). Time, space, and the evolution of Afro-American society in British mainland North America. *American History Review, 85*, 44.

BERLIN, I. (1998). *Many thousands gone: The first two centuries of slavery in North America.* Cambridge, MA: Harvard University Press.

BERLOW, A. (1999). The wrong man. *Atlantic Monthly, 66*.

BLASSINGAME, J. (1972). *The slave community: Plantation life in the antebellum south.* New York: Oxford University Press.

BOHM, R. (2003). *Deathquest II: An introduction to the theory and practice of capital punishment in the United States.* Cincinnati, OH: Anderson.

BOWERS, W. (1984). *Legal homicide: Death as punishment in America, 1864–1982.* Boston: Northeastern University Press.

BOWERS, W., & PIERCE, G. (1980). Arbitrariness and discrimination under post-*Furman* capital statutes. *Crime and Delinquency, 26*, 563.

BOWERS, W., STEINER, B., & SANDYS, M. (2001). Death sentencing in black and white: An empirical analysis of the role of jurors' race and racial jury composition. *University of Pennsylvania Journal of Constitutional Law, 3*, 171–274.

BREWER, E. (2001). Let's play Jeopardy: Where the question comes after the answer for stopping prosecutorial misconduct in death penalty cases. *Northern Kentucky Law Review, 28*, 34.

BRIDGEWATER, P. (2001). Un/Re/Dis covering slave breeding in Thirteenth Amendment jurisprudence. *Washington and Lee Race and Ethnic Ancestry Law Journal, 7*, 11–43.

BRIGHT, S. (1995). Discrimination, death and denial: The tolerance of racial discrimination in infliction of the death penalty. *Santa Clara Law Review, 35*, 433–483.

BRIGHT, S., & KEENAN, P. (1995). Judges and the politics of death: Deciding between the Bill of Rights and the next election in capital cases. *Boston University Law Review, 75*, 759.

BRODERICK, R. (1992). Why the peremptory challenge should be abolished. *Temple Law Review, 65*, 369.

BROWN, D. (2000). Criminal procedure entitlements, professionalism, and lawyering norms. *Ohio State Law Journal, 61*, 801–865.

BROWNMILLER, S. (1975). *Against our will: Men, women and rape.* New York: Bantom Books.

BROWNWORTH, V. (1992, June 16). Dykes on death row. *The Advocate.*

BRUNDAGE, W. (1993). *Lynching in the New South: Georgia and Virginia, 1880–1930.* Urbana: University of Illinois Press.

BURNSIDE, F. (1999). Dying to get elected: A challenge to the jury override. *Wisconsin Law Review, 1999*, 1017–1049.

BUSH, J. (1996). The first slave (and why he matters). *Cardozo Law Review, 18*, 599–629.

BUTLER, P. (1995). Racially based jury nullification: Black power in the criminal justice system. *Yale Law Journal, 105*, 677–725.

CARRIGAN, W. (2003). The lynching of persons of Mexican origin or descent in the United States, 1848 to 1928. *Journal of Social History, 37*, 411–440.

CARRIGAN, W. (2004). *The making of a lynching culture: Violence and vigilantism in central Texas, 1836–1916.* Urbana: University of Illinois Press.

CARTER CENTER SYMPOSIUM ON THE DEATH PENALTY. (1997). *Georgia State University Law Review, 14*, 329–445.

CENTER FOR PUBLIC INTEGRITY: INVESTIGATIVE JOURNALISM IN THE PUBIC INTEREST. (2003). *Harmful error: Investigating America's local prosecutors.* Retrieved from http://www.publicintegrity.org/pm/default.aspx

CHAMBLISS, W. (1977). *Law, order and power.* Reading, MA: Addison-Wesley.

CHRISTOPHER COMMISSION REPORT. (1991). *Report of the Independent Commission on the Los Angeles Police Department.*

CLARKE, J. (1998). Without fear or shame: Lynching, capital punishment and the subculture of violence in the American South. *British Journal of Political Science, 28*, 269–189.

COHEN, D. (1996). Official oppression: A historical analysis of low-level police abuse and a modern attempt at reform. *Columbia Human Rights Law Review, 28*, 165–199.

COLE, G. (1970). The decision to prosecute. *Law and Society Review, 4*, 331–344.

CONRAD, C. (1998). *Jury nullification: The evolution of a doctrine.* Durham, NC: Carolina Academic Press.

COOPER, W., & TERRILL, T. (1996). *The American South: A history.* New York: McGraw-Hill.

CROCKER, P. (2001). Is the death penalty good for women? *Buffalo Criminal Law Review, 4*, 917–965.

CURTIN, P. (1998). *The rise and fall of the plantation complex: Essays in Atlantic history.* New York: Cambridge University Press.

DAVIS, A. (1981). *Women, race, and class.* New York: Vintage Books.

DAVIS, A. (1996). Benign neglect of racism in the criminal justice system. *Michigan Law Review, 94*, 1660–1686.

DAVIS, A. (1998). Prosecution and race: The power and privilege of discretion. *Fordham Law Review, 67*, 13–67.

DAVIS, A. (2000). The color of violence against women. *Colorlines, 3*(3). *Color of violence: Violence Against Women of Color* conference held in Santa Cruz, California, in April 2000. Retrieved from http://www.arc.org/C_Lines/CLArchive/story3_3_02.html.

DEATH PENALTY INFORMATION CENTER. (2005a). *Women and the death penalty*. Retrieved from http://www.deathpenaltyinfo.org/article.php?did=230&scid=24#facts.

DEATH PENALTY INFORMATION CENTER. (2005b). *Race of death row inmates executed since 1976*. Retrieved from http://www.deathpenaltyinfo.org/article.php?scid=5&did=184.

Developments in the law: Race and the criminal process: IV. Race and the prosecutor's charging decision. (1988). *Harvard Law Review, 101*, 1520–1557.

DIETER, R. (1998). The death penalty in black and white: Who lives, who dies, who decides. Death Penalty Information Center. Retrieved from http://www.deathpenaltyinfo.org/article.php?scid=45 &did=539.

DINOS, A. (2001). Custodial sexual abuse: Enforcing long-awaited policies designed to protect female prisoners. *New York Law School Law Review, 45*, 281–296.

EARLE, E. (1992). Banishing the thirteenth juror: An approach to the identification of prosecutorial racism. *Columbia Law Review, 92*, 1212–1242.

EITZEN, D., & BACA-ZINN, M. (1992). *Social problems*. Boston: Allyn & Bacon.

ERLICH, S. (1996). Comment: The jury override: A blend of politics and death. *American University Law Review, 45*, 1403–1452.

ESPY, W., & SMYKLA, J. (2004). *Executions in the United States, 1608–2002: The Espy File* [Computer file]. 4th ICPS ed. Compiled by M. Watt Espy and John Ortiz Smykla, University of Alabama. Ann Arbor, MI: Inter-University Consortium for Political and Social Research [Producer and distributor].

FAGAN, J. (2005). *Deterrence and the death penalty: A critical review of new evidence*. Testimony to the New York Assembly Standing Committee on Codes, Assembly Standing Committee on Judiciary, and Assembly Standing Committee on Corrections. Hearings to the Future of Capital Punishment in the State of New York. (January 21, 2005). Retrieved from http://www. deathpenaltyinfo.org/ FaganTestimony.pdf.

FEAGIN, J.R., (2001). *Racist America: Roots, current realities, and future reparations*. Massena, NY: Kagleighbug Books.

FEDE, A. (1996). Gender in the law of slavery in the antebellum United States. *Cardozo Law Review, 18*, 411–432.

FINKELMAN, P. (1993). The color of race. *Tulane Law Review*, 67, 2063–2112.

FINS, D. (2005, Winter). *Death row USA: A quarterly report by the Criminal Justice Project of the NAACP Legal Defense and Educational Fund, Inc*. Retrieved from http://www.naacpldf.org /content/pdf/pubs/drusa/DRUSA_Winter_2005.pdf.

FITZPATRICK, P. (1999). Always more to do: Capital punishment and the (de)composition of law. In A. Sarat (Ed.), *The killing state: Capital punishment in law, politics, and culture* (p. 118). New York: Oxford University Press.

FLANNIGAN, J. C. (1974). The Virgina collection. Frederickburg, VA: Central Rappahannock Regional Virginia State Library.

FLOWERS, R. (1988). *Minorities and criminality*. New York: Greenwood Press.

FOGEL, W. (1989). *Without consent or contract: The rise and fall of American slavery*. New York: Norton.

FOGELMAN, M. (2002). Justice asleep is justice denied: Why dozing defense attorneys demean the Sixth Amendment and should be deemed per se prejudicial. *Journal of the Legal Profession, 26*, 67–100.

FONER, E. (1988). *Reconstruction: America's unfinished revolution*. New York: Harper & Row.

FORMAN, J. (2004). Juries and race in the nineteenth century. *Yale Law Review, 113*, 895–938.

FRANKLIN, J., & MOSS, A. (2000). *From slavery to freedom: A history of Negro Americans*. New York: Knopf.

FRIEDMAN, L. (1987). *A history of American law*. New York: Simon & Schuster.

FRIEDMAN, L. (1993). *Crime and punishment in American history*. New York: Basic Books.

GEER, M. (2000). Human rights and wrongs in our own backyard: Incorporating international human rights protections under domestic civil rights law—A case study of women in United States prisons. *Harvard Human Rights Journal, 13*, 71–134.

GELLER, W., & TOCH, H. (1996). *Police violence: Understanding and controlling police abuse of Force*. New Haven, CT: Yale University Press.

GENOVESE, E. (1974). *Roll, Jordan, roll: The world the slaves made*. New York: Basic Books.

GEORGES-ABEYIE, D. (1990). The myth of a racist criminal justice system? In B. MacLean & D. Milovanovic (Eds.), *Racism, empiricism, and criminal justice*. Vancouver: Collective Press.

GOLDSTEIN, R. (2001, March14,). Queer on death row. *The Village Voice*. Retrieved from http://www.villagevoice.com/news/0111,goldstein,23066,1.html.

GORDON, N. (2003). *Misconduct and punishment: State disciplinary authorities investigate prosecutors accused of misconduct*. Harmful Error: Investigating America's Local Prosecutors. The Center for Public Integrity. Retrieved from http://www.publicintegrity.org/pm/default.aspx?sID=sidebarsb&aID=39.

GRANT, D. (1975). *The anti-lynching movement: 1883–1932*. San Francisco: R and E Research Associates.

GREEN, D. (1998). Racial inequality in the criminal justice system: Native Americans, Asian Americans, blacks, Hispanics and whites. In W. Velez (Ed.), *Race and ethnicity in the United States: An institutional approach* (pp. 82–99). Dix Hills, NY: General Hall, Inc.

GRIFFIN, P. (1997). Jumping on the ban wagon: *Minetos v. City University of New York* and the future of the peremptory challenge. *Minnesota Law Review, 81*, 1237–1270.

GROSS, S. (1985). Race and death: The judicial evaluation of evidence in discrimination in capital sentencing. *University of California Davis Law Review, 18*, 1275–1325.

GRUNEWALD, K. (2002). *Atkins v. Virginia. Capital Defense Journal, 15,* 117.

HADDEN, S. (2001). *Slave patrols: Law and violence in Virginia and the Carolinas*. Cambridge, MA: Harvard University Press.

HARRIES, K. (1992). Gender, execution, and geography in the United States. *Geografiska Annaler, Series B, Human Geography, 74* (1), 21–29.

HARRISON, P., & BECK, A. (2004, November). *Prisoners in 2003*. U.S. Department of Justice, Bureau of Justice Statistics. Retrieved from http://www.ojp.usdoj.gov/bjs/pub/pdf/p03.pdf.

HAWKINS, D. (1987). Beyond anomalies: Rethinking the conflict perspective on race and criminal punishment. *Social Forces, 65*, 719–745.

HBO Documentary (Producer). America Undercover, Welcome to the Other Side. [Documentary series]. *The execution of Wanda Jean*. Retrieved from http://www.hbo.com/docs/programs/wanda/.

HELLER, R. (1997). Selective prosecution and the federalization of criminal law: The need for meaningful judicial review of prosecutorial discretion. *University of Pennsylvania Law Review, 145*, 1309.

HIGGINBOTHAM, A. (1978). *In the matter of color: Race and the American legal process—The colonial period*. New York: Oxford University Press.

HIGGINBOTHAM, A. (1996). *Shades of freedom: Racial politics and presumptions of the American legal process*. New York: Oxford University Press.

HIGGINBOTHAM, L., & JACOBS, A. (1992). The "law only as an enemy": The legitimization of racial powerlessness through the colonial and antebellum criminal laws of Virginia. *North Carolina Law Review, 70*, 969–1070.

HIGGINBOTHAM, L., & KOPYTOFF, B. (1989a). Racial purity and interracial sex in the law of colonial and antebellum Virginia. *Georgetown Law Review, 77*, 1967–2028.

HIGGINBOTHAM, A., & KOPYTOFF, B. (1989b). Property first, humanity second: The recognition of the slave's human nature in Virginia civil law. *Ohio State Law Journal, 50*, 511–540.

HINDUS, M. (1976). Black justice under white law: Criminal prosecutions of blacks in antebellum South Carolina. *Journal of American History, 63*(3), 575–599.

HINDUS, M. (1980). *Prison and plantation: Crime, justice, and authority in Massachusetts and South Carolina, 1767–1878.* Chapel Hill: University of North Carolina Press.

HOFSTADTER, R. (1973). *America at 1750: A social portrait.* New York: Vintage Books.

HOLDEN-SMITH, B. (1996). Lynching, federalism, and the intersection of race and gender in the Progressive Era. *Yale Journal of Law and Feminism, 8,* 31–78.

HOOKS, B. (1981). *Ain't I a woman: Black women and feminism.* Boston: South End Press.

HOWARD, R. JR., (1999). Changing the system from within: An essay calling for more African Americans to consider being prosecutors. *Widener Law Symposium, 6,* 139.

HOWARTH, J. (1994). Deciding to kill: Revealing the gender in the task handed to capital jurors. *Wisconsin Law Review, 1994,* 1345–1424.

HOWARTH, J. (2002). Executing white masculinities: Learning from Karla Faye Tucker. *Oregon Law Review, 81,* 183–229.

HUMAN RIGHTS WATCH. (1996a). *All too familiar: Sexual abuse of women in U.S. state prisons.* Retrieved from http://hrw.org/reports/1996/Us1.htm.

HUMAN RIGHTS WATCH. (1996b). *Sexual abuse of women in U.S. state prisons: A national pattern of misconduct and impunity.* Retrieved from http://hrw.org/english/docs/1996/12/07/usdom4164.htm.

HUMAN RIGHTS WATCH. (1998a). *Human Rights Watch challenges Michigan's subpoena to reveal confidential information.* Retrieved from http://www.hrw.org/press98/oct/michig1015.htm.

HUMAN RIGHTS WATCH. (1998b). *No where to hide: Retaliation against women in Michigan state prison.* Retrieved from http://www.hrw.org/reports98/women/.

HUMAN RIGHTS WATCH. (1998c). *Shielded from justice: Police brutality and accountability in the United States.* Retrieved from http://www.hrw.org/reports98/police/index.htm.

HUMAN RIGHTS WATCH. (1998d). *Women raped in prisons face retaliation. Michigan failing to protect inmates, says rights group.* Retrieved from http://www.hrw.org/press98/sept/women921.htm.

HUMAN RIGHTS WATCH. (1999). *U.S. Department of Justice bargains away rights of women prisoners: Settlement agreement lacks adequate protections for female inmates sexually abused by prison staff.* Retrieved from http://hrw.org/english/docs/1999/06/11/usdom931.htm.

HUMAN RIGHTS WATCH. (2001). *Beyond reason: The death penalty and offenders with mental retardation.* Retrieved from http://www.hrw.org/reports/2001/ustat/.

HUMAN RIGHTS WATCH. (2002). *Race and incarceration in the United States.* Retrieved from http://www.hrw.org/backgrounder/usa/race/race-bck-onepage.htm.

HUMAN RIGHTS WATCH. (2003). *Incarcerated America.* Human Rights Watch Backgrounder. Retrieved from http://www.hrw.org/backgrounder/usa/incarceration/.

IFILL, S. (1997). Judging the judges: Racial diversity, impartiality and representation on state trial courts. *Boston College Law Review, 39,* 95.

INIKORI, J., & ENGERMAN, S. (1994). A skeptical view of Curtin's and Lovejoy's calculations. In D. Northrup (Ed.), *The Atlantic slave trade* (pp. 665–666). Lexington, KY: D.C. Heath.

JOHNSON, H., & WOLFE, N. (2003). *History of criminal justice.* Cincinnati, OH: Anderson.

JOHNSON, P. (1997). At the intersection of injustice: Experiences of African American women in crime and sentencing. *The American University Journal of Gender and the Law, 4,* 1–76.

JOHNSON, S. (1985). Black innocence and the white jury. *Michigan Law Review, 83,* 1611–1708.

JOHNSON, S. (1988). Unconscious racism and the criminal law. *Cornell Law Review, 73,* 1016.

JOHNSON, S. (1993). Racial imagery in criminal cases. *Tulane Law Review, 67,* 1739–1805.

JOHNSON, S. (1998). Symposium on race and criminal law: *Batson* ethics for prosecutors and trial court judges. *Chicago-Kent Law Review, 73,* 475–507.

JOHNSON, S. (2001). Racial derogation in prosecutors' closing arguments. In D. Milovanoic & K. Russell (Eds.), *Petite apartheid in the U.S. criminal justice system: The dark figure of racism* (pp. 79–102). Durham, NC: Carolina Academic Press.

JOHNSON, T. (1994). When prosecutors seek the death penalty. *American Journal of Criminal Law, 22,* 280.

JONES, M. (1993). Darkness made visible: Law, metaphor, and the racial self. *Georgetown Law Journal, 82*, 437–511.

JORDAN, E. (2000). Crossing the river of blood between us: Lynching, violence, beauty, and the paradox of feminist history. *Journal of Gender, Race and Justice, 3*, 545–580.

JORDAN, W. (1968). *White over black: American attitudes toward the Negro, 1550–1812*. New York: Norton.

KENNEDY, R. (1997). *Race, crime, and the law*. New York: Pantheon Books.

KENNEDY, R. (2003). *Interracial intimacies: Sex, marriage, identity, and adoption*. New York: Pantheon Books.

KLARMAN, M. (2001). The white primary rulings: A case study in the consequences of Supreme Court decisionmaking. *Florida State University Law Review, 29*, 55–107.

KOEPKE, J. (2000). Note: The failure to breach the blue wall of silence: The circling of the wagons to protect policy perjury. *Washburn Law Journal, 39*, 211–242.

KOLCHIN, P. (2003). *American slavery: 1619–1877*. New York: Hill and Wang.

KOPEC, J. (2003). Avoiding a death sentence in the American legal system: Get a woman to do it. *Capital Defense Journal, 15*, 353–382.

KOUSSER, M., & GRIFFIN, L. (1998). Revisiting a festival of violence. *History Methods, 31*, 171–180.

KROLL, M. (1992). *Killing justice: Government misconduct and the death penalty*. Retrieved from http://www.deathpenaltyinfo.org/dpic.r10.html#sxn6.

LADERBERG, A. (1998). The "dirty little secret": Why class actions have emerged as the only viable option for women inmates attempting to satisfy the subjective prong of the Eighth Amendment in suits for custodial sexual abuse. *William and Mary Law Review, 40*, 323–363.

LANGAN, P. (1994). No racism in the justice system. *Public Interest, 117*, 48–52.

LAUMANN, E. (1994). *The social organization of sex: Sexual practices in the United States*. Chicago: University of Chicago Press. Cited in *Amicus Curiae* in support of petitioners. *Lawrence and Garner v. State of Texas*, No. 02–102 (U.S. March 26, 2003), p. 16.

LAWRENCE, F. (2003). Enforcing bias-crime laws without bias: Evaluating the disproportionate-enforcement critique. *Law and Contemporary Problems, 66*, 49–69.

LEADERSHIP CONFERENCE ON CIVIL RIGHTS, LEADERSHIP CONFERENCE EDUCATION FUND. (2000). *Justice on trial: Racial disparities in the American criminal justice system*. Retrieved from http://www.civilrights.org/publications/reports/cj/intro.html.

LEADERSHIP CONFERENCE ON CIVIL RIGHTS, LEADERSHIP CONFERENCE EDUCATION FUND. (2003). The Bush administration takes aim: Civil rights under attack. Retrieved from http://www. civilrights.org/publications/reports/taking_aim/bush_takes_aim.pdf.

LEADERSHIP CONFERENCE ON CIVIL RIGHTS, LEADERSHIP CONFERENCE EDUCATION FUND. (2004). *Cause for concern: Hate crime in America*. Retrieved from http://www.civilrights.org/ publications/reports/cause_for_concern/.

LEAGUE OF WOMEN VOTERS. Brief of *Amici Curiae* in *Miller-El v. Cockrell*, 123 S. Ct. 1029 (2003). Retrieved from http://www.deathpenaltyinfo.org/MillerElAmicus.pdf.

LEE, K. (1996). Race and self-defense: Toward a normative conception of reasonableness. *Minnesota Law Review, 81*, 367–500.

LEIPOLD, A. (1997). Race-based jury nullification: Rebuttal (Part A). *John Marshall Law Review, 30*, 923.

LERNER, B. (2003, October 28,), Scholars argue over legacy of surgeon who was lionized, then vilified. *New York Times*, F7.

LIEBERMAN, M. (2000). Statement of the Anti-Defamation League on bias-motivated crime and the Hate Crimes Prevention Act. *Chicano-Latino Law Review, 21*, 53–77.

LIEBMAN, J., FAGAN, J., WEST, V., & LLOYD, J. (2000). Capital attrition: Error rates in capital cases, 1973–1995. *Texas Law Review, 78*, 1839.

LITTLE, R. (2004). What federal prosecutors really think: The puzzle of statistical race disparity versus specific guilt, and the specter of Timothy McVeigh. *DePaul Law Review, 53*, 1591–1644.

LITWACK, L. (1961). *North of slavery: The Negro in the free states, 1790–1860*. Chicago: University of Chicago Press.

LITWACK, L. (1979). *Been in the storm so long: The aftermath of slavery*. New York: Random House.

LOFQUIST, W. (2002). Putting them there, keeping them there, and killing them: An analysis of state-level variations in death penalty intensity. *Iowa Law Review, 87*, 1505–1557.

LOS ANGELES POLICE COMMISSION. (1991). *Five years later*. Author.

LOS ANGELES POLICE DEPARTMENT. (2000). *Board of inquiry into the rampart area corruption incident: A public report*. Author.

LYON, A. (2001). Setting the record straight: A proposal for handling prosecutorial appeals to racial, ethnic or gender prejudice during trial. *Michigan Journal of Race and Law, 6*, 319.

MACNAMARA, D., & SAGARIN, E. (1977). *Sex, crime, and the law*. New York: Free Press.

MANN, C. (1989). Racism, powerlessness, and justice: Minority and female: A criminal justice double bind. *Social Justice: A Journal of Crime, Conflict & World Order, 16* (4), pp. 95–114.

MANN, C. (1993). *Unequal justice: A question of color*. Bloomington: Indiana University Press.

MARABLE, M. (1985). *How capitalism underdeveloped black America*. Boston: South End Press.

MARONEY, T. (1998). The struggle against hate crime: Movement at a crossroads. *New York University Law Review, 73*, 564–620.

MARSHALL, T. (1986). Remarks on the death penalty made at the Judicial Conference of the Second Circuit. *Columbia Law Review, 86*, 1.

MCADAMS, J. (1998). The ABA's proposed moratorium on the death penalty: Racial disparity and the death penalty. *Law and Contemporary Social Problems, 61*, 153.

MCDONOUGH, M. (2003). *Atkins'* impact: States need standard for determining who is mentally retarded, ineligible for death sentence. *American Bar Association Journal*, Report 3.

MCFEELY, W. (1997). A legacy of slavery and lynching: The death penalty as a tool of social control. *Champion, 21*, 30–32.

MCGOVERN, J. (1982). *Anatomy of a lynching: The killing of Claude Neal*. Baton Rouge: Louisiana State University Press.

MCMILLEN, N. (1989). *Dark journey: Black Mississippians in the age of Jim Crow*. Urbana: University of Illinois Press.

MCMILLIAN, T., & PETRINI, C. (1990). *Batson v. Kentucky*: A promise unfulfilled. *University of Missouri, Kansas City Law Review, 58*, 361.

MCPHERSON, J. (1999, February 26). Comparing the two reconstructions. *Princeton Alumni Weekly, 16*, 18–19.

MILOVANOIC, D., & RUSSELL, K. (2001). Introduction—Petite apartheid. In D. Milovanoic & K. Russell (Eds.), *Petite apartheid in the U.S. criminal justice system: The dark figure of racism* (pp. xv–xxiii). Durham, NC: Carolina Academic Press.

MINTZ, J. (1987). Note: *Batson v. Kentucky*: A half step in the right direction (racial discrimination and peremptory challenges under the heavier confines of equal protection). *Cornell Law Review, 72*, 1026.

MORGAN, E. (2003). Women on death row. In R. Muraskin (Ed.), *It's a crime: Women and justice* (pp. 289–304). Upper Saddle River, NJ: Prentice Hall.

MORRIS, T. (1996). *Southern slavery and the law: 1619–1860*. Chapel Hill: University of North Carolina Press.

MUHAMMAD, P. (2004). The Trans-Atlantic slave trade: A forgotten crime against humanity as defined by international law. *American University International Law Review, 19*, 883–947.

MURPHY, D. (2004, March 16). Case stirs fight on Jews, juries and execution. *New York Times*, p. 1.

MYRDAL, G. (1944). *An American dilemma: The Negro population and modern democracy*. New York: Harper & Brothers.

NAACP LEGAL DEFENSE AND EDUCATION FUND. Brief of Amici Curiae, *Miller-El v. Cockrell*, 123 S. Ct. 1029 (2003). Retrieved from http://www.deathpenaltyinfo.org/MillerElAmicus.pdf.

NASH, G. (1988). *Forging freedom: The formation of Philadelphia's Black Community, 1720–1840.* Cambridge, MA: Harvard University Press.

NORTON, A. (1999). After the terror: Mortality, equality, fraternity. In A. Sarat (Ed.), *The killing state: Capital punishment in law, politics, and culture.* New York: Oxford University Press.

NUNN, K. (2000). The "Darden Dielemma": Should African Americans prosecute crime? *Fordham Law Review, 68,* 1473.

OBERMAN, M. (1996). Mothers who kill. *American Criminal Law Review, 34,* 1.

OGLETREE, C. (2002). Black man's burden: Race and the death penalty in America. *Oregon Law Review, 81,* 15–38.

PAGE, A. (2005). Batson's blind-spot: Unconscious stereotyping and the peremptory challenge. *Boston University Law Review, 85,* 155–262.

PARKER, L. (2004, March 11). Justice pursued for Emmett Till. *USA Today,* p. 3A.

PATERSON, O. (1998). *Rituals of blood: Consequences of slavery in two American centuries.* New York: Basic Civitas.

PELOSO, W. (1997). Les Miserables: Chain gangs and the cruel and unusual punishments clause. *Southern California Law Review, 70,* 1459–1511.

PEREA, J., DELGADO, R., HARRIS, A., & WILDMAN, S. (2000). *Race and races: Cases and resources for a diverse America.* St. Paul, MN: West Group.

PHILLIPS, U. (1915). Slave crime in Virginia. *American Historical Review, 20,* 336–340.

POKORAK, J. (1998). Probing the capital prosecutor's perspective: Race of the discretionary actor. *Cornell Law Review, 83,* 1811.

POOLE, E., & REGOLI, R. (1983). The decision to prosecute in felony cases. *Journal of Contemporary Criminal Justice, 2,* 18.

PRESIDENT'S COMMISSION ON LAW ENFORCEMENT AND ADMINISTRATION OF JUSTICE. (1967). *The Courts, 28.*

QUARLES, B. (1987). *The Negro in the making of America.* New York: Macmillan.

QUINNEY, R. (1970). *The social reality of crime.* Boston: Little, Brown.

QUINNEY, R. (1977). *Class, state, and crime: On the theory and practice of criminal justice.* New York: D. McKay.

RADELET, M., LOFQUIST, W., & BEDAU, H. (1996). Prisoners released from death rows since 1970 because of doubts about their guilt. *Thomas M. Colley Law Review, 13,* 907.

RAFTER, N. (2004). *Partial justice: Women, prisons, and social control.* New Brunswick, NJ: Transaction.

RAGONE, P., & WILLIAMS, J. (1995). Conference: The death penalty in the twenty-first century, *American University Law Review, 45,* 239.

RANDALL, V. (1996). Bioethics and law symposium deconstructing traditional paradigms in bioethics: Race, gender, class and culture: Slavery, segregation and racism: Trusting the health care system ain't always easy! An African American perspective on bioethics. *Saint Louis University Public Law Review, 15,* 191–235.

RAPAPORT, E. (2000). Equality of the damned: The execution of women on the cusp of the 21st century. *Ohio Northern University Law Review, 26,* 581–600.

RAPAPORT, E. (2001). Staying alive: Executive clemency, equal protection, and the politics of gender in women's capital cases. *Buffalo Criminal Law Review, 4,* 967–1007.

RAPER, A. (1933). *The tragedy of lynching.* Chapel Hill: University of North Carolina Press.

RASKIN, J. (1995). Affirmative action and racial action. *Howard Law Journal, 38* 521–559.

RAWLEY, J. (1981). *The Transatlantic slave trade.* New York: Norton.

REED, J. (1972). Percent black and lynching: A test of Blalock's theory. *Social Forces, 50,* 356.

REICH, J. (1989). *Colonial America*. Upper Saddle River, NJ: Prentice Hall.

REISS, O. (1997). *Blacks in colonial America*. Jefferson, NC: McFarland.

REYNOLDS, E. (1985). *Stand the storm: A history of the Atlantic slave trade*. New York: Allison and Busby.

RICHELLE, V. (1993). Racism as a strategic tool at trial: Appealing race-based prosecutorial misconduct. *Tulane Law Review, 67*, 2357.

RIZER, A. (2003). Justice in a changed world: The race effect on wrongful convictions. *William Mitchell Law Review, 29*, 845–867.

ROBERTS, D. (1991). Punishing drug addicts who have babies: Women of color, equality, and the right of privacy. *Harvard Law Review, 104*, 1419–1482.

ROBERTS, D. (1993a). Crime, race, and reproduction. *Tulane Law Review, 67*, 1945–1977.

ROBERTS, D. (1993b). Racism and patriarchy in the meaning of motherhood. *American University Journal of Gender and Law, 1*, 7.

ROBERTS, D. (1997). Symposium: On representing race: Unshackling black motherhood. *Michigan Law Review, 95*, 938–964.

ROMNEY, L. (2005, April 19). Outside prosecutors feel urban–rural rift. *Los Angeles Times*, pp. B1, B10.

RUETER, T. (1996). Why women aren't executed: Gender bias and the death penalty. *Human Rights, 23*, 10.

RUSSELL, K. (1994). The constitutionality of jury override in Alabama death penalty cases. *Alabama Law Review, 46*, 5.

SALMON, M. (1986). *Women and the law of property in early America*. Chapel Hill: University of North Carolina Press.

SAVAGE, D. (2005, April 19). Justices weigh state's jury selection law. *Los Angeles Times*, p. A12.

SCHAEFER, R. (2004). *Racial and ethnic groups*. Upper Saddle River, NJ: Prentice Hall.

SCHECK, B., NEUFELD, P., & DWYER, J. (2000). *Actual innocence: Five days to execution and other dispatches from the wrongfully convicted*. BDD Audio.

SCHEFLIN, A. (1972). Jury nullification: The right to say no. *Southern California Law Review, 45*, 168.

SCHULBERG, D. (2000). The execution of females. *Orange County Lawyer, 42*, 25–32.

SCHULBERG, D. (2003). Dying to get out: The execution of females in the post-*Furman* era of the death penalty in the United States. In R. Muraskin (Ed.), *It's a crime: Women and justice* (pp. 273–288). Upper Saddle River, NJ: Prentice Hall.

SCHMALL, L. (1996). Forgiving Guin Garcia: Women, the death penalty and commutation. *Wisconsin Women's Law Journal, 11*, 283.

SCHWARZ, P. (1996). *Slave laws in Virginia*. Athens: University of Georgia Press.

SCHWARTZ, P. (1997). *Twice condemned: Slaves and the criminal laws of Virginia, 1705–1865*. Union, NJ: Lawbook Exchange.

SCOTT, P. (1989). Jury nullification: An historical perspective on a modern debate. *West Virginia Law Review, 91*, 389.

SHAPIRO, A. (2000). Unequal before the law: Men, women and the death penalty. *American University Journal of Gender, Social Policy and the Law, 8*, 427–470.

SHIPMAN, M. (2002). *The Penalty is death: U.S. newspaper coverage of women's executions*. Columbia: University of Missouri Press.

SIEBERT, A. (1999). *Batson v. Kentucky*: Application to whites and the effect on the peremptory challenge system. *Columbia Journal of Law and Social Problems, 32*, 307–330.

SIEGEL, R. (1997). Why equal protection no longer protects: The evolving forms of status-enforcing state action. *Stanford Law Review, 49*, 1111–1148.

SILVERSTEIN, K. (2001, May 7). The judge as lynch mob: How Alabama judges use judicial override to disregard juries and impose death sentences. *The American Spectator*.

Sitkoff, H. (1981). *The struggle for black equality, 1954–1980*. New York: Hill & Wang.

Smallwood, A. (1998). *The atlas of African-American history and politics: From the slave trade to modern times*. Boston: McGraw-Hill.

Snead, H. (1986). *Blood justice: The lynching of Mack Charles Packer*. New York: Oxford University Press.

Stampp, K. (1956). *The peculiar institution: Slavery in the antebellum South*. New York: Vintage Books.

Staples, R. (1975). White racism, black crime and American justice: An application of the colonial model to explain crime and race. *Phylon, 36*, 14–22.

Steiker, C. (2002). Things fall apart, but the center holds: The Supreme Court and the death penalty. *New York University Law Review, 77*, 1475.

Streib, V. (1994). Death penalty for lesbians. *National Journal of Sexual Orientation Law, 1*, 104–126.

Streib, V. (1990). Death penalty for female offenders. *University of Cincinnati Law Review, 58*, 845–880.

Streib, V. (2003). Executing women, juveniles, and the mentally retarded: Second class citizens in capital punishment. In J. Acker, R. Bohm, & C. Lanier (Eds.), *America's experiment with capital punishment: Reflections on the past, present and future of the ultimate penal sanction*. Durham, NC: Carolina Academic Press.

Streib, V., & Sametz, L. (1989). Executing female juveniles. *Connecticut Law Review, 22*, 3–16.

Tabak, R. (1999). Racial discrimination in implementing the death penalty. *Human Rights, 26*, 5.

Tarpley, J. (1996). Black women, sexual myth, and jurisprudence. *Temple Law Review, 69*, 1343–1388.

Teeters, N., & Zibulka, C. (1984). Executions under state authority. In W. Bowers (Ed.), *Executions in America* (Appendix 1). Lexington, KY: D.C. Heath.

The Tennessean. (2001, July 27). 1 in 4 blacks condemned by all-white juries.

Texas Defender Service. (2000). *A state of denial: Texas justice and the death penalty*. Retrieved from http://www.texasdefender.org/publications.htm.

Thorton, J. (1998). *Africa and Africans in the making of the Atlantic world, 1400–1680*. New York: Cambridge University Press.

Tolnay, S., & Beck, E. (1995). *A festival of violence: An analysis of southern lynchings, 1882–1930*. Courtroom Television Network, LLC.

Tonry, M. (1995). *Malign neglect: Race, crime, and punishment in America. Studies in Law, Politics, and Society*. New York: Oxford University Press.

Tran, J. (1997). Death by judicial overkill: The unconstitutionality of overriding jury recommendations against the death penalty. *Loyola of Los Angeles Law Review, 30*, 863.

Troutt, D. (1999). Screws, koon, and routine aberrations: The use of fictional narratives in federal police brutality prosecutions. *New York University Law Review, 74*, 18–122.

Turk, A. (1969). *Criminality and legal order*. Chicago: Rand McNally.

Turner, J., Singleton, R., & Musick, D. (1984). *Oppression: A socio-history of black-white relations in America*. Chicago: Nelson Hall.

Uelmen, G. (1997). Crocodiles in the bathtub: Maintaining the independence of state supreme courts in an era of judicial politicization. *Notre Dame Law Review, 72*, 1133.

Underwood, B. (1992). Ending race discrimination in jury selection: Whose right is it anyway? *Columbia Law Review, 92*, 725.

U.S. Commission on Civil Rights, Office of Civil Rights Evaluation. (2004). *Redefining rights in America: The civil rights record of the George W. Bush administration, 2001–2004*, Draft Report of the Commissioners' Review. Retrieved from http://www.usccr.gov/pubs/bush/bush04.pdf.

U.S. Department of Commerce, Bureau of the Census. (1975). *Historical statistics of the United States, colonial times to 1970—Bicentennial edition, Part 2. Estimated population of American colonies: 1610–1780*, Washington, DC: Author.

U.S. DEPARTMENT OF JUSTICE. (1996). *CRIPA investigation of Arizona women's prisons.* Author.

U.S. DEPARTMENT OF JUSTICE. (2003). *Fact sheet for hate crime statistics, 2002.* Retrieved from http://www.fbi.gov/pressrel/pressrel03/02hcfactsh.htm.

U.S. DEPARTMENT OF JUSTICE. (2000). *Conduct of law enforcement agencies investigations. Los Angeles Police Department.* Washington, DC: U.S. Government Printing Office.

U.S. GENERAL ACCOUNTING OFFICE. (1990). *Death penalty sentencing: Research indicates pattern of racial disparities.*

VANDIVER, M., & COCONIS, M. (2001). Sentenced to the punishment of death: Pre-*Furman* capital crimes and executions in Shelby County, Tennessee. *University of Memphis Law Review, 31,* 861–918.

VICK, D. (1995). Poorhouse justice: Underfunded indigent defense services and arbitrary death sentences. *Buffalo Law Review, 43,* 329.

VORENBERG, J. (1981). Decent restraint of prosecutorial power, *Harvard Law Review, 94,* 1521, 1555.

WALKER, S., SPOHN, C., & DELONE, M. (2000). *The color of justice: Race, ethnicity and crime in America.* New York: Sage.

WARDEN, R. (2001). *Center on wrongful convictions, eyewitness study, how mistaken and perjured eyewitness identification testimony put 46 innocent Americans on death row.* Retrieved from http://www.law.nwu.edu/depts/clinic/wrongful/causes.htm.

WEINBERG, S. (2003). *Shielding misconduct: The law immunizes prosecutors from civil suits.* Harmful Error: Investigating America's Local Prosecutors. The Center for Public Integrity. Retrieved from http://www.publicintegrity.org/pm/default.aspx?sID=sidebarsb&aID=36.

WEINSTEIN, H. (2002, June 16). Judges ignore juries to impose death. *Los Angeles Times,* A21.

WHITE, P. (2001). Errors and ethnics: Dilemmas in death. *Hofstra Law Review, 29,* 1265.

WHITE, W. (1969). *Rope and faggot: Biography of Judge Lynch.* New York: Arno Press.

WHITE, W. (1989). Fact-finding and the death penalty: The scope of a capital defendant's right to jury trial. *Notre Dame Law Review, 65,* 1.

WIECEK, W. (1996). The origins of the law of slavery in British North America. *Cardozo Law Review, 17,* 1711–1792.

WILLIAMS, K. (2000). The deregulation of the death penalty. *Santa Clara Law Review, 40,* 677.

WILLIAMS, K. (2002). Mid-Atlantic People of Color Legal Scholarship Conference, The death penalty: Can it be fixed? *Catholic University Law Review,* 51, 1177–1226.

WOODWARD, C. (1965). *The strange career of Jim Crow.* New York: Oxford University Press.

WRIGGINS, J. (1983). Rape, racism, and the law. *Harvard Women's Law Journal, 6,* 103.

WRIGHT, D. (1991). *African Americans in the colonial era: From African origins through the American Revolution.* Arlington Heights, IL: Harlan Davidson.

ZANGRANDO, R. (1980). *The NAACP crusade against lynching, 1909–1950.* Philadelphia, PA: Temple University Press.

CASES

Atkins v. Virginia, 536 U.S. 304 (2002).

Batson v. Kentucky, 476 U.S. 79 (1986).

Brady v. Maryland, 373 U.S. 83 (1963).

Brown v. Board of Education, 347 U. S. 483 (1954).

Butler v. Cooper, 554 F.2d 645 (1977).

The Civil Rights Cases, 109 U.S. 3 (1883).

Edmonson v. Leesville Concrete Company, 500 U.S. 614 (1991).

Furman v. Georgia, 408 U. S. 238 (1972).

Georgia v. McCollum, 505 U.S. 42 (1992).
Gregg v. Georgia, 428 U.S. 153 (1976).
Hernandez v. New York, 500 U.S. 352 (1991).
J.E.M v. Alabama, 511 U.S. 127 (1994).
Penry v. Lynaugh, 492 U.S. 302 (1989).
Plessy v. Ferguson, 163 U.S. 537 (1896).
Ring v. Arizona, 536 U.S. 584 (2002).
Schriro v. Summerlin, 524 U.S. (2004). Slip Opinion No. 03-526.
Strauder v. West Virginia, 100 U.S. 303 (1880).
Swain v. Alabama, 380 U.S. 202 (1965).
Taylor v. Louisiana, 419 U.S. 522 (1975).
United States v. Clary, 34 F.3d 709 (1994).
Williams v. Mississippi, 170 U.S. 213 (1898).

25

African American Ph.D. Women in Criminal Justice Higher Education

Equal Impact or the Myth of Equality?

Elvira M. White and Laura B. Myers

L imited research has been conducted to determine the impact of African American Ph.D. women in criminal justice, criminology, and juvenile justice. Separate studies have examined African American academicians and African American female doctoral students in the pipeline. There is a void in the literature in the study of African American Ph.D. women as a separate group. This study will examine and compare the impact and influence in the discipline of African American female academicians who received degrees pre-1998 with those who graduated post-1998 to determine if the numbers have substantially increased and if their experiences have positively changed since the last study was conducted. It will examine the perceptions of African American women to include experiences within the academic environment, mentoring junior faculty, their influence on female African American doctoral students, and upward mobility in rank and scholarship.

INTRODUCTION

In the last half of the twentieth century, the field of higher education in the United States, which had been historically composed of white males, became more diverse. With the Civil Rights Movement, the Women's Movement, and the desegregation of schools in the United States, the number of women and minorities who graduated from high school, earned college degrees, and obtained graduate degrees began to increase. With the turn of the century, the expectation was that women and minorities would hold positions in the workplace in equal numbers to their white, male counterparts. They would also earn equivalent pay. However, this has not been the case.

The number of women and minorities in higher education has grown at an even slower rate than in most career fields. The demands of tenure-track employment, such as publication rates, journal prestige, and the collegial expectations of senior faculty, have made it especially difficult for women to succeed in higher education. With many of these women trying to have and raise children and maintain their marriages, little latitude is given in the tenure-track process (Caplan, 1995). The story for minorities, and especially minority women, is a lack of mentorship and sponsorship needed to achieve the higher ranks of the professorship. Minorities often find it difficult to get the same co-authorship opportunities, networking opportunities, and critical recommendations that benefit their white and male counterparts.

In the discipline of criminal justice and criminology, the impact of this dearth of women and minorities in our professor ranks is having substantial impact. Criminal justice professionals are increasingly accused of diversity errors leading to grievances, lawsuits, and scandals from the public and fellow personnel. The lack of diversity at the higher ranks of the criminal justice profession, including policing and corrections, could be impacted through the education of personnel at the college level. An appreciation of diversity and the management of diversity can be taught in the college curriculum. Women and minorities teaching in criminal justice and criminology would provide role models for a more diverse population to enter the field of criminal justice. At the same time, a diversity of professors would create the pipeline necessary to produce women and minorities with graduate degrees to return to higher education.

Very little attention has been paid to the low numbers of women and minorities in criminal justice higher education. It is important to understand whether the situation is improving and what the issues might be facing the women and minorities currently in the discipline. This study focuses on African American women specifically because the research that does exist indicates that these women have experienced extreme difficulties with higher education employment.

This study is a follow-up to a previous study published in 1999 that indicated that African American women were experiencing these difficulties. The authors of this article decided it was time to see if any significant changes had occurred.

PREVIOUS RESEARCH

The limited study of African American female Ph.D.s in general and those in the criminal justice discipline suggest that there has been little progress made in numbers or impact in the discipline since an original study was conducted in 1994 (Gilbert & Tatum, 1999). That study suggested that African American women in criminal justice are subjected to both race and gender stratification and have experiences that differ significantly from those of their white female and African American male counterparts. Another study conducted about the same time (Bing, Heard, & Gilbert, 1995) examined African American faculty members in criminal justice and criminology programs. Perceptions in treatment, experiences, and attitudes were examined in both studies. The results were similar to the Gilbert and Tatum study (1999). The only other relevant literature that remotely addressed the subject of African American female Ph.D.s in criminology and criminal justice was conducted to examine African Americans in doctoral programs in criminology and criminal justice to determine if those persons in degree programs were actually matriculating out of the programs with a Ph.D. (Edwards, White, Bennett, & Pezzella, 1998a; Edwards, White, Bennett, & Pezzella, 1998b). This research did not focus on the experiences and perceptions of the African American female population, but did give the indication that growing numbers of African Americans were graduating from doctoral programs. This would mean a population of African American graduates would be finding employment in the teaching and research field, creating the opportunity to assess whether the higher education environment had improved from the early 1990s and whether African American women were making an impact on the field.

Even with this hope of affecting the underrepresentation of African American women in criminal justice higher education, the picture for women and minorities has not improved much in other career fields. Another discipline that is closely related in terms of experience, numbers of women, and its traditionally being a white-male-dominated discipline—chemistry and chemical engineering—continues to suffer from the same issues of diversity and lack numbers of African American female Ph.D.s (Nelson, 2005). A study was conducted to determine the relative success of minority women in chemistry and chemical engineering and whether they were seeking opportunities in academia or industry. In the case of those women obtaining a Ph.D. in chemistry, the research revealed that they were more likely to seek employment in the industry rather than in higher education where they had seen the inhospitable environment for women and minority faculty.

In 2005, evidence abounds that women and minority faculty in the hard sciences still suffer inhospitable environments, lack of opportunities, and even pay differentials (*MIT Newsletter*, 1999). The president of Harvard University came under fire recently regarding his statements regarding women in science, giving the impression that he concurred with sentiments that women were inferior to men when it came to scientific ability (Bombardieri, 2005). It is no wonder, then, that many women and minorities are anxious about their treatment in higher education. The problems often begin while in graduate school. While graduate assistantships sometimes provide the only means of financial support for women of color, the manner in which they are treated can oftentimes determine if they will successfully matriculate to completion (Malveaux, 2004).

The question remains whether the situation has improved for African American women in criminal justice higher education. Since the research of the 1990s, has the environment for graduate students and faculty improved? That previous research was the call for improvement. Has it been done? Has diversity management improved in criminal justice higher education or is equality still just a myth for African American women?

METHODS

A survey was sent via email to 54 African American women in criminal justice higher education who had been identified from the *Directory of Minority Ph.D. Criminologists* (Heard & Penn, 2000) and from snowballing and personal contacts who gave additional names. The directory was the most recent compilation of names and contact information that could be obtained. The survey was sent via email so the researchers could track the number of emails that had been misdirected. Once the researchers determined that the respondent was no longer at that email address, contacts and additional evidence were used to determine the current location of the respondent. If the researchers had used traditional snail mail, it would have been impossible to track the transitions of the respondents.

The researchers had hoped to get a significant response rate and be able to analyze quantitative data. However, the response rate was very low and changed the entire nature of the methodology. The researchers were unable to locate many of the respondents and those who were located were fearful about doing the survey. At that point, the researchers decided to turn to a qualitative methodology to interpret their findings. An analysis of the emailing of the surveys, the surveys that were completed, and a forum discussion with African American women in the discipline were conducted. This new methodology actually provided more insight and answers to the researchers' questions than the original methodology.

RESULTS

Analysis of the Emails

Fifty-four emails were sent out and immediately messages returned indicating that many of the respondents were no longer at that location. Some of those messages told us where that person had relocated. Messages also were received indicating that the person was no longer in higher education or that she was not interested in completing the survey. It also was learned that 3 of the women had died in recent months, 2 of them at a relatively young age. In the end, only 22 of the original 54 could be located and were still employed in higher education. Of those 22, nearly half of the respondents sent messages that they were afraid to participate.

Completed Surveys

The first completed surveys received came from African American women who also held the J.D. degree. This information would become useful in the later analysis of the evidence obtained.

At the end of the data collection phase and after numerous attempts to locate respondents and to encourage their participation, only six completed surveys had been obtained. The researchers decided to turn to a qualitative assessment of that data and to the email analysis to determine how to proceed with the research.

The assessment revealed that African American women with both the J.D. and the Ph.D. were more willing to respond to the survey. From their responses, the researchers interpreted that their willingness was based on their knowledge of the legal system and their reduced fear of their employment situation because of that knowledge. The researchers believed that some of the lack of response from other respondents might be from fear of the employer learning their responses. This interpretation would be confirmed later.

The responses from those who did complete the survey confirmed that their particular experiences were no different from the experiences of African American women cited in the previous research from the 1990s. The women in this study focused on poor relationships with their colleagues, the lack of information provided to them in the job interview process regarding salary and other opportunities, a lack of mentors, bad graduate school experiences, and, most important, their difficulties in achieving rank and tenure. Many of these women were older and had children, but were still at the assistant professor rank and had not been granted tenure at previous institutions. These women had left these previous institutions and some were considering leaving their current institutions. Some of these women indicated they were much happier at their current institutions than at previous institutions. The good news was that these women were doing well with their students and had been able to mentor students of all races and genders. Their students supported them and respected them.

Forum Discussion

The researchers decided to take the information obtained so far to present at a national conference. It was hoped that more respondents could be located at the conference to obtain additional surveys. Nearly 20 African American women attended the conference and were approached by the researchers about completing the survey. The researchers were able to confirm that the lack of response was due primarily to fear of retaliation. Many of these women shared their stories with the researchers. The older women had experienced discrimination to the extent that some of them had been forced to resign or been denied tenure. Others had left positions before receiving tenure because they perceived the environment to be inhospitable. Some of the younger women were trying to achieve tenure and were worried about their futures.

The researchers invited these women to the conference presentation which became a forum on diversity issues in higher education and the criminal justice field. The African American women who attended the presentation included both graduate students and professors. The presentation became a unique situation where these women and others felt comfortable to express their concerns and share some of their experiences. Those women who had served in faculty positions confirmed the data obtained from the completed surveys: African American women were not getting the same access to opportunities in their jobs. Many of them felt unwelcome and out of the flow of communication. They perceived they had few mentors and very little assistance in their development as faculty. They also felt that there was little concern about the problem. In fact, a recent study confirms those feelings. Hart (2005) conducted a study at the University of Missouri–Columbia which indicated that women and minority faculty are often not taken seriously when they voice their concerns about work environments and pressures.

The graduate students asked many questions about their futures. They had experienced various levels of discrimination while in graduate school. One student was angry that she had been labeled as a teacher of the race course, not because of her interest, but because of her minority status. Another student was angry that white students did not understand her experiences as a minority or the importance of minority issues in criminal justice.

These graduate students were very concerned about how they were going to deal with the issues that their older African American female colleagues had experienced. They wanted to know whether they should delay marriage and children so they could face discrimination from a stronger position. The discussion focused on whether delaying personal commitments or eliminating them altogether might help. The consensus was that it would make no difference. Veteran faculty with and without family commitments had experienced similar discriminatory experiences.

The discussion then turned to the changes that would be necessary to reduce discrimination and allow African American women to impact criminal justice higher education. Immediately, the focus was broadened to include African American males who are even more underrepresented in criminal justice higher education. The audience included not only the minority women discussed earlier, but also white males, white females, Asian females, Caribbean females, gay males, and lesbians. Almost everyone involved themselves in the discussion and provided suggestions and examples.

The consensus of the group was the need to overcome the lack of communication necessary for everyone to be successful in criminal justice higher education. It was clear that for criminal justice higher education to become more welcoming to not just African American females but to all those who had been disenfranchised, including gays, lesbians, women, and other minority males and females, greater attention to the issues and creative solutions would be necessary.

The issue of communication was perceived by the group to be the primary problem. Over the years, attempts had been made with the Heard and Penn directory and the Women and Minorities Sections of American Society of Criminology (ASC) and Academy of Criminal Justice Sciences (ACJS) to increase networking and to enhance communication. Yet, these efforts really have only served to connect people who are part of those efforts. Communication has to go further. Suggestions were made to create a "council" of schools with minority faculty and students, including historically black colleges and universities (HBCUs). This "council" would serve to support faculty and students, enhance networking, and help strengthen people for the higher education employment process. By bringing numerous schools together rather than just individuals, the efforts would be stronger and more visible. Using email, faculty and students could share information on how to interview, the questions to ask, and the pitfalls to avoid. The tenure and promotion process, as well as the publication and research process, could be discussed and would be less threatening and navigation of the process would be easier. More mentoring and coaching via email could occur and people could help each other like never before.

The other significant issue raised was how to support graduate students so they would not postpone their personal lives in the belief that they could be successful if they only made the ultimate sacrifices. The group made it very clear that the students should not become "work nuts" with the idea that overcompensating would solve their problems. More experienced faculty made it clear that those who discriminate are counting on that overcompensation. Such people will take advantage of the work nut. However, they are not likely to reward that work with tenure and promotion. It will take a more unique solution. The council concept with coaching and mentoring from a diversity of people, both nationally and internationally could make a difference and allow not just African American women, but all others to live a normal life and be successful in the career of criminal justice higher education.

CONCLUSION

The goal of this research was to determine whether the situation for African American women in criminal justice higher education had improved from the late 1990s when the last research was undertaken. Are African American women finally making their impact on the field?

In the previous research, locating respondents and getting a good response rate was very difficult. The responses that were obtained in the late 1990s indicated that African American women were not progressing in rank. They were having difficulty getting tenure.

The hope of the researchers in this current project was to find that some improvement had occurred for African American women. It was clear almost from the outset that little had changed and perhaps had become somewhat worse. Just locating the women for the study proved difficult. The Heard and Penn directory's intent had been to make it easier, but very few of these women could be located from that compilation. In the last five years many of these women had changed jobs. This is an indicator of the lack of employment stability for these women.

The researchers were amazed at the fear of the women who declined to respond to the survey. Their discrimination experiences had caused them much harm, anxiety, and frustration. They perceived that answering the survey might jeopardize their futures. If criminal justice researchers are unwilling to respond to surveys that might benefit them, then that fear is very real and indicates the reality for these women. There is a major problem of discrimination facing African American women in criminal justice higher education.

One implication of this discrimination is that African American women are still underrepresented in faculty ranks. Undergraduate and graduate criminal justice students do not see diversity in their educators. They are not benefiting from the perspectives these women would bring to the teaching process. This also impacts the criminal justice profession where diversity problems abound. The only way to change the perspective of insensitive criminal justice professionals is to educate them with different perspectives and to grow new leaders in criminal justice with an appreciation of diversity.

The pipeline to send more women and minorities into higher education is affected as well. Fewer undergraduate women and minorities will decide to earn graduate degrees. Those who do pursue graduate degrees may decide to become work nuts because they want to avoid the problems their predecessors faced. Forcing people to become work nuts to overcompensate for a state of inequality only perpetuates the problem.

While this research confirmed that inequality for African American women in criminal justice higher education is still alive and well, the great benefit of the research was learning that so many people are concerned about these issues and want to help resolve the problem. The forum discussion that emerged within the national conference presentation brought people together from all over the world to discuss the problem. The researchers had never before seen an academic presentation become such an educational focus group. The idea that emerged to create a council of schools is unique and has never been attempted before. It is an idea with a great deal of potential because of the plan to mentor and coach people via email across the world to help strengthen faculty and graduate students. It has a great deal of potential because coaching and mentoring in other fields have created substantial success. It could work for criminal justice higher education.

The reduction of inequality in criminal justice higher education is a myth. Inequality is still a problem and may be even more of a problem since the last research on the subject. The African American women in this study have clearly revealed the nature of discrimination for them and their careers. The effect on criminal justice students and criminal justice professionals is even greater because African American women are still being denied their ability to impact the field.

REFERENCES

BOMBARDIERI, M. (2005, January 17). Summers' remarks on women draw fire. *Boston Globe*. Retrieved April 28, 2005, from http://www.boston.com/news/education/higher/articles/2005/01/17/summers_remarks_on_women_draw_fire/.

BING, R., HEARD, C., & GILBERT, E. (1995). The experiences of African Americans and whites in criminal justice education: Do race and gender differences exist? *Journal of Criminal Justice Education, 6*(2), 123–145.

CAPLAN, P. J. (1995). *Lifting a ton of feathers: A woman's guide to surviving in the academic world*. Toronto: University of Toronto Press.

EDWARDS, W., WHITE, N., BENNETT, I., & PEZZELLA, F. (1998a). Who has come out the pipeline? African Americans in criminology and criminal justice. *Journal of Criminal Justice Education, 9*(2), 249–265.

EDWARDS, W., WHITE, N. BENNETT, I., & PEZZELLA, F. (1998b). Who's in the pipeline? A survey of African Americans in doctoral programs in criminology and criminal justice. *Journal of Criminal Justice Education, 9*(1), 1–18.

GILBERT, E., & TATUM, B. (1999). African American women in the criminal justice academy: Characteristics, perceptions, and coping strategies. *Journal of Criminal Justice Education, 10*(3), 231–246.

HART, J. (2005). Study finds women faculty experience more stress than men in higher education. *Black Issues in Higher Education, 22*(3), 12.

HEARD, C., & PENN, E. (2000). *Directory of Minority Ph.D. Criminologists*. Prairie View, TX: Prairie View A&M University.

MALVEAUX, J. (2004). Do graduate assistants get a fair deal? *Black Issues in Higher Education, 21*(19), 34.

MIT NEWSLETTER. (1999). A study on the status of women faculty in science at MIT. Retrieved April 28, 2005, from http://web.mit.edu/fnl/women/women.html.

NELSON, D. (2005). *Contrasts in chemistry and chemical engineering: The supply vs. the summit, industry vs. academia*. Retrieved March 30, 2005, from http://awis.org/smag01nelson.html.

26

Factors Affecting the Internal and External Relationships of African-American Policewomen within an Urban Police Department

Mark R. Pogrebin, Lyn Taylor, and Harold Chatman

This chapter explores the professional, job-related relationships of African-American policewomen. The difficulties black women police officers face are often exacerbated by the intersection of race and gender that influence their self-perceptions and perceptions of those with whom they interact, including their officers and members of the community. Additionally, job-related issues and interactions appear to impact community relations, particularly in circumstances involving minorities. The experiences of these women suggest that the marginalization continues to be problematic for some minorities working in law enforcement. The research is based on qualitative data obtained from black female police officers in a large urban city.

INTRODUCTION

The experience of African-American women in a largely white male-dominated occupation is almost entirely lacking from the research literature. Overall, research on the experiences of minority women has been limited in number and restricted in scope (Gilkes, 1981). Studies of black women have been regarded as deviant cases or incorporated into studies of women in general with the primary focus on white women's universal experiences (Collins, 1986; Gilkes, 1981). Few systematic studies have focused on discrimination against minority women (Nkomo, 1988; Schroedel, 1985). This research explores gender and race discrimination as experienced by black female police officers.

Historically, occupational norms have been linked to work segregation by sex (Coser & Rockoff, 1971; Jacobs, 1989; Laws, 1979; Stockard & Johnson, 1980). Sex typing by specific jobs, though arbitrary, follows one basic rule: Men and women are different and should be doing different things. Such stereotypical thinking has long sustained the stigmatization of those who violate norms of occupational segregation, thus reinforcing sex-role typing in the workplace. Sex-role stereotypes function to keep women in ancillary and supportive roles, rather than in positions of independence, authority, and leadership (Safilos-Rothschild, 1979).

Early studies and contemporary literature reveal that women who have entered a variety of traditional male occupations have faced discriminatory hiring assignments and practices, opposition from coworkers, and inadequate on-the-job training (Gray, 1984; Gruber & Bjorn, 1982; Kanter, 1977; Meyer & Lee, 1978; O'Farrell & Harlan, 1982; Swerdlow, 1989; Walshok, 1981). Policewomen remain a marginalized, unaccepted minority, not only in the United States but also in other countries, despite a long history of involvement in policing (Brown, 1997, 2000; Dene, 1992; Heidensohn, 1992; Reiner, 1992). Women officers may be labeled by their male counterparts as interlopers who have invaded male territory. By entering an occupation that is perceived as masculine in nature, women may be seen as courageous protectors of the community (Yoder, 1991). Women who enter the profession and hold their own as good police officers often present a threat to the masculine self-perception and image that male police wish to maintain. The cop culture, described by Reiner (1992, p. 124) is one of "old-fashioned machismo."

The marginalization of policewomen is well documented, but generally ignored within law enforcement agencies. The informal "canteen" cop culture is entrenched in offensive humor, sexual stereotypes, and harassment (Balkin, 1988; Brown, 1997; Fielding, 1994; Heidensohn, 1992; Hunt, 1990; Martin, 1990; Reiner, 1992; Young, 1991). Reiner (1992) suggests that internal solidarity among police officers coupled with social isolation masks conflicts within the organization. Consequently, the divisions between male and female officers are rarely addressed by administrators and are exacerbated by informal rules embedded in the masculine subculture. The "cult of masculinity" continues to denigrate, condescend, and deny full access to women who seek policing careers (Young, 1991).

The problems of acceptance for African-Americans in police work appear to be particularly acute. Alex (1969) argued that African-American males often experience "double marginality" as a result of the expectations held by the dominant majority for their dual roles as minority group members and as police officers. Belknap and Shelley (1992) concluded from their study of policewomen that race played a role in how minority females were perceived within their departments. Further, they suggest that black women were less likely than white policewomen to believe that male police recognized them for good police work. Belknap and Shelley also found that black female police officers experienced double marginality as a result of being women and members of a racial minority. Black female police officers, who face the additional obstacles associated with gender discrimination, seem to suffer from marginality to a much greater degree than their male minority counterparts.

Minority police and women also are subject to special stressors such as exclusion from the informal channels of support and information, as well as ostracism and overt racial or sexist comments by white offices (Ellison & Genz, 1983; Morash & Haarr, 1995).

Martin (1994), who studied the social and work relations of black policewomen, found that the forms of exclusion black females experienced were poor instruction in communication; peer hostility and ostracism through the silent treatment; oversupervision; exposure to dangerous situations; and inadequate back-up by male officers. Strained relationships among officers cause additional stress for many black policewomen (Pogrebin & Poole, 1998; Yoder, Adams, & Prince, 1983). Additionally, black women often experience degrading stereotyping (Dill, 1979). According to Doener (1995) in a study of police officer retention patterns, black females leave the job at a much higher rate compared to all other police—on average leaving during their fourth year. One important reason for early termination may be the direct result of exclusionary practices that black women experience in a white male environment.

Black police officers often experience marginality as a result of the expectations held by the dominant majority for their dual roles as minority group members and as police officers (Alex, 1969; Belknap & Shelley, 1992). Milutinovich (1977) argues that racism and the lack of common experience between the races in the workplace can lead whites to be psychologically and socially distant from blacks. The lack of acceptance by both members of his or her own social group and his or her white peers on the police department places an enormous strain on a variety of relationships. Martin (1994) noted that black women have limited expectations of becoming one of the boys. Haarr (1997) concluded from her study of race and gender in a police patrol bureau that the vast majority of black male and female officers expressed feelings of social distance from the organization.

With the arrival of black women in policing, black males traded on their masculinity to distance themselves from both black and white female police and aligned themselves with the dominant majority of white males (Martin, 1994). Distancing themselves from women provided the means for acceptance of black male officers by white male officers. Black men who provide mentoring and support for black women officers do so at the expense of exclusion by the dominant majority (Yoder & Aniakudo, 1997). According to Pike (1985), black male officers do not challenge the masculine police role in the same way women do. Because black men are seen as physically strong, streetwise, and masculine, they fit well with the attributes that white male police believe are important to be an effective police officer. White women officers racially distanced themselves from minority women police, thereby providing themselves with the opportunity to utilize their racial similarity to align themselves with white male officers.

In general, the literature suggests a lack of unity between black and white women in the police world. This, notes Martin (1992, 1994), can be attributed to racial differences. Martin further claims that white women police, like black male officers, are perceived to trade on their racial and gender solidarity with higher status white policemen. Yoder and Aniakudo (1997), in their study of black women firefighters, found women were often divided along racial lines. They concluded that racial similarity between white women and men was the most important variable that caused the separation between black and white women firefighters. This is an important observation, which may serve to explain why black females are near the bottom of the police occupational stratification structure.

Our focus in this study describes and analyzes the informal, organizational, and external social relationships that African-American women experience as a result of their occupational profession.

METHODS

This research was a qualitative study with African-American female officers who work in an urban police department. The department has approximately 1,400 sworn law enforcement officers. Minorities and women on the force are represented by 126 African-American males, 224 Hispanic/Latino males, 37 Hispanic/Latina females, 93 white females, and 21 African-American females. The entire black female population served as respondents in this study. The median age of the women was 37 (range = 21–51). Their police employment ranged from 1 to 22 years. Their educational background varied from high school to postgraduate degrees, with more than half having attended or graduated from college.

Interviews were conducted at the respondents' homes, in restaurants, on ride-alongs, and at off-duty jobs. Each interview lasted approximately 90 minutes and was tape-recorded with the subject's consent. A semistructured interview format was used, which relied on sequential probes to pursue leads provided by the subjects, allowing the officers to identify and elaborate on important domains they perceived to characterize their experiences in police work. The interview tapes were transcribed for qualitative data analysis. The data were analyzed for general statements about relationships among categories of observations (Schatzman & Strauss, 1973) and grouped into conceptual domains (Glaser & Strauss, 1967). This research focuses on areas related to the internal and external experiences that commingle with gender and race to define on-the-job relationships for African-American policewomen. The accounts of these women may not be reflective of all African-American police officers, but their narratives add voice and depth to our understanding of the issues they face (Ragin, 1994; Seidman, 1998).

FINDINGS

Relationships with White Policewomen—Internal

Many of the respondents reported that often they view their white female peers as needing protection from male officers when involved in threatening street encounters. The women interviewed prided themselves on not having to be as dependent on male officers to rescue them in similar situations. A shared pride in their ability to handle tough circumstances as the result of their lifelong experiences exists among these officers and is exemplified by the following statement: "It's like black women, since they have been on the bottom for so long, are a lot stronger than white women. Just internally stronger." The respondents also felt that white women were overly concerned with being accepted by higher status white males, often at the expense of other women, as noted by the following statement: "I've seen some women really go at it. I mean not physically, but I'm talking about backstabbing, the rumors, the cutthroatness. . . . Well, if they can't get ahead then nobody else [can] either."

Numerous differences exist between the treatment of white and black women working in a masculine world where women are placed at the bottom of the status hierarchy. Because black women police must constantly battle perceptions by peers that they are not good enough to be on the force and face both negative racial and female stereotypes, they must prove themselves as worthwhile employees. As one woman related, "You really have to work twice as hard for the same recognition as your white coworkers."

Black and white women officers clearly are not unified by gender to demand equal treatment to that of their male peers. In addition, other issues confronting female officers are not addressed with a united female voice. It is apparent from the respondents' views that relations with white female officers can best be described as based on self-interest first and unification as women with common employee problems as a distant second. The reasons for the lack of unification of women on the force was related by the following participant:

> Because of the things that go on as far as sexual harassment, it's not the in thing to do, to be supportive of one another because we are in a sense dividing the pie. We are going against our male counterparts, and we are labeling them or branding them or letting them know that their union is not good enough for us because you are not supportive of women, because you harass women or whatever you do.

Relations with Black Policemen

Our findings concerning the perception of support by black male officers for black women officers varied widely by respondent. Some of the women officers believe that their presence on the police department actually improved black males' status position among the white male officers of the department. Yoder and Aniakudo (1997) discovered that black females in the firehouse felt that black and white male bonding was increased by their presence and reduced social distance between the two groups. Black and white men became unified to some degree by the common attributes of being male and having similar attitudes that generally opposed the entrance of women into their profession. Yoder and Aniakudo concluded that from a black woman firefighter's perspective, relations with black male co-workers reflected their lower position within the existing race–gender status hierarchy.

From the perspective of some black policewomen, many black male officers are deliberately not supportive of black women as a result of their own minority status in the department. One minority woman explained her viewpoint of the situation: "The black men, even on this job, are just a little bitty cut of society, and they don't support black women." Another offered a functional explanation for the lack of support black females receive from their black male counterparts:

> We would be on the same detail for a month. I found them nonsupportive, self-interested. It was like they were, I don't know if they were that conscious about it, they had gone into a protective stance, and that's where they stayed. So it was to protect themselves and you had to deal with looking after yourself.

Protecting one's self-interest in the above situation can be directly linked to the conscious perceptions that black male police have concerning their desire for inclusion within the police organization. Black men who provide mentoring and support for black women officers do so at the expense of exclusion by the dominant majority (Yoder & Aniakudo, 1997). In short, being overtly and enthusiastically supportive of black female police may not be beneficial to a minority male's occupational status due to gender prejudice on the part of many white males who control the politics of the department. According to Pike (1985), black male officers do not challenge the masculine police role in the same way women do. Because black men are seen as physically strong, streetwise, and masculine they fit well with the attributes that white male police believe are important to be an effective policeman.

The other perspective of our respondents was that black men have a more difficult time than black women in the police organization. One respondent voiced her belief that black women police officers are perceived as less threatening to white police than black males: "I think that for some, black women are higher on the hierarchy than black men. Because I think that for some reason they [white males] feel that we're not as much a threat to them as black males are."

The perceived threat the above respondent is discussing is the ever-present issue of promotion. It is in this circumstance that competition for the few promotional positions becomes a highly emotional issue and everyone who competes is seen as a threat. Black women pose little organizational threat to white police officers, as compared to black male police, which may explain why black males are thought to be more discriminated against within the department than black women, as suggested by some of our respondents. The following statement explains one respondent's perception of the differences of stereotyping by whites between black female and black male officers:

> But when racial discrimination comes in, it has to do with black men. There is a lot of discrimination directed toward them [b]ecause the black woman in the past has always been the white man's maid, slave, or bed keeper. So they don't look negatively toward us. Discrimination-wise, I feel in this department, as far as I have seen, that you get more discrimination toward black males than black females for those reasons.

Although there existed a difference of opinion among our participants in the area of which gender group experienced more racial discrimination, it appears that very few black policewomen perceived any advantage in being a minority employee within the department. Since white male officers play such a dominant role in the actual operation and control of the organization, it is imperative that we understand the relationship between white officers and black policewomen.

Relations with White Policemen

Hurtado (1989) notes that white women are subordinate in their relations with white men through seduction as a result of their socialization to docility, passiveness, and internalized social controls. Black women's subordination to white males is through experienced rejection as a result of physical separation with few opportunities for interaction. Black women officers believe that white policemen, who had few social interactions with blacks as children and later as adults, see them as an unknown entity:

> The majority of white officers are kind of afraid of black women. They don't know what to do with us. How to categorize us. Where to put us. They don't understand us.

Black female officers seem to feel that white policemen stereotype white women to keep them subordinate. Policemen resolve the ambiguity of women's presence by placing them into separate categories such as seductress, mother, or lesbian (Hunt, 1990). A black female officer who perceives white policemen's interests as centered on the physical appearance of white policewomen discussed one type of categorical stereotype:

> But there's always something they are looking for. Unless you are a little blonde headed, beautiful looking floozy with a nice ass and good boobs. You know they don't want anything to do with you for showing that you are a Tarzan and you can pick up a stolen car or shoot 20 rounds. It don't mean shit to them.

The fact that both black male and female police officers are such a small percentage of the overall organization may explain why some white policemen feel free to openly verbalize racial slurs about minority citizens without fear of reprisals. Obviously such derogatory statements do little to help improve relations between black and white police officers:

> You hear it all the time in the way they describe suspects. For people that are supposed to be trained, intelligent people, who feel that blacks can't do the job and aren't educated enough, they themselves are blatantly ignorant when they try to describe different ethnic groups or when they use a lot of ethnic slang when they are on the radio or off the radio or just out on a call out of the ear shot of the commanders. They figure, what the hell, what are they going to do? Fire me? A lot of them are senior officers and that's their attitude or younger arrogant officers or whatever. They really don't give a shit.

Such a racial insensitivity on the part of many white male police can result in black officers of both genders feeling degraded and isolated from the white majority. Haarr (1997) concluded from her study of race and gender in a police patrol bureau that the vast majority of black male and female officers expressed feelings of social distance from the organization as compared to their white peers.

The disrespect for minority citizens on the part of some white officers obviously has caused many minority police to feel estranged from the department. Police managers who use derogatory slang words and are unaware that such adjectives are extremely offensive to their minority subordinates represents an even greater insult:

> It's serious when administrators are not aware of certain words and terms that are sensitive to black people. Because they are not aware of it they perpetuate the problem.

From the viewpoint of black police, the use of derogatory racial statements about citizens with whom they interact results in negative feelings toward white police in general. One must ask why some white officers continue to practice racism toward the black community. In addition, are they unaware of the effects such behavior has on their black peers? Milutinovich (1977) offers an explanation for such insensitivity. He argues that racism and the lack of common experience between the races in the workplace can lead whites to be psychologically and socially distant from blacks. Extreme psychological and social distance may provide some explanation for why some white officers behave in such a seemingly offensive manner.

Based on our interview data, it appears that black women officers remain distant from their white counterparts. From our viewpoint, those interviewed wish to maintain a good working relationship with whites, but one cannot characterize those relationships as comradely. It is not our intent to leave the impression that all white and all black police officers fail to form lasting relationships during the course of their work. The data provided by our black female participants, however, indicate that they clearly perceive white officers with skepticism and usually appear to distrust their intentions. Until the organizational culture of the police department becomes more accepting of women and minorities and allows for their inclusion as equals, relations between white and black police of both genders will likely continue to be distant and suspicious.

Relations with the Black Community—External

When interacting with members of the black community, black female officers realize that citizens may respond to their authority in unpredictable ways. Martin (1994) notes that black officers do not behave as aggressively as white policemen because of the awareness that law enforcers are perceived as oppressors by minority citizens. Instead, they attempt to understand the people they encounter in predominately black areas. This point is clearly made by one officer who stated, "I think that having a black background you have better insight as to why or how they react whereas my white counterpart may not be able to see that."

During police and minority-citizen encounters, the ability to understand a fellow minority member's social situation enables minority officers to empathize with the problems and the circumstances of the minority citizen. Muir (1977, p. 54) contends that empathy is an integral part of the worldview of good police officers: "If he [the officer] felt morally reconciled to using coercion and at the same time he reflected empathetically upon the conditions of mankind, he measured up to being a professional, a good policeman."

All of the women whom we interviewed acknowledged the importance of sensitivity to the feelings of minority citizens. They utilized their racial background experiences when interacting with minority citizens. One woman related the differences between how black and white police treat black male citizens:

> Black men typically are very proud. They have a lot of pride and a lot of the times it hurts because I can see their pride, I can see their pain, I can see it all. . . . But they [white police] cannot see the pain that I can see from being a black person. It's something you can't describe to them because unless they are them, unless they experience that kind of discrimination and stuff, it's underlying, it is invisible and it's there and unless you have been exposed to it, you can't see it.

The majority of the officers we interviewed were raised in the black community and have a realistic view of what it is to be a minority in a predominantly white world. Many of them still reside in predominantly black areas of the city. Perhaps, because of their experiences as black women, they offer a more compassionate view for the plight of minority people. One respondent stated, "A lot of the times a black officer will be more understanding of black issues in the black community." Allowing minority citizens to preserve some dignity during their encounters with police demonstrates an understanding of the pride of minority people. Goffman (1955, p. 215) notes:

> Just as a member of any group is expected to have self-respect, so also is he expected to sustain a standard of considerateness; he is expected to go to certain lengths to save the feelings

and the face of others present, and he is expected to do this willingly and spontaneously because of emotional identification with others and their feelings.

Our sample of officers stressed the importance of respect and empathy in their interactions with minority citizens—two attributes they believed white police officers do not exhibit when confronting members of the black community. Our respondents viewed themselves as more effective in most police–minority encounters. One woman expressed this point:

> The worst thing they [white police] would say about me is that I'm too nice and I tell them it's not about niceness, it's about "respect." I think a lot of black females give more respect to black people whenever possible and the white females don't.

Another female officer discussed empathy with black citizens in her interaction as an authority figure: "I like people a lot and have a lot of compassion for them. I don't know, I've been through a lot of hard times myself so I'm really sensitive to a lot of things that happen to people."

The subject of trust was also discussed with our respondents. Questions were asked to determine if the respondents thought black citizens have more trust in and are more willing to cooperate with black police rather than white police. Many of the black female officers expressed a belief that there was much more trust between black citizens and black police. A woman officer related her experience when white police officers tried to get information from black witnesses:

> Black people gravitate towards black people. When I was in homicide I would have experiences where black people would give white officers a hard time, but they would treat me great. They would totally go off with white officers, but if I showed up, it was like they trusted me.

We generally were discussing witness cooperation in most cases where trust between minority citizens and minority police was an issue. We doubt that cooperation with police officers by minority suspects with prior criminal records would be greatly enhanced by the presence of minority officers. However, even in felony circumstances, black suspects may feel more comfortable talking to a black officer. Overall, our respondents were of the opinion that racial likeness proved to be beneficial in interacting with the black community.

Policing in a predominantly black neighborhood offers minority female officers the opportunity to influence the community in a positive way. Many of our study group commented on their desire to go beyond their law enforcement roles and somehow help to improve the community. A woman officer who perceived her role as beyond the standard police model expressed this desire:

> I kind of wanted to make a difference in our community and give back to the community and also be a black person on the force who cares, because the people are always complaining about how the police mistreat them. I felt a black person on the department could help stop whatever bad was going on.

Our respondents also thought that another aspect of helping black citizens involved demonstrating that treatment of minority community members by black woman officers differs from treatment by white officers. In comparing herself to white officers, this participant claimed that whites "sometimes do things that we wouldn't do because I'm black and I'm a woman and I would give somebody a break whereas they [white police] wouldn't."

Interaction with members of the black community in a more positive manner with the hope of improving police–community relations was expressed by one respondent. She stated: "As black officers, we have a chance to come and maybe somewhat even up the score instead of forming a partnership with white police and doing equally as bad in our community." This officer, along with the majority of respondents, expressed the feeling that white police of both genders do not treat black citizens in a manner that black female police believe to be effective. For them, the goal is not to emulate the white–black police police–citizen encounters they see, but rather to treat black community members with more respect and empathy than do their white peers. Our respondents, however, were aware that in situations where white officers acted disrespectfully toward black people, they were also viewed negatively by black citizens.

Occasionally citizens in predominantly black areas of the city express appreciation and admiration for black women police. Here we see the only ranking black woman in the entire department relating an incident in which a minority man recognized her accomplishments for attaining rank:

> I stopped at this restaurant. Now this guy, he was a black guy and really unfriendly. I was in uniform. I had my police car and stuff so he's looking at me, he wasn't saying to much at all, and then as he's getting his order he says, "Well, I didn't think they had any black lieutenants on this police department," and I said "I'm the only one." This guy says, shouting, "Go, sister, YES!"

Police–citizen encounters often are negative experiences for minority citizens. Therefore, many minority people resent any authority figures working in their neighborhood. A veteran black female officer expressed this point: "Sometimes when you get to a scene, the blacks, whether they be male or female, they are automatically on you, period. You know, you're 'the man,' you're the law." In some instances it appears that members of the black community perceive all police as oppressive and that black officers in positions of authority may be viewed as traitors.

Many of the study participants said that they have more conflict with black women citizens than they do with black males in official police interactions. The following description of encounters between black female officers and black female citizens illustrates this perception:

> I can't get along with black women. I mean, we can go to a call and if I have any problems, if I have any resistance, if I have any arguments, nine times out of ten it's with a black female. The reason they attack me is because they want me to be on their side. They expect me to understand their position.

However, if a white female officer is involved in a crisis with a black female complainant or suspect, the black citizen often is much less hostile and treats the white policewoman as an authority figure:

> A white female officer, they could probably accept a little bit more because she is white. They may not like her, they might probably give her a little bit of grief, but for me, another sister,

you know, we are at the bottom of the totem pole. Thus, you have the bottom of the totem pole telling the bottom of the totem pole what to do and with some women, it doesn't go over well. And you bump heads. They will curse you. They will call you call a black bitch, black ho!

Another woman police officer noted "They will call me a lesbian, or if I have to pat them down 'Are you getting a good feel? I hope you're getting your rocks off' or things to get to you, and you feel like choking them." The exhibition of disrespectful behavior by these citizens, primarily from the lower socioeconomics stratum, is likely a class-based reaction to an authority figure who is perceived as also being at the "bottom of the totem pole."

White police officers often expect black police to control black people who have come in contact with the criminal justice system. Many of the respondents resented their perceived obligation. One black woman observed: "You get tired of always being responsible for every black person arrested, that kind of thing. I would always be expected to quiet down the black people." White police appear to stereotype all blacks as bonded by race and often fail to differentiate between black police and black offenders. In summary, white officers seem to believe that black police, because of race, are somehow obligated to know and understand black people who violate the law. The assumption that both black police and black offenders share similar traits and culture is particularly offensive to black officers as a group. Such assumptions by white officers of both genders seem to provide an additional factor that prevents inclusion of black women in the police organization.

INTERNAL AND EXTERNAL STRESSORS

Informal Organizational Stress

The stressful effects of police work are exacerbated for minority women because of their low status and exclusionary practices within the organization. Our respondents agreed that women officers have more difficulty being accepted into the organization as compared to men. Research also shows that women police endure additional stress-related factors (Morash & Haarr, 1995; Wexler & Logan, 1983). These factors include a lack of acceptance as competent officers, denial of information, lack of mentors, little protection, sexual harassment, and exposure to profanity. The time and energy devoted to enduring these factors creates additional stress.

Minority women appear to experience unique stressors that are a result of workplace problems (Morash & Haar, 1995). Important causes of additional stress for minority police include a perceived lack of influence on the daily operations of the department, poor equipment, lack of opportunity to advance, the experience of being "set up" or ridiculed, and feelings of being invisible. Stress is increased for racial minorities who have to work with white peers who frequently exhibit negative reactions toward minorities.

One respondent described how her minority status creates additional stress for her:

There is an extra added stress that you cannot make a mistake not only for yourself but because of what you represent to other people in this job. If I was to do something or something was to go extremely wrong, it would be a very long time before you would see another black in that position.

The perception that as a black officer you represent all black police appears to place enormous pressure on individual minority police. One participant stated: "I would say that your actions are held accountable to a higher standard, and it affects not only you, but it affects the whole race."

Parenting

Work for policewomen does not end when the shift is over. The conflicting demands of home and job can prove to be very stressful for policewomen (Grennan,1988; Pogrebin, 1986). An example of the conflict between the parent and police roles and the difficulty policewomen often have in determining the reason for certain reactions by colleagues is illustrated by the following story told by a black police woman. She was informed by her mother, her children's caregiver, that her son had cut himself. The respondent felt it was necessary to go home to check on her son's condition:

> My son was in that experimental stage. So the sergeant says, "Well, you know I can't really afford to give you the day off." I went in there and I didn't even ask for the day off. I just wanted to be able to go home, to check on him to make sure he didn't have to go to the hospital, 'cause my mother was home with my daughter who is an infant and I did not want to have that extra added stress of trying to pack them all up in the car if he needed to go to the hospital. I figured I would run him there, bring him home and that's that. Well, he didn't need to go and they were kind of shocked that I was back in service within hours. My sergeant said, "Well, I thought you needed more time," and I said, "No, I wanted to make sure that he was okay." So I don't know if it's just that he's male or that he's just insensitive, or maybe he's like that to everyone. I don't know.

The majority of women in our study who had children were single, creating an additional burden of the parental responsibilities of a single parent. Police departments do not make accommodations for female employees who are single parents and the policewomen typically find themselves caught between their jobs and their obligations as parents. Comparing her roles as police officer, wife, and mother, a respondent explained why she thinks being a police officer can be more difficult for women than for men:

> I spent a lot of time trying to keep my family and so I would go to work and run home and try to leave dinner prepared in order to keep some little order going with my family and find out what they had done that day, so that it wouldn't look like I really was not there. But as a female, it's very hard to be married and still be the little woman and have supper fixed for you and everything. I am that little woman that my family is expecting to come home and have dinner done, with dishes done, the laundry done and then sit down and have a talk about how bad it's been for them that day. So, from a female perspective, it's a lot harder for us on the job than men.

The majority of male police officers of all races do not have the primary responsibility for child rearing. Additionally, men also are not responsible for most of the domestic tasks that many women perform. Female police, who are head of the household, rarely have the time to participate as frequently in off-duty social interactions as their male counterparts. Socializing in the police department is necessary to form the bonds and trust that are crucial for promotional opportunities. Therefore, female officers who are single parents are at a distinct disadvantage when it comes to promotion:

> I just think that the men have more opportunities for promotion than the women, because the majority of women are mothers and are raising children, or helping raise grandchildren, or whatever the circumstances may be. We don't have time to be going hanging out with the guys and meeting Joe and Joe knows chief so-and-so, and they all go out and have a drink at the bar.

Despite their inability to socialize after hours, it is unlikely that many single black female officers would be invited to off-duty social occasions. As a result, they are left out of the off-duty informal organizational network that appears to be an important element for occupational advancement.

Personal Relationships

The majority of the respondents in our study were single parents who were divorced, often because of the stress police work places on marriage. They found their occupation an obstacle in sustaining meaningful relationships with civilian males. Many of their problems with men appear to be based on the perception of police as being authoritative and masculine. This is especially true for black males who have had emasculating experiences during police–citizen encounters. Because many members of minorities often perceive police as oppressive, having any type of relationship with a woman in law enforcement can prove to be conflicting for many black men. This view is expressed by a black woman who related the difficulty of being accepted as a person and not as a police officer in her private life.

> Everybody always relates to you as the "man," or "you be the man." So then nobody wants to sleep with the man, you want to sleep with a woman. If I'm being pegged as the man, then it's hard for me to find a real man who can just identify me as a person. I never became a person, I'm always a police officer first or the man. So until you can meet someone who can just see who you are as an individual, and then realize you have a job as a police officer, and they're both not the same thing, then it affects you a lot. That's why I don't have a man right now.

For many black women being a police officer appears to affect their opportunities for establishing relationships with men who would not prejudge them as police officers first and women second:

> If you are a single black female raising children, it is even harder because now you are not only relying on outside people to help you take care of your children, but the chances of you finding a man that is very secure and comfortable with himself is very slim.

Police patrol entails shift and weekend work that also limits female police from meeting men who work normal business hours. As one single women commented, "It's harder to meet people. I hardly date."

Working for a police department can create problems for women in their marriages. One respondent described the role her work played in the breakup of her marriage. After she started working for the department, her husband became troubled by her role as a police officer. She felt that his pride as the male head of the family was threatened by her position as an authority figure outside the home. It is likely that this is not a uniquely black male phenomenon and presumably applies to white males as well. A respondent described her perception of her husband's view of his role as a man after she became a police woman:

> But for a man to sit back and to let his wife take on a part of his role that in the past had been solely reserved for him, and that being the protector, not only of the public but in some sense your family, is like giving up a part of your manhood or a part of how you were raised as far as taking care of your family is concerned.

When a black female officer is a single parent and has a relationship with a man additional problems often surface that are direct results of police work. Not only are children an important consideration but shift work, overtime, childcare, and a host of other responsibilities contribute to the lack of time and energy necessary to maintain a long-term relationship with a man. A respondent described the difficulties in maintaining a relationship while working as a police officer:

> I came on the department divorced and with one child and then later had a relationship with a man I was serious about. I had another child and decided not to get married because it was too difficult to carry on a relationship with this kind of job.

Female police officers must also be aware of the background of males with whom they associate. Fraternization with a person who engages, even peripherally, in illegal behaviors can threaten the career of a police officer. Many of the study participants stated that they often meet men who are involved in questionable behavior or who are good citizens but have associates who engage in criminal activity. A younger respondent related the circumstances surrounding her boyfriend's behavior when they were not together:

> He had lifestyle problems, where when he was with me he was one way, he was somebody okay. But he had all these friends that were on the fringe of going to jail, being involved with drugs, forgery, illegal kinds of things. I just felt that if I stayed around him it would only be a matter of time before he got burned, consequently I would get burned, just by knowing him.

After she initiated a breakup, she stated: "I think he lied about his feelings toward me and this job. I think that he was always someone else when he was not with me." The study participants alluded to the difficulty in meeting professional middle-class black males socially.

CONCLUSIONS

The difficulties that African-American women face as police officers often involve relationships with others. Like other research on social organization, the results show that officers adjust their working relationships and interactions with their own perceptions of the social and political departmental environment as well as their own interests and experiences in the organization (Fielding, 1988; Haarr, 1997). The traditional masculine organizational norms contribute to the continuing marginalization of minorities and women in law enforcement. The demands of police work often result in individual and group isolation.

The exclusion of black women is apparent in their relationships with fellow officers: black and white, male and female. In contrast to the findings of Yoder & Aniakudo 1997), the isolation experienced by our respondents was not a self-imposed coping mechanism, but rather a deliberate proscription based on their low status within the organizational hierarchy. The voices of "outsiders within" rarely are heard because of preconceived and prejudicial notions of who should be a police officer.

Based on the interview data, it appears that black women officers remain distant from their white counterparts. The women wished to maintain a good working relationship with whites, but many of those relationships can scarcely be characterized as camaraderie. In some cases, white and black police officers do form lasting relationships during the course of their work. The general consensus among the women interviewed, however, indicates that they clearly perceive white officers with skepticism and usually appear to distrust their intentions. Until the organizational culture of the police department becomes more accepting of women and minorities and allows for their inclusion as equals, relations between white and black police of both genders will likely continue to be distant and suspicious.

Occupational obstacles that African-American policewomen face may diminish as an increasing number of women enter the workforce, though support of their peers, both off and on the job, is a crucial element for reducing isolation and discrimination. Martin (1994) asserts that white and minority women see acceptance by male officers of the same race as more important than the support of other women, for both work-related and social reasons. Respondents in this organization overwhelmingly focused on the need for racial solidarity. One woman believed, for example, that "there is an understanding that we need to look out for each other; that we need to take care of each other." Some officers also noted positive change and increased support among minorities. One respondent stated:

> You see more blacks dealing with each other instead of trying to pull each other down but trying to lift each other up. I don't know if that was the case before [in the department]. But there's not that many of us so I think it's important for us to do for each other.

Despite affirmative action mandates and research that show women make satisfactory police officers, females comprise only 10 percent of all municipal police officers in America (Dulaney, 1996; Reaves, 1989). Female police often experience hostility and resentment from their male peers (Balkin, 1988; Belknap & Shelley, 1992; Herrington, 1993; Townsay, 1982). Even in recent years, women officers claim that sexual harassment is prevalent and continuous (Erez & Tontodonato, 1992). This negative treatment is thought to be an important stress factor for women officers (Poole & Pogrebin, 1988; Wexler & Logan, 1983).

It is unlikely that the opportunities for black female officers will improve unless police departments hire more black women and improve retention rates. According to Doener's (1995) study of police officer retention patterns, black females leave the job at a much higher rate compared to all other police—on average leaving during their fourth year. One important reason for early termination may be the direct result of exclusionary practices that black women experience in a white male working environment. The organizational subculture must change from within before minority groups will gain acceptance, fair treatment and job satisfaction. Meanwhile, African-American policewomen seem to accept the inherent difficulties of the job; as noted by one woman:

> Black women know how to struggle. So when you, as a black woman, meet an adversary or meet a situation that's going to cause you grief, you know you got to struggle, so you don't have to do the little things that maybe a white woman would do. I know my job is often hard, and I know it's very trying at times, but [for] me, as a black woman, life is like that.

REFERENCES

ALEX, H. (1969). *Black and blue*. New York: Appleton-Century-Crofts.

BALKIN, J. (1988). Why policemen don't like policewomen. *Journal of Police Science and Administration, 16*, 24–38.

BELKNAP, J., & SHELLEY, J. (1992). The new lone ranger: Policewomen on patrol. *American Journal of Police, 12*, 47–75.

BERGER, J., FISK, H., NORMAN, R., & ZEIDITCH, M., JR. (1997). *Status characteristics in social interaction: An expectation status approach*. New York: Elsevier.

BROWN, J. (1997). European policewomen: A comparative research perspective. *International Journal of the Sociology of Law, 12*, 1–19.

BROWN, J. (2000). Discriminatory experiences of police women. A comparison of officers serving in England and Wales, Scotland, Northern Ireland and the Republic of Ireland. *International Journal of the Sociology of Law, 28*, 91–111.

BROWN, J., & HEIDENSOHN, F. (2000). *Gender and policing: Comparative perspectives*. New York: St. Martin's Press.

BUZAWA, E., AUSTIN, T., & BANNON, J. (1994). The role of selected sociodemographic and job-specific variables in predicting patrol officer job satisfaction: A reexamination ten years later. *American Journal of Police, 13*, 51–75.

COLLINS, P. (1986). Learning from the outsider within: The sociological significance of black feminist thought. *Social Problems, 33*, 14–30.

COSER, R., & ROCKOFF, G. (1971). Women in the occupational world: Social disruption and conflict. *Social Problems, 19*, 535–554.

DENE, E. (1992). A comparison of the history of entry of women into policing in France and England and Wales. *Police Journal, 65*, 236–242.

DILL, B. (1979). The dialectics of black womanhood. *Signs, 4*, 543–555.

DOENER, W. G. (1995). Officer retention patterns: An affirmative action concern for police agencies? *American Journal of Police, 14*, 197–210.

DULANEY, W. M. (1996). *Black police in America*. Bloomington: Indiana University Press.

ELLISON, K., & GENZ, J. (1983). *Stress and the police officer*. Springfield, IL: Charles Thomas.

EREZ, E., & TONTODONATO, P. (1992). Sexual harassment in the criminal justice system. In I. Moyer (Ed.), *The changing roles of women in the criminal justice system* (pp. 227–252). Prospect Heights, IL: Waveland Press.

FELKNES, G., & SCHROEDEL, J. (1993). A case study of minority women in policing. *Women and Criminal Justice, 4*, 65–89.

FIELDING, N. (1988). *Joining forces: Police training, socialization, and occupational competence*. New York: Routledge.

FIELDING, N. (1994). Cop canteen culture. In T. Newburn & E. Stanko (Eds.), *Just boys doing the business: Men, masculinity and crime*. London: Routledge.

GILKES, C. (1981). From slavery to social welfare: Racism and the control of black women. In A. Swerdlow & H. Lessing (Eds.), *Class, race and sex* (pp. 288–300). Boston: G.K. Hall.

GLASER, B., & STRAUSS, A. (1967). *The discovery of grounded theory: Strategies for qualitative research.* Chicago: Aldine.

GOFFMAN, E. (1955). On face work: An analysis of ritual elements in social interaction. *Psychiatry, 18,* 213–231.

GRAY, S. (1984). Sharing the shop floor: Women and men on the assembly line. *Radical America, 18,* 69–88.

GRENNAN, S. (1988). Findings on the role of officer gender in violent encounters with citizens. *Journal of Police Science and Administration, 15,* 78–85.

GRUBER, J., & BJORN, L. (1982). Blue-collar blues: The sexual harassment of women autoworkers. *Work and Occupation, 4,* 271–298.

HAARR, R. (1997). Patterns of interaction in a police patrol bureau: Race and gender barriers to integration. *Justice Quarterly, 14,* 53–85.

HEIDENSOHN, F. (1992). *Women in control? The role of women in law enforcement.* Oxford: Clarendon Press.

HERRINGTON, N. (1993). Female cops. In R. Dunham & J. Alpert (Eds.), *Critical issues in policing* (pp. 361–366). Prospect Heights, IL: Waveland Press.

HUNT, J. (1990). The logic of sexism among police. *Women and Criminal Justice, 2,* 3–30.

HURTADO, A. (1989). Relating to privilege: Seduction and rejection in the subordination of white women and women of color. *Signs, 14,* 833–855.

JACOBS, J. (1989). *Revolving doors: Sex segregation and women's careers.* Stanford, CA: Stanford University.

KANTER, R. (1977). *Men and women of the corporation.* New York: Basic Books.

LAWS, J. (1979). *The second X: Sex role and social role.* New York: Elsevier.

LEINEN, S. (1984). *Black police, white society.* New York: New York University Press.

MARTIN, S. (1979). POLICEwomen and policeWOMEN: Occupational role dilemmas and choices of female officers. *Journal of Police Science and Administration, 2,* 314–323.

MARTIN, S. (1990). *On the move: The status of women in policing.* Washington, DC: Police Foundation.

MARTIN, S. (1992). The interactive affects of race and sex on women police officers. *The Justice Professional, 6,* 155–172.

MARTIN, S. (1994). Outsider within the station house: The impact of race and gender on black women police. *Social Problems, 41,* 383–400.

MEYER, H., & LEE, M. (1978). *Women in traditionally male jobs: The experience of ten public unity companies.* U.S. Department of Labor, Employment, and Training Administration. Washington, DC: U.S. Government Printing Office.

MILUTINOVICH, J. (1977). Black-white differences in job satisfaction, group cohesiveness, and leadership style. *Human Relations, 12,* 113–140.

MORASH, M., & GREENE, J. (1986). Evaluating women on patrol: Critique of contemporary wisdom. *Evaluation Review, 10,* 230–255.

MORASH, M., & HAARR, R. (1995). Gender, workplace problems and stress in policing. *Justice Quarterly, 12,* 113–135.

MUIR, W. (1977). *Police: Street corner politicians.* Chicago: University of Chicago Press.

NKOMO, S. (1988). Race and sex: The forgotten case of the black female manager. In S. Rose & L. Larwood (Eds.), *Women's careers: Pathways and pitfalls.* New York: Praeger.

O'FARRELL, B., & HARLAN, S. (1982). Craftworkers and clerks: The effect of male coworker hostility on women's satisfaction with nontraditional jobs. *Social Problems, 29,* 252–265.

PAK, A., DION, K. L., & DION, K. K. (1991). Social psychology correlates of experienced discrimination: Test of the double jeopardy hypothesis. *International Journal of Intercultural Relations, 14,* 243–254.

PIKE, D. (1985). Women in the police academy training: Some aspects of organizational response. In J. Moyer (Ed.), *The changing roles of women in the criminal justice system* (pp. 250–270). Prospect Heights, IL: Waveland Press.

POGREBIN, M. (1986). The changing role of women: Female police officers occupational problems. *The Police Journal, 59*, 26–35.

POGREBIN, M., DODGE, M., & CHATMAN, H. (2000). Reflections of African-American women on their careers in urban policing. Their experiences of racial and sexual discrimination. *International Journal of the Sociology of Law, 28*, 311–326.

POGREBIN, M., & POOLE, E. (1998). Sex, gender, and work: The case of women jail officers. In J. Ulmer (Ed.), *The sociology of crime, law, and deviance* (pp. 105–124). Greenwich, CT: JAI Press.

POOLE, E., & POGREBIN, M. (1988). Factors affecting the decision to remain in policing: A study of women officers. *Journal of Police Science and Administration, 16*, 49–55.

POTTS, C. (1983). *Responsible police administration.* Montgomery: University of Alabama Press.

PRICE, B., & GAVIN S. (1982). A century of women in policing. In B. Price & N. Sokoloff (Eds.), *The criminal justice system and women* (pp. 399–412). New York: Clark Boardman.

RAGIN, C. C. (1994). *Constructing social research.* Thousand Oaks, CA: Pine Forge Press.

REINER, R. (1992). *The politics of the police* (2nd ed.). Toronto: University of Toronto Press.

RHODE, D. (1989). *Justice and gender: Sex discrimination and the law.* Cambridge, MA: Harvard University Press.

SAFILOS-ROTHSCHILD, C. (1979). *Sex role stereotypes and sex discrimination: A synthesis and critique of the literature.* U.S. Department of Health, Education, and Welfare, National Institute of Education. Washington, DC: U.S. Government Printing Office.

SCHATZMAN, L., & STRAUSS, A. (1973). *Field research strategies for a natural sociology.* Upper Saddle River, NJ: Prentice Hall.

SCHROEDAL, J. (1985). *Alone in a crowd: Women in the trades tell their stories.* Philadelphia: Temple University.

SEIDMAN, T. E. (1998). *Interviewing as qualitative research: A guide for research in education and social sciences.* New York: Teachers College Press.

STOCKARD, J., & JOHNSON, M. (1980). *Sex roles.* Upper Saddle River, NJ: Prentice Hall.

SWERDLOW, M. (1989). Men's accommodations to women entering a nontraditional occupation: A case of rapid transit operatives. *Gender and Society, 3*, 373–387.

TOWNSEY, R. (1982). Black women in American policing: An advancement display. *Journal of Criminal Justice, 10*, 455–468.

WALSHOK, M. (1981). *Blue-collar women: Pioneers on the male frontier.* New York: Anchor Books.

WEST, C., & FENSTERMAKER, S. (1995). Doing difference. *Gender and Society, 5*, 178–192.

WEXLER, J., & LOGAN, D. (1983). Sources of stress among women police officers. *Journal of Police Science and Administration, 11*, 46–53.

YODER, J. (1991). Rethinking tokenism: Looking beyond numbers. *Gender and Society, 55*, 178–192.

YODER, J., ADAMS, J., & PRINCE, H. (1983). The price of a token. *Journal of Political and Military Sociology, 11*, 327–337.

YODER, J., & ANIAKUDO, P. (1997). Outsiders within the firehouse: Subordination and difference in the social interactions of African American woman firefighters. *Gender and Society, 11*, 324–341.

YOUNG, M. (1991). *An inside job.* Oxford: Clarendon Press.

27

Victims of Domestic Stalking

A Comparison of Black and White Females

Janice Joseph

Stalking has gained recognition and credibility as a serious crime in the United States. Victims of stalking include those currently at risk of physical and/or emotional harm, and those in constantly pending danger but not immediately at risk. Women are the victims of stalking in disproportionate numbers (Puente, 1992).

The actions of stalkers can be extremely threatening and dangerous to their victims. Stalking can escalate to violence, so stalking victims frequently live in fear and terror. Often, they are forced to alter their lives significantly in attempts to find safety and freedom from the harassing behavior of former spouses, ex-partners, or strangers (National Institute of Justice, 1996). In this chapter we focus on the extent and nature of domestic stalking among black and white victims, critically examine New Jersey's stalking legislation, and make some recommendations.

DEFINITIONS OF STALKING

Legal definitions vary from state to state, but most states define stalking as willful, malicious, threatening, and repeated conduct for the purpose of causing fear in the victim. The types of acts that states identify as stalking behaviors include the following: terrorism, surveillance, harassment, nonconsensual communication, trespass, and threats. It can also include written and verbal communication; unsolicited and unrecognized claims of romantic involvement; loitering, following, or appearing within the sight of another; contacting the victim by telephone; sending mail or electronic mail; and appearing at the workplace or residence of the victim.

EXTENT OF STALKING

Unlike most violent crimes, the Federal Bureau of Investigation and many state law enforcement officials do not categorize the incident of stalking as a separate offense. Consequently, no one knows just how common stalking is in the United States. With the passage of the 1994 Crime Bill by the U.S. Congress, which mandated the tracking and compilation of stalking crime statistics, experts will be able to determine the prevalence of this crime in the future.

It is estimated that 200,000 people in the United States stalk someone each year, and this figure is rising (Guy, 1993). Five percent of women in the general population will be a victim of stalking at some time in their lives, 51 percent of stalking victims are ordinary citizens, and 75 to 80 percent of stalking is domestic-related. Ninety percent of the stalkers suffer from some kind of mental disorder, 9.5 percent suffer from erotomania, and 43 percent have love obsession with their victims (U.S. Congress Senate Committee on the Judiciary, 1992).

The first national survey on stalking was recently conducted by the U.S. Justice Department. The study was conducted on 8,000 women and 8,000 men regarding their experiences with stalking. The study found that stalking was more prevalent than previously thought: 8 percent of women and 2 percent of men have been stalked at some time in their lives. Eighty percent of the stalking victims were women and most were between 18 and 29 years old. About 87 percent of the stalkers were men. The study estimated that about 1 million women and 400,000 men are stalked every year and that women were more likely to be stalked by their male intimate partners, while men were more likely to be stalked by a stranger or an acquaintance. In most cases, the episodes lasted a year or less. Less than half of the victims were directly threatened, although the victims experienced a high level of fear. The results also indicated that there was a strong relationship between stalking and other forms of violence in intimate relationships (Tjaden & Thoennes, 1998).

DOMESTIC STALKING

Most victims of stalking are victimized by acquaintances. This represents 70 to 80 percent of all stalking cases and is distinguished by the fact that some previous personal or romantic relationship existed between the stalker and the victim before the stalking behavior began. The victims may be ex-spouses, ex-lovers, relatives, or coworkers. Perpetrators are often out for revenge and will stop at nothing to get it (Zona, Sharma, & Lane, 1993). The majority of stalking victims are victims of domestic stalking.

Domestic stalking cases that arise from domestic violence situations constitute the most common type of stalking and usually culminate in violent attacks against the victims. Victims of domestic stalking at one time shared a personal relationship with the perpetrators as an intimate or member of the same household. This includes common-law relatives as well as long-term acquaintances. The domestic stalker is often motivated by a desire to continue or reestablish a relationship after it has ended, or is out for revenge. In addition, there is usually a history of prior abuse or conflict between the victim and the stalker. The stalker intends to hurt the victim physically, and the confrontation between the two often results in tragic consequences. Domestic stalkers are most dangerous when they are first deprived of their source of power and self-esteem (Holmes, 1994); in other words, the time when their victims determine to remove themselves physically from the offender's presence on a permanent basis by leaving the relationship is very critical for victims.

The Cycle of Domestic Stalking

Schaum and Parrish (1995) identified a cycle of domestic stalking that is similar to the cycle of domestic violence. The first phase, the tension-building phase, may move from relatively innocuous invasions to more dangerous efforts to control the victim. In this phase, the victim is harassed, threatened, and terrorized by behaviors such as annoying phone calls, unsolicited letters, odd gifts, actual threats, surveillance of the victim, following the victim, and acts of vandalism.

In the second phase, the explosive or acutely violent phase, the stalker uses violence against the victim, including physical assault, kidnapping, rape, violence against family members and friends, and the perpetrator's final act of control: murder, suicide, or both.

The third phase is the hearts and flowers phase, in which the stalker either changes his techniques and asks for forgiveness or may leave the victim alone for a period of time, making the victim feeling temporarily safe. The victim may even take this to mean that the stalking is over. However, this phase is often only a new tactic in the cycle of stalking, and the stalking starts all over again.

This cycle of domestic stalking may continue for years. In some cases, the stalker may murder the victim in an attempt to have control over her. Some stalkers, however, abandon their current victim and redirect their fixation to more challenging and vulnerable females (Schaum & Parrish, 1995). Although this progression of the stalking cycle is common, no stalker is completely predictable. Some stalkers may never escalate past the first stage. Others move from the first stage to the last stage with little warning. Still others regress to previous stages before advancing to the next. Some stalkers may engage in episodes of threats and violence with alternating flowers and love letters. A few stalkers will progress to later stages in only a few weeks or even days. In other cases, some stalkers who have engaged in the most serious stalking behaviors may go months or even years without attempting a subsequent contact (National Victim Center, 1995). It is this unpredictability that makes stalkers very dangerous to their victims.

VICTIMS OF DOMESTIC STALKING: THE STUDY

In this section we present information from a sample of 86 female stalking victims. Some victims were interviewed at a courthouse. Others were referred to the researchers by other victims and were interviewed at their homes or a place that was convenient for them.

Measuring Instrument

The items on the interview schedule were developed from research of the literature on stalking. The interview schedule was divided into three parts: part I focused on the nature and extent of the stalking experienced by the victims; part II included items on the response of the victims to the stalking; and part III examined the effects of the stalking on the victims.

Description of Sample

More of the victims (41 percent) were between 25 and 29 years old than other ages. Sixty-eight percent were Catholics, 26 percent Protestant, and 6 percent of other religions. The average annual income was between $20,000 and $29,999. Fifty-three percent were African-Americans and 47 percent were white. None of the victims were living with the stalker, but 48 percent were ex-wives, 22 percent of them were still legally married to the stalker, 17 percent were former girlfriends, and 13 percent were strangers.

Nature of Stalking

The nature and extent of the stalking are shown in Table 1, which indicates that the most common activities of the stalker were following the victim (78 percent), intruding on the victim (73 percent), sending unwanted gifts to the victim (72 percent), stalking the victim's children (65 percent), and verbally threatening the victim (64 percent). Most stalkings lasted over seven months (68 percent). Table 1 also indicates that significantly more white victims than black victims were harassed on the telephone and followed. On the other hand, significantly more blacks than whites were threatened verbally and had their children stalked.

Responses to Stalking

Victims of stalking responded in several ways to their stalking, including preventive measures against the stalking. In responding to the stalking, many of the victims used preventive measures. Table 1 indicates that many of the victims bought a security system (61 percent), changed their address (60 percent), changed their behavior (54 percent), alerted the neighbors (52 percent), and documented the stalker's behavior (50 percent). The data indicate that more whites than blacks alerted their neighbors or bought a security system. On the other hand, more blacks than whites purchased caller identification for their telephones.

The majority of the victims (94 percent) said that they believed that they were stalked because the stalker wanted to control them or instill fear in them. In addition, 21 percent of the victims believed that their stalker was psychotic or delusional. Many of the victims clearly stated that the stalker knew what he was doing. Fifty-four percent of the victims also experienced domestic violence when they were intimately involved with the stalker.

Effects of Stalking

The experience of being stalked over a period of time can be described as psychological terrorism. Victims live in constant fear and are often forced to alter their lifestyle (change their address, move, and give up social activities). The results of the survey indicated that

TABLE 1   Characteristics of the Stalking by Race (Percent)

	Total (n = 87)	White (n = 40)	Black (n = 47)	χ^2 (df = 1)
Nature of the stalking				
Invade privacy	39	28	49	3.12
Intrude	73	75	68	0.49
Threaten verbally	64	50	80	8.85**
Harass on the telephone	48	66	25	13.70***
Threaten physically	29	3	40	21.13***
Show up unexpectedly	60	53	66	1.47
Perform surveillance	49	53	46	0.29
Hurt victim physically	52	50	53	0.08
Send unwanted gifts	72	100	51	24.37***
Follow victim	78	75	81	0.73
Stalk children	65	53	75	4.14*
Duration of the stalking				
Less than 1 month	8	11	4	
1–6 months	25	17	30	
7–12 months	35	46	28	
1–4 years	32	26	38	5.53
Responses to the stalking				
Documented stalker's behavior	50	54	50	0.15
Alerted neighbors	52	75	36	12.34***
Used caller ID	41	25	53	6.70**
Bought security system	61	98	34	37.90***
Got bodyguard	10	15	3	3.44
Bought dog	51	49	52	0.75
Bought a gun	25	30	21	0.93

*Significance at .05.
**Significance at .01.
***Significance at .001.

the stalking had a negative impact on many of the victims, as shown in Table 2. The majority of victims experienced sleeplessness (81 percent), anger (82 percent), fear (73 percent), self-blame (70 percent), anxiety (62 percent), and depression (62 percent). Sixty percent were forced to changed their address, and 54 percent had to change their behaviors, such as walking late at night or going certain places alone. Table 2 also shows that whites were significantly more likely than blacks to change their address, be fearful, and experience sleeplessness, nightmares, and anxiety.

TABLE 2   Social and Psychological Effects of Stalking by Race (Percent)

	Total ($n = 87$)	White ($n = 40$)	Black ($n = 47$)	χ^2 ($df = 1$)
Changed address	60	77	50	6.20**
Changed behavior	54	64	47	2.40
Self-blame	70	51	85	11.28***
Anger	82	77	84	0.77
Fear	73	100	51	24.93***
Nightmare	41	57	28	6.88**
Sleeplessness	81	95	65	15.17***
Anxiety	62	74	50	4.91*
Depression	62	51	70	2.77
Posttraumatic syndrome	41	49	34	1.83

*Significance at .05.
**Significance at .01.
***Significance at .001.

Use of Social Services

The majority of the victims utilized social service agencies to deal with the stalking. Sixty percent of the respondents reported the stalking to the police; 74 percent obtained a restraining order, 69 percent took the stalker to court, 61 percent went to a battered women shelter, 41 percent were counseled, and 31 percent went to a psychiatrist (Table 3). Many of the victims who reported the perpetrator to police indicated that arrest by the police

TABLE 3   Use of Social Services (Percent)

Agency	Total ($n = 87$)	White ($n = 40$)	Black ($n = 47$)	χ^2 ($df = 1$)
Police	60	78	27	14.06***
Restraining order	74	74	74	1.00
Court	69	77	58	3.16
Shelter	61	70	50	4.04*
Counselor	41	52	26	5.76**
Psychiatrist	31	51	15	12.87***

*Significance at .05.
**Significance at .01.
***Significance at .001.

(94 percent) did not deter the stalker. Similarly, the majority of those who took out a restraining order against the stalker (91 percent) said that the stalker continued his stalking.

The data indicate that whites were more likely than blacks to call the police, go to a shelter, or visit a counselor or psychiatrist. The reason for this disparity could be that blacks are distrustful of the social system, including the police, and so are reluctant to seek help from these agencies.

Perceptions of the Stalking Legislation

The victims were asked to assess the effectiveness of the state of New Jersey's stalking legislation, which was enacted in 1993. In 8 percent of cases, the legislation was not enacted during the stalking incidents. In 13 percent of the cases, the legislation did not exist at the onset of the stalking. Over three-fourths (83 percent) of the victims claimed that they did not believe that the legislation was effective in protecting them. Of those who took the perpetrator to court (69 percent), 41 percent claimed that the charges were downgraded to a lesser offense, such as harassment, 23 percent reported that the perpetrator spent only a few weeks in jail, 28 percent that the charges were dropped because of insufficient evidence, and only 8 percent felt that the perpetrator was justly punished.

CRITICAL ANALYSIS OF NEW JERSEY STALKING LEGISLATION

Since the passage of that first antistalking law in 1990 in California, all 50 states have enacted stalking statutes. These new laws were intended to give law enforcement agencies more powerful tools to arrest and prosecute stalkers and to offer victims of stalking much greater protection than was previously available for them (National Institute of Justice, 1993).

The New Jersey antistalking law went into effect on January 5, 1993. It is intended to protect victims who are repeatedly followed and threatened and is modeled after the 1990 California statute. The bill states that a person is guilty of stalking if he or she purposely and repeatedly follows or harasses another person and makes a credible threat with the intent to place that person in reasonable fear of death or serious bodily injury (New Jersey Statute Annotated, 1995). There are, however, some problems with the law.

Legal Elements of State Antistalking Legislation

There are certain legal elements in New Jersey's state antistalking legislation, including a course of conduct requirement, a purposeful or intentional behavior requirement, a threatening behavior requirement, a fear of physical harm requirement, and a reasonable person requirement.

Course of Conduct.   New Jersey's antistalking law requires that the alleged perpetrator engage in a "course of conduct involving repeatedly maintaining a visual or physical proximity to a person or repeatedly conveying verbal or written threats or threats implied by conduct or a combination thereof directed at or toward a person" (New Jersey Statute Annotated, 1995, p. A1). New Jersey does not clearly identify the behaviors that constitute a course of conduct, although the law was intended to prosecute persons who follow or harass others. The definition of course of conduct should have been much more precise and broader. Many states specify the prohibited behaviors and include surveillance, following, "lying in wait," harassing, approaching, pursuing, and intimidating of a victim, trespassing, showing a weapon, vandalizing, disregarding warning by a victim, and confining or restraining another person (U.S. Department of Justice, 1998). Statutes that narrowly define the course of conduct and the circumstances that constitute stalking may provide only limited protection for female victims. The New Jersey legislation defines "repeatedly" as two or more occasions. What this seems to imply is that one act of stalking, no matter how serious it may be, does not constitute stalking.

Purposeful or Intentional Behavior Requirement.   According to New Jersey, stalking is "purposeful," "reckless," and "negligent." What this law requires is criminal, that is, the perpetrator is aware of what he or she is doing and has a conscious desire or objective to engage in the conduct or engages in the behavior irresponsibly. This requirement of criminal intent creates a loophole for the mentally disturbed offender. A stalker with erotomania, psychosis, or an antisocial personality disorder (all suffering, therefore, from mental disturbances) may well believe that he is merely showing the victim how much he loves her, despite the fact that his intentions may be creating fear in the victim. A prosecutor may have difficulty establishing such a stalker's guilt through criminal intent (Schaum & Parrish, 1995).

Threatening Behavior Requirement.   Like most states, New Jersey requires that the stalker pose a threat or act in a way that causes a person to be fearful. These threats could be verbal or written. This is an important element because nonverbal acts can be as threatening as written threats. The context in which certain gestures are made can make them suggestive and frightening. For example, a stalker can convey a threat by forming his hand into the form of a gun and pointing it a woman, or delivering a dead animal on a victim's doorstep. These cues are subtle but powerful enough to cause fear, especially in domestic stalking cases (National Institute of Justice, 1996).

Fear of Physical Harm Requirement.   The New Jersey statute stipulates that the stalker's acts must cause the victim to be fearful of bodily harm or death to "himself" or a member of "his" immediate family. This requirement means that the victim has to believe that the stalker will injury, disfigure, or even kill him or her or his or her immediate family before the behavior can be considered stalking. Such a restrictive requirement ignores behaviors that may not be perceived as causing such extreme violence but, nevertheless, are frightening. Why should a threat of such extreme violence be required before a victim can be protected? What is also interesting about this legislation is that it uses the terms himself and his when the majority of the victims of stalking are women (New Jersey Statute Annotated, 1995).

Reasonable Person Requirement.   In New Jersey the victims of stalking have to meet the reasonable fear or reasonable person's standard of fearfulness for their perpetrator to be charged with stalking. The statute states that the behavior should cause a "reasonable person" to fear bodily injury (New Jersey Statute Annotated, 1995, p. B1). The reasonable standard requirement is based on what a reasonable person would feel rather than on the victim's personal feelings and experiences. This is a critical element for many victims, especially victims of domestic stalking. An ex-wife, for example, who has had a prior violent relationship with the perpetrator may react fearfully to minor harassing incidents, whereas others might ignore similar incidents. Does this mean that the ex-wife's fear is unreasonable? Not necessarily, but she could be viewed as overly sensitive, and thus a judge could consider her fear unreasonable. A stalker may whisper to his former wife: "Remember the gift I gave you last year for your birthday?" To a casual listener this may seem nonthreatening, but only the victim would be able to understand the real meaning of this statement, which could be: "Remember the beating that I gave you on that day." The determination as to who is a reasonable person or what is reasonable fear is left to the discretion of the judge. However, the victim's perception of reasonable fear should be taken into consideration rather than how a reasonable person would respond to threats of a stalker. Lawmakers are now beginning to realize that the victim's perception of possible violence is the most accurate indicator of whether such violence will occur and are amending their laws (Schaum & Parrish, 1995). In addition to the criticism noted above, the term "reasonable" is not defined in New Jersey's legislation.

Persons Covered by the Antistalking Legislation.   New Jersey extends its antistalking legislation to the victim's immediate family members. The statute defines immediate family as spouse, child, sibling, or any person who regularly resides in the household or who within the preceding six months resided regularly in the household (New Jersey Statute Annotated, 1995). This restrictive definition therefore does not apply to anyone who has not resided in the household for over six months. Ten states mention stalking or harassing of a minor in their antistalking statutes, and nine of them provide for enhanced penalties against persons who stalk or harass minors. In five of these states, minors under the age of 16 are covered by the law; in three other states, coverage is extended to minors under the age of 18; and in the ninth state, only minors under the age of 12 are covered (U.S. Department of Justice, 1998). New Jersey does not cover minors in its legislation. Sometimes victims of stalking seek the assistance of close friends and coworkers who themselves may become victims of the stalker as well. However, none of the states' antistalking legislation covers close friends and coworkers of the victims.

Criminal and Civil Remedies

In New Jersey, stalking is a crime of the fourth degree, which is punishable by a term of imprisonment of up to 18 months, a fine of up to $7,500, or both. A second or subsequent offense of stalking that involves an act of violence or a credible threat of violence against the same victim would be punishable as a crime of the third degree. If the defendant commits the crime of stalking in violation of an existing court order prohibiting the behavior, the offense would be classified as a crime of the third degree, which is punishable by a term of imprisonment of three to five years, a fine of up to $7,500, or both (New Jersey Statute Annotated, 1995). New Jersey has both misdemeanor and felony classifications of stalking, but felony penalties for stalking are restricted to stalking where there is bodily harm, the presence of a weapon, or where the stalking constituted a violation of a protective order. It does appear, then, that the state takes the crime of stalking seriously only when the stalker threatens the victim violently.

In 1996, the New Jersey Stalking Law was amended to allow "victims" to obtain permanent restraining orders against stalkers. The permanent order can (1) restrain the defendant from entering the residence, property, school, or place of employment of the victim and require the defendant to stay away from any specified place that is named in the order and is frequented regularly by the victim; and (2) restrain the defendant from making contact with the victim, including an order forbidding the defendant from personally or through an agent initiating any communication likely to cause annoyance or alarm, including, but not limited to, personal, written, or telephone contact with the victim, the victim's employers, employees, or fellow workers, or others with whom communication would be likely to cause annoyance or alarm to the victim (New Jersey Statute Annotated, 1995). This amendment is an improvement over the original legislation passed in 1993, but restraining orders are very limited. Protective orders allow the women partial protection in that they can go to court to get the orders before anything violent actually happens as long as there is a sufficient likelihood that it will happen. These orders can serve as the first formal means of intervention in a stalking situation, but protective orders have several inherent limitations, especially if they are not enforced.

Challenges to New Jersey's Legislation

Like most stalking legislation, New Jersey's statute is open to constitutional challenges that can make it difficult to prosecute successfully perpetrators of stalking and to protect victims. The legislation can be challenged on the grounds of vagueness and overbreadth.

Vagueness and Overbreadth.   The vagueness doctrine under the due process clauses for the Fifth and Fourteenth Amendments of the U.S. Constitution requires that all persons be given fair notice of what conduct is against the law and may subject them to criminal liability. This doctrine provides that a statute is void if the conduct forbidden by it is so poorly defined that persons of common intelligence must guess at its meaning and differ as to its application. Further, courts condemn vague statutes because they may result in arbitrary enforcement of the statutes.

A similar, yet distinct ground for voiding statutes as unconstitutional is the concept of overbreadth. The doctrine of overbreadth states that the government may not pursue satisfaction of a proper governmental purpose by means that sweep unnecessarily broadly and thereby invade protected freedoms. The danger of overly broad statutes is twofold: that they may deter citizens from engaging in constitutionally privileged activities and that they give law enforcement officials the power to select certain citizens and punish them. The test for determining overbreadth is whether the statute substantially restricts constitutionally protected conduct.

Many of the elements in the state's stalking legislation can be viewed as being too vague. For example, such words as "followed," "threatened," "knowingly," "recklessly," and "negligently" are not clearly defined in New Jersey's law. Similarly, such phrases as "explicit or credible threat," "visual or physical proximity," or "threats implied by conduct" have been used without sufficient definition or clarity. The statute also prohibits behaviors that can be considered protected constitutionally.

In 1999, Anthony Cardell, who was convicted of stalking, appealed his conviction on the grounds that the 1996 amended New Jersey's stalking law was too broad and too vague. He argued also that the present New Jersey's stalking law limited his First Amendment rights to freedom of speech, association, and assembly, specifically in its definition of course of conduct, which makes reference to "maintaining a visual or physical proximity to a person" and to "conveying verbal threats." His arguments were that these conditions duly restrict his ability to go where he wishes and to say what he wants to say.

The defendant also argued that the antistalking statute was unconstitutionally vague in general and as applied to his conduct in this case. His argument again focused on the phrase "repeatedly maintaining a visual or physical proximity" to the victim. In essence, he complained that the phrase fails to inform how close one must get to be in violation of the law. The court ruled against both his arguments on the vagueness and overbreadth of the statute, thereby upholding the law as constitutional (*State v. Cardell*, 1999). In *State v. Saunders* (1997), the court also upheld the stalking legislation on the grounds that it was not vague or or too broad.

Despite the fact that challenges to New Jersey's stalking legislation have failed, if challenges continue, it may one day be struck down as being unconstitutional. It appears that in responding to the concerns of stalking victims, New Jersey, like so many other states, has had to walk a narrow line. On the one hand, it has to protect individuals' rights and freedoms of expression and travel and movement, and on the other hand, it cannot permit one person to place another person or his or her family in fear of physical or emotional harm. In trying to reconcile these two issues, New Jersey may have failed to balance these competing interests properly by drafting legislation that may have legal and constitutional problems. More constitutional challenges to this law are to be expected. Unless New Jersey amends its stalking law, it will be subjected to constitutional scrutiny. A challenge to this law, if successful, would result in further victimization of stalking victims.

RECOMMENDATIONS

Based on the problems in New Jersey's stalking statute, New Jersey should enact stalking legislation that:

- Is comprehensive, enforceable, and not open to constitutional scrutiny. To accomplish this, New Jersey needs to revise the present antistalking law, removing all legal loopholes.
- Protects a broad category of persons, including extended family members, minors, acquaintances, coworkers, friends, or anyone who is likely to assist the victim.
- Reforms the procedures that impede victims from taking legal actions against perpetrators of stalking, especially in the case of protection orders. States should provide easy access to long-term protection orders that prohibit the perpetrator from stalking the victim.

- Establishes severe penalties, both criminal and civil, for the crime of stalking, but at the same time avoids the possibility of any constitutional challenges under the Eighth Amendment.

One of the major difficulties with the prosecution of stalkers appears to be the lack of clear procedures, training, and the seriousness given to the crime by criminal justice professionals. Therefore, New Jersey should:

- Develop clear and comprehensive procedures for the filing, investigation, and prosecution of complaints involving the crime of stalking.
- Provide law enforcement officers, attorneys, judges, and other professionals, such as physicians and social workers, with proper training on the crime of stalking. With comprehensive training, criminal justice professionals and other professionals can become important sources of assistance for stalking victims.
- Penalize officials who do not follow the proper procedures and protocols for the enforcement of antistalking legislation.
- Utilize a collaborative approach to stalking by developing a multidisciplinary team of professionals from the criminal justice system, social services, mental health system, victim advocates, legal services, and other agencies. Multidisciplinary teams are more effective in preventing crimes and protecting victims.

The foregoing recommendations are not a panacea for preventing the crime of stalking or for protecting stalking victims but if implemented, can be useful and helpful to victims of stalking. Stalking is a serious crime and should be treated as such if states want to deal with it effectively and protect victims from stalkers.

SUMMARY

In the past several decades, the crime of stalking has gained attention due primarily to the victimization of some well-known celebrities. It is a crime of terrorism and obsession. The most common victims of stalking have had an intimate relationship with the perpetrator—they are victims of domestic stalking. The results of this small sample of stalking victims clearly indicated that stalking involves a variety of behaviors, which can range from mild to serious. The study also indicated that stalking had a physical and psychological impact on the victims. In comparing the white victims with the black victims, the study indicated that the nature of the stalking differed among the two groups and that the two groups responded differently to the stalking. One of the interesting findings is that significantly more white victims than black victims used social services. It would appear that the black victims were distrustful of social services.

In an attempt to deal with stalking, states like New Jersey have enacted antistalking legislation designed to provide protection for victims of stalking. However, there is some question as to whether these laws can be effective in protecting victims. New Jersey's stalking legislation is open to constitutional challenges and could someday be found unconstitutional. New Jersey's stalking law needs to be amended so that stalkers can be prosecuted and convicted successfully and their victims protected effectively.

REFERENCES

Guy, R. A. (1993). Nature and constitutionality of stalking laws. *Vanderbilt Law School, 46*, 991–1029.

Holmes, R. M. (1994, May). Stalking in America. *Law and Order, 12*, 89–92.

National Institute of Justice. (1993). *Project to develop a model of antistalking code for states. Final summary report*. Washington, DC: U.S. Department of Justice.

National Institute of Justice. (1996). *Domestic violence, stalking, and antistalking legislation*. Washington, DC: U.S. Department of Justice.

National Victim Center. (1995). *Stalking: Questions and answers*. Arlington, VA: INFOLINK.

New Jersey Statute Annotated, 2C:12-10, § B (1) (1995).

Puente, M. (1992, July 21). Legislators tackling the terror of stalking. *USA Today*, p. 9.

Schaum, M., & Parrish, K. (1995). *Stalked: Breaking the silence on the crime of stalking in America*. New York: Simon & Schuster.

Tjaden, P., & Thoennes, N. (1998). *Stalking in America: Findings from the national violence against women survey*. Washington, DC: U.S. Government Printing Office.

U.S. Congress Senate Committee on the Judiciary. (1992). *Antistalking legislation hearing before the Senate Judiciary Committee*. Washington, DC: U.S. Government Printing Office.

U.S. Department of Justice. (1998). *Stalking and domestic violence: Third annual report to Congress under the Violence Against Women Act*. Washington, DC: U.S. Government Printing Office.

Zona, M. A., Sharma, K. K., & Lane, J. (1993). A comparative study of erotomanic and obsessional subjects in a forensic sample. *Journal of Forensic Sciences, 38*, 894–903.

CASES

State v. Cardell, 318 N.J. Super. Ct. App. Div., 175 (1999).

State v. Saunders, 302 N.J. Super. Ct. App. Div., 509 (1997).

SECTION VI

Women and Prison

28

The Daily Adult Interactive Learning Experience Program

Evaluating the Needs of Lower-Functional Female Adult Offenders in Prison

Rosemary L. Gido and Danielle McDonald

In the last 30 years, the research literature on incarcerated women has slowly begun to focus on the special needs of female offenders. Advocacy groups have noted that U.S. prison systems remain *particularly deficient in the provision of medical and mental health care*, even as the increase in female offenders with histories of trauma, substance abuse, mental challenge and disorder, and other co-occurring disorders pose tremendous challenges for correctional systems at all levels. This chapter presents an evaluation of a model program for female inmates with limited coping and functioning skills. The Daily Adult Interactive Learning Experience (DAILE), a program in a northeastern state female correctional facility, focuses on improving daily living skills, medical compliance, and coping skills, as well as educational/vocational and substance abuse program participation. Process and outcome evaluations of DAILE are discussed. Best practices elements from this program are recommended for dissemination to other female prison settings.

INTRODUCTION

In the last 30 years, the research literature on incarcerated women has slowly begun to focus on the special needs of female offenders. Due largely to the "war on drugs," the number of imprisoned women in the United States increased 125% between 1990 and 2000. Moreover, this increase was due primarily to admissions of women of color convicted for drug offenses (Kruttschnitt & Gartner, 2003, pp. 1–9). According to the most recent Bureau of Justice statistics, the number of women in U.S. state and federal prisons continued to rise at a rate greater than that of imprisoned males. From June 30, 2003, to June 30, 2004, the rate of increase for incarcerated women was 2.9%; the rate of increase for men was 2% (Harrison & Beck, 2005).

As female prison and jail populations have grown, the significant physical and mental health care needs of these women have become apparent (Ross & Lawrence, 2002). Yet, advocacy groups and researchers have noted that prison systems have not been able to develop adequate facilities for women at varying levels of security and *remain particularly deficient in the provision of medical and mental health care* (Belknap, 2003, p. 99; Human Rights Watch, 2003). Female offenders with histories of trauma, substance abuse, mental challenge and disorder, and other co-occurring disorders pose tremendous challenges for correctional systems across the country.

Indeed, the research on these issues is sporadic, with the most study focused on offenders with mental illness[1] (Danzer, 2003; Sacks, Sacks, & Stommel, 2003; Minnesota Department of Corrections, Minnesota Department of Human Services, 2002). Lurgio and Swartz (2000), in a comprehensive monograph on *persons with serious mental illness (PSMIs)* in the criminal justice system, note that both deinstitutionalization and criminalization of persons who are mentally ill since the 1960s, combined with rigorous drug enforcement policies since the 1980s, have increased the numbers of drug-using inmates who are mentally ill in jails and prisons. By 1999, 29% of white females, 20% of black females, and 22% of Hispanic females in state prisons were identified as mentally ill (Human Rights Watch, 2005). The study *Caught in the Net* (American Civil Liberties Union, Break the Chain, & the Brennan Center for Justice, 2005) notes the increasing number of "dual diagnosed" offenders—mental illness coupled with addiction (p. 19).

INCARCERATED OFFENDERS WITH MENTAL RETARDATION AND LOWER INTELLECTUAL FUNCTIONING

In 2002, the American Association on Mental Retardation (AAMR) offered the following definition of *mental retardation*:

> [Mental retardation is] a disability, which is characterized by significant limitations both in intellectual functioning and in adapting behavior or skills prior to age 18. Specifically, an IQ score below the level of 70–75 is considered an important indicator of mental retardation. (Taiping Ho, 2003, p. 1)

A review of the literature finds no comprehensive studies of inmates who are mentally retarded (MR), have lower IQ functioning, or are developmentally disabled.[2] Nichols, Bench, Morlok, and Liston (2003) conducted phone surveys with 42 states to determine the type and level of specialized services for offenders with mental retardation. Only 18 states had programs specifically for inmates who had lower intellectual functioning; another 23 grouped inmates who were mentally ill with those who were mentally retarded for treatment services.

While researcher Joan Petersilia has built a case for intermediate sanction sentencing for offenders with MR/lower functioning (1997), in-prison programs are largely referenced in articles in *Corrections Today* magazine. A program in Washington State accepts inmates during their final six months of imprisonment, focusing on reintegration into the community (Maddess & Hooper, 2000). Similarly, the Connections program of Oregon State Penitentiary operates a satellite program in the women's prison. The 6-to-8-month program is to prepare offenders for integration into the general population and participation in regular education and work programming, with follow-up monitoring to ensure their safety (*Gaseau*, 2004).

A search of the Web for current programs specifically for mentally retarded female inmates finds such programs in North Carolina, Arizona, and Oklahoma. Again, given the small numbers of incarcerated women compared to men, state correctional departments are most likely to combine treatment resources for inmates with a variety of mental disorders.

Both Nichols et al. (2003) and Petersilia (1997) note the higher risk factors for inmates who are mentally challenged in prison settings. These include higher rates of sexual and physical victimization, violent behavior incidents stemming from a lack of communication skills, and an inability to adjust to and integrate into general population programming. The American Association on Mental Retardation found no empirical evidence for linking mental retardation to violent behavior (Taiping Ho, 2003, p. 2). Yet, "mentally retarded persons are likely to have low self esteem, poor tolerance, be easily influenced by others, and be eager to please authorities such as the police" (p. 2). It is clear that there is a need for the type of program described in the remainder of this chapter.

PROGRAM DESCRIPTION AND HISTORY

The Daily Adult Interactive Learning Experience (DAILE) program was developed in 2001 to meet the needs of an increased number of women inmates with lower intellectual functioning entering a northeastern state's correctional system. The program targeted women with *mental health*, *mental retardation*, and *co-occurring disorders*, as well as *substance abuse* problems. Funded by a grant, the program has been run by two outside private mental health care providers since its inception.

The DAILE program was developed after a noticeable increase in misconducts among women inmates who had a history of mental illness. These women had a difficult time adjusting to the structured environment of prison, which often resulted in a long stay within the facility's Restricted Housing Unit. In segregation, many of these women deteriorated further, and some engaged in self-injurious behavior, causing them to spiral even more out of control.

Central to the DAILE program philosophy is its positive interactive approach to learning, based on a comprehensive assessment of individual client needs. Drawing on "best practices" from community professionals working with people who are mentally challenged, the DAILE program utilizes a "positive approaches model" that includes intensive support and learning opportunities to model change behaviors. This program focus thus shifts the emphasis to rewards to shape behaviors, rather than punishment for rule breaking.

Female inmates admitted to the DAILE program have an IQ in or below the low-average range; maladaptive behaviors or identified deficits in daily functioning (with priority given to self-injurious actions and a history of substance dependence or abuse); dual diagnosis; medical problems that interfere with treatment; and an inability to benefit from general population programming (work detail, school, and alcohol and other drug special needs groups). The program discourages admissions of individuals who engage in predatory behavior, exhibit a pattern of unpredictable violent behavior toward others, and who have a diagnosis of antisocial personality disorder. DAILE admissions discharges are rare.

Five broad goals have been established and are the basis for the DAILE program operational components:

1. A structured support program that offers a daily schedule of learning activities for program participants.

2. Flexible individualized treatment plans for each participant that are based on a comprehensive psychiatric, medical, substance abuse, social, behavioral, and cognitive needs assessment. Each service plan is developed following program admission and includes continual plan adjustment as well as coordination with the Department of Corrections' unit team and security staff.

3. Structured learning programming in the areas of substance abuse, medical, psychological/psychiatric, social (daily living), cognitive/educational, and vocational/prevocational. Individual and group sessions, as well as daily living and vocational training activities, are coordinated with the department's treatment and security staff and entire DAILE treatment team.

4. Active involvement of staff and other long-term inmates as learning mentors in the alcohol and drug education groups.

5. Accountability to the Department of Corrections with an established system of program documentation and adherence to program objectives.

The current private vendor supports a program staff that includes a program director, registered nurse, licensed social worker, four mental health workers, and one administrative assistant. Given the stresses of an aging, overcrowded facility, the program is located in the basement of the Special Needs Housing Unit.

EVALUATION METHODOLOGY

With support from a Department of Corrections grant, the researchers made five on-site visits to the DAILE program in fall 2004 to collect data and formulate a process and outcome evaluation. Institutional Review Board approval was obtained prior to study initiation.

A process evaluation basically traces how a program is conceptualized and implemented. In this study, the *process evaluation* sought to determine *whether the program was implemented as designed*. Specific evaluation questions included:

1. Is the program running as planned—are goals being met?

2. What is the general process that clients follow through the program?

3. How are program objectives being delivered?

4. How are program objectives and program operations being documented?
   - What information is collected and how is it used in decision making?
   - How are individual records utilized to support individual treatment goals? How are aggregate data utilized to keep the program directed to goals and objectives?

5. What are the program's strengths and weaknesses?

Outcome-based evaluation strategies were focused on DAILE program *impacts on inmate participants*. Here, documentation was sought to determine program:

1. Reduction in participant misconduct rates
2. Improvements in medication compliance
3. Reduction in mental health unit admissions
4. Improvements in basic living and social skills
5. School and alcohol and drug program attendance

Evaluation Strategies

Site visits were based on a data and information access plan developed with the program director during the first visit. The objective was to collect DAILE program data and information without program interference or staff and client distraction. The following evaluation tasks were completed:

1. Program director interview and program overview
   - Review of sample client file for documentation of "typical" records in place for recording client progress
   - Identification and understanding of program components and "delivery systems"

2. Program process "mapping"
   - Director and researcher mapped the process that program participants follow once admitted to the program
   - Process "key points" were documented and matched to records/forms in place for each client as she moves through the program process
   - Program goals/objectives were matched to reports/forms; collected to document individual and "group" progress

3. Data on inmate participants were collected for the Department of Corrections data system to develop a profile of DAILE current and past participants ($N = 57$).

4. Information and data were collected on school and alcohol and drug programming. The director updated statistics and clarified the data collection process on misconducts, mental health unit admissions, psychiatric observation cell

admissions, school attendance, alcohol/drug program participation, and medication compliance.

5. The researchers conducted a focus group comprised of all DAILE staff and the Special Needs Unit counselor and psychologist.

PROGRAM EVALUATION FINDINGS

DAILE Participant Profile

- The age of program participants ranged from 23 to 74, with 54% 40 years of age or older. The average age was 43.
- Sixty percent of the women in the program were not married—only 9% reported being married; 20% were divorced.
- Forty-nine percent of DAILE participants were African American; 49% were Caucasian; 2% were Hispanic.
- The offenses for which the women are serving time range from theft to murder in the first degree. The two most common offenses were aggravated assault (20%) and drug offenses (14%). Thirty-one percent are serving time for a nonviolent offense, while 69% are imprisoned for a violent offense.
- Only 11 of the 57 DAILE participants have been parole violators.

Process Evaluation Findings

- The DAILE program clearly adheres to the goals and objectives established for the program. The goals and objectives are met at all levels of program delivery—for individual clients and day-to-day program operations.
- A careful mapping of the DAILE program operational structure and process indicates there is *rigorous* monitoring and documentation of individual progress through treatment plans. Standard reporting forms tally and document DAILE program operations and provide measures of adherence to goals and objectives.
- The program delivery system is fluid and adaptable—achieved through staff teamwork and feedback from individual observational and compliance records, including treatment plans, daily meetings, individual conferences, behavioral observations, and so on.

Outcome Evaluation Findings

The DAILE program has had several impacts as measured by institutional indicators as follows.

- *Misconducts.* The number of cell restrictions for women in the DAILE program decreased by 49%. The number of days spent in the Restricted Housing Unit

(RHU) increased after the start of the program by 9%. This increase can be explained by the inclusion of inmates with borderline personality disorder and women diagnosed with schizophrenic disorders. Overall, 4.5% of the DAILE population is responsible for 87% of time spent in the RHU.

- *Mental health unit admissions.* Many of the women in the DAILE program have serious psychological problems. Before this program, many of the participants did not take their medication as prescribed, which ultimately meant they would be admitted to the mental health unit. With the inception of the DAILE program, Mental Health Unit admissions decrease by 43%.

- *School attendance.* School attendance is mandatory for those women who function below an eighth-grade level. Overall, 81% of the women did attend school on a regular basis.

- *AOD and dual diagnosis groups.* Women who have substance abuse problems, as determined during their intake into the institution, attend an alcohol and drug program modeled after Alcoholics Anonymous and Narcotics Anonymous. The Dual Diagnosis Group includes three months of education and therapy as a treatment, with attendance required. Peer inmate mentors lead these groups that take place three times a week. Attendance for these programs is good, with the majority of women participating.

- *Medication compliance.* Medication compliance is carefully monitored and recorded by the DAILE nurse. Medication compliance for the DAILE participants has clearly improved and is reported to have achieved 96% compliance.

Daile Focus Group Observations

The researchers led the DAILE staff team in a discussion of participants' social skills, barriers to program delivery, and "best practices" from the program that could be disseminated in establishing the program at other facilities.

Social Skills

1. The greatest improvements have come in personal hygiene and keeping the unit clean. Personal pride is encouraged, and the "shame" label is displaced—"you are taking your meds and taking care of yourself." There is clearly less teasing from other inmates.

2. There is an improvement in manners and civility. An officer commented on the difference in behavior during Thanksgiving Day dinner this past year compared to last.

3. Much of the behavioral improvements have come about due to a bonding with DAILE staff (particularly mental health workers) and a desire of the participants to please the staff with respectful behaviors and less "acting out."

4. The Department of Corrections support has been excellent. In the institution, there was initial doubt and concern that participants were getting items not

available to other inmates. There is now a sense that there are fewer problems with these women and recognition that MHU and RHU admissions are down due to the DAILE program.

Barriers to Program Delivery

5. Staff are working to improve the system of medication distribution. Dispensed and monitored outside the unit, there is still the potential for critical psychiatric and medical medications not to be taken.

6. The greatest obstacle to current and future program delivery is lack of space generally and the quality of the current space in particular. The program cannot expand under current space constraints, and the physical layout interferes with program delivery. Plans are in place for expansion, with an additional back room approved for this purpose.

EVALUATION CONCLUSIONS—BEST PRACTICES

The process and outcome evaluations of the DAILE program document a program delivery system that is fluid and adaptable. This was achieved through staff teamwork and feedback from individual observations and compliance records including treatment plans, daily meetings, individual conferences, behavioral observation, and so on. The DAILE program's strengths were clearly the director and staff's expertise, work ethic, and devotion to the participants of the program.

A number of program best practices emerged from the focus group and researchers' observations. These were recommended to the Department of Corrections as essential program elements for dissemination to other facility sites:

- Program delivery that is based on a teamwork structure
- Program staff rapport and communication with security staff
- Adaptable and fluid program operations as directed by ongoing monitoring of client needs
- Documentation and standardization of program operations through formalized procedures and information/data collection systems

NOTES

1. President George Bush signed the Mentally Ill Offender Treatment and Crime Reduction Act into law on October 30, 2004. The legislation created a $50 million federal grant program to "expand prisoners' access to mental health treatment while incarcerated and upon re-entry into the community" (American Psychological Association, 2004).

2. These terms, as well as "mentally challenged," are found in the literature and program descriptions.

REFERENCES

American Civil Liberties Union, Break the Chains, and the Brennan Center for Justice. (2005). *Caught in the net: The impact of drug policies on women and families.* Retrieved from http://www.aclu.org

American Psychological Association. (2004, November). *Mentally Ill Offender Treatment and Crime Reduction Act becomes law* [Press release]. Retrieved from http://www.apa.org/releases

Belknap, J. (2003). Responding to the needs of women prisoners. In S. F. Sharp (Ed.), *The incarcerated woman: Rehabilitative programming in women's prisons* (pp. 93–106). Upper Saddle River, NJ: Prentice Hall.

Danzer, A. (2003). *Erie County community reintegration of offenders with mental illness and substance abuse (CROMISA) program: Program evaluation.* Erie, PA: Mercyhurst College Civic Institute.

Harrison, P. M., & Beck, A. J. (2005). *Prison and jail inmates at mid-year 2004.* Rockville, MD: U.S. Department of Justice/Bureau of Justice Statistics.

Gaseau, M. (2004). *Protection and access: Managing inmates with disabilities.* People Aligned to Replace Injustices & Cruelty with Knowledge. Retrieved from http:// www.patrickcrusade.org/ PROTECTION_AND_ACCESS.html

Kruttschnitt, C., & Gartner, R. (2003). Women's imprisonment. In M. Tonry (Ed.), *Crime and justice: A review of research* (Vol. 30, pp. 1–81). Chicago: University of Chicago Press.

Lurigio, A., & Swartz, J. A. (2000). Changing the contours of the criminal justice system to meet the needs of persons with serious mental illness. In J. Horney (Ed.), *Criminal justice 2000: Policies, processes and decisions of the criminal justice system* (Vol. 3, pp. 45–108). Washington, DC: National Institute of Justice.

Maddess, P., & Hooper, D. (2000). Washington state's transitional program helps special needs offenders. *Corrections Today, 62*(7), 80–83.

Human Rights Watch. (2003). *Mental health trends and women prisoners.* Retrieved from http://www.hrw.org/reports/2003

Minnesota Department of Corrections, Minnesota Department of Human Services. (2002). *Symposium on offenders with mental illness: Understanding and hope.* St. Paul, MN: Minnesota Department of Corrections.

Nichols, M., Bench, L. L., Morlok, E., & Liston, K. (2003). Analysis of mentally retarded and lower-functioning offender correctional programs. *Corrections Today, 65*(1), 119–121.

Petersilia, J. (1997). Justice for all? Offenders with mental retardation and the CA corrections system. *The Prison Journal, 77*(4), 358–380.

Ross, P. H., & Lawrence, J. E. (2002). Health care for women offenders: Challenge for the new century. In R. L. Gido & T. Alleman (Eds.), *Turnstile justice: Issues in American corrections* (pp. 73–88). Upper Saddle River, NJ: Prentice Hall.

Sacks, S., Sacks, J. Y., & Stommel, J. (2003). Modified therapeutic community programs for inmates with mental illness and chemical abuse disorders. *Corrections Today, 65*(6), 90–99.

Taiping Ho. (2003). Complex issues about mentally retarded defendants. *International Encyclopedia of Justice Studies.* Retrieved from http://www.iejs.com/Mental_Health/mentally_retarded_ defendants.htm

29

Disparate Treatment in Correctional Facilities

Women Incarcerated

Roslyn Muraskin

❖

As of June 30, 2003, "the nation's prisons and jails held 2,078,570 men and women" (Bureau of Justice Statistics, 2004a, p. 1). This is an increase of 57,600 more inmates than state, local and federal officials held on the same day one year earlier. During this year (2002–2003) the "number of female state and federal inmates grew by 5.0 percent, compared to a 2.7 percent male inmate growth. By June 30, 2004, the female inmate population reached 103,310" (p. 1).

Three out of four violent female offenders commit simple assault. An estimated 28 percent of violent female offenders are juveniles. An estimated 4 in 10 women who commit violent crimes are perceived as being under the influence of alcohol and/or drugs at the time the crime was committed. In 1998 alone there were an estimated 3.2 million arrests of women. And since 1990 the number of female defendants convicted of felonies in state courts has grown at more than twice the rate of increase in male defendants (U.S. Department of Justice, 2000).

The providing of services and programs is all part of good correctional practice. It ensures that those inmates returned to society can be be reintegrated into society. With the number of women incarcerated there exists the need for proper treatment within the correctional facilities. In this chapter we review the problems and cases of the past, demonstrating that services legally mandated have not been fully delivered.

OVERVIEW

Based on the self-reports of victims of violence, women account for about 14 percent of violent offenders—this is an annual average of about 2.1 million violent female offenders.

493

It is estimated that three out of four violent female offenders commit simple assault. There is an estimated 28 percent of females who are violent and who are classified as juveniles. It is also likely that an estimated 4 in 10 women who commit acts of violence have been perceived by their victims to have been under the influence of either alcohol or drugs at the commission of the crime. What is noted is that the per capita rate of women who murdered in the year 1998 (latest date figures are available) was the lowest since 1976. Overall the rate by which women commit murder has been declining since 1980. In 1998 there were an estimated 3.2 million arrests of women which accounts for about 22 percent of all arrests during that year. The per capita rate of arrest among juvenile females has been estimated to be nearly twice the adult female rate. It is a fact that since 1990 the number of female defendants who have been convicted of felonies in various state courts has been growing at more than two times the rate of increase in male defendants. As of 1998 (latest figures available) there were an estimated 950,000 women who were under the care, custody, or control of correctional agencies—probation or parole agencies supervising 85 percent of these offenders in the community. This total equals out to a rate of about 1 woman involved with the criminal justice system for every 109 adult women in the U.S. population. Disturbing about these statistics is the factor that women who are under the supervision of criminal justice agencies were mothers of approximately 1.3 million minor children (Greenfeld & Snell, 1999, p. 1).

In examining the racial and ethnic composition of the general population, we find that "non-Hispanic black females outnumber non-Hispanic black males by nearly 1.9 million, accounting for more than a quarter of the total difference in the number of males and females in the general population" (Bureau of Justice Statistics, 2000). The average age of females in the general population is about 2½ years higher than that of males. See Table 1 for a comparison of violent crimes committed by females and males. It is interesting to note that among females, Hispanic females have the lowest average age, that of 29.6 years, while white non-Hispanic women have the highest, 39.6 years (Greenfeld & Snell, 1999, p. 1).

About 1 out of 7 violent offenders described by victims was a female. Women accounted for 1 in 50 offenders committing a violent sex offense, including rape and

TABLE 1   Comparison of Violent Crimes by Gender

Offense	Average Annual Number of Offenders Reported by Victims, 1993–1997		Women as a Percentage of Violent Offenders
	Female	Male	
All	2,135,000	13,098,000	14%
Sexual assault	10,000	442,000	2
Robbery	157,000	2,051,000	7
Aggravated assault	435,000	3,419,000	11
Simple assault	1,533,000	7,187,000	18

TABLE 2   Characteristics of Violent Female Offenders

Offense	Percent by Race of Female Offenders		
	White	Black	Other
Violent offenses	55%	35%	11%
Robbery	43	43	14
Aggravated assault	45	46	10
Simple assault	58	31	10

sexual assault; 1 in 14 robberies; 1 in 9 offenders committing aggravated assault; and more than 1 in 6 offenders described as having committed a simple assault. Black and white offenders accounted for nearly equal proportions of women committing robbery and aggravated assault; however, simple assault offenders were more likely to be described as white (see Table 2).

With regard to women who murder: "Since 1993 both male and female rates of committing murder have declined. Rates of committing murder in 1998 were the lowest since statistics were first collected in 1976. The estimated rate for murder offending by women in 1998 was 1.3 per 100,000, about 1 murderer for every 77,000 women. The male rate of murder offending in 1998 was 11.5 per 100,000, about 1 murderer for every 8,700 males" (Bureau of Justice Statistics, 2000, p. 10).

"In 1998 there were an estimated 3.2 million arrests of women, accounting for about a fifth of all arrests by law enforcement agencies. Women were about 17% of those arrested for Part I violent crimes (murder, rape, robbery, and aggravated assault) and 29% of those arrested for Part I property crimes (burglary, larceny, and motor-vehicle theft). Women accounted for about 16% of all felons convicted in State Courts in 1996. Women were 8% of convicted violent felons, 23% of property felons, and 17% of drug felons. Women defendants accounted for 41% of all felons convicted of forgery, fraud, and embezzlement" (Bureau of Justice Statistics, 2000, p. 11).

According to Julie Samuels, acting director for the National Institute of Justice, there exists the common observation that the criminal behavior of women is not to be deemed an important problem. For many years it has been believed that if women were to commit any crimes, they would commit only minor crimes and therefore have always constituted a small fraction of the correctional population. But these facts have veiled a trend that has attracted everyone's attention. It is well known that although crime rates are down, there is a growing population within correctional facilities as a result of tougher and longer sentences. For women, however, the number of female inmates is growing at a rate higher that than of men. Among academics there has been a call to redefine justice.

According to Samuels, "Whether justice should promote unalloyed equality, be blind to the circumstances in which crime is committed, and consider only the gravity of offense and prior record, is still a matter of debate. In the current sentencing environment, the view of those who favor equity above all other considerations has won the day. There is another perspective, the belief that sanctions ought to be tailored to the specific characteristics and circumstances of individual offenders" (U.S. Department of Justice, 2000, p. 2).

LOOKING BACK INTO HISTORY

In the United States, no constitutional obligation exists for all persons to be treated alike. The government frequently does, in fact, treat disparate groups differently. However, this does not excuse invidious discrimination among potential recipients (Gobert & Cohen, 1981, pp. 294–295). What is required is that where unequal treatment exists, the inequalities must be rational and related to a legitimate interest of the state (Pollack & Smith, 1978, p. 206). Laws have created categories in which some people may be treated unequally. These categories have always included women incarcerated in correctional facilities. The question that still arises is "whether the inequalities by the law are justifiable—in legal terms whether the person upon whom the law's burden falls has been denied equal protection of the law" (pp. 206–207).

Since the decision in *Holt v. Sarver* (1970), in which the court declared an entire prison to be in violation of the Eighth Amendment and imposed detailed remedial plans, the judiciary has taken an active role in the administration of correctional facilities. Many of the landmark cases challenged the inequity of treatment between male and female prisoners.

Ostensibly, the needs of male and female prisoners would appear to be the same. They are not. Although some inmate interests are similar, others are separate and distinct. In many institutions, criteria developed for men were applied automatically to women, with no consideration given for gender differences. Research has shown that female offenders have always experienced more medical and health problems than do male inmates. Classification officials have noted that female offenders have needed help in parenting skills, child welfare, pregnancy and prenatal care, home stability, as well as an understanding of the circumstances of their crime. But typically, assignments to programs and treatment resources within correctional facilities have always been based on what is available rather than on what should be available.

A review of the literature of the cases and issues that have dealt with disparate treatment has revealed that each takes note of the fact that women historically have represented a small minority in both prisons and jails. Yet the effects of incarceration have been in many but not all respects similar for men and women. Each has suffered the trauma of being separated from family and friends. When either a man or a woman becomes imprisoned, he or she experiences a loss of identity as well as a devaluation of his or her status. Regardless of the inmate's gender, prison life has coerced conformity to an environment alien to the individual, where one's every movement is dictated each and every minute (Muraskin, 1989).

Most challenges to prison conditions have neglected the special needs of female prisoners, especially the jails, where both males and females are located together. Traditionally, correctional facilities for women have not received funding comparable to that of correctional facilities for men. Education and vocational-training programs for women have been historically and seriously underfunded. "Benign neglect [has] . . . created a situation of unequal treatment in many states" (Hunter, 1984, p. 133). Correctional administrators have insisted that "the small number of female offenders [has] made it too expensive to fund such programs." The courts, however, have ruled that "cost is not an acceptable defense for denying equal treatment" (pp. 133–134). Historically, females have been subject to policies designed for the male offender. Just as "women have deferred to males in the economic, social, political spheres of life, [i]n the legal realm, more specifically in the imprisonment of the female, women have been forced into the status of being less than equal" (Sargent, 1984, p. 83).

REVIEW OF CASES: WOMEN AND EQUALITY/PARITY

When inmates similarly situated find themselves being treated differently, there may exist a violation of equal protection. A review of the cases discussed below demonstrates what established the discrimination against women who are incarcerated.

Constitutionally, no obligation exists for the government to provide any benefits beyond basic requirements. However, this principle should not be an excuse for invidious discrimination among potential recipients (Gobert & Cohen, 1981, pp. 294–295). Case law has held that benefits afforded some cannot be denied solely on race or gender. In any equal protection challenge, the central question that has been raised is the "degree of state interest which can justify disparate treatment among offenders" (*Reed v. Reed*, 1971). As established, the "classification must be reasonable, not arbitrary and must bear a fair and substantial relation to the object of the legislation or practice" (*Reed*). Courts, for example, have found sex classifications to be irrational because they appear to be enacted solely for the convenience of correctional administrators (see *Craig v. Boren*, 1976;[1] *Weinberger v. Wisenfeld*, 1975;[2] *Eslinger v. Thomas*, 1973).[3] Existing differences in conditions, rules, and treatment among inmates have proven fertile ground for equal protection challenges. Administrative convenience is not an acceptable justification for disparity of treatment (*Cooper v. Morin*, 1979, 1980), nor is lack of funds an acceptable justification for disparate treatment (*State ex rel Olson v. Maxwell*, 1977).

Legal uprisings against intolerable conditions in correctional facilities and prisoners' rights litigation were initiated by male attorneys and male prisoners. In the early stages of this litigation, female inmates did not turn to the courts, nor did officials at female institutions fear lawsuits, condemnation by the public, or inmate riots. With so few women incarcerated, there was little the women felt they could do. This situation has changed. Female prisoners sued and demanded parity with male prisoners. The Fourth Amendment has been the source for issues of violation of privacy, and the Eighth Amendment is used for cases involving cruel and unusual punishment.

Differential sentencing of similarly situated men and women convicted of identical offenses has been found to violate the equal protection clause. A review of cases dealing generally with sentencing in correctional institutions includes prior rulings in the case of *United States ex rel Robinson v. York* (1968), which held that it was a violation of the equal protection clause for women who were sentenced to indeterminate terms under a Connecticut statute to serve longer maximum sentences than those of men serving indeterminate terms for the same offenses. In *Liberti v. York* (1968), the U.S. Supreme Court held that the female plaintiff's indeterminate sentences of up to three years violated the equal protection clause because the maximum term for men convicted of the same crime was one year. In *Commonwealth v. Stauffer* (1969), a Pennsylvania court held the practice of sentencing women to state prison on charges for which men were held in county jail to be a violation of a woman's right to equal protection.

In *Williams v. Levi* (1976), dealing with disparate treatment in the issue of parole, male prisoners in the District of Columbia were placed under the authority of the D.C. Board of Parole, whereas women prisoners were placed under the authority of the U.S. Board of Parole's stricter parole standards of violence. In *Dawson v. Carberry* (1973), it was held that there must be substantial equivalence in male and female prisoners' opportunities to participate in work-furlough programs.

In *Barefield v. Leach* (1974), women at the Women's Division of the Penitentiary of New Mexico claimed that conditions there violated their rights to an uncensored press, to have their persons free from unreasonable searches, to be free from cruel and unusual punishment, and to be allowed due process and equal protection of the law regarding disciplinary procedures and rehabilitative opportunities, respectively. The court held that "[w]hat the equal protection clause requires in a prison setting is parity of treatment as contrasted with identity of treatment, between male and female inmates with respect to the conditions of their confinement and access to rehabilitative opportunities." Barefield is especially important, as it was the first case to enunciate the standard against which disparity of treatment of men and women in prison was to be measured.

Still further, in *McMurray v. Phelps* (1982), there was a challenge to conditions for both men and women at the Quachita County jail, where the jail ordered an end to the disparate treatment of female detainees. And in *Mary Beth G. v. City of Chicago* (1983), a strip-search policy under which female arrestees underwent a full strip search without reason to believe that a weapon or contraband was present was ruled to be a violation of the equal protection clauses as well as the Fourteenth Amendment.

In *Bounds v. Smith* (1977), the Court held that access to the courts by prisoners was a fundamental constitutional right. The Court noted that there existed an affirmative obligation on the part of state officials to ensure court access by providing adequate law libraries or some alternative involving a legal-assistance program. It was noted further in the Court's decision that females had less access to library facilities than did male inmates. This situation was ordered remedied. In *Cody v. Hillard* (1986), the Court held that inmates at the state women's correctional facility, which had neither a law library nor law-trained assistants, were denied their constitutional right of meaningful access to the courts.

In a case dealing with the transfer of female inmates out of state because of a lack of facilities (*State ex rel Olson v. Maxwell*, 1977), female inmates filed a petition for a supervisory writ challenging the North Dakota practice of routinely transferring them to other states to be incarcerated, alleging a denial of equal protection and due process. It was held that North Dakota must not imprison women prisoners outside the state unless and until a due process waiver hearing was held or waived and the state admitted that it could not provide women prisoners with facilities equal to those of male prisoners.

"From a policy perspective, discriminatory distribution of prison privileges . . . will appear counter-rehabilitative, fueling inmate administration animosity and generating inmate peer jealousies" (Gobert & Cohen, 1981, p. 295). In *Canterino v. Wilson* (1982, 1983), it was indicated that "restrictions imposed solely because of gender with the objective of controlling lives of women inmates in a way deemed unnecessary for male prisoners" would not be tolerated. The Court concluded that "males and females must be treated equally unless there is a substantial reason which requires a distinction be made" (1982). Case law has established that discriminatory selection for work release when based on race, religion, gender, or even mental impairment is not an acceptable practice. Any arbitrary or capricious selection for participation in work programs has been prohibited by the courts.

Due to the small numbers of women in men's correctional facilities, services and treatment programs have appeared to have been reduced. Such reduced services included medical services. Generally, there has always been a wider range of medical services provided for male inmates than female inmates. Thus in both *Todaro v. Ward* (1977) and *Estelle v. Gamble* (1976), the issues were medical. In the former case, the medical system in the Bedford Hills Correctional Facility was found to be unconstitutionally defective, while in the latter, there was found to be deliberate indifference to the medical needs of the females. This was a violation of the Eighth Amendment.

In *Bukhari v. Huto* (1980), it was held that no justification existed for disparate treatment based on the fact that women's prisons serviced a smaller population and the cost would be greater to provide programs equivalent to the men's institutions. Cost could not be claimed as an excuse for paucity of services.

The landmark case on women's prison issues was *Glover v. Johnson* (1979). This was a comprehensive case challenging a disputed system of educational, vocational, work, and minimum security programs in the Michigan prison systems based on due process and equal protection. The Court ruled that female prisoners must be provided program opportunities on a parity with male prisoners. The case resulted in an order requiring the state to provide postsecondary education, counseling, vocational programs, and a legal education program (in companion case *Cornish v. Johnson*, 1979) as well as other relief. "Institutional size is frankly not a justification but an excuse for the kind of treatment afforded women prisoners" (Glover, 1979).

In a facility in Nassau County, New York, in the case of *Thompson et al. v. Varelas* (1985), the plaintiffs asked for

> [d]eclaratory and injunctive relief regarding the discriminatory, oppressive, degrading and dangerous conditions of . . . their confinement within the Nassau County Correctional Center. . . . [A]lleged in their action was the existence of inadequate health care, lack of private attorney visiting facilities, inadequate and unequal access to employment, recreation and training; unequal access to library facilities and newspapers, and excessive confinement; unsanitary food preparation and service; and, inadequate and unequal access to religious services.

They claimed that lack of these facilities and services violated their rights as guaranteed by the First, Fifth, Sixth, Eighth, Ninth, and Fourteenth Amendments to the Constitution of the United States, but it was not until September 1985 that a consent was entered in the *Thompson* case. *Thompson* makes a further argument for the needs of a checklist of standards against which to assess what constitutes disparate treatment in the correctional facilities.

Prior to these cases the female prisoner was the "forgotten offender." Testimony by a teacher in the *Glover* case indicated that whereas men were allowed to take shop courses, women were taught at a junior high level because the motto of those in charge was "keep it simple, these are only women."

In the twenty-first century, we find that those cases that involve sex discrimination in the correctional facilities, jails or prisons, educational and vocational programs as well as employment opportunities, the interstate transfer of inmates and visiting privileges, the courts generally held that the discrimination in such cases was unconstitutional or unlawful. However, in those cases that involve regulations such as grooming, the cases have been held not to be unconstitutional. Where we have cases regarding disparate treatment involving inmates criminally committed to a mental hospital as well as disparate treatment regarding recreational programs offered to both men and women, there is legal authority that holds such treatment to be unequal and unlawful. Most of the cases previously discussed are based on the Fourteenth Amendment to the constitution as well as its counterparts in the states.

As for example in the case of *Batton v. State Government of North Carolina* in 1980,

> the court denied the government defendants' motion for summary judgment as to the female inmates' claim that they were offered vocational training opportunities only in low-paying, dead-end, traditionally female jobs while male inmates were afforded training in a wide variety of occupations. Stating that it had to employ an intermediate level of judicial scrutiny to the inmates' equal protection claims, the court added that a parity of treatment standard provided instructive guidance for analyzing these claims. Although the court noted that the government defendants produced the results of preference polls taken of samples of the female inmate population which indicated a continuing preference for traditionally female jobs, the court stated that the polls were suspect because no systematic explanations were offered of the job characteristics of many of the occupations listed, adding that it would not assume that the survey accurately reflected the desires of the female inmates. (501 F. Supp. 1173)

Subsequently in the case of *Davie v. Wingard* (1997), the differences in the regulations that govern the length of the hair of male and female inmates, it was held that such differences were justified by much lower incidence of contraband concealment, escape, gang participation, and the violence by women inmates as compared to male inmates (958 F. Supp. 1244).

In *Klinger v. Department of Corrections* (1994), "female state prison inmates could not maintain class action against [a] prison system on the basis of an equal protection challenge to disparities between services and facilities made available to male and female prison populations, where differences between male and female institutions, such as size, average length of stay, and security levels resulted in women inmates not being similarly situated to males" (31 F.3d 727).

Still in cases that dealt with the unlawfulness of unequal treatment, in the case of *Clarkson v. Coughlin* (1995), it was held that though there may be a larger number of male deaf and hearing-impaired inmates held in state prisons, this was not a justification for the lack of availability for such services to deaf and hearing-impaired female inmates. They were also entitled to interpretive services as well as assistive communicative devices as needed as part of the normal medical and mental healthy treatment (898 F. Supp. 1019).

In an interesting decision, the Ninth Circuit Court of Appeals held (*Gerber v. Hickman*) in 2001 "as a matter of first impression that a prisoner's right to procreate survives his incarceration but was subject to restriction based on legitimate penological interests. The court found that a prison's refusing to allow a male prisoner from artificially inseminating his wife was not reasonably related to the asserted legitimate penological interest of treating men and women inmates equally to the extent possible, for purposes of determining whether the prison had violated the prisoner's due process rights. Likewise, the court also rejected the prison's asserted legitimate penological interest in avoiding liability from women prisoners asserting their equal protection rights to challenge the denial of an opportunity for artificial insemination" (2001 WL 1008205).

And interestingly, in what is somewhat of a continuance of the *Glover* case, in 1999, it was held that "apprenticeship opportunities provided to male and female inmates of state prison were sufficiently comparable and, therefore, did not constitute gender discrimination in violation of [the] equal protection clause, despite [the] fact that male inmates were offered twelve different types of apprenticeships and female inmates were offered seven types; all eligible female inmates could participate in apprenticeship, while only [a] small portion of eligible male inmates could participate" [*Glover v. Johnson*, 35 F. Supp. 1010 (E.D. Mich 1999)].

And in another issue, that of visiting privileges, it was held that whereas over 90 percent of the jail population consists of males, the county was justified in allowing more total visiting time to males than females, especially since no prisoner, male or female, could be visited for more than 15 minutes at a time. To have allowed a greater percentage of time for the public to visit would have constituted differential treatment (*Morrow v. Harwell*, 768 F.2d 619, 1985).

And so it continues.

Although litigation has provided the opportunity for inmates to have a role in altering their conditions of confinement, a judicial opinion does not necessarily bring about change, then or now. Viewed from a nonlegal perspective, litigation is simply a catalyst for change rather than an automatic mechanism for ending wrongs. All the cases held that invidious discrimination cannot exist.

REVIEW OF THE LITERATURE

The first penal institution for women opened in Indiana in 1873. By the beginning of the twentieth century, women's correctional facilities had opened in Framingham, Massachusetts, in Bedford Hills, New York, and in Clinton, New Jersey. The Federal Institution for Women in Alderson, West Virginia, opened in 1927, and the House of Detention for Women (the first separate jail for women) opened in New York City in 1931. These institutions all shared one thing in common, "traditional values, theories and practices concerning a woman's role and place in society. . . . The staffs, architectural design and programs reflected the culturally valued norms for women's behavior" (Feinman, 1986, p. 38).

Historically, disparate treatment of male and female inmates started when state penitentiaries first opened. "Female prisoners . . . were confined together in a single attic room above the institution's kitchen. [They] were supervised by the head of the kitchen below. Food was sent up to them once a day, and once a day the slop was removed. No provision was made for privacy or exercise and although the women were assigned some sewing work, for the most part they were left to their own devices in the 'tainted and sickly atmosphere'" (Rafter, 1983, p. 135). Female convicts were morally degraded to a greater extent than male convicts. The reformatories built for female prisoners "established and legitimated a tradition of deliberately providing for female prisoners treatment very different from that of males" (p. 148).

"From Lombroso to the present, criminological thought has been wrought with the sexism inherent in assuming that there exist only two distinct classes of women—those on pedestals and those in the gutter" (Lown & Snow, 1980, p. 195). "The differential law enforcement handling seems to be built into our basic attitudes toward women. The operation of such attention can be called euphemistically the chivalry factor" (Reckless, 1967).

The chivalry factor meant that women should be treated more leniently than men. The nature of treatment and programs for female inmates appears to indicate the assumption of such a theory. Theories have always abounded concerning the causes of criminality by female offenders. The chivalry factor, once accepted, does not appear to be held in favor today. Once a woman enters the correctional facility, she has not necessarily benefited from the benevolence of the criminal justice system. Theories of female crime have always emphasized the natural differences between men and women but have failed to explain why women commit the crimes they do. It is clear that female prisoners have historically been treated differently and sometimes worse than male prisoners. Often, as an alternative to differential treatment, the model followed has been that of the male prisons, which has frequently ignored the obvious physical differences of female inmates. An almost total lack of enforcement of standards exists for the confinement of women.

In addition to the historically poor quality and minimal services that have been made available to female inmates, they have continued to suffer the same miserable conditions of incarceration as those of male inmates. Women have suffered even more in the jails, because of the failure to classify them according to the seriousness of their crime. Women have always lived in crowded facilities, often finding themselves under squalid conditions, lacking privacy, faced with insensitive visiting rules, callous treatment, and the threat of, or actual, sexual abuse. Stress on the female inmate also continues to stem from being separated from her family and children.

Much of the neglect in assessing disparate treatment has been attributed by writers believing that the experiences in prison for both men and women are the same and are not areas calling for special investigation. As Rafter indicated in 1983, it was not until the 1970s that literature dealing with women's prisons began to take notice of their specialized problems (p. 130). Feinman (1982) indicated that for the most part, programs in correctional facilities for women continued to be based on the belief that "the only acceptable role for women is that of wife/mother" (p. 12). The female offender continues to be described as being poor, African-American, Hispanic, or other; undereducated; and lacking in both skills and self-confidence. Whereas nearly two-thirds of the women under probation supervision are white, nearly two-thirds of those confined in local jails and state and federal prisons are minority: black, Hispanic, and other races. The majority of the women who are incarcerated have graduated from high school. About 7 in 10 women who are in the correctional facilities have minor children. These women are reported to have an average of 2.1 children. These estimates convert into more than 1.3 million children who are the offspring of women incarcerated. Female prisoners demonstrate more difficult economic circumstances than do their male counterparts: About 4 in 10 women in state prison reported that they were employed full time prior to being arrested, while nearly 6 in 10 males had been working full time. The up-to-date figures show that about 44 percent of women who are incarcerated had been physically or sexually assaulted. About half of the women have used alcohol or drugs at the time they were caught. "About 6 in 10 women in State prisons described themselves as using drugs in the month before the offense, 5 in 10 described themselves as a daily user of drugs, and 4 in 10 were under the influence of drugs at the time of the offense" (Bureau of Justice Statistics, 2000, p. 19). In the year 1998, the highest per capita rate of women who were confined was in Oklahoma (1,222), and the lowest was in Maine and Vermont (9 in each) (p. 21). There are currently about 138,000 women confined in correctional facilities, which represents a "tripling of the number of incarcerated women between the years 1985 and 1997" (latest available figures) (p. 8).

Indications are that in the twenty-first century, more women will be involved in committing crimes than ever before. Yet when women are released back into the community, studies continue to show that men still represent a disproportionate majority in community programs. The way that community programs continue to be structured continues to provide evidence of the lack of sensitivity and the differential treatment afforded women.

Historically, the women's correctional system was not to replicate that of the men's but rather was to differ along a "number of key dimensions, including its historical development, administrative structures, some of its disciplinary techniques and the experience of inmates" (Rafter, 1983, p. 132). Today's women's facilities have changed little from those at the beginning of the twentieth century. Today, women's prisons appear to be smaller and fewer in number (Pollock-Byrne, 1990, p. 97). Characteristically women's prisons are located farther from friends and families, their numbers being relatively small compared to that of men prisoners, with the "relatively small number of women in prison and jail [being] used to 'justify' low levels of specialization in treatment and failure to segregate the more serious and mentally ill offenders from the less serious offenders" (as is done in men's prisons and jails) (p. 97).

The attitude that has persisted throughout the literature over these many years illustrates that women have been regarded as moral offenders, whereas men have continued to assert their masculinity. "[I]nstitutional incarceration needs to become more reflective of the ongoing changing social climate" (Sargent, 1984, p. 42). Most states continue to have one (in some cases, two) facilities for women, which of necessity must be of maximum security; local jails house both men and women. Population size has become a justification for ignoring the plight of women prisoners. However, as pointed out in the decision in *Glover*, size is but "an excuse for the kind of treatment afforded women prisoners" (p. 1078). The disparate treatment of female and male prisoners "is the result of habitual and stereotypic thinking rather than the following of a different set of goals for incarceration" (Lown & Snow, 1980, p. 210).

If administrators in corrections continue to assign women's corrections low priority in budget allocation, staff development, and program development, continued conflict can be expected between the needs of the correctional facilities and such treatment afforded women in this century. It may well be that because of overcrowding in both types of facilities, men's and women's equality will become less of an issue, thereby producing equally undesirable conditions for both. Regardless, disparate treatment continues to permeate correctional institutions. Adequate care and continuity in the delivery of services to all inmates is important. Standards must be applied equally. Such standards as developed over the years are meant to serve efficiency, provide greater cost-effectiveness, and establish better planning than we have at present.

According to Richie, Tsenin, and Widom (2000), "there is a common perception that the criminal behaviors of women and girls are not serious problems. Women are more likely to commit minor offenses and have historically constituted a very small proportion of the offender population. But these facts mask a trend that is beginning to attract attention. The dramatic rise in the number of prison and jail inmates is fairly well known; less so is that the ranks of women inmates are increasing much faster than are those of their male counterparts. The pace at which women are being convicted of serious offenses is picking up faster than the pace at which women are convicted" (p. 2). These researchers have asked for a redefining of justice. "Whether justice should promote unalloyed equity, be blind to the circumstances in which crime is committed, and consider only gravity of offense and prior record, is still a matter of debate. In the current sentencing environment, the view of those who favor equity above all other considerations has won the day. . . . [W]omen and girls who are caught up in the justice system enter it as a result of circumstances distinctly different from those of men, and so find themselves at a distinct disadvantage" (p. 3).

If the cases are the catalyst for change, change must occur. Words have little meaning if actions do not follow (Muraskin, 1989, p. 126).

NOTES

1. In *Craig v. Boren* (1976) it was held to "withstand [a] constitutional challenge under the equal protection clause of the Fourteenth Amendment, classification by gender must serve important governmental objectives and must be substantially related to achievement of those objectives."
2. *Weinberger v. Wisenfeld* (1975) was a case in which a widower was denied benefits for himself on the ground that survivors' benefits were allowable only to women under 42 USCS sec. 4029g: "a provision, heard, 'Mother's insurance benefits,' authorizing the payment of benefits based on the earnings of a deceased husband and father covered by the Social Security Act, to a widow who has a minor child in her care." The Court held that "(1) the sex-based distinction of 42 USCS sec. 402(g), resulting in the efforts of women workers required to make social security contributions producing less protection for their families than was produced by the efforts of men, violated the rights to equal protection under the due process clause of the Fifth, and (2) the distinction could not be justified on the basis of the 'non-contractual' character of social security benefits, or on the ground that the sex-based classification was one really designed to compensate women beneficiaries as a group for the economic difficulties confronting women who sought to support themselves and their families."
3. *Eslinger v. Thomas* (1973) was an action brought by a female law student who alleged that she was denied employment as a page because of her gender. Citing *Reed*, the Court indicated that the "Equal Protection Clause (denies) to States the power to legislate that different treatment be accorded to persons placed by a statute into different classes on the basis of criteria wholly unrelated to the objective of that statute." The Court quoted from an article by Johnson and Knapp (1971) that "on the one hand, the female is viewed as a pure, delicate and vulnerable citizen who must be protected from exposure to criminal influences; and on the other, as a brazen temptress, from whose seductive blandishments the innocent must be protected. Every woman is either Eve or Little Eva—and either way she loses." The decision of the lower court was reversed, there being no "fair and substantial 'relation between the object of the resolution' which was to combat the appearance of impropriety, and the ground of difference, which was sex."

REFERENCES

ALLEN, H. E., & SIMONSEN, C. E. (1978). *Corrections in America: An introduction* (Criminal Justice Series). Encino, CA: Glencoe.

AMERICAN CORRECTIONAL ASSOCIATION. (1985, April). *Standards for adult local detention facilities* (2nd ed.). In cooperation with the Commission on Accreditation for Corrections. Lanham, MD: Author.

ARDITI, R. R., GOLDBERG, F., JR., PETERS, J., & PHELPS, W. R. (1973). The sexual segregation of American prisons. *Yale Law Journal, 6*(82), 1229–1273.

ARON, N. (1981). Legal issues pertaining to female offenders. In N. Aron (Ed.), *Representing prisoners.* New York: Practicing Law Institute.

BELKNAP, J. (1996). *The invisible woman.* Belmont, CA: Wadsworth.

BUREAU OF JUSTICE STATISTICS. (2004a, June 30). *Prison statistics.* Retrieved from http://www.ojp. usdoj.gov/bjs

BUREAU OF JUSTICE STATISTICS. (2004b, May 27). *Nation's prison population increase largest in four years.* www.ojp.usdoj.gov/bjs

FABIAN, S. L. (1980). Women prisoners' challenge of the future. In N. Aron (Ed.), *Legal rights of prisoners.* Beverly Hills, CA: Sage.

FEINMAN, C. (1982). Sex role stereotypes and justice for women. In B. R. Price & N. J. Sokoloff (Eds.), *The criminal justice system and women* (pp. 131–139). New York: Clark Boardman.

FEINMAN, C. (1986). *Women in the criminal justice system.* New York: Praeger.

GIBSON, H. (1973). Women's prisons: Laboratories for penal reform. *Wisconsin Law Review.*

GOBERT J. J., & COHEN, N. P. (1981). *Rights of prisoners.* New York: McGraw-Hill.

GREENFELD, L. A., & SNELL, T. L. (1999). *Bureau of Justice Statistics special report, women offenders.* Washington, DC: U.S. Department of Justice.

HUNTER, S. (1984, Spring–Summer). Issues and challenges facing women's prisons in the 1980's. *Prison Journal, 64*(1).

INCIARDI, J. A. (1984). *Criminal justice.* Orlando, FL: Academic Press.

LEWIS, D. K. (1982), Female ex-offenders and community programs. *Crime and Delinquency: Rights of Prisoners*, 28.

LOWN, R. D., & SNOW, C. (1980). Women, the forgotten prisoners: *Glover v. Johnson.* In S. L. Fabian (Ed.), *Legal rights of prisoners.* Beverly Hills, CA: Sage.

MURASKIN, R. (1989). Disparity of correctional treatment: Development of a measurement instrument. Doctoral dissertation, City University of New York. *Dissertation Abstracts International.*

MURASKIN, R. (2000). *It's a crime: Women and justice.* Upper Saddle River, NJ: Prentice Hall.

POLLACK, H., & SMITH, A. B. (1978). *Civil liberties and civil rights in the United States.* St. Paul, MN: West.

POLLACK-BYRNE, J. (1990). *Women, prison and crime.* Belmont, CA: Brooks/Cole.

RAFTER, N. (1983). Prisons for women, 1790–1980. In M. Tonry & N. Morries (Eds.), *Crime and justice: An annual review of research* (Vol. 5). Chicago: University of Chicago Press.

RECKLESS, W. (1967). *The crime problem.* New York: Appleton-Century-Crofts.

RICHIE, B. E., TSENIN, K., & WIDOM, C. S. (2000, September). *Research on women and girls in the justice system.* Washington, DC: National Institute of Justice.

SARGENT, J. P. (1984, Spring–Summer). The evolution of a stereotype: Paternalism and the female inmate. *Prison Journal*, 1.

SARRI, R. (1979). Crime and the female offender. In E. S. Gomberg & V. Frank (Eds.), *Gender and disordered behavior: Sex differences in psychopathology.* New York: Brunner/Mazel.

SINGER, L. (1979). Women and the correctional process. In F. Adler & R. Simon (Eds.), *The criminality of deviant women.* Boston: Houghton Mifflin.

U.S. DEPARTMENT OF JUSTICE. (2000), http://www.ojp.usdoj.gov/bjs.pub/ascii/wo.txt

WILLIAMS, V. L., FORMBY, W. A., & WATKINS, J. C. (1982). *Introduction to criminal justice.* Albany, NY: Delmar.

WOOD, D. (1982). *Women in jail.* Milwaukee, WI: Benedict Center for Criminals.

CASES

Barefield v. Leach, Civ. Action No. 10282 (1974).

Batton v. State Government of North Carolina, Executive Branch 501 F. Supp. 1773 (1980 ED NC).

Bounds v. Smith, 430 U.S. 817 (1977).

Bukhari v. Huto, 487 F. Supp. 1162 (E.D. Va. 1980).

Canterino v. Wilson, 546 F. Supp. 174 (W.D. Ky. 1982) and 562 F. Supp. 106 (W.D. Ky. 1983).

Clarkson v. Coughlin, 898 F. Supp. 1019 (S.D.N.Y. 1995).

Cody v. Hillard, 799 F.2d 447 (1986).

Commonwealth v. Stauffer, 214 Pa. Supp. 113 (1969).

Cooper v. Morin, 49 N.Y. 2d 69 (1979), cert. denied, 446 U.S. 984 (1980).

Cornish v. Johnson, No. 77-72557 (E.D. Mich. 1979).

Craig v. Boren, 429 U.S. 190 (1976).

Davie v. Wingard, 958 F. Supp. 1244 (S.D. Ohio 1997)

Dawson v. Carberry, No. C-71-1916 (N.D. Cal. 1973).

Eslinger v. Thomas, 476 F.2d (4th Cir. 1973).

Estelle v. Gamble, 429 U.S. 97 (1976).

Gerber v. Hickman, 2001 WL 1008205 (9th Cir. 2001).

Glover v. Johnson 35 F. Supp. 2d 1010 (E.D. Mich. 1999).

Glover v. Johnson, 478 F. Supp. 1075, 1078 (1979).

Holt v. Sarver, 309 U.S. F. Supp. 362 (E.D. Ark. 1970).

Klinger v. Department of Corrections, 31 F.3d 727 (1994, CA8 Neb.).

Liberti v. York, 28 Conn. Supp. 9, 246 A.2d 106 (S. Ct. 1968).

Mary Beth G. v. City of Chicago, 723 F.2d 1263 (7th Cir. 1983).

McMurray v. Phelps, 535 F. Supp. 742 (W.D.L.A. 1982).

Molar v. Gates, 159 Cal. Rptr. 239 (4th Dist. 1979).

Morrow v. Harwell, 768 F.2d 619 (1985).

Reed v. Reed, 404 U.S. 71 (1971).

State ex rel Olson v. Maxwell, 259 N.W.2d 621 (Sup. Ct. N.D. 1977).

Thompson et al. v. Varelas, Sheriff, Nassau County et al., 81 Civ. 0184 (JM) (September 11, 1985).

Todaro v. Ward, 431 F. Supp. 1129 (S.D.N.Y. 1977).

United States ex rel Robinson v. York, 281 F. Supp. 8 (D. Conn. 1968).

Weinberger v. Wisenfeld, 420 U.S. 636, 43 L. Ed. 2d 514 (1975).

William v. Levi, Civ. Action No. Sp. 792–796 (Sup. Ct. D.C. 1976).

RELATED CASES NOT IN CHAPTER

Casey v. Lewis, 834 F. Supp. 1477 (1993, DC Ariz.) Issue of Mental Hospital Commitment.

Forts v. Malcolm, 426 F. Supp. 464 (1977, SD NY) Issue of Grooming.

Pargo v. Elliott, 894 F. Supp. (1995, S.D. Iowa) Issues of Employment, Recreation, Visiting.

Women Prisoners of District of Columbia Dept. of Corrections v. District of Columbia, 93 F.3d 910 (D.C. Cir. 1996) Issue of Employment.

30

From the Inside

Patterns of Coping and Adustment among Women in Prison

Zina T. McGee, Ebone' Joseph, Ina Allicott,
Trudy-Ann Gayle, Asha Barber, and Ashley Smith

Using a sample drawn from female jail inmates in four states, this project seeks to understand the experiences of women in jail and prisons, particularly with regard to coping with separation from children. The project examines the extent to which familial background characteristics (i.e., living situation while growing up, family history of incarceration, and parental abuse of drugs and alcohol) relate to the female inmate's own circumstances including abuse prior to incarceration, history of drug and/or alcohol abuse, and physical illness. Specific race differences regarding familial background characteristics (i.e., living situation while growing up, family history of incarceration, and parental abuse of drugs and alcohol) and/or the female inmate's own patterns of abuse prior to incarceration, history of drug and/or alcohol abuse, and physical illness are also examined. The project describes the patterns of treatment including drug/alcohol treatment, mental health counseling, medical attention, group counseling, parenting classes, and reunification counseling, and the differences that exist regarding the presence of treatment and the offender's race. Emphasis is placed on the mechanisms that the female inmates use to cope with their incarceration, and the specific factors that relate to the female inmate's use of drugs/alcohol, including prior sexual, emotional, and physical abuse. Racial differences regarding the type of drugs used prior to incarceration among the female jail inmates are explored in addition to policy implications for criminal justice processing of female inmates with children.

LITERATURE REVIEW

In the United States, rates of female arrests and subsequent incarceration are increasing. Recent figures suggest that although there are fewer female offenders than male offenders, the rate at which women are being arrested, convicted, and sentenced has steadily increased, with an estimated 1 in every 109 women in the United States under some form of correctional supervision and confinement (Masters, 2004). Over the past few years, more attention has been given to women's encounters with the criminal justice system, primarily because of the backlash of wars waged against drugs and crime, determinate sentencing, mandatory sentencing, and judicial practices, all of which continue to adversely affect women who often find themselves in dire circumstances because of their participation in low-level drug offenses (Simon & Ahn-Redding, 2005). It has been estimated that half of incarcerated females engaged in either drug or alcohol abuse at the time their offense was committed, and although they are more likely to display significant substance abuse problems, they are often less likely to receive substance abuse treatment. In other instances, substance abuse treatment may be all that is offered to women suffering from a range of other problems that often speak to the need for increased group therapy, family counseling, reunification programs, and mental health treatment. Further, issues of multicultural counseling awareness, sensitivity, and training are rarely focused on discussions of what happens to many women who will ultimately be released from jails and prisons, only to recidivate because of the lack of proper aftercare (Morton, 2004). This poses a particular problem for women offenders since many of them are more likely to have been sexually abused as children with mental health issues that were not properly diagnosed and treated prior to incarceration (Alexander, 2000). Yet, research continues to show that when handling female offenders within a correctional setting, less emphasis is placed on dealing with issues of incest, childhood sexual abuse, and neglect despite the fact that many of these women are also mothers with children under the age of 18 (Alemagno, 2001; Kristine & Myers, 2003; Kubiak, Young, Siefert, & Stewart, 2004; Sharp & Ericksen, 2003; Voorhis, Braswell, & Lester, 2004). Instead, the correctional approach continues to focus less on issues of empowerment and reunification and more on the notion that "she should have thought of her children before she committed the crime," prompting many scholars to argue that since parenting is seen as more of a privilege that must be earned, fewer programs will be developed to help women to properly reunite with their children and to assume responsibility for their lives (McGee, 2000; McGee & Baker, 2003; Morris & Wilkinson, 1995; Young, 1998). Female offenders are rarely liberated, and have been forced into subservient positions where they feel powerless and dependent. Many of them have been physically and psychologically battered by husbands and boyfriends and are devoid of the necessary skills to rebuild relationships and provide effective parenting after their release from jails and prisons. While many researchers have suggested that the female criminal is no longer a "forgotten offender" since more attention has been given to her involvement in the criminal justice system, they have also noted that the system continues to ignore the dimensions of prior experiences and trauma that often serve as precursors to her crimes (Chesney-Lind, 2002; Enos, 2001; Johnston, 1997; Pollock, 1998; Richie, 2002).

Regarding motherhood and confinement, almost 60% to 80% of all incarcerated female offenders have minor children. Most of these women have at least 2 children, and it is estimated that 1 out of 12 women are pregnant during their incarceration (Masters, 2004). Prior to their confinement, many women were either single, divorced, or separated, and the sole providers for their children. Separation from children is deemed one of the worst situations a female offender can endure as she is faced with the disintegration of her family on the outside while attempting to adjust to a new environment inadequately prepared to give her proper medical care, counseling, and mental health treatment (Enos, 2001). Moreover, she is often denied the ability to acquire parenting skills to support her children, survival training to face her reintegration into society, and the needed services to assist her with personal responsibility and independence. Studies continue to indicate that the incarceration of a mother disrupts a family more than the incarceration of a father, although only 6% of women with children have been convicted of a violent crime compared to 45% of men with children (Morton, 2004). More than half of all incarcerated mothers have reported no personal visits with their children, creating even more emotional barriers that force many women to experience diminished feelings of control and personal worth (Henriques & Manatu-Rupert, 2001; McGee & Baker, 2003). The negative consequences among children with mothers in confinement are often influenced by the age of the child at the time of the separation, the length of the mother's incarceration, the strength and resiliency of the mother–child bond, the type of crime committed by the mother, the level of family and community support, and the child's relationship with the custodian. These children, like their mothers, will experience a host of emotions such as fear, anxiety, loneliness, anger, and guilt, while researchers have also noted that the incarceration of mothers may produce similar crime patterns among their daughters in that an estimated 44% to 64% of all girls detained in the juvenile justice system have mothers who have either been arrested or incarcerated (Morton, 2004).

Richie (2002), in her assessment of the impact of mass imprisonment, suggests that the obstacles to parenting that women face are exacerbated by the fact that the separation is unexpected and fast, and when children are able to visit their mothers, they often encounter difficulties in transportation, visitor hour changes, and financial burdens, while their mothers must deal with limited communication with lawyers and less access to parole boards compared to men. The experiences of prison isolation, depression, and guilt over being separated from children continue to surface as women are faced with adverse family situations, unresolved emotions, physical illness, drug dependency, abandonment from husbands, and the frequent loss of privileges within the correctional setting. All of these factors strip them of their self-concept and self-esteem as they must participate in a series of self-degradation ceremonies involving their hygiene, clothing, appearance, day-to-day living, and most important, the loss of contact with their children. Although some women enter the system pregnant and are confronted with child custody matters, women of color remain the most impacted since their primary problem centers around drug addiction. The focus of the criminal justice system is not on the middle- to upper-income white women addicted to prescribed medications, but on the disproportionate number of lower-income women of color, African American women in particular, who abuse illegal substances (Alexander, 2000). Women are often denied comprehensive services including transition programs, alternatives to violence training, aftercare, counseling, mental health treatment, life skills training, parenting skills training, and vocational preparation, and even less emphasis is placed on specialized programs that incorporate women's victimization as part of their treatment for drug abuse and criminal behavior. Strategies for successful intervention often do not include a holistic approach, and fewer programs address the impact of domestic violence on substance abuse, a problem which is more pronounced for African American women, who are more likely to be the victims of severe husband-to-wife violence (Johnston, 1997; Morton, 2004; Pollock, 1998). Situations for these women are worsened by their poor educations, limited resources, and their location in high-crime neighborhoods. While many of their crimes are nonviolent, they are more likely to face charges of child abuse and neglect, much of which is due to the impact of race and gender oppression on addiction, which is often not addressed in counseling approaches (Henriques, 1995, 1996; McGee & Baker, 2003). This is particularly problematic since it has been suggested that the children of incarcerated women may be the next generation of prisoners without access to successful intervention programs and the necessary financial resources to escape poverty and violence.

As noted earlier, women of color remain the most impacted by increased levels of mass incarceration. These women are more often mothers of dependent children, and they are vastly overrepresented in the incarcerated female population. While they are more likely to be nonviolent offenders, they are still viewed as a threat to the moral conscience of the dominant society since they fail to meet the standards of appropriate motherhood (Sharp & Ericksen, 2003). However, what is often overlooked is that upon the release of many of these women, they are deprived of the opportunity to learn the necessary skills to fully integrate into society. They are forced to struggle with issues relating to finding permanent housing and suitable employment, regaining custody of children, and obtaining adequate services. Even less attention is placed on the need for extensive follow-up and proper case management. Richie (2002) persuasively argues that increased drug-related incarceration of disadvantaged women of color with a history of traumatic experiences is senseless and cruel, and is perpetuated by a vicious cycle that lures them into an illegal drug trade to escape abuse and support their addictions, only to be denied services upon their release because of a felony conviction. Their cases with child protective services frequently remain opened and they are more vulnerable to losing their children to foster care, producing devastating consequences for their well-being and the well-being of their children. Chesney-Lind's (2002) description of the criminal justice system's attempt to provide "vengeful equity," whereby criminal women are treated in manners similar to criminal men, is further supported here in that women with drug convictions are often prohibited from receiving welfare benefits for life. Further, minimal consideration is given to the idea that gender can often propel one into crime, particularly because of the high rates of physical and sexual abuse experienced by many women prior to the age of 18. Although the rates of prior abuse are high for both male and female offenders, men are more likely to report abuse during childhood, whereas women are more likely to report abuse both as juveniles and as adults, further supporting research linking traumatic experiences to criminal involvement among women (Chesney-Lind, 2002). Additionally, female offenders are less likely to negotiate plea reductions since their drug crimes are normally at the lowest level of the drug hierarchy. Many of the drug crimes committed by women, most of whom have small children, are not for adventurous purposes but are instead committed to self-medicate in an effort to escape a traumatic experience. This, coupled with the fact that minority women with children are more likely to be economically marginalized and disadvantaged, severely affects public policy decisions, many of which are not based on providing greater opportunities to women and effective treatment, but are instead based on a series of "get-tough policies" that only serve to further dismantle the family structure of many women confined for nonviolent offenses.

Discussions of drug abuse and incarceration among women prompted many criminologists to declare the "war on drugs" as a war on women, specifically minority women who are more likely to be lower income with limited education, and the sole providers of their children, further compelling them to a life of criminal involvement (Mann, 1995; McGee, 2000; Pollock, 1999). The changes in justice policies already discussed have increased the number of women confined for nonviolent offenses (Mumola, 2000), and although the penal system has toughened its laws on female offenders, little consideration has been given to the distinctive characteristics of the female offender when discussions of treatment programs to prevent recidivism occur. The female offender faces burdens that are interconnected by race, class, and gender; however, fewer correctional programs recognize the unique and complex issues that she encounters. Her incarceration experience is marked by the lingering effects of domestic violence, substance abuse, addiction, and sexual abuse, further prohibiting her to effectively parent and deal with the day-to-day experiences of motherhood.

Regarding the treatment of female offenders, characteristics that are important to note when developing programs further illustrate the need for gender-specific programs. When considering mental health issues, for example, studies indicate that 33% of female offenders are diagnosed with posttraumatic stress disorder, 12.2% are diagnosed with a serious mental illness, and 72% present a dual diagnosis. However, despite these statistics, many inmates report inadequate mental health treatment. Research also suggests that 45.8% of female offenders have had at least some high school education, 53.5% were unemployed prior to arrest, and 50.4% were between the ages of 25 and 34 at the time of their arrest (American Correctional Association, 1994; Madem, Swinton, & Gunn, 1994; Snell & Morton, 1990). Unlike the traditional male inmate, women bring a variety of unique health and relationship issues to the prison experience, but without understanding the many characteristics of female offenders, treatment programs cannot be appropriately tailored to address their needs.

According to the Bureau of Justice Statistics, 115,000 minor children had mothers incarcerated in state prisons in addition to 10,600 in federal prisons (Mumola, 2000). While there is limited research on the impact of separation, studies have indicated that the separation and limited mother–child contact are contributing factors to the mental health of both mother and child. The current argument is that because females comprise such a small percentage of the prison population, there is less of a need for increased funding, further perpetuating the multiple problems confronting incarcerated mothers and their children. Major barriers that exist for mothers and their children include distance and insufficient funding for treatment. A study conducted by Beck and Kernberg (2001), for example, found that on average, children of incarcerated mothers must travel 100 miles to state facilities and over 250 miles to federal facilities. More than 30% of dependent children travel over 500 miles to visit their mothers. Sharp (2003) points toward a greater need for further research on the impact of overnight visits with children in an effort to reduce the likelihood of recidivism. Effective programs designed to treat the female offender must also address all aspects of the parent–child relationship. This is particularly important since the emerging literature suggests that forced parent–child separations are extremely traumatic and the effects of parental crime, arrest, and incarceration on children are profound. Children are affected in various ways including emotionally and behaviorally as a direct result of maternal incarceration (Gabel, 1992). Following short-term separations, parents and children experience grief and a sense of loss (Johnston, 1995a). Young children who are developmentally unable to understand their mother's absence are usually affected the most. For these children, the parent's absence is perceived as voluntary. While children at these ages are particularly susceptible to "survivor's guilt" following the arrest and removal of a parent, most children of offenders report some feelings of inferiority or unworthiness and a sense of responsibility for the separation (Johnston, 1995b). Children are typically concerned with the physical well-being and safety of arrested parents. Indeed, some children believe that their parent is dead following arrest (Johnston, 1995b).

Although children experience the incarceration of a father more frequently than the incarceration of a mother, the children of incarcerated mothers are more likely to be displaced from their homes and to experience problems associated with the separation from their parent (Bloom & Steinhart, 1993). Children of female inmates suffer even more trauma since the mother is usually their primary caregiver (Fishman, 1983). Most children, especially young children, are in the primary care of their mother when she is arrested. The degree of disruption in these children's lives upon the arrest of their mothers depends largely on where they go and who takes care of them while she is incarcerated. When fathers go to jail or prison, their children's mothers typically continue to care for them (United States Department of Justice, 1993). This is less often the case when mothers are incarcerated. Mothers in state prisons report that their children are in the care of the father, while the rest report that the child is with a grandmother, another close relative, a family friend, or in a foster home or agency (U.S. Department of Justice, 1993). Children of incarcerated mothers are more likely to engage in lawbreaking behavior and are at significantly increased risk for second generation incarceration (Johnston, 1991, 1992, 1995a, 1995b). A frequently cited figure notes that children of incarcerated parents are six times more likely than their peers to be incarcerated (U.S. Department of Justice, 1993). In a sample of 100 women in a California jail, it was reported by mothers that 11.4% of children had been arrested and 10% had been incarcerated (Johnston, 1991). Incarcerated mothers in Trice's (1997) study of 229 adolescent children reported that 29% of their children had been arrested. Despite the degree of trauma these children experience and the amount of research that clearly establishes a linkage between the criminality of children and their parents, the well-being of children of incarcerated mothers is often ignored in policy discussions relating to female offending. Further, maternal health care in the prison system remains limited. Gynecological exams are not routinely performed, and nearly all correctional facilities lack programs for prenatal or postpartum treatment, prenatal nutrition, allocation for methadone treatment, educational support for childbirth and rearing, or preparation for mother–child separation. Maternal incarceration has detrimental effects on children, families, and society. Women and children affected by maternal incarceration are among the most oppressed and vulnerable populations in the United States (Luke, 2002), and maternal incarceration damages children during the developmental stages as well as the parent's overall well-being. Children are more likely to enter into the criminal justice system than their peers who do not have incarcerated parents, and a mother who is separated from her children is more likely to recidivate within a short period of time (Crawford, 2003).

In this chapter, we focus on several factors that are of concern when studying female offenders, particularly African American women. Issues central to the current study are the experiences of women in jail and prison particularly with regard to coping with separation from children. Our intent is to explore the linkage between familial history of incarceration, drug addiction, sexual abuse, mental illness, and treatment among a sample of female inmates studied over a one-year period. Special attention is paid to the degree of contact with children, prior history of substance abuse, mental illness, treatment for drug and alcohol problems, and coping with separation from children. The study uses two primary sources of information: survey data collected from 200 female inmates and in-depth interviews conducted on 20 women who were either incarcerated at the time of the interview or had been released from the correctional setting.

RESEARCH METHODOLOGY

During the fall of 2004 and the spring of 2005, surveys were conducted with 200 women incarcerated in jails in Virginia, Maryland, District of Columbia, and New York. Twenty interviews were also conducted on some of the women currently housed in the jails and a few who had been released from the correctional institution. We recruited women to the study by requesting volunteers within the female housing unit and obtaining information on other women who would be willing to address their experiences after incarceration. We specifically recruited women with children, and the study reports on a convenience sample since random sampling was not available due to considerable transition and court dates. We are unable to report on the participation rate because of the transition within the units and the anonymity of respondents. We obtained informed consent, and research assistants conducted the interviews and distributed the surveys to the women in a private setting within the jails. They also interviewed females released from prison in community centers that provided services to ex-offenders. There was no compensation provided for data collection within the jails; however, women in the community centers who were former jail inmates received $20 for each interview.

Questionnaire items examined familial background characteristics (i.e., living situation while growing up, family history of incarceration, and parental abuse of drugs and alcohol), the inmate's own situations including abuse prior to incarceration, history of drug and/or alcohol abuse, physical illness, patterns of treatment including drug/alcohol treatment, mental health counseling, medical attention, group counseling, parenting classes, and reunification counseling. Items also addressed the mechanisms that female inmates used to cope with their incarceration, particularly in instances where extended separation from children was involved. To further understand the experiences of women in jail and the manner in which they coped with being away from their children, we used a series of open-ended questions for interviews addressing how the female inmates felt about being away from home, the impact that incarceration had on their lives, the degree to which they received support in jail to assist with rehabilitation, the factors that contributed to their ability to cope while in jail, their goals in life prior to incarceration, and the dynamics of dealing with criminal justice personnel. The questions were later modified as a follow-up interview on released offenders to explore how they adjusted to life after incarceration. For this study, women receiving drug abuse and mental health treatment were compared with women who did not.

RESEARCH RESULTS

Quantitative Findings

Table 1 presents background characteristics of the female inmates in the sample. Results show that at the time of their arrest, most women were between the ages of 35 and 44 (42%), were divorced (36%), had completed high school (38%), and were employed full time (34%). Most of the women were black (55%), and a vast majority of the women had children under the age of 18 (71%). They were more likely to have been charged with drug possession (46%), followed by larceny theft (34%), fraud (22%), other offenses relating to drugs (20%), and other property offenses (10%). None of the women reported involvement in violent offenses such as murder, negligent manslaughter, and assault. The findings are

TABLE 1   Demographic Characteristics and Criminal History of Female Jail Inmates

Characteristic	%
Race/Ethnicity	
Black	55%
White	45
Age	
18–24	20%
25–34	10
35–44	42
45–54	28
Marital Status	
Married	24%
Divorced	36
Separated	5
Never Married	35
Highest Level of Education	
Some High School	29%
High School Graduate	38
Some College or More	33
Employment Status	
Employed Full Time	34%
Employed Part Time	23
Unemployed, Looking for Work	15
Unemployed, Not Looking for Work	28
Children Under 18 Years of Age	71%
Charged with Larceny/Theft	34
Charged with Fraud	22
Charged with Other Property Offenses	10
Charged with Drug Possession	46
Charged with Other Drug Offenses	20

consistent with previous studies that suggest that many of the women processed through the criminal justice system are nonviolent, first-time offenders (Crawford, 2003; Kubiak et al., 2004; Morris & Wilkinson, 1995).

Table 2 presents a description of the specific experiences of the women in jail, including information on their family background, history of abuse, relationships with their children, drug addiction, mental health status, physical health, the extent of treatment for drugs and mental illness, participation in specific programs, and patterns of coping with incarceration. Results show that most of the female offenders lived with both parents while growing up (56%), although a substantial number also lived with their mothers in single family households (34%). Fewer respondents lived in a foster home (10%), and consistent with research that has indicated generational patterns of abuse and incarceration, most reported that they had incarcerated family members (77%), while 44% reported having parents who abused drugs (Morton, 2004). Ten percent of the respondents reported having parents who were treated for mental conditions, and a large number of them reported having been physically or sexually abused before their incarceration (70%), with half of them being abused before the age of 18. Consistent with previous research that has examined the extent to which women are faced with a variety of parenting issues from concerns about their children's well-being to their level of contact with their children, the findings show that most of the respondents lived with their children before incarceration (70%), and the majority of them reported that their children were living with a grandparent during their incarceration (35%). While the mothers did report frequent contact with their children (71%), they were less likely to receive visits from their children (41%) compared to phone calls (76%) and mail (76%). This finding is supported by current studies suggesting that one of the major barriers that women face while in prison is maintaining contact with their children, particularly in terms of visitation, which has been linked to the likelihood of recidivism (Beck & Kernberg, 2001; Sharp, 2003).

Regarding substance abuse and treatment, results in Table 2 also reveal that most women had a history of prior drug or alcohol abuse (75%), were under the influence of drugs or alcohol at the time of their arrest (52%), and had committed an offense to get money for drugs (60%). Fewer women reported a history of mental illness or psychiatric condition (28%), although it should be noted that the question did not ask if they had been previously diagnosed with any type of mental disorder or mental illness. Eighteen percent of the women reported being under the influence of psychiatric medication at the time of their arrest. Regarding specific types of drugs, the majority of women reported having used marijuana (80%) and/or cocaine (65%) compared to other drugs such as heroin, stimulants, depressants, hallucinogens, antidepressants, and drugs such as crack. These figures are supported by research suggesting that women offenders with histories of substance abuse present complex clinical profiles with a range of medical, psychological, and social problems (Alemagno, 2001). However, fewer programs have assessed the specific needs of these women and have focused more on the observations of clinicians. In that regard, results from the current study show that while the majority of women have received drug or alcohol treatment at some point in their lives (62%), fewer have received mental health counseling (41%). Additionally, these women were less likely to report that they had received drug or alcohol treatment while in jail (35%) and mental health counseling while in jail (10%). Less than one-fourth of the women received a gynecological examination in jail (23%), while a small percentage reported that

TABLE 2   Profile History and Treatment Needs of Female Jail Inmates

Characteristic	%
Respondent's Living Status While Growing Up	
Both Parents	56%
Mother Only	34
Grandparents	5
Other Relatives	5
Respondent Lived in a Foster Home While Growing Up	10%
Respondent Has Had Incarcerated Family Members	77
Respondent's Parents Have Abused Drugs/Alcohol	44
Respondent's Parents Were Treated for a Mental Condition	10
Physically or Sexually Abused Prior to Incarceration	70
Physically or Sexually Abused Before the Age of 18	50
Respondent Has Been Physically Abused	60
Respondent Has Been Sexually Abused	60
Respondent Has Been Emotionally Abused	46
Respondent Lived with Children Prior to Jail	70
Children's Current Living Status	
Father	25%
Grandparent	35
Other Relative	14
Foster Home	26
Contact with Children	71%
Calls to/from Children	76
Mail to/from Children	76
Visits by Children	41
History of Prior Drug or Alcohol Abuse	75
History of Mental Illness or Psychiatric Condition	28
Under the Influence of Drugs/Alcohol at Arrest	52
Under the Influence of Psychiatric Medication at Arrest	18
Committed an Offense to Get Money for Drugs	60
Has Used Marijuana	80
Has Used Cocaine	65
Has Used Heroin	29
Has Used Stimulants	33
Has Used Depressants	36
Has Used Hallucinogens	28
Has Used Antidepressants	31

Has Used Other Drugs	10
Has Participated in Drug/Alcohol Treatment	62
Has Participated in Mental Health Counseling	41
Has Participated in Drug/Alcohol Treatment in Jail	35
Has Participated in Mental Health Counseling in Jail	10
Diagnosed with a Physical Illness	28
Treated by a Doctor in Jail for Physical Illness	18
Received a Gynecological Exam in Jail	23
Pregnant When Admitted into Jail	5
Received Gynecological Care/Prenatal Care in Jail	5
Has Participated in Individual/Group Counseling	33
Is Participating in Individual/Group Counseling in Jail	5
Has Received Prescription Medications in Jail	28
Admitted Overnight to Mental Hospital for Treatment	33
Has Been Treated for a Diagnosed Mental Condition	36
Has Been Treated for a Mental Condition in Jail	23
Has Received Counseling or Treatment for Family Issues	28
Has Received Parenting Classes	48
Family Helps with Coping in Jail	90
Friends Help with Coping in Jail	79
Child Helps with Coping in Jail	32
Counselor Helps with Coping in Jail	11
Physician Helps with Coping in Jail	11
Pastor Helps with Coping in Jail	44

they were pregnant at the time that they entered the correctional facility (5%). Few of them reported having received prenatal care while incarcerated (5%).

With reference to family counseling and treatment for mental health conditions, the findings suggest that only one-third of the women have participated in some form of individual/group counseling, with 5% reporting that they had received this type of counseling while incarcerated. Twenty-eight percent of the female inmates reported receiving prescription medications while in jail, while 33% indicated that they had been admitted overnight to a mental health facility. Fewer of the women offenders in the sample had been treated for a diagnosed mental condition (36%), had been treated for a diagnosed mental condition in jail (23%), had received family counseling or treatment (28%), and had received parenting classes (48%). It must also be noted that none of the women reported that they had participated in a family reunification program. While all of the respondents reported that they were able to use some mechanism to cope with their imprisonment, the majority of them indicated that they relied on their family to help them cope (90%), followed by their friends (79%), their pastor (44%), and their children (32%). Fewer of the women reported that they relied on a counselor (11%) or a physician (11%) to help them cope with their circumstances.

As expected, these findings have treatment policy implications. Although there has been an expansion of drug treatment opportunities, fewer women are given access to other services such as mental health counseling, family reunification, parenting classes, and group counseling. Many of these women will ultimately be released without stable housing or legal sources of income. Discussions of the treatment of released jail detainees continue to utilize a pathological framework while denying the multidimensional needs of women who have been victimized by physical abuse and drug addictions. Johnston (1997), for example, argues that the greatest risk for female inmates is their loss of parental rights, which results primarily from maternal substance abuse and the lack of reunification services for women offenders. The likelihood of mother–child reunification declines with prior maternal incarceration, and as women are arrested, convicted and incarcerated multiple times, the rates at which they will be permanently separated from their children are quickly rising, further suggesting the need to explore additional treatment options for these women beyond the traditional substance abuse programs. The needs of these women are multidimensional, and research findings continue to show that effective treatment programs should be designed to address all aspects of their incarceration and subsequent release.

Table 3 presents a description of the specific racial differences among the women in jail, including information on their family background, history of abuse, relationships with their children, drug addiction, mental health status, physical health, the extent of treatment for drugs and mental illness, participation in specific programs, and patterns of coping with incarceration. Chi-square tests of independence (χ^2) were conducted for this portion of the analysis, and the study reports all relationships that were significant at the .05 level. Results show that white women were more likely than their black counterparts to report a prior history of drug or alcohol abuse (100%), report a prior history of mental illness or psychiatric condition (40%), indicate that they were under the influence of drugs or alcohol at the time of their arrest (82%), indicate that they were under the influence of psychiatric medication at the time of their arrest (40%), and report that they committed an offense to get money to buy drugs (89%). Compared to black women, they were also more likely to indicate that at some point in their lives they had used marijuana (100%), cocaine (100%), heroin (42%), stimulants (51%), depressants (69%), hallucinogens (51%), and antidepressants (58%). However, with regard to the use of crack which was categorized as a separate drug from cocaine, black women were more likely to report usage (18%). This finding is consistent with Alexander's (2000) argument that crack cocaine has had a major impact on African American women, particularly those who maintain their own households and are currently receiving Aid to Families with Dependent Children (AFDC). In this regard, he suggests that the unique experiences of African American women are often dismissed and proposes a feminist model to examine the full context of their lives since successful intervention requires a holistic approach. Further, Alexander (2000) notes that the oppressive intersection of race, class, and gender must be examined within the context of domestic violence and addiction among females, women of color in particular. This is an issue that must be addressed by counselors in an effort to provide effective treatment.

As stated earlier, fewer of the female inmates reported participation in a variety of programs other than those addressing substance abuse. The findings in Table 3 suggest

TABLE 3   Racial Differences in Profile History and Treatment Needs of Female Jail Inmates

Characteristic	% Black	% White
History of Prior Drug or Alcohol Abuse	55%	100%
History of Mental Illness or Psychiatric Condition	18	40
Under the Influence of Drugs/Alcohol at Arrest	27	82
Under the Influence of Psychiatric Medication at Arrest	0	40
Committed an Offense to Get Money for Drugs	36	89
Has Used Marijuana	64	100
Has Used Cocaine	36	100
Has Used Heroin	18	42
Has Used Stimulants	18	51
Has Used Depressants	9	69
Has Used Hallucinogens	9	51
Has Used Antidepressants	9	58
Has Used Other Drugs	18	0
Has Participated in Mental Health Counseling	27	58
Has Participated in Drug/Alcohol Treatment in Jail	55	11
Has Participated in Mental Health Counseling in Jail	18	0
Diagnosed with a Physical Illness	18	40
Treated by a Doctor in Jail for Physical Illness	0	40
Received a Gynecological Exam in Jail	9	40
Pregnant When Admitted into Jail	9	0
Received Gynecological Care/Prenatal Care in Jail	9	0
Has Participated in Individual/Group Counseling	27	40
Is Participating in Individual/Group Counseling in Jail	0	11
Has Received Prescription Medications in Jail	18	40
Has Been Treated for a Diagnosed Mental Condition	18	58
Has Been Treated for a Mental Condition in Jail	9	40
Has Received Counseling or Treatment for Family Issues	9	51
Family Helps with Coping in Jail	80	100
Friends Help with Coping in Jail	60	100
Child Helps with Coping in Jail	50	11
Pastor Helps with Coping in Jail	30	60

specific racial differences with regard to women's participation in these programs. For example, white women were more likely than their black counterparts to report participation in mental health counseling (58%), to report being diagnosed with a physical illness (40%) and treated by a doctor (40%), to report receiving a gynecological examination in jail (40%), to report participation in individual/group counseling prior to jail (40%) and while in jail (11%), to have received prescription medications in jail (40%), to have been treated for a diagnosed mental condition prior to jail (58%) and while in jail (40%), and to have received family counseling (51%). However, results also show that a large number of black women were more likely to report participation in drug/alcohol treatment in jail (55%). Fewer reported participation in mental health counseling in jail (18%), although the percentage of participation remained higher than that of white women. Additionally, white women reported greater reliance on the following to cope with detainment: family (100%), friends (100%), and a pastor (60%). Black women were more likely to report reliance on their children (50%) in their efforts to cope with their situation. Concepts of familial bonds and kinship care among women of color are supported here, although it must also be noted that the cumulative effects of poverty, racism, and sexism experienced by many black mothers will ultimately become the experiences of their children, thus creating a new generation of youth at risk. Findings of racial differences regarding the types of treatment and services offered to female inmates are further supported by Richie's (2002) assertion that minority women continue to face collateral damage within the penal system as they are forced to bear the burden of punitive policies and extreme sentencing, only to find themselves facing another plight as they are denied effective treatment for the problems that they may experience beyond drug addictions. Their consistent lack of participation in programs such as family/individual counseling and mental health treatment is further supported by the discriminatory practices that will prevent them from achieving outcomes relating to economic independence, family reunification and reduced criminal involvement.

In an effort to examine the extent to which familial background characteristics (i.e., living situation while growing up, family history of incarceration, and parental abuse of drugs and alcohol) relate to the female inmate's own circumstances such as history of victimization prior to incarceration, history of drug and/or alcohol abuse, and physical illness, bivariate correlations were conducted and suggest that (1) a moderate association exists between prior victimization of the female inmate and having parents who abused drugs and/or alcohol ($r = .415, p < .01$); (2) a weak association exists between prior victimization of the female inmate and having grown up in a foster care setting ($r = .347, p < .01$); and (3) a negligible association exists between prior victimization of the female inmate and having parents who were incarcerated ($r = .166, p < .05$). In other words, female inmates who reported being the victim of abuse prior to their incarceration were also more likely to have grown up in a foster home, and were also more likely to have parents who had been incarcerated and had abused drugs and/or alcohol. Findings also indicate that a negligible relationship exists between the female inmate's abuse of drugs and/or alcohol and having grown up in a foster home ($r = .192, p < .01$). Those reporting abuse of drugs and/or alcohol were also more likely to report that they grew up in a foster care setting. Finally, results show that a negligible association exists between the female inmate's health status and having grown up in a foster care setting ($r = .163, p < .01$), and that a weak association exists between the female inmate's health status and having parents who abused drugs and/or alcohol ($r = .328, p < .01$). Hence, women reporting physical illness were more likely to have grown up in a foster home and were also more likely to have parents who abused drugs and/or alcohol. In order to examine race differences, a separate analysis was conducted to control for the effects of race, and with the exception of the correlation between the female inmate's illness and parental abuse of drugs and/or alcohol, all other correlations increased in value when the race variable was held constant. These findings suggest that race may be a determining factor in the association between physical illness and parental abuse of drugs and/or alcohol among female inmates in the sample. This is further supported by the contention that many minority women are almost unilaterally denied medical services and assessments that address the linkage between their family histories and their present conditions, and that programs addressing childhood events, family history and traumatic experiences would be more cost effective than incarcerating women in adulthood.

Finally, chi-square tests of independence (χ^2) were conducted to illustrate the need for services and treatment, and the extent to which limited programs can be linked to a variety of problems experienced by female inmates. Results from these analyses reveal the following:

1. Female inmates who did not participate in drug/alcohol treatment programs reported having incarcerated family members (87%).

2. Female inmates who did not participate in individual/group counseling in jail reported having incarcerated family members (86%).

3. Female inmates who did not participate in mental health counseling reported having parents who abused drugs and/or alcohol (58%).

4. Female inmates who did not participate in individual/group counseling in jail reported having parents who abused drugs and/or alcohol (49%).

5. Female inmates who did not receive family counseling or treatment reported having parents who abused drugs and/or alcohol (54%).

6. Female inmates who did not receive parenting classes reported having parents who abused drugs and/or alcohol (65%).

7. Female inmates who did not participate in drug treatment programs in jail reported being physically or sexually abused prior to incarceration (77%).

8. Female inmates who did not participate in mental health counseling in jail reported being physically or sexually abused prior to incarceration (72%).

9. Female inmates who did not participate in individual/group counseling reported being physically or sexually abused prior to incarceration (78%).

10. Female inmates who did not participate in mental health counseling in jail reported a history of prior drug or alcohol abuse (78%).

11. Female inmates who did not receive parenting classes reported a history of prior drug or alcohol abuse (90%).

12. Female inmates who did not participate in drug/alcohol treatment reported a history of mental illness or psychiatric condition (47%).

13. Female inmates who did not participate in individual/group counseling in jail reported a history of mental illness or psychiatric condition (31%).

Thus, the findings of these analyses clearly suggest that successful intervention must encompass the full context of women's lives, and programs that inadequately determine the needs of women offenders will prevent them from receiving the comprehensive services necessary to develop the whole person, one who will eventually return to her children to assume responsibility for their lives and her own.

Qualitative Findings

A variety of themes surfaced from the participants' interview responses. Among them were concerns about their children and visitation, having limited support and treatment for mental health and substance abuse, being undereducated with few resources, and facing lengthy sentences for nonviolent crimes. The voices of these women made it apparent that regardless of their race, educational status, criminal involvement, income level, and addictions, these women were still mothers. While incarcerated they remained clean and sober, giving them the opportunity to recognize the pain that they had inflicted on their children, a realization that left many of these women with feelings of shame and hopelessness. During an interview with a group of inmates at one of the jails, Mary, a 38-year-old white mother of four, said as her eyes filled with tears,

> I want to do things differently now. My kids have been adopted out, I have no contact with my children, no pictures, they took them, I can't visit them, and I'm depressed. It's a terrible, horrible experience here, the loneliness . . . being away from my family.

Mary's words represent the thoughts and feelings of many incarcerated women with children, feelings of embarrassment and helplessness, not knowing what to do, yet still knowing that something must be done. Although they were uncertain about their futures upon release, these women still held on to the hopes of reuniting with their children and having a second chance to be mothers again to their children. Mary was not alone in her thoughts as Sandra, a 34-year-old black mother of five, said in a disheartened tone,

> My older ones are angry, the younger ones are confused, two of them are in foster care, and my three-year-old baby has been adopted out. It was a nightmare, a life-changing nightmare. I didn't know I needed papers in court to keep my child; my mother had the papers, I didn't know. I'm in a deep depression, I refuse medication, there's no counseling here, and I'm making it by the grace of God.

Another participant in the same facility, Sylvia, a 50-year-old white mother of twins who has been in and out of the system for 20 years, sadly recounted her life as she explained,

> My twins are 23 now. I lost contact with them when they were 13 . . . Years later we established a relationship. . . . Well, my son, he's angry; he has no contact with me, but my daughter, she writes sometimes. I'll never do anything again. I'm alone without my family.

The voices of Mary, Sandra, and Sylvia illustrate the impact that incarceration has on children who can appropriately be characterized as the "voiceless victims." The urgency in their stories reinforces the need for programs that will embrace the mother–child bond by increasing the amount of contact and visitation among women and their children. The need for greater contact was a consistent theme that also emerged from other interviewees who expressed concern for their children and were fearful that their children would suffer from feelings of confusion, being misunderstood, anger, hurt and resentment. While there has been minimal research on the reunification process, the words of each of the women provided additional insight into the painful experiences that many incarcerated mothers encounter as they prepare to be released into a society that will immediately expect them to effectively raise their children.

In addition to the concerns of the mother–child separation, a critical component to the unique experiences of incarcerated women is the pervasive issue of lack of treatment for mental health problems and drug abuse. With conditions that have often been misdiagnosed or untreated, some of the women indicated that substance abuse was the primary factor that caused them to return to jail or prison several times. They also discussed feeling uneducated and unaware about their addictions. During additional interviews with women who had been released from prison, Vicki, a 52-year-old black woman who served time for shoplifting and drug charges, said in a raspy voice,

> Prison taught me nothing . . . it was a waste of my time, it did not treat the problem, I am now clean for 10 years because of Narcotics Anonymous (NA). My help came from learning how to deal with my disease. I was not educated on the disease . . . it made me numb . . . it made me feel good. But through NA I have learned how to deal with my problems and face them . . . prison taught me nothing!

Vicki, who has been out of the system for 11 years, also said,

> I wanted the feeling everybody else had, I used drugs to numb feelings from my abusive husband. Heroin, coke, I did it all, I had to have it! I even tried to commit suicide. The drugs weren't taking anymore, everything I did, stealing, prostitution, it was for drugs. I was worthless, penniless . . . the drugs tear you down, they make you worn out, but now . . . I'm worth more than all the gold in the world.

As Vicki spoke it became even more evident that the hopelessness that once controlled her mind and her life resulted from excessive drug abuse precipitated by domestic violence. This is supported by empirical studies, and understanding the nexus between domestic violence incidents and substance abuse is a critical factor in treating and healing the female offender. As with Vicki's circumstance, other women interviewed in jail expressed the same concerns with inadequate treatment and limited knowledge of their addictions. Felicia, a 38-year-old black mother, discussed in an angry tone her feelings toward the lack of resources within prisons and jails compared to the resources provided to male inmates. She said,

> They have courses for men here. They are cared for here. There is nothing for women . . . no parenting skills, no reunification programs, nothing. The other local jail has more programs for women but most of us are on the waiting list to get there where we could get better help.

Kathy, a 45-year-old biracial woman dealing with a shoplifting addiction, said that she found herself misdiagnosed, misunderstood, and frustrated with limited support and assistance. Only recently had her shoplifting problem been linked to severe clinical depression after several years of being arrested and detained in jails. She said,

> I am good away from home; it's a safe haven for me here. I have never abused drugs or alcohol. I was placed on antidepressants but that is not what I need. I need help with my shoplifting problem, they say I'm a kleptomaniac. They never looked at me to see what was wrong until I asked them, so I'm safe here.

The themes that emerged from the interviews with these women were consistent with the literature and supported the notion that a woman's experience in jail may be affected by the multiple dimensions of her life such as past abuse, domestic violence, separation from children, and other concerns unique to women in our society. Despite the limited research on the linkage between diminished contact with children while incarcerated and repeat offending, scholars continue to note that the issue of mother–child contact is critical to the understanding of women's criminality after incarceration. Many of the respondents reported feelings of depression, shame, and guilt, yet reported receiving no counseling to assist them with their mental health status. Many of the women also indicated that the only treatment they had received in jail was for substance abuse, and very few services had been provided to them that addressed group counseling, family reunification, mental health treatment, and postrelease counseling. Pollock (1998) contends that where there is a lack of appropriate counseling and treatment, women will never be able to experience the normal aspects of parenting because of the haze of addiction or because they have transferred their responsibilities to other family members. The findings of this research demonstrate the need for effective intervention programs that must be made accessible to women in jails and prisons if they are to reunite with their families and become successful in their efforts to become resocialized within society.

SUMMARY AND DISCUSSION OF RESULTS

The release of an incarcerated mother can be a joyous occasion, but for many mothers, it can also be characterized by extreme disappointment. Upon release, many mothers discover that their children have grown and changed in their absence. Additionally, many realize that their children have become adjusted to new settings and caretakers. Unfortunately, many mothers find their children difficult to handle. Research suggests that this occurs because some children are fearful of repeated separations from their mothers (Kristine & Myers, 2003). Additionally, many children who have been separated for a long period of time are more likely to view their mothers as weak authority figures and are unable to understand or sympathize with her situation, forcing them to act inappropriately. Research has also indicated that children of incarcerated mothers have an array of developmental problems, further suggesting the need for increasing programs that identify the multiple risks and issues of children of incarcerated women. Factors such as age during time of maternal incarceration and duration of incarceration are critical to understanding the development of children of incarcerated mothers (Trice, 1997).

Effective programs in prison can combat physical and psychological problems of women in the prison system. Presently, correctional institutions at a minimum provide legally mandated levels of medical resources and services that target only physical health concerns and not mental health concerns. The programs that are most effective include a combination of substance abuse programs, work training, parenting classes, child visitation programs, work release programs, and education and health care programs (Crawford, 2003; Luke, 2002). Women inmates also need a strong network of supportive peers and programs that also deal with experiences of child sexual abuse, domestic violence, and negative relationships with men. To effectively reduce recidivism and promote healthy life choices and environments among women in the prison systems upon release, it is imperative to address past histories of victimization while dealing with current behaviors involving drug and alcohol abuse.

Correctional rehabilitative programs must become tailored to the subjective experience of the female offender. Alexander (2000) suggests that the characteristics of promising programs for women in prison must include substance abuse awareness, empowerment with basic life skills, parenting skills, vocational and educational training, as well as relationship empowerment. Other components of effective treatment are well-trained staff, individualized and structured programs, sufficient resources, victimization services, and program participation. Because substance abuse is so prevalent among female offenders, programs for those on probation should also provide adequate childcare, which has been a significant hindrance to many women trying to meet probation requirements. When addressing substance abuse, it is equally important to note the racial and economic differences that accompany usage. Most minority and lower-income women are not addicted to legal substances, but are instead battling addictions to hard drugs such as crack-cocaine (McGee, 2000; McGee & Baker, 2003).

The findings of this research project support the contention that although there are programs that aim to treat the female offender and her addictions, there are fewer that incorporate family reunification, developing parenting skills, and counseling and treatment for mothers and their children. If the criminal justice system will not provide additional alternatives to incarceration, there must be an increase in funding for gender-specific treatment programs and greater emphasis on family-based correctional programs in order to successfully treat the female offender. The findings of this research study have clearly indicated a need for parenting programs, substance abuse treatment, mental health counseling for posttraumatic experiences, vocational/educational training, basic life skills training, and perhaps most important, programs for reuniting the mother and child and maintaining contact while she is incarcerated. Only then can we lay the foundation for treating and rehabilitating women in the "concrete womb," many of whom are forced to parent their children behind bars. Additionally, there is a dire need for the critical evaluation of existing programs to further determine what is effective, what contributes best to the reduction of recidivism, and what promotes the greatest mental health outcomes among the diverse population of women in prison and the children that they leave behind.

REFERENCES

ALEMAGNO, S. (2001). Women in jail: Is substance abuse treatment enough? *American Journal of Public Health, 91*, 798–801.

ALEXANDER, R. (2000). Counseling, treatment, and intervention methods with juvenile and adult offenders. Belmont, CA: Brooks/Cole/Thomson Learning.

AMERICAN CORRECTIONAL ASSOCIATION. (1994). The female offender: What does the future hold? Lanham, MD: St. Mary's Press.

BECK, A. J., & KERNBERG, J. C. (2001). *Prisoners at midyear 2000*. Washington, DC: U.S. Department of Justice.

BLOOM, B., & STEINHART, D. (1993). Why punish the children: A reappraisal of the children of incarcerated mothers in America. San Francisco: National Council on Crime and Delinquency.

CHESNEY-LIND, M. (2002). Imprisoning women: The unintended victims of mass imprisonment. In M. Chesney-Lind & M. Mauer (Eds.), *Invisible punishment: The collateral consequences of mass imprisonment*. New York: New Press.

CRAWFORD, J. (2003). Alternative sentencing for female inmates with children. *Corrections Today, 65*, 708–812.

ENOS, S. (2001). *Mothering from the inside: parenting in a women's prison*. Albany: State University of New York Press.

FISHMAN, S. H. (1983). Impact of incarceration on children of offenders. *Journal of Children in Contemporary Society, 15*, 89–99.

GABEL, S. (1992). Behavioral problems in sons of incarcerated or otherwise absent fathers: The issue of separation. *Family Process, 31*, 303–314.

HENRIQUES, Z. (1995). African-American women: The oppressive intersection of gender, race, and class. *Women and Criminal Justice, 7*, 56–79.

HENRIQUES, Z. (1996). Imprisoned mothers and their children separation-reunion syndrome dual impact. *Women and Criminal Justice, 8*, 77–95.

HENRIQUES, Z., & MANATU-RUPERT, N. (2001). Living on the outside: African American women before, during, and after imprisonment. *The Prison Journal, 8*, 145–163.

JOHNSTON, D. (1991). *Jailed mothers*. Pasadena, CA: Pacific Oaks Center for Children of Incarcerated Parents.

JOHNSTON, D. (1992). *Helping children of offenders through intervention programs*. Lanham, MD: American Correctional Association.

JOHNSTON, D. (1995a). Effects of parental incarceration. In K. Gabel & D. Johnston (Eds.), *Children of incarcerated parents*. Boston: Lexington Books.

JOHNSTON, D. (1995b). Parent–child visits in jail. *Children's Environments, 12*, 25–38.

JOHNSTON, D. (1997). Developing services for incarcerated mothers. In C. Blinn (Ed.), *Maternal ties: A selection of programs for female offenders*. Lanham, MD: American Correctional Association.

KRISTINE, H., & MYERS, B. (2003). The effects of secrecy and social support on behavioral problems in children of incarcerated women. *Journal of Child and Family Studies, 12*, 229–242.

KUBIAK, S. P., YOUNG, A., SIEFERT, K., & STEWART, A. (2004). Pregnant, substance abusing, and incarcerated: Exploratory study of a comprehensive approach to treatment. *Families in Society: The Journal of Contemporary Human Services, 85*, 177–198.

LUKE, K. (2002). Mitigating the ill effects of maternal incarceration on women in prison and their children. *Child Welfare, 81*, 692–702.

MADEM, A., SWINTON, M., & GUNN, J. (1994). A criminological and psychiatric survey of women serving a prison sentence. *British Journal of Criminology, 342*, 172–191.

MANN, C. R. (1995). Women of color and the criminal justice system. In B. R. Price & N. Sokoloff (Eds.), *The criminal justice system and women: Offenders, victims and workers* (2nd ed.). New York: McGraw-Hill.

MASTERS, R. E. (2004). *Counseling criminal justice offenders* (2nd ed.). Thousand Oaks, CA: Sage.

McGEE, Z. T. (2000). The pains of imprisonment: Long-term incarceration effects on women in prison. In R. Muraskin (Ed.), *It's a crime: Women and justice* (2nd ed.). Upper Saddle River, NJ: Prentice Hall.

McGee, Z. T., & Baker, S. R. (2003). Crime control policy and inequality among female offenders: Racial disparities in treatment among women on probation. In R. Muraskin (Ed.), *It's a crime: Women and justice* (3rd ed.). Upper Saddle River, NJ: Prentice Hall.

Morris, A., & Wilkinson, C. (1995). Responding to female prisoners' needs. *Prison Journal, 75,* 295–306.

Morton, J. B. (2004). *Working with women offenders in correctional institutions.* Lanham, MD: American Correctional Association.

Mumola, C. (2000). *Incarcerated parents and their children.* Washington, DC: U.S. Department of Justice.

Pollock, J. (1998). *Counseling women in prison.* Thousand Oaks, CA: Sage.

Pollock, J. (1999). *Criminal women.* Cincinnati, OH: Anderson.

Richie, B. (2002). The social impact of mass incarceration on women. In M. Chesney-Lind & M. Mauer (Eds.), *Invisible punishment: The collateral consequences of mass imprisonment.* New York: New Press.

Sharp, S. F. (2003). Mothers in prison: Issues of parent–child contact. In S. Sharp (Ed.), *The incarcerated woman: Rehabilitative programming in women's prisons.* Upper Saddle River, NJ: Prentice Hall.

Sharp, S. F., & Ericksen, M. E. (2003). Imprisoned mothers and their children. In B. H. Zaitzow & J. Thomas (Eds.), *Women in prison: Gender and social control.* Boulder, CO: Lynne Rienner.

Simon, R. J., & Ahn-Redding, H. (2005). *The crimes women commit and the punishments they receive* (3rd ed.). Lanham, MD: Lexington Books.

Snell, T., & Morton, D. (1994). *Women in prison.* Washington, DC: Bureau of Justice Statistics.

Trice, A. D. (1997). *Risk and protective factors for school and community problems for children of incarcerated women.* Paper presented at the biennial meetings of the Society for Research in Child Development, Indianapolis, IN.

United States Department of Justice. (1993). *Jail inmates.* Washington, DC: Bureau of Justice Statistics.

Voorhis, P. V., Braswell, M., & Lester, D. (2004). *Correctional counseling and rehabilitation.* Cincinnatti, OH: Anderson.

Young, D. (1998). Health status and service use among incarcerated women. *Family and Community Health, 21,* 3–19.

31

"Love Doesn't Solve All Problems"

Incarcerated Women and Their Significant Others

Theresa A. Severance

While several scholars have focused on the impact of incarceration on parent–child relationships, less is known about relationships between inmates and their significant others. The few existing studies, moreover, have been based on male inmates' experiences. Prior to incarceration, many women inmates are married or have boyfriends and live with their partners, but little is known about the nature of these relationships or the impact incarceration may have on them. Open-ended, unstructured interviews were utilized to explore such themes as whether and how partners support women while they are incarcerated, and the perceived future of these relationships. Significant others differed in their willingness and ability to support women during incarceration, but women were equally ambivalent about the decision to reunite with partners when they are released.

INTRODUCTION

This chapter explores issues concerning incarcerated women and the individuals they identify as their "significant other" (e.g., husband, boyfriend, or girlfriend). While several researchers have focused on the relationships between incarcerated parents and their children (e.g., Bloom, 1993; Hale, 1988; Hawkins, 1995), less is known about relationships with significant others. The few studies that have examined these relationships, moreover, are based on male inmates' experiences (e.g., Carlson & Cervera, 1991; Girshick, 1996; Kepford, 1994). For example, the plight of inmates' wives has been studied (Fishman, 1990; Girshick, 1996) as well as the quality and quantity of male inmates' visitation (Carlson & Cervera, 1991; Jackson, Templer, Reimer, & LeBaron, 1997).

Roughly 20% of incarcerated women are married and about 30% are separated or divorced (Greenfeld & Snell, 1999). Prior to incarceration, about 20% of women inmates resided with their spouses and children and an additional 19% lived with their spouses or boyfriends (Owen & Bloom, 1995). Statistics on marital or parental status, however, fail to capture the variety or nature of women's romantic relationships before, during, and after prison. According to Hairston (2003), researchers have been too limited in their definitions of family as they relate to inmates. By focusing almost exclusively on married couples with children (i.e., wives and children of incarcerated men) and incarcerated single mothers and their children, researchers have neglected other family arrangements, such as relationships between women inmates and their partners. As a result, we know little about the nature of these relationships, how they might relate to the experiences of imprisoned women, and the impact they may have on reintegration efforts.

It's commonly assumed that partners of female inmates will break off the relationship immediately upon her incarceration (Watterson, 1996). This belief, however, is short-sighted and fails to acknowledge the influence such relationships may have on pre-prison behavior, the likelihood that some relationships will continue after imprisonment, the possibility that some women will find new significant others while in prison, and the probability they will rekindle or seek out new relationships soon after release. Learning more about the relationships among imprisoned women and their significant others may enhance our understanding of the circumstances preceding incarceration as well as strengthen our ability to provide programs and services to prepare women for reintegration into the community and prevent future involvement in criminal activities.

SIGNIFICANT OTHERS IN CONTEXT

Research concerning postrelease experiences of male inmates suggests a strong family bond during and after incarceration is linked to lower rates of recidivism and fewer parole violations (Hairston, 1988, 1991). Maintaining a relationship during imprisonment, however, is difficult. As Hairston (2003) points out, "Couples are usually denied sexual intimacy and are unable to engage in day-to-day interactions, experiences, and sharing that sustain marital and other intimate relationships" (p. 270). Communication and contact are vital components of relationship maintenance, yet as Hairston (2003) notes, "The correctional policies and practices that govern contact between prisoners and their families often impede, rather than support, the maintenance of family ties" (p. 274), as evidenced by the rate structures of prisoner telephone systems and rules concerning visitation. Reuniting with spouses and children after prison can also prove challenging, as indicated by Rose and Clear (2003), as relationships have strained over time or former inmates and their significant others must relearn or negotiate their respective roles.

While male inmates may continue to receive support from the outside, many women in prison believe their partners will not be there when they are released (Watterson, 1996). For example, men who go to prison typically receive more visits than do their female counterparts (Girshick, 1996; Owen, 1998). Girshick (1996) attributes this disparity to differential gender socialization in which females are expected to assume and maintain caregiving and support roles. Differences in visitation are not limited to frequency of contact, however. According to Girshick (1996), men often receive visits from their wives and mothers, while women inmates' visitation is generally limited to sisters and mothers. Owen (1998) also observed that male inmates were more likely to be visited by female partners, while incarcerated women typically receive visits from family members and caretakers of their children.

Another explanation for the gendered disparity in spousal or partner support may include the personal qualities of partners. For example, the partners of women inmates are often themselves involved in criminal activity or are incarcerated (Jones, 1993; Zalba, 1964). The relationship between women inmates and their partners prior to confinement, moreover, is often characterized by abuse and exploitation (Belknap, 2001; Girshick, 1999; Sheridan, 1996). In light of this, one might suggest women are better off without their significant others and indeed might find imprisonment brings a "respite from crime-partner relationships" (Welle & Falkin, 2000). However, this view fails to address what Owen (1998) refers to as the " 'Prince Charming Myth' that a man will arrive to provide the care and support promised by the myth of motherhood" (p. 12), a recurring theme among the women she interviewed. Many incarcerated women continue to be rather traditional in their gender role beliefs and much of their self-worth and coping revolves around their relationships (Girshick, 1999; Owen, 1998). Furthermore, without adequate resources and financial and social support after release, finding a man becomes an attractive alternative to homelessness and despair (Severance, 2004).

METHOD

Participants in this study were incarcerated at the Ohio Reformatory for Women (ORW) in Marysville, Ohio. Located in a rural area northwest of Columbus, the facility opened in 1916 and houses all security levels of inmates; included on the grounds is Camp Meridian, Ohio's first female boot camp. At the time data was collect during the fall of 1998, the prison population totaled approximately 1,800 women. A total of 40 women participated in in-depth interviews, which were tape-recorded with the permission of the participants. This chapter focuses on the issues pertaining to women inmates and their significant others, though the interviews included questions regarding a wide range of inmate issues, including the impact of incarceration on their relationships with family and friends outside the institution and relationship networks among inmates.

Inmates from three different groups—admissions, general population, and pre-release—were included in the study. This strategy provided a diverse sample in terms of sentence length (ranging from 1 year to life) and sentence phase (ranging from 2 days to 12 years spent at the institution). Overall the sample included 47.5% white and 52.5% black inmates, with ages ranging from 19 to 62 years (the mean age was 34). The sample contains an overrepresentation of whites; according to the Ohio Department of Rehabilitation and Correction, the institution's end-of-month tallies for October 1998 included approximately 60% black inmates and 40% white with an approximate mean age of 34 years.

Institutional restrictions influenced the sampling strategy for each group, but all inmates were given the opportunity to select the most convenient time to be interviewed. In the rigid structure of the prison environment, the aspect of choice was believed to encourage participation by allowing participants to be interviewed if and when they chose. All potential participants were given a written project description indicating that the purpose of the study was to learn more about the experiences of women who to go prison and that this information may help develop future programs and services for women with experiences similar to their own. Written descriptions were followed by a brief oral explanation by the researcher reiterating the purpose of the study and the voluntary nature of their participation.

Inmates in pre-release were interviewed first. All inmates at ORW must complete a three-week release program prior to their release date. Pre-release classes typically include approximately 40 inmates. During the first week of a new session, the researcher attended a pre-release class. At this time the researcher presented each inmate-student with a written project description, then addressed the entire pre-release class to explain the purpose of the project and to solicit volunteers for the study. Inmates were asked to indicate on a sign-up sheet if they were interested in participating. The sheets were posted on a wall outside the pre-release coordinator's office. A total of 15 inmates from the pre-release class agreed to participate and all were included in the sample.

The size and nature of the general population required a different sampling strategy. The warden's office agreed to generate a 5% random sample of the general population, which produced a list of 83 inmates. From this list, every third inmate was called for a group meeting and given project descriptions by the researcher along with a brief presentation and the opportunity to volunteer their participation. Participants were asked to sign a sheet indicating what day and time would be most convenient for their interviews. Inmates in both Camp Meridian and solitary confinement were excluded from the sample at the administration's request for either programmatic (boot camp) or disciplinary (solitary confinement) reasons. Sixteen inmates from the general population agreed to be interviewed and all were included in the sample.

The prison's Admissions area—by inmates' accounts and the researcher's own observations—was a particularly chaotic site. This portion of the prison population was the most problematic to study, in part because inmate classification was still in progress, the limited programming meant time was less structured, and the entire Admissions population (approximately 300 inmates) was housed in two large halls within the same dormitory. The Admissions supervisor agreed to assist the researcher in recruiting volunteers, largely on the basis of convenience. Indeed, this group largely consisted of inmates who happened by while the researcher was available and seeking a participant. The researcher, however, carefully explained to each potential participant the nature of the study and noted that participation was strictly voluntary. Most of the newly admitted inmates appeared "shell-shocked" by the noise and confusion around them and seemed to welcome the chance to talk to someone who was not wearing the uniform of either a prison inmate or corrections officer. Nine interviews were conducted with newly admitted inmates.

Data collection involved open-ended unstructured interviews lasting between one-half hour and two hours. To guide the interviews, inmates were given substantive topic areas including personal background, perceptions of prison experiences, and expectations for release. Subjects were given laminated cards indicating topics to be discussed—such as "Life at ORW," "Family Outside," and "Significant Other"—and asked to begin with the topic or theme of their choice. Probes were utilized as needed to keep subjects on task and to facilitate brevity. Participants were interviewed in private rooms with only the researcher present. Institutional restrictions, however, resulted in different interview locations for each sample group. Interviews with pre-release participants were conducted in the public defenders' office directly adjacent to the pre-release classroom. General population subjects were primarily interviewed in the administrative captain's office or in a nearby conference room when the administrative captain's office was unavailable. Finally, interviews in Admissions were conducted in an administrator's office, a counselor's office, or a library, all allowing much privacy. Regardless of the physical location, no prison staff members were in a position to overhear the interviews.

The current study sought to explore several issues of importance to women inmates. While the concerns of the women in this sample may not represent those in other institutions, the information provided here may instruct future efforts. Limitations of this study relate to sample size, which was limited to 40 subjects for both temporal and practical reasons, and the selection process for participants from the Admissions group. While the sample was approximately representative of the institutional population in terms of race and age, subjects were not recruited on the basis of such characteristics. Additionally, participation in the study was strictly voluntary. The experiences of women who chose to participate in this project may be different from women who did not participate in the study.

Data analysis was rooted in the "grounded theory" approach suggested by Glaser and Strauss (1967). Interviews were transcribed verbatim in a process that occurred simultaneously with data collection. Categorization of themes developed as the interviews and resulting transcriptions were completed. Examination of interview data revealed several issues pertaining to significant others; these themes are the focus of this chapter.

FINDINGS

When asked about a significant other outside, most inmates had someone who fit the category, regardless of the particular term used to describe the relationship (e.g., husband, boyfriend, or girlfriend). Separation and solitude led many women to reflect on their relationships with their partners left behind. The significance of these individuals was threefold. First, they often played a critical part in the activities that led to incarceration. Second, significant others sometimes provided much-needed support for women while they were imprisoned. Finally, the anticipated impact of these relationships on reintegration efforts was also discussed and will be presented.

Influence

For many inmates, a male partner was a factor in the activities leading to incarceration. At times the role of the significant other was clear, as the inmate and her partner were co-defendants. Often the significant other's influence was less direct; as an enabler, he or she may have supported, or contributed to, drug and alcohol abuse preceding incarceration. Infrequently, a significant other was the victim of a woman's offense.

Co-Defendants.   Whether women and their significant others were legally found to be co-defendants, or just acted in that capacity, many women talked about their partners' direct involvement in their commitment offenses.

> I was charged with a Felony 1 and a Felony 2. I was charged with the same thing as he was and I was named co-defendant. Well, he left and I'm here. . . . It was a drug charge. [She was charged with drug possession and drug trafficking.]

I: Are you still married?

R: That's an iffy question. . . . According to the thing I have, no, we're not . . . the ladies up front [administration], they said, no, we're not. So I'm not sure. He's incarcerated too. . . . So I don't know. . . . He's my co-defendant. [She was charged with robbery.]

[My husband] is in [prison]. He's my co-defendant. . . . He has to do life without parole. [She was charged with aggravated murder.]

My fiancé. . . . He's mainly the problem that I got in trouble. My dad says if I go back with him, he'll kill him [laugh]. . . . He's also incarcerated. . . . He did a breaking and entering and he tried to get me involved in it, so I got the same time as he got.

It was myself and my co-defendant, which was my lover on the street. . . . I've been a lesbian all my life. . . . I let [a guy] stay with us. . . . He had got on drugs and him and a dope dealer got in a fight and he killed [the dealer] in my house. . . . I panicked when I came in and this is what I saw. I didn't call the police. I panicked, you know? I panicked for myself and for her. It was a year after that before he got picked up on something— some ol' bullshit charge. Then he said that this lesbian couple had killed somebody and blah, blah, blah. . . . And that's how the story goes. I ended up here and so did she.

I took a case for a man, so he wouldn't go to jail. He was supposed to be my boyfriend. . . . I thought I loved him, but I loved the fact that he would supply me with my dope. It wasn't love. . . . It was just dopin' and when I went to jail he left me for dead. When I came home, I went out and found him and told him not to leave me for dead after I just took a case for him. . . . We got into a big ol' fight and I got charged with escape because I didn't go back to the halfway house. [She was originally charged with drug possession.]

Enablers.   In many cases, a significant other was not directly implicated in the offense that led to a woman's incarceration. This did not mean, however, the individual was entirely without blame; a partner was often instrumental in drug and/or alcohol abuse associated with the offense. Many significant others, moreover, were involved in their own criminal activity. Indeed, references to a boyfriend's or husband's incarceration were common.

I'm not going to say the reason why I got high was because of him, but he played a part in me getting high because he kept using and I chose to stay with him regardless and while trying to stop him, ended up taking [drugs] myself. It's like if a person sees someone drowning and they go out in the water and they end up drowning too. Well, that's what I felt like I was doing to myself. Now that I'm in here and I'm thinking about it, I know that there ain't no sense in me setting myself up for that. . . . Being in here has made me think about this cycle that I keep going through with him. 'Cause, like I said, I usually be the strength and be the one to stop using. I be the one to turn to God because he never did. . . . I would be the one to go through rehab or get tired of using or whatever. I'm not going to repeat that same cycle. It's over. My children mean more to me than that, and God means more to me than that, and I mean more to me than that. You know, it's not worth it.

He's a big dope dealer. He just got convicted, or actually charged, with three conspiracy charges and the Feds got him for that. He's a Federal case. The only reason, I'm sure, that I wasn't brought down in that mess is because I was locked up. It helped me in the long run. I pray to God now that I'm glad I was here because there were worse things to come. [She said she robbed an old lady to get money to buy drugs.]

I got a couple of letters from [my boyfriend], but I told him if he couldn't quit doing drugs, then there wasn't no way [I would go back with him]. . . . And he made it clear that he

> wasn't ready to stop, so I had to quit . . . let him go if I wanted to try to stay out of this place.

> My other friend I know from the street, her husband and my husband were best friends. Me and my husband spent $30,000 in three weeks with her and her husband getting high.

> My first marriage was an abusive one and I was the abused. Now that I'm on my second marriage, I'm the abuser. I would go get high, get drunk, to escape so I wouldn't have to be there and look at him, talk to him. . . . Anything he would say would make me mad and I would just trash the whole house. . . . Things would be broke, laying out in the street. We would buy brand-new things every day to replace the things that I broke so that when my mom would come to the house, she wouldn't say, "Oh, what's going on. . . . You having some marital problems? Did she have another temper tantrum?"

> I had a bad influence behind me . . . a very bad influence. . . . I had a spouse. . . . I wasted so many years with him. . . . Nothing was ever there. I would go to prison, he would be out. I would be out, he would go to prison. That's how it was. . . . It was a choice to go separate ways. He was locked up, but I had a choice and that was to either keep on towards that force, or just turn my back. . . . I had to turn my back. I did better. I stayed out of here three years. . . . Even though I ended up doing something wrong. . . . I didn't keep that cycle going. . . . I had to turn my back on that relationship in order to get some strength in myself. That's sad, but that's what happened.

Victims.   Generally when a woman strikes out violently against another, the victim is an intimate (Dobash, Dobash, & Guttridge, 1986). Indeed, the victims of nearly every woman in the sample charged with a violent offense were familiar, and, usually, a partner. Some claimed these acts were in self-defense:

> It was an assault case . . . over a self-defense, though. It was self-defense. My ex-boyfriend, he just kept jumping on me. . . . We both was intoxicated. I had had enough of it and so I picked up something to defend myself and he got cut. They charged me with felonious assault.

> My charges were for voluntary manslaughter and they were related to a domestic violence case. . . . The odd thing about it was there were two people involved in my case. One was a fellow I had been living with at the time, and the other one was one of his friends. . . . We had gotten involved in a situation. . . . Unfortunately both him and the other fellow that were involved with my case both died the night of the incident.

Self-defense, however, was not always the case:

I'm here for the murder of my lesbian lover of [many] years. . . . I was in two mental hospitals previously. They let me out and [several] days later I killed her. I just lost my mind. I had had several nervous breakdowns before.

Social Support

An inmate's need for support—social, emotional, and economic—while incarcerated is well known. Significant others, however, vary in both their willingness and ability to provide assistance while a partner is in prison. While the wives and girlfriends of male inmates often maintain their caregiving and support roles, men are perceived as more reluctant to stand by while a wife or girlfriend goes to prison (Girshick, 1996). As one inmate, five months into her seven-month sentence, explained:

> I would say that [a significant other] might stick around if they are married, stay around and support them. But I'd say if you just have a boyfriend or you're coming to prison for awhile, you can say good-bye because he is gone. He's got himself another girlfriend and they're having fun somewhere. I've been married for 6 years. He's gone having fun somewhere, probably with 3 or 4 women.

The reported behaviors of several male partners were consistent with this belief. Although factors such as relationship type (husband versus boyfriend) and sentence length might influence whether partners maintain their relationships with incarcerated women, no clear pattern emerged. Even women in relatively long-term relationships and those with rather short sentences were soon abandoned by the men in their lives:

> I was seeing this guy for four and a half years before I came here. . . . Well, he sort of did a, "Oh, you're going to be doing time?" desertion thing. [She had served 6 months of a 1-year sentence.]
>
> My husband is trying to file for divorce and get me for abandonment because I am here. I haven't heard from my husband the whole time I've been here, so I don't know what's going on. The only thing I heard from him is when he called my mom and said he wanted my address. He wanted to get a hold of me so he could file for divorce. [She had served 5 months of a 7-month sentence.]

Several women were frustrated by the lack of assistance provided by partners they had supported during a period of incarceration. In several instances, the same men whom these women had supported did not respond in kind:

> [My husband] like, turned me off and on . . . if he doesn't want to be bothered . . . or if his relationship with who he's with go wrong, then he wants to be bothered. . . . It's a hurting feeling because he was once locked up too. [She had served nearly 4 years of an 8-to-15-year sentence.]
>
> I had a boyfriend. He just got out when I got locked up. He was out for like a month and a half. I called him and some other girl answered the phone and I just never called back. [She had served just over 3 years of a 1½-to-5-year sentence.]
>
> We don't communicate much because I am here and he got a little girl and got her pregnant. He don't love her. He still writes me and wants to be with me, but [he] got this other female pregnant. . . . So it made me feel so bad because I had been with him 5 years and he just go and do this. But I got to also blame myself 'cause I shouldn't have been in the predicament I was in and came here. I talked to him on Thanksgiving Day and he was doing all right. He don't do as much as he supposed to like I was there when he was in jail. [She was 8 months into a 5-to-25-year sentence.]

Perhaps anticipating the difficulty of maintaining ties with a significant other, one woman was especially pragmatic in her approach to the situation:

> When I found out I was coming to prison, there was no use to keep my boyfriend. [She was recently sentenced to 5 to 25 years.]

Abandonment by a boyfriend or husband, however, may not be an experience shared by all incarcerated women, at least in the early stages of imprisonment. Several inmates talked about boyfriends or husbands who maintained contact through phone calls, letters, and visits. A few women had partners who provided care and assistance for their children (some shared and some not) or other family members. In fact, a few male partners were described as the "only one" who had stood by as the women progressed through the criminal justice system to jail, then prison. This continued support was viewed as vital to the women's survival.

> I tell him that's what keeps me going. Other than that, I would just give up in this joint. I know once you get there, once they get you in the system, it's hell getting out. So I'm just really hoping that my out date is [soon] and hopefully even before then. [Her sentence was 7 months. At the time of the interview, she had been at the institution 17 days.]

> My boyfriend, he's the only one that's really been there, [through my] going to jail, everything. [She was 43 days into a 6-month sentence.]

> He's the one who took me downtown, because I turned myself in. Every time I call, he says, "I'll be glad when you get home, get out of that place" . . . me too. [She was 9 days into a 6-month sentence.]

> My husband has stood by me, which in 99% of the cases, they don't stand behind you. So I'm very, very lucky he's stood by me. He's been there and he's defended me and he's defended my case and he believes in me totally. I'm glad I have that support. . . . I think God knows that I can't. . . . I can't lose my support system. I couldn't make it. I feel undeserving of [my husband's] love. He says to me, "How many times do I have to show you that I'm committed to you? How many times do I have to prove myself to you? I am here. I am responsible for you and I will take care of you." And he does. [She had served 4 months of a 15-year sentence.]

When a woman goes to prison for a long time, uncertainty plagues even the most steadfast relationship. The aforementioned inmate spoke of the dedication and support her husband had given for nearly 3 years as she waited in jail for her case to be resolved, but underlying skepticism and concern about the future was revealed later in the discussion:

> He's doing what he can to save up money and get things together because he knows he has five years and there's a chance in five years that I may get out. . . . *If he's there.* I'm so lucky because there's so many women out here who, when they go to prison, their husbands leave them. And my husband's been behind me to two and a half years now. And you know, he may have to wait fifteen years. But I know he'll be there. I know he'll be the one waiting for me when I walk out those doors. He's the one who will be there. [Italics added]

Release and Reintegration

Although significant others varied in their willingness and ability to support women while they were incarcerated, the women were equally ambivalent about the decision to reunite with partners when they are released. The extent to which the other was "significant" may determine, in part, whether a woman wished to resume the relationship, especially when the relationship was deemed troublesome.

Relationships perceived as beneficial were most likely to include plans for reunification. Such relationships generally included partners who had provided support or encouragement during incarceration as well as those less involved with crime and drugs.

> I'll be getting married. He's a nice person. He's a nice guy. He helped me every step of the way. . . . He always took me back to court and everything and he said there ain't no sense in running no more. He uplifts me. When I'm down, he brings me up. We were like friends, but it's been closer than that. We've been together for 6 years.

> [I look forward to] getting back to my new-found love. So in the letters, we're going to start, like I said, try to pick up where it stopped and go on. . . . We'll be getting our house together and everything. . . . Just go on loving each other and doing for each other. . . . He's real good for me. He really is. He makes me happy. He does for me. He sees about me. He cares about me.

> I'm going to start a new relationship. I just happened to keep in touch with a real good friend of mine and since I've been here, we've gotten together and plan on getting together on the outside. . . . I'm sort of nervous about that, but he's a real nice guy. He don't do drugs. He goes to church. I'm lucky I got one that goes to church. . . . It's going to be a lot different from any other relationship I've had. . . . We eventually want to get our own place. He's got two boys and I've got two girls, so it will probably be a "Brady Bunch" scene. We've been talking about marriage, maybe later on down the line. . . . We're not just going to hop out and get married, but I have a lot of high hopes.

Life behind bars may give some women the courage and the strength to sever ties to significant others whose influence was perceived as harmful or negative. Prison may also offer an escape from an abusive relationship; for some the physical separation of imprisonment provided the safety and security needed to leave an abusive partner. In either case, several inmates claimed to have made a complete break and had no intention of reuniting with their partners:

> He wanted to get on my visitation list, but I was strong enough to tell him no, because he was not going to come visit me and abuse me—verbally abuse me. I know he wouldn't physically abuse me in front of people, but he would verbally do it and I don't need that because I am in recovery. This is about change . . . he needs help himself; he's got issues.

> I'm not going to say the reason why I got high was because of him, but he played a part in me getting high because he kept using and I chose to stay with him regardless and while trying to stop him, ended up taking [drugs] myself. It's like if a person sees someone drowning and they go out in the water and they end up drowning too. Well, that's what I felt like I was doing to myself. Now that I'm in here and I'm thinking about it, I know that there ain't no sense in me setting myself up for that. . . . Being in here has made me think about this cycle that I keep going through with him. 'Cause, like I said, I usually be the strength and be the one to go through with rehab or get tired of using or whatever. I'm not going to repeat that same cycle. It's over. My children mean more to me than that, and God means more to me than that, and I mean more to me than that. You know, it's not worth it.

> I got a couple of letters from him, but I told him if he couldn't quit doing drugs, then there wasn't no way . . . and he made it clear that he wasn't ready to stop, so I had to quit. . . . Let him go if I wanted to try to stay out of this place.

> It was for the best that I came here because he was very abusive towards me. He beat on me all the time and I was very young. . . . I was his "prized possession" as he would put it. I couldn't do anything that I wanted to. I couldn't go out with my friends. I was 18 years old and a hostage basically is what I felt like.

For many women, the future with a significant other was more ambiguous. A boyfriend's or husband's involvement in drugs and crime, a woman's long prison sentence, and changes in the inmate's own attitudes and behavior may contribute to her uncertainty about maintaining a relationship. When the problems that brought a woman to prison are intertwined with her relationship with a boyfriend or husband, the decision to reunite is often difficult. Several women seemed torn between feelings for their partner and the desire to stay out of trouble, as illustrated by the following accounts:

> [My boyfriend] said that he had been off drugs for three weeks and he planned to stay off drugs, but I haven't heard from him since, so I know he's back on drugs. But God gave me a chance, so I'm going to go back home to him and give him a chance. I already told him, "Look, this is what's going down. I'm not going home to that same old bull- shit." I'm going to give him at least two months and if he hasn't gotten himself together, I'm sorry, but I'm going to have to just go on about my business. My priority these days is to get my kids back and if he can't . . . if drugs is more important to him than the two boys I have by him, well so be it. I'm going to go on and get my life back in order. But I'm going to give him a chance to get himself together because it's like I come to the penitentiary, it's like he don't care no more.

> I'm telling [my boyfriend] it's going to take two to maintain an apartment, just the neces- sary things. We fight. I've had a lot of domestic violence charges—never convicted— but, you know, a lot of charges and I'm tired of that. I don't want to do that anymore. Being here has really made me think and calm my temperament. I've grown up. I'm sorry to say that this is maybe what it took for me to realize that life is short and I don't want to live that way anymore. I don't want to have to be constantly going to court, lay- ing out fines because I won't pay them, or didn't pay them, and doing community service.

> I talk to my boyfriend about twice a week. I don't know if he will be able to handle me now, being that I'm sober. The new me, the controlled me, I'm not as outspoken as I was.

Whether separation continues after release, however, is unclear. The emotional pull of a relationship can be difficult for some women to resist. Several inmates spoke of past relationships characterized by abuse and exploitation, and their persistent desire to help or change the men with whom they were involved. The complexities of reunification were illustrated by one inmate who described her plan to avoid moving back in with her husband when she was released:

> Well, he got the place, but like I said, I can't go there. I'm going to write some shelters and stuff like that, trying to see if I can have something set up for when I leave. With the relation- ship with him, I haven't really handled that relationship at all. But I know I'm not going to that house because I choose not to. I don't want to lie, but I'm thinking that I might have to lie to him and tell him that the court is making me stay with my family, not him because of his addiction. It might help clear the air so he don't think I'm just totally cutting him off

or whatever. Because I don't want to hurt him, but at the same time I can't hurt myself anymore.

DISCUSSION

The significant others left behind when women go to prison may affect how women adjust to incarceration, how they do their time, and the plans they make for reintegration. Simply assuming these men cease to exist upon incarceration may impede prison adjustment and rehabilitation efforts for some women. Programs and policies for women inmates should be informed by the influence of their relationships with significant others.

Even if an inmate's boyfriend or husband abandons her upon incarceration, someone else likely will assume this role when she is released. Indeed, as Girshick (1996, p. 24) states, "women's sense of self-worth and morality is embedded in social relationships," an observation supported by the following accounts:

> Before I came in here, I was the type of person that didn't really think a whole lot about myself. Never really thought I was worth much unless I could make a difference in somebody's life. . . . With the relationship that I was in, one of the reasons I stuck it out was that I thought if I could just stick it out and help him, then I will be worth something because I have a made a difference in somebody's life.

> I got involved with this guy and one thing led to another and things just got out of hand. . . . He told me that he would never get me in any kind of trouble. . . . When you're with somebody, when you live with somebody, you really trust them with your whole heart and your whole life. . . . You think you really know people, but you really don't. . . . If you can't trust somebody to take care of you and not lie to you and get in trouble. . . . Look where it got me. . . . I wasn't focusing on myself and my life. . . . I think I just didn't want to lose him. I was hoping that he'd get better, but he never did. Me thinking it and wishing it and wanting it didn't make it happen. Love doesn't solve all problems.

The attitudes and behaviors resulting from women's socialization as caregivers and companions may present unique challenges for developing effective programs and services for female inmates. Neutralizing the effects of past relationships and painful lessons learned—or not—is no easy task. As Owen (1998) noted,

> Sexual activity and motherhood are often the only bargaining chips in society available to these marginalized women. Such activity has negative consequences for their life chances. Ironically, these activities are the very things that most women are socialized to do, and the consequences, particularly the birth of children, further limit their participation in viable economic activities. (p. 12)

Programs can be developed, however, to encourage critical examination of relationship patterns and their influence on behavior. Enhancing a woman's ability to identify harmful influences and recognize them as potential "triggers" to involvement in crime and drugs may aid in her recovery efforts. Finally, society must provide support and assistance to women as they attempt to reintegrate. Empowerment strategies that prepare women to be less dependent on others and giving women the tools they need to prevail are desperately needed to ensure their success upon release.

ACKNOWLEDGMENTS

The author would like to acknowledge Dr. Joseph E. Jacoby (Bowling Green State University) for his support and suggestions, as well as the Ohio Department of Rehabilitation and Correction and the Ohio Reformatory for Women for their cooperation and assistance.

REFERENCES

BELKNAP, J. (2001). *The invisible women: Gender, crime, and justice* (2nd ed.) Belmont, CA: Wadsworth.

BLOOM, B. (1993). Incarcerated mothers and their children: Maintaining family ties. In J. A. Gondles, Jr. (Ed.), *Female offenders: Meeting the needs of a neglected population* (pp. 60–68). Baltimore: United Book Press.

CARLSON, B. E., & Cervera, N. (1991). Inmates and their families: Conjugal visits, family contact, and family functioning. *Criminal Justice and Behavior, 18*(3), 318–331.

DOBASH, R. P., EMERSON DOBASH, R., & GUTTRIDGE, S. (1986). *The imprisonment of women.* New York: Basil Blackwell.

FISHMAN, L. T. (1990). *Women at the wall.* Albany: State University of New York Press.

GIRSHICK, L. (1996). *Soledad women: Wives of prisoners speak out.* Westport, CT: Praeger.

GIRSHICK, L. (1999). *No safe haven: Stories of women in prison.* Boston: Northeastern University Press.

GLASER, B. G., & STRAUSS, A. L. (1967). *Discovery of grounded theory: Strategies for qualitative research.* Chicago: Aldine.

GREENFELD, L. A., & SNELL, T. L. (1999). *Bureau of Justice Statistics special report, women offenders.* Washington, DC: U.S. Department of Justice.

HAIRSTON, C. F. (1988). Family ties during imprisonment: Do they influence future criminal activity? *Federal Probation, 52*(1), 48–52.

HAIRSTON, C. F. (1991). Family ties during imprisonment: Important to whom and for what? *Corrective and Social Psychiatry, 22*(4), 21–27.

HAIRSTON, C. F. (2003). Prisoners and their families: Parenting issues during incarceration. In J. Travis & M. Waul (Eds.), *Prisoners once removed: The impact of incarceration and reentry on children, families, and communities* (pp. 259–282). Washington, DC: Urban Institute Press.

HALE, D. C. (1988). The impact of mothers' incarceration on the family system: Research and recommendations. In F. Hagan & M. Sussman (Eds.), *Deviance and the family* (pp. 143–154). New York: Halworth Press.

HAWKINS, R. (1995). Inmate adjustments in women's prisons. In K. C. Haas & G. P. Alpert (Eds.), *The dilemmas of corrections* (pp. 103–122). Prospect Heights, IL: Waveland.

JACKSON, P., TEMPLER, D. I., REIMER, W., & LeBARON, D. (1997). Correlates of visitation in a men's prison. *International Journal of Offender Rehabilitation, 41*(1), 79–85.

JONES, R. S. (1993). Coping with separation: Adaptive responses of women prisoners. *Women and Criminal Justice, 5*(1), 71–97.

KEPFORD, L. (1994). The familial effects of incarceration. *International Journal of Sociology and Public Policy, 14*(3/4/5), 54–90.

OWEN, B. (1998). *In the mix: Struggle and survival in a women's prison.* Albany: State University of New York Press.

OWEN, B., & BLOOM, B. (1995). Profiling women prisoners: Findings from national surveys and a California sample. *The Prison Journal, 75*(2), 165–185.

ROSE, D. R., & CLEAR, T. R. (2003). Incarceration, reentry, and social capital: Social networks in the balance. In J. Travis & M. Waul (Eds.), *Prisoners once removed: The impact of incarceration and reentry on children, families, and communities* (pp. 313–341). Washington, DC: Urban Institute Press.

SEVERANCE, T. A. (2004). Concerns and coping strategies of women inmates concerning release: "It's going to take somebody in my corner." *Journal of Offender Rehabilitation, 38*(4), 73–97.

SHERIDAN, M. J. (1996). Comparison of the life experiences and personal functioning of men and women in prison. *Families in Society, 77*(7), 423–434.

WATTERSON, K. (1996). *Women in prison: Inside the concrete womb.* Boston: Northeastern University Press.

WELLE, D., & FALKIN, G. (2000). The everyday policing of women with romantic co-defendants: An ethnographic perspective. *Women and Criminal Justice, 11*(2), 45–65.

ZALBA, S. (1964). *Women prisoners and their families.* Albany, NY: Delmar.

32

Women in Prison

Vengeful Equity

Barbara Bloom and Meda Chesney-Lind

The number of women in U.S. prisons has increased dramatically in recent decades, rising nearly sixfold since 1980. In addition, the increase in women's imprisonment has outstripped the male increase every year since the mid-1980s. As a result, women's share of the correctional population has also increased significantly. In the face of such increases, the authors question whether changes in the character of women's crime, measured either by arrest or commitment data, signal a change in the seriousness of women's offenses. A review of these data suggests a significant increase in the proportion of women with drug offenses serving time in state and federal prisons. Additionally, large numbers of women are imprisoned for property offenses.

A review of the conditions that women experience in prison suggests that they are experiencing the "worst of both worlds" correctionally. On the one hand, recent "parity"-based litigation has been deployed to justify treating women inmates the same as men—resulting in women on chain gangs and in boot camps. On the other hand, details of women's experience of prison underscore the persistence of gender as a theme in their situations both inside the prison and in their relationships with their families. Finally, the need to seek actively to reduce our nation's reliance on imprisonment as the primary response to women's crime is discussed.

In recent years, movie audiences have been entertained by Hollywood's newest construction of women, "the rampaging female" (Birch, 1994, p. 1). Films such as *Thelma and Louise*, *Fatal Attraction*, *Basic Instinct*, *Set It Off*, and *Bound*, among others, have introduced images of women—African-American and white, heterosexual and lesbian, working and middle class—seeking and apparently getting revenge, money, excitement, control, and "liberation" through criminal activity. While notions of womanhood that appear in popular culture, particularly movies, have always been problematic (Douglas, 1994; Haskell, 1973), the last two decades have seen a particular and determined focus on the lethally violent woman, who has become the "new cliché of Hollywood cinema, stabbing and shooting her way to notoriety" (Birch, 1994, p. 1; Holmlund, 1995). There is no denying the fact that women's violence fascinates the general public at the same time that it perplexes feminist scholars (White & Kowalski, 1994), but its chief attribute is its relative rarity. As an example, women killers have accounted for about 10 to 15 percent of all homicides for centuries (Holmlund, 1994, p. 131), and there is even some evidence that the number of adult women killing men actually decreased rather sharply in the last few years. One estimate of this decline is 25 percent (Holmlund, 1994, p. 131). Hollywood's female crime wave has occurred in the absence of a dramatic change in the level of women's violence or serious crime for that matter (see also Chesney-Lind, 1997). It has, however, accompanied a different change, one that may explain the need to construct women as more culpable, blameworthy, and aggressive: a dramatic increase in the number of imprisoned women.

THE NATIONAL CONTEXT: GETTING TOUGHER ON WOMEN'S CRIME

Historically, women under criminal justice supervision were correctional afterthoughts, often ignored because their numbers were extremely small in comparison to those of men under supervision (Rafter, 1990). Indeed, in the mid-1970s, only about half the states and territories had separate prisons for women, and many jurisdictions housed women inmates in male facilities or in women's facilities in other states.

This pattern shifted dramatically during the 1980s, and since then, the nation has seen the number of women in U.S. prisons increase sixfold. In 1980 there were just over 12,000 women in U.S. state and federal prisons. By 1996 there were almost 75,000 (Bureau of Justice Statistics, 1997a). Since 1985 the annual rate of growth of female prisoners averaged 11.2 percent higher than the 7.9 percent average increase in male prisoners.

Women's share of imprisonment has also increased. At the turn of the century, women were 4 percent of those imprisoned; by 1970 this had dropped to 3 percent, and women accounted for only 3.9 percent of those in prison in 1980; but by 1996, women accounted for 6.3 percent of those in prison (Bureau of Justice Statistics, 1997a, p. 6; Callahan, 1986).

California led the nation with 10,248 women in prison, followed by Texas, with 9,933, New York with 3,728, and Florida with 3,302 incarcerated women (Bureau of Justice Statistics, 1997a, p. 6). As of October 12, 1997, the number of women incarcerated in California state prisons reached over 11,000 (California Department of Corrections, 1997).

The rate of women's imprisonment is also at an historic high, increasing from a low of 6 sentenced female inmates per 100,000 women in the United States in 1925 to 51 per 100,000 in 1996 (Bureau of Justice Statistics, 1997a, p. 5; Callahan, 1986). As we shall see, the soaring increase in the imprisonment of women is not explained by changes in the character and seriousness of women's offending. In fact, despite media images of violent women offenders, the proportion of women serving sentences in state prisons for violent offenses declined from 48.9 percent in 1979 to 32.2 percent in 1991. In states such as California, which operates the two largest women's prisons in the nation, the decline is even sharper. In 1992, only 16 percent of the women admitted to the California prison system were incarcerated for violent crimes, compared to 37.2 percent in 1982 (Bloom, Chesney-Lind, & Owen, 1994).

What does explain the increase? The war on drugs has become a largely unannounced war on women, particularly women of color, and this has clearly contributed to the explosion in the women's prison population (Bloom et al., 1994). Over two decades ago (1979), 1 in 10 women in U.S. prisons was serving time for drugs. Now it is 1 out of 3 (32.8 percent), and while the intent of "get tough" policies was to rid society of drug dealers and "kingpins," over a third (35.9 percent) of the women serving sentences for drug offenses in the nation's prisons are serving time solely for "possession" (Bureau of Justice Statistics, 1988, p. 3).

Under current punishment philosophies and practices, women are also increasingly subject to criminalization of noncriminal actions and behaviors. For example, large numbers of poor and homeless women are subject to criminalization as cities across the nation pass ordinances prohibiting begging and sleeping in public places. Many of these women are mothers. Additionally, pregnant drug-addicted women are increasingly being sentenced to prison. Possibly the most dramatic targets of the war on drugs are pregnant women using illegal drugs, who are characterized as "evil women" willing to endanger the health of their unborn children in pursuit of drug-induced highs.

PROFILE OF WOMEN PRISONERS

The characteristics of U.S. women prisoners reflect a population that is triply marginalized by race, class, and gender. Imprisoned women are low income, disproportionately African-American and Latina, undereducated and unskilled with sporadic employment histories. Moreover, they are mostly young, single heads of households, with at least two children (Owen & Bloom, 1995). Women prisoners have a host of medical, psychological, and financial problems and needs. Substance abuse, compounded by poverty, unemployment, physical and mental illness, physical and sexual abuse, and homelessness, often propels women through the revolving door of the criminal justice system.

Table 1 describes the characteristics of state female inmates as follows: African-American women comprise 46 percent of women prisoners, white women 36.2 percent of women in prison, and Hispanic women 14.2 percent of women in prison. The median age of women in prison is approximately 31 years.

The majority of imprisoned women were unemployed prior to arrest (53.3 percent) and 22.7 percent had completed high school. The majority of incarcerated women were also unmarried (45 percent never married). More than three-fourths have children, two-thirds of whom are under age 18 (Bureau of Justice Statistics, 1994). The majority of the children of imprisoned mothers live with relatives, primarily grandparents. Approximately 10 percent of the children are in foster care, a group home or other agency. About 8 to 10 percent of women are pregnant when they are incarcerated (Bloom & Steinhart, 1993).

Women under criminal justice supervision frequently have histories of childhood or adult abuse. Forty-three percent of women inmates reported being physically or sexually

TABLE 1   Characteristics of Female State Prison Inmates, 1991

Characteristic	Percent
Race/origin	
White non-Hispanic	36.2%
Black non-Hispanic	46.0
Hispanic	14.2
Other	3.6
Age	
17 or younger	0.1%
18–24	16.3
25–34	50.4
35–44	25.5
45–54	6.1
55 and older	1.7
Median age	31.0%
Marital status	
Married	17.3%
Widowed	5.9
Divorced	19.1
Separated	12.5
Never married	45.1
Education	
Eighth grade or less	16.0%
Some high school	45.8
High school graduate	22.7
Some college or more	15.5
Prearrest employment	
Employed	46.7%
Full-time	35.7
Part-time	11.0
Unemployed	53.3

Note: Total number of inmates for 1991 was 38,796.

Source: Snell and Morton (1994).

abused at some time in their lives prior to incarceration. More than four in every ten women reported that they had been abused at least once before their current admission to prison (Snell & Morton, 1994, p. 5). Compared to men, imprisoned women were at least three times more likely to have been physically abused and at least six times more likely to

TABLE 2   Childhood Households of Female Inmates and Abuse Experienced before Prison, 1991

	Percent of Female Inmates
Grew up in a household with both parents present	58%
Ever lived in a foster home or institution	17
Parents or guardians abused alcohol or drugs	34
Immediate family member ever incarcerated	47
Ever physically or sexually abused	43

Source: Snell and Morton (1994).

have been sexually abused since age 18. For most women under correctional supervision, their problems began as girls; another national study of women in U.S. prisons and jails indicated that nearly half (46.7 percent) had run away as girls—and two-thirds of these women ran away more than once (American Correctional Association, 1990). Table 2 illustrates the family lives of women inmates prior to prison.

Incarcerated women use more drugs and use them more frequently than do men. About 54 percent of the women used drugs in the month before their current offense, compared to 50 percent of the men. Women prisoners are also more likely than their male counterparts to use drugs regularly (65 versus 62 percent), to have used drugs daily in the month preceding their offense (41 versus 36 percent), and to have been under the influence at the time of the offense (36 versus 31 percent). Nearly one in four female inmates reported committing their offense to get money to buy drugs, compared to one in six males (Bureau of Justice Statistics, 1994, p. 7).

The rate of HIV infection is higher for women prisoners than for men prisoners. At the end of 1995, 4.0 percent of female state prisoners were infected with HIV compared to 2.3 percent of male prisoners. From 1991 to 1995, the number of male state inmates infected with HIV increased 28 percent, while the number of female inmates infected with HIV increased at the much faster rate of 88 percent (Bureau of Justice Statistics, 1997b, p. 6).

MOTHERS BEHIND BARS

It is estimated that between 75 and 80 percent of women prisoners are mothers (Bloom & Steinhart, 1993) and that two-thirds of those who are mothers have at least one child under age 18 (Snell & Morton, 1994). A similar percentage of male prisoners, approximately 65 percent, are fathers (Bureau of Justice Statistics, 1994). When a father is incarcerated, responsibility for his children is typically assumed by their mother.

The problems facing incarcerated mothers and their children have been the focus of studies spanning more than three decades. The research has consistently shown that mothers who are prisoners face multiple obstacles in maintaining their relationships with their children. In addition to correctional systems, mothers in prison must also deal with child welfare agencies.

A mother's incarceration is more disruptive to children since mothers are frequently the primary caretakers of their children prior to incarceration. The majority of these mothers are single parents who had custody of their children (73 percent) prior to incarceration. Many of these women never see their children during the period that they are incarcerated. According to a national study (see Bloom & Steinhart, 1993), over 54 percent of the children of incarcerated mothers never visited their mothers during incarceration. For mothers who were separated from their children prior to arrest, the no-visit rate was 72 percent.

Bloom and Steinhart (1993) found that 17 percent of children whose mothers were incarcerated lived with their fathers, nearly half (47 percent) lived with their grandparents, 22 percent were with relatives or friends, and about 7 percent had been placed in foster care. Incarcerated mothers whose children are in foster care must overcome numerous obstacles to maintain their parental rights (Barry, 1995). Children are often in multiple-foster-care placements and siblings are separated, making it difficult for mothers to determine the whereabouts of their children. This situation is exacerbated when the social services caseworker does not maintain timely communication with the mother. Distance from the prison, lack of transportation, and limited economic resources on the part of the caregiver can pose barriers to regular visitation by children. This, coupled with inadequate family reunification services during incarceration and inability to meet contact requirements and statutory schedules for reunification, put many incarcerated mothers at considerable risk of losing custody of their children (Gabel & Johnston, 1995).

A mother who is incarcerated may not have access to resources such as parent education, drug treatment, counseling, and vocational training to meet the other reunification requirements commonly imposed by dependency courts. Additionally, whereas continuing contact between mother and child may be the most significant predictor of family reunification following incarceration, as mentioned previously, mothers in prison often have little or no contact with their children while incarcerated.

Although no studies have systematically examined the extent of this issue, the Center for Children of Incarcerated Parents has found that involuntary termination of parental rights occurs disproportionately among women. About 25 percent of women offenders whose children participate in the center's therapeutic programs lost their parental rights (Johnston, 1992).

The Personal Responsibility and Work Opportunity Reconciliation Act of 1996 (PRA) is likely to cause further disruption to incarcerated women and their families. For example, PRA specifically denies federal assistance to two categories of women offenders, drug felons and probation and parole violators. First, PRA imposes a lifetime ban on receiving food stamps or assistance from the federal grant for anyone convicted of a drug felony. Pregnant women can receive benefits while pregnant but not after the child is born. PRA also prohibits benefits to persons violating the conditions of probation and parole. In 1996 there were 515,600 women on probation and 79,300 on parole (Bureau of Justice Statistics, 1997a), and many of them are at high risk of technical violations due to failure to report or drug relapse. The ban does not distinguish between minor technical violations and serious violations such as committing a new crime. These provisions pose significant consequences for women in prison and their families since women incarcerated for drug offenses are the fastest-growing population in women's prisons (Katz, 1997).

CURRENT OFFENSES

Studies have consistently shown that women generally commit fewer crimes than men and that their offenses tend to be less serious. Gilfus (1992); Bloom, Chesney-Lind, and Owen (1994); and Pollock (1994) argue that women's patterns of criminal activity differ from those of men in both the type and amount of crime committed by women. Nearly half of all women in prison are currently serving a sentence for a nonviolent offense and have been convicted in the past only of nonviolent offenses (Snell & Morton, 1994, p. 1). The offenses for which women are arrested and incarcerated are primarily property and drug offenses. When women do commit acts of violence, it is most likely against a spouse or partner and in the context of self-defense (Browne, 1987; Bureau of Justice Statistics, 1994).

As noted earlier, contrary to media-spawned images of the "new violent female criminal," the proportion of women imprisoned for violent offenses continues to decline. Meanwhile, the proportion of women in prison for drug-related offenses has increased substantially. When women do commit violent offenses, they often do so in self-defense and as a response to domestic violence. Additionally, women prisoners are far more likely to kill intimates or relatives (49 percent) than strangers (21 percent), whereas men are more likely to kill strangers (50.5 percent) than intimates or relatives (35.1 percent) (Bureau of Justice Statistics, 1994). The nature of women's violence is often intertwined with their own histories and experiences of abuse, and consequently, their acts of violence take on a different significance than men's violence (Stark & Flitcraft, 1996; Websdale & Chesney-Lind, 1997).

The war on drugs, coupled with the development of new technologies for determining drug use (e.g., urinalysis), plays another less obvious role in increasing women's imprisonment. Many women parolees are being returned to prison for technical parole violations because they fail to pass random drug tests. Of the 6,000 women incarcerated in California in 1993, approximately one-third (32 percent) were imprisoned due to parole violations. In Hawaii, 55 percent of the new admissions to the Women's Community Correctional Center during a two-month period in 1991 were being returned to prison for parole violations, due largely to drug violations. Finally, in Oregon, during a one-year period (October 1992–September 1993), only 16 percent of female admissions to Oregon institutions were incarcerated for new convictions; the remainder were probation and parole violators. This pattern was not nearly so clear in male imprisonment; 48 percent of the admissions to male prisons were for new offenses (Anderson, 1994).

Nowhere has the drug war taken a larger toll than on women sentenced in federal courts. In the federal system, the passage of harsh mandatory minimums for federal crimes, coupled with new sentencing guidelines intended to "reduce race, class and other unwarranted disparities in sentencing males" (Raeder, 1993), have operated in ways that distinctly disadvantage women. They have also dramatically increased the number of women sentenced to federal institutions. In 1989, 44.5 percent of the women incarcerated in federal institutions were being held for drug offenses. Only two years later, this increased to 68 percent. Twenty years ago, nearly two-thirds of the women convicted of federal felonies were granted probation, but in 1991 only 28 percent of women were given straight probation (Raeder, 1993, p. 927). The mean time to be served by women drug offenders increased from 27 months in July 1984 to a startling 67 months in June 1990

(Raeder, 1993, p. 929). Taken together, these data explain why the number of women in federal institutions has skyrocketed since the late 1980s. In 1988, before full implementation of sentencing guidelines, women comprised 6.5 percent of those in federal institutions; by 1992 this figure had jumped to 8 percent. The number of women in federal institutions increased by 97.4 percent over a three-year period (Bureau of Justice Statistics, 1989, p. 4; 1993, p. 4).

Snell and Morton (1994) found many women are serving time in state prisons for larceny–theft. Indeed, of the women serving time for property offenses (28.7 percent of all women in prison), well over a third (36.7 percent) are serving time for larceny–theft. This compares to only 18 percent of men who are serving time for property crimes. Fraud is another significant commitment offense for women, accounting for 35 percent of women's but only 9.7 percent of men's most serious property offenses. Men serving time for property offenses are more likely to be serving time for burglary (52.4 percent).

California again gives us a closer look; over a third (34.1 percent) of women in California state prisons in 1993 were incarcerated for property offenses for which "petty theft with a prior" is the most common offense. This generally includes shoplifting and other minor theft. One women in ten in California prisons is doing time for petty theft. In total, one women in four is incarcerated in California for either drug possession or petty theft with a prior (Bloom et al., 1994, p. 3).

ARREST PATTERNS

The pattern of women's arrests provides little evidence that women's crimes are increasing in seriousness and frequency, which would, in turn, explain the dramatic increase in women's imprisonment. As an example, arrests of adult women increased by 36.5 percent between 1986 and 1995 (Federal Bureau of Investigation, 1996, p. 213). During that same period, the number of women held in state and federal prisons increased by 179 percent (Bureau of Justice Statistics, 1997a).

Most of the increase in women's arrests is accounted for by more arrests of women for nonviolent property offenses such as fraud, forgery, and theft, as well as for drug offenses. The arrest data also support the notion that the war on drugs has translated into a war on women. Between 1986 and 1995, arrests of adult women for drug abuse violations increased by 91.1 percent compared to 53.8 percent for men (Federal Bureau of Investigation [FBI], 1996, p. 213). In the last decade, arrests of women for drug offenses and other assaults have replaced fraud and disorderly conduct as the most common offenses for which women are arrested (see Table 3). Women's share of arrests for serious violent offenses went from 10.8 percent to 12.3 percent between 1983 and 1992 (FBI, 1992).

These figures, however, should not be used to support notions of dramatic increases in women's crime. As an example, while the number of adult women arrested between 1994 and 1995 did increase, it was only by 4 percent (FBI, 1996, p. 216). Turning specifically to trends in the arrests of women for Part One or "index" offenses (murder, rape, aggravated assault, robbery, burglary, larceny–theft, motor vehicle theft, and arson), these did increase by 16.2 percent (compared to an increase in male arrests of 4.5 percent) between 1986 and 1995 (FBI, 1993, p. 222). While these figures may appear to be

TABLE 3   U.S. Rank Order of Adult Male and Female Arrests, 1986 and 1995

	Male				Female			
1986 Arrests	Percent of Total	1995 Arrests	Percent of Total	1986 Arrests	Percent of Total	1995 Arrests	Percent of Total
(1) Other offenses	24.3%	(1) Other offenses	28.7%	(1) Other offenses	21.0%	(1) Other offenses	26.2%
(2) DUI	17.1	(2) DUI	11.3	(2) Larceny–theft	18.0	(2) Larceny–theft	14.5
(3) Drunkenness	9.4	(3) Drug abuse	11.0	(3) DUI	11.3	(3) Drug abuse	9.7
(4) Drug abuse	7.9	(4) Other assaults	8.8	(4) Fraud	8.4	(4) Other assault	8.1
(5) Larceny–theft	7.4	(5) Larceny–theft	6.8	(5) Drug abuse	6.8	(5) DUI	8.0

Source: Compiled from the Federal Bureau of Investigation (1996, p. 213).

dramatic, recall that this category includes larceny–theft, which some contend often involves such minor offenses that it should not be confused with serious crime (see Steffensmeier & Allan, 1995).

Moreover, looking at these offenses differently reveals, if anything, a picture of stability rather than change over the past decade. Women's share of these arrests as a proportion of all those arrested for these offenses rose from 21.8 percent to 23.4 percent between 1986 and 1995. Women's share of arrests for serious violent offenses moved from 11 percent to 15 percent during this same period (FBI, 1996, p. 213).

Overall, the increase in women's arrests is largely accounted for by more arrests of women for nonviolent property offenses such as shoplifting (larceny–theft), which was up 8.1 percent; check forgery (forgery or counterfeiting), which was up 41.9 percent; welfare fraud, which was up 13.5 percent; and most important, drug offenses, which were up 100.1 percent (FBI, 1996, p. 213). Here the increases in arrests are real, since the base numbers are large, and as a result, these offenses comprise a large portion of women's official crime. Whether they are the product of actual changes in women's behavior over the last decade or changes in law enforcement practices is an important question to which we now turn.

THE NATURE AND CAUSES OF WOMEN'S CRIME

As represented in official arrest statistics, women's crime is remarkably similar to the pattern seen in girls' arrests. Essentially, adult women have been, and continue to be, arrested for minor crimes and what might be called "deportment" offenses (prostitution, disorderly conduct, and "driving under the influence"). Their younger counterparts are arrested for essentially the same crimes, as well as status offenses (running away from home, incorrigibility, truancy, and other noncriminal offenses for which only minors can be taken into custody). Like arrests of girls, arrests of adult women have shown an increase in both aggravated and other assaults. Finally, and most important, adult women's arrests for drug offenses have surged.

Where there have been increases in women's arrests for offenses that appear to be nontraditional, as in the case of assault or drug offenses, careful examination of these trends reveals the connections between these offenses and women's place.

English (1993) approached the issue of women's crime by analyzing detailed self-report surveys that she administered to a sample of 128 females and 872 male inmates in Colorado. She examined both the participation rates and crime frequency figures for a wide array of offenses. She found few differences in the participation rates of men and women, with the exception of three property crimes. Men were more likely than women to report participation in burglary, while women were more likely than men to have participated in theft and forgery. Exploring these differences further, she found that women "lack the specific knowledge needed to carry out a burglary" (English, 1993, p. 366).

Women were far more likely than men to be involved in forgery. Follow-up research on a subsample of high-crime rate female respondents revealed that many had worked in retail establishments and therefore "knew how much time they had between stealing the checks or credit cards and having them reported" (English, 1993, p. 370). The women said that they would target strip malls, where credit cards and bank checks could be stolen easily and used in nearby retail establishments. The women reported that their high-frequency theft was motivated by a "big haul," which meant a purse with several hundred dollars in it as well as cards and checks. English concludes that women's overrepresentation in low-paying, low-status jobs increases their involvement in these property crimes (English, 1993, p. 171).

English's findings with reference to two other offenses where gender differences did not appear in participation rates are worth exploring. She found no difference in the participation rates of women and men in drug sales and assault. However, when examining these frequency data, English found that women in prison reported significantly more drug sales than men reported, but this was not because they were engaged in big-time drug selling. Instead, the high number of drug sales was a product of the fact that women's drug sales were "concentrated in the small trades (i.e., transactions of less than $10)" (English, 1993, p. 372). Because they made so little money, English found that 20 percent of the active women dealers reported 20 or more drug deals per day (English, 1993, p. 372).

A reverse of the same pattern was found when she examined women's participation in assault. Here, slightly more (27.8 percent) of women than men (23.4 percent) reported an assault in the last year. However, most of these women reported only one assault during the study period (65.4 percent) compared to only about a third of the men (37.5 percent).

In sum, English found that both women's and men's crime reflected the role played by economic disadvantage in their criminal careers. Beyond this, though, gender played an important role in shaping women's and men's response to poverty. Specifically, women's criminal careers reflect "gender difference in legitimate and illegitimate opportunity structures, in personal networks, and in family obligations" (English, 1993, p. 374).

WOMEN AND THE DRUG CONNECTION

The majority of female arrests are for drug offenses and crimes committed to support a drug habit, particularly theft and prostitution. According to Drug Use Forecasting (DUF) data, more than half of women arrestees test positive for drugs. Drug-related arrests contribute to increases in the female prison population (Bureau of Justice Statistics, 1991). Federal Bureau of Investigation (FBI) data suggest that women accounted for 20 percent of the increase in drug arrests between 1980 and 1989. From 1982 to 1991, the number of women arrested for drug offenses increased by 89 percent, compared with an increase of 51 percent for men during the same period (Mauer & Huling, 1995).

Studies show that women are more likely to use drugs, use more serious drugs more frequently, and are more likely than men to be under the influence of drugs at the time of their offenses (Bureau of Justice Statistics, 1991, 1992). Although it is commonly assumed that women addicts will probably engage in prostitution to support their drug habits, their involvement in property crimes is even more common. In their sample of 197 female crack/cocaine users in Miami, Inciardi, Lockwood, and Pottieger (1993) found that in the women's last 90 days on the street, 76 percent engaged in drug-related offenses, 77 percent committed minor property crimes, and 51 percent engaged in prostitution (p. 120). The reliance on prostitution to support drug habits was also not confirmed in Anglin and Hser's sample (1987). According to the FBI, arrests for prostitution decreased between 1983 and 1992 (FBI, 1993). Anglin and Hser (1987) found that the women in their sample supported their habits with a variety of crimes, in addition to property crimes, to raise money. Although theft is the crime of choice for women drug users, the researchers found that drug dealing was one of the criminal activities in which their respondents engaged (p. 393).

Data from state and federal court convictions also suggest that women are being arrested, convicted, and sentenced to prison for drug and property crimes but that both crime categories appear to be related to drug use. Felony conviction data for most serious offenses from state courts in 1990 illustrate that the highest percentage of women were convicted of fraud, which includes forgery and embezzlement (38 percent), followed by drug possession (17 percent) and trafficking (15 percent) (Maguire, Pastore, & Flanagan, 1993, p. 528). In terms of the numbers of offenders sentenced in the federal courts in 1992 under the U.S. Sentencing Commission Guidelines, the largest numerical category for females was drug offenses.

SENTENCE LENGTH AND TIME SERVED

Because female prisoners tend to receive shorter sentences than men overall, it has been assumed that women benefit from chivalrous treatment by sentencing judges. Recent research and available data suggest that shorter sentences for women are in fact a result in gender differences in the offenses for which women are incarcerated, criminal histories, and crime roles. On average, women incarcerated in state prisons in 1991 had fewer previous convictions than men, and their record of past convictions was less violent. Women were more likely than men to be in prison for drug and property offenses, and less likely than men to be incarcerated for violent offenses (Mauer & Huling, 1995).

The Bureau of Justice Statistics (1991, 1994) provides some information on time served and sentence length. Overall, average time served for those released in 1986 was 16 months. Violent offenders served an average of 27 months, with property offenders serving about 13 months on average and drug offenders serving around 14 months. In the 1991 sample, women received somewhat shorter maximum sentences than men, with half of the female prisoners serving a sentence of 60 months or less versus half of the men serving a sentence of 120 months or less. Twenty-four percent of the female prison population received sentences of less than 36 months. For women's drug offenses, the median sentence received was 54 months (with a mean of 79 months); property offenders received a median sentence of 44 months (with a mean of 74 months); and violent offenders received a median sentence of 180 months (mean 178 months). For all female prisoners, the median sentence received was 60 months, with a mean of 105 months (Bureau of Justice Statistics, 1994).

RACE, CLASS, AND GENDER DISPARITIES

Contemporary feminist theorists argue for the integration of race, class, and gender in any analytic framework used to study the experiences of women in the criminal justice system. Without such a framework it is impossible to draw a truly accurate picture of their experiences.

Only a few research efforts, however, have focused on the combined effects of race, class, and gender disparities among women in the criminal justice system. The stark realities of race, class, and gender discrimination touch the lives of all women and appear throughout the criminal justice process. Racial bias is a factor in arrests, pretrial treatment, and differential sentencing of women offenders. Women of color are disproportionately incarcerated in the United States. African-American women are incarcerated at a rate seven times that of white women (143 versus 20 per 10,000), and women of color represent more than 60 percent of the adult women in state and federal prisons nationwide (American Correctional Association, 1990). Women of color are also disproportionately represented on the death rows of this country relative to their proportion in the general population.

Mann (1995) documents disproportionality in prison sentences by comparing arrest rates with sentencing rates of women offenders in three states, California, Florida, and New York. She found that in all three states, women of color, particularly African-Americans, were disproportionately arrested. Mann asserts that women of color face double discrimination because of their gender and race/ethnicity. When class level is included, these women often face triple jeopardy.

A recent review of the literature addressing differential sentencing of African-American women and men notes the dearth of research on the possible interactive effects of gender and ethnicity and the inconclusiveness of the available information on the influence of race and ethnicity on criminal justice dispositions (Odubekun, 1992). The few studies that do report race-specific gender differences indicate more punitive treatment of women of color.

Foley and Rasche (1979) found that African-American women received longer sentences (55.1 months) than white women (52.5 months) in their study of one Missouri institution over a 16-year period. When the same offense was committed, Foley and Rasche found differences based on race. For example, white women imprisoned for murder served one-third less time than African-American women incarcerated for the same offense.

According to Mann (1989), in 1979, 32 percent of the women arrested and sentenced to prison in California were African-American, 14.9 percent were Hispanic, 0.8 percent were Native American, and 52.4 percent were white. By 1990, felony prosecutions of women of color in California had increased to 34.4 percent for African-Americans, 19 percent for Hispanics, and 2.5 percent for other women of color; prosecutions of white female felons had decreased to 43.8 percent. California female convictions in 1990 were fairly consistent across racial and ethnic subgroups.

In a study of sentencing outcomes for 1034 female defendants processed in a northern California county between 1972 and 1976, Kruttschnitt (1980–1981, p. 256) reports that in three of the five offense categories studied, a defendant's race or income affected her sentence. "Specifically, African-American women convicted of either disturbing the peace or drug law violations are sentenced more severely than their white counterparts."

In a study of gender differences in felony court processing in California in 1988, Farnsworth and Teske (1995) found that white women defendants were more likely to have charges of assault changed to nonassault than were women of color. Also, class and race often come together, as defendants are often African-American or Latina, and poor. Similar to arrest figures, sentencing statistics may also reflect the race and gender bias that occurred in the earlier decision-making stages of the criminal justice process.

THE WAR ON DRUGS: A WAR ON WOMEN OF COLOR

The declared intention to get rid of drugs and drug-related crime has resulted in federal and state funding being allocated for more police officers on the streets, more federal law enforcement officers, and the building of more jails and prisons rather than funds for prevention, education, and treatment. Poor women of color have become the main victims of these efforts in two ways. As mothers, sisters, daughters, and partners, they are trying to hold their families and communities together while so many men of color are incarcerated, and in addition, they are increasingly imprisoned themselves.

The incarceration of women of color, especially African-Americans, is a key factor in the increase in the number of women in prison. Women serving sentences for possession and possession for sale constitute the majority of women in prison for drug offenses.

According to a recent study by the Sentencing Project, from 1989 to 1994, young African-American women experienced the greatest increase in criminal justice control of all demographic groups studied. The 78 percent increase in criminal justice control rates for black women was more than double the increase for black men and for white women, and more than nine times the increase for white men (Mauer & Huling, 1995). Nationally, between 1980 and 1992 the number of black females in state or federal prisons grew 278 percent while the number of black males grew 186 percent; overall, the inmate population increased by 168 percent (Mauer & Huling, 1995).

Mauer and Huling (1995) present compelling evidence to support their contention that much of this increase can be laid at the door of the war on drugs, which many now

TABLE 4   State Prisoners Incarcerated for Drug Offenses by Race or Ethnic Origin and Gender, 1986 and 1991

	1986		1991		Percent Increase	
	Male	Female	Male	Female	Male	Female
White (non-Hispanic)	12,868	969	26,452	3,300	106%	241%
Black(non-Hispanic)	13,974	667	73,932	6,193	429	828
Hispanic	8,484	664	35,965	2,843	324	328
Other	604	70	1,323	297	119	324
Total	35,930	2,370	137,672	12,633	283	433%

Source: Mauer and Huling (1995).

assert has become a war on women, particularly women of color. Their analysis of Justice Department data shows that between 1986 and 1991, the number of black non-Hispanic women in state prisons for drug offenses nationwide increased more than eightfold, from 667 to 6,193. This 828 percent increase was nearly double the increase for black non-Hispanic males and more than triple the increase for white females (see Table 4).

"EQUALITY WITH A VENGEANCE": IS EQUAL TREATMENT FAIR TREATMENT?

Pollock (1994) asks if women are receiving more equal treatment in the criminal justice system today. If equal treatment relates to equal incarceration, the answer appears to be a resounding yes. It is certainly true that many more women offenders are likely to be incarcerated than at any other time in U.S. history. The criminal justice system appears to be more willing to incarcerate women.

There is a continuing debate among feminist legal scholars about whether equality under the law is necessarily good for women. To recap this debate (see Chesney-Lind & Pollock-Byrne, 1995, for a full discussion), some feminist legal scholars argue that the only way to eliminate the discriminatory treatment and oppression that women have experienced in the past is to push for continued equalization under the law, that is, to champion equal rights amendments and to oppose any legislation that treats men and women differently. It is argued that while equal treatment may hurt women in the short run, in the long run it is the only way to guarantee that women will ever be treated as equal partners in economic and social realms. For example, MacKinnon (1987, pp. 38–39) states: "For women to affirm difference, when difference means dominance, as it does with gender, means to affirm the qualities and characteristics of powerlessness." Even those who do not view the experience of women as one of oppression conclude that women will be victimized by laws created from "concern and affection" that are designed to protect them (Kirp, Yudof, & Franks, 1986).

The opposing argument maintains that women are not the same as men and that because it is a male standard that equality is measured against, women will always lose. Therefore, the position calls for recognizing the differential or "special" needs of women. This would mean that women and men might receive differential treatment as long as it did not put women in a more negative position than the absence of such a standard.

Yet another position points out that both the equal treatment and special needs approaches accept the domination of male definitions. For example, equality is defined as rights equal to those of males, and differential needs are defined as needs different from those of males. In these cases, women are the "other" under the law; the "bottom line" is a male one (Smart, 1989). Eisenstein (1988) writes: "Difference in this instance is set up as a duality: woman is different from man and this difference is seen as a deficiency because she is not man" (p. 8).

While these scholars are identifying the limitations of an equal-treatment model in law or in research in legal practices, that model and the evidence on which it is based are the centerpiece for sentencing reforms throughout the United States. These gender-neutral sentencing reforms aim to reduce sentencing disparity by punishing like crimes in the same way. By emphasizing parity, and then utilizing a male standard, more women are losing their freedom (Daly, 1994).

PRISONS AND PARITY

Initially, the differential needs approach was the dominant correctional policy. From the outset, the correctional response to women offenders was to embrace the Victorian notion of "separate spheres" and to construct and manage women's facilities based on what were seen as immutable differences between men and women (Rafter, 1990; Singer, 1973). Women were housed in separate facilities, and programs for women prisoners represented their perceived role in society. Thus they were taught to be good mothers and housekeepers; vocational education to prepare for employment was slighted in favor of domestic training. Women were hired to supervise female prisoners in the belief that only they could provide for the special needs of women prisoners and serve as role models to them. To some degree, this legacy still permeates women's prisons.

Sentencing practices also treated women and men differently. Women typically were much less likely to be imprisoned unless the woman offender did not fit the stereotypical female role; for example, she was a bad mother or did not have a family to care for (Chesney-Lind, 1987; Eaton, 1986).

The differential treatment of women in sentencing and prison programming was challenged by an emerging "parity" perspective during the 1970s. As a result of prisoner rights' litigation based on the parity model (see Pollock-Byrne, 1990), women offenders are being swept up in a system that seems bent on treating women "equally." This equity orientation translated into treatment of women prisoners as if they were men. Since this orientation did not change the role of gender in prison life or corrections, women prisoners receive the worst of both worlds.

For example, boot camps have become very popular as an alternative to prison for juvenile and adult offenders. New York operates a boot camp for women that is modeled on boot camps for men. This includes uniforms, short hair, humiliation for disrespect of staff, and other militaristic approaches.

Chain gangs for women have also become fashionable. In Alabama, male chain gangs were reinstated and corrections officials in that state were threatened with a lawsuit brought by male prisoners suggesting that the practice of excluding women from chain gangs was unconstitutional. The response from the Alabama Corrections Commissioner was to include women in chain gangs (Franklin, 1996). The corrections commissioner was ultimately forced to resign, but the debate about the value of male chain gangs continues in the state.

A serious and persistent allegation that has been associated with women's imprisonment is sexual abuse of women inmates at the hands of male correctional officers. The sexual victimization of women in U.S. prisons is the subject of increasing news coverage and, more recently, international scrutiny. Scandals have erupted in Georgia, Hawaii, California, Ohio, Louisiana, Michigan, Tennessee, New York, and New Mexico (Craig, 1996; Curriden, 1993; Lopez, 1993; Meyer, 1992; Sewenely, 1993; Stein, 1996; Watson, 1992). This issue is of such concern that it has attracted the attention of organizations such as Human Rights Watch (1996).

Institutional subcultures in women's prisons, which encourage correctional officers to "cover" for each other, coupled with inadequate protection accorded women who file complaints, make it unlikely that many women prisoners will formally complain about abuse. Additionally, the public stereotype of women in prison as "bad girls" also makes it difficult for a woman inmate to support her case against a correctional officer in court. Finally, what little progress has been made is now threatened by recent legislation that has curtailed the ability of prisoners and advocates to sue about prison conditions (Stein, 1996, p. 24; see also Human Rights Watch, 1996).

Reviewing the situation of women incarcerated in five states (California, Georgia, Michigan, Illinois, and New York) and the District of Columbia, Human Rights Watch (1996) concluded:

> Our findings indicate that being a woman prisoner in U.S. state prisons can be a terrifying experience. If you are sexually abused, you cannot escape from your abuser. Grievance or investigatory procedures, where they exist, are often ineffectual, and correctional employees continue to engage in abuse because they believe that they will rarely be held accountable, administratively or criminally. Few people outside the prison walls know what is going on or care if they do know. Fewer still do anything to address the problem. (p. 1)

Human Rights Watch (1996) also noted that investigators were "concerned that states' adherence to U.S. anti-discrimination laws, in the absence of strong safeguards against custodial sexual misconduct, has often come at the fundamental rights of prisoners" (p. 2).

Ironically, despite the superficial emphasis on equity in contemporary corrections, it appears that women today are also recipients of some of the worst of old separate spheres abuses, particularly in the area of social control. As an example, McClellan (1994) examined disciplinary practices at prisons housing Texas male and female inmates. McClellan constructed two samples of inmates (271 males and 245 females) from Texas Department of Corrections records and followed them for a one-year period. She found gender-related differences in treatment between the sexes. For example, she documented that while most men in her sample (63.5 percent) had no citations or only one citation for a rule violation, only 17.1 percent of the women in her sample had such records. McClellan (1994) noted that women prisoners were more likely to receive numerous citations and for different sorts of infractions than men. Most frequently, women were cited for "violating posted rules," while males were cited most often for "refusing to work" (p. 77). Women were more likely than men to receive the most severe sanctions.

McClellan (1994) notes that the wardens of the women's prisons in her study state quite frankly that they demand total compliance with every rule on the books and punish violations through official mechanisms. She concluded that there exist "two distinct institutional forms of surveillance and control operating at the male and female facilities" (p. 87).

DOING TIME: ADAPTATION AND COPING IN CONTEMPORARY WOMEN'S PRISONS

Very little research has been conducted on women prisoner subcultures in over two decades since the classic research of Ward and Kassebaum (1965), Giallombardo (1966), and Heffernan (1972). Owen (1998) describes the world of women's prisons today. As Owen explains, the day-to-day world of female prisons now requires a new description and analysis. She attempts to answer several critical questions: How do women in prison do time? How has prison culture for women changed from the findings of earlier research? How have the contemporary problems of overcrowding, the war on drugs, gangs, and racial division among prisoners affected the way women do time? Owen observed that women prisoners organize their time and create a social world that is quite different from contemporary men's prisons. She suggests that imprisonment and its subsequent response are gendered.

As cited in Owen (1998), the early work of Ward and Kassebaum (1965) and Giallombardo (1966) focused on a social structure based on the family, traditional gender roles, and same-gender relationships. Later studies (Larsen & Nelson, 1984; Leger, 1987; Propper, 1982) described the female prisoner culture in terms of pseudofamily structure and homosexual relations, following themes developed by Ward and Kassebaum and Giallombardo. These studies suggest that women create lives in prison that reflect elements of traditional family roles and the street life. This social structure revolves around their sexual identify and attendant social roles, mirroring their relations with males on the outside.

Owen explains that Heffernan (1972) found that the existing descriptive and theoretical models of prison culture were based on a male version of the prison and therefore were inadequate for describing life in a women's prison. Employing Syke's (1958) hypotheses, Heffernan looked for key roles and norms that enable the prisoner social system to act cohesively and to reject those who don't adopt the roles and norms. Although she found no support for Syke's role adaptations among the women prisoners in her study, Heffernan described adaptation to the inmate world in terms of three orientations: "the square," a woman who was tied to conventional norms and values; "the cool," a person doing time in a way that involved control and manipulation; and "the life," someone who embraced a more deviant criminal identity based on the culture of the streets.

Similar to Irwin (1970), Heffernan argues that a woman's initial orientation to prison was often based on preprison identities. She found that women who created a family life in prison were most apt to adapt to prison life and that the family was a critical element to the social order of the prison.

The imprisonment of women is tied directly to their status under patriarchy (Kurshan, 1992). Kurshan states that while prisons are used as social control for both men and women, the imprisonment of women "as well as all other aspects of our lives, takes place against a backdrop of patriarchal relationships" (p. 230). Following this theme, Owen (1998) suggests that "the study of women in prison must be viewed through the lens of patriarchy and its implications for the everyday lives of women."

According to Owen (1998), little has changed in women's prison culture. Personal relationships with other prisoners, both emotionally and physically, connections to family and loved ones, and commitments to preprison identities continue to shape the core of prison culture among women. "The world of the women's prison is shaped by pre-prison experiences, the role of women in contemporary society, and the ways women rely on personalized relationships to survive their prison terms" (p. 7). Economic marginalization, histories of abuse, and self-destructive behavior form the pathway to women's imprisonment. The degree to which these behaviors continue to shape their lives, in turn, is dependent on the nature of one's experience in the prison and attachment to competing systems and identities (p. 8).

Contemporary women's prisons also differ from men's prisons in terms of gang activity. Owen (1998) found a lack of organized gangs at her study site, the Central California Women's Facility. She attributed this to the prison family structure and the activities surrounding this structure, which may meet the survival needs of women prisoners that are often met by street gangs.

CONCLUSIONS: PROGRAM AND POLICY IMPLICATIONS

The expansion of the women's prison population has been fueled primarily by increased rates of incarceration for drug law violations and other less serious offenses. The majority of imprisoned women in the United States are sentenced for nonviolent crimes, which often reflect their marginalized status. Women prisoners share many of the problems of their male counterparts, but they also endure unique issues as a result of their race, class, and gender. This threefold jeopardy is manifested in several ways: (1) women offenders are more likely to be victims of physical, sexual, and emotional abuse; (2) they are at greater risk of incarceration due to substance abusing behavior; and (3) they are most likely to be the sole caretakers of dependent children and they are economically marginalized.

Women prisoners have a host of medical, psychological, and financial problems and needs. Substance abuse, compounded by poverty, unemployment, physical and mental illness, physical and sexual abuse, and homelessness often propels women through the revolving door of the criminal justice system. Rather than affording an ameliorative approach to these complex issues, the law enforcement response often exacerbates these problems, causing further psychological and social stress.

Changes in criminal justice policies and practices over the last decade have clearly contributed to dramatic growth in the female prison population. Mandatory prison terms and sentencing guidelines are gender-blind, and in their crusade to get tough on crime, policymakers have gotten tough on women, drawing them into jails and prisons in unprecedented numbers.

The data summarized in this chapter, as well as other research, suggest that women may be better served in the community due to the decreased seriousness of their crimes and their amenability to treatment. By focusing on strategies that directly address the problems of women in conflict with the law, the overuse and overcrowding of women's prisons can be avoided.

Women prisoners have experienced a history of neglect in the development and implementation of correctional programming targeted to their situations. Historically, programs for women offenders were based on male program models without consideration as to their appropriateness for women. Thus we have very little empirical evidence indicating what works for female offenders.

Research supported by the National Institute of Corrections by Austin, Bloom, and Donahue (1992) identified a series of effective strategies for working with women offenders in community settings. This study reviewed limited program evaluation data and found that "promising approaches" are multidimensional and deal with the gender-specific needs of women. Austin et al. found that promising community programs combined supervision and services to address the specialized needs of female offenders in safe, structured environments. These programs and strategies use an "empowerment" model of skill building to develop competencies to enable women to achieve independence.

A recent study (Koons, Burrows, Morash, & Bynum, 1997) provides characteristics of promising programs serving women offenders. "A sizable number of promising models approached the treatment of women offenders using a comprehensive and holistic strategy for meeting their needs" (p. 521). Program components included elements such as the use of continuum of care, individualized and structured programming, and an emphasis on skill building.

A review of the backgrounds of women in prison suggests more effective ways to address their problems and needs. Whether it be more funding for drug treatment programs, more shelters for the victims of domestic violence, more family-focused interventions, or more job training programs, the solutions are available. However, changes in public policy are needed so that the response to women's offending is one that emphasizes human needs rather than focusing solely on punitive sanctions. The tax dollars saved by reducing women's imprisonment could be reinvested in programs designed to meet their needs, which would enrich not only their lives but the lives of their children and future generations.

REFERENCES

American Correctional Association. (1990). *The female offender: What does the future hold?* Washington, DC: St. Mary's Press.

Anderson, S. (1994). *Comparison of male and female admissions one year prior to the implementation of structured sanctions.* Salem: Oregon State Department of Corrections.

ANGLIN, M., & HSER, Y. (1987). Addicted women and crime. *Criminology, 25,* 359–394.

AUSTIN, J., BLOOM, B., & DONAHUE, T. (1992). *Female offenders in the community: An analysis of innovative strategies and programs.* Washington, DC: National Institute of Corrections.

BARRY, E. (1995). Legal issues for prisoners with children. In K. Gabel & D. Johnston (Eds.), *Children of incarcerated parents* (pp. 147–156). New York: Lexington Books.

BIRCH, H. (ED.). (1994). *Moving targets: Women, murder and representation.* Berkeley. University of California Press.

BLOOM, B., CHESNEY-LIND, M., & OWEN, B. (1994). *Women in California prisons: Hidden victims of the war on drugs.* San Francisco: Center on Juvenile and Criminal Justice.

BLOOM, B., & STEINHART, D. (1993). *Why punish the children? A reappraisal of the children of incarcerated mothers in America.* San Francisco: National Council on Crime and Delinquency.

BROWNE, A. (1987). *When battered women kill.* New York: Free Press.

BUREAU OF JUSTICE STATISTICS. (1988). *Profile of state prison inmates, 1986.* Washington, DC: U.S. Department of Justice.

BUREAU OF JUSTICE STATISTICS. (1989). *Prisoners in 1988.* Washington, DC: U.S. Department of Justice.

BUREAU OF JUSTICE STATISTICS. (1991). *Women in prison in 1986.* Washington, DC: U.S. Department of Justice.

BUREAU OF JUSTICE STATISTICS. (1992). *Women in jail in 1989.* Washington, DC: U.S. Department of Justice.

BUREAU OF JUSTICE STATISTICS. (1993). *Prisoners in 1992.* Washington, DC: U.S. Department of Justice.

BUREAU OF JUSTICE STATISTICS. (1994). *Women in prison.* Washington, DC: U.S. Department of Justice.

BUREAU OF JUSTICE STATISTICS. (1997a). *Prisoners in 1996.* Washington, DC: U.S. Department of Justice.

BUREAU OF JUSTICE STATISTICS. (1997b). *HIV in prisons and jails, 1995.* Washington, DC: U.S. Department of Justice.

CALIFORNIA DEPARTMENT OF CORRECTIONS. (1997, October 15). *Weekly report of population.* Data Analysis Unit, Offender Information Services Branch. Sacramento, CA: CDC.

CALLAHAN, M. (1986). *Historical corrections statistics in the United States, 1850–1984.* Washington, DC: Bureau of Justice Statistics.

CHESNEY-LIND, M. (1987). Female offenders: Paternalism reexamined. In L. Crites & W. Hepperele (Eds.), *Women, the courts and equality* (pp. 114–140). Newbury Park, CA: Sage.

CHESNEY-LIND, M. (1997). *The female offender: Girls, women and crime.* Thousand Oaks, CA: Sage.

CHESNEY-LIND, M., & POLLOCK-BYRNE, J. (1995). Women's prisons: Equality with a vengeance. In J. Pollock-Byrne & A. Merlo (Eds.), *Women, law and social control* (pp. 155–175). Boston: Allyn & Bacon.

CRAIG, G. (1996, March 23). Advocates say nude filming shows need for new laws. *Rochester Democrat and Chronicle,* pp. A1, A6.

CURRIDEN, M. (1993, September 20). Prison scandal in Georgia: Guards traded favors for sex. *National Law Journal,* 8.

DALY, K. (1994). *Gender, crime and punishment.* New Haven, CT: Yale University Press.

DOUGLAS, S. (1994). *Where the girls are: Growing up female with the mass media.* New York: Random House.

EATON, M. (1986). *Justice for women?* Milton Keynes, England: Open University Press.

EISENSTEIN, Z. (1988). *The female body and the law.* Berkeley: University of California Press.

ENGLISH, K. (1993). Self-reported crime rates on women prisoners. *Journal of Quantitative Criminology, 9,* 357–382.

FARNSWORTH, M., & TESKE, R. (1995). Gender differences in felony court processing: Three hypotheses of disparity. *Women and Criminal Justice, 6*(2), 23–44.

FEDERAL BUREAU OF INVESTIGATION. (1992). *Crime in the United States, 1991*. Washington, DC: U.S. Department of Justice.

FEDERAL BUREAU OF INVESTIGATION. (1993). *Crime in the United States, 1992*. Washington, DC: U.S. Department of Justice.

FEDERAL BUREAU OF INVESTIGATION. (1996). *Crime in the United States, 1995*. Washington, DC: U.S. Department of Justice.

FOLEY, L., & RASCHE, C. (1979). The effect of race on sentence, actual time served and final disposition on female offenders. In J. Conley (Ed.), *Theory and research in criminal justice*. Cincinnati, OH: Anderson.

FRANKLIN, R. (1996, April 26). Alabama to expand chain gangs—adding women. *USA Today*, p. 3A.

GABEL, K., & JOHNSTON, D. (EDS.). (1995). *Children of incarcerated parents*. New York: Lexington Books.

GIALLOMBARDO, R. (1966). *Society of women: A study of a women's prison*. New York: Wiley.

GILFUS, M. (1992). From victims to survivors: Women's routes of entry and immersion into street crime. *Women and Criminal Justice, 4*(1), 62–89.

HASKELL, M. (1973). *From reverence to rape: The treatment of women in the movies*. New York: Holt, Rinehart and Winston.

HEFFERNAN, E. (1972). *Making it in prison: The square, the cool, and the life*. New York: Wiley.

HOLMLUND, C. (1995). A decade of deadly dolls: Hollywood and the woman killer. In H. Birch (Ed.), *Moving targets: Women, murder and representation*. Berkeley: University of California Press.

HUMAN RIGHTS WATCH. (1996). *All too familiar: Sexual abuse of women in U.S. state prisons*. New York: Holt, Rinehart & Winston.

INCIARDI, J., LOCKWOOD, D., & POTTIEGER, A. (1993). *Women and crack cocaine*. New York: Macmillan.

IRWIN, J. (1970). *The felon*. Upper Saddle River, NJ: Prentice Hall.

JOHNSTON, D. (1992). *The children of offenders study*. Pasadena, CA: Pacific Oaks Center for Children of Incarcerated Parents.

KATZ, P. (1997). The effect of welfare reform on incarcerated mothers and their families. *Family and Corrections Network Report, 14*, 3, 6.

KIRP, D., YUDOF, M., & FRANKS, M. (1986). *Gender justice*. Chicago: University of Chicago Press.

KOONS, B., BURROWS, J., MORASH, M., & BYNUM, T. (1997). Expert and offender perceptions of program elements linked to successful outcomes for incarcerated women. *Crime and Delinquency, 43*(4), 512–532.

KRUTTSCHNITT, C. (1980–1981). Social status and sentences of female offenders. *Law and Society Review, 15*(2), 247–265.

KURSHAN, N. (1992). Women and imprisonment in the U.S. In W. Churchill & J. VanDer Wall (Eds.), *Cages of steel* (pp. 331–358). Washington, DC: Maisonneuve Press.

LARSEN, J., & NELSON, J. (1984). Women, friendship, and adaptation to prison. *Journal of Criminal Justice, 12*(5), 601–615.

LEGER, R. (1987). Lesbianism among women prisoners: Participants and nonparticipants. *Criminal Justice and Behavior, 14*, 463–479.

LOPEZ, S. (1993, July 8). Fifth guard arrested on sex charge. *Albuquerque Journal*, pp. A1, A2.

MACKINNON, C. (1987). *Feminism unmodified: Discourse on life and law*. London: Harvard University Press.

MAGUIRE, K., PASTORE, A., & FLANAGAN, T. (1993). *Sourcebook of criminal justice statistics, 1992*. U.S. Department of Justice, Bureau of Justice Statistics. Washington, DC: U.S. Government Printing Office.

MANN, C. (1989). Minority and female: A criminal justice double bind. *Social Justice, 16*(3), 95–114.

MANN, C. (1995). Women of color and the criminal justice system. In B. Price & N. Sokoloff (Eds.), *The criminal justice system and women* (pp. 118–135). New York: McGraw-Hill.

MAUER, M., & HULING, T. (1995). *Young black Americans and the criminal justice system: Five years later.* Washington, DC: The Sentencing Project.

McCLELLAN, D. (1994). Disparity in the discipline of male and female inmates in Texas prisons. *Women and Criminal Justice, 5*(2), 71–97.

MEYER, M. (1992, November 9). Coercing sex behind bars: Hawaii's prison scandal. *Newsweek*, pp. 23–25.

ODUBEKUN, L. (1992). A structural approach to differential gender sentencing. *Criminal Justice Abstracts, 24*(2), 343–360.

OWEN, B. (1998). *In the mix: Struggle and survival in a women's prison.* Albany: State University of New York Press.

OWEN, B., & BLOOM, B. (1995). Profiling women prisoners: Findings from national surveys and a California sample. *Prison Journal, 75*(2), 165–185.

POLLOCK, J. (1994, April). *The increasing incarceration rate of women offenders: Equality or justice?* Paper presented at Prisons 2000 conference, Leicester, England.

POLLOCK-BYRNE, J. (1990). *Women, prison, and crime.* Pacific Grove, CA: Brooks/Cole.

PROPPER, A. (1982). Make-believe families and homosexuality among imprisoned girls. *Criminology, 20*(1), 127–139.

RAEDER, M. (1993). Gender and sentencing: Single moms, battered women and other sex-based anomalies in the gender-free world of federal sentencing guidelines. *Pepperdine Law Review, 20*(3), 905–990.

RAFTER, N. (1990). *Partial justice: Women, prisons, and social control.* New Brunswick, NJ: Transaction Books.

SEWENELY, A. (1993, January 6). Sex abuse charges rock women's prison. *Detroit News*, pp. B1, B7.

SINGER, L. (1973). Women and the correctional process. *American Criminal Law Review, 11*, 295–308.

SMART, C. (1989). *Feminism and the power of law.* London: Routledge & Kegan Paul.

SNELL, T., & MORTON, D. (1994). *Women in prison. Special report.* Washington, DC: Bureau of Justice Statistics.

STARK, E., & FLITCRAFT, A. (1996). *Women at risk: Domestic violence and women's health.* London: Sage.

STEFFENSMEIER, D., & ALLAN, E. (1995). Gender, age and crime. In J. Sheley (Ed.), *Handbook of contemporary criminology* (pp. 88–116). New York: Wadsworth.

STEIN, B. (1996, July). Life in prison: Sexual abuse. *The Progressive*, pp. 23–24.

SYKES, G. (1958). *Society of captives.* Princeton, NJ: Princeton University Press.

WARD, D., & KASSEBAUM, G. (1965). *Women's prison: Sex and social structure.* Chicago: Aldine-Atherton.

WATSON, T. (1992, November 16). Georgia indictments charge abuse of female inmates. *USA Today*, p. A3.

WEBSDALE, N., & CHESNEY-LIND, M. (1997). Doing violence to women: Research synthesis on the victimization of women. In L. Bowker (Ed.), *Masculinities and violence.* Thousand Oaks, CA: Sage.

WHITE, J., & KOWALSKI, R. (1994). Deconstructing the myth of the nonaggressive woman: A feminist analysis. *Psychology of Women Quarterly, 18*, 487–508.

33

The Reentry Process for Women

Dale J. Brooker

Women's role in the reentry process is complex and not always at the forefront of research agendas. This chapter focuses on women who are getting out of prison and the various issues and challenges that face them as they attempt to reintegrate into the community. In addition, there will be a discussion on the women who must deal with the process of reentry because of their relationship(s) with recently released inmates (both men and women). There has been some current research done to assess the effects that the reentry process has on the family members and significant others (many of whom are female—the grandmothers, mothers, partners, daughters, and sisters) dealing with a loved one being released from incarceration and will be highlighted here, but there still remains much to be done in the area. The final part of this chapter will outline what areas of research should be focused on to assist in the understanding of this complex phenomenon: the reentry process for women.

Women's rates of incarceration have increased significantly over the last decade. According to the Bureau of Justice Statistics (2003a), during 2002 the number of women under the jurisdiction of state or federal prison authorities increased 4.9%, compared to a 0.2% drop in 2001. The number of men in prison rose 2.4%, up from 1.2% the previous year. At year-end 2002 there were 97,491 women and 1,343,164 men in state or federal prisons. Furthermore, statistics indicated that women in 1999 constituted 9.9% of those returning from prison to parole, up from 7.9% in 1990 (Bureau of Justice Statistics, 2003b). With this increase there are a number of consequences to consider that are specific to women. One of the consequences concerns what will be done with those women who will be returning to society after their incarceration is over. Another has to do with the specific problems they face that are unique because of the specific gender roles they play, what awaits them upon reentry, and how society will respond.

Recent literature in the field of reentry has focused almost exclusively on men who are returning to society without any real concrete discussion on women who are being released. Even when women are studied they tend to be simply included rather than focused upon. Nelson, Deess, and Allen (1999) examined the experiences of people (male and female) released from prison for one month. While women made up 33% of the sample, the research did little to address the differences or similarities in experiences of those men and women in the reentry process. Another failure in this expanding area of research has been the exploration into the women who play a role in the reentry process for those males being released. These women are the wives, girlfriends, mothers, sisters, aunts, daughters, and friends who share the consequences of incarceration. This chapter explores both of these crucial dynamics to gain a better understanding of how women's lives are impacted by the reentry process and proposes a more comprehensive research agenda when it comes to women, crime, and justice.

WOMEN COMING HOME

Scores of women will be released from prison this year, some will be "off paper" having done their full sentence, but a majority will be placed on parole for a period of time ("on" paper). Women face a number of trials and tribulations that are part of the reentry process, whether on or off paper. Even prior to being incarcerated, many women have had long life histories of drug use and abuse along with being abused and victimized (physically and sexually). Women face physical and emotional problems as well, and the stress of being incarcerated can be compounded with the reality that the reentry process presents. Employment opportunities may be hard to come by, especially if there was limited education and limited employment experience prior to incarceration. Those women who are mothers face even more challenges in the reentry process; reestablishing the bond that may have been lost during the reentry process is crucial for mothers and their children. Five areas will be the focused on in this section: (1) issues related to the health and well-being of women going through the reentry process; (2) family issues, including children and reconciling broken relationships; (3) the stigma associated with being a female ex-felon; (4) issues surrounding employment and employability of women being released; and (5) the access to social capital and positive reciprocal relationships.

HEALTH AND WELL-BEING

The idea of health and well-being of recently released female inmates is crucial to understand to get a better sense of what must be considered by policymakers, social service organizations, and the communities where these women will reside. Health and well-being includes the mental, physical, and emotional health of women who have been released from prison as well as understanding the previous history of substance abuse that many have dealt with in the past and are likely to deal with again upon release. The reality is that higher percentages of women are convicted for drug offenses and are more likely to report drug usage prior to incarceration than their male counterparts (Greenfeld & Snell, 2000). In many instances, women have also been abused by someone in their lives whether physically, sexually, or both and this too must be considered in any discussion on the reentry process. As Greenfeld and Snell (2000) note, 44% of women under correctional authority have reported either being physically or sexually assaulted at some point in their lives. This life history of women prior to incarceration allows the discipline to fully grasp what it means to be a woman in the criminal justice system, and furthermore, what it means to be a woman in today's society.

As Covington (2003) points out, women are faced with a number of issues upon reentry that are different than their male counterparts: substance abuse, trauma, and mental health. Substance abuse can be a serious barrier for women, considering the likelihood of use and abuse prior to incarceration. In conjunction with substance abuse, Covington (2003) highlights research that suggests women who have substance abuse issues also are dealing with depression and anxiety, as well as other mood disorders. There is growing research that suggests women have higher rates of psychosis, severe affective disorder, posttraumatic stress disorder, substance abuse and dependence, and cognitive impairment (Swanson, Morrissey, Goldstrom, Rudolph, & Manderscheid, 1993; Teplin, Abram, & McClelland, 1997). This presents a significant problem if not addressed either during the incarceration process through proper programming or upon release. The idea of trauma is derived from the notion that many women in the system (and out of the system) have gone through very traumatic life events (including physical and sexual abuse) and are aggravated by the prison experience itself. Women in prison have higher rates of mental illness, which if not properly diagnosed or treated can present another major barrier to successful reintegration. Without proper care and treatment women's experiences can be horrific and detrimental to the families of the ex-offenders, especially the children.

FAMILY

Rafter (1985) notes, "unlike men sentenced to prison, women seldom have been able to rely on a spouse to care for their children; therefore they have suffered more anxiety about the welfare of their families" (p. 179). Rafter's commentary gets to the heart of the idea that women's familial experiences are different from men's and research must recognize this in order to fully grasp the incarceration and reentry to women in this society. Women with children may feel a sense of worry above and beyond their male counterparts because of the interactions they have with their children prior to incarceration and this sense of worry or concern follows them through the imprisonment period up to the day of release and beyond. Especially problematic is the incarceration period itself where criminal justice policies and the rules and regulations within prison make it difficult for mothers and children to have any meaningful interaction with one another, thereby contributing to the anxiety felt by many inside. Although men and women are equal in reporting the amount of contact they have with their children during prison, women are far more likely to go home and actually live with their children upon release. The release and reentry of a woman is filled with significant barriers including the attempts to restore harmony among children and other family members. The reunification of mother and child is difficult and can be complex. Complications can and do arise as women try to reintroduce themselves into their children's lives.

While many women rely on a grandparent (usually the grandmother, see section below) to take on the role of caregiver while they are incarcerated, men who are in prison are more likely to have their children reside with the other parent (Mumola, 2003). Furthermore, women, more than men in prison, will have to rely on the foster care system to support their children. Travis, Cincotta, and Solomon (2003) indicated reunification of parents with children can be especially difficult for women because of the fact that about 10% had their children placed in foster care during their incarceration period. Added to this is the fact that the 1997 Adoption and Safe Families Act may present women who have been locked up for over 18 months with the possibility of losing their parental rights. Once again, the issue is compounded by the fact that getting them out of foster care is a process that can be strenuous because parents must show they can care and provide for the child, which means they must have gainful employment, housing, and child care in place even before the child can be placed back with the parent.

STIGMA

Those individuals leaving prison understand and are well aware of the stigma that is associated with being an ex-felon and this awareness affects a number of the decisions that are made. It also reflects societal response to those individuals. The response is one that makes it difficult to find jobs and housing, and to engage in positive, healthy relationships that could be the key to being successful in the reentry process. A sense of self beyond the identity of a felon is needed to assist those who are attempting to reintegrate. Uggen, Manza, and Behrens (2004) studied both men and women who were inmates, parolees, and probationers. A major component in their work had to do with how the participants viewed themselves, where they were in their lives, and how society perceived them. This research highlighted the fact that the stigma that felons are faced with affects many parts of their lives including their confidence level when searching for a job, dealing with family members, and being accepted again by society. They concluded that "their felony convictions made them outsiders, occupying a status that is 'less than the average citizen'" (p. 288). Attempts to change roles during the reentry process can be compromised by the labels applied to ex-felons. Reentry also means a shift in identity from a prison number to a person who is expected to find employment, have a good family life, and stay clean and sober, as well as be part of the community. The problem in many cases is that this shift is difficult and hindered by the fact that society and the criminal justice system are harsh when it comes to dealing with ex-offenders. Women may face an even more difficult time if they had children prior to incarceration. Perceptions of female offenders with children could be distorted by the public because of the traditional view (with regard to gender roles) that women are not fulfilling their motherly duty if they "went and got locked up."

EMPLOYMENT

Women reentering society are faced with the reality that many of them did not have legitimate employment prior to incarceration, much of which has to do with the gender stratification that exists in society. Women are likely to be faced with a lack of opportunities because of the many obstacles in gaining meaningful employment. According to Greenfeld & Snell (2000), women offenders are less likely to be employed prior to prison than their male counterparts; when employed they make less money than men and are more likely to be on welfare prior to their incarceration. More specifically the study notes that prior to incarceration 4 in 10 women versus 6 in 10 men were working full time; 37% of women and 28% of men had incomes less than $600 a month before arrest; and 30% of women offenders reported receiving welfare assistance compared with 8% of male offenders. This translates into a very difficult situation for those being released back into the community. Compounding this is the lack of adequate vocational and educational programs in female correctional facilities. In their extensive research on women offenders, Reisig, Holtfreter, and Morash (2002) found that 34% of the women in their sample were on welfare prior to incarceration while 30% were employed full time.

One recent, nonacademic portrayal of life after prison highlights the economic plight of one woman, but gives great insight into the post-incarceration experiences of a woman. *Life on the Outside* by Jennifer Gonnerman tells the story of Elaine Bartlett, a New York woman incarcerated for 16 years. Her journey from prison to life back in society provides a valuable account of what many women face through the reentry process. Despite the fact that Bartlett's release was well publicized, she still struggled with finding a job and a place to live, keeping her family together, being a parent to children she had not seen since they were very young, and dealing with the ins and outs of the parole system. Gonnerman (2004) noted specifically that placing a human face on the phenomenon that has been kept from people is a "way to expose the hidden consequences of our nation's punishment policies" (p. 350).

SOCIAL CAPITAL

Emerging in the reentry literature is the focus on social capital as a predictor of success. The concept of social capital (see Bourdieu, 1980; Coleman, 1990) is relevant in that it allows researchers to understand that there are more severe consequences for recently released inmates than just the inability to acquire a job. As Hagan and Coleman (2001) note, "there is little doubt about the decline in social capital available to persons returning to communities from prison" (p. 362). Reisig et al. (2002) examined the issues surrounding the availability of social capital among women offenders. In so doing, they illustrate the importance of this concept in the women's reentry literature. Their research found that income prior to incarceration was correlated with the types of social networks that they associated with upon release. Those women who made more money annually from legal sources of income prior to incarceration were more apt to have larger social networks which translated into more available resources for the women being released. The research also noted that young, poor, and less educated women have fewer available resources that could facilitate the acquisition of further education and employment. This in turn could lead them to what Reisig and colleagues (2002) call "negative human capital" or "criminal capital" (p. 181). This type of capital is sought out after legitimate forms of capital cease to be available, a condition that is brought on by a stressful reentry process.

EXPERIENCES OF WOMEN AFFECTED BY MASS INCARCERATION

Focusing exclusively on female prisoners overlooks the millions of women whose lives are directly affected by the criminal justice system on a daily basis: the wives, girlfriends, mothers, daughters and other female kin and kith of prisoners. (Comfort, 2003, p. 79)

Over the past two decades incarceration rates have increased and during this time, many women have had their husbands, boyfriends, fathers, and sons imprisoned only to be left with the hardships of being another family without a male figure in the home. For many, this shift in family dynamics and social relationships has had significant consequences for the women who are disproportionately left with the responsibilities for maintaining the family's health, finances, and overall cohesiveness. The experiences of women who are affected by and are the victims of mass incarceration can present researchers with meaningful accounts that get to the essence of this phenomenon.

Comfort (2003) presents research that details women's experiences as they begin the process of visiting their partners in prison. The research identifies the visiting area of San Quentin primarily as a female space, due to the fact that almost all who enter are women. It is revealed that the women go through what Comfort notes as a "secondary prisonization" by experiencing firsthand how the penal system operates when it comes to the process of visitation. This process, with its elaborate regulations, rules, procedures, and deprivations, is perceived by the female visitors as harsh, unfair, and a barrier to being able express their true selves. The value of this research is that it contributes greatly to an understanding of how women are affected by the incarceration process.

Another critical area of women's experiences is explored by research which focuses on the roles they play when a family member is incarcerated. The grandmother is an essential member of the extended family network and represents the matriarch in many minority familial settings. It is the grandmother who often becomes the primary caregiver when a family member is incarcerated. Mumola (2003) reported that of those women (with children) incarcerated in state and federal institutions in 1999, 53% indicated the current caregiver of their children was a grandparent. As parents become separated from their children during the incarceration process, it is the grandmother who looks to ensure her grandchildren are fed, clothed, and have proper shelter, education, and emotional support. Ruiz (2002) points out that the steady rise of female (who are disproportionately of color) incarcerations has left many grandmothers with increased responsibilities as caregivers and this has had a significant impact on their health and well-being. Dressel and Barnhill (1994) studied African American grandmothers and noted in their case study that not only is the day-to-day care of grandchildren stressful, so too are the transitional periods of arrest, conviction, and the eventual release of their daughters. Furthermore, a number of health problems and psychological issues arise for these caregivers. The stress and strain of being a caregiver can also be compounded if there is a financial burden. Grandmothers who have to care for their grandchildren can incur numerous expenses that, if the women are not working or receiving assistance from other kin, can create serious amounts of distress and in effect impact the children as well.

Braman (2004) writes extensively in his ethnography about women's experiences as the wives, mothers, and daughters of men who are incarcerated. The stigma of being the family member of someone who is incarcerated can affect daily interactions with others. Braman (2004) points out, "female relatives of prisoners also bear a significant burden as a result of gender differences in their reactions to stigma" (p. 175). The internalization of these shameful feelings oftentimes overcomes the women in these situations and makes it apparent that the punishment of a loved one creates a significant hardship. The hardship is also recognized in Braman's work (2004) on his discussion of "prison worries." These worries are the feelings that loved ones have when thinking of what a prisoner is going through while incarcerated and what they will go through upon release. When they receive correspondence from a prisoner, mothers, daughters, and other family members have to process what is being said and while many letters may be upbeat, there is the reality that is prison life—one that is sometimes filled with unfair treatment, poor conditions, and a less than positive atmosphere.

A RESEARCH AGENDA FOR STUDYING WOMEN IN THE REENTRY PROCESS

Research in the field of reentry is growing considerably and while much is left to do quantitatively, qualitative research has provided insights into a number of issues particularly crucial to understanding how women are affected by the process. Braman (2004) recommends looking beyond what the numbers tell us and focusing on how people on the outside (the kin of those incarcerated) construct meanings about their lives. It is one thing to provide people with a statistical analysis of the number of families affected by mass incarceration; it is an entirely different endeavor to extract the meaning out of people's life experiences. Therefore, I propose a more rigorous qualitative research agenda for studying women's lives and experiences that surround the process of incarceration and reentry. To do this, life histories and case studies should be utilized in an effort to explore this underresearched phenomenon with an emphasis on the complex roles of gender, race/ethnicity, and socioeconomic status. Furthermore, it would be useful to examine not only women who are going through the process itself, but also other women who suffer the consequences of having a growing number of people placed into the prison industrial complex. Policymakers, social welfare workers, community leaders, criminal justice officials, and academics alike can benefit if more attention is given to the variety of women who must deal with incarceration and the reentry process.

REFERENCES

BOURDIEU, P. (1980). Le capital social [Social capital]. *Actes de la Recherche en Sciences Sociales, 31*, 2–3.

BRAMAN, D. (2004). *Doing time on the outside: Incarceration and family life in urban America.* Ann Arbor: University of Michigan Press.

BUREAU OF JUSTICE STATISTICS. (2003a). *Prisoners in 2002: Bulletin* (revised August 27, 2003). Washington, DC: U.S. Department of Justice.

BUREAU OF JUSTICE STATISTICS. (2003b). *Reentry trends in the United States: Inmates returning to the community after serving time in prison* (revised August 20, 2003). Washington, DC: U.S. Department of Justice.

COLEMAN, J. (1990). *Foundations of social theory.* Cambridge, MA: Harvard University Press.

COMFORT, M. (2003). In the tube at San Quentin: The "secondary prisonization" of women visiting inmates. *Journal of Contemporary Ethnography, 32*(1), 77–107.

COVINGTON, S. (2003). A woman's journey home: Challenges for female offenders. In J. Travis & M. Waul (Eds.), *Prisoners once removed: The impact of incarceration and reentry on children, families and communities* (pp. 67–103). Washington, DC: Urban Institute Press.

DRESSEL, P., & BARNHILL, S. (1994). Reframing gerontological thought and practice: The case of grandmothers with daughters in prison. *The Gerontologist, 34*, 685–690.

GONNERMAN, J. (2004). *Life on the outside: The prison odyssey of Elaine Bartlett*. New York: Farrar, Strauss and Giroux.

GREENFELD, L., & SNELL, T. (2000). *Bureau of Justice Statistics special report, women offenders*. Washington, DC: U.S. Department of Justice.

HAGAN, J., & COLEMAN, J. P. (2001). Returning captives of the American war on drugs: Issues of community and family reentry. *Crime and Delinquency, 47*(3), 352–367.

MUMOLA, C. (2003). *Incarcerated parents and their children*. Washington, DC: U.S. Department of Justice.

NELSON, M., DEESS, P., & ALLEN, C. (1999). *The first month out: Post-incarceration experiences in New York City*. New York: Vera Institute of Justice.

RAFTER, N. (1985). *Partial justice: Women in state prisons, 1800–1935*. Boston: Northeastern University Press.

REISIG, M., HOLTFRETER, K., & MORASH, M. (2002). Social capital among women offenders: Examining the distribution of social networks and resources. *Journal of Contemporary Criminal Justice, 18*(2), 167–187.

RUIZ, D. (2002). The increase in incarcerations among women and its impact on the grandmother caregiver: Some racial considerations. *Journal of Sociology and Social Welfare, 28*(3), 179–197.

SWANSON, J., MORRISSEY, J., GOLDSTROM, I., RUDOLPH, J., & MANDERSCHEID, R. (1993). *Demographic and diagnostic characteristics of inmates having mental health services in state adult correctional facilities: United States, 1988*. Statistical Note No. 209. Washington, DC: U.S. Department of Health and Human Services.

TEPLIN, L., ABRAM, K., & MCCLELLAND, G. (1997). Mentally disordered women in jail: Who receives services? *American Journal of Public Health, 87*(4), 604–609.

TRAVIS, J., CINCOTTA, E., & SOLOMON, A. (2003). *Families left behind: The hidden costs of incarceration and reentry*. Washington, DC: Urban Institute Press.

UGGEN, C., MANZA, J., & BEHRENS, A. (2004). "Less than the average citizen": Stigma, role transition and the civic reintegration of convicted felons. In S. Murana & R. Immarigeon (Eds.), *After crime and punishment: Pathways to offender reintegration* (pp. 261–293). Portland, OR: Willan.

34

Dying to Get Out

The Execution of Females in the Post-*Furman* Era of the Death Penalty in the United States

David E. Schulberg

In this chapter we examine the subject of women and the death penalty in the modern era of American capital punishment jurisprudence. Proceeding from the unusual perspective of the death penalty itself, as opposed to the more frequently referenced experiences of women on death row, we bring a unique context to an important subject deserving of careful attention.

While providing an overview of the highlights of U.S. death penalty history, we examine briefly the constitutional underpinnings of modern capital punishment jurisprudence, including Eighth and Fourteenth Amendment–related Supreme Court decisions. Attention is given to several key Supreme Court cases that have had a startling effect on the present capital punishment scheme in the United States. Particular emphasis is given to a review of several important feminist theories purporting to explain gender-centric patterns in capital punishment jurisprudence involving women, including chivalry, evil woman, and equality theory.

We discuss several gender-based factors involved in the cases of the only women executed to date in the modern death penalty era in the United States and outline the facts surrounding the offenses that caused them each to be executed. Finally, we will draw conclusions and make recommendations concerning the present and future state of female death penalty jurisprudence in the United States.

Velma Barfield asked for cheese doodles, a Kit Kat bar, and a Coke (B. Bass, personal communication, April 13, 2000). Karla Fay Tucker requested a banana, a peach, and a garden salad with ranch dressing (Texas Department of Criminal Justice, 2000). Judias Buenoano wanted steamed broccoli, steamed asparagus with tomato and lemon wedges, black pepper, fresh strawberries, and hot tea (Debra Buchanan, personal communication, March 3, 2000). Betty Lou Beets (Texas Department of Criminal Justice, 2000), apparently having little appetite, made no special request whatsoever (Texas Department of Criminal Justice, 2000). Christina Riggs selected supreme pizza, garden salad with ranch dressing, pickled okra, strawberry shortcake, and cherry limeade (D. Taylor, personal communication, May 1, 2000). Wanda Jean Allen, also apparently lacking appetite, asked for nothing (A. Taylor, personal communication, May 31, 2001). Marilyn Kay Plantz, comparing only with Christina Riggs in the appetite department, ordered a chicken taco salad, a Mexican pizza, two encharitos, two chicken soft tacos, an order of cinnamon twists, a piece of pecan pie, and two cans of Coca-Cola (A. Taylor, personal communication, May 31, 2001).

What made each of these meals unique, even macabre, and each of the women eating them noteworthy, was not, however, what they ate—nor, perhaps, even where they ate. What was special was what these meals themselves were. Each woman, although time separated their fate from one another, was about to be executed for murder, and these meals were their last.

Barfield, Tucker, Buenoano, Beets, Riggs, Allen, and Plantz remain the only women put to death in the United States since the Supreme Court cleared the way for executions to resume, with the 1976 decision in *Gregg v. Georgia* (Death Penalty Information Center, 2000b).

THE DEATH PENALTY: AN OVERVIEW

As the new millennium dawns, capital punishment remains our society's ultimate ritual for reclaiming power from those who murder (Carroll, 1997). Capital punishment also remains one of society's two most hotly debated topics, comparing, in this regard, only with abortion (Maloney, 2000). When questioned concerning their opinion on capital punishment, the average person is either definitely for or against it (Smith, 1999, p. 5).

Capital punishment remains part of our national crime control policy even as we find ourselves the only Western nation still to execute its own citizens (Maloney, 2000). From a low of 42 percent in 1966 (Death Penalty Information Center, 2000a), the death penalty has steadily climbed in popularity to between 66 percent (Death Penalty Information Center, 2000d) and 77 percent (Maloney, 2000), although this approval drops to 50 percent when life without the possibility of parole is introduced as an alternative (Death Penalty Information Center, 2000d).

Historical Highlights

The number of executions conducted in American history is not known. Executions were often local affairs, and permanent records were generally not centrally kept. Despite the national shift to prisons, some states conducted official hangings at local jails well into the twentieth century (Maloney, 2000).

Official statistics on lawful executions were first collected in the United States in the 1930s (University of Alaska–Anchorage, 2000). Between 1930 and 1967, when an unofficial moratorium on executions was agreed to by those jurisdictions having a death penalty, a total of 3859 had taken place, of which 32 women were lawfully executed in the United States (Smith, 1999). These figures do not include extrajudicial executions—lynching—which, in the United States between 1882 and 1951 accounted for at least 4,730 additional deaths (Maloney, 2000). Such factors preclude a complete and accurate account of persons executed, officially and otherwise, much less the number of women (Schmall, 1996).

Although one report "confirmed" 18,309 executions, including those of 501 women (Schmall, 1996), another estimated 18,000 to 20,000 executions, with 400 believed to be of women (Rapaport, 1990). Victor Streib, a noted writer on women and the death penalty, estimates that fewer than 400 females were lawfully executed in the history of U.S. capital punishment (Carroll, 1997). Although the number of executions in the United States remains unclear (Carroll, 1997), the first and last executions of women in the earlier era of death penalty jurisprudence is known. In 1632, Jane Champion became the first woman executed in the new colonies (Death Penalty Information Center, 2000a), with Elizabeth Ann Duncan, in August 1962, the last (Streib, 2000a).

CONSTITUTIONAL UNDERPINNINGS OF THE DEATH PENALTY

The Eighth Amendment

In *Trop v. Dulles*, the U.S. Supreme Court noted that the contours of what constituted cruel and unusual punishment were not clearly defined but could not be limited to harms the framers had experienced (*Trop v. Dulles*, 1958). Although *Trop* was not a capital case (Reggio, 2000), opponents of the death penalty applied the court's logic to their cause, arguing that capital punishment should no longer be allowed (Death Penalty Information Center, 2000b). Following closely on *Trop*, the Supreme Court entered a watershed period in the history of capital punishment jurisprudence, beginning in 1962 when the Court held that the Eighth Amendment was "incorporated" and applied to the states. This case, *Robinson v. California* (1962), profoundly affected capital jurisprudence, leading to increased federal appeals, and a noticeable decline in executions (Smith, 1999). This culminated in the previously mentioned unofficial moratorium on executions, which lasted from 1967 (Death Penalty Information Center, 2000a) until 1977 (Streib, 2000a), while the federal courts decided the constitutionality of existing death penalty statutes (Smith, 1999).

Fine-Tuning the Death Penalty

In 1968 the U.S. Supreme Court began to "fine-tune" the way in which capital punishment was administered (Death Penalty Information Center, 2000c). The Court held that a law mandating death, upon jury recommendation, was unconstitutional in that it encouraged waiving a jury trial (*U.S. v. Jackson*, 1968) and also held that a juror could be disqualified only where the person's attitude toward capital sentencing would prevent an impartial decision (*Witherspoon v. Illinois*, 1968).

In 1970, again addressing jurors and juror discretion in capital cases (Death Penalty Information Center, 2000a), the Court considered two cases consolidated under *McGautha v. California* (under *Crampton v. Ohio* and *McGautha v. California*, 1971). Both cases were premised on Fourteenth Amendment claims of violation of due process (Death Penalty Information Center, 2000a). Rendering its decision, the Court approved of unfettered jury discretion and nonbifurcated trials (McGautha, 1971).

Although the Court has been active over the past 20 years defining the relationship of the Eighth and Fourteenth Amendments to capital punishment (Smith, 1999), it seems clear that the present Court remains strongly supportive of capital punishment and will remain so for at least the foreseeable future (Maloney, 2000). But this was not always so.

SUPREME COURT GUIDANCE

Furman v. Georgia

In 1972 the Supreme Court heard three cases that rocked the underpinnings of the U.S. criminal justice system (Smith, 1999). Consolidated under *Furman v. Georgia* (1972), these cases considered the Eighth Amendment–based argument that unfettered jury discretion resulted in arbitrary and capricious sentencing (Death Penalty Information Center, 2000b). All nine justices tried to define the contours of "cruel and unusual" punishment, each filing separate opinions and thus leaving no clear standard with which states could harmonize their death penalty laws (Smith, 1999). Justice White, concurring in *Furman*, neatly summed up the capital punishment situation, noting that "there was no meaningful basis for distinguishing the few cases in which it was imposed from the many cases in which it was not" (Maloney, 2000, p. 14).

Furman held punishment to be cruel and unusual if the sanction was too severe, applied arbitrarily, offended the sense of justice, or was no more effective than a less severe penalty (Reggio, 2000). Although over 600 death sentences were commuted as a direct result, the number of persons sentenced to death built again, as states revised their laws to conform to *Furman* (University of Alaska, 2000). A new and invigorated death penalty era was taking shape (Streib, 1990).

Gregg v. Georgia

In 1976, the Supreme Court consolidated the cases (University of Alaska, 2000) of *Gregg v. Georgia*, *Jurek v. Texas*, and *Proffitt v. Florida*, reinstating the death penalty under the model of guided discretion. The Court ruled that the death penalty did not violate the Eighth Amendment (Death Penalty Information Center, 2000d) if it was administered so as to protect against arbitrariness and discrimination (Maloney, 2000). *Gregg* confirmed the constitutionality of new capital punishment statutes in Florida, Georgia, and Texas (Death Penalty Information Center, 2000).

On January 17, 1977, Gary Gilmore became the first person to be executed (Death Penalty Information Center, 2000b) in the modern death penalty era (Streib, 1990). Although capital punishment was again an American legal reality, several key Supreme Court decisions modifying its application were to follow (Smith, 1999).

Additional Key Decisions

In the related cases of *Woodson v. North Carolina* (1978) and *Roberts v. Louisiana* (1976), the Court declared that statutes mandating the death penalty for certain offenses were unconstitutional. These two decisions invalidated mandatory capital punishment statutes in

21 states and reduced the capital sentences of hundreds of inmates to life imprisonment (University of Alaska, 2000).

In *Coker v. Georgia* (1977), the Court held that the death penalty for rape of an adult female was disproportionate to the offense and therefore unconstitutional. The decision lead to the reduction of 20 rape-based death sentences across the United States. The 1978 Supreme Court decision in *Lockett v. Ohio* (1978) required sentencing authorities to consider broadly every possible mitigating factor relating to the offense before them rather than being limited to those on a specified list. Lockett resulted in the release of 99 condemned inmates from Ohio's death row (University of Alaska, 2000).

In unrelated challenges between 1986 and 1989 (University of Alaska, 2000), the Supreme Court held it unconstitutional to execute the mentally insane (*Ford v. Wainwright*, 1986) as well as those under 16 at the time they killed (*Thompson v. Oklahoma*, 1988). The Court also held it not categorically unconstitutional to put to death the mentally retarded (*Penry v. Lynaugh*, 1989), although it has recently agreed to revisit this issue later this year (Death Penalty Information Center, 2001a).

THE DEATH PENALTY AND GENDER

Feminist Theories and Capital Punishment

Although scholarly writing sometimes concerns itself with women on death row, little has been written about females and the death penalty (Carroll, 1997). This may have to do with the few women sentenced to death, or the cultural anomaly of actually executing them (Rapaport, 1990). As deftly indicated by Carroll (1997, p. 1413): "Why focus on capital punishment when death row is roughly as open to women as is the United States Senate?"

Although the number of women contemporarily sentenced to die, or actually executed, is perhaps too low to be of much statistical interest (Carroll, 1997), the disparity between the risk of male and female execution might support the belief that there is "a chivalrous disinclination to sentence women to die" (Rapaport, 1990, p. 504). If true, however, this disinclination dissipates rapidly and in proportion to the type and degree of violent conduct exhibited by these females.

Concentrating on prosecutorial discretion and juror disposition to sentence women to death, gender-based theories account for much discussion as to why some women are executed and others not. No gender-based theory, however, can boast the long and detailed support that race- or class-based theories enjoy (Carroll, 1997), although theories based on race or class may not consider gender-centric causative factors unique to female criminality.

The Chivalry Theory

The chivalry theory argues that women are safeguarded by traditional and protective notions of femininity, which preclude jurors from seeing women as "death eligible" despite the vicious nature of the act with which they are charged. Gender assumptions that stereotype women as being weak, passive, submissive, and dependent on men are viewed as creating a protective shield that makes females less attractive to imprison and less eligible to execution (Carroll, 1997).

As Victor Streib notes: "It's like a girl playing on the football team. Knocking her on her butt doesn't give you the same thrill as it would if it was a big guy. The death penalty is partly man against man" (Phillips, 2000), a notion echoed by Leigh Beinen, a Northwest University law professor who studies death-penalty related gender bias (Rueter, 1996). Beinen believes that few women face execution because of the symbolism central to capital punishment, saying: "Capital punishment is about portraying people as devils, but women are usually seen as less threatening."

The Evil Woman Theory

The basis of the evil woman theory is that a female who acts particularly violently, or in gender-defying or forbidden ways, is denied the protections of gender afforded others of her gender, making her more eligible for death sentencing if she commits a capital crime. To fit this model, a woman must violate the important social values of humanity with her criminal act, and the strictures of femininity with her "unladylike" conduct. Such behavior allows judges and juries to put aside notions of these defendants as the "gentler sex" and to see them as dangerous monsters (Carroll, 1997).

Chivalry versus Evil Woman: A Commonality

According to Carroll (1997), supporters of the chivalry and evil woman theories agree that the death penalty really acts to enforce the outer boundaries of acceptable feminine behavior by marking gender-acceptable boundaries. The penalty of death and the act of execution are viewed by these proponents as proof that the law enforces social conformity. To be executed, murderers must represent the power of evil. Because women rarely descend to such levels, and because of the ritualistic, reclaiming aspects associated with execution, women are rarely put to death. It is the rare woman, and the rare act of evil by women, that is sufficiently powerful to make executing her reassure us about our own personal safety. To reach this level, these theorists agree, a woman must frighten, behaving completely in opposition to the female norm expectations of others. Death eligibility for women implies not only the cessation of womanly conduct, but also the taking on of typically male violence (Carroll, 1997).

The Equality Theory

Women tend to commit different kinds of crime and have less extensive criminal records than men, which might account for fewer women being sentenced to death and ultimately executed. These factors suggest that forces other than gender may influence which women are subject to capital sanction, and that a theory of equality may be more representative than either the chivalry or evil woman theories as a reason why women receive the death penalty (Carroll, 1997).

The equality theory proposes that females are sentenced to death only when their offenses are particularly egregious and uses their scarcity on death row to suggest that few women commit the type of offense that warrants capital punishment for either gender. Noted gender researcher Elizabeth Rapaport suggests that equality theory may be the most accurate explanation concerning women on death row, given the limited information available, because it most neatly reflects the stories of men on death row, suggesting an overall equality in sentencing (Carroll, 1997).

Putting Theory to the Test

Five of the women executed in the present death penalty era clearly fit the mold agreed upon by experts as providing "a better chance of being sentenced to death" (Streib, 2000a), having committed "Bonnie and Clyde types of things" (Streib, 2000b, p. 3), "coldblooded [sic], very atrocious type of crime" (Phillips, 2000, p. 3). Juries and judges who might otherwise have found mitigation related to gender (Rueter, 1996) were unable or unwilling to in their cases. The cases of Velma Barfield, Christina Riggs, and Wanda Jean Allen, however, are arguably different in these respects.

Evidence that gender-neutral factors may account for the same results as those more gender-centric exists (Rueter, 1996), although the continuing sociolegal migration toward actual gender equality may eventually make all gender-based factors concerning women and capital punishment moot (Streib, 1990). As for Karla Fay Tucker, Judias Buenoano, Betty Lou Beets, and Marilyn Kay Plantz, the sheer brutality of their crimes appears to have done that for them.

Velma Barfield's execution, on the other hand, may have resulted as much from incredibly poor timing as any other factor, including the nature of her crime. Support for the death penalty was high in North Carolina and the governor was running for a hotly contested senatorial seat, the election for which was just four days after the scheduled execution date (Rapaport, 1990). Barfield may have been as much a victim of politics as of her own bad acts.

As for Christina Riggs, her execution remains a bizarre anomaly of the U.S. justice system. Initially, Riggs requested the trial jury to sentence her to death (Death Penalty Information Center, 2000a) and later mounted a very limited appeal of her murder conviction, but not her sentence (*Riggs v. Arkansas*, 1999), and finally chose to actively decline all further appeals of both her conviction and sentence (Death Penalty Information Center, 2000a).

Although it fits the rubric of the evil woman theory, Wanda Jean Allen's case arguably does so more due to her own nature than that of the murder for which she was put to death. Unlike Tucker, Buenoano, Beets, and Plantz, Allen's violation of the strictures of femininity hurt her at least as much, and probably more, than any perceived violation of the objective rules of humanity. Joanne Bell, executive director of the Oklahoma chapter of the American Civil Liberties Union, pointed out that had Allen been part of a straight couple, she probably would have been tried for manslaughter, not murder, and therefore not faced the death penalty (Simo, 2001). Allen was a lesbian convicted of killing her live-in lesbian lover. This was a fact exploited by the prosecution during her trial (Kirby, 2001) and used by the gay and lesbian media to point out perceived homophobic attitudes, but rarely mentioned outside that forum (Simo, 2001). As Tonya McClary, program director for the National Coalition to Abolish the Death Penalty said, "Oklahoma is in the Bible

Belt; it's very homophobic" (Kirby, 2001). None of this, however, minimizes the cold-blooded nature of the murder for which Allen was put to death.

SEVEN WOMEN

Velma Barfield

Velma Barfield, executed in North Carolina on November 2, 1984 (Death Penalty Information Center, 2001c), was the first woman to die in the United States in the modern era of the death penalty and the first woman to be executed in 22 years. Put to death for killing her boyfriend with arsenic, Barfield admitted to poisoning three other persons, including her mother, and was suspected in the poisoning death of her husband (Death Penalty Information Center, 2000a).

Barfield poisoned her boyfriend to prevent his filing forgery charges related to checks for prescription drugs to which she had long been addicted. This followed a pattern evidenced in several of her previous murders. Her jury found aggravating circumstances in that the murder was based on pecuniary gain as well as the desire to avoid criminal liability (Death Penalty Information Center, 2000a).

Barfield's sentence was not only carried out—unique enough, regardless of gender, when so many death sentences are commuted for a variety of reasons—but also went forth despite what was characterized as her "miraculous" transformation while in prison (Carroll, 1997). This "born-again christian [sic] grandmother, now drug free, well adjusted and extraordinarily well liked, even loved, at Women's Prison," perhaps should have been granted clemency, and indeed might have been were it not, many believe, for the proximity of the election (Rapaport, 1990).

Karla Fay Tucker

Karla Fay Tucker became the second woman put to death in the modern death penalty era and the first executed in Texas since the Civil War (CNN Interactive, 1998). Although there is no doubt of her readily admitted guilt (Gwynne, 1998), it remains unclear whether the enormous coverage surrounding her case was due more to her gender or profound conversion to Christianity (Agitator, 1998b), or to the fact that she was "an attractive young woman" (Maloney, 2000, p. 8). Tucker may not have been "the same person who had coldly participated in two murders 15 years earlier" (Maloney, 2000, p. 9), but the facts surrounding her case epitomize her as perhaps the very essence of the "evil woman" (Carroll, 1997, p. 1421). Her crimes have been characterized as "particularly brutal" (Horn, 1998).

Tucker and her boyfriend, after consuming "an astonishing quantity of heroin, Valium, speed, percodan, mandrax, marijuana, dilaudid, methadone, tequila and rum" (Gwynne, 1998), broke into an occupied apartment, where Tucker's boyfriend struck the male victim with a hammer (*Tucker v. Texas*, 1988). As the victim begged for his life, Tucker struck him repeatedly with a pickax until he was dead, the pair later repeating the process on a female found hiding under a blanket in the apartment (Rapaport, 1990). Afterward, Tucker told her sister that "she got a thrill while 'picking' Dean," and that "every time she 'picked' Jerry, she looked up and she grinned and she got a nut and hit him again." Both bodies suffered over 20 wounds (CNN Interactive, 1998), and the female victim still had the pickax embedded in her when later discovered (Rapaport, 1990).

Were the details of the two murders not enough to seal Tucker's fate, her own penalty phase testimony most certainly was. Tucker's admission of a personal history of vicious fights, planned robbery-murders, and two planned witness killings clearly showed that she represented a continuing danger to society (Rapaport, 1990). Despite the perhaps meritorious argument that she found religion and changed remarkably since her conviction (Maloney, 2000), Karla Fay Tucker was executed on February 3, 1998 (CNN Interactive, 1998). The following month, Judias Buenoano became the third woman executed in the modern death penalty era.

Judias Buenoano

Judias Buenoano might never have been suspected of murder were it not for her 1983 attempt to kill her fiancé by a car bomb (Agitator, 1998a). He survived, had some pills she had previously given him analyzed, and discovered that they contained deadly poison (*Buenoano v. Florida*, 1988). When police investigated the bombing they realized that "Buenoano" was Spanish for "Goodyear," learned of her previous marriage under that name, and discovered that her former husband's body contained lethal amounts of arsenic (Agitator, 1998a).

Testimony at Buenoano's murder trial revealed that she had told two friends how to kill with poison, admitting to them that this was how she murdered Goodyear. One of these women also testified that Buenoano told her that she should heavily insure her husband and then poison him, to escape her poor marriage (*Buenoano v. Florida*, 1988).

Although convicted only of murdering Goodyear, there was evidence that Buenoano had poisoned a previous boyfriend, as well as her own son (Agitator, 1998a). Buenoano had her mortgage paid, and additionally collected $118,000 in insurance and other compensation from money gained from the three murders. Had she succeeded in killing her fiancé, Buenoano would have received over $510,000 in life insurance, plus 60 percent of his estate (*Buenoano v. Florida*, 1988).

Executed by Florida on March 30, 1998 (Death Penalty Information Center, 2001c), Buenoano holds the dubious distinction of being the first woman to die in that state's electric chair (Florida Department of Corrections, 2000). Arguably, she could also be the poster-child for the evil woman theory. Her conviction resulted in virtually no publicity (Maloney, 2000). The same was not true, however, for Betty Lou Beets. Beets was a great-grandmother, and virtually none of the rather extensive international coverage of her execution let the world forget it.

Betty Lou Beets

When executed by Texas (British Broadcasting Corporation [BBC], 2000) on February 24, 2000 (Death Penalty Information Center, 2000d), Betty Lou Beets was a 62-year-old great-grandmother, a fact that the world media mentioned prominently in almost every report concerning her (Time.com, 2000). Also mentioned, although less prominently, were unsubstantiated allegations by Beets that she had been a battered wife (BBC, 2000).

Mentioned as an afterthought in many articles, however, was that Beets had been convicted of murdering her fifth husband (Yahoo!News, 2000) for his insurance and pension (BBC, 2000), shooting her second husband and charged but not tried for the murder of her fourth husband. Dubbed the "Black Widow" (APB News, 2000) due to her fatal propensity toward eliminating her mates, Beets's two dead husbands were found buried around her home, both encased in sleeping bags and both shot in the backs of their heads (BBC, 2000). Beets was the second woman executed in Texas since statehood and the fourth in the modern death penalty era (Yahoo!News, 2000).

Christina Riggs

Christina Riggs's execution came about so suddenly that virtually no news coverage or protests resulted from it. Foregoing additional appeals that may have preserved her life indefinitely, and refusing to ask the governor for clemency (Death Penalty Information Center, 2000b), Riggs became the first woman ever executed by the state of Arkansas and the fifth woman in the United States to be executed since *Furman* (Death Penalty Information Center, 2001c), succumbing to lethal injection on May 2, 2000 (D. Tyler, personal communication, May 1, 2000).

Convicted of the premeditated murders of her five-year-old son and two-year-old daughter in November 1997, Riggs readily admitted to suffocating each child when drugs she had administered failed to kill them. Admittedly despondent due to personal problems over which she planned to kill herself, Riggs admitted to killing her children to prevent them from thinking she did not love them and to prevent a custody battle that might have separated the children due to their differing fathers (*Riggs v. Arkansas*, 1999).

Wanda Jean Allen

When executed by the state of Oklahoma on January 11, 2001, Wanda Jean Allen became the sixth woman put to death since U.S. executions resumed in 1977 (Death Penalty Information Center, 2001c). She also became a woman of many dubious firsts. The first lesbian executed in the United States in the twenty-first century (Simo, 2001), Allen was also the first woman executed by Oklahoma since statehood (Death Penalty Institute of Oklahoma, 2001) and the first black woman put to death in the United States since Betty Jean Butler was executed in Ohio in 1954 (Fight the Death Penalty in USA, 2001).

Ending their relationship after a domestic dispute, Gloria Leathers left the house that she and Allen shared and rode with her mother to the police station to file a report arising from the breakup. Allen followed, and after trying unsuccessfully to reconcile (Pro Death Penalty.com, 2001), shot Leathers once in the abdomen with a handgun she held concealed under her sweatshirt. Allen fled but was arrested four days later, the same day that Leathers succumbed to her wound (Pro Death Penalty.com, 2001).

Approaching the execution, much of the world's media (Simo, 2001) focused on the defense contentions that Allen had an IQ of 69, which placed her within the range of mental retardation (Kirby, 2001). Ignored was that a psychologist placed her IQ at 80 in the mid-1990s (Fight the Death Penalty, 2001). Also ignored was Allen's mother's testimony that Allen had done well in school (Rueter, 1996).

Virtually ignored was the manslaughter conviction (Carroll, 1997) that Allen was on probation for when she killed Leathers (Fight the Death Penalty, 2001), her written threat to kill Leathers were she to end their relationship, and her having told Leathers's son, on the day of the shooting, that she would not rest until Leathers was dead (Carroll, 1997).

Marilyn Kay Plantz

Marilyn Kay Plantz, the seventh woman executed since *Furman*, ushered in the present U.S. death penalty era (Death Penalty Information Center, 2001c). The second female put to death by Oklahoma in less than four months (Yahoo!News, 2001), remains as of this writing, the last woman executed in the United States (Death Penalty Information Center, 2001c).

Executed May 1, 2001, for the murder of her husband Jim Plantz, the death was planned to look like an accident (Doucette, 2001a) in order to cash in on approximately $219,000 in life insurance (*Plantz v. Oklahoma*, 1994). Marilyn Kay Plantz epitomizes all that the evil woman theory implies. After several failed attempts to have her husband killed (*Plantz*), Marilyn Plantz arranged for her lover (Doucette, 2001a) and another man (*Plantz*) to ambush Jim Plantz as he entered the house that he and Marilyn shared. Both men beat Plantz repeatedly with baseball bats that she provided (*Plantz*). Although the victim cried out for her as he was being struck, his cry went ignored. Marilyn Plantz was waiting in her bedroom for the attackers to finish (Doucette, 2001b).

After severely beating Jim Plantz, the assailants carried their now-moaning victim outside, where Marilyn commented that her husband's "head was busted open" and that his injuries did not appear accidental. Marilyn then ordered the men "to burn him" (*Plantz*) and returned to the house to clean up the blood (Doucette, 2001a).

With one assailant driving Jim Plantz's pickup, and the other following in Marilyn's car, the killers drove to a rural area (Doucette, 2001a), placed the victim behind the truck's steering wheel, doused him and the cab with gasoline, and set him on fire. Both men admitted seeing the victim rise up as they drove away, and evidence indicated that Jim Plantz had tried to escape from the burning truck before being felled by smoke and flames (*Plantz v. Oklahoma*, 1994).

The killers returned to find Marilyn still cleaning up blood, and at her direction, exchanged their bloody clothing for that of their victim. The killers left the Plantz home, disposed of the bloody clothing, which had been put into a sack by Marilyn, and then bought sandwiches and drinks with money from Jim Plantz's trouser pockets (*Plantz*).

The Plantz's then nine-year-old daughter and five-year-old son, asleep in the next room throughout the attack, reacted to their mother's death sentence quite differently. Whereas her daughter reconciled with her and appealed for mercy on her behalf, Plantz's son visited her but without reconciliation. In fact, her son wrote the following to the Oklahoma Pardon and Parole Board: "Can you even try to imagine in your worst nightmares, having your father killed in the very next room with the T-ball bat he taught you to hit with the day before?" (Doucette, 2001a).

One of the killers that Marilyn Plantz hired testified for the prosecution in exchange for his life (Peebles, 2001). Her former lover (Doucette, 2001a), later executed for his part in the murder (Mullen, 2001), testified that while he had no particular reason to kill Jim Plantz, he thought of the abuse Marilyn told him she suffered at the hands of her husband, including blackened eyes which he himself had seen (Peebles, 2001). Although Marilyn Plantz told the police that she and her husband had enjoyed a perfect marriage, and during her trial steadfastly denied any role in the murder of her husband (Peebles, 2001), she eventually confessed to her part in the killing (Yahoo!News, 2001).

Although mounting questions continue to develop concerning the forensic work and related testimony of Oklahoma City police chemist Joyce Gilchrist (Yahoo!News, 2001), neither Gilchrist nor her work were seen as a deciding factor in Plantz's conviction (ChannelOklahoma, 2001b) or execution (Yahoo!News, 2001). Any controversy which might have been raised in the Plantz case became, as noted by Oklahoma Governor Frank Keating, outweighed by the damning testimony of one of her co-conspirators, additional and unchallenged evidence of her guilt, and her own confession (Yahoo!News, 2001).

CONCLUSIONS

One recent death-penalty-related study showed that not only was there lack of evidence of any deterrent effect following Oklahoma's reinstitution of the death penalty after a 25-year moratorium, but killings between strangers actually increased significantly after that state again began executions. Strikingly similar results were shown in a California study, following the first execution in that state in 25 years, although the increased murder rate was more modest than in Oklahoma and was studied for only eight months following the particular executions. Research in Texas found that the infliction of capital punishment had no effect on the number of murders in that state despite the fact that Texas had been conducting executions at a relatively steady rate for many years (*Riggs v. Arkansas*, 1999).

As for gender, the issue becomes even murkier. The United States holds the dubious distinction of housing more women condemned to death than any other country in the world, although this population remains virtually invisible unless a woman is scheduled for imminent execution. This comparatively small population, coupled with its invisibility (Thompson, 1997), are two major reasons why gender is not studied more, and this lack of study is why gender-centric reasons for women committing capital crimes, and being put to death for these crimes, are still, to this day, greatly unknown. If these reasons are to become known, research must be undertaken to pinpoint the reasons why women commit capital offenses, especially in light of the few gender-centric theories that purport to account for what is a varied and growing death row population in the United States.

What has been a much hidden and ignored problem must not be permitted to remain so (Thompson, 1997), at least if we, as a society, are not to have this population continue to grow until, by sheer numbers, it forces us to conduct such important research. By then, of course, any steps taken will have been too little and too late for the even larger number of women who find themselves on this country's death rows, as well as their victims.

Although the population of women on death rows in the United States is infinitesimal compared with similarly situated males (Thompson, 1997), it remains inconceivable, especially in this so-called modern age, that such a unique and identifiable population can simply be ignored. Their identifiability, if not also their low numbers, make them an almost ideal class for particularly accurate and effective research and for results implementation.

The worst crime may not be the comparatively few murders committed by these women, although each in itself is tragic, as much as the almost larger evil represented by our ignorance of why they were committed. This is especially true in considering a population as generally nonthreatening, well adjusted to incarceration, and unbelievably amenable to rehabilitation, as are the vast majority of females sentenced to death row.

Perhaps their very amenability, adjustment, and nonthreatening status is their worst enemy, robbing these women of the possibility of advanced treatment modalities that could better support their approach to normalized, if not also productive lives while remaining imprisoned. This would almost assuredly be the result if this population were larger, or their behavior more noticed.

As for the women executed since the reinstitution of the death penalty, excluding Velma Barfield, Christina Riggs, and possibly Wanda Jean Allen, for the reasons stated earlier, each stands apart as a stark exception that reinforces the probability of the points noted above. Tucker, Buenoano, Beets, and Plantz each killed while not needing to kill. They killed out of evil intent and design, not from necessity; and in each of the cases described, these women did so particularly coldbloodedly. These four women stand as stark exceptions to every stricture that would have allowed them to remain indistinguishable within the limited "crowd" that are women sentenced to die in the United States. They set themselves apart from the group by their overt viciousness, and they paid for this ferocity with their lives.

POSTSCRIPT

Since this chapter was originally published, three more women have been executed in the United States (Death Penalty Information Center, 2005a): Lois Nadean Smith, in Oklahoma on December 4, 2001; Lynda Lyon Block, in Alabama on May 10, 2002; and Aileen Carol Wuornos, in Florida on October 9, 2002 (Prosecuting Attorney, Clark County, Indiana, 2005).

Lois Nadean Smith was put to death for the torture-killing of her son's former girlfriend (Pro Death Penalty.com, 2005a). "Mean Nadine," as she was referred to during an Oklahoma Pardon and Parole Board hearing (Amnesty International, 2001), killed her son's girlfriend over rumors the girl was going to report the son's involvement with illegal drugs to authorities (Pro Death Penalty.com, 2005a).

Trial testimony indicated Smith stabbed her victim in the throat, twisting the knife before removing it; repeatedly told the victim she was going to be killed; and jumped repeatedly on her victim's throat, before the victim succumbed to the last of eight gunshot wounds (Pro Death Penalty.com, 2005a). Smith testified that she had stabbed and shot at the victim, but had not intended to kill her (Pro Death Penalty.com, 2005a).

Issues raised unsuccessfully during Smith's appeal included an alleged conflict of interest in that her trial attorney represented both she and her co-defendant, and failure of counsel to introduce, as a mitigating factor, Smith's lack of criminal history (National Coalition to Abolish the Death Penalty, 2005).

Smith, 61, was the third and last woman executed in the United States in 2001, all from Oklahoma, emptying that state's women's death row (COURTTV.com, 2001). This was the highest number of women executed in one year during the modern era of the death penalty (Death Penalty Information Center, 2005a).

Lynda Lyon Block, 54, was executed by the State of Alabama for her part in the murder of an on-duty Opelika police sergeant (Dead Man Eating.com, 2005). Block's common-law husband, George Sibley, Jr., with whom she was fleeing a pending criminal complaint in Florida, was approached by the sergeant as he was waiting for Lynda to finish a call at a nearby public telephone booth (Pro Death Penalty.com, 2005).

Witnesses testified that Sibley began firing at the sergeant, and that Block then approached and began firing (Pro Death Penalty.com, 2005a). Although Block and Sibley maintained they fired in self-defense after the officer touched his holster, witnesses said Sibley fired at the sergeant first, with Block joining in after the sergeant was already wounded (Pro Death Penalty.com, 2005a). Both were sentenced to death partially because ballistics experts could not determine who actually fired the fatal shots (Pro Death Penalty.com, 2005a).

Although listed by several sources as a "volunteer"—a condemned person who chooses to forgo appeals to hasten execution—it appears Block's death was not so much the result of volunteerism as it was of liberal political fanaticism. Block and her husband, both antigovernment zealots, maintained that Alabama never regained statehood again following the Civil War, that it therefore lacked the authority to try them, and steadfastly refused to participate or assist in any appeals (Pro Death Penalty.com, 2005a).

That Block was not a true volunteer is reflected in the fact that, shortly before her execution, she sent a handwritten letter requesting clemency from Alabama Governor Don Siegelman, which was denied (Robinson, 2002).

Block, the first woman executed by Alabama since 1957 (Pro Death Penalty.com, 2005a), will almost certainly be the last woman—and probably the last condemned of either gender—to die in Alabama's electric chair. The state has since legislated lethal injection as the preferred method of execution, unless electrocution is specifically requested by a condemned person (Dead Man Eating.com, 2005).

Aileen Carol Wuornos, 46 (Koch, 2002), is arguably the most well-known female condemned of the modern death penalty era. Her story has been made into at least three books, a television movie, a documentary, and an opera (Pro Death Penalty.com, 2005a). In fact, within weeks of her arrest Wuornos and her attorney had sold the movie rights to her story (Prosecuting Attorney, 2005), and three top investigators on the case hired lawyers to field Hollywood offers (National Coalition to Abolish the Death Penalty, 2002).

Traced through her thumbprints on pawn tickets of items taken from some of the victims (Prosecuting Attorney, 2005), Wuornos was convicted of one murder, pled guilty to five others, and was suspected in the disappearance of a seventh man, all whom she met as a roadside prostitute (Pro Death Penalty.com, 2005a).

Although she initially maintained her innocence, even after her conviction, Wuornos eventually admitted to the murders (Pro Death Penalty.com, 2005), fired her attorneys, and actively opposed all appeals and efforts of mitigation made by others on her behalf (Koch, 2002).

Many sources have labeled Wuornos America's first female serial killer (UPI, 2005). Although not definitive, that development alone set Wuornos apart from the already unique group that are female murderers in America.

Unlike any of the other women executed in the modern era of the death penalty, however, Wuornos aggressively and repeatedly sought out complete strangers for victimization, coldly killed and robbed them, and admittedly would have continued to do so if she had not been stopped (Pro Death Penalty.com, 2005a), her own words chillingly reflecting this reality: "I killed those men, robbed them as cold as ice. And I'd do it again, too. There's no chance in keeping me alive or anything, because I'd kill again. I have hate crawling through my system" (Pro Death Penalty.com, 2005a).

Wuornos, at least at this writing, has the dubious distinction of being the last woman executed in the United States (Death Penalty Information Center, 2005a).

Without exception, each of these women, their crimes and their fates, seems to match, almost too well, those that have come before. Each of these women was a fervent participant in the crimes for which condemned, and committed acts heinous in both violence and brutality—at least in the cases of Block and Wuornos—continuing to bring attention to themselves beyond the point of their convictions. By their own doing these women set themselves apart from women who could seek the protection of their own femininity as insulation from execution.

As of this writing, there are no female executions scheduled imminently anywhere in the United States (Death Penalty Information Center home page, 2001). This could change at any time, however, depending on the progress of individual cases. There remains no moratorium on public execution in the United States, including the execution of women, and no such moratorium, formal or informal, is projected.

Retired Supreme Court Justice Harry Blackmun, commenting on the effectiveness of capital punishment, said he felt "morally and intellectually obligated to concede that the death penalty experiment has failed" (Maloney, 2000). Although this may or may not be true intellectually, realistically such concerns are made virtually mute by the polemic that the death penalty inspires.

Immediately after the execution of Barbara Graham and two accomplices following an infamous 1950s murder, reporter Al Martinez told the arresting detective outside the execution area that their deaths would make little overall difference. "Others will go on killing," Martinez said. The detective looked at Martinez for some time before he replied: "But they won't" (Martinez, 2000).

Although neither side involved in the death penalty debate may ever prove that theirs is the right argument, or perhaps even the better argument, one fact seems undeniable. As long as states continue to spend more money on prisons than on education, there will remain a need to argue the effectiveness of capital punishment, with or without regard to the issue of gender.

Frances Elaine Newton, executed for the murders of her husband, 7-year-old son, and 21-month-old daughter, never wavered from her claim of innocence, saying the killings may have been the result of a drug debt owed by her husband, a longtime drug addict (Carson, 2005). This prospect, although corroborated by the victim's brother, who told authorities where the dealer lived, was never investigated by authorities (Smith, 2005), who built a largely circumstantial case against Newton.

Newton and her husband were having marital problems and seeing others at the time of the murders (Smith, 2005), and her husband told his girlfriend on the day of the killings that he did not trust Newton. Damming, too, was the fact that Newton had purchased life insurance on her husband and daughter—a policy already existing on her son (Carson, 2005)—forging her husband's signature on insurance purchased only months before the murders (Pro Death Penalty.com, 2005d). Newton was arrested and charged with murder the next day (Carson, 2005).

As for other evidence, Newton told police she had removed a pistol from the family home the day of the murders (Smith, 2005) and hid it inside an abandoned house owned by her parents (Carson, 2005), in plain view of her cousin, saying she did so to keep her husband from getting into trouble with it (Smith, 2005). Problems arose later in that prosecutors and other law enforcement personnel seem to differ as to how many similar firearms had been recovered and tested in connection with the case, thus clouding the evidentiary value of the resulting ballistic evidence. Nitrites, possibly from contact with either gunpowder or fertilizer, and present near the hem of Newton's skirt (Smith, 2005) though not on her hands or sweater (Democracy Now!, 2005), raised more questions about whether Newton had merely held or actually fired a gun. The case was further jeopardized in that the forensics tests were conducted at the Houston Police Crime Lab—a facility in which results have been repeatedly and successfully challenged as incompetent, resulting in a number of embarrassing exonerations. This reputation contributed to Governor Perry's granting of a 120-day reprieve to retest the physical evidence (Smith, 2005).

Although the gun was retested and was found to have fired the fatal shots, the skirt Newton wore could not be retested (Carson, 2005). Tests performed in 1987 had destroyed any nitrites on the garment, and court officials had contaminated it by sealing it in a bag that also contained the victim's bloody clothing (Smith, 2005). No trace of blood was ever found on Newton's person, clothing, or car, despite the gory nature of the murder scene, as evidenced by the large amount of blood tracked from room to room by the murderer (Democracy Now!, 2005).

None of this, however, seems to have raised doubt with the trial jury, primarily because no defense really materialized at her trial. Newton's trial attorney reportedly told a colleague he was "burned out" and unenthusiastic at the time of her trial (Carson, 2005) and never thoroughly examined the evidence against her (Democracy Now!, 2005). This poor performance was noted in the several complaints Newton filed with the trial judge concerning her representation and in an affidavit filed in the course of appeals by another attorney involved in the original trial, attesting to the trial attorney's provision of ineffective legal assistance (Pro Death Penalty.com 2005d).

Newton's execution does not mesh comfortably with any feminist theories so much as it does genderless theories involving geography, race, and class. Newton was not executed because she had allegedly committed particularly egregious, unique, or disquieting murders—women have been known to murder their mates and children—so much as because those murders took place in Texas, and because testimony and evidence in her case were not fully challenged or tested. Newton was the first black woman executed by the state of Texas since the Civil War (Smith, 2005).

REFERENCES

AGITATOR. (1998a). Case of Judias V. Buenoano, execution of Judias V. Buenoano. Accessed February 2000. http://www.agitator.com/dp/98/judibuen.html.

AGITATOR. (1998b). Case of Karla Faye Tucker, execution of Karla Faye Tucker. Accessed February 2000. http://www.agitator.com/dp/98/karlatuck.html.

AMNESTY INTERNATIONAL. (2001, December 7). USA: Further information on death penalty, Lois Nadean Smith, Sahib al-Mosawi. Retrieved June 13, 2005, from http://web.amnesty.org/library.index.ENGAMR511782001?open&of=ENG2AM.

APB NEWS. (2000, February 24). Texas executes "Black Widow." Accessed February 24, 2000. http://www.apbnews.com/cjsystem/justicenews/2000/02/24BEETS0224_01.html.

BRITISH BROADCASTING CORPORATION. (2000, February 25). U.S. grandmother executed for murder. Accessed February 25, 2000. http://news.bbc.co.uk/hi/english/world/Americas/newsid_655000/655686.stm.

CARROLL, J. E. (1997). Images of women and capital sentencing among female offenders: Exploring the outer limits of the Eighth Amendment and articulated theories of justice. *Texas Law Review*, *75*, 1413.

CARSON, D. (2005, September 15). *Texas Executions.Org*. Retrieved September 15, 2005, from http://www.txexecutions.org/reports/349.asp.

CHANNELOKLAHOMA. (2001a, January 12). State executes Wanda Jean Allen. Accessed April 30, 2001. http://www.channeloklahoma.com/okl/news/stories/news-20010111-165311.html.

CHANNELOKLAHOMA. (2001b, May 1). Gilchrist problems won't stop Plantz execution. Accessed June 18, 2001. http://www.channeloklahoma.com/okl/news/stories/news-74885020010501-110518.html.

CNN INTERACTIVE. (1998). Profile: Facing death with memories of murder. Accessed March 3, 2000. http://www.cnn.com/SPECIALS/1998/tucker.execution/profile.

COURTTV.COM.(2001). Oklahoma puts third woman to death, passes Texas for number of executions this year. Retrieved June 13, 2005, from http://www.courttv.com/news/death_penalty/120501_okla_ap.html.

DEAD MAN EATING.COM. (2005). Alabama last meal Lynda Lyon Block. Retrieved June 13, 2005, from http://deadmaneating.com/dme2002.html.

DEATH PENALTY INFORMATION CENTER. (2000a). Arkansas executes despondent woman. http://www.deathpenaltyinfo.org/index.html.

DEATH PENALTY INFORMATION CENTER. (2000b). Facts about deterrence and the death penalty. Accessed April, 2000. http://www.deathpenaltyinfo.org/index.html

DEATH PENALTY INFORMATION CENTER. (2000c). History of the death penalty. Accessed February 2000. http://www.deathpenaltyinfo.org/index.html.

DEATH PENALTY INFORMATION CENTER. (2000d). What's new (last updated February 25, 2000). Accessed February 25, 2000. http://www.deathpenaltyinfo.org/index.html.

DEATH PENALTY INFORMATION CENTER. (2001a). Upcoming executions. Accessed May 26, 2001. http://www.deathpenaltyinfo.org/index.html.

DEATH PENALTY INFORMATION CENTER. (2001b). What's new (last updated June 15, 2001). Accessed June 18, 2001. http://www.deathpenaltyinfo.org/index.html.

DEATH PENALTY INFORMATION CENTER. (2001c). Women and the death penalty. Accessed May 26, 2001. http://www.deathpenaltyinfo.org/index.html.

DEATH PENALTY INFORMATION CENTER. (2005a). Executions scheduled for 2005. Retrieved July 2, 2005, from http://www.deathpenaltyinfo.org/article.php?scid=8&did=190.

DEATH PENALTY INFORMATION CENTER. (2005b). Searchable database of executions. Retrieved June 20, 2005, from http://www.deathpenaltyinfo.org/getexecdata.php.

DEATH PENALTY INFORMATION CENTER. (2005c). Women and the death penalty. Retrieved June 20, 2005, from http://www.deathpenaltyinfo.org/getexecdata.php.

DEATH PENALTY INFORMATION CENTER. (2005d). Number of executions by state and region since 1976. Retrieved September 18,2005, from http://www.deathpenaltyinfo.org/article.php?scid=8&did=186.

DEATH PENALTY INSTITUTE OF OKLAHOMA. (2001, February 27). Wanda Allen executed January 11, 2001. Accessed April 30, 2001. http://www.dpio.org/inmates/Allen_Wanda.html.

DEMOCRACY NOW! (2005). From Death Row: Texas set to execute first African-American woman since Civil War. Retrieved September 17, 2005, from http://www.democracynow.org/article.pI?sid=05/08/25/1342238.

DOUCETTE, B. (2001a, May 1). Woman awaits her execution. *Oklahoma Online.* Accessed May 1, 2001. http://www.oklahoman.com/cgi-bin/show_article?ID=677729&pic=none&TP=getarticle.

DOUCETTE, B. (2001b, May 2). Woman dies for husband's 1988 slaying. In the news: Corrections news from around the world. Accessed May 26, 2001. http://www.doc.state.ok.us/DOCS/News/010502itn.htm.

FIGHT THE DEATH PENALTY IN USA. (2001). Executions, 1996–2000. Accessed June 18, 2001. http://fdp.dk/uk/exec/exe-0101.htm.

FLORIDA DEPARTMENT OF CORRECTIONS. (2000). Death row fact sheet: Facts and fallacies. Accessed February 2000. http://www.dc.state.fl.us/oth/deathrow.

GWYNNE, S. C. (1998, January 19). Why so many want to save her. *Time.Com.* Accessed March 3, 2000. http://www.time.com/time/magazine/1998/dom/900119/crime.a_time_investigati7.html.

HORN, R. (1998, January 20). Outspoken jurist says death penalty needs to be consistent. http://www.reporternews.com/local/poe0120.html.

KIRBY, D. (2001). Was justice served? *Advocate.* Accessed April 30, 2001. http://www.advocate.com/html/stories/832/832_wandajean.asp.

KOCH, J. (2002, October 9). Serial killer Aileen Wuornos executed. United Press International. Retrieved June 22, 2005, from http://www.upi.com/view.cfm?StoryID=20021009-104131-9199r.

MALONEY, J. J. (2000). The death penalty. *Crime magazine: An encyclopedia of crime.* Accessed March 3, 2000. http://www.crimemagazine.com/cp101.htm.

MARTINEZ, A. (2000, March 12). The long, cold mile. *Los Angeles Times*, p. B1.

MULLEN, T. (2001, April 18). Board rejects woman's bid for clemency. *Daily Oklahoman.* Accessed June 18, 2001. http://www.ocadp.org/plantz.html.

NATIONAL COALITION TO ABOLISH THE DEATH PENALTY. (2001). Execution alert, Oklahoma, Lois Nadean Smith. Retrieved June 19, 2005, from http://ncadp.org/html/decalertok01.html

NATIONAL COALITION TO ABOLISH THE DEATH PENALTY. (2002, October 9). Retrieved June 22, 2005, from http://www.ncadp.org/html/oct_02-florida.html.

PEEBLES, R. (2001). Clemency denied on April 17. Death Penalty Institute of Oklahoma. Accessed June 20, 2001. www.dpio.org/inmates/Plantz_Marilyn.html.

PHILLIPS, R. A. (2000, February 25). No gender equality on death row. *APBNews.* Accessed February 25, 2000. http://www.apbnews.com/cjsystem/findingju_/women0226_01.html?s=syn.yahoofc_women022,1,2.

PRO DEATH PENALTY.COM. (2001). January 2001 executions. Accessed June 1, 2001. http://prodeathpenalty.com/Pending/01/jan01.htm.

PRO DEATH PENALTY.COM. (2005a). December 2001 executions. Retrieved June 13, 2005, from http://www.prodeathpenalty.com/Pending/01/dec01.htm.

PRO DEATH PENALTY.COM. (2005b). May 2002 executions. Retrieved June 13, 2005, from http://www.prodeathpenalty.com/Pending/02/may02.htm.

PRO DEATH PENALTY.COM. (2005c). October 2002 executions. Retrieved June 13, 2005, from http://www.prodeathpenalty.com/Pending/02/oct02.htm.

PRO DEATH PENALTY.COM. (2005d). September 2005 executions. Retrieved September 20, 2005, from http://www.prodeathpenalty.com/pending/05/sep05.htm.

PROSECUTING ATTORNEY, CLARK COUNTY, INDIANA. (2005). Aileen Carol Wuornos. Retrieved June 22, 2005, from http://www.clarkprosecutor.org/html/death/US/wuornos805.htm.

RAPAPORT, E. (1990) Some questions about gender and the death penalty. *Golden Gate University Law Review, 20*, 501–538.

REGGIO, M. H. (2000). History of the death penalty. Frontline: The execution. Accessed March 2000. http://www.pbs.org/wgbh/pages/frontline/shows/execution/readings/history.html.

ROBINSON, C. (2002, May 10). *Birmingham News*. p. 1-A.

RUETER, T. (1996). Why women aren't executed: gender bias and the death penalty. www.abanet.org/irr/hr/genderbias.html.

SCHMALL, L. (1996). Forgiving Guin Garcia: Women, the death penalty and commutation. *Wisconsin Women's Law Journal, 11*, 283–315.

SIMO, A. (2001). Oklahoma kills black lesbian. *The Gully*. Accessed April 30, 2001. http://www.thegully.com/essays/gaymundo/010115allen.html.

SMITH, J. (2005, September 8). *Austin Chronicle*. Retrieved September 16, 2005, from http://disc.server.com/discussion.cgi?disc=207906;article=10095;title=Against%20Death.

SMITH, S. C. (1999, December 2). Capital punishment in the United States. *Close Up Foundation: Capital Punishment in the United States*. www.closeup.org/punish/org.

STREIB, V. (1990). Death penalty for female offenders. *University of Cincinnati Law Review, 58*, 845–867.

STREIB, V. (2000a). Death penalty for female offenders: January 1973 to June 1999. http://www.law.onu.edu/faculty/streib/femdeath.htm.

STREIB, V. (2000b, February 26) No gender equality on death row. *APBNews*. Accessed March 2000. http://www.apbnews.com/cjsystem/findingjustice/2000/02/26/women0226_02.html.

TEXAS DEPARTMENT OF CRIMINAL JUSTICE. (2000). Final meal requests. Accessed March, 2000. http://TDCJ.ST.TX.US/stat/finalmeals.htm.

THOMPSON, C. (1997). The invisibility of women on death row: A personal view. *Lifelines Ireland Newsletter*. Accessed April, 2000. http://www.sun.soci.niv.edu/~critcrim/dp/dp-wom1.

TIME.COM. (2000, February 24). Improbably, Betty Lou Beets' death is news. Accessed February 24, 2000. http://www.time.com/time/daily/0,2960,39849-101000224,00.html.

UNIVERSITY OF ALASKA–ANCHORAGE. (2000). Focus on the death penalty. *Justice Center Web site*. Accessed March 2000. http://www.uaa.alaska.edu/just/death/history.html.

YAHOO!NEWS. (2000, February 25). Texas executes grandmother. sg.dailynews.yahoo.com/headlines/world/afp/article.H..../Texas_executes_evidence.htm.

YAHOO!NEWS. (2001, May 1). Oklahoma executes woman despite evidence dispute. Accessed May 28, 2001. http:/dailynews.yahoo.com/h/nm/20010501/ts/usa_execution_oklahoma_dc_1.html.

CASES

Allen v. Oklahoma, No. 99-6033 (1999) WL 49284 (10th Cir., July 13, 1999). Unpublished opinion.

Buenoano v. Florida, 527 So. 2d 194 (Fla. Sup. Ct., 1988).

Coker v. Georgia, 433 U.S. 584 (1977).

Crampton v. Ohio & McGautha v. California (consolidated under) 402 U.S. 183 (1971).

Ford v. Wainwright, 477 U.S. 399 (1986).

Furman v. Georgia, 408 U.S. 238 (1972).

Gregg v. Georgia, 428 U.S. 153 (1976).

Jurek v. Texas, 428 U.S. 262 (1976).

Lockett v. Ohio, 438 U.S. 586 (1978).

Penry v. Lynaugh, 492 U.S. 302 (1989).

Plantz v. Oklahoma, 876 P.2d 268 (1994).

Proffitt v. Florida, 428 U.S. 242 (1976).

Riggs v. Arkansas, 3 S.W. 3d 305 (1999).

Roberts v. Louisiana, 428 U.S. 325 (1976).

Robinson v. California, 370 U.S. 660 (1962).

Thompson v. Oklahoma, 487 U.S. 815 (1988).

Trop v. Dulles, 356 U.S. 86 (1958).
Tucker v. Texas, 771 S.W. 523 (1988).
U.S. v. Jackson, 390 U.S. 570 (1968).
Witherspoon v. Illinois, 391 U.S. 510 (1968).
Woodson v. North Carolina, 428 U.S. 280 (1978).

35

Women on Death Row

Etta F. Morgan

Capital punishment is a controversial issue in society, yet it is the most severe punishment that our courts can administer. The purposes of this chapter are to (a) provide a historical overview of capital punishment; (b) explain capital punishment using Girard's theory of culture; (c) examine the influence of the Supreme Court regarding capital punishment; (d) discuss the importance of gender in the criminal justice process; and (e) review the literature on executed females as well as share some of the experiences and problems of female death-row inmates.

INTRODUCTION

Ironically, every aspect of our society is influenced by the social and cultural perspectives that dominate our being. These influences are also prevalent in the administration of our prisons. Women, as second-class citizens in society, carry this status into the penal system, which openly ignores their needs in more ways than one. One prime example would be that most states have only one prison for women, and some have none. Female criminality and experiences have often been described based on men's experiences. Previous research (Erez, 1989; Kruttschnitt, 1982; Mann, 1984; Pollock-Byrne, 1990; Visher, 1983; Zingraff & Thompson, 1984) suggests that, as a group, women have been treated more leniently in the criminal justice system than men. If this is true, then it may explain the disproportionate number of women sentenced to death in relation to the number of men sentenced to death. Female offenders have often been a forgotten population in research as well as in reality.

Limited research has focused on women sentenced to death. Victor Streib publishes a quarterly report, which details demographics about the offender, a brief statement about the offense, and the current status of the inmates (i.e., reversals, commutations). Gillespie

(1997), O'Shea (1999), and O'Shea (2000) provide historical data about the lives of women sentenced to death, their crimes and trials, various legislation affecting women sentenced to death, and the period leading up to the executions and the actual executions. Other authors (Fletcher, Dixon, Shaver, & Moon, 1993; Mann, 1984) tend to devote only a few pages in textbooks to a discussion of women on death row. Perhaps this is due to the fact that women do not commit violent crime at the same rate as men.

There appears to be an increase in female crime based on the current *Uniform Crime Reports (UCR)*, but it is unclear as to whether this increase is due to actual offenses or changes in reporting practices by law enforcement agencies. Cautiously interpreting the *UCR* data, there seems to be an increase in violent crimes by females, but basically, female crime is still concentrated in the area of property crimes. Upon closer examination of violent crimes, it is found that women homicide offenders tend to kill persons of the same race, usually an intimate male associate. As a group, women murderers are not as common as their male counterparts, which could possibly influence the treatment they receive in the criminal justice system. In examining the imposition of death sentences in this country, it is obvious that women are not sentenced to death or executed at the same rate as men.

The death penalty has and continues to be a controversial issue in the United States. It is the ultimate sentence that can be imposed for a criminal offense. Proponents of the death penalty suggest that it is needed in order to deter would-be criminals, while opponents believe that it is an inhumane act on the part of society in administering justice. In the past, the death penalty was withdrawn because some states were unfairly targeting specific populations of offenders. Although it was reinstated by the Supreme Court in 1976, the controversy has not been settled as to whether the death penalty should be used as a form of punishment.

HISTORICAL OVERVIEW

Capital punishment is a controversial issue nationally as well as internationally. It is believed to have been in existence before societies became organized. After the organization of society, legal codes were established in an attempt to provide rules and regulations for social control. Capital punishment has been included in legal codes since the period of the Old Testament continuing on to the Code of Hammurabi, Assyrian laws, Athenian codes, European laws, and the code established in the 13 colonies (Koosed, 1996).

Capital punishment in the United States has been greatly influenced by English traditions and research has shown it to be an Anglo-American custom (Paternoster, 1991). The practice of capital punishment in the colonies reflected the ideology of the American people in regard to the types of crime that were considered capital offenses. Because there was no uniform criminal code throughout the colonies, each state had different capital statutes (Kronenwetter, 1993; Paternoster, 1991). In some instances, states declared fewer offenses (5–8) capital offenses if committed by whites while identifying 70 offenses as capital offenses if committed by blacks (Paternoster, 1991). After the American Revolution, states begin to restrict the number of offenses that could be classified as capital offenses. States also narrowed the application of capital punishment by establishing degrees of murder and giving juries more discretion in sentencing, thereby permitting the jury to sentence people to death in only the most serious murders (Paternoster, 1991).

Along with the passage of discretionary statutes for capital crimes, this period of American capital punishment has two distinct characteristics. First, executions were public events and second, local authorities were responsible for performing all executions. Executions were performed as public events until the end of the 1800s, although some public executions were performed as late as 1936 and 1937 (Paternoster, 1991). At the turn of the century we find a shift from public executions controlled by local authorities to executions controlled and conducted by the state (Paternoster, 1991).

Capital punishment's historical significance is not only related to punishment but also to social control. Capital punishment was often administered upon those identified as members of problem populations. It was believed that these populations did not respect established authority. In many instances, these populations were viewed as threatening or dangerous to established authority. Capital punishment also had an extralegal form that was lynching. According to Paternoster (1991), "[l]ynching, primarily by vigilante groups, was frequently used by majority groups to keep minorities oppressed" (p. 8). The use of this extralegal form of capital punishment claimed more lives than legal executions (Paternoster, 1991). Although we experienced a decline in lynchings with the centralization of the death penalty, there were more executions between 1930 and 1940 than were noted for the following 20 years. During the 1960s and 1970s, there was a decline followed by a moratorium on capital punishment (Paternoster, 1991).

Over time, there have been regional differences in the imposition of the death penalty. Historically, the South has performed more executions than any other region. In examining capital offenses and capital statutes during the premodern era, Paternoster (1991) states, "one interesting feature about the imposition of capital punishment for different offenses is that the region of the country and the race of the offender has been, at least in the past, an important correlate" (p. 15). Statistics (Flanagan & Maguire, 1989) suggest that race may have been an overriding factor in the imposition of the death penalty for particular offenses in the South resulting in racially biased applications of the death sentence. It has also been suggested, as in previous years, that capital punishment continued to be used as a form of social control for specific groups.

Capital punishment, as the ultimate sentence, has also created problems for juries. Specifically, juries were at odds with the harshness of the laws and as a result found themselves mitigating that fact instead of the case. In later years, juries were given discretionary powers with the understanding that they were to consider any and all factors related to the case that could support a death sentence as well as factors supportive of a noncapital sentence (Paternoster, 1991). This unbridled reign led to irrational and discriminatory practices in the imposition of death sentences. The uncontrolled sentencing freedom enjoyed by juries and the misapplication of death sentences "led to the temporary suspension of the death penalty in the United States" (Paternoster, 1991, p. 17).

The modern era of capital punishment represents the return to the imposition of death sentences. During the moratorium on capital punishment, the Supreme Court ruled that the discretionary powers given to juries were unconstitutional along with the procedures used for the imposition of death sentences. A thorough examination of the Supreme Court's position as it relates to capital punishment will be examined in more detail later using Girard's theory of culture.

THEORETICAL ANALYSIS

The debate over capital punishment remains unresolved in American society. Some believe that capital punishment deters would-be criminals while others contend that persons should be punished based on the doctrine of retribution. Another possible explanation for the existence of capital punishment in our society may be the need for ritualized violence as a method of social control. Although controversial, Rene Girard's theory of culture (1977) based on religious thought, anthropology, psychology, literary criticism, and other social sciences appears to explain the importance of the death penalty in our society. According to Girard (1987):

> In the science of man and culture today there is a unilateral swerve away from anything that could be called mimicry, imitation, or mimesis. And yet, there is nothing, or next to nothing, in human behavior that is not learned, and all learning is based on imitation. If human beings suddenly ceased imitating, all forms of culture would vanish. . . . The belief is that insisting on the role of imitation would unduly emphasize the gregarious aspects of humanity, all that transforms us into herds. There is a fear of minimizing the importance of everything that tends toward division, alienation, and conflict. If we give a leading role to imitation, perhaps we will make ourselves accomplices of the force of subjugation and uniformity. (p. 7)

The theory that human behavior is, to some extent, learned behavior resulting from imitating the behavior of others has also been advanced by theorists such as Aristotle, Plato, Tarde, and Sutherland. Although Plato's description of imitation, as well as his followers, failed to identify specific behaviors involved in appropriation, Girard (1987) states that "if imitation does indeed play the fundamental role for man, as everything seems to indicate, there must certainly exist an acquisitive imitation, or, if one prefers, a possessive mimesis whose effects and consequences should be carefully studied and considered," not overlooked (p. 9). It is indisputable that imitation brings about conflict but, in many instances, persons have learned to control and dispense imitated behavior in acceptable ways.

Society determines which behaviors are authorized, thereby identifying behaviors that may or may not be imitated. In other words, there are restricted imitations. These prohibitions exist because some behaviors are just plain absurd or they threaten the safety of society (Girard, 1987). It has been suggested that primitive societies understood that there was a relationship between mimesis and violence unlike modern society (Girard, 1987). The theory of culture advanced by Girard claims that:

> [T]here is a connection between conflict and acquisitive mimesis. Modern society tends to view competition and conflict differently from primitive society mainly because we tend to see difference emerge from the outcome of a conflict. . . . [W]e tend to focus on the individual act. (pp. 11–12)

By focusing on the individual act, instead of the act and its context, we (modern society) are able to view violence as an isolated crime. In doing so, we fail to truly understand the context in which the act was committed and its relationship to the violence experienced. Instead, we depend upon the power of our judicial institutions to mandate adherence to the rules of social order which does little, if anything, to increase our understanding of imitative violence or the importance of external factors to violent behavior(s). The purpose of these judicial institutions seems to imply that all persons in a society will abide by the laws that have been established and agreed upon by the members of society, but this is not true—especially since laws tend to represent the wishes of those persons who have power and wealth in society (the elite) in an attempt to control the masses.

It has been suggested that without these institutions, "the imitative and repetitious character of violence becomes manifest once more; the imitative character of violence is in fact most manifest in explicit violence, where it acquires a formal perfection it had not previously possessed" (Girard, 1987, p. 12). For example, in previous societies, a murder expanded substantially in the form of blood feuds. Violent acts, such as the blood feuds and other rivalries, had to be curtailed in order to reunite the community and the solution had to be dramatic and violent. Basically, the idea was and remains violence begets violence.

In *McGautha v. California* (1971) a violent solution was also suggested by one justice as the only means by which violence could be ended even though it was noted that violence is self-propagating. Fortunately or unfortunately, our society has established a judicial institution in the form of the death penalty as a means to end violence (sanctioned self-propagating violence). Society has proscribed the method, time, and deliverer of the punishment for the sanctioned ritualized killing of another individual (Girard, 1987). As such, the death penalty is a dramatic and violent solution used to reunite the community, but fails, unless the targeted community is the victim's family, not society as a whole. Beschle (1997) states, "[M]odern legal systems seek to break the cycle of imitative violence by directing the punitive urge of all members of society toward a common enemy" (p. 521). The common enemy becomes the "new victim" in the community-sanctioned ritualized violence.

In order to proceed through the various phases of the ritualized killing, there must first be some type of relationship established between the "new victim" and the community. As part of the ritualized killing, it is important that the person to be executed (the new victim) is viewed as the cause of the community's discord and that his or her death will somehow restore peace in the community. Girard (1987) also suggests that "at the moment when violence ceases and peace has been established, the community has the whole of its attention fixed on the victim it has just killed" (p. 81) which leads one to surmise that, in some instances, there is a fascination with some executed individuals such as Gary Gilmore and Ted Bundy.

In addition to the symbol of intense interest in the executed victim, there are many symbols associated with the death process. For example, the tradition of the *last meal* is viewed as a special privilege or a ritualized privilege granted by the community to one who, for a brief period, is perceived as special and worthy of this treatment. Additionally, the person who has received the death sentence most often is a typical member of the community, but is also significantly different because of his or her criminal act. This being the case, most members of the community lack compassion for and do not identify themselves with the offender. Having used Girard's theory of culture to explain the symbolism in the death process, we will now use his theory to examine the shift in the rulings of the Supreme Court.

Girard's (1987) theory can be used as a plausible explanation for the shift in the courts from being concerned with guilt to focusing more on expediting executions. As justices are replaced on the Court, we find that the new member is expected to bring to the

Court a particular view that is shared by the controlling political party. The justice, then, merely advances the opinions shared by those who are not in office who share the same beliefs. In many instances, justices have been accused of relying on personal feelings or previous policy decisions that purportedly expressed the public's desires, in order to write opinions for various cases. This being the case, it is safe to assume that some of the opinions rendered by the Court have not only been influenced by public opinion but also mirror public opinion, thereby extending the theory of imitation to the Court. For this reason, we are able to link Girard's theory of culture to the shift in Supreme Court decisions based on the makeup of the Court and the political climate under which it has operated. Girard (1987) noted that society does not desire to be perceived as in a state of constant revenge, but is more interested in providing an effective judicial system that allows permissible social constraints. The apparent shift in the Supreme Court suggests that some, if not all, of the justices believe that there must be little or no interference from the Supreme Court in lower court decisions. This "hands off" approach has evolved over time as the Supreme Court has decided various cases. In the following sections, we will briefly discuss this evolutionary process of the Supreme Court.

THE INFLUENCE OF THE SUPREME COURT

One phase that the Supreme Court entered into can be identified as the period of constitutionality. By this we mean that the Court was concerned with the issue of whether or not the death penalty itself was against the Constitution of the United States. *Powell v. Alabama* (1932) (the right to appointed counsel in capital cases) is said to represent the beginning of the Court's reform efforts concerning the death penalty. It is during this period that the Court used broad interpretations of the Fourteenth Amendment to bring about changes in criminal justice systems throughout the states in relation to capital cases. However, the main issue of whether the death penalty was in violation of the Constitution was often *not discussed*. It was not until Justice Goldberg's dissenting opinion in *Rudolph v. Alabama* (1963) that there was even any hint of a constitutional issue.

The Court continued to avoid the issue of constitutionality until there was an active campaign against the death penalty initiated by the NAACP Legal Defense Fund, which resulted in a moratorium against executions. During this period, the Court, in *Witherspoon v. Illinois* (1968), ruled that juror exclusion could not be based solely on an individual's personal objections to the death penalty. It is also in *Witherspoon* that we find the first written opinion (by Justice Stewart) in a case decision that questions the propriety of the death penalty. Without ruling specifically on whether the death penalty was against the Constitution of the United States, the Court suggested that morally sound jurors would not impose the death penalty upon another human and, therefore, a decision concerning the matter was unwarranted by the Court (Burt, 1987). The Court presumed that American society was harmonious and stable and would work in such a manner as to maintain social order (Burt, 1987). The implication was that the maintenance of social order would deter and/or reduce crime and there would be no need for administering the death penalty. Therefore, the Court would not have to address the constitutionality issue concerning the death penalty.

However, four years later in *Furman v. Georgia* (1972), the majority of the justices declared that the death penalty as administered was in violation of the Eighth Amendment protection against cruel and unusual punishment. The rationale for this conclusion varied among the justices, but the main concern was the application of the death penalty under the existing standards. However, the Court failed to declare the death penalty unconstitutional based on a different set of standards. By 1976, the Court in *Craig v. Boren* (1976), *Proffitt v. Florida* (1976), and *Jurek v. Texas* (1976) ruled that the sentence of death was not an unconstitutional punishment and for a brief period began scrutinizing imposed death sentences upon appellate review. According to Burt (1987), "this kind of closely detailed, sustained observation by the Supreme Court was itself 'aberrational'" (p. 1780).

Beginning in 1983, the Court turned resolutely away from this pursuit, instead appearing intent on affirming capital punishment in order to suppress "'the seeds of anarchy—of self help, vigilante justice, and lynch law'" (Burt, 1987, p. 1780). The Court not only seemed to support capital punishment, but it also began closing avenues previously open to inmates seeking federal constitutional relief. State appellate courts were encouraged to (a) spend less time reviewing cases, (b) overlook admitted errors in death penalty proceedings, and (c) disregard the proportionality review process (Burt, 1987). Then, in 1985, the Court made another shift in the capital punishment debate.

In *Wainwright v. Witt* (1985) the Court dismantled the opinion it rendered in *Witherspoon* concerning death-qualified jurors and instead concluded that there was a presumption of correctness on the part of state judges in excluding jurors. This action by the Court blocked federal constitutional review unless the defense attorney could show that the trial judge had erred. Given the resources available to defense attorneys in capital cases, the likelihood of a challenge to the presumption of correctness lies moot. The Court continued to tear down the tenets of the *Witherspoon* decision in its ruling of *Lockhart v. McCree* (1986). It ruled that even if a death-qualified jury is more conviction prone than other juries, that fact alone *does not* raise a constitutional issue for review by the Court. According to Burt (1987), the Court's ruling in *Lockhart* reveals that "the Court is content on suppressing rather than exploring doubts about capital punishment" (pp. 1788–1789).

The twenty-first century has been interesting to say the least in regard to the Supreme Court's rulings on death penalty cases. In *Atkins v. Virginia* (2002), the Court held that "executions of mentally retarded criminals are 'cruel and unusual punishments' prohibited by the Eighth Amendment" (pp. 5–17). The Supreme Court in its ruling suggested that society no longer approves of executing mentally disabled offenders noting that consistently states are passing legislation declaring that death is not an acceptable punishment for these individuals. In another landmark decision, the Supreme Court ruled in *Roper v. Simmons* (2005), "the Eighth and Fourteenth Amendments forbid imposition of the death penalty on offenders who were under the age of 18 when their crimes were committed" (pp. 6–25). Again, the Court notes that its decision is based upon the evolving standards of decency that have been expressed by enactments of legislatures and the Court's own judgment, adding that "the death penalty is a disproportionate punishment for juveniles" (pp. 10–21). It is apparent that some state legislatures and the Supreme Court have begun to listen to the voice of the people in regard to certain legal issues; however, we must also remember that each case that comes before the Court must stand on its own merit. The debate over capital punishment is not over; for now, two crucial issues have been resolved until they are once again challenged in the courts.

It is not surprising that the controversy surrounding capital punishment continues when the justices of the Supreme Court cannot effectively deal with the issue. If there are constitutional safeguards to ensure that inmates are afforded those rights, why should judges be instructed to overlook such safeguards? Does this mean that the justices of the Supreme Court view persons convicted and sentenced to death as less than human and, therefore, should not be afforded the rights guaranteed by the Constitution? It seems fair to say that the chaos that has plagued the Court concerning capital punishment is representative of the con-fusion and inconsistencies that prevail in society about capital punishment. Perhaps, the chaos that plagues us (society) could be diffused by simply treating those persons sentenced to death as human beings until death, if an execution is forthcoming. After all, what does society have to lose, if death is what one seeks? Does acknowledging that these people are human stir up emotions that one tries hard to suppress? Is that why we prefer not to read or hear about the conditions of incarceration? Facing the reality that death-row inmates are humans, just like any of us, makes it hard to accept the inadequacies of prison life.

THE ADMINISTRATION OF LAW

Laws, in any society, define behaviors that are deemed unacceptable based on the morals and values of the community at large. They also determine who will be punished (Price & Sokoloff, 1995). In societies that are not very complex, informal rather than formal methods are used as means of social control. Both society and individuals are presumably protected by the laws. These laws may prescribe punishments, direct or restrain certain actions, and access financial penalties. Price and Sokoloff (1995) state "the law protects what those in power value most" (p. 14). Laws are created and passed by legislative bodies composed mainly of rich, white men and persons who share their interests (Price & Sokoloff, 1995). Laws are the mechanism by which the dominant class ensures that its interests will be pro-tected (Quinney, 1975). However, challenges to specific laws are not uncommon (Price & Sokoloff, 1995).

Historically, women have been considered the property of their fathers or husbands without full acknowledgment of them as individuals with rights granted by the Constitution (Price & Sokoloff, 1995). Several cases have come before the Supreme Court concerning the rights of women. In the landmark case of *Reed v. Reed* (1971), the Supreme Court ruled that women were indeed persons and should be treated as such under the United States Constitution. The Court stated that the Fourteenth Amendment clause:

> does not deny to States the power to treat different classes of persons in different ways. . . . [It] does, however, deny to States power to legislate that different treatment be accorded to per-sons placed by a statute into different classes on the basis of criteria wholly unrelated to the objective of that statute. A classification "must be reasonable, not arbitrary, and must rest upon grounds of difference having a fair and substantial relation to the object of the legislation. . . ." (*Reed v. Reed*, 1971)

According to the justices, preference based on sex that is used merely to reduce the number of court hearings that could arise because two or more persons are equally entitled is directly in violation of the Fourteenth Amendment clause forbidding arbitrariness, nor can sex be used as a preventive measure against intrafamily controversies (*Reed*, 1971). Based on this ruling, the Court recognized women as individuals with the right to individualized treatment, but it did not identify sex in relation to the suspect-classification argument under the Fourteenth Amendment.

It was not until *Frontiero v. Richardson* (1973) that the Court attempted to rule that sex was a suspect-classification that "must be subjected to strict judicial scrutiny" (p. 677). This case involved differential treatment of men and women in the military in regard to their respective spouses being classified as dependents. The ruling by the Court also stated that the current statute was in violation of the Due Process Clause of the Fifth Amendment. Justice Powell suggested that the Court should not rule on sex as a suspect-classification because the Equal Rights Amendment (ERA) had been approved by Congress and it would eliminate the need for such a classification (*Frontiero*, 1973). Unfortunately, the states did not ratify the ERA. Sex discrimination would have evolved had there not been a plurality decision.

Women were still seeking equal rights during the Ford and Carter administrations, although the Court ruled in *Craig* (1976) that "classification by gender must serve important governmental objectives and must be substantially related to achievement of those objectives." Yet, this case did not have a true impact on constitutional law; instead, it most notably suggested that there were changes in alliances among the justices. These cases represent only small legal gains by women.

According to Hoff (1991):

> [S]ome of the most disturbing gender-biased decisions the Supreme Court has reached in the last seventeen years have involved pregnancy cases. . . . [O]ther recent decisions are either discouraging or disquieting for the cause of complete female equality, especially where redistributive economic issues are at stake. (p. 251)

Knowing that many households are now headed by women has not moved Congress or the Supreme Court to properly address the comparable worth issue. Instead, they avoid the comparable worth issue as though it were a plague. Women must decide "whether they prefer equal treatment as unequal individuals (when judged by male standards) or special treatment as a protected (and thus implicitly) inferior group" (Hoff, 1991, p. 274). The legal system has not always treated women and girls fairly and this could be due in part to the perceptions men (who are the majority in the legal system) have of females (Price & Sokoloff, 1995). Roberts (1994) states, "the criminal law most directly mandates socially acceptable behavior. Criminal law also helps to shape the way we perceive women's proper role" (p. 1). Women who do not adhere to prescribed gender roles and commit criminal offenses are viewed differently by our criminal justice system. This issue will be discussed more fully in the following section.

Female Criminality

Female crime is not as prevalent as that of males and previously had not been considered a social problem (Belknap, 1996). Women are also more likely to commit fewer and less serious violent crimes than males (Belknap, 1996; Mann, 1984; Pollock-Byrne, 1990;

Simon & Landis, 1991). Yet, we have been led to believe that female crime has reached outlandish proportions and far exceeds male crime. The basis for this information has been the *Uniform Crime Reports (UCR)* compiled by the Federal Bureau of Investigation (FBI) from data supplied by law enforcement agencies.

According to Steffensmeier (1995), these data (*UCR*) are problematic in assessing female crime patterns. Steffensmeier (1995) suggests the following: (a) the changes in arrest rates may be related more to "public attitudes and police practices . . . than actual behaviors"; (b) because of the broadness of categories they include "dissimilar events and . . . a range of seriousness"; and (c) the definition of serious crime as used by the *UCR* tends to lead one to believe that serious female crime has risen dramatically, when in fact, women have been arrested more for the crime of larceny, "especially for shoplifting" (p. 92) than any other Type I offense. Previous research (Mann, 1984; Naffine, 1987; Simon & Landis, 1991; Steffensmeier, 1980) has revealed that overall female crime rates have remained fairly stable in most areas. The notable changes are in the areas of "less serious property offenses and possibly drugs" (Belknap, 1996, p. 58).

In order to better assess the rate of female crime, Steffensmeier (1995) completed a 30-year study of arrest statistics. Although the study examined trends in individual offenses, of particular importance here are the trends by type of crime based on male and female arrests. The type of crimes chosen to develop trends for male and female arrests were "violent, masculine, Index [serious], and minor property" (Steffensmeier, 1995, p. 94). He found that female participation in masculine crimes increased slightly which led to more arrests, but this was not the case for violent crimes. Steffensmeier (1995) again attributes the increase in arrests for index crimes to an increase in the number of women committing larcenies. Women have also had an increase in arrest rates for minor property crimes (Belknap, 1996; Steffensmeier, 1995). Simpson (1991) suggests that violent behavior varies among females and it is difficult to separate the individual influences of race, class, and gender because they are so intermingled. For the purposes of this chapter, we will only examine the influence of gender in the administration of law.

Having examined briefly female criminality, we will now turn our attention to the processing of female criminal cases by the criminal justice system. It has been suggested (Chesney-Lind, 1982; Farnworth & Teske, 1995; Frazier, Bock, & Henretta, 1983; Harvey, Burnham, Kendall, & Pease, 1992; Spohn & Spears, 1997; Steffensmeier, 1980) that women receive differential treatment during the processing of criminal cases. The differential treatment may be negative or positive. For example, Steffensmeier (1980) suggested that the likelihood of future offending and the perceived danger to the community influenced the preferential treatment of women in the criminal justice process and as a result increased their chances of receiving probation instead of prison. Yet, Chesney-Lind (1982) discovered that female juveniles have always received negative differential treatment. She noted that the females were processed into the juvenile justice system as a result of status offenses and received institutionalization more often than male juveniles.

Frazier and colleagues (1983) examined the effect of probation officers in determining gender differences in sentencing severity. In their study, they collected data from presentence investigation reports with various information concerning the offender as well as recommendations from the probation officers regarding sentences. According to Frazier et al. (1983), "there is a strong relationship between gender of offender and final criminal court disposition. . . . [P]robation officers' recommendations have major effects and . . . being female greatly increases the likelihood of receiving a nonincarceration sentence recommendation" (pp. 315–316). Harvey et al. (1992) in an international comparison of gender differences in criminal justice found that women were processed out of the criminal justice system more often than men. Their study also revealed that men who were processed through the criminal justice system were convicted and imprisoned at a higher rate than women worldwide. Harvey, et al. (1992) note that "criminal justice worldwide operates differentially by gender (but not necessarily in a discriminatory way)" (p. 217).

In another study, Farnworth and Teske (1995) found some evidence of gender disparity in relation to charge reductions if there was no prior criminal history. The absence of prior offending was noted to increase the possibility of probation for females. Based on the selective chivalry thesis, Farnworth and Teske (1995) discovered that "white females were twice as likely as minority females to have assault charges changed to nonassault at sentencing" (p. 40). There was also supportive evidence, which suggested that the use of discretionary powers influenced informal rather than formal decisions (Farnworth & Teske, 1995).

More recently, Spohn and Spears's (1997) study of the dispositions of violent felonies for both men and women revealed that more men (71.4%) than women (65.0%) were prosecuted, but their conviction rates were very similar and major differences appeared in sentencing. For example, males were incarcerated 77.4% of the time versus 48.2% for females. Overall, females normally served 428 fewer days in prison (p. 42) than males. This study also found that charge reduction or total dismissal of charges was more likely for females than males. Spohn and Spears (1997) state:

> Females were more likely than males to have injured their victims. . . . Female defendants were much less likely than male defendants to have a prior felony conviction. Females were charged with and convicted of less serious crimes and were less likely . . . to be charged with or convicted of more than one offense . . . less likely than males to have used a gun to commit the crime or to have victimized a stranger. . . . [F]emales were more likely to have private attorneys and to be released prior to trial. (p. 42)

Based on their findings, Spohn and Spears (1997) suggest that violent female offenders are looked upon differently by judges for various reasons such as (1) females may be perceived as less dangerous to the community; (2) females may have acted as an accomplice instead of being the primary perpetrator; (3) the risk of recidivism is less for females; and (4) there is better chance of rehabilitating female offenders.

WOMEN AND CAPITAL PUNISHMENT

The imposition of the death penalty is not just racially biased, but it is also gender biased. Streib (1990) states that gender bias is associated with two main sources: "(a) the express provisions of the law and (b) the implicit attitudes, either conscious or subconscious, of key actors involved in the criminal justice process" (p. 874). Although gender is not mentioned specifically in state statutes, there are certain considerations that may be applied differently based on gender (Streib, 1990). For example, most male criminals have prior criminal histories that include violent acts while women, on the other hand, do not have significant prior criminal histories and they tend to be less violent than their male counterparts. When women are arrested for murder, it is usually their first offense. Because there tends to be an absence of criminal behavior on the part of women, Mann (1984) and Steffensmeier (1980) suggest that women are not viewed as a threat to society. Another factor considered in capital cases is the defendant's mental state. Allen (1987) suggests that a commonly held belief is that female murderers are emotionally unbalanced at the time of the crime. Additionally, women are usually not the primary perpetrator; therefore, they are able to request consideration for this mitigating factor. According to Streib (1990), "even when all of the specific aggravating and mitigating factors are the same for male and female defendants, females still tend to receive significantly lighter sentences in criminal cases generally" (p. 879).

In examining the treatment of female defendants in the criminal justice system, Gillespie and Lopez (1986) found:

> in one area, however, women have constantly been treated with unquestionable deference because of their sex—that of the death penalty. Women have been traditionally been considered a separate class, deserving of a brand of "justice" all their own. Rather than execute them, they have been lectured, even released to the supervision of their husbands, and often never brought to trial. (p. 2)

It has been suggested that this deference is directly related to the paternalistic attitudes of male power brokers in the criminal justice system. However, this idea explains only why some women receive preferential treatment. It is not useful in explaining the absence of this same treatment toward other women. It is this difference in the treatment received by other female defendants that makes them susceptible to harsh treatment in the criminal justice system. Research (Mann, 1984; Streib, 1990) has shown that women who are uneducated, poor, members of a racial minority group, and of a lower socioeconomic group tend not to receive preferential treatment in the criminal justice system. It is the women who have any or all of the aforementioned factors who are more likely to be condemned to death and, in some instances, executed in our society.

Historically, we find that there is and has been an acceptance of executing female offenders in this country. Although executions of female defendants are rare, there have been 533 confirmed executions of women since 1632. This represents 2.7% of all executions in this country. Yet, when we examine executions of females from other centuries, we find that fewer executions take place today than in the past. For example, women comprised only 0.5% of the executions during the twentieth century (Streib, 1998). In the following section, we will briefly discuss the characteristics of executed women.

We find that 68% of the women who have been executed were white and 32% were black. Although some defendants were over 50, the average age was 38.7 years old. In terms of previous criminal history, one had a prior homicide conviction while the others had only minor criminal histories. The motivation for the crimes was profit and emotion, but they were not always domestic situations (Gillespie & Lopez, 1986). Several patterns emerged related to executed women and the crimes. First, there was usually nothing unique or particularly heinous about the crime. Second, collecting insurance was the primary motive for the murder in many cases and in most instances, there was a male accomplice. Next, there seemed to be no established relationship between the victim and the defendant. Finally, the South has executed more women than any other region while New York leads the states in the execution of women (Gillespie & Lopez, 1986).

In examining death sentences from 1973 to 1997, we find that women received only 117 death sentences compared to over 6,210 death sentences for men (Streib, 1998). During the seventies women received only 21 death sentences, but there was a dramatic increase (29) in the number of death sentences imposed on women in the eighties for an overall total of 50 death sentences in the two decades following the resurgence of the death penalty. During 1989, there were 11 death sentences given to women representing the single highest total of death sentences given women in any one year from 1973 to 1997 (Death Penalty Information Center, 1998). In the nineties, 45 death sentences were imposed and the number of death sentences imposed on women exceeded the combined total of the two preceding decades. It is interesting to note that 72 of the death sentences imposed during 1973–1997 were either commuted to life imprisonment or reversed while three of the death sentences were actually fulfilled (Death Penalty Information Center, 1998; Streib, 1998). Since 1998 there have been 31 death sentences imposed on women: 7 in both 1998 and 2000; 5 in both 1999 and 2002; 2 in both 2001 and 2003; and 3 in 2004 (Streib, 2004). According to Streib, "the wide fluctuations in annual death sentencing rates (from one to eleven in a given year) are unexplained by changes in statutes, court rulings, or public opinion" (p. 6).

As of January 1, 2005 there were 3,401 males and 54 females on death row. Women constituted 1.56% of the total death-row population (Criminal Justice Project of the NAACP Legal Defense and Educational Fund, Inc., 2005). Some women are no longer legally under a death sentence (approximately four) but may continue to be housed on death row pending additional appeals and are therefore counted in the above total (Streib, 2004). Since capital punishment was reinstated in 1976, there have been 944 executions. Of these executions, only 10 women (Velma Barfield, 1984; Karla Faye Tucker, 1998; Judy Buenoano, 1998; Betty Lou Beets and Christina Riggs, 2000; Wanda Jean Allen, Marilyn Kay Plantz, and Lois Nadeen Smith, 2001; and Lynda Lyon Block and Aileen Wuornos, 2002) have been executed representing 1.06% of the total number of executions. Oklahoma leads the nation in executing women with 3 in 2001, followed by Texas and Florida with 2 each (Streib, 2004).

Upon closer examination, we find that the women on death row range in age from 25 to 75. Thirty-five percent of the women on death row were between the ages of 20 and 29 at the time of the criminal act. Thirty-six percent of the women were between 30 and 39 years old at the time of the crime. The racial breakdown of defendants reveals that 54% of the inmates are white while 32% are black. Latinas represent only 6% of the female death-row population (Streib, 2004). Briefly, we should note that the victims were 60% white, 13% black, 23% Latina, and 4% Asian. The majority of victims were male (56%) with females representing 44% of the victims. Most of the victims can be placed into two age categories: 0–10 (32%) and 18–49 (47%) (Streib, 2004).

The women who are currently serving a death sentence are subjected to the same inadequate environmental conditions as other women in prison, namely, poor medical care, inhumane treatment, and isolation from family. In many instances, people who are in correctional facilities become socialized to believe that they are (a) not human, (b) worthless, and (c) cannot be rehabilitated. In other words, they will always be criminals. Some critics also suggest that we should not permit persons on death row access to rehabilitative programs because they are serving a death sentence. I disagree, especially since the reversal rate on appeal for women is 97%.

Although the reversal rate for women is high, until their sentences are reversed, these women must survive within the confines of the institution. A major concern for death-row inmates is medical care. First, a death-row inmate has to wait until an officer makes a security check in order to secure a form requesting a doctor's visit. Then a nurse decides whether or not the request will be granted. In many instances, this decision is based solely on the nurse's opinion, not on a preliminary evaluation of the inmate's medical condition. Inmates state that they often do not seek medical assistance because the officers accuse them of trying to get attention. One inmate was so worried that the officers were going to accuse her of trying to get attention that she did not seek medical assistance at the onset of a heart attack. Her cellmate finally called an officer against the sick woman's wishes to take her to the infirmary. Unfortunately, the nurse in the infirmary said there was nothing wrong with her and had the inmate returned to her cell. The inmate died later that night of a massive heart attack. This is only one story of the lack of concern shown by some people who are employed to provide medical care to inmates. Yet, the media suggests that inmates have the best medical care available.

Death-row inmates, like other inmates, are seldom treated like persons by correctional officers and staff. Instead, they are made to feel like a burden that everyone wishes would go away. Because death row is isolated from general population, the correctional officers are the only people these inmates interact with during the day. If an inmate is housed in the same cell unit as another death-row inmate, they may visit and talk to each other. Some correctional officers speak to inmates in a manner that creates problems. By this I mean that inmates expect to be treated like humans, not animals or objects. Although their daily activities are programmed by the institution, some correctional officers add to the humiliation of the inmates by their conduct and handling of the inmate. It is times like these that inmates need to be able to turn to family to cope with the dehumanization characteristic of prison life.

In some instances, families cannot withstand the pressures associated with having a family member incarcerated. In far too many cases, family relationships are strained because there is little to no contact with the incarcerated person. Research (Mann, 1984; Pollock-Byrne, 1990) shows that women tend to lose contact with their families more often than men because women's facilities are in rural, remote areas of the state. As a result, visitation is more difficult and more restricted for death-row inmates. Women also experience a severe emotional separation from family and friends due to their socialization process. Family support adds to the inmate's sense of humanity. Without this support, inmates do not have a buffer from the institutional process of dehumanization.

CONCLUSION

The reversal rate on appeal for women sentenced to death is approximately 97% (Streib, 1998). Because of the high reversal rate associated with female offenders, we have been lulled into believing that women would not be executed. Given the current attitude toward executing women, we can expect an increase in the number of women executed. We believe that this increase is inevitable because of the "ever lingering get tough on crime" mentality presently dominant in our society along with recent legislation in Congress limiting appeals for defendants.

REFERENCES

ALLEN, H. (1987). Rendering them harmless: The professional portrayal of women. In P. Carlen & A. Worrell (Eds.), *Gender, crime and justice*. Milton Keynes: Open University Press.

BELKNAP, J. (1996). *The invisible woman: Gender, crime and justice*. Belmont, CA: Wadsworth.

BESCHLE, D. (1997). What's guilt (or deterrence) got to do with it?: The death penalty, ritual, and mimetic violence. *William and Mary Law Review, 38*(2), 487–538.

BURT, R. (1987). Disorder in the court: The death penalty and the Constitution. *Michigan Law Review, 85*, 1741–1819.

CHESNEY-LIND, M. (1982). Guilty by reason of sex: Young women and the juvenile justice system. In B. Price & N. Sokoloff (Eds.), *The criminal justice system and women* (pp. 77–105). New York: Clark Boardman.

CRIMINAL JUSTICE PROJECT OF THE NAACP LEGAL DEFENSE AND EDUCATIONAL FUND, INC. (2005, Winter). *Death row U.S.A.* New York: Author.

DEATH PENALTY INFORMATION CENTER. (1998). Facts about the death penalty. Washington, DC: Author.

EREZ, E. (1989). Gender, rehabilitation, and probation decisions. *Criminology, 27*(2), 307–327.

FARNWORTH, M., & TESKE, R., JR. (1995). Gender differences in felony court processing: Three hypotheses of disparity. *Women and Criminal Justice, 6*(2), 23–44.

FLANAGAN, T., & MAGUIRE, K. (1989). *Sourcebook of criminal justice statistics*. Washington, DC: U.S. Department of Justice, Bureau of Justice Statistics.

FLETCHER, B., DIXON SHAVER, D., & MOON, D. (1993). *Women prisoners: A forgotten population*. Westport, CT: Praeger.

FRAZIER, C., BOCK, E., & HENRETTA, J. (1983). The role of probation officers in determining gender differences in sentencing severity. *The Sociological Quarterly, 24*, 305–318.

GILLESPIE, L. (1997). *Dancehall ladies: The crimes and executions of America's condemned women*. New York: University Press of America.

GILLESPIE, L., & LOPEZ, B. (1986). *What must women do to be executed: A comparison of executed and non-executed women*. Paper presented at the American Society of Criminology, Atlanta, GA.

GIRARD, R. (1977). *Violence and the sacred* (Patrick Gregory, translator). Baltimore: Johns Hopkins University Press.

GIRARD, R. (1987). *Things hidden since the foundation of the world*. London: Athlone Press.

HARVEY, L., BURNHAM, R., KENDALL, K., & PEASE, K. (1992). Gender differences in criminal justice: An international comparison. *British Journal of Criminology, 32*(2), 208–217.

HOFF, J. (1991). *Law, gender & injustice: A legal history of U.S. women*. New York: New York University Press.

KOOSED, M. (1996). *Capital punishment: The philosophical, moral, and penological debate over capital punishment*. New York: Garland.

KRONENWETTER, M. (1993). *Capital punishment: A reference handbook*. Santa Barbara, CA: ABC-CLIO.

KRUTTSCHNITT, C. (1982). Respectable women and the law. *The Sociological Quarterly, 23*(2), 221–234.

MANN, C. (1984). *Female crime and delinquency*. Tuscaloosa: University of Alabama Press.

NAFFINE, N. (1987). *Female crime: The construction of women in criminology*. Sydney, Australia: Allen & Unwin.

O'SHEA, K. (1999). *Women and the death penalty in the United States, 1900–1998*. Westport, CT: Praeger.

O'SHEA, K. (2000). *Women on the row: Revelations from both sides of the bars*. Ithaca, NY: Firebrand Books.

PATERNOSTER, R. (1991). *Capital punishment in America*. New York: Lexington Books.

POLLOCK-BYRNE, J. (1990). *Women, prison, and crime*. Pacific Grove, CA: Brooks/Cole.

PRICE, B., & SOKOLOFF, N. (1995). The criminal law and women. In B. Price & N. Sokoloff (Eds.), *The criminal justice system and women: Offenders, victims, and workers* (pp. 11–29). New York: McGraw-Hill.

QUINNEY, R. (1975). *Class, state and crime: On the theory and practice of criminal justice*. New York: Longman.

ROBERTS, D. (1994). The meaning of gender equality in criminal law. *The Journal of Criminal Law and Criminology, 85*(1), 1–14.

SIMON, R., & LANDIS, J. (1991). *The crimes women commit, and the punishments they receive*. Lexington, MA: Lexington Books.

SIMPSON, S. (1991). Caste, class, and violent crime: Exploring differences in female offending. *Criminology, 29*(1), 115–135.

SPOHN, C., & SPEARS, J. (1997). Gender and case processing decisions: A comparison of case outcomes for male and female defendants charged with violent felonies. *Women & Criminal Justice, 8*(3), 29–59.

STEFFENSMEIER, D. (1980). Assessing the impact of the women's movement on sex-based differences in the handling of adult criminal defendants. *Crime and Delinquency, 26*, 344–357.

STEFFENSMEIER, D. (1995). Trends in female crime: It's still a man's world. In B. Price & N. Sokoloff (Eds.), *The criminal justice system and women: Offenders, victims, and workers* (pp. 89–404). New York: McGraw-Hill.

STREIB, V. (1988). *American executions of female offenders: A preliminary inventory of names, dates, and other information* (3rd ed.). Cleveland: Author.

STREIB, V. (1990). Death penalty for female offenders. *University of Cincinnati Law Review, 58*(3), 845–880.

STREIB, V. (1998). *Capital punishment for female offenders, names, dates, and other information* (3rd ed.). Cleveland: Author.

STREIB, V. (2004). *Death penalty for female offenders, January 1, 1973 through September 30, 2004*. Ada, OH: Author.

VISHER, C. (1983). Chivalry in arrest decisions. *Criminology, 21*(1), 5–28.

ZINGRAFF, M., & THOMSON, R. (1984). Differential sentencing of men and women in the U.S.A. *International Journal of the Sociology of Law, 12*, 401–413.

CASES

Atkins v. Virginia, 000 U.S. 00-8452 (2002).

Craig v. Boren, 429 U.S. 190, 197 (1976).

Frontiero v. Richardson, 411 U.S. 677 (1973).

Furman v. Georgia, 408 U.S. 238 (1972).

Jurek v. Texas, 428 U.S. 262 (1976).

Lockhart v. McCree, 106 S. Ct. 1758 (1986).

McGautha v. California, 402 U.S. 183 (1971).

Powell v. Alabama, 287 U.S. 45 (1932).

Proffitt v. Florida, 428 U.S. 242 (1976).

Reed v. Reed, 404 U.S. 71, 92 S. Ct. 251, 30 L. Ed. 2d, 255 (1971).

Roper v. Simmons, 000 U.S. 03-633 (2005).

Rudolph v. Alabama, 375 U.S. 889 (1963).

Wainwright v. Witt, 469 U.S. 412 (1985).

Witherspoon v. Illinois, 391 U.S. 510 (1968).

36

Home Confinement and Intensive Supervision as Unsafe Havens

The Unintended Consequences for Women[1]

Cortney A. Franklin and Faith E. Lutze

Existing research has documented the gendered nature of U.S. correctional institutions and their effect on men and women in prison. Many scholars suggest that community corrections environments may be safer for women offenders. Research has not, however, specifically identified the effect of home confinement and community supervision policies on the lives of female offenders. A host of empirical evidence concludes that female offenders share similar attributes including substance abuse, chronic sexual and physical victimization, and a lack of self-esteem or self-worth. We argue that these characteristics, combined with the nature of home confinement and community supervision policies, may put women at risk for continued abuse, victimization, and criminal involvement.

The expanding population of female inmates, in combination with their diverse and distinct needs, has prompted criminal justice policy makers to explore alternatives to incarceration for nonviolent female offenders. In doing so, some states have begun to divert women into community-based supervision programs (see Chesney-Lind & Pasko, 2004). Feminist scholars and women's advocates for years have argued that treating women within a community context, as opposed to an institutional setting, will more effectively address the unique and diverse needs of women offenders (Chesney-Lind & Pasko, 2004; Pollock, 2002).

Existing research has established that female offenders share a host of similar attributes such as histories of physical or sexual victimization, substance abuse, mental illness, and high-risk medical concerns (Belknap, 2001; 2003; Chesney-Lind & Pasko, 2004; Fearn & Parker, 2005; Franklin, Fearn, & Franklin, 2005; Marcus-Menoza & Wright, 2003; Pollock, 2002; Van Wormer & Bartollas, 2000). Women's prisons have been continually criticized as inadequate in treating and housing female offenders as a result of the gendered nature of institutional corrections compounded by overcrowding and a lack of resources, funding, and appropriate programming (Belknap, 2001; Chesney-Lind & Pasko, 2004; Lutze, 2003; Pollock, 2002; Schram, 2003). Further, researchers have consistently argued that institutional environments "replicate and reinforce the victimization and marginalization of women" through harassment, discrimination, and sexual violation (Belknap, 2003, p. 95; also see Lutze, 2003). While it is proposed that community options appear to more effectively serve women by keeping them connected to the community, their children, and to social service alternatives, there may be unforeseen outcomes for women that revolve specifically around the nature of community correctional strategies such as home confinement and intensive supervision.

In this chapter, we identify the extent to which community corrections options may result in unintended negative consequences for female offenders. Although we agree with other scholars that female offenders should be treated in the community, we are cautious about the positive outcomes of such approaches. This is a result of the masculine-gendered orientation of correctional policies compounded with the reality of poverty and violence in which many women offenders live. We argue that intensive supervision and home confinement alternatives may replicate the powerlessness of the prison experience by confining female offenders to the place of their preoffense victimization as well as to a lifestyle in which they have little control and one that may have contributed to their criminal behavior.

The treatment of women offenders, whether in prison or the community, must first be understood in the broader social context of patriarchy and how it influences the design and implementation of correctional policies. Recent correctional policy indicates that we are successful in instituting greater control through increased incarceration and supervision in the community (see Irwin & Austin, 1997), but do little to address women's prior and future victimization, violence within the home, male-dominated and oftentimes violent relationships, personal consequences of drug and alcohol addiction, demands of parenting in a less than adequate environment, and dependence on inadequate public services.

THE GENDERED NATURE OF U.S. CORRECTIONS

We have argued elsewhere that prisons are designed by men to punish other men and that this narrowly defined, gendered approach to corrections has negative consequences for both men and women (Lutze, 2003; Lutze & Bell, 2005; Lutze & Murphy, 1999). The purpose of this chapter is to add a note of caution to the potential reliance upon community corrections as a panacea in the treatment of female offenders because of the inattention paid to the unique circumstances of many female offenders. To understand the influence of current correctional policy on women's lives, however, it is first important to understand the broader social context in which correctional policy is designed.

Patriarchy and Masculinity

The role and importance of masculinity must be understood according to its place in patriarchal society where patriarchy is defined as a social system that is "male-dominated, male-centered, and male identified" (Johnson, 1997, p. 5). Patriarchy is male-dominated to the extent that positions of power and authority are exclusively reserved for men (e.g., business executives, religious leaders, political decision makers). Patriarchy is male-centered where the focus of society revolves around men and men's lives. Finally, patriarchy is male-identified where the male norm defines human existence. In other words, the male experience is the benchmark society uses to measure all human experience (Johnson, 1997). It is this final element of male-identification in patriarchal society that plays a central role in understanding how society is organized and how it directly affects the lives of men and women.

According to the definition of patriarchy, it follows that masculinity is related to possessing power and control. Further, masculinity is narrowly defined as "a socially constructed set of values and practices that glorify status, aggression, independence, and dominance" (Franklin, in press; Johnson, 1997; Kilmartin, 2000). Such characteristics are stereotypically masculine in that they represent the male experience.[2] In general, this translates into policies that tend to ignore the life experiences of women who, within patriarchal structures, are expected to be nurturing, passive, dependent, and subservient to males. This gender dichotomy has been linked to perpetuating male violence, economic marginality for women and children, inequality in health care and housing, and other quality of life issues (see Lorber, 2001).

For female offenders, male-identified justice means that correctional programs are first designed to control and punish men and then are extrapolated to the control and punishment of women. Thus, policies designed from a masculine perspective are deemed appropriate to control young, single, aggressive (and often violent), poor males. These same policies are applied to women who are more likely to be poor, young, nonviolent, single parents. This results in policies that often overcontrol nonviolent women and ignore their underemployment, poverty, and their dependence upon others because of their sole responsibility to provide for their children. Therefore, the differences of women are invisible and subjugated when equality is based on a narrowly defined male experience.[3]

Correctional policies aimed at the general male offending population have negative outcomes for women where they are designed to accommodate the motivations, offending patterns, and lifestyles of the male offender (see Belknap, 2001; Chesney-Lind, 2003; Chesney-Lind & Pasko, 2004; Lutze, 2003; Pollock, 2002). For example, research has cited three-strikes laws and other tough on crime policies (Danner, 2003), the war on drugs (Bush-Baskette, 2004a, 2004b), shock incarceration programs (Marcus-Mendoza, Klein-Saffran, & Lutze, 1998), institutional corrections (Hannah-Moffat, 1995), gendered prison programming (Schram, 2003), and narrowly defined treatment programs grounded in male-identified theory (Covington, 2004) as having harmful and potentially detrimental consequences for women. Correctional programs designed to "get tough" on male offenders place women in environments that keep them in a state of dependence, subordination, and marginality whether in an institutional or community setting (see Eaton, 1993; Zaplin, 1998).

To compensate for the detrimental effects of male-identified prisons and programs on women, feminist scholars have traditionally advocated sanctioning and treating women within the community context. Although we strongly agree that prison should be considered only as a last resort, we argue that community corrections options must be reevaluated based on the reality of women's lives within offender populations. It remains that intermediate sanctions and community options such as home confinement and intensive supervision are also organized around the male experience, thus ignoring the powerful influence of patriarchy and limited systems of support (both public and private) on the lives of female offenders. Failure to consider systems that are male-identified in their pursuit of justice and punishment can be potentially lethal to women and their ability to remain free from state control.

ATTRIBUTES OF THE FEMALE OFFENDER

Female inmates share a host of similar preincarceration characteristics that define both their experiences as offenders and their chances of postrelease success. Current research has established that the average female offender is plagued with poverty and a lack of education and job-related skills, resulting in primarily minimum- or low-wage jobs and a reliance on social service and welfare programs. Additionally, she is generally young, under- or unemployed, unmarried, and is the lone caregiver of her children (see Chesney-Lind & Pasko, 2004; Kelley, 2003; Pollack, 2002; Zaitzow & West, 2003, for a review).

Moreover, research indicates that as many as half of female offenders have a history of severe physical and sexual abuse experienced both as children and as adults (see Chesney-Lind & Pasko, 2004; Chesney-Lind & Sheldon, 1998; Marcus-Mendoza & Wright, 2003; Silbert & Pines, 1981). In addition, the abuse is generally perpetrated by male relatives or intimate male partners (Fletcher, Rolison, & Moon, 1993; Greenfield & Snell, 1999; Sargent, Marcus-Mendoza, & Yu, 1993). This violence has devastating psychological consequences that may affect behavioral adjustment and treatment outcomes in prison (Girshick, 2003; Marcus-Mendoza & Wright, 2003). The aftermath brought on by the abuse results in the experience of trauma-related mental health problems (Cauffman, Feldman, Waterman, & Steiner, 1998) such as posttraumatic stress disorder (PTSD) (Zlotnick, 1997), among other negative psychiatric conditions and antisocial/borderline personality disorders (Eppright, Kashani, Robinson, & Reid, 1993). For example, women experience low self-esteem, ongoing emotional stress, anxiety, self-hatred, depression, and impulsive behavior (Zaplin, 1998), all of which have devastating effects on the ability to effectively respond to treatment efforts and community reintegration techniques (Marcus-Mendoza & Wright, 2004).

To add insult to misery, most female offenders disproportionately suffer from substance abuse and drug addiction problems (Kelley, 2003; Pollack, 2002). Scholars have argued that this is in part a coping response to the high rate of abuse and victimization (Belknap, 2003; Chesney-Lind & Rodriguez, 1983; Pollock, 2002; Sargent et al., 1993). Notably, prior to their incarceration, women report using more drugs and using drugs more frequently than their male offending counterparts (Kelley, 2003). Further, a majority of women report that they were under the influence at the time of their offense or committed the offense with the goal of obtaining drugs and sustaining their addiction (see Pollock, 2002; Zaitzow & West, 2003 for a brief review). Further, women report engaging in or having engaged in prostitution as a way to obtain drugs or money on a regular or semiregular basis (Polonsky et al., 1994; Steel & Haverkos, 1992). Prostitution, in addition to other high-risk behaviors such as the use of intravenous drug and needle sharing, poses substantial threats to the health and medical well-being of this female population (Franklin et al., in press; Guyon, Brochu, Parents, & Desjardins, 1999; Leh, 1999; Lurigio, Swartz, & Jones, 2003; Marquart, Brewer, Mullings, & Crouch, 1999). With that said, incarcerated women have a host of growing health-care and medical needs. Most notably, women often require medical attention resulting from reproductive-related health problems, tuberculosis, high-risk pregnancies, and HIV/AIDS (Acoca, 1998; Fearn & Parker, 2005; Franklin et al., 2005; Kassira et al., 2001; Zaitzow & West, 2003).

The Role of the Male Intimate Partner

While the general female offending population is plagued with special needs resulting from prior experiences and preincarceration life circumstances, a surprising number of these factors are directly connected to their male intimate partners. For example, as previously mentioned, a startling number of female offenders are victims of physical violence, battery, and sexual victimization. This is increasingly the result of abuse perpetrated in the context of the home by both male relatives and male intimate partners (Fletcher et al., 1993; Greenfeld & Snell, 1999; Sargent et al., 1993). Thus, trauma-related mental health problems resulting from the abuse (e.g., PTSD, depression, lack of self-esteem or self-worth, anxiety) can logically be attributed to their male intimate partners and other family members.

Further, research indicates that a majority of at-risk women are introduced to drugs and other addictive substances through male partners. Additionally, research has cited past physical and sexual victimization as motivation for substance use and addiction (Arnold, 1990; Chesney-Lind & Rodriguez, 1983; Pollock, 2002; Sargent et al., 1993). Women who are victims of battery and sexual violence may respond through self-destructive behaviors such as illicit substance use culminating as drug addiction and chemical dependency (see Belknap, 2003; Chesney-Lind & Rodriguez, 1983; Sargent et al., 1993). Moreover, female offenders are most often involved in drug-related crimes whether they are economic crimes (stealing money to buy drugs) or illegal drug usage (Chesney-Lind, 2003; Chesney-Lind & Pasko, 2004). This regularly occurs either with or for male offending partners (see Robinson, 1992, for a brief review).

The argument logically follows that the substance addiction, in addition to the behavior undertaken to sustain the addiction (e.g., prostitution, nonviolent drug crimes, and petty theft) is a result of behavior perpetrated by male intimates (such as abuse and victimization). In addition, research has documented the extent to which women's involvement in crime is in response to conditions of abuse (physical and sexual) and addiction (see Robinson, 1992). While such a statement does not excuse the actions of the female offender, it does understand that antisocial behaviors may be related to outside influences and recidivism may be simply a direct result of exposure to high-risk intimate others and environments that are highly correlated with criminal behavior.

The use of community correctional options needs to be evaluated with the conditions of women's experiences in mind. Further, institutional correctional environments tend not to alter the negative outcomes of preincarceration life conditions for women. In fact, these institutional environments may even exacerbate them (see Lutze, 2003). Thus, it is important to consider how intensified, sanction-oriented community corrections may adhere to similar male-identified organizing principles, thus resulting in similar outcomes for women living in the community.

INTENSIVE SUPERVISION AND HOME CONFINEMENT

A review of the literature suggests that community corrections has shifted away from its origins of reintegration and rehabilitation to a greater emphasis on accountability and control of offenders (Petersilia, 2003). It is this shift that causes concern for female offenders. Intensive supervision and home confinement correctional strategies evolved as intermediate sanctions in response to an overburdened correctional system where a lack of resources and prison overcrowding prompted innovative and alternative punishment options in U.S. corrections (Cullen, Wright, & Applegate, 1996; Dean-Myrda & Cullen, 1998; Lurigio & Petersilia, 1992; Petersilia, Lurigio, & Byrne, 1992). Initially, these correctional sanctions were deemed advantageous for their rehabilitative and community-attachment, treatment-oriented contexts (Renzema, 1992) particularly as they relate to nonviolent and drug-involved offenders (Petersilia, Turner, & Deschenes, 1992). Offenders would carry out their sentence confined to their place of residence where they could take advantage of treatment and rehabilitative programming options while remaining in contact with family, peer, and employment attachments (Cullen et al., 1996). Thus, these options gave a punishment as well as a treatment-oriented focus with the hopes of rehabilitation, reduction in future recidivism, and reintegration into the community.

Criticism from the general public, however, labeled intermediate community sanctions as "soft on crime" and punishment advocates demanded tougher penalties for breaking the law (see Byrne, 1989; Clear, 1994; Ellsworth, 1996; Irwin & Austin, 1997; Lutze, Smith, & Lovrich, 2000; Petersilia, 1996). Currently, home confinement and intensive supervision policies rely primarily on a deterrence-based sentencing model that downplays their treatment-oriented potential (Lurigio & Petersilia, 1992). This is the case as offenders are presented with threats of criminal detection through intensive case monitoring and electronic surveillance, arrest, custody revocation, and the consequences of incarceration (Baumer & Mendelsohn, 1992; Lurigio & Petersilia, 1992). Recent research supports this philosophical shift from identifying these community sanctions as a primarily rehabilitative approach to ones viewed in light of their short-term crime control focus (Lurigio & Petersilia, 1992).

Research evaluating the success of intermediate sanctions has demonstrated that intensive supervision probation programs (ISPs) increase surveillance but studies have yielded conflicting results as to whether or not high levels of surveillance can decrease recidivism (see Cullen et al., 1996, for a review). For instance, research conducted in Georgia and New Jersey indicates that ISP offenders have lower reincarceration rates and a 10 percent reduction in the number of offenders sentenced to prison (Cullen et al., 1996). The researchers concluded that high levels of surveillance decreases recidivism among offenders. Critics argue that these evaluations are methodologically flawed because of incompatible comparison groups (see Cullen et al., 1996).

Multisite studies, however, suggest that ISPs do not affect recidivism. For instance, a RAND evaluation of 14 ISPs in nine states indicates that they are successful in increasing surveillance, but do not seem to affect offender recidivism (Cullen et al., 1996). A seven-state study, by Petersilia, Turner, et al. (1992), on the effectiveness of ISPs with drug offenders also found that ISP offenders received higher levels of surveillance but there were no significant differences in recidivism rates. Interestingly, none of these studies appear to have considered the effect of intensive supervision on women's recidivism rates.

Research has also attempted to identify the success of home confinement (HC) in reducing recidivism as compared to traditional incarceration. In general, home confinement programs target low-risk offenders. Studies indicate no differences between recidivism among HC offenders and those sentenced to traditional incarceration (Cullen et al., 1996; Smith & Akers, 1993). Researchers have argued that home confinement remains a valuable sentencing option as it diverts offenders from prison, decreases crowding, and offers community-based treatment and rehabilitative services (Cullen et al., 1996; Petersilia, Turner, et al., 1992; Smith & Akers, 1993).

Scholars have criticized intensive probation supervision and home confinement sanctions that exclude a rehabilitative component and focus primarily on deterrence as an outcome, especially as related to female offenders (see Robinson, 1992). Criticisms stem from the differences in both motivation and crime-type contexts between male and female offending populations where women have a host of special and diverse needs that relate specifically to their propensity to engage in criminality (Chesney-Lind & Pasko, 2004).

Those who have proposed potential harms associated with community sanctions have focused on punishment outcomes and neglected to identify problems associated with the specific *nature* of home confinement and community supervision options to the degree that such sanctions may be harmful to women in terms of exposing female offenders to abuse and violence in the home. This is a direct result of the special circumstances and shared attributes of the female offender. These characteristics, combined with the nature of home confinement and intensive supervision policies, have the potential to put women at risk.

COMMUNITY SUPERVISION PUTS WOMEN AT RISK

One might argue that community supervision, namely, confinement to the home (with its gateway to potential victimization and introduction to addiction), may not be as positive or protective an influence as previously suggested, especially for the general female offending population. In addition, further consideration of community correctional policies is necessary to fully grasp their effect on women under correctional supervision.

Confinement to the Home: Perpetuating the Problem

While the current political climate surrounding home confinement and community supervision policies focuses on deterrence and the punitive nature of behavioral monitoring and crime detection, such policies possess both positive and negative consequences for women depending upon the home and the community in which women are subjected. Many have argued that women benefit from maintaining community attachment to family networks, positive peer connections, housing, employment, and from receiving social service options (Chesney-Lind & Pasko, 2004; Zaplin, 1998). As the following review will show, however, this is an optimistic view of the communities and services available to most female offenders. It assumes homes that are free from domestic violence and drug use, communities that provide positive peer networks, access to social service agencies with adequate services, and correctional officers with a treatment orientation. Unfortunately, this is not a reality for the majority of female offenders and especially for those offenders who are plagued with poverty. As previously mentioned, violence, drug addition, and economic marginality are all interwoven to put women at high risk for continued victimization and reoffending.

Abusive Environments.   Research has established that physical, sexual, and mental abuse and violation generally takes place within the home and is perpetrated by male intimate partners (Fletcher et al., 1993; Greenfield & Snell, 1999; Sargent et al., 1993). In addition, women are typically introduced to substance abuse and addiction through male intimates. It is also clear that a large number of female offenders are victims of domestic violence and will be exposed to high-risk violent environments upon their release. Women offenders, due to economic marginality and poverty, will be subjected to living in public housing where violence toward women is perpetuated in marginal communities with high crime rates and a constant exposure to drugs and other criminal activity (see Clear & Cardora, 2003; DeKeseredy & Schwartz, 2002; Freudenberg, 2001; Renzetti & Maier, 2002). If public housing is unavailable resulting from a drug-related conviction, then many women are forced to live with relatives who are often financially stressed. Additionally, they may rely upon finding refuge with others who are often living in similar circumstances.

Given this situation, it logically follows that home confinement and intensive supervision policies, where women are punished through sanctions that require them to remain under house arrest, open the opportunity for more abuse by confining female offenders to the place of their victimization. Additionally, confining at-risk women to the home will have the potential to further the problems associated with their abuse such as negative mental, medical, and physical health outcomes. Where men are socialized to respond externally to mental degradation and physical confrontation, women are taught and reinforced to internalize abuse (Kilmartin, 2000; Simmons, 2002). This behavior pattern may create a damaging cycle of violence, thus recreating the very problems that community corrections and intervention programs are designed to treat.

Family Networks and Peer Connections.   Extended family networks and positive peer connections have also been considered to be important conditions for women's success after release from prison or for keeping women from going to prison (see Belknap, 2001). Although this is true, the reality for many women offenders, especially those who violate the conditions of their supervision or who reoffend, is that their networks are limited and their peers are in similarly stark situations (Holtfreter, Reisig, & Morash, 2004). In addition, victims of domestic violence are often isolated and solely dependent upon their perpetrator for survival, thus further hindering and preventing social networks and relationships that would help establish freedom from both private and state forms of control (see LaViolette & Barnett, 2000).

Social Services.   The presence of domestic violence, drug abuse, economic marginality, and limited peer networks strongly suggests that publicly funded services must be provided to support change. With this in mind, it is appropriate to argue that social service agencies can adequately provide support that will lead to positive life change. This, however, assumes access to social services. If access is achieved, it assumes programs that are designed to suit the needs of the offender population. It also assumes community corrections (probation and parole) officers who will advocate on their clients' behalf. Unfortunately, this is often not the case as a result of a number of legal and political factors that tend to interfere with providing services.

For instance, many women cannot get access to housing because of laws that prohibit offenders with drug-related convictions to live in public housing. In addition, welfare to work laws push many women into low-paying menial jobs that transition them from welfare to members of the working poor (see Holtfreter, et al., [2004] for a review). Further, convicted offenders are often legally prohibited from working in many jobs such as nursing, are barred from possessing a state license for many occupations (i.e., cosmetology), and are excluded from receiving education grants and federal loans for postsecondary education. Thus, their economic marginality is legally coerced and politically maintained.

Even when social services exist, access is often limited or may be delayed for lengthy periods of time. For example, women who need shelter to escape domestic violence are left with limited access depending upon where they live, the age of their children, and the type of services that the agency provides (LaViolette & Barnett, 2000). Women who need drug treatment are often subjected to treatment programs that have been designed for men and thus ignore the different causes of women's addiction (see Zaplin, 1998). Further, access to drug treatment may be postponed while waiting for a vacancy at a drug treatment facility. Although women are expected to remain drug and crime free in the interim, this is often unrealistic to accomplish without timely access to support and treatment services and increased exposure to violence and high-risk behaviors related to survival.

When social service agencies step in to help, they can also play a role in disempowering women. Strict guidelines often come with the acceptance of social services in which women must acquiesce in order to receive benefits. Women are limited in where they may live, receive medical services, work, spend or save money, send their children to school, and other personal decisions that guide their basic lives. Thus, the institutional dependency established during prison is reinforced after prison (see Eaton, 1993). Although many of these conditions of social services can be positive, especially during the initial crises (see Holtfreter et al., 2004), continuation may perpetuate a cycle of dependency that is also difficult to escape.

Community Supervision Officers.   Female offenders must also contend with the ever present community supervision officer and the court-imposed conditions of their supervision while reestablishing their lives. Many conditions of supervision are obviously positive. Offenders should not be consuming drugs and alcohol, associating with criminal peers, and participating in behaviors related to criminal offending. Offenders should be encouraged to work, have a permanent residence, and care appropriately for their children. It is often not the conditions of supervision that are problematic, but the way in which offenders are supervised (Clear & Latessa, 1993; Gaarder, Rodriguez & Zatz, 2004). For instance, many community corrections officers support rehabilitation, understand offenders' needs, and are active advocates for connecting offenders to the appropriate community resources (see Drapela & Lutze, 2005; Lutze et al., 2004, for a review). Other officers, however, are more punitive and less likely to advocate on the behalf of offenders. This increased focus on monitoring generally results in reacting to problems by increasing surveillance and holding offenders accountable through tougher sanctions versus advocating support services directly related to reducing criminogenic needs (see Murphy & Lutze, 2005). In a political climate focused on "getting tough" through male-identified correctional approaches this skews community corrections toward ignoring the needs of women and focusing on sanctions. Even officers who are oriented toward advocacy are often frustrated by a poor relationship with social service agencies and multiple barriers to getting the client timely access to services (see Lutze et al., 2004).

Reintegration after Prison.   The complicated nature of reintegration into the family (especially with children) and the community can be overwhelming for women who spend time in prison before release to the community. Women under correctional supervision are not prepared to alter negative life events outside prison. Research has identified the problems that lie in creating institutional dependence among high-risk female offenders (Eaton, 1993; Lutze, 1994, 2003). This occurs among incarcerated women who have a history of abuse as well as financial and emotional dependency on their male partners. Eaton (1993) argues that prison reinforces this disempowerment, as women who are under supervision are not properly prepared for reintegration but rather are socialized into dependence and thus disempowered. Women who do not develop strategies to deal with life after prison may be unsuccessful and have a tendency to reoffend (Eaton, 1993; Lutze, 1994). Community correctional sanctions run the risk of creating this same form of institutional dependence. When social service agencies and community punishment sanctions perpetuate dependency among women, they are unable and unprepared to effect change.

Rather than benefiting from advantageous social service options, women are forced to endure additional victimization, thus affecting their chances of postrelease success and community reintegration. Further, they are stripped of their control and limited in their ability to alter or change the negative aspects of their lives. For example, physical and sexual abuse among women leads to mental health disorders and self-medication through chemical dependency which plays a defining role in criminal involvement. When this volatile combination of attributes is combined with poverty, single motherhood, and a lack of support networks and social resources, women are bound to fall miserably into a life plagued by poverty, criminality, and antisocial behaviors.

Similar to so many policies in criminal justice designed to treat, deter, and punish offenders, the outcomes for women are not thoroughly examined and often result in unintended and/or harmful consequences (see Belknap, 2001; Bush-Baskette, 2004a, 2004b; Chesney-Lind, 2003; Chesney-Lind & Pasko, 2004; Covington, 2004; Eaton, 1993; Hannah-Moffat, 1995; Lutze, 2003; Marcus-Mendoza et al., 1998; Schram, 2003). Further, while community sanctions appear to provide the greatest opportunity for this population of at-risk offenders, the potential for increased violence and respective abuse may negate positive outcomes.

SUGGESTIONS FOR CHANGE

It is evident that the existing male-identified structure of U.S. corrections plays a defining role in terms of the way female offenders are punished and treated in addition to their respective chances for postrelease success. While the harms associated with community correctional sanctions remain virtually unexplored, it appears that women may be in danger of further victimization as a result of intensive supervision and home confinement policies that sanction women through house arrest.

It is important to consider how women-identified (free from patriarchal influence) correctional policies may be developed to punish and treat female offenders. Feminist scholars are not misguided in their quest to divert women to community-based sanctions as such punishment alternatives have definite advantages when compared to traditional incarceration. It appears, however, as if criminal justice policies neglect to account for the differences in attributes and needs of female versus male offenders. This is a direct result of the way in which the structure of corrections continues to function within a patriarchal framework where the focus and goals of punishment sanctions are male-identified and male-centered in their quest for justice.

One possible suggestion lies in the use of a gender impact statement. This phenomenon is simply a new take on the old idea of an environmental impact statement where political decision makers identify the real-life policy implications of correctional legislation designed to affect the general female offending population (see Barak, Flavin, & Leighton, 2001, for a related discussion). While such a strategy may not fully eliminate unintended correctional outcomes, by identifying the risks to women offenders, policy makers may begin to direct attention to an increasingly powerless and often ignored population.

Additional ideas for change stem from the earlier notion of institutional dependency. At-risk populations of offending women should be sanctioned and treated in ways that empower them to alter the negative life events that are so highly correlated with criminal involvement (Eaton, 1993; Zaplin, 1998). Instead of perpetuating disempowerment and stripping them of control, community sanctions should provide treatment and rehabilitative resources that teach and prepare women for life after correctional supervision.

All offenders, but especially women with children, need immediate access to housing, medical care, and basic life support if we hope to keep them from relying upon abusive males, drugs, property crime, and prostitution to escape the immediate hardships of poverty (see Holtfreter et al., 2004). Community corrections officers need to proactively address issues of violence within the home (past and present) and how this is directly linked to the ultimate failure of women to remain crime free. It is no longer acceptable for community corrections officers or female offenders to view domestic violence and sexual abuse as an unchangeable aspect of women's lives when research clearly indicates the long-term negative effects for all who are exposed to violence—especially children (see LaViolette & Barnett, 2000, for a review).

It is also necessary to begin to see drug abuse as a curable disease in which people fully recover. Offenders who establish sobriety for a reasonable period of time should be granted the trust of the public in restoring the right to work in professions that currently deny access to convicted offenders. Further consideration should also be directed toward allowing successfully treated drug-involved offenders access to federal educational loans and grants in order to further skills-related development. This will help to offset the desperation of a life of poverty with no realistic way into a stable middle-class lifestyle. Additionally, this may play a role in aiding the social mobility of the dreadfully poor.

Community corrections officers need to be encouraged and educated in terms of when to sanction and when to support the behavior of offenders. There is plenty of evidence to suggest that if the goal is to reduce recidivism and to protect the community from further victimization, then a balance must be achieved between offender accountability and support if change is to be successfully achieved (see Van Voorhis, Braswell, & Lester, 2000; Zaplin, 1998). Punitive approaches alone do not work except for the most extreme offenders.

Finally, there needs to be a recognition that narrowly defined masculine approaches that continue to fail miserably to reduce male recidivism will work just as poorly to change women's criminal offending. It is time that male-centered and male-identified correctional policies be recognized for their biased outcomes for both men and women. As long as correctional policies continue to operate within a male-identified model of punishment and treatment, the respective effects of such policies have the potential to result in damaging outcomes for women. Thus, community correctional strategies need to be rethought in order to effectively punish while simultaneously meeting the unique treatment and rehabilitative needs of women.

NOTES

1. An earlier version of this chapter was presented at the annual meetings of the Academy of Criminal Justice Sciences in Chicago, Illinois, March 2005.
2. For instance, public and private business dictate schedules and demand time commitments from workers that often cannot accommodate single-parent households or women with small children (Lorber, 2001). Such expectations are created around the notion that there is a "wife" at home who is responsible for domestic duties and child-rearing. This expectation reflects the male experience and neglects to accommodate the working woman or single parent who is forced to juggle family responsibilities and full-time employment. Similar assumptions that revolve around the male experience are often extrapolated to women's lives through politics, education, criminal justice, and in this case, corrections policy.
3. Research has suggested that prisons are among the most masculine organizations where men are disproportionately represented as inmates and correctional staff (see Lutze & Bell, 2005; Lutze & Murphy, 1999; Newton, 1994). Further, the structure and hierarchy of prisons reflect the male-dominated and masculine nature of its organization (Newton, 1994; Sims, 1994). Existing research documenting gender in organizations looks specifically at the way masculinity and femininity become institutionalized through the design and procedures of the organization (Mills, 1992). As such, masculinity and the cultural values associated with maleness are generally preferred characteristics desired by organizations (Morgan, 1986). The gendered nature of organizations plays a role in perpetuating gender and gender dichotomies in society (Witz & Savage, 1992). Carrabine and Longhurst (1998) address the importance of power relations in the context of institutional settings. They argue that such relations involve the "construction and reproduction of masculinities" (Carrabine & Longhurst, 1998, p. 164). As a masculine organization, the prison reinforces masculine gender roles and the male-identified model for human experience (see Lutze, 2003; Lutze & Bell, 2005; Lutze & Murphy, 1999; Morash & Rucker, 1990; Toch, 1977).

REFERENCES

Acoca, L. (1998). Defusing the time bomb: Understanding and meeting the growing health care needs of incarcerated women in America. *Crime & Delinquency, 44,* 49–69.

Arnold, R. (1990). Processes of victimization and criminalization of black women. *Social Justice, 17,* 153–166.

BARAK, G., FLAVIN, J., & LEIGHTON, P. (2001). *Class, race, gender, and crime: Social realities of justice in America.* Los Angeles: Roxbury.

BAUMER, T. L., & MENDELSOHN, R. (1992). Electronically monitored home confinement: Does it work? In J. M. Byrne, A. J. Lurigio, & J. Petersilia (Eds.), *Smart sentencing: The emergence of intermediate sanctions* (pp. 54–67). Newbury Park, CA: Sage.

BELKNAP, J. (2001). *The invisible woman: Gender, crime, and justice* (2nd ed.). Belmont, CA: Wadsworth.

BELKNAP, J. (2003). Responding to the needs of women prisoners. In S. Sharp (Ed.), *The incarcerated woman: Rehabilitative programming in women's prisons* (pp. 93–106). Upper Saddle River, NJ: Prentice Hall.

BUSH-BASKETTE, S. R. (2004a). The war on drugs and the incarceration of mothers. In P. J. Schram & B. Koons-Witt (Eds.), *Gendered (in)justice: Theory and practice in feminist criminology* (pp. 236–244). Long Grove, IL: Waveland Press.

BUSH-BASKETTE, S. R. (2004b). The war on drugs as a war against black women. In M. Chesney-Lind & L. Pasko (Eds.), *Girls, women and crime: Selected readings* (pp. 185–194). Thousand Oaks, CA: Sage.

BYRNE, J. (1989). Reintegrating the concept of community into community-based corrections. *Crime & Delinquency, 35,* 471–499.

CARRABINE, E., & LONGHURST, B. (1998). Gender and prison organisation: Some comments on masculinities and prison management. *The Howard Journal, 37,* 161–176.

CAUFFMAN, E., FELDMAN, S., WATERMAN, J., & STEINER, H. (1998). Posttraumatic stress disorder among female juvenile offenders. *Journal of the American Academy of Child & Adolescent Psychiatry, 37,* 1209–1216.

CHESNEY-LIND, M. (2003). Reinventing women's corrections: Challenges for contemporary feminist criminologists and practitioners. In S. F. Sharp (Ed.), *The incarcerated woman: Rehabilitative programming in women's prisons* (pp. 3–14). Upper Saddle River, NJ: Prentice Hall.

CHESNEY-LIND, M., & PASKO, L. (2004). *The female offender: Girls, women and crime* (2nd ed.). Thousand Oaks, CA: Sage.

CHESNEY-LIND, M., & RODRIGUEZ, N. (1983). Women under lock and key. *The Prison Journal, 63,* 47–65.

CHESNEY-LIND, M., & SHELDON, R. G. (1998). *Girls, delinquency, and juvenile justice* (2nd ed.). Belmont, CA: Wadsworth.

CLEAR, T. (1994). *Harm in American penology: Offenders, victims, and their communities.* Albany: State University of New York Press.

CLEAR, T., & CARDORA, E. (2003). *Community justice.* Belmont, CA: Wadsworth.

CLEAR, T., & LATESSA, E. (1993). Probation officers' roles in intensive supervision: Surveillance versus treatment. *Justice Quarterly, 10,* 441–460.

COVINGTON, S. S. (2004). Women in prison: Approaches in the treatment of our most invisible population. In P. J. Schram & B. Koons-Witt (Eds.), *Gendered (in)justice: Theory and practice in feminist criminology* (pp. 341–353). Long Grove, IL: Waveland Press.

CULLEN, F., WRIGHT, J. P., & APPLEGATE, B. K. (1996). Control in the community: The limits of reform? In A. T. Harland (Ed.), *Choosing correctional options that work: Defining the demand and evaluating the supply* (pp. 69–116).Thousand Oaks: Sage.

DALY, K., & CHESNEY-LIND, M. (1988). Feminism and criminology. *Justice Quarterly, 5,* 101–143.

DANNER, M. J. E. (2003). Three strikes and it's *women* who are out: The hidden consequences for women of criminal justice policy reforms. In R. Muraskin (Ed.), *It's a crime: Women and justice* (pp. 209–219). Upper Saddle River, NJ: Prentice Hall.

DEAN-MYRDA, M., & CULLEN, F. (1998). The panacea pendulum: An account of community as a response to crime. In J. Petersilia (Ed.), *Community corrections: Probation, parole, and intermediate sanctions* (pp. 3–19). New York: Oxford Press.

DeKeseredy, W., & Schwartz, M. (2002). Theorizing public housing woman abuse as a function of economic exclusion and male peer support. *Women's Health and Urban Life: An Interdisciplinary Journal, 1,* 26–45.

Drapela, L., & Lutze, F. (2005). *Considering the other side of prisoner re-entry: An in-depth study of the personal and professional attributes of community corrections officers in Washington State.* A paper presented at the annual meetings of the Academy of Criminal Justice Sciences, Chicago, IL.

Eaton, M. (1993). *Women after prison.* Philadelphia: Open University Press.

Ellsworth, T. (1996). *Contemporary community corrections* (2nd ed.). Prospect Heights, IL: Waveland Press.

Eppright, T. D., Kashani, J. H., Robinson, B. D., & Reid, J. C. (1993). Comorbidity of conduct disorder and personality disorders in incarcerated juvenile populations. *American Journal of Psychiatry, 150,* 1233–1236.

Fearn, N. E., & Parker, K. (2005). Health care for women inmates: Issues, perceptions, and policy considerations. *California Journal of Health Promotion, 3*(2), 1–22.

Fletcher, B. R., Rolison, G. T., & Moon, D. G. (1993). The woman prisoner. In B. R. Fletcher, L. D. Shaver, & D. G. Moon (Eds.), *Women prisoners: A forgotten population* (pp. 15–26). Westport, CT: Praeger.

Franklin, C. A. (in press). Male peer support and police culture: Understanding the resistance and oppression of women in policing. *Women and Criminal Justice.*

Franklin, C. A., Fearn, N. E., & Franklin, T. W. (2005). HIV/AIDS among female prison inmates in correctional institutions: A public health concern. *California Journal of Health Promotion, 3*(2), 99–112.

Freudenberg, N. (2001). Jails, prisons, and the health of urban populations: A review of the impact of the correctional system on community health. *Journal of Urban Health: Bulletin of the New York Academy of Medicine, 78,* 214–235.

Gaarder, E., Rodriguez, N., & Zatz, M. S. (2004). Criers, liars, and manipulators: Probation officers' view of girls. *Justice Quarterly, 21,* 547–578.

Girshick, L. B. (2003). Abused women and incarceration. In B. H. Zaitzow & J. Thomas (Eds.), *Women in prison: Gender and social control* (pp. 95–117). London: Lynne Reinner.

Greenfeld, L. A., & Snell, T. L. (1999). *Women offenders: Special report.* Washington DC: Bureau of Justice Statistics.

Guyon, L., Brochu, S., Parents, I., & Desjardins, L. (1999). At-risk behaviors with regard to HIV and addiction among women in prison. *Women & Health, 29,* 49–66.

Hannah-Moffat, K. (1995). Feminine fortresses: Women-centered prisons? *The Prison Journal, 75,* 135–164.

Holtfreter, K., Reisig, M., & Morash, M. (2004). Poverty, state capital, and recidivism among women offenders. *Criminology & Public Policy, 3,* 185–208.

Irwin, J., & Austin, J. (1997). *It's about time: America's imprisonment binge* (2nd ed.). Belmont, CA: Wadsworth.

Johnson, A. G. (1997). *The gender knot: Unraveling our patriarchal legacy.* Philadelphia: Temple University Press.

Johnson, A. G. (2001). *Privilege, power, and difference.* Mountain View, CA: Mayfield.

Karissa, E. N., Bauserman, R. L., Tomoyasu, N., Caldeira, E., Swetz, A., & Solomon, L. (2001). HIV and AIDS surveillance among inmates in Maryland prisons. *Journal of Urban Health: Bulletin of the New York Academy of Medicine, 78,* 256–263.

Kelley, M. S. (2003). The state-of-the-art substance abuse programs for women in prison. In S. F. Sharp (Ed.), *The incarcerated woman: Rehabilitative programming in women's prisons* (pp. 119–148). Upper Saddle River, NJ: Prentice Hall.

Kilmartin, C. T. (2000). *The masculine self* (2nd ed.). Boston: McGraw-Hill.

LaViolette, A., & Barnett, O. (2000). *It could happen to anyone: Why battered women stay* (4th ed.). Thousand Oaks, CA: Sage.

Leh, S. K. (1999). HIV infection in U.S. correctional systems: Its effect on the community. *Journal of Community Health Nursing, 16*(1), 53–63.

Lorber, J. (2001). *Gender inequality: Feminist theories and politics* (2nd ed.). Los Angeles: Roxbury.

Lurigio, A. J., & Petersilia, J. (1992). The emergence of intensive supervision programs in the United States. In J. M. Byrne, A. J. Lurigio, & J. Petersilia (Eds.), *Smart sentencing: The emergence of intermediate sanction* (pp. 3–17). Newbury Park, CA: Sage.

Lurigio, A. J., Swartz, J. A., & Jones, C. (2003). HIV disease and women offenders. In R. Muraskin (Ed.), *It's a crime: Women and justice* (pp. 152–171). Upper Saddle River, NJ: Prentice Hall.

Lutze, F. E. (1994). Women after prison. *International Criminal Justice Review, 4*, 103–104.

Lutze, F. E. (2003). Ultramasculine stereotypes and violence in the control of women inmates. In B. H. Zaitzow & J. Thomas (Eds.), *Women in prison: Gender and social control* (pp. 183–204. Boulder, CO: Lynne Reinner.

Lutze, F. E., & Bell, C. A. (2005). Boot camp prisons as masculine organizations: Rethinking recidivism and program design. *Journal of Offender Rehabilitation, 40*(3/4), 133–152.

Lutze, F. E., & Murphy, D. (1999). Ultramasculine prison environments and inmates' adjustment: It's time to move beyond the "boys will be boys" paradigm. *Justice Quarterly, 16*, 709–734.

Lutze, F. E., Smith, P., & Lovrich, N. (2000). Premises for attaining more effective offender accountability through community involvement: Washington State's new approach. *Corrections Management Quarterly, 4*(4), 1–9.

Lutze, F. E., Smith, P., & Lovrich, N. (2004). *A practitioner-initiated research partnership: An evaluation of Neighborhood-Based Supervision in Spokane, Washington.* Washington, DC: U.S. Department of Justice, Office of Justice Programs (NIJ grant #1999-CE-VX-0007).

Marcus-Mendoza, S. T., Klein-Saffran, J., & Lutze, F. (1998). A feminist examination of boot camp prisons for women. *Women and Therapy, 12*(1), 173–185.

Marcus-Mendoza, S. T., & Wright, E. (2003). Treating the woman prisoner: The impact of a history of violence. In S. Sharp (Ed.), *The incarcerated woman: Rehabilitative programming in women's prisons* (pp. 107–117). Upper Saddle River, NJ: Prentice Hall.

Marquart, J. M., Brewer, V. E., Mullings, J., & Crouch, B. M. (1999). The implications of crime control policy on HIV/AIDS related risk among women prisoners. *Crime & Delinquency, 45*, 82–98.

Mills, A. J. (1992). Organization, gender, and culture. In A. J. Mills & P. Tancred (Eds.), *Gendering organizational analysis* (pp. 93–111). Newbury Park, CA: Sage.

Morash, M., & Rucker, L. (1990). A critical look at the idea of boot camp as a correctional reform. *Crime & Delinquency, 36*, 204–222.

Morgan, G. (1986). *Images of organization.* London: Sage.

Murphy, D., & Lutze, F. (2005). *Power imbalances in police-probation partnerships: Analyzing the threat of mission distortion.* A paper presented at the annual meetings of the Academy of Criminal Justice Sciences, Chicago, IL.

Newton, C. (1994). Gender theory and prison sociology: Using theories of masculinities to interpret the sociology of prisons for men. *The Howard Journal, 33*, 193–202.

Pearl, N. (1998). Use of community-based social services by women offenders. *Journal of Offender Rehabilitation, 26*, 91–110.

Petersilia, J. (1996). Measuring the performance of community corrections. In T. Ellworth (Ed.), *Contemporary community corrections* (2nd ed., pp. 312–326). Prospect Heights, IL: Waveland Press.

Petersilia, J. (2003). *When prisoners come home: Parole and prisoner reentry.* New York: Oxford University Press.

PETERSILIA, J., LURIGIO, A. J., & BYRNE, J. M. (1992). The emergence of intermediate sanctions. In J. M. Byrne, A. J. Lurigio, & J. Petersilia (Eds.), *Smart sentencing: The emergence of intermediate sanctions* (pp. ix–xv). London: Sage.

PETERSILIA, J., TURNER, S., & DESCHENES, E. P. (1992). Intensive supervision programs for drug offenders. In J. M. Byrne, A. J. Lurigio, & J. Petersilia (Eds.), *Smart sentencing: The emergence of intermediate sanctions* (pp. 18–37). Newbury Park, CA: Sage.

POLLOCK, J. (2002). *Women, prison, and crime.* Belmont, CA: Wadsworth/Thomson Learning.

POLONSKY, S., KERR, S., HARRIS, B., GAITER, J., FICHTNER, R., & KENNEDY, M. (1994). HIV prevention in prisons and jails: Obstacles and opportunities. *Public Health Reports, 109,* 615–625.

RENZEMA, M. (1992). Home confinement programs: Development, implementation, and impact. In J. M. Byrne, A. J. Lurigio, & J. Petersilia (Eds.), *Smart sentencing: The emergence of intermediate sanctions* (pp. 41–53). Newbury Park, CA: Sage.

RENZETTI, C., & MAIER, S. (2002). "Private" crime in public housing: Violent victimization, fear of crime and social isolation among women public housing residents. *Women's Health and Urban Life: An Interdisciplinary Journal, 1,* 46–65.

ROBINSON, R. A. (1992). Intermediate sanctions and the female offender. In J. M. Byrne, A. J. Lurigio, & J. Petersilia (Eds.), *Smart sentencing: The emergence of intermediate sanctions* (pp. 245–260). Newbury Park, CA: Sage.

SARGENT, E., MARCUS-MENDOZA, S., & YU, C. H. (1993). Abuse and the woman prisoner. In B. R. Fletcher, L. D. Shaver, & D. G. Moon (Eds.), *Women prisoners: A forgotten population* (pp. 55–64). Westport, CT: Praeger.

SCHRAM, P. J. (2003). Stereotypes and vocational programming for women prisoners. In S. F. Sharp (Ed.), *The incarcerated woman: Rehabilitative programming in women's prisons* (pp. 17–28). Upper Saddle River, NJ: Prentice Hall.

SILBERT, M. H., & PINES, A. M. (1981). Sexual child abuse as an antecedent to prostitution. *Child Abuse and Neglect, 5,* 407–411.

SIMMONS, R. (2002). *Odd girl out: The hidden culture of aggression in girls.* New York: Harcourt.

SIMS, J. (1994). Tougher than the rest? Men in prison. In T. Newburn & E. A. Stanko (Eds.), *Just boys doing business? Men, masculinities, and crime* (pp. 100–117). London: Routledge.

SMITH, L., & AKERS, R. (1993). A comparison of recidivism of Florida's community control and prison: A five-year survival analysis. *Journal of Research in Crime and Delinquency, 30,* 267–292.

STEEL, E., & HAVERKOS, H. W. (1992). Epidemiologic studies of HIV/AIDS and drug abuse. *American Journal of Drug and Alcohol Abuse, 18,* 167–175.

TOCH, H. (1977). *Living in prison: The ecology of survival.* New York: Free Press.

VAN VOORHIS, P., BRASWELL, M., & LESTER, D. (2000). *Correctional counseling & rehabilitation* (4th ed.). Cincinnati, OH: Anderson.

VAN WORMER, C. S., & BARTOLLAS, C. (2000). *Women and the criminal justice system.* Boston: Allyn & Bacon.

WITZ, A., & SAVAGE, M. (1992). The gender of organizations. In M. Savage & A. Witz (Eds.), *Gender and bureaucracy* (pp. 3–62). Oxford: Blackwell.

ZAITZOW, B. H., & WEST, A. D. (2003). Doing time in the shadow of death: Women prisoners and HIV/AIDS. In S. F. Sharp (Ed.), *The incarcerated woman: Rehabilitative programming in women's prisons* (pp. 73–90). Upper Saddle River, NJ: Prentice Hall.

ZAPLIN, R. (1998). *Female offenders: Critical perspectives and effective interventions.* Gaithersburg, MD: Aspen.

ZLOTNICK, C. (1997). Posttraumatic stress disorder (PTSD), PTSD comorbidity, and childhood abuse among incarcerated women. *The Journal of Nervous and Mental Disease, 185*(12), 761–763.

SECTION VII

Women and Professions

37

The Impact of Women on the Police Subculture

Kim M. Lersch and Thomas Bazley

❖

INTRODUCTION

The occupation of policing is quite unique. It is the job of police officers to make arrests, detain individuals accused of criminal activity and, under certain circumstances, deprive individuals of their constitutionally guaranteed freedoms. They also have the right to use deadly force, if need be, in order to gain compliance. Police officers, most of whom still possess only a high school education, have an incredible amount of authority and influence over the daily lives of citizens. In addition to their unique powers, officers charged with street-level law enforcement see a world that many of us can only imagine, one filled with human suffering, violence, exploitation, and constant challenges to their authority.

Because of the unique characteristics of police work, a distinct subculture has evolved, one that permeates every aspect of policing including recruitment and selection, behavioral aspects of officers in the field, and overall acceptance of officers into the profession. In this subculture, the display of attributes associated with masculinity and toughness are rewarded; physical and emotional weakness, fear, compassion, and other qualities labeled as "feminine" are devalued. Given the nature of the police subculture, it is not surprising that women have had limited representation among law enforcement personnel. The occupation of policing has been described as one of the most resistant to the acceptance of women, who have summarily been denied access to the informal policing peer groups (Bartollas & Hahn, 1999; Belknap & Shelley, 1992; Lanier, 1996). In this chapter we begin with a discussion of the elements of the police subculture. We then explore the impact of this subculture on women entering police work. We close with an examination of the resultant changes in the subculture and occupation of policing as women enter the profession in larger numbers.

THE SUBCULTURE OF POLICING

A very popular sociological explanation that is often provided to better understand police behavior involves the subculture of policing. Proponents of this perspective (Herbert, 1998; Skolnick, 1966, 2002; Stark, 1972; Westley, 1970) discuss the law enforcement officer as being affected by the norms, values, expectations, and regulatory principles of their occupation. While the term *subculture* is usually applied to lower-class youth gangs, a subculture may be defined as a group that maintains a distinctive set of values, norms, and lifestyles that sometimes differs from the overall culture of society. For a variety of reasons, the distinct occupational characteristics of the law enforcement officer tend to be in conflict with and isolated from the community in which they are employed.

From the very beginning, individuals seeking employment as law enforcement officers are a distinctive group. Prospective officers are carefully screened using a variety of mechanisms, including extensive background checks. Applicants must demonstrate that they possess "good moral character" and have no felony convictions, nor any misdemeanor convictions related to perjury or providing false statements. They must pass a physical examination and demonstrate that they are physically able to perform the required tasks. Some researchers have argued that the screening mechanisms used to select appropriate candidates for law enforcement employment are designed to weed out those who have not demonstrated a clear adherence to middle-class norms and values. Successful candidates form a homogeneous cohort of individuals who, from the very start, have been selected because they share a common worldview. As a result of the selection process, law enforcement personnel tend to be white, conservative, middle-class males (Kappeler, Sluder, & Alpert, 1998).

Once employed, young recruits find themselves in a different lifestyle from most of their nondepartmental friends. Because they are low in seniority, many new officers must work the night shift. At a time when most young couples or individuals are developing friendships and socializing, the pool of available people declines due to the odd hours that the officer works. Officers are forced to rely heavily on their coworkers for companionship, which further serves to isolate them from society.

The dangerous nature of law enforcement work fosters an environment based on friendship and trust. While violent police–citizen encounters are rare, the threat of danger is always present and the authority of the officer is always being challenged (Skolnick & Currie, 1970). Officers must rely on each other for protection; norms that stress the importance of teamwork, cooperation, and mutual responsibility are extremely high among officers (Stark, 1972; Westley, 1970). Officers turn to each other for support and understanding. Outsiders from mainstream society are viewed as unsympathetic and hostile toward officers, and the officers must have someone to turn to in order to alleviate the stress of their occupation (Stark, 1972).

Officers are thrust into the personal lives of complete strangers and rarely see people under the best of conditions. Officers tend to become cynical and hardened, and the conversations tend to focus on violence and crime (Van Maanen, 1980). They tend to develop a distinctive way of looking at the world that sets them off from normal citizens and further contributes to their social isolation. Ultimately, a sort of "bunker mentality" develops in which the officers view the world in an "us versus them" fashion. Officers can only trust other officers for friendship, support, understanding, and loyalty.

MASCULINITY AND THE POLICE SUBCULTURE

One of the consistent themes that has emerged among policing scholars in research on the police subculture is that of masculinity. In order to be accepted into the police ranks, an officer must exhibit "macho" traits, including toughness, confidence, bravery, emotional detachment, and aggressiveness (Crank, 1998; Garcia, 2003; Martin, 1980). Kappeler et al. (1998), in an oft-cited essay, stated that bravery was a central component of the police subculture. Bravery has been defined as a special form of masculine behavior (Crank, 1998). Throughout their tenure on the streets, exhibitions of bravery can "make or break" an officer. New officers are not truly accepted until they have successfully maneuvered their way through a dangerous situation. When faced with hazardous challenges and threats to their authority, police officers must never back down. Instead, the officers must "show balls" and deal with the situation head-on. In the worldview of patrol officers, backing down is a sign of weakness that reflects poorly not only on the individual officer but on the entire force as well. Officers who demonstrate cowardice face ostracism from the informal peer groups and are not accepted as "good" police officers.

Herbert (1998) described several normative orders that characterize the social world of the police. Included among these normative orders, which Herbert defined as "a set of rules and practices centered around a primary value," was adventure/machismo. In his ethnographic study of the Los Angeles Police Department, Herbert described two labels that the officers applied to other officers: "hardchargers" and "station queens." Hardchargers aggressively seek out dangerous situations such as vehicle pursuits and crime-related calls for service. These officers enjoy the adrenaline high that accompanies such unpredictable, potentially explosive encounters. According to Herbert (1998, p. 356), "Hardchargers are police warriors and exemplify such typically masculine characteristics as courage and strength."

Conversely, officers who tend to avoid danger are labeled as "station queens," a term that is less than flattering given the masculine nature of the occupational culture. As noted by Herbert, the use of the term "queens" feminizes these officers who prefer the safety of the station house to the dangerous environment of the streets. Femininity, therefore, is associated with weakness, fear, and cowardice. While acts of bravery are revered and rewarded, expression of "feminine" traits violates the rules and expectations for behavior. It was perhaps Crank who summarized it best in his essay appropriately titled "No Place for Sissies." According to Crank (1998, p. 180), "Masculinity is a theme that runs through the occupation, affects social status, reinforces group solidarity, and infuses officers' self-images as men's men."

MAINTAINING MASCULINITY: NO GIRLS ALLOWED

The masculine theme that defines the occupational culture of policing has flourished because of (1) the demographics of police departments, and (2) the misconceptions surrounding the true nature of police work. Together, these factors have kept women from enjoying full status in law enforcement circles.

One of the primary reasons that the masculinity theme has prospered relates to the demographics of police agencies, especially in the early years. Prior to the early 1970s, it was quite difficult to find women among the ranks of sworn law enforcement officers. A survey of the largest municipal police agencies in 1967 revealed that there were less than 1,800 females with full law enforcement powers (Roberg, Novak, & Cordner, 2005). The 1972 Equal Employment Opportunity Act (EEOA), which extended the protections provided by the 1964 Civil Rights Act to state and local governments, marked the beginning of a new era in many law enforcement agencies (Martin & Jurik, 1996). Discrimination was now prohibited based on race, color, and gender. Some have gone so far as to say that without benefit of the 1972 EEOA mandate and other protections such as affirmative action, women would have been denied entry to police patrol duties (Hale & Lanier, 2002).

In theory, the act would open many doors to persons of color and to women who wished to pursue a career in law enforcement. In practice, it has been difficult to undo the impact of nearly 150 years of an all-white, all-male occupational culture. It was not uncommon for agencies to have formal policies restricting the employment and advancement of women as police officers. Highly respected policing experts, including O. W. Wilson, spoke out on the abilities of women to fully serve as police officers. In his influential textbook on police management (which Walker & Katz, 2002, described as the "informal bible" of police administration), Wilson and his coauthor stated that men were more effective administrators who were better able to perform under stressful conditions (see Wilson & McLaren, 1963, cited in Roberg et al., 2005).

Despite the EEOA protections, women continue to be underrepresented as police officers. According to the latest statistics, women hold a mere 14.3 percent of all sworn law enforcement positions in this country (National Center for Women and Policing, 1999). In a study of the distribution of women in Florida police agencies, Poulos and Doerner (1996) found that 20 percent of the smaller agencies in the state did not employ a single female officer. While it should be mentioned that there have been gains in the representation of women in law enforcement, the growth has been slow, with an average annual increase of 0.5 percent. If the representation of women continues to grow at this same slow rate, it will take about 70 years for women to reach equal standing in the police profession (Bureau of Justice Assistance and National Center for Women and Policing, 2000).

Hiring standards are often blamed for maintaining gender imbalances on police agencies. As argued by Kappeler, Sluder, and Alpert (1998), police employment standards are designed to screen out candidates who do not possess certain values, traits, and characteristics. Among other things, these hiring standards may assist in determining an applicant's "physical prowess, sexual orientation and gender identification" (1998, p. 89). Applicants who fail to demonstrate their conformity to traditional, conservative ideals were excluded from employment, as were those who did not fit the "macho" expectations associated with the image of a "good" cop.

Physical agility tests were also an effective means of maintaining a masculine force. Because of the potentially dangerous nature of police work, it was felt that we would need very large, imposing individuals to serve as police officers (Haarr, 1997). For many years, police agencies screened for these characteristics. First and foremost, applicants for positions as law enforcement officers had to meet a minimum height requirement in order to be considered for employment. For the majority of agencies, the minimum height was 5 feet 8 inches. This was significantly higher than the average height for females, thereby eliminating the majority of women from employment consideration (Holladay, 2002; President's Commission on Law Enforcement and Administration of Justice, 1967; Walker & Katz, 2002). Even if a woman was tall enough to meet the minimum standards, she would then face a rather imposing physical ability test that for years overemphasized upper body strength. Applicants were asked to complete a variety of military-style physical challenges in a specified amount of time, such as push-ups, sit-ups, and bench-presses of one's own weight. Women failed these exams at significantly higher rates than their male peers, and thus were eliminated from the "qualified" applicant pool (Hale & Wyland, 1993; Swanson, Territo, & Taylor, 1998).

MAINTAINING MASCULINITY: THE MYTH OF THE CRIME FIGHTER

The question remains: Why were such big and strong men needed in order to perform the duties of police officers? This need is largely based on erroneous assumptions about the everyday duties of a patrol officer. The public often assumes that police work is dangerous, violent, and unpredictable (Austin & Hummer, 1999). Popular movies and television shows regularly portray officers in precarious situations dealing with criminals who are often brutal and dangerous. Similarly, in their quest for ratings, newspapers and television news shows overemphasize the violent aspects of policing. Officer-involved shootings are front-page news stories, fueling the belief that police work is much more dangerous than it actually is. Police officers themselves tend to exaggerate the danger of their work, telling and retelling "war stories" and focusing their conversations on crime and violence (Manning, 1977; Skolnick & Currie, 1970; Westley, 1970).

Additionally, the need for big, strong aggressive men was fueled by the traditional crime control model of law enforcement. Under this model, police work is defined by a constant war on crime and little else. The crime control model has been credited with maintaining a subculture that encourages police to view their jurisdiction as a combat zone where only the aggressively masculine can survive (Appier, 1998). Walker and Katz (2002) describe the inaccurate assumptions regarding the police work as "the myth of police officers as crime fighters."

In reality, instead of being focused on fighting crime, most police work is concerned with service-related issues (Garcia, 2003; Hale & Wyland, 1993). In an analysis of more than 26,000 calls for service to three metropolitan police agencies, only 2 percent of the calls were related to what would be considered serious violent crime: murders, rapes, robberies, and so on. Conversely, a third of the calls were related to various information or minor assistance problems, such as citizens needing directions, complaints over barking dogs, or other relatively trivial, often noncriminal events (Walker & Katz, 2002; see also Scott, 1981). Similarly, Parsons and Jesilow (2001) stated that only about 10 percent of policing work involves the law enforcement component, and dangerous activities involve less than 1 percent of citizen-initiated complaints.

Despite evidence to the contrary, the myth of the "police as crime fighters" has persisted, and police work has been summarily categorized as "man's work." The maintenance of the crime-fighting image has undermined most attempts to reform the police.

For example, a great deal of research has examined the resistance of the police subculture to reforms associated with community policing, a form of policing that has not been viewed as "real" police work (see, for example, Moore, 1992; Wood, Davis, & Rouse, 2004). Furthermore, the crime-fighting image has been particularly detrimental to the integration of women into the occupation.

IMPACT OF THE POLICE SUBCULTURE

When women first entered patrol work, they were met with open hostility and organized resistance from their male peers. It was not unheard of for male supervisors to refuse to train female recruits, or for female officers to be denied back-up in dangerous situations (Hunt, 1984; Martin, 1980; Martin & Jurik, 1996).

Today, many female officers continue to face discrimination and prejudice in the workplace (Barker, 1999; Haarr, 1997; Hale & Lanier, 2002; Hunt, 1990; Martin, 1994). Barker (1999), in a 20-year ethnographic study of the Los Angeles Police Department, observed that officers noted clear distinctions between the "Old Police," or those hired prior to 1972, and the "New Police." The New Police, which included many women and minority officers, were viewed by the Old Police as being less competent, not as committed, and less qualified to hold their positions.

Barker's findings are not atypical. The literature is consistent with respect to reports of prejudice and disparate treatment of women in patrol by their male counterparts. Despite the gains made by women, male coworkers and supervisors continue to resist females on patrol (Hale & Wyland, 1993; Lanier, 1996). The hostility has been so great that a report published by the U.S. Department of Justice concluded that "research consistently demonstrates that the negative attitude of male colleagues is the single most significant problem reported by female officers" (Bureau of Justice Assistance and National Center for Women and Policing, 2000, p. 22).

The boys-only clubhouse mentality has contributed to a climate in which sexual harassment is commonplace and acceptable. The majority of women in law enforcement have reported incidents of sexual harassment, which include being the target of inappropriate jokes and sexually charged comments, being exposed to pornography, and experiencing unwanted sexual advances (Haarr, 1997; Martin, 1980, 1992; National Center for Women and Policing, 1999).

This chapter began with an overview of the stressors experienced by all law enforcement personnel, including danger, hostility from the general public, and the requirement to handle calls for service involving human tragedies and suffering. In fact, policing is often described as one of the most stressful occupations (He, Zhao, & Archbold, 2002). Female officers experience additional stress due to the fact that they have been marginalized within the field (Haarr, 1997; Lanier, 1996; Wexler & Logan, 1983). Because they are denied access to the informal social structure that exists among law enforcement officers, women do not benefit from the support male officers enjoy from the company and camaraderie of other officers. While sporting clubs and other recreational activities are common among male police officers, women are often denied access to these informal gatherings. For example, in a qualitative study of a midwestern police department, Haarr (1997) observed that officers segregated themselves based on race and gender. During roll call, white male officers sat at tables and interacted with other white male officers. Additionally, Haarr noted that female officers were disproportionately assigned to "A cars," or a one-person patrol car. Not only were these women isolated from social interactions with other officers, but they were also relegated to more menial patrol functions, such as writing tickets and responding to calls regarding stolen vehicles.

The unique stress placed on female law enforcement officers manifests itself in a number of ways. Due to their marginalization, women become less likely to assert themselves and engage in self-directed activities. This lack of initiative may lead to a negative downward cycle as male officers then view the women as lazy and unmotivated, which only adds to the disparate treatment of the female officers (Haarr, 1997). Ni He and colleagues (2002) found that female officers reported higher levels of depression and somatization, or the level of discomfort related to physical problems such as aches and pains, as well as complaints related to cardiovascular and gastrointestinal disorders than their male counterparts. Occupation-related stress may spill over into officers' private lives. Rates of divorce and separation are higher among female officers than their male counterparts (Kirschman, 1997). As a result of the special problems facing female officers, the turnover rate of women exceeds that of men (Peak, 2003).

THE FUTURE OF WOMEN POLICE: CHANGING THE SUBCULTURE

More contemporary research studies on the subculture of policing have begun to question the absolute, unwavering existence of a single, unified value system held by all officers (Barker, 1999; Cochran & Bromley, 2003; Herbert, 1998; Morrison, 1993; Wood et al., 2004). As law enforcement agencies become more and more diverse, values and attributes of the more traditional police subculture may be on the wane. While the greater influx of women and people of color to the ranks of police officers has had an impact, other factors influencing changes in the occupational culture within police agencies include the leadership of the agency; changing political climates; lawsuits concerning hiring practices and the treatment of citizens; and the evolving mission of the police from a crime control philosophy to community-oriented, problem-solving policing (Herbert, 1998; Wood et al., 2004). Instead of a single value system identified among early all-male police departments, researchers have identified multiple subcultures that compete with and, in some cases, may be more influential than the more traditional model.

In a four-year ethnographic study, Wood and his colleagues (2004) identified seven competing police subcultures in the "Sunbelt City Police Department." While some officers still held fast to the traditional norms, the existence of other subcultures, including the "opportunistic," "paramilitary," "administrative," "civilian," "expert COP," and "community-oriented policing" subcultures ensured that front-line officers were no longer indoctrinated into a single worldview. Interestingly, women had gained some level of acceptance by the more traditionally minded officers, although their entry into the paramilitary subculture was largely denied. The paramilitary subculture embodies many of the same values as the traditional subculture, only it is much more aggressive. Officers in this group were described as "competitive soldiers" and "one-dimensionally masculine."

Subcultures associated with community policing models, while present, did not exert a particularly strong influence on the department personnel as a whole.

Similarly, in an analysis of a southern sheriff's department, Cochran and Bromley (2003) identified three different subcultures: "Subcultural Adherents," "COP Cops," and "Normals." Subcultural adherents comprised a relatively small group within the agency, with only one-sixth of the officers aligning themselves with more traditional beliefs. The COP Cops were more likely to report support of the service-oriented functions of police agencies and accounted for nearly one-third of the respondents. Finally, the Normals, who comprised nearly one-half of the deputies, were not strongly committed to either subculture.

Clearly, the influence of a single, traditional normative order among police officers is being challenged. The successful acceptance of women into policing as full, equal professionals may ultimately rest upon which subculture becomes dominant. Will the more traditional subculture that is based on a crime control model regain its singular dominance, or will the influence of community policing elicit lasting change on the value systems of officers? Certainly, no one can argue that the popularity of community-oriented, problem-solving policing has grown exponentially over the past 20 years. This form of policing is built on communication and mutual respect between officers and local citizens. It is in this type of policing that women may find unique success (Miller, 1999). A number of researchers have concluded that female police officers are less authoritarian, less brutal, more nurturing, better communicators, and that due to differential socialization, possess a greater pacifying quality than do their male counterparts (Bell, 1982; Grennan, 1987; Rivlin, 1981; Van Wormer, 1981; Weldy, 1976). Furthermore, a recent report by the Bureau of Justice Assistance and National Center for Women and Policing (2000) concluded that because of their unique traits, female officers may be especially suited to perform the type of policing functions associated with community policing (see also Bazley, Lersch, & Mieczkowski, 2004).

If community policing remains popular, it would follow that female police officers would be more accepted and achieve greater success in this type of policing function. Additionally, the traditional police subculture, which is based on "us versus them" distrust of citizens and fueled by a crime control doctrine, is incompatible with the underlying philosophy of community policing. It would be more and more difficult to follow the doctrine of a traditional police subculture in an agency that has truly seized upon the community policing model. Of course, the question remains: Will community policing last, or is it simply another flash in the pan? The question is open for debate (see Skogan, 2004). Only time will tell which police service model—and which subculture—will emerge as the dominant value system among law enforcement personnel.

CONCLUSION

As Waddington (1999) notes, sexism is not a trait that is exclusive to police culture. The police simply are a reflection of the patriarchal beliefs of the larger society in which masculine traits are valued over femininity (Garcia, 2003). Traditionally, through our laws and cultural standards, men have had the power to dictate which positions women are allowed to hold in society (Bartollas & Hahn, 1999; Martin & Jurik, 1996). It was not all that long ago that women were prohibited from attending college, owning property, managing their own financial affairs, or voting. Clearly, sexism among the police is not unique. It exists not only in male-dominated occupations, but across society as well. While great advancements for women have been made, there is still room for improvement. This is especially true in the field of policing.

REFERENCES

APPIER, J. (1998). *Policing women: The sexual politics of enforcement and the LAPD*. Philadelphia: Temple University Press.

AUSTIN, T., & HUMMER, D. (1999). What do college students think of policewomen? An attitudinal assessment of future law enforcement personnel. *Women and Criminal Justice, 10*(4), 1–24.

BARKER, J. (1999). *Danger, duty, and disillusion: The worldview of the Los Angeles police officers*. Prospect Heights, IL: Waveland Press.

BARTOLLAS, C., & HAHN, L. (1999). *Policing in America*. Boston: Allyn & Bacon.

BAZLEY, T., LERSCH, K. M., & MIECZKOWSKI, T. (2004, November). *Female patrol officers and use of force: Community policing considerations*. Paper presented at the annual meetings of the American Society of Criminology, Nashville, TN.

BELKNAP, J., & SHELLEY, J. K. (1992). The new Lone Ranger: Policewomen on patrol. *American Journal of Police, 12*, 47.

BELL, D. (1982). Policewomen: Myths and realities. *Journal of Police Science and Administration, 10*(1), 112–120.

BUREAU OF JUSTICE ASSISTANCE AND NATIONAL CENTER FOR WOMEN AND POLICING. (2000). *Recruiting and retaining women: A self-assessment guide for law enforcement*. Washington, DC: U.S. Department of Justice.

COCHRAN, J. K., & BROMLEY, M. L. (2003). The myth(?) of the police subculture. *Policing: An International Journal of Police Strategies & Management, 26*, 88–118.

CRANK, J. P. (1998). *Understanding police culture*. Cincinnati, OH: Anderson.

GARCIA, V. (2003). "Difference" in the police department: Women, policing and "doing gender." *Journal of Contemporary Criminal Justice, 19*, 330–344.

GRENNAN, S. (1987). Findings on the role of officer gender in violent encounters with citizens. *Journal of Police Science and Administration, 15*, 78–85.

HAARR, R. (1997). Patterns of interaction in a police patrol bureau: Race and gender barriers to integration. *Justice Quarterly, 14*(1), 53–85.

HALE, D., & LANIER, M. (2002). New millennium: Women in policing in the twenty-first century. In R. Muraskin & A. R. Roberts (Eds.), *Visions for change: Crime and justice in the twenty-first century* (3rd ed., pp. 480–497). Upper Saddle River, NJ: Prentice Hall.

HALE, D., & WYLAND, S. (1993). Dragons and dinosaurs: The plight of patrol women. *Police Forum, 3*(2), 1–6.

HE, N., ZHAO, J., & ARCHBOLD, C. (2002). Gender and police stress: The convergent and divergent impact of work environment, work-family conflict, and stress coping mechanisms of female and male police officers. *Policing: An International Journal of Police Strategies & Management, 25*, 687–708.

HERBERT, S. (1998). Police subculture reconsidered. *Criminology, 36*, 343–369.

HOLLADAY, A. (2002, December). *Wonderquest*. Retrieved February 1, 2004, from http:www.wonderquest.com/size-women-us.htm.

HUNT, J. (1984). The development of rapport through negotiation of gender in field work among police. *Human Organization, 43*, 283–296.

HUNT, J. (1990). The logic of sexism among police. *Women and Criminal Justice, 1*, 3–30.

Kappeler, V. E., Sluder, R. D., & Alpert, G. P. (1998). *Forces of deviance: Understanding the dark side of policing* (2nd ed.). Prospect Heights, IL: Waveland Press.

Kirschman, E. (1997). *I love a cop: What police families need to know.* New York: Guilford.

Lanier, M. (1996). Evolutionary typology of women police officers. *Women and Criminal Justice, 8*(2), 35–57.

Manning, P. (1977). *Police work.* Cambridge, MA: MIT Press.

Martin, S. (1980). *Breaking and entering: Policewomen on patrol.* Berkeley: University of California Press.

Martin, S. (1992). The changing status of women officers: Gender and power in police work. In I. L. Moyer (Ed.), *The changing role of women in the criminal justice system* (pp. 281–305). Prospect Heights, IL: Waveland Press.

Martin, S. (1994). "Outsider within" the station house: The impact of race and gender on black women police. *Social Problems, 41,* 383–400.

Martin, S., & Jurik, N. (1996). *Doing justice, doing gender: Women in law and criminal justice occupations.* Thousand Oaks, CA: Sage.

Miller, S. (1999). *Gender and community policing: Walking the talk.* Boston: Northeastern University Press.

Moore, M. (1992). Problem solving and community policing. In M. Tonry & N. Morris (Eds.), *Crime and justice: An annual review* (pp. 99–158). Chicago: University of Chicago Press.

Morrison, R. D. (1993). The police subculture: Myth or reality? *Law & Order, 41,* 87.

National Center for Women and Policing. (1999). *Equality denied: The status of women in policing.* Retrieved January 15, 2004, from http://www.womenandpolicing.org/Final_1999StatusReport.htm.

Parsons, D., & Jesilow, P. (2001). *In the same voice: Women and men in law enforcement.* Santa Ana, CA: Seven Locks Press.

Peak, K. J. (2003). *Policing America: Methods, issues, challenges* (4th ed.). Upper Saddle River, NJ: Prentice Hall.

Poulos, T., & Doerner, W. (1996). Women in law enforcement: The distribution of females in Florida police agencies. *Women in Criminal Justice, 8*(2), 19–33.

President's Commission on Law Enforcement and Administration of Justice. (1967). *Task force report: The police.* Washington, DC: U.S. Government Printing Office.

Rivlin, G. (1981). The last bastion of macho. *Update on Law-Related Education, 5,* 22–24, 65–67.

Roberg, R., Novak, K., & Cordner, G. (2005). *Police and society* (3rd ed.). Los Angeles: Roxbury.

Scott, E. (1981). *Calls for service: Citizen demand and initial police response.* Washington, DC: U.S. Government Printing Office.

Skogan, W. G. (2004). *Community policing: Can it work?* Belmont, CA: Wadsworth/Thomson Learning.

Skolnick, J. (1966). *Justice without trial.* New York: Wiley.

Skolnick, J. (2002). Corruption and the blue code of silence. *Police Practice and Research, 3*(1), 7–19.

Skolnick, J., & Currie, E. (1970). *Crisis in American institutions.* Boston: Little Brown.

Stark, R. (1972). *Police riots: Collective violence and law enforcement.* Belmont, CA: Wadsworth.

Swanson, C., Territo, L., & Taylor, R. (1998). *Police administration: Structures, processes, and behavior* (4th ed.). Upper Saddle River, NJ: Prentice Hall.

Van Maanen, J. (1980). Beyond account: The personal impact of police strategies. *Annals of the Academy of Political and Social Science, 452,* 145–156.

Van Wormer, K. (1981). Are males suited to police patrol work? *Police Studies, 3,* 41–44.

Waddington, P. A. J. (1999). Police (canteen) sub-culture: An appreciation. *British Journal of Criminology, 39,* 287–309.

Walker, S., & Katz, C. (2002). *The police in America: An introduction* (4th ed.). Boston: McGraw-Hill.

WELDY, W. (1976). Women in policing: A positive step toward increased police enthusiasm. *The Police Chief, 43*, 46–47.

WESTLEY, W. (1970). *Violence and the police*. Boston: MIT Press Books.

WEXLER, J. G., & LOGAN, D. D. (1983). Sources of stress among women police officers. *Journal of Police Science and Administration, 13*, 98–105.

WILSON, O. W., & McLAREN, R. C. (1963). *Police administration* (3rd ed.). New York: McGraw-Hill.

WOOD, R. L., DAVIS, M., & ROUSE, A. (2004). Diving into quicksand: Program implementation and police subcultures. In W. Skogan (Ed.), *Community policing: Can it work?* (pp. 136–162). Belmont, CA: Wadsworth/Thomson Learning.

38

Women in State Policing

An Assessment[1]

Trina Rose and N. Prabha Unnithan

We examine several issues associated with the participation of women in policing, specifically at the state level. Based on an extensive literature review, we find that the passage of the Equal Opportunity Act of 1972 was crucial in enhancing the incorporation of females into state police forces. Further, all state departments now include the equal opportunity employer clause in their recruitment materials. However, the effects that this rhetoric has had on the "real" numbers of women in state highway police departments have remained uninvestigated. We examine (1) recruitment policies for males and females, (2) testing policies for males and females, and (3) whether and/or how these policies affect the numbers of sworn female officers in the 49 U.S. state highway patrol departments. The information was gathered by contacting relevant personnel in all 49 states and by visiting every state patrol Web site. Preliminary analysis indicates that there are very few state departments that have more than 10% female force, and almost half (48.93%) of all state departments have less than 5% sworn female officers. We provide several reasons for these low numbers and proportions.

The subject of women in the law enforcement profession has garnered a good deal of attention (see the references at the end of this chapter). Similar to police studies in general, most of the research focuses on local municipal police departments. As a result, systematic and specific information that addresses the hiring of women into uniformed positions in various state highway patrol departments around the United States is hard to come by. What are the various policies that affect the hiring of women into state police forces? How do they compare to each other? How do they impact women in state policing? How much progress has been made in incorporating women into a profession that has always had a decidedly "male" profile? This chapter is an initial attempt at gathering and analyzing information aimed at answering these and other questions that pertain to female state police officers.

To answer these questions, first, a comprehensive literature review of women in policing before and after the Equal Opportunity Act of 1972 (or EOA, a crucial piece of legislation that has affected the hiring of women in all occupations in the United States) was carried out. Further, relevant personnel in all 49 departments (except for Hawaii which does not have a state police force) in the United States that have sworn state officers were contacted and interviewed by telephone for the purpose of examining their most recent recruitment and testing procedures. Information gathered in this manner was supplemented by visiting each state patrol's Web site. In addition, the most recent numbers of sworn officers each state department had, and how many of those were female, were also collated. In doing so, we compare and contrast various state policies and procedures against each other, and against the percentage of women within their respective departments.

Many larger municipalities have long ago noted some of the advantages to hiring women, such as their wider range of communication techniques and the psychological tendencies of suspects toward female as opposed to male officers (Melchionne, 1967). Some of the state departments in this study have gone out of their way to actively recruit females, and some departments just let those who are interested find their way to them. Due to the fact that there is very little other research on state policing (see Bechtel, 1995), it is not possible to compare these results to research by others. However, we do discuss the implications of these findings, and make suggestions for future policing research and departmental practice at the state level.

LITERATURE REVIEW

Policing Literature Before the Equal Opportunity Act of 1972

In the 21st-century United States, we rarely hear the term "policemen" anymore. Instead police personnel are referred to as police officers or officers of the peace, and the profession is referred to as law enforcement or policing. These terms, however, have only recently been widely accepted and used. Previously, even if officers were simply referred to as "police" instead of "policemen," many times one could still see gendered language when the author referred to the police as "he" (Cook, 1967; Devlin, 1966; Guernsey, 1966; McNamara, 1967; Somerville, 1969; Vandall, 1971; Vega, 1968).

Thus, it should come as no surprise that literature that addresses women in policing is very rare before the 1980s, and literature on policies regarding recruitment and testing female candidates is therefore nonexistent. While the early literature is limited, it is easy to deduce the social perception of policing as a masculine profession. One article of interest here is Melchionne (1967) who described the status of women in policing five years prior to the passage of the EOA, at the 73rd Annual Conference of the International Association of Chiefs of Police (IACP). Theresa Melchionne, a pioneering female officer of the New York Police Department who went on to become commissioner (and also an educator at John Jay College of Criminal Justice), makes an attempt to redefine the role of a policewoman as having all the same rights and duties as a policeman. She pointed out that at first, women were hired as juvenile officers and community officers to embellish the numbers of individuals (in these generally less prestigious aspects of police work, we should add). Though Melchionne (1967, p. 258) still included the statement, "permits use of her unique resources along the entire spectrum of police work, without diminishing the importance of her primary mission with respect to women and children," we suspect she was quite the spectacle that day, making such "irrational" projections as empowering policewomen with arresting authority.

Melchionne's (1967) paper is an early illustration of women's struggles to become police officers. It is also significant in that it was published only one year after Guernsey's (1966) pioneering research on state troopers in Florida. The dichotomy created by these two articles is telling; one from the perspective of a very large metropolis (New York) that had been hiring female police officers at least since 1946; and the other from a still very small state department that was still struggling to overcome the perception that only "maladjusted personality types gravitated to the work" of state troopers (Guernsey, 1966, p. 56). In practically the same year that Melchionne (1967) redefines policing to include "policewomen," Guernsey argues "a man could choose this job in the same way that other men choose other jobs" (Guernsey, 1966, p. 56). This small bit of early evidence suggests that state police departments were, at least at one point, behind larger municipalities in accepting women into their ranks.

Wilson (1952) states that minimum standards of citizenship, residence, education, age, height, and weight should be placed on all candidates, and those who do not meet those standards should be deemed as ineligible. In a scoring table provided alongside, a candidate can rank high above 90% only if she or he is 5 feet 10 inches or taller, has a four-year degree, and is 24 years or younger. It is possible for a woman to meet these qualifications, but highly unlikely. We see the gendered language mentioned above when Wilson writes about these standards: "The younger man is less likely to have . . . skills that may tempt him to leave the police service" (1952, p. 232). Wilson states that "height has advantages in police service that justify a minimum standard of 5 feet 9 inches" (1952, p. 233), but does not explain what those advantages are.

Later, Eastman and Eastman (1969) write on personnel issues in policing. By this time they were concerned with making policing a competitive and attractive career-oriented field. In addition, Heisel (in Eastman & Eastman, 1969) encourages recruiters to make a special effort to convince minority groups to apply for police work. Thus, there has been at least an ideological shift in the recruiting of racial and ethnic minorities. Education and intelligence are still requirements of selection: "He must be able to absorb readily the constantly expanding volume of material with which a policeman must be familiar" (Heisel in Eastman & Eastman, 1969, p. 177). Once again, however, we witness the gendered language regarding policing. Under "physical requirements," Heisel started by saying that "the era of brute strength . . . is over; brain, not brawn, is required" (cited in Eastman & Eastman, 1969, p. 177). Just a little later, however, Heisel confirms that not much has changed with regard to excluding women physically. The height requirement is not as stringent, but remains at 5 feet 9 inches. To his credit, however, he at least defends this requirement stating that there is a presumable psychological advantage for taller, bigger men. Height and weight requirements have changed (but not disappeared) to allow recruiting and hiring women into the police. More significantly, following the EOA of 1972, it became illegal to discriminate based on one's gender. Let us take a look at what the contemporaneous literature had to say about women entering a profession that had been dominated by men for so long.

Reactions to the Implementation of the Equal Opportunity Act of 1972

Although there is significantly more literature on women in policing after the passage of the EOA in 1972, much of it began appearing in the 1980s and focused on analyzing the effectiveness of women in policing a decade later. Powers (1983) expressed frustration with how to target women for recruitment into policing. Steel and Lovrich (1987, p. 53) found "little if any effect upon police agency performance can be attributed to differing levels of female police officers." But it was later noted that, even "when female officers graduated from police academies, it was not uncommon for male officers to continue their hostility" (O'Connor in Muraskin, 2003, p. 444). According to Martin (1989), the proportion of women increased between 1978 and 1986, but they still constituted only 20% of the applicant pool. The same year, Warner, Steel, and Lovrich (1989, p. 562) suggested that "progress toward social equity for women in such male-dominated occupations as policing is highly dependent upon a formal administrative structure established specifically to achieve this goal." Have policies been adopted to address this? And, if so, have they been successful? We shall see in the following pages.

Recent Literature on Women in Policing in the United States

Following the passage of the EOA in 1972, police departments adopted policies that were more open and inclusive to the hiring of women. In sheer numbers, their impact has been significant. Martin (1989) sent mail survey questionnaires to 319 police departments serving populations of 50,000 and above to examine the impact of the EOA. Her findings indicate that the proportion of women in large and medium-sized police departments increased from 4.2% of sworn personnel in 1978 to 8.8% in 1986. Simultaneously, the proportion of women in supervisory roles also increased. Martin (1989, p. 21) concluded that affirmative action policies "have had a major impact on the current entry rate and overall representation of women in policing." Public acceptance of female officers has also been forthcoming (see Leger, 1997, regarding patrol officers).

At the same time, the literature is divided on the impact of women in policing with one smaller faction suggesting that this process has been less stressful than expected, while another larger one disputes this assertion. On the "less of a problem than expected" side, Felkenes and Lasley (1992) argue that administrative concerns regarding hiring women may not be justified given that there are generally positive attitudes (regardless of race or gender of the respondent) after the introduction of affirmative action into a police department. Similarly, Bartol, Bergen, Volckens, and Knoras (1992) found that while women reported more stressors than men, it did not affect their job performance. Worden (1993) found that there are not many differences in the way men and women see their role as police officers. We speculate, however, that this may be because those who might view their role differently, male or female, are weeded out during the recruitment, testing, and selection processes.

On the other hand, many researchers have reached the opposite conclusion—that incorporating women in policing has been difficult. O'Connor (in Muraskin, 2003, p. 445) notes that "policing continues to be an overwhelmingly masculine enterprise" and points out that some still believe "that widespread bias in police hiring, selection practices, and recruitment policies keep women out of law enforcement." Similarly, Jacobs (1987) notes the coping mechanisms used by female officers in a traditional male occupation. This subject has not been confined to journal articles; entire chapters in textbooks have also been devoted to women in policing. Ollenburger and Moore (1998) note in one of their chapters that there was general hostility from male officers when women took on exchange value in policing. Flynn (in Muraskin, 1999, p. 25) more recently calls this a "staunch resistance to the employment of women" in law enforcement. She also notes three barriers working against the full integration of women into law enforcement as being sociocultural perceptions of police work, characteristics of the organizational structure of the police subculture, and the pervasive stereotyping of women police. Finally, Muraskin (2003) speculates that female turnover in departments could be eliminated if these departments would take the time to create an affirmative work environment for both genders. And so, we see that the adopted departmental policies have allowed some women into uniformed positions, but studies show that their quality of life on the job may be suffering because of their choice to pursue police work.

Let us turn our attention to the representation of women in state policing today, the primary focus of this paper. As can be seen from the above literature review, we know little about the recruitment mechanisms and resulting proportions of women in policing at the state level. This lack of information, however, is also reflective of the overall neglect (Bechtel, 1995) of state policing as a research arena.

STUDY FINDINGS

State Patrol Recruitment Mechanisms

Based on our discussions with highway patrol officials in 49 states, it is clear that recruitment procedures do not differ formally across these departments for males and females. By "formally," we mean having existing written procedures for advertising, disseminating information regarding openings, encouraging individuals who inquire to apply, determining initial eligibility, testing criteria, selection procedures etc. Further, there are no differences in terms of the usual selection stages themselves, such as written examinations, physical examinations, oral board interviews, polygraph tests, psychological evaluations, and intensive background checks. However, many departments have informal recruitment techniques directed toward getting women to apply. Some departments use direct recruitment strategies to get women to apply for jobs. For example, the Idaho, Michigan, and South Carolina state patrols volunteered the information that they send female recruiting officers on as many recruitment trips as possible to appeal to possible female candidates. The Idaho police also elaborated to say that they use target groups to help recruit women, and they are members of the National Center for Women & Policing, which "conducts and disseminates original research on the status of women in policing and the impact of gender on police operations" (National Center for Women & Policing, 2005). South Carolina sends recruiters to colleges with large minority populations and women's colleges specifically to get minorities and women to apply. Finally, the Michigan patrol stated that the females in their executive branches (i.e., captains and lieutenants) do much of the recruitment of women to show promotional possibilities for women in their department.

While Ohio, New Jersey, Kansas, and Colorado did not volunteer such information when contacted by telephone, their Web sites clearly showed a different kind of "direct" recruitment strategy. Because the Internet is increasingly used to access information, it could be very advantageous for a department to target underrepresented groups for recruitment via the World Wide Web. Each of these state departments had links to pages on their official Web sites dedicated to women in sworn positions. These specific pages displayed testimonies from female troopers who enjoyed their career; provided information on women who had made it to "ranking" positions within the department (e.g., "Uniformed Women in the KHP," at http://www.kansashighwaypatrol.org/womeninkhp.htm); and included pictures of female officers on the job. (Our own state of Colorado, unfortunately, had only a "Coming Soon" notification on the Web page dedicated to women in the Colorado State Patrol.) In addition to the above-discussed states, others are placing recruitment videos on their Web pages, so that potential police candidates can be recruited from home. Particularly noteworthy is Louisiana's recruitment video that depicts a little girl who dresses up in her father's uniform, and is shown growing up to be a trooper herself.

Finally, direct recruitment messages being sent to women interested in a state badge are often supplemented by implied and indirect communications. Departments such as Georgia, Texas, and Vermont specifically displayed pictures of a uniformed female officer on the front page of their recruitment Web page. Furthermore, Arkansas, Nevada, Oregon, Virginia, and West Virginia portrayed group pictures of officers, each with a female somewhere in the group.

State Testing Policies

Testing policies, on the other hand, must be strictly adhered to for the sake of fairness and also to avoid litigation. The data accumulated in this study show that there is a dichotomy among state testing policies: either states have no differences at all in their testing procedures and qualifying marks for males and females across all testing administered, or they base their physical testing criteria on the age and gender standards authored by the Cooper Institute of Aerobics Research (CIAR), the institute that sets the standards for military agencies. A little over one-third of the states continue to use the so-called Cooper standards (see the Table 1).

However, it is interesting to note that the Cooper Institute Web site itself states the following, on its "Law Enforcement" link:

> According to legislation (Civil Rights Act of 1991), separate standards are against the law. The principle is expressed as **Same Job = Same Standard**. Consequently, in our opinion, age and gender standards are in conflict with this law if applied as *mandatory* standards for selection (academy entrance), completion of training (academy exit) or maintenance programs (for incumbents). . . .
>
> The age and gender based norms were used in the past . . . because they did appear reasonable and they minimized adverse impact against protected classes. However, with a required

TABLE 1   State Departments Using Cooper Standards

State	Percent Females
Connecticut*	6.40%
Georgia	2.90
Illinois	10.10
Maine	7.38
New Hampshire	8.57
New Mexico	4.12
New York	8.44
North Carolina	2.46
North Dakota	4.44
Ohio	9.97
Oregon	10.00
Rhode Island	7.66
South Dakota	1.27
Utah	4.78
Vermont*	8.08
Washington	8.25

*Official estimate by state personnel.

emphasis on job relatedness brought about by the Civil Rights Act of 1991 and the ADA, the age and gender based norms (**as mandatory standards**) are currently not recommended. . . .

Absolute standards . . . are recommended. Same Job = Same Standards makes the most sense. Absolute standards, however, will probably demonstrate adverse impact especially against females. (Cooper Institute, 2005)

Even though standards were originally researched and set up specifically for law enforcement agencies, according to its Web site, CIAR clearly no longer suggests the usage of these standards for law enforcement personnel.

Actual Percentages of Women in State Departments

The results show a large range of percentages of women in state departments, not exceeding 12.40%, but as low as 1.27%. Melchionne (1967, p. 257) wrote, "the percentage of policewomen to male officers in ten of the larger cities of the country ranged from a high of 2¼% to a low of 1/20 of 1% of the force." Thirty-five years later, the IACP administered a survey of large municipalities (but no state departments) and found that 17% of the agencies surveyed had no female officers, while 55% had only between one and four female officers (O'Connor in Muraskin, 2003). In the literature, O'Connor remarks in grim hindsight, in that "it has taken almost 150 years for women to represent 14% of our nation's police forces" (in Muraskin, 2003, p. 447). Powers (1983, p. 63) predicts that there will have to be significant increases in the number of women police officers to match their numbers in the general population and that this "may be a long time coming." Echoing this literature, our data show there are no state departments that lack females on their force, as in the IACP study, and only one of the states fits into the second category of having only one to four female officers. Unfortunately, the state with the highest percentage of females (Michigan at 12.4%) still does not amount to the national average of the percentage of women in *all* uniformed police positions, of 14% (see Table 2).

Recruitment and Results

Martin (1989, p. 39) suggested that "increases in the number of women in recruitment and training assignments as well as high visibility supervisory positions" would help with recruitment and retention of women. At first glance it would seem that these suggested recruiting techniques work, since as discussed in the previous section, Michigan, using aggressive recruitment techniques, had the highest percentage of sworn women for all 49 states surveyed at 12.40%. However, that prospect does not seem to be uniformly accurate when we realize that South Carolina, despite its active and direct techniques at recruitment, had only 3.3% ($N = 788$) women on their force (less than one-quarter of that of Michigan). Idaho falls between the two with 6.9% ($N = 200$) uniformed females, and though this is significantly lower than Michigan's rate, it still ranks Idaho at number 17 out of 49. However, these three states by no means reflect the totality of states that use these types of active, aggressive, and direct recruitment strategies, as this was volunteered information only.

Moving on to the states that exemplified direct recruitment through their Web site, we see a similar phenomenon. Ohio, which had a link directly to its pamphlet designed specifically for women, had a resounding 9.97% ($N = 1,525$) sworn female officers, whereas Kansas with its link to "Uniformed Women in the KHP" had a women's component amounting to only 3.36% ($N = 535$) of its force. New Jersey also fell short (but above Kansas) at 3.93% women, but Colorado, even though its link led to only a "Coming Soon" message, fell between the extremes at 5.86% ($N = 666$) females. And, though it was our favorite recruitment technique, Louisiana came in between Kansas and New Jersey with 3.63% ($N = 1,020$) women on its force.

Georgia, Texas, and Vermont, distinguished by having a picture of a female officer displayed on the front of their recruitment Web page, had the following statistics when surveyed in 2005: Georgia had 2.90% ($N = 793$) females, Texas had 6.13% ($N = 3,407$) females, and Vermont had 8.08% ($N = 297$) women. While not as drastic, we see one state in the upper percentages, one state in a much lower percentage, and one in the middle.

Arkansas, Nevada, Oregon, Virginia, and West Virginia display group pictures of officers with at least one female somewhere in the group. Arkansas had 4.98% ($N = 502$) female officers, Nevada had 5.23% ($N = 421$) uniformed women, Oregon had 10% ($N = 600$) sworn females, Virginia had 5.33% ($N = 1,163$) women officers, and West Virginia had 2.77% ($N = 650$) uniformed females.

Perhaps another important fact is that only 15 (30%) of the states mentioned above directly or indirectly recruited females into uniformed positions with their state. However, not all states were asked about their more informal recruitment techniques. After visiting all 49 state patrol Web sites, we may state that only 25% (12) of the states directly or

TABLE 2   Percent Sworn Females by State

State	Total Sworn Troopers	Total Female Troopers	Percent Female Troopers
Alabama	659	13	1.97%
Alaska*	300	20	6.67
Arizona	1,115	75	6.73
Arkansas	502	25	4.98
California	7,194	654	9.09
Colorado**	666	39	5.86
Connecticut*	1,156	74	6.40
Delaware	649	68	10.48
Florida*	1,800	180	10.00
Georgia	793	23	2.90
Idaho	200	13	6.50
Illinois	2,060	208	10.10
Indiana	1,331	65	4.88
Iowa	370	13	3.51
Kansas	535	18	3.36
Kentucky	984	32	3.25
Louisiana	1,020	37	3.63
Maine	298	22	7.38
Maryland	1,519	139	9.15
Massachusetts	2,199	204	9.28
Michigan	1,774	220	12.40
Minnesota	500	49	9.80
Mississippi	515	10	1.94
Missouri	1,070	41	3.83
Montana	204	9	4.41
Nebraska	510	26	5.10
Nevada	421	22	5.23
New Hampshire	280	24	8.57
New Jersey	2,800	110	3.93
New Mexico	558	23	4.12
New York	4,669	394	8.44
North Carolina	1,465	36	2.46
North Dakota	135	6	4.44

(*Continued*)

TABLE 2   Continued

State	Total Sworn Troopers	Total Female Troopers	Percent Female Troopers
Ohio	1,525	152	9.97
Oklahoma	802	11	1.37
Oregon	600	60	10.00
Pennsylvania	4,178	189	4.52
Rhode Island	222	17	7.66
South Carolina	788	26	3.30
South Dakota	157	2	1.27
Tennessee	1,000	43	4.30
Texas	3,407	209	6.13
Utah	418	20	4.78
Vermont*	297	24	8.08
Virginia	1,163	62	5.33
Washington	1,055	87	8.25
West Virginia	650	18	2.77
Wisconsin	492	59	11.99
Wyoming	189	7	3.70

* Official estimate by state personnel.
** As of October 2004.

indirectly recruit females using their Web pages. Having analyzed direct and indirect recruitment policies and strategies, let us look at testing policies.

The Impact of Testing Policies

Testing policies are also crucial with regard to the number of women in sworn positions with various states. As seen above, some states continue to use the Cooper standards (see Table 1). Note that with the exception of North Carolina and Georgia, none of the states that continue to use the Cooper standards are in what has traditionally been defined as the "South." In addition, with the exception of South Dakota, the only states that continue to use the Cooper standards that have fewer than 3% females are southern states. This may indicate a regional bias, which will be discussed later. Because the testing policies are a dichotomy, it is difficult to speculate further, only with regard to the testing policy alone, without further data. In addition, use of the Cooper standards as testing policy appears to be diminishing, probably due to the recommendations for law enforcement agencies from the CIAR itself. Thus, if these standards are having an effect (increasing female representation), we may see these effects disappear with movement away from the CIAR standards.

TABLE 3   States with Equal or More than 10% Females

State	Total Sworn Troopers	Total Female Troopers	Percent Female Troopers
Delaware	649	68	10.48 %
Florida*	1,800	180	10.00
Illinois	2,060	208	10.10
Michigan	1,774	220	12.40
Oregon	600	60	10.00
Wisconsin	492	59	11.99

*Official estimate by state personnel.

TABLE 4   States with Less than 3% Females

State	Total Sworn Troopers	Total Female Troopers	Percent Female Troopers
Alabama	659	13	1.97 %
Georgia	793	23	2.90
Mississippi	515	10	1.94
North Carolina	1,465	36	2.46
Oklahoma	802	11	1.37
South Dakota	157	2	1.27
West Virginia	650	18	2.77

As noted earlier, according to the Web site, going to testing procedures that are completely equal for males and females may have "adverse effects" on female candidates.

Other Impacts and Analyses

For further analytic purposes, the states are divided into two categories: (1) states with equal or more than 10% uniformed females, and (2) states with less than 3% sworn females.

Table 3 depicts the states with more than 10% sworn females. With the exception of Florida, which is not necessarily understood to be the "traditional South" because of its influx of elder populations (and which is also an estimate), none of these states is located in the South. In addition, half of these states are located in the upper Midwest region of the United States. Finally, as a matter of curiosity, all states with at least 10% females (again, except Florida, which was a "contested" state) were "blue" (or Democratic) states in the 2000 and 2004 presidential elections.

Table 4 shows the states that have fewer than 3% uniformed females in their departments. Again, four of the six states with under 3% sworn women are located in areas defined traditionally as belonging to the South. However, the state with the lowest number and percentage of females is South Dakota. But South Dakota is the only one of these six states that has less than 500 total officers (in fact, its state police force is significantly smaller at 157 officers). Yet, in terms of partisan identification, these are all states that were "red" (or Republican) in the 2000 and 2004 elections.

CONCLUSIONS AND DISCUSSION

In this chapter, we attempted to gauge the nature and extent of participation of women in state police forces. The literature on the overall topic of women in policing has noted increasing numbers of females in American police departments and the crucial impact of the EOA of 1972 in enhancing their participation. It has also been divided on the question of departmental resistance and related difficulties involved in such integration. At the same time, we have not been able to find research that focuses specifically on female participation in state-level policing.

The above analyses indicate some regional and political patterns. The traditional South is known for its conventional and conservative attitudes toward women (and minorities). According to our survey, all of the police forces traditionally in states thought of as the South had less than 5% uniformed females. In addition, four of the six states with less than 3% females were also in the South. Because of these conventional attitudes, the low percentages may simply reflect the overall lack of female participation in the labor force, as opposed to discriminatory attitudes toward women in a traditionally male career, such as policing.

At the other extreme, almost all of the state police forces that had more than 10% women were "blue states" in the 2000 and 2004 presidential election. From this, one can deduce that a more progressive orientation and a supportive attitude toward women in the labor force may result in acceptance of women holding previously "masculine" positions in society, such as policing. However, the above could also reflect a religious pattern as well. It is no secret that the South is known as the religious conservative "Bible Belt." It is possible that the religiosity of the state as a whole is more reflective of that state's likelihood to have a larger population of women in state law enforcement.

One added piece of speculation: South Carolina volunteered the information that it had been on a hiring freeze since the year 2003. This information suggests that the percentages found in this study could be a combination between the high turnover rate for females in law enforcement (Martin, 1989) and state hiring freezes (given widespread state budget difficulties in recent times). At another level this would negate the arguments supporting discrimination against females in law enforcement careers or lower levels of female attraction toward such positions.

We further speculate that a combination of the above reasons may result in the distribution seen in the various states. In some cases, testing and recruitment policies have been shown to result in lower or higher number of females in the state departments. However, regional (and possibly religious) factors and female participation in the labor force may affect state percentages. In addition, factors not discussed here, such as the economic status of a state and its population characteristics (e.g., age distribution and gender ratio), may play a part in the numbers of females represented in state law enforcement. These ideas could be tested by analyzing the effects of population, age distribution, gender ratio, and indicators of state economic status, as well as the relative religiosity of the state, on the numbers and percentages of women in policing. Whatever the reasons underlying female underrepresentation in state police forces (hovering at below 13% for even the states with the best records in a nation where women constitute more than half the population) could stand improvement.

Suggestions for Departments

What could be done to improve these low numbers and proportions at the level of individual state police departments? Pendergrass and Ostrove (1984, p. 308) suggest "improvement in status and income associated with entry into male-dominated employment may ameliorate stress consequences for policewomen in comparison to other employed women." By reducing these possible stresses, perhaps highway patrol positions may become more attractive to women. Poole and Pogrebin (1988, p. 54) found that it is well known after only three years on the force that "few women actually get promoted . . . [and] those few women who have beaten the odds and have been promoted may be perceived by other female officers as exceptional cases." Thus, Martin's (1989) suggestion to increase the visibility of women in supervisory positions might also increase the recruitment and retention of women. Ten years later, Martin (1999) provides a different view, finding that women's emotional labor in policing is often exploited and undervalued by other officers who use female officers to play mother roles or serve as confidantes. At the same time, if emotions are expressed on the job, male officers are quick to criticize that. Perhaps training officers appropriately could lower the effects of this confusing and contradictory phenomenon. The point is that there are many different suggestions that could help increase the numbers of women, but even those that are relatively easy to do (e.g., displaying pictures of female officers on a Web page), are carried out by only a small percentage of state departments.

NOTE

1. A version of this chapter was presented at the Annual Meetings of the Western Social Science Association in Albuquerque, New Mexico, in April 2005.

REFERENCES

BECHTEL, K. H. (1995). *State police in the United States: A socio-historical analysis.* Westport, CT: Greenwood.

BARTOL, C. R., BERGEN, G. T., VOLCKENS, S., & KNORAS, K. M. (1992). Women in small-town policing—Job-performance and stress. *Criminal Justice and Behavior, 19*(3), 240–259.

COOK, W. (1967). Policemen in society: Which side are they on? *Berkeley Journal of Sociology, 12,* 117–129.

COOPER INSTITUTE. (2005). *Common questions regarding physical fitness tests, standards and programs for public safety.* Retrieved from http://www.cooperinst.org/lawstand.pdf

DEVLIN, P. (1966). Police in a changing society. *The Journal of Criminal Law, Criminology, and Police Science, 57*(2), 123–129.

EASTMAN, G. D., & EASTMAN, E. M. (1969). *Municipal police administration.* Washington, DC: International City Management Association.

FELKENES, G. T., & LASLEY, J. R. (1992). Implications of hiring women police officers: Police administrators' concerns may not be justified. *Policing and Society, 3*(1), 41–50.

GUERNSEY, E. (1966). The state trooper: A study of men and attitudes in law enforcement. *Research Reports in Social Science, 9*(2), 36–58.

JACOBS, P. (1987). How female police officers cope with a traditionally male occupation. *Sociology and Social Research, 72*(1), 4–6.

LEGER, K. (1997). Public perceptions of female police officers on patrol. *American Journal of Criminal Justice, 21*(2), 231–249.

MARTIN, S. E. (1989). Women on the move? A report on the status of women in policing. *Women and Criminal Justice, 1*(1), 21–40.

MARTIN, S. E. (1999). Emotional labor in the service economy: Emotional labor on the job: Police force or police service? Gender and emotional labor. *The Annals of the American Academy of Political and Social Science, 111*, 561.

MCNAMARA, J. (1967). Uncertainties in police work: The relevance of police recruits' backgrounds and training. In David Bordua (Ed.), *Police: Six sociological essays.* New York: Wiley.

MELCHIONNE, T. (1967). Current status of problems of women police. *The Journal of Criminal Law and Criminology, 58*(2), 257–260.

MURASKIN, R. (1999). Women professionals in criminal justice: A global perspective. In R. Muraskin (Ed.), *Women and justice: Development of international policy.* Philadelphia: Taylor and Francis.

MURASKIN, R. (2003). *It's a crime: Women and justice.* Upper Saddle River, NJ: Prentice Hall.

NATIONAL CENTER FOR WOMEN & POLICING. (2005). *NCWP publications.* Retrieved from http://www.women and policing.org/publications.asp

OLLENBURGER, J. C., & MOORE, H. A. (1998). *A sociology of women: The intersection of patriarchy, capitalism, and colonialism* (2nd ed.). Upper Saddle River, NJ: Prentice Hall.

PENDERGRASS, V., & OSTROVE, N. (1984). A survey of stress in women in policing. *Journal of Police Science and Administration, 12*(3), 303–309.

POOLE, E., & POGREBIN, M. (1988). Factors affecting the decision to remain in policing: A study of women officers. *Journal of Police Science and Administration, 16*(1), 49–55.

POWERS, M. (1983). Employment motivations for women in policing. *The Police Chief, 50*(11), 60–63.

SOMERVILLE, B. (1969). Double standards in law enforcement with regard to minority status. *Issues in Criminology, 4*(1), 35–44.

STEEL, B. S., & LOVRICH, N. P., JR. (1987). Equality and efficiency tradeoffs in affirmative action—real or imagined? The case of women in policing. *The Social Science Journal, 24*(1), 53–70.

VANDALL, F. (1971). Training to meet the police function. *Wisconsin Law Review, 2*, 547–575.

VEGA, W. (1968). The liberal policeman: A contradiction in terms? *Issues in Criminology, 4*(1), 15–34.

WARNER, R. L., & STEEL, B. S. (1989). Affirmative action in times of fiscal stress and changing value priorities: The case of women in policing. *Public Personnel Management, 18*(3), 291–309.

WARNER, R. L., STEEL, B. S., & LOVRICH, N. P. (1989). Conditions associated with the advent of representative bureaucracy: The case of women in policing. *Social Science Quarterly, 70*(3), 562–578.

WILSON, O. W. (1952). *Police planning.* Springfield, IL: Charles C. Thomas.

WORDEN, A. P. (1993). The attitudes of women and men in policing—Testing conventional and contemporary wisdom. *Criminology, 31*(2), 203–241.

39

Early Policing in the United States

"Help Wanted—Women Need Not Apply!"

Martin L. O'Connor

In the early nineteenth century the United States was a collection of agriculturally based communities. Although these communities employed sheriffs, constables, and a night watch (Bartollas & Hahn, 1999, p. 7), there were no police departments per se. Nevertheless, these communities were strongly influenced by English traditions and practices. Therefore, in 1829, when the English Parliament created the London Metropolitan Police Department and organized a paid police force, the United States took notice. The need and desire for a paid police force in U.S. communities became apparent. In 1833, the city of Philadelphia created its first police department, and in 1844 the New York State Legislature authorized municipalities to create police forces. Soon police departments were created throughout New York (Bartollas & Hahn, 1999). Similar police departments were created in Baltimore, Boston, Cincinnati, Newark, and New Orleans (Richardson, 1974). The personnel policies of the newly created police departments mirrored the discrimination in U.S. society. Simply stated, all police departments were composed exclusively of white males (Bouza, 1992). During the nineteenth and most of the twentieth centuries, the recruitment efforts of American police agencies with respect to women could be summarized as: "Help wanted—women need not apply!"

WOMEN BEGIN TO KNOCK AT THE POLICE DOOR

In the mid-nineteenth century the prison system in the United States was staffed almost exclusively by males. Their male guards sexually exploited a number of female inmates and the attendant publicity created efforts for change. Under pressure from the American Female Moral Reform Society to reform the system, in 1845 the city of New York hired six matrons for its jails (Schultz, 1995). Later, the same effort to place matrons in police stationhouses to assist in processing female arrestees was opposed by the Men's Prison Association (Berg & Budnick, 1986). Although women were not welcome in the male club of policing, the growing need for women to assist police agencies with some of the problems of delinquent children and prostitutes led to the police appointment of a woman "safety worker" in Portland, Oregon, in 1905. Safety worker Lola Baldwin, although not classified as a police officer, was the first documented appointment of a woman with some police power (Bartollas & Hahn, 1999). In 1910, Alice Stebbins Wells, a social worker, was appointed by the Los Angeles Police Department as a detective to work with women and children. Soon thereafter, police departments throughout the country began employing policewomen in support positions to assist in police work associated with women and children. These women were welcomed into police departments in their support roles (Hale, 1992). In 1922, there were 500 policewomen in the United States, and by 1960 their number had grown to 5,617 (Schultz, 1995). Although women began to see a crack in the police personnel door, the resistance of the male police culture to an expanded role for women in policing was strong and well organized (Martin, 1994). Most of the 17,000 U.S. police agencies did not employ women. Sixty years after the appointment of Alice Stebbins Wells as the first policewoman, the role of women in policing was still confined to support functions or work with juveniles and women. Furthermore, women employed in these positions were frequently required to have greater education than male police officers, and women were not permitted to compete with male officers for promotions (Milton, 1972). Some major U.S. police departments did not employ female officers in any capacity until 1966.[1]

During the 1960s a great wave of social change took place in the United States. The civil rights movement, the antiwar movement, the due process revolution, and the feminist movement were seriously questioning the nation's values. The patriarchal order that dominated society for thousands of years was under sustained attack.

> The resistance toward women in policing must be ultimately viewed in terms of the patriarchal society. . . . Western society, as well as most other cultures, has been based on social, philosophical, and political systems in which men by force, direct pressure, or through tradition, ritual, custom, language, etiquette, education, and law determine what part women shall or shall not play. . . . In policing, women had the "audacity" to desire entrance to an all male occupation, one that male officers perceived to demand the traditionally masculine attributes of dominance, aggressiveness, superiority and power. (Bartollas & Hahn, 1999, p. 286)

In the United States, women were kept in check by social norms, and legislatures created statutes embodying social values that restricted various opportunities for women. These statutes were generally approved by the courts (*Minor v. Happersett* [1875]: women do not have the right to vote in federal elections; *Hoyt v. Florida* [1961]: women can be exempted from jury service and do not have to fulfill the duties of citizenship; *Bradwell v. Illinois* [1873]: qualified women can be excluded from certain occupations, such as lawyer, simply because of their gender; *Goesaert v. Cleary* [1948]: access of women to certain occupations can be limited; *Radice v. New York* [1924]: women can be prohibited from working nights; *U.S. v. St. Clair* [1968]: women can be exempted from the responsibilities of military service). In the 1960s and 1970s a feminist wave began sweeping the United States. The feminist movement gained the attention of the U.S. Supreme Court when it ruled for the first time that sex-based classifications were "subject to scrutiny under the equal protection clause" (*Reed v. Reed*, 1971). In addition, the feminist movement was given powerful impetus by Betty Friedan, who touched a nerve by what she called "The Problem That Has No Name." In essence, she described the role of American women and their dissatisfaction with a nation that limited their roles in society. She raised the question: "Is this all?" (Friedan, 1963). The same question "Is this all?" could be applied to the second-class role of women in policing where they were principally confined to clerical positions and working with children. The issue was: Are woman going to be able to compete in a police career on an equal footing with their male counterparts? The resounding answer from the police organizational culture in the United States was clear, direct, and powerful. No! In the late 1960s, police officers in the New York City Police Department were asked what they thought about women becoming patrol officers. Some of their responses included the following: "Ptl. Paul DiStephano said, 'The idea of a woman driving a radio car is enough to make you want to quit the job. . . .' Ptl. James Miller said, 'It's a bad arrangement. A woman just isn't built to handle situations that confront policemen. They're not physically equipped to do a job that sometimes demands muscle. . . .' Ptl. George Hall said, 'A woman's place is definitely not in a radio car—it's in an office. I'll even go a little further than that—a woman belongs at home, taking care of the kids.'" (Fyfe, Greene, Walsh, Wilson, & McLaren, 1997). The attitude voiced by these officers in the 1960s fairly reflects the overwhelming sentiment of the U.S. police culture of its day. Women were simply not wanted as full partners in the policing enterprise.

LEGAL FORCES BEGIN TO OPEN POLICE DOORS TO WOMEN

In 1964, Congress passed the most historic and sweeping civil rights legislation ever enacted, 42 U.S.C., § 2000. Title VII of this legislation dealt with discrimination in employment on the basis of race, color, religion, national origin, and sex. It is of interest to note that the legislation was designed primarily to address racial discrimination and the word "sex" was added to the bill at the last minute on the floor of the House of Representatives by opponents of the measure in an attempt to prevent its passage (Freeman, 1991, p. 163). Notwithstanding enormous opposition in Congress, the Civil Rights Bill became law in July 1965. The legislation did not affect discrimination against women in most police departments immediately because the act exempted municipal governments from its coverage. However, the act was a very important legal force with respect to discrimination in U.S. society. Women began to believe that it might be possible for the barriers to equal employment in policing to be removed. In 1968, two women in Indianapolis became the first in the nation to be appointed to regular patrol duties in a marked police car (Lord, 1995). Very few municipalities followed the Indianapolis lead. In fact, in some states legal statutes still prohibited women from becoming patrol officers.[2] Therefore, even if an enlightened police official in these states wanted to appoint a female to patrol duties, state statutes and civil service requirements prevented such action. Finally, in 1972, Title VII was amended to apply to state and municipal governments, thereby providing protection against discrimination in employment for women seeking entry to police departments. However, the legal battle was not yet over. Women soon found that there were additional barriers preventing them from assuming the role of police officer. These hurdles were the numerous police height, weight, and physical fitness standards that were in effect in police departments across the nation. It was not uncommon for these standards to require that applicants be 5 feet 7 inches to 5 feet 10 inches in height. In addition, it was not uncommon to require applicants to pass an obstacle course requirement, a standing broad jump, pull-ups, a sit-up while holding a weight on one's shoulders, and one-handed dumbbell presses (Fyfe et al., 1997). These standards excluded most women from entering the police profession. The relevancy of these standards was highly questionable and almost all of these standards were eliminated as a result of the U.S. Supreme Court decision in *Griggs v. Duke Power Company* (1971). In *Griggs*, the Court unanimously approved the disparate impact method of analyzing discrimination claims. Therefore, a policy or practice may be discriminatory if it has a disproportionate effect upon a particular group and is not job related or justified by business necessity. Hence, height, weight, and physical fitness standards that were facially neutral in their treatment of different groups but, in fact, fell more harshly on women violated Title VII because these standards could not meet the test of *Griggs*. Since *Griggs*, law enforcement agencies have repeatedly tried to justify some measure of height, weight, and physical fitness requirements but have been unable to do so (see also *Dothard v. Rawlinson*, 1977).[3]

THE POLICE DOOR IS LEGALLY OPEN TO WOMEN

After state laws banning women from policing were overturned by the mandates of Title VII and height, weight, and physical fitness standards were removed because they could not meet the test of *Griggs*, women began entering the police profession in increasing numbers. Some women entered police departments and did not encounter great difficulties.[4] Nevertheless, many women encountered enormous resistance from the police organizational culture. Women experienced this resistance very early in their police careers and frequently upon their entry to police academies. In some police academies the physical fitness routine that was geared to male officers was used to demonstrate that females lack the physical strength to be police officers. The lack of upper body strength prevented many female recruits from doing as well as their male counterparts on some physical fitness regimes. In addition, some police academy trainers reluctantly agree to provide remedial firearms training to female recruits because of a female's unfamiliarity with weapons and a lack of hand strength. It has been said that inequality in police training may also be fostered by "an emphasis on meeting physical fitness standards that do not have to be maintained beyond the academy . . . [thus magnifying] the importance of physical differences. [In addition], informal coddling of women by some physical education instructors who are protective or unable to deal with some women's manipulative efforts also negatively affects all women. . . . It also undermines the confidence of male officers in women officers in general, and divides the women."

Occasionally, police academy instructors have stood in front of police academy classes and stated, "I don't care what they say, women don't belong on the job."[5] In police academy role-play exercises, female recruits who did not act in an aggressive manner like their male counterparts were considered to have "no command presence." Civility by female recruits was viewed as a sign of weakness. In some police academies it was required that recruits get into a boxing ring with boxing gloves and actually fight a male officer. One training officer in a major police agency suggested that this was necessary to see if a female officer "could take a punch."[6] Some women claimed that they were boxed right out of the police academy (*Newsday*, December 1986).

When female officers graduated from police academies and assumed their role as patrol officers, it was not uncommon for male officers to continue their hostility. Male officers viewed patrol work as "men's work" (Balkin, 1988; Milton, 1974). The hostility toward women on patrol has been based primarily on stereotypes regarding the ability of women to do what is considered a man's job (Bell, 1982). A number of studies were conducted in several cities throughout the United States to determine whether women can perform patrol work as effectively as men. The results of these studies demonstrated overwhelmingly that women are capable of successful performance as patrol officers (Bartell & Associates, 1978; Bartlett & Rosenblum, 1977; Bloch & Anderson, 1974; Sherman, 1975). The problem with these studies is the question that is raised: Can women perform patrol work as successfully as men? This question presupposes that there is a male way of policing. There is not. Although some males may be more aggressive than some females, both males and females bring their own individuality to the problems of policing. Some males are not suited for police work and some females are not suited for police work. Individual knowledge, skills, and abilities are the most important determinants of whether a person can be an effective patrol officer, not gender.

WOMEN IN POLICING: THE TWENTY-FIRST CENTURY

In 2001 the Bureau of Labor Statistics indicated that women account for almost 47 percent of the workforce in the United States. Approximately 30 percent of the legal profession is now comprised of women. Yet in policing, women hold approximately 14 percent of our nation's law enforcement positions, 8.8 percent of supervisory positions and just 7.4 percent of the top command positions (International Association of Chiefs of Police [IACP], 1998). Policing continues to be an overwhelmingly masculine enterprise. Some argue that the gains for women in policing have been very slow and that women will not reach a gender balance in policing for another seventy years (Martin, 1990, p. 3). There are those who believe that widespread bias in police hiring, selection practices, and recruitment policies keep women out of law enforcement. The National Center for Women & Policing argues that entry exams with an overemphasis on upper body strength still wash out many qualified women and that women are discouraged from entering policing because of the aggressive authoritarian outdated paramilitary model of law enforcement. In addition, it is suggested that once on the job, women face discrimination, harassment, intimidation, and are maliciously thwarted as they attempt move up in rank. There is no question that the military model of policing is still widespread in the United States. Furthermore, some large police agencies employ the psychoauthoritarian stress-training model of recruit training that is closely associated with the training in some military boot camps. This "in-your-face" training model frequently involves screaming, extraordinary profanity, and demeaning actions by police trainers toward police recruits and it turns off a certain number of males and females who may be interested in police careers. This psychoauthoritarian training model has been criticized by some of the most prominent members of the police community.[7] Hopefully, during the twenty-first century, police administrators will finally realize that this Neanderthal model of police training keeps talented men and women from the police profession, is incompatible with the concept of community policing, and is detrimental to effective policing in a free society. There is an urgent need for improved police training, with a focus on human communication to develop officers who are capable of helping citizens identify and solve problems in their communities (Birzer & Tannehill, 2001). Hopefully, in the near future, job-related police training programs will be instituted so that more women will be encouraged to bring their exceptional skills to our nation's policing problems.

Recently, the International Association of Chiefs of Police (IACP) established an Ad Hoc Committee on Women in Policing to examine the role of women in policing. The committee, utilizing the resources of the Gallup Organization, conducted a survey of some of its 14,000 members. The survey confirmed critical information regarding the status of women in policing. While recognizing that the number of women in policing is growing, it also revealed:

- There are few women in policing compared to their male counterparts.
- Women still face bias from male officers.
- Many police departments lack strategies for recruiting women.
- Women officers may face gender discrimination and a "glass ceiling" that inhibits promotion.
- Sexual harassment still occurs in many police departments.
- Although the need is great, there are very few mentoring programs for women officers.

Early in the twentieth century, the IACP supported women only in support roles in policing, not in patrol functions. Therefore, it is an extraordinary change for this major international police organization to now state that "it is essential to strengthen the position of women in policing—their professional development, their progress to positions of leadership, and their contribution to the public service and safety" (IACP, 1998).

Some of the specific recommendations of the IACP study are as follows:

1. Police agencies should be educated regarding the value of gender diversity in policing.
2. Police agencies should advertise and recruit qualified women.
3. Police agencies should train members regarding gender discrimination and sexual harassment and adopt a zero-tolerance approach to discrimination and sexual harassment.
4. Police agencies should establish policies to improve the role of women in policing.
5. Police agencies should mentor female officers and strengthen their potential for longevity.
6. Police agencies should improve promotional strategies for women and move women into police leadership positions.

The IACP has concluded that while a number of agencies have welcomed women officers, "many simply have not . . . [and] women have often had to bring litigation against departments to overcome resistance" (IACP, 1998). The IACP survey disclosed that 17 percent of the agencies surveyed had no female officers and 55 percent of the agencies surveyed had between one and four female officers. Ninety-one percent of the police departments surveyed had no female officers in policymaking positions. In addition, 28 percent of the departments surveyed express concern that "women lack sufficient physical strength, capacity for confrontation, size, strength and force" (p. 13). This finding is troubling in light of the overwhelming evidence that policing is more cerebral than physical and it suggests that the myth that one must be big, strong, and physical to be a police officer still has support in the police organizational culture.[8] Perhaps that is why women continue to be disproportionately assigned to support positions rather than patrol (Martin, 1990). Another factor may be paternalism, which involves male officers protecting or excusing women from undesirable tasks. This practice of assigning women to nonline functions suggests that women can't be "real cops," and it stigmatizes female officers in general and creates resentment among male officers (Padavic & Reskin, 1990).

It has taken almost 150 years for women to represent 14 percent of our nation's police forces. The police road they have traveled in the latter half of the twentieth century has been difficult for many. Nevertheless, despite the pessimistic views of some regarding the future of women in policing, there is much to be optimistic about in the twenty-first century. A number of legal and cultural barriers to women in policing have been jettisoned. Women are showing increasing interest in police careers. Research regarding the role of women in policing is very positive. Research has demonstrated that women rely on a policing style that uses less physical force, and women excel at defusing and deescalating potentially violent confrontations with citizens and are less likely to become involved in problems of excessive force. In addition, female officers often possess better communication skills than their male counterparts and are better able to facilitate the cooperation and trust required to implement community policing (Lonsway, 2000). Furthermore, in the later half of the twentieth century, for the first time women became chiefs of police in several major police departments, including Houston, Atlanta, and Portland. At least one study found that female police executives were more flexible, emotionally independent, self-assertive, self-confident, and creative than their male counterparts (Price, 1974). A number of studies demonstrate that female officers utilize a less authoritarian style of policing and rely less on physical force (Worden, 1995). The cult of machismo in policing is changing, albeit at a glacial pace. Unlike their predecessors, it is now not uncommon for male officers to recognize reluctantly that women make "good cops." Major police departments and police organizations have expressed the desire to recruit, employ, and promote more women in policing.[9] The U.S. Supreme Court has established guidelines regarding sexual harassment that significantly increase the chance of employer liability if employers do not rid their workplace of sexual harassment (*Burlington Industries v. Ellerth*, 1998; *Faragher v. City of Boca Raton*, 1998). The Court has said that even a sitting president of the United States is not immune from charges of sexual harassment (*Clinton v. Jones*, 1997). Almost all police departments have established sexual harassment policies (IACP, 1998). In some areas of the country, the wages, fringe benefits, and working conditions have improved significantly, thereby making policing a very attractive profession for both men and women. With these changes, it is almost certain that during the twenty-first century the number of women in policing will grow exponentially. The increased representation of women is almost certain to transform the authoritarian military climate of police agencies and hopefully make American policing kinder, gentler, and more sensitive to individual rights and the envy of the world.

NOTES

1. The Nassau County Police Department in New York is the seventh largest police department in the United States, with a force of more than 3,000 sworn officers. This department did not hire women in any supporting role until the mid-1960s.
2. See New York Civil Service Law, § 58, which specifically provided that only a "male" could become a patrol officer in New York. The male restriction was not removed by the New York state legislature until 1972, when Title VII of the Civil Rights Act of 1964 was amended so that it applied to state and municipal governments.
3. The Civil Rights Act of 1991 further strengthened Title VII after the decision of the U.S. Supreme Court in *Wards Cove Packing Co. v. Antonio* (1989).
4. The author has interviewed several female officers in different police departments who believe that they were treated quite fairly. However, some women in the same police academy class have had very different experiences and perceptions regarding their acceptance by the male police culture.
5. The author was involved as a police administrator in two major police agencies in the United States. During a career of more than 30 years there were several occasions in which statements like this were reported to have occurred during formal training sessions. In some cases, police instructors readily admitted making the statements. In addition, anecdotal information of similar statements being made in other police academies across the country was not uncommon.
6. By parity of reasoning, one police observer suggested (tongue in cheek) that trainers should shoot police recruits to see if they can take a shot.
7. Herman Goldstein, former chief of police Joseph McNamara, and the late Daniel P. Guido, the former commissioner of police of the Nassau County New York Police Department, and the Suffolk County New York Police, the Westchester County New York Police Department, the Yonkers New York Police Department, and the Stamford Connecticut Police Department. Numerous other police officials have also condemned this extreme paramilitary model of police training.
8. Physical strength has not been shown to predict general police effectiveness (Sherman, 1975), or the ability to handle dangerous situations successfully (Bell, 1982).
9. Police departments in Albuquerque and Tucson have dramatically increased their female recruits (Polisar & Milgram, 1998) and 25 percent of the Madison, Wisconsin, Police Department now is composed of female officers. In addition, the International Association of Chiefs of Police is making a major effort to encourage its members to recruit, employ, and promote women in policing.

REFERENCES

BALKIN, J. (1988). Why policemen don't like policewomen. *Journal of Police Science and Administration, 16*(1), 29–38.

BARTELL & ASSOCIATES. (1978). *The study of police women competency in the performance of sector police work in the city of Philadelphia.* Author.

BARTLETT, H. W., & ROSENBLUM, A. (1977). *Policewomen effectiveness in Denver.* Denver, CO: Civil Service Commission.

BARTOLLAS, C., & HAHN, L. D. (1999). *Policing in America.* Needham Heights, MA: Allyn & Bacon.

BELL, D. J. (1982). Policewomen: Myths and reality. *Journal of Police Science and Administration, 16*(1), 29–38.

BERG, B. L., & BUDNICK, K. J. (1986). Defeminization of women in law enforcement: A new twist in the traditional police personality. *Journal of Police Science and Administration, 314.*

BIRZER, M. L., & TANNEHILL, R. (2001, June). A more effective training approach for contemporary policing. *Police Quarterly, 4*(2), 233–252.

BLOCH, P. B., & ANDERSON, D. (1974). *Policewomen on patrol: Final report.* Washington, DC: Urban Institute, pp. 1–67.

BOUZA, A. V. (1992). *The police mystique: An insider's look at cops, crime and the criminal justice system.* New York: Plenum Press.

FREEMAN, J. (1991). How "sex" got into Title VII: Persistent opportunism as a maker of public policy. *J.L. & Equality, 9,* 163.

FRIEDAN, B. (1963). *The feminine mystique.* New York: Norton.

FYFE, J. J., GREENE, J. R., WALSH, W. F., WILSON, O. W., & MCLAREN, R. C. (1997). *Police administration* (5th ed.). New York: McGraw-Hill.

HALE, D. C. (1992). Women in policing. In G. W. Cordner & D. C. Hale (Eds.), What works in policing? Operations and administration examined. Cincinnati, OH: Anderson/Academy of Criminal Justice Sciences.

INTERNATIONAL ASSOCIATION OF CHIEFS OF POLICE. (1998). *The future of women in policing: Mandates for action.*

LONSWAY, K. A. (2000, Summer). *Hiring and retaining more women: The advantages to law enforcement agencies.* Washington, DC: National Center for Women & Policing.

LORD, L. K. (1995). Policewomen. In *The Encyclopedia of Police Science* (2nd ed.). New York: William Bailey.

MARTIN, S. E. (1990). *On the move: The status of women in policing.* Washington, DC: Police Foundation.

MARTIN, S. E. (1994, August). Outsider within the station house: The impact of race and gender on black women police. *Social Problems, 41.*

MILTON, C. (1972). *Women in police.* Washington, DC: Police Foundation.

MILTON, C. (1974). *Women in policing: A manual.* Washington, DC: Police Foundation.

PADAVIC, I., & RESKIN, B. (1990). Men's behavior and women's interest in blue-collar jobs. *Social Problems, 37,* 613–628.

POLISAR, J., & MILGRAM, D. (1998, October). Recruiting, integrating and retaining women police officers: Strategies that work. *Police Chief.*

PRICE, B. R. (1974). *A study of leadership strength of female police executives: Police perspectives, problems, prospects.* New York: Praeger, pp. 96–107.

RICHARDSON, J. F. (1974). *Urban police in the United States.* Port Washington, NY: Kennikat Publishing.

SCHULTZ, D. M. (1995). *From social worker to crime fighter: Women in United States municipal policing.* Westport, CT: Praeger.

SHERMAN, L. J. (1975). An evaluation of policewomen on patrol in a suburban police department. *Journal of Police Science and Administration, 3*(4), 434–438.

WORDEN, R. E. (1995). The causes of police brutality: Theory and evidence on police use of force. In *And justice for all: Understanding and controlling police abuse of force.* Washington, DC: Police Executive Research Forum.

CASES

Bradwell v. Illinois, 88 U.S. 130 (1873).
Burlington Industries v. Ellerth, 524 U.S. 742 (1998).
Clinton v. Jones, 520 U.S. 681 (1997).
Dothard v. Rawlinson, 433 U.S. 321 (1977).
Faragher v. City of Boca Raton, 524 U.S. 775 (1998).
Goesaert v. Cleary, 335 U.S. 464 (1948).
Griggs v. Duke Power Co., 401 U.S. 424 (1971).
Hoyt v. Florida, 368 U.S. 57 (1961).
Minor v. Happersett, 88 U.S. 162 (1875).
Radice v. New York, 264 U.S. 292 (1924).
Reed v. Reed, 404 U.S. 71 (1971).
U.S. v. St. Clair, 291 F. Supp. 122 (1968).
Wards Cove Packing Co. v. Antonio, 490 U.S. 642 (1989).

40

Who's Afraid of Johnny Rotten?

Assessing Female Correctional Staff's Perceived Fear and Risk of Victimization in a Juvenile Male Institution

Jill A. Gordon and Laura J. Moriarty

While there is a great deal of research on correctional staff attitudes for a variety of issues that range from job satisfaction to support for punitive ideology, there has been relatively little focus on staff's perceived fear and risk of victimization within the institution. Likewise, when research is conducted, it typically examines gender differences and rarely looks more closely at females as a group to isolate any within-group variation that might be lost by focusing on comparing gender. In this chapter, we argue that a better understanding is needed of female correctional officers and their perceived levels of fear and risk of victimization. A survey measuring perceived fear and risk of victimization within the institution was administered to a sample of female juvenile correctional officers employed at an all-male juvenile facility. The chapter reports the findings of this study: Primarily we found very low levels of perceived fear and risk of victimization among the women sampled. While the fear and risk levels were low, they were still higher than the male levels in the sample. Relying on the correctional literature, we propose some explanations for these findings.

INTRODUCTION

We know that violence and victimization exist not only in society but also within the correctional system. Official reports of both underestimate the actual figures occurring in society and prisons. Additionally, women are more fearful of crime (and so it is thought, violence) and victimization than men. What is unknown is whether women report higher levels of workplace violence and victimization if they work in a correctional setting. Does the highly volatile work environment and daily contact with inmates curb or intensify the level of perceived fear of violence and victimization among female employees within a male institution? Such a provocative question has received little to no attention within the available literature. The literature does look at similar issues, but it does so from the inmate's perspective (see Hemmens & Marquart, 1999).

This chapter examines female correctional officers' levels of perceived fear and risk of violence and victimization within the prison environment. First, an understanding of the foundation and background on these issues must be addressed. Therefore, we will begin the chapter with a discussion on the historical involvement of women within a correctional setting, then proceed to discuss issues related to correctional officers and institutional corrections in general, and conclude this section with a general discussion of the fear of crime literature.

This chapter reports the results of a study conducted at two juvenile detention centers where female correctional officers work. We are interested in gauging their overall perceived fear and risk of victimization in the institution by inmates and other staff members to determine if female juvenile correctional officers are more or less fearful than their counterparts in terms of both females in general and their male counterparts at the institution where they are employed. The chapter reports the results of this inquiry.

REVIEW OF THE LITERATURE

Female Correctional Officers: A Historical Examination

Females have worked in corrections throughout history; however, their role was predominately clerical in nature. It was not until the early 1970s that women began to penetrate into the role of correctional officer, which was exclusively reserved for men prior to this time (Cheeseman, Mullings, & Marquart, 2001). The expansion of employment opportunities for women in corrections was possible due to the extension of Title VII of the Civil Rights Act (Flynn 1982; Jurik, 1985a; Morton 1981). The infiltration of females as correctional officers was met with many doubts and reservations, uncertainty, and legal challenges.

These concerns focus (as many are still present today) on several areas: Male correctional personnel are concerned with the reliability of a female officer to appropriately respond in a violent situation (Holeman & Krepps-Hess, 1983; Jurik 1985a); even though it has been found that female correctional officers are more likely to dissipate potentially violent situations (Kissel & Katasampes, 1980; Zimmer, 1986). Another concern is the mere presence of female officers in an institution reduces the perception that prisons are inherently dangerous (Crouch, 1985). Females are also questioned on their psychological adjustment and ability to work effectively in the institutional setting (Jurik, 1985a). Finally, it was presumed that women would become emotionally attached and overly involved in the personal lives of inmates (Etheridge, Hale, & Hambrick 1984; Jurik 1985a; Pollock-Byrne 1990). The result of these apprehensions has been both overt and covert opposition to the female correctional officer (Horne 1985; Jurik 1985a; Owen 1985; Zimmer, 1986).

The resistance to female correctional officers occurred more so with other male staff rather than with the inmates (Holeman & Krepps-Hess, 1983; Holland, Levi, Beckett, & Holt, 1979; Peterson 1982). The degree of support and confidence in the job performance of female officers has varied greatly (Hemmens, Sothr, Scholeler & Miller, 2002; Jurik, 1988; Jurik & Halemba, 1984; Lawrence & Mahan, 1998; Zimmer 1986). Still today a review of the current literature finds some opposition among male officers who are more experienced (Lawrence & Mahan, 1998) and among those with a military background (Hemmens et al., 2002).

The hiring of female correctional officers has resulted in several legal challenges focusing on an inmate's right to privacy. The courts have determined that the female's right to employment in an all-male facility supersedes the inmate's right to privacy (see *Bagley v. Watson*, 1983; and *Grummet v. Rushen*, 1984). Although a common grievance still is the reduction of privacy (Zimmer, 1986), studies examining inmates directly reveal that many inmates do not see the presence of female personnel as an invasion of privacy (Holeman & Krepps-Hess, 1983). Furthermore, inmates report female officers are more understanding and supportive than male officers (Peterson, 1982; Zimmer, 1986) and female officers positively influence the institutional environment (Peterson, 1982).

From a historical perspective, it can be said that the acceptance of women in "nontraditional" roles regardless of the organization or agency has improved. However, female correctional officers are still relatively small in number and like with many other employment areas where females are the minority, tokenism and harassment still occur in such settings.

Correctional Officer Research

There is a vast amount of research focusing on correctional officers' attitudes. Many studies have examined demographic variables in relation to correctional officers' attitudes regarding job satisfaction, work stress, inmates, and support for various correctional philosophies (Britton, 1997; Cullen, Link, Wolfe, & Frank, 1985; Cullen, Lutze, Link, & Wolfe, 1989; Dowden & Tellier, 2004; Hepburn & Knepper, 1993; Jackson & Ammen, 1996; Jacobs & Kraft, 1978; Johnson & Price, 1981; Jurik & Halemba, 1984; Kasselbaum, Ward, & Wilner, 1964; Lindquist & Whitehead, 1986; Poole & Regoli, 1980; Robinson, Porporino, & Simourd, 1993, 1997; Toch & Klofas, 1982; Van Voorhis, Cullen, Link, & Wolfe, 1991; Whitehead & Lindquist, 1989). The degree to which demographic factors affect the attitudes varies within the literature, from a direct effect to no effect. Britton (1997) emphasized that the results of gender and racial differences vary by the procedures used to evaluate the issues. For example, gender and racial differences are revealed when a qualitative approach is used (Jurik, 1985b, 1988; Owen, 1988; Zimmer, 1986), revealing that women and racial minorities are still challenged in their ability to operate as correctional officers and are discriminated against. However, few relationships between attitudes and race and gender are uncovered in quantitative analyses of the issue (Blau, Light, & Chamlin, 1986; Cullen et al., 1985; Gordon, 1999; Jackson & Ammen, 1996; Jurik & Halemba, 1984; Jurik & Winn, 1987; Van Voorhis et al., 1991).

What is evidenced in the quantitative studies are correlations between job stress and job satisfaction which is influenced by a variety of factors such as security level of the facility, years of experience, and assignment (Britton, 1997; Cullen et al., 1985; Van Voorhis et al., 1991). Taken in whole, however, we do not have definitive evidence of the predictors of a variety of correctional work-related issues. And as espoused by Britton (1997), "If individual characteristics are not the primary influences shaping officer perceptions of the work environment (an issue by no means resolved), one must look to elements of that environment for explanation" (p. 87). We suggest one individual factor that has been neglected is officer perception of violence and victimization within their environment.

Over the past decade the demographic characteristics of the correctional staff have changed. There are currently more women and racial minorities entering the institutional setting. In addition, the overall level of education appears to be increasing. Such changes support the efforts to continue considering institutional staff attitudes. Interestingly, with all the changes in both the officer and inmate characteristics, studies have not focused on perceived violence or victimization from a staff member's perspective. It seems essential to examine the concept as a possible factor to assist in the explanation of job satisfaction and officer burnout, especially given that the two factors are related to the number of physical ailments and mental anguish officers experience (Cheek & Miller, 1983).

Perceived dangerousness is a related concept and has been "operationalized by inverse scoring the correctional officers' satisfaction level with their personal safety" (Dowden & Tellier, 2004, p. 34). This measure was considered within a single study and a meta-analysis on work stress (Dowden & Tellier, 2004; Tellier & Robinson, 1995). The meta-analysis reveals a relationship between perceived dangerousness, as defined above, and job stress especially among the Canadian workforce and not necessarily in the United States. An explanation offered on the discrepancy between cultural differences in the relationship was due to the increased exposure to violence and victimization experienced in U.S. institutions. We believe the conceptual nature of perceived dangerousness as defined by Dowden and Tellier (2004) is limited in scope and that a more robust measure of the general concept that includes perceived levels of fear and risk of violence and victimization might yield more informative results on the concept.

Institutional Violence

Violence and victimization exist in many forms within the institutional setting, ranging from inmate-on-inmate violence to large-scale violence among groups. There was a 20 percent increase in inmate-on-inmate and a 32 percent increase in inmate-on-staff violence at the national level within a five-year period between 1990 and 1995 (Stephans, 1997). Additional research reports correctional officers were subjected to 58,000 nonfatal violent incidents between 1992 and 1996 (Warchol, 1998). Within juvenile institutions 6,900 staff members were injured and 24,200 institutionalized juveniles were injured within a 12-month time frame (Parent, et al., 1993). It is important to note that these official statistics most likely underreport the inmate-on-inmate incidents in comparison to self-report data (Bowker, 1980). Four hundred and sixty incidents of collective violence were reported from 1900 to 1983 (Montgomery & MacDougall, 1984).

A variety of factors are related to institutional violence and victimization: the inclusion of a younger or juvenile population (Bowker, 1980; Ellis, Grasmick, & Gilman, 1974;

Light, 1991; Malbi, Holley, Patrick, & Walls, 1979; McShane & Williams, 1996), prison crowding (Gaes & McGuire, 1985), inmate deprivation and disorganization (Useem, 1985; Useem & Kimball, 1989), and organizational transformation (Useem, 1985). Moreover, when daily conflict is continuous, the likelihood of collective victimization occurring also increases (Lombardo, 1994).

In addition to official reports of violence and victimization some studies discuss or examine inmates' perception of violence. Research indicates inmates have a high level of fear of victimization and consistently feel vulnerable (Hemmens & Marquart, 1999; McCorkle, 1993; Toch, 1977). The level of fear fluctuates by sociodemographic characteristics (Hemmens & Marquart, 1999, McCorkle, 1993), prior incarceration history (Wright, 1991), and not surprisingly the levels of fear among the inmate population were higher than found in the general population of society (McCorkle, 1993). The importance of looking at fear within an institutional setting is linked to both inmate physical and mental health (McCorkle, 1993; Zamble & Porporino, 1988). Given the established relationship between high levels of inmate fear and poor health, one pauses to ponder whether the same is true among correctional staff.

Fear of Crime

Decades of research on fear of crime has revealed a consistent finding: Females are more fearful of crime than males. This relationship is even stronger when we add age to the equation; elderly females have some of the highest levels of fear (see Gordon, Moriarty, & Grant, 2003; Hale, 1996; Roundtree & Land, 1996, for a complete list of citations from previous studies). There have been a few studies where this relationship was not substantiated. For example, Akers and his colleagues found that elderly females in their sample were less fearful than was the tradition (Akers, LaGreca, Sellers, & Cochran, 1987). Akers et al. rationalized that this lower level of fear, as compared to what other studies have consistently found, was directly related to the vulnerability of the sample. The authors concluded that this sample was less vulnerable as compared to other more traditional samples of elderly people. The authors purposely oversampled elderly individuals and used drivers' license listings to draw their sample. The authors surmised that the sample was more mobile than the typical elderly sample where subjects are drawn from other sampling frames. The assumption was that those who could drive (assumed by the fact that the person had a valid drivers' license or he or she would not have been on the sampling frame) resulted in a sample who felt less vulnerable because they were more mobile. Other researchers have not found this relationship, but they failed to oversample the elderly.

Explanations for the higher levels of fear among women have been attributed to vulnerability, environmental cues, and victimization (Sutton & Farrall, 2005). Another interesting explanation for these differences has been advanced by Smith and Torstensson (1997) who found that women tend to exaggerate their fear of crime levels while men tend to suppress theirs. Sutton and Farrall (2005, p. 213) infer that "the difference between men and women on fear-of-crime measures occurs because men are less willing than women to report their fears." They conducted research to determine whether social pressures associated with masculine gender roles (e.g., "big boys don't cry") tend to prohibit men from accurately reporting fear of crime. They found that the "data showed that for men, but not women, reported fear levels are inversely related to scores on a so-called 'lie scale,' which measures the tendency to provide socially desirable rather than totally candid responses. This pattern holds irrespective of age and (it) suggests that the genders are affected differently by social pressure to downplay fears about crime" (p. 212).

Other explanations for the differences in fear of crime are ascribed to direct (e.g., being a victim of a crime) and indirect victimization (e.g., sometimes referred to as vicarious victimization where knowledge or information about a criminal act is learned). Both are directly and positively related to fear of crime.

Last, structural factors (i.e., social disorganization) have been found to increase fear of crime. Such factors include high community crime indexes, low social cohesion, high population density, civic disengagement, and political apathy (Sampson, 2001).

METHOD

The purpose of this chapter is to identify if female correctional officers are fearful of juvenile male detainees and if their levels of fear and perceived risk are different than male officers. This is a salient position for a few reasons. First, the general fear of crime literature reflects a difference in fear and perceived risk by gender. Specifically, females feel more vulnerable than males. Second, a similar line of argument found in the institutional correctional literature can be applied. Research has shown that sex and race compositions among officers and inmates have influenced the level of job satisfaction (Blau et al., 1986; Kanter, 1977; Van Voorhis et al., 1991). The general point here is that minority officers' level of comfort is higher within a prison with most of the inmates being minorities and female staff members enjoy their jobs to a higher extent when the number of female officers is higher. Given this general logic, it may be assumed that more female officers would report varying levels of fear and perceived risk of violence and victimization within an all-male juvenile facility than the male officers.

This descriptive study examines perceived fear and risk of victimization among juvenile correctional staff at two male juvenile correctional facilities. The primary focus of this research is to depict the level of fear and risk among female correctional staff at all-male juvenile facilities.

This research stems from a larger study investigating variations among officers by facility type[1] (Gordon et al., 2003). The two facilities are similar in that they both are located in Virginia, in close proximity to the greater metro-Richmond area, are medium security facilities, house about the same number and type of youth, and have similar designs and structure (i.e., several independent buildings surrounded by secure fencing and a central secure entry point). They function differently in that one provides a residential substance abuse treatment program to all youth and the other operates more as a traditional institution emphasizing public safety while meeting the needs of the offenders.

Design and Sample

A cross-sectional design was used to investigate the levels of fear and risk. A self-report survey was administered to those who had daily contact with the detainees; this included juvenile correctional officers, psychologists, case managers, and rehabilitation counselors (both private and state). The survey was distributed at the beginning of the shift during the summer of 2000 and was collected by a fellow correctional employee within an hour. Participation was voluntary. This method yielded an overall response rate of 98 percent for Barrett and 67 percent for Hanover. Although the current study will compare male and female response to the levels of fear and risk, the primary emphasis is on female staff members. Therefore, the response rate for female staff at Barrett was 86 percent and 56 percent at Hanover. So, while the response rate for the study is acceptable and the percentages reflect what is often found in other all-male juvenile detention centers, the actual number of female officers is small ($n = 33$ females).

Table 1 reveals the majority of women were white (82 percent), approximately 35 years of age with most having been enrolled in some college (54 percent). Fifty-eight percent of the respondents worked at Barrett Juvenile Correctional center with most women (79 percent) being correctional officers who report working approximately 5.7 years in corrections.[2]

Instrument and Measures

The self-report survey consisted of 76 questions that included measures of demographic and work history characteristics; attitudinal statements regarding rehabilitation, autonomy, and job satisfaction; and statements addressing perceived fear and risk of victimization.

The theoretical rationale for the measures of perceived fear and risk can be found in detail elsewhere (see Gordon et al., 2003); however, a brief discussion is still warranted here. The measures created were based on Bowker's (1980) theoretical analysis of violence and victimization experienced by correctional staff. Bowker (1980) offered five probable victimizing circumstances that correctional officers may experience; he calls these experiences "analytical victimization." The situations (or analytical victimizations) were categorized as the (1) *daily grind*, (2) *riots*, (3) *patterned spontaneous attacks*, (4) *unexpected attacks*, and (5) *victimization by other correctional officers*. Each encompasses an individual level and collective level of victimization. Bowker's work fully describes each area but he never measured or tested his propositions. Figure 1 presents the items used to measure fear and risk of victimization on both the individual and collective level.

The goal of the prior study was to examine the measures' theoretical relevance and to identify if there were variations in individual and collective victimization based on the type of juvenile institution where an officer is employed. Because this current analysis is limited to female respondents each item will be examined independently rather than in the manner that was conducted in the prior study (we developed aggregate measures for each area of interest). There are 10 items[3] measuring perceived fear of victimization ("How afraid are you of . . .") and perceived risk of victimization ("How likely do you think it is that . . ."), where the attributes ranged from 1 to 5, with 1 indicating the least amount of fear or risk and 5 indicating the highest amount of fear or risk.

This study therefore provides a descriptive examination of female correctional officers' levels of perceived fear and perceived risk of victimization. In addition, a comparison between male and female responses is considered.

TABLE 1   Demographic and Work History Characteristics

Variable	Number	Percent
Age		
20–29	5	15%
30–39	10	30
40–49	5	15
50 or older	1	3
Missing	12	36
Mean	34.9	
Race		
White	27	82%
Non-White	5	15
Missing	1	3
Education		
High School Diploma/GED	8	24%
Some College	18	54
Bachelor or Graduate Degree	7	21
Years of Employment		
in Corrections		
Less than 3	20	61%
4–6	6	18
7–9	2	6
10 or more	5	15
Mean	5.7	
Shift		
Days Only	13	40%
Evenings Only	9	27
Nights Only	8	24
Rotating Days and Nights	3	9
Current Position		
Correctional officer	26	79%
Treatment staff	7	21
Facility		
Hanover	14	42%
Barrett	19	58

Fear of Victimization—Individual Level

(How afraid are you of . . .)

Patterned Spontaneous

1. Being hurt when transferring youth between cells?
2. Being hurt when breaking up a fight?
3. Being hurt when conducting a cell search?

Staff-to-Staff

1. Being attacked by a fellow officer?

Unexpected Attacks

1. Being attacked by an inmate?

Daily Grind

1. Personal threats from inmates toward you?
2. Personal threats from inmates toward your family?

Risk of Victimization—Individual Level

(How likely is it that . . .)

Patterned Spontaneous

1. You will be hurt when transferring youth between cells?
2. You will be hurt when breaking up a fight?
3. You will be hurt when conducting a cell search?

Staff-to-Staff

1. You will be attacked by a fellow officer?

Unexpected Attacks

1. You will be attacked by an inmate?

Daily Grind

1. You will have personal threats from inmates toward you?
2. You will have personal threats from inmates toward your family?

Fear of Victimization—Collective Level

(How afraid are you of . . .)

Riot

1. Being taken hostage?
2. A riot occurring in this institution?
3. Of not staying on the good side of certain inmates because you want them to defend you during a violent situation?

Patterned Spontaneous

1. Being hurt when transferring youth between cells?
2. Being hurt when breaking up a fight?
2. Being hurt when conducting a cell search?

Staff-to-Staff

1. Being attacked by a fellow officer?

Unexpected Attacks

1. Being attacked by an inmate?

Risk of Victimization—Collective Level

(How likely is it that . . .)

Riot

1. You will be taken hostage?
2. A riot will occur in this institution?
3. You will stay on the good side of certain inmates because you want them to defend you during a violent situation?

Patterned Spontaneous

1. You will be hurt when transferring youth between cells?
2. You will be hurt when breaking up a fight?
3. You will be hurt when conducting a cell search?

Staff-to-Staff

1. You will be attacked by a fellow officer?

Unexpected Attacks

1. You will be attacked by an inmate?

FIGURE 1   Conceptualization and Operationalization of Perceived Fear and Risk of Victimization Combining Bowker's Typology with Individual and Collective Levels of Victimization (Gordon, Moriarty, and Grant, 2003, p. 75)

ANALYSIS

Table 2 presents the frequency responses for the items measuring fear. In general, the women report relatively low levels of being afraid for most items. To illustrate, approximately half of all women (52 percent) had a low response to *How afraid are you of personal threats towards your family*; 52 percent had a low response to *How afraid are you of staying on the good side of certain inmates so they will defend you in violent situations*; and 64 percent low response to *How afraid are you of being attacked by a fellow officer.* Additionally, combining response categories one and two reveals females have lower levels of fear with regard to being taken hostage (54 percent), being hurt when transferring between cells (51 percent) or conducting a cell search (58 percent), and personal threats towards them (54 percent). Whereas, the remaining items in Table 2 show a rather even or split distribution of fear. Specifically 39 percent report a low, 21 percent a medium, and 33 percent a high level of fear when asked about being hurt when breaking up a fight; 42 percent report a low, 15 percent a medium, and 36 percent a high level of fear concerning being attacked by an inmate.

Table 3 investigates the perceived risk of an event happening. In general the responses are relatively consistent with their reported fear (reported above), with most responses being in categories 1 and 2—low likelihood that an incident will occur. A couple of slight changes are noteworthy. While the level of fear and risk for being taken hostage is relatively low (response categories 1 and 2), their fear of this happening is slightly higher with 54 percent scoring into the low category where examination of perceived risk reveal 64 percent of the respondents falling into the low category. That is, 36 percent of the women perceive the risk of being taken hostage as moderate to high and only 46 percent fear this will happen.

TABLE 2   Frequency of Response for Single Item Measures of Fear

	Low		Medium		High
Variable	1	2	3	4	5
How afraid are you of . . .					
being taken hostage	15 (45%)	3 (9%)	7 (21%)	2 (6%)	4 (12%)
a riot occurring	10 (30%)	5 (15%)	9 (27%)	4 (12%)	5 (15%)
being hurt when transferring between cells	12 (36%)	5 (15%)	6 (18%)	4 (12%)	1 (3%)
being hurt when breaking up a fight	9 (27%)	4 (12%)	7 (21%)	5 (15%)	6 (18%)
being hurt while conducting a cell search	16 (49%)	3 (9%)	4 (12%)	3 (9%)	2 (6%)
being attacked by a fellow officer	21 (64%)	5 (15%)	2 (6%)	0 (0%)	2 (6%)
being attacked by an inmate	6 (18%)	8 (24%)	5 (15%)	9 (27%)	3 (9%)
personal threats from inmates toward you	11 (33%)	7 (21%)	6 (18%)	4 (12%)	3 (9%)
personal threats from inmates toward your family	17 (52%)	2 (6%)	5 (15%)	2 (6%)	2 (6%)
"staying on the good side" of certain inmates so they will defend you in violent situations	17 (52%)	2 (6%)	3 (9%)	2 (6%)	2 (6%)

TABLE 3   Frequency of Response for Single Item Measures of Perceived Risk

	Low		Medium		High
Variable	1	2	3	4	5
How likely do you think it is that you will . . .					
be taken hostage	17 (52%)	4 (12%)	5 (15%)	4 (12%)	1 (3%)
witness a riot	7 (21%)	5 (15%)	10 (30%)	6 (18%)	3 (9%)
be hurt when transferring between cells	11 (33%)	6 (18%)	5 (15%)	4 (12%)	2 (6%)
be hurt when breaking up a fight	7 (21%)	6 (18%)	6 (18%)	5 (15%)	7 (21%)
be hurt while conducting a cell search	14 (42%)	4 (12%)	7 (21%)	2 (6%)	2 (6%)
be attacked by a fellow officer	22 (68%)	1 (3%)	1 (3%)	1 (3%)	1 (3%)
be attacked by an inmate	6 (18%)	9 (27%)	6 (18%)	9 (27%)	6 (18%)
receive personal threats from inmates toward you	8 (24%)	5 (15%)	6 (18%)	5 (15%)	7 (21%)
receive personal threats from inmates toward your family	15 (46%)	3 (9%)	4 (12%)	4 (12%)	3 (9%)
"stay on the good side" of certain inmates so they will defend you in violent situations	16 (49%)	1 (3%)	4 (12%)	2 (6%)	2 (6%)

A comparison of gender difference by single item measures is presented in Tables 4 and 5. The tables reveal consist gender differences across fear and risk with females' average level of fear and perceived risk being higher than males for the majority of items. There are also several items that are statistically significant: riot, attack by inmate, and personal threats from inmates. Specifically, females are more fearful and perceive their risk as higher than men when focusing on the variable "a riot occurring." Women also have a higher fear and perceived risk of being attacked by an inmate than men. One other item is statistically significant only with regard to perceived risk, suggesting females perceive their risk of personal threats from inmates toward them as higher than male correctional staff.

DISCUSSION

In general this study reveals relatively low levels of fear and perceived risk of violence and victimization occurring at both the individual and collective levels. That said, what is also evident is slightly higher mean levels of fear and perceived risk of victimization and violence between genders among the majority of the single items measures examined, with

TABLE 4   An Examination of Mean Difference of Fear by Gender

Variable	Female	Male	t-value
How afraid are you of . . .			
being taken hostage			
Mean	2.12	1.76	1.24
Sd	1.51	1.40	
a riot occurring			
Mean	2.67	2.04	2.33*
Sd	1.42	1.27	
being hurt when transferring between cells			
Mean	1.85	1.93	-0.352
Sd	1.39	1.13	
being hurt when breaking up a fight			
Mean	2.67	2.53	0.467
Sd	1.61	1.40	
being hurt while conducting a cell search			
Mean	1.75	1.53	0.934
Sd	1.43	1.01	
being attacked by a fellow officer			
Mean	1.44	1.25	0.821
Sd	1.26	1.05	
being attacked by an inmate			
Mean	2.67	2.16	1.79**
Sd	1.45	1.36	
personal threats from inmates toward you			
Mean	2.24	1.90	1.30
Sd	1.43	1.22	
personal threats from inmates toward your family			
Mean	1.69	1.99	-1.03
Sd	1.40	1.48	
"staying on the good side" of certain inmates so they will defend you in violent situations			
Mean	1.45	1.21	1.16
Sd	1.41	0.88	

*Significant at the .05 level.
**Level of significance is .076.

TABLE 5   An Examination of Mean Difference of Perceived Risk by Gender

Variable	Female	Male	t-value
How likely do you think it is that you will . . .			
be taken hostage			
Mean	1.91	1.66	0.961
Sd	1.27	1.24	
witness a riot			
Mean	2.69	2.13	2.00*
Sd	1.35	1.34	
be hurt when transferring between cells			
Mean	2.00	1.88	0.465
Sd	1.45	1.19	
be hurt when breaking up a fight			
Mean	2.88	2.56	1.03
Sd	1.56	1.44	
be hurt while conducting a cell search			
Mean	1.91	2.10	−0.631
Sd	1.37	1.52	
be attacked by a fellow officer			
Mean	1.13	1.13	−0.038
Sd	1.07	0.81	
be attacked by an inmate			
Mean	2.71	2.07	2.26*
Sd	1.48	1.35	
receive personal threats from inmates toward you			
Mean	2.84	2.32	1.67**
Sd	1.58	1.50	
receive personal threats from inmates toward your family			
Mean	2.00	2.08	−0.254
Sd	1.54	1.47	
"stay on the good side" of certain inmates so they will defend you in violent situations			
Mean	1.50	1.38	0.449
Sd	1.45	1.17	

*Significant at the .05 level.
**Level of significance is .097.

some differences being significant. Also, when looking at only the women the items that have more variation are those related to being physically attacked by the youth. Such findings are both surprising and somewhat not surprising. What is unexpected is the relatively low level of fear among the women, but what is not surprising is the difference found between the genders.

Considering the general fear of crime literature, we may find an explanation for these findings. Sutton and Farrall (2005) point to vulnerability, environmental cues, and victimization as antecedents to higher levels of fear and risk. This may be why we see differences between the genders in the current study. There may be differences in the influence of these antecedents on female perceived fear and risk of victimization. However, given the highly volatile nature of the prison environment and the few women employed in direct line staff with the inmates, one would assume that higher levels of fear and risk should be present. Since this is not the case, it may be possible that as the daily interaction within the environment becomes normalized, the general routine reduces the feelings of vulnerability among women.

Also, a female correctional officer or treatment staff role within the institutional setting is different than within society. So where she may have felt a sense of fear if one of the juvenile inmates were walking within her neighborhood one evening, she is the authority figure and perhaps the routine is more predictive than on the outside. Another possible confounding factor is the presence of a female superintendent who was at one of the selected facilities for a decade and was the current superintendent at the other facility. It is possible that the female staff members feel a sense of security given that a female is leading the institution. Similar lines of arguments have been made regarding the number of female personnel in nontraditional job roles, where it has been shown that such increases in the numbers of females in these types of jobs influences job satisfaction. It is therefore plausible that as the number of female-headed institutions increases, the perception among female employees that their voices are heard increases, and thus impacts their perception, in a positive way, of their own fear and risk of victimization.

The exploratory nature of the measures within the study should be addressed. The issue at hand is whether or not expansion of the conceptualization of fear and perceived risk to include notions of feelings of safety or perceptions of dangerousness would yield similar or different results. The literature suggests male responses will vary when asked about their level of feeling safe or unsafe in a given situation, rather than do they fear a given situation (Walklate, 1998). Given the fact that we know psychological and physical violence and victimization occur in prisons, it is recommended that the measures be expanded to not only include the dimensions of fear and risk but also to inquire about concerns of safety.

Another dimension to consider is perceived dangerousness. We would argue that such a concept needs to be operationalized differently than in the past where personal safety was tied into job satisfaction (Dowden & Tellier, 2004; Tellier & Robinson, 1995). Rather, such a concept should consider situations or areas of a prison in which officers' awareness of danger is more or less acute. It is expected that such measures would be correlated with fear or perceived risk; however, more variability may be uncovered because the wording of the concept may produce more anxiety in men than simply asking about fear (Lupton & Tulloch, 2000).

Future research must examine a larger group of correctional officers to verify the current findings. Additionally, it would be important to examine female correctional officers within the adult male prison environment. We suspect that the levels of fear and risk for the females would be greater because the current study deals with juveniles. The focus on juveniles may be attributing to the lower levels of fear and risk given the maternal instinct is more innate with a younger group. The gender differences found in this study may or may not be present if the focus is on the adult system due to the philosophical differences underpinning the juvenile justice system and criminal justice system.

So, who's afraid of Johnny Rotten? Apparently not the female officers in either of the two institutions where this research was conducted. It remains to be seen whether these findings can be replicated in other similar (juvenile) institutions and in adult correctional facilities.

NOTES

1. The two facilities examined were Barrett Juvenile Correctional Center and Hanover Correctional Center.
2. For a description of the entire sample see Gordon, Moriarty, and Grant (2003).
3. Fear and risk variables included "being taken hostage," "a riot occurring," "being hurt when transferring between cells," "being hurt when breaking up a fight," "being hurt while conducting a cell search," "being attacked by a fellow officer," "being attacked by an inmate," "personal threats from inmates toward you," and "staying on the good side of certain inmates so they will defend you in violent situations."

REFERENCES

AKERS, R., LaGRECA, A., SELLERS, C., & COCHRAN, J. (1987). Fear of crime and victimization among the elderly in different types of communities. *Criminology, 25,* 487–505.

BLAU, J. R., LIGHT, S. C., & CHAMLIN, M. (1986) Individual and contextual effects on stress and job satisfaction: A study of prison staff. *Work and Occupations, 13,* 131–156.

BOWKER, L. (1980). *Prison victimization.* New York: Elsevier/North-Holland.

BRITTON, D. (1997). Perceptions of the work environment among correctional officers: Do race and sex matter? *Criminology, 35,* 85–106.

CHEEK, F., & MILLER, M. (1983). The experience of stress for correction officers: A double-blind theory of correctional stress. *Journal of Criminal Justice, 11,* 105–120

CHEESEMAN, K. A., MULLINGS, J., & MARQUART, J. (2001). Inmate perceptions of security staff across various custody levels. *Corrections Management Quarterly, 5,* 41–48.

CROUCH, B. (1985). Pandora's box: Women guards in men's prisons. *Journal of Criminal Justice, 13,* 535–548.

CULLEN, F., LINK, B., WOLFE, N. T., & FRANK, J. (1985). The social dimensions of correctional officer stress. *Justice Quarterly, 2,* 505–533.

CULLEN, F., LUTZE, F., LINK, B., & WOLFE, N. T. (1989). The correctional orientation of prison guards: Do officers support rehabilitation? *Federal Probation, 53,* 33–42.

DOWDEN, C., & TELLIER, C. (2004). Predicting work-related stress in correctional officers: A meta-analysis. *Journal of Criminal Justice, 32,* 31–47.

ELLIS, D., GRASMICK, H., & GILMAN, B. (1974). Violence in prisons: A sociological analysis. *American Journal of Sociology, 80,* 16–43.

ETHERIDGE, R., HALE, C., & HAMBRICK, M. (1984). Female employees in all-male correctional facilities. *Federal Probation, 48,* 54–65.

FLYNN, E. (1982). Women as criminal justice professionals: A challenge to tradition. In N. Rafter & E. Stanko (Eds.), *Judge, lawyer, victim, thief* (pp. 305–340). Stroughton, MA: Northeastern University Press.

GAES, G., & McGUIRE, W. (1985). Prison violence: The contribution of crowding versus other determinants of prison assault rates. *Journal of Research in Crime and Delinquency, 22,* 41–65.

GORDON, J. A. (1999). Do staff attitudes vary by position? A look at one juvenile correctional center. *American Journal of Criminal Justice, 24*(1), 81–94.

GORDON, J. A., MORIARTY, L. J., & GRANT, P. (2003). Juvenile correctional officers' perceived fear and risk of victimization: Examining individual and collective levels of victimization in two juvenile correctional centers in Virginia. *Criminal Justice and Behavior, 30*(1), 62–84.

HALE, C. (1996). Fear of crime: A literature review. *International Review of Victimology, 4,* 79–150.

HEMMENS, C., & MARQUART, J. (1999). Straight time: Inmates' perceptions of violence and victimization in the prison environment. *Journal of Offender Rehabilitation, 28,* 1–21.

HEMMENS, C., STOHR, M., SCHOELER, M., & MILLER, B. (2002). One step up, two steps back: The progression of perceptions of women's work in prisons and jails. *Journal of Criminal Justice, 20,* 473–489.

HEPBURN, J., & KNEPPER, P. (1993). Correctional officers as human services workers: The effects on job satisfaction. *Justice Quarterly, 10*(2), 315–337.

HOLEMAN, H., & KREPPS-HESS, B. (1983). *Women correctional officers in the California Department of Corrections.* Sacramento: California Department of Corrections.

HOLLAND, T., LEVI, M., BECKETT, G., & HOLT, N. (1979). Preferences of prison inmates for male versus female institutional personnel. *Journal of Applied Psychology, 64,* 564–568.

HORNE, P. (1985). Female correctional officers. *Federal Probation, 49,* 46–54.

JACKSON, J., & AMMEN, S. (1996). Race and correctional officers' punitive attitudes toward treatment programs for inmates. *Journal of Criminal Justice, 24* (2), 153–166.

JACOBS, J., & KRAFT, L. (1978). Integrating the keepers: A comparison of black and white prison guards in Illinois. *Social Problems, 25,* 304–318.

JOHNSON, R., & PRICE, S. (1981). The complete correctional officer: Human service and the human environment of prison. *Criminal Justice and Behavior, 8,* 343–373.

JURIK, N. C. (1985a). An officer and a lady: Organizational barriers to women working as correctional officers in men's prisons. *Social Problems, 32,* 375–388.

JURIK, N. C. (1985b). Individual and organizational determinants of correctional officers' attitudes toward inmates. *Criminology, 23,* 523–539.

JURIK, N. C. (1988). Striking a balance: Female correctional officers, gender role stereotypes, and male prisons. *Sociological Quarterly, 58,* 291–305.

JURIK, N. C., & HALEMBA, G. (1984). Gender, work conditions and the job satisfactions of women in a non-traditional occupation: Female correctional officers in men's prisons. *Sociological Quarterly, 25,* 551–566.

JURIK, N. C., & WINN, R. (1987). Describing correctional security dropouts and rejects: An individual or organizational profile? *Criminal Justice and Behavior, 14,* 5–25.

KANTER, R. (1977). *Men and women of corporations.* New York: Basic Books.

KASSELBAUM, G., WARD, D., & WILNER, D. (1964). Some correlates of staff ideology in the prison. *Journal of Research on Crime and Delinquency, 1,* 96–109.

KISSEL, P., & KATSAMPES, P. (1980). The impact of women correction officers in the functioning of institutions housing male inmates. *Journal of Offender Counseling, Services, and Rehabilitation, 4,* 213–231.

LAWRENCE, R., & MAHAN, S. (1998). Women corrections officers in men's prisons: Acceptance and perceived job performance. *Women and Criminal Justice, 9,* 63–88.

LIGHT, S. C. (1991). Assaults on prison officers: Interactional themes. *Justice Quarterly, 8,* 243–261.

LINDQUIST, C. A., & WHITEHEAD, J. T. (1986). Burnout, job stress and job satisfaction among southern correctional officers: Perceptions and causal factors. *Journal of Offender Counseling, Service, and Rehabilitation, 10*, 5–26.

LOMBARDO, L. (1994). Stress, change, and collective violence in prison. In M. Braswell, R. Montgomery, & L. Lombardo (Eds.), *Prison violence in America* (2nd ed., pp. 291–306). Cincinnati, OH: Anderson.

LUPTON, D., & TULLOCH, J. (2000). Theorizing fear of crime: Beyond the rational/irrational opposition. *British Journal of Sociology, 50*, 507–523.

MALBI, J., HOLLEY, C., PATRICK, J., & WALLS, J. (1979) Age and prison violence: Increasing age heterogeneity as a violence-reducing strategy in prison. *Criminal Justice and Behavior, 6*, 175–186.

MCCORKLE, R. C. (1993). Living on the edge: Fear in a maximum-security prison. *Journal of Offender Rehabilitation, 19*, 27–41.

MCSHANE, M. D., & WILLIAMS, F. P. III (1996). *Encyclopedia of American prisons*. New York: Garland.

MONTGOMERY, R., & MACDOUGALL, E. (1984). *American prison riots 1971–1983* [monograph]. Columbia, SC: University of South Carolina.

MORTON, J. (1981). Women in correctional employment: Where are they now and where are they headed? *Women in Corrections, 1*, 7–16.

OWEN, B. A. (1985). Race and gender relations among prison workers. *Crime and Delinquency, 31*, 147–159.

OWEN, B. A. (1988). *The reproduction of social control: A study of prison workers at San Quentin*. New York: Wiley.

PARENT, D., LEITER, V., KENNEDY, S., LEVINS, L., WENTWORTH, D., & WILCOX. S. (1993). *Conditions of confinement in juvenile detention and correctional facilities: Crowding pervasive in juvenile facilities*. Washington, DC: Bureau of Justice Statistics, U.S. Department of Justice.

PETERSON, C. (1982). Doing time with the boys: An analysis of women correctional officers in all-male facilities. In B. Price & N. Sokoloff (Eds.), *The criminal justice system and women* (pp. 437–460). New York: Clark Boardman.

POLLOCK-BYRNE, J. (1990). *Women, prison, and crime*. Pacific Grove, CA: Brooks/Cole.

POOLE, E. D., & REGOLI, R. (1980). Role stress, custody orientation and disciplinary actions: A study of prison guards. *Criminology, 18*, 215–226.

ROBINSON, D., PORPORINO, F., & SIMOURD, L. (1993). The influence of career orientation on support for rehabilitation among correctional staff. *The Prison Journal, 73*(2), 162–177.

ROBINSON, D., PORPORINO, F., & SIMOURD, L. (1997). The influence of educational attainment on the attitudes and job performance of correctional officers. *Crime and Delinquency, 43*(1), 60–77.

ROUNDTREE, P. W., & LAND, K. C. (1996). Perceived risk versus fear of crime: Empirical evidence of conceptually distinct reactions in survey data. *Social Forces, 74*(4), 1353–1376.

SAMPSON, R. J. (2001). Crime and public safety: Insights from community-level perspectives on social capital. In S. Saegert, J. P. Thompson, & M. R. Warren (Eds.), *Social capital and poor communities* (pp. 89–114). New York: Russell Sage Foundation.

SMITH, W. R., & TORSTENSSON, M. (1997). Gender differences in risk perception and neutralizing of fear of crime: Towards resolving the paradoxes. *British Journal of Criminology, 37*, 608–634.

STEPHANS, J. (1997). *Census of state and federal correctional facilities, 1995*. Washington, DC: Bureau of Justice Statistics, U.S. Department of Justice.

SUTTON, R. M., & FARRALL, S. (2005). Gender, socially desirable responding and the fear of crime. Are women really more anxious about crime? *British Journal of Criminology, 45*(2), 212–224.

TELLIER, C., & ROBINSON, D. (1995). *Correlates among front-line correctional staff*. Paper presented at the annual convention of the Canadian Psychological Association, Charlottetown, PEI, Canada.

TOCH, H. (1977). Social climate and prison violence. *Federal Probation, 4*, 21–25.

TOCH, H., & KLOFAS, J. (1982). Alienation and desire for job enrichment among correction officers. *Federal Probation, 46,* 35–44.

USEEM, B. (1985). Disorganization and the New Mexico prison riot of 1980. *American Sociological Review, 50,* 677–688.

USEEM, B., & KIMBALL, P. (1989). *State of siege: U.S. prison riots, 1971–1986.* New York: Oxford University Press.

VAN VOORHIS, P., CULLEN, F., LINK, B., & WOLFE, N. T. (1991). The impact of race and gender on correctional officers' orientation to the integrated environment. *Journal of Research in Crime and Delinquency, 28*(4), 472–500.

WALKLATE, S. (1998). Crime and the community. *British Journal of Sociology, 49,* 550–569.

WARCHOL, G. (1998). *Workplace violence, 1992–96—National Crime Victimization Survey.* Washington, DC: Bureau of Justice Statistics, U.S. Department of Justice.

WHITEHEAD, J. T., & LINDQUIST, C. A. (1989). Determinants of correctional officers' professional orientation. *Justice Quarterly, 6*(1), 69–85.

WRIGHT, K. (1991). A study of individual environmental and interactive effects in explaining adjustment to prison. *Justice Quarterly, 8,* 217–242.

ZAMBLE, E., & PORPORINO, F. (1988). *Coping, behavior, and adaptation in prison inmates.* New York: Springer-Verlag.

ZIMMER, L. E. (1986). *Women guarding men.* Chicago: University of Chicago.

CASES

Bagley v. Watson, 579 F. Supp. 1099 (C. Ore. 1983).

Forts v. Ward, 621 F.2d 1210 (2nd Cir. 1980).

Grummet v. Rushen, 587 F. Supp. 913 (N.D. Cal. 1984).

41

From the Bassinet to the Bar

The Effect of Motherhood on Women's Advancement in the Legal Profession

Jody Clay-Warner and Jennifer McMahon

Women have made great advances in the legal profession in recent years. They have entered the profession in record numbers, leading some to conclude that the law is a profession in which gender equality has been attained. In order to investigate this claim, we review recent studies that examine women's position in the profession, paying particular attention to those that examine the ways in which parenthood impacts women's opportunities. Evidence indicates that while women have made great strides, gender inequity remains. In particular, women face significant wage and partnership gaps, as well as a substantial professional penalty for motherhood. We conclude by suggesting ways in which the legal profession could address these issues.

There is no question that women have made significant advances in the legal profession since the American Bar Association admitted its first female members in 1918 (Feinman, 1986). Consistent with the history of other elite professions, however, once women were admitted to practice they experienced discrimination in hiring, salary, and promotion. Even after gains in the 1970s, women continued to face barriers both to entry and advancement. The 1980s and 1990s saw both the growth of the profession, as well as the growth of task forces designed to study and address women's disadvantaged position. In the 21st century, women are now visible and vocal members of the legal profession and have reached near parity with men in admissions to law school (Glater, 2001). In fact, scholars now talk of the "feminization" of the profession and ask what effect this large influx of women will have on the practice of law itself (Chiu & Leicht, 1999; Menkel-Meadow, 1988). Research reveals, however, that despite great progress gender equality in the legal profession has not been reached.

In attempting to understand the barriers that women attorneys continue to face, scholars have begun to examine the effects that motherhood might have on women's advancement. Research indicates that caretaking in general and motherhood in particular are devalued in our society. As a result, women in many professions pay a significant penalty for motherhood and the temporary leaves often associated with motherhood (Folbre, 2001). Women's dedication to their careers is also questioned when they become mothers. Thus, they often are penalized even when they do not take leave and when their work hours remain unchanged. Men's careers, however, often benefit from fatherhood. As Coltrane (2004) states, men are viewed as more stable once they become fathers and "are assumed to possess the mature leadership qualities that qualify one to be a manager or a CEO" (p. 215).

A variety of factors, of course, potentially affect women's position in the legal profession. In examining gender bias it is therefore necessary to consider the array of challenges that women have faced. Though our focus is on parenthood, we begin by reviewing women's recent experiences in the legal profession more generally by examining the gendered wage gap and barriers to partnership. We then highlight the role that parenthood plays in differentially shaping women's experiences as legal professionals.

SALARY DISCRIMINATION

Though sex differences in salary today are certainly smaller than they were in the past, men's earnings continue to outpace those of women (Adam & Baer, 1984; Gellis, 1991; Glancy, 1970; Hagan, 1990; White, 1967). According to 2004 data from the Bureau of Labor Statistics, the median earning of female lawyers is 73 percent that of male lawyers. Evidence of a wage gap is not sufficient to demonstrate discrimination, however. To determine whether or not women are disadvantaged in their earnings, we must consider studies that include years of experience, hours worked, and other human capital variables.

Huang (1997) considered human capital arguments in her examination of why the gender gap in attorneys' earnings existed. She found that female attorneys earned approximately the same as their male counterparts upon graduation, but that a wage gap soon emerged and that the gap grew over time. Huang reports that though the wage gap is smaller for more recent graduates, men continue to receive significantly greater compensation than do women for attending a prestigious law school, and receive a much less severe penalty for time taken out of the labor force. Interestingly, marriage is also correlated with increased earnings for men but is associated with decreased earnings for women. Hersch (2003) also finds that the marriage "premium" for men explained a large proportion of the wage gap in earnings among respondents to the 1990 and 1993 National Survey of College Graduates. Thus, human capital and associated family variables operate differently in predicting earnings of male and female attorneys. In each case, these differences favor men.

Occupational segregation may also explain a substantial proportion of the wage gap. As Epstein discusses (1993), women are more likely to work in lower paid specialties, such as public interest and family law, than are men. Hersch (2003) finds, however, occupational segregation exists primarily for older cohorts of attorneys, which in her study were defined as those who obtained J.D.s prior to 1990. Many women, though, begin their careers in high-prestige settings, but turn to lower-paid specialties later in their career.

Thus, we cannot determine from Hersch's study whether the decreasing effects of occupational segregation will endure. Interestingly, though, the wage gap also appears to be more pronounced at upper income levels, which suggests that a "glass ceiling" limits women's earnings in the upper echelon of the profession and that occupational segregation is only part of the story (Chiu & Leicht, 1999).

BARRIERS TO PARTNERSHIP AND PROMOTION

Not only does a gendered wage gap continue to exist, but there also appears to be a "partnership" gap. An early illustration of this partnership gap is Elizabeth Anderson Hishon's attempt to be made partner at King & Spalding, a prestigious Atlanta firm, which in 1984 had yet to have a female partner. After being denied a partnership, Hishon filed a complaint with the Equal Employment Opportunity Commission and sued King & Spalding. The lower court concluded that partnership decisions were private relationships that must be entered into under mutual agreement and, as a result, did not fall under the purview of the Civil Rights Act (Morello, 1986). The Supreme Court unanimously reversed the lower court's decision, however, and ruled that partnership decisions were covered under the 1964 Civil Rights Act, giving Hishon permission to take legal action against the law firm (Morello, 1986).

Despite the impact of the Hishon case, women continue to be underrepresented as partners. As late as 2001, fewer than 16 percent of partners at major U.S. law firms were women (National Association for Law Placement, 2001). Research continues to find that not only are women making partner at lower rates than are men, but that women are judged by different standards than are men when partnership decisions are being made. Kay and Hagan (1998) found in their survey of Canadian attorneys in law firm practice that 46 percent of the men who had begun their careers on a partnership track had made partner while only 25 percent of the women had done so. Human capital variables did not explain the different partnership rates between men and women, leading Kay and Hagan to conclude that "women associates are required to embody standards that are an exaggerated form of the partnership ideal, and these standards are imposed uniquely on women" (p. 741). In a longitudinal study of attorneys from 1990 to 1996, Kay and Hagan (1999) confirm that women must be exceptional in order to be made partner, as men received a greater return on their billable hours, client recruitment, and service to clients than did women when going up for partner.

Many women, of course, leave the firm before a partnership decision is made, as they perceive the barriers to be too great to overcome (Epstein et al., 1995). Others recognize the difficulties they would face in a private firm and choose to pursue other employment options. These women are not willing to make the sacrifices necessary to reach the superstar status often necessary for women to make partner and, as a result, they either retreat into government work or into the less stressful world of in-house counsel (see Hull & Nelson, 2000). These sectors are generally considered to be less prestigious than are private firms, and salary levels are certainly lower. As Hull and Nelson (2000) find, the segregation of women into such lower paying areas of practice is only partly a result of personal preference. They suggest that the constraints law firms place on employees disproportionately affect women, further contributing to the exodus of women from private firms. As

Epstein et al. (1995) note, one of the most significant ways in which this problem manifests itself is in the perceived inability of women to combine motherhood with an elite
legal career.

CAREER AND MOTHERHOOD

It is widely recognized that child and family responsibilities differentially affect male and
female attorneys (Blodgett, 1988; Coltrane, 2004; Epstein et al., 1995; Foster, 1995;
French, 2000). Addressing these differential effects, Foster (1995) describes the dominant,
one-dimensional paradigm of the legal profession as conflicting with the multidimensional
requirements of the family. The legal profession demands complete devotion and commitment to an uninterrupted career (Foster, 1995; French, 2000; Korzec, 1997). Given that law
practice has been based on male norms and "patterned around the traditional male life
cycle" (Korzec, 1997, p. 140), the current standards of success in the legal profession are
more attainable for male attorneys than for female attorneys who feel that they must also
meet conventional standards of success in the family (Rhode, 2001).

According to the traditional standards of the legal profession, to be a successful
attorney one must work long hours both during the week and on the weekends (Foster,
1995). Indeed, there is a premium put on maximizing billable hours. Findings from a 1991
ABA report indicate that 45 percent of lawyers in private practice bill over 1,900 hours a
year and 50 percent work over 2,400 hours a year (American Bar Association, 1991). For
attorneys, the typical work week far exceeds the traditional 40 hours at the office, and commitment to the firm and to the practice of law in general is often measured by "face-time"
or time spent in the office (Reichman & Sterling, 2001). Additionally, a successful attorney
must be constantly available to clients and be able to go out of town, come into the office
on short notice, and be available for business and social outings to generate clients (Foster,
1995).

With such standards, the demands of the legal profession often conflict with the
demands of children and the family. Given that the legal profession is based upon male
norms, it comes as no surprise that women may find it difficult to achieve work–family
balance. Due to the premium placed on time spent at the office, high billable hours, and
around-the-clock availability, women attorneys with children are often at a disadvantage
(Reichman & Sterling, 2001). Even if women attorneys are willing and able to put their
work responsibilities ahead of their family and childcare responsibilities, their colleagues
often "assume that they will not be available or *should not* be available" (Reichman &
Sterling, 2001, p. 951).

Although male attorneys express dissatisfaction with not having enough time to
spend with their families, significantly more married male attorneys compared to married
female attorneys have a stay-at-home spouse to take care of home and childcare responsibilities; most married female attorneys have a spouse who also has a demanding full-time
career (Rhode, 2001). Using data from the 1990 and 1993 National Survey of College
Graduates, Hersch (2003) found that only 40 percent of the male attorneys had wives who
worked full-time outside the home, whereas 90 percent of female attorneys had spouses
who were employed full time. Given that societal expectations still place child and family
responsibilities primarily on women, trying to balance work and family obligations poses

a much bigger problem for female attorneys compared to male attorneys. Female attorneys with children must constantly struggle between being a dedicated lawyer and being a devoted mother (Rhode, 2001). Cunningham (2001) explains the "double-bind" for a female attorney with children—she is either viewed as an uncommitted lawyer or an uncommitted mother— "if she is a good lawyer, she must be a bad mother, or vice versa. She can only be a successful lawyer at the expense of her children, and she is often seen as failing on both fronts" (p. 997). Many female attorneys hire full-time live-in childcare in order to meet the demands of work and home. Epstein and colleagues (1995) reported that 80 percent of female partners and 65 percent of female associates in their study had full-time live-in help compared to only 40 percent of male partners and 22 percent of male associates. They explain that a high percentage of male attorneys have stay-at-home spouses, which makes it unnecessary to hire childcare. This, however, is not the case for most female attorneys.

THE MOMMY-TRACK AND PART-TIME WORK

In a controversial attempt to offer a solution to work–family conflicts for women, Schwartz (1989) suggested that employers offer "career and family women" opportunities to work part time or to utilize an alternative work schedule. According to Schwartz, such arrangements enable companies to retain their high-performing "career and family women," and enable these women to play an active role in their children's lives while continuing to pursue their careers. Although Schwartz seems to offer a possible solution to work–family conflict for women, there is a paradox of the "mommy-track"—while enabling women to balance work and family responsibilities, it actually negatively affects their career advancement and earnings (Korzec, 1997). Especially for attorneys, "'mommy-tracking' can be viewed as leading to second class status" (Korzec, 1997, p. 127).

Beyond just being perceived as less committed to the legal profession, "mommy-trackers" face some serious negative consequences (Korzec, 1997). Although there is variation, most attorneys who work part time are removed from the partnership track (Epstein et al., 1995). Even if an attorney consistently worked a 40-hour work week, her official status as a part-time employee would make her ineligible for partnership at many firms (Foster, 1995; Reichman & Sterling, 2001). Firms also discount part-time work when making partnership decisions by focusing on hours billed instead of efficiency (Reichman & Sterling, 2001). While working part time, it is also often assumed that female attorneys with children will not be available on short notice and as a result they receive lower quality assignments (Reichman & Sterling, 2001). In fact, attorneys who work part time or take a leave risk losing their clients altogether (Reichman & Sterling, 2001). In a climate in which "rainmaking" is highly valued, even the possibility of client loss may be enough to dissuade many women from pursuing part-time work arrangements. As a result, many female attorneys leave large law firms to work for smaller firms or for the government (Foster, 1995; Reichman & Sterling, 2001).

Working part time or taking a leave to take care of children has been viewed as a "women's issue" due to male attorneys' reluctance to utilize family-friendly policies and alternative work arrangements (Cunningham, 2001). According to Cunningham, this reluctance is due to the nature of the law firm culture. Those who control the law firm culture—

especially in regard to the policies, goals, and measures of success—are primarily older male attorneys who were able to dedicate the majority of their time to legal practice because they had stay-at-home spouses who took care of home and childcare responsibilities. As a result, younger male attorneys feel discouraged from working part time or taking a leave to care for their children (Cunningham, 2001). Furthermore, most large law firms have gender-specific family leave policies that allow women to take a paid family leave, but they do not offer the same benefits to male attorneys. Instead, male attorneys must prove that they are the primary caregiver in order to qualify for such benefits. No such "proof" is required for women (Cunningham, 2001). These policies reflect the assumption that women are primarily responsible for providing childcare and men are primarily responsible for providing the family with financial support.

Due to the difficulties and/or negative effects of trying to balance work and childcare obligations, deciding when (or if) to have children is often a very difficult decision for female attorneys (Epstein et al., 1995). The issue is even more complicated when women are on the partnership track. Partnership decisions are typically made 7 to 10 years after an attorney has been working at a law firm, which for many women also happens to encompass the prime childbearing years. Female attorneys who wish to have children are, as one female attorney explained in an interview with Nancy Blodget (1988), "caught between the brass ring and the biological clock" (p. 58).

Indeed, there are risks associated with any choice that a female attorney may make regarding motherhood. Women who decide to have children prior to partnership may be viewed as less committed to the firm, a perception that may adversely affect partnership decisions (Coltrane, 2004; Cunningham, 2001). Such women may also need to work part time or on an alternative work schedule, which may remove the women from the partnership track altogether (French, 2000). On the other hand, while choosing to delay or forgo motherhood allows female attorneys to devote more time toward making partner, French (2000) points out that firms may deny these women partnerships anyway because it is often assumed that women will have a child shortly after making partner. Thus, it is not necessarily the choice that a woman makes regarding whether or when to become a mother that adversely affects her becoming a partner. Instead, women lawyers are disadvantaged because society tends to view all women as either mothers or potential mothers. This results in statistical discrimination, which occurs when the future productivity of a particular worker is assessed in terms of the perceived average future productivity of others who are like the worker in question (Arrow, 1972; Phelps, 1972).

When women do choose motherhood and take time off to care for children, they may pay an additional penalty. In a study of graduates from the University of Michigan Law School, Noonan and Corcoran (2004) found that taking time out from work for childcare responsibilities decreases a lawyer's chance of making partner and decreases their earnings if they do become partner. For men, a one-year family leave reduced the probability of making partner from .58 to .00 and working part time for 42 months reduced the probability from .58 to .39. For women, their chances of becoming a partner dropped from .35 to .22 for taking a one-year leave for childcare purposes and from .35 to .28 if they worked part time for 42 months. Although the effects of taking a leave and working part time appear to be more severe for male attorneys, it is important to note that very few men actually take a leave or work part time. In fact, in Noonan and Corcoran's (2004) study only 1 percent of the male attorneys with children had taken childcare leave compared to 42 percent of the female attorneys with children. Similarly, just 1 percent of the fathers had worked part time compared to 47 percent of the mothers.

Noonan and Corcoran (2004) point out that their results do not suggest that there is a direct penalty for motherhood. In fact, they find that having children does not reduce women's likelihood of making partner when controlling for other factors, such as experience and leave-taking. Their results indicate, though, that it is taking time off from work to care for children, and not simply having children, that negatively affects women's chances for partnership, as well as their earnings. Given limited options for childcare, however, having children often requires women to take leave, which translates into an indirect penalty for motherhood.

ACHIEVING WORK–FAMILY BALANCE

The question remains as to if and how female attorneys will be able to achieve work–family balance while gaining equality in the legal profession. Most researchers recognize that there must be a change in the law firm culture before this can be achieved (Cunningham, 2001; Foster, 1995; French, 2000; Korzec, 1997; Reichman & Sterling, 2001; Rhode, 2001). French (2000) proposes that time will correct the problem. He argues that as older cohorts of male partners age out of the profession, they will be replaced by younger cohorts that include an increasing number of women. As a result, there will be more women on partnership committees and subsequently more females promoted to partner. Even if these younger cohorts include only a small number of women, according to French (2000), younger male attorneys will have been more exposed to female attorneys in law school and while practicing law. As a result, this younger cohort of males will be more sensitive to the needs of female attorneys.

Reichman and Sterling (2001), however, criticized this attrition hypothesis because it fails to take into account the fact that many women are choosing to leave law firms prior to making partner. Indeed, with large numbers of women leaving before making partner, partnership committees will continue to be dominated by men. Also, many of the women who have made partner have assimilated to the one-dimensional paradigm of the law firm, thus perpetuating the existing norms of the law firm culture (Foster, 1995). As Reichman and Sterling (2001) state, "women will not rise in substantial percentages to partners in law firm practice until law firms recognize the gendered nature of these organizations and provide avenues for women to accumulate the professional assets necessary to advance" (p. 962).

According to Cunningham (2001), changing the law firm culture is going to take the efforts of both male and female attorneys advocating for a more realistic work–family balance. As long as only female attorneys are offered and/or utilize part-time or alternative schedules as a mechanism for balancing the demands of the firm and their children, female attorneys are going to continue to be marginalized in the legal profession (Cunningham, 2001; Rhode, 2001). Instead of waiting until the older male attorneys age out of the profession, Cunningham (2001) believes that the senior partners need to be convinced that adopting more family-friendly policies for both males and females would serve the firm's economic interests. Specifically, Cunningham (2001) points to the increasing dissatisfaction with the current legal culture and the increasing desire among younger cohorts, both male and female, to achieve work–family balance. In competing with other firms for the most talented lawyers, the firms with the most family-friendly policies are going to benefit the most. Also, addressing the high rate of attrition, Cunningham (2001) states, "if law firms wish to acquire and retain talented lawyers in the emerging economy, they must look for ways such as modified work schedules to lure lawyers in and keep them from leaving. Thus, flexible work arrangements should be presented to upper-management not in terms of 'morality' but rather in terms of 'money'" (p. 1003). Cunningham (2001) adds that job satisfaction can increase productivity, and he points to research that indicates that many part-time attorneys work more efficiently than full-time attorneys.

In sum, changing the culture of the legal profession requires that law firms adopt gender neutral policies and practices (Cunningham, 2001; Foster, 1995; Korzec, 1997; Rhode, 2001). Such policies should allow both male and female attorneys to take a family leave without penalty (Cunningham, 2001; Reichman & Sterling, 2001). Also, researchers stress the importance of law firms allowing attorneys to utilize alternative work arrangements (which allow for flexible work schedules and part-time hours) while on the partnership track (Cunningham, 2001; Foster, 1995; Korzec, 1997; Reichman & Sterling, 2001). Furthermore, calls for changes in the law firm culture have included recommendations for eliminating the emphasis on billable hours (Cunningham, 2001; Foster, 1995; Rhode, 2001). In fact, researchers (Cunningham, 2001; Foster, 1995) point out that focusing on billable hours as a measure of success actually discourages efficiency, causes burnout, lowers the quality of work, and may cause the firm to lose clients. Alternative billing methods, such as value billing or a fixed fee, would take the emphasis off of time and place it on the quality of service provided, thus encouraging efficiency and increasing opportunities for work–family balance (Korzec, 1997). According to Foster (1995), changing the culture of the legal profession is key to accommodating multidimensional attorneys. Furthermore, these changes will help to break down the separate spheres ideology and stereotypes regarding the different roles for men and women (Cunningham, 2001; Rhode, 2001).

CONCLUSION

Historically, women have faced discrimination in the legal profession, and even today a substantial salary gap exists. Nonetheless, women have made impressive advances, largely owing to the tremendous expansion of the legal profession in the last two decades. Currently, 34 percent of attorneys practicing in the United States are female (Bureau of Labor Statistics, 2004), and women now comprise 49 percent of law school students in this country (American Bar Association, 2003). The Bureau of Labor Statistics (2000), however, predicts that growth within the profession will slow at least through 2008 and suggests that competition for jobs will increase substantially. Thus, there is a risk that women's gains will be lost due to changes in the labor market. Considerable challenges also face women who hope to combine motherhood with a legal career. Women may even be penalized for being "potential mothers," whether they actually choose to become parents or not. The result is a pattern of gender discrimination based upon cultural expectations for motherhood and the incompatibility of these expectations with a high prestige legal career.

Thus, challenges remain for women entering the legal profession in the 21st century. The *Judges' Journal* recently asked the Honorable Margaret H. Marshall, Chief Justice of the Supreme Judicial Court of the Commonwealth of Massachusetts, whether or not gender bias still exists in the legal system. Judge Marshall replied that women lawyers today "will face far fewer obstacles than the women pioneers who came before them; but they will receive far fewer breaks than my generation. They are coming into their own; but they will be on their own" ("Gender Bias in the Legal System," 2000, p. 8).

REFERENCES

ADAM, B., & BAER, D. (1984). The social mobility of women and men in the Ontario legal profession. *Canadian Review of Sociology and Anthropology, 21*, 22–46.

AMERICAN BAR ASSOCIATION. (1991). *The report of At the Breaking Point: A National Conference on the Emerging Crisis in the Quality of Lawyers' Health and Lives—Its impact on law firms and client services.* Chicago: Author.

ARROW, K. (1972). The theory of discrimination. In O. Ashenfelter & A. Rees (Eds.), *Discrimination in labor markets.* Princeton, NJ: Princeton University Press.

BLODGETT, N. (1988, June 1). Whatever happened to the class of '81? *American Bar Association Journal*, 56–60.

BUREAU OF LABOR STATISTICS. (2000). *Occupational Outlook Handbook 2000–01.* (Bulletin 2520). Washington, DC: U.S. Government Printing Office.

BUREAU OF LABOR STATISTICS. (2004). *Current Population Survey.* Washington, DC: U.S. Government Printing Office.

CHIU, C., & LEICHT, K. T. (1999). When does feminization increase equality? The case of lawyers. *Law & Society Review, 33*, 557–583.

COLTRANE, S. (2004). Elite careers and family commitment: It's (still) about gender. *The Annals of the American Academy of Political and Social Science, 596*, 214–220.

COMMISSION ON WOMEN IN THE PROFESSION (AMERICAN BAR ASSOCIATION). (2003). *A current glance of women in the law.* Chicago: Author.

CUNNINGHAM, K. (2001). Father Time: Flexible work arrangements and the law firm's failure of the family. *Stanford Law Review, 53*, 967–1008.

EPSTEIN, C. F. (1993). *Women in law* (2nd ed.). New York: Basic Books.

EPSTEIN, C. F., SAUTE, R., OGLENSKY, B., & GEVER, M. (1995). Glass ceilings and open doors: Women's advancement in the legal profession. *Fordham Law Review, 64*, 291–449.

FEINMAN, C. (1986). *Women in the criminal justice system* (2nd ed.). New York: Praeger.

FOLBRE, N. (2001). *The invisible heart: Economics and family values.* New York: New Press.

FOSTER, E. (1995). The glass ceiling in the legal profession: Why do law firms still have so few female partners? *UCLA Law Review, 42*, 1631–1688.

FRENCH, S. (2000). Of problems, pitfalls and possibilities: A comprehensive look at female attorneys and law firm partnership. *Women's Rights Law Reporter, 21*, 189–216.

GELLIS, A. J. (1991). Great expectations: Women in the legal profession, a commentary on state studies. *Indiana Law Journal, 66*, 941–976.

Gender bias in the legal system: Does it still exist? (2000, Spring). *The Judges' Journal*, 6–8.

GLANCY, D. (1970). Women in law: The dependable ones. *Harvard Law School Bulletin, 21*(5), 23–33.

GLATER, J. D. (2001, March 26). Women are close to being majority of law students. *New York Times.*

HAGAN, J. (1990). The gender stratification of income inequality among lawyers. *Social Forces, 63*, 835–855.

HERSCH, J. (2003). The new labor market for lawyers: Will female lawyers still earn less? *Cardozo Women's Law Journal, 10*, 1–59.

HUANG, W. R. (1997). Gender differences in the earnings of lawyers. *Columbia Journal of Law and Social Problems, 30*, 267–311.

HULL, K. E., & NELSON, R. L. (2000). Assimilation, choice, or constraint? Testing theories of gender differences in the careers of lawyers. *Social Forces, 79*, 229–264.

KAY, F. M., & HAGAN, J. (1998). Raising the bar: The gender stratification of law firm capital. *American Sociological Review, 63*, 728–743.

KAY, F. M. & HAGAN, J. (1999). Cultivating clients in the competition for partnerships: Gender and the organizational restructuring of law firms in the 1990's. *Law & Society Review 33*, 517–555.

KORZEC, R. (1997). Working on the "Mommy-Track": Motherhood and women lawyers. *Hastings Women's Law Journal, 8*, 117–140.

MENKEL-MEADOW, C. (1988). The feminization of the legal profession: The comparative sociology of women lawyers. In R. Abel & P. Lewis (Eds.), *Lawyers in society* (vol. 3, pp. 196–255). Berkeley: University of California Press.

MORELLO, K. B. (1986). *The invisible bar: The women lawyer in America, 1638 to the present.* New York: Random House.

NATIONAL ASSOCIATION FOR LAW PLACEMENT. (2001, December). Dearth of women and attorneys of color remain in law firms. Washington, DC: National Association for Law Placement.

NOONAN, M., & CORCORAN, M. E. (2004). The Mommy track and partnership: Temporary delay or dead end? *The Annals of the American Academy of Political and Social Science, 596*, 130–150.

PHELPS, E. S. (1972). The statistical theory of racism and sexism. *American Economic Review, 62*, 659–666.

REICHMAN, N., STERLING, J. S. (2001). Recasting the brass ring: Deconstructing and reconstructing workplace opportunities for women lawyers. *Capital University Law Review, 29*, 923–977.

RHODE, D. (2001). *Balanced lives: Changing the culture of legal practice.* A report by the American Bar Association's Commission on Women in the Profession. Washington, DC: American Bar Association.

SCHWARTZ, F. (1989). Executives and organizations: Management women and the new facts of life. *Harvard Business Review, 67*, 65–76.

WHITE, J. (1967). Women in law. *Michigan Law Review, 65*, 1051–1118.

42

The Dislike of Female Offenders among Correctional Officers

A Need for Specialized Training

Christine E. Rasche

Work with *women* offenders? Oh, they are the *worst!* I hate to admit it, but I would rather have a caseload of male rapists than a caseload of WOMEN petty offenders! (female community corrections officer)

There is a widespread phenomenon in corrections that has not been well researched scientifically. Anecdotally, this phenomenon shows up in conversations with correctional line staff, both those who work in prisons and in community corrections. While correctional leaders seem to mostly regard it as a curiosity with little real relevance to correctional practice, I think this phenomenon *does* have an impact on correctional officers and administrators alike. More important, it also has an direct impact on inmates at prison facilities for *women*. This phenomenon is the pervasive tendency among correctional workers to *dislike* working with female offenders or to *avoid* working at women's prisons, and to view such duty as undesirable.

This dislike of female offenders appears to be very widespread in corrections and is well known by almost all who work in the field. As Pollack (1984) has noted, "There is informal agreement among correctional personnel that female offenders are somehow 'harder to work with' than male offenders" (p. 84). One has only to ask correctional officers whether they *prefer* working with male or female offenders. Spontaneously, most correctional officers (both male and female) tend to state a clear preference for working with *male* offenders.

Logically, this preference might seem somewhat counterintuitive. After all, male inmates are much more likely than female inmates to be housed in very large facilities where supervision is somewhat more difficult, and male inmates are also more likely to physically attack and injure correctional staff. A layperson might well expect that correctional staff would prefer to work in smaller facilities with inmates who are unlikely to physically harm them. However, all the available evidence suggests that the opposite is true.

The layperson might also expect that a such preference for working with male inmates would be widespread only among *male* correctional officers, given the macho-oriented nature of our culture in general and criminal justice professions in particular. A layperson might easily assume that at least *female* correctional officers would prefer working with female inmates, either for ideological reasons or because of a desire for less physically risky work. Again, however, this does not seem to be true. With a few notable exceptions discussed below, most female correctional officers also seem to express a clear preference for working with male inmates instead of female inmates. For the purposes of this discussion, I call this widespread phenomenon the *male inmate preference*.

As far as can be determined, this male inmate preference is found among both male and female correctional officers, among both high- and low-ranking officers, among officers working at both male and female inmate facilities, and among officers in all regions of the country. It appears among both those correctional personnel working in prisons and those in community corrections. Baines and Alder (1996) also found it among juvenile justice practitioners who almost completely agreed that "girls are more difficult to work with." When this sort of male bias is expressed, it usually seems to be articulated *immediately*, seeming to require little or no thought on the part of respondents. Indeed, a question about their working preferences usually elicits from correctional staffers a prompt, strong, even passionate response, such as the quotation that opened this chapter. Laughter and boisterous exclamations about their working experiences often result, along with unsolicited explanations for their preferences in the form of horror stories.

In fact, often the only correctional staff who do *not* seem to express the male inmate preference, at least in my experience, are long-time female staff members working at female-only correctional facilities. Such staff are often women who began their careers before institutional staffs were gender-integrated, and many have spent their entire careers working at institutions for female offenders. In general, their preference for working with *female* inmates seems to arise from long and successful experience in working with female offenders. However, some also express a strong ideological commitment to working with women offenders. This ideological commitment among the older, long-time female staffers is sometimes feminist in nature but it can also be religious. It should be noted that some *younger* correctional female staff members at female facilities (as well as a few *male* staffers) also express such an ideological commitment to working with female offenders. But outside of these comparatively few ideologically committed or long-time women's prison staff members, my experience is that most other correctional personnel clearly express the male inmate preference—even though they will often simultaneously agree that male inmates are more likely to represent a hazard to their own personal safety.

The fact that the male inmate preference has not been well researched scientifically does *not* mean that it represents a new phenomenon. Observations about the comparatively greater difficulty of working with female inmates appear in literature dating back at least to the mid-nineteenth century. For example, Pollack (1986) cites one prison matron's description of female inmates in the 1860s:

> It is a harder task to manage female prisoners than male. . . . They are more impulsive, more individual, more unreasonable and excitable than men; will not act in concert, and cannot be disciplined in masses. Each wants personal and peculiar treatment, so that the duties fall much more heavily on the matrons than on the warders; matrons having thus to deal with units, not aggregates, and having to adapt themselves to each individual case, instead of simply obeying certain fixed laws and making others obey them, as in the prison for males. (Pollack, 1986)

Somewhat more recently Charles Turnbo, who served as the warden of the female prison at Pleasanton, California from the late 1970s to the early 1980s, recalled that when he was made the warden in 1978 he "received as many condolences as congratulations" (Turnbo, 1993, p. 13). He was also subjected to hearing the war stories of other colleagues who had pulled duty in women's facilities, since "many wardens want nothing to do with an all-female prison population" (Turnbo, 1993, p. 13). By way of explanation, Turnbo quoted Heffernan in observing that "Women are seen as a persistent and continuing problem in corrections for two reasons: one, their small numbers, and two, their perceived nature" (Turnbo, 1993, p. 13).

By far the most extensive scientific research on this phenomenon to date has been done by Pollack (1984, 1986). Her research on correctional officers' attitudes revealed that what I call the male inmate preference is a real component of what she calls the prevailing modern "CO culture." Two-thirds (68%) of her sample of 45 experienced correctional officers who had worked in both male and female facilities stated preferences for working with male inmates, and two-thirds (67%) also agreed that female inmates were harder to supervise. Interestingly, female correctional officers generally expressed a *stronger* preference for working with male inmates than did male correctional officers ($f = 72\%$, $m = 66\%$) and were *more* likely than their male colleagues to agree that women inmates were more difficult to manage ($f = 83\%$, $m = 55\%$) (Pollack, 1986).

However, male and female correctional officers may not always have the same reasons for holding the same preference. As shown on Table 1, Pollack (1986) found that the reasons given by *male* officers for a male inmate preference included perceived difficulties in supervising the opposite sex and fear of being framed for rape. Male officers also perceived the need to modify their normal behavior when working with women inmates (e.g., curbing their speech, being careful about the use of force). By contrast, the reasons given by *female* officers for a male inmate preference included perceptions that male inmates were more likely to treat women officers with respect and that male inmates seemed to appreciate them as women, which made the job more enjoyable. In short, male correctional officers were likely to perceive more potential penalties for working with female inmates, while female correctional officers saw more rewards in working with male inmates. Interestingly, however, reasons given by *both* male and female officers for disdaining work with female inmates included perceptions that women inmates are more demanding and tended to complain more than male inmates, and that women inmates are more likely to refuse orders.

TABLE 1   Reasons Given by Correctional Officers for the Male Inmate Preference

Reasons given by male officers for preferring to work with male inmates included:

1. Difficulties in supervising the opposite sex and fear of being framed for rape.
2. The need to modify their behavior toward women inmates (e.g., curb their speech, be careful about the use of force).

Reasons given by female officers for preferring to work with male inmates included:

1. Male inmates were seen as more likely to treat women officers with respect.
2. Male inmates were seen as appreciating them as women, which made the job more enjoyable.

Reasons given by both male and female officers for the male inmate preference included:

1. Women inmates are more demanding.
2. Women inmates complain more.
3. Women inmates are more likely to refuse orders.

Source: Pollack (1986).

Pollack (1986) also found that there were a few correctional officers in her sample who preferred to work with *women* inmates, even though they agreed that women inmates were more difficult to supervise. These officers indicated that they enjoyed the challenge of trying to deal with the demands and problems of female inmates. These atypical correctional officers also stated that they enjoyed the "variety, unpredictability, and constant turmoil that was likely to be present in settings for women" (Pollack, 1986, p. 99). Normally, qualities such as "constant turmoil" are *not* listed as desirable job attributes!

As part of her research, Pollack (1984, 1986) explored correctional officers' views of male and female inmates by giving officers lists of adjectives that they apply to different types of inmates. As Table 2 shows, Pollack found that some adjectives were applied frequently to *both* male and female inmates. Thus, both male and female prisoners were seen as being defensive, distrustful, and manipulative (1986).

However, *female* inmates specifically were characterized as emotional, temperamental, moody, manipulative, quarrelsome, demanding, changeable, complaining, argumentative, excitable, immature, and noisy. By comparison, choosing from this same list of adjectives, *male* inmates were characterized by correctional officers as active, defensive, boastful, aggressive, and manipulative. Pollack noted that "only three adjectives for males were agreed upon by more than 60 percent of the officers, whereas 60 percent or more officers agreed on twelve adjectives for females" (1986, pp. 34–35). This greater consensus among the correctional officers about which adjective labels to apply to female inmates

> raises the possibility that officers possess a stereotype of females. It is not unusual to obtain a high rate of agreement among those who possess a common stereotype of a group; likewise, one is less likely to get consensus on a description of any group for which a stereotype is not operating, since people interact and perceive each other differently. (Pollack, 1986, p. 35)

Ultimately, Pollack found three "themes" emerging from the adjective descriptions of female inmates selected by correctional officers. As shown in Table 3, the first theme

---

TABLE 2   Adjectives Used by Correctional Officers to Describe Female and Male Inmates

---

Some adjectives were applied frequently to both male and female inmates:

Defensive (54.5%)

Distrustful (50%)

Manipulative (65%)

But female inmates also were characterized as:

Emotional (83%)

Tempermental (76%)

Moody (74%)

Manipulative (71%)

Quarrelsome (64%)

Demanding (69%)

Changeable (67%)

Complaining (81%)

Argumentative (69%)

Excitable (64%)

Immature (62%)

Noisy (64%)

By comparison, male inmates were characterized as:

Active (64%)

Defensive (60%)

Boastful (57%)

Aggressive (55%)

Manipulative (60%)

Source: Pollack (1986).

was "defiance," which involved selecting descriptions of women inmates as being likely to oppose the officers in various ways. This included descriptions of women inmates as being argumentative, less likely to follow rules, demanding, and harder to handle. In the closed world of the prison, *defiant* inmates are uniformly disliked by correctional officers, whose jobs often hinge on the degree to which they are able to manage inmates smoothly.

The second theme Pollack (1986) found emerging from the adjectives correctional officers chose to describe female offenders was "open display of emotion." This involved characterizations of women inmates as expressing more feeling, being louder and noisier, having a greater tendency to cry, erupting in spur-of-the-moment outbreaks, fighting spontaneously and easily, and losing their tempers easily. Clearly, such boisterous displays are viewed by correctional officers as management problems, particularly when the emotional outburst of one inmate can result in emotional displays among others.

TABLE 3   Themes in the Description of Female Inmates by Correctional Officers

---

1. *Defiance:* descriptions of the women as opposing the officers, which included women inmates described as being argumentative, less likely to follow rules, demanding, harder to handle, questioning rules, more troublesome, more complaining, confronting verbally, more critical, less respectful, and harder to reason with.

2. *Open display of emotion:* descriptions of women inmates as expressing more feelings, being louder/noisier, screaming/hollering more, having a greater tendency to cry, having spur-of-the-moment outbreaks, fighting spontaneously and easily, being ready to explode, being crybabies, being explosive, losing their tempers easily.

3. *Gratification seeking:* described women as needing and wanting more from their environment, needing/wanting both material and personal commodities such as attention, friendship, or sympathy, wanting things with little or no patience, emotionally demanding, less independent, more childish, having critical demands, and having a greater need for friends.

Source: Pollack (1986).

The third theme characterizing female offenders in the eyes of correctional officers, according to Pollack (1986), was that female inmates were seen as "gratification seeking." This described women inmates as needing and wanting both material and personal commodities such as attention, friendship, or sympathy more than males, and wanting things immediately with little or no patience or willingness to wait. Such impatient and demanding inmates are, once again, viewed by correctional officers as "management problems," who tend to create a major fuss over minor problems and who, therefore, make supervision more difficult. Overall, Pollack (1986) found that there was strong agreement among her respondents that men and women inmates required different styles of supervision (91%), and that there could be situations where they as correctional officers needed to respond to men and women in different fashions (73%).

Interestingly, when asked to account for why these perceived differences between male and female inmates exist, Pollack (1984, 1986) found that correctional officers referred to general "sex differences (whether biological or socialization) rather than institutional factors" (1986, p. 116). In other words, women *inmates* and women *in general* were seen as being similar.

> The inmates' behavior, in other words, is taken for granted, and the officers see themselves as doing their best within the confines of that assumption. Attempts to change behavior by changing procedures, policies, or other situational components are unlikely to be viewed as effective since it is assumed that the behavior is not situationally induced. We could, therefore, expect the officers to view inmate-generated problems with exasperated resignation, which indeed, appears to be their attitude. (Pollack, 1986, p. 116)

In short, correctional officers did not think there was anything they could do about the greater difficulty posed by female inmates because it was a product of nature. Women inmates were just being *women*.

Pollack's (1984, 1986) reports on correctional officer's different attitudes toward male and female inmates are by far the most scientific analysis of a sentiment which both experienced correctional workers and outside observers readily assert runs throughout the field. This tendency to view female inmates as more difficult to manage leads to the perpetuation of the male inmate preference.

PERCEPTIONS VERSUS REAL DIFFERENCES

The question that follows is whether there are *real* differences between male and female inmates in terms of supervision and management requirements, or whether correctional officers are merely articulating unfounded prejudices and stereotypes. As it turns out, there is a considerable literature on the differences between men and women in captivity. Not the least of this difference, of course, is that by year-end 2003 men continued to outnumber women in state and federal prisons by 15 to 1 (Harrison & Beck, 2004). Beyond that, however, there are at least three dimensions of difference between male and female prison inmates.

The first dimension of difference between male and female inmates is their *demographic profiles*. The demographic characteristics of women who are in prison are different in some important ways from those of males who are in prison. First, African Americans are clearly overrepresented in American prisons compared to their proportion of the population in general. While there have been several reports of larger percentages of African Americans among women in prison than among men (Binkley-Jackson, Carter, & Rolison, 1993; Goetting & Howsen, 1983; Rafter, 1985; Sarri, 1987), this appears to be true only in slightly more than a dozen states as of 2003. In most states, there is a somewhat lower proportion of African American and minority women than men, or the numbers are almost equivalent (American Correctional Association [ACA], 2003). Overall, women inmates have tended to be slightly older as a group than male inmates. Women inmates have also tended to be slightly better educated than their male counterparts—though this is not saying much, since both male and female inmates tend to be less academically skilled when tested than their respective completed years of formal education would suggest.

The vast majority of women in prison are mothers. Women inmates are highly likely to have minor children in the home prior to imprisonment and were usually the primary caregivers for their dependent children, which is much less true of male inmates with dependent children (Koban, 1983). Compared to male inmates, female inmates are imprisoned more often for economic and drug-related crimes than violent or assaultive crimes (Greenfeld & Snell, 1999; James, 2004). Women inmates are less likely to have been legitimately employed compared to their male counterparts, despite the fact that they were often the sole support for their minor children. Of those women who were employed prior to prison, most were at very low-level jobs at low pay; two-thirds had never held a job paying more than $6.50 an hour (Greenfeld & Snell, 1999).

About 80% of all women in state prisons have problems with substance abuse (Center for Substance Abuse Treatment, 1997). Women prisoners have been shown to have a higher likelihood of drug addiction/abuse than males, especially addiction to heroin, cocaine and other intravenous drugs. In the light of this, it is perhaps not so surprising to find out that female inmates are more likely to be known HIV-positive than male inmates (Maruschak, 2004). Women prisoners also have many other physical health problems, more than male prisoners. It has been gauged that up to a third of incarcerated women go on sick call each day compared to 10% or less for incarcerated men (Bloom, Owen, & Covington, 2003).

Also, women prisoners have been found to have high levels of sexual and/or physical abuse as either children or adults, or both; usually these are much higher levels than even the high levels sometimes reported for male prison inmates (ACA, 1990; Arnold, 1990; Carlen, 1983; Chesney-Lind & Rodriguez, 1983, Fletcher, Shaver, Moon, 1993; Gilfus, 1992; Immarigeon, 1987a, 1987b; Sargent, Marcus-Mendoza, & Yu, 1993). Thus, in 2002 over half of all women jail inmates said they had been physically or sexually abused, compared to only about 13% of males in jail (James, 2004). And imprisoned women had triple the likelihood of reporting an abuse history than male prisoners (Harlow, 1999). With this history, it is perhaps not surprising to learn that women in prison are also highly likely to have had prior experience with the mental health care system. Women prison inmates have a higher likelihood of mental disorder than women in the outside world (Bureau of Justice Statistics, 2001).

In short, a national profile of women offenders reveals that they are:

- Disproportionately women of color.
- In their early to mid-30s.
- Most likely to have been convicted of a drug-related offense.
- From fragmented families that include other family members who also have been involved with the criminal justice system.
- Survivors of physical and/or sexual abuse as children and adults.
- Individuals with significant substance abuse problems.
- Individuals with multiple physical and mental health problems.
- Unmarried mothers of minor children.
- Individuals with a high school or general equivalent diploma (GED) but limited vocational training and sporadic work histories. (Bloom et al., 2003, p. 8).

In addition to such differences in their *demographic profiles*, a second dimension of difference between male and female inmates is that they have quite dissimilar *needs during incarceration*. Some differences between the sexes are obvious and expected. For example, women have needs for gynecologically related goods and services, such as menstrual supplies, annual gynecological check-ups, prenatal care for those who are pregnant, and postnatal care and counseling for those who give birth in prison. Only recently have prison systems begun to acknowledge that such prenatal and postnatal care and counseling needs to be both of the *normal* variety, which might be given to any woman before and after giving birth, and somewhat *specialized* care, given to women with greater needs. Such specialized care is needed partly because of the large proportion of prison pregnancies that are "high-risk" in nature. That is, women who are pregnant in prison are more like than those in the general population to have been in ill health previously, to have received little prior prenatal care, and to suffer from a variety of chronic conditions that increase risk during pregnancy or afterward (Acoca, 1998; Resnick & Shaw, 1980; Ross & Fabiano, 1986). However, specialized care is also required because following a prison birth there is (in all but a few women's prisons) an inevitable "loss" of the newborn, who will be immediately taken away from the mother and placed outside the prison with foster caregivers. Though the child lives, its physical loss immediately following birth may be experienced as almost "deathlike" by the imprisoned mother. Special health care, both physical and mental, is required under such considerations. Male inmates, obviously, do not require such services.

Also among the obvious and expected differences between the sexes in needs during incarceration are that women inmates need different sorts of routine health and beauty aids, and different types of clothing. Women prisoners also express a much higher need for privacy than do male inmates. Furthermore, women generally need a different kind of diet, with fewer calories and carbohydrates overall and more of certain vitamins and minerals than men require. Ironically, the growing trend in over the past two decades to standardize treatment of male and female inmates has reduced or eliminated some of the individualized food service, clothing options, and commissary health and beauty choices that used to be accorded to women in smaller female facilities.

Less obviously, it is only recently that have we begun to realize that women inmates need specialized counseling for sexual and/or physical abuse that most received as children or adults. Indeed, women are more likely than men to be in prison precisely for the killing an adult abuser, particularly a spouse, lover, or other family member. They are also somewhat more likely to be imprisoned for having killed their own children; many women who kill their own children explain their actions as a form of "mercy" killing in the face of what they saw as intolerably brutal conditions. Also, because they were often the primary caregivers to their minor children prior to their imprisonment, women inmates seem to need more help than do male inmates in dealing with the separation from their children, which many view as the harshest single aspect of being imprisoned. There is now considerable evidence that for all these reasons women inmates need more counseling and psychiatric services overall than do male inmates. Certainly women inmates receive far more psychotropic drugs than do male inmates.

In part because of all these unique stressors, women inmates seem to need different kinds of supervision techniques from correctional officers. Because so many women inmates have an abusive history, correctional staff may unwittingly trigger "flashbacks" of painful past abuses if they utilize the common in-your-face confrontational approach favored for handling male inmates. Male correctional staff may be more likely to run into this problem, since women inmates are likely to have been abused primarily by the males in their lives, but it should be noted that even female staff can employ supervisory tactics that backfire when used with female offenders.

In discussing these first two dimensions of difference between male and female inmates, demographic profile differences and different needs during incarceration, it is noteworthy that we have not made any references to the third dimension, *differences in personality*. This is important because we have already seen that there are big differences in the ways staff *perceive* the personalities and behaviors of incarcerated men and women in general. As it turns out, there is evidence to suggest that some of these perceived differences are real. For example, some researchers (Joesting, Jones, & Joesting, 1975; McKerracher, Street, & Segal, 1966) found women prisoners are more likely than male prisoners to engage in what is usually called "acting out" behaviors (e.g., extreme emotional outbursts). A higher level of emotionality is indeed a consistent theme among writers describing women prisoners, including higher levels of emotional attachment *between* female inmates than is usually found between male inmates (Giallombardo, 1966; Lekkerkerker, 1931; Ward & Kassebaum, 1965). This higher level of emotionality is perceived by correctional officers as problematic because "emotions displayed by the inmates may translate into hostility toward the officer" (Pollack, 1984).

It seems clear that there are many *real* differences between male and female offenders in prison that could translate into differences in required management and supervisory approaches. If we add the third dimension, differences in personality, it would seem that not only must the overall management of an institution be revised in certain significant ways to accommodate female offenders, but the day-to-day business of direct inmate supervision might need to be altered significantly in order for things to go as smoothly as possible.

SHOULD INMATE DIFFERENCES LEAD TO SPECIALIZED STAFF TRAINING?

In 2003 there were 213 state public and private correctional facilities in the United States that housed adult and juvenile female offenders only, plus another 309 state cogender facilities handling both male and female adult and juvenile offenders. Four additional female-only institutions are run by the Federal Bureau of Prisons, which also operates 22 cogender facilities (ACA, 2003). In short, at least 548 correctional institutions in the United States house female inmates, either alone or in conjunction with male inmates. This is a remarkable expansion of women's prisons if you consider that in 1996 there were only 68 female-only and 97 cogender correctional facilities in the United States (ACA, 1998). Of particular note is the spectacular increase in privately contracted facilities, particularly in the area of youth services and juvenile justice, the vast majority of which seem to be cogender.

While men still vastly outnumber women behind bars in the United States, the *number* of women incarcerated by the states and the federal government has increased at a much faster rate than did the number of men since the 1980s. This has resulted in most states now having record-high numbers of women prisoners in their custody. Prior to 1980, most states had only one separate women's prison facility—and some states did not even have that, continuing instead to house women in small separate units within larger men's prisons or in coeducational facilities, or even sending them to women's prisons in adjoining states. A few states still do not have female-only adult institutions (Alaska, Hawaii, Maine, North Dakota, and Vermont) but, due to the huge population growth of prisoners in the 1980s and 1990s, many states have now opened *multiple* women's institutions. By year-end 2003 there were over 101,000 women in state and federal prisons, with an average annual increase of 5% between 1995 and 2003 (compared to 3.3% for men) (Harrison & Beck, 2004). Indeed, by 2003 at least 21 states had two or more adult women's prisons, seven states had at least three adult female-only prisons, and another seven states had four or more female-only adult institutions (ACA, 2003). Most female-only adult correctional institutions today house hundreds of inmates each, though in 2003 the numbers ranged from as few as 32 female inmates in Wilmington, North Carolina, to as many as 3,095 in Chowchilla, California (ACA, 2003).

Most states added to their correctional workforce exponentially in the 1980s in the effort to keep pace with burgeoning prison populations, and thousands of correctional staff are now employed by these women's institutions and cogender facilities. Add to this the correctional officers in the thousands of jails, prerelease centers, work release centers, halfway houses, medical facilities, forestry camps, detention centers, and other facilities around the nation that house one or more women detainees, and the numbers of correctional officers affected by the management differences required for female versus male inmates is enormous.

Furthermore, the inmate population boom of the 1980s led to some remarkable and dramatic facilities changes. In some states, within the span of just a few years, facilities changed from housing males inmates only to housing co-correctional inmate populations, to then housing females only as inmate populations grew or shifted. This meant that correctional officers who were experienced in working with male inmates have sometimes found themselves suddenly supervising female offenders with little advanced preparation.

Given all the differences between male and female inmates noted above, we might expect that correctional systems would be concerned about providing specialized preparation to those correctional staff members assigned to work with female offenders. However, there seems to be little evidence of specialized training for correctional staff assigned to female facilities. The American Correctional Association recognized this in the mid-1980s when it noted that the "requirements and opportunities for staff development often overlook the needs of administration and staff for professional, on-going training in managing the female offender" (ACA, 1986, p. 29). Modern researchers on women in prison, likewise, have also noted the lack of specialized training for staff in women's prisons:

> Typically, state correctional systems have moved from an approach that isolates and differentiates the women's institution to an approach that alleges that all inmates and all prisons are the same in terms of rule, supplies, assignments and other factors. This latter approach is no more helpful than the benign neglect that previously characterized the central office's attention to facilities for women; women's prisons obviously have unique needs, different from men's institutions. (Pollack-Byrne, 1990, p. 115)

Of course, the counterargument to the claim that specialized training is needed for staff working in women's prisons is that regular correctional training is sufficient. That is, if the routine training given to new correctional officers includes training for the different supervisory requirements of female versus male inmates, then no specialized training would be needed for those assigned to women's institutions.

THE CONTENT OF ROUTINE CORRECTIONAL TRAINING

The idea of requiring any training *at all* for correctional officers to prepare them for their duties is not a very old one. The first correctional training school was begun in New York in 1930 by the Federal Bureau of Prisons (Schade, 1986). Both prior to and after that, the states apparently hired correctional officers directly into their jobs, with little or no formal training of any kind except that received on the job. Official reviewers and reform-minded critics of corrections often complained about the quality of the correctional staff, but they usually recommended remedies in the form of taking more care about *who* was hired—rather than expressing concern about what preparation was given to that individual *after* hiring.

Thus, for example, shortly after the Civil War, prison reformers Wines and Dwight (1867) set forth guidelines for the hiring of prison officers, in which they asserted that:

> Prison officers should be men of strict and uniform sobriety. . . . They should be men of mild temper, quiet manners, and pure conversation. . . . They should be men of decision and energy. . . . They should be men of humane and benevolent feelings. . . . They should be men having a sincere interest in those placed under their care. . . . They should be men of high moral principle, and distinguished by habits of industry, order and cleanliness. . . . They should be men possessing a knowledge of human nature in its various aspects and relations. . . . They should be men of sterling and incorruptible honesty. . . . They should be men of experience. . . . They must be men of a just and steadfast purpose, free from prejudice and partiality. . . . They should be men of untiring vigilance. . . . They should have a liking for the occupation in which they are employed. . . . Finally, prison officers should be men duly impressed with religious principles; men who fear God, and are in the habit, as the expression of that reverence, of attending the services of some religious body. (Wines & Dwight, 1867, pp. 120–122)

It is only after this long recitation about what kind of *men* corrections should seek to hire that Wines and Dwight provide a brief paragraph on *female* officers, about whom they recommend:

> The qualifications of female officers are, in many respects, the same as those of males. It is especially important, however, that female officers should be distinguished for modesty of demeanor, and the exercise of domestic virtues, and that they should possess that intimate knowledge of household employment, which will enable them to teach the ignorant and neglected female prisoners how to economize her means, so as to guard her from the temptations caused by waste and extravagance. (Wines & Dwight, 1867, pp. 123–24)

These are certainly descriptions of outstanding prospective employees. Such exemplary persons, both then and now, might possibly be attracted to high-paying high-prestige jobs. But what was the likelihood that corrections was able to attract large numbers of such inherently good and skilled workers in the 1800s—or could even do so now? Modern writers Hawkins and Alpert (1989) have provided a much more brutally frank description of a modern correctional officer's job:

> A candid job description for a correctional officer position would read something like this: Excellent employment opportunity for men and women who are willing to work eight-hour shifts at varying times (early morning, afternoon, and late nights) on a rotating basis. Applicants must enforce numerous rules with few guidelines. They must be willing to risk physical harm, psychological harassment, and endure the threat of inmate law suits, which could involve civil liability. They must be willing to spend eight hours each day among people who do not like them. They will not be allowed to fraternize with these people, but are expected to control as well as help them. Applicants must accept that they have little or no input into the rules they will be asked to enforce, not will they be privy to the policy rationale for these rules. They should realize that management will probably not listen to their complaints. Work superiors, located in a military chain of command, are likely to have a great deal of time invested in organizational rules and therefore will resist employee innovations. The person at the top of the chain of command is likely to be a political appointment, but applicants are not allowed to engage in political activity. Promotion is infrequent and opportunities for advancement in the organization are very limited. All applicants are considered

untrustworthy: frequent questioning and searches of private possessions are designed to reduce corruption. Applicants must give up some civil rights for employment to continue. Women and minority groups are encouraged to apply, but will be discriminated against once on the job. (Hawkins & Alpert, 1989, pp. 338–339)

This "job description" of a correctional officer is exaggerated, of course, but there is some evidence that persons who seek correctional employment are entering into an employment area which does *not* have much inherent attractiveness. For example, Smith (cited in Farmer, 1977, p. 239) found that the social position of the correctional officer had very little prestige with compared with other occupations or careers. This low prestige may be not so much a reflection of the low pay and minimal qualifications which corrections work has traditionally involved as it is a reflection of the *object* of that work: prison inmates. Jacobs and Retsky observed that the job of prison guard is not entirely unlike other guard jobs, except that

> bank guards and Secret Security Agents derive some measure of esteem from the objects they guard, while "close contacts with convicted felons seems morally profaning for the (prison) guard (p. 10)." (Cited in Farmer, 1977, p. 238)

There is ample evidence that the commitment to the job at the lower levels of correctional work is not generally very great and that the field suffers from relatively high turnover rates (Williamson, 1990, p. 79). This may be because of the lower prestige of the field and its less desirable working conditions. But it also may be because there is some evidence that a significant proportion of persons who enter correctional work do so out of *economic necessity* (Crouch, 1980; Shannon, 1987); in other words, most people do not enter correctional work out of a zeal to work with prisoners. Interestingly, the degree to which economic necessity plays a role in correctional recruitment may vary somewhat by gender. In at least one study, a much larger proportion of women indicated that they had sought correctional employment because they were interested in human service work ($f =$ 55%, $m = 14\%$) whereas males more frequently indicated that they took the job because there was not alternative work available to them ($m = 14\%, f = 3\%$) (Jurik & Halemba, 1984). Overall, however, it may be concluded that the dedication of correctional officers to their work varies greatly, and that there is little internal incentive to seek more difficult or challenging posts, such as assignment to women's prisons.

There has been little analysis of the training afforded to staff working in women's prisons. As of 1993, preservice correctional training in general in the United States varied from a minimum of two weeks (in Louisiana, North Dakota, and Wyoming) to a maximum of 16 weeks (only in Michigan), with the average being about $5\frac{1}{2}$ weeks (for 48 states that reported plus the Federal Bureau of Prisons) (Maquire & Pastore, 1994, pp. 101–107). What is the content of that training? Wicks (1980) has noted that the emphasis in recent decades has been on *standardizing* correctional training in the United States, so that there can be some assurance that all correctional officers have received basic training in certain skills and knowledge areas that are consistent with state policies and procedures. Shaver (1993) observed that training in Oklahoma, for example, consisted of 4 weeks of intensive, centralized group training of new recruits, followed by another three to five days of in-house training and orientation once new correctional officers arrived at their actual work site. However, "very little of this training is directly related to their new positions. Rather, the training focuses on the policies, rules, regulations and values of the correctional agency" (p. 122).

There is no reason to assume that Oklahoma is a training aberration in this regard. Shannon (1987) found that only 85% of his Ohio correctional officer respondents reported that they had received 40 hours of training prior to starting their position, though the ACA has stipulated that 40 hours of preservice training should be the *minimum*. Only 60% of Shannon's respondents indicated that they had received 120 hours of training during their first year on the job as required by the ACA. Even fewer (42%) indicated that they had received the required 40 hours of in-service training per year since starting their jobs (see Table 4).

When asked about the content of the training they had been given, Shannon's respondents indicated that the training they most frequently received had to do with firearms training, housing and body searches, contraband hunting, report writing, rules and regulations of the institution, self-defense training, key and tool control, riot control tactics, and CPR certification (Shannon, 1987, p. 174). In general, Shannon notes that:

TABLE 4   Specific Training Reportedly Received by Correctional Officers[a]

Subject	Percent
Firearms training	97
Housing and body searches	93
Contraband hunting	92
Training in report writing	88
Rules and regulations of the institution	85
Self-defense training	84
Key and tool control	78
Riot control tactics	67
Valid CPR certification	66
Legal authority training	64
Suicidal inmate recognition	62
Emergency prevention training	61
Techniques for protecting prison property	59
Inmate's rights training	57
Valid first-aid certification	56
How to behave if taken hostage	56
Radio communications	54
Identifying mental illness	52

[a]All other specific training was completed by less than half of respondents.

Source: Shannon (1987, p. 174).

> The officer's formal training consists primarily of instruction in the skills and mechanics of security procedures and the handling of inmates to maintain order and prevent trouble. The real learning (training) occurs on the job under inmate testing and manipulation attempts. (Shannon, 1987, p. 173)

Of course, it is after formal preservice training that the new correctional officer learns about and enters into the "officer subculture," which may well train the recruit somewhat differently than did the academy. For example, while the academy trains rookies in approved ways to handle inmates, the officer subculture "encourages officers to use intimidating behavior to establish authority over inmates" (Shannon, 1987, p. 173). It also provides working definitions of kinds of inmates the new correctional officer can expect to confront, and anecdotal evidence of what techniques work best with different kinds of inmates.

In short, while most academy training focuses on mechanical skills and operational procedures, the real "wisdom" about inmate handling comes from on-the-job inculcation into an officer subculture that may emphasize stereotypes and extreme examples. It is perhaps not at all surprising that such training leaves most correctional officers ill-prepared to deal with the unique needs and demands of working with female offenders in custody.

THE NEED FOR SPECIALIZED TRAINING FOR STAFF WORKING WITH FEMALE OFFENDERS

So far, we have seen that there are a variety of circumstances that combine to produce the widespread presence of the male inmate preference among correctional officers: the perceptions of and stereotypes about female inmates that are conveyed in the correctional officer subculture; the very real supervisory differences posed by the needs of female inmates compared to their male counterparts; and the limited and largely operations-oriented training given to officer recruits. All these conspire to virtually ensure that most correctional officers are somewhat biased against, and certainly unskilled in dealing with, female offenders in custody.

Little wonder, then, that so many correctional officers report unsatisfactory experiences in working with female offenders or, in the absence of any actual experience in female prisons, much anticipatory prejudice against such assignments. Little wonder, additionally, that women inmates continue to be viewed as more difficult to manage, since little (if any) routine training is aimed at helping correctional officers understand their female inmate charges or what supervisory techniques might be more effective with this population. And finally, little wonder that charges of sexual harassment and inappropriate behavior from correctional officers toward inmates has emerged in the 1990s as one of the more problematic features of managing female institutions. Many state correctional systems have found themselves facing such charges—either in the media or in the courtroom—from individual inmates, interest groups representing inmates, or the federal government.

Suffice it to say that confronting the problem of male inmate preference and all that it means *should* become a high priority of all correctional systems housing female offenders. The costs of defending the system against lawsuits and media reports are high. But there is little evidence that, absent media attacks or lawsuits, most correctional systems are taking preventive measures by providing appropriate specialized training to their correctional staff members in women's institutions. Though the costs of such specialized training would be comparatively modest, it appears that most correctional leaders still regard the male inmate preference as the norm, or an anecdotal curiosity with little effect on daily operations. Since their systems are always populated predominantly by male inmates, the fact that correctional officers overwhelmingly prefer duty with male inmates does not seem to be a problem. Those comparatively few correctional officers assigned to women's institutions, and their discontent with such duty, seems like a small problem in an ocean of correctional difficulties facing the modern correctional administrator. The result, however, is that those correctional staff members who *are* assigned to women's prisons continue to work with inmates about whom they hold highly negative perceptions and for whose management they have never been properly trained. If nothing else, it is these correctional officers and the female inmates they supervise who are the losers.

REFERENCES

ACOCA, L. (1998). Defusing the time bomb: Understanding and meeting the growing health care needs of incarcerating women in America. *Crime and Delinquency, 44*(1), 49–70.

AMERICAN CORRECTIONAL ASSOCIATION. (1986). *Public policy for corrections: A handbook for decision makers.* College Park, MD: Author.

AMERICAN CORRECTIONAL ASSOCIATION. (1990). *The female offender: What does the future hold?* Arlington, VA: Kirby Lithographic Company.

AMERICAN CORRECTIONAL ASSOCIATION. (1998). *Directory: Juvenile and adult correctional departments, institutions, agencies and paroling authorities, United States and Canada, 1997.* College Park, MD: Author.

AMERICAN CORRECTIONAL ASSOCIATION. (2003). *2003 directory: Adult and juvenile correctional departments, institutions, agencies and probation and paroling authorities* (64th ed.). Lanham, MD: Author.

ARNOLD, R. (1990). Processes of victimization and criminalization of black women. *Social Justice, 17*(3), 153–166.

BAINES, M., & ALDER, C. (1996). Are girls more difficult to work with? Youth workers' perspectives in juvenile justice and related areas. *Crime and Delinquency, 42*(3), 467–485.

BINKLEY-JACKSON, D., CARTER, V. L., & ROLISON, G. L. (1993). African-American women in prison. In B. R. Fletcher, L. D. Shaver, & D. G. Moon (Eds.), *Women prisoners: A forgotten population* (pp. 65–74). Westport, CT: Praeger.

BLOOM, B., OWEN, B., & COVINGTON, S. (2003, June). *Gender-responsive strategies: Research, practice, and guiding principles for women offenders* (NIC 018017). Washington, DC: National Institute of Corrections, U.S. Department of Justice.

BUREAU OF JUSTICE STATISTICS. (2001). *Mental health treatment in state prisons, 2000.* Washington, DC: U.S. Department of Justice.

CARLEN, P. (1983). *Women's imprisonment: A study in social control.* London: Routledge and Kegan Paul.

CENTER FOR SUBSTANCE ABUSE TREATMENT. (1997). *Substance abuse treatment for incarcerated offenders: Guide to promising practices.* Rockville, MD: U.S. Department of Health and Human Services.

CHESNEY-LIND, M., & RODRIGUEZ, N. (1983). Women under lock and key. *Prison Journal, 63*(2), 47–65.

CROUCH, B., & ALPERT, G. (1980). An exploration of the prison guards' attitudes toward correctional components. *International Journal of Offender Therapy.*

FARMER, R. E. (1977). Cynicism: A factor in corrections work. *Journal of Criminal Justice, 5,* 237–246.

FLETCHER, B. R., SHAVER, L. D., & MOON, D. G. (1993).*Women prisoners: A forgotten population.* Westport, CT: Praeger.

GIALLOMBARDO, R. (1966). *Society of women: A study of a women's prison.* New York: Wiley.

GILFUS, M. E. (1992). From victims to survivors to offenders: Women's routes of entry and immersion into street crime. *Women and Criminal Justice, 4*(1), 63–90.

GOETTING, A., & HOWSEN, R. M. (1983). Women in prison: A profile. *The Prison Journal, 63*(2), 27–46.

GREENFELD, L. A., & SNELL, T. L. (1999). *Women offenders.* Bureau of Justice Statistics Special Reports (NCJ 175688). Washington, DC: U.S. Department of Justice.

HARLOW, C. W (1999). *Prior abuse reported by inmates and probationers.* Bureau of Justice Statistics Selected Findings (NCJ 172879). Washington, DC: U.S. Government Printing Office.

HARRISON, P. M., & BECK, A. J. (2004, November). *Prisoners in 2003. Bureau of Justice Statistics Bulletin* (NCJ 205335). Washington, DC: U.S. Department of Justice.

HAWKINS, R., & ALPERT, G. P. (1989). *American prison systems: Punishment and justice.* Upper Saddle River, NJ: Prentice Hall.

IMMARIGEON, R. (1987a). Women in prison. *Journal of the National Prison Project, 11,* 1–5.

IMMARIGEON, R. (1987b). Few diversion programs are offered female offenders. *Journal of the National Prison Project, 12,* 9–11.

JAMES, D. J. (2004, July). *Profile of jail inmates, 2002.* Bureau of Justice Statistics Special Report (NCJ201932). Washington, DC: U.S. Government Printing Office.

JOESTING, J., JONES, N., & JOESTING, R. (1975). Male and female prison inmates' differences on MMPI scales and revised beta I.Q. *Psychological Reports, 37,* 471–474.

JURIK, N. (1985). Individual and organization determinants of correctional officer attitudes toward inmates. *Criminology, 23*(3), 523–539.

JURIK, N., & HALEMBA, G. J. (1984, Autumn). Gender, working conditions and job satisfaction of women in non-traditional occupations: Female correctional officers in men's prisons. *The Sociological Quarterly, 25,* 55–556.

KOBAN, L. (1983). Parent in prison: A comparative analysis of the effects of incarceration on the families of men and women. *Research in Law, Deviance and Social Control, 5,* 171–183.

LEKKERKERKER, E. (1931). *Reformatories for women in the United States.* Groningen, The Hague: J. B. Wolters.

MAQUIRE, K., & PASTORE, A. L. (Eds.). (1994). *Sourcebook of criminal justice statistics: 1993.* U.S. Department of Justice, Bureau of Justice Statistics. Washington, DC: U.S. Government Printing Office.

MAQUIRE, K., & PASTORE, A. L. (Eds.). (1997). *Sourcebook of criminal justice statistics: 1996.* U.S. Department of Justice, Bureau of Justice Statistics. Washington, DC: U.S. Government Printing Office.

MARUSCHAK, L. (2004). *HIV in prisons and jails, 2002.* Bureau of Justice Statistics Bulletin (NCJ 205333). Washington, DC: U.S. Government Printing Office.

McKERRACHER, D. W., STREET, D. R. K., & SEGAL, L. S. (1966). A comparison of the behavior problems presented by male and female subnormal offenders. *British Journal of Psychiatry, 112,* 891–899.

POLLACK, J. M. (1984). Women will be women: Correctional officers' perceptions of the emotionality of women inmates. *The Prison Journal, 64*(1), 84–91.

POLLACK, J. M. (1986). *Sex and supervision: Guarding male and female inmates.* New York: Greenwood Press.

Pollack-Byrne, J. M. (1990). *Women, prison and crime*. Pacific Grove, CA: Brooks/Cole.

Rafter, N. H. (1985). *Partial justice: Women in state prisons, 1800–1935*. Boston: Northeastern University Press.

Resnick, J., & Shaw, N. (1980). Prisoners of their sex: Health problems of incarcerated women. In I. P. Robbins (Ed.), *Prisoners' rights sourcebook* (pp. 319–413). New York: Clark Boardman.

Ross, R. R., & Fabiano, E. A. (1986). *Female offenders: Correctional afterthoughts*. Jefferson, NC: McFarland.

Sarri, R. (1987). Unequal protection under the law: Women and the criminal justice system. In J. Figueira-McDonough & R. Sarri (Eds.), *The trapped woman: Catch-22 in deviance and control* (pp. 55–64). Newbury Park, CA: Sage.

Sargent, E., Marcus-Mendoza, S., & Yu, Chong Ho. (1993). Abuse and the woman prisoner. In B. R. Fletcher, L. D. Shaver, & D. G. Moon (Eds.), *Women prisoners: A forgotten population* (pp. 55–64). Westport, CT: Praeger.

Schade, T. (1986). Prison officer training in the United States: The legacy of Jesse O. Stutsman. *Federal Probation, 50*(4), 40–46.

Shannon, M. J. (1987, April). Officer training: Is enough being done? *Corrections Today, 49,* 172–175.

Shaver, L. D. (1993). The relationship between language culture and recidivism among women offenders. In B. R. Fletcher, L. D. Shaver, & D. G. Moon (Eds.), *Women prisoners: A forgotten population*. Westport, CT: Praeger.

Turnbo, C. (1993). Differences that make a difference: Managing a women's correctional institution. In American Correctional Association, *Female offenders: Meeting the needs of a neglected population* (pp. 12–16). Laurel, MD: American Correctional Association.

Ward, D. A., & Kassebaum, G. G. (1965). *Women's prison: Sex and social structure*. Chicago: Aldine.

Wicks, R. J. (1980). *Guard! Society's professional prisoner*. Houston, TX: Gulf.

Wines, E. C., & Dwight, T. W. (1867). *Report on the prisons and reformatories of the United States and Canada*. Albany, NY: Van Benthuysen and Sons Steam Printing House. Reprinted by AMS Press Inc., New York, 1973.

43

Women on the Bench: Mavericks, Peacemakers, or Something Else?

Research Questions, Issues, and Suggestions

Susan L. Miller and Michelle L. Meloy

Judicial sentencing is the outcome of a cumulative process reflecting many earlier decisions and stages. One question raised by researchers is whether or not male and female judges bring different perspectives and methods of case resolution to the bench. Most of the research conducted on sentencing outcomes thus far has been quantitative, and as such, may mask subtle distinctions between how male and female judges operate. What may be needed in studying gender and judicial decision making, then, is a deeper, qualitative examination of the social context of the judiciary through an exploration of individual attitudes of female judges and their role orientations, as well as of the organizational/social factors that affect them. There are two related parts to this chapter: First, we examine what we know about women judges in general according to studies conducted by state and federal gender task forces and related literature; and second, we explore what "woman judge" means and what this experience implies as described by a sample of women judges.

Despite the unprecedented numbers of women judges at the local, state, and federal level today, including two U.S. Supreme Court justices, women on the bench remain a token percentage of the judiciary. In 2004, 22 percent of state appellate court justices were women, and 10 to 15 percent of federal judgeships are currently held by women[1] (Neubauer, 2002). For most elective state judiciary positions, women had to wait until after passage of the Nineteenth Amendment to be eligible (Cook, 1978; Feinman, 1986). The first attorney-trained woman in the United States was elected to a state trial court (Ohio) in 1920, and the first woman was appointed to the federal bench in 1934. Even after that, the numbers remained small and it was not until 1979 that all states had at least one attorney-trained woman on their courts (Berkson, 1981–1982). For the state in which our sample of female judges was selected, the number of female attorney-judges increased from 8 in 1980 to 20 in 1990.

The chapter begins with an overview of the state and federal gender task force findings and an examination of factors and circumstances that have shaped many of the contemporary beliefs, behaviors, and working environments of women judges. In particular, we explore the ramifications of a male-dominated justice profession for women who join, the dynamics of personal and professional conflicts, and gender-related issues in judicial decision making. Within this broader framework, we also specifically examine women's own words about their judicial experiences and actions.

GENDER TASK FORCES

Fighting the war against gender bias is nothing new for women, and the battles won have afforded them the right to vote, to enter traditionally male-dominated occupations, and lifted legal prohibitions against sex-based discrimination. Although progress has been made on many fronts, the courts and the legal profession remain one of the most impervious bastions of patriarchy and bias. If women do not yet enjoy fair and equitable treatment under the law and in the justice system, their struggles and triumphs remain "bittersweet and incomplete" (Kearney & Sellers, 1996, p. 586).

Beginning in 1983, under the urging of the National Organization for Women's Judicial Educational Program, publication of the first gender task force (New Jersey Task Force on Women and the Courts) was released. To date, more than 40 states and 9 of the 13 federal circuits have established task forces to study the degree to which gender bias exists within the court system and to propose ways of eliminating it. The primary questions the task forces sought to answer include: Is justice gender blind? Is equal treatment extended to all players? Does the context in which women fight against injustices ironically engage in its own discriminatory practices?

Generally, the task force findings can be categorized into two groups. The first dealt with gender bias as a constant factor in the daily operations of the courtroom and in the judicial decision-making process. In other words, the gender task forces of the state and federal judiciary closely examined how the perceptions of and about women (i.e., as jurors, witnesses, attorneys, judges, plaintiffs, defendants, etc.) affect not only women's experience in the courtroom but potentially the legal outcome as well. The second category looked at how gender bias affected the occupational positions available to women within the legal profession and court administration. Stated differently, the gender task forces investigated the extent to which professions within judicial circles remained segregated by gender (Kearney & Sellers, 1997).

Time and again, the reports cited the "pervasiveness" of gender bias in the judiciary specifically, in regard to issues of domestic violence, divorce economics, child custody, courtroom dynamics (Riger, Foster-Fishman, Nelson-Kuna, & Curran, 1995), sexual harassment and discrimination, occupational and pay range segregation, haphazard commitment to affirmative action principles, and employee benefit packages that are insensitive to the needs of women (Kearney & Sellers, 1997, p. 8). Therefore, rather than being a repository of justice and fairness, the courts, at times, engage in their own form of discrimination (Resnik, 1996).

Traditionally, the courts have viewed women in stereotypical fashion. For instance, according to the task force findings, many courts continue to believe that women are partially, if not primarily, responsible for their own domestic violence and sexual harassment victimization and also prejudge the type of juror or witness a woman will be based solely on her gender. Additionally, women's performance as mothers and wives are critiqued by the courts according to conventional expectations. These images of women remain apparent today, in that the "sex of females somehow defines their role and nature" (Kearney & Sellers, 1996, p. 9).

Gender stereotypes may help explain the courtroom insensitivity male professionals exhibit toward female professionals. The task force reports revealed a consistent pattern: women employed by the court, including those sitting on the bench, stated that men addressed them by terms of endearment (i.e., honey, sweetheart, dear), and subjected women to jokes, at their own expense, emphasizing gender and sexuality (Rosenberg, Perlstadt, & Phillips, 1993). Female lawyers and judges were often referred to by their first name, whereas men of equal or lower stature were called "your honor" or "counselor" (Kearney & Sellers, 1997, p. 10). Therefore, women are seen as women, first and foremost, regardless of their formal or actual powers. "That women judges and lawyers who possess the privilege of formal authority can still be subjected to minor and major harassment bears testament to the pervasive modes by which [male] domination continues" (Resnik, 1996, p. 972).

Gender bias and sexism in the courts are enduring despite the fact that women enter law school at nearly the same rate as those of their male counterparts, come from similar backgrounds, attend the same law programs, and perform equally well in their academic endeavors. However, the similarities between female and male lawyers end after graduation. Female lawyers are overrepresented in lower-prestige ranks (government, legal aid, and public defender work), and males are overrepresented in the higher-prestige positions (large law firms and the judiciary) (Coontz, 1995). The higher echelons of the court remain dominated by white men (Resnik, 1996). Unfortunately, this trend does not appear to be dissipating, and law, as an occupation, remains highly stratified by gender. For instance, one study found that as more women enter the profession, the career gap between women and men deepened (Tienda, Smith, & Ortiz, 1987).

This career gap is true not only for attorneys but also for other female court employees. Court personnel systems are plagued by rampant gender bias, with some states (Rhode Island, Connecticut, Utah, Colorado, and Massachusetts) reporting upward of 95 percent of female court personnel sharing in the lowest seven pay grades and none in the top seven. Men dominate key administrative positions throughout the court system, whereas the low-paying "clerical ghetto" is reserved, almost exclusively, for women (Kearney & Sellers, 1996).

The task force reports have made a significant impact on the administration of justice at the state and federal level and offer many recommendations to eliminate gender bias in the courts. Several states have published follow-up reports that track the court's progress in implementing change.[2] Some examples of these judicial revisions are: education and training highlighting gender bias, new sexual harassment policies, revamped personnel procedures designed to include family-sensitive measures for court employees and witnesses, increased emphasis on affirmative action procedures to encourage the recruitment of minorities and women, and the elimination of gender bias terminology in legal statutes and court documents. Some jurisdictions have also initiated "court watching programs" to serve as overseers of gender bias in courtrooms (Kearney & Sellers, 1996). However, perhaps the single greatest achievement of the task force movement has been its ability to make women's voices heard and to illustrate that women suffer from gender bias in courts and the legal system differently than men (Resnik, 1996). We turn now to an overview of the organizational and professional barriers that women face when entering the legal and judicial professions.

Breaking into All-Male Domains: Women's Entrance into the Criminal Justice Profession

The far-reaching influence of "separate spheres" mentality (which divided the world into the public sphere of economic and intellectual pursuits for men, and the private sphere of [supposedly] tranquil domesticity for women) confined women—both perceptually and structurally—to differential utilization in the labor market (Flynn, 1982). Rigid gender-role expectations, socialization practices, and institutionalized exclusionary practices operate to perpetuate the dearth of job opportunities for women in the criminal justice and legal fields, with the notable exception of supportive roles such as staff positions. These practices were eventually challenged by women who sought entrance into policing, corrections, and the courts in the 1970s (see Belknap, 1991; Martin, 1980; Price & Sokoloff, 1995; Zimmer, 1986).

Even when successful, as in the past 20 years, women often have found that once inside, their roles and advancement opportunities are severely curtailed because of stereotypes, differently applied performance and evaluation standards, and lack of access to the "old boys' network" (see Epstein, Saute, Oglensky, & Gever, 1995; Schafran, 1987). "Although these problems are not peculiar to criminal justice, they are keenly felt among women in this area, perhaps because crime and crime control are so closely associated with traditionally 'masculine' values" (Flynn, 1982, p. 344). Masculine traits, such as power, force, authority, and aggressiveness, are seen as belonging only to men and as the central qualifications for professions such as police officers, lawyers, judges, and correctional officers, and therefore used to justify maintaining them as male-only domains: "The link between masculinity and criminal justice is so tightly bound that we may say it is true not merely that only men can be crime fighters, but even that to be a crime fighter means to be a man" (Wilson, 1982, p. 361). Some scholars suggest, however, that the most resistance to admitting women to positions of traditional male power has been by the courts due to the law degree requirement (Baunach & Rafter, 1982). Mandating additional educational credentials—when structural access to law schools has not been equal for men and women until recently—exacerbates an already lopsided gatekeeping process. Nowhere is women's underrepresentation more glaring than in the courts (Githens, 1995).

Access to the Old Boys' Network and Gatekeeping of Political Power

There is an inclination on the part of male gatekeepers to maintain judicial selection criteria that favor men. For instance, the American Bar Association embraces career paths that are typically male dominated. Older, wealthy, corporate attorneys are awarded high judicial selection ratings at the expense of women who are less likely to share similar background characteristics, career patterns, and political activism (Beiner, 1999; Githens, 1995). "No doubt the key to judicial selection lies in the political system. Since federal and state bar associations exert substantial influence over judicial appointments, it is significant that women are largely excluded from the boards of governors of bar associations and from executive positions within these organizations. Rather, political party leaders who slate judicial candidates tend to follow value systems that invariably favor the selection of male candidates" (Flynn, 1982, p. 319).

Criminal justice agencies generally are regarded as "bastions of classical male chauvinism which operate in a variety of unspoken ways to effectively exclude women" (Lamber & Streibe, 1974; see also Martin & Jurik, 1996). One way that antiwomen attitudes emerge is through the operating stereotypical assumption that the "male" characteristics of brute force, physical prowess, and toughness are the desirable characteristics of the job. These stereotypical characteristics are emphasized in the courts as well: Women are viewed as not being tough, analytical, or unemotional enough to function successfully as attorneys, or make the hard decisions that judges face (Merlo & Pollock, 1995).

Another way that such attitudes emerge is through development of the "all-male clubhouse," where "[i]n such work environments, participants often value the exclusivity of totally male companionship as a desirable goal in itself" (Wilson, 1982, p. 366). The process is informal, with old boys' networks established through which favors are exchanged, barriers to inclusion are constructed, and bonding among the dominant male players is facilitated (Farr, 1988). Socializing and other informal interactions with colleagues contribute to a more satisfying working environment. Women are typically more isolated than men in the criminal justice profession, given the scarcity of female colleagues. This isolation is exacerbated for women occupying high positions in their professions, such as judgeships (Merlo & Pollock, 1995). Apart from the job morale/satisfaction issue, informal exchanges with colleagues also offer opportunities to learn important job-related information. Women become disadvantaged if they are excluded from these: "[I]f you don't sit down and talk with your colleagues, you miss an awful lot of information: What's going on? What bills are pending in the legislature? Who's going to be the next director or something or other? If you just go about your business, you'll be the only one who doesn't know that something critical is about to happen and you'll look foolish because you ask stupid questions. It's a big dilemma" (Baunach & Rafter, 1982, pp. 351–352).

Unfortunately, despite growth in the numbers of women entering criminal justice professions today, in the decade and a half since these early studies were conducted, not much has changed in the restructuring of gendered patterns in male-dominated organizations (Belknap, 1996; Martin & Jurik, 1996; Messerschmidt, 1993; Moyer, 1992).

LISTENING TO THE WORDS OF FEMALE JUDGES

In this section we explore the perceptions and experiences of a small sample of female judges. A total of 20 active female judges were identified in 1990 using state bar association information on all attorney-judgeships in any capacity (civil, criminal, administrative, appellate, etc.) in the state under investigation.[3]

These 20 female judges represent 8.4 percent of the available attorney-judgeships in the state. Although all 20 judges were invited to participate by responding to a written survey and to in-depth interviews, only five judges comprised the final sample.[4] The sample of judges who participated include an illustrious group: an appellate court judge, two district court judges, and two circuit court judges, some of whom hold high-ranking positions in the state bar association. We explored judges' demographic characteristics, educational experiences, aspects of their private lives, political and legal philosophies, and other attitudes concerning the intersection of their personal and professional lives.

The judges are all white, range in age from 41 to 68, represent various religious orientations, are either currently married or were married, and have children. In addition, the judges come from families steeped in the legal professions, which may play a role in facilitating the women's interest in law. This type of familial influence may be typical of the women who headed for higher education before the great changes of the 1970s.

Parents, teachers, and Eleanor Roosevelt were most often cited as people who served as role models for the participants as they were growing up. However, when asked specifically about who the role models were who encouraged and supported their decision to enter law school, those most often mentioned were male family members, male bosses, and male lawyers and judges. Despite current statistics indicating that 40 to 50 percent of all students enrolled in law schools are women, the judges in this sample remember the numbers of women in their graduating law school class (between the years of 1951 and 1975) never exceeding more than 10 percent. Survey responses indicate that none of these judges encountered a female law professor or advisor. Male classmates and male professors gave no support or only moderate support. For instance, one respondent was asked while in law school why she was taking up a chair that "rightly" belonged to a male.

All of the judges self-identified as feminists, Democrats, and liberal in philosophy. The political or social causes in which they indicated the most interest include women's rights, domestic violence, gender bias in the courts, women in the law, and financial problems experienced by economically dependent spouses. We focus on three areas revealed as significant to the judges: first, we examine the women's entrance process into the judiciary. Next, we explore the intricacies involved in balancing public and private lives and the isolating effects of the bench. Finally, we examine the judges' own perceptions of how being female might affect judicial decision making as well as their opinion on criminal justice/legal issues.

Impressions of the Gatekeeping Process

The judges were asked if they faced any gender-related difficulties in becoming a judge (including earlier phases of their legal careers) and whether or not their access to the bench was limited in any way.[5] All judges indicated that they faced discrimination; actions addressing these instances of discrimination, however, were rarely taken because of the possibility of jeopardizing one's future. Several were also unwilling to risk financial security by challenging such discrimination. One judge said she took no action "although I could have. I knew it would ruin my reputation if I did." Another judge said: "Depending on the circumstances, I would ignore it or respond with humor or challenge the treatment." Still another judge said that her strategy was to find a different job. These discriminatory experiences are confirmed by the findings of the state committee formed to study gender bias in the courts. Specifically, the committee found that 13 percent of the male attorneys, 20 percent of the female attorneys, 15 percent of the male judges, and 69 percent of the female judges responded that they were aware of gender bias in the selection process.[6]

In contrast to the obstacles identified that curtailed or discouraged women from pursuing the bench, judges were also asked to identify the specific factors that helped them to become judges and what kinds of support or reactions they received from their male colleagues:

> First, a plan. The plan was to cultivate the Judicial Nominating Committee, place myself in a position of prominence, in continuing legal education and in Bar Association and cultivate the person best known to have the Governor's ear. (Judge A)

> Motherhood! Of course, being a Master because it was a courtroom situation; also, being the first woman Bar president, having worked around the judges for years, political activities, affiliations with individuals and groups. (Judge E)

> I always knew that they did not want the women getting, you know, these positions. But, they were always very cordial. . . . I find that the younger lawyers (when I say younger I mean in their 40s and younger) don't have, I don't think, the hang-ups as much. You know, they went through law school together, accept women, and are just used to women being in everything they do and it's just a very normal thing. But [the older men] are falling back and re-grouping. In other words, the women have a very tough time. . . . Every time a woman tried to get on the Circuit Court, they kind of close forces and really resist because you're getting to the top of the pinnacle, see, and they're very afraid that they're going to lose their stronghold. Gender bias is still there. We're breaking down the barriers, you know, it takes time. I see these young women coming on, 35, 38 years old, you know, it's going to be a different world for them as they go through, I think. (Judge C)

These statements demonstrate that the women are "savvy" to the political networking process even if their access to this network is more restricted than members of the male political in-group. Overall, three of the judges believed that their gender played a role to get them on the bench because "those in power" finally agreed to consider women and began to search deliberately for qualified female candidates. In fact, the state committee explicitly recognized the harm created when the number of female appointments were limited: It "reinforces the discriminatory environment women face" (based on the state's Special Joint Committee, 1989), and this recognition may have stimulated judicial nominations of female candidates.[7]

Reconciliation of Personal and Public Lives and the Isolating Effects of the Bench

The judges discussed at length the difficulties in juggling and combining career and family roles. Without prompting, the judges indicated that motherhood was one of the best preparatory jobs they could have experienced before becoming a judge. The judges repeatedly stressed that "motherhood" prepared them best for the bench, for it taught them "to be patient, to listen, to be firm, and to be fair." One judge said:

> I think that being a mother has got to be a good background for being a judge. You do a lot of decision-making when you're raising a family—all the time. I raised a family from a desk.

Also, at the dinner table, when you're trying to find out something, you learn never to act surprised. You learn skills that are very, very useful on the bench. (Judge C)

Similarly, being a "working mother" helped the following judge to appreciate the dilemmas that many women face when balancing family and professional responsibilities.

Child care problems. I am certainly very sympathetic to child care problems. And I've had women write to me thanking me for understanding that they have to go, for example, at 5:00 pm because they have to have their kids picked up by 5:30 pm and they've gone in front of other judges who don't understand. And I understand that, and I would never make a lawyer who couldn't stay for those reasons really stay. I'm almost shocked, this is the 21st century, I mean, we've got to get in line here. Not everybody can afford care in the house and they don't choose that method and kids need to be dealt with and it's a societal issue. So, in that respect, I certainly think my gender and experience as a working mother have played a big role. . . . I've had people thank me profusely and I think other magistrates they wouldn't even ask, but they somehow know they can ask me. (Judge C)

The judges were also queried about whether they found their positions socially isolating as well as the reaction they received from strangers upon discovering their occupation. The judges responded as follows:

The black robe is isolating. . . . Reactions I received from others? Surprise. You go into a group with a man and someone will say you know Judge _____. They will invariably look at the man and shake his hand. (Judge A)

I feel less isolated because there is fairly good representation of women and blacks. But I do feel isolated from my former lawyer friends and bar associate friends. People are standoffish and reserved about what they say in my presence. . . . Some men are disrespectful or don't show deference. They are usually litigants. Some lawyers make inappropriate jokes to ingratiate themselves. (Judge B)

Isolated? Yes. Appearance of impropriety rules mandate isolation; only lawyers you know have no chance of appearing before you can you see socially on a court day (e.g., lunch!). Reaction from others? Surprise, dismay, respect. . . . What I enjoy least about being a judge is the isolation from other lawyers; isolation from my friends, particularly lawyers. (Judge D)

This isolation may be related to both professional position and gender. Increased professional envy of female judges by their male colleagues may also be a factor related to women's isolation.

Gender-Related Attitudes and Justice-Based Philosophies

The judges were asked to discuss a variety of topics related to gender, such as: Does being a woman play a role in decision making? Do women judges impose harsher sentences to overcompensate for any stereotype that women are more lenient? The judges explicitly acknowledged that being a woman did play a positive role in how they responded to some cases. The judges generally felt that they behaved more patiently, more humanely, and possessed the ability to admit when they don't always have all the answers. These traits were not perceived as weaknesses, however, but as positive skills and strengths that women judges bring to the bench to complement their legal knowledge and professional experiences.

> We're all a product of who we are, and I think there's a difference somehow in the way we do our jobs as judges. I'm not unhappy, as being perceived to be reasonable, I think it's what I really am. I am quite willing to admit when I don't know the answer. I don't feel hung up on not being able to admit that. I don't feel I have to pretend that I know everything. (Judge C)

> I think any woman has an empathy for a woman that comes before her who has been beaten. I think that we can relate to what this woman is going through; how embarrassed she is to stand up in front of the world and talk about being beaten by her husband. . . . I feel like my gender helps me a lot in criminal cases; you have these young people who come before you, you know, first time offenders, I look at them, I see my children, or their friends. I'm sure men have their skills and I think women look at things—we make just as good decisions, but, many times we're not as objective as the men because we have that emotional quotient that comes in there just naturally. It gives us a different view. You know, I think we all come up with the same decision at the end, but we come to it from a different way. (Judge E)

> I do sometimes have a reflection . . . that I am being tough because I don't want to be perceived as being soft and I try to examine whether that is what I am doing and I usually decide that it is not. I enumerate the reasons for my sentence. I write down what the sentence is and the basis. But I'm just giving myself a margin of error and I'm suggesting that I don't think we know ourselves absolutely and that there is a possibility that sometimes that concern about how others perceive us is more weighty than I think it is. But I believe and I hope that generally my sentences are fair and are based on objective reasons and not on any fear that I have on how people will perceive me. (Judge B)

During the in-depth interviews, judges responded to a variety of questions pertaining directly to issues of law that affect women. Time after time, the judges responded that although gender should not play a role, nonetheless, it might. They expressed that women judges may be able to empathize more, particularly with female victims. Actions by male judges, on the other hand, particularly the ones who continue to operate within a historical and stereotypical context of victim blaming when facing violent crimes committed by men against women, might reflect their own (male) assumptions and experiences in a culture that often trivializes women's experiences and victimizations. For instance, the women were asked if they believed that it makes a difference for male judges or female judges to preside over rape cases.

> I don't know. I would hope not. I would hope that any judge would be able to look at the evidence fairly and impartially and direct the jury in the same way. It's not as much of an issue if you realize that 99 percent of the time rape cases are going to be tried by a jury. And, a jury is made up, generally, of both men and women and we assume that all members of that jury will decide the case fairly and impartially according to the evidence presented. If we can assume that in laypeople, why should we not assume that of judges who are not only trained in the law, but through their experience as judges, expected to behave in a fair and impartial manner? (Judge D)

> Whether it does or not, I don't know. I suppose that the reality is I suppose on some level, it's probably even on a subconscious level more frightening for a female because you can imagine it happening to yourself. (Judge C)

Yes I do. Now there again, there are of course I think our new breed of males may be a little different, but so many men I've heard them say "oh, she asked for it," or "what's the big deal" and things like that. I don't know that the men have caught on yet that rape is such a violent act, it's not really a sexy act; it's an act of violence against the woman. . . . I can only tell you of how I can translate these into domestic violence cases that we hear all the time and some of my own colleagues, some of the comments they make, make me realize how insensitive they are. You know, I've even heard them say [she pretends to sound like a man while saying this], "well, you know, women like to be roughed up," and "you don't understand—a lot of women like that." Until they get away from that attitude, until they realize, then, we have a problem. (Judge E)

Domestic violence had been earlier identified as an area in which all of the judges expressed strong interests. The judges focused on the enforcement aspect, reflecting the trend to arrest batterers rather than relying on alternatives to law enforcement, such as separation, and mediation. The female judges' responses sharply contradicted empirical research that has shown in the past that the male judiciary has not treated domestic violence cases with any more seriousness than other players in the criminal justice system (i.e., police and prosecutors) (see Dobash & Dobash, 1992; Price & Sokoloff, 1995).

Well, it depends on the circumstances. I think that the arrest option must be available to the victim. In other words, we have fought for many years now to finally get a law on the books that requires an officer to make the arrest and that permits such cases to be brought into criminal court in a manner that's workable and effective. That's not to say that there aren't other alternatives, or that other alternatives aren't appropriate in many cases. But sometimes, nothing short of arrest is going to work. And I think that that has to absolutely be available. (Judge A)

If someone has committed an act of domestic violence or if the victim has legitimate reasons of being in imminent danger or fear of imminent danger, then absolutely—we can't find out later that we should have had a warrant. . . . If I have a domestic violence case on my docket and I put someone on probation and an order as a condition he has to move or stay away from the victim, not threaten, intimidate, harass or annoy.

If I get a call, I don't take a chance. We've learned, I think, we have to make sure. I think, too, too many times these cases are not taken seriously, and people are really injured. (Judge E)

I have for years felt that it was important that victims of those kinds of crime be treated like victims of other crimes. I don't think just because it's between people who know one another that the option shouldn't be available. . . . But I think that the option of an arrest and a trial and conviction is one that ought to be accessible to victims of domestic violence. And it ought to be used. (Judge B)

Overall, our interview data reveal a marked difference in judges' philosophies about gender-crime issues that may be atypical of traditional male judicial attitudes. (For in-depth discussions of feminist jurisprudence related to gender differences in philosophical orientations, see Fineman & Thomadsen, 1991; Frug, 1992; Hoff, 1991). For years, advocates of women's rights, lawyers, and others have opposed and challenged the manner in which the criminal justice and legal systems treat female victims of violent crimes committed by male offenders. The extant literature demonstrates that the enforcers (police), interpreters (lawyers and judges), and punishers (corrections) are primarily male and have been socialized and trained to believe assumptions and expectations about appropriate gender roles in society (Price & Sokoloff, 1995; Stanko, 1985). The judges in this sample seem to recognize the results of this institutionalized and systemic sexism: victim blaming and differential treatment of women. Part of this heightened understanding is shaped by their own experiences.

In summary, the judges' responses indicate the salience of the role that gender plays not only in the dynamics of specific crimes but also in the responses to these crimes by members of our social and legal institutions (Allen & Wall, 1993; "Different Voices," 1990; Merlo & Pollock, 1995). These beliefs are consistent with findings revealed in research on state supreme court justices which suggested that female judges tend to have a "pro-woman" stance on a large range of issues that directly affect women and often vote against the male majority on matters related to sex discrimination, sexual conduct and abuse, medical malpractice, and property settlements (Allen & Wall, 1987, 1993). The data in this series of research indicated that female judges held steadfast to their beliefs when it came to expanding women's rights, even in the face of opposition from the majority of the court (Allen & Wall, 1993). Future research could explore whether or not judges respond to consciousness raising about general social problems identified by society at large, or whether judges highlight specific issues because of their personal backgrounds, experience, and world views (see Tobias, 1990, 1991).

DISCUSSION AND CONCLUSIONS

In this chapter we explored women judges in light of the gender task force findings as well as offered insight into the way that women judges view themselves within social and judicial contexts. For the component relating to women judges, the depth and richness of the interview data, despite its small sample size, provides more detailed information than that typically collected by close-ended survey instruments. The judges describe their own experiences and perceptions, which serves as a starting point in refining questions that should also be asked of male judges in future comparative studies, as well as providing a complementary data set to quantitative research exploring sentencing decisions and gender.[8]

Most prior research that has identified gender-related differences among judges has focused exclusively on the types of sentences they impose. This kind of research hides the importance of background factors and experiences that shape one's world views and also ignores differences in the social construction of gender roles and expectations in our society. Gender alone may not exert significant influences on sentencing decisions per se, but the different experiences and philosophies that men and women have create a contextualized construct that may exert distinctions in judicial decision making (Davis, 1992–1993; Rush, 1993; Sherry, 1986; West, 1991). The differences that men and women may bring to the bench typically remain unacknowledged because they contradict the model of the "impartial" arbiter. The information gleaned from the judges' voices here lend support to hopes that women's "emphasis on connection and contextuality might similarly transform law" (Sherry, 1986, p. 165), as well as to hopes of interrupting gender bias operating against women in the courts.

The judicial gender task forces succeeded in prioritizing the issue of gender bias at the state and federal levels. The reports and follow-up studies generated by this movement emphasize women's experiences in the court system and legal profession and portray how these experiences differ by gender. Collectively, the task force findings have demanded that the "halls of justice" take judicial notice of the problems created by gender discrimination within its courtrooms, administrative organizations, and the legal profession as well as validating the perceptions of women (Resnik, 1996, p. 963).

For the women judges interviewed here, several important findings emerge. First, the voices of the women judges indicate that although they experience multiple obligations, they have succeeded in reconciling these diverse role-strain pressures. The judges have reconceptualized the "traditional" caretaking role of motherhood to be one that offers excellent preparation for the bench. This interpretation differs greatly from "male" attributes of detachment and autonomy because it explicitly recognizes the benefits of familial and intimate experiences (Anleu, 1995).[9] This kind of characterization permits women judges to use their conventional sexual roles to claim legitimacy in their nontraditional career choice.

The women assert that they have been successful at negotiating and balancing their personal and professional obligations. In fact, by imbuing women's traditional female roles with honor, and insisting that these attributes are the reason for their greater clarity of judicial vision, the women judges present themselves as innovative mavericks who are more sensitive to situations of personal, familial, and/or economic injustice.

A second important finding that emerged concerns the judges' explicit perceptions about how they believe that being a woman contributes to their decision making. Although the judges are quick to emphasize that their decisions are fair, equal, strict, and just, they recognize that being female may bring a uniquely feminine understanding to the situation. The judges interviewed in this study stressed that they believe that both male and female judges ultimately reach the same legal conclusion but that they follow different paths to get there—paths that are indeed related to gender.[10] The judges describe their judicial style as patient, empathic, reasonable, with a willingness and openness to hear all sides, and they recognize that these characteristics may be misperceived or misunderstood by others as indicating that they are lenient or coddle criminals (i.e., are "soft" on crime). The judges, however, insisted that this was not the case. Their rulings were simply shaped by different understandings of the situations and were enhanced by these understandings, not harmed or weakened. It is likely that defendants and victims felt that they were treated with more respect because of the judges' demeanor and style, regardless of case outcome. In fact, other research suggests that offenders treated with more respect perceive greater levels of procedural justice and satisfaction (Paternoster, Brame, Bachman, & Sherman, 1997). Nowhere are these unique understandings more apparent than when we examine the judges' opinions concerning women's rights. Their willingness to resist assimilation pressures to adopt male professional norms when confronting women's issues is noteworthy. Unlike the younger "careerist" women lawyers studied by Rosenberg, Perlstadt, and Phillips (1990), who rejected feminist objectives and labels and viewed gender as "inconsequential to their careers," the women judges in this study self-labeled as feminists and endorsed the centrality of gender and its role in shaping legal discourse and judicial action.[11]

Similar to the task force findings, the judges in our sample believed that the sexist comments and actions they experienced did contribute to an inhospitable working environment throughout their legal and judicial careers. They also described feeling isolated and alienated from males in the field as well as from other lawyers and judges. These working conditions may reflect the consequences of being treated as tokens due to their scarcity in numbers and heightened visibility, so that their "non-achievement characteristics . . . eclipse performance" (MacCorquodale & Jensen, 1993, p. 583). As such, these findings echo those of Rosenberg et al. (1993) in their research on sexist work experiences of women lawyers: Gender disparagement and sexual harassment are manifestations of "gendered systems that maintain and reinforce inequalities between men and women on the job" (p. 415).

By bringing their personal and professional experiences into the courtroom, the women revealed that they were able to dispense justice with a gentleness as well as a firmness that belied their own imaginings and expectations of a more humane courtroom setting. In fact, these views are consistent with findings reported in other studies which demonstrate that women judges opt for more participatory management styles, in contrast to men's preference for more hierarchical courtroom styles, and that women judges are more likely to acknowledge others' emotions and fears than are male judges (Martin, 1990). Although quantitative studies may demonstrate that female judges' sentencing outcomes could be comparable or dissimilar to male judges' outcomes, the gendered paths that these follow—paths that are strikingly apparent in qualitative research, yet masked in statistical analyses—are distinctly different. Furthermore, an analysis of the task force findings provides insight into the "gendered machinery" of the court system and complements the interviews of the female judges. Hearing the voices of women and the nature of their thinking and experiences offers a much richer context in which to explore the judicial process.

POSTSCRIPT

As of this writing, a new Supreme Court justice sits on the bench, John Roberts. Justice Sandra Day O'Connor has retired and we await word on her replacement. The question will be how the makeup of the Supreme Court will impact women.

N O T E S

1. According to the National Center for State Courts, there are no current hard data on the percentage of female judges at the state trial level (personal communication, 2001). Furthermore, the 1995 data cited here on the percentage of women justices serving at the federal level represent the most accurate information available. However, since these statistics are not updated annually and because many federal judgeships are vacant due to judges retiring or leaving office for other reasons (Beiner, 1999), it is difficult to ascertain precisely the current demographics of the federal judiciary.
2. Colorado, Connecticut, Florida, Kentucky, Maryland, Massachusetts, New York, Minnesota, Vermont, and the state of Washington have all published procedural guidelines on how to address various types of gender bias. Additionally, judicial education programs, designed to eliminate gender bias and sexual harassment in the courts, have been enacted in at least 26 different states.
3. The state of this study will not be identified, to ensure confidentiality of the judges.
4. The other judges declined to participate because they were either too busy or because they were too concerned about confidentiality. Being approached to reveal examples of gender bias may have been perceived as threatening to their professional positions.

5. In the state of this study, the judicial selection process follows two steps: first, a nominating committee screens candidates and develops a list that is sent to the governor for each judicial vacancy. The nominating committees are comprised of attorney and lay members. Next, the governor makes appointments from these lists within a year of the occurrence of the vacancy.

6. Whereas the females indicated that the nominating committee discriminates against women in terms of initial selection and criteria, the males contended that women have been given preferential treatment in the appointment process. The data reflect, however, that despite sufficient numbers of eligible women lawyers who are of an appropriate age for appointment, women are consistently overlooked at judicial appointment time.

7. According to the state committee, many lawyers and judges believed that a quota system applied to women judges in that "once 'enough' women have been appointed, no more need apply" (Special Joint Committee, 1989). The women believed that higher standards (especially with respect to professional experience) applied to women, and inappropriate questions concerning family responsibilities, financial need, and spouse's occupations were asked of female candidates but not of male candidates, and these criteria disadvantaged women. Male attorneys, however, believed that women were selected over males who were far better qualified, and women were favored "out of a misplaced sense of imbalance on the bench" (Special Joint Committee, 1989). The committee found no substantiation for these claims, and in fact, discovered that the opposite was true. (Due to honoring the request of the judges for confidentiality, the state special joint committee is not identified or listed in the references.)

8. Obviously, our research does not attempt to compare women's experiences and perceptions with those of their male counterparts on the bench, although this avenue may be a potentially fruitful inquiry to pursue in future studies.

9. Feminist scholars no doubt recognize that just as essentialist positions about women are problematic, there are also potential problems when introducing essentialist characteristics of men.

10. This is a puzzling contradiction: At the same time that the women judges admit that they may have greater insight and empathy related to women's legal issues, they maintain that these strengths do not influence their final outcomes.

11. It may also be the case that as women attain higher-status positions, such as judgeships, they feel "safe" in being more outspoken compared to aspiring "careerist" lawyers.

REFERENCES

ALLEN, D., & WALL, D. (1987). The behavior of women state supreme court justices: Are they tokens or outsiders? *Justice System Journal, 12*(1), 232–244.

ALLEN, D., & WALL, D. (1993). Role orientations and women state supreme justices. *Judicature, 77*, 156–161.

ANLEU, S. L. R. (1995). Women in law: Theory, research, and practice. In B. R. Price & N. J. Sokoloff (Eds.), *The criminal justice system and women offenders, victims, and workers.* New York: McGraw-Hill.

BAUNACH, P. J., & RAFTER, N. H. (1982). Sex-role operations: Strategies for women working in the criminal justice system. In N. H. Rafter & E. A. Stanko (Eds.), *Judge, lawyer, victim, thief.* Boston: Northeastern University Press.

BEINER, T. (1999). What will diversity on the bench mean for justice? *Michigan Journal of Gender and Law, 6*(113), 1–36.

BELKNAP, J. (1991). Women in conflict: An analysis of women correctional officers. *Women and Criminal Justice, 2*, 89–115.

BELKNAP, J. (1996). *The invisible woman: Gender, crime and justice.* Cincinnati, OH: Wadsworth.

COOK, B. B. (1978). Women judges: The end of tokenism. In W. Hepperle & L. Crites (Eds.), *Women in the courts*. Williamsburg, VA: National Center for State Courts.

COONTZ, P. (1995). Gender bias in the legal profession: Women "see" it, men don't. *Women and Politics, 15*(2), 1–22.

DAVIS, S. (1992–1993). Do women judges speak "in a difference voice"?—Carol Gilligan, feminist legal theory, and the Ninth Circuit. *Wisconsin Women's Law Journal, 7–8,* 143–173.

DAVIS, S., HAIRE, S., & SONGER, D. R. (1993). Voting behavior and gender on the U.S. courts of appeals. *Judicature, 77*(3), 129–133.

Different voices, different choices? The impact of more women lawyers and judges on the judicial system. (1990). *Judicature, 74*(3), 138–146.

DOBASH, R. E., & DOBASH, R. P. 1992. *Women, violence and social change*. New York: Routledge.

EPSTEIN, C. F. (1981). *Women in law*. New York: Basic Books.

EPSTEIN, C. F. (1983). The role strain of balancing political and professional responsibilities with family and personal responsibilities. In W. Hepperle & L. Crites (Eds.), *Women in the courts*. Williamsburg, VA: National Center for State Courts.

EPSTEIN, C. F. (1988). *Deceptive distinctions: Sex, gender, and the social order*. New Haven, CT: Yale University Press.

EPSTEIN, C. F. (1990). Faulty framework: Consequences of the difference model for women in the law. *New York Law School Law Review, 35,* 309–336.

EPSTEIN, C. F., SAUTE, R., OGLENSKY, B., & GEVER, M. (1995). Glass ceilings and open doors: Women's advancement in the legal profession. *Fordham Law Review, 64*(2), 291–449.

FARR, K. A. (1988). Dominance bonding through the good old boys sociability groups. *Sex Roles, 18,* 259–277.

FEINMAN, C. (1986). *Women in the criminal justice system* (2nd ed.). New York: Praeger.

Final report of the Special Committee on Gender to the D.C. Circuit Task Force on Gender, Race and Ethnic Bias. (1996). *Georgetown Law Review, 84*(5), 1657.

FINEMAN, M. A., & THOMADSEN, N. S. (1991). *At the boundaries of law: Feminism and legal theory*. New York: Routledge.

FLANGO, C. (1998). *Appellate court procedures*. Williamsburg, VA: National Center for State Courts.

FLYNN, E. E. (1982). Women as criminal justice professionals: A challenge to tradition. In N. H. Rafter & E. A. Stanko (Eds.), *Judge, lawyer, victim, thief*. Boston: Northeastern University Press.

FRUG, M. J. (1992). *Postmodern legal feminism*. New York: Routledge.

GILLIGAN, C. (1982). *In a different voice*. Cambridge, MA: Harvard University Press.

GITHENS, M. (1995). Getting appointed to the state court: The gender dimension. *Women and Politics, 15*(4), 1–24.

HOFF, J. (1991). *Law, gender, and injustice*. New York: New York University Press.

KEARNEY, R., & SELLERS, H. (1996). Sex on the docket: Reports of state task forces on gender bias. *Public Administration Review, 56*(6), 587–593.

KEARNEY, R., & SELLERS, H. (1997). Gender bias in court personnel administration. *Judicature, 81*(1), 8–14.

LAMBER, J. S., & STREIBE, V. L. (1974). Women executives, managers, and professionals in the Indiana criminal justice system. *Indiana Law Review, 8,* 353.

MACCORQUODALE, P., & JENSEN, G. (1993). Women in the law: Partners or tokens? *Gender & Society, 7,* 582–593.

MACKINNON, C. (1982). Towards a feminist jurisprudence. *Stanford Law Review, 34,* 703–737.

MARTIN, E. (1990). Men and women on the bench: Vive la difference? *Judicature, 73*(4), 204–208.

MARTIN, S. E. (1980). *Breaking and entering: Policewomen on patrol*. Berkeley: University of California Press.

MARTIN, S. E., & JURIK, N. C. (1996). *Doing justice, doing gender: Women in law and criminal justice occupations*. Thousand Oaks, CA: Sage.

McCormick, P., Job, T., & Brockman, J. (1993). Do women judges make a difference? An analysis by appeal court data. *Canadian Journal of Law and Society, 8*(1), 135–148.

Menkel-Meadow, C. (1985). Portia in different voice. *Berkeley Women's Law Journal, 1,* 39.

Merlo, A. V., & Pollock, J. M. (1995). *Women, law, and social control.* Boston: Allyn & Bacon.

Messerschmidt, J. W. (1993). *Masculinities and crime: Critique and reconceptualization of theory.* Lanham, MD: Rowman & Littlefield.

Moyer, I. L. (1992). *The changing roles of women in the criminal justice system.* Prospect Heights, IL: Waveland Press.

Murray, F. K. (1990). Women and the law: Have we really come a long way? *Judge's Journal,* 19–23.

Neubauer, D. (2002). *America's courts and the criminal justice system.* Belmont, CA: Wadsworth.

Paternoster, R., Brame, R., Bachman, R., & Sherman, L. (1997). Do fair procedures matter? The effect of procedural justice on spouse assault. *Law and Society Review, 31*(1), 163–204.

Price, B. R., & Sokoloff, N. J. (1995). *The criminal justice system and women: Women offenders, victims, and workers.* New York: McGraw-Hill.

Resnik, J. (1996). Asking about gender in courts. *Signs: Journal of Women in Culture and Society, 21*(4), 952–990.

Riger, S., Foster-Fishman, P., Nelson-Kuna, J., & Curran, B. (1995). Gender bias in courtroom dynamics. *Law and Human Behavior, 19*(5), 465–480.

Rosenberg, J., Perlstadt, H., & Phillips, W. R. F. (1990). Politics, feminism and women's professional orientations: A case study of women lawyers. *Women and Politics, 10,* 19–48.

Rosenberg, J., Perlstadt, H., & Phillips, W. R. F. (1993). Now that we are here: Discrimination, disparagement, and harassment at work and the experience of women lawyers. *Gender and Society,* 7, 415–433.

Rush, S. E. (1993). Feminist judging: An introductory essay. *California Review of Legal and Women's Studies, 609,* 627–632.

Schafran, L. H. (1987). Practicing law in a sexist society. In L. L. Crites & W. L. Hepperle (Eds.), *Women, the courts, and equality.* Newbury Park, CA: Sage.

Sherry, S. (1986). The gender of judges. *Law and Inequality, 4,* 159.

Stanko, E. A. (1985). *Intimate intrusions: Women's experience of male violence.* London: Routledge & Kegan Paul. The effects of gender in the federal courts: The final report of the Ninth Circuit gender bias task force. (1994). *Southern California Law Review, 8,* 745.

Tiedna, M., Smith, S., & Ortiz, V. (1987). Industrial restructuring, gender segregation, and sex differences in earning. *American Sociological Review, 52,* 195–210.

Tobias, C. (1990). The gender gap on the federal bench. *Hofstra Law Review, 19*(1), 171–184.

Tobias, C. (1991). More women named federal judges. *Florida Law Review, 43,* 477–486.

West, C., & Zimmerman, D. H. (1987). Doing gender. *Gender and Society, 1,* 125–151.

West, R. L. (1991). The difference in women's hedonic lives: A phenomenological critique of feminist legal theory. In M. A. Fineman & N. S. Thomadsen (Eds.), *At the boundaries of law: Feminism and legal theory.* New York: Routledge.

Wikler, N. J. (1987). Educating judges about gender bias in the courts. In L. L. Crites & W. L. Hepperle (Eds.), *Women, the courts, and equality.* Newbury Park, CA: Sage.

Wikler, N. J., & Schafran, L. H. (1991). Learning from the New Jersey Supreme Court task force on women in the courts: Evaluation, recommendations and implications for other states. *Women's Rights Law Reporter, 12,* 313–385.

Wilson, N. K. (1982). Women in the criminal justice professions: An analysis of status conflict. In N. H. Rafter & E. A. Stanko (Eds.), *Judge, lawyer, victim, thief.* Boston: Northeastern University Press.

Zimmer, L. E. (1986). *Women guarding men.* Chicago: University of Chicago Press.

44

Three Strikes and It's *Women* Who Are Out

The Hidden Consequences for Women of Criminal Justice Policy Reforms[1]

Mona J.E. Danner

❖

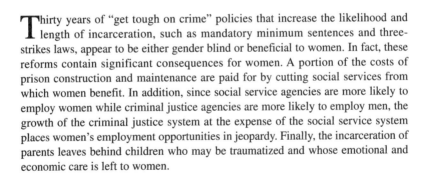

Thirty years of "get tough on crime" policies that increase the likelihood and length of incarceration, such as mandatory minimum sentences and three-strikes laws, appear to be either gender blind or beneficial to women. In fact, these reforms contain significant consequences for women. A portion of the costs of prison construction and maintenance are paid for by cutting social services from which women benefit. In addition, since social service agencies are more likely to employ women while criminal justice agencies are more likely to employ men, the growth of the criminal justice system at the expense of the social service system places women's employment opportunities in jeopardy. Finally, the incarceration of parents leaves behind children who may be traumatized and whose emotional and economic care is left to women.

The 1994 Federal Crime Control Act marks the 26th year of the get tough on crime movement initiated with the passage of the 1968 Crime Control and Safe Streets Act (Donziger, 1996, p. 14). The 1984 crime bill increased penalties for drug offenses thereby engaging the war on drugs and initiating the centerpiece of law-and-order legislative efforts to control crime—mandatory minimum and increased sentence lengths. "Three strikes and you're out" laws in particular captured the imagination of the public, the press, and the politicians. State legislators in 37 jurisdictions proposed three-strikes laws in 1993 and 1994, often as part of their own state crime bills. By the end of 1995, 24 state jurisdictions and the federal government had enacted these laws, and California voters had made three strikes part of their Constitution (Clark, Austin, & Henry, 1997; Turner, Sundt, Applegate,

723

& Cullen 1995). The new sentencing laws contained in the federal and state crime bills increased the dramatic expansion of the criminal justice system already under way, especially in corrections.

At the end of 2003, the United States recorded over 6.9 million adults in the correctional population, that is, on probation or parole, in jail or prison. By mid-year 2003, our nation incarcerated over 1.3 million of its citizens in federal and state prisons, more than a fourfold increase in just 20 years; another 691,000 people were in local jails (U.S. Department of Justice, 2004). Over 182,000 of those imprisoned were women and another 1 million women were on probation or parole (Glaze & Palla, 2004; Harrison & Karberg, 2004). In the 1980s, the rate of women's imprisonment increased nearly twice as much as that of men's, and 34 new women's prison units were opened (Immarigeon & Chesney-Lind, 1992). African Americans, who account for 13 percent of the population, are 45 percent of those incarcerated (Beck & Karberg, 2001); 25 years ago they were 35 percent of those locked up (Maguire, Pastore, & Flanagan, 1993, p. 618). Black men are seven times and black women are over four and one-half times more likely to be imprisoned than are white men and women (Harrison & Karberg, 2004); the expansion of mandatory and increased sentences for drug law violations accounts for much of the increase (Mauer, 1990). The numbers of black women imprisoned for drugs has increased more than three times that of white women (Bush-Baskette, 1998). Young African American men are particularly hard hit by the rhetoric and ensuing policies associated with the war on drugs and three-strikes laws (Tonry, 1995). Nearly all of those behind bars are poor.

The result of "lock 'em up" policies is that state and federal prisons currently operate at, respectively, up to 117 and 133 percent capacity (Harrison & Karberg, 2004). Across the country, federal and state governments are engaged in an enormous and costly prison construction program. In fact, prisons represent "the only expanding public housing" in our country ("The Prison Boom," 1995, p. 223). One truism of prison and jail construction remains: "If you build it, they will come." And so, the costs associated with maintaining these facilities and incarcerating citizens—especially geriatrics as lifers age—will quickly dwarf the costs of construction.

The rationale behind the crime bills and the resulting expansion of the criminal justice system cannot be found in the crime rate. Despite political rhetoric at the national and state levels and the carnage presented daily and repeatedly in all forms of news and entertainment media, the violent crime rate remained relatively stable or decreased over the last 30 years as measured by the National Crime Survey (Catalano, 2004).

Throughout it all, however, the consequences for women of the expansion of the criminal justice system remain largely unconsidered and invisible in public policy discussions. This chapter makes women visible in the identification of the hidden costs to women of the expansion of the criminal justice system. In brief, I argue that one way or another it is *women* who will pay the lion's share of criminal justice reform.

LOOKING FOR WOMEN

The feminist revolution in society and the academy is about making women visible, interrogating and deconstructing the manner in which women do appear, and calling for progressive action to benefit women. In criminal justice, feminist analysis has largely focused on women as offenders, victims, and workers (Price & Sokoloff, 1995) with the issues and debates centered around building theory, containing men's violence against women, and the equality/difference concern (Daly & Chesney-Lind, 1988). This chapter advances feminist perspectives in criminal justice in the analysis of the ways in which supposedly gender-blind crime control writ large affects *all* women.

Women are not readily visible in current criminal justice policy debates. The use of a baseball analogy—"three strikes and you're out"—to refer to the policy of mandatory life sentences for those persons convicted of three felonies illustrates the exclusion of women from the crime debates. Although it's called "the national pastime," women don't identify with baseball much, have no significant presence in the sport, and reap few of its economic benefits (facts true of all professional sports). Yet it is in this sense that baseball represents an excellent analogy to the crime bills since women remain largely invisible from the debates surrounding criminal justice reforms. When women do appear, it is often as diversionary props that only barely resemble the realities of the lives of women and girls. Recent public debates in some states regarding increasing the availability of concealed weapons provide one illustration of this phenomenon.

During the 1995 legislative year, Virginia enacted a "right to carry" law requiring that judges grant permits for concealed weapons to nearly anyone who applies (Snider, 1995). Lobbyists for the National Rifle Association (NRA) along with sympathetic legislators repeatedly invoked the image of the lone woman walking to her car at night who might need a gun to protect herself from the lurking stranger ready to pounce on her at any moment. This image of a woman served as a diversionary prop to obscure the protests of police and judges who objected to the law because of safety concerns and the restriction on judicial discretion. The image also diverted attention away from the vested interests of the NRA and state politicians who benefit from NRA contributions. This is simply one example of the way in which women are used in debates surrounding criminal justice policies. Women's lives and the realities of potential dangers are distorted, and in the process, women are left out of the debate and policies are enacted that will not only fail to benefit most women, but will, in fact, harm many women.

Nearly all of the political rhetoric about crime focuses on making our streets and neighborhoods safe again and protecting our homes from vicious, dangerous intruders. The focus on stranger crimes ignores the fact that it is the ones whom they know and love who represent the greatest danger to women's lives. Although women are much less likely than men to become victims of violent crimes in general, when women are assaulted, robbed, or raped, the best guess is to look to their loved ones. Of these violent crimes that women experience, the perpetrator is a husband, boyfriend, ex-husband, or ex-boyfriend 19 percent of the time; the comparable figure for men is 3 percent. Adding in other relatives increases the figure for women to 29 percent; for men, it is 8 percent. Expanding the definition to include other persons known reveals that 67 percent of the times that women are the victims of violent crimes the assailant is known to the victim as either an acquaintance, a friend, relative, or an intimate partner; for men this figure is 42 percent (Catalano, 2004). The offender is a stranger in less than one-quarter of the occasions when women are victims of violent crime by a lone offender (Bachman & Saltzman, 1995). In violent crimes occurring between spouses, lovers, ex-spouses, and ex-lovers, nearly 90 percent of the time, the victim is a woman. And a woman is the victim in 70 percent of murders between intimate partners (Greenfeld et al., 1998).

Women need far less protection from strangers than from supposed protectors, especially intimate partners, relatives, and acquaintances. But the debates surrounding the crime bills and recent research demonstrate that women are also at risk from the lawmakers and even some law enforcers (Kraska & Kappeler, 1995), most of whom are men, nearly all of them white, and with respect to politicians, legislators, and judges, members of the elite social classes. Lawmakers do not pay attention to the data but, like the public, fall victim to popular myths about crime, especially the myth that it is strangers who are most responsible for violent victimizations, particularly those committed against women. The result is that this myth and others like it are used to shape public debate and craft public policies that ignore women's lives and force women to bear the brunt of the financial and emotional costs for such policies.

The New York Times called women the "quiet winners" in the U.S. Crime Bill because of the inclusion of the Violence Against Women Act (Manegold, 1994). This portion of the national crime bill budgeted $1.6 billion dollars for a national hotline for domestic violence victims and education programs aimed at police, prosecutors, and judges. It includes provisions that encourage mandatory arrests in domestic violence complaints, sex offender registration programs, and the release to victims of the results of rapists' HIV tests. It had also allowed women to file civil suits in cases of sex bias crimes, although this provision was overturned by the U.S. Supreme Court in *U.S. v. Morrison* (2000).

The Violence Against Women Act makes women's victimization visible and crafts public policies to assist women. The act represents an important step in public recognition of, and response to, male violence against women. But examination of the crime bills and their accompanying public debate reveals no sign of women other than as victims of domestic violence.

Feminist interrogation about how criminal justice policies affect women's lives calls us to make visible more of the ways in which the criminal justice policies affect women. Considering the unintended consequences and hidden costs of the crime bills and current public policies suggests that women are less likely to be quiet winners in criminal justice reforms as a whole, than to be quiet and big-time losers.

And so we return to the baseball analogy. "Three strikes and you're out" doesn't just refer to the policy of mandatory life sentences following a third felony conviction. It also refers to three ways in which women will be hurt by, and forced to pay for, criminal justice reform.

STRIKE ONE: OFF THE ROLLS

The first strike against women comes in the decisions regarding which government services will be sacrificed to pay for the expansion of the criminal justice system. The emphasis on budget balancing and deficit reduction at the national and state levels means that money targeted for tough-on-crime proposals comes at the expense of other government programs. RAND researchers concluded that implementation of California's three-strikes law would require cuts in other government services totaling more than 40 percent over eight years—a move that would leave the State of California "spending more money keeping people in prison than putting people through college" (Greenwood et al., 1994, p. 34).

The hardest hit programs, however, are those in social services, especially those targeted to the poor, most of whom are women and children.[2]

Discussion about entitlements to the poor is to some limited extent a separate debate about the causes of poverty and the state's responsibility, or lack thereof, to help alleviate misfortune and suffering. But, it is also a debate that remains close to the debates about crime and criminal justice. Like criminal offenders and prisoners, women on welfare and their families are demonized as lazy, unwilling to work for their keep, immoral, and criminal. Both groups—composed disproportionately of poor and minority persons—are scapegoated as the source of numerous social ills while public attention draws away from inequitable economic and political conditions (Sidel, 1996). Blaming the victims of structural conditions justifies cutting welfare for the poor and funneling savings elsewhere.

Social services that benefit women are sacrificed to accommodate the expenditures associated with the expansion of the criminal justice system. Chesney-Lind (1995) notes that New York continued to build beds in women's prisons at the same time that it had an insufficient number of beds for women and children in shelters. Adequate social services can reduce those life stressors associated with criminality; legal changes and battered women's shelters helped reduce the rates of women's homicide of male partners (Browne, 1990, cited in Chesney-Lind, 1995).

The rhetoric surrounding cuts in social programs reveals class, as well as race/ethnic and gender, bias. The Welfare Reform Bill of 1996 imposed a limitation on the length of time that poor women may receive welfare assistance. After two years most women will be kicked off the rolls under the assumption that they will find work. Overall, few provisions are made for ensuring that either jobs or day care are available. We see social class operating here. Politicians, pundits, and religious leaders commonly argue that children should be cared for at home by the mother. Apparently, this is true, however, only for middle-class mothers and their children; poor mothers are admonished and will be legally required to leave their children so that they may return to work in order to save the tax coffers.

In 1994, at the same time that Virginia first instituted welfare reform, the state also passed its crime bill and accompanying criminal justice reforms. Plans called for the building of 27 new prisons at a cost of $1 billion over 10 years (later estimates placed these costs at $2–4 billion) as well as three strikes and other provisions for increasing the length of sentences for violent offenses and repeat offenses. The bill also called for the abolition of parole as of January 1, 1995, but the governor's new parole board had already, in effect, abolished parole as it drastically reduced the number of paroles granted—at a cost of $77 million in just 6 months (LaFay, 1994). Virginia prisons were so overcrowded that they could not accept new inmates housed in local jails awaiting transfer to the state system. This, in turn, led to such pressures in the jails that sheriffs sued the state to force it to assume its responsibility and take custody of its charges (Jackson, 1995). One way in which Virginia, like all states, deals with the problem of overcrowding is to ship inmates to other states and pay them the costs associated with incarceration (LaFay, 1995).

The expenditures associated with the expansion of the criminal justice system are being paid for in part by the savings to come from reforms that cut the social safety net of welfare. Further, an "iron triangle" of interests—politicians, job-starved communities, and businesses that build and service prisons—benefits from tough-on-crime rhetoric and policies (Thomas, 1994). Neither military, corporate, nor middle-class subsidy programs are targeted for payment in support of the prison industrial complex; rather, social service programs—with their disproportionately poor, minority, and female recipients—remain those responsible for picking up the check.

Women are the majority of direct beneficiaries of various social service programs, but we know that they steer nearly all of those benefits to their dependents, especially their children but also elderly people and adults with disabilities in their lives. Simply put, women and those who depend upon them will lose their economic and social safety net, in part so that politicians can appear to be tough on crime and imprison more men and women. It is poor women—who are also disproportionately minority, especially African American women—and their families who in this way will pay a disproportionate share of the hidden costs associated with the war on crime and drugs. Strike one.

STRIKE TWO: JOBS FOR WHOM?

Women are not only more likely than men to be the recipients of social services, women are also more likely to be employed in social service agencies as social workers, case workers, counselors, and support staff. The implications of this fact represent the second strike against women. Seventy-one percent of social workers are women, and women comprise an even larger portion of front-line case workers and clerical personnel (U.S. Bureau of the Census, 2000, p. 416). Thus, as social services are cut back, women workers will be disproportionately affected.

Critics will respond that the expansion of the criminal justice system means increased employment opportunities for women. After all, 26 percent of law enforcement employees in the United States are women (Pastore & Maguire, 2000, Table 1.56). Even greater opportunities appear to exist in corrections, where 29 percent of employees in adult corrections are women (Maguire & Pastore, 1999, p. 81). However, most women employed in law enforcement and corrections agencies work in traditional pink-collar ghettos as low-wage clerical or support staff. Practically speaking, the *only* way to advance to upper levels of administration in either policing or corrections is through line employment as a police or correctional officer. And although 71 percent of law enforcement employees are police officers, only 11 percent of police officers are women (Pastore & Maguire, 2000, Table 1.56), and women make up just 19 percent of correctional guards (Maguire & Pastore, 1999, p. 81).

There remains a long-standing bias against women in policing and corrections. Even after more than 20 years of proven effectiveness as officers on the streets and in the prisons, male coworkers and supervisors persist in their bias against women. They use harassment and masculine work cultures that marginalize women to resist efforts to increase the representation of women on these forces (Martin & Jurik, 1996; Morash & Haarr, 1995).

The attacks on affirmative action in the current political climate further endanger women's employment possibilities in the criminal justice system (Martin, 1995). In addition, the definition and nature of work in criminal justice is being restructured to emphasize punitiveness and dangerousness. In Virginia, probation and parole counselors were renamed officers and may now carry weapons (Sec. 53.1–145 of the Code of Virginia). Virginia's Director of Corrections since 1994 insists that probation and parole clients as well as inmates be called "convicts" or "felons." These moves emphasize punishment and the untrustworthiness of offenders; they stand in sharp contrast to the need to develop positive relationships in order to encourage social adjustment. Such practices also emphasize masculinity as a requirement for the job, thereby creating a climate that further discourages women in the work.

Three-strikes and no-parole policies have at least three implications for police and correctional officers. For the police, three strikes may influence people likely to be caught in the web of these laws to take more desperate measures than ever to evade arrest. For correctional guards, abolishing parole first means overcrowding in the prisons; it also means the loss of incentives and rewards for good behavior and the loss of faith in the future. In turn, these conditions produce an increase in the likelihood of prison violence and uprisings.

Thus, real increases in fear and the loss of hope among offenders become coupled with politically inspired attitudes about the dangerousness of offenders and the punitive goals of the work. Combined with attacks on affirmative action, bias against women in traditionally male occupations and the resulting stress on women employees, these factors may be surprisingly effective in bringing about actual *decreases* in women's employment in precisely those positions in policing and corrections that lead to advancement and higher pay.

The crime bills represent a government jobs program—criminal justice is, in fact, "the only growing public-sector employment" ("The Prison Boom," 1994, p. 223)—but the new jobs created come at the cost of other public sector jobs, such as those in social services, which are more likely to be held by women. And the new jobs created by the expansion of the criminal justice system are overwhelmingly jobs for men. Strike two.

STRIKE THREE: FAMILY VALUES?

Men and women who commit crimes for which they are convicted and sentenced to prison have not lived their lives solely in criminal gangs; they do not structure their entire days around illegal activity; they are not *only* criminals. They are also sons and daughters, fathers and mothers. In short, they are responsible for caring for others who depend on them, and most of them do their best to meet these responsibilities because they do, in fact, love their families.

Sixty-five percent of women and 55 percent of men in state prisons in 1997 had children under the age of 18; most of these women (64 percent) and many men (44 percent) lived with their children before entering prison (Mumola, 2000). Imprisoned adults cannot contribute to their families' financial or psychological well-being. In a few cases children are committed to foster homes or institutions. But most of the time another family member takes over care of those children and any elderly persons or adults with disabilities left behind—and that family member is usually a woman. This fact represents the third strike against women.

Because most of those imprisoned are men, it is the women in their lives—wives, girlfriends, and mothers—who are left with the responsibility for providing for the economic and emotional needs of the children and any dependent adults, a task these women must accomplish on their own. When women are imprisoned, it is generally their mothers who take over the care of the children.

As we imprison increasing numbers of men and women, we saddle more women with sole responsibility for care of the next generation. The problem is exacerbated when the state, due to overcrowding, moves prisoners out of its system and to other states, thereby leaving the women and children bereft of even emotional support from incarcerated parents.

Today in the United States, "there are at least 1.5 million children of prisoners and at least 3.5 million children of offenders on probation or parole" (Johnston, 1995a, p. 311). The women who care for these children, as well as the children themselves, must be recognized as paying some of the hidden costs of punitive criminal justice policies. Parental arrest and incarceration endures as a traumatic event for all involved. It can lead to inadequate child care due to persistent and deepening poverty. In addition, children may suffer from problems with which the women who care for them must cope: developmental delay, behavioral and emotional difficulties, feelings of shame and experiences of stigmatization, distrust and hatred of police and the criminal justice system, and subsequent juvenile delinquency (Carlson & Cervera, 1992; Fishman, 1990; Johnston, 1995b). In effect, children suffer from posttraumatic stress disorder when their parents are imprisoned (Kampfner, 1995). Effective programs to address the needs of children of incarcerated parents and their caregivers remain few in number and endangered.

As politicians get tough on crime, it is women and children who do the time, alone. Remembering the first two strikes against women discussed earlier, it emerges as strikingly clear that women will not be able to look to the federal or state government for either public assistance or public employment. Strike three. It's *women* who are out.

FINAL THOUGHTS: AN EVERY WOMAN'S ISSUE

It remains far too easy to be lulled into complacency when it comes to women and criminal justice. After all, women represent a very small number of offenders. And in spite of male violence against women, most victims of crime are men. Yet, the social construction of crime and criminals and the political nature of their control are neither gender blind, nor gender neutral. We are finally and fully confronted by the harsh reality that criminal justice *is* about women, *all* women. Although it occasionally operates as an important resource for women, the criminal justice system most frequently represents a form of oppression in women's lives. It attacks most harshly those women with the least power to resist it. As Jean Landis and I wrote a decade ago:

> it is time to recognize that in real life . . . offenders do not exist as exclusive objects. They are connected in relationships with other people, a major portion of whom are women—mothers, wives, lovers, sisters and daughters. Any woman who fights to keep her wits, and her roof, about her as she helplessly experiences a loved one being swept away by the currents of criminal justice "knows" the true brutality of the system and the extensiveness of its destruction. If she is a racial/ethnic minority person, which she is likely to be, and/or if she is poor, which she surely is, she intuitively knows the nature of the interaction between criminal justice practices and the racist and/or classist [as well as sexist] structure of her society, as well as its impact on her life, her family, and her community. (Danner & Landis, 1990, pp. 111–112)

She also knows that precious little assistance exists for her, and those who depend on her, in the form of either welfare or employment from the larger community as represented by the state. In addition, it is every woman, no matter who she is, who will pay for the dramatic expansion of the criminal justice system. Growing the criminal justice system in an era of tax cuts and budget reduction requires shrinking other government services, such as education, health care, and roads, that benefit all members of the public. Clearly, criminal justice *is* a women's issue.

The get-tough, lock 'em up, and three-strikes policies will not reduce crime nor women's pain associated with crime. They will only impoverish communities as they enrich politicians and those corporations associated with this new prison industrial complex. Although women have been largely left out of the debate, it is women who are the quiet losers—the big-time losers—in the crime bills. Criminal justice reforms such as these are politically motivated, unnecessary, ineffective, and far, far too costly. Finally, and most important, it is women who receive the least from the wars on crime and drugs, and it is women who bear most of their hidden burdens.

ACKNOWLEDGMENTS

This chapter was originally prepared as the *1995 Women's Studies Junior Faculty Lecture,* Old Dominion University; I thank Anita Clair Fellman, director of Women's Studies, for that invitation. Thanks to Marie L. VanNostrand (formerly of Virginia Department of Criminal Justice Services) and Lucien X. Lombardo (Old Dominion University) who were most gracious in providing me with materials. The members of Our Writing Group and COOL provided much encouragement and entertainment. An earlier version was presented at the 1995 American Society of Criminology meetings, Boston, Massachusetts.

NOTES

1. This chapter is an updated adaptation from the author's chapter in *Crime Control and Women: Feminist Implications of Criminal Justice Policy* edited by Susan L. Miller (Newbury Park, CA: Sage 1998).
2. Entitlements to the poor include Temporary Assistance to Needy Families (TANF) formerly known as Aid to Families with Dependent Children (AFDC); the Women, Infants and Children (WIC) nutritional program; food stamps; school breakfast and lunch programs; Medicaid; public housing and emergency grants; and social security for persons who are disabled and dependent, as well as other programs. Each of these programs is under attack and will almost certainly be cut back, just as has welfare.

REFERENCES

BACHMAN, R., & Saltzman, L. E. (1995). *Violence against women: Estimates from the redesigned survey.* Washington, DC: U.S. Department of Justice.

BECK, A. J., & Karberg, J. C. (2001). *Prison and jail inmates at midyear 2000.* Washington, DC: U.S. Department of Justice.

BROWNE, A. (1990, December 11). *Assaults between intimate partners in the United States.* Testimony before the United States Senate, Committee on the Judiciary, Washington, DC.

BUSH-BASKETTE, S. R. (1998). The war on drugs as a war against Black women. In S. L. Miller (Ed.), *Crime control and women: Feminist implications of criminal justice policy* (pp. 113–129). Thousand Oaks, CA: Sage.

CARLSON, B. E., & CERVERA, N. (1992). *Inmates and their wives: Incarceration and familiy life.* Westport, CT: Greenwood Press.

CATALANO, S. M. (2004). *Criminal victimization, 2003.* Washington, DC: U.S. Department of Justice.

CHESNEY-LIND, M. (1995). Rethinking women's imprisonment: A critical examination of trends in female incarceration. In B. R. Price & N. J. (Eds.), *The criminal justice system and women: Offenders, victims, and workers* (2nd ed., pp. 105–117). New York: McGraw-Hill.

CLARK, J., AUSTIN, J., & HENRY, D. A. (1997). *"Three strikes and you're out": A review of state legislation.* Washington, DC: U.S. Department of Justice.

DALY, K., & CHESNEY-LIND, M. (1988). Feminism and criminology. *Justice Quarterly, 5,* 497–538.

DANNER, M., & LANDIS, J. (1990). Carpe diem (Seize the day!): An opportunity for feminist connections. In B. D. MadLean & D. Milovanvovic (Eds.), *Racism, empiricism and criminal justice* (pp. 109–112). Vancouver, British Columbia, Canada: Collective Press.

DONZIGER, S. A. (ED.) (1996). *The real war on crime: The report of the national criminal justice commission.* New York: HarperPerennial.

FISHMAN, L. T. (1990). *Women at the wall: A study of prisoners' wives doing time on the outside.* New York: State University of New York Press.

GLAZE, L. E., & PALLA, S. (2004). *Probation and parole in the United States, 2003.* Washington, DC.: U.S. Department of Justice.

GREENFELD, L. A., RAND, M. R., CRAVEN, D., KLAUS, P. A., PERKINS, C. A., RINGEL, C., et al. (1998). *Violence by intimates: Analysis of data on crimes by current or former spouses, boyfriends, and girlfriends.* Washington, DC: U.S. Department of Justice.

GREENWOOD, P. W., FYDELL, C. P., ABRAHAMSE, A. F., CAULKINS, J. P., CHIESA, J., MODEL, K. E., et al. (1994). *Three strikes and you're out: Estimated benefits and costs of California's new mandatory-sentencing law.* Santa Monica, CA: RAND.

HARRISON, P. M., & KARBERG, J. C. (2004). *Prison and jail inmates at midyear 2003.* Washington, DC: U.S. Department of Justice.

IMMARIGEON, R., & CHESNEY-LIND, M. (1992). *Women's prisons: Overcrowded and overused.* San Francisco, CA: National Council on Crime and Delinquency.

JACKSON, J. (1995, January 11). Sheriffs suing state to relieve overcrowding in city jails. *The Virginian-Pilot,* pp. A1, A6.

JOHNSTON, D. (1995a). Conclusion. In K. Gabel & D. Johnston (Eds.), *Children of incarcerated parents* (pp. 311–314). New York: Lexington Books.

JOHNSTON, D. (1995b). Effects of parental incarceration. In K. Gabel & D. Johnston (Eds.), *Children of incarcerated parents* (pp. 59–88). New York: Lexington Books.

KAMPFNER, C. J. (1995). Post-traumatic stress reactions in children of imprisoned mothers. In K. Gabel & D. Johnston (Eds.), *Children of incarcerated parents* (pp. 89–100). New York: Lexington Books.

KRASKA, P. B., & KAPPELER, V. E. (1995). To serve and pursue: Exploring police sexual violence against women. *Justice Quarterly, 12,* 85–111.

LAFAY, L. (1994, December 9). New, low parole rate has cost Va. $77 million. *The Virginian-Pilot,* pp. A1, A24.

LAFAY, L. (1995, February 17). State sends 150 inmates to Texas. *The Virginian-Pilot,* pp. A1, A9.

MAGUIRE, K., & PASTORE, A. L. (EDS.). (1999). *Sourcebook of criminal justice statistics 1998.* Washington, DC: U.S. Department of Justice.

MAGUIRE, K., PASTORE, A. L., & FLANAGAN, T. J. (EDS.). (1993). *Sourcebook of criminal justice statistics 1992.* Washington, DC: U.S. Department of Justice.

MANEGOLD, C. S. S. (1994, August 25). Quiet winners in house fight on crime: Women. *New York Times,* p. A19.

MARTIN, S. E. (1995). The effectiveness of affirmative action: The case of women in policing. *Justice Quarterly, 8,* 489–504.

MARTIN, S. E., & JURIK, N. D. (1996). *Doing justice, doing gender: Women in law and criminal justice occupations.* Thousand Oaks, CA: Sage.

MAUER, M. (1990). *Young black men and the criminal justice system: A growing national problem.* Washington, DC: The Sentencing Project.

MORASH, M., & HAARR, R. N. (1995). Gender, workplace problems, and stress in policing. *Justice Quarterly, 12,* 113–140.

MUMOLA, C. J. (2000). *Incarcerated parents and their children.* Washington, DC: U.S. Department of Justice.

PASTORE, A. L., & MAGUIRE, K. (EDS.). (2000). *Sourcebook of criminal justice statistics.* Retrieved May 4, 2001, from http://www.albany.edu/sourcebook/.

PRICE, B. R., & SOKOLOFF, N. J. (1995). *The criminal justice system and women: Offenders, victims, and workers* (2nd ed.). New York: McGraw-Hill.

RENNISON, C. M. (2000). *Criminal victimization 1999.* Washington, DC: U.S. Department of Justice.

SIDEL, R. (1996). *Keeping women and children last: America's war on the poor.* New York: Penguin Books.

SNIDER, J. R. (1995, December 13). Have gun, will travel. *The Virginian-Pilot.*

The prison boom. (1995, February 20). *The Nation,* pp. 223–224.

THOMAS, P. (1994, May 12). Making crime pay. *Wall Street Journal,* pp. A1, A6.

TONRY, M. H. (1995). *Malign neglect: Race, crime, and punishment in America.* New York: Oxford University Press.

TURNER, M. G., SUNDT, J. L., APPLEGATE, B. K., & CULLEN, F. T. (1995). "Three strikes and you're out" legislation: A national assessment. *Federal Probation, 59,* 16–35.

U.S. BUREAU OF THE CENSUS. (2000). *Statistical abstract of the United States 2000.* Washington, DC: U.S. Government Printing Office.

U.S. DEPARTMENT OF JUSTICE. (2004, July 25). *Almost 6.9 million on probation or parole or incarcerated in U.S. prisons or jails* (press release). Retrieved February 1, 2005, from http://www.ojp. gov/bjs/pub/press/ppus03pr.htm.

CASE

U.S. v. Morrison, 529 U.S. 598, 2000.

SECTION VIII

Women, Terrorism, and Beyond

45

Femmes Fatales

The Evolution and Significance of Female Involvement in Terrorist Networks and Suicide Bombings

Elizabeth Schafluetzel-Iles and Jeffrey P. Rush

This research explored the evolution and significance of female involvement in terrorist networks. A historical context and evolution of female involvement in terrorist networks was presented and reviewed for emerging trends in the transition in type of female participation. Current examples of female involvement in terrorist networks, specifically homicide bombings, are quantified over a four-year period from 2000 to 2003, and then compared to prior periods. Analysis showed an increasing trend to use females as homicide bombers within terrorist networks. The significance of this trend was considered in relation to the educational levels of female homicide bombers. This research concluded that homicide bombings, in general, are becoming an increasingly common tactic used by terrorist networks, and that using females as homicide bombers has emerged as a coinciding phenomenon. Overall, this investigation directs avenues for future research regarding the significance of female participation in terrorist networks, both domestically and abroad, and how that might relate to females' educational levels.

INTRODUCTION

Rudy Giuliani, "America's mayor," says that the suicide threat is the worst threat we face (Morgenstern, 2005). This comment becomes all the more important when we consider three "flaws" regarding suicide threats (e.g., suicide bombers):

- Only crazy or deranged people do this (suicide terror) and they strike at random.

- They don't devote resources to it.
- It's not happening in my neighborhood.

Adding to this list, no doubt for most people, is the unthinkable of the unthinkable: that women could possibly be involved in such acts. Although it is difficult for many to understand or even accept the idea of suicide bombers, it is all the more improbable that a woman could be involved in such an activity. And yet they are, and it appears their involvement is increasing.

Investigating the evolution and significance of female involvement in terrorist networks is important because it appears to be a new and growing trend in the tactics utilized by terrorist networks, particularly in regard to using females as suicide or homicide bombers. Recently, Commemorating Martyrs of the Global Islamic Movement in Iran announced that close to 450 individuals have volunteered to engage in suicide bombing tactics in Iraq and elsewhere. Of this number, over half were identified as female (My Way news, 21, 2005). With the United States Department of Homeland Security's primary purpose being "to protect the nation against future terrorist attacks [and to] analyze threats . . . and coordinate the response of our country," it would seem that the need to examine the possibility of this trend is necessary for practitioners to stay abreast of the potential trends in terrorist tactics (U.S. Department of Homeland Security [DHS], 2003, Organization section, para. 3). In fact, regarding the war on terrorism, the Central Intelligence Agency (CIA) cites that "the greatest challenge is to penetrate these terrorist networks" in an attempt to better understand and thwart their tactics, and furthermore, that "these challenges are the focus of our efforts" in combating terrorism (CIA, 2003, FAQ section, para. 5).

Given the relatively limited amount of analysis regarding the occurrence and significance of female involvement in terrorist networks, it is the general intent of this investigation to generate a comprehensive base from which future research might draw and/or emerge; and, more specifically, to explore the significance and some of the possible implications of this emerging trend among terrorist networks to utilize female involvement—particularly regarding suicide or homicide bombings. To better understand why this trend might be emerging, it is necessary to first define the current concept of terrorism in general and identify some of its emerging tactics; second, to give an illustration of some of the historical female participation in terrorist networks; third, to detail some of the more recent examples of female involvement in terrorist activities as evidence of the increasing use of females to perpetrate such terrorist acts as suicide or homicide bombings; fourth, to examine the evolution of the female role in terrorist networks; and finally, to examine the significance behind increasing female involvement within terrorist networks.

TERRORISM: DEFINING ITS GOALS, TACTICS, AND TRENDS

According to the CIA (2003), "the intelligence community is guided by the definition of terrorism contained in Title 22 of the United States Code, Section 2656f (d)," which states, in part:

> The term "terrorism" means premeditated, politically motivated violence perpetrated against noncombatant targets by subnational groups or clandestine agents, usually intended to influence an audience. The term "international terrorism" means terrorism involving the territory

or the citizens of more than one country. The term "terrorist group" [or network] means any group that practices, or has significant subgroups that practice, international terrorism. (FAQ section, para. 6)

Furthermore, Boaz Ganor, director of the International Policy Institute for Counter-Terrorism (ICT), defines suicide terrorism specifically as "the operational method in which the very act of the attack is dependent upon the death of the perpetrator," an act that is aimed at "striking a blow to public morale" (Ganor, 1998, pp. 12–17; 2001, pp. 140–145). Generally, as White (2003) points out, it is often "more helpful to examine the meaning of terrorism within specific frameworks . . . [because] the definition of terrorism changes within political and social contexts" (pp. 5–7). While there has been difficulty in the world community in identifying a uniform definition of terrorism, the International Counter-Terrorism Academic Community (ICTAC, 2005) agrees on the following:

> "Terrorism is the deliberate use of violence against civilians in order to achieve political goals (ideological, nationalist, social, religious etc.)." In light of this definition, terrorism is always an illegitimate strategy for any group of people, just as targeting civilians is defined as a war crime in conflicts between states.

In addition, there is a rationale behind the additional usage of term "homicide bombing" when addressing suicide bombings in this investigation. In April of 2002, "the term 'homicide bombing' was coined by the press secretary of President George W. Bush as a synonym for suicide bombing" (Wikipedia, 2003, Usage, para. 2). The motivation of the Bush administration is to "de-emphasize the self-sacrificial connotations of suicide bombing and emphasize the contention that suicide bombers are committing murder" (Wikipedia, 2003, Usage, para. 2). While the use of the term is not as common as that of *suicide bombing*, both *Fox News* and the *New York Post* have made attempts to convert to using the term. This conversion is definitely worthwhile, particularly regarding reshifting the focus of these bombings away from the perpetrators and onto the impact of their violent crimes.

Regarding the goals of terrorist networks, Robert Pape (2003) suggests that "terrorism has two purposes—to gain supporters and to coerce opponents" (p. 345). Of particular interest here are the tactical methods that these terrorist networks employ to gain attention to their political cause (support), and how they are able to manipulate popular perceptions to effectuate the political changes they desire (coercion) by committing such criminal acts as suicide or homicide bombings (terror). It is possible that homicide bombings have become the most effective "weapon" that the terrorist networks now have available to accomplish their political goals (Gunaratna, 2000). As Pape (2003) also states, "terrorist organization are increasingly relying on suicide attacks to achieve major political objectives . . . [because] suicide terrorism follows a strategic [and tactical] logic" (pp. 343–344). This logic is not without merit. Sprinzak (2000) identifies the following as some of the advantages of suicide terror:

- It is a simple and low-cost operation (requiring no escape route or rescue mission).
- It increases the likelihood of mass casualties and extensive damage (since the bomber can choose the exact time, location, and circumstances of the attack).

- There is no fear that interrogated terrorists will surrender important information (because their deaths are certain).
- It has an immense impact on the public and the media (because it precipitates an overwhelming sense of helplessness).

In using females as homicide bombers, Beyler (2003b) points out, "terrorist organizations have added a new focus to terrorism by placing the emphasis on the perpetrators . . . opening the stage for the entry of [even more] female combatants" (Introduction, para. 1). Beyler continues, "female participation is being manipulated by terrorist organizations, which intend to use the image of a female suicide bomber to distort worldwide public opinion" (Worldview, para. 3). Sheikh Ahmed Yassin, the spiritual leader of Hamas, in commenting about their use of a female suicide bomber said, "Women are like the reserve army—when there is a necessity, we use them" (Regular, 2004). Oftentimes, "the media [also] becomes a victim of this strategy by describing female bombing actions as the only way for these women to express their frustration; a testimony of utter despair" (Beyler; Worldview, para. 4). Therefore, in an effort to garner public and political support, these terrorist organizations are using homicide bombings and, more specifically, female homicide bombers to shock the conscience of democratic ideologies via the influence of the media in order to coerce concessions from their opponents.

Zedalis (2004) notes that terrorist organizations use women as weapons because they provide:

- Tactical advantage: stealthier attack, element of surprise, hesitancy to search women, female stereotype (e.g., nonviolent)
- Increased number of combatants
- Increased publicity (greater publicity = larger number of recruits)
- Psychological effect

"It is the ultimate asymmetric weapon," explained Magnus Ranstorp, director of the Center for the Study of Terrorism and Political Violence. "You can assimilate among the people and then attack with an element of surprise that has an incredible and devastating shock value" (Van Natta, 2003, sec. 4, p. 1). Women, it would seem, have been "discovered" as advantageous for terrorist groups and organizations to use.

Given the wave of investigation into terrorist networks in general since September 11, 2001, it is essential to review three emerging suppositions regarding the modern tactics of terrorism before narrowing the focus to female participation specifically. First, we will examine the insightful common denominators put forth by Robert Pape (2003) in an article published by the *American Political Science Review* called "The Strategic Logic of Suicide Terrorism" that examines why homicide terrorism works and why it will continue to increase. Second, we will explore the role of media usage by terrorist networks. Finally, this chapter will review the adaptive nature of terrorist networks as reported by the CIA in the *National Strategy for Combating Terrorism* (2003).

Pape (2003) contends that the tactical common denominator for utilizing the tactic of homicide terrorism among terrorist networks transcends the most common explanations of why "suicide terrorism is rising around the world (e.g., religious fanaticism or psychological explanations)" (p. 343). His research argues that "over the past two decades, suicide terrorism has been rising largely because terrorists have learned that it pays . . . [and that] the terrorist's political causes have made more gains after they resorted to suicide operations than they had before" (p. 343). As the title of Pape's work implies, homicide terrorism has a strategic and tactical logic, "one specifically designed to coerce modern liberal democracies to make significant concessions" (p. 343). Furthermore, these "modern liberal democracies," or the terrorist's targets, are also "democratic occupying entities" such as, for example, the United States, Israel, and the Russian Federation (Gordon, 2003)—a characteristic, we would note, that is also highly conducive to media influence and attention. It is also a characteristic that empowers terrorist networks with the ability to shock the conscience of democratic ideology via the media to achieve their political concessions.

It would seem that the media has become a key tool in the tactics of terrorist networks as well. Terrorist networks use the media to gain public and political support—to make their cause known, to coerce the concessions made by "democratic occupying entities," and to reinforce the successful tactic of utilizing homicide bombers in the first place. In fact, while not the specific focus of this study, an observation that is perhaps worthy of future research is the increase in occurrence and effectiveness of homicide terrorism as found in Pape's (2003) research between the years of 1980 to 2001, and how that corresponds to the dawn of cable television, the Internet, and the advent of globalization. However, for the sake of this investigation, it is enough to state that technology and media influence is a "force multiplier" for terrorist networks (White, 2003, pp. 16–17). "In military terms, a force multiplier increases striking power without increasing the strength of a unit" (White, 2003, p. 16). Regarding the media's influence in relation to the terrorist network's tactics, "[media] coverage can enhance the aura of the event . . . twenty-four hour news coverage leads to sensationalist filler" (White, 2003, pp. 16–17). All of which only serves to reinforce the support and acknowledgment of a terrorist network's cause, and shift the focus away from the brutal crimes they have committed.

Furthermore, the CIA, in its *National Strategy for Combating Terrorism* (2003), also states that "[t]he international environment defines the boundaries within which terrorists' strategies take shape. As a result of freer, more open borders this environment unwittingly provides access to havens, capabilities, and other support to terrorists" (p. 6). Therefore, the defenders of democracy must also stay abreast of the adaptive environment and "changing nature of terrorism" (CIA, 2003, p. 6). The CIA report continues, "the terrorist challenge has changed considerably over the past decade and likely will continue to evolve. Ironically, the particular nature of the terrorist threat we face today springs in large part from some of our past successes" (p. 6). Furthermore, speaking to the end of the Cold War, a period that corresponds to Pape's (2003) research and the rise of media influence, the CIA report concurs that:

> We also saw dramatic improvements in the ease of transnational communication, commerce, and travel. Unfortunately, the terrorists adapted to this new international environment and turned the advances of the 20th century into the destructive enablers of the 21st century. (p. 7)

Once again, the adaptive nature of terrorist networks builds on modern technology and the media to further their political cause (Gunaratna, 2000).

Ironically, "terrorists often seek out states [and countries] where they can operate with impunity. . . . More audaciously, foreign terrorists also establish cells in the very open, liberal, and tolerant societies that they plan to attack" (CIA, 2003, p. 8). By utilizing the very freedoms of democratic society, terrorist networks use the very system they seek to thwart as a means to their end. Shrewdly, these terrorists adapt to whatever works best and change tactics to whatever is most effective at accomplishing their goals. For example, when guerilla tactics began to be viewed as too militant and producing less effective results for terrorist networks in the late 1970s, they began to use homicide bombings, which produced more effective and beneficial results (Gordon, 2003). Furthermore:

> Today's terrorist threat is different from that of the past. Modern technology has enabled terrorists to plan and operate worldwide as never before. With advanced telecommunications, they can coordinate their actions among dispersed cells while remaining in the shadows. Today's terrorists increasingly enjoy a force-multiplier effect by establishing links with other like-minded organizations around the globe. (CIA, 2003, p. 10)

So, while Saddam Hussein may be able to "eradicate a 'problem' by killing tens of thousands of Kurds . . . democratic society's liberal notions and horror at such tactics preclude equally combative suppression philosophies" (Gordon, 2003).

This adaptive nature of terrorist networks has also been mirrored in two recent presentations regarding the tactics of terrorism: first, by Robert Ruth in his presentation of *Town and Country Terrorism* at the annual Southern Criminal Justice Association's meeting on September 24, 2003, in Nashville, Tennessee, regarding domestic terrorism and the infiltration of foreign factions; and second, by Major Andy Dietz, United States Marine Corps, in his address to the Southeastern Command and Leadership Academy at the University of Tennessee at Chattanooga on November 12, 2003. Both gentlemen reported similar observations regarding the adaptive nature of terrorist networks, but in different ways and from different viewpoints.

In his study, Ruth (2003) reported a trend of terrorist networks to migrate toward and infiltrate rural areas to avoid detection (specifically North Carolina), a tactic that generally required recruitment of sympathetic locals. Furthermore, Ruth observed that as one terrorist tactic was discovered or revealed to authorities, the terrorist networks would modify their next attack accordingly (e.g., a philosophy reminiscent of a line from the 1987 film *The Untouchables*: "You send one of ours to the hospital, we'll send one of yours to the morgue."). Conversely, from his military experience in the most recent war in Iraq, Major Dietz (2003) reported high levels of specific tactical adaptations by terrorist networks. Whereas attacks used to focus on taking out a single target, such as one military vehicle, now, through observation by terrorists regarding the spacing between vehicles, several targets (vehicles) are attacked at once. Furthermore, Dietz (2003) observed, the terrorists are becoming stealthier by hiding explosives in Coke cans and among debris on the street.

With the definition, goals, and purpose of terrorist networks reviewed, and after examining the current tactics and trends of terrorist networks, we now turn to why females historically have been considered an unlikely threat, even in the face of conflicting historical evidence.

HOW COULD SHE?

There has been perhaps no concept as readily dismissed by popular contention as that of a willfully violent woman—the operative assumption being that even if a woman is violent, she could not have wanted, deliberately, to cause harm (Pearson, 1997). This inherent disbelief seems to know no boundaries. As a demographic, it would appear that women have successfully convinced the world that they are practically incapable of *willfully* perpetrating violence, much less commit an act of terrorism. Quite simply, the mortal threat of a female foe is rarely, if ever, taken seriously. These dismissive assumptions are the greatest strength behind making an argument for the increasing likelihood of terrorist networks to utilize female participants to perpetrate terrorist acts—specifically regarding homicide bombings.

Society's primordial block regarding the capacity of females to commit violent acts may be the most glaring example of denial ever recorded. So why does this phenomenon prevail? It is perhaps the deeply engrained ideology of women as life-givers, not life-takers, which does the most to prevent any legitimate notion of the willfully violent female offender (Adler, 1981; Chesney-Lind, 1997; MacDonald, 1991; Mann, 1984; Pollak, 1977). However, it is typically the physiology factors that are the first to be argued against any female involvement in violent or terrorist acts. Our species cannot seem to shake the gender roles of men being the stronger *protector* and women being the weaker *protectee*. Sure, in primordial days when physical strength was a requirement to defend the tribe in combat it could be argued that men had the physical edge of brute force. However, those days are long gone. Today, merely squeezing a trigger or flipping a switch is all that is *physically* required to be able to commit a violent act of terrorism.

How could she? This emblematic response to violent female offenders in general reflects the belief that women are not psychologically wired for aggression (Adler, 1981; Chesney-Lind, 1997; MacDonald, 1991; Mann, 1984; Pearson, 1997; Pollak, 1977). It automatically assumes that the violent female offender is an anomaly, or, at the very least, an involuntary participant. Even when a violent female offender or terrorist has been identified, it has often been in the light of secondary support to a larger male-dominated campaign (MacDonald, 1991) and not, for example, as the brains behind the brawn, or as a willing and eager participant. Furthermore, most female offenders or terrorists are routinely labeled as crazed, hypermasculine Lomobrosian atavists, feminist man-hating lesbians, or merely brainwashed little girls who just happened to fall in with the wrong guy (MacDonald, 1991).

Little credence has ever been given to the genuine involvement of women in violent criminal acts or terrorist activities. As Pollak (1977) points out, "women have received more commendations for their seemingly low criminality than practically any other population group . . . [and] it is a grave mistake not to challenge that assumption" (p. 1). The more likely scenario, as Pollak (1977) continues, "is a statistical deception of the masked character of female crime" (p. 1). Female offenders, particularly violent female offenders, are underreported, less often detected than their male counterparts, and, if apprehended, shown more leniency in sentencing (Adler, 1981; Chesney-Lind, 1997; Mann, 1984; Pollak 1977).

By not taking seriously this even darker figure of underreported violent female crime, and perhaps consequently the increased potential for female involvement in terrorist activities, the criminal justice system may be leaving the back door wide open for surprise exploitation. Freda Adler (1981) puts this notion into perspective:

> The historical perception of women as more dependent and emotional than men, and less aggressive and defiant of authority, has carried over to the criminal justice system . . . where the functionaries have chivalrously treated women more protectively than men. (p. 4)

All of which is quite disadvantageous in today's reality where society demands that practitioners and the government be as prepared as possible against any future acts of terrorism. If the criminal justice system is unwilling to examine, or does not believe in the viability of the female terrorist, then perhaps the inevitable will be as shocking as a commercial airliner being used as a bomb.

THE HISTORICAL CONTEXT

The following are but a few examples of the historical involvement of females in terrorist networks. Many, if not all, terrorist networks are known to covertly recruit women specifically because of the ease with which females are able to circumvent detection by security when carrying out a mission (Beyler, 2003b; Copeland, 2002; Gunaratna, 2000; Lloyd, 2000; MacDonald, 1991; MFA, 2003; Schweitzer, 2003). The following groups historically have maintained largely unrecognized and unexamined female memberships. These examples are by no means exhaustive. A brief synopsis of each group will be given first, with an analysis of the evolution, transition, and significance of female involvement to follow.

The Baader-Meinhof Gang

This group was the forerunner of a Germany terrorist organization that would become known as the Red Army Faction (RAF), and whose heyday of terror was primarily during the 1970s. Two females, Gundrun Ensslin and Ulricke Meinhof, are credited with being the brains and revolutionary heart behind the brawn of Andreas Baader, a male, who was reported as being more interested in the criminal lifestyle and the "adventure" of terrorist activities than the predominately feminist and Marxist ideology that drove the faction (MacDonald, 1991). Numerous women were drawn to join the various incarnations of the RAF and commit terrorist attacks for their anticapitalist cause. In fact, 10 years ago (circa 1991), five of the eight most wanted German terrorists were women from the RAF (MacDonald, 1991). Most of the original leaders of this group were captured, including both female founders who later died while incarcerated. The fall of the Soviet Union is generally credited with the demise of this terrorist network (Schweitzer, 2003).

The ETA

"ETA" stands for Euskadi Ta Askatasuna (meaning "homeland and freedom"), but is more commonly referred to as the Basque Nation and Liberty, emerged from the Basque region of Spain during the 1950s. It is one of the largest nationalistic terrorist groups in Europe (White, 2003). Currently, the ETA is an active terrorist organization whose traceable funds, along with many other groups, were frozen by the United States Treasury Department in the wake of the September 11 attacks ("U.S., EU Freeze ETA Group Assets," 2002). This group has always recruited women and had a large female commando division. An associated feminist political movement called Egizan (meaning "Act Women") collaborates with the ETA to commit terrorist acts for both groups and is reported as having some of the most ruthless female members among terrorist networks (MacDonald, 1991; White, 2003).

Lebanon/Hezbollah

The first female homicide bombing was committed on April 8, 1985, in a car bombing against the Israeli Defense Forces (IDF) in Lebanon, Khyadali Sana, killing four soldiers and wounding two others (Beyler, 2003a, Chronology, para. 1; Pape, 2003, p. 357). Six more female homicide bombers would strike the Southern Lebanon Army (SLA) over the next two years (see Appendix A). The SLA was backed primarily by the IDF and assisted by the United States, France, and the United Nations (Pape, 2003).

In fact, the very first homicide bombing happened in 1983 against the U.S. Embassy in Beirut. It was perpetrated in response to the insurgence of Israeli forces into Lebanon, and is perhaps the event that led to the withdrawal of democratic entities in the area (Pape, 2003). While it was perhaps the shock of the first occurrence of homicide terrorism that led to democratic concessions in Beirut, the fact that a female perpetration of a homicide bombing barely two years later in the same campaign cannot be overlooked. The two phenomena appear to be growing in effectiveness along simultaneous timelines and, it would appear, for similar reasons—to coerce moderate gains against "occupying democratic entities" (Pape, 2003).

North Korea and Kim Hyon Hui

Perceiving the selection of Seoul for the 1988 Olympics as a political affront, and seeking to frighten countries away from the international games, the North Korean government activated one of its terrorist operatives to bomb Korean Air Flight 858. That operative was Kim Hyon Hui, a woman who was specifically recruited and brainwashed by her government to commit a terrorist act because of the unassuming nature inherent to her being a female—a female who would have killed herself when caught if her cyanide cigarette had worked properly, a female who took eight days to break under intense interrogative techniques, a female who intended to blow up an airline full of people for her country (MacDonald, 1991).

Liberation Tigers for Tamil Eelam (LTTE)

This Tamil separatists group began utilizing homicide terrorism tactics in its fight for independence from Sri Lanka in the late 1980s and female suicide bombers in early 1990s (Gunaratna, 2000; White, 2003). Nearly half of all the LTTE members are female, as well as comprising about half of the elite homicide division called the Black Tigers (Lloyd, 2000; MacDonald, 1991; White, 2002). The most notorious female homicide attack by the LTTE occurred on May 21, 1991, when a woman known as Dhanu assassinated Rajiv Gandhi and killed 16 other people in the process. After garlanding Gandhi and kneeling down to touch his feet, Dhanu detonated the explosives hidden under her traditional cultural gown. Dhanu had been specifically chosen by the LTTE because of the perceived lack of suspicion regarding women by Gandhi's security (Lloyd, 2000; MacDonald, 1991).

Nearly a third of the 168 homicide bombings committed by the LTTE between 1980 and 2000 have been perpetrated by female guerrillas (Gunaratna, 2000; Schweitzer, 2003). An attempt was made on President Chandrika Kumaratunga on December 18, 1999, that killed 23 people and nearly blinded the president. Another female homicide bomber detonated her explosives in front of the office of Prime Minister Sirimavo Bandaranaike on January 5, 2000, killing 13 people (Lloyd, 2000). However, after two decades of fighting and homicide bombings, the Liberation Tigers of Tamil Eelam began a ceasefire in December 2001when the Sri Lankan government agreed to peace negotiations and concessions for the LTTE's political cause.

The Intifada

This group was an uprising of Palestinians, primarily women and children, begun in October of 1987 as a subgroup of the Palestinian Liberation Organization (PLO), and set against the Israeli military occupation of the West Bank and the Gaza Strip (MacDonald, 1991; White, 2003). The young girls involved were treated as equals by their compatriot boys and the Israeli soldiers in their tactics, deadly aim and stealth. These young girls also made up at least half of the *shebab*—the terrorist army of young people that attacked the soldiers. The function of the older women in the group was to organize the riots and stand in front of the male and children rebels because the Israeli soldiers were less likely, and in fact ordered not to shoot them. In addition, the older female members of the group used traditional female clothing to hide and transport a variety of armor and weapons. Even though the Israelis were aware of this female participation, the reluctance to manhandle these women was further deterred by the soldiers' fear of fighting off a mob of outraged Palestinian Muslim men for physically violating their women (MacDonald, 1991).

The most notorious Intifada woman was Leila Khaled, the leader of the Black September faction. "Khaled led a daring hijacking of four airliners on September 6, 1970, which resulted in the destruction of three of the aircraft, the near overthrow of the Jordanian government, and her own capture" (Westerman, 2003). Khaled continues to be an outspoken activist against the "continued Israeli occupation" from her jail cell, and a proponent of the potential of Al-Qaida utilizing female homicide bombers ("Al-Qaida set to Unleash," 2003). It would seem that the young girls who threw rocks in the first Intifada have now evolved into the homicide bombers of the second Intifada.

The Palestinian Liberation Organization (PLO), Hamas/Hezbollah

In addition to the Intifada, several officially sanctioned women's committees were founded with the guidance of Yasser Arafat and the PLO under the guise of educational and vocational training, charity work, and health services. In reality, these committees were to train the Intifada, run guns and launder money for al-Fatah (the military branch of the PLO), and indoctrinate fedayeen or holy warriors (MacDonald, 1991; White, 2003). The Palestinian female members used this heavy reliance on their services to pressure the men of the movement into passing an Equal Rights for Women bill, "the men . . . relying as heavily as they do on the women's crucial roles, agreed . . . albeit reluctantly" (MacDonald, 1991, p. 67).

Ironically, this increased "liberation" of Palestinian women may have very well paved the way for the greater proportional increase in female perpetration of homicide bombings against Israeli targets for the terrorist network seen today (Beyler, 2003b; Copeland, 2002; MacDonald, 1991; Schweitzer, 2003). This is a contrasting rationale to Beyler's notion that these women have been left with no other way to express their frustrations of utter despair, for why else would *women* resort to such terrorist tactics—the *how could she* mentality. While an analysis will follow, other than among the Chechnya rebels, the Israeli/Palestinian conflict has seen the greatest insurgence of female homicide bombers over the last three years (see Appendixes A and B).

The catalyst for increased female homicide bombings in Palestine occurred on January 27, 2002, when Wafa Idris became the first Palestinian female homicide bomber.

Since that time over a dozen Palestinian women have perpetrated or facilitated suicide bombings against Israeli targets, as opposed to only three known facilitators in the two years prior to Wafa's attack (see Appendix A). Furthermore, these "female bombers have been absorbed into a growing Palestinian cult of martyrdom," their images appear on posters, they are glorified in poems and songs, and they have come to be viewed as "folk heroes" and "martyrs" (Copeland, 2002, para. 4).

The Chechen Rebels

After the collapse of the Soviet Union in 1991, Chechnya (again) sought its independence from what would become known as the Russian Federation. On December 11, 1994, President Boris Yeltsin ordered Russian troops to invade Chechnya to disarm illegal armed formations (e.g., terrorist networks). However, by spring of 1996, Chechen fighters had forced Russian troops to sign a peace agreement, which, in effect, recognized Chechnya's independence. However, feuding for power between Chechen warlords led to a series of bombings in Moscow and Volgodonsk that killed upward of 217 people (Waal, 2002). Russian Prime Minister Vladimir Putin seized on the anti-Chechen publicity to order an extensive and heavy aerial bombardment of Chechnya. In February 2000, the rebel separatists who had fled to the mountains reinflamed the terrorist network operations of the Chechen rebels (Waal, 2002).

Scarcely a year later, on November 21, 2001, the first female Chechen homicide bomber struck in an attack on the Russian Federation's (RF) Grozny military commander Gaidar Gajiyev (Schweitzer, 2003). Less than a year after that, in October 2002, approximately half of the 41 terrorists (all with explosives strapped to their bodies) who seized some 700 hostages in a Moscow theater were women; approximately 170 hostages were killed in this attack. Over a dozen Chechen female homicide bombers have struck RF targets since that time (see Appendix A). It should also be noted that there were several women involved in the terrorist takeover of the school in Beslan.

Much like their Palestinian counterparts, Chechen women are being recruited because they are female and less suspicious than men when targeting marks, not to mention the shocking nature of female combatants to the Russian populace and subsequent media attention—albeit somewhat less so than the Palestinian women. While the increase of Chechen women in terrorist networks might be due to the sheer depletion of Chechen male rebels from "cleanings sweeps" conducted by the RF, the increasing occurrence of female Chechen rebels cannot be denied (Waal, 2002).

The Taliban and Al-Qaida

By way of the Arabic newspaper *A-Sharq Al-Awsat*, a woman named Umm Osama, which means mother of Osama (as in Bin Laden), announced her leadership of a women's homicide division now working within the terrorist network. Umm reports that the Taliban and Al-Qaida have trained her "women warriors" in weaponry to battle U.S. forces in Afghanistan, and will be utilizing these women to carry messages from Afghani leaders to the frontlines. Umm explains that:

Islamic law permits the woman to stand by the man and to support him in the holy war [and] warns the U.S. that members of her women warriors unit will be arriving very shortly to deliver its first blow, which has been "declared by their leader" to be a strike that will knock the September 11th attacks into oblivion ("Al-Qaida set to Unleash," 2003; "Code Pink," 2003).

While there have been no overt acts perpetrated thus far by these women warriors, the fact that this terrorist network utilized the threat of this type of tactic is significant to the evolution of the female participation in terrorist networks, particularly regarding homicide bombers. First, the terrorist networks are purposely using the threat of female homicide bombers or women warriors; second, the occupying democratic entities or targets of these potential actions are receiving these threats as credible; and third, the media is seizing on the sensationalism of potential female homicide terrorists, thus providing increased attention to the terrorists' political cause.

In fact, approximately a month after Umm's announcement, the Federal Bureau of Investigation (FBI) issued its first "be on the lookout" for a female in the war on terrorism ("FBI Warns," 2003). Two days later, Aafia Siddiqui was detained by Pakistani authorities under the suspicion of being a "fixer" for Al-Qaida, meaning she allegedly funneled money for the terrorist network ("Woman Sought", 2003). Subsequently, on June 21, 2003, three other women were also arrested in Saudi Arabia for participation in an alleged plot by Al-Qaida to attack Mecca ("Reports: At Least Three Women," 2003).

THE EVOLUTION AND TRANSITION

To sensationalize a cause, particularly when the focus remains on the perpetrator because she is a female, seems to have become a coercive technique utilized by terrorist networks that occupying democratic entities are even less able to tolerate than homicide terrorism in general. After all, what better way to attract media attention to a political cause and to shift the focus off the violent criminal acts of terrorism, than to place the focus on the perpetrator because she is a woman (Beyler, 2003b). The horrific nature and loss of life associated with homicide bombings shock the conscience of modern democracies. Excessive media attention inflames the public's outrage, and sometimes sympathy, toward these terrorist networks—all of which pressures governments into making concessions they hope will stop the killing, but not because they have had a particular change of politics.

To reiterate, terrorist networks now seem to be purposely using the threat of female homicide bombers or women warriors to coerce concessions. Additionally, the occupying democratic entities or targets of these potential actions are receiving these threats as credible, and the media is sensationalizing the potential for, and occurrence of female terrorists as a thrilling news angle, which only provides increased attention to the terrorists' political cause. Modern terrorist networks seem to be rolling all the emerging trends in terrorist tactics into one with female participation and perpetration of homicide bombings.

When viewed in the historical context, the evolution of female participation in terrorist networks seems to correspond to the research of Robert Pape regarding the increased usage of homicide terrorism in general (2003). This was a tactical change perhaps encouraged by the concessions made by the Reagan administration in Beirut after the homicide bombing of the U.S. embassy in 1983 (Pape, 2003). Since that time, "there have been at least 188 separate suicide terrorist attacks worldwide . . . increasing from 31 in the 1980s, to 104 in the 1990s, to 53 in 2000–2001 alone" (Pape, 2003, p. 343). Homicide bombings have increased and will continue to increase because they work.

Correspondingly, an examination of the frequency of female homicide bombers from 1980 to 2000 in comparison to 2000 to 2003 reveals that similar conclusions may be made regarding the increased usage of female homicide bombers by terrorist networks. This trend has increased dramatically when compared to prior periods, one that will perhaps continue to increase because of media influence and for similar reasons indicated by Pape's (2003) research on the increase of homicide terrorism in general because it works.

METHODOLOGY

There are four main terrorist networks that have used or are currently using female homicide bombers: Hezbollah and the Palestinian resistance in Lebanon during the 1980s against Israel, the United States, and the South Lebanon Army; the Tamil Tigers (LTTE) between 1980 and 2000 against Sri Lanka; Hezbollah, Hamas, and the PLO since 2001 against Israel; and the Chechen rebels since 2000 against the Russian Federation.

There were seven individual females involved in seven separate bombings during Hezbollah's Lebanon campaign between 1985 and 1987. While exact occurrences and specific cases of female bombings by the LTTE were unavailable other than the sensationalized attacks, it is generally reported and accepted by experts in the field that approximately 50 of the 168 homicide bombings committed by the LTTE between 1980 and 2000 were perpetrated by females (Cronin, 2003; Gunaratna, 2000; Lloyd, 2000; MacDonald, 1991). There have been 18 individual females involved in 18 separate homicide bombings, or facilitation of homicide bombings, by Hezbollah/Hamas/PLO against Israel between 2001 and 2003. There have been 32 individual females involved in 10 separate homicide bombings against the Russian Federation by Chechen rebels between 2000 and 2003 (see Appendixes A and B).

A simple generation of the yearly average of female participation in homicide bombings in the four terrorist networks is given in Table 1. The four campaigns that have used female bombers can be divided into two separate time periods: one that is prior to year 2000 and in which the campaigns have ended (Hezbollah/Lebanon and the LTTE); and the other, post-2000 in which the campaigns are ongoing (Hezbollah/Hamas/PLO and the Chechen rebels). Furthermore, when comparing the two time periods, the instance of female participation nearly triples for the current Hezbollah/Hamas/PLO campaign and

TABLE 1   Female Participation in Homicide Bombings

Campaign	Time Period	Females	Yearly Average
Hezbollah/Lebanon	1985–1987	7	2.34
LTTE/Sri Lanka	1980–2000	50	2.5
Hezbollah/Hamas/PLO/Jihad	2001–2003	18	6
Chechen Rebels	2000–2003	32	8

nearly quadruples for the Chechen rebel campaign, going from a combined pre-2000 average of 2.42 per year to 6 per year and 8 per year, respectfully.

It was perhaps the flurry of media attention surrounding Wafa Idris as the first "martyred" Palestinian female homicide bomber in 2002 that would seem to be the turning point for terrorist networks to increase the tactical usage of female homicide bombers. Since Wafa's bombing in 2002, there have been 14 Palestinian and 30 Chechen females involved in either the perpetration or facilitation of homicide bombings, or arrested for intending to carry out such bombings (see Appendixes A and B). Furthermore, during the three-year period between 2000 and 2003, there have been 50 females involved in 28 incidents of homicide terrorism on behalf of terrorist networks (killing at least 422), more than half the total number of female homicide bombings committed by the LTTE alone over a 20-year period (see Appendix B).

This analysis and comparison seems to show an increasing trend to use females as homicide bombers within terrorist networks, particularly over the last four years (2000–2003). This increasing trend to tactically use female homicide bombers by terrorist networks seems to correspond directly to the findings of Pape's research on the increasing instance of suicide terrorism in general (2003). Thus, this research also concludes that homicide bombings, in general, are becoming an increasingly common trend and tactic used by terrorist networks to garner concessions from their targets, and that the tactical use of females as homicide bombers is emerging as a coinciding phenomenon that might inevitably spill over into the domestic arena or, at the very least, continue to rise abroad.

THE SIGNIFICANCE

So, why might this trend to utilize female participation be significant to practitioners regarding the future of terrorist activities and attacks, particularly in the domestic arena? In an examination of the Palestinian women perpetrating or facilitating homicide bombings, the Israeli Ministry of Foreign Affairs (MFA) states that "the terrorist organizations behind the attacks want to exploit the advantages of dispatching females to perpetrate them" (MFA, 2003, para. 1). Furthermore, the MFA noted that these terrorist networks utilized females "under the assumption that a female is thought of as soft, gentle, and innocent and therefore will arouse less suspicion . . . [meaning] terrorists were aware of their need for camouflage" (para. 1).

Also, in citing the common characteristics of Palestinian females involved in these homicide bombings, the MFA states that these females "were from two poles of Palestinian society . . . well-educated professionals and common young women lacking education and a profession," with the preponderance coming from the top, or well-educated pole among Palestinian females (MFA, 2003, para. 2). When compared to the Chechen rebels, the only other currently active terrorist network to use female homicide bombers, the female faction found among the rebels corresponds well to the lower or uneducated pole of females cited by the MFA.

The increased occurrence of female involvement in homicide bombings among these two terrorist networks found in Palestine and Chechnya over the last four years provides an educational-level dichotomy for examination, particularly regarding the future of possible terrorist activities or attacks in the United States. There are primarily two reasons for the increase: (1) the level of education among women in the United States and their participation in gangs or radical extremist organizations that may or may not be currently involved in the perpetration of terrorist type activities; and (2) the recruitment and infiltration by foreign terrorist networks into domestic groups predisposed to such subversive activities such as gangs and radical extremist organizations.

While little hard data exist regarding the exact number of female members in radical or extremist organizations in the United States such as the Earth Liberation Front (ELF) and the Animal Liberation Front (ALF), both are generally considered to maintain high levels of female participation. Moreover, whereas radical factions of these organizations may not represent the official dogma of the groups from which they emerge, in some instances, particularly in regard to ELF, some of these groups have perpetrated terrorist-type activities. For example, "ELF takes credit for arsons at a ski resort in Vail, CO, inspiring four teens to torch housing developments in Long Island, and recently, fire-bombing sport-utility vehicles at an auto dealership outside Erie, PA" (Malkin, 2003, para. 4). However, what is of particular interest here is the generally accepted notion that women who become members of these groups are well educated and typically become members while attending college, not so unlike their educated Palestinian counterparts.

Also, female membership in gangs across the United States is perhaps as epidemic as the gang problem itself and could quite possibly be seen as correlating to the low or uneducated pole of female involvement found among the Chechen rebels. "Although the percentage of gang members who [are] female is difficult to ascertain, all sources agree the numbers [are] significant" ("Number of Female Gang Members," 2001, para. 1). Couple that with the fact that Jeff Fort sought to offer the services of the Black P. Stone Nation to Moammar Gadhafi in 1986, and more recently Jose Padilla of the Latin Kings was linked as an operative for Al-Qaida, is it really so far-fetched to predict that eventually terrorist networks might utilize U.S. gangs to perpetrate operations, and that those operations might inevitably include the participation of female gang members?

Furthermore, gangs are also increasingly embracing the Islamic principles that underlie the motivational philosophy of most terrorist networks ("Gangs and Terrorism," 2003, para. 2). Louis Farrakhan has been working with the Bloods in Los Angeles and the Vice Lords in Chicago regarding the adoption of Islamic principles and ideology. What's more, many gang legends who have been incarcerated, such as Sanyika Shakur (aka "Monster" Kody Scott), have converted to this militant brand of Islam and continue to influence their respective gang members toward uniting with this militant faction of Islamic rationale ("Gangs and Terrorism," 2003, para. 5). Not to mention that gangs, like all organizations, but most particularly those of the socially excluded, are supported by the underground economy. Untraceable and prolific funds from the sale of drugs and other illegal activities provide a wealth of untapped power for these gangs ("Gangs and Terrorism," 2003, para. 10). This is a potential outlet that has not yet been explored or exploited by terrorist networks, but one that may very well be on the horizon.

Additionally, well-known gangster tactics have long since used females as stealthy perpetrators of illegal endeavors; for example, using women as mules to smuggle drugs or even "using sex as ploy to distract victims" (Valdez, 2000, p. 403). Beyond that, the number of female gang members and outright female gangs has consistently been on the rise. What is to preclude these female gangsters from cutting out the middleman, both figuratively and literally, and start doing it for themselves? In examining current trends among female gang members, Valdez (2000) states "female gang members will also be involved in crimes for profit as they expand their criminal behavior" (p. 403). Furthermore, "you can anticipate an increasing number of female gang members to carry guns and commit more violent crimes" (Valdez, 2000, p. 403).

DISCUSSION

It is perhaps no coincidence that the social revolution and feminist movement of the 1960s and 1970s gave birth to the first insurgence of female participation in terrorist networks (e.g., the Baader-Meinhof Gang, Intifada, ETA, LTTE, and PLO). Criminologists have long predicted that the progression of social equalization between the sexes, particularly the entrance of women into economic pursuits, would lead to an increase in the volume of female crime (Adler, 1981; Chesney-Lind, 1997; Mann, 1984; Pollak, 1977). While this emancipation theory is intriguing, it can account for only some middle- to upper-class involvement of females in criminal or terroristic activities such as those female members of ELF, ALF, and some of the Palestinian suicide bombers. It certainly does not consider the sociodemographics associated with the women who did not benefit from the primarily middle-class U.S.-led social revolution in the first place (Adler, 1981; Chesney-Lind, 1997; Mann, 1984; Pollak, 1977).

The opposite pole of women prone to terrorist involvement would seem to be the marginalized, poverty-laden, oppressed, sublower class of uneducated women who have nothing to lose but everything to gain, such as those female members found among the Chechen rebels and potentially among U.S. gangs. These women tend to become doubly committed to a cause because they have to be twice as tough as the men whose ranks they infiltrate (MacDonald, 1991). "The real question," as Chesney-Lind (1997) points out, "is why so *few* women resort to violence in the face of such horrendous victimization" in the first place (p. 98). Given the constant outcry from feminist organizations regarding the continual oppression, victimization, and violence against women, why should the increasing emergence of female terrorists be shocking at all? After all, women have the denial of society to believe, the covert means to accomplish, an ample motive to commit, and the stealthy opportunity to become some of the most deadly of terrorists. Instead of disbelieving it could happen, practitioners should perhaps be preparing for when it does.

In fact, during the final month of this analysis (December 2003), three of the most deadly homicide bombings committed by females to date were perpetrated, one by a Palestinian female and the other two by Chechen females. These homicide bombings were significant for yet another reason. In the Palestinian bombing:

> The Jihadi bomber engaged the first defense perimeter, i.e. the security guard, eliminated him, then burst into the restaurant and triggered her mini-doomsday device . . . a new weapon has been used: Human Precision Bombs. . . . They will fight their way into their targeted locations. The so-called "weapon of the weak" has been upgraded further. It has become a smart weapon of precision. (Phares, 2003, para. 5, 8, & 10)

The Chechen bombings also used this two-point attack. These attacks may mark yet another adaptive tactic beginning to be utilized by terrorist networks. In an insightful commentary, Dr. Walid Phares (2003) further observes that suicide bombings have traditionally been one-dimensional, in that the moment the bombers encountered the first perimeter of a target, usually security, they blew themselves up. Now, they are becoming two-dimensional attacks, "two missions, two stages and two results" (para. 6).

Indeed, it would seem that homicide terrorism, the so-called weapon of the weak, continues to adapt, and it is perhaps not surprising that women, the supposed weaker sex, are increasingly being used to utilize these new techniques. In fact:

> We do not know whether women have been successfully committing [these crimes] because few female criminals were considered important enough to study . . . [perhaps] the female criminal has just never been caught and is laughing all the way to the bank—if she isn't robbing it. (Mann, 1984, p. 97)

Society cannot continue to deny that *she* is capable of violent terrorist acts; there is no empirical evidence available to suggest that *she* is any less likely than *he* to perpetrate these acts. In fact, as this research has shown, *she* is increasingly being used to perpetrate terrorist activities, particularly homicide bombings. "Female offenders are no longer an insignificant subset of the criminal population, nor are they merely an appendage to a system devised for processing and confining men" (Adler, 1981, p. 5). Maybe a common (although officially unadmitted) instruction given to the counterterrorist squads in Europe is the most prudent of advice: "shoot the women first" (MacDonald, 1991, p. xiv).

CONCLUSIONS

There is no question that homicide terrorism, in general, is an increasingly common tactic used by terrorist networks to achieve moderate concessions from their targets, and that utilizing females as homicide bombers is emerging as a coinciding phenomenon that might inevitably spill over into any future occurrences of domestic terrorism by way of gangs or extremist groups, as well as, at the very least, continue to rise abroad. Counterterrorist strategies must accept the idea that females can and are being used as homicide bombers. It should also be understood that homicide bombings do not occur at an individual level (Zedalis, 2004); that is, individuals do not suddenly decide to strap a bomb to themselves and go kill thousands of people. Homicide bombers are recruited by terrorist organizations to engage in such an attack. Therefore unrelenting pressure must be placed on the organizations that support, encourage, and manage terrorism.

Additionally, tactics and techniques must be developed and used "against" the communities that support the use of homicide bombings, for without the support of the communities, the homicide bombings are less likely to be sustained.

Agencies (public and private) should increase the hiring of females so that suspicious-looking females will be more likely to be detained and searched without the usual accusations of misconduct (which are far less likely to occur when females are involved). Training for all personnel should be increased so that everyone is aware of the warning signs and what action to take or not take.

Future research might explore the two educational poles of female involvement, and examine the female membership of domestic extremist groups and gangs as they may or may not relate to future occurrences of terrorist-type activities or infiltration by foreign terrorist networks.

Finally, the NIMBY ("not in my back yard") mindset must be eliminated. The fact is that homicide bombings can and do occur, and females are an increasingly large part of that. We must also realize that anything can be a target, and that the terrorists seem to be changing their focus to soft targets (e.g., malls, schools, hospitals). Nothing should be overlooked, and the idea that it can happen here and might happen anywhere needs to become far more prevalent. We must assume a 9/12 mindset rather than the 9/10 mindset so many people seem to have. Without the proper mindset we run the risk of being unprepared for the lovely young woman hanging out in the food court at the local mall, and realize too late that yes, she was in fact a homicide bomber.

REFERENCES

ADLER, F. (1981). *The incidence of female criminality in the contemporary world.* New York: New York University Press.

Al-Qaida set to unleash female suicide bombers: Group carries out bin Laden orders, poised for major attack in America. (2003, March 12). *WorldNetDaily.* Retrieved March 12, 2003, from http://www.wnd.com/news/article.asp?ARTICLE_ID=31488.

BEYLER, C. (2003b, February 12). Messengers of death: Female suicide bombers. *International Policy Institute for Counter-Terrorism—International Terrorism.* Retrieved June 1, 2003, from http://www.ict.org.il/inter_ter/frame.htm.

BEYLER, C. (2003a, February 12). Chronology of suicide bombings carried out by women. *International Policy Institute for Counter-Terrorism—International Terrorism.* Retrieved October 13, 2003, from http://www.ict.org.il/.

CENTRAL INTELLIGENCE AGENCY (CIA). (2003, February). *National strategy for combating terrorism.* Retrieved July 2, 2003, from http://www.cia.gov/terrorism/publications/Counter_Terrorism_Strategy.pdf.

CHESNEY-LIND, M. (1997). *The female offender: Girls, women, and crime.* Thousand Oaks, CA: Sage.

Code pink: Al Qaida announces women's suicide division. (2003, March 18). *World Tribune Online.* Retrieved March 18, 2003, from http://216.26.163.62/2003/me_terror_03_18.html.

COPELAND, L. (2002, April 27). Female suicide bombers: The new factor in the Mideast's deadly equation. *Washington Post Online.* Retrieved November 22, 2003, from http://www.washington-post.com/ac2/wpdyn?pagename=article&node=&contentId=A57052-2002Apr26&notFound=true.

CRONIN, A. K. (2003, August 28). Terrorists and suicide attacks. *Congressional Research Service: The Library of Congress.* Retrieved January 29, 2004, from http://www.fas.org/irp/crs/RL32058.pdf.

DIETZ, A. (2003, November 12). *The fight for freedom: Defending democracy.* Paper presented at the weekly meeting of the Southern Command and Leadership Academy at the University of Tennessee, Chattanooga.

FBI WARNS OF AL QAEDA WOMEN. (2003, April 1). *CBS News Online.* Retrieved April 23, 2003, from http://www.cbsnews.com/stories/2003/04/01/attack/main547237.shtml.

GANGS AND TERRORISM. (2003). *GangResearch.Net.* Retrieved November 29, 2003, from http://www.gangresearch.net/Globalization/terrorism/terrorism.html.

GANOR, B. (1998). Defining terrorism, is one man's terrorist another man's freedom fighter? In the annual presentation of the International Policy Institute for Counter-Terrorism publication *Herzlia* (pp. 12–17). Herzlia: ICT Publication.

GANOR, B. (2001). Suicide attacks in Israel. In the annual presentation of the International Policy Institute for Counter-Terrorism publication *Herzlia* (pp. 140–145). Herzlia: ICT Publication.

GORDON, D. (2003, September 11). *Human artillery* [NPR Radio Broadcast]. WBUR Boston: The Connection. Retrieved and heard September 11, 2003, from http://www.theconnection.org/shows/ 2003/09/20030911_b_main.asp.

GUNARATNA, R. (2000, October 20). Suicide terrorism: A global threat. *Jane's Intelligence Review Online.* Retrieved November 4, 2003, from http://www.janes.com/security/international_security/news/usscole/jir001020_1_n.shtml.

INTERNATIONAL COUNTER-TERRORISM ACADEMIC COMMUNITY (ICTAC). (2005). A community of internet. Retrieved April 7, 2005, from http://www.ict.org.il/.

LLOYD, M. (2000, April 2). Exploring the heart of a female assassin: Indian filmmaker inspired by attack on Gandhi. *Boston Globe Online.* Retrieved September 14, 2003, from http://www.operationsick.com/articles/20000402_exploringtheheartofafemaleassassin.asp.

MACDONALD, E. (1991). *Shoot the women first.* New York: Random House.

MALKIN, M. (2003, March 21). American eco-terrorist declare war. *WorldNetDaily.* Retrieved March 29, 2003, from http://www.wnd.com/news/article.asp?ARTICLE_ID=31638.

MANN, C. R. (1984). *Female crime and delinquency.* Birmingham: University of Alabama Press.

MFA (ISRAELI MINISTRY OF FOREIGN AFFAIRS). (2003, January). *The role of Palestinian women in suicide terrorism.* Retrieved July 29, 2003, from http://www.mfa.gov.il/mfa/go.asp?MFAH0n210.

MORGENSTERN, H. Suicide terror—An overview of the threat [web cast]. (2005, April 19).

MY WAY NEWS. (2005, April 21).

NUMBER OF FEMALE GANG MEMBERS. (2001, March). *Office of Juvenile Justice Delinquency and Prevention.* Retrieved September 3, 2003, from http://www.ncjrs.org/html/ojjdp/jjbul2001_3_3/page2.html.

PAPE, R. A. (2003, August). The strategic logic of suicide terrorism. *American Political Science Review, 97,* 343–361.

PEARSON, P. (1997). *When she was bad: Violent women and the myth of innocence.* New York: Viking Penguin Putnam.

PHARES, W. (2003, October 6). Lessons learned from the Hafia attack (Part I). *Townhall.com: Conservative News and Information.* Retrieved October 7, 2003, from http://www.townhall.com/columnists/GuestColumns/Phares20031006.shtml.

POLLAK, O. (1977). *The criminality of women.* Westport, CT: Greenwood Press.

REGULAR, A. (2004, January 16). Mother of two becomes first female suicide bomber for Hamas. *Haaretz.*

REPORTS: AT LEAST THREE WOMEN ARRESTED IN MECCA PLOT. (2003, June 21). *Fox News Channel Online.* Retrieved June 21, 2003, from http://www.foxnews.com/story/0,2933,90080,00.html.

RUTH, R. (2003, September 24). *Town and country terrorism.* Paper presented at the annual meeting of the Southern Criminal Justice Association, Nashville, TN.

SCHWEITZER, Y. (2003, October 9). Female suicide bombers for God. *Tel Aviv University: The Jaffee Center for Strategic Studies.* Retrieved on October 13, 2003, from http://www.imra.org.il/story.php3?id=18478.

SPRINZAK, E. RATIONAL FANATICS. (2000, September–October). *Foreign Policy,* 68.

U.S. DEPARTMENT OF HOMELAND SECURITY (DHS). (2003). *DHS Homepage: DHS Organization.* Retrieved November 22, 2003, from http://www.dhs.gov/dhspublic/theme_home1.jsp.

U.S., EU FREEZE ETA GROUP ASSETS. (2002, May 2). *CNN Online.* Retrieved March 21, 2003, from http://www.cnn.com/2002/US/05/03/eta.assets/index.html.

VALDEZ, A. (2000). *Gangs: A guide to understanding street gangs* (3rd ed.). San Clemente, CA: Law Tech Publishing.

VAN NATTA, D., JR. (2003, August 24). Big bang theory: The terror industry fields its ultimate weapon. *New York Times,* sec. 4, p. 1.

WAAL, THOMAS DE. (2002, July 25). *Fighting for Chechnya: Is Islam a factor?* [PBS Television broadcast]. Wide Angle: Public Broadcast System. Retrieved, read, and viewed May 23, 2003, from http://www.pbs.org/wnet/wideangle/shows/chechnya/index.html.

WESTERMAN, T. (2003, January 31). Cheerleader for female suicide bombers: Lady terrorist welcomes participation by Palestinian women. *WorldNetDaily*. Retrieved January 31, 2003, from http://www.wnd.com/news/article.asp?ARTICLE_ID=26261.

WHITE, J. R. (2003). *Terrorism: An introduction* (4th ed.). Belmont, CA: Wadsworth/Thompson Learning.

Wikipedia: The free online encyclopedia. (2003). Suicide bombing. Retrieved November 22, 2003, from http://en.wikipedia.org/wiki/Suicide_bombing.

WOMAN SOUGHT BY FBI REPORTEDLY ARRESTED IN PAKISTAN. (2003, April 3). *NBC News Online: Chicago*. Retrieved April 5, 2003, from http://www.nbc5.com/news/2088397/detail.html.

ZEDALIS, D. D. Female suicide bombers. (2004, June). Monograph. Strategic Studies Institute of the U.S. Army War College.

APPENDIX A: INCIDENCES OF FEMALE PARTICIPATION, 1980–2003

Lebanon: Hezbollah vs. Israel, United States, and South Lebanon Army

Date	Weapon	Target	Killed
April 9, 1985	Car bomb	IDF convoy	4
July 9, 1985	Car bomb	SLA post	22
September 12, 1985	Car bomb	SLA post	21
November 26, 1985	Car bomb	SLA post	20
July 17, 1986	Car bomb	Jezzine	7
November 11, 1987	Bag bomb	AUB hospital	7
November 14, 1987	Suitcase bomb	Beirut airport	6

Note: The names of these women in corresponding order are: Khyadali Sana, Kharib Ibtisam, Khaierdin Miriam, Al Taher Hamidah, Shagir Karima Mahmud, and Sahyouni Soraya.

Source: Beyler, 2003, Chronology; Pape, 2003, p 357.

Chechnya: Chechen Rebels vs. the Russian Federation

Date	Weapon	Target	Killed
June 9, 2000	Car bomb	Russian Special Forces building	27
November 29, 2001	Belt bomb	Gaidar Gajiyev, RF military leader	3
October 26, 2002	Belt bombs/hostages	Moscow Theater	170
May 12, 2003	Car bomb	Znamenskoye, RF compound	59
May 14, 2003	Belt bomb	Akhmad Kadyrov, RF leader	17
June 5, 2003	Belt bomb	Mosok, Russia bus w/soldiers	17
July 5, 2003	Belt bomb	Moscow rock festival	16
July 11, 2003	Bag bomb	Near Moscow café	1
December 5, 2003	Belt/bag bomb	Commuter train	44
December 9, 2003	Belt/bag bomb	Kremlin	6

Note: To the best of our knowledge, the names of these women have not been published.

Israel: Hezbollah/Hamas/PLO/Islamic Jihad vs. Israel

Date	Weapon	Target	Killed
August 3, 2001	Attempted to place a bomb	Tel Aviv bus station	
August 9, 2001	Led bomber to site	Sbarro pizzeria	15
August 31, 2001	Transported bomb	Hadera restaurant	1 (self)
January 27, 2002	Belt bomb (Wafa)	Jaffa market, Jerusalem	2
February 27, 2002	Belt bomb	Maccabim checkpoint	1 (self)
March 21, 2002	Led bombers to site	King George St, Jerusalem	3
March 29, 2002	Belt bomb	Kiryat Hayovel, Jerusalem	2
April 11, 2002	Arrested—was to participate in attack that occurred the next day		
April 12, 2002	Belt bomb	Mahane Yehuda market	6
April 25, 2002	Arrested crawling toward Israeli settlement in Gaza to blow self up		
May 19, 2002	Led bomber to site	Netanya marketplace	3

Israel: Hezbollah/Hamas/PLO/Islamic Jihad vs. Israel (Continued)

Date	Weapon	Target	Killed
May 22, 2002	Backed out/attested	Rishon Lezion mall	2
June 14, 2002	Would-be bomber arrested	Target unknown	
July 1, 2002	Would-be bomber arrested	Target unknown	
July 17, 2002	Arrested on way to commit bombing in Jerusalem		
July 27, 2002	Arrested on way to commit bombing in Jerusalem		
May 18, 2003	Bag bomb	Afula's Amakim mall	6
October 3, 2003	Belt bomb	Hafia Maxim restaurant	21

Note: The names of these women in corresponding order are: Iman Asha, Ahlam Tamini, Abir Hamdan, Wafa Idris, Dareen Abu Aisheh, Kahira As'sdi and Sana'a Shahada, Ayat al-Akras, Shfaa al-Koudsi, Andaleeb Taquataqah, Iman Abu Housa, Da'a Jiusi, Arin Ahmed, Tahani Titi, Leila Bahari, Thawiya Hamour Umaya, and Mohammed Danaj. The last two have not yet been identified.

Source: Beyler, 2003a, Chronology; MFA, 2003.

APPENDIX B: NUMBER OF FEMALES INVOLVED IN INCIDENCES, 2000–2003

Israel: Hezbollah/Hamas/PLO/Islamic Jihad vs. Israel

Year	Number of Females	Number of Incidences	Number Killed
2001	3	3	16
2002	13	13	19
2003	2	2	27
Total	18	18	62

Chechnya: Chechen Rebels vs. the Russian Federation

Year	Number of Females	Number of Incidences	Number Killed
2000	1	1	27
2001	1	1	3
2002	20	1	170
2003	10	7	160
Total	32	10	360

Combined Total			
2000–2003	50	28	422

46

Women's Attitudes toward the Threat of Terror

Ramona Brockett, Jonathan C. Odo, and Peter C. Ezekwenna

❖

The fear of terrorism is a reality that had not been a part of the social landscape in America until September 11, 2001. America was victimized. Even further, America waged a "war on terror" in response to this victimization against those in the Middle East and others around the world who despise the philosophy and way of life that America calls "freedom." Having done so, this has given rise to a social problem and new form of violence in America—terrorism. While victimization and threat are not new criminological phenomena for people in America, especially women who have suffered domestic abuse and rape, the fear or threat of terrorism presents yet another crease in the analysis of victimization that affects the coping mechanisms of those who have historically been victims.

The four major objectives of this chapter are (1) to measure the fear of the threat of terrorism and its impact on American women who have traditionally suffered violence and domestic abuse; (2) to analyze whether the threat of terrorism has had more or less of an effect on American women who have chronically suffered from the victimization of violence and domestic abuse—as opposed to those who have not had a history of domestic abuse or violence; (3) to establish an understanding of the reaction of those women who have been victimized through domestic abuse or violence; and (4) to distinguish the reasoning behind difference in the reactions of these women to the threat of terrorism brought on by the acts of 9/11.

DOMESTIC ABUSE AND PATRIARCHAL TERRORISM

Analyzing the impact of the threat of global terrorism on women in America who have suffered domestic abuse must include an analysis of "terrorism" and its impact on victims of violence. In 1995, Johnson defined two types of domestic abuse and violence while using data from the 1985 Second National Family Violence Survey—couple violence and patriarchal terrorism. According to Johnson, "couple violence" is common among both men and women. He found that this type of domestic violence does not occur frequently. In fact, his findings concluded that this type of domestic abuse is illusive in that there is not a pattern of escalation; further, it tends not to be physically injurious (Johnson, 1995).

Johnson's second finding of "patriarchal terrorism" differs from the first. This is the first instance where he uses the term *terrorism* to define a violent domestic occurrence. Here, this type of violence, or domestic terrorism, is perpetrated by men toward women escalating over time in both frequency and severity. This violence is not only physical, but, through the use of control, it includes threats, isolation, and economic subordination (p. 284). Further, the roots or historical aspect of this violence comes from a Western family tradition that is rooted in patriarchy, where the home is dominated by the male.

Carlson, in 1997, similarly describes woman abuse as patriarchal terrorism as defined by Johnson. That definition includes patterns of behavior that involve physical, emotional, psychological, verbal, and sexual abuse for the purpose of controlling and demeaning a woman (Carlson, 1997). The definition in itself is synonymous with the act of terrorism. Emotionally, the result of this type of terrorism perpetrated against women produces specific cognitive and behavioral responses that include anger, anxiety, fear, low self-esteem, depression, risk of suicide, confusion, feelings of being overwhelmed, memory loss, poor concentration, suspicion, paranoia, and the recurring trauma of abuse and avoidance of the emotions associated with it (Dutton-Douglas & Dionne, 1991). Further, this type of abuse, albeit terrorism, causes a condition known as posttraumatic stress disorder (Thomas, 2003). Dissociation is a resulting symptom associated with domestic violence and, as a contributing result of posttraumatic stress disorder, it allows the battered woman to separate from her emotional, mental, and physical self (Abel, 2001). In essence, this type of abuse causes the woman to separate from her emotions in order to cope with the trauma. Hence, the definition of patriarchal terrorism and the resulting psychological disorders that affect the victims' cognitive and behavioral patterns of reaction lay the groundwork for understanding the post-9/11 effect global terrorism may have in the lives of those American women who have historically, albeit chronically, suffered domestic abuse.

Similarly, the effects of global terrorism have been found to have a similar effect on the psychological and cognitive behaviors of women in America (Thomas, 2003). In a study conducted by Thomas measuring the reactions of "midlife women" to the 9/11 tragedy, she found that four to six months after 9/11, 61 percent of the women in the study were still distressed, exhibiting symptoms of fear, sadness, anger, powerlessness, distrust, and vigilance (p. 853). Further, in the aftermath it was found that there was an increased incidence of posttraumatic stress disorder, depression, stress-related physical illness, generalized anxiety disorder, and an unfamiliar sense of vulnerability regarding the safety of the home (Pyszczynski, Solomon, & Greenberg, 2003). The theoretical framework upon which these studies of women's stress were premised included terror management theory. Terror management theory, which was formulated in 1984, posits that events that produce acute awareness of death will cause humans to buffer existential anxiety through proximal and distal defenses due to death anxiety brought about by terrorist threat (Thomas, 2003). Theoretically, this seems to explain the similarity in the cognitive reactions of women who have been abused by their spouses and those who react to the potential threat of terror. Actually, both forms of "terrorism" bring about the same result—fear, anxiety, and helplessness. This further aids in explaining the benign reaction to the threat of global terrorism brought on by the events of 9/11 by women who have suffered abuse in the home.

Women who have historically suffered chronic domestic abuse reacted differently to the fear of terrorism than and those who have not. While a comparison of abuse suffered by those women who are victimized in their homes and those who suffer from the threat of victimization as a result of the actions perpetrated against the United States after the 9/11 attacks may seem spurious, the fear of threat is strikingly similar. Further, knowing and understanding the abused woman's fear of post-9/11 global terrorism must be understood within the context of paternal terrorism. The woman who has been abused in the home reacts differently to the threat of 9/11 terror than the woman who has never suffered abuse. Further, because the same mechanisms for coping with abuse occur within the domestic sphere of patriarchal terrorism as occur in the global sphere of post-9/11 terrorism, the similarities between them are characterized by the cognitive reaction of the women as victims of these types of violence.

In the studies conducted by researchers, findings show that earlier life trauma heightens susceptibility to posttraumatic stress disorder when these victims are exposed to subsequent trauma (Brewin, Andrews, & Valentiner, 2000). Further, researchers found that women who had suffered previous trauma and violence in their lives had a "tempered" response to the 9/11 tragedy (Thomas, 2003). Several factors influence this tempered reaction including cultural background, age, economic circumstances, sexual orientation, experiences in the victim's family of origin, and the victim's level of intelligence (Carlson, 1997). The abused woman reacts to the stress of the violence actually occurring in the home as well as the anticipated stress (Mitchell & Hodson, 1983). In fact, women who had backgrounds of previous trauma and violence felt as though these experiences helped them cope with the trauma of the 9/11 incidents because they are familiar with the trauma associated with terrorism in domestic violence.

On the other hand, researchers found that women who had never suffered domestic violence or patriarchal terrorism had a hard time coping with the anticipated threat of another post-9/11 attack. In fact, in the Thomas study (2003) the findings showed an increased incidence of posttraumatic stress disorder, generalized anxiety disorder, fear, sadness, anger, distrust, and other psychopathology among women who had not previously been abused. This finding is relevant as women who had never suffered abuse react to the potential threat of a post-9/11 terrorism attack in the same way the abused woman reacts to the threat of patriarchal terrorism in the home. In fact, it has been found that the abused woman reacts to the stress of the violence actually occurring in the home as well as the anticipated stress associated with the possibility of its reoccurrence (Mitchell & Hodson, 1983). What emerges from these findings is the difference between those who have traditionally suffered terrorism in the form of domestic violence, and those whose experience with terrorism came about as a result of the 9/11 events. While women who have suffered violence in the home react to the threat of post-9/11 terror as survivors of domestic violence, women who have never suffered patriarchal terrorism react to the threat of post-9/11 terror similarly to those women who react toward those who perpetrate patriarchal terrorism in the home.

TERRORISM AND THE OPPRESSION OF WOMEN

One common theme within patriarchal terrorism and the threat of post-9/11 terrorist threat is the effect it has on the oppression of women. Patriarchal terrorism is based in the Western philosophy of patriarchy, with the cornerstone of its philosophy lying in the oppression or secondary citizenship of women (Johnson, 1995). The result is the justification of the act of violence in the home because that sphere is controlled by the man through subjugation of the woman. Further, in patriarchal terrorism through emotional, physical, and economic oppression the woman is victimized and rendered helpless through the act of domestic violence. The result is a feeling of fear, lack of control, helplessness, and hopelessness on the part of the victim who, in the case of patriarchal terrorism, is the woman. The resulting fear comes from the basis of the justification of oppression as the woman's classification is that of a secondary citizen who neither has power, legitimacy, or authenticity within the framework of the home or society.

Interestingly, in an article written by Dr. Karla Cunningham comparing cross-regional trends in terrorism, and specifically in female terrorism, something very similar to patriarchal terrorism happens with women in these societies. Cunningham notes terrorist organizations who are practicing global terrorism tend to come from societies where the women are oppressed and treated as secondary citizens (2003, p. 172). She notes that similar to the Ku Klux Klan (KKK) and the Third Reich, terrorist networks like Al-Qaeda tend to be male dominated and discriminatory toward women. Although the terrorist organization may use women to carry out its terrorist acts, these women who are used as suicide bombers are invisible within the terrorist organizations, and their roles deeply embedded within the constructs of their social networks make them marginally important (Cunningham, 2003). When these organizations use women to carry out their terrorist regimens, these women's participation is less authentic and less legitimate because they are politically peripheralized due to their status as women (p. 175). Further, their status as women prevents them from having a voice subjecting them to doing what they are told and renders them inconsequential and unimportant. The consequences of the terrorist actions they are forced to participate in may result in death, and because of their status that result is again of no importance. This, in itself, is a form of violence similar to domestic violence or patriarchal terrorism because the use of women for such acts (i.e., suicide bombers) represents violence perpetrated toward women; they are merely being used as a tool to promote the terrorist mission.

A comparison of patriarchal terrorism and global terrorism or terrorist threat provides an interesting comparison of similarities between the actors—the perpetrator and the victim. As illustrated by the definition of patriarchal terrorism, oppression and victimization are the cornerstone of male domination and violence toward the female victim. Further, Western patriarchal philosophy is embedded within the operationalization of the terrorism resulting in fear. Women—who are considered secondary citizens and ancillary because they are not seen as an authentic part of legitimate society rendering them helpless, hopeless, and unimportant—allow the resulting domestic violence to occur. Terrorist networks similar to Al-Qaeda, which have threatened the United States since the 9/11 tragedy—view the roles of women in society similarly, using their women in violent, destructive, and life-threatening ways to promote their networks of terror.

The purpose of this chapter is to analyze the reaction of American women who suffer from domestic violence, or patriarchal terrorism to the perceived threat of post-9/11 terrorism. As we see from a review of the literature and an analysis of theoretical perspectives, it appears American women who have suffered trauma, violence, or domestic violence have a benign reaction to the threat of terrorism. Further, those who have never suffered trauma prior to 9/11 suffer the same symptoms as those women who have experienced domestic violence or patriarchal terrorism. What becomes more interesting and even complex is that women who fear the threat of potential post-9/11 terrorism experience a cognitive response to trauma similar to those victims of domestic violence.

AMERICA'S ASSAULT ON DOMESTIC VIOLENCE VERSUS ITS WAR ON TERROR

It is apparent from the literature that patriarchal terrorism and the threat of terrorism evoke the same cognitive response by American women. In order to rescue women who experience trauma either by the hand of a patriarchal terrorist or the threat of a post-9/11 global terrorist attack, there must be significant intervention tools in place to prevent the violence from continuing to occur, ultimately providing an intervention for the victim. With regard to the nation's "assault on domestic violence," a combination of external and internal factors such as policing strategies along with mental health services have been employed to address this assault (Hamilton & Coates, 1993). The message to the victim and the perpetrator is that the impact of the violence does not end when the victim leaves the relationship; instead, as this trauma impacts society at large it must be addressed as a major public and mental health problem. Similarly, the war on terror must be approached in terms of intervention.

Prior to the early 1990s, domestic violence left untreated resulted in police visiting the domicile of the assault and walking away, often leaving the perpetrator and victim in the same home with deadly results (Neilsen, Endo, & Ellington, 1992). Analysis of intervention strategies led to an assault on domestic violence, which promotes coping and stress mechanisms that help promote not only the protection of the victim, but also cognitive strategies to move beyond violence and toward safety. This intervention strategy promotes cooperation with police, health care workers, and mental health professionals.

Similarly, with regard to the war on terror, Sarbin (2003) notes that successful suppression of terrorism requires continuous, patient, undramatic civilian work and cooperation with other countries including coordination within American government for "a systematic approach addressing what to do before, during and after a potential terrorist attack" (p. 153). Sarbin points specifically to the 1993 terrorist plot to bomb the New York Lincoln and Holland tunnels, along with their attempt to destroy 11 American passenger planes in Asia in 1995 (p. 154). Therefore, intervention strategies have been successful in thwarting terrorism both in domestic violence, or patriarchal terrorism, and global terrorism. These types of strategies can ultimately serve as successful coping tools and mechanisms for American women who experience trauma resulting from terrorism.

The next portion of this chapter will analyze the results of a survey taken of women on the East Coast and their response to the threat of terrorism. This analysis seeks to establish the validity of the literature and its significance for women's cognitive response to patriarchal terrorism and the threat of global terrorism, determining whether American women who have previously experienced trauma and domestic violence have a benign response to the threat of terror post-9/11.

METHODOLOGY

Data for this study was analyzed by the second and third authors. The data were taken from a 23-item administered survey created to measure American women's perception of the threat of a post-9/11 terrorist attack on the United States. The measuring instrument was given to a random sample of women at various locations on the East Coast who were asked to complete the questionnaire.

Of all the participants, 11 percent were Caucasoid, 86 percent were Negroid, and, "other" represented the remaining 3 percent. The age of respondents varied from 17 to 60. Most of the participants were single (89 percent), while the married (10 percent), and divorced (2 percent), made up the rest of the participants. When asked if they feel safe since 9/11, the categories and percentages of response included: "no" (68 percent), "somewhat" (31 percent), and "yes" (2 percent). Of the participants, 81 percent were not victims of domestic violence, while 18 percent were victims of domestic violence. When measuring violence, in general, the question "Have you been a victim of violence in general?" received a response of "no" (55 percent) and "yes" (44 percent).

Next, in order to determine whether women who had experienced domestic violence felt safe, or less safe since the attacks on 9/11, 53 percent of the women who were victims of domestic violence expressed that they felt "less safe," while 15 percent of these same women indicated that they felt "safe." Those women who were victims of violence in general responded that they felt "less safe" (35 percent) and that they felt "safe," (32 percent) since the attacks.

In order to determine whether women who had not experienced domestic violence felt "safe," or "less safe," since the attacks on 9/11, the data indicated 50 percent of the women who were not victims of domestic violence expressed feeling "less safe," whereas 27.4 percent of these same women indicated feeling "safe." Those women who were not victims of violence in general responded by indicating that 36 percent of them felt "less safe," and 12 percent of these same women felt "safe" since the 9/11 attacks. Finally, when all of these women—those who suffered violence and domestic abuse along with those who did not—were asked, "Do you think America will suffer another terrorist attack?" 86 percent responded "yes" and 11 percent responded "no."

DISCUSSION

Overall, results from the data gave a sense of insecurity among the subjects that participated in the study. The 9/11 terrorist attack on America has undermined a great feeling of safety and confidence in their environment. Further, it is clear that indications from the literature correspond with the survey. Women who have not experienced domestic abuse and violence tend to react to the threat of terrorism differently than those who have experienced patriarchal terrorism and violence. While these surveys seem to indicate that women regardless of their experience with domestic abuse and violence seem to feel less safe since the 9/11 attacks, their feeling of safety seems to vary. For instance, those who never suffered domestic violence had a greater feeling of safety than those who were abused. Further, those women who suffered a form of violence felt safer than those who had not suffered violence. Hence, these findings would indicate that the experience of violence determines the extent to which the American woman may cognitively experience the threat of a post-9/11 attack. This may influence her ability to cope.

CONCLUSION

America is a nation whose experience with terrorism coming from outside its borders is limited. In fact, as seen by the literature, the experience of terrorism has been through domestic violence in the form of paternal terrorism. Terrorism is violence, and the data seem to indicate that those American women who experienced violence may experience the threat of a post-9/11 terrorist attack differently than those who have not experienced violence. As the literature indicates, their cognitive ability to cope is vastly different than those women who have not had the same experiences with violence.

REFERENCES

ABEL, E. M. (2001, December). Comparing the social service utilization, exposure to violence, and trauma symptomology of domestic violence female "victims" and female batterers. *Journal of Family Violence, 16*(4), 401–420.

BREWIN, C. R., ANDREWS, B., & VALENTINER, J. D. (2000). Meta-analysis of risk factors for posttraumatic stress disorder in trauma exposed adults. *Journal of Consulting and Clinical Psychology, 68*(5), 748–766.

CARLSON, B. E. (1997). A stress and coping approach to intervention with abused women. *Family Relations, 46*(3), 291–299.

CUNNINGHAM, K. J. (2003). Cross-regional trends in female terrorism. *Studies in Conflict & Terrorism, 26*, 171–195.

DUTTON-DOUGLAS, M. A., & DIONNE, D. (1991). Counseling and shelter services for battered women. In M. Steinman (Ed.), *Woman battering: Policy responses* (pp 113–130). Cincinnati, OH: Anderson.

HAMILTON, B., & COATES, J. (1993). Perceived helpfulness and Use of professional services by abused women. *Journal of Family Violence, 8*, 313–324.

JOHNSON, M. P. (1995). Patriarchal terrorism and common couple violence: Two forms of violence against women. *Journal of Marriage and Family, 7*, 283–294.

MITCHELL, R. E., & HODSON, C. A. (1983). Coping with domestic violence: Social support and psychological health among battered women. *American Journal of Community Psychology, 11*, 629–654.

NEILSEN, J. M., ENDO, R. K., & ELLINGTON, B. L. (1992). Social isolation and wife abuse: A research report. In E. C. Viano (Ed.), *Intimate violence: Interdisciplinary perspectives* (pp. 49–59). Washington, DC: Hemisphere.

PYSZCZYNSKI, T., SOLOMON, S., & GREENBERG, J. (2003). In the wake of 9/11: The psychology of terror. Washington, DC: American Psychological Association.

SARBIN, T. R. (2003). The metaphor-to-myth transformation with special reference to the "war on terrorism." *Peace and Conflict: Journal of Peace Psychology, 9*(2), 149–157.

THOMAS, S. P. (2003). None of us will ever be the same again. Reactions of American midlife women to 9/11. *Health Care for Women International, 24*, 853–867.

47

Images of Serial Murderers among College Students

Druann Maria Heckert, Daniel Alex Heckert, and Mark A. Ferraiolo

❖

It has been argued that conceptualizations of crime are socially created and constitute a core process of the social reality of crime (Quinney, 1970). Such constructions, in turn, influence criminal justice decisions (Surrette, 1998). Serial murderers have been heavily portrayed in the mass media in the past several decades. We surveyed 224 college students to assess how they visualized male and female serial murderers. We found that media constructions have a powerful impact on images of serial murderers among college students. The typical image of a serial killer was that they were mentally ill, white, and the product of family dysfunction and/or abuse, which reflect typical media portrayals. Constructions of female serial murderers tended to mimic the constructions of male serial killers.

Quinney (1970, p. 22) proposed that conceptualizations of crime are socially created and constitute a core process of the social reality of crime: "Wherever we find the concept of crime, there we will find conceptions about the relevance of crime, the offender's characteristics and the relation of the crime to the social order." These constructions are mediated by popular culture and mass media, a predominant influence in modern society (see Ferrell, 1995; Ferrell & Sanders, 1995; Ferrell & Websdale, 1999). Neither inconsequential nor benign, popular culture profoundly shapes society and potentially influences policy. For example, the successful construction of the serial murderer problem and cultural attention to movies such as *Silence of the Lambs* influenced three-strikes legislation (Surrette, 1998). Consequently, images created—even if based on at least partially false information contained in media images—need to be understood (Clear, 1998).

Among interpersonal crimes, serial murder is the gravest. The construction of this criminal is also severe, as well, in that this type of criminal has not been completely humanized. In her examination of 172 serial murder movies, Epstein (1995) suggested that serial murderers have become modern "mythic monsters"; in fact, 20 percent were portrayed as supernatural (e.g., werewolves or demons) and 60 percent were pictured as superhuman (e.g., not merely mortal in terms of the extraordinary effort required to subdue or kill them). Fox and Levin (2001) contended that an alternate movie image—that of a charming, brilliant, and handsome serial killer figure—now exists. Nevertheless, neither image matches a real serial killer—an "extraordinarily ordinary" mortal (Fox & Levin, 2001, p. 104). As Arendt (1964) suggested so long ago, there is a "banality of evil" and it certainly emerges in human forms.

Jenkins (1994) noted that serial killers have become ubiquitous in various media such as television shows and various genres of books, in addition to movies. More recently than the Epstein study, Hickey (2002) identified 69 additional movies appearing from 1995 until 2002. In addition to not being portrayed as completely human, myths have been created (see Fox & Levin, 1999; Hale & Bolin, 1998; Hickey, 2002; Jenkins, 1998). These myths are varied and include, but are not limited to the following: Serial killers are all male, all intelligent, all white, all sexual sadists, and so numerous that there is an epidemic of them. Certainly, culture has created notions about this most heinous type of criminal, notions that are not always entirely accurate.

This exploratory study attempts to elucidate images and their internalization by members of the public. Survey data were collected from college students at a college in the northeast. The primary aim of this chapter is to analyze, in a preliminary fashion, the construction of the image of serial murderers.

SERIAL MURDER

Multicide, or mass murder, includes simultaneous killers, or those murderers who kill all their victims at once, and serial killers, or those murderers who kill their victims on separate occasions (Levin & Fox, 1985). Definitional differences are fairly minor. Holmes and Holmes (1998, p. 18) defined serial murder as "the killing of three or more people over a period of more than thirty days, with a significant cooling-off period between the killings." Hickey (2002, p. 19) noted that a serial murder denotes "any offenders, male or female, who kill over time" with a minimum of three to four victims and some discernible pattern.

While multiple murder is not solely a modern phenomenon, the proliferation of serial murder has emerged in recent decades as an uncommon—yet all too common—form of crime that constitutes a problem in modern American society (Holmes & DeBurger, 1985). Hickey (2002) collected a sample of 337 male serial murderers; 94 percent of these criminals began their killing after 1900. As the century progressed, the percentage increased significantly as is evidenced by the fact that 45 percent of these individuals began their killings in the two-decade period between 1975 and 1995. Leyton (1986, p. 22) explained this "meteoric rise": "The mid-1980's were years of unprecedented growth, experimentation, and innovation among multiple murderers, years in which all previous 'records' were broken and sacrosanct social barriers were pierced." The crime continues, unabated.

Furthermore, academic study of homicide is not new as social scientists have analyzed homicide for a lengthy period of time (see Brearly, 1932, 1935; Guttmacher, 1960; Hackney, 1969; Palmer, 1960, 1968; Redfield, 1880; Wolfgang, 1958; Wolfgang & Ferracuti, 1967). Jenkins (1993) commented that social scientific research on multiple murder did not commence until the 1980s; currently, a significant body of social scientific literature exists (see Egger, 1984, 2002; Hickey, 1997, 2002; Holmes & Holmes, 1998; Levin & Fox, 1985; Leyton, 1986; Norris, 1998). Clearly, the academic perception of serial murder as a serious criminological issue is fairly recent.

In addition to academic interest, Jenkins (1994) argues that public interest in the crime has created a "serial murder boom." In fact, the social problem of serial murder has been socially constructed, primarily through popular culture (i.e., although not solely a new element of cultural representations) and the Department of Justice. Fox and Levin (2001) also noted that serial killers are so ensconced in popular culture that they have appeared in trading cards, comic books, and t-shirts. Or, as Jenkins (1994, p. 97) described, "It is scarcely too much to describe multiple murder in the last decade as a cultural industry in its own right, with serial killers as a pervasive theme in television, the cinema, and the publishing world."

MALE SERIAL MURDERERS: CHARACTERISTICS AND ETIOLOGY

Hickey (2002, p. 129) noted that male serial murderers compose the "darkest, most sinister side of human existence." What are the characteristics of these individuals? Empirical examinations of serial killers have established certain patterned characteristics of those who engage in serial murder (see Hickey, 2002; Keeney & Heide, 1994). In perhaps the most significant accumulation of data, Hickey (2002) collected information about 337 male serial killers and drew the following composite. The offenders were an average age of 27.5 years at the beginning of their crime sprees. When identifiable (in 226 cases), serial murderers had the following race/ethnicity: 73 percent white; 22 percent African American (more common, more recently); 3 percent Hispanic; 1 percent Asian; and 1 percent other race or ethnicity. The victim-to-offender relationship was primarily that of stranger to stranger. Females were more often victimized than males and other vulnerable victims (children, etc.) were frequent victims. Educational background and occupation were varied, but male serial killers tended to have low educational achievement (e.g., few were college graduates; high school or less was common) and blue-collar jobs. In relation to the crimes themselves, the crimes were more often processual. As Hickey (2002, p. 154) concluded:

> Consequently, offenders were frequently found to have used a variety of nonlethal, potentially lethal, and lethal attacks on the victim. . . . In this study, firearms were used in approximately 40 percent of the cases, but not as the main mode of death. The victims in this study may have actually died from strangulation, a bullet to the head, or a stab to the heart, but these often were the final acts committed after the victim had been successfully tortured, mutilated, and/or beaten by the offender.

The offenders tended to have prior encounters with trouble—at least in the 198 cases that Hickey (2002) was able to assemble. In fact, 67 percent had either been confined to prison or a mental institution. A significant portion did have criminal pasts (e.g., 37 percent sex-related crimes, 13 percent homicide, 45 percent property crimes, 17 percent illegal drugs). In relation to their biographical backgrounds, 62 cases existed where offenders had experienced trauma(s) prior to adulthood including the following: rejection, 48 percent;

unstable home, 37 percent; physical abuse, 35 percent; mental/emotional abuse, 34 percent; divorce, 19 percent; alcoholic parent, 18 percent; adopted, 13 percent; sexual abuse, 13 percent; parents deceased, 11 percent; illegitimate, 10 percent; poverty, 8 percent; prostitute mother, 6 percent. Thus, Hickey (2002) has provided a most comprehensive accounting of the patterns of male serial killers.

The vital sociological/criminological question remains the etiological one. There is perhaps an exasperating difficulty in accounting for the most heinous of interpersonal crimes. Holmes and DeBurger (1985) contend that the psychogenic is the most explanatory of the three levels of explanation—sociogenic, psychogenic, and biogenic—and maintain that etiology is primarily intrinsic within the personality of the offender. At a psychological level, most researchers maintain that psychopathy is the more common denominator, not mental illness (see Hickey, 2002; Holmes & DeBurger, 1985; Holmes & Holmes, 1998; Levin & Fox, 1985). Thus, the psychology of the offender has been proposed as paramount; psychopathy has been most often utilized as the explanation.

Hickey (2002) has also proposed an etiological model—the trauma-control model—that attempts to provide causal insight by examining a multitude of factors that are typical in serial killers. Predispositional factors, such as an extra Y chromosome, may be present. A traumatic event, or multiple traumatizations, may occur to the offender during childhood and adolescent socialization, such as abuse or death of parents. In some people, the traumas may cause feelings of rejection and may be dealt with in a negative manner; a profound lowering of self-esteem can surface. Dissociation could occur and the psychopathy is a means of restoring some psychological semblance of control. Additionally, facilitators—including psychoactive substances, pornography, and the occult—are often utilized by the offender. Violent fantasy is also a common pattern in serial killers. The interactive elements of this model compose the theoretical framework for explaining commonalities among serial killers.

As outlined above, social scientists have been able to collect vital information about the actual commonalities of serial killers and have been able to provide some theoretical insight into pivotal factors that shape them. This profile is that of a human rather than a mythic monster.

FEMALE SERIAL MURDERERS: CHARACTERISTICS AND ETIOLOGY

Egger's (1990) belief that women were basically not serial killers and the FBI claim in the 1990s that Aileen Wuornos was the first female serial killer were simply wrong (Hickey, 2002; Holmes & Holmes, 1998). This misconception might have been rooted in a cultural disinclination to perceive women as capable of committing the worst of the interpersonal crimes (Hickey, 2002). Still, Hale and Bolin (1998, p. 57) concluded, "But one thing is without doubt: the final result is as deadly as any act committed by her male counterpart."

A profile of female serial murderers has emerged (Hickey, 2002; Keeney & Heide, 1994). In the most comprehensive sample, Hickey (2002) analyzed 62 cases of female serial murderers and made the following conclusions. The average age at first lethal offense was thirty, but the range was great (15 to 69). Around one-third (32 percent) did not act alone; the rest acted alone. Their lethality was significant; as the average number of victims was in the 7 to 9 range. Whites are overrepresented at 93 percent; the remaining

7 percent are African American. While the information was not available on every killer, when known, female serial killers were of various occupational orientations. Thus, the following diversity emerges: 8 percent unemployed, 10 percent unskilled, 15 percent semi-skilled, 5 percent skilled, 10 percent professional, 11 percent other, and 41 percent unknown. The victim selection was such that strangers were less likely to be murdered than family, but the percentage of strangers killed has risen since 1975. Thus, one-fourth killed strangers only and one-third killed family only. When killing family, husbands were the most common victims. Children were most commonly victimized if the offender did not know the victim; nevertheless, solo killers were especially prone to victimize patients. Overall, when strangers were the target, the vulnerable were at the most risk. Poison was the most common method of killing, either alone or with some other method; other methods included either alone or in combination with some other method: shooting, bludgeoning, suffocation, stabbing, and drowning (some only). Solo killers tended to use poisoning more frequently, and those who did not act alone often used the more violent means listed above. Unlike male serial murderers, money (partially or only) was by far the most common motivation. Other motivations included, partially or primarily, the following: control, enjoyment, sex, drug addiction, cults, covering up other crimes, self-perceiving children to be a burden, feelings of being an inadequate parent, and other ones as well. Like male serial murderers, female serial killers are commonly psychopathic. All in all, these constitute core characteristics of female serial murderers.

Regarding etiology, as most explanations have been developed in relation to males, the issue of generalizability is of concern, as it is in much criminology (Daly & Chesney-Lind, 1988; Jensen, 2001). To reiterate, psychopathy is the explanation most commonly advanced at the individual level and Hickey (2002) does conclude that psychopathy was common among female serial killers, as well. Additionally, Hickey (2002) has proposed the most in-depth theoretical explanation as the trauma-control model. Social science has primarily focused on patterns and motivations of female serial killers (Hale & Bolin, 1998; Holmes & Holmes, 1998). As money is the primary motivator and lust is most rare (Hale & Bolin, 1998), it might be that Hickey's last element of violent fantasy is missing among female serial killers. Hale and Bolin (1998) also describe various traumas—such as loss—as common and thus, other elements of the model might hold up. At any rate, the etiology of female serial killers has been relatively ignored.

MEDIA REPRESENTATIONS

The most in-depth study completed of images of serial murderers was conducted by Epstein (1995) of 172 movies, of various genres, featuring a solo serial killer. Some accurate information was conveyed in this particular media format. Information that was accurately portrayed included the following: Serial killers are slightly older than many criminals, predominately white, predominately male, and are prone to engage in some type of criminal pattern (e.g., targeting similar victims). On the other hand, movies have also presented inaccuracies, as well. In the first place, a major fallacy occurs in that movie serial killers are not portrayed as concretely human; rather, they are portrayed as superhuman or supernatural. There is a virtual absence of homosexual serial killers in film. Also, motivation is not presented to reflect reality. In reality, male serial killers are often motivated to commit a sexual crime or to exercise complete power over another person. In the movies, while male serial killers are often shown as misogynistic, it often becomes infused with the more sublime or romantic love/family motivations. For example, the killer is motivated by love, in the abstract. Another inaccurate portrayal is that actual victims tend to be overrepresented by women, children, and young men; film victims are approximately equally represented by males and females. A glaring misrepresentation occurs when females are portrayed—albeit rarely—on film. Undoubtedly, the presentation does not reflect reality. As Epstein (1995) concluded:

> Also notably inaccurate is the representation of female serial killers. Actual murders by women who meet the definitional requirements of serial killing frequently involve the killing of children, the elderly, or the sick. This type of serial murder is not depicted in film. Rather, female serial killer characters are typically presented as avenging a gang rape, as reacting to a wrong that they feel has been committed against a significant male character, or as motivated by an evil, supernatural force.

In essence, the movie imagery of this type of criminal is complicated in that both factual and fictional information is included. Epstein (1995) concluded that since some imagery is portrayed correctly in the movies, the viewer may be left with the perception that they have an overall realistic image.

HYPOTHESES

Images rooted in popular culture are profound and have great propensity to shape the perception that people have of the actual category. A further understanding of these processes is needed. Based on the preceding literature review, we developed the following hypotheses.

1. The percentage of respondents specifying various racial categories will reflect the prevailing media constructions, as articulated by Epstein's (1995) analysis. Specifically, nearly all of the respondents will visualize the typical male and female serial murderer as white.
2. Based on prevailing media constructions, the majority of respondents will visualize the typical male serial murderer as mentally ill (as opposed to psychopathological). Our assumption is that the lay understanding of psychopathology (antisocial personality disorder) is inaccurate and confused with other types of mental illness, such as schizophrenia. Because media constructions of female serial murderers are sparse, we hypothesize that respondents will visualize the typical female serial murderer similarly to the typical male serial murderer.
3. Based on media representations of serial murderers as nearly superhuman and Fox and Levin's (2001) notion of the myth of the brilliant serial killer, we hypothesize that respondents will overestimate the typical intelligence of serial murderers for both male and female serial murderers.
4. Based on prevailing media constructions (Epstein, personal correspondence, July 28, 2004), we hypothesize that respondents will underestimate the degree to which male serial murderers have previous criminal records. Again, with regard to

visualization of criminal records, we hypothesize that respondents will visualize the typical female serial murderer similarly to the typical male serial murderer.

5. Based on prevailing media constructions, we hypothesize that the respondents will overestimate the degree to which the typical male and female serial murderer was motivated by family trauma in childhood, such as dysfunctional or abusive family lives.

6. We hypothesize that exposure to social science information, through taking courses in criminology and criminal justice, reading nonfiction accounts, and reading social science research, will increase the accuracy of visualizations of typical serial murderers.

7. We hypothesize that exposure to mass media information on serial murder, such as movies and novels, will decrease the accuracy of visualizations of typical serial murderers.

METHODS

Data were collected from a convenience sample of 224 college students at a northeastern college. Obviously, the ability to generalize from a convenience sample is limited. Nonetheless, as little to no previous research has been done on this topic, the current study is intended to be an exploratory study. The questions included both close-ended questions and open-ended questions. The close-ended questions were asked to garner background information on the respondents, such as age, year in school, sex, and extent of exposure to social science and media portrayals of serial murder. Several open-ended questions were then asked about male and female serial murderers (separately) to assess participants' views of the demographic characteristics and appearance of the typical serial murderer; beliefs regarding the overall psychological profile of the typical serial murderer; perceptions of the typical criminal background of serial murderers; the typical pattern and methods of serial murder; and the causes that motivate the typical serial murderer. A close-ended question asked what state best described male and female serial murderers (insane, evil, monster, satanic, or other).

Responses to open-ended questions were coded thematically. Two graduate assistants coded responses to all the open-ended questions for all respondents. To assess reliability, the two coders independently coded all the open-ended questions for twenty respondents and had over a 90 percent agreement on all items.

Because of the exploratory nature of this study, we use simple descriptive statistics to address the seven hypotheses. Because we have a convenience sample, we do not use inferential statistics (tests of statistical significance). To assess the first five hypotheses, data are presented as frequency distributions. Cross-tabular analysis, with appropriate measures of association, is used to assess the last two hypotheses.

RESULTS

As stated above, the convenience sample consisted of 224 students enrolled in various sociology/criminology classes at a northeastern college. As Table 1 shows, the sample was almost equally divided between females (55 percent) and males (45 percent). A question

TABLE 1   Frequency Distributions for Independent Variables ($n = 224$)

Variable	Percentage
Sex	
female	54.5%
male	45.5
Year in School	
freshman	16.1%
sophomore	31.7
junior	32.6
senior	19.6
Courses in Criminology or CJ	
no	58.0%
yes	42.0
Social Class	
upper class	8.1%
upper-middle class	32.4
middle class	41.9
lower-middle (working) class	17.6
Watch Serial Murder Movies	
no	5.8%
yes	94.2
Ever Read Materials Regarding Serial Murder	
no	42.5%
yes	57.5
Ever Read Non-Fiction Regarding Serial Murder	
no	62.1%
yes	37.9
Ever Read Novels Regarding Serial Murder	
no	64.3%
yes	35.7
Ever Read Social Science Studies	
no	75.9%
yes	24.1

about self-identified class background was asked and resulted in the following: upper class (8 percent); upper-middle class (32 percent); middle class (42 percent); lower-middle (working) class (18 percent); and lower class (0 percent). Almost half (42 percent) had taken one or more courses in criminology. While 58 percent had read material on serial murder, only 38 percent had read nonfiction work on the topic and around a fourth (24 percent) had read criminological or social scientific (i.e., academic) accounts of the topic. The sample was more likely to be familiar with popular cultural interpretations of serial murderers. Ninety-four percent had seen a movie or many movies on the topic (with the modal category being 4–6 movies) and 36 percent had read a novel about serial murder. Clearly, the sample was more immersed in popular culture interpretations than in academic research.

Table 2 shows the results for the open-ended coding with regard to the typical visualization of male and female serial murderers. The first hypothesis is supported. To the extent that race is mentioned in the responses to the question regarding what male and female serial murderers would look like, the overwhelming response was white. Only 3 percent of the participants specified that male serial murderers were typically black and only 1 percent specified that female serial murderers were typically black. Interestingly, race was almost twice as likely to be visualized for male serial murderers as for female serial murderers, which probably reflects the lower representation of female serial murderers in media accounts.

Hypothesis two is also supported. The majority of respondents either had no visualization regarding the typical psychological profile of serial murderers (37 percent for males; 46 percent for females) or visualized the typical serial murderer as having a mental illness other than schizophrenia (48 percent for males; 41 percent for females). Less than 10 percent of the respondents (9 percent for males; 7 percent for females) visualized the typical serial murderer as being psychopathic or sociopathic, which contrasts with the actual reality demonstrated by social science and corresponds more to typical media representations of serial murderers. As predicted, respondents did visualize the typical female serial murderer similarly to the typical male serial murderer (Cramer's V = .85).

Additional psychological factors emerged in the open-ended responses to the question asking about the typical psychological profile of serial murderers. The responses included descriptions of the typical serial murderer as lonely (37 percent for males serial murderers; 25 percent for females), insecure (5 percent for both); and angry or aggressive (15 percent for males; 17 percent for females). Interestingly, approximately 10 percent (11 percent for males; 9 percent for females) of the participants cited biological causes (chromosomal/genetic, chemical, or neurological) of serial murderer, and 4 percent of respondents described serial murderers as normal.

Hypothesis two is also supported by responses to the partially close-ended question that asked what state best describes serial murderers. The overwhelming majority of participants responded insane (42 percent for male serial murderers; 44 percent for female serial murderers) or other type of mental illness (43 percent for male serial murderers; 42 percent for female serial murderers). A small percentage checked evil (8 percent for male; 11 percent for female), which is the category that probably most closely corresponds to the construct of psychopathy or sociopathy that characterizes the majority of serial murderers according to Hickey (2002) and Levin and Fox (1985). Finally a small percentage responded that serial murderers were monsters (7 percent for males; 2 percent for females) or satanic (1 percent for both). Again, as predicted, participants gave very similar responses for female serial murderers as they did to male serial murderers (Cramer's V = .66).

TABLE 2   Frequency Distributions for Dependent Variables ($n = 224$)

Variables	Male Serial Murderers Percentage	Female Serial Murderers Percentage
Race Mentioned for Males		
white	62.8%	33.9%
black	2.8	0.9
other	0.0	1.3
none mentioned	34.4	63.8
Psychological Profile		
schizophrenia, etc.	3.8%	3.6%
psychopathology/sociopathology	9.0	7.1
general/other mental illness	47.6	40.6
no mental illness	2.9	3.0
none mentioned	36.7	45.7
IQ Mentioned in Psychological Profile		
high IQ	21.4%	14.2%
average IQ	0.5	1.0
low IQ	1.4	1.5
none mentioned	76.7	83.2
Descriptions of Serial Murderers in Psychological Profile		
lonely	36.7%	24.9%
insecure	5.2	5.1
angry	13.3	14.7
aggressive	1.9	2.5
biological issues	10.5	8.6
normal	3.8	4.1
State That Best Describes Serial Murderers		
insane	41.7%	44.1%
evil	8.3	10.8
monster	6.9	2.3
satanic	0.5	0.9
other mental illness	42.6	41.8
Criminal Background		
no criminal record	39.2%	39.4%
unspecified juvenile delinquency	5.1	4.3
limited property	6.0	11.1

TABLE 2   (Continued)

extensive property	0.0	0.5
limited violent	9.2	7.7
limited combination	7.8	7.2
extensive violent	17.1	12.5
extensive combination	12.0	9.1
none mentioned	3.7	8.2
Causes—Dysfunctional Family/Abuse		
not mentioned	25.5%	24.9%
mentioned	74.5	75.1
Other Causes Mentioned		
alienation, loneliness, self-esteem	18.5%	12.2%
poverty	7.4	5.4
racism	1.9	1.0
homophobia	0.5	0.5
gender	2.3	0.5

Hypothesis three was supported. Although the vast majority of respondents did not mention intelligence in their open-ended responses, the overwhelming majority of respondents who did mention intelligence posited the typical serial murderer as having a high IQ (21 percent for males; 14 percent for females). Very few respondents indicated that the typical serial murderer has an average (1 percent) or low (1.4 percent for males; 1.5 percent for females) IQ.

Hypothesis four, which posits that the criminal background of serial murderers will be underestimated, is supported. Hickey (2002) documents that fully two-thirds of male serial murderers had been confined either in prison or a mental institution, suggesting that the typical serial murderer has an extensive criminal background. Yet, 39 percent of the students posited that the typical serial murderer had no criminal record at all. In addition, another 11 percent (for males) to 15 percent (for females) of students stated that the typical serial murderer had only unspecified juvenile delinquency or limited property crime in their past. Thus, less than one-third (29 percent for males; 22 percent for females) of the respondents posited that the typical serial murderer had a history of extensive violent crime (by itself or in combination with property crime). As predicted, responses were similar for the typical female serial murderer to the responses for the typical male serial murderer (Cramer's V = .58).

Hypothesis five, which stated that respondents would overestimate the degree of family trauma when asked what causes or explains serial murder, is supported. According to Hickey (2002), the percentage of male serial murderers who experienced family trauma and/or abuse is less than one-third, whereas three-fourths of the respondents (75 percent for both male and female serial murderers) listed dysfunctional family and/or abuse as a primary causative agent in the past of the typical serial murderer. Again, responses were similar for the typical female serial murderer to the responses for the typical male serial murderer (Phi = .70).

Although family dysfunction/abuse was by far the most cited cause or explanation for serial murder, other factors were also listed. The second most common factor cited was alienation, loneliness, and low self-esteem (19 percent for male serial murderers; 12 percent for females). A small percentage of respondents cited poverty (7 percent for males; 5 percent for females), racism (2 percent for males; 1 percent for females), homophobia (1 percent for both), or gender issues (2 percent for males; 1 percent for females).

Hypothesis six predicted that exposure to social science information will increase accuracy of visualizations of typical serial murderers. To assess this hypothesis, whether the respondent had taken courses in criminology or criminal justice, whether they had ever read social science or criminology studies, and whether they had read nonfiction accounts were cross-tabulated with visualizations regarding race, psychological profile, psychological state, criminal background, and family trauma for male and female serial murderers. Because these analyses result in 30 tables and only three of the relationships were statistically significant (and the effects were weak) the results are not shown. Essentially, these analyses fail to support hypothesis six. Exposure to social science information did not significantly alter visualizations of typical male and female serial murderers.

Hypothesis seven predicted that exposure to mass media information will decrease the accuracy of visualizations of typical serial murderers. To assess this hypothesis, whether the respondent had ever watched serial murderer movies, ever read materials on serial murder, or had ever read novels about serial murder were cross-tabulated with visualizations regarding race, psychological profile, psychological state, criminal background, and family trauma for male and female serial murderers. Again, 30 tables were generated, and only three of the relationships were statistically significant (with very weak effects); the results are not shown. Thus, hypothesis seven was not supported.

To rule out additional sources of variation, we also cross-tabulated sex, year in school, and self-perceived social class with the main visualization variables. Only sex produced significant and interpretable differences. Specifically, as Table 3 shows, sex was associated with speculations regarding family trauma. Male respondents were less likely (17 percent difference) to posit family dysfunction or abuse as existing in the background of the typical female serial murderer. Sex also had a weak effect on the responses to the partially close-ended question that assessed mental health state of serial murderers. As Table 3 reveals, female respondents were more likely than male respondents to check the typical serial murderer as being insane, while male respondents were more likely to check the typical serial murderer as having an other mental illness.

DISCUSSION

In summary, the first five hypotheses were supported. Together, they support our contention that media constructions have a powerful impact on images of serial murderers held by college students. The last two hypotheses, however, were not supported. Apparently, exposure to social science and nonfiction accounts of serial murder do not fundamentally alter the images of serial murderers. Mass media constructions would appear to be potent and

TABLE 3   Family Trauma and State of Typical Serial Murderer by Sex of Respondent

	Sex of Respondent		
Independent Variable	Male	Female	Effect
Dysfunctional/Abusive Family in			
Background of Female Serial Murderer			
no	34%	18%	
yes	66	83	phi = .19
Best Description of Mental Health			
State of Male Serial Murderer			
insane	35%	47%	
evil	10	7	
monster	3	10	
satanic	1	0	Cramer's
other mental illness	51	36	V = .22
Best Description of Mental Health			
State of Female Serial Murderer			
insane	37%	50%	
evil	12	10	
monster	0	4	
satanic	2	0	Cramer's
other mental illness	49	36	V = .23

permeating in shaping images of criminals. Image can be more powerful than fact. Despite this finding, it is intriguing that greater exposure to mass media information, such as movies and novels, did not influence images of serial murderers. Perhaps our failure to tap additional sources of mass media exposure, such as television and newspaper news accounts, explains this finding. The ambient nature of mass media constructions are such that additional exposure through novels and movies does not result in changing constructions of serial murder.

A limitation of this study was that it was conducted on a small convenience sample of college students, limiting the generalizability of these results. Also, the open-ended questions utilized made it harder to directly compare the descriptions of the students to descriptions from social science and media description; nevertheless, these open-ended questions proved to be advantageous in terms of allowing students to generate their own understanding in an undirected format.

Other interesting conclusions emerge in this study. For example, the creation of the category of the female serial killer is limited and is demonstrated by the fact that student constructions of female serial killers primarily tended to mimic the construction of male serial killers. This factor is probably rooted in the paucity of both media imagery and the accumulation of social science information on this topic.

Another finding that emerges is that these students constructed images of serial killers as primarily mentally ill. There are cases of mentally ill serial murderers as Holmes and Holmes (1998) describe the visionary serial murderer as a mentally ill person who kills in response to voices. Nevertheless, psychopathy is the common description of a serial killer. This phenomenon—to view serial killers as mentally ill—is probably partially explained by what Conrad and Schneider (1980) describe as a medicalization of deviance that results in a tendency for modern humans to exclude evil and medicalize the explanation of deviance. According to Conrad and Schneider (1980, p. 251), "there is little to be gained by deploying such a medical vocabulary of motives. It only hinders us from comprehending the human element in the decisions we make, the social structures we create, and the actions we take." Mental illness is perhaps the easiest explanation to that which appears unexplainable.

Trauma is part of the modeling advanced by Hickey (2002) and family dysfunctions constitute common traumas. Interestingly, the most commonly cited etiological factor was family dysfunction and/or abuse. Perhaps, the work of researchers and practitioners in the field of domestic violence (see Straus, Gelles, & Steinmetz, 1980; Straus, Hotaling, Finkelhor, & Kirkpatrick, 1988) has been partially responsible for constructing this issue as a major social problem.

Quinney (1970) sagely contended that the conceptualizations of crime are fundamental to the social reality of crime. Furthermore, as previously noted, images do have the capability of influencing criminal justice policy (Surrette, 1998) and individuals within a cultural context who compose juries and other actors in the criminal justice system. Images, internalized by the public, need to be understood and the role of the media in shaping those images needs to be further studied.

Further study would prove beneficial, as well. For example, while composing a major element of media presentation, serial murder is obviously a fairly rare crime in relation to other crimes. Studies could be conducted on the internalization of images of other, more common, types of crime. To what extent do movies and other popular culture formats provide factual information about crimes such as robbery, burglary, and rape and to what extent do these formats present fictional information? To what extent does the public internalize fact and to what extent does the public internalize fiction about these crimes? These are important questions that impact public involvement in the criminal justice system and thus impact criminal justice policy.

ACKNOWLEDGMENTS

The authors would like to thank Kristen Hughes and Veronica Simms for coding the open-ended questions.

REFERENCES

ARENDT, H. (1964). *Eichmann in Jerusalem*. New York: Viking Press.

BREARLY, H. (1932). *Homicide in the United States*. Chapel Hill: University of North Carolina Press.

BREARLY, H. (1935). The pattern of violence. In W. T. Couch (Ed.), *Culture in the south* (pp. 678–692). Chapel Hill: University of North Carolina Press.

CLEAR, T. (1998). Foreword. In F. Bailey & D. Hale (Eds.), *Popular culture, crime and justice*, (pp. ix–x). Belmont, CA: West/Wadsworth.

CONRAD, P., & SCHNEIDER, J. W. (1980). *Deviance and medicalization*. St. Louis: C.V. Mosby.

DALY, K., AND CHESNEY-LIND, M. (1988). Feminism and criminology. *Justice Quarterly 5*, 497–533.

EGGER, S. A. (1984). A working definition of serial murder. *Journal of Police Science and Administration, 12*, 348–357.

EGGER, S. A. (1990). Serial murder: A synthesis of literature and research. In S. A. Egger (Ed.), *Serial murder: An elusive phenomenon* (pp. 3–34). New York: Praeger.

EGGER, S. A. (2002). *The killers among us: An examination of serial murder and its investigation* (2nd ed.). Upper Saddle River, NJ: Prentice Hall.

EPSTEIN, S. (1995). The new mythic monster. In J. Ferrell & C. R. Sanders (Eds.), *Cultural criminology*. (pp. 66–79). Boston: Northeastern University Press.

EPSTEIN, S. (2004, July 28). Personal correspondence.

FERRELL, J. (1995). Culture, crime and cultural criminology. *Journal of Criminal Justice and Popular Culture, 3*, 25–42.

FERRELL, J., & SANDERS, C. (EDS.). (1995). *Cultural criminology*. Boston: Northeastern University Press.

FERRELL, J., & WEBSDALE, N. (1999). *Making trouble: Cultural constructions of crime, deviance, and control*. Hawthorne, New York: Aldine De Gruyter.

FOX, J., & LEVIN, J. (1999). Serial murder: Myths and reality. In M. D. Smith & M. A. Zahn (Eds.), *Studying and preventing homicide* (pp. 79–96). Thousand Oaks, CA: Sage.

FOX, J., & LEVIN, J. (2001). *The will to kill: Making sense of senseless murder*. Boston: Allyn & Bacon.

GUTTMACHER, M. S. (1960). *The mind of the murderer*. New York: Farrar, Straus, and Giroux.

HACKNEY, R. D. (1969). Southern violence. In H. D. Graham & T. R. Gurr (Eds.), *The history of violence in America* (pp. 2–27). New York: Bantam.

HALE, R., & BOLIN, A. (1998). The female serial killer. In R. M. Holmes & S. T. Holmes (Eds.), *Contemporary perspectives on serial murder* (pp. 33–58). Thousand Oaks, CA: Sage.

HICKEY, E. (1997). *Serial murderers and their victims* (2nd ed.). Belmont, CA: Wadsworth.

HICKEY, E. (2002). *Serial murderers and their victims* (3rd ed.). Belmont, CA: Wadsworth.

HOLMES, R. M., & DEBURGER, J. (1985). Profiles in terror: The serial murderer. *Federal Probation, 53*, 29–34.

HOLMES, R. M., & HOLMES, S. T. (1998). *Serial murder* (2nd ed). Thousand Oaks, CA: Sage.

HOTALING, G. T., FINKELHOR, D., KIRKPATRICK, J. T., & STRAUS, M. (1988). *Family abuse and its consequences: New directions in research*. Beverly Hills: Sage.

JENKINS, P. (1993). Chance or choice? The selection of serial murder victims. In A. V. Wilson (Ed.), *Homicide: The victim-offender connection* (pp. 461–478). Cincinnati, OH: Anderson.

JENKINS, P. (1994). *Using murder*. New York: Aldine De Gruyter.

JENKINS, P. (1998). African-American and serial homicide. In R. M. Holmes & S. T. Holmes (Eds.), *Contemporary perspectives on serial murder* (pp. 17–32). Thousand Oaks, CA: Sage.

JENSEN, V. (2001). *Why women kill: Homicide and gender equality*. Boulder, CO: Lynne Rienner.

KEENEY, B. T., & HEIDE, K. M. (1994). Gender differences in serial murderers: A preliminary analysis. *Journal of Interpersonal Violence, 9*, 383–398.

LEVIN, J., & FOX, J. A. (1985). *Mass murder: America's growing menace*. New York: Plenum Press.

LEYTON, E. (1986). *Compulsive killers*. New York: New York University Press.

NORRIS, J. (1998). *Serial killers*. New York: Dolphin.

PALMER, S. (1960). *A study of murder*. New York: Crowell.

PALMER, S. (1968). Murder and suicide in forty non-literate societies. *Journal of Criminal Law, Criminology, and Police Science, 56*, 320–324.

QUINNEY, R. (1970). *The social reality of crime*. Boston: Little, Brown.

REDFIELD, H. V. (1880). *Homicide: North and south*. Philadelphia: Lippincott.

STRAUS, M., GELLES, R. J., & STEINMETZ, S. K. (1980). *Behind closed doors*. New York: Doubleday/Anchor.

SURRETTE, R. (1998). Prologue: Some unpopular thoughts about popular culture. In F. Bailey & D. Hale (Eds.), *Popular culture, crime and justice* (pp. xiv–xxiv). Belmont, CA: West/Wadsworth.

WOLFGANG, M. (1958). *Patterns in criminal homicide*. Philadelphia: University of Pennsylvania Press.

WOLFGANG, M., & FERRACUTI, F. (1967). *The subculture of violence*. London: Tavistock.

SECTION IX
Girls and Delinquency

48

The Impact of Gender on Juvenile Justice Decisions

Michelle Inderbitzin

❖

INTRODUCTION

In spite of efforts to ensure that sentencing decisions are based solely upon legally relevant variables rather than on social characteristics of offenders, gender remains an important factor in juvenile justice decisions. While many studies have documented gender differences in punishment, there remains uncertainty as to how and why such differences occur and whether we should be striving for equal treatment at all. This chapter addresses two central questions about the impact of gender on juvenile justice decisions. First, are boys and girls punished differently for "like crimes" (Daly, 1994a)? To date, there is relatively little research comparing juvenile court decisions for boys and girls charged with serious offenses. Second, if gender disparities are found within a system of determinate sentencing, how is gender discrimination put into play? What are the mediating factors and justifications? With sentencing guidelines in place in juvenile courts in many states, there is much less room for judicial discretion. How then is gender discrimination occurring?

REVIEW OF THE LITERATURE AND THEORETICAL PERSPECTIVES

A major concern in the study of law and social control is whether boys and girls who commit similar crimes are treated equitably by the juvenile justice system. Daly (1994a) claims that justice scholars must recognize that crime and punishment are sexed and gendered; measures of the process should thus reflect those qualities. Daly frames the basic question as follows: "there has been much conjecture on gender and punishment, but research to date has not answered a simple question: Are men and women punished differently for 'like crimes' and for reasons we find unacceptable?" (Daly, 1994a, p. 117).

Previous research on gender and punishment has revealed an apparent paradox: Females are generally either viewed as receiving preferential treatment as they are assigned lenient sentences by chivalrous judges (or other actors earlier in the system, such as the police or prosecutors), or females who break the law are thought to be punished for breaking sex-role stereotypes, thus resulting in harsher sanctions than those received by their male counterparts (Kruttschnitt & Green, 1984; Visher, 1983). This paradox has been particularly visible in the field of juvenile justice where girls have historically been punished much more severely than boys for juvenile-only status offenses (which would not be crimes if committed by adults), even as they have generally been viewed as less culpable than boys for their more serious crimes (Bishop & Frazier, 1992; Chesney-Lind & Shelden, 2004; Willemsen & van Schie, 1989; Wundiersitz, Naffine, & Gale, 1988). This sexual double standard meant that girls were less likely to be charged with criminal offenses, but were more likely to be committed to institutions (Chesney-Lind & Shelden, 2004).

The Juvenile Justice and Delinquency Prevention Act of 1974 (JJDP Act) changed the face of juvenile justice agencies across the country when it required states receiving federal funds for delinquency prevention to begin deinstitutionalizing and diverting status offenders. As a result, the incarceration of young women in detention centers and training schools fell dramatically (Chesney-Lind & Shelden, 2004).

When studying gender and punishment, critical consideration must be given to the type of crime committed and to the offender's prior record. It may simply be that gender inequality in punishment occurs because legally relevant characteristics of the offender are different. Previous research has found male delinquency to be more serious, more frequent, and longer-lasting than female delinquency (Shelden & Chesney-Lind, 1993); if this is still the case, we should generally expect males to receive harsher sanctions than females.

Several lines of reasoning are used to explain potential gender and punishment disparities. Belknap (2001) offers three competing hypotheses for explaining gender effects in sentencing: the first possibility is that there will be equal treatment for males and females in the justice system. This is the null hypothesis, where there is no gender effect. The second possibility is that there will be chivalry or paternalism in the justice system, where there is sex discrimination against male offenders, and females are treated more leniently. Although the effect is the same, the reasoning behind chivalry and paternalism is a bit different. With chivalry, actors in the justice system behave gallantly toward young women; paternalism is more about taking care of the powerless and dependent. The third possibility for explaining gender disparity in punishment is the evil woman hypothesis. In this case, female offenders are viewed as violating gender roles as well as laws; thus, they will be punished more harshly than their male counterparts for similar offenses (Belknap, 2001, pp. 131–132).

Because much of the research on the impact of gender on juvenile justice sentencing decisions is focused on status offenses and the differential treatment of female status offenders, the present study is an attempt to look at serious offenses in a juvenile court system that has undergone a radical shift from its original goals and practices. Washington state provides an excellent case study for this analysis: the focus of the juvenile court in Washington state is on serious person and property offenses; status offenders have been removed from the jurisdiction of juvenile justice agencies. By placing jurisdiction of status offenders with Child Protective Services or the Department of Social Health and Services, Washington state's juvenile court has moved away from "child-saving" (Platt, 1977), and has adopted a criminalized juvenile court that operates much like adult criminal courts. One important part of this system is the adoption of determinate sentencing guidelines to be applied to all juveniles processed through the juvenile justice system. Under the mandates of determinate sentencing, judges simply do not have the freedom to exercise a great deal of personal discretion; thus, only legally relevant variables should be considered in sentencing offenders. As such, by the time cases have made it in front of the judge, juvenile court sentences should be gender neutral.

DATA AND METHOD

Quantitative Data and Method

This study uses data from the Washington state juvenile justice system.[1] Unlike adults, juveniles do not have the right to a jury trial (Bernard, 1992). Instead, juvenile cases are tried and sentenced by a judge. With the revision of the juvenile justice system in Washington state in 1978, judges are now required to work within sentencing guidelines that assign points based on the offender's age, the seriousness of the present crime, the number and seriousness of past crimes, and the length of time between past offenses and the current offense. Under these sentencing guidelines, the judge must utilize the standard range unless he or she declares "manifest injustice," a rare occurrence used in less than 10 percent of the cases to come before the court. The goal behind such sentencing guidelines is to hold juvenile offenders accountable for their actions and to sentence them to like punishments for like crimes. Within this system, gender differences in sentencing should be proportionate; there should be no gender discrimination.

Qualitative Data and Method

For the qualitative analysis, I followed the lead of Kathleen Daly (1994b) and analyzed the social files of juvenile offenders as prepared by the probation officers working with them. These presentence investigation reports gave a description of the current offense as well as a description of the youth, his or her family background, his or her academic and social history, and the probation officer's sentencing recommendation. Based on Daly's work matching cases of male and female offenders who had committed like crimes (Daly, 1994b), I compared the cases of 30 girls and 30 boys who had committed generally similar crimes. In doing so, I hoped to be able to take into account the histories of the individual offenders, the reasons given for the probation officer's recommendations, and a general sense of the "gestalt of the harm."

ANALYSIS AND FINDINGS

Quantitative Analysis

In looking at the numbers, the quantitative analyses suggest there is a double standard still very much in place for boys and girls, but it is not easily interpreted. Table 1 shows the means of males and females for key variables.[2] A quick glance at this table suggests that males seem to generally receive harsher sanctions than females. For example, boys in this sample were significantly more likely than girls to be detained in secure facilities after arrest, to be charged with a felony, and to be sentenced to confinement in a juvenile correctional facility.

Table 2 shows correlation coefficients for those same variables.[3] In terms of gender, being male was significantly and positively correlated with prior offenses (.135), pre-adjudication diversions (.115), being charged with a felony (.131), being detained prior to adjudication (.110), and being sentenced to confinement (.137). On the whole, males were more likely than females to be slightly older, to commit and be charged with more serious crimes, to have official records of past offenses, to be detained after arrest, and to subsequently be sentenced to confinement in a juvenile correctional facility.

Qualitative Analysis

In looking at the presentence investigation reports and comparing the "gestalt of the harm" (Daly, 1994b), rather than just the offense as charged, boys seemed to do more damage and cause more injury in committing their crimes than did girls. In addition, the circumstances of girls' lives and their crimes are generally different than those of boys. The probation

TABLE 1   Sample Mean Differences in Offender Characteristics by Gender

Variables	Males	Females	Total	t-value	Sig.
Age	15.797	15.443	15.734	3.07	.002
	($N = 1,254$)	($N = 267$)	($N = 1521$)		
Race	.457	.505	.466	1.52	.129
	(1,452)	(307)	(1,759)		
Violent Offense	.230	.182	.222	1.83	.068
	(1,425)	(307)	(1,732)		
Priors	3.169	1.478	2.871	5.74	.000
	(1,458)	(312)	(1,770)		
Previous Diversions	.815	.423	.746	4.86	.000
	(1,458)	(312)	(1,770)		
In School	.670	.714	.677	1.18	.236
	(969)	(192)	(1,161)		
Detained	.461	.303	.433	4.80	.000
	(1,274)	(271)	(1,545)		
Charged w/Felony	.579	.407	.549	5.53	.000
	(1,446)	(307)	(1,753)		
Sentenced to Confinement	.554	.344	.529	4.39	.000
	(888)	(122)	(1,010)		

TABLE 2 Zero-Order Correlations, Means, and Standard Deviations

	Gender	Race	Age	Violent	Priors	Prediv.	Felony	Detained	School	Confined
Gender	1.00	.036	-.079	-.044	-.135*	-.115*	-.131*	-.110*	.035	-.137*
Race		1.00	-.009	-.065	-.089*	.017	.013	-.046	.031	.010
Age			1.00	.068	.224*	.218*	.085*	.185*	-.261*	.121*
Violent				1.00	.052	.081*	.176*	.256*	-.071	.263*
Priors					1.00	.502*	.179*	.304*	-.323*	.336*
Prediv.						1.00	.059	.224*	-.196*	.142*
Felony							1.00	.476*	-.219*	.315*
Detained								1.00	-.361*	.566*
School									1.00	-.326*
Confine										1.00
Mean	.82	.47	15.73	.22	2.86	.74	.55	1.09	.68	.53
Std. Dev.	.38	.50	1.71	.41	4.76	1.30	.50	1.41	.47	.50

*$p < .001$ (2-tailed)

officers' responses to boys and girl were different in tone, as well, although they varied widely; there are echoes of child-saving, paternalism, chivalry, and purely punitive attitudes in their reports to the judges.

The social files give us the tools to answer the question of whether the survival of girls is being criminalized. In this sample, as in much previous research (Chesney-Lind, 1989), it did seem to be the case. As can be seen in Figure 1, girls were much more likely than their male counterparts to have been sexually and physically abused, to be described as "incorrigible" or out of the control of their parents, and to have run away from home. Girls were also more likely to be described as depressed and to have a history of place-ments in psychiatric units, another extreme form of social control. Many had run away from profound victimization and had turned to crime as a means of survival.

Probation officers in their presentence reports were more likely to attribute girls' delinquent behavior to the influence of bad peers, while males were more often character-ized as affiliated with gangs. In addition, males used weapons, particularly guns, more fre-quently in the commission of their crimes. The gestalt of the harm was considerably higher in the offenses committed by males; they did significant damage to their victims. Males in this sample were involved in shootings, stabbings, and unsolicited attacks. They were involved in severe beatings, multiple robberies, and several were charged with child rape or molestation.

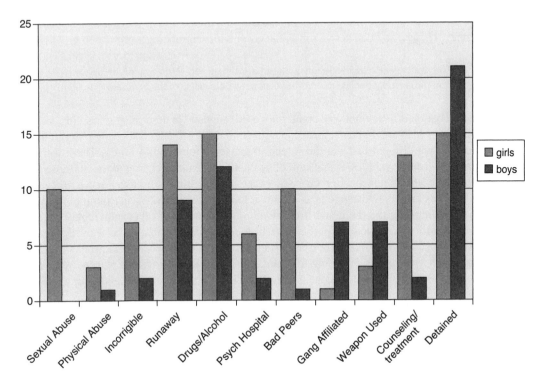

FIGURE 1   Social History, Attributions, and the Gestalt of the Harm

In recommending a ruling of manifest injustice, urging judges to impose a sentence outside of the standard range, probation officers' presentence reports on girls were more likely to claim that particularly severe punishment was "for their own good or protection." The idea seemed to be that juvenile correctional facilities could provide mandated counseling and treatment that would benefit female offenders. Reports on boys more often emphasized individual accountability, dangerousness of the offender, and the protection of the community. Child-saving ideals were still very much in place for girls, but were much less apparent in the boys' files. This, then, may be how paternalism seeps into a juvenile justice system that operates under determinate sentencing guidelines. Judges are compelled to take seriously the recommendations made by others, including probation officers, social workers, and psychiatrists; these actors often view the behavior and needs of male and female offenders quite differently.

Examples of paternalistic statements from the juvenile court files of girls will help to illustrate the point. A psychiatrist's report on Kim, 17, charged with first-degree arson, is interpreted as follows (all names have been changed):

> He does not believe that Kim was motivated to commit the crime out of a desire to inflict pain and to do damage. He believes her motivation was "to get attention," to be heard and to make a cry for help.

Probation officers often made attributions about the motives and thought processes of female offenders. Standard language in their reports at times seemed inconsistent with the circumstances of the crime; for example, the following comment was made in a report on Sydney, 18, who stabbed her victim in the chest with scissors:

> The respondent's conduct neither caused nor threatened serious bodily injury or the respondent did not contemplate that his/her conduct would cause or threaten seriously bodily injury.

The probation officer employed commonly used language in describing mitigating factors, which may lead to a lighter sentence, but given that the offender stabbed her victim in the chest, it would seem that she did intend to cause serious bodily injury. There were no examples from boys' files of this kind of sympathetic reinterpretation of the offense.

From the statements in their presentence reports, boys were much more likely than girls to be considered dangerous and a threat to the community. As an example, Brad, 16, shot his victim in the thigh and fired his gun at a number of other individuals. He was charged with assault and the probation officer recommended that he be waived from the juvenile justice system and be tried as an adult. The file had a heading "Reasons for declining jurisdiction and transferring to adult status" and eight different reasons were then listed. The probation officer concluded: "Brad is well aware of right and wrong and has allegedly committed an aggressive, violent act against another person . . . it was the unanimous decision to support a declination of jurisdiction and transfer Brad to adult status." Similarly, Max, 15, was charged with reckless endangerment after he discharged a firearm from a moving vehicle. The probation officer outlined 9 reasons why the "respondent is a serious and clear danger to society" and added 15 supporting documents for a finding of manifest injustice and a longer than standard sentence. While the presentence reports characterized a number of males as dangerous and a threat to society, such language was rarely used to describe female delinquents. Girls, instead, were more likely to be viewed as a threat to themselves.

Because they were viewed as more of a threat to themselves than to others in the community, probation officers frequently recommended that female offenders be sentenced to confinement or "treatment" in secure facilities for their own protection and good. For example, in a report on Jane, 17, charged with assault and taking a motor vehicle without permission, the officer made the following statement:

> Jane is a product of a very dysfunctional family with a long history of substance and physical abuse. . . . Jane's physical aggression and drug use are not surprising given the environment she was raised in. Unfortunately, there is little chance that things will change given the present dynamics in the family . . . a period of confinement appears to be the best option at this time. . . . It is feared that only a very long term inpatient and follow up treatment program has any chance to overcome her drug/alcohol malady. It is felt that she needs treatment, not punishment.

Even more extreme is a statement from a report on Allison, 16, charged with possession of cocaine; the probation officer recommended a finding of manifest injustice and a particularly long sentence:

> Alleged in this incident is a Class C felony, which is not a serious offense. Allison is actually more of a victim of her own addiction and the risks involved are actually greater to her than to the community at large. . . . There are services in the juvenile system that would be of benefit to both her and the community . . . her actions in obtaining and using drugs place Allison at a very high risk for drug overdose, AIDS, or becoming a crime victim and it could be estimated that her life expectancy, without effective intervention, is approximately age 21 years. . . . Allison's only hope for treatment—and perhaps for saving her life—is to remain in the juvenile justice system and be placed in long term, secure drug/alcohol treatment program where the controls for her behavior are externally enforced till such time as her addiction is effectively addressed.

Even as they recognized the poor family environments the girls came from and the abuse that they suffered, probation officers repeatedly recommended confinement in juvenile correctional facilities as a way for the girls to get out of their homes and to get counseling and treatment. A final example illustrates the point, from a report on Amanda, 18, charged with violation of the Uniform Substances Act:

> Amanda has an exceptional attitude and has proved to be quite remarkable. . . . Amanda has been badly abused emotionally and became an adolescent who has resorted to injecting hardcore drugs such as heroin and cocaine. She was experimenting with ways of deadening her own pain from the emotional and physical abuse. . . . Amanda through her efforts has earned the privilege to remain at a halfway house and become the productive citizen she was meant to be . . . she is involved in her own salvation.

On the whole, in the matched cases, there were more sympathetic attributions made for female offenders. Child-saving attitudes were much in evidence in the files of the girls, much less so in the files of the boys. The language in the boys' files more often focused on the threat they posed to the community and the need to hold them accountable for their delinquent activities.

Looking just at the statistics, girls do appear to be getting lighter sentences than their male counterparts, much of which can be attributed to the level of seriousness of their crimes and the perception of the threat they pose. When examining the qualitative data, however, a slightly different picture emerges. The tone in the boys' files tends to be more punitive; the tone in the girls' files is much more paternalistic. The best intentions of probation officers and judges end up looking a lot like punishment at the time of sentencing; one misses the logic and the reasoning when just analyzing the quantitative data.

FINAL THOUGHTS

This chapter addressed the question of whether boys and girls are treated differently for "like crimes." In this sample, the answer appears to be yes, although the circumstances of seemingly comparable crimes were still quite different, with males wreaking more havoc on the community and girls' destructive behavior more often aimed inward. The factors mediating gender discrimination in punishment are complex. Justice research has been criticized for too often using an "add women and stir" approach. Feminist scholars argue that we must evaluate women and girls using standards based on their own unique life circumstances. In this study, there did seem to be a double standard at play. When punished severely, the issue for boys seemed to be to hold them accountable for their offenses, while girls were more often seen as needing help, counseling or protection that the juvenile justice system could theoretically provide. Ultimately, even in a state where discretion has been largely taken from the hands of judges, gender remains an important variable in sentencing decisions.

Whether the reasons for such disparate treatment are acceptable or not is open to debate. Juvenile justice decisions still seem to be influenced by the good intentions of the actors, even in a state that utilizes determinate sentencing guidelines. Depending on the goal of the institution, this child-saving attitude may help to justify gender disparities in punishment. If and when girls' survival is being criminalized (Acoca, 1998; Chesney-Lind, 1989), perhaps equal treatment should not be the goal.

NOTES

1. Data for this analysis were taken from the five largest counties in Washington state. For all counties except King County (which includes Seattle), information on the youth processed through the juvenile courts was obtained from the 1991 JUVIS data on all cases referred to juvenile courts in Washington state. For King County, data were taken from the 1991 King County data on referrals to the King County Juvenile Court. The data were collected by Bridges et al. (1993) for a study funded by the Office of Juvenile Justice and Delinquency Prevention of the United States Department of Justice and the Department of Social and Health Services. For further information on the data, see Bridges et al. (1993), *Racial Disproportionality in the Juvenile Justice System* (Appendix One).
2. The cases for this study are individuals, or specifically juveniles that have entered the juvenile justice system. In order to make the sample representative by race and seriousness of the crime, the researchers oversampled minorities, felony referrals, and cases confined to juvenile

correctional facilities. The weighted sample was then used for analysis. For individuals who had committed or were charged with more than one offense, the data for sentencing were taken on the most serious offense. The full sample is 1,777 cases, including 1,458 males and 312 females (with 7 missing cases in which the individual's gender was not clearly stated in the records). As the focus of this study is on gender and because there is a relatively small group of females, the broader category of nonwhite was used for minorities rather than an attempt at a racially specific analysis.

3.   Gender was coded male = 0; female = 1.

REFERENCES

ACOCA, L. (1998). Outside/Inside: The violation of American girls at home, on the streets, and in the juvenile justice system. *Crime & Delinquency, 44*, 561–589.

BELKNAP, J. (2001). *The invisible woman: Gender, crime, and justice* (2nd ed.). Belmont, CA: Wadsworth.

BERNARD, T. J. (1992). *The cycle of juvenile justice*. New York: Oxford University Press.

BISHOP, D. M., & FRAZIER, C. E. (1992). Gender bias in juvenile justice processing: Implications of the JJDP Act. *Criminology, 82*, 1162–1186.

BRIDGES, G. S., ENGEN, R. L., & BERETTA, G. (1993). *Racial disproportionality in the juvenile justice system: Final report*. Prepared for the Department of Social and Health Services and the Washington State Legislature.

CHESNEY-LIND, M. (1989). Girls' crime and woman's place: Toward a feminist model of female delinquency. *Crime & Delinquency, 35*, 5–29.

CHESNEY-LIND, M., & SHELDEN, R. G. (2004). *Girls, delinquency, and juvenile justice* (3rd ed.). Belmont, CA: Wadsworth.

DALY, K. (1994a). Gender and punishment disparity. In G. S. Bridges & M. A. Myers (Eds.), *Inequality, crime, and social control* (pp. 117–133). Boulder, CO: Westview Press.

DALY, K. (1994b). *Gender, crime, and punishment*. New Haven, CT: Yale University Press.

KRUTTSCHNITT, C., & GREEN., D. E. (1984). The sex-sanctioning issue: Is it history? *American Sociological Review, 49*, 541–551.

PLATT, A. M. (1977). *The child savers: The invention of delinquency* (2nd ed., enlarged). Chicago: University of Chicago Press.

SHELDEN, R. G., & CHESNEY-LIND., M. (1993). Gender and race differences in delinquent careers. *Juvenile and Family Court Journal*, 73–89.

VISHER, C. A. (1983). Gender, police arrest decisions, and notions of chivalry. *Criminology, 21*, 5–28.

WILLEMSEN, T. M., & VAN SCHIE, E. C. M. (1989). Sex stereotypes and responses to juvenile delinquency. *Sex Roles, 20*, 623–638.

WUNDIERSITZ, J., NAFFINE, N., & GALE, F. (1988). Chivalry, justice or paternalism?: The female offender in the juvenile justice system. *ANZJS, 24*, 359–376.

49

Developing Gender-Specific Services for Delinquency Prevention

Understanding Risk and Resiliency

Barbara Bloom, Barbara Owen, Elizabeth Piper Deschenes, and Jill Rosenbaum

❖

INTRODUCTION

Within the last few years the proportion of female youthful offenders has increased, while there has been a decrease in crime among male juvenile delinquents (Acoca, 1999). Despite the increase in the number of girls and young women arrested and placed within the juvenile justice system over the last several decades, female youthful offenders remain a small proportion of the juvenile justice population (Belknap, 1996; Chesney-Lind & Shelden, 1998). The nature of female delinquency is generally less threatening to the public order than that of male juveniles, who are more likely to be arrested for violent crimes and serious property crimes (Chesney-Lind & Shelden, 1998). Consequently, girls and young women have been relatively invisible in the juvenile justice system. This invisibility affects every aspect of the juvenile justice system and results in a lack of attention to girls in juvenile justice research and theory and a lack of programs and services for female youthful offenders (Belknap, 1996).

Until recently, few resources within the juvenile justice system have been directed toward the needs of at-risk girls, despite their unique situation. For example, a report issued by the Law Enforcement Assistance Administration in 1975 indicated that only 5 percent of federally funded juvenile delinquency projects and only 6 percent of all local funds were directed toward girls (Chesney-Lind & Shelden, 1998). More recently, a meta-analysis of program evaluations conducted since 1950 on 443 delinquency programs reported that 34.8 percent were exclusively for males and an additional 42.4 percent served mostly males; only 2.3 percent served girls exclusively, and only 5.9 percent served a majority of females (Lipsey, 1990). Within the last few years the Office of Juvenile Justice and Delinquency Prevention (OJJDP) launched a multilevel approach, which has resulted in publication of an inventory of state efforts (Community Research Associates, 1998), an inventory of best practices and training curricula (Greene, Peters & Associates, 1997), and a variety of program development activities (Budnick & Shields-Fletcher, 1998).

Although social scientists have studied delinquency and other high-risk behaviors of male adolescents for decades, most research has not focused specifically on high-risk girls. This has resulted in little insight into the reasons for their involvement in the juvenile justice system (Belknap, 1996; Chesney-Lind & Shelden, 1992; Leonard, 1982; Naffine, 1987; Smart, 1976). Many studies of delinquency included few girls and young women in their samples, and this has set a precedent for most of the research on juvenile delinquency (Calhoun, Jurgens, & Chen, 1993; Miller, Trapani, Fejes-Mendoza, Eggleston, & Dwiggins, 1995; Minnesota Advisory Task Force on the Female Offender in Corrections, 1994). Belknap (1997) describes the lack of research related to females as a telling indicator of "girls' and women's invisibility in theories [which] has doggedly followed them in every way imaginable" (p. 2). This is also true of policy research and development, as well as institutional and programmatic responses. When the major sociological theories of delinquency focus almost exclusively on males, it raises a concern as to whether these theories should be used to explain girls' delinquent behavior as well.

Feminist theorists suggest that the focus on gender goes beyond simply adding another variable to the study of female crime and delinquency (e.g., "add women and stir"). Contemporary feminist research has contributed to our understanding of the female experience in a way that does not simply contrast it to that of men. Feminist criminology, particularly when informed by concern for sexual victimization, offers a great deal to the study of female crime and delinquency (Chesney-Lind, 1992; Owen & Bloom, 1995). From this perspective, exploitation by men acts as a trigger for behavior by females, causing them to run away or begin abusing drugs at an early age. These behaviors are often referred to as survival strategies that ultimately result in girls' involvement in the juvenile justice system (Chesney-Lind, 1992). However, even feminist criminology has failed to fully explore the intersection of race, class, and gender in girls' and women's offending until recently (Bloom, 1996).

Interest has begun to shift to the unique issues of female delinquency, the nature and causes of girls' involvement in crime, and the biological and developmental issues that are particular to girls and young women. The ways in which girls develop their identity and relationships with others have begun to influence theory and research about female crime and delinquency. According to Gilligan (1982), boys develop their identity in relation to the world, while girls develop their identity in relation to others. For girls, moral decisions are based on specific personal situations, in contrast with the more common male focus on assertive decision making and exercising judgments based on absolutes. Gilligan asserts that in women's lives, attachment, interdependence, and connectedness are critical issues that form the foundation of their identity; and female moral development is often based on personal views and a commitment to others. Often, this commitment involves giving up or sacrificing one's own well-being for the benefit of others.

Professionals working with women and girls are articulating the need to recognize the centrality of relationships as a central tenet in the female's psychological life

(Covington, 1998; Gilligan, 1982; Pipher, 1994). This approach recognizes that women's and girls' psychological profile differs from that of men, including the accumulated effects of exposure to abuse and trauma, battering, and an overemphasis on gender-based expectations such as caretaking and docility. Further, female behaviors are seen as reactions to multiple sources of marginalization and as expressions of resistance. This shift has profound implications for treatment and services for those who work with girls and women in the criminal justice system (Bloom, 1997).

Developing gender-specific programs for females requires a better understanding of the unique situation of girls and the risk factors relating to juvenile delinquency and their involvement in the juvenile or criminal justice system, but to date there have been relatively few studies. Risk and resiliency factors are associated with various spheres of influence, such as family, peer, and individual characteristics, school and social environments, and community status. How, and to what extent, these factors are present and interact can significantly increase the likelihood of involvement in delinquency and subsequent treatment by the juvenile justice system. Traditionally, researchers have focused on risk factors that are likely to result in negative or self-destructive behaviors among youth. More recently, experts have also endeavored to identify resiliency or protective factors described by Scott (1994) as "those characteristics or circumstances which enable individuals to grow, thrive, and succeed in spite of what appear to be insurmountable odds" (p. 5).

Through a review of the literature, in this chapter we discuss various factors within the following domains for risk and resiliency in relationship to girls' delinquent behavior: community, school, family, individual and peers. The review of the existing research on girls in the juvenile justice system identified the following themes: (1) the increased involvement of girls in the juvenile justice system; (2) risk factors for their involvement in the juvenile justice system; and (3) differential treatment of girls once they are in the system (Girls Inc., 1996). These findings are summarized to provide suggestions for gender-specific programming for the prevention of female delinquency.

PROFILE OF AT-RISK ADOLESCENT FEMALES

Female adolescents at risk or involved in the juvenile justice system often come from impoverished, urban, inner-city environments; have been reared in female-headed, single-parent households; or have experienced foster care placement. They have a higher likelihood than their male counterparts of being channeled into the juvenile justice system as a result of fleeing physically and/or sexually abusive home environments, and they are more likely to have abused drugs and/or alcohol than adolescent girls in the general population (Washington, 1997). Several studies have identified the following common characteristics of at-risk adolescent females (American Correctional Association [ACA], 1990; Chesney-Lind & Shelden, 1998; Girls Inc., 1996; Greene, Peters & Associates, 1997; Minnesota Advisory Task Force on the Female Offender in Corrections, 1994):

- Age 13 to 18 years
- History of victimization, especially physical, sexual, and emotional abuse
- School failure, truancy, and dropout
- Repeated status offenses, especially running away

- Unstable family life, including family involvement in the criminal justice system, lack of connectedness, and social isolation
- History of unhealthy dependent relationships, especially with older males
- Mental health issues, including history of substance abuse
- Overrepresentation among communities of color
- Economically marginalized populations

COMMUNITY RISK AND RESILIENCY FACTORS

Community risk factors include social and structural factors that influence the environment in which girls are raised. The literature has focused on racial or ethnic background, socioeconomic status, and issues of immigration or acculturation. Research also suggests that communities that provide extracurricular and social activities can foster resiliency for young women. To this end, communities need to provide a continuum of opportunities for drug and alcohol education, abuse and sex education, nontraditional job training, social skills development, places to go (e.g., safe havens), and mentoring opportunities.

Race and Ethnicity

Girls from racial/ethnic minority groups are caught in the double bind of the gender and racial expectations of their communities of origin and those of the dominant culture. Moreover, racial and ethnic minority girls have different experiences with the dominant institutions in this society (West, 1994). Although it is essential to identify and correct gender bias in the juvenile justice system, attending to gender alone is not an adequate response for girls of color in detention.

Even though arrest and incarceration rates have increased for girls in general during the past decade, girls of color are overrepresented in the juvenile justice population. Girls of color constitute the largest and fastest-growing segment of female adolescents in secure detention, and race and class play as significant a role as gender in girls' development and life choices, as well as in their treatment (Amaro, 1995; Anderson, 1996; LaFramboise & Howard-Pitney, 1995; Martin, 1993; Nelson, 1997; Orenstein, 1994; Washington, 1997). Using data collected in 29 states, the National Council on Crime and Delinquency reported that African Americans comprise nearly 50 percent of all girls in secure detention, Hispanics 13 percent, and Caucasians 34 percent.

There are disparities in the treatment of girls involved in the juvenile justice system. Minority families are viewed as "less interested in their children" than are white families (Frazier & Bishop, 1995, p. 43). This may result in a style of response that reflects stereotypes of the dominant culture when dealing with minority families (Washington, 1997). For example, Miller (1994) found that African American and Latina girls were 70 to 80 percent more likely than white girls to be recommended for detention-oriented placement. The behavior of African American girls was often typified as being the result of inappropriate lifestyle choices, whereas the behavior of white girls was framed in terms of self-image problems, peer pressure, and abandonment issues (p. 20). Girls of color are at particular risk for inadequate treatment of prior sexual abuse (Washington, 1997).

Socioeconomic Status

Socioeconomic background is a strong predictor of female, as well as male, adolescents' risk for involvement in the juvenile justice system (Washington, 1997). Poor youth are more likely to be processed through the official criminal justice system, while their more affluent counterparts are more likely to be diverted into private treatment programs (Belknap, 1996; Frazier & Bishop, 1995; Girls Inc., 1996; La Free cited in Washington, 1997).

The proportion of U.S. children living in poverty varies significantly by race and ethnicity: 12 percent white; 30 percent African American; 27 percent Latino/Hispanic; 20 percent Asian/Pacific Islander; 26 percent Native American (Brindis, Peterson, & Brown, 1997) as well as geography. At 25 percent, California has the 10th highest proportion in the nation of children and youth living in poverty (California Department of Finance, 1993).

To a large extent, socioeconomic status is a factor in girls' committing certain types of crimes (e.g., girls steal things they need or think they need but cannot afford). Girls and young women are particularly susceptible to these temptations because they believe that their popularity is linked to physical appearance and fashion during adolescence. Once arrested, socioeconomic status also limits their ability to post bond or pay for a private attorney, as well as the types of services they receive (Belknap, 1996). On the other hand, if a delinquent girl's family has money or insurance, she may be diverted out of the juvenile justice system and placed in a private facility for services such as a drug treatment or mental health counseling or therapy. If a girl or young woman comes from a low-income family, these options may not exist. As a result, there is more of a chance that delinquent girls from low-income families will end up in the juvenile justice system and may not receive the services that they need (Girls Inc., 1996).

SCHOOL RISK AND RESILIENCY FACTORS

Studies of school performance of girls and boys suggest that the marginalization and stereotyping of women in popular culture are unintentionally reinforced in schools (American Association of University Women [AAUW], 1992). Shortchanging girls of classroom attention, the emphasis on competitive (rather than cooperative) learning, a shortage of the use of women as role models in texts and lesson plans, sexual harassment by fellow students, and reinforcing gender stereotypes of abilities all have a negative impact on girls' aspirations. Declining school performance is related to a decrease in self-esteem among preadolescent and adolescent girls (AAUW, 1992). Although girls begin their school years with skills and ambitions comparable to those of boys, by the time they are in high school, "most have suffered a disproportionate loss of confidence in their academic abilities" (p. 5). Even though there is no strong evidence that single-sex education is better for girls than coeducation, some of the positive results are a heightened regard by girls for math and science, an increase in girls' risk taking, and a gain in girls' confidence from academic competence (AAUW, 1998).

Despite the unintentional negative effect of the school environment on many girls, studies have shown that school performance continues to be important to them, and school failure can contribute to their delinquency (Adler, 1975; Cernkovich & Giordano, 1979b). Other studies found that a positive outlook and performance in school-related activities, and an emphasis on the importance of math, science, and computer skills were strong correlates for academic success and a reduction in delinquent behavior for girls (AAUW, 1992; Chesney-Lind & Shelden, 1998).

Truancy contributes to delinquency, drug use, and dropout (Garry, 1996). A recent report from the Los Angeles County Office of Education concluded that "chronic absenteeism is the most powerful predictor of delinquent behavior—(for) behavior involving drugs, alcohol, or violence" (Shuster, 1995, p. 1). In California, approximately 15 percent of all students drop out during their four years of high school (Rothenbaum, 1998). Girls and young women who drop out are less likely than boys to return to school or to obtain a GED (Posner, 1990).

The educational system seldom takes into account the psychosocial construction of girls' lives, especially during middle adolescence. Evidence points to the difference in school cultures between girls (adult and teacher oriented) and boys (group and peer oriented), and the importance of designing school programs that take these differences into account (Block, cited in Chesney-Lind & Shelden, 1998).

School environments that recognize the unique learning styles of girls (e.g., cooperative learning and group problem solving versus individual competitiveness) and have high expectations for academic performance, especially in the math and sciences, are especially able to provide for resiliency in young women. These schools foster community partnerships and provide extracurricular activities not only to the student but to the entire family, including education on issues of abuse, sexuality, drug and alcohol use, and job training. Gender-specific nontraditional vocational job training for girls is also an important school component.

FAMILY RISK AND RESILIENCY FACTORS

The family environment of many at-risk or delinquent girls includes parental substance abuse and violence as well as physical, sexual, and emotional abuse. Additional characteristics of family dysfunction, which place girls at risk for future delinquency, include parental rejection and/or abandonment (e.g., experiencing little love, affection, or warmth), inadequate supervision, witnessing or experiencing conflict, marital discord, and violence in the home. Studies indicated that the majority of California Youth Authority (CYA) female wards came from single-parent and multiproblem families (Owen & Bloom, 1997; Rosenbaum, 1989). Both parents had deserted one out of every 10 CYA wards in the 1960s. Even fewer girls in the 1990s grew up in two-parent families than in the 1960s (25 percent versus 15 percent). Windle (1997) focused on the adverse effects of parental drinking on adolescents, including the contribution made by disruptive, alcohol-influenced parenting behaviors to internalizing (e.g., depression, anxiety) and externalizing problems (e.g., delinquency) by their children.

Family Criminality

Familial involvement in crime is another correlate for delinquency. Family characteristics, which appear to have more of an impact on girls than on boys, include the involvement of a family member in the criminal justice system (Dembo et al., 1998). An ACA (1990) study indicated that 64 percent of juvenile girls in detention had a family member who was or had been incarcerated.

Two studies of girls incarcerated in the California Youth Authority indicated that the vast majority came from families where criminality was common. Seventy-six percent of female CYA wards in the 1960s (Rosenbaum, 1989) and 89 percent of female CYA wards in the 1990s (Owen & Bloom, 1997) had family members who had been arrested. Owen and Bloom (1997) indicated that nearly one-half of the respondents reported that their father had been incarcerated and one-fourth reported that their mother had been incarcerated. About three-fourths of the girls in the 1960s had at least one family member with a criminal record, and half of the time it was the girls' mothers who had felony arrest records. The girls reported that 71 percent of their parents fought regularly with the children. Family conflict over alcohol was noted in 81 percent of the families; 34 percent of the fathers were known alcoholics, as were 31 percent of the mothers. Owen and Bloom note that although records were not kept on domestic violence unless a specific charge was filed, in the 1960s " a number of the known fathers had spent time in jail for fighting with their wife." Nearly one-third of parents of the CYA wards in the 1960s had histories of mental illness.

Foster Care and Out-of-Home Placement

An examination of the living situations of incarcerated girls prior to detention provides additional insight into another dimension of their family situations. In a study of girls' living situations prior to incarceration in the California Youth Authority, Owen and Bloom (1997) found that 40.6 percent lived with a parent or guardian, 12.3 percent with a spouse or partner, 11.8 percent with a grandparent or other relative, and 9.9 percent with a friend or roommate. An additional 9.8 percent reported living alone or in a program, and 9.9 percent reported having no permanent address or being homeless.

Statistics of public juvenile facilities indicate that 69,075 juveniles were in residential custody in 1995. California had the highest number, 19,567, 28 percent of the nation's total (Poe-Yamagata & Butts, 1996). A study by the ACA (1990) indicated that over half (54 percent) of juvenile females in detention indicated that they lived with parents or grandparents prior to their incarceration.

The increase in the number of juvenile girls committing certain categories of delinquent acts has resulted in more out-of-home placements. On the national level, the increase in the number of girls and young women involved in person offenses (e.g., homicide, robbery, aggravated assault, simple assault), which resulted in out-of-home placement, is nearly twice that of boys (Poe-Yamagata & Butts, 1996). The California Department of Social Services (1998) reports that approximately 5 percent of the 100,000 youth in out-of-home placement are referrals from probation.

Data from the California Department of Social Services (1998) also provides information on the numbers and reasons for removal from the home for girls and boys ages 10 through 18 during 1997. In 1997, 26,004 boys and 25,038 girls were removed from their homes. The vast majority of both boys and girls were removed for neglect (boys 36 percent; girls 39 percent) and physical/sexual abuse (boys 13 percent; girls 20 percent). Only 4 percent of the girls and 17 percent of the boys were removed for law violations.

Family Dysfunction, Substance Abuse, Physical and Sexual Abuse

Research has consistently shown childhood abuse and neglect and family disruption to be significant factors related to female delinquency (ACA, 1990; Calhoun et al., 1993; Chesney-Lind, 1995; Daniel, 1994; Minnesota Advisory Task Force on the Female Offender in Corrections, 1994; Robinson, 1994; Schwartz, Willis, & Battle, 1991). Childhood abuse and family dysfunction manifest themselves in a variety of ways, including physical and sexual abuse, physical neglect, lack of supervision, and emotional maltreatment. In addition, there may be negative role modeling by one or both substance-abusing parents, with the presence of drugs within the home contributing to an unsafe environment from which girls attempt to escape by running away.

Family dysfunction is another characteristic in the lives of female delinquents. Parenting styles tended to be chaotic and inconsistent, and youths were victims of abuse and neglect. Positive feedback and nurturance from parents were noticeably lacking. Nearly 40 percent of the mothers of the CYA wards in the 1960s had been charged with child abuse and/or neglect, some within the first six months of their daughter's life (Rosenbaum, 1989). This proportion was even higher by the 1990s, when two-thirds of the wards interviewed reported that they were victims of child abuse or emotional abuse by a family member (Owen & Bloom, 1997). Nearly one-half reported that they were victims of sexual abuse, and over one-third had experienced sexual assault by peers or a stranger. Over half of the wards in the 1960s were mothers themselves by the time they left CYA. For the most part, they lacked the supports and resources needed to raise children and cope with their environment.

Research has shown that girls respond differently than boys to family dysfunction. For example, Dornfeld and Kruttschnitt (1992) found that marital discord, marital stability, and change influence the lives of boys and girls differently. These responses were not limited to gender stereotypes, however. The study found only minimal support for a commonly held hypothesis that in response to a given stressful event, boys act out and girls internalize their feelings. Girls and young women residing with an unmarried parent for a prolonged period of time were more likely than boys to report having used alcohol. Males were more likely than females to appear depressed and anxious as a result of divorce. The study results suggest that marital dissolution places boys at risk for depression and girls for delinquency.

Childhood abuse and neglect play a significant role in girls' involvement in the juvenile justice system, especially if the abuse occurs within the family (Dembo, Schmeidler, Sue, Bordon, & Manning, 1995; Dembo, Williams & Schmeidler, 1993). The resulting problem behaviors are often related to these traumatic home events and can include sexual acting out, often in defiance of parents and guardians. Dembo et al. (1995) describe this as a representation of "culturally conditioned expression of aggression against society" (p. 88). The interpersonal problems and corresponding coping behaviors (e.g., running away, sexual promiscuity) of girls result in status offenses and adjustment problems (e.g., dropping out of school) rather than delinquent behavior.

According to Kelley, Thornberry, and Smith (1997), childhood maltreatment is a significant, high predictor of all types of delinquent behavior; and the seriousness or violence level of delinquency increases with the severity of maltreatment experienced. Official records of delinquent behavior show a 13 percent higher rate for maltreated youth than for those without such a history (Kelley et al., 1997). In addition to serious delinquent behavior and violence, childhood maltreatment was found to be strongly correlated with teen pregnancy, drug use, lower school performance, and mental health problems.

Research data consistently point to a strong link between abuse and juvenile female delinquency (ACA, 1990; Culross, 1997; Girls Inc., 1996; Miller et al., 1995). Although boys have a greater risk of emotional neglect and serious physical injury from abuse, girls are sexually abused three to four times more often than boys but have a lower risk of emotional neglect and serious physical injury than boys (Kilpatrick & Saunders, 1997; Sedlak & Broadhurst, 1996). Victimization starts at an early age. For girls, sexual abuse starts earlier and lasts longer than abuse of boys and is more likely to be perpetrated by a family member.

As many as two-thirds to three-fourths of delinquent girls report a history of sexual abuse, and 60 percent of young women involved in the juvenile justice system report physical abuse (ACA, 1990; Chesney-Lind, 1989; Chesney-Lind & Shelden, 1992). Owen and Bloom's 1997 study of girls in the California Youth Authority found that 85 percent indicated abuse of some type during their lives. Another study by the ACA (1990) found that 47 percent of girls reporting physical abuse indicated that they were abused ten or more times. Over half (54 percent) of girls who told someone that they were being abused indicated that reporting it made things worse, or at best, the abuse continued with no change. Only 25 percent of girls who reported abuse to someone indicated that the abuse stopped (ACA, 1990).

Often, abuse in the home prompts adolescent girls to run away, which is one of the most prevalent risk factors for girls' involvement in the juvenile justice system. The high incidence of runaway incidents bears a closer look, as this survival strategy may lead to incarceration (Calhoun et al., 1993; Chesney-Lind, 1995). Girls and young women often run away, not only to escape abuse but also to protect family relationships. Often, they believe that they somehow deserved, encouraged, or invited abuse; and running away and the subsequent delinquent survival behaviors are easier to deal with than feelings of complicity in their own abuse.

Actual arrest rates show that girls and boys run away from home in about equal numbers, but parents and police may respond differently to the same behavior. Parents may be more likely to call the police when their daughters do not come home, and police may be more likely to arrest a female than a male runaway (Chesney-Lind, 1997).

Chesney-Lind (1997) describes the situation of girls who repeatedly run away to escape physical or sexual abuse, and subsequently engaging in street crime to survive. "Some girls resort to panhandling and shoplifting, other theft for money, food, and clothes. Some exchange sex for these necessities and become involved in prostitution and drug abuse. Girls' situations often are worsened by patriarchal law enforcement and justice systems that require girls to obey parents and stay at home. In many cases girls are sent back to their victimizers. Even when taken out of their homes, courts have few placement alternatives for girls and sometimes are left only with returning them home" (p. 5).

Once a girl is on the street, her exposure to other risk factors is increased. A study by Iwamoto, Kameoka, and Brasseur (1990) of homeless youth in Waikiki, about half of whom were girls, revealed that their most urgent needs are housing, jobs, and medical services. Exposure to violence is greatly increased for homeless adolescents, who are also more likely to suffer from poor nutrition, sexual exploitation, and exposure to human immunodeficiency virus (HIV) infection and sexually transmitted diseases (Deisher & Rogers, 1991). Because runaways are out of school, they are also at risk for arrest for truancy, and their educational advancement opportunities are affected.

Many abused girls who are picked up for status offenses such as running away or being truant are returned to the abusive home environment—the runaway girl is seen as the problem, while the parents' problems, including physical and sexual abuse, are not discovered. For many years these girls' accounts of abuse were ignored, and they were institutionalized in detention centers and training schools inappropriately as delinquents. If group homes or other out-of-home placement options are lacking or full, judges have no alternative but to keep girls in secure facilities until placement becomes available. Placement in secure detention facilities may be inappropriate given the circumstances that led to their running away (Anderson, 1994). Furthermore, research indicates that many workers in the juvenile justice system lack experience with and knowledge about sexual abuse (Baines & Alder, 1996). Thus, even though it is widely recognized that most girls entering the juvenile justice system have been sexually abused, the workers in the system may be ill prepared to respond appropriately to this issue.

Resiliency Factors

Grossman, Beinashowitz, and Anderson (1992) noted that cohesion and communication with a mother were important predictors of resiliency and delinquency avoidance for both boys and girls. Collectively, the findings of these authors concluded that although girls and boys respond differently to family events, the responses couldn't be predicted along gender lines.

Ideally, youth would acquire resiliency traits at home. However, they can also be learned and reinforced outside the home. Other external factors, besides the involvement of a caring adult, can help youth to increase their resiliency. Benard (1991) cited positive and high expectations of the youth from adults and others around them, and opportunities for meaningful involvement within the school, family, or community as important factors. Brooks (1994) believes that it is important for adults to help children build on their current skills and abilities, or islands of competence (i.e., areas that are, or could be, sources of pride and accomplishment), as a way of helping them to take pride in themselves, thereby increasing their resiliency. By taking a strength-based perspective of youth, the focus becomes one of assisting youth in developing support systems and skills that will help them meet their needs and overcome difficulties (Brendtro & Ness, 1996).

Specific resiliency factors in any given case often depend on the particular context of the person's life and are related to other factors. For young people, a key factor is the presence of a caring adult with whom the youth has developed a significant relationship based on trust and mutual respect. Such persons could be a parent or primary caregiver, but other family members, teachers, and members of the community can also fill this role.

Families that encourage connectedness and child centeredness provide positive role models and social messages regarding risky behaviors such as drug and alcohol abstinence. Access to services such as drug and alcohol treatment, and parenting and family management skills, can positively affect the nurturance factor within troubled families.

INDIVIDUAL AND PEER RISK AND RESILIENCY FACTORS

Hawkins, Catalano, and Miller (1992) have identified two categories of risk factors for adolescents: broad societal, cultural, and contextual factors, which provide legal and normative expectations for behaviors, and factors found within the individuals and their interpersonal environments (e.g., families, schools, and peer groups). Contextual factors include laws and norms favorable to the availability of drugs and alcohol, and extreme economic deprivation and neighborhood disorganization. Individual and interpersonal factors include physiological factors, family alcohol and drug behavior and attitudes, poor or inconsistent family management, family conflict, low bonding to the family, early and persistent problem behaviors, academic failure and poor school commitment, peer rejection in elementary grades, association with drug-using peers, alienation and rebelliousness, attitudes favorable to drug use, and early onset of drug use (Hawkins et al., 1992).

Substance Abuse

Studies of juveniles in the criminal justice system reveal higher rates of illicit drug use than that of adolescents among the general population (Rolf, Nanda, Baldwin, Chandra, & Thompson, 1991; Sigda & Martin, 1996, in Monahan, 1997). Substance abuse plays a role in how girls engage in delinquent behavior in two ways. First, if a girl comes from a family in which one or both parents are substance abusers, she may feel the need to run away from a home in which substance abuse is prevalent. Alternatively, she may stay in the home and take advantage of the lack of parental supervision due to substance abuse by violating curfews or skipping school. Second, girls who have been victims of physical and/or sexual abuse may turn to drugs or alcohol as a way to "self-medicate" and block out the trauma of the abuse. By turning to drugs and alcohol, girls put themselves at risk for arrest (Dembo, Williams & Fagan, 1994).

The vast majority of runaway and homeless youth in Los Angeles reported substance use during the preceding month (Young, Gardner, & Lopez, 1997). In a study of San Francisco teenagers, Shorter, Schaffner, Shick, and Frappier (1996) identify ways in which older drug dealers recruit runaway girls to handle street sales. Young girls, often girlfriends of older dealers, are convinced to take the risks of dealing because they will probably face lighter consequences if caught. Drug use, especially crack cocaine, affects girls who become prostitutes by increasing their risk of contracting sexually transmitted diseases and HIV, and, if they are mothers, losing their children to the foster care system.

Some of the risk factors for adolescent females' involvement in alcohol and drug use identified by Bodinger-de Uriarte, Austin, and Thomas (1991, p. 29) are early alcohol and drug use; parents, especially mothers, who are alcohol and drug abusers; victims of physical and/or sexual abuse; poor family and school bonds; unconcern with traditional feminine norms; numerous social opportunities for alcohol and drug use; poor self-concept, especially with physical appearance; difficulties coping with stress and life events, especially in the areas of dating and sexual activity; and involvement in other problem behaviors. Childhood exposure to violence, sexual abuse, and physical maltreatment lead to an increased likelihood of drug and alcohol problems for girls later in life (Rosenbaum & Murphy, 1995).

The ACA (1990) study of female juveniles in detention reported the types of substances abused included alcohol (59 percent), marijuana (50 percent), and cocaine (20 percent). Over half reported abusing more than one type of substance. A recent study of 668 adolescents detained in juvenile facilities in 13 California counties found that of the 78 females in the study, 69 percent reported alcohol use and 70 percent reported tobacco use in the 30 days prior to the interview (Monahan, Gil-Rivas, Danila, & Anglin, submitted). Thirty-one percent of the 67 females who agreed to be tested for illicit drugs were positive for at least one drug (marijuana, amphetamines, and cocaine), and 10.4 percent tested positive for two or more drugs (Monahan et al., submitted). Owen and Bloom's study (1997) of 162 female CYA wards found evidence of significant, widespread drug use among this population. The study found the mean age for first use of alcohol was 11 years old. Eighty-three percent of the respondents indicated drug use at age 14 or younger, with half using before they were 12, and 70 percent by age 13. About 15 percent reported use of three or more illegal substances during their youth.

Victimization

A history of victimization is often a precursor to involvement in the juvenile justice system. According to data from the National Crime Victimization Survey and the Federal Bureau of Investigation, females 12 to19 years old have higher rates of violent victimization (murder, sexual and physical assault, robbery) than do females in any other age group (Craven, 1997). Homicide is the second-leading cause of death for females 15 to 19 years old (Anderson, Kochinek & Murphy, 1996). A study of intentional injury in a primary care pediatric setting found that 10 percent of injuries to adolescent females resulted from violence in dating relationships and 45 percent were inflicted by other adolescent girls (Sege, Stigol, Perry, Goldstein, & Spivak, 1996). Another study found that 31 percent of girls interviewed had been in a physical fight in the past 12 months (Kann et al., 1996). National data indicate that adolescents are nearly three times as likely as adults to be victims of violent crimes (Sickmund, Snyder, & Poe-Yamagata, 1997).

Delinquent Peer Factors and Gangs

The significance of peer influence cannot be underestimated. A socialization process centered on peer relationships and experimentation, generally through joining and participating in groups, characterizes adolescence. The role of delinquent peer relationships in encouraging delinquency and how a young person associates or avoids association with delinquent peers has been examined (Agnew, 1993; Snyder, Dishion, and Patterson, 1986; Thornberry, Krohn, Lizotte, & Chard-Wierschem, 1993; Warr, 1993).

Association with delinquent peers often leads to gang membership or association that puts youth at risk for engaging in criminal activities. Little is known about whether gangs attract adolescents who are already highly delinquent or whether they create highly delinquent adolescents as a part of the gang process (Thornberry et al., 1993). The fact remains that gang members are significantly more likely to engage in delinquent behaviors than are nongang members (Esbensen, Huizinga, & Wieher, 1993). Thornberry et al. (1993) agree and add that gang participation is a more important factor in predicting delinquency than is the type of person who is being recruited into the gang.

There is little research on the role of delinquent peers that is specific to girls and young women. Female gangs are typically viewed as extensions of male gang membership. However, studies have found that between 10 and 46 percent of gang members are female (Campbell, 1991; Esbensen et al., 1993; Esbensen & Winfree, 1996; Fagan, 1990; Moore, 1991). Esbensen and Deschenes (1997) attribute the wide range of estimates to the fact that most studies have been ethnographic rather than quantitative in design and have tended to focus on adult women rather than adolescent girls.

Several studies suggest that females join gangs in an attempt to escape the reality of being victims of poverty (Fagan, 1996; Hagedorn, 1988; Vigil, 1988; Wilson, 1987). Thus the potential for gang involvement is heightened for marginalized girls, where lack of education and employment opportunities and lives of poverty leave them with few resources or alternatives. These studies describe the lives of these girls as characterized by instability, exposure to violence in the home and community, fear of abuse, and the experience of watching other family members, especially their mothers, being victimized. These multiple factors heighten the need for attachment and a sense of belonging for marginalized girls and young women that can lead to gang involvement. At-risk young women tend to be isolated from society and alienated from social institutions (Felkenes & Becker, 1995). Consequently, they drop out of school at an early age and engage in violent or other criminal behavior, including gang membership.

Esbensen and Deschenes (1997) have identified other differences between female gang and nongang members. Compared to other girls, the female gang members are less committed to school, more inclined to report limited opportunities, more socially isolated, and less likely to disapprove of and feel guilty for violent behavior. Girls in gangs who engage in violent crime appear to have low social control and to learn the criminal behavior from their peers. They are more likely than nongang girls to have lower self-esteem and higher levels of risk seeking and impulsivity.

Sexual Activity and Maturity

Traditionally, female delinquency has been equated with female sexuality. Patriarchal society has made a concerted effort to control female sexuality, both socially and legally. This has fostered a double standard: boys are expected to explore and "sow wild oats," while girls are expected to remain chaste (Belknap, 1996; Girls Inc., 1996).

Young women are not only monitored and controlled vis-à-vis their sexuality but also by their physical appearance. A study by Rosenbaum and Chesney-Lind (1994) found that male intake personnel at the California Youth Authority noted physical appearance in terms of cultural standards. This was particularly the case if the girl had a charge of "immorality" on her record. Physical attractiveness was least likely to be noted for girls detained for serious offenses.

Early physical development may be linked to engagement in delinquency among some girls (Caspi, Lynam, & Moffit 1993). Girls who mature early may be more vulnerable to peer pressure because others attribute greater social maturity to them than is warranted by their chronological age. Thus these girls tend to associate with older peer groups. Furthermore, the onset of puberty adds pressures for entering into relationships with boys. As a result, girls who mature early may feel the need to engage in delinquent acts to impress boys, or alternatively, they may join delinquent peer groups, such as gangs, to have greater access to boys. Also, girls who have been physically or sexually abused have earlier and higher rates of sexual activity and are more likely to have multiple partners and engage in a wider range of sexual behaviors (Levitt, 1994).

Teen Pregnancy and Parenting

During the past two decades the United States experienced a dramatic increase in the number of teenagers becoming pregnant. Levitt (1994) found that over 1 million of the estimated 11 million sexually active teenage girls in the United States will become pregnant every year. Teen mothers are disproportionately poor young women of color. Black and Latina teenagers are 67 percent more likely to get pregnant than are white teens (Levitt, 1994). Teen pregnancy and related child care responsibilities account for approximately 47 percent of girls who drop out of school. Dropouts who do not receive a high school diploma lack many of the necessary life skills to survive in the world (Chesney-Lind & Shelden, 1992). Davidson's (1983) survey of teenage mothers found that approximately 90 percent receive no financial aid from the fathers of their children.

Unintentional pregnancy is a major risk factor for juvenile female offenders (Monahan, (1997). Data from a survey of 430 juvenile facilities found that 68 percent had one to four pregnant teens among their correctional population at any time, despite the fact that they could not provide adequate prenatal care services for high-risk pregnancies (Breuner & Farrow, 1995).

Health

According to Monahan (1997), the physical and mental health needs of adolescents have only recently been a source of concern within the juvenile justice system. Historically, resources were used primarily to support the health needs of males, who constitute the majority of the juvenile offender population. As a result, little information is available regarding the physical and mental health needs of female delinquents, a small but growing and important subpopulation of juveniles at risk for serious health-related problems. The lack of access to health care is a significant risk factor for marginalized girls and young women.

A study of 156 randomly selected juvenile offenders in the King County Youth Facility in Seattle, Washington identified the following acute and chronic health problems among them: asthma and other respiratory illnesses, seizure disorders, allergies, diabetes, sexually transmitted diseases, conditions associated with stress and trauma, poor nutritional status and obesity, dermatological problems, and dental cavities (Farrow, 1991). "Chronic health conditions are common and have often gone untreated prior to entry in the juvenile justice system" (Owens, 1991, in Monahan, 1997, p. 3). Few had received a physical or dental examination within the past two years and a majority (83 percent) had a lifetime history of treatment in an emergency room for a traumatic injury (Farrow, 1991).

Monahan (1997) found that the majority of girls in correctional settings have gone without primary health care during their lifetime and suffer from preventable and/or treatable health problems (e.g., inadequate nutrition, dental caries, and asthma). As stated elsewhere, many female offenders come from low-income urban communities. Young female offenders are also exposed to high levels of violence associated with gang involvement, weapons possession, and other delinquent activities prevalent in their communities (Ash, Kellermann, Fuqua-Whitley, & Johnson, 1996; Rhodes & Fischer, 1993).

Numerous studies have documented higher-than-average risk behaviors and levels of sexually transmitted diseases (STDs) among incarcerated youth and a correlation between the level of substance abuse and these behaviors (Alexander-Rodriguez & Vermund, 1987; Boudov, 1997; Canterbury et al., 1995; McCabe, Jaffe, & Diaz, 1993; Morris, Baker, & Huscroft, 1992; Rolf, Nanda, Baldwin, Chandra, & Thompson, 1991; Shew & Fortenberry, 1992; Wood & Shoroye, 1993).

Monahan et al. (submitted) asked 78 adolescent female arrestees for information related to sexual activity for the 30 days prior to their interviews. About half of the females indicated that they had sex while under the influence of drugs or alcohol. The majority of respondents (86 percent) had been sexually active and had used condoms inconsistently or not at all (73 percent), with over half of females reporting that they had two or more sexual partners, and 14 percent having contracted a sexually transmitted disease at some time in the past.

With a higher-than-average risk for HIV infection, another study of 113 incarcerated males and females revealed that they had less knowledge of preventive strategies for HIV and reported high rates of HIV risk behaviors than did a comparison group of students attending a public high school (DiClemente, Lanier, Horan, & Lodico, 1991). Despite the elevated risk for HIV and STDs among juveniles in detention, HIV has not yet become as widespread as other STDs among this population. A review of available information on results of HIV testing of confined juveniles resulted in less than 1 percent testing positive (Widom & Hammett, 1996).

Mental Health

The developmental tasks faced by females during puberty, including understanding and coping with menarche, adjusting to ongoing physical, psychological, and social changes, and exploring their sexual identity contribute to the risk for mental health disorders (Woods, 1995). Juvenile female offenders are exposed to additional levels of stress and other threats to their ability to cope with and meet the tasks associated with normal psychological and social development, including childhood abuse (Hutchinson, 1992). Early sexual exploitation is associated with disturbances in self-esteem and self-concept, the development of high-risk behaviors, academic failure, and the inability to establish and maintain healthy relationships in adulthood (Hutchinson, 1992). In addition to abuse and neglect, many adolescents have been exposed to physical violence, such as witnessing assaults against their mothers, other family members, or other people within their surrounding communities (Dembo, Williams, Wothke, Schmeidler, & Brown, 1992; Lake, 1993).

Psychopathology, particularly depression, among female juvenile offenders has been reported by numerous researchers (Armistead, Wierson, Forehand, & Frame, 1992; Milin, Halikas, Meller, & Morse, 1991). Unlike males, who tend to express depression externally by aggression or other forms of acting-out behaviors, females are more likely to become socially isolated or engage in self-destructive behaviors (Dembo et al., 1993).

Several studies have documented mental health disorders are more common in juvenile justice facilities than among the general population (Greenbaum, Foster-Johnson,

& Petrila, 1996; Melton & Pagliocca, 1992; Myers, Burket, Lyles, Stone & Kemph, 1990; Otto, Greenstein, Johnson, & Friedman, 1992). Mental health problems are present for between 10 percent and 60 percent of the referrals. Among incarcerated adolescents there is a high incidence of conduct disorder, but more females than males diagnosed with both anti-social and borderline personality disorders (Eppright, Kashani, Robinson, & Reid, 1993).

Trauma.   As a result of abuse, neglect, and exposure to violence, research has indicated that many juvenile female offenders suffer from undiagnosed and untreated posttraumatic stress disorder (PTSD), which, without treatment, may have long-term adverse effects (Steiner, Garcia, & Matthews, 1997; Vermund, Alexander-Rodriguez, Macleod, & Kelley, 1990). Posttraumatic stress disorder has been linked to maladaptive behaviors such as delinquency, drug use, and increased sexual activity. A study by Waterman (1997) of 42 girls and young women in the California Youth Authority found that 52 percent suffered from PTSD secondary to some form of abuse, a greater rate than those of girls from other environments and boys from the same environment. Many of the subjects had been exposed to family and community violence.

Suicide.   Contributors to adolescent suicide include feelings of helplessness and hope-lessness, loneliness, impulsivity, the lack of a stable environment, and increased external and internal stressors. Davis, Bean, Schumacher, and Stringer (1991) found that 13.5 per-cent of adolescents had a history of suicide attempts and 21.3 percent had made threats, indicating high rates of suicidal risk factors among adolescent detention populations.

A national study by the ACA (1989) found 57 percent of female juveniles in deten-tion had attempted suicide, the majority of whom exhibited symptoms of depression. Only 22 percent indicated that they had received mental health services. Mental health problems can be exacerbated by the social isolation associated with incarceration (Hutchinson, 1992; Mitchell & Varley, 1990; Parent et al., 1994). When girls and young women are con-fined in detention facilities, detention staff often lack the experience and training needed to provide appropriate services for the mental health needs of this population (Baines & Alder, 1996). The ACA (1989) found only 355 juvenile facilities contracted for psycholog-ical services for detainees. Thirty percent of juvenile detention facilities reported the need for substance abuse treatment for detainees, indicating that between 60 and 80 percent of juvenile females required substance abuse treatment at intake. The ACA study also found that 41 percent of juvenile detainees indicated that the type of help they felt they needed most during their first detention was psychological counseling, followed by drug counsel-ing (19 percent). Of those who received program services during detention, 35 percent indicated that the program that helped them most was mental health counseling.

National correctional and public health associations have recently recognized the need for reform within the juvenile health services system (ACA, 1989; American Medical Association, 1984; Child Welfare League of America and the American Academy of Pediatrics, 1988; Dubler, 1986; National Commission on Correctional Health Care, 1992). Although improved health care standards are widely supported, inadequate resources fre-quently inhibit or delay their implementation (Owens, 1991). A national study of juvenile detention facilities by the Office of Juvenile Justice and Delinquency Prevention reported that (1) the majority of adolescents were not receiving a full assessment within one hour of admission as set forth in national standards, (2) fewer than one-fifth of the adolescents had such an assessment within one week, (3) one-third of the adolescents were screened by unqualified staff, (4) approximately one-fourth had no access to tuberculosis screening, (5) fewer than half had access to screening for sexually transmitted diseases, and (6) many institutions did not provide sufficient staff to monitor suicidal youth adequately (Parent et al., 1994). Notification of medical staff prior to release of juveniles can assure that necessary treatment has been provided or arrangements are made for follow-up in the community. However, in many facilities, adolescents are frequently discharged without this being done (Thompson, 1992).

Juvenile facility health services have been described as deficient in many areas (American Medical Association, 1990; Anno, 1984; Bazemore & McKean, 1992; Brown, 1993; Farrow, 1991; Office of Juvenile Justice and Delinquency Prevention, 1996). Monahan (1997) found that the health care services provided to adolescent and young adult women in detention settings is episodic and often does not include health promotion or prevention. The American Academy of Pediatrics (1989) conducted a study of medical services in 79 juvenile facilities and found that the majority were below community standards in health assessment, physical examinations, care provided by staff during "sick calls," and screening for mental health problems. The study noted that many correctional health professionals held low opinions of the adolescents under their care, sometimes violating patients' rights to privacy during examinations and treatments, or interpreted complaints as manipulative or malingering behaviors, which could result in unnecessary delays in providing care.

The deficiencies found in juvenile health services may be related to the fact that facility staff are often not adequately trained to intervene in the multiple and complex risk behaviors commonly found among the youth in their care (Alexander-Rodriguez & Vermund, 1987; Dembo, 1996). Professional staff training and support within juvenile health services has been described as below standard and in need of reform (Feinstein, 1992; Jameson, 1989).

Although deficiencies in the quality of care provided to adolescent females and inadequate training of correctional staff to intervene on their behalf can unintentionally cause harm, some correctional policies and procedures perpetrate harm directly. These include the use of social isolation as a sanction, which can exacerbate stress and anxiety and contribute to self-destructive behaviors; and the danger of sexual assault by staff or other detainees (Chesney-Lind & Rodriguez, 1983; Faith, 1993). Excessive and improper use of physical restraints while in custody is another harmful practice that can result in psychological trauma and physical injury (Mitchell & Varley, 1990). Other potentially harmful medical practices include standing orders for delousing, body cavity searches for drugs or other prohibited items, and the use of sedatives for behavior control and exposure to communicable diseases such as tuberculosis (American Academy of Pediatrics, 1989; Owens, 1991).

Resiliency Factors

Aspects of a person's personality can make them more resilient to stressors and better able to avoid participation in delinquent behaviors. For instance, resilient people "see obstacles as something that can be overcome, endured, or changed; persevere in finding ways to improve situations; develop a range of strategies and skills to address a situation; and have a broad range of interest and goals" (Scott, 1994, p. 5). Benard (1991) identified resiliency factors that include social competence, problem-solving ability, autonomy, and a sense of purpose and belief in the future. Certain community and individual factors can protect against the adverse effects of exposure to violence (Osofsky, 1995). These include access to a supportive adult, having a safe place in the neighborhood that is protected from violence, and having the individual resources to find alternatives to violence.

With a focus on youth development, individual resilience/protective factors incorporate positive self-concept and gender identification with feelings of competency, spirituality, healthy risk taking, and adaptability. Girls with strong verbal skills, who are willing to articulate and discuss issues and explore creative solutions, including developing their own support systems, are especially resilient. As their own self-concept grows, these young women are more able to incorporate an awareness of social norms and their intuitive ability to "read the scene" into their repertoire of survival skills. Their ability to explore multiple options, make plans, and accept responsibility for the outcome of those plans is enhanced.

PROMISING PROGRAM COMPONENTS

Programming for girls and young women needs to be shaped by their unique situations. In other words, programs and services should be gender-specific. Girls Inc. (1996) describes gender-specific services for young women as those designed "to meet the unique needs of female offenders; that value the female perspective; that celebrate and honor the female experience; that respect and take into account female development; and that empower young women to reach their full potential" (p. 24). However, Bloom (1997) notes that specific direction on how to achieve these objectives is not readily apparent from the existing literature. Historically, research, programs, and treatment have been based on the male experience, and often neglect women's needs. Effective programming for girls and women should be shaped by and tailored to their unique situations and problems. To do this, there is a need to develop a theoretical approach to treatment that is gender sensitive and addresses the realities of girls' and young women's lives (Bloom, 1997).

Austin, Bloom, and Donahue (1992) identified promising programs and intervention strategies for supervising female offenders in the community. Austin et al. (1992) found that "promising community programs combined supervision and services to address the specialized needs of female offenders in highly structured, safe environments where accountability is stressed" (p. 21). Austin et al. stated that promising programs often use an empowerment model, in which skills are developed to allow women to gain independence and multidimensional strategies that address specific women's needs (e.g., substance abuse, parenting, relationships, gender bias, domestic violence, and sexual abuse).

Bloom (1997) argues for rigorous evaluation to measure the effectiveness of gender-specific interventions in terms of client outcomes, given the fact that information on the long-term effectiveness of these gender-specific strategies is nonexistent. This would allow researchers to move away from impressionistic data and toward empirically based documentation of program effectiveness.

Appropriate services for girls and young women must have multiple components that address the complex issues that adolescent females face. They consist of educational opportunities, employment and vocational training, placement options, and mental and physical health services, all of which must be delivered in a culturally sensitive manner. Bloom (1997) discusses the need to incorporate the idea of females' sense of self, which manifests and develops differently in female-specific groups as opposed to coed groups; and how the unique needs and issues (e.g., physical/sexual emotional victimization, trauma, pregnancy and parenting) of women and girls can be addressed in a safe, trusting, and supportive female-focused environment.

Covington (1998) argues for a holistic approach to develop gender-specific services for this population. An approach based on relational theory would incorporate "physical, psychological, emotional, spiritual, and sociopolitical issues" (p. 18), including theories of treatment of addiction and trauma. A holistic model of treatment should include a comprehensive case management approach along a continuum of care, ranging from community-based prevention, intervention, and treatment to aftercare. This continuum could include residential and day treatment as well as other female-focused inpatient or outpatient services.

Girls Inc. (1996) describes essential elements for effective prevention programs for juvenile females. First, juvenile females should have employment and vocational training that presents a wide array of career opportunities and is not constrained by gender stereotypes. In addition, girls should be provided with adequate and appropriate physical and mental health care, accurate information about sex, eating disorders, HIV and acquired immunodeficiency syndrome (AIDS), and strategies on how to protect themselves from sexual, physical, and substance abuse. Finally, girls and young women need access to opportunities where they can feel safe to explore and learn from each other about the issues they face as young women.

The Girls Inc. (1996) study also stresses that early intervention programs could help girls resolve many of the problems that place them at risk for engaging in delinquent behavior. The study suggests that almost every girl would benefit from good prevention programs that help them acquire the skills, knowledge, and values that promote health, happiness, and productivity. Furthermore, early intervention programs could address risk factors for juvenile delinquency, such as alcohol and drug use, school problems, abuse, and association with delinquent peers.

Belknap, Holsinger, and Dunn (1997) describe key issues from a series of focus groups with delinquent girl detainees, which are important to consider when identifying components for promising gender-specific interventions. For these girls and young women, the important issues are gaining and keeping respect and counseling to address traumatic experiences. Many express concerns on how they will "make it" once they were released.

Researchers agree that the most effective approaches should be holistic, client-centered, and empowering (Austin et al., 1992; Chesney-Lind & Shelden, 1992; Greene, Peters & Associates, 1997; Mayer, 1995). Responses should employ a strengths-based approach rather than attempting to "cure" the client of pathology.

Bloom (1997) argues that treatment should be based on a theory of female psychological development emphasizing the centrality of relationships, connectedness, and mutuality as fundamental aspects of healthy, growth-promoting relationships. Treatment and services should build on girls' and women's strengths/competencies and avoid focusing on their deficiencies. Cultural awareness and sensitivity should be promoted, and the cultural resources and strengths in various communities should be utilized. Female development should be addressed within a context of race, class, gender, and sexual orientation. Female physical and mental health and wellness should be promoted, including raising awareness about HIV/AIDS, STDs, eating disorders, family planning, nutrition, relaxation, and exercise. Educational and vocational training opportunities should be commensurate with girls' and women's interests and abilities so as to garner their potential (including traditional and nontraditional career options). Program staff should be representative in terms of gender, race/ethnicity, and sexual orientation. She suggests that girls and women can benefit from mentors from their particular communities who exemplify survival and growth, as well as resistance and change.

As the information above indicates, there is a growing body of research and program information available that speaks to the issues and situation of at-risk girls and young women. Program developers and service providers should consider the multidimensional issues faced by girls and young women and develop a multidisciplinary response. To do this, policymakers must take into consideration the need to bridge systems and coordinate a variety of public- and private-sector resources.

ACKNOWLEDGMENTS

This research was supported by Grant 96-JF-FX-0006 from the California Office of Criminal Justice Planning (OCJP). The opinions, findings, and conclusions in this report are those of the authors and not necessarily those of OCJP.

REFERENCES

Acoca, L. (1999, October). Investing in girls: A 21st century strategy. *Juvenile Justice*, 6(1).

Adler, F. (1975). *Sisters in crime: The rise of the new female criminal*. New York: McGraw-Hill.

Agnew, R. (1993). Why do they do it? An examination of the intervening mechanisms between social control variables and delinquency. *Journal of Research in Crime and Delinquency, 30*, 245–266.

Alexander-Rodriguez, T., & Vermund, S. H. (1987). Gonorrhea and syphilis in incarcerated urban adolescents: Prevalence and physical signs. *Pediatrics, 80*, 561–564.

Amaro, H. (1995). Love, sex and power: Considering women's realities in HIV prevention. *American Psychologist, 50*(6), 437–447.

American Academy of Pediatrics. (1989). Health care for children and adolescents in detention centers, jails, lock-ups, and other court-sponsored residential facilities. *Pediatrics, 84*, 1118–1120.

American Association of University Women. (1992). *How schools shortchange girls*. Washington, DC: Author.

American Association of University Women. (1998). *Separated by sex: A critical look at single-sex education for girls*. Washington, DC: Author.

American Correctional Association. (1989). *Certification standards for health care programs*. Laurel, MD: Author.

American Correctional Association. (1990). *The female offender: What does the future hold?* Washington, DC: St. Mary's Press.

American Medical Association. (1984). *Standards for health services in juvenile correctional facilities*. Chicago: Author.

AMERICAN MEDICAL ASSOCIATION. (1990). Health status of detained and incarcerated youths. *Journal of the American Medical Association, 263*, 987–991.

ANDERSON, G. (1994). Juvenile justice and the double standard. *America, 170*, 13–15.

ANDERSON, M. (1996) *Race, class and gender: Common bonds, different voices.* Thousand Oaks, CA: Sage.

ANDERSON, R. N., KOCHINEK, K. D., & MURPHY, S. L. (1996). *Report of final mortality statistics, 1995.* Hyattsville, MD: National Center for Health Statistics.

ANNO, B. J. (1984). *The availability of health services for juvenile offenders: Preliminary results of a national survey.* Chicago: National Commission on Correctional Health Care.

ARMISTEAD, L., WIERSON, M., FOREHAND, R., & FRAME, C. (1992). Psychopathology in incarcerated juvenile delinquents: Does it extend beyond externalizing problems? *Adolescence, 27*, 309–314.

ASH, P., KELLERMANN, A. L., FUQUA-WHITLEY, D., & JOHNSON, A. (1996). Gun acquisition and use by juvenile offenders. *Journal of the American Medical Association, 275*, 1754–1758.

AUSTIN, J., BLOOM, B., & DONAHUE, T. (1992). *Female offenders in the community: An analysis of innovative strategies and programs.* Washington, DC: National Institute of Corrections.

BAINES, M., & ALDER, C. (1996). Are girls more difficult to work with? Youth workers perspectives in juvenile justice and related areas. *Crime & Delinquency, 42*, 467–485.

BAZEMORE, G., & MCKEAN, J. (1992). Minority overrepresentation. In L. S. Thompson & J. A. Farrow (Eds.), *Hard time, healing hands: Developing primary health care services for incarcerated youth* (pp. 99–119). Arlington, VA: National Center for Education in Maternal and Child Health.

BELKNAP, J. (1996). *The invisible woman: Gender, crime, and justice.* Cincinnati, OH: Wadsworth.

BELKNAP, J. (1997). *Gender specific services workshop: A report to the governor.* Cincinnati, OH: University of Cincinnati.

BELKNAP, J., HOLSINGER, K., & DUNN, M. (1997). Understanding incarcerated girls: The results of a focus group study. *Prison Journal, 77*, 381–404.

BERNARD, B. (1991). *Fostering resiliency in kids: Protective factors in the family, school, and community.* San Francisco: Far West Laboratory for Educational Research and Development.

BLOOM, B. (1996). *Triple jeopardy: Race, class, and gender as factors in women's imprisonment.* Unpublished doctoral dissertation. University of California–Riverside.

BLOOM, B. (1997). *Defining "gender-specific": What does it mean and why is it important?* Paper presented at the National Institute of Corrections' Intermediate Sanctions for Women Offenders National Project Meeting, September, Longmont, CO.

BODINGER-DE URIARTE, C., AUSTIN, G., & THOMAS, C. (1991). *Substance abuse among adolescent females* (pp. 1–29). Portland, WA: Western Regional Center for Drug-Free Schools and Communities.

BOUDOV, M. (1997). *Juvenile hall STD prevalence monitoring project: Progress report.* Los Angeles: Los Angeles County STD Program.

BRENDTRO, L., & NESS, A. (1996). Fixing flaws or building strengths? *National Educational Service Newsletter*, 4.

BREUNER, C. C., & FARROW, J. A. (1995). Pregnant teens in prison: Prevalence, management, and consequences. *Western Journal of Medicine, 162*, 328–330.

BRINDIS, C., PETERSON, S., & BROWN, S. (1997). *Complex terrain: Charting a course of action to prevent adolescent pregnancy: An analysis of California's policy landscape.* San Francisco: UCSF Center for Reproductive Health Policy Research.

BROOKS, R. B. (1994). Children at risk: Fostering resiliency and hope. *American Journal of Orthopsychiatry, 64*, 545–553.

BROWN, R. T. (1993). Health needs of incarcerated youth. *Bulletin of the New York Academy of Medicine, 70*, 208–218.

BUDNICK, K. J., & SHIELDS-FLETCHER, E. (1998). *OJJDP Fact Sheet #84: What about girls?* Washington, DC: U.S. Department of Justice.

CALHOUN, G., JURGENS, J., & CHEN, F. (1993). The neophyte female delinquent: A review of the literature. *Adolescence, 28*, 461–472.

CALIFORNIA DEPARTMENT OF FINANCE. (1993). *County population projections for 1996.* Sacramento, CA: Author.

CALIFORNIA DEPARTMENT OF JUSTICE. (2001). *Adult and juvenile arrests reported, sex and law enforcement disposition by specific offense statewide: January through December 1999.* Sacramento: California Department of Justice, Division of Law Enforcement, Law Enforcement Information Center.

CALIFORNIA DEPARTMENT OF SOCIAL SERVICES. (1998). *Foster care information system.* Sacramento, CA: Information Services Bureau.

CAMPBELL, A. (1991). *The girls in the gang* (2nd ed.). Cambridge, MA: Basil Blackwell.

CANTERBURY, R. J., MCGARVEY, E. L., SHELDON-KELLER, A. E., WAITE, D., REAMS, P., & KOOPMAN, C. (1995). Prevalence of HIV-related risk behaviors and STDs among incarcerated adolescents. *Journal of Adolescent Health, 17*, 173–177.

CASPI, A., LYNAM, D., & MOFFITT, T. (1993). Unraveling girls' delinquency: Biological, dispositional and contextual contributions to adolescent misbehavior. *Developmental Psychology, 29*, 19–30.

CERNKOVICH, S., & GIORDANO, P. (1979a). Delinquency, opportunity and gender. *Journal of Criminal Law and Criminology, 70*, 141–151.

CERNKOVICH, S. & GIORDANO, P. (1979b). A comparative analysis of male and female delinquency. *Sociological Quarterly, 20*, 131–145.

CHESNEY-LIND, M. (1989). Girl's crime and women's place: Toward a feminist model of female delinquency. *Crime & Delinquency, 35*, 5–29.

CHESNEY-LIND, M. (1992). *Rethinking women's imprisonment: A critical examination of trends in female incarceration.* Unpublished manuscript. University of Hawaii at Manoa.

CHESNEY-LIND, M. (1995). Girls, delinquency, and juvenile justice: Towards a feminist theory of young women's crime. In B. Price & N. Sokoloff (Eds.), *The criminal justice system and women* (2nd ed., pp. 71–88). New York: McGraw-Hill.

CHESNEY-LIND, M. (1997). *Female offenders: girls, women and crime.* Thousand Oaks, CA: Sage.

CHESNEY-LIND, M., & RODRIGUEZ, N. (1983). Women under lock and key. *Prison Journal, 63*, 47–65.

CHESNEY-LIND, M., & SHELDEN, R. (1992). *Girls, delinquency and juvenile justice.* Pacific Grove, CA: Brooks/Cole.

CHESNEY-LIND, M., & SHELDEN, R. (1998). *Girls, delinquency and juvenile justice* (2nd ed.). Belmont, CA: Wadsworth.

CHILD WELFARE LEAGUE OF AMERICA AND THE AMERICAN ACADEMY OF PEDIATRICS. (1988). *Standards for health care services for children in out-of-home care.* Washington, DC: Authors.

COMMUNITY RESEARCH ASSOCIATES. (1998). *Juvenile female offenders: A status of the states report.* Washington, DC: Office of Juvenile Justice and Delinquency Prevention.

COVINGTON, S. (1998). The relational theory of women's psychological development: Implications for the criminal justice system. In R. Zaplin (Ed.), *Female offenders: Critical issues and effective interventions* (pp. 113–131). Gaithersburg, MD: Aspen.

CRAVEN, D. (1997). *Sex differences in violent victimization* (NCJ-164508). Washington, DC: Bureau of Justice Statistics.

CULROSS, P. (1997). *Relationships between victimization and offending among female adolescents.* Background paper for OCJP Modeling Gender-Specific Services in Juvenile Justice: Policy and Program Recommendations Project.

DANIEL, M. (1994). *Models for change: National juvenile female offenders conference* (pp. 106–109). Laurel, MD: American Correctional Association.

DAVIDSON, S. (1983). *The second mile: Contemporary approaches to counseling young women.* Tucson, AZ: New Directions for Young Women.

DAVIS, D. L., BEAN, G. J., SCHUMACHER, J. E., & STRINGER, T. L. (1991). Prevalence of emotional disorders in a juvenile justice institutional population. *American Journal of Forensic Psychology, 9,* 1–13.

DEISHER, R. W., & ROGERS, W. M. (1991). The medical care of street youth. *Journal of Adolescent Health, 12*(7), 500–503.

DEMBO, R. (1996). Problems among youth entering the juvenile justice system: Their service needs and innovative approaches to address them. *Substance Use and Misuse, 31,* 81–94.

DEMBO, R., PACHECO, K., RAMIREZ-GARMICA, G., SCHMEIDLER, J., GUIDA, J., & RAHMAN, A. (1998). A further study of gender differences in service needs among youth entering a juvenile assessment center. *Journal of Child and Adolescent Substance Abuse, 7*(4), 49–77.

DEMBO, R., SCHMEIDLER, J., SUE, C., BORDEN, P., & MANNING, D. (1995). Gender differences in service needs among youth entering a juvenile assessment center: A replication study. *Journal of Correctional Health Care, 2,* 191–216.

DEMBO, R., WILLIAMS, L., & FAGAN, J. (1994). Development and assessment of a classification of high risk youths. *Journal of Drug Issues, 24,* 25–53.

DEMBO, R., WILLIAMS, L., & SCHMEIDLER, J. (1993). Gender differences in mental health service needs among youths entering a juvenile detention center. *Journal of Prison and Jail Health, 12,* 73–101.

DEMBO, R., WILLIAMS, L., WOTHKE, W., SCHMEIDLER, J., & BROWN, C. H. (1992). The role of family factors, physical abuse, and sex victimization experiences in high-risk youths' alcohol and other drug use and delinquency: A longitudinal model. *Violence and Victims, 7,* 245–246.

DICLEMENTE, R. J., LANIER, M. M., HORAN, P. F. & LODICO, M. (1991). Comparison of AIDS knowledge, attitudes, and behaviors among incarcerated adolescents and a public school sample in San Francisco. *American Journal of Public Health, 81,* 628–630.

DORNFELD, M., & KRUTTSCHNITT, C. (1992). Do the stereotypes fit? Mapping gender-specific outcomes and risk factors. *Criminology, 30,* 397–419.

DUBLER, N. N. (1986). *Standards for health services in correctional institutions* (2nd ed.). Washington, DC: American Public Health Association.

EPPRIGHT, T. D., KASHANI, J. H., ROBINSON, B. D., & REID, J. C. (1993). Co-morbidity of conduct disorder and personality disorders in an incarcerated juvenile population. *American Journal of Psychiatry, 150,* 1233–1236.

ESBENSEN, F., & DESCHENES, E. (1997). *Boys and girls in gangs: Are there gender differences in behavior and attitudes?* (Grant 94-IJ-CX-0058). Washington, DC: National Institute of Justice.

ESBENSEN, F., DESCHENES, E., & WINFREE, L. T., JR. (1998, March). *Differences between gang girls and gang boys: Results of a multi-site survey.* Paper presented at the annual meeting of the Academy of Criminal Justice Sciences, Albuquerque, NM.

ESBENSEN, F., & HUIZINGA, D. (1993). Gangs, drugs, and delinquency in a survey of urban youth. *Criminology, 3,* 565–589.

ESBENSEN, F., HUIZINGA, D., & WIEHER, A. (1993). Gang and non-gang youth: Differences in explanatory factors. *Journal of Contemporary Criminal Justice, 9*(2), 94–116.

ESBENSEN, F., & WINFREE, L. (1996). *Race and gender differences between gang and non-gang youth: Results from a national survey.* Paper presented at the annual meeting of the Academy of Criminal Justice Sciences.

EVALUATION AND TRAINING INSTITUTE. (1996). *Study of gender specific services: Initial review of the literature.* Sacramento, CA: Office of Criminal Justice Planning.

FAGAN, J. (1990). Social processes of delinquency and drug use among urban gangs. In C. R. Huff (Ed.), *Gangs in America* (pp. 183–219). Newbury Park, CA: Sage.

FAGAN, J. (1996). Gangs, drugs and neighborhood change. In R. Huff (Ed.), *Gangs in America* (2nd ed., pp. 39–74). Thousand Oaks, CA: Sage.

FAITH, K. (1993). *Unruly women: The politics of confinement and resistance.* Vancouver, Canada: Press Gang.

FARROW, J. A. (1991). Health issues among juvenile delinquents. In L. S. Thompson (Ed.), *The forgotten child in health care: Children in the juvenile justice system* (pp. 21–33). Washington, DC: National Center for Education in Maternal and Child Health.

FEINSTEIN, R. A. (1992). Training. In L. S. Thompson & J. A. Farrow (Eds.), *Hard time, healing hands: Developing primary health care services for incarcerated youth* (pp. 37–47). Arlington, VA: National Center for Education in Maternal and Child Health.

FELKENES, G., & BECKER, H. (1995). Female gang members: A growing issue for policy makers. *Journal of Gang Research, 2,* 1–10.

FRAZIER, C., & BISHOP, D. (1995) Reflections on race effects in juvenile justice. In K. Leonard, C. Pope, & W. Feyerherm (Eds.), *Minorities in juvenile justice* (pp. 16–46). Thousand Oaks, CA: Sage.

GARRY, E. (1996, October). Truancy: First step to a lifetime of problems. *Juvenile Justice Bulletin.* Washington, DC: Office of Juvenile Justice and Delinquency Prevention.

GILLIGAN, C. (1982). *In a different voice: Psychological theory and women's development.* Cambridge, MA: Harvard University Press.

GILLIGAN, C. (1992). *Meeting at the crossroads.* New York: Ballantine.

GIRLS INCORPORATED NATIONAL RESOURCE CENTER. (1996). *Prevention and parity: Girls in juvenile justice.* Indianapolis, IN: Author.

GREENE, PETERS & ASSOCIATES. (1997). Materials presented at annual meeting of American Society of Criminology, San Diego, CA.

GREENBAUM, P. E., FOSTER-JOHNSON, L., & PETRILA, A. (1996). Co-occurring addictive and mental disorders among adolescents: Prevalence research and future directions. *American Journal of Orthopsychiatry,* 52–60.

GROSSMAN, F. K., BEINASHOWITZ, J., & ANDERSON, L. (1992). Risk and resilience in young adolescents. *Journal of Youth and Adolescence, 21,* 529–550.

HAGEDORN, J. M. (1988). *People and folks: Gangs, crime, and the underclass in a rustbelt city.* Chicago: Lake View Press.

HAWKINS, J. D., CATALANO, R. F., & MILLER, J. Y. (1992). Risk and protective factors for alcohol and other drug problems in adolescence and early adulthood: Implications for substance abuse prevention. *Psychological Bulletin, 112,* 64–105.

HUTCHINSON, J. (1992). Mental health. In L. S. Thompson & J. A. Farrow (Eds.), *Hard time, healing hands: Developing primary health care services for incarcerated youth* (pp. 121–133). Arlington, VA: National Center for Education in Maternal and Child Health.

IWAMOTO, J. J., KAMEOKA, K., & BRASSEUR, Y. C. (1990). *Waikiki homeless youth project: A report.* Honolulu, HI: Catholic Services to Families.

JAMESON, E. J. (1989). Incarcerated adolescents. The need for the development of professional ethical standards for institutional health care providers. *Journal of Adolescent Health Care, 10,* 490–499.

KANN, L., WARREN, C. W., HARRIS, W. A., COLLINS, J. L., WILLIAMS, B. I., ROSS, J. G., et al. (1996). Youth risk behavior surveillance: United States, 1995. *Morbidity and Mortality Weekly Report, 45*(SS-4), 1–83.

KELLEY, B. T., THORNBERRY, T. P., & SMITH, C. A. (1997). *In the wake of childhood maltreatment.* Washington, DC: Office of Juvenile Justice and Delinquency Prevention.

KILPATRICK, D., & SAUNDERS, B. (1997). *The prevalence and consequences of child victimization.* Washington, DC: National Institute of Justice.

LAFRAMBOISE, T., & HOWARD-PITNEY, B. (1995). Suicidal behavior in American Indian female adolescents. In S. Canetto & D. Lester (Eds.), *Women and suicidal behavior* (pp. 157–173). New York: Springer.

LA FREE, G. (1989). *Rape and criminal justice: The social construction of sexual assault.* Belmont, CA: Wadsworth.

LAKE, E. S. (1993). An exploration of the violent victim experiences of female offenders. *Violence and Victims, 8,* 41–51.

LEONARD, E. B. (1982). *Women, crime, and society.* New York: Longman.

LEVITT, D. (1994). *Teen families and welfare dependency in California.* Sacramento: California Family Impact Services.

LINDGREN, S. (1996). *Gender specific programming for female adolescents.* Unpublished master's thesis. Augsburg College, Minneapolis, MN.

LIPSEY, M. (1990). *Juvenile delinquency treatment: A meta-analytic inquiry into the variability of effects.* New York: Russell Sage.

MARTIN, T. (1993). From slavery to Rodney King: Continuity and change. In H. Madhubuti (Ed.), *Why L.A. happened: Implications of the 1992 Los Angeles rebellion* (pp. 27–40). Chicago: Third World Press.

MAYER, J. (1995). *Taking girls into account: Changing a juvenile services agency from within.* Baltimore: Maryland Department of Juvenile Services.

MCCABE, E., JAFFE, L. R., & DIAZ, A. (1993). Human immunodeficiency virus positivity in adolescents with syphilis. *Pediatrics, 92,* 695–698.

MELTON, G. B., & PAGLIOCCA, P. M. (1992). Treatment in the juvenile justice system: Directions for policy and practice. In J. J. Cocozza (Ed.), *Responding to the mental health needs of youth in the juvenile justice system.* Seattle, WA: National Coalition for the Mentally Ill in the Criminal Justice System.

MILIN, R., HALIKAS, J. A., MELLER, J. E., & MORSE, C. (1991). Psychopathology among substance-abusing juvenile offenders. *Journal of the American Academy of Child and Adolescent Psychiatry, 30,* 569–574.

MILLER, J. (1994) Race, gender and juvenile justice: An examination of disposition decision-making for delinquent girls. In M. Schwartz & D. Milovanovic (Eds.), *The intersection of race, gender and class in criminology* (pp. 219–246). New York: Garland.

MILLER, D., TRAPANI, C., FEJES-MENDOZA, K., EGGLESTON, C., & DWIGGINS, D. (1995). Adolescent female offenders: Unique considerations. *Adolescence, 30,* 429–435.

MINNESOTA ADVISORY TASK FORCE ON THE FEMALE OFFENDER IN CORRECTIONS. (1994). *Needs assessment and recommendations for adolescent females in Minnesota.* St. Paul: Minnesota Department of Corrections.

MITCHELL, J., & VARLEY, C. (1990). Isolation and restraint in juvenile correctional facilities. *Journal of the American Academy of Child and Adolescent Psychiatry, 2,* 251–255.

MONAHAN, G. (1997). *The physical and mental health needs of female adolescents at risk or involved in the juvenile justice system.* Los Angeles: UCLA Drug Abuse Research Center.

MONAHAN, G., GIL-RIVAS, V., DANILA, B., & ANGLIN, D. A. (in press). *Health-risk behaviors of adolescents in the juvenile justice system.*

MOORE, J. (1991). What leads sexually abused juveniles to delinquency. *Corrections Today, 42.*

MORRIS, R. E., BAKER, C. J., & HUSCROFT, S. (1992). Incarcerated youth at risk for HIV infection. In R. DiClemente (Ed.), *Adolescents and AIDS: A generation in jeopardy* (pp. 52–70). Newbury Park, CA: Sage.

MYERS, W. C., BURKET, R. C., LYLES, B., STONE, L., & KEMPH, J. P. (1990). DSM-III diagnoses and offenses in committed female juvenile delinquents. *Bulletin of the American Academy of Psychiatry and the Law, 18,* 14–54

NAFFINE, N. (1987). *Female crime: The construction of women in criminology.* Sydney, Australia: Allen & Unwin.

NATIONAL COMMISSION ON CORRECTIONAL HEALTH CARE. (1992). *Standards for health services in juvenile confinement facilities.* Chicago: Author.

NELSON, J. (1997). *Straight, no chaser*. New York: Putnam.

OFFICE OF JUVENILE JUSTICE AND DELINQUENCY PREVENTION. (1993). *Juvenile justice and delinquency prevention act of 1974*. Washington, DC: Author.

OFFICE OF JUVENILE JUSTICE AND DELINQUENCY PREVENTION. (1996). *Prevention and parity: Girls in juvenile justice*. Washington, DC: Author.

ORENSTEIN, P. (1994). *School girls*. Garden City, NJ: Doubleday.

OSOFSKY, J. D. (1995). The effects of exposure to violence in young children. *American Psychologist, 50*(9), 782–788.

OTTO, R. K., GREENSTEIN, J. J., JOHNSON, M. K., & FRIEDMAN, R. M. (1992). Prevalence of mental disorders in the juvenile justice system. In J. J. Cocozza (Ed.), *Responding to the mental health needs of youth in the juvenile justice system*. Seattle, WA: National Coalition for the Mentally Ill in the Criminal Justice System.

OWEN, B., & BLOOM, B. (1995). Profiling women prisoners. *Prison Journal, 75*, 165–185.

OWEN, B., & BLOOM, B. (1997). *Profiling the needs of young female offenders: Final report to executive staff of the California Youth Authority* (Grant 95-IJ-CX-0098). Washington, DC: National Institute of Justice.

OWENS, J. W. (1991). The importance of standards in providing health care for incarcerated youth. In L. S. Thompson (Ed.), *The forgotten child in health care: Children in the juvenile justice system* (pp. 49–53). Washington, DC: National Center for Education in Maternal and Child Health.

PARENT, D., LEITER, V., LIVENS, L., WENTWORTH, D., WILCOX, S., & STEPHEN, K. (1994). *Conditions of confinement: Juvenile detention and corrections facilities*. Washington, DC: Office of Juvenile Justice and Delinquency Prevention.

PIPHER, M. (1994). *Reviving Ophelia*. New York: Ballantine Books.

POE-YAMAGATA, E., & BUTTS, J. A. (1996). *Female offenders in the juvenile justice system: Statistics summary*. Washington, DC: Office of Juvenile Justice and Delinquency Prevention, pp. 1–6.

POSNER, M. (1990, March). Female dropouts: The challenge. *Women's Educational Equity Act Digest*.

RHODES, J., & FISCHER, K. (1993). Spanning the gender gap: Gender differences in delinquency among inner-city adolescents. *Adolescence, 28*, 879–890.

ROBINSON, R. A. (1994). Private pain and public behaviors: Sexual abuse and delinquent girls. In C. K. Riessman (Ed.), *Qualitative studies in social work research*. Thousand Oaks, CA: Sage.

ROLF, J., NANDA, J., BALDWIN, J., CHANDRA, A., & THOMPSON, L. (1991). Substance misuse and HIV/AIDS risks among delinquents: A prevention challenge. *International Journal of Addiction, 25*, 533–559.

ROSENBAUM, J. (1989). Family dysfunction and female delinquency. *Crime & Delinquency, 35*, 31–44.

ROSENBAUM, J. (1993). The female delinquent: Another look at the family's influence on female offending. In R. Muraskin & T. Alleman (Eds.), *It's a crime: Women and justice* (pp. 399–416). Upper Saddle River, NJ: Prentice Hall.

ROSENBAUM, J., & CHESNEY-LIND, M. (1994). Appearance and delinquency: A research note. *Crime & Delinquency, 40*, 250–261.

ROSENBAUM, M., & MURPHY, S. (1995). *An ethnographic study of pregnancy and drug use. Final Report to the National Institute on Drug Abuse* (Grant RO1-DA 06832).

ROTHENBAUM, D. (1998). Phone interview. Sacramento: Educational Demographics Unit, California Department of Education.

SCHWARTZ, I. M., WILLIS, D. A., & BATTLE, J. (1991). *Juvenile arrest, detention, and incarceration trends 1979–1989*. Ann Arbor: University of Michigan's Center for the Study of Youth Policy.

SCOTT, J. L. (1994). The victor's crown of resiliency. In C. M. Todd (Ed.), *Child care center connections* (pp. 5–7). Urbana: University of Illinois Cooperative Extension Service.

SEDLAK, A. J., & BROADHURST, D. D. (1996). *Executive summary of the third national incidence study of child abuse and neglect.* Washington, DC: Administration for Children and Families, U.S. Department of Health and Human Services.

SEGE, R., STIGOL, L. C., PERRY, C., GOLDSTEIN, R., & SPIVAK, H. (1996). Intentional injury surveillance in a primary care setting. *Archives of Pediatrics and Adolescent Medicine, 150,* 277–283.

SHEW, M. L., & FORTENBERRY, J. D. (1992). Syphilis screening in adolescents. *Journal of Adolescent Health*, 13, 303–305.

SHORTER, A. D., SCHAFFNER, L., SHICK, S., & FRAPPIER, N. S. (1996). *Out of sight, out of mind: The plight of adolescent girls in the San Francisco Juvenile Justice System.* San Francisco: Center on Juvenile and Criminal Justice.

SHUSTER, B. (1995, June 28). L.A. school truancy exacts a growing social price. *Los Angeles Times,* p. 12.

SICKMUND, M., SNYDER, H. N., & POE-YAMAGATA, E. (1997). *Juvenile offenders and victims: 1997 update on violence.* Washington, DC: Office of Juvenile Justice and Delinquency Prevention.

SIGDA, K. B., & MARTIN, S. L. (1996). Substance use among incarcerated adolescents: Associates with peer, parent, and community use of substances. *Substance Use and Misuse, 31,* 1433–1445.

SMART, C. (1976). *Women, crime, and criminology: A feminist critique.* London: Routledge & Kegan Paul.

SNYDER, J., DISHION, T.J., & PATTERSON, G. R. (1986). Determinants and consequences of associating with deviant peers during preadolescence and adolescence. *Journal of Early Adolescence, 6,* 29–43.

STEINER, H., GARCIA, I. G., & MATTHEWS, Z. (1997). Post-traumatic stress disorder in incarcerated juvenile delinquents. *Journal of the American Academy of Child and Adolescent Psychiatry, 36,* 357–365.

THOMPSON, L. S. (1992). Health status and health care issues. In L. S. Thomspon & J. A. Farrow (Eds.), *Hard time, healing hands: Developing primary health care services for incarcerated youth* (pp. 21–36). Arlington, VA: National Center for Education in Maternal and Child Health.

THORNBERRY, T. P., KROHN, M., LIZOTTE, A., & CHARD-WIERSCHEM, D. (1993). The role of juvenile gangs in facilitating delinquent behavior. *Journal of Research in Crime and Delinquency, 30,* 55–87.

VERMUND, S. H., ALEXANDER-RODRIGUEZ, T., MACLEOD, S., & KELLEY, K. F. (1990). History of sexual abuse in incarcerated adolescents with gonorrhea or syphilis. *Journal of Adolescent Health Care, 11,* 449–452.

VIGIL, J. D. (1988). *Barrio gangs: Street life and identity in southern California.* Austin: University of Texas Press.

WARR, M. (1993). Parents, peers, and delinquency. *Social Forces, 72,* 247–264.

WARREN, M. (1982). Delinquency causation in female offenders. In N. Hahn-Rafter & E. Stanko (Eds.), *Judge, lawyer, victim, thief.* Boston: Northeastern University Press.

WASHINGTON, P. (1997). *Policy and program considerations for racial-ethnic minority girls at risk or involved in the juvenile justice system.* Background paper for OCJP Modeling Gender-Specific Services in Juvenile Justice, Policy and Program Recommendations Project.

WATERMAN, J. D. (1997). *Post-traumatic stress disorder and incarcerated female juvenile delinquents.* Unpublished doctoral dissertation.

WEST, C. (1994). *Race matters.* New York: Vintage Books.

WIDOM, R., & HAMMETT, T. (1996, April). HIV/AIDS and STDs in juvenile facilities. *Research in Brief.*

WILSON, W. J. (1987). *The truly disadvantaged: Inner city, the underclass, and public policy.* Chicago: University of Chicago Press.

WINDLE, M. (1997). Effect of parental drinking on adolescents. *Research in Brief*, 97.

WOOD, V., & SHOROYE, A. (1993). Sexually transmitted disease among adolescents in the juvenile justice system of the District of Columbia. *Journal of the National Medical Association, 85*, 435–439.

WOODS, N. F. (1995). Young women's health. In C. I. Fogel & N. F. Woods (Eds.), *Women's health care: A comprehensive handbook*. Thousand Oaks, CA: Sage.

YOUNG, N. K., GARDNER, S. L., & LOPEZ, J. (1997). *Alcohol and other drug use among California's adolescent population and the current systems' responses* (pp. 6–20). Fullerton: California State University, Department of Alcohol and Drug Programs.

50

Gender Differences in Delinquency Career Types and the Transition to Adult Crime

Kimberly Kempf-Leonard and Paul E. Tracy

There are few topics that rival the research and policy attention currently bestowed on serious, violent, and chronic juvenile offenders. Major efforts are under way to identify these threatening offenders, develop effective intervention strategies to stop their criminality, and initiate prevention programs that will ensure that subsequent youth do not follow in such delinquency career paths. Unfortunately, little attention has been devoted to females in this important policy arena. In this chapter we examine gender differences in serious, violent, and chronic offending among the 1958 Philadelphia birth cohort. With a large number of subjects and extensive criminal history information through age 26, these data enable us to make gender comparisons across delinquent and criminal careers that are unavailable in many other investigations. Based on our findings, we offer suggestions on how knowledge about gender differences might affect future research and policy efforts.

PRIOR RESEARCH

Serious, violent, chronic juvenile offenders first gained notice in the 1970s with the publication of *Delinquency in a Birth Cohort* (Wolfgang, Figlio, & Sellin, 1972), *The Violent Few* (Hamparian, Schuster, Dinitz, & Conrad, 1978), and Shannon's (1978, 1980) research on three cohorts in Racine, Wisconsin. These studies identified a very small proportion of juvenile offenders that were responsible for the majority of juvenile crime, including the most serious acts of delinquency. More recently, Tracy, Wolfgang, and Figlio (1990) reported an even greater involvement by chronic offenders in the 1958 Philadelphia birth cohort, and Tracy and Kempf-Leonard (1996) extended the research on the 1958 cohort to include the transition from delinquency career to adult crime. These studies have provided significant descriptions of juvenile careers, and according to Walker (1985), Delinquency in a Birth Cohort, in particular, is "the single most important piece of criminal justice research in the last 25 years and a major influence on crime control thinking" (p. 39).

The widespread interest in the topic of career criminals and criminal careers led the National Academy of Sciences to convene a Panel on Research on Criminal Careers in 1983 to assess the evidence and recommend directions for future research. According to panel chairperson Al Blumstein, "members were in general agreement about the findings and conclusions of the scientific evidence on criminal careers, but there were divergent views on the ethics of how such information should be used in dealing with offenders." Views among panelists ranged from objections to any criminal justice action based on anticipated future offending to a desire to see even weak results put to use as quickly as possible (Blumstein, Cohen, Roth, & Visher, 1986, p. x). A better understanding of the ethical issues associated with measurement difficulties and various intervention ideas may be the major legacy of the panel's two published volumes.

Of relevance here is the fact that females were included in fewer studies reviewed by the panel. Based on those studies and concerning gender differences in criminal careers, it was reported that "[I]n general, patterns of participation among females parallel those among males: higher estimates for broad crime domains and low thresholds of involvement. The most consistent pattern with respect to gender is the extent to which male criminal participation in serious crimes at any age greatly exceeds that of females, regardless of source of data, crime type, level of involvement, or measure of participation" (Blumstein et al., 1986, p. 40). There was reportedly "substantial debate" over causes of the strong empirical associations between demographic variables and aggregate arrest rates, but "the panel did not attempt to resolve those theoretical debates" (p. 26). Concluding comments about gender differences included: "much ambiguity surrounds the underlying theoretical meaning of differences," and "these differentials reflect relationships with other variables that are not yet well understood" (pp. 24–25).

More recently, the Office of Juvenile Justice and Delinquency Prevention initiated a Comprehensive Strategy for Serious, Violent, and Chronic Juvenile Offenders (Howell, 1995; Wilson & Howell, 1993), and established a study group on serious and violent juvenile offenders. In a volume published in 1998, this study group reviewed knowledge about serious, violent, and chronic juvenile offenders and the types of interventions that can reduce their level of offending (Loeber & Farrington, 1998).

Perceptions of gender differences in offending are clearly evident among members of the study group. One chapter begins with the contention that "in any birth cohort, the incidence and prevalence of violent and serious delinquency are more frequent among males than females" (Lipsey & Derzon, 1998, p. 86). The only chapter devoted to demographic descriptions of serious juvenile offenders is based on data for which information on females are available, and therefore it includes discussion only on issues pertaining to race and ethnic differences in offending. In a footnote, the authors comment that gender differences are beyond the scope of their paper and refer to a study based solely on young black women (Hawkins, Laub, & Lauritsen, 1998, p. 46).

A few descriptive findings of similar gender patterns are reported. For example, among the 524 females and 580 males in the Denver Youth Study, problem use of both alcohol and marijuana was higher among both male and female serious offenders than among other delinquents. (Huizinga & Jakob-Chien, 1998, pp. 50–51). The finding of higher rates of violence among male adolescents with histories of abuse and neglect compared to other males in the Rochester Youth Study also held for females (Smith & Thornberry, 1995). Prevalence of serious offending across multiple years for females in the National Youth Survey data was 3.8 percent for late-onset females versus 15.4 percent for early-onset females and 2.5 percent for late-onset males versus 12.7 percent for early-onset males (Tolan & Gorman-Smith, 1998, p. 76).

Among efforts to identify different pathways of development, a primary focus of the study group, findings based on females have either not been reported or have been discounted. For example, Loeber and Hay (1994) reported that their conceptual model of three pathways based on 1,500 males in the Pittsburgh Youth Study can account for most delinquency career patterns. There has been, however, only one subsequent test of this model using data from the National Youth Survey and 1,102 boys in the Chicago Youth Development Study, and no gender comparisons were made (Tolan & Gorman-Smith, 1998, pp. 80–84).

In reporting on relationships between predictor variables and outcome measures for serious or violent offending among the prospective longitudinal studies in their meta-analysis, Lipsey and Derzon (1998) identify that most of the studies include samples that are primarily male (p. 89). It is interesting that they still identify gender as a significant predictor of subsequent violent and/or serious delinquency, more than any other personal characteristics examined (pp. 96–98). In their assessment of potential targets for preventative intervention, they note that although gender and race are not "malleable," the prediction models suggest that male gender is "not a feasible target" among the 6 to 11 and 12 to 14 age groups (p. 100).

The link between early aggression and conviction and subsequent behavior is cited as "among the most stable characteristics, when measured for populations" (Tolan & Gorman-Smith, 1998, p. 73). The correlations for this relationship, however, are identified as "0.25 to 0.40 for males and lower for females" in two studies (i.e., Cairns, Cairns, Neckerman, Geist, & Gariepy, 1988; Coie & Dodge, 1983) and as "nonsignificant for females" in one other (i.e., Huesmann, Eron, Lefkowitz, & Walder, 1984; Tolan & Gorman-Smith, 1998, p. 73). Violence at age 15 predicted violence in later years among the 205 males, but less consistently and strongly among the 219 females in the Rutgers Health and Human Development Project (White, 1992). Similar findings from the Seattle Social Development Project show that gender is significantly able to predict self-reported violent behavior at age 18, with the likelihood of violence among males double that of females (Hawkins et al., 1998, p. 144). Other gender differences were reported for the Seattle Social Development Project. Inverse relationships between violent behavior and both parent–child communication and school bonding were weak for females, but strong for males (Williams, 1994, pp. 136, 138). The influence of delinquent siblings, however, was stronger for girls than for boys (p. 140).

Among other findings reviewed by the study group, Denno (1990) reported an inverse relationship between academic achievement and subsequent violent offending for both males and females, and the relationship was strongest for females. For both males and females, leaving home before age 16 was linked to increased levels of violence in McCord and Ensminger's Woodlawn Study of African American Children in Chicago (Hawkins et al.,

1998, pp. 137–138). Finally, in the only report on gender differences among factors associated with gang membership, Thornberry (1998) provided the following account for the 250 females and 750 males in the Rochester Youth Study: "On the one hand, school variables, access to and values about drugs, and prior delinquency operate in generally similar ways for males and females. On the other hand, neighborhood characteristics appear to be much more important in increasing the likelihood of gang membership for the females than for the males. In contrast, family, peer, and psychological states (depression, stress, and self-esteem) are more potent predictors of gang membership for the males than the females" (p. 156).

Apart from the relatively small number of comparisons identified here, no other gender-based predictions of behavior are reported in the OJJDP study group volume. We do not posit that gender bias is responsible for the omission of gender differences in this research, as measurement difficulties associated with observing the low-base-rate phenomena of serious, violent, and chronic juvenile offenders in general, and for females in particular, are clearly noted. For example, Huizinga & Jakob-Chien (1998) contend that "because statistical significance is dependent on sample sizes, some differences that appear to be substantively significant are not statistically different, especially for girls" (p. 53). It also is reported that "estimates for females are less stable," but there is some suggestion of (a) a lower proportion of high aggression but (b) a higher proportion of serious criminal behavior among the more aggressive (Tolan & Gorman-Smith, 1998, p. 74). These authors conclude that because most studies have focused on males, there are substantial limitations in applying knowledge based only on males, and much of what can be concluded about serious, violent, and chronic juvenile offenders may apply only to males (p. 70).

The notable exception to research based on small numbers of subjects is analysis of 151,209 juvenile court careers by Howard Snyder. He provides interesting evidence that the large majority of youth handled by the juvenile court were referred only once. Most of the delinquents were never charged with a serious offense. Delinquents born later were not more frequent, more serious, or more violent than their earlier counterparts. Most chronic offenders did not commit violence, although most violent delinquents were also chronic offenders. Further, the majority of chronic and violent offenders also were involved in serious but nonviolent offending. In these findings, Snyder (1998) finds "comfort in the fact that the juvenile justice system is largely achieving its goal of successfully intervening in the lives of delinquent youth" (p. 442). He also contends, however, that "the juvenile justice system may be spreading its net wider, bringing in more juveniles, not more serious juvenile offenders because much of the recent growth in referrals was due to nonserious offenses" (p. 443). Regrettably absent in this interesting work is an indication of gender differences, although females presumably are included among the large number of cases spread across 15 cohorts that Snyder examined.

Of course, it is nothing new to ignore gender differences. Omission of how males and females differ actually is more the routine than the exception (Bergsmann, 1989; Chesney-Lind, 1997, pp. 17–21). A recent reminder of this situation appears in the aptly named book, *The Invisible Woman*, in which Belknap (1996) comments: "[I] found it frustrating to search through mainstream journals (and some books) to find out if women and/or girls were included in the research questions or samples. For example, studies with male-only samples rarely identified this in the title, while studies with female-only or female and male samples almost consistently reflected this in their titles. If women were excluded from the study, then most authors perceived no need to include 'male' in the title" (p. 4).

Although seldom questioned, the justification usually offered for not conducting gender-specific analyses is that too few females are available for observation. Indeed, a plethora of convincing evidence exists that both the male prevalence and incidence of offending far exceed that of females. But beyond these two basic parameters of offending, the knowledge base is more limited about the nature of other aspects of offending that might be characterized by gender differences. In fact, we know little about female offending in general. The irony, of course, is that by ignoring gender differences in offending, prior research may be failing to focus on the demographic factor that may actually have the greatest ability to distinguish crime; it is at least better than age, race, or social class, which are far more common in scientific inquiries about offending (Hagan, Gillis, & Simpson, 1985; Leonard, 1982).

Another problem with the lack of attention paid to female offending is that considerable unfounded speculation exists in place of accumulated research. Both historically and today, there is a tendency to view female offenders and offending as aberrations, abnormal even among society's deviants, and certainly not feminine. For example, Lombroso's beliefs in the late nineteenth century that females are less developed on the evolutionary scale and that female criminals exhibit male characteristics are no longer appreciated, but support for his contention that female delinquency is linked to biological traits can certainly still found today. Similarly, Pollack's contention in 1950 that the onset of menstruation, pregnancy, and menopause are linked to criminality has been widely cast aside, but his idea that females use their sexuality to obtain deferential treatment reappears today as the chivalry hypothesis in some explanations of differential treatment. Freud's concept of penis envy has been strongly questioned, but the influence of his views is evident in psychological theories that trace gender differences in personality development and adaptations.

The influence of these early theorists is evident among the criminal career panel debates on explanations based on "biological differences, differences in moral training, differences in socialization experiences, and fewer criminal opportunities for girls because they are more closely supervised" (Blumstein, Cohen, Roth, & Visher, 1986, p. 25). Although there is no consensus on the relative influence of nature or nurture, and most explanations integrate popular elements, prevailing theories include themes that gender differences in offending can be explained by corresponding gender differences in socialization, cognitive abilities, personality adaptations, neurological functioning, and hormonal and biochemical composition (Weisheit & Mahan, 1988). The most common diminished views of female offending continue to relegate it to a symptom of moral, emotional, or family problems and not "real" [male] delinquency and crime (Caine, 1989; Chesney-Lind, 1997; Naffine, 1987).

More important than presumptions about the inherent causes of crime, however, is the lack of attention and the misguided responses that females receive from criminal justice agencies. The range of behavior generally considered acceptable is narrower for females (Chesney-Lind, 1973, 1995; Dembo, Williams, & Schmeidler, 1993; Kempf-Leonard & Sample, 1998), and different factors appear to affect how females are processed (Chesney-Lind & Shelden, 1992; Gelsthorpe, 1989; Krohn, Curry, & Nelson-Kilger, 1983;

Rosenbaum & Chesney-Lind, 1994; Visher, 1983). Females may receive from police more restrictive, harsher, and longer interventions than do comparable males (Visher, 1983), courts, and correctional facilities (Bishop & Frazer, 1992; Chesney-Lind, 1973; Krisberg, Schwartz, Fishman, Eisikovits, & Guttman, 1986; Rhodes & Fischer, 1993). Females are also sent for treatment to mental hospitals in lieu of traditional juvenile justice facilities more often than males (Chesney-Lind, 1995; Miller, 1994; Weithorn, 1988). Further, some female-specific treatment programs dictate stereotypical feminine behavior (Chesney-Lind & Shelden, 1992; Gelsthorpe, 1989; Kersten, 1989), and even new reform efforts in this area may be problematic (Kempf-Leonard & Sample, 1998).

Some of these situations no doubt exist because inadequate resources are allocated and too few programs attend to the prevention and treatment of girls and women who offend (Chesney-Lind, 1997, p. 90; Lipsey, 1992, p. 106; Valentine Foundation, 1990, p. 5). Even among those criminal justice agencies that do try to respond to females, there are many inappropriate services, interventions, and sanctions. According to Chesney-Lind (1997), "there have been major changes in the way that the United States has handled girls' and women's crime in recent decades that do not necessarily bode well for the girls and women who enter the criminal justice system" (p. 3). In placing blame, Chesney-Lind says, "[the silence about females] has hidden key information from public view and allowed major shifts in the treatment of women and girls—many on the economic margins—to occur without discussion and debate."

The "forgotten few" female offenders (Bergsmann, 1989) may be small in number, but their ability to help us understand wider behaviors should not be discounted. Even differential treatment by juvenile and criminal justice has been attributed to paternalism prevalent in general society (Chesney-Lind, 1995; Odem, 1995; Price & Sokoloff, 1995), which itself merits better understanding. Indeed, our understanding of crime and criminal justice would be much less, and criminology might not have become the large and growing field it now has if its "parent disciplines" had forestalled attention to deviants among investigations of routine behaviors. It is for these reasons that we believe it is important to examine gender differences among serious, violent, and chronic juvenile offenders and their transition to adult crime.

DATA

In this chapter we utilize the data files from the 1958 Philadelphia Birth Cohort Study. Records from all public and private schools in Philadelphia were used to identify the population of 27,160 males and females born in 1958 who resided in Philadelphia at least from ages 10 through 17. Together with the criminal history data that were collected for the cohort through age 26, these data are superior to those on which many previous investigations have been based. The present data permit the systematic structuring of the longitudinal sequence of police contacts and thereby help to facilitate the identification of youths, both delinquents and nondelinquents, who are most likely to proceed to adult crime.

The 1958 Philadelphia birth cohort comprises a population and, as such, is not vulnerable to the usual threats of external validity posed by sampling procedures because every available subject is included regardless of their delinquency or adult crime status. This cohort of 13,160 males and 14,000 females is the largest of its kind and includes detailed information drawn from several sources able to identify characteristics of its members. Further, the requirement of Philadelphia residence between ages 10 and 18 for defining the cohort provides a uniform time frame and setting within which cohort members were at risk of offending. Sample mortality is not problematic in this longitudinal investigation because the retrospective data collection involved unobtrusive archival examination of records that are maintained routinely by the Philadelphia Police Department and area schools.

The crime measures are drawn from police rap sheets and the associated investigation reports that were provided by the Juvenile Aid Division of the Philadelphia Police Department. These records were used to characterize police encounters that the cohort experienced before age 18. In addition to official arrests, the rap sheet data also contain "police contact" information. The police maintain records of these contacts that result in "remedial," or informal, handling of the youth by an officer whereby youth are generally remanded to the custody of their parents. Thus the juvenile delinquency data contain both official arrests and informal contacts that did not result in an arrest, thus representing a total record of official delinquency, and further, representing a much better record of delinquency than data that were based solely on arrest information. The police investigation reports were used to supplement information provided in the rap sheets with detailed descriptions of the criminal event in which the subject was involved. The Municipal and Court of Common Pleas of Philadelphia served as data sources for offenses committed by the cohort after reaching the legislatively imposed adult status of age 18. Adult criminal history data are available through December 31, 1984, or through age 26 for all cohort members. The 1958 Philadelphia Birth Cohort Study is rich in the criminal history and offense data available to assess important criminological issues. Further description of the 1958 Philadelphia Birth Cohort Study data collection procedures and the results of a comparison study of the juvenile delinquency careers for males in the 1958 and 1945 Philadelphia cohorts may be found in Tracy and Kempf-Leonard (1996) and Tracy et al. (1985, 1990).

It is important to note that an assumption was made that the residential status of subjects remained stable after age 17. FBI rap sheets on adult offending were obtained to capture even migratory adult crime, but those data were not used because it was too difficult to identify subjects accurately. Married females with new surnames were lost because the distinct federal numbering system necessitated identification based on the subject's name.

RESULTS

Delinquency

Female subjects (n = 14,000) comprise 51.5 percent of the 27,160 persons in the 1958 Philadelphia birth cohort. Yet they comprise just 14.1 percent of the 6,287 delinquents, and 14.9 percent of the cohort members who committed offenses as adults. Collectively, these females were responsible for 3,897 juvenile offenses and 909 adult crimes. In this chapter we investigate gender differences and similarities in the nature and distribution of these offenders and offenses. We first examine the prevalence of delinquency, which refers to the proportion of a subject group that has been recorded officially as delinquent.

Table 1 shows 4,315 males and 1,972 females were officially recorded as delinquent; thus the prevalence of delinquency is 32.8 percent for males and 14.1 percent for females

TABLE 1   **Frequency and Percentage of Delinquents by Gender**

	Males		Females		
	Number	Percent	Number	Percent	M/F Ratio
Nondelinquents	8,845	67.2%	12,028	85.9%	0.78:1
Delinquents	4,315	32.8	1,972	14.1	2.33:1
Total	13,160	100.0%	14,000	100.00%	

in the 1958 cohort. Given the smaller number of females, a gender comparison based merely on frequencies or counts would be inappropriate—the males would predominate and comparisons would be misleading. However, the percentage of delinquents adjusts for the population size at risk. Thus, in calculating the ratio of males to females, we rely on the percentage rather than the frequency. The ratio of the percentage of male delinquents to that of female delinquents indicates that for each female delinquent, there were about 2.3 male delinquents. As would be expected from prior research, males are much more likely than their female peers to become officially involved with the juvenile justice system.

Gender differences in the frequency, or incidence, of delinquency are shown in Table 2. We first provide data for all officially recorded delinquent acts, followed by only those delinquent acts that were law violations or crimes (i.e., status offenses were excluded). The largest proportion of both male delinquents (41.8 percent) and female delinquents (59.9 percent) had only one officially recorded delinquent offense of any kind. Roughly one-third each of the males and females exhibited moderate recidivism and had from two to four delinquent offenses. High recidivism, five through nine offenses, were observed for 15.2 percent of the males and 6.2 percent of the females. The smallest proportion of both males (7.6 percent) and females (1.2 percent) had very high recidivism and accumulated ten or more official contacts with police.

The male/female ratios for these percentages indicates a distinct gender effect. That is, as delinquency becomes more frequent, or more chronic, each female offender has a much higher percentage of male counterparts. The ratios start at 0.69:1 at the level of one-time offender, then increase consistently as we move to two to four offenses (1.09:1), and then five to nine offenses (2.45:1). Among the group responsible for the highest incidence of delinquency—10 or more offenses—there were 6.3 male delinquents for each female.

When delinquents who committed only status offenses are excluded and only criminal law violations are considered, the pattern shown above becomes even more pronounced. The group with no law violations, or status offenders only, includes just 11.7 percent of the male delinquents compared to 44.7 percent of the female delinquents. Similarly, the offender group with but one single crime encounter includes 40.3 percent of the females and 39.3 percent of the males. Thus, taken together, a substantial proportion of females, 85 percent, committed either no crimes or at most one crime in their delinquency career as compared to 51 percent of male delinquents.

When we examine recidivists, we see that at the level of two through four criminal law violations, only 13.9 percent of the females compared to 32.1 percent of the males

TABLE 2   Number and Percentage of Delinquent Offense Groups by Gender

	Males		Females		
	Number	Percent	Number	Percent	M/F Ratio
Nondelinquents					
All offenses					
(including status)					
1	1,804	41.8%	1,182	59.9%	0.69:1
2–4	1,529	35.4	643	32.6	1.09:1
5–9	654	15.2	123	6.2	2.45:1
10+	328	7.6	24	1.2	6.33:1
Total	4315	100.0%	1,972	99.9%	
Criminal law violations					
0	504	11.7%	876	44.7%	0.26:1
1	1,697	39.3	794	40.3	0.98:1
2–4	1,383	32.1	274	13.9	2.31:1
5–9	515	11.9	24	1.2	9.92:1
10+	216	5.0	4	0.2	25.0:1
Total	4,315	100.0%	1,972	100.3%	

were so classified. At the level of high criminal violations, five through nine offenses, this group included 11.9 percent of the males but only 1.2 percent of the females. Finally, at the highest recidivism level of criminal violations, ten or more offenses, we find 5 percent of the male delinquents but less than 1 percent of the females (0.2 percent).

The ratio of these percentages indicate that about four female delinquents for each male delinquents with no law violation and approximately one-to-one among the group with a single crime. However, there were 2.3 males per female among delinquents with two to four offenses, 9.9 males per female for five to nine offenses, and 25 males per female for 10 or more offenses. These ratios clearly indicate that as the levels of crime-related delinquency (as opposed to any type of offending, which includes status offenses) increase, fewer and fewer females are found compared to males.

In Table 3 we turn to data concerning gender differences in the probabilities of recidivism at each offense rank in the delinquency career, from the first to the nth offense. The probability estimate for male delinquents making the transition from a single offense to a second one is 0.58, compared to 0.40 for female delinquents, or looked at another way, about 42 percent of males compared to 60 percent of females commit only one delinquent offense. Male delinquents have a higher probability of recidivism than do female delinquents at each offense rank. The exception to this pattern occurs for the transition between 19 and 20 offenses for which the probability for females stays at 1.0 until the twenty-fourth offense. But these higher scores are unreliable, as they are based on only one female delinquent.

TABLE 3   Juvenile Recidivism Probabilities: All Delinquent Acts

Offense Rank	Males			Females		
	Career Frequency	Total Frequency	Probability	Career Frequency	Total Frequency	Probability
1	1,804	4,315	1.0000	1,182	1,972	1.0000
2	705	2,511	0.5819	379	90	0.4006
3	502	1,806	0.7192	163	411	0.5203
4	322	1,304	0.7220	101	248	0.6034
5	212	982	0.7531	51	147	0.5927
6	174	770	0.7841	32	96	0.6531
7	119	596	0.7740	18	64	0.6667
8	74	477	0.8003	13	46	0.7188
9	75	403	0.8449	9	33	0.7174
10	56	328	0.8139	6	24	0.7273
11	46	272	0.8293	6	18	0.7500
12	40	226	0.8309	3	12	0.6667
13	37	186	0.8230	2	9	0.7500
14	25	149	0.8011	2	7	0.7778
15	16	124	0.8322	1	5	0.7143
16	10	108	0.8710	1	4	0.8000
17	12	98	0.9074	1	3	0.7500
18	13	86	0.8776	1	2	0.6667
19	16	73	0.8488		1	0.5000
20	11	57	0.7808		1	1.0000
21	8	46	0.8070		1	1.0000
22	2	38	0.8261		1	1.0000
23	2	36	0.9474		1	1.0000
24	6	34	0.9444	1	1	0.0000
25	3	28	0.8235			
26	4	25	0.8929			
27	1	21	0.8400			
28	2	20	0.9524			
29	3	18	0.9000			
30	3	15	0.8333			
31	1	12	0.8000			
32	2	11	0.9167			
33		9	0.8182			

TABLE 3   (Continued)

| | Males | | | Females | | |
Offense Rank	Career Frequency	Total Frequency	Probability	Career Frequency	Total Frequency	Probability
34	3	9	1.0000			
35		6	0.6667			
36		6	1.0000			
37	1	6	1.0000			
38		5	0.8333			
39	1	5	1.0000			
40		4	0.8000			
41	2	4	1.0000			
42		2	0.5000			
43		2	1.0000			
44		2	1.0000			
45		2	1.0000			
46		2	1.0000			
47		2	1.0000			
48	1	2	1.0000			
49		1	0.5000			
50		1	1.0000			
51		1	1.0000			
52		1	1.0000			
53	1	1	1.0000			

Although Table 3 confirms the greater involvement of males in delinquent recidivism, and that the distribution of career totals is smaller and more constrained for the females, these results also indicate that female recidivists, like males, exhibit a pattern of escalating recidivism probabilities as offense rank increases. That is, while far fewer female delinquents recidivate at each offense rank, the pattern of such recidivism follows a probabilistic process that is very similar to that for males, thus suggesting a difference of degree rather than of kind.

Of the 19,145 officially recorded offenses, male delinquents were responsible for 15,248 (79.6 percent) and female delinquents for 3,897 (20.4 percent). The distribution of these offenses across specific offense categories is shown in Table 4. The most common offense categories among male delinquents were truancy (13 percent), disorderly conduct (12 percent), burglary (11 percent), theft (11 percent), drugs (5 percent), and simple assault (5 percent). By comparison, female delinquents were most actively involved in runaway (39 percent), theft (13 percent), truancy (9 percent), disorderly conduct (8 percent), and simple assault (5 percent). As would be expected from prior research, males predominate

TABLE 4   Number, Percent, and Rate (per 1,000) of All Delinquent Acts by Gender

	Males			Females			
	Number	Percent	Rate	Number	Percent	Rate	M/F Ratio
Index offenses							
Homicide	55	0.4%	4.18	5	0.1%	0.36	11.61:1
Rape	101	0.7	7.67	2	0.1	0.14	54.79:1
Robbery	1,290	8.5	98.02	43	1.1	3.07	31.93:1
Aggravated assault	561	3.7	42.63	107	2.7	7.64	5.58:1
Burglary	1,673	11.0	127.13	52	1.3	3.71	34.27:1
Theft	1,671	11.0	126.98	500	12.8	35.71	3.56:1
Vehicle theft	640	4.2	48.63	18	0.5	1.29	37.70:1
Nonindex offenses							
Males predominate							
Simple assault	698	4.6	53.04	209	5.4	14.93	3.55:1
Arson	42	0.3	3.19	7	0.2	0.50	6.38:1
Receive stolen goods	69	0.5	5.24	7	0.2	0.50	10.48:1
Weapons	457	3.0	34.73	23	0.6	1.64	21.18:1
Vandalism	813	5.3	61.78	63	1.6	4.50	13.73:1
Drugs	714	4.7	54.26	100	2.6	7.14	7.60:1
Drunk driving	40	0.3	3.04	1	0.0	0.07	43.43:1
Liquor laws	211	1.4	16.03	43	1.1	3.07	5.22:1
Truancy	1,987	13.0	150.99	347	8.9	24.79	6.09:1
Disorderly	1,837	12.0	139.59	319	8.2	22.79	6.13:1
Trespass	603	4.0	45.82	93	2.4	6.64	6.90:1
City ordinance	534	3.5	40.58	82	2.1	5.86	6.92:1
Sex offenses	66	0.4	5.02	9	0.2	0.64	7.84:1
Gambling	8	0.1	0.61	1	0.0	0.07	8.71:1
Vagrancy	35	0.2	2.66	4	0.1	0.29	9.17:1
Drunkenness	166	1.1	12.61	17	0.4	1.21	10.42:1
Prostitution	11	0.1	0.84	1	0.0	0.07	12.00:1
Escape	205	1.3	15.58	14	0.4	1.00	15.58:1
Conspiracy	31	0.2	2.36	2	0.1	0.14	16.86:1
Incorrigible	6	0.0	0.46	4	0.1	0.29	1.59:1
Explosives	8	0.1	0.61	n/a			
Disturbance	5	0.0	0.38	n/a			
Fraud	6	0.0	0.46	6	0.2	0.43	1.07:1

TABLE 4   (Continued)

	Males			Females			
	Number	Percent	Rate	Number	Percent	Rate	M/F Ratio
Females predominate							
Runaway	467	3.1	35.49	1,518	39.0	108.43	0.33:1
Invest. person	235	1.5	17.86	296	7.6	21.14	0.84:1
Forgery	3	0.0	0.23	4	0.1	0.29	0.79:1
Total	15,248	100	1158.6	3,897	100.0	278.36	4.16:1

significantly among index crimes for which the male/female ratios are quite substantial. Further, the gender ratios show similarities for the offenses of runaway, forgery, fraud, investigation of person, and incorrigibility, while the biggest differences occur for rape, drunk driving, auto theft, burglary, robbery, and weapon offenses, for which the male/female ratios are substantial.

The overall estimate for male/female percent ratio based on total number of offenses indicates that over four male delinquents were apprehended for every female delinquent. Similarly, the offense rate for males, 1.158.66, is about four times higher (4.16) than the rate, 278.36, for females. Clearly, these offense data demonstrate, as expected, that delinquency of males far exceeds that of females when frequency of violations is the operative measure.

In Table 5 we examine gender differences among delinquents who could be classified as serious, violent, and/or chronic offenders. Violent offenders had delinquency records that included homicide, rape, robbery, aggravated assault, or aggravated sexual intercourse. These violent delinquents included 1,128 males, or 26 percent of the 4,315 male delinquents, and 140 females, or 14 percent of the 1,972 female delinquents. Thus for every violent female delinquent there were nearly four males who could be classified as violent.

The serious offenders include all violent offenders, plus those with burglary, theft, vehicle theft, arson, and vandalism in excess of $500. In this category there were 2,182 males (50.6 percent) and 326 females (16.5 percent). The male/female ratio is about 3:1. Serious crime specialists committed over half of their total career offenses in that category.

TABLE 5   Percent of Offenders by Delinquency Career Type

	Males		Females		
	Number	Percent	Number	Percent	M/F Ratio
Violent offender	1,128	26.1%	140	7.1%	3.68:1
Serious offender	2,182	50.6	326	16.5	3.07:1
Serious specialist	112	2.6	3	0.2	13.0:1
Chronic offender	982	22.8	147	7.5	3.04:1

There were 112 male specialists in serious crime (2.6 percent) but only 3 females, for a male/female ratio of 13:1.

The familiar classification of chronic offenders is those with a career total of five or more offenses. There were 982 chronic male delinquents (22.8 percent) and 147 chronic female delinquents (7.5 percent) for a male/female ratio of 3:1.

Adult Crime

It is important to move beyond the delinquency dimension and examine the transition to the adult sphere of criminality. Whatever may be the differences in youthful misbehavior, it is instructive to investigate the nature of the relationship between delinquency career types and adult crime by gender. Do males and females make the transition in the same way? Do the same delinquency factors put females and males at risk for adult crime, or is there a gender interaction with delinquency patterns? These issues need to be addressed.

The intersection among serious, violent, and chronic juvenile offenders, and the proportion of each that subsequently became adult offenders is depicted in Tables 6 and 7 and in Figure 1. In Table 6 we note that there were 895 males who were classified as both

TABLE 6   Number and Percent of Career Types by Gender[a]

Career Type	Males		Females		M/F Ratio
	Number	Percent of Delinquents	Number	Percent of Delinquents	
Total delinquents	4,315	100.0%	1,972	100.0%	n/a
Serious delinquents	2,182	50.6	326	16.5	3.07:1
Violent delinquents	1,128	26.1	140	7.1	3.68:1
Chronic delinquents	982	22.8	147	7.5	3.04:1
Serious and chronic	895	20.7	69	3.5	5.91:1
Percent of serious		41.0		21.2	1.93:1
Percent of chronic		91.1		46.9	1.94:1
Violent and chronic	612	14.2	39	2.0	7.10:1
Percent of violent	54.2		27.9		1.94:1
Percent of chronic		62.3		26.5	2.35:1
Not delinquents	8,845	67.2[b]	12,028	85.9[b]	0.78:1

[a]There is no consensus on the optimal cutoff to define chronic offenders, or whether the same definition should apply to males and females. One argument offered against a gender-neutral definition is that it is likely to capture a much smaller proportion of female offenders than male offenders, who also would "probably represent a more extreme group" (Blumstein et al., 1986; Loeber, Farrington, & Waschbusch, 1998, pp. 15–16). Having already addressed high incidence separately, however, the traditional definition of five or more offenses is adopted here.

[b]Rather than all delinquents, this percentage is based on the population total of 13,160 males and 14,000 females.

TABLE 7 Number and Percentage of Career Types by Gender[a]

Career Type	Males			Females			
	Number of Delin-quents	Number Adult Crimes	Percent of Row	Number of Delin-quents	Number Adult Crimes	Percent of Row	M/F Ratio
Total delinquents	4,315	1,805	41.8%	1,972	236	12.0%	3.48:1
Serious delinquents	2,182	1,123	51.5	326	81	24.8	2.08:1
Violent delinquents	1,128	634	56.2	140	36	25.7	2.19:1
Chronic delinquents	982	619	63.0	147	42	28.5	2.21:1
Serious and chronic	895	571	63.8	69	30	43.5	1.47:1
Violent and chronic	612	394	64.4	39	17	43.6	1.48:1
Not delinquents	8,845	1,273	14.4	12,028	304	2.5	5.76:1

[a]There is no consensus on the optimal cutoff to define chronic offenders, or whether the same definition should apply to males and females. One argument offered against a gender-neutral definition is that it is likely to capture a much smaller proportion of female offenders than male offenders, who also would "probably represent a more extreme group" (Blumstein et al., 1986; Loeber et al., 1998, pp. 15–16). Having already addressed high incidence separately, however, the traditional definition of five or more offenses is adopted here.

serious and chronic offenders. Although comprising only one-fifth of all male delinquents, this group represents 91.1 percent of the total chronic subset and 41.0 percent of the serious male delinquents. In contrast, the 69 serious and chronic female delinquents comprised less than 4 percent of the total, 46.9 percent of the chronic group, and 21.2 percent of the serious female delinquents. For each such female delinquent, there were approximately two male delinquents. Delinquents who were both violent and chronic offenders included 612 males, or 14 percent, and 39 females, or 2 percent. This career type represented two-thirds of the male chronic offenders, one-fourth of the female chronic offenders, just over half of the violent males, and just over one-fourth of violent females. The male/female percent ratio was again 2:1.

The prevalence of subsequent adult offending through age 26 is shown in Table 7 separately by gender for each delinquency career type. Among both males and females, adult offending was least prevalent among nondelinquents (14 percent males, 3 percent females) and most prevalent among chronic offenders who also had records of either violent or serious crimes (64 percent males, 44 percent females). Although parallel patterns of adult prevalence exist among the delinquency career types for males and females, the lower prevalence among females is very clearly evident. The male/female ratio of nearly 6:1 suggests the most variation among virgin adult offenders, those with no juvenile record. The ratio for overall delinquents is 3.5:1, and for each of the serious, violent, and chronic delinquency careers the adult offending ratios identify males/females 2:1.

Figure 1 provides a useful display of the information given in Tables 6 and 7, using the familiar Venn diagram approach with intersecting circles to represent the proportion of delinquents in each of the significant delinquency career types. All delinquents are

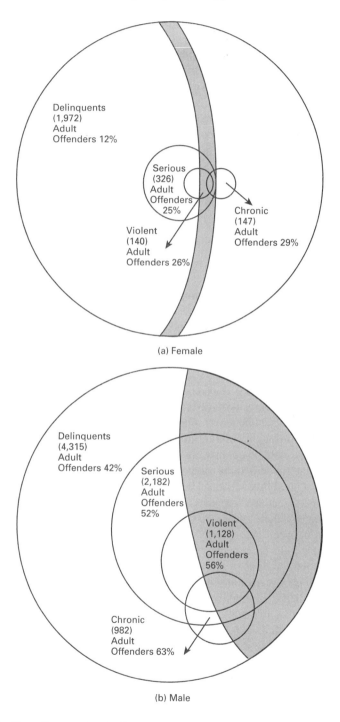

(a) Female

(b) Male

FIGURE 1   Venn diagram showing intersection between delinquency career types: (a) female; (b) male.

encompassed within the outer circle. Those delinquents who had no record of any serious offense, and fewer than five official encounters with the police, are included in the proportion of the larger circle outside the other circles. Overlapping areas between the circles represent delinquency careers with attributes from two or more groups. The shaded portion of each circle represents the percentage of each delinquency career subgroup that also committed adult crime.

In comparison to Snyder's analysis of multiple court cohorts, we use a more conservative definition of chronic offending, the traditional five or more police contact, whereas he relied on a cutoff of four or more delinquency referrals to court (Snyder, 1998, p. 437). We had no cases of kidnapping and include rape as a violent offense. We also include vandalism of property in excess of $500 as a serious offense, which Snyder does not, and he includes drug trafficking and weapons as serious nonviolent offenses (p. 429). Despite these differences, there is value in comparing our findings of the intersecting career paths of delinquents.

In Snyder's career paths, 33.6 percent were serious delinquents, 14.5 percent were chronic delinquents, 8.1 percent were violent, 12.1 percent were serious and chronic, and 1 percent was violent and chronic. Although based on a single earlier cohort and in some cases a more conservative definition, each significant career path included a higher proportion of delinquents in our study. For example, in comparison to Snyder's 33.6 percent, we had 50.6 percent of the males and 16.5 percent of the females identified as serious delinquents. In comparison to his 14.5 percent, we found chronic delinquents among 22.8 percent of the males and 7.5 percent of the females. In comparison to his 8.1 percent, 26.1 percent of the males and 7.1 of the females in our cohort were violent delinquents. Similarly, his finding of 12.1 percent as serious and chronic delinquents corresponded to our finding of 20.7 percent of the males and 3.5 percent of the females. Finally, 1 percent violent and chronic delinquents for him, compared to 14.2 of the males and 2 percent of the males for us. Although variation in delinquent behavior across geographic locations or birth year may yield some answers to these difference in delinquency career paths, it is also likely that Snyder's failure to control for gender differences provides at least a partial explanation. Our ability to control for adult offending illustrates further the extent to which observations of gender differences are important.

Ultimately, there is value in specifying the statistical strength and significance of the connection between delinquency career types and making the transition to adult crime. Thus in Table 8 we provide the results from a logistic regression model that predicts adult crime status on the basis of the three delinquency career types. These multivariate results present the highly interesting finding that the type of career a delinquent had as a juvenile is highly predictive of adult status for both males and females and in almost exactly the same way. That is, a violent delinquency career is not significant for females and does not quite reach significance for males. Yet, for both males and females having been either a serious delinquent or a chronic delinquent is highly predictive of adult status. Each of the effects was significant for males and females and produced substantial odds ratios. However, the odds ratios observed were strongest for females. If a female delinquent was a serious offender, she was 2.7 times more likely than nonserious females to move on to adult crime. The corresponding score was 1.5 among males. Similarly, among females, chronics were 2.4 times more likely to have a record of adult crime than nonchronic offenders, while the odds were slightly less among males (2.3:1). Of importance here is the

TABLE 8   Prediction of Adult Status by Juvenile Career Types and Gender

Juvenile Career Types	Coefficient	Standard Error	p-Value	Odds Ratio
Females				
Violent delinquent	−0.034	0.264	0.898	0.967
Serious delinquent	1.012	0.195	0.000	2.750
Chronic delinquent	0.888	0.210	0.000	2.430
Males				
Violent delinquent	0.176	0.090	0.052	1.192
Serious delinquent	0.424	0.080	0.000	1.528
Chronic delinquent	0.834	0.086	0.000	2.302

fact that although females are less likely to become serious delinquent or chronic juvenile offenders, when they do reflect these career types, these effects are more pronounced in producing adult crime status among females than among males.

In Table 9 we present a few details on the gender differences in the type of adult criminals in the cohort just to highlight the fruitful lines of research that can be conducted on male and female offending across the life course. We focus on offenders rather than offenses because we want to highlight the qualitative dimension rather than the mere quantitative extent of the adult criminality. It is readily apparent that there are more similarities than differences in the adult offending careers. Females and males have similar percentages for index crimes, theft offenses, and offenses involving weapons. Yes, males predominate, but not as substantially as is the case for other crimes, such as robbery, drugs, and alcohol. These results surely indicate that females are almost as likely as males to become

TABLE 9   Number and Percent of Adult Offender Types by Gender

Offender Type	Females Number	Females Percent	Males Number	Males Percent
Any type	236	100.0%	1,805	100.0%
Index	51	63.9	1,364	75.6
Violence	96	40.7	854	47.3
Robbery	21	8.8	515	28.5
Theft	81	34.3	916	50.7
Weapon	58	24.6	661	36.6
Drugs	37	15.7	534	29.6
Alcohol	13	5.5	221	12.2

certain types of adult criminals. We would expect, however, that the frequency with which males commit these acts would be far greater than for females. Yet it is the propensity itself that holds almost equal interest to the more usual inquiry surrounding the frequency of offending.

SUMMARY AND IMPLICATIONS

We have investigated a number of topics surrounding gender differences in delinquency. The following summarize the major findings with respect to the topic areas of interest: prevalence, incidence, and juvenile delinquent subgroups.

The prevalence data clearly indicated that the phenomenon of delinquency is very different among girls than among boys. Of the 14,000 girls in the 1958 cohort, 1,972, or about 14 percent, had at least one delinquent offense before reaching age 18. The boys were almost two and one-half times more likely to be delinquent than were their female counterparts. When prevalence was broken down by level of delinquency status, the gender differences were pronounced. Among females, 60 percent of the delinquents were one-time offenders, whereas only 7 percent were chronic recidivists. Thus the girls were about one and one-half times more likely to be delinquents with but one delinquent offense, while boys were about three times more likely to have been a chronic offender with five or more offenses. In particular, therefore, chronic delinquency was a very different phenomenon among girls than among boys in the 1958 cohort. Of the 1972 female delinquents, 147 were classified as chronic offenders. These chronic females represented just 1.4 percent of the girls at risk, 7.5 percent of the delinquent subset, and 18.5 percent of the recidivists. The proportion of male chronics exceeded that of females by factors of 7.5:1 among subjects, 3:1 among delinquents, and 2:1 among recidivists.

The 1,972 female delinquents were responsible for a total of 3,897 delinquent acts. The offense rate (per 1,000 cohort members) was 278.36. Seven hundred and twenty-seven, or 18 percent of the female offenses, were UCR Index offenses, with a rate of 52.0 per 1,000 cohort girls. One hundred and fifty-seven of the female offenses were violent index offenses (4 percent of the total delinquent acts and 22 percent of the index crimes) with a rate of 11 per 1,000 girls in the cohort.

The gender effects shown among these data were quite pronounced. The offense rate for boys was four times greater than that for girls. The gender disparity increased to a factor of almost 9:1 for UCR Index offenses. The male/female ratio increased even further, to 14:1 for violent offenses. The most glaring differences occurred for the following serious offenses: 14:1 for homicide, 33:1 for robbery, 10:1 for aggravated assault, 34:1 for burglary, and 37:1 for vehicle theft.

We also examined the intersection among various classifications of delinquency to determine the extent to which the categories of the serious offender, the violent offender, and the chronic offender were capturing the same group of delinquents. We found that males were much more likely than females to be serious and chronic (about six times more likely), and violent and chronic (about seven times more likely).

Finally, however, we also examined the prevalence of adult crime in association with the various offender classifications in order to detect the extent to which a history of a particular type and/or frequency of juvenile delinquency was predictive of adult crime status.

We found first that females had comparatively low adult crime status compared to males. That is, 236 (12 percent) of the 1,972 female delinquents and 304 (2.5 percent) of the females at risk went on to commit a crime as an adult. These findings were overshadowed by the male results, which showed that 1805 (41.8 percent) of the 4,315 male delinquents and 1,273 (14.4 percent) of the males at risk had records of adult crime. However, we also found that when we examined the intersection of the offender classifications and their association with adult crime, the gender disparity diminished. That is, male delinquents were about 3.4 times as likely as female delinquents and male subjects were 5.76 times as likely as female subjects to go on to adult crime, but the results for serious, violent, and chronic offenders were generally in the range of twice as likely. More interestingly, when we examined the intersections, we found that the male predominance declined even further, to about 1.5:1 for both the serious and chronic and violent and chronic intersections. Clearly, these findings indicate that a combined history of frequent and serious, or frequent and violent, places a female a substantial risk of adult crime that is closer to her male counterpart than when such combined traits are missing from the juvenile career. Thus, a female who uncharacteristically has a delinquency career that is similar to her male counterpart rather than her female peers (who generally have a limited involvement in delinquency) exhibits a substantially higher risk of continuing the offense career as she becomes an adult, just like her chronic male counterpart. In fact, our multivariate model indicated that the connection between delinquency career type and adult crime was strongest for females.

Overall, our results produce the finding that males are far more involved in offending than females. However, when analysis of recidivism and seriousness of offending are extended to females, the findings show that females are indeed found among the small group of offenders present at the limited end of the continuum of those who behave most badly.

Our findings have highlighted many differences; still others remain to be examined. For gender differences to be understood, research must attend to offending over the criminal career, or life course, and focus on crime-specific modeling. For example, a better understanding of the links between crime and responses to victimization, including how juvenile justice processing serves to label the responses of female victims as offenses, would help illuminate the criminal career pathways that flow from such victimization. Important contextual differences across age, race, social class, and geographic location also merit a lot more attention (Chesney-Lind, 1997; Simpson, 1991). We must examine gender similarities to understand better the differences. We will, and we urge other researchers, to take seriously Chesney-Lind's contention that "[g]irls' pathways into crime, even into violence, are affected by the gendered nature of their environments and particularly their experiences as marginalized girls in communities racked by poverty" (p. 176).

While Feld (1997, p. 132) argues that juvenile courts go to great lengths to evade the unpleasant topic of punishment and its "disagreeable qualities," it is the contention of Chesney-Lind (1997) that such feelings of avoidance and discomfort are directed even more acutely at females. Meanwhile, disproportionate media accounts of serious juvenile crime approaching epidemic proportions (Blumstein, 1995; DiIullio, 1996; Fox, 1996) have given rise to the notion of the "superpredator" (DiIullio, 1996), including the liberated "female gangsta" (Chesney-Lind, 1997, pp. 34–37; Maher & Curtis, 1995). Such media portrayals have affected public perception of juvenile offenders and the corresponding "feeding frenzy" of policy responses (Howell, 1998; see also Doi, 1998; Zimring, 1996b).

Issues about the social construction of childhood and adolescence have been raised (Bernard, 1992; Feld, 1997). It has also been argued that teenagers, in general, tend to be demonized in contemporary American society, and that serious, violent, and chronic juvenile offenders exist because society has not acted responsibly toward youth in other important arenas (Males, 1996). Concerning females, criticism has been advanced that "those who tout these 'crime waves' use a crude form of equity feminism to explain the trends observed and, in the process, contribute to a 'backlash' against the women's movement" (Chesney-Lind, 1997, p. 56; Faludi, 1991).

The policy debate and legislative action has resulted in harsher, more restrictive codes and procedures for processing juvenile offenders, especially serious, violent, and chronic delinquents, in nearly every state (Torbet et al., 1996; Walker, 1995). Some policy initiatives aim to limit discretion, standardize court decisions, and classify offenders for correctional supervision and treatment (Weibush, Baird, Krisberg, & Onek, 1995; Wilson & Howell, 1993). Other changes couple juvenile justice with criminal justice, typically through greater use of juvenile transfer to criminal court (Fagan, 1995; Howell, 1997; Singer, 1996; Tracy & Kempf-Leonard, 1998). Accountability is a recurrent theme, with changes aimed at holding juvenile offenders—and sometimes also their parents—responsible for their actions (Albert, 1998). In some areas, the accountability objective links with treatment (Bazemore & Day, 1996; Bazemore & Umbreit, 1995; Wilson & Howell, 1993), but more often the focus is on punishment and retribution (Feld, 1997). According to Feld, "[t]hese recent changes signal a fundamental inversion in juvenile court jurisprudence from treatment to punishment, from rehabilitation to retribution, from immature child to responsible criminal. . . . The common over-arching legislative strategy reflects a jurisprudential shift from the principle of individualized justice to the principle of offense, from rehabilitation to retribution, and an emphasis on the seriousness of the offenses rather than judges' clinical assessments of offenders' 'amenability to treatment'" (p. 79). Feld subsequently advocates abolition of the juvenile court in favor of a single explicitly punitive criminal justice process in which culpability and sanctions are discounted for youth (Feld, 1997). Although Feld might appear the lone advocate of this position, it is clearly implicit in much of the public and policy debate.

In terms of effectiveness, it is important to note that a purely punitive response to serious juvenile offenders discounts advances made in the area of treatment. According to Lipsey (1992), "It is no longer constructive for researchers, practitioners, and policymakers to argue about whether delinquency treatment and related rehabilitative approaches work. As a generality, treatment clearly works. We must get on with the business of developing and identifying the treatment models that will be most effective and providing them to the juveniles they will benefit" (p. 85). In their review of programs, Lipsey and Wilson (1998) identify reductions in recidivism as high as 40 percent among the best programs for serious juvenile offenders, a larger effect than shown for delinquents in general. They conclude: "If anything, then, it would appear that the typical intervention in these studies is more effective with serious offenders than with less serious offenders" (p. 23). Characteristics of the most effective treatment programs were intensive services, more contact hours, longer stays, multiple services, consistent implementation, and external evaluation teams. Most important, not only has treatment been found far more effective in reducing recidivism than punishment (Gendreau, 1996), but it is also clearly more cost-effective (Greenwood, Model, Rydell, & Chiesa, 1996).

We know that effective treatment can be administered by the juvenile courts. Rates of recidivism tend to be lower in juvenile courts than in criminal courts (Howell, 1997, p. 3). Moreover, our own research shows that early routine probation intervention is effective, even for serious chronic juvenile delinquents, whereas the same may not be true of routine commitment to correctional facilities (Tracy & Kempf-Leonard, 1996, pp. 109–142). Similarly, Dean, Brame, and Piquero (1996) attributed lower recidivism to early probation intervention among several hundred North Carolina youth they followed for six years. Howell (1997, p. 5) also reports on a 12-month follow-up evaluation, in which reductions as high as 50 percent in arrests, court petitions, probation violations, and new facility commitments were attributed to an early intervention program in a California probation department.

Of course, as might be expected, attention to females is noticeably absent among the policy discussion and most of the policy initiatives. Two notable exceptions appear under provisions of the JJDP Act of 1974, as reauthorized in 1992:

1. To be eligible for federal funding, each state must provide "an analysis of gender-specific services for the prevention and treatment of juvenile delinquency, including the types of such services available and the need for such services for females and a plan for providing the needed gender-specific services" (Public Law 102-586, 1992).

2. As part of the challenge grant program for state advisory groups, additional funds are available to examine policies for gender bias and to develop female-specific programs. Based on the number of responses from states, the gender area has been the most popular among those available in the challenge grant program (Girls Inc., 1996, p. 26).

In the larger policy arena, however, these two initiatives make barely a mark.

In light of our observations that policy responses to serious, violent, and chronic juvenile offenders have not attended to gender differences although our research findings suggest that they should, we offer four recommendations. First, most policy reforms are predicated on notions of individual responsibility and accountability, which should require that we know more about the high incidence of delinquency that involves adolescents' miscalculation of risk (Bernard, 1992; Feld, 1997; Matza, 1964). Zimring, 1996a (pp. 90–99) equates the "self-autonomy" of adolescence with a "learner's permit" that provides youth with the opportunity to make choices and learn responsibility, yet "preserves the life chances for those who make serious mistakes." Although gender is not mentioned, Feld (1997, p. 121) acknowledges that "youthful development is highly variable." It is age which explains his view that "the ability to make responsible choices is learned behavior, and the dependent status of youth systematically deprives them of chances to learn to be responsible" (p. 114). Given prevailing arguments that girls are more sheltered and closely supervised than boys, yet their prevalence also is lower, gender differences in response to independence and in learning responsibility could prove very valuable in the policy arena. Fortunately, many scholars research gender differences in development (e.g., Bem, 1993; Chesney-Lind & Shelden, 1992; Messerschmidt, 1993, Orenstein, 1994; Osgood, Wilson, O'Malley, Bachman, & Johnson, 1996; Sadker & Sadker, 1994), and their contributions need to be targeted appropriately and included in the policy responses to juvenile offenders.

Second, Feld (1997) relies on knowledge gleaned from delinquency career research that desistance, maturation, or "aging out" typically occur, which he interprets as a natural phenomenon, to justify the feasibility of his system as follows: "Unlike a rehabilitative system inclined to extend its benevolent reach, an explicitly punitive process would opt to introduce fewer and more criminally 'deserving' youths into the system. . . . In allocating scarce resources, [this system] would use seriousness of the offense to rationalize charging decisions and 'divert' or 'decriminalize' most of the 'kids' stuff' that provides the grist of the juvenile court mill until it became chronic or escalated in severity" (pp. 128–129). This stance in favor of ignoring problem juvenile behavior until it reaches an intolerable level, however, also ignores research findings showing success associated with early intervention. Further, it creates a system in which the needs of economically and culturally outcast populations are conveniently ignored. Not only does this omission seem contrary to Feld's own concern for social justice (pp. 72, 132–136), but it is likely to adversely affect females, who are disproportionately represented among the socially marginalized populations (Chesney-Lind, 1997, p. 115). Thus we recommend rejection of Feld's abolition idea.

Third, although we strongly advocate a better understanding and more awareness of gender similarities and differences in delivering services, we currently find ourselves in opposition to gender-specific policy developments. Because justice should equate to equity, female-specific services seem likely to perpetuate stereotype and diminished aid to girls and women (Chesney-Lind, 1997, p. 162). In this area, we agree with Feld (1997, p. 121) that fairness and the objectivity of law are sacrificed when dispositions reflect subjective explanations of behavior and personal responsibility. Indications to this effect in the form of well-intentioned but premature or poorly conceived programming efforts, already exist among the new policy initiatives (Kempf-Leonard & Sample, 1998).

Our findings indicate gender differences in degree of serious, violent, and chronic offending, but gender similarities in general career patterns of interest. These findings lend support to suggestions that status offenders should be reintegrated as a feasible target of mainstream juvenile justice (Krisberg & Austin, 1993). Gender similarities in behavior, coupled with evidence of gender bias or differential processing, serve to remind us of the warning that criminal justice functions to maintain the modern patriarchy (Chesney-Lind, 1997, p. 4). How this occurs would be the important first step in helping to abolish it. Of course, obstacles to equity presented by the greater social stratification of rights and privileges remain (Simpson, 1991). Fortunately, the progressive ideas found within the new strategy for a comprehensive juvenile justice system are consistent with our findings and with other research on gender differences, and on male serious, violent, and chronic juvenile offenders (Howell, 1995, 1997; Wilson & Howell, 1993). Thus we support a balanced approach of prevention, early intervention, and graduated sanctions that provides for treatment, just as it aims to strengthen the family, support core institutions in their supporting roles of youth development, and identify and control the small group of serious, violent, and chronic juvenile offenders.

Criminology must confront the fact that both theory and research have not fully appreciated the full range of issues surrounding male and female involvement in delinquency and crime. The offending behavior of females cannot be dismissed as merely a less frequent or less serious analog to that of males. Such a dismissal has two noteworthy consequences. First, it precludes the development of common explanations, where they are appropriate, but more important, it prevents the conceptualization and investigation of gender-specific perspectives where they are warranted and very necessary. Second, it precludes the investigation of the differential processing that females receive in the juvenile and criminal justice systems and the effects of such processing on subsequent offending. Criminologists must therefore heed the caution expressed by Chesney-Lind and Shelden (1992) that girls experience a childhood and adolescence heavily colored by their gender, and it is simply not possible to discuss their problems, their delinquency, and what they encounter in the juvenile justice system without considering gender in all its dimensions (p. 212).

REFERENCES

ALBERT, R. L. (1998). *Juvenile accountability incentive block grants program.* OJJDP Fact Sheet 76. Washington, DC: Office of Juvenile Justice and Delinquency Prevention.

BAZEMORE, G., & DAY, S. E. (1996). Restoring the balance: Juvenile and community justice. *Juvenile Justice, 3*(1), 3–14.

BAZEMORE, G., & UMBREIT, M. (1995). Rethinking the sanctioning function in juvenile court: Retributive or restorative responses to youth crime. *Crime & Delinquency, 49,* 296–316.

BELKNAP, J. (1996). *The invisible woman.* Belmont, CA: Wadsworth.

BEM, S. (1993). *The lenses of gender.* New Haven, CT: Yale University Press.

BERGSMANN, I. (1989). The forgotten few: Juvenile female offenders. *Federal Probation, 53,* 73–78.

BERNARD, T. J. (1992). *The cycle of juvenile justice.* New York: Oxford University Press.

BISHOP, D., & FRAZER, C. (1992). Gender bias in the juvenile justice system: Implications of the JJDP Act. *Journal of Criminal Law and Criminology, 82*(4), 1162–1186.

BLUMSTEIN, A. (1995, August). Violence by young people: Why the deadly nexus? *NIJ Journal,* 1–9.

BLUMSTEIN, A., COHEN, J., ROTH, J. A., & VISHER, C. A. (1986). *Criminal careers and "career criminals."* Washington, DC: National Academy Press.

CAINE, M. (ED.). (1989). *Growing up good: Policing the behavior of girls in Europe.* Newbury Park, CA: Sage.

CAIRNS, R. B., CAIRNS, B. D., NECKERMAN, H. J., GEIST, S. D., & GARIEPY, J. L. (1988). Social networks and aggressive behavior: Peer support or peer rejection? *Developmental Psychology, 24,* 815–823.

CHESNEY-LIND, M. (1973). Judicial enforcement of the female sex role. *Issues in Criminology, 8,* 51–71.

CHESNEY-LIND, M. (1995). Girls, delinquency, and juvenile justice: Toward a feminist theory of young women's crime. In B. R. Price & N. J. Sokoloff (Eds.), *The criminal justice system and women* (2nd ed., pp. 71–88). New York: McGraw-Hill.

CHESNEY-LIND, M. (1997). *The female offender: Girls, women, and crime.* Thousand Oaks, CA: Sage.

CHESNEY-LIND, M., & SHELDEN, R. (1992). *Girls delinquency and juvenile justice.* Pacific Grove, CA: Brooks/Cole.

COIE, J. D., & DODGE, K. A. (1983). Communities and changes in children's socioeconomic status: A five-year longitudinal study. *Merrill-Palmer Quarterly, 29,* 261–282.

DEAN, C. W., BRAME, R., & PIQUERO, A. R. (1996). Criminal propensities, discrete groups of offenders, and persistence in crime. *Criminology, 34,* 547–574.

DEMBO, R., WILLIAMS, L., & SCHMEIDLER, J. (1993). Gender differences in mental health service needs among youths entering a juvenile detention center. *Journal of Prison and Jail Health, 12,* 73–101.

DENNO, D. (1990). *Biology and violence: From birth to adulthood.* Cambridge: Cambridge University Press.

DiIULLIO, J. J. (1996, Spring). They're coming: Florida's youth crime bomb. *Impact*, 25–27.

DOI, D. J. (1998, April). The MYTH of teen violence. *State Government News*, 17–19.

FAGAN, J. (1995). Separating the men from the boys. In R. Howell, R. Hawkins, B. Krisberg, & J. Wilson (Eds.), *Sourcebook on serious violent juvenile offenders* (pp. 238–257). Thousand Oaks, CA: Sage.

FALUDI, S. (1991). *Backlash: The undeclared war against American women*. New York: Anchor Books.

FELD, B. C. (1997). Abolish the juvenile court: Youthfulness, criminal responsibility, and sentencing policy. *Journal of Criminal Law and Criminology, 88*(1), 68–136.

FOX, J. A. (1996). *Trends in juvenile violence: A report to the U.S. attorney general on current and future rates of juvenile offending*. Boston: Northeastern University.

GELSTHORPE, L. (1989). *Sexism and the female offenders: An organizational analysis*. Aldershot, Hants. England: Gower.

GENDREAU, P. (1996). The principles of effective interventions with offenders. In A. T. Harland (Ed.), *Choosing correctional options that work* (pp. 117–130). Thousand Oaks, CA: Sage.

GIRLS INCORPORATED NATIONAL RESOURCE CENTER. (1996). *Prevention and parity: Girls in juvenile justice*. Indianapolis, IN: Girls Inc.

GREENWOOD, P. W., MODEL, K. E., RYDELL, C. P., & CHIESA, J. (1996). *Diverting children from a life of crime: Measuring costs and benefits*. Santa Monica, CA: RAND Corporation.

HAGAN, J., GILLIS, A. R., & SIMPSON, J. (1985). The class structure of gender and delinquency: Toward a power-control theory of common delinquent behavior. *American Journal of Sociology, 90*, 1151–1178.

HAMPARIAN, D. M., SCHUSTER, R., DINITZ, S., & CONRAD, J. (1978). *The violent few*. Lexington, MA: Lexington Books.

HAWKINS, J. D., HERRENKOHL, T., FARRINGTON, D. P., BREWER, D., CATALANO, R. F., & HARACHI, T. W. (1998). A review of predictors of youth violence. In R. Loeber & D. P. Farrington (Eds.), *Serious and violent juvenile offenders* (pp. 106–146). Thousand Oaks, CA: Sage.

HAWKINS, D. F., LAUB, J. H., & LAURITSEN, J. L. (1998). Race, ethnicity, and serious juvenile offending. In R. Loeber & D. P. Farrington (Eds.), *Serious and violent juvenile offenders* (pp. 30–46). Thousand Oaks, CA: Sage.

HOWELL, J. C. (ED.). (1995). *Guide for implementing the comprehensive strategy for serious, violent, and chronic juvenile offenders*. Washington, DC: Office of Juvenile Justice and Delinquency Prevention.

HOWELL, J. C. (1996). Juvenile transfer to the criminal justice system: State of the art. *Law and Policy, 18*, 17–60.

HOWELL, J. C. (1997). *Juvenile justice and youth violence*. Thousand Oaks, CA: Sage.

HOWELL, J. C. (1998). *Juvenile justice and youth violence*. Thousand Oaks, CA: Sage.

HUESMAN, L. R., ERON, L. D., LEFKOWITZ, M. M., & WALDER, L. O. (1984). Stability of aggression over time and generations. *Developmental Psychology, 20*, 1120–1134.

HUIZINGA, D., & JAKOB-CHIEN, C. (1998). The contemporaneous co-occurrence of serious and violent juvenile offending and other problem behaviors. In R. Loeber & D. P. Farrington (Eds.), *Serious and violent juvenile offenders* (pp. 47–67). Thousand Oaks, CA: Sage.

KEMPF-LEONARD, K., & SAMPLE, L. (1998). *Disparity based on sex: Is gender-specific treatment warranted?* Paper presented at the annual meetings of the Academy of Criminal Justice Sciences.

KERSTEN, J. (1989). The institutional control of girls and boys: An attempt at a gender-specific approach. In M. Caine (Ed.), *Growing up good: Policing the behavior of girls in Europe* (pp. 129–144). Newbury Park, CA: Sage.

KRISBERG, B., & AUSTIN, J. F. (1993). *Reinventing juvenile justice*. Newbury Park, CA: Sage.

KRISBERG, B., SCHWARTZ, I. M., FISHMAN, G., EISIKOVITS, Z., & GUTTMAN, E. (1986). *The incarceration of minority youth*. Minneapolis, MN: Hubert Humphrey Institute of Public Affairs.

KROHN, M., CURRY, J., & NELSON-KILGER, S. (1983). Is chivalry dead? *Criminology, 21,* 417–439.

LEONARD, E. (1982). *Women, crime, and society.* New York: Longman.

LIPSEY, M. W. (1992). Juvenile delinquency treatment: A meta-analytic inquiry into the variability of effects. In T. D. Cook, H. Cooper, D. S. Cordray, H. Hartman, L. V. Hedges, R. J. Knight, et al. (Eds.), *Meta-analysis for explanation* (pp. 83–127). New York: Russell Sage.

LIPSEY, M. W., & DERZON, J. H. (1998). Predictors of violent or serious delinquency in adolescence and early adulthood: A synthesis of longitudinal research. In R. Loeber & D. P. Farrington (Eds.), *Serious and violent juvenile offenders* (pp. 86–105). Thousand Oaks, CA: Sage.

LIPSEY, M. W., & WILSON, D. B. (1998). Effective intervention for serious juvenile offenders: A synthesis of research. In R. Loeber & D. P. Farrington (Eds.), *Serious and violent juvenile offenders* (pp. 315–335). Thousand Oaks, CA: Sage.

LOEBER, R., & FARRINGTON, D. P. (EDS.). (1998). *Serious and violent juvenile offenders* (pp. 106–146). Thousand Oaks, CA: Sage.

LOEBER, R., FARRINGTON, D. P., & WASCHBUSCH, D.A. (1998). In R. Loeber & D. P. Farrington (Eds.), *Serious and violent juvenile offenders* (pp. 13–29). Thousand Oaks, CA: Sage.

LOEBER, R., & HAY, D. F. (1994). Developmental approaches to aggression and conduct problems. In M. Rutter & D. F. Hay (Eds.), *Development through life: A handbook for clinicians* (pp. 488–516). Oxford: Blackwell.

MAHER, L., & CURTIS, R. (1995). In search of the female urban "gangsta": Change, culture, and crack cocaine. In B. R. Price & N. J. Sokoloff (Eds.), *The criminal justice system and women* (2nd ed., pp. 148–166). New York: McGraw-Hill.

MALES, M. A. (1996). *The scapegoat generation: America's war on adolescents.* Monroe, ME: Common Courage Press.

MATZA, D. (1964). *Delinquency and drift.* New York: Wiley.

MESSERSCHMIDT, J. (1993). *Masculinities and crime: Critique and reconceptualization.* Lanham, MD: Rowman & Littlefield.

MILLER, J. (1994). Race, gender and juvenile justice: An examination of disposition decision-making for delinquent girls. In M. D. Schwartz & D. Milovanovic (Eds.), *The intersection of race, gender and class in criminology* (pp. 219–246). New York: Garland.

NAFFINE, N. (1987). *Female crime: The construction of women in criminology.* Sydney, Australia: Allen & Unwin.

ODEM, M. E. (1995). *Delinquent daughters.* Chapel Hill: University of North Carolina Press.

ORENSTEIN, P. (1994). *School girls.* New York: Doubleday.

OSGOOD, W., WILSON, J., O'MALLEY, P., BACHMAN, G., & JOHNSON, L. (1996). Routine activities and individual deviant behavior. *American Sociological Review, 61,* 635–655.

PRICE, B. R. & SOKOLOFF, N. J. (EDS.). (1995). *The criminal justice system and women* (2nd ed.). New York: McGraw-Hill.

PUBLIC LAW 102-586. (1992, November 4). Juvenile justice and delinquency prevention, fiscal years 1993–96. 106 Stat. 4982.

RHODES, J., & FISCHER, K. (1993). Spanning the gender gap: Gender differences in delinquency among inner city adolescents. *Adolescence, 28,* pp. 880–889.

ROSENBAUM, J., & CHESNEY-LIND, M. (1994). Appearance and delinquency: A research note. *Crime & Delinquency, 40,* 250–261.

SADKER, M., & SADKER, D. (1994). *Failing at fairness: How America's schools cheat girls.* New York: Scribner's.

SHANNON, L. (1978). A longitudinal study of delinquency and crime. In C. Wellford (Ed.), *Quantitative studies in criminology.* Beverly Hills, CA: Sage.

SHANNON, L. (1980). *Assessing the relationship of adult criminal careers to juvenile careers.* Washington, DC: U.S. Government Printing Office.

SIMPSON, S. (1991). Caste, class, and violent crime: Explaining difference in female offending. *Criminology, 29*(1), 115–135.

SINGER, S. (1996). *Recriminalizing delinquency.* Cambridge: Cambridge University Press.

SMITH, C., & THORNBERRY, T. P. (1995). The relationship between childhood maltreatment and adolescent involvement in delinquency. *Criminology, 33*, 451–481.

SNYDER, H. N. (1998). Serious, violent, and chronic juvenile offenders: An assessment of the extent of and trends in officially recognized serious criminal behavior in a delinquent population. In R. Loeber & D. P. Farrington (Eds.), *Serious and violent juvenile offenders* (pp. 428–444). Thousand Oaks, CA: Sage.

THORNBERRY, T. (1998). Membership in youth gangs and involvement in serious and violent offending. In R. Loeber & D. P. Farrington (Eds.), *Serious and violent juvenile offenders* (pp. 147–166). Thousand Oaks, CA: Sage.

TOLAN, P. H., & GORMAN-SMITH, D. (1998). Development of serious and violent offending careers. In R. Loeber & D. P. Farrington (Eds.), *Serious and violent juvenile offenders* (pp. 68–85). Thousand Oaks, CA: Sage.

TORBET, P., GABLE, R., HURST, H., MONTGOMERY, I., SZYMANSKI, L., & THOMAS, D. (1996). *State reponses to serious and violent juvenile crime.* Washington, DC: Office of Juvenile Justice and Delinquency Prevention.

TRACY, P. E. & KEMPF-LEONARD, K. (1996). *Continuity and discontinuity in criminal careers.* New York: Plenum.

TRACY, P. E., & KEMPF-LEONARD, K. (1998). Sanctioning serious juvenile offenders: A review of alternative models. *Advances in Criminological Theory, 8*, 135–171.

TRACY, P. E., WOLFGANG, M. E., & FIGLIO, R. M. (1985). *Delinquency in two birth cohorts: Executive summary.* Washington, DC: U.S. Government Printing Office.

TRACY, P. E., WOLFGANG, M. E., & FIGLIO, R. M. (1990). *Delinquency careers in two birth cohorts.* New York: Plenum.

VALENTINE FOUNDATION. (1990). *A conversation about girls.* Bryn Mawr, PA: The Foundation.

VISHER, C. (1983). Gender, police arrest decisions, and notions of chivalry. *Criminology, 21*, 5–28.

WALKER, S. (1985). *Sense and nonsense about crime: A policy guide.* Monterey, CA: Brooks/Cole.

WALKER, S. (1995). *Sense and nonsense about crime: A policy guide* (2nd ed.). Monterey, CA: Brooks/Cole.

WEIBUSH, R. G., BAIRD, C., KRISBERG, B., & ONEK, D. (1995). Risk assessment and classification for serious, violent, and chronic juvenile offenders. In J. C. Howell, B. Krisberg, J. D. Hawkins, & J. J. Wilson (Eds.), *A sourcebook: Serious, violent, and chronic juvenile offenders* (pp. 171–212). Thousand Oaks, CA: Sage.

WEISHEIT, R., & MAHAN, S. (1988). *Women, crime and criminal justice.* Cincinnati, OH: Anderson.

WEITHORN, L. A. (1988). Mental hospitalization of troublesome youth: An analysis of skyrocketing admission rates. *Stanford Law Review, 40*, 773–838.

WHITE, H. R. (1992). Early problem behavior and later drug problems. *Journal of Research in Crime and Delinquency, 29*, 412–429.

WILLIAMS, J. H. (1994). *Understanding substance use, delinquency involvement, and juvenile justice system involvement among African American and European-American adolescents.* Unpublished dissertation. University of Washington–Seattle.

WILSON, J. J., & HOWELL, J. C. (1993). *A comprehensive strategy for serious, violent, and chronic juvenile offenders.* Washington, DC: Office of Juvenile Justice and Delinquency Prevention.

WOLFGANG, M. E., FIGLIO, R. M., & SELLIN, T. (1972). *Delinquency in a birth cohort.* Chicago: University of Chicago Press.

ZIMRING, F. E. (1996a). *American youth violence.* New York: Oxford University Press.

ZIMRING, F. E. (1996b, August 19). Crying wolf over teen demons. *Los Angeles Times,* p. B5.

SECTION X

Conclusions

Conclusions

Roslyn Muraskin

According to Catherine MacKinnon, "[e]quality in human societies is commonly affirmed but rarely practiced. As a principle, it can be fiercely loved, passionately sought, highly vaunted, sentimentally assumed, complacently taken for granted, and legally guaranteed. Its open detractors are few. Yet despite general consensus on equality as a value, no society is organized on equality principles. Few lives are lived in equality, even in democracies. As a fact, social equality is hard to find anywhere" (2001, p. 2).

Then how do we conclude? Women are committing crimes at a higher rate than ever before. Have we failed to remember the women? Are women not deserving of the same rights and privileges as men?

According to the *Universal Declaration of Human Rights* (1948):

> Article 1. All human beings are born free and equal in dignity and rights. They are endowed with reason and conscience and should act toward one another in a spirit of brotherhood.
> Article 6. Everyone has the right to recognition everywhere as a person before the law.

This Declaration of Human Rights is a document of international rights and is a component of international law. But are all human beings born free and equal? "Sex equality is often guaranteed by law, including where sex inequality is pervasive in society. More imagined than real in life, sex equality guarantees varies dramatically, its observance ranging from obvious to anathema. Around the world and throughout history, in settings from the institutional to the intimate, sex equality remains more promise than fact" (MacKinnon, p. 3).

In the words of Justice Ruth Bader Ginsburg, "[t]he classification man/dependent woman is the prototypical sex line in the law and has all the earmarks of self-fulfilling prophecy." That discrimination against women is a long tradition is an understatement.

> Words are more than a collective art; they are simultaneously a collective cage. Unconscious and unquestioned obedience to established meanings bind humankind with steel bands to both the good and bad of yesterday. Law is called upon to serve goals other than predictability and certainty, which logic being what it is, walk backwards. The paramount obligation of

law is to secure, to make safe, equal rights and justice under the law. This is the daunting task of the remarkably few words which comprise the United States Constitution. (Thomas, 1991, p. xx)

We have come a long way since the days of Rousseau[1] (1906) when he wrote that "[t]he whole education of women ought to be relative to men. To please them, to be useful to them, to make themselves loved and honored by them, to educate them when young, to care for them when grown, to counsel them, to console them, and to make his life sweet and agreeable to them—these are the duties at all times, and what should be taught to them (*women*) from their infancy."

Even a longer way since Napoleon Bonaparte spoke, "nature intended women to be our slaves; . . . they are our property, we are not theirs. They belong to us, just as a tree that bears fruit belongs to a gardener. . . . Women are nothing but machines for producing children."

And from Lord Chesterfield, "women, then, are only children of larger growth: they have an entertaining tattle, and sometimes wit; but for solid, reasoning good sense, I never knew in my life one that had it or who reasoned or acted consequentially for four and twenty hours together."

In the words of Aristotle, "we may thus conclude that it is a general law that there should be naturally ruling elements and elements naturally ruled . . . the rule of the free-man over the slave is one kind of rule; that of the male over the female another . . . the slave is entirely without the faculty of deliberation; the female indeed possesses it, but in a form which remains inconclusive." Remember that the word *man* meant human being; the males appropriated it.

As we have learned throughout this work, women have had to struggle to be considered persons under the law and to be afforded the same opportunities as men before the law. The struggle continues. Men may have been considered to be the protector of woman, but in the world in which we live today, every woman and man deserves to be given the same opportunity to succeed. The criminal justice system has an obligation to treat both sexes on a par with each other. There is no room for disparate treatment. History has taught us that women have suffered as much and perhaps more than men. As confirmed in the Declaration of Seneca Falls in 1848, "[T]he history of mankind is a history of repeated injuries and usurpations on the part of man toward woman, having in direct object the establishment of an absolute tyranny over her."

The Fourteenth Amendment to the Constitution of the United States declares that "no state . . . shall . . . deny to any person within its jurisdiction the equal protection of the laws." That amendment is to be applied equally to women and men. Hopefully in today's world, we no longer adhere to the tenets of the words of Justice Brenner as he delivered the majority opinion in the 1908 case of *Muller v. Oregon:*

> That woman's physical structure and the performance of maternal functions place her at a dis-advantage in the struggle for subsistence is obvious. This is especially true when the burdens of motherhood are upon her. . . .
>
> [H]istory discloses the fact that woman has always been dependent upon man. He established his control at the outset by superior physical strength, and the control in various forms. . . . She is properly placed in a class by herself, and that legislation designed for her pro-tection may be sustained, even when like legislation is not necessary for men, and could not be sustained.

Admittedly, laws can discriminate, but such discrimination becomes unconstitutional when it is judged to be arbitrary and serves no legitimate purpose. *Frontiero v. Richardson* (1973) needed one more vote to declare that *sex was a suspect classification*, although it did concede that differential treatment accorded men and women serves no practical purpose. Today, the attitude of the criminal justice system seems to have changed. We recognize that women are victims of crime and that they, too, perpetuate crime. We recognize that equal treatment is demanded and is an absolute necessity. Having moved from traditional homebound social roles into positions of power and influence, women have become more assertive and aggressive while being capable of competing with men in all realms of life. As noted throughout this work, litigation, changes in law, and constitutional amendments have held our criminal justice system to task in demanding that women are properly defined as people and are deserving of all the rights and privileges of men. To do otherwise would make our system of law a public disgrace.

From cases of domestic violence, where traditionally the abuser was taken for a walk around the block, to now where there are mandatory and pro-arrest policies, to maternal drug use during pregnancy and the complex legal and ethical questions that pit the rights of pregnant women against the rights of the fetus (rights that are nonexistent under *Roe*), to the systematic white racism that exists in this country with regard to executed black women, to woman serial killers, to the impact of gender decisions with regard to young girls and juvenile delinquency, to female involvement in acts of terrorism, and to the days of history when we were faced with the factor of the Salem Witch Trials, for women who were not witches, to cases of rape that are treated differently than any other crime, we find ourselves overwhelmed with women's rights and factors of privacy.

In the words of MacKinnon (2001), "[u]nless something is done, even if recent rates of measurable progress for elite women continue, no American now alive will live in a society of sex equality nor will their children or their children's children" (p. 2). MacKinnon continues: "More imagined than in real life, sex equality in law tends to be more formal or hypothetical than substantive and delivered. In legal application, the meaningfulness of sex equality guarantees varies dramatically, its observance ranging from obvious to anathema. Around the world and throughout history, in settings from the institutional to the intimate, sex equality remains more promise than fact" (p. 3).

In the words of philosopher Richard Rorty, to be a woman "is not yet the name of a way of being human" (Person, 1992). "His formulation at once recognizes that woman's lives would not be 'human' by the standard set by men, and that women's reality has not been reflected in the standard for what 'human' is. It invites redefinition of the human standard in the image of women's realities and unrealized possibilities, as well as proposes change in women's situation to meet the existing standard of a 'human' life. Can one challenge the validity of a standard and assert a right to the benefits of its application at the same time? Are women 'human'?" (MacKinnon, p. 3).

Although litigation provides an opportunity for all persons to have a role in altering their conditions of life, a judicial opinion requiring such comprehensive changes does not necessarily bring about such change. We have found that litigation is but a catalyst for change rather than an automatic mechanism for ending wrongs found. We know that within the criminal law, litigation indicates that disparate treatment of any kind is not permissible absent meaningful and objective justification. From Lombroso to the present, "criminological thought has been wrought with the sexism inherent in assuming that there exist two distinct classes of women—those on pedestals and those in the gutter" (Muraskin, 1989).

Throughout history, we have lived with a double standard. Disparate treatment can no longer exist, for it is all about women and men, justice and fairness. And we must never forget the ladies, for then it *will be a crime.*

NOTE

1. These following quotes can be found referenced in a work by Barbara Sinclair Deckard, *The Women's Movement*, published in 1979.

REFERENCES

DECKARD, B. S. (1979). *The women's movement: Political, socioeconomic, and psychological issues* (2nd ed.). New York: Harper & Row.

MACKINNON, C. A. (2001). *Sex equality*. New York: Foundation Press.

MURASKIN, R. (1989). *Disparity of correctional treatment: Development of a measurement instrument*. Unpublished doctoral dissertation. City University of New York.

PERSON, G. B. (ed.). (1992). Feminism and pragmatism. *Tanner Lectures of Human Values*, 1(7).

ROUSSEAU, J. J. (1906). *Emile, or a treatise on education*. (W. H. Payne, ed.) As found in Cynthia Ozick, "Women and Creativity" in Vivian Gornick and Barbara Moran, eds., *Women in Sexist Society*. New York: Signet 1971.

THOMAS, C. S. (1991). *Sex discrimination in a nutshell* (2nd ed.) St. Paul, MN: West.

UNITED NATIONS. (1948, December 10). *Universal declaration of human rights*. Adopted and proclaimed by General Assembly Resolution 217 A (111).

CASES

Frontiero v. Richardson, 411 U.S. 677 (1973).

Muller v. Oregon, 208 U.S. 412 (1908).

Index